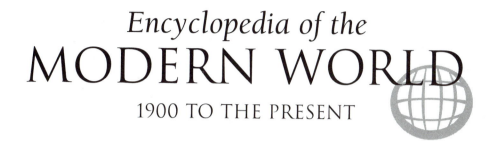

Encyclopedia of the
MODERN WORLD
1900 TO THE PRESENT

Encyclopedia of the
MODERN WORLD

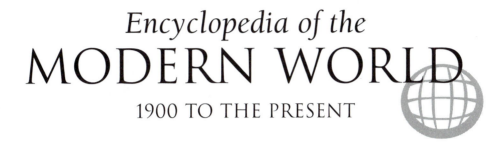

1900 TO THE PRESENT

VOLUME III
P–Z

William R. Keylor
GENERAL EDITOR

Michael McGuire
ASSOCIATE EDITOR

Facts On File
An imprint of Infobase Publishing

Encyclopedia of the Modern World: 1900 to the Present

Facts On File, Inc.
An imprint of Infobase Publishing
132 West 31st Street
New York NY 10001

Library of Congress Cataloging-in-Publication Data

The encyclopedia of the modern world: 1900 to the present / William R. Keylor, general editor ; Michael McGuire, associate editor. p. cm.
ISBN 0-8160-4872-X (HC. : alk. paper)
1. History, Modern—20th century—Encyclopedias. 2. World politics—20th century—Encyclopedias. 3. Twentieth century—Encyclopedias. I. Keylor, William R., 1944– II. McGuire Michael (Michael E.), 1976–
D419.E53 2005
909.82′03—dc22   2004061975

Facts On File books are available at special discounts when purchased in bulk quantities for businesses, associations, institutions, or sales promotions. Please call our Special Sales Department in New York at
(212) 967-8800 or (800) 322-8755.

You can find Facts On File on the
World Wide Web at http://www.factsonfile.com

Text design by Dorothy M. Preston
Cover design by Nora Wertz
Illustrations by Dale Williams

Printed in the United States of America

VB Hermitage 10 9 8 7 6 5 4 3 2 1

This book is printed on acid-free paper.

To James Arthur Keylor
with brotherly love

Contents

Entries P to Z

P

Pacific Islands, Trust Territory of the Several island chains in the western Pacific under U.S. administration; includes the CAROLINES (as well as the Palaus), the MARSHALLS and the MARIANAS (except GUAM), in Micronesia. A Japanese LEAGUE OF NATIONS mandate from 1919 to 1945, in 1944 the islands were seized by the U.S. during WORLD WAR II; in 1947 they became a trust territory with the approval of the UNITED NATIONS. The trusteeship ended in 1990.

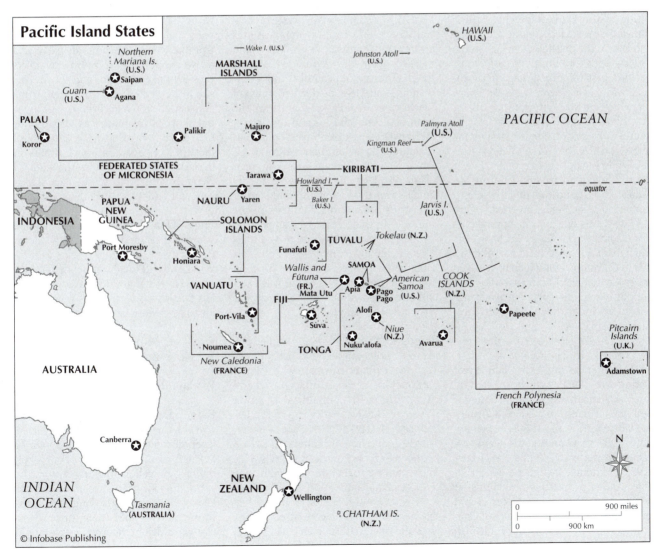

Pacific Island States

957

Actor Al Pacino in . . . And Justice for All. 1979
(PHOTOFEST)

Pacino, Al (1940–   ) American stage and motion picture actor and winner of the Academy Award for Best Actor (1993). Born in New York City, studied acting at the Herbert Berghof Studio under drama coach Charlie Laughton and later at the prestigious Actors Studio in New York City under LEE STRASBERG. Pacino's first important stage performance was in *The Indian Wants the Bronx,* for which he won an Obie Award for Best Actor in 1967. Two years later he won a Tony Award for his supporting role in the play *Does a Tiger Wear a Necktie?* While Pacino's success in the theater led to his motion picture debut in *Me, Natalie* (1969) and to a small role as a junkie in *The Panic in Needle Park* (1971), it was not until he appeared in *The Godfather* (1972) as Michael Corleone that Pacino became a star. After his role in *Godfather*—for which he received an Academy Award nomination for Best Supporting Actor—Pacino generally appeared in independent feature films, such as *Serpico* (1973) and *Dog Day Afternoon* (1975). He also reprised his role as Corleone in *The Godfather, Part II* (1974). After his impressive film career during the 1970s, which resulted in three Academy Award nominations for Best Actor, Pacino's career took a turn for the worse during the 1980s. It was not until 1989 that moviegoers again saw Pacino in the crime drama *Sea of Love* (1989). Although the film did not garner any Academy Award nominations, it reinvigorated Pacino's acting career and led to his appearances in *The Godfather: Part III* (1990), *Dick Tracy* (1990),

Frankie and Johnny (1991) *Glengarry Glen Ross* (1992) and *Scent of a Woman* (1992), for which he won an Academy Award for Best Actor in 1993. Since the resurgence of his career, Pacino has appeared in several blockbuster pictures, such as *Heat* (1995), *The Devil's Advocate* (1997), *Any Given Sunday* (1999), *The Insider* (1999) and *The Recruit* (2002).

Pact of Paris See KELLOGG-BRIAND PACT.

Paderewski, Ignace Jan (1860–1941) Polish pianist, composer and statesman. Born in Kurylowka in Russian Poland, Paderewski began playing the piano at an early age. He entered the Warsaw Conservatory in 1872 and later studied with Theodor Leschetizky. Paderewski debuted in Vienna in 1887, in Paris in 1888 and in the U.S. in 1891. His technical virtuosity and brilliant style soon made him the most celebrated and beloved pianist since Franz Liszt. Also a composer, he wrote orchestral pieces, an opera, a cantata, songs and chamber music, as well as piano pieces, notably the well-known Minuet in G. Touring repeatedly and commanding huge fees, he donated much of his fortune to Poland, mainly in the form of aid to refugees and musicians. Paderewski was a passionate Polish nationalist and patriot. After World War I, when the new Polish state was proclaimed in 1918, he briefly served as its ambassador to Washington and shortly afterward became his country's prime minister. In this capacity, he signed the VERSAILLES Peace Treaty and served until 1920. Retaining an interest in Polish affairs, he later devoted most of his time to music. But in 1940–41 he was head of POLAND's government-in-exile during the Nazi occupation.

Page, Ruth (1899–1991) American dancer, choreographer and ballet director. A dynamic performer who gained international acclaim in solo concerts and with such companies as Anna PAVLOVA's classical ballet and Serge DIAGHILEV's BALLETS RUSSES, Page was one of the first choreographers to create works based on American themes. Her most famous ballet in this vein was *Frankie and Johnny* (1938) in collaboration with Bentley Stone. Some of her most popular ballets were based on operas and operettas, such as *Vilia* (1953),

adapted from *The Merry Widow.* In 1928 she created the role of Terpsichore in the world premiere of Igor STRAVINSKY's *Apollo,* as choreographed by Adolph Bolm. She founded the Chicago Opera Ballet in 1956, which became Ruth Page's International Ballet (1966–69), then the Chicago Ballet (1972–present). Rudolph NUREYEV made his New York City debut with her company in 1962.

Page, Walter Hines (1855–1918) American author, publisher and ambassador. After attending Duke University, Randolph-Macon College and Johns Hopkins University, Page began his literary career in 1880 as a reporter for the *Gazette* in St. Louis. In later years he either reported for or edited the *New York World,* the *Raleigh State Chronicle,* the *New York Evening Post,* the *Forum,* the *Atlantic Monthly* and *World's Work.* In 1900 Page joined Frank N. Doubleday in establishing Doubleday-Page, a publishing company that later became Doubleday and Company. Page became an early and active supporter in Woodrow WILSON's presidential campaign, and when Wilson was elected, he appointed Page ambassador to Great Britain. Throughout most of his tenure as ambassador (1913–18), Page strongly advocated that the U.S. abandon its neutrality in WORLD WAR I and join the side of Great Britain. On this issue Page was at constant odds with President Wilson.

Pagis, Dan (1931–1986) Israeli poet. A scholar of medieval Hebrew literature, Pagis spent three years during WORLD WAR II in a NAZI CONCENTRATION CAMP. He emigrated to ISRAEL in 1946. His poetry was regarded as a significant literary response to the HOLOCAUST.

Pahlavi, Mohammad Reza Shah See MOHAMMAD REZA SHAH PAHLAVI.

Pahlavi, Reza See REZA SHAH PAHLAVI.

Paige, Leroy "Satchel" (c. 1906–1982) American baseball player. A legendary pitcher, Paige was noted for his fastball and his variety of curveball pitches, as well as his longevity in the sport. Starting in baseball's Negro Leagues in the 1920s, Paige spent his prime playing years there, prior to entering the Major Leagues as a 42-year-old "rookie" with the Cleveland Indians (1948). Paige was brought to Cleveland a year after the Brooklyn Dodgers broke the color barrier with second baseman Jackie ROBINSON. Despite his late beginning, the 6-foot-3-inch pitcher was a deceptive, powerful addition to the Major Leagues and completed a relatively long career when he retired in 1965, while in his late fifties. The first black pitcher in major league baseball, Paige's birth records were so obscure that even he was able only to estimate his date of birth. Some authorities have added as much as a decade to his age. Paige was inducted into the Baseball Hall of Fame in 1971.

Paine, Thomas (*1921–1992*) U.S. space administrator. Best known in later years as the chair of the National Commission on Space and before that as administrator of NASA from 1968 to 1970, Paine had a strong impact on the U.S. space program. Charged in 1985 with setting out the nation's goals in space, the Paine Commission consisted of more than a dozen space-age luminaries, ranging from Nobel Prize-winning physicist Luis ALVAREZ to X-1 pilot Charles YEAGER. The publication of their report came right on the heels of the January 1986 *CHALLENGER* disaster, giving all the more impact to its bold visions. They called for an ambitious agenda of exploration, development, and eventual settlement of new worlds in the next 50 years, "from the highlands of the Moon to the Plains of Mars." From October 1968 to September 1970, when Paine served as acting administrator and then as NASA's third administrator, the first seven manned APOLLO missions were launched. It was a time when the nation was galvanized by the excitement of seeing 21 astronauts orbit the Earth over the span of two years, with 15 of them traveling to the Moon and four of them walking on its surface.

Paisley, Ian Richard Kyle (*1926– *) Northern Irish politician and Protestant clergyman. A fundamentalist minister, Paisley founded the Free Presbyterian Church of Ulster in 1951 and the Martyrs' Memorial Free Presbyterian Church in 1969. In both the pulpit and the political arena, he is an outspoken activist against Catholic dominance in Ulster and against interference in NORTHERN IRELAND from either Britain or Dublin. Paisley entered Parliament as a Protestant Unionist member in 1970. A year later he helped form the Democratic Unionist Party, which has become Northern Ireland's second largest party. Paisley won a seat in the European Parliament in 1979, to which he was re-elected in 1984, although he consistently opposed British membership in the EUROPEAN ECONOMIC COMMUNITY. He denounced the 1985 HILLSBOROUGH ACCORD designed to foster cooperation from all parties on Northern Ireland. Although ostensibly opposed to violence, Paisley has earned a reputation as a demagogue; he has organized numerous Protestant protests, and his rhetoric is widely seen as a divisive force in the province. In 1988, when Pope JOHN PAUL II visited Northern Ireland, Paisley interrupted him, calling out "antichrist," and was subsequently ejected from the European Parliament. Paisley and the Democratic Unionist Party were involved in the 1998 Good Friday Agreement that sought to create a joint power-sharing government for Catholic and Protestant leaders in Northern Ireland. However, his party left the negotiations when Sinn Féin entered the talks.

Pakistan Country in south Asia; bordered by Afghanistan on the north and west, China on the northeast, India on the east and southeast, Iran on the southwest and the Arabian Sea on the south. Pakistan, scene of countless invasions over the centuries, is approximately 90 percent Muslim, and its official language is Urdu. From 1857 to independence in 1947 it was a part of British INDIA; in 1956 it became a republic in the British Commonwealth. Formation of the Muslim League in 1906 led to increased demands for Muslim political freedom in the face of India's dominant Hindu population. By 1930 a national separatist movement had evolved, led by the poet and statesman Muhammad Iqbal, and in 1940 Muhammad Ali JINNAH took over as leader of the Muslim League, later serving as Pakistan's first head of state in 1947.

The abrupt division of British India into the new nations of Pakistan and India caused bloody riots and warfare among hundreds of thousands of Hindus and Muslims, who uprooted themselves to be among their own people. At independence, West Pakistan (present-day Pakistan) was separated from East Pakistan (now known as BANGLADESH) by approximately 1,000 miles of territory

under India's jurisdiction. Further, in 1947–48 divided Pakistan went to war with India over the mountain provinces of JAMMU and KASHMIR; disputes erupted again in 1965, but in December 1972 a boundary was firmly established.

Growing dissatisfaction in East Pakistan accused the government of favoring the West; although the East won a majority in parliament in December 1970, its legislature was not allowed to convene. In March 1971 East Pakistan declared itself independent as Bangladesh. West Pakistani troops were unsuccessful in their attempts to crush the rebellion, and they were defeated when India entered the war in December (see INDO-PAKISTANI WAR OF 1971). In February 1974, Pakistan was forced to recognize independent Bangladesh. Further tension broke out on the Pakistani border in December 1979, during the Soviet invasion of neighboring AFGHANISTAN. Zulfikar Ali BHUTTO, leader of the Pakistan People's Party, became president in December 1971; with the introduction of a new constitution (1973), he became prime minister. Bhutto followed a policy of Islamic socialism, strengthening relations with other Islamic (mainly Arab) countries and nationalizing key industries. He won reelection in 1977 but was overthrown in a coup led by Gen. Zia al-Haq, who assumed the presidency and declared martial law. Bhutto was executed. Because of his anticommunism, Zia received strong support from the U.S. Zia was killed when his airplane exploded in August 1988. Bhutto's daughter, Benazir BHUTTO, was elected president at the end of the year but faced severe economic and political problems. She was defeated in a 1990 election, and soon after charged with corruption. In 1998 following India's testing of nuclear weapons, Pakistan followed suit by conducting two underground nuclear tests. The United States promptly imposed economic sanctions on the two countries. In 1999 General Pervez MUSHARRAF overthrew the government of Prime Minister Nawaz Sharif and assumed the presidency. Since the start of the U.S. president George W. BUSH's "War on Terror," President Musharraf has attempted to cooperate with U.S. forces

seeking to capture the Saudi-born terrorist Osama BIN LADEN and his top associates in AL-QAEDA, while seeking to avoid angering his own Islamic constituency. In October 2005 a powerful earthquake in Pakistan killed almost 100,000 people and left more than 3 million people homeless as the frigid winter approached.

Pal, George (1908–1980) HOLLYWOOD producer-director of animated and science fiction films. Born in Hungary, he immigrated to the U.S. in 1939. Early in his film career he was primarily a cinema cartoonist. His series of "Puppetoons" for PARAMOUNT in the 1940s won him a special ACADEMY AWARD (1943) for his innovations in "stop-motion" animation techniques. In the 1950s he became one of Hollywood's foremost masters of science fiction and fantasy films. He won eight Academy Awards for the productions of such classics as *Destination Moon* (1950), *When Worlds Collide* (1951), *War of the Worlds* (1953) and *The Seven Faces of Dr. Lao* (1964). Perhaps his greatest achievement was his adaptation of H. G. WELLS's *The Time Machine* (1960), which he also directed and for which he realized many of the cinematic implications embedded in the original book.

Palade, George Emil (1912–) Romanian-American physiologist and cell biologist; educated at Bucharest University, he was a professor of physiology during World War II. Palade immigrated to America in 1946, becoming a naturalized citizen in 1952. He worked at the Rockefeller Institute for Medical Research, New York, becoming professor of cytology there (1958–72). In 1972 he became director of studies in cell biology at Yale University's medical school. Although Palade's work has been primarily concerned with studies of the fine structure of animal cells, he has also investigated the nature of plant chloroplasts. His discovery of small bodies called "microsomes," which function independently of the mitochondria (of which they were previously thought to be a part), showed them to be rich in ribonucleic acid (RNA) and therefore the site of protein manufacture. The microsomes were subsequently renamed ribosomes. For his work in cel-

lular biology, Palade received, with Albert CLAUDE and Christian DE DUVE, the NOBEL PRIZE for physiology or medicine (1974).

Palar, Lambertus N. (1902–1981) Indonesian statesman and diplomat, prominent in INDONESIA's struggle for independence. Palar served as Indonesia's chief delegate to the UNITED NATIONS from 1950 to 1953. Later he was ambassador to India, Canada and the U.S. A leading spokesman for the nonaligned nations of Asia and Africa, he denounced "neocolonialism," called for neutral and nuclear-free zones and advocated strong sanctions against SOUTH AFRICA because of that nation's policy of APARTHEID.

Palau This group of islands is part of the western Caroline Islands located in the western Pacific Ocean. The Palau archipelago is 458 square kilometers and consists of more than 200 islands, many of them coral atolls. Spain ruled the islands in the late 19th century but then sold them to Germany in 1899. At the outbreak of World War I the islands were seized by Japan, which was given a mandate over Palau by the League of Nations in 1920. The Japanese were removed during World War II, and in 1947 Palau became part of the UN Trust Territory of the Pacific Islands administered by the United States. Palau became a self-governing republic in 1981 but suffered from a troubled political history in the 1980s. The republic's first president, Haruo Remeliik, was assassinated in 1985, and the third president, Lazarus E. Salii, committed suicide in 1988 amid allegations of fraud. In 1994 Palau became an independent nation in free association with the United States, which is responsible for its defense, and a member state of the UN. In 2003 Palau signed the Comprehensive Test Ban Treaty.

Palchinsky, Peter Ioakimovich (1875–1929) Russian engineer and politician. During World War I Palchinsky was a leading member of the central war industries committee. Following the 1917 FEBRUARY REVOLUTION he was appointed the provisional government's deputy minister of trade and industry and defended the Winter Palace against the BOLSHEVIKS. A tech-

nical expert of GOSPLAN, he was accused of sabotage and shot at the beginning of the purges. He was said to have founded the underground league of engineering organizations.

Palestine Though there is no official Palestinian state at present, historically the biblical land of Palestine covered the general area of the modern State of ISRAEL and its occupied territories of GAZA and the WEST BANK. Part of the OTTOMAN EMPIRE, Palestine became a British Mandate after WORLD WAR I until its partition into Arab and Jewish zones by the UNITED NATIONS in 1947. The Palestinians, Arabs who trace their origins to the biblical Palestine, have fought against Jewish settlement of the area, especially after the State of Israel was established in 1948. Feeling dispossessed of their land, thousands left during the Israeli War for Independence (see ARAB-ISRAELI WAR OF 1948–49) and are scattered throughout the Middle East, with large numbers in JORDAN and the Israeli-occupied territories. Attempts to settle the problems of Palestinian displacement have failed, and Arab-Israeli tensions have escalated with wars in 1956, 1967, 1973, and 1982. The situation has been exacerbated by the PALESTINE LIBERATION ORGANIZATION (PLO; founded 1964), which has used terrorist attacks to push for Palestine's liberation, and by the INTIFADA, which broke out in the occupied territories in 1987. In 1988 the PLO acceded to a 1967 UN resolution, thereby implicitly recognizing Israel, renouncing terrorism and accepting a two-state solution based on Israeli withdrawal from the occupied territories. Although the PLO also declared the independent state of Palestine (recognized only by Arab states), the problem of a Palestinian homeland remains unresolved. The signing of the Oslo Accords by Israeli prime minister Yitzak RABIN and PLO leader Yasir ARAFAT in 1993 created the PALESTINIAN AUTHORITY (PA), an institution scheduled to receive greater domestic control over the Gaza Strip and the West Bank. In 1994 PA president Yasir Arafat relocated to the West Bank city of Ramallah. In 2000 U.S. president Bill Clinton hosted a meeting at Camp David between Arafat and Israeli prime minister Ehud BARAK which came very close to, but ultimately failed to reach, an agreement on the borders and political status of a proposed Palestinian state. Soon, a second Palestinian uprising (INTIFADA II) began, prompting the new hard-line Israeli prime minister Ariel SHARON to place Arafat under house arrest in Ramallah and break off all negotiations with the PA leader. After Arafat's death in 2004, Sharon reopened talks with the new head of the Palestinian Authority, Mahmond Abbas, on the basis of U.S. president George W. BUSH's "roadmap for peace." Sharon unilaterally withdrew Israeli military forces and settlements from the Gaza Strip in summer 2005, while resuming construction of a barrier separating Israel from the West Bank that incorporated several Jewish settlements along the western fringe of that territory.

PALESTINE

1917	British Balfour Declaration promising a national home for Jews in Palestine encourages Jewish immigration.
1922	Britain is given League of Nations mandate over Palestine.
1948	Britain leaves Palestine; State of Israel proclaimed in Tel Aviv.
1948–49	Israeli war of independence drives 780,000 Palestinians from their homeland.
1964	Palestine National Council (PNC), "a parliament-in-exile," is formed and establishes the Palestine Liberation Organization.
1987	Intifada (uprising) breaks out.
1988	PNC votes to support UN resolution 242 (1967), which recognizes Israel and calls for Israeli withdrawal from the West Bank and Gaza. It also declares the existence of an independent state of Palestine with Jerusalem as its capital; (December) with the PLO's renunciation of terrorism, dialogue is opened with the U.S.
1993	Oslo Accords create Palestinian Authority to govern portions of the West Bank and Gaza.
2000	Meeting of Palestinian Authority president Yasir Arafat and Israeli prime minister Ehud Barak with U.S. president Bill Clinton at Camp David fails to produce agreement on borders and political status of proposed Palestinian state.
2000	Second intifada begins.
2003	Israel reoccupies almost all of the West Bank.
2004	Yasir Arafat dies.
2005	Israel completes a full withdrawal from all settlements in the Gaza Strip.
2006	Hamas wins majority of seats in legislative elections, defeating the ruling Fatah party.

Jewish children on their way to Palestine after being liberated from Buchenwald Concentration Camp. 1945 (LIBRARY OF CONGRESS, PRINTS AND PHOTOGRAPHS DIVISION)

Palestine Liberation Organization (PLO) Coordinating organization, including several separate Arab groups, that aims at the "liberation" of PALESTINE from the Israeli regime and the creation of a homeland for Palestinians. It was widely considered the political spokesman and military arm of the Palestinian people. Founded in 1964, it is dominated by the Al Fatah guerrillas led by Yasir ARAFAT, who was named PLO head in 1969. The UNITED NATIONS recognized it as the legitimate Palestinian government in 1974. The group was forced out of Jordan in 1971, moving to BEIRUT, LEBANON, until expelled by the Israeli invasion of 1982. The PLO regrouped at its new headquarters in Tunis, Tunisia. In 1993 the Oslo Accords created the PALESTINIAN AUTHORITY (PA), a quasi-autonomous organization designed to govern increasing portions of the West Bank and Gaza Strip. The group has engaged in many acts of terrorism throughout the world in attempts to further its cause, but claims to have largely abandoned violence in favor of political action. After his death in 2004, Arafat was succeeded by Mahmoud Abbas.

Palestinian Authority (PA) The quasi-autonomous governing body of several predominantly Palestinian Arab regions in the Israeli-occupied territories of the West Bank and the Gaza Strip. Created in 1993 as part of the Oslo Accords between the PALESTINE LIBERATION ORGANIZATION (PLO) and ISRAEL, the PA was designed to be the successor organization to the PLO, which renounced its historic hostility to the State of Israel and its open and tacit support of terrorist attacks upon Israeli citizens. According to the precepts of the Oslo Accords, the PA would control administrative and security affairs in several urban districts and their rural hinterlands inhabited by Palestinians in the West Bank and Gaza Strip. To facilitate the continued pacification of the territories under PA control, the accords permitted the PA to have a security force of 15,000, which had tripled in size by 2003. PA leader Yasir ARAFAT established his headquarters in the West Bank town of Ramallah, and the PA assumed political control of several West Bank cities and towns. Although the Oslo Accords did not establish a timetable for the creation of a Palestinian state, statements immediately following the Oslo Accords by Israeli prime minister Yitzhak RABIN and Arafat implied that, if the agreement proved successful, the PA would become the official government of a Palestinian state.

Between 1993 and 2003 Arafat functioned as the authority's president and prime minister and hand-picked the cabinetlike structure that oversaw the PA's administrative and security operations. Although Arafat scheduled, administered and won an election for the position of PA president in 1996, he indefinitely suspended future elections following his victory. In response to an outbreak of terrorist attacks on Israelis in 2001 (see INTIFADA II) and Israeli allegations that Arafat used the offices of the PA to mastermind such attacks, international pressure forced Arafat to remove himself from the prime ministry. He chose Mahmoud Abbas to replace him in this office. However, Arafat retained control over the appointment of cabinet officials and regularly limited the degree of influence Abbas exercised within the PA. This led to Abbas's resignation within a few months of his selection. Arafat then nominated Ahmed Qurei, the chief member of the PA's parliament, to replace Abbas in September 2003. After Arafat's death in 2004, Abbas was elected as his successor. In 2006 the militant Islamist Hamas organization won the majority of seats in the legislative election, defeating the ruling Fatah party, causing Qurei and his cabinet to resign.

Paley, William S. *(1901–1990)* U.S. broadcast entrepreneur. He created the CBS network out of a handful of ailing radio stations he purchased in 1928. The network branched out into television in the 1950s and was the dominant force in U.S. broadcasting into the 1970s. He signed such popular performers as Lucille BALL, Jack BENNY, Jackie GLEASON and Ed SULLIVAN, as well as newsmen Edward R. MURROW, William L. SHIRER, Howard K. Smith and Eric SEVAREID. CBS produced such popular successes as *Gunsmoke, I LOVE LUCY, The Mary Tyler Moore Show, ALL IN THE FAMILY* and *M*A*S*H**. Paley was a noted socialite and art collector, as well as a powerful, and often ruthless, businessman.

Palme, Olof *(1927–1986)* Swedish premier. Born into an aristocratic family, Palme attended Kenyon College in Ohio and in 1951 earned a law degree at the University of Stockholm. In 1969, after serving in parliament and as a government minister, Palme became leader of the Social Democratic Party and then premier. For the next two decades he dominated Swedish politics. On the international scene, he was a vocal critic of the U.S. role in VIETNAM as well as of the Soviet invasion of CZECHOSLOVAKIA. On the domestic front, Palme levied high taxes to provide generous medical, educational and recreational programs for Swedish citizens. On February 28, 1986, Palme was assassinated by an unknown gunman as he and his wife were leaving a Stockholm movie theater, shocking Sweden and the world. An unemployed laborer named Carl Gustav Christer Pettersson was convicted of the crime, but his conviction was later overturned by a court of appeals.

Palmer, Arnold *(1929–)* U.S. golfer. A dominant golfer from the 1950s to the 1980s, he is one of the greatest golfers of all time. In 1981 the PGA championship trophy was renamed the Arnold Palmer Award. As golf became a popular televised sport, viewers watched Palmer's fans, dubbed "Arnie's Army," follow him through every round. His 60 tour victories included four Masters titles and a 1959 U.S. Open. The winner of 19 foreign titles, he played on six Ryder Cup teams and seven World Cup teams. As a member of the Senior PGA Tour, Palmer continued to play well, winning 10 Senior Tour tournaments until illness and age slowed him down after the beginning of the 21st century.

Palmer, Geoffrey *(1942–)* NEW ZEALAND politician; educated at the Victoria University of Wellington (B.A. in political science, 1964; LL.B., 1965) and the University of Chicago (doctor of laws, 1967). Before entering parliament, Palmer practiced as a solicitor and taught at Victoria University, the University of Iowa and the University of Virginia. He entered the House of Representatives at a by-election in August 1979 and became deputy leader of the LABOUR PARTY in February 1983. Palmer became deputy prime minister in 1988, heading the ministries of justice and the environment as well. He became prime minister in mid-1989. Palmer's tenure as prime minister, and his career as a

member of Parliament, ended in September 1990. Following his departure from politics Palmer spent a year teaching political science at the University of Iowa in the U.S. and the Victoria University of Wellington in New Zealand. In 1994 he helped found Chen and Palmer, a legal firm in Wellington, New Zealand.

Palmer, Jim *(1945–)* American professional baseball player (1965–84, winner of the Cy Young award (1973, 1975, and 1976) and member of the Baseball Hall of Fame. In 1965, Palmer began his 20-year career with the American League (AL) team the Baltimore Orioles. During the 1966 season, he led the Orioles to the American League pennant, with a personal record of 15 wins and 10 losses and helped pitch his team to a World Series championship against the Los Angeles Dodgers. Palmer recorded impressive statistics for the 1970, 1971, 1972 and 1973 seasons, averaging 20 wins per season. He helped the Orioles win another World Series title against the Cincinnati Reds in 1970 and earned the AL earned run average (ERA) title and the Cy Young Award in 1973. Between 1975 and 1977, Palmer led all AL starting pitchers in wins and earned two additional Cy Young Awards in 1975 and 1976. In 1983 he won his third and final World Series with the Orioles, when he helped them defeat the Philadelphia Phillies in five games. During the 1984 seasons, after losing three games Palmer retired from the Orioles, with a career 2.86 ERA average and 2,212 strikeouts. In 1990, Palmer was elected to the Baseball Hall of Fame on the first ballot.

Palmer Raids See RED SCARE.

PAN (National Action Party) Mexican political party. Founded in 1939 by members of the INSTITUTIONAL REVOLUTIONARY PARTY (PRI) who were dissatisfied with their party's domestic policies, PAN has since emerged as a conservative political force in Mexican elections. Its appeal as a party in opposition to the continuously ruling PRI largely stemmed from PAN's pledge to end corruption within the Mexican federal and state governments, which PAN repeatedly accused PRI of tolerat-

ing, and in some cases, organizing. On economic issues, it often exhibited a fiscal conservatism. For instance, PAN regularly called for the sale of certain government-owned and -run businesses, such as Mexican Petroleum (PEMEX), and also favored cutting government expenditures on social welfare programs. Although it competed with the PRI in national, state and local elections, PAN delegates in Mexico's national legislature regularly cooperated with the PRI leadership on some bills on which they have voted, such as the NORTH AMERICAN FREE TRADE AGREEMENT (NAFTA). On July 2, 2000, the PAN candidate for president of Mexico, Vicente FOX, became the first non-PRI candidate elected to that office.

Pan, Hermes (Hermes Panagiotopulos) *(1910–1990)* U.S. choreographer. He created the dances for all but one of the 10 films starring Fred ASTAIRE and Ginger ROGERS in the 1930s and 1940s; among the films were *Flying Down to Rio* (1933), *Top Hat* (1935) and *Swing Time* (1936). He won an ACADEMY AWARD in 1937 for *A Damsel in Distress*. His other films included *Kiss Me Kate* (1953), *Cleopatra* (1963) and *My Fair lady* (1964).

Panama (Republic of Panama) Covering an area of 30,185 square miles, Panama is located on the southern part of the Central American isthmus, which joins North and South America. Much of Panama's history in this century has been dominated by its relationship with the UNITED STATES and the importance of the PANAMA CANAL (completed in 1914). With U.S. support Panama became independent from Colombia in 1903. Opposition to U.S. influence led to revisions of the Canal Treaty (originated in 1903) in 1936 and 1955 revoking U.S. rights of intervention in Panamanian affairs. Anti-U.S. sentiment led to riots in 1959. Politically unstable, Panama had elected governments overthrown in 1941, 1949, 1951 and 1968. Colonel Omar TORRIJOS came to power in 1968, initiating reforms and negotiating new canal treaties with the U.S. that abolished the Canal Zone and paved the way for transition of the canal to Panamanian control by the year 2000. General Manuel Antonio

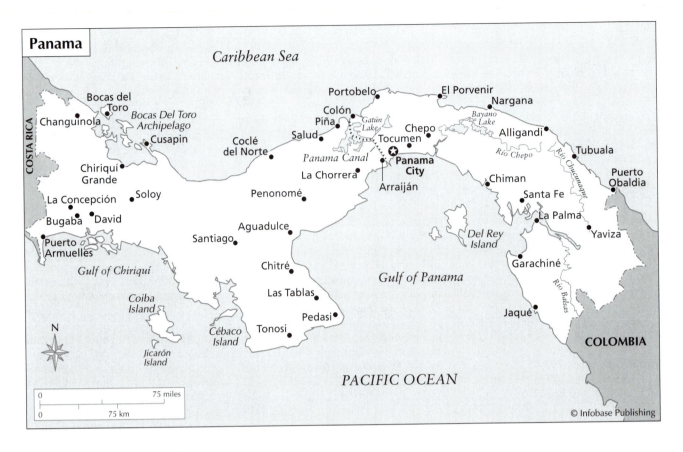

Panama

Caribbean Sea

COSTA RICA

Bocas del Toro
Changuinola
Bocas Del Toro Archipelago
Cusapin
Chiriquí Grande
Soloy
La Concepción
Bugaba   David
Puerto Armuelles
Gulf of Chiriquí
Coiba Island
Santiago
N
Jicarón Island
Cébaco Island
Tonosi
Las Tablas
Chitré
Pedasi
Aguadulce
Penonomé
Coclé del Norte
Salud
Piña
Colón
Portobelo
Gatún Lake
Panama Canal
La Chorrera
Arraiján
Tocumen
Panama City
Chepo
El Porvenir
Nargana
Bayano Lake
Alligandi
Río Chepo
Chiman
Santa Fe
La Palma
Garachiné
Del Rey Island
Gulf of Panama
Jaqué
Río Balsas
Tubuala
Puerto Obaldia
Río Chucunaque
Yaviza
COLOMBIA

PACIFIC OCEAN

0   75 miles
0   75 km

© Infobase Publishing

Noriega Morena, who rose to power in the 1980s, was accused of political fraud and assassination and of ties to drug smuggling. Attempts to remove him from power culminated in the U.S. military invasion in 1989 and the installation of Guillermo Endara as president. Noriega surrendered in 1990 and in a trial in Miami, Florida, in 1992 was found guilty of drug trafficking and sentenced to 40 (later reduced to 30) years in prison. On December 31, 1999, Panama gained full control over the canal zone, and its first female president, Mireya Moscoso, was elected. In 2004 Martin Torrijos, son of Colonel Torrijos, was elected president but faced opposition in 2005 to his reform plans for the pension system.

Panama Canal Canal across the Isthmus of Panama, connecting the Caribbean Sea and the Atlantic Ocean with the Pacific Ocean. Some 50 miles long, the Panama Canal is one of the engineering marvels of the 20th century. It is also of immense strategic and commercial importance. The French attempted to dig a canal across Panama in 1881, but this effort failed because of disease (malaria), poor planning and lack of funds. The U.S. obtained rights to dig a canal in 1901; when Colombia (of which Panama was then a part) refused permission to continue in 1903, U.S. President Theodore ROOSEVELT encouraged a successful Panamanian independence movement. Under the Hay-Bunau-Varilla Treaty between the U.S. and Panama, the U.S. obtained the 10-mile-wide PANAMA CANAL ZONE in exchange for $10 million and an annual rent of $250,000. Meanwhile, U.S. Army doctors Walter REED and William C. GORGAS took measures to eliminate the mosquitos whose transmission of yellow fever and malaria had plagued the earlier French effort. U.S. construction of the canal began in 1904. Because the sea level is not the same on the Atlantic and Pacific ends of the canal, three sets of locks had to be constructed to raise and lower ships as they pass from one ocean to the other. The canal was officially opened on August 15, 1914.

The U.S. ownership of the canal has often been a source of friction between Panama and the U.S. The PANAMA CANAL TREATY (1977) provided for the return of the Canal Zone to Panama; the canal was turned over to Panama in 1999. The U.S. exercised its right to protect the canal when U.S. forces invaded Panama in December 1989 to arrest Panamanian strongman Manuel Noriega. On December 31, 1999, the canal was transferred to Panamanian control. (See also PANAMA.)

Panama Canal Zone A strategically significant ribbon of territory 10 miles wide, stretching along both sides of the PANAMA CANAL. The zone was created in 1903 and assigned to U.S. supervision by treaty, but the surrounding country of PANAMA complained about this arrangement as early as 1926. American control of the zone was a sore point for Panamanian nationalists. In a move that caused controversy in the U.S., President Jimmy CARTER formally transferred the Canal Zone to Panama in 1978. On December 31, 1999, the canal was transferred to Panamanian control.

Panama Canal Zone Treaty Agreement of September 7, 1977, between U.S. president CARTER and Panamanian general Torrijos that the U.S. would evacuate its five-mile-wide zone (on each side of the PANAMA CANAL) on De-

PANAMA

1903	Independence from Colombia.
1914	Panama Canal completed; U.S. accorded "sovereign rights" in Canal Treaty.
1925	U.S. troops land to protect U.S. interests during strikes and rent riots.
1936	Canal Treaty revised, rent paid to Panama increased, right of U.S. intervention revoked.
1959	Riots in Panama City protest U.S. flag flying in Canal Zone and not Panama flag.
1972	Brigadier General Omar Torrijos is vested with virtually unlimited power as "Supreme Leader of the Panamanian Revolution."
1977	U.S. promises to turn over canal zone to Panama by the end of 1999.
1980	Former shah of Iran is granted asylum, triggering demonstrations and student violence; shah is persuaded to leave for Egypt.
1988	General Manuel Antonio Noriega, head of Panama Defense Forces, indicted on drug charges in U.S.; President Eric Arturo Delvalle ousted by National Assembly after attempt to dismiss Noriega.
1989	Noriega captured in U.S. invasion of Panama; a Democratic Opposition Alliance candidate who lost election when results were annulled by Noriega, Guillermo Endara, is installed as president with U.S. support.
1992	Noriega is found guilty of drug offenses in a trial in the U.S. and is given a 40-year prison sentence.
1994	Ernesto Pérez Balladares is elected president.
1999	In national elections, Mireya Moscoso, widow of former president Arnulfo Arias and leader of the opposition Arnulfista Party, becomes Panama's first woman president. Panama gains full control of the Panama Canal Zone on December 31.
2004	Martin Torrijos, son of the former dictator Omar Torrijos, wins the presidential election.
2005	President Torrijos seeks to reform the funds-depleted social security system, sparking protests and strikes over proposed increases in pension contributions.

cember 31, 1999. On December 31, 1999, the canal was transferred to Panamanian control.

Panamanian Revolution of 1903 By the Hay-Herrán Treaty, COLOMBIA was to lease the U.S. land across the isthmus of Panama to build a canal. Colombian president José Manuel Moarroquín favored this action, but the Colombian congress rejected the treaty. Phillippe Jean Bunau-Varilla, who held canal-building rights, organized a revolt in PANAMA against Colombia on November 3–4, 1903. The rebels proclaimed independence, the U.S. cruiser *Nashville* deterred landing of Colombian troops to suppress the uprising and U.S. president Theodore ROOSEVELT recognized Panamanian independence on November 6, 1903, and received Bunau-Varilla as its minister. On November 18, 1903, the U.S. and Panama signed the Hay-Bunau-Varilla Treaty, giving the U.S. a lease in perpetuity of a 10-mile-wide strip of land across the isthmus for payments to Panama of $10 million, plus $250,000 annually.

Pan American World Airways (Pan Am) American airline, founded in 1927 by Juan TRIPPE. In the first few decades of its existence, Pan Am established important international air routes and made long-distance passenger air travel an everyday reality. In the late 1950s it was one of the first airlines to introduce jet service, and it was the first airline to have the BOEING 747 jumbo jet in regular service (1970). Following the deregulation of the U.S. airline industry in the 1980s, Pan Am suffered financial losses and ceased operation in 1991. Pan Am later became a regional airline focusing on low-cost flights from the United States to the Caribbean.

Pan Am 103 On December 21, 1988, Pan American flight 103 crashed near the village of Lockerbie, Scotland. All 244 passengers and 15 crew members aboard the 747 jumbo jet were killed in the crash, which also claimed the lives of 11 people on the ground. The flight had originated in Frankfurt, Germany, had stopped over at London's Heathrow Airport and was headed for Kennedy Airport in New York City when the disaster occurred. British and U.S. investigators soon established that the crash was caused by a plastic bomb hidden inside a radio casette recorder placed in passenger luggage. It was further disclosed that the U.S. government had alerted airlines, airports and embassies in Europe of a threat to bomb

Pan Am planes flying from Frankfurt to the U.S. during this period, but that authorities had not informed the flying public. After the crash, responsibility was claimed by a pro-Iranian group calling itself the Guardians of the Islamic Revolution; investigators later identified a group called the Popular Front for the Liberation of Palestine-General Command as the likely criminals. The disaster provoked a tightening of airline security for U.S. airliners operating abroad. The bombing of Pan Am flight 103 is regarded as one of the most heinous of the many terrorist attacks on innocent civilians in the late 20th century. On May 3, 2000, a specially convened Scottish court began the trial of Abdelbaset Ali Mohmed al-Mergrahi and Al Amin Khalifa Fhimah, who stood trial for their involvement in the terrorist attack. The trial ended on January 31, 2001, with the Scottish judges in attendance convicting al-Mergrahi and sentencing him to life imprisonment. The same judges acquitted Fhimah and allowed him to return to Libya. Al-Megrahi and his lawyers immediately appealed the verdict, but that appeal was denied in March 2002.

Pandit, Vijaya Lakshmi (*1900–1990*) Indian diplomat. She was the sister of the first prime minister of INDIA, Jawaharlal NEHRU. When the country gained its independence from Britain in 1947, Nehru appointed her ambassador to the USSR, a post she held from 1947 to 1949. She then served as ambassador to the U.S. from 1949 to 1952. She was the first woman to serve as president of the UNITED NATIONS General Assembly (1953–54). From 1954 to 1961 she was India's high commissioner to Britain. During the 1970s, she became alarmed by the authoritarian character of her niece Indira GANDHI's rule and became a staunch critic of the regime.

Pankhurst, Emmeline Goulden (*1858–1928*) British suffragist. With her husband, the barrister Richard Pankhurst, she founded the Women's Franchise League in 1889. When the LIBERAL PARTY failed to support women's rights, she formed (1903) the more militant Women's Social and Political Union. Joined in the movement by her daughters Christabel Harriette Pank-

British suffragette and women's rights leader Emmeline Pankhurst. 1913 (LIBRARY OF CONGRESS, PRINTS AND PHOTOGRAPHS DIVISION)

hurst (1880–1958) and (Estelle) Sylvia Pankhurst (1882–1960), she and other members engaged in a number of militant actions to further the cause. Repeatedly arrested, she used hunger strikes as a tactic. After the outbreak of WORLD WAR I, she devoted herself to the war effort. She moved to Canada after the war, returning to England in 1926. A revered figure in Great Britain, she died while running for election to Parliament a few weeks after full voting rights had been granted to women.

Panofsky, Erwin (*1892–1968*) German-American art historian. Born in Germany, he received a Ph.D. from the University of Freiburg and taught at the University of Hamburg from 1921 to 1933. Panofsky fled Germany and emigrated to the U.S., where he became a professor of fine arts at New York University and in 1935 joined the faculty at the Institute for Advanced Study, Princeton, New Jersey. One of the most important art historians of the 20th century, he took an early interest in the Italian Renaissance and gradually turned his attention to northern European art of the 15th and 16th centuries. A rigorous scholar, he was intensely concerned with the iconography of the various periods he studied. Among his many works are *Studies in Iconology* (1939, 2nd ed. 1962), *Albrecht Dürer* (1943,

4th ed. 1955), *Early Netherlandish Painting* (1953) and *Renaissance and Renascences in Western Art* (1960).

Papadopoulos, George (*1919–1999*) Greek military officer and political leader. A career officer, Papadopoulos attained the rank of colonel and was a member of the military junta that seized control of the Greek government in 1967. Resigning from the army, Papadopoulos became premier later that year and soon established himself as a harsh and dictatorial ruler. He became regent in 1972, abolished the monarchy and created a republic the following year and named himself president. An unpopular ruler, he was ousted by yet another military coup late in 1973.

Papagos, Alexander (*1883–1955*) Greek military and political leader, prime minister (1952–55). A career officer commissioned in 1906, he was appointed minister of war (1935) and army chief of staff (1936). Commander in chief of the Greek army in WORLD WAR II, he repelled invasion by Italy in 1940, but his forces were defeated by Germany in 1941. After the war he directed the 1949 campaign against communist guerrillas. Again appointed chief of the armed forces in 1950, he resigned to form the conservative Greek Rally Party and became prime minister in 1952. During his term in office, Papagos strengthened Greek ties with the West.

Papal States See the VATICAN.

Papandreou, Andreas (*1919–1996*) Greek political leader. Son of George PAPANDREOU, who served as GREECE's premier from 1963 to 1967, Papandreou immigrated to the U.S. in 1940, where he served in the navy and taught economics at the University of Minnesota and the University of California until returning to Greece in 1959. After his father became premier he renounced his U.S. citizenship and held several government posts, eventually enduring imprisonment and self-imposed exile when his father was overthrown in 1967. He returned to Greece in 1974 and founded a new political party that espoused controversial socialist ideas and opposed U.S. influence and military presence. He was elected premier in 1981, but lost the 1989 election because of charges of misconduct and a marital scandal. Papandreou again served as prime minister from 1993 to 1996, when he retired from politics because of failing health.

Papandreou, George *(1888–1968)*

Greek statesman, three-time premier (1944–45, 1963, 1964–65). Born in Salonika, he became a lawyer and entered political life as an antiroyalist moderate socialist. He served as a member of parliament and was interior minister (1923), was exiled briefly in 1926 and then served in a number of government posts. Again exiled in 1936, he was active in the resistance movement and headed a Greek government-in-exile from 1944 to 1945. Returning to GREECE after WORLD WAR II, he held office in various Social Democratic cabinets from 1946 to 1952. In 1961 he formed the liberal Center Union Party, serving as premier for 55 days in 1963 and again becoming premier the following year. Disputes with King CONSTANTINE II led to his dismissal in 1965. In 1967, after a military coup d'état, Papandreou was arrested and briefly imprisoned. Constantly at odds with the government, he was placed under house arrest a number of times thereafter until his death.

Papen, Franz von *(1879–1969)*

German politician. A military attaché to Washington (1913–15), he was posted to Turkey during World War I, after which he began his political career. A Catholic Center Party member of the Prussian parliament from 1921 to 1932, he was appointed chancellor by Paul von HINDENBURG in 1932 but was soon succeeded by Kurt von Schleicher. Remaining close to Hindenburg, von Papen was instrumental in persuading the aging president to name Adolf HITLER as chancellor in 1933, while Papen himself was appointed vice chancellor. Afterward, he served as German ambassador to Austria (1936–38), helping to prepare for the ANSCHLUSS. For the duration of WORLD WAR II he was ambassador to Turkey. Tried at the NUREMBERG WAR CRIMES TRIALS (1946), von Papen was acquitted, but he was later imprisoned by a German denazification court. He was freed in 1949. Von Papen's memoirs were published in 1952 (Eng. tr., 1953). (See also GERMANY.)

Papp, Joseph (Joseph Papirefsky) *(1921–1991)*

American theatrical director and producer. Born in New York City, Papp was trained at the Actor's Lab in Los Angeles. Since the 1950s he has been one of the most innovative and influential figures in American theater. In 1954 he founded the New York Shakespeare Festival, and in an attempt to make Shakespearean plays available to the general public he staged a variety of productions in Central Park from 1957 to 1962. In 1967 Papp founded the Public Theater, and in 1973 he was appointed director of the Vivian Beaumont and Mitzi C. Newhouse theaters at Lincoln Center. Papp was responsible for introducing a wide array of new playwrights, directors and actors in Broadway and off-Broadway productions. Among his most memorable plays are *Hair* (1967), a musical version of *Two Gentlemen of Verona* (1971), *That Championship Season* (1972), *A Chorus Line* (1975) and *Pirates of Penzance* (1980).

Papua New Guinea

Nation in the southwestern Pacific Ocean, east of Indonesia and north of the northeastern tip of Australia. It occupies the eastern half of the island of New Guinea as well as a number of adjacent islands, including Bougainville in the Solomon Islands and New Britain in the Bismarck Archipelago. Much of this tropical country is mountainous and heavily forested, with exotic fauna and flora. In 1906 British New Guinea became the Territory of Papua, as control was transferred to newly independent Australia. With the outbreak of WORLD WAR I, Australia also took control of German New Guinea, and in 1920 this became a LEAGUE OF NATIONS Mandated Trust Territory under Australian trusteeship. Following Japanese occupation during WORLD WAR II, the eastern half of New Guinea reverted to Australian control as a single colony, the Territory of Papua and New Guinea. In 1963 INDONESIA took control of Dutch New Guinea and incorporated it into the Indonesian state as the territory of Irian Jaya. Papua New Guinea achieved self-government in 1973 and full independence in 1975, with a parliamentary system of government. The country has been ruled by a series of unstable coalitions composed of political parties based on patronage rather than ideology. At independence Papua New Guinea faced serious secessionist threats. Problems of law and order led to the declaration of states of emergency in PORT MORESBY (the capital) in 1979 and 1985, and in the Highlands (where there was severe ethnic unrest) in 1979. Unrest resurfaced on Bougainville island in late 1988, when local landowners demanded compensation for damage done to their land by the island's giant copper mine. Bougainville separatists continued to struggle for independence despite the national government's agreeing to accept a transitional Bougainville government in 1994. Both sides signed a truce in 1997, and in 2001 promised to hold an islandwide referendum in Bougainville as early as 2011. Over 80 percent of the population of 3,800,000 is Papuan; less

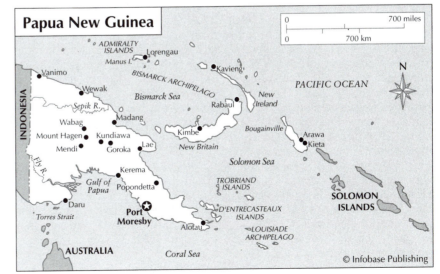

Papua New Guinea

1906	Britain transfers its rights to Australia, which renames the lands Papua.
1914	German New Guinea is occupied by Australia at the outbreak of World War I; from the merged territories, Papua New Guinea is formed.
1920–42	Papua New Guinea is held as a League of Nations mandate by Australia.
1942–45	Papua New Guinea is occupied by Japan.
1973	Achieves self-government.
1975	Papua New Guinea achieves full independence as a dominion within the Commonwealth.
1979	Owing to rioting, a state of emergency is declared in Port Moresby and the Highlands.
1988	The secessionists fight for the independence of the island of Bougainville.
1994	Fighting between the secessionists and the government ends when the opposing parties sign a peace agreement.
1997	A truce ends the hostilities.
2001	Both sides agree to hold a referendum in Bougainville by 2011.

than 15 percent is Melanesian, while Polynesian, Chinese and European minorities comprise the remainder.

Paracel Islands A group of 130 islands located in the South China Sea initially controlled by FRANCE (1932–54), then by VIETNAM (1954–74), and later disputed among China, TAIWAN, and Vietnam (1974–   ). The islands were originally claimed by French troops in Indochina for the construction of an advanced weather station. They were transferred to the control of the interim South Vietnamese government following the 1954 Geneva Conference that ended French control of Indochina. Between 1954 and 1974 the islands were administered by the successive governments of South Vietnam, until military forces from the PEOPLE'S REPUBLIC OF CHINA invaded the islands in 1974 and imprisoned the small South Vietnamese garrison on the archipelago. Since 1974 the island chain has been claimed by

Vietnam, Taiwan, and the People's Republic of China because of its abundant fishing waters and because geological surveys have indicated the presence of major natural gas and oil deposits on the ocean bottom surrounding the islands. The islands themselves have no indigenous inhabitants, although China has maintained small garrisons on the islands since occupying them. In July 2001, at the meeting of the ASEAN REGIONAL FORUM, Vietnam alleged that these military forces and their naval patrol boats were responsible for the illegal seizure of 17 Vietnamese fishing boats and the detaining of their collective crews of 200 men.

In 1997 China announced its plans to transform the island chain into a tourist attraction and has since improved the port facilities on two of the larger islands, Woody Island and Duncan Island. Chinese contractors began construction in the mid-1990s on a military airport to service the island

chain. The airport's construction was completed in 2001.

Parade Landmark French cubist ballet, the collaboration of impresario Serge DIAGHILEV, composer Erik SATIE, designer Pablo PICASSO and choreographer Leonide MASSINE. Begun in 1915, it was premiered by the BALLETS RUSSES at the Théâtre du Châtelet in Paris on May 18, 1917. The stage action depicts the street efforts by a number of circus performers—magicians, acrobats, cowboys and animals—to lure passersby into the show. Even if the pedestrians on stage are ultimately unimpressed by it all, the production itself exploded like a grenade in the face of the ballet world. Subsequent performances were jeered, and Satie almost came to blows with a hostile critic. Singled out for derision were Picasso's nine-foot-tall, wooden Cubist sculpture; costumes that included mobile skyscrapers; and Satie's use of sound effects in the orchestra—typewriters, police sirens and airplane engines. (See also CUBISM.)

Paraguay (Republic of Paraguay) Located in central South America, Paraguay covers an area of 157,006 square miles. From 1900 to 1935 Paraguay suffered economic chaos and violence from power struggles between two opposing political parties. Paraguay was united only when it defeated Bolivia during the CHACO WAR (1932–35), fought over Bolivia's attempt to control the upper Paraguay River. The untimely death of popular president Marshall José Félix Estigarribia (1939–40) led to the provisional presidency of General Higinio Moringo, which ended in the 1947 revolts, leaving thousands dead. After six presidents in as many years, General Alfredo STROESSNER became dictator in 1954, establishing economic and political stability during his 35-year rule. He was overthrown in 1989, and new elections were held, bringing General Andrés Rodríguez to the presidency. Under a new constitution that was approved in 1992, the National Republican Association (Colorado) Party won the 1993 parliamentary and presidential elections. However, the government has been continually beset by corruption, leading to the resignation of President Raúl Cubas (1998–99), and the near impeachment of President

Paraguay

1904	Argentine-backed liberals take control from Brazilian-backed Colorado Party.
1932	Chaco War; Bolivia attempts conquest of huge jungle area with rumored oil reserves and access to navigable rivers; Paraguay holds out against an army three times the size of its own; economy is exhausted.
1935	Treaty with Bolivia; Paraguay gains territory, grants access to rivers.
1936	Army ejects liberals.
1939	War hero General Estigarribia elected; begins building state-dominated society in line with national traditions of authoritarianism.
1940	Estigarribia killed in plane crash.
1944	Paraguay allows wide activity by Axis powers, but still receives massive U.S. military aid.
1945	Declares war on Axis, just prior to end of war.
1947	Liberals revolt; thousands killed.
1954	After six presidents attempt to govern in six years, General Alfredo Stroessner seizes power; establishes brutal dictatorship.
1959	Invasion of exiles from Brazil and Argentina crushed; agreement with Japan brings settlers to forested regions.
1960	Stroessner cements ties with U.S., which aids development projects.
1961	Friendship Bridge completes first direct road link to Atlantic ports.
1973	World's largest hydroelectric project completed at Itaipu, in partnership with Brazil.
1980	Former Nicaraguan dictator Somoza, granted asylum by Stroessner, is assassinated in Asunción; relations with Nicaragua broken off.
1987	Under pressure from Catholic Church and U.S., Stroessner relaxes martial law.
1989	Military coup overthrows Stroessner; free elections put General Rodríguez, coup leader, in power.
1993	National Republican Association (Colorado) Party wins national elections.
1995	President Juan Carlos Wasmosy forcibly retires two senior military officials who question his authority.
1996	President Wasmosy dismisses General Lino César Oviedo for engaging in political activity; Oviedo refuses dismissal and is arrested for insurrection.
1997	General Oviedo wins the Colorado Party nomination for president.
1998	General Oviedo sentenced to 10 years in prison for coup attempt; Oviedo's running mate, Raúl Cubas Grau, is chosen Colorado Party candidate for president; Cubas is elected president and pardons Oviedo.
1999	Congress impeaches Cubas, who resigns and flees the country with Oviedo. Luis González Macchi becomes president.
2000	Julio César Franco of the Liberal Party is elected vice president, breaking the 50-year-old hold on power of the Colorado Party.
2003	Presidential elections won by the Colorado Party and Nicanor Duarte Frutos is sworn in. His predecessor, Luis González Macchi, is put on trial for corruption charges.
2004	Peasants invade landholding demanding redistribution. More than 400 are killed in Asunción shopping center fire.

Paraguay

Luis González Macchi (1999–2003) in 2002. In 2003 Nicanor Duarte Frutos was elected president and, in the same year, Macchi was put on trial for corruption. Disaster struck in 2004 when more than 400 people were killed in a fire at a shopping center in Asunción.

Paramount Pictures One of HOLLYWOOD's "Big Five" production/exhibition motion picture studios (along with METRO-GOLDWYN-MAYER, WARNER BROS., RKO and 20TH CENTURY-FOX). In 1912 Adolph ZUKOR, a furrier turned entrepreneur, incorporated the Famous Players Film Company, which successfully launched a series of prestige movie adaptations of popular stage plays, including *Queen Elizabeth* with Sarah BERNHARDT. In 1916 Famous Players merged with the Jesse L. Lasky Feature Play Company, which boasted a roster of stage and screen talent including David BELASCO, Samuel GOLDWYN and Cecil B. DE MILLE. (The Lasky-De Mille *The Squaw Man* [1913] had been one of the first

feature-length movies made in the Hollywood/Los Angeles area.) The distribution network for Famous Players-Lasky was Paramount, formed in 1914 by W.W. Hodkinson. By 1917 other production companies began releasing through Paramount, including Artcraft, which had two of the biggest movie stars in the world under contract, Mary PICKFORD and Douglas FAIRBANKS. Acquisition of more movie theaters began in the 1920s. Zukor took over the business operations in New York City and Jesse Lasky oversaw the productions in Hollywood. In 1930 the corporate name became the Paramount Publix Corporation. Although Paramount was by now one of the biggest studios in the U.S., GREAT DEPRESSION-related difficulties forced it into bankruptcy in 1933. Lasky was forced out. Zukor became chairman of the board when it was reorganized in 1935 as Paramount Pictures. The 1930s and '40s were Paramount's peak period as the studio continued the policy originated by Famous Players of

utilizing talent developed in other media, radio, recording, vaudeville and the legitimate stage. Top directors included Ernst LUBITSCH, Rouben MAMOULIAN, Josef von STERNBERG and Billy WILDER. Stars included Mae WEST, Jeanette MacDonald, the MARX BROTHERS, W.C. FIELDS, Bing CROSBY, Gary COOPER and Martin and LEWIS. Some of the most successful pictures were Preston STURGES comedies (*The Lady Eve,* 1941), musicals (*Holiday Inn,* 1942) and the Crosby-Hope "Road" pictures (*Road to Zanzibar,* 1943). Later releases included several Alfred HITCHCOCK pictures (*Vertigo,* 1958, and *Psycho,* 1960); the Francis Ford COPPOLA *GODFATHER* series; the *Star Trek* series; and the Indiana Jones series. In 1949, along with other major Hollywood studios, Paramount was forced by government action to divest itself of its theater chains. Gulf and Western Industries acquired the studio in 1966.

Pâris de Bollardière, Jacques-Marie-Roch-André (*1907–1986*) French pacifist. He was a hero of the French RESISTANCE during WORLD WAR II who became a general in the French army. He caused an uproar in 1957, when he asked to be relieved of his command in ALGERIA to protest the torture of Algerian rebels. In 1961 he retired from active duty and began to emerge as an outspoken pacifist. His participation in a 1973 protest expedition to France's South Pacific nuclear testing site of Mururoa led to his being struck from the French army reserve list.

Parish, Mrs. Henry (Sister) II (*1910–1994*) Leading American interior decorator best known for the development of an informal or casual style in large and often elaborate residential projects. Parish (widely known by the familiar "Sister," as she was called by her family) began practice in 1933 without formal training, taking on projects for friends and, as her reputation grew, for many wealthy and well-known clients. Her style was eclectic, her rooms comfortably cluttered with a profusion of antiques and accessories. During the 1960s she took on the redecoration of the White House for the KENNEDYs, working toward historic restoration with the use of appropriate antiques and decorative elements. From 1962, Mrs. Parish continued in practice, with Albert Hadley as a partner, in the firm of Parish-Hadley Associates, Inc.

Paris Peace Accord (1973)

A cease-fire agreement intended to end the VIETNAM WAR. The pact was formally signed on January 27, 1973, by representatives of the four parties directly involved in the conflict—the U.S., North Vietnam, South Vietnam and the VIET CONG. The battlefield truce went into effect at 8 A.M., January 28, Saigon time. The pact also called for the withdrawal of all American troops from South Vietnam, the communist release of all U.S. PRISONERS OF WAR and a four-nation commission to police the truce. It did not provide a political solution to the conflict, but allowed North Vietnamese troops to remain in the south and called for an eventual reunification of the country "through peaceful means." The pact was worked out by U.S. National Security Advisor Henry KISSINGER, North Vietnamese foreign minister LE DUC THO and other negotiators at the Paris peace conference over a number of months. (Kissinger and Le Duc Tho were subsequently awarded the 1973 NOBEL PRIZE for peace. The choice met with much controversy.) Kissinger and Le Duc Tho initialed the plan on January 23. That day, U.S. president Richard M. NIXON announced the end of the war, calling the peace plan "an honorable agreement." South Vietnamese

U.S. Secretary of State William P. Rogers signs the agreement to end the Vietnam War. 1973. (LIBRARY OF CONGRESS, PRINTS AND PHOTOGRAPHS DIVISION)

president Nguyen Van THIEU simultaneously announced the pact in South Vietnam but expressed doubt about the permanence of the agreement. Many historians believe that the Paris agreement was intended solely to allow an orderly, face-saving U.S. withdrawal from VIETNAM and to create the semblance of a peaceful solution. The last American troops were withdrawn on March 29, 1973. In January 1975 the North Vietnamese launched their final offensive, capturing SAIGON and forcing South Vietnam to surrender (April 30). The North Vietnamese thus achieved the victory they had sought from the beginning of the war.

Paris Peace Conference

Multinational post–WORLD WAR I congress held by the victorious countries, 27 in all, led by the "Big Four"—Great Britain's LLOYD GEORGE, France's CLEMENCEAU, Italy's Orlando and the U.S.'s WILSON. It convened on January 18, 1919, and held its last session on January 16, 1920. The results of this often tumultuous and conflict-ridden conference were embodied in a number of treaties that officially terminated the war and fixed postwar settlement terms for each of the defeated nations. They were the VERSAILLES TREATY (Germany), St. Germain (Austria), Neuilly (Bulgaria), Trianon (Hungary) and SÈVRES (Turkey). The most significant of these, the Versailles Treaty of May 1919, forced Germany to admit its guilt in the war; severely limited German rearmament; ceded territory (Alsace and Lorraine restored to France, Prussian Poland and a majority of West Prussia to Poland); provided for many of the reparations demanded by France; placed the Saar and the Rhineland under allied occupation and called for a number of plebiscites in freed territories. The Paris Peace Conference largely rejected Woodrow Wilson's FOURTEEN POINTS, but it did accept his proposed LEAGUE OF NATIONS, which was officially approved in April 1919. The conference was marred by the squabbling of countries that sought their own national goals rather than a reasoned consensus and by the forced lack of participation of the defeated powers, who came to bitterly resent terms that were not agreed upon by

all the parties but dictated by the victors to the vanquished.

Paris Peace Treaties

Post–WORLD WAR II treaties signed in Paris on February 10, 1947, between the Allies and the principal European supporters of Germany. They were the result of a 21-nation Allied conference that began in July 1946. In separate documents, treaties were signed between the Allies and Italy, Romania, Hungary, Bulgaria and Finland. Terms of the treaties included the ceding of some territory by Italy, Finland and Hungary, colonial losses by Italy, the creation of Trieste as a free city and various border agreements. These terms were not harsh, largely because the nations involved had made separate peace agreements with the Allies and had opposed Germany by the time WORLD WAR II ended.

Paris student demonstrations

Protest demonstrations held by French students in the spring of 1968 to protest the government's large expenditure on the military and lack of funding for education and social programs and to demand curriculum reform. A massed group of students demonstrated on the Left Bank on May 2 and was attacked by police. Rioting ensued, with the students supported by workers, who staged the longest general strike in French history. The ferment did not cease until late June and almost destroyed the Gaullist government and the Fifth Republic. As a result of the demonstrations, the students were promised reforms and the workers were given a large pay increase.

Park Chung Hee (1917–1979)

Korean general and politician; president of SOUTH KOREA (1963–79). Park began his military career in the Japanese army in WORLD WAR II. At the war's end he joined the South Korean army. Rising to major general, in 1961 he led a coup that deposed the South Korean government. Park was elected president in 1963 and pursued a successful policy of economic modernization. However, intolerant of any dissent, he declared martial law in 1971 and imprisoned opposition leaders. A failed assassination attempt in 1974 killed his wife. In 1979 he was assassinated by the head of the Korean Central Intelligence Agency during a meeting.

Parker, Bonnie See BONNIE AND CLYDE.

Parker, Charlie "Bird" *(1920–1955)* American alto saxophonist. Charlie Parker is a prime exemplar of the archetypal and inspired jazz virtuoso. His advanced technique, soaring sound and constant quest for extending jazzdom's basic theme-and-variation approach led him to the sophisticated, post–World War II style best known as BEBOP. Parker's musical roots were in Kansas City, whose easygoing, bluesy swing was based on slightly altered repetitions of "riffs," or motifs. His unique contribution came with his capacity to invent ever new and complex motivic variations at innovatively brisk tempos; also significant was his ability to swing with a free-flowing yet insistent momentum. Indeed, throughout the 1950s, Parker's transcendent solo style became the benchmark against which other improvisors were measured.

Historically, Parker and his fellow boppers are pivotal because of their role in transforming jazz from an essentially popular, big band dance music to a small group affair in which inspired, sound-of-surprise virtuosity became the prime value. Parker also contributed to the repertory of jazz standards with "Ornithology," "Now's the Time" and "Scrapple from the Apple." In the conformist postwar period of the late 1940s–50s, Parker became a major cult figure, a larger-than-life icon whose genius was seen as expressed not only in his music, but also in an unorthodox and tragic lifestyle influenced by drug and alcohol addiction. Parker's story is the subject of two important films, the documentary *Celebrating Bird* (1987) by Gary Giddins, and Clint EASTWOOD's docu-drama feature, *Bird* (1988).

Parker, Dorothy (Dorothy Rothschild) *(1893–1967)* American poet, short story writer and one of the outstanding satirists and wits of her generation. While working as the drama critic for *Vanity Fair* magazine (1917–20) and theater critic/book reviewer for *The NEW YORKER* (1927–33), she became a legendary figure in the New York literary scene, noted for her acid quips and wry comebacks. A member of the famous Round Table of wits at the Algonquin Hotel during the 1920s and '30s, she soon established a reputation for plangent lyrics and ironic short stories, all beautifully crafted literary miniatures. Among her poetry collections are *Enough Rope* (1926), *Death and Taxes* (1931) and *Deep as a Well* (1936). Her short story collections include *Laments for the Living* (1930) and *After Such Pleasures* (1933), which contains "Big Blonde," her single most famous story. Parker was also a playwright, screenwriter and correspondent. Her *Collected Stories* were published in 1942, the *Collected Poetry* in 1944.

Parks, Gordon *(1912–2006)* American photographer and filmmaker. After working as a photographer for the Farm Security Administration and for Standard Oil, Parks worked as a staff photographer for *Life* magazine from 1948 to 1968. In 1969 he directed the film based on his novel *The Learning Tree*, and in 1971 he began making his *Shaft* detective films, making him the first black director of major Hollywood releases.

Parks, Rosa (Rosa Louise McCauley Parks) *(1913–2005)* American Civil Rights heroine. Born in Tuskegee, Alabama, Rosa Louise McCauley attended the Montgomery Industrial School for girls and Alabama State Teachers College before marrying Raymond Parks and becoming an activist in the local chapter of the NATIONAL ASSOCIATION FOR THE ADVANCEMENT OF COLORED PEOPLE in Montgomery, Alabama. On December 1, 1955, she was arrested and fined for refusing to give up her seat to a white man on a municipal bus in the rigidly segregated city. The young pastor of the Dexter Avenue Baptist Church, Dr. MARTIN LUTHER KING, JR., organized a boycott of the city-owned bus company that dramatized the plight of black people in the Deep South and led to a Supreme Court decision that reversed her conviction and outlawed racial segregation in public transportation. The MONTGOMERY BUS BOYCOTT is regarded by most historians as the beginning of the modern Civil Rights movement in the United States. In later life Rosa Parks became a symbol of the opposition to racial discrimination in America. She was awarded the Presidential Medal of Freedom by President Bill CLINTON in 1996 and a Congressional Gold Medal 1999. After her death in Detroit in 2005, her casket lay in state in the rotunda of the United States Capitol, as thousands of admirers of her courageous act 50 years earlier paid their last respects to this early pioneer of the American Civil Rights movement.

Parra, Nicanor *(1914–)* Chilean poet. Educated at the University of Chile, Brown and Oxford, Parra has had a career as a teacher of mathematics and physics. His first book was *Cancionero sin nombre* (1937), but he achieved his fame with *Poemas y antipoemas* (1954), which has been translated both as *Antipoems* (1960) and *Poems and Antipoems* (1967). As an "antipoet"—a freewheeling iconoclast who seeks to deflate the intellectual pretensions of poetry as a form—Parra's influence and stature in Chilean letters are second only to Pablo NERUDA, his collaborator for the prose work *Discuros* (1962). His *Obra gruesa* (1969) has also been translated as *Emergency Poems* (1972).

Parri, Ferruccio *(1889–1981)* Italian politician. During the 1930s Parri played a leading role in the underground opposition to Benito MUSSOLINI. He later led the largest Italian partisan group in the guerrilla war against German occupation at the end of WORLD WAR II. He founded the short-lived Action Party and was named premier of ITALY in June 1945. His six-party coalition lasted only five months before two of the groups withdrew in protest over his plan to dismantle some large corporations. He was later a founding member of the Italian Republican Party. In 1963, as an independent leftist, he was appointed senator for life.

Parrish, Frederick Maxfield *(1870–1966)* American painter known for his murals and commercial illustrations. "The work of no American artist," writes Coy Ludwig, "was . . . more familiar in the United States during the first three decades of this century than that of Maxfield Parrish." Born in Philadelphia, Parrish traveled widely during his youth and received artistic encouragement from his father, entering the Pennsylvania Academy of Fine Arts in 1892. From his studio, "The Oaks," in New Hampshire he took advantage of the flourishing print media of the day. Around the turn of the 20th century he began producing the numerous book illustrations, calendars and posters that quickly established him as one of America's most prominent illustrators. His most famous book illustrations include those for Kenneth Grahame's *Dream Days* (1900), Eugene Field's *Poems of Childhood* (1904) and *The Arabian Nights* (1907). He regularly worked for such major magazines as *Harper's Weekly, Scribner's Magazine* and *Collier's*. His elegant whimsies contributed to the advertising of products such as Jello-O, Fisk tires and General Electric Mazda Lamps.

Parrish also dominated the art-print market. *Garden of Allah* (1918) and *Daybreak* (1922), for example, made him, as reported by TIME magazine in 1936, one of the three most popular artists in the world (with Van Gogh and Cézanne). His extraordinary murals, including the 18 panels he painted for the Curtis Publishing Company in Philadelphia, are among his most significant achievements. His work is distinguished by monumental, draped figures, Greco-Roman architectural elements—particularly pillars—luminous light (particularly the color blue) and a determined theatricality that balances the graceful with the grotesque. "My theory is that you should use all the objects of nature . . . as stage properties on which to hang your idea." He worked until his 91st year, when arthritis forced him to lay aside his brushes.

Parsons, Talcott *(1902–1979)* American sociologist and social theorist. Parsons's 46-year teaching career at Harvard University (1927–73) helped to mold three generations of sociologists. His theory of human behavior, once described as "vast and tangled, a veritable jungle of fine distinctions and intertwining classifications," was not fully understood by many sociologists.

Parti Québécois (Canada) Separatist political party in the province of Quebec, CANADA. The Parti Québécois (or PQ) rose to power in Quebec in the 1970s behind its energetic leader, René LEVESQUE. The separatist movement had gained momentum and some credibility when Charles de Gaulle, president of France, announced "Vive le Québec libre" during a visit to Montreal. However, once in power the party's referenda to begin negotiations to secede from Canada were twice rejected by provincial voters, and the party lost the next election to the Liberals. A newer generation of PQ separatists tried to prevail where the older generation failed, in light of voter disappointment with the rejection of the so-called Meach Lake agreement that would have given Quebec a special status within the Canadian confederation. The Parti campaigned vigorously during a 1995 referendum on independence; however, the measure lost narrowly, with 50.58% voting to remain with Canada.

Partisan Review American literary quarterly, founded in 1934. The *Partisan Review* has long been one of the leading "little magazines" of America, but it exercised an especially great influence from the 1930s to the 1950s, when its liberal-to-left political viewpoints and its combination of sociological analysis and literary criticism made it an intellectual focal point. Coedited by Philip Rahv for over 30 years, its leading writers included critic Lionel TRILLING, poets Randall JARRELL and Delmore SCHWARTZ and fiction writer Saul BELLOW. In 2003 the *Partisan Review* created a controversy when it published "Tolerating Intolerance: The Challenge of Fundamentalist Islam in western Europe," which suggested that the presence of a large Islamic minority in western European nations was a potential future threat to the security of Western societies.

Partnership for Peace An intergovernmental organization created in January 1994 by members of NORTH ATLANTIC TREATY ORGANIZATION (NATO) to preserve and improve Europe's security and political and economic stability, both within the alliance and between NATO nations and the formerly communist states of eastern Europe. By 1997 the Partnership for Peace encompassed 27 states in eastern, central and western Europe. The partnership was originally designed to assuage Russian security concerns about the repercussions for Russian security interests of the admission of former WARSAW PACT members to NATO; it also provided for greater political and military cooperation between NATO forces and those former nations intent on preserving their independence from Russia. The partnership was put under strain by NATO's decision in 1997 to admit POLAND, the CZECH REPUBLIC and HUNGARY—three former Warsaw Pact members—to membership. Since then, the Partnership for Peace has helped reduce the animus between RUSSIA and NATO. The U.S., which strongly supported the addition of eastern European states in 1997, arranged for Russia's designation as a consultative member of NATO.

Partsalides, Dimitrios *(1901–1980)* Greek politician. Born in the Turkish port of Trabzon, Partsalides went to GREECE as a refugee after the GRECO-TURKISH WAR OF 1921–22. He became involved in the Greek communist movement in the 1930s. During the GREEK CIVIL WAR (1946–49) he was designated prime minister by the communist insurgent movement but never actually held the post.

Pascin, Jules (Julius Pincas) *(1885–1930)* American painter. Born in Vidin, Bulgaria, Pascin first became known for the sketches he did around 1903 for Munich's satirical newspaper *Simplicissimus*. He moved to Paris in 1905, settled in the U.S. and became a citizen in 1914. Pascin traveled widely and was a well-known bohemian figure in Paris, where he again settled in 1922 and where he committed suicide eight years later. He was a splendid draftsman, and his sensuous paintings have an elegant line and pastel tonality. Among his characteristic works are *Young Woman in Red* (1924, Musée d'Art Moderne, Paris) and *Ginette and Mireille* (1929, Petit Palais, Paris). Pascin was also a talented printmaker and book illustrator.

Pashtun A Pashto-speaking ethnic group in Pakistan and Afghanistan that assumed great political and diplomatic importance during the reign of the Taliban-controlled government of Afghanistan (1996–2001) and after the TALIBAN's overthrow (2001–). In Afghanistan, Pashtuns make up approximately 45 percent of the nation's population (and 11 percent of the population in Pakistan), making them the most important constituency from which any government in AFGHANISTAN must derive support. During the civil war in Afghanistan between the Soviet-supported People's Democratic Party (PDP) and the various factions of the MUJAHIDEEN (1979–91), both sides were in large part dominated by Pashtuns. Between 1994 and 2001, key Pashtun elements lent their support to the Taliban, a political-religious movement that began in KANDAHAR and espoused ISLAMISM, which called for strict Islamic law throughout the country. Following the overthrow of the Taliban by American military forces in 2001, one of the key international concerns of American officials was to ensure that the successor government would obtain and retain the support of the Pashtuns. In an effort to curry favor among Pashtun communities, the U.S. supported the selection of HAMID KARZAI, an ethnic Pashtun living in exile among the Pashtun community of PAKISTAN, as the interim leader of the Afghanistan state.

Pašić, Nikola (1845–1926) Serbian statesman. He was trained as an engineer but soon turned to politics and was elected to the Serbian parliament in 1878. That year he formed the Serbian Radical Party, a group dedicated to the creation of a greater Serbia, which he headed for the rest of his life. Exiled from 1883 to 1889, he returned and became premier of Serbia in 1891, the first of many times he was to serve in that office. He was extremely powerful in Serbia during the years preceding WORLD WAR I and led the country throughout it. After the 1917 overthrow of the Russian monarchy, which he had supported, Pašić negotiated the formation of the Kingdom of the Serbs, Croats and Slovenes (later YUGOSLAVIA). A delegate at the PARIS PEACE CONFERENCE, he was the increasingly conservative premier of Yugoslavia during most of the years from 1921 until his death.

Pasolini, Pier Paolo (1922–1975) Italian director and writer. Often controversial, Pasolini was a gifted film director and writer who focused on the seamier side of life and used nonprofessionals to play his characters. He published his first novel, *Ragazzi di vita* (*Children of Light*), in 1954 and

wrote his first screenplay, for *Woman of the River,* in 1955. In 1961 he directed his first film, *Accattone.* International acclaim came with his award-winning film *The Gospel According to St. Matthew* (1964). Pasolini's evocation of the sensuality and richness of the medieval world was seen in *The Decameron* (1971), *The Canterbury Tales* (1972) and *The Arabian Nights* (1974). He was murdered in 1975.

Pass Laws Legislation in SOUTH AFRICA requiring black South Africans to carry passbooks (internal passports) at all times. Instituted in the 1950s, the laws severely restricted blacks' freedom of movement and were a source of black discontent. The pass laws were repealed in 1986.

Pasternak, Boris (1890–1960) Russian poet and novelist widely acknowledged as one of the greatest Russian writers of the 20th century. The son of the noted portrait painter Leonid Pasternak and his wife, pianist Rosa Pasternak, Pasternak grew up in a comfortable Moscow household. His parents entertained such famous figures as Leo Tolstoy, Rainer Maria RILKE and Aleksandr SCRIABIN, who made a lasting impression on the young Pasternak. Educated in Russia and at Heidelberg, he studied art, music and philosophy be-

Russian author Boris Pasternak (LIBRARY OF CONGRESS. PRINTS AND PHOTOGRAPHS DIVISION)

fore turning to literature. His first collection of poetry was *A Twin in the Clouds* (1914), but it was his third volume, *Sister, My Life* (1922), that established his reputation, which he was to maintain with many subsequent poetic works. Pasternak experienced the RUSSIAN REVOLUTION as an observer rather than as a participant, and for most of his life he remained as apolitical as he was prudent. During the 1920s and into the early '30s he received official approval to go with his critical acclaim. However, following differences with Joseph STALIN in the mid-1930s, Pasternak was unable to publish his own work for several years. (Stalin's apparent respect for and fear of Pasternak, whom he could have easily destroyed, remains one of the fascinating mysteries of the Soviet dictator's behavior.) During this time he occupied himself with translating the works of Shakespeare, Shelley and others into Russian. Sometime after WORLD WAR II Pasternak began writing the work for which he is best known in the West, the novel *DOCTOR ZHIVAGO.* The manuscript was smuggled into Italy for publication in 1957. Awarded the NOBEL PRIZE for literature in 1958, Pasternak was denounced by the Soviet government and forced to refuse the award. *Doctor Zhivago* remained unpublished in the USSR until 1987. Yevgeny Pasternak, the author's son, accepted his father's Nobel Prize medal at a ceremony in Stockholm on December 10, 1989. Among Pasternak's other books is *Safe Conduct* (1931).

Pastrana, Andrés (1958–) Conservative Colombian politician and president of COLOMBIA (1998–2002). After winning election to the Colombian Senate in 1991, Pastrana was defeated for the presidency of the country by Ernesto Samper in 1994. In 1998 he won election to the presidency based in part on his campaign promise that, if elected, he would meet with leaders from the Colombian leftist guerrilla group FARC, in an effort to end the ongoing civil war between the rebels and the government.

Pastrana and his subordinates repeatedly met with FARC representatives, and in November 1998 he agreed to give FARC a safe haven within Colombia roughly the size of Switzerland that would be completely free of government interference. Although Pastrana's policies initially resulted in better relations between the government and FARC, by February 2002 FARC had resumed its insurgency, kidnapping high-level politicians. Pastrana responded with military strikes on FARC strongholds. Pastrana's valiant efforts to negotiate with the leftist guerrillas both improved Colombia's standing in the international community, and resulted in increased financial aid from the U.S., as President George W. BUSH proclaimed Colombia an ally in the "War on Terrorism." Barred constitutionally from seeking reelection, Pastrana was succeeded in the presidency by independent candidate Álvaro Uribe Vélez in 2002.

Pastrone, Giovanni (*1883–1959*) Italian motion picture pioneer, director and producer at the turn of the 20th century. Born in Montechiaro d'Asti, he began his film career in one of Italy's first studios, Rossi (later ITALA FILMS), in Turin. Quickly he distinguished himself as both a studio manager and a filmmaker. He created a chain of movie theaters throughout Italy to show the Itala product and with his one-reel *La caduta di Troia* (*The Fall of Troy*) displayed the traits that would make him world famous— a flair for spectacle and skill at handling crowds. His most important film was the feature-length *Cabiria* (1914), a landmark mixture of historical spectacle and revolutionary camera work that had an enormous impact upon the epic ambitions of American director D.W. GRIFFITH. Made under the nominal imprimatur of esteemed Italian playwright Gabriele D'ANNUNZIO, it established Italy as the dominant country in film production at the time. Its central character, the strongman "Maciste" (Bartolomei Pagano), starred in several subsequent Pastrone-directed vehicles. Under the pseudonym "Piero Fosco" he also directed several intimate chamber dramas, including *Hedda Gabler* (1919). He was Italy's first great impresario/filmmaker. Today he is less well-known for his technical innovations, which included camera supports and projection lamps. He left Itala Films in 1919 and retired from the business, devoting the rest of his life to medical research.

Patasse, Ange (*1937– *) Prime minister (1976–78) of the Central African Empire under Emperor BOKASSA. Patasse held a variety of cabinet posts from 1965 until he became prime minister in 1976. Ousted in July 1978, he formed an opposition council in exile in Paris. He later opposed President Kolinba and was again forced into exile. (See also CENTRAL AFRICAN REPUBLIC.)

Pathet Lao Communist guerrilla movement in LAOS. From 1954 to 1973 the Pathet Lao were involved in a civil war against pro-American, royalist army officers. Following the ceasefire of 1973 a royalist-communist coalition government held office until the communist victory in VIETNAM (1975) led to a complete communist takeover of Laos.

Paton, Alan Stewart (*1903–1988*) South African author. Paton was educated as a physicist and mathematician at the University of Natal and subsequently taught at various South African institutions. Paton established his reputation with his first and best-known novel, CRY, THE BELOVED COUNTRY (1948; filmed 1951), which was an early and eloquent plea for racial equality in SOUTH AFRICA. This was followed by *Too Late the Phalarope* (1953, adapted as a play, 1965), another successful social commentary in which a young, white South African is imprisoned because of his love affair with a black woman. Paton wrote many works of nonfiction, including *The Land and People of South Africa* (1955) and the autobiography *Towards the Mountain* (1980), before his next novel, *Ah, But Your Land Is Beautiful,* appeared in 1981. The novel, which depicts the beginning of the antiapartheid movement, includes details about the Liberal Party of South Africa, of which Paton was founder and president from 1958 to 1968, when it was banned. A second volume of autobiography, *Journey Continued,* was published in 1988.

Patterson, Floyd (*1935–2006*) American boxer. In 1952 Patterson won an Olympic gold medal as a heavyweight. He then turned professional and began the three-year climb that would lead to a shot at the title left open by Rocky MARCIANO's retirement. He took the title in 1956 and successfully defended it until a 1959 loss to Ingemar Johans-

son of Sweden. The following year, Patterson became the first man ever to retake the title as he defeated Johansson in a rematch. He lost the title for the last time to Sonny Liston in 1962 but continued to fight until he was defeated by Muhammad ALI in 1972.

Patterson, William A. (*1899–1980*) American pioneer in the commercial aviation industry. Patterson was the first president of United Airlines (1934–66) and helped build the company into what at the time was the world's largest private airline. He introduced a number of major innovations that transformed passenger flying from a hazardous adventure into a routine occurrence. In the 1930s he introduced the use of female flight attendants and guaranteed monthly pay for pilots. In the 1950s he made United the first airline to commit itself to the jet aircraft.

Patton, George S(mith), Jr. (*1885–1945*) American general noted for his exploits during WORLD WAR II. Born into a distinguished military family in San Gabriel, California, he attended West Point, was commissioned in 1909 and commanded a tank brigade in France during WORLD WAR I. A swashbuckling figure and daring tactician, he became a master of armored warfare. During World War II he was a corps commander (1942–43) in the invasions of North Africa and Sicily. As commander of the 3rd Army (1944–45) after the invasion of NORMANDY, Patton spearheaded the brilliant sweep of American troops from Normandy, through France and into Germany. He was instrumental in stopping the

U.S. general George Patton (LIBRARY OF CONGRESS, PRINTS AND PHOTOGRAPHS DIVISION)

German offensive in the battle of the BULGE (December 1944–January 1945) and relieving the besieged American troops at BASTOGNE. He later sped across the Rhine, through Germany and into Czechoslovakia. Briefly military governor of Bavaria at the end of the war, he headed the 15th Army in 1945 but was fatally injured in an automobile accident soon after his appointment. Patton's brilliant record was somewhat marred by a much-publicized incident in which he slapped a combat-weary soldier during a hospital visit, an incident for which he later apologized. His unfavorable views on the USSR, then a U.S. ally, were also outspoken and controversial. Patton's memoirs, *War as I Knew It,* were published posthumously in 1947; his wartime service was later the basis of the motion picture *Patton* (1970).

Paul VI **(Giovanni Montini)** *(1897–1978)* Supreme pontiff of the Roman Catholic Church. Montini was born in Concesio, Italy, the son of a member of the Italian parliament who also edited a Catholic newspaper. Ordained as a priest in 1920, he was papal secretary of state from 1924 to 1954 and was subsequently named archbishop of Milan. In 1958 he became a cardinal. Montini—taking the name Paul VI—succeeded Pope JOHN XXIII in June 1963 and oversaw the final work of the ecumenical SECOND VATICAN COUNCIL that had been initiated by his papal predecessor. Paul VI broke with historical tradition by becoming the first pope to travel to non-European nations—including visits to Israel and India in 1964, the UNITED NATIONS headquarters in New York City in 1965, a tour of Latin America in 1968 and missions to Uganda in 1969 and Australia and the Philippines in 1970. As to matters of dogma, Paul VI was conservative on the controversial issue of birth control but advocated a liberalized usage of the vernacular in church ritual. He died of a heart attack in 1978.

Paul, Robert William *(1869–1943)* Pioneering British motion picture director, producer and inventor at the turn of the century. Born in Highbury, England, he studied engineering. Learning about the Edison recording and peep-show devices (the Kinetoscope and Kinematograph) used in America, he devised similar machines himself—

the first such machines in England. A year later, in collaboration with Great Britain's first cameraman, Birt Acres, he began experimenting and filming actualities and music hall acts. The effects of fast, slow and reverse motion, he claimed, were inspired in part from a novel by his friend H.G. WELLS, *The Time Machine.* By 1895 Paul was making short films in the first British film studio, located in North London, and projecting them in music halls with his own patented Theatrographe (later renamed the Animatographe). *The Twins' Tea Party* (1897) contains an early use of the closeup. A trick film called *The Motorist* (1905) has a simple plot where, in Paul's words, a motorcar eludes a pursuing policeman by climbing up the side of a house and "goes motoring right across the clouds, makes a friendly call on the sun . . . then resumes its cloudy journey, and reaches the planet Saturn." He made his last film, *The Butterfly,* in 1910 and then, disinterested in the growing sophistication of story films, retired from the business and spent his remaining years in instrument making.

Pauli, Wolfgang *(1900–1958)* Austrian-Swiss physicist; educated at the University of Munich, where he obtained his Ph.D. in 1922. After further study in Copenhagen with Niels BOHR and at Göttingen with Max BORN, Pauli taught at Heidelberg before accepting the professorship of physics at the Federal Institute of Technology, Zurich. Apart from the war years, which he spent in the U.S. at the Institute of Advanced Studies, Princeton, Pauli remained at Zurich until his death and was respected for his deep insight into the newly emerging quantum theory. His initial reputation was made in relativity theory with his publication in 1921 of his *Relativitätstheorie.* His name is mainly linked with two substantial achievements. The first, formulated in 1924, is known as the "Pauli exclusion principle." It follows from this that as an electron can spin in only two ways, each quantum orbit can hold no more than two electrons. Once both vacancies are full, further electrons can fit only into other orbits. With this principle the distribution of orbital electrons at last became clear, that is, it could be explained and predicted in purely quantum terms. For his introduction of the exclusion

principle, Pauli was awarded the 1945 NOBEL PRIZE for physics. Pauli's second great insight was in resolving a problem in beta decay—a type of radioactivity in which electrons are emitted by the atomic nucleus.

Pauling, Linus Carl *(1901–1994)* American chemist. Born in Portland, Oregon, he attended Oregon State Agricultural College and received a Ph.D. from the California Institute of Technology in 1925, teaching there until 1964. His early research dealt with the nature of chemical bonding and molecular structure, as he applied the quantum theory to chemistry. His ideas were published in the landmark scientific study *The Nature of the Chemical Bond* (1939). Pauling also conducted research on biological molecules. In 1940 he and Max DELBRÜCK introduced a molecular-based theory of antibody-antigen reactions, and later that decade he did extensive studies of sickle cell anemia. Using magnetic measurements, he studied the hemoglobin molecule, work that later led to extensive explorations of the helical structure of proteins conducted with R. B. Corey. In 1954 Pauling was awarded the NOBEL PRIZE for chemistry in recognition of his work on chemical bonding. After WORLD WAR II, he became increasingly concerned with the dangers of radioactivity and nuclear testing and actively campaigned against the U.S. testing program. He has also been a committed and vocal proponent of world disarmament and international peace, concerns he expressed in *No More War* (1958). He became one of the few individuals to win two Nobel Prizes when he was awarded the Nobel Prize for peace in 1962. In the 1960s Pauling developed an interest in the biological effects of large doses of vitamin C, advocating its use in preventing the common cold. He continued to conduct research on vitamin theory throughout the 1970s.

Pavarotti, Luciano *(1935–)* Italian tenor; one of the greatest bel canto singers of this century and perhaps the most popular tenor since Enrico CARUSO. Pavarotti was born in Modena and was originally a school teacher. After winning the first prize in the Concorso Internazionale in Reggio Emilia, Pavarotti debuted in that city as Rodolfo in PUCCINI's *La Bohème,* a role that is one of his finest. He made his first appearance at Covent Garden in the same part in 1963 and at the Metropolitan Opera in 1968. His performances in the 1960s and '70s opposite soprano Joan SUTHERLAND were especially memorable. Specializing in the great lyric tenor roles, he was a featured singer at the Met, at La Scala and at many other major opera houses throughout the world. Among his other notable roles are Edgardo in *Lucia di Lammermoor,* Nemorino in *L'Elisir d'Amore,* Tonio in *The Daughter of the Regiment,* the duke in *Rigoletto* and Riccardo in *Un Ballo in Maschera.* A romantic leading man despite his considerable bulk and his wooden acting, Pavarotti is known as "the King of the High Cs." He is an enormously popular figure, with legions of loyal fans even among the non-opera-going public, and has starred in numerous television specials. In addition to singing in many opera recordings, he has also made solo albums featuring operatic selections, Neapolitan songs and Christmas music. Some critics have questioned his taste and dismissed his many galas and television extravaganzas as contrived media events. Nonetheless, Pavarotti has been almost universally acclaimed for the lyrical purity of his voice and the stylistic verve of his performances. In the mid-1990s Pavarotti collaborated with fellow tenors Plácido Domingo and José Carreras in releasing a series of recordings of all three men called *The Three Tenors.* In 2004 Pavarotti made his last appearance at the Metropolitan Opera in New York City. His vocal powers had been in decline for a number of years, and he had suffered from numerous health problems.

Pavese, Cesare *(1908–1950)* Italian novelist, poet, translator, and editor. Pavese was educated in Turin; he graduated in 1930 with a thesis on Walt Whitman, whose influence was evident in *Lavorare stanca* (1936, *Hard Labor*). After 1933 he was an editor and reader for a publishing house. In 1935 he was imprisoned by the fascists; confinement and solitude were prominent themes in his work. His first novel, *Paesi tuoi* (1941, *Your Country*) portrayed Piedmontese peasants, whereas his second, *La spiaggia* (1942, *The Beach*), was a portrait of the bourgeois Italian Riviera reminiscent of F. Scott FITZGERALD. His best novel was *La luna e ifalo* (1950, *The Moon and the Bonfires*). His work reflects a transitional age as the rural Italian countryside gives way to modern technological urbanism. He translated his favorite book, *Moby-Dick,* as well as works by John STEINBECK, James JOYCE and Gertrude STEIN. Not long after his receipt of the prestigious Strega Prize, he committed suicide in a Turin hotel room. Many of his writings were published posthumously.

Pavlov, Ivan Petrovich *(1849–1936)* Russian physiologist; discoverer of the conditioned reflex. In 1870, Pavlov entered the University of St. Petersburg, where he studied chemistry and animal physiology. In 1883 he received his M.D. from the Medico-Chirurgical Academy, where he continued to work for virtually the rest of his life. Until 1902, Pavlov studied blood pressure and respiration in dogs and the animal's digestive system; for the latter work he received the 1904 NOBEL PRIZE for medicine or physiology. From 1902 until his death, Pavlov conducted his famous research on conditioned reflexes, a term he coined. Working again with dogs, Pavlov demonstrated that the animals had learned to associate certain stimuli (such as their attendant) with their feedings and had come to exhibit the same physiological responses to these stimuli as to the food itself. That is, the dogs demonstrated a learned, or conditioned, reflex in addition to their store of innate, or unconditioned, reflexes. Through these experiments, Pavlov believed he had established the fundamentally physiological nature of psychological phenomena, although he was never able to adequately explain the exact mechanism of the connection.

Pavlova, Anna Pavlovna *(1881–1931)* Russian prima ballerina. Having trained under Per Christian Johansson and Paul Gerdt at the Imperial Theater School, Pavlova danced with the Maryinsky Theater in 1899, and was made prima ballerina in 1906. In 1909 she joined DIAGHILEV'S BALLETS RUSSES, but in 1911 she left the company after becoming a traditionalist and rejecting the innovations of Diaghilev. She settled in London, formed her own company and toured extensively with it. She is considered one of the greatest prima ballerinas of all time.

Payne, Melvin Monroe *(1911–1990)* U.S. scientific research director. He served as an executive director and scientific research director with the NATIONAL GEOGRAPHIC SOCIETY for 55 years and was also the society's president (1967–76) and chairman (1976–87). He was chairman of the society's committee for research and exploration (1975–89), in which he supported such research as the underwater expeditions of Jacques-Yves COUSTEAU, Louis LEAKEY's search for early man in East Africa and Jane GOODALL's study of wild chimpanzees.

Payton, Walter Jerry *(1954–1999)* American football player. One of the greatest running backs of all time, Payton initially planned on a career in music, taking up football late in high school. During his college career at Jackson State University, he scored a record 464 points in an abbreviated three-and-a-half-year career. In 1975, he was drafted by the Chicago Bears, who went on to compile their first winning record in a decade. Two years later, Payton set a single-game rushing record with 275 yards, and later that year was named the league's most valuable player. He was near or at the top in all rushing categories, including touchdowns scored. Payton died in 1999 because his contraction of bile duct cancer made it impossible for him to receive a liver transplant. His NFL rushing record was broken in 2002 by Dallas Cowboys' running back Emmit Smith.

Paz, Octavio *(1914–1998)* Mexican poet, critic, essayist, diplomat. Although Paz was born and educated in Mexico City, his world travels immersed him in many different cultural traditions. He published his first poems at the age of 17. In 1937 he visited Spain and was strongly affected by the SPANISH CIVIL WAR. In 1943–45 he traveled in the U.S. on a Guggenheim fellowship. In 1945 he met André BRETON and the surrealists in Paris (see SURREALISM). He entered the diplomatic service and was posted to San Francisco, New York, Paris, Tokyo, Geneva and Delhi. In the early 1970s he taught at Cambridge and Harvard. *Sun Stone* (1957) and *Blanco* (1966) are recognized as his finest poetry. His many influential prose works include *The Labyrinth of Solitude* (1950; revised

1959), *The Bow and the Lyre* (1956), *Quadrivium* (1965), *Alternating Current* (1967) and *Conjunctions and Disjunctions* (1969). Although he had left-wing sympathies, Paz was extremely critical of the USSR and Cuba. Paz was awarded the NOBEL PRIZE in literature in 1990.

Peace Corps Independent agency of the U.S. government, established by President John F. KENNEDY in 1961. The Peace Corps sends American volunteers to developing countries that request its services. These volunteers teach basic skills and give advice about such subjects as agriculture, engineering and nutrition. Often, volunteers directly participate in construction projects, planting and harvesting, or in the provision of medical care. Since it was founded, more than 170,000 Americans—many of them recent college graduates—have served two-year terms in the Peace Corps.

peaceful coexistence Term referring to the state of relations between socialist and capitalist countries. At the Allied Supreme Council at Cannes in 1922 the Allies endorsed Georgy Chicherin's coexistence thesis, stating that each nation should choose its own system of government and economy. KHRUSHCHEV pursued a foreign policy of so-called peaceful coexistence, acknowledging the existence of noncommunist social systems but believing that communism would ultimately triumph.

Peacock, Andrew (*1939– *) Australian politician. Educated at Melbourne University, Peacock entered the house of representatives in 1966 as the Liberal member for Kooyong. He held ministerial office in the closing years of Liberal domination in the late 1960s and early 1970s and again when the LIBERAL PARTY regained power in 1975. Between 1975 and 1980 he was minister of foreign affairs. When the Liberals lost power in 1983, Peacock succeeded Malcolm FRASER as Liberal leader; in 1985 he was removed by John Howard, after a bitter party feud, but in May 1989 returned to leadership of the Liberal Party. In 1996, when the Liberal and National Parties formed a coalition government, Peacock became the minister for foreign affairs. (See also AUSTRALIA.)

Peake, Mervyn Laurence (*1911–1968*) British writer, poet and artist. Peake remains best known as a writer of Gothic fantasy literature. His most famous work is the Gormenghast trilogy—*Titus Groan* (1946), *Gormenghast* (1950) and *Titus Alone* (1959)—which recounts the memories of Titus, the aging 77th earl of Groan, as he sits in his slowly crumbling ancestral castle. Critics have rated the Gormenghast trilogy as the only serious rival, in fantasy literature, to the Lord of the Rings trilogy of J.R.R. TOLKIEN. Peake was born in China, the son of a British medical missionary. He was educated at Oxford. In addition to his fantasy fiction, Peake was a poet whose volumes include *The Glassblowers* (1950) and *The Rhyme of the Flying Bomb* (1962). He was also a renowned book illustrator who illustrated his own works and produced illustrated editions of *The Rime of the Ancient Mariner* by Samuel Taylor Coleridge (1943) and *Treasure Island* by Robert Louis Stevenson (1949).

Pearl Harbor, Japanese attack on (*December 7, 1941*) At 7:55 A.M. on Sunday, December 7, 1941, a swarm of Japanese aircraft swooped out of the sky and attacked the U.S. naval and air bases at Pearl Harbor on Oahu Island, HAWAII. This attack was a complete surprise, although tensions between the U.S. and Japan had been building

The USS Arizona shown after the Japanese attack on Pearl harbor. 1941 (LIBRARY OF CONGRESS. PRINTS AND PHOTOGRAPHS DIVISION)

up for some time (see WORLD WAR II). No one was prepared to do battle early on a Sunday morning in Hawaii, and for two hours the Japanese planes, aided by SUBMARINES and midget submarines, wreaked havoc on the U.S. fleet. Of the eight battleships present, three were sunk, another capsized and the remainder badly damaged; three cruisers, three destroyers and five other vessels were sunk or seriously damaged; and 247 planes, 175 of which were destroyed on the ground, were lost. Only 29 of the 360 Japanese planes were shot down before the rest returned to their distant aircraft carriers. About 4,500 persons were killed or wounded, including 2,300 U.S. military personnel. The next day the U.S. Congress declared war against Japan; U.S. president Franklin D. ROOSEVELT declared that December 7, 1941, was a "day that shall live in infamy." (See also WORLD WAR II IN THE PACIFIC.)

Pears, Sir Peter (*1910–1986*) British tenor. Pears was a founder member of the English Opera Group and an active director of the Aldeburgh Festival, which he cofounded with Benjamin BRITTEN and Eric Crozier in 1948. Britten created some of Pears's most notable roles, in such works as *Peter Grimes, Billy Budd* and *Death in Venice.* They were professional partners from the 1930s until the composer's death in 1976. Pears also participated in the premiers of such major nonoperatic works by Britten as the *Serenade for Tenor, Horn and Strings,* and the *War Requiem.* He was also an outstanding interpreter of music by other 20th-century British composers and of music by classical masters ranging from Heinrich Schuetz to Franz Schubert.

Pearse, Patrick Henry (**Padraig Pearse**) (*1879–1916*) Irish nationalist and revolutionary. Born in Dublin, Pearse was the son of an Englishman and an Irish woman. He was educated in law but became interested in Irish language and culture, which had been suppressed by the British. He became a schoolteacher and also edited *An Claidheamh Soluis,* the journal of the Gaelic League. In his writings, Pearse developed the idea of blood sacrifice, calling for the Irish to shed their blood in order to achieve independence from the British. In 1913 Pearse became active in the paramilitary Irish Volunteers. He directed the group during the 1916 EASTER RISING against British rule and proclaimed IRELAND's independence from the steps of the General Post Office in Dublin. After the rebellion was put down he was tried by a military court and executed. Pearse is considered a martyr and national hero by many Irish, but his romantic ideas about the necessity of violence have been widely blamed for contributing to the allure of the IRISH REPUBLICAN ARMY and for impeding a peaceful solution to the troubles of NORTHERN IRELAND.

Pearson, Drew (Andrew Russell Pearson) *(1896–1969)* American journalist. As a staff member of the *Baltimore Sun,* Pearson became known in 1931 for his article "The Washington Merry-Go-Round," on which he collaborated with Robert Allen. In 1932 the two started a column of the same name that specialized in exposing the private lives of public figures and unearthing government corruption. The enormously popular but not always completely accurate column was syndicated in 350 newspapers by 1942. Pearson conducted an exclusive interview with Soviet premier Nikita KHRUSHCHEV in 1961, and Pearson's influence was manifest when his exposure of the financial misconduct of Senator Thomas DODD led to Senate hearings and Dodd's eventual censure. When Pearson died in 1969, his column was the most widely read in the U.S. He was succeeded by columnist Jack ANDERSON.

Pearson, Lester Bowles *(1897–1972)* Canadian diplomat and statesman, prime minister of CANADA (1963–68). Born in Ontario, he attended the University of Toronto and Oxford. Entering the diplomatic service, he held a variety of posts and served as ambassador to Washington (1944–46). During his tenure in the U.S., he was Canada's adviser at the conferences at DUMBARTON OAKS (1944) and San Francisco (1945), playing an important part in the establishment of the UNITED NATIONS and leading Canada's UN delegation from 1946 to 1956. Also serving as Canada's secretary of state for external affairs from 1948 to 1957, he became the first Canadian to win the NOBEL PRIZE for peace (1957) in recognition

of his efforts in mediating the SUEZ CRISIS of 1956. An important figure in the COMMONWEALTH OF NATIONS, Pearson was also important in the formation of the NORTH ATLANTIC TREATY ORGANIZATION (NATO). He led the opposition in the Canadian parliament from 1958 to 1963 and after the Liberal victory in 1963 became prime minister, serving in that office until 1968. His books include *Democracy in World Politics* (1955), *Words and Occasions* (1970) and three volumes of memoirs (1972–75).

Peary, Robert Edwin *(1856–1920)* American explorer. Peary is famous for his discovery of the North Pole in 1909. A civil engineer in the U.S. Navy by profession, Peary made his first expedition to Greenland in 1891 accompanied by Matthew Henson, who was his assistant on all his Arctic expeditions. He discovered new land and proved that Greenland is an island. He failed twice to reach the North Pole (1898–1902; 1905–06) before achieving his goal in 1909. He led 24 men who guided 19 sledges pulled by 133 dogs over 400 miles of drifting ice floes. Finally on April 6, Peary, Henson and four Eskimos reached the Pole. A later controversy over whether Frederick A. COOK had reached the Pole first was settled in Peary's favor.

Pechstein, Max *(1881–1955)* German painter. He began his career as an apprentice to a decorative artist in 1896 and later taught art in Dresden. An expressionist, he joined DIE BRÜCKE in 1906. An interest in the exotic in art prompted him to visit the South Seas in 1913–14. A member of the Prussian Academy of Arts from 1922 to 1933, he was expelled by the Nazis, who condemned him as a "degenerate" artist and forbade exhibition of his work. Pechstein taught at the Berlin School of Fine Arts from 1945 until his death. His work is bold in color and composition, but less dramatic and more decorative than that of his fellow German expressionists. He is also well-known for his graphics and for the stained glass and mosaics that he executed late in his career. (See also EXPRESSIONISM.)

Pedersen, William *(1938–)* American architect. Educated at the Univer-

sity of Minnesota and the Massachusetts Institute of Technology and a winner of the Rome Prize in Architecture, he is the chief design architect at Kohn Pedersen Fox in New York City. He is known for contextual buildings that relate strikingly to their environments, relating them to their setting and their streets, and emphasizing human and social elements in their designs. He is best known for two office high-rise buildings on Wacker Drive in Chicago and for the Cincinnati headquarters for Proctor & Gamble. In 1998 Pederson received the National Architectural Honor Society's Gold Medal in recognition of his lifetime achievements in architecture.

Peerce, Jan (Jacob Pincus Perelmuth) *(1904–1984)* American operatic tenor and concert performer. Born in New York City, Peerce gained his earliest musical experience singing in a synagogue choir; he also studied violin and became an accomplished performer during his teens. However, his fame came as a principal singer at RADIO CITY MUSIC HALL (1932–40) and as a singer on the radio. In 1938 he made the first of many appearances with conductor Arturo TOSCANINI when he sang the tenor solo in Beethoven's *Ninth Symphony* with the New York Philharmonic. He made his opera debut as the Duke in *Rigoletto* with the Columbia Opera Company in 1938 and his Metropolitan Opera debut as Alfredo in *La Traviata* in 1941. For the next 26 years he sang with the Met and was guest artist with major opera companies in Europe, appearing in such roles as Edgardo in *Lucia di Lammermoor* and Rodolfo in *La Bohème*. He also appeared in films, including *Carnegie Hall* (1947) and on Broadway as Tevye in the musical *Fiddler on the Roof* (1971).

Pegler, (James) Westbrook *(1894–1969)* American newspaper columnist. Born in Minneapolis, Minnesota, Pegler was a working journalist by the age of 16. He wrote for the United Press for many years, then, in 1933, began writing his *New York World-Telegram* column "Fair Enough," in which he caustically attacked public figures. Ultraconservative, Pegler lambasted Franklin D. ROOSEVELT and his NEW DEAL policies; yet he also showed his hatred for European fascists. In 1941

Pegler won a PULITZER PRIZE for his exposure of racketeering in labor unions. From 1944 to 1962 he wrote for King Features Syndicate and from 1962 to 1964 for the JOHN BIRCH SOCIETY publication *American Opinion*. In 1954, he lost a highly publicized libel case to writer Quentin Reynolds.

Péguy, Charles Pierre *(1873–1914)* French poet. Péguy, a Roman Catholic, was one of the major French poets of the first decades of the 20th century. Raised in abject poverty, Péguy succeeded in winning academic scholarships and thereby educating himself to take a major role in French literary life. In 1900 he founded the journal *Cahiers de la Quinzane,* which became the leading French literary quarterly of its era. An ardent patriot, Péguy wrote several lengthy prose poems that combined nationalistic fervor and Catholic piety. Some of these were translated into English as *Basic Virtues* (1943) and *Men and Saints* (1944). Péguy was killed during WORLD WAR I at the Battle of the MARNE.

Pei, I(eoh) M(ing) *(1917–)* Chinese-American architect. Born in Canton, he emigrated to the U.S. in 1935, studied at the Massachusetts Institute of Technology and Harvard University, where he taught from 1945 to 1948, and became an American citizen in 1954. In 1948 he moved to New York City, where he executed a number of major projects for Webb and Knapp. In 1955 he opened his own firm. His influential works, in which buildings are sensitively integrated into their surroundings, include Mile High Center, Denver (1956); Place Ville Marie, Montreal (1963); and Kips Bay Plaza apartments, New York City (1960–65). Noted for their monumentality, simplicity and beauty, Pei's other commissions include the National Center for Atmospheric Research, Boulder (1967); two buildings at M.I.T. (1964; 1970); the Everson Museum of Art, Syracuse, New York (1968); the East Building at the National Gallery of Art, Washington, D.C. (1978); the Bank of China Building, Hong Kong; and the Fragrant Hill Hotel, Beijing. One of his best known and most controversial structures is Le Grand Louvre in Paris (1989). This set of three glass and steel pyramids, one large and two subsidiary, covers an underground visitors' center, stores and other facilities in the courtyard of the world-renowned Louvre Museum.

Pei, Mario *(1901–1978)* Italian-born linguist and educator. Pei, who was born in Rome, came to the U.S. as a youth and was educated at the City College of New York. A facility for languages led Pei to make the study of the history of human languages his special scholarly province. His major works include *The Story of Language* (1949), a widely read general survey, and *Words in Sheep's Clothing* (1969). Pei taught at Columbia University for over three decades and also served as a special adviser on language training for U.S. Army personnel.

Pei, Wenzhong *(1904–1982)* Chinese archaeologist. In 1929 he discovered the skull of Peking Man, estimated to be half a million years old. The discovery furnished the first strong evidence of man's evolution from less-advanced life forms.

Pele **(Edson Arantes do Nascimento)** *(1940–)* Brazilian soccer player. Considered to be the greatest soccer player ever, Pele is the only person to have played on three World Cup–winning teams (1958, 1962 and 1970). Discovered by Brito, a former Brazilian international player, Pele joined the Santos club in 1956 at 16. The following year he starred in Brazil's first World Cup triumph, scoring two goals in the final. During his career with Santos and Brazil (1956–74), he scored 1,216 goals in 1,254 games, the highest goal scoring rate in soccer history; his 1,000th goal was scored on November 19, 1969. Pele first played for Brazil in 1957; he retired from international play following the 1970 World Cup victory having scored a record 97 goals for Brazil. He played his final club game for Santos on October 2, 1974, but came out of retirement in 1975 to play for the New York Cosmos of the North American Soccer League. Pele retired on October 1, 1977, having scored 1,281 goals in 1,363 games. In 1999 the National Olympic Committees of the world voted Pele the premier athlete of the 20th century.

Pelée, Mount Volcano on island of MARTINIQUE in the West Indies. Mount Pelée erupted in 1902 and 1929. The 1902 eruption destroyed the entire town of Saint Pierre, along with all of its 40,000 inhabitant—except for one, a prisoner in the local jail.

Pelli, Cesar Antonio *(1926–)* American architect. Born in Argentina, he studied at the University of Illinois. He has devoted himself to a public architecture that "celebrates life," creating large buildings that have a feeling of great lightness and an inherent humanity. From 1968 to 1976 he headed the architectural design division of Gruen Associates in California. Among the outstanding works of this period are the 1967 headquarters of Comsat in Clarksburg, Virginia, and of Teledyne in Northridge, California. In 1977 he opened his own office in New Haven, Connecticut, and became the chairman of the department of architecture at Yale. Among his notable later buildings are the World Financial Center, New York City, the Northwest Center, Minneapolis and the Pacific Design Center, Los Angeles.

Penderecki, Krzysztof *(1933–)* Polish composer. Associated with the avant-garde movement, Penderecki developed a highly individual style of composition in which he utilizes all resources of sound, such as shouting and striking the piano strings with mallets. He developed his own system of optical notation, using symbolic ideograms to indicate the desired sound. He has taught at the Superior School of Music in Cracow (1958–66), the Folkwang Hochschule für Musik in Essen, Germany (1966–68), and part-time at Yale University (since 1973). His best-known work is *Threnody in Memory of the Victims of Hiroshima* (1959–60). Other important works include the choral-orchestral piece *The Resurrection of Christ* (1971). Penderecki received several international honors throughout the 1990s, including the Great Cross of Merit from Germany (1999), and the United Nations Educational Scientific and Cultural Organization (UNESCO) International Music Council Award (1993).

Pendergast, Thomas Joseph *(1872–1945)* American politician and Democratic Party leader. He rose to power as a political boss in the Missouri Democratic Party after serving in various state positions. He aided in Harry TRUMAN's U.S. Senate victory (1934), but was imprisoned in 1939 after being convicted for income tax violations; his political machine collapsed.

Pendray, G. Edward *(1901–1987)* One of the founders of the American Interplanetary Society (later called the American Rocket Society). A science reporter for the *New York Herald Tribune,* Pendray was also a fellow member of the British Interplanetary Society, elected a few months after the society was formed in 1933. After visiting Europe in 1931 and observing the work of the German Rocket Society a month after it had successfully launched it first liquid-propellant rocket, Pendray urged the AIS to follow suit. The American Interplanetary Society launched its first liquid-propellant rocket May 14, 1933. The rocket cost a grand total of $30.60 with an additional cost of $28.80 for launch expenses. But Robert GODDARD, working independently, had already beaten the AIS to the punch and, by the time of the AIS launch, was already working on more advanced models of the liquid-propellant rocket.

penicillin Generic term for a group of antibiotic agents that were the first to be used in the treatment of bacterial infections in human beings. The effect of penicillin on bacteria was first observed by Sir Alexander FLEMING in 1929, but the substance did not become widely useful in clinical treatment until after it had been purified by various biologists, notably H.W. FLOREY and E.B. CHAIN, in 1941. Penicillin was first obtained from the *Penicillium notatum* molds observed by Fleming but is now more frequently produced from large, aerated fermentation vats of *P. chrysogenum.* Penicillin works by breaking down the walls of bacterial cells and is effective against many gram-positive bacteria. Penicillin has been used to treat syphilis, meningococcal meningitis, gas gangrene and pneumococcal pneumonia, as well as many staph and strep infections. Although some gram-negative bacteria, such as those causing gonorrhea, are susceptible to penicillin, most gram-negative infections cannot be treated by the antibiotic. However, such synthetic versions of the antibiotic as ampicillin, methicillin and oxacilin have been used against both kinds of bacteria. The use of penicillin is limited by its tendency to cause allergic reactions in some people and by the ability of a number of microorganisms to become penicillin-resistant.

Penkovsky, Oleg *(1919–1963)* Soviet double agent. After serving in World War II, Penkovsky went to work for Soviet military intelligence. In 1961, he became a double agent for the West and began to pass top-secret information concerning Soviet military strategy and preparedness. His activities exposed in 1963, Penkovsky was tried by Soviet officials and sentenced to death. The information he provided is credited with helping to determine American responses to Soviet actions during the BERLIN WALL and the CUBAN MISSILE crises in the early 1960s.

Penn, Irving *(1917–   )* American photographer. Born in Plainfield, New Jersey, Penn attended the School of Industrial Art in Philadelphia from 1934 to 1938. On the staff of *Vogue* magazine since 1943, he is best known for his dramatically stylish high-fashion photography. His work has been exhibited at a number of leading museums, notably the Metropolitan Museum of Art and the Museum of Modern Art, New York City.

Penney, J(ames) C(ash) *(1875–1971)* American department store tycoon. Penney founded J.C. Penney Company, Inc., in 1902. The company eventually operated more than 2,000 domestic and foreign retail outlets, including 1,700 stores in the U.S.

Penney, William George *(1909–1991)* Creator of the British ATOMIC BOMB. A mathematician and physicist who specialized in measuring the force of explosions, Penney was sent by the British to work with the U.S. team that was assembling the world's first atomic bomb in LOS ALAMOS, New Mexico, in 1944. Following its use of two atomic bombs against Japan in 1945, the U.S. ended its atomic weapons research collaboration with the British in 1946. Penney returned to England, where he began from scratch to design the first British atomic bomb, successfully tested in 1952. He later became direc-

tor of the British government's Atomic Weapons Research Establishment. He was made a life peer in 1967.

Pentagon Papers See *NEW YORK TIMES v. UNITED STATES.*

People v. Simpson See O.J. SIMPSON MURDER TRIAL.

Pepper, Claude Denson *(1900–1989)* American politician. A liberal Democrat from Florida, Pepper's congressional career began in the Senate, where he served from 1937 until 1951. During his Senate years, he was a close ally of President Franklin D. ROOSEVELT and a passionate advocate of such NEW DEAL programs as Social Security, health care insurance and minimum wage legislation. In 1951 he lost a bitter Democratic primary contest to a former protege who branded him "Red Pepper" for his supposedly pro-Soviet attitudes. Pepper returned to Congress in 1962, serving in the House of Representatives. In his later years he was a champion of legislation on behalf of the elderly. Shortly before his death, President George BUSH awarded him the U.S. Medal of Freedom, the nation's highest civilian award. At the time of his death he was the oldest member of the U.S. Congress. Congress voted to have his body lie in state in the Capitol Rotunda, an honor usually granted only to U.S. presidents and national heroes.

Percy, Walker *(1916–1990)* American author. Percy's novels portrayed the spiritual despair of upper-middle-class life in the post–World War II American South. Trained as physician and psychiatrist, he published his first book in 1961. That book, *The Moviegoer,* won him a National Book Award for Fiction. His later works included *The Thanatos Syndrome* (1987), *Love in the Ruins* (1971), *The Last Gentleman* (1966) and *The Second Coming* (1980).

Perelman, S(idney) J(oseph) *(1904–1979)* American humorist, author and scriptwriter. Perelman's brilliant talent for wordplay, spoofs and madcap comedy helped shape American humor in the 20th century. He wrote parts of the early MARX BROTHERS movies *Monkey Business* (1931) and *Horse Feathers* (1932). Among his other credits were numerous essays, books, and plays. He wrote the book for the 1943 Broadway musical hit *One Touch of Venus* as well as the script for the ACADEMY AWARD–winning film *Around the World in Eighty Days* (1956). He also contributed short humor pieces to THE NEW YORKER magazine.

Peres, Shimon (*1923– *) Israeli political leader and prime minister (1984–86). Peres was born in Poland and immigrated to Palestine in 1934. He was educated at a youth village and at Tel Aviv University. During the 1948 war he was put in charge of naval supplies and then of major arms purchases. In 1965 Peres followed his mentor, David BEN-GURION, into the breakaway Rafi Party but later rejoined Labor and served as minister of communications and transport (1970–74). He was minister of defense from 1974 until Labor's 1977 election defeat. In 1984 he became prime minister in the government of national unity but handed over the post to Yitzhak SHAMIR in late 1986. An organization man with a flair for international public relations, Peres is renowned for his vision of IS-RAEL as a technological power. He was the driving force behind the establishment of Israel's aircraft industry and its nuclear reactor in Dimona, and he is committed to the development of the country's electronics industry. Peres speaks fluent French and was the architect of the "French connection," leading to the secret pact with France and Britain before the Suez War and to Israel's acquisition of an unprecedented military arsenal. Peres became Israeli foreign minister following the July 1992 victory of the Labor Party in national elections. He helped negotiate the 1993 Oslo Accords, which allowed for limited Palestinian self-government in the West Bank and Gaza Strip. In recognition of his involvement in the Palestinian-Israeli peace process, Peres shared the 1994 Nobel Peace Prize with Israeli prime minister Yitzhak RABIN and PALESTINIAN LIBERATION OR-GANIZATION (PLO) leader Yasir ARAFAT. Peres became prime minister following the November 5, 1995, assassination of Rabin and held that post until losing to Likud Party candidate Benjamin NE-TANYAHU in 1996. Peres began a two-year term as foreign minister in a government of national unity with

Likud prime minister Ariel Sharon. In 2003 he resigned his position to protest Sharon's support for the expansion of Jewish settlements in the occupied territories. In 2005 Peres was defeated for the leadership of the Labor Party by Amir Peretz. Peres later joined Prime Minister Sharon's new party, Kadima.

perestroika (Russian for "restructuring") Shortly after he came to power in 1985, Soviet leader Mikhail GORBACHEV acknowledged that the USSR faced grave economic problems. Under its traditional Marxist-Leninist policies, which emphasized central planning and control of all phases of production and distribution, the Soviet economy had stagnated. The country was burdened by a lethargic bureaucracy, inefficient state-run industries, poor quality of manufactured goods, lack of consumer products, food shortages and a generally low standard of living. Gorbachev stressed the need for wide-ranging economic reforms, some of which ran counter to the accepted Marxist-Leninist economic doctrine. These included opening the economy to market forces, allowing competition and a limited amount of private ownership. Gorbachev's program of perestroika was hailed in the West as a sign of movement away from the USSR's hard-line communist past, although Gorbachev seemed reluctant to abandon Marxist principles altogether. Given the continuing decline of the Soviet economy and the possibility of economic and political upheaval, many economists wondered whether Gorbachev's reforms would be too little and too late to revive the nation's economy. Boris YELTSIN and other reformers claimed that Gorbachev's approach was too cautious; they pushed for more radical reforms. As of early 1991, the fate of perestroika was uncertain.

Pérez Alfonzo, Juan Pablo (*1904–1979*) Oil minister of VENEZUELA and cofounder of the ORGANIZATION OF PE-TROLEUM EXPORTING COUNTRIES (OPEC). Perez drafted the revolutionary policies that led to the nationalization of the Venezuelan oil industry in 1976.

Pérez de Cuéllar, Javier (*1920– *) Peruvian diplomat, UN secretary-general (*1982–   *). Pérez de Cuéllar held various posts from 1944 to 1978. He

represented Peru at the UNITED NATIONS from 1971 to 1975 and was president of the Security Council in 1974. He served as undersecretary-general for special political affairs from 1979 to 1981. As secretary-general, in August 1988 he succeeded in negotiating a cease-fire between Iran and Iraq, ending the bloody IRAN-IRAQ WAR OF 1980–88. In January 1991 he went to Baghdad in a last-ditch effort to persuade Iraqi leader Saddam HUSSEIN to withdraw Iraqi forces from Kuwait by the UN deadline of January 15, 1991. Hussein rebuffed Pérez, and UN coalition forces led by the U.S. subsequently initiated OPERATION DESERT STORM against Iraq. His term as secretary general expired in December 1991. He was succeeded by Boutros BOUTROS-GHALI. He received the Presidential Medal of Freedom from President George H. W. Bush in 1991. In 1995 he failed to unseat Peruvian president Alberto FUJIMORI.

performance art Art form utilizing live performance as a medium. While the term *performance art* first came to prominence in the 1960s, the cabaret performances of DADA artists in the World War I era constitute the real beginning of performance art as an accepted cultural form. Performance art views itself as a form of visual art that uses human movement and theatrical effects, as well as spoken lines and music. In the 1960s, performance art played a key role in the HAPPENINGS of the era. Performance art is often a vehicle for social protest.

Perkins, Frances (*1882–1965*) American public official and U.S. secretary of labor. As part of his NEW DEAL reform program aimed at pulling the U.S. out of the GREAT DEPRESSION, President Franklin D. ROOSEVELT envisioned a stronger role for organized labor. The president shocked many by appointing Frances Perkins as secretary of labor in 1933, the first woman to be appointed to a cabinet post. Perkins had previously served as New York state's industrial commissioner under then-governor Roosevelt. In her influential post Perkins lobbied for strong labor legislation and oversaw the revitalization of the Department of Labor to enforce the new statutes. She served for the duration of the Roosevelt administration.

Perkins, Maxwell (*1884–1947*) Legendary American book editor. Born in New York City, he was educated at Harvard University and worked as a reporter for *The New York Times* before becoming an editor at Charles Scribner's Sons in 1910. There he became famous as an advocate of contemporary U.S. fiction. A sensitive reader with a superb ear for language and an uncanny ability to shape a brilliant but undisciplined manuscript into literature, he was important in editing and publishing the works of such eminent American writers as F. Scott FITZGERALD, Ernest HEMINGWAY, J.P. MARQUAND and Thomas WOLEE.

Perlman, Itzhak (*1945–   *) Israeli-born concert violinist. Left permanently crippled from poliomyelitis at the age of four, Perlman overcame his handicap to become probably the best known violin virtuoso of his generation. After appearances on the *Ed SULLIVAN Show* (1959) and winning the Leventritt competition at CARNEGIE HALL in 1964, he performed with several orchestras, including the New York Philharmonic. Perlman toured the United States in 1965–66 and Europe in 1966–67. He has made many acclaimed recordings, often in collaboration with pianist Vladimir ASHKENAZY, violinists Isaac STERN and Pinchas Zukerman and conductor Zubin Mehta. He received a Grammy in 1978 for his album of Vivaldi's *The Four Seasons*. In addition, Perlman has taught and performed at the Aspen Music Festival in Colorado and has served on the faculty of Brooklyn College School of the Performing Arts (since 1975). He has been featured in numerous television specials. Perlman received the National Medal of Arts in 2000 from President Bill Clinton.

Perls, Frederick Solomon and Laura Posner Married couple, both German-born, who were the key founders of the psychological school of GESTALT psychotherapy. Fritz (c. 1894–1970) and Laura Perls (1905–90) met as university students in Frankfurt in 1930. They left Germany in 1933 to escape the emergent Nazi rule and, after a stay in South Africa, went to the U.S. in 1948. In the late 1940s and 1950s, they combined to produce a number of writings (sometimes published with only Fritz listed as the author) that established gestalt psychotherapy as a leading influence on therapeutic practice in America and Europe. They also founded the New York Institute for Gestalt Therapy in 1952. The gestalt approach rejected the psychoanalytic emphasis on early childhood trauma to focus instead on the present-time patterns of perception and emotional attachments of patients. The Perls borrowed from the gestalt perception researches of German psychologist Kurt Goldstein as well as from EXISTENTIALISM and the theatrical acting-out techniques of psychodrama. Fritz became a widely known figure in the 1960s for his teaching work at the Esalen Institute in California.

Perón, Eva (Duarte de) (**"Evita"**) (*1919–1952*) Argentinian political figure. Born Eva Duarte, she was a well-known actress before marrying Juan PERÓN in 1945. After Perón was elected president in 1946, the glamorous Evita, a superb public speaker, became the virtual coruler of ARGENTINA. The unofficial minister of health and labor and founder of the Eva Perón Social Aid Foundation, she was influential in securing voting rights for women and in providing educational and social reforms. She was particularly popular with Argentina's poor, many of whom regarded her as a near saint. Opposed by the military, she failed in an attempt to become vice president in 1951. Her death from cancer a year later was an enormous blow to Perón's first regime. Eva Perón's legend was perpetuated in the musical *Evita* (1976) by Tim RICE and Andrew LLOYD WEBBER. *Evita* was later adapted for a 1996 motion picture of the same name in which pop music star MADONNA played the title role, for which she received a Best Actress Golden Globe Award.

Perón, Juan Domingo (*1895–1974*) Two-time president of ARGENTINA (1946–55, 1973–74). Born in Buenos Aires, Perón became a professional military officer and, in travels to Germany and Italy, was impressed by the fascist regimes there. In 1943 he was an important figure in the right-wing coup that toppled President Ramón S. Castillo. After the installation of Edelmiro Farrell as president, Perón first became secretary of labor and social welfare, then minister of war and vice president, thereby assuming the most powerful position in the ruling military junta. His support of labor unions and social reform won him widespread, almost fanatical, support among Argentina's workers. When the leaders of a 1945 coup imprisoned him, mass demonstrations by the *descamisados* ("shirtless ones") organized by his second wife, Eva Duarte PERÓN, won his release. He was subsequently elected president in the 1946 landslide. Perón's massive reform program, known as *PERONISMO,* was a mixture of strong nationalism and a fascist-influenced TOTALITARIANISM in which all opposition was quashed. His attempt to provide economic stability and self-sufficiency to the nation lost momentum in the late 1940s and early '50s, as demand for Argentinian wheat and beef waned and the economy lagged. The death of the enormously popular Eva in 1952 further weakened his position, disputes with the Roman Catholic Church led to his excommunication in 1955 and that same year he was deposed by a military coup. Fleeing the country, he settled in Spain in 1960. The hold of *peronismo,* which had united workers, nationalists, industrialists and the military, remained strong, and Perón continued to direct it from exile. In 1971 he returned to Argentina, and two years later he was again elected president. He died in office nine months later and was succeeded by his vice president, his third wife, Isabel Martínez de Perón. She was overthrown in a military coup in 1976.

peronismo (also called *justicialismo*) Political, economic and social program pursued by Argentinian dictator Juan PERÓN between 1946 and 1955. In some ways similar to FASCISM, it involved a five-year economic plan, extensive government control of economy and society and an end of British influence on the economy.

Perret, Auguste (*1874–1954*) French architect and engineer whose work moved French architecture toward MODERNISM early in the 20th century. Perret was born in Brussels and joined his father and brothers in the family construction firm. He was a student at the Ecole des BEAUX-ARTS in Paris and first became known for his 1903 apartment house at Paris' 25 bis, rue Franklin, a building that expresses its reinforced concrete frame externally, while incorporating decorative tile ornament of an ART NOUVEAU character. The Théâtre des Champs Elysées of 1911–13 was completed by Perret with visible concrete framing. The emphasis on structure in these works places them in a historical line that leads directly to modernism. The church of Notre Dame du Raincy (1922–23) uses concrete framing with walls largely filled by modern stained glass—a striking and much imitated approach to a modern form of ecclesiastical architecture. His plans for the postwar rebuilding of Le Havre (1949–56) were among his last works. Perret's strong influence was extended by his role as a teacher in several ateliers and schools, including, in 1940, at the Ecole des Beaux-Arts.

Perry, Frederick John *(1909–1992)* British tennis player. A world-renowned player during the 1930s, Perry was the first player to win all four grand slam tournaments (although not in the same year)—he won Wimbledon (1934–36), the U.S. Open (1933–34), the French Open (1935) and the Australian Open (1934). He was the first non-American to win the U.S. Open and the first Britisher to win the French and Australian Opens.

Perse, Saint-John (Marie-René-Auguste-Aléxis Saint-Léger Léger) *(1887–1975)* French poet and diplomat. Born in the West Indies, he and his family moved to France in 1899. A career diplomat, he was posted to the French embassy in Beijing, served at the 1921 arms limitation talks in Washington, D.C., and was secretary general of the French Ministry of Foreign Affairs from 1933 to 1940. A staunch opponent of FASCISM, he went into self-imposed exile in the U.S. from 1940 until the end of WORLD WAR II. His poetry is at once arcane and lyrical, difficult and evocative. Perse published his first poem in 1909. It was followed by the volumes *Eloges* (1911, tr. 1944) and *Amitié du Prince* (1921). He attracted his first significant critical attention with the publication of *Anabase* (1924), a symbolic history of humanity that was translated as *Anabasis* by T. S. ELIOT in 1930. His other volumes of verse include *Exil* (1944, tr. 1949), *Vents* (1946; *Winds*, 1953) and *Amers* (1957; *Seamarks*, 1958). Widely considered one of the most original

poets of the 20th century, he was awarded the NOBEL PRIZE in literature in 1960.

Pershing, John Joseph "Black Jack" *(1860–1948)* American general, commander in chief of the American Expeditionary Force in WORLD WAR I. A graduate of the Military Academy at West Point (1886), Pershing served in several Indian wars and in the Spanish-American War. He was adjutant general in the Philippine Islands (1906–13) and defeated the Philippine Moros in 1913. In 1916–17 he commanded the U.S. raid into Mexico against Pancho VILLA (see VILLA'S RAIDS). In 1917 President Woodrow WILSON chose Pershing to command the American forces in Europe. His army was never totally self-sufficient, but the Americans distinguished themselves in several major engagements, and Pershing returned to a hero's welcome in the U.S. in 1919. That year he was named General of the Armies, the first American general to hold that rank. Pershing later served as army chief of staff (1921–24). He won the PULITZER PRIZE for his memoirs, *My Experiences in the World War* (1931).

Persia See IRAN.

Persian Gulf (Arabian Gulf) During the 20th century the Persian Gulf region has gradually become one of the most sensitive parts of the world, both economically and militarily. The gulf itself is an arm of the Arabian Sea, extending some 600 miles from the Shatt el-Arab delta to the Strait of Hormuz.

General John Pershing. 1918 (LIBRARY OF CONGRESS. PRINTS AND PHOTOGRAPHS DIVISION)

Its maximum width is approximately 200 miles. The oil-rich nations of BAHRAIN, QATAR, the UNITED ARAB EMIRATES, SAUDI ARABIA, KUWAIT, IRAQ and IRAN all have some coastline on the gulf. Much of the oil exported from these countries is transported by tankers through the gulf. At the turn of the century, Britain was a dominant force in the region. An international agreement in 1907 formally recognized the gulf as part of the British sphere of influence. The realization in the 1930's that the gulf region contained the largest petroleum reserves in the world made the Persian Gulf a vital shipping lane. Regional conflicts in the last quarter of the century made the gulf a center of worldwide attention. The Islamic revolution in Iran (1979), the Soviet invasion of AFGHANISTAN (1979), the IRAN-IRAQ WAR OF 1980–88 and Iraq's invasion of Kuwait (1990) and the subsequent PERSIAN GULF WAR (1991) all emphasized Western and Japanese dependence on imported oil and underlined the strategic importance of the Persian Gulf.

Persian Gulf War Conflict (1990–91) between IRAQ and an allied coalition sponsored by the UNITED NATIONS and largely directed by the UNITED STATES. On August 2, 1990, on the orders of its dictator, Saddam HUSSEIN, Iraq launched a surprise invasion of the small neighboring country of KUWAIT. Kuwait was quickly overwhelmed and occupied, and Iraq announced that Kuwait was no longer an independent country but a province of Iraq. The occupying Iraqis systematically plundered the country. A number of nations, including the U.S., denounced the invasion and called for Iraqi troops to withdraw. The U.S. swiftly sent armed forces to SAUDI ARABIA to deter an Iraqi attack on that country; the U.S. operation, involving some 250,000 troops, was dubbed **Operation Desert Shield.** Other nations in the coalition who sent troops to the region included the UNITED KINGDOM, FRANCE, EGYPT and SYRIA; Saudi Arabia, as the host country for the coalition forces, also provided major facilities and manpower. The coalition forces were under the command of U.S. general Norman SCHWARZKOPF. In the following months, the UN passed a series of resolutions calling for Iraq's total withdrawal from Kuwait and imposing sanctions on that country. In November 1990, President BUSH ordered more U.S. forces to the region, bringing the total of U.S. troops in Operation Desert Shield to some 500,000.

Bush also won international support for a UN resolution imposing a deadline of January 15, 1991, for the withdrawal of all Iraqi forces from Kuwait. If the Iraqis did not comply, the resolution authorized the U.S. and its allies to use force to remove them. After debate, the U.S. Congress also authorized the president to use force if necessary. Despite negotiations, including last-minute diplomatic moves by the USSR (which supported the resolution) to persuade Iraq to withdraw, Hussein refused to budge. Hussein warned that there would be dire consequences if his forces were attacked, implying the use of chemical weapons. Less than 17 hours after the UN Security Council's deadline expired, the U.S. and its allies—notably Britain and France—launched a massive air and missile assault on Iraq (January 16, 1991).

This attack was code-named **Operation Desert Storm.** Using high-technology equipment in combat for the first time—CRUISE MISSILES, laser-guided "smart" bombs and other ordnance—the Allies achieved rapid air superiority and scored hits against key military targets in Iraq. Although the Iraqis shot down several Allied aircraft, they otherwise put up little resistance; much of the Iraqi air force fled to Iran or to bases in the north. Hoping to bring ISRAEL into the conflict and split the Western-Arab coalition, Iraq also intermittently launched Soviet-built Scud missiles against Israel (as well as against Saudi Arabia). However, these did not cause any military damage, and the U.S. successfully persuaded Israel not to counterattack.

After six weeks of round-the-clock bombardment, the Allies launched a multipronged ground offensive against Iraqi forces in Kuwait and in Iraq (February 24). The Allies swiftly outflanked and overwhelmed the Iraqis; by the third day of the invasion, more than 50,000 Iraqis had surrendered. Hussein's much-vaunted Republican Guards—the elite Iraqi forces—failed to slow the Allied advance. However, the Iraqis did set fire to hundreds of oil wells in Kuwait and (earlier) also dumped millions of gallons of crude oil into the Persian Gulf. These acts served no military purpose but caused the worst environmental contamination in history. Kuwait was liberated on February 27, and a cease-fire took effect on February 27–28. The destruction of Kuwaiti oil wells and Iraq's plundering of the country left Kuwait's infrastructure severely damaged. In the aftermath of the war, meanwhile, various rebel groups in Iraq attempted to overthrow Saddam Hussein, but by the end of 1991 Hussein had gained the upper hand against opponents of his regime.

Persian Revolution of 1906–09

Persia was in financial straits when the ailing shah succumbed to popular pressure for a constitution, signing the Fundamental Law in 1906, establishing a constitutional monarchy. He died soon after, succeeded by his son, Muhammed Ali (1872–1925). Using a Persian Cossack brigade formed with Russian help, Ali prorogued the assembly. A second assembly developed an absolutist constitution, without abrogating the previous one. Ali's reactionary prime minister was murdered, however, and a liberal prime minister upheld the 1906 document until his arrest in December 1907. The assembly was dispersed by Cossacks in June 1908. A third assembly abolished the 1906 constitution, after which Muhammed Ali attempted to rule absolutely. Rebellions erupted in Tabriz (1908), Rasht and Isfahan (1909), and despite Russian aid, Bakhtiari tribesmen and troops from Rasht captured Tehran in July 1909, forcing Ali's abdication in favor of his 12-year-old son, Ahmed Mirza (1898–1930).

Persian Revolution of 1921

Persia was on the verge of collapse, its ruler corrupt, when Reza Khan PAHLEVI (1877–1944), an army officer, led Cossacks in a coup d'état on February 21, 1921. Pahlevi made himself minister of war and commander in chief and gained control of the country. He introduced reforms, remodeled the army, induced the Russians to withdraw their troops (1921) and Britain as well (1923), became prime minister (1923) and, after gaining dictatorial powers, had the shah deposed (1925). In late 1925 he changed his name to Reza Shah Pahlevi and founded the Pahlevi dynasty.

Person to Person Innovative American television interview program of the 1950s. Edward R. MURROW hosted the first six years of the show, from October 1953 to June 1959, and Charles Collingwood took over until the show's demise in September 1961. By contrast to Murrow's news-oriented SEE IT NOW program, *Person to Person* was a relaxed, informal visit via live television into the homes of celebrities. Wreathed in cigarette smoke, Murrow would sit in the studio before a wall screen and converse with celebrities conducting tours of their homes. The range of guests was amazing—politicians and world leaders like Fidel CASTRO and then-senator John F. KENNEDY, scientists like Margaret MEAD, authors like John STEINBECK, and entertainers like Marilyn MONROE. For all its avowed informality, the complexities of the live transmissions were enormous, and Murrow frequently seemed ill at ease. Purportedly, he did the show to ensure that *See It Now* could remain on the air. "To do the show I want to do," he once said, "I have to do the show I don't want to do." The series was seldom controversial, concludes historian Erik Barnouw, and depended upon "a *Vogue* and *House Beautiful* appeal, along with a voyeuristic element." Needless to say, its ratings were always much higher than those of *See It Now.*

Pertini, Alessandro "Sandro"

(1896–1990) Italian politician, president of ITALY (1978–85). A hero of WORLD WAR II, Pertini was a founder of the Italian Socialist Party. As president of Italy, he was widely hailed for restoring credibility to the Italian government following a period marked by urban terrorism, economic troubles and corruption.

Peru

Western South American nation, bordered by ECUADOR and COLOMBIA on the north, BRAZIL and BOLIVIA on the east, CHILE on the south, and the Pacific Ocean on the west. Its capital is Lima. Peru emerged from the 19th century involved in border disputes with its neighbors. In the early 1900s its politics were dominated by Augusto B. Leguía, who was president from 1908 to 1912 and again from 1919 to

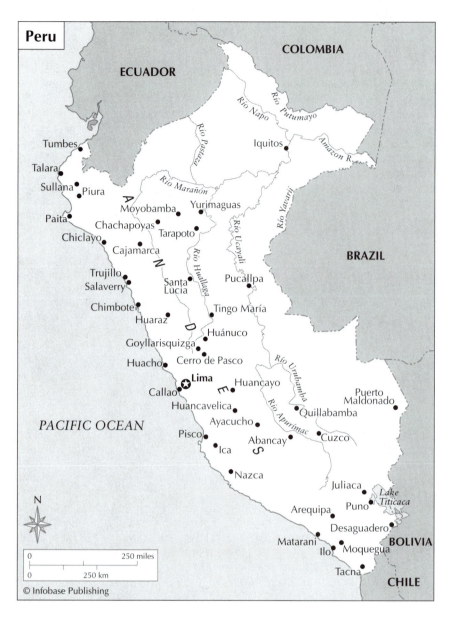

Peru

ECUADOR

COLOMBIA

Tumbes
Talara
Sullana
Piura
Paita
Chiclayo
Trujillo
Salaverry
Chimbote
Huaraz
Goyllarisquizga
Huacho
Cerro de Pasco
Callao
Lima
Huancayo
Huancavelica
Ayacucho
Pisco
Ica
Nazca

Moyobamba
Chachapoyas
Tarapoto
Cajamarca
Santa
Lucía
Huánuco
Tingo María

Yurimaguas

Iquitos

Pucallpa

BRAZIL

Puerto
Maldonado
Quillabamba
Abancay
Cuzco

Juliaca
Arequipa
Puno
Desaguadero
Matarani
Ilo
Moquegua
Tacna

Lake
Titicaca

BOLIVIA

Río Napo
Río Putumayo
Amazon R.
Río Pastaza
Río Marañón
Río Ucayali
Río Huallaga
Río Yavarí
Río Urubamba
Río Apurímac

A N D E S

PACIFIC OCEAN

N

0   250 miles
0   250 km

© Infobase Publishing

CHILE

1930. A virtual dictator, Leguía courted U.S. investments, with little regard for the economic welfare of the Peruvian people. During the 1920s a new political party, APRA (American Popular Revolutionary Alliance), was formed to fight imperialism and to better the treatment of the Indian population. By the 1940s it had taken hold, and in 1945 a free election was held. The elected government was toppled in 1948 in a military coup led by General Manuel Odria. APRA was temporarily banned, and Odria served as president from 1950 to 1956, when Manuel Prado, who had served as president from 1939 to 1945, was reelected. The moderate Fernando Belaúnde Terry was elected in 1963 but was overthrown in a coup led by General Juan Velasco Alvarado in 1968. Velasco installed a military junta that was deposed in a bloodless coup in 1975 by his premier, General Francisco Morales Bermúdez, who promised a gradual return to civilian government. In 1980 elections were held, and Belaúnde Terry was reelected. His government faced increasingly dire economic conditions and threats of a border war with Ecuador, but he managed to last out his term. In 1985 Alán García Pérez became president. A young Social Democrat, García Pérez set out to clean up the government and boost the economy by limiting its payment of foreign debt and price controls. In 1987 he announced his intention to nationalize Peru's banks. García Pérez voiced support for the Sandinistas and was critical of U.S. policy in Central America. Peru continued to struggle with its economy—in 1987 and '88 there were widespread workers' strikes—and with Maoist insurgents such as the Sendero Luminoso (Shining Path) guerrillas. Peru is also a major grower of coca, which is used to produce COCAINE. In 1990 García Pérez was succeeded by Alberto Fujimori, who refused U.S. military aid and attempted to replace coca crops with other agricultural production. Fujimori cracked down on the insurgents and established an authoritarian regime, but his tenure in office ended prematurely in 2000 amid corruption scandals. He fled to Japan to a life of self-imposed exile in Tokyo. The government of Peru tried to extradite him from Japan, where he had become a citizen, to face charges of murder and kidnapping supposedly perpetrated during his days in power. In 2001 Alejandro Toledo is elected as Peru's first president of native Indian origin. A commission set up to investigate the 20-year war against the Shining Path rebels issued a report in 2003 claiming that over 69,000 people were killed in that time. Toledo was found guilty of electoral fraud in 2004, but was allowed to remain in office until his term expired in 2006.

Perutz, Max Ferdinand (1914–2002) Austrian-British biochemist. In 1937 Perutz began investigating the structure of hemoglobin, the oxygen-carrying protein of the blood. He set up the molecular biology laboratory at Cambridge University in 1946; seven years later, Perutz was still hard at work trying to find an underlying regularity in the structure of protein molecules. In 1953 he seized upon a solution by applying the isomorphous replacement technique, which alters the diffraction patterns of a molecule, making it easier to compute the positions of atoms. This technique allowed him to determine the structure of hemoglobin, which contains some 12,000 atoms. In 1962 he was awarded the NOBEL PRIZE in chemistry, along with his colleague John C. Kendrew, who conducted X-ray studies of the muscle protein myoglobin. After receiving the Nobel Prize, Perutz further refined his model of the

PERU	
1919	Augusto Leguía becomes president and gives U.S. companies extensive rights to exploit Peruvian mineral and oil deposits.
1924	The American Revolutionary Popular Alliance is formed (APRA).
1931	Military junta led by Colonel Luis Sánchez Cerro takes over the country.
1956	Former president Manuel Prado (1939–45) becomes president and through austerity measures helps create economic stability.
1968	General Juan Velasco Alvarado in a self-styled military junta seizes power and institutes land reforms and nationalizes U.S. assets.
1975	General Francisco Morales Bermúdez takes over the country and institutes austerity measures in hopes of obtaining aid from the International Monetary Fund.
1985	Alán García, head of APRA, is elected president. As triple-digit inflation devastates wages and civil war is threatened, García declares a state of emergency.
1990	Alberto Fujimori, an agricultural engineer of Japanese descent who had no previous political experience, defeats novelist Mario Vargas Llosa, also a political novice, for the presidency.
1995	President Fujimori wins a second term.
1996	Fourteen rebels of Tupac Amaru Revolutionary Movement invade the Japanese ambassador's residence in Lima, taking hundreds of hostages.
1997	A commando attack ends the four-month embassy siege, killing all the rebels and rescuing alive 72 remaining hostages.
1999	Presidents Fujimori and Jamil Mahuad of Ecuador sign an agreement fixing a new border. Oscar Ramírez Duránd, the sole remaining commander of Shining Path, is captured.
2000	Fujimori is elected to a third term as president; while Fujimori is in Japan, opposition parties take control of congress; Fujimori resigns.
2001	In presidential elections, Alejandro Toledo is elected.
2003	A Truth and Reconciliation Commission report on atrocities during the 20-year war of the government against the Shining Path rebels affirms that approximately 69,280 people were killed.
2005	A four-day uprising by nationalist army reservists in the south fails. A congressional commission finds President Toledo guilty of fraud; Congress votes not to impeach.

hemoglobin molecule, depicting how oxygen is transported in the blood.

Pessoa, Fernando (*1888–1935*) Portuguese poet and literary critic. Pessoa stands as the major Portuguese literary figure to emerge in the modern era. Relatively little of his work was published in his lifetime, and his critical reputation has grown slowly but steadily. Born in Lisbon, Pessoa was educated in South Africa after the death of his father. While there Pessoa became fluent in English. He wrote noteworthy verse in both Portuguese and English. A poetical technique for which Pessoa is especially noted is the use of heteronyms, or alternative authorial personalities, resembling the verse personae of Ezra POUND. As a literary critic, Pessoa was influenced by the tenets of FUTURISM. His books of verse include *Antinous* (1918), *Inscriptions* (1920) and *Mensagem* (1935).

Pétain, Henri-Philippe (*1856–1951*) French army officer and head of France's VICHY government during WORLD WAR II. A graduate of the military academy at St. Cyr, he was commissioned in the infantry in 1878 and subsequently taught at the Ecole de Guerre. In WORLD WAR I he became a military hero, stopping German advances at the battle of VERDUN (1916). Appointed commander in chief of the French forces in 1917, he was promoted to the rank of marshal the following year. After the war he was posted to MOROCCO, where he joined Spain in the campaign against ABD EL-KRIM (1926). After the fall of FRANCE in 1940, Pétain was recalled from his post as ambassador to Spain and made vice premier. Succeeding Paul REYNAUD as premier, he concluded an armistice with GERMANY and assumed the title of chief of state in the new Vichy government of occupied France. Pétain sought an "honorable" collaboration with Germany in order to protect French citizens and prisoners, but his status as hero crumbled as harsh fascist policies were brought to bear. At the end of 1941 he dismissed Prime Minister Pierre LAVAL, who urged total collaboration with the Nazis. However, the following year, at the Germans' insistence, he was forced to recall Laval to office. Laval assumed the bulk of power, and Pétain became a virtual figurehead. After the defeat of Germany in 1945, Pétain was tried for treason, found guilty and sentenced to death. That penalty was commuted to life imprisonment by Charles DE GAULLE, and Pétain died in prison.

Peter II *(1923–1970)* King of YUGOSLAVIA (1934–45). Yugoslavia's second and last king, he succeeded to the throne under the regency of his cousin, Prince Paul, after the assassination of his father, King Alexander. Peter assumed power in 1941 after a coup d'état overthrew the regency. Weeks later he was forced to flee his country for England when GERMANY invaded Yugoslavia (see WORLD WAR II IN THE BALKANS). After the war, in 1945 TITO's communist regime abolished the monarchy and deposed Peter. The ex-king settled in the U.S., where his autobiography, *A King's Heritage,* was published in 1955. He died in the U.S. 15 years later.

Peter, Paul & Mary American folk group. Comprised of Peter Yarrow, Paul Stookey and Mary Travers, the group's roots are in the protest movement of the 1960s, even as their political activism continues today. Their early albums, such as *Peter, Paul & Mary* (1962) and *In the Wind* (1963), influenced such artists as Bob DYLAN. Among their hit singles in the early 1960s were such songs as "If I Had a Hammer" and "Puff the Magic Dragon," a perennial children's favorite. They had an unexpected number-one hit in 1969 with the romantic ballad "Leaving on a Jet Plane."

Peter Pan Long-running fantasy play by Sir James BARRIE about a boy who refused to grow up and ran away to a life of adventure in the Never, Never Land. The play has been an international success since its first English production on December 27, 1904, with Nina Boucicault in the title role. The first American production quickly followed on November 6, 1905, with Maude ADAMS. It has been estimated that in its first 50 years in England alone the play was presented over 10,000 times. The genesis of the play is long and complex. It contains scenes and characters from Barrie's boyhood in Kirriemuir and Dumfries, Scotland. Peter himself was a composite of the four children of Arthur and Sylvia Davies, whom Barrie

had met in Kensington Gardens in 1898 and with whom Barrie remained closely associated the rest of his life. The character first appears by name in Barrie's novel for adults, *The Little White Bird* (1901), and was later developed in 1903 under the title *The Great White Father.* The title was changed from the 1904 premiere.

The central roles of Pan and Captain Hook have attracted numerous stage and screen luminaries over the years. Traditionally, Peter has been played by an actress, and the list includes Maude Adams, Margaret Lockwood, Jean Arthur, Mary MARTIN and gymnast Cathy Rigby. Since Gerald Du Maurier first played Hook, the role has been taken on by the likes of Charles LAUGHTON, Alastair Sim, Boris KARLOFF and Cyril Ritchard. Barrie rewrote the play in novel form in *Peter and Wendy* in 1911. In America producer Herbert Brenon adapted it for the movies in 1924 with Betty Bronson in the title role. Subsequent versions include a musical version by Leonard BERNSTEIN in 1950, the Walt DISNEY animated film in 1953 and the Mary Martin television/stage musical in 1954, which has undergone several revivals with other actresses.

"Peter Principle" A rule that states that every employee tends to rise to his or her level of incompetence, then remain there. The principle was set forth and popularized in the satirical best-selling book *The Peter Principle: Why Things Always Go Wrong* (1969) by Canadian educator and psychologist Peter J. Laurence. The book explained that if an employee does a good job, he or she is repeatedly promoted until he or she eventually reaches a level where he or she cannot do the work—and there he or she remains. Although the "Peter Principle" was conceived tongue-in-cheek, it undoubtedly has a large element of truth.

Peters, Roberta (Roberta Peterman) *(1930–)* American coloratura soprano. Born in New York City, Peters spent her teenage years studying voice, languages, dancing and drama. By age 19 she had learned 20 opera roles. Her first professional appearance and Metropolitan Opera debut came unexpectedly when, with six hours notice, she sang the role of Zerlina in *Don*

Giovanni (1950). Over the next quarter century Peters excelled in the bel canto repertory at the Met. Her most distinguished and often-sung roles (in addition to Zerlina) included Gilda in *Rigoletto,* Queen of the Night in *The Magic Flute* and Despina in *Cosi fan tutte.* Peters has also won the Bolshoi medal (usually given to Russian artists only), sung at the White House six times, been a highly successful recitalist and made numerous recordings and TV appearances. Since her two-year term as a member of the National Council on the Arts (1991–93) Peters has received several honors, including the National Medal of Arts presented to her by William Jefferson CLINTON in 1998 and New York City's Handel Medallion presented to her in 2000 by New York City Mayor Rudolph GIULIANI in recognition of her cultural contributions to the city.

Peterson, Forrest *(1922–1990)* U.S. test pilot. Peterson flew the X-15 in five flights between 1960 and 1962 to a top altitude of 101,800 feet and was the only Navy pilot to fly the experimental rocket plane. Having spent four years in the program, Peterson left in 1962 to pursue what became a highly successful career in naval aviation, during which he served as captain of the aircraft carrier USS *Enterprise,* commander of the Sixth Fleet's Carrier Group Two and vice chief of naval operations for air at the Pentagon. He retired in 1980.

Petlyura, Semyon Vasilyevich *(1879–1926)* Ukrainian patriot who worked tirelessly to gain independence for the UKRAINE. In 1905 Petlyura helped found the Ukrainian Social Democratic Workers' Party. Having served in the Russian army in World War I, in 1917 he joined the Ukrainian central council, and was minister of defense in the first Ukrainian government. In 1920 he fought not only the Red Army in the north but also the anti-Soviet forces of General Anton Ivanovich DENIKIN. He spent some months in Warsaw, but after the peace of Riga he moved his government to Paris and was assassinated by a communist agent.

Petri, Elio *(1929–1982)* Italian film director and a leader of the neorealist movement in cinema. His 10 films satirized Italian society and challenged the established political order. Among his best-known films were *The Working Class Goes to Heaven,* which shared the Grand Prize at the 1972 CANNES FILM FESTIVAL, and *Investigation of a Citizen Above Suspicion,* which won the 1970 ACADEMY AWARD for best foreign film.

Pevsner, Anton *(1886–1962)* Russian constructivist artist. Having spent a year at the St. Petersburg Academy of Art in 1910, Pevsner went to Paris and then Norway, where he painted in the cubist style. In the early 1920s Pevsner began working on constructions and, together with his brother Naum GABO, joined the antiproductionist group Inkhuk.

Pevsner, Nikolaus Bernhard *(1902–1983)* German-born British architectural historian and critic. He established his career at the University of Göttingen. When Adolf HITLER became chancellor in 1933, Pevsner escaped from NAZI GERMANY to England, where he lectured at Cambridge and Oxford Universities and at the University of London. He was best known for editing the monumental 46-volume series *The Buildings of England* (1951–74).

P-40 See FLYING TIGERS.

Pham Van Dong *(1906–2000)* North Vietnamese official. Born in the French protectorate of Annam, which later became part of North Vietnam, Pham Van Dong was a close associate of HO CHI MINH both before and after the FRENCH INDOCHINA WAR OF 1946–54. During the VIETNAM WAR, he served as minister of foreign affairs and later as prime minister of North Vietnam. In July 1976 he was named prime minister of the newly unified Socialist Republic of VIETNAM.

Phantom of the Opera British and American musical stage production (1986–). On October 9, 1986, Andrew Lloyd Webber premiered *Phantom of the Opera* at Her Majesty's Theater in London. An adaptation of a novel by Gaston Leroux, *Phantom* chronicled the obsession of a disfigured opera connoisseur in 1861 who lived in the catacombs of the Paris Opera House, became obsessed with a young singer and understudy named

Christine and endeavored to advance her career through a variety of underhanded methods. In January 1987 *Phantom* opened on Broadway in New York City and proceeded to win seven Tony Awards, including Best Musical, at the 1987 ceremonies. It continued a long run on Broadway, and with the closing of *Cats* in 2002, it holds the distinction of being the current longest-running Broadway show in New York City. Since its debut, it is estimated that over 52 million people have seen *Phantom* in New York and London, as well as performances by touring companies throughout the world. Additionally, *Phantom's* total box office sales have exceeded $3 billion, making it the most profitable musical in history.

Phao Sriyanond *(1910–1960)* Thai army leader of the 1947 coup that restored Field Marshal Pibul Songgram to power in THAILAND. He served as chief of the Thai national police from 1947 to 1957. In 1957 he was exiled by Field Marshal Thanarat for alleged secret dealings with the government of communist CHINA. He spent the remainder of his life in Switzerland.

Phat Huynh Tan *(1913–1989)* Vietnamese communist leader. He was the chief theoretician of the VIETCONG, the communist-led political movement in South Vietnam that was backed by North Vietnam during the VIETNAM WAR. Following the communist victory in South Vietnam (1975), he became one of the few South Vietnamese to hold a leadership position in the HANOI government.

phenomenology School of philosophical thought that emerged in the early 1900s. Phenomenology—literally, the study of phenomena—has had a tremendous influence on psychology, sociology, theology, historical analysis and literary criticism in the 20th century. The key figures behind its formulation in the first decades of the century were three Germans—historian Wilhelm Dilthey, philosopher Edmund HUSSERL and sociologist Max Scheler. Phenomenology borrowed from 18th-century philosopher Immanuel Kant the notion of phenomena (perceived and experienced reality) as being distinct from noumena (ultimate

reality). Phenomena alone may be comprehended by human observers. The method of phenomenology emphasized that the task of an intellectual observer was to achieve a reconstructive identification with the phenomena under study, with the understanding that perfect objectivity was impossible while blatant bias was to be shunned. Phenomenology had a major influence on EXISTENTIALISM.

Philby, H(arold) A(drian) R(ussell) "Kim" *(1912–1988)* British-born Soviet spy, considered the most notorious double agent of the COLD WAR, if not of the 20th century. Philby was educated at Cambridge University in the early 1930s and recruited there as a Soviet KGB agent in 1933. He joined the British intelligence agency MI6 at the outbreak of World War II, becoming head of the service's anti-Soviet section in 1944. This key post enabled him to pass top secret information to Moscow. In the late 1940s Philby betrayed a secret Anglo-American plan to overthrow the communist government of ALBANIA. In 1949, he became MI6's liaison officer with the U.S. CENTRAL INTELLIGENCE AGENCY and was thus in an ideal position to compromise every MI6/CIA operation against the Soviet Union. In 1951 he warned fellow Cambridge graduates and Soviet spies Guy BURGESS and Donald MACLEAN that they were under suspicion, giving them time to defect to the Soviet Union. The CIA believed that Philby was the "third man" in the spy ring, but MI5, the British counterintelligence unit, was unable to prove any connection. Philby's activities were not fully exposed until he himself defected to the Soviet Union in 1963 just before his planned arrest. In Moscow, Philby continued his life as a KGB general; he never expressed regret for his treason.

Philippine election of 1986 Historic election that led to the fall of the regime of President Ferdinand MARCOS. Marcos had made an apparently impromptu announcement of upcoming elections while being questioned on an American news program. The election was held as promised, amid allegations of widespread fraud, with Corazon AQUINO, the widow of assassinated opposition leader **Benigno**

Aquino, as Marcos's main challenger. Both Marcos and Aquino claimed victory, but independent observers declared that Aquino had actually won the election. Less than three weeks later, U.S. president Ronald REAGAN called on Marcos to resign and offered him a haven in the U.S. On February 25 Marcos and Aquino each held their own inauguration ceremonies. Several hours later, Marcos went into exile. His 20-year reign as president was brought to an end after two leading military allies resigned from their posts—Lieutenant General Fidel RAMOS and Defense Minister Juan Ponce Enrile. The departure of Marcos, his wife **Imelda Marcos** and their entourage was widely hailed by Filipinos who felt that the Marcos regime had been thoroughly corrupt.

Philippine Insurrection of 1899–1902.

The Philippines led by Emilio Aguinaldo had declared independence from Spain on June 12, 1898, but Spain ceded the islands to the U.S. by the treaty of Paris. Aguinaldo refused U.S. control, establishing an independent government under the Malolos constitution. Hostilities against American rule began February 4, 1899. After several battles, American forces pushed the Filipinos back from Manila, capturing their capital at Malolos. Aguinaldo carried on guerrilla war until captured on March 23, 1901. The guerrilla war continued until May 6, 1902, when civil government was established under American control with William Howard TAFT as the first governor.

Philippines (Republic of the Philippines)

The Philippines consist of 7,100 islands that cover a total land area of approximately 115,800 square miles in the west Pacific Ocean about 497 miles off the southeast Asian coast. Formally ceded to the United States under terms of the Treaty of Paris, which ended the Spanish-American War, the country became the Commonwealth of the Philippines in 1935. JAPAN invaded the country in 1941, exploiting and brutalizing the people until U.S. forces liberated the country in 1944. The Republic of the Philippines was declared in 1946. After two decades of one-term presidents, Ferdinand MARCOS became president in 1965. During the next 20 years he

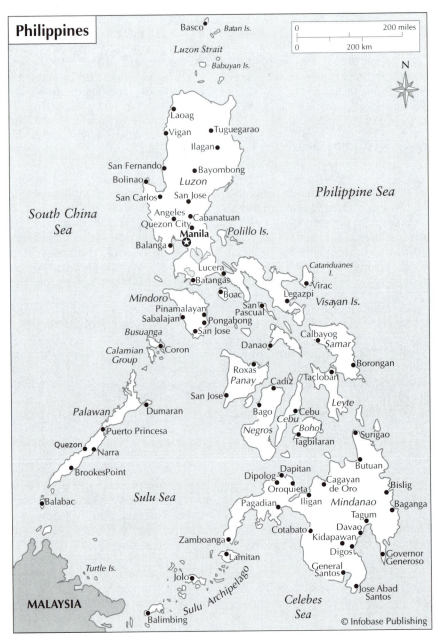

crushed all opposition and quelled insurrections by communist and Muslim guerrilla groups. He was ousted in 1986 with the election of Corazon AQUINO, widow of opposition leader Benigno Aquino, who had been murdered on his return to the country in 1983. A new constitution was approved in 1987. The Aquino government continued to battle guerrilla groups and survived several attempted coups, the most serious of which occurred in 1989. Although the Philippines remained free from autocratic rule with the elections of Fidel Ramos (1992–98) and Joseph Estrada (1998–

2001) and the inauguration of Gloria Macapagal-Arroyo (2001–   ), the country has been plagued by an insurrection by the Islamic separatist movement since 1994. In 2006 President Arroyo declared a state of emergency after a coup attempt was discovered.

Phillips, Rev. Channing E. (1928–1987)

American CIVIL RIGHTS activist. A United Church of Christ clergyman, he was Washington, D.C., Democratic national committeeman from 1968 to 1972. He became the first black nominated for president by a major political party when the Washington delegation

PHILIPPINES

1898	Philippines ceded to U.S. after Spanish-American War.
1899	Philippine nationalists who fought with Americans against Spanish in the Spanish-American conflict now fight U.S. domination in the Philippine-American War.
1941–45	Japan invades and subjects Philippines to brutal occupation.
1945	U.S. forces invade Philippines and liberate Manila.
1946	Republic of Philippines proclaimed independent sovereign state.
1965	Ferdinand Marcos wins presidency; attendant economic stagnation, rampant inflation and endemic corruption fuel popular opposition to his administration.
1972	Marcos imposes martial law.
1983	Prominent opposition leader Benigno Aquino returns from exile and is shot dead in the airport terminal as he disembarks plane.
1986	Under U.S. pressure, Marcos calls election, is defeated by Corazon Aquino, widow of Benigno; Aquino vows to recover national assets looted by Marcos and his allies, wipe out corruption and affirm civilian supremacy over military.
1987	One hundred thousand people visit Malacañang Palace to view luxury goods abandoned by Marcos family, among which are 1,060 pairs of Imelda Marcos's shoes.
1989	Ferdinand Marcos dies in exile in Hawaii.
1990	Earthquake on island of Luzon kills 1,621 people; President Aquino asks U.S. Congress for aid; Imelda Marcos charged with stealing $200 million from Philippine treasury, is acquitted in U.S. federal court for lack of evidence.
1994	Islamic separatist movement launches insurrection.
1998	President Ramos does not run for reelection; Joseph Estrada, a well-known actor, is elected president.
2001	Estrada is ousted amid charges of corruption; Vice President Gloria Macapagal-Arroyo is sworn in as president.
2003	A cease-fire between the government and the Moro Islamic Liberation Front (MILF) breaks down (February) and resumes (July).
2004	Arroyo wins the presidential elections.
2005	The cease-fire ends as heavy fighting resumes between government troops and MILF rebels. President Arroyo comes under fire to resign over allegations of vote rigging.
2006	President Arroyo declares state of emergency after a failed coup attempt.

to the 1968 Democratic National Convention nominated him as its favorite son candidate in place of the slain Robert F. KENNEDY.

Phony War (*German: Sitzkrieg*) Term given to a brief period in WORLD WAR II that followed Germany's BLITZKRIEG attack on Poland. Lasting from late 1939 until early 1940, the Phony War (also known as the "*Sitzkrieg*") was a time of inaction during which the French and British maintained a defensive position behind the MAGINOT LINE and the USSR turned its attention to the RUSSO-FINNISH WAR. Given over to strategizing, this period of military malaise was ended by Adolf HITLER's invasion of NORWAY on April 9, 1940, and the subsequent replacement of Neville CHAMBERLAIN with Winston CHURCHILL as British prime minister on May 10.

photojournalism Technique of journalistic reporting that relies heavily on incisive and exemplary photographic images. While photography has served as a component of journalism since the mid-19th century, it stepped to the forefront only in the 20th century. The first key development of the modern era was German inventor Alfred Korn's 1907 technique of sending photographic images by wire. By the 1920s, German magazines such as the *Münchner Illustrierte Presse* (MIP) had won an audience by letting photographs do much of the narrative work in their articles. In the U.S., this approach was successfully emulated by two magazines founded in the mid-1930s, *LIFE* and *Look*. Photojournalists who have won renown for their work since the 1930s include Margaret BOURKE-WHITE, Robert CAPA, Walker EVANS and W. Eugene Smith.

Photo-Secession A loose-knit group of American photographers formed at the beginning of the 20th century by Alfred STIEGLITZ. As propounded in 1902 in its journal *Camera Work*, the general mandate was the promotion of the higher forms of photography as a fine art. At the time, argues historian William Innes Homer, American photography was "embarrassingly awkward," a collection of stereotypical studio portraits and "superficial imitations of the conventions of painting."

Photo-Secession's original members included Edward STEICHEN, Gertrude Kasebier, Clarence H. White, Joseph T. Keiley, Frank Eugene and Alvin Langdon COBURN. There were many exhibitions over the next few years, notably in "291," Stieglitz's famous exhibition space on Fifth Avenue. Dissension soon eroded the ranks of the society. Stieglitz grew increasingly dissatisfied at those members whose pictorial effects imitated with soft-focus lenses the hazy effects of Impressionist paintings. He demanded that photography pursue the course of a "straight," unmediated expression. Other members were disgruntled at Stieglitz's increasing use of the exhibition space for contemporary painters. By the time the group sponsored the International Exhibition of Pictorial Photography in Buffalo in 1910, a schism with Stieglitz was imminent. After his withdrawal, the Photo-Secessionists organized a "second" Secession, the Pictorial Photographers of America, in 1916. Its gradual dissolution came, writes Homer, from a preponderance of "bland, soft-focus pictorialism."

Piaf, Edith (Giovanna Gassion) (1915–1963) French singer. *Piaf* is the French word for sparrow, and this adopted name became the symbol of Edith Piaf's immense popularity with the French people. She was known as The Little Sparrow because of her slight build and plaintive singing style that could wring the heights of emotion from the ballads that dominated her musical repertoire. In the 1940s and '50s, at the height of her fame, Piaf was a familiar figure not only in her native land but also in England and the U.S. She was admired not only by her fans but by literati such as Jean COCTEAU. Her life was in many ways a tragic one, marred by failed marriages and drug abuse. The hit Broadway play *Piaf* (1980), written by Pam Gens and starring Jane Lapotaire, was a musical re-creation of her legend.

Piaget, Jean (1896–1980) Swiss psychologist, renowned for his groundbreaking studies of child development and theories of human intelligence. Piaget was initially interested in the natural sciences, and received his doctorate in science in 1918. However, he became increasingly fascinated by the question of how children learn and by the 1920s had shifted his energy to this as-yet undeveloped field. He theorized that all children learned by passing through a series of distinct intellectual stages and that each child was a significant agent in that process. He also proposed that children, starting from birth, were constantly constructing and reconstructing their own model of reality, revising their conceptions of the world around them through their own self-discoveries. Piaget was active in research for more than 60 years; during this time he exercised a profound influence on the field of child psychology in Europe and the U.S. He wrote more than 50 books and monographs and received honorary degrees from more than 30 universities. He worked at the Universities of Geneva (1929–54), Lausanne (1938–51) and the Sorbonne (1952–63).

Piano, Renzo (1937–) Italian-born architect and winner of the Pritzker Prize for architecture (1998). Born in Genoa, Piano studied architecture at the Milan Polytechnic under renowned Italian architect Franco Albini. In 1964 Piano graduated from Milan Polytechnic, and began to work as an architect with Louis Khan in Philadelphia and A. S. Makowsky in London. In 1971 Piano joined with Richard Rogers to form Piano & Rogers, an architectural studio that, between 1971 and 1977, was in charge of designing and overseeing the construction of the Centre Georges Pompidou, a modern art museum in Paris. In 1977 he ended his collaboration with Rogers to start Piano & Rice, an architectural firm with engineer Peter Rice, which from 1978 to 1982 was primarily known for its construction of a residential complex in Corciano, Italy. In 1981 Piano formed his own independent architectural agency, the Renzo Piano Building Workshop in Genoa, with the goals of producing more innovative architectural designs and of serving as a mentor to aspiring Italian architects. He later established branches of his workshops in Paris (1987) and Osaka (1989). Throughout his career, Piano has been responsible for designing and overseeing the construction of a variety of projects ranging from Genoa subway stations (1983) to the San Nicola Stadium in Bari, Italy (1987) to the Kansai International Airport terminal in Osaka, Japan (1988) to the London Bridge Tower in London, England (2000). In 1998, in recognition of his contributions to the field of architecture, Piano received the Pritzker Prize, the highest honor in the architectural field.

Picasso, Pablo (1881–1973) Spanish-born painter, sculptor and potter, widely regarded as the greatest visual artist of the 20th century. Trained at an early age by his Spanish painter father, Picasso moved to PARIS as a young man and spent most of his life there and in the Midi region of France. In the early 1900s, Picasso produced noteworthy portraits during what are known as his Blue and Rose Periods. With fellow painter Georges BRAQUE, Picasso founded the highly influential artistic movement known as CUBISM in the late 1900s. His famous painting *Les Demoiselles d'Avignon* (1907)—which depicts five women in diverse geometric poses and incorporates the influence of African art—is regarded as the first true cubist painting. Picasso's painting styles continued to evolve throughout his career, ranging from strong realism to extreme abstraction. In the 1940s he produced a series of "found object" sculptures. In the 1950s and after, he devoted considerable energy to his pottery works in the Midi.

Piccard, Auguste (1884–1962) Swiss physicist. A pioneer in the exploration of the atmosphere and the ocean floor, Piccard taught in the U.S. and Switzerland before becoming professor of physics at Brussels Polytechnic (1922–56). To explore the atmosphere he developed a pressurized cabin attached to a balloon; he successfully tested it in 1931, ascending approximately 11 miles into the atmosphere. Next he designed a maneuverable craft to explore the ocean deeps, which reached a depth of about a mile when tested in 1948. A second craft descended to 2.5 miles in the Mediterranean. It was later sold to the U.S. Navy and used to plumb the Marianas trench in the Pacific (seven miles deep) in 1960.

Piccolo, Lucio (1903–1969) Italian poet. A native son of Palermo, Piccolo led a relatively isolated life at his home in Sicily and often focused on

Sicilian subjects. *Nove liriche (Nine Poems)* was privately printed in 1954. He owes his critical discovery to Eugenio MONTALE's praise of his 1956 *Canti barocchi (Baroque Songs)*. Other works include *Gioco a nascondere* (1960, *Hide and Seek*) and *Plumela* (1967). His poems are filled with rich and exotic imagery and attempt to achieve a sense of timelessness.

Pickford, Mary *(1893–1979)* The most popular motion picture star in screen history. She was a rare combination of dramatic actress, comedienne, entrepreneur and businessperson. Born Gladys Smith in Toronto, she toured with various theater road companies as "Baby Gladys," the primary breadwinner in her family. By the age of 16 she had not only conquered the Broadway stage (winning over producer David BELASCO to star in his *The Warrens of Virginia*) but had begun appearing in short films directed by D. W. GRIFFITH for the BIOGRAPH company. The next seven years consolidated her position as the number-one box-office star and highest-paid contract player in the business. "The Little Girl with the Curls," as her fans dubbed her, became "The Girl with the Cash-Register Brain," as her boss at Famous Players, Adolph ZUKOR, described her. She went from $40 a week at Biograph to $10,000 a week in 1916. With the creation that year of the Pickford Film Corporation, she became the first star to produce her own pictures and win a degree of control over her work. These

Silent film star and founding member of United Artists Mary Pickford (LIBRARY OF CONGRESS, PRINTS AND PHOTOGRAPHS DIVISION)

were the years of her quintessential image, a radiant, sprightly little girl with plenty of courage and daring. With her favorite directors, Marshall Neilan and Maurice Tourneur, she made many classics, including *Poor Little Rich Girl* (1917), *Pride of the Clan* (1916) and *Daddy Long Legs* (1919); and some genuine masterpieces such as *Rebecca of Sunnybrook Farm* (1917) and *Stella Maris* (1918). After her marriage to Douglas FAIRBANKS Sr. in 1920 and her involvement in the founding of UNITED ARTISTS, her work began to change. Bigger budgets and more mature roles produced *Dorothy Vernon of Haddon Hall* (1925), *The Taming of the Shrew* (1929) and *Coquette,* for which she won an ACADEMY AWARD as best actress in 1929. Her famous curls were cut off for that role, creating a sensation with the press and the public. After making *Secrets* in 1933, she retired from acting and devoted the rest of her life to business affairs, charitable activities, a book of memoirs (*Sunshine and Shadow*, 1955) and presiding over Beverly Hills society at her home, Pickfair, with her third husband, Charles "Buddy" Rogers. Before her death in 1979 she donated more than 50 of her Biograph-period films to the American Film Institute and received a special Academy Award in 1975 in recognition of her contributions to American film.

Piggott, Lester *(1935–)* British jockey. Piggott is widely regarded as the leading British jockey of the 20th century. Born to a father who was a steeplechase rider and a mother from a racing family, Piggott scored the first of his record seven Epsom Derby wins in 1954 when he was only 19. He was the British champion jockey in 1960, and continuously from 1964 to 1971. His best year was 1966 when he booted home 191 wins. Always popular with racing fans for his intense style, his rough riding tactics rendered him less so with his fellow jockeys. His 3,000 wins over 25 years included victories in the Irish Sweepstakes, the Arc de Triomphe and the Washington International. In the 1980s, Piggott ran afoul of the law and served a prison term for tax evasion. However, he made a spectacular comeback when he won a major race in the 1990 Breeders' Cup at Belmont at age 55. Piggott retired in 1995.

"Pig War" *(1905–1909)* SERBIA, in an attempt to reduce dependence on Austria-Hungary, imported French (instead of Austrian) munitions and established a customs union with BULGARIA, making Austrian goods uncompetitive. AUSTRIA responded by closing off Serbian pork imports. Serbia refused to bow, pressuring for a trade outlet on the Adriatic Sea through Austrian administered BOSNIA-HERZEGOVINA, and was supported by Russia. War between RUSSIA and Austria was averted by a German ultimatum (1909) demanding cessation of Russian aid to Serbia. Austria and Serbia developed a new commercial treaty, but Serbia covertly agitated among Slavs in newly Austrian annexed Bosnia-Herzegovina, contributing to the start of WORLD WAR I.

pill, the Method of oral contraception that became widely available in 1961. Early forms of the pill contained artificial forms of the female hormones estrogen and progesterone. Taken for 21 days during a menstrual cycle, they suppress the production of the pituitary hormones that normally cause ovulation. The lack of ovulation prevents the possibility of pregnancy. More recent versions of the pill have contained only the progesterone-like hormone. It does not prevent ovulation but does prevent fertilization. The contraceptive pill is extremely popular because of its ease of use and comparative safety. However, it has been shown to cause some health risks, including cardiac or cardiovascular problems, and blood clots in some women who smoke, are overweight or are above the age of 35. Among the less serious side effects that the pill may produce are nausea, headache and weight gain.

Pilnyak, Boris (B. A. Vogaul) *(1894– 1937)* Russian writer. Pilnyak's novel *The Naked Year* (1922) was the first novel to deal with the revolution and its effects on Russian life. Pilnyak became disillusioned with the regime, and the publication of *Mahogany* (1929) caused him to be expelled from the author association. His novel about the FIVE-YEAR PLAN, *The Volga Flows into the Caspian Sea*, was an attempt to reinstate himself in official favor. He survived the purges by publicly denouncing his "antirevolutionary" writings.

Piłsudski, Józef *(1867–1935)* Polish soldier and nationalist leader. Piłsudski began his political career agitating against Russian rule of POLAND. At age 20 he was sent to Siberia for several years as punishment for his anti-Russian activities. Returning to Poland (1892), he founded and edited a socialist-nationalist newspaper. During the RUSSO-JAPANESE WAR (1904–05) he went to Tokyo to appeal for Japanese aid for a Polish revolt against RUSSIA, but this mission failed. At the start of WORLD WAR I he organized a force of some 10,000 Polish volunteers to fight alongside the Austrians against Russia. However, he earned the mistrust of the Germans, who interned him in 1917. He returned to newly independent POLAND at the end of the war (1918). With the title of marshal he assumed command of all Polish troops and was made provisional head of state. He successfully defended Poland against a Soviet invasion (1919–20). He retired as head of the army in 1923 but led a military coup three years later (May 12–15, 1926) after a breakdown of the democratic government. He was officially prime minister from 1926 to 1928 and again briefly in 1930; but as minister of war from 1926 on, he remained the virtual dictator of Poland until his death. Piłsudski was one of the first European leaders to recognize the dangers of NAZISM, but his warnings went largely unheeded.

Pinhiero de Azevedo, José Baptista *(1917–1983)* Portuguese naval officer and politician. He was a member of the ruling **Junta of National Salvation,** a coalition of leaders who governed PORTUGAL following a military coup in April 1974 that ousted the authoritarian government of Premier Marcelo Caetano. Pinheiro de Azevedo served as premier in a provisional government from September 1975 until June 1976, when he oversaw the country's first democratic elections in 48 years.

Pink Floyd British ROCK and roll band. Pink Floyd, which achieved great commercial success in the 1970s, was founded in London in 1966. Featuring a psychedelic style, the original lineup of musicians included Syd Barrett, vocals and guitar; Roger Waters, bass; Richard Wright, keyboards; and Nick Mason, drums. Pink Floyd enjoyed its first British hit with the single "Arnold Layne" (1967). In 1968 David Gilmour joined the band as a replacement for Barrett. Pink Floyd became known for its dramatic and inventive use of large-scale sound systems, electronic music and vocal choruses. Its album *The Dark Side of the Moon* (1973) remained on the American album charts for over a decade—the longest run in recording history. Its 1979 album *The Wall* featured the hit single "Another Brick in the Wall." In 1995 Pink Floyd was inducted into the Rock and Roll Hall of Fame.

Pinochet, Augusto *(1915–)* A career Chilean army officer, Pinochet rose to general and was commander in chief of CHILE's armed forces from 1973 to 1980. He led the right-wing coup that deposed President Salvador ALLENDE in 1973. President of the Government Council of Chile (1973–74), he subsequently became president of Chile in 1974. An authoritarian though not totalitarian leader, he followed a strict policy of repression against opponents of his regime. In October 1988 a referendum calling for new elections was adopted by popular vote; Pinochet agreed to abide by the result. A democratic civilian government was elected in 1989, and Pinochet stepped down upon the inauguration of the new president, although he remained as commander in chief of the army. In October 1998 Pinochet traveled to Britain to receive medical treatment, but was taken into custody for extradition to Spain, where he was scheduled to stand trial on charges that he committed atrocities against Spanish citizens. However, in 2000, a British court ruled that he was not physically and mentally fit to stand trial, and Pinochet was sent back to Chile. In 2005 a court in Chile placed Pinochet under indictment and house arrest in connection with the slaying of 119 dissidents in 1975.

Pinter, Harold (Harold Da Pinta) *(1930–)* British playwright, screenplay writer and theatrical director. Pinter is the leading British playwright of the postwar era, with a unique gift—for which admiring critics coined the term "Pinteresque"—for portraying psychological anguish through subtly revelatory dialogue. His first success, the one-act play *The Room* (1957), was followed by several acclaimed full-length plays including *The Birthday Party* (1958), *The Dumb Waiter* (1958) and *The Caretaker* (1960), which was adapted into an acclaimed British film, titled *The Guest* (1964), featuring Alan Bates, Donald Pleasance and Robert Shaw. A more recent play, *Betrayal* (1978), was adapted by Pinter himself into screenplay form for the film *Betrayal* (1982), starring Jeremy Irons, Ben Kingsley and Patricia Hodge and concerning a tortured love triangle. Pinter has written frequently for films—including the screenplay for *The French Lieutenant's Woman* (1981)—while continuing his involvement with the theater. Pinter continued to produce plays throughout the 1990s, including *Moonlight* (1993), *Ashes to Ashes* (1996) and *Celebration* (1999). He is married to the British writer Lady Antonia Fraser.

Pinza, Ezio *(1892–1957)* Italian bass opera singer and actor. Pinza was considered one of the greatest bass voices of the opera stage from the 1920s to the 1940s. He was a regular performer with the Metropolitan Opera in New York, although he toured regularly in Europe and South America as well. Pinza appeared often in Verdi basso roles and also triumphed in the lead role of Mozart's *Don Giovanni*. Late in his career, Pinza turned to less demanding vocal roles in Broadway musicals and enjoyed great success in Richard RODGERS and Oscar HAMMERSTEIN II's *South Pacific* (1949). He thereafter enjoyed a brief HOLLYWOOD career in films such as *Tonight We Sing* (1953).

Pioneer Early U.S. spacecraft and program, developed in response to the Soviet Luna missions, which had orbited and photographed the moon at close range. *Pioneer 1,* which attained an altitude of 70,171 miles, was launched on October 11, 1958. A month later, the launch of *Pioneer 2* failed; *Pioneer 3,* launched on December 6, reached an altitude of 63,580 miles. *Pioneer 4,* launched March 3, 1959, completed the first lunar fly-by at a distance of 37,300 miles from the moon. The Pioneers were succeeded by the RANGER missions, but continued to be used into the '70s for long-range probes to Jupiter, Saturn and beyond.

Pioneers Group for young Soviets between the ages of 10 and 14 to 15 years, founded as an auxiliary to the KOMSOMOL in 1922. The aim of the movement was outlined in the Komsomol statute: It should make its members "convinced fighters for the Communist Party cause, inculcate in them the love of labor and knowledge, and assist the formation of the younger generation in the spirit of communist consciousness and morality." Regular meetings were held; visits were arranged to places of revolutionary interest; and Pioneers paraded and took part in summer camps. Pioneer activities often provided a useful addition to the school curriculum. Those wishing to join had to take the Pioneer oath and undertake to obey the Pioneer laws. Nearly all children in this age range were Pioneers.

Piotrovsky, Boris B. *(1908–1990)* Russian archaeologist and museum director. Piotrovsky was one of the leading archaeologists of the 20th century. His most famous project was the discovery, in 1939, of remains of the ancient civilization of Urartu in what is now Armenia. Through his excavations in Karmir Blur in Armenia, Piotrovsky unearthed an Urartu fortress and town. During his career, he published over 200 scholarly works. In 1964 he was named director of the Hermitage, the famous St. Petersburg museum that houses one of the world's great collections of art and archaeological artifacts. Piotrovsky was an honorary member of numerous Western academies of science, including those of France and England.

Pirandello, Luigi *(1867–1936)* Italian playwright, actor, story writer, novelist and literary critic. Pirandello, who won the NOBEL PRIZE for literature in 1934, was a prolific and versatile writer who remains best known for his works for the stage. An important precursor of the Theater of the ABSURD movement, Pirandello was a theatrical pioneer in dealing with existential themes including the tenuous nature of sanity, the loss of secure personal identity in modern society and the absurd cruelties occasioned by political ambition. He was also influential by virtue of his discarding of standard dramatic plot structure. Pirandello's first success came with the play *Right You Are (If You Think So)* (1917). His major theatrical works include *Enrico IV* (1922), *The Man with a Flower in His Mouth* (1923), *Lazarus* (1929) and the trilogy of *Six Characters in Search of an Author* (1922), *Each in His Own Way* (1924) and *Tonight We Improvise* (1929).

Pire, Jules-Joseph *(1878–1953)* Belgian general and WORLD WAR II RESISTANCE leader. At the time of the Nazi invasion of BELGIUM in May 1940, Pire was an infantry commander. Joining the forces resisting Germany, Pire entered the Belgian Legion in 1941 and was widely known by the code name "Pygmalion." In collaboration with other Resistance groups, he executed a number of important sabotage raids in 1944. Leading the underground Belgian army, he aided British and American troops in the liberation of Belgium in September 1944, preventing the retreating German army from destroying such key installations as the port facilities at Antwerp and protecting Belgian armored divisions that were actively supporting Allied activities.

Piro, Frank "Killer Joe" *(1920–1989)* American dancer and dance instructor who taught popular dance steps to scores of high-society figures. Among Piro's students were the Duke and Duchess of WINDSOR (see EDWARD VIII), Luci Baines Johnson (daughter of Lyndon Baines JOHNSON), and Dame Margot FONTEYN. He also helped popularize many of the discotheque-style dances of the 1960s and '70s. He was known as "Killer Joe" for his ability to outlast any partner of the dance floor.

Piston, Walter *(1894–1976)* American composer and teacher. As a composer, Piston is noted for his sophisticated, balanced, neoclassical style and his use of harmony and counterpoint. As a teacher, he was admired for his musical knowledge and ability to inspire such students as Leonard BERNSTEIN. He taught music at Harvard University from 1926 until he retired in 1960. His most famous compositions include Symphony No. 3 (1947) and Symphony No. 7 (1960), for which he received PULITZER PRIZES, and a Viola Concerto (1957) and String Quartet No. 5 (1962), for which he received New York Music Critics Circle Awards.

Pius X (Giuseppe Melchiorre Sarto) *(1835–1914)* Supreme pontiff of the Roman Catholic Church. Born Giuseppe Sarto in Riese, Italy, Pius X reigned from 1903 to 1914. As pope, he condemned religious modernism, reformed the church's system of religious instruction, opposed anticlerical laws in Italy and France and began the process of recodifying canon law and retranslating the Bible. Renowned for his concern for the poor, Pius X was canonized a saint in 1954 by Pope PIUS XII.

Pius XI (Ambrogio Damiano Achille Ratti) *(1857–1939)* Supreme pontiff of the Roman Catholic Church. Achille Ratti, born in Desio, Italy, reigned as pope from February 6, 1922, to February 10, 1939. As pope, Pius XI promoted missionary activities, criticized laissez-faire capitalism and denounced MUSSOLINI and HITLER. In 1929, he signed with Italy the Lateran Agreement, which granted independent status to Vatican City and recognized Catholicism as Italy's official religion.

Pius XII (Eugenio Pacelli) *(1876–1958)* Supreme pontiff of the Roman Catholic Church (1939–58). Born in Rome, Pacelli was ordained a Roman Catholic priest in 1899 and entered the papal diplomatic service in 1901, serving in various capacities therein for 38 years. He became both a cardinal and a papal secretary of state in 1930. Pacelli became acquainted with German politics as a nuncio to the WEIMAR REPUBLIC during the 1920s, and in 1933 he negotiated a diplomatic agreement between the Vatican and the newly formed Nazi government. In 1939 he was elected as pope and took the name Pius XII. During WORLD WAR II Pius XII failed to make any public protest against the Nazi genocide efforts against the Jews, thereby earning a great deal of public criticism. After the war Pius XII condemned the new communist regimes in Poland, Romania, Hungary and Yugoslavia.

Plague, The Novel (1947) by French NOBEL PRIZE–winning author Albert CAMUS, widely regarded as one of the great novels of the 20th century. Written in post–WORLD WAR II France, it shows the influence of the painful occupation of France by the Nazis, during which time Camus was active in the French RE-SISTANCE. The story is set in the Algerian city of Oran, in which a plague (interpreted by many critics as symbolizing the invading Nazi forces) has broken out. As the city is cordoned off and dwindles in population and resources, the inner resources of each resident are tested. Some, such as heroic Dr. Bernard Rieux, give themselves over to helping their fellow humans and succeed in spiritually transcending their formerly shallow lives to become, in the terms of Camus's existential philosophy, saints without a God. Other persons retreat into selfishness and are likened unto the rats that scamper in the plague-ridden streets. (See also EXISTENTIALISM.)

Plaid Cymru Welsh name for the Party of Wales, or Welsh Nationalist Party, formed by intellectuals who merged several small groups in August 1925. Its program favors Welsh language and culture. It gained publicity with involvement in the terrorist bombings of a Royal Air Force (RAF) base in 1938. In 1966 disillusionment with the LABOUR PARTY gained Plaid Cymru its first House of Commons seat, which increased to three by 1974. The party is also represented in local governments and councils. After the defeat of Welsh autonomy in the 1979 referendum, the party lost ground, but managed to retain two seats in Parliament in that year's election. Its members are mostly from the middle class, favoring a moderate economic program and opposing English-language signs and migration to Wales by wealthy English people.

Planchon, Roger (1931–) French stage director, actor and playwright. Planchon is best known as an innovative theatrical visionary who succeeded, in his native land, in drawing substantial popular and critical attention to productions staged outside of Paris. His own theater, first founded in Lyon in 1950 and subsequently located in Villeurbanne as the Théâtre National Populaire, has become one of the leading centers of French drama. Influenced by Antonin ARTAUD and Bertolt BRECHT, Planchon has tended to avoid the classic French theater repertoire in favor of innovative stagings of modern European playwrights as well as iconoclastic reinterpretations of Shakespeare. His

own plays include *Bleus, blancs, rouges* (1967), *Le Cochon noir* (1974) and *Gilles de Rais* (1976). In 1998 Planchon helped produce *Lautrec,* a film depicting the Parisian life of the artist Henri de Toulouse-Lautrec.

Planck, Max Karl Ernst Ludwig (1858–1947) German physicist. Planck is the originator of quantum theory and therefore the father of 20th-century physics. He received his Ph.D. in 1879 from the University of Munich, and from 1889 to his retirement in 1928, he was affiliated with the University of Berlin. In 1900, while investigating the radiation given off by hot bodies, Planck discovered that the radiation was not emitted consistently over all wave lengths, as predicted by classical physics, but in "jumps"; this led him to suggest that energy was released in small packets, or quanta. Planck's revolutionary theory was soon put to the test by other researchers, including Albert EINSTEIN, who used the quantum theory to explain the photoelectric effect in 1905; Niels BOHR, who based his model of the hydrogen atom on the principle in 1913; and Arthur COMPTON, who used it to investigate X-ray scattering in 1923. In 1918 Planck won the NOBEL PRIZE for physics.

Plante, Joseph Jacques Omer (1929–1986) French-Canadian athlete. He was one of the greatest goaltenders in the history of the National Hockey League. During his 17–year career he played with five teams but was best known as the goalie of the Montreal Canadiens in the 1950s, when the team won five successive Stanley Cups. His career goals against average was 2.37, with 82 shutouts. He won the Vezina Trophy seven times for the lowest goals against average. He emerged from a three-year retirement in 1968, lending credibility to the expansionist St. Louis Blues. He was the first modern goaltender to wear a face mask and was one of the first to establish the modern style of roaming beyond the goal crease.

plastics Plastics are synthetic materials that can be turned into a variety of usable products through such processes as heating and molding. As a result of their molecular structure (plastic molecules are called poly-

mers), plastics soften when heated but become rigid when cooled, and are tough and lightweight. The term *plastic* is derived from the Greek *plastikos,* meaning "to form." In 1910 American chemist Leo H. Baekeland made the first completely synthetic plastic, called BAKELITE. The plastics industry exploded after 1920 with the growth of the chemical industry and development of necessary equipment for its manufacture. Such raw materials as cellulose, coal and petroleum products are combined with a variety of chemicals and additives to make durable plastic. Plastics can be made by molding, extrusion, lamination, casting and foaming, and are used in everything from rigid foam for refrigerator insulation and flexible foam for clothing to nylon films for medical use.

Plate, Battle of the River Naval engagement between the British and Germans that took place on December 13, 1939, in the early part of WORLD WAR II. The German pocket battleship *Graf Spee,* which had already sunk nine Allied ships, was sighted in the South Atlantic by a British cruiser squadron under the command of Commodore Henry Harwood (later admiral). The three-ship squadron inflicted considerable damage on the German vessel, which was forced into Montevideo for repairs. Meanwhile, a large naval force gathered at the Plate estuary. The Germans were forced to scuttle the *Graf Spee* off the coast of Uruguay on December 17, rather than face the British ships. The Battle of the River Plate was the first direct encounter between British and German forces during the war, and was an important naval victory and morale-booster for the British.

Plath, Sylvia (1932–1963) American poet. The daughter of an elderly German-American entomologist who died when she was eight and of an ambitious mother, Plath was a star student in high school. In the summer of 1954, along with Anne SEXTON, she studied with Robert LOWELL at Boston University. Plath's autobiographical novel, *The Bell Jar* (1961), describes her years at Smith College (B.A., 1955), an unhappy stint as a guest editor for *Mademoiselle* in 1953 and her hospitalization after her first suicide attempt. She attended Newnham College, Cambridge, where she married the poet Ted HUGHES in 1956. In 1959 she settled in England. She published only two books before her suicide at the age of 31, but her posthumous *Ariel* (1965) stunned the literary world with its starkly powerful and horrific imagery. Her poetry continued to appear for a decade while her reputation and influence burgeoned, particularly among feminists (see FEMINISM). Plath is considered among the strongest and most original of the CONFESSIONAL POETS, although her work continues to stir controversy.

Playboy of the Western World, The Play (1907) by the Irish playwright John Millington SYNGE. Though it is now acknowledged as a classic, *The Playboy of the Western World* was a highly controversial play when it was first performed, sparking riots by audiences in Dublin in 1907 and in New York City upon its American premiere in 1911. What aroused the audience so was the bold portrayal of its protagonist, the randy and charismatic Christy Mahon, who wins the heart of the lovely Pegeen Mike and the esteem of an entire Irish village due to his false bragging as to how he murdered his tyrant of a father. When Christy's father—still alive and healthy—arrives in search of his son, Christy feels compelled to try to kill him to save his honor. But a murder attempt pursued in their own environs leads the once-admiring villagers to call for Christy's death. Christy's father begs for clemency, however, and he and his son depart from the village reunited in spirit. The central theme of *Playboy* is the ease by which people are swayed by superficial appearances and assumptions.

Player, Gary Jim *(1935–   )* South African golfer. Arnold PALMER, Jack NICKLAUS and Gary Player had a virtual lock on tournament play during the 1960s. In 1959, at the age of 23, Player became the youngest player ever to win the modern British Open, an event he was to capture again in 1968 and 1972. He twice won the U.S. Masters at Augusta: first, in a thrilling one-stroke victory over Arnold Palmer and again 13 years later. Despite his preference for playing in Europe, Asia and Africa, Player finished his career sixth on the American career earnings list.

Plekhanov, Georgi Valentinovich *(1857–1919)* Russian politician. When the organization Zemlya i Volya, of which Plekhanov was a member, split into violent and nonviolent factions, Plekhanov became leader of the new, nonviolent Cherny Peredel (Black Repartition). Having become a Marxist in Western Europe, in 1883 he founded the Liberation of Labor group. Collaborating with LENIN, Plekhanov at first supported the BOLSHEVIKS, but in 1903 joined the MENSHEVIKS, and in 1910 he established the faction of "party-minded" Mensheviks. He played a unique part in converting the Russian intelligentsia to Marxism. After the FEBRUARY REVOLUTION of 1917, Plekhanov set up the right-wing Social Democratic organization Unity, but died shortly after the Bolshevik seizure of power.

Plisetskaya, Maya *(1925–   )* Russian ballerina. Having studied at the Bolshoi School, Plisetskaya was considered one of the greatest ballerinas of her time. She is noted particularly for her interpretation of the role of Odette-Odile in *Swan Lake*.

Plomley, Roy *(1914–1985)* British radio personality who created and hosted what was believed to be the world's longest-running radio series, *Desert Island Discs*, broadcast on the BBC since 1942. Each week, he asked his guest celebrities to choose eight records, one book and one luxury item they would like to have with them if marooned on a desert island. He would then chat with them about their lives and intersperse the conversation with recordings of their musical selections. Over the years he had close to 1,800 guests on the show, including Princess Margaret and Prime Minister Margaret Thatcher.

PM See Ralph McAllister INGERSOLL.

Pocket Book American publishing company, founded in 1939 by Robert F. de Graff *(1895–1981)*. It was the first U.S. publisher to specialize in paperback editions. Beginning with 10 inexpensive reprints, it marketed these books by selling them at newsstands, in grocery stores and in drugstores for 25 cents apiece. Pocket Book revolutionized the U.S. publishing industry and opened the way for what became a standard practice in the publishing and book-selling industry. By the time de Graff retired in 1957, Pocket Book's annual sales totaled $15 million.

Podhoretz, Norman See COMMENTARY.

Podoloff, Maurice *(1890–1985)* American sports executive. Podoloff was president of the Basketball Association of America (BAA) from 1946 to 1949 and, from 1949 until his retirement in 1963, first president of the National Basketball Association (NBA). That league was created through a merger of the BAA and the old National Basketball League. Only 5 feet 2 inches tall himself, he never played basketball but was one of the game's great innovators. He invented the 24–second clock and the six-foul rule and implemented the use of professional referees. He was responsible for the NBA landing its first TV contract in 1954.

Podvoysky, Nicholas Ilich *(1880–1948)* Soviet politician. Having joined the Social Democratic Labor Party in 1901, Podvoysky later adhered to its BOLSHEVIK faction. He was the owner of a publishing house specializing in Social Democratic literature before World War I. Following the FEBRUARY REVOLUTION of 1917, he was a member of the executive branch of the first legal Bolshevik St. Petersburg committee and chairman of the military commission of the central committee and of the military revolutionary committee of the Petrograd Soviet. After the seizure of power, Podvoysky set about the task of organizing the Red Army. In spite of the fact that he served as a commissar in the RUSSIAN CIVIL WAR, he fell out of favor and from the 1930s was relegated to serving on the staff of the Marx-Engels-Lenin Institute.

pogrom (devastation) An attack on JEWS and Jewish property, especially in the Russian Empire. Russian pogroms, which were condoned by the government, were particularly common in the years immediately after the assassination of Alexander II in 1881 and again from 1903 to 1906, although mob persecution of Jews continued until the 1917 Russian Revolution.

Poincaré, Raymond *(1860–1934)* French statesman, president of FRANCE (1913–20). A Parisian lawyer, he was a member of the Chamber of Deputies from 1887 to 1912, holding various cabinet posts, and served as a senator from 1903 to 1913. He became premier and foreign minister in 1912. Perceiving the threat of war from Germany, he strengthened ententes between France and both Russia and England, while attempting to prepare his nation for hostilities. Becoming president in 1913, he extended service in the military to three years. During WORLD WAR I he supported a personal and political foe, Georges CLEMENCEAU, as head of the government in order to secure French unity. After the war Poincaré called for stringent punishment of Germany and felt that the terms of the TREATY OF VERSAILLES were overly lenient. Leaving the presidency, he once more served as a senator from 1920 to 1929. Again named premier and foreign minister in 1922, he attempted to force continued German reparations by sending French troops into the RUHR in 1923. Forced out of office in 1924, he returned in 1926 during a period of financial crisis and carried out policies that stabilized the franc. He retired in 1929.

Poitier, Sidney *(1924–)* American actor and director. Known for his subtle and powerful performances, Poitier was the first black American to become a major HOLLYWOOD star. Born in Florida of Bahamian parents, he received his training at the American Negro Theater in New York in the late 1940s. Poitier broke into film in the 1950s, starring in several important pictures dealing with racism: *Cry, the Beloved Country* (1952, based on the novel by Alan PATON), *The Blackboard Jungle* (1955) and *The Defiant Ones* (1958), which earned him an ACADEMY AWARD nomination as best actor. He won the best actor award for his performance in *Lilies of the Field* (1963). In 1967 he played leading roles in three hits: a schoolteacher in inner-city London in *To Sir, with Love;* a black detective from the North investigating a murder in the deep South in *In the Heat of the Night;* and a man about to enter an interracial marriage in *Guess Who's Coming to Dinner.* In the 1970s he directed and costarred in several films with Bill COSBY. After an absence from

the screen, he reemerged in 1988, directing and starring in the chase thriller *Shoot to Kill.* Poitier received a lifetime achievement award from the Academy of Motion Picture Arts and Sciences in 2002.

Poland Eastern European nation bordered on the north by the Baltic Sea; the east by Russia (Kaliningrad), Lithuania, Belarus and Ukraine; the south by Slovakia and the Czech Republic; and the west by GERMANY. Divided among Russia, Prussia and AUSTRIA after 1795, Poland did not gain independence until 1918 under the leadership of Józef PIŁSUDSKI, who had led Polish forces in WORLD WAR I for Austria against Russia. In 1920, taking advantage of Russia's internal upheaval, Poland fought for and regained additional territory, which was ceded in a 1921 treaty. In August of 1939 NAZI Germany and the USSR signed a treaty containing a covert agreement to divide Poland between them. In September the German inva-

sion of Poland was quickly followed by a Soviet invasion from the east. Poland fell and WORLD WAR II began. Władysław Raczkiewicz formed an exile government in Paris, which moved to London when France was occupied in 1940. In 1941 Germany attacked the USSR and took all of Poland. Polish communists fought alongside the Soviets. The Poles formed an alternate government in 1944, the Polish Committee of National Liberation, which the Soviets recognized. Declaring itself the Provisional Government of Poland, it moved to Lublin, where it was joined by some of the exiled government from London. The Allies recognized it at the YALTA CONFERENCE in 1945. A 1944 treaty between Poland and the USSR established their border at the CURZON LINE, but Poland gained territory from Germany to the west in an Allied agreement after the war, so the country was effectively shifted westward and millions of Poles resettled. Elections in 1947 established a "people's republic" in

POLAND

1918	An independent Polish republic is established after World War I, with Marshal Józef Piłsudski elected president
1919–21	Poland mounts an advance into Lithuania and Ukraine. Treaty of Riga ends the war, and Poland regains much territory.
1939	Russia and Germany agree to share Poland. Poland is invaded by Germany from the west and Russia from the east.
1940	An exile government is based in Paris and then moved to London.
1941	Germany attacks the Soviet Union and takes all of Poland.
1944–45	Poland is liberated from Nazi rule by the Soviet Union's Red Army; boundaries are redrawn westwards at the Potsdam Conference. One half of "old Poland," 70,000 square miles in the east, is lost to the USSR; 40,000 square miles of ex-German territory in Silesia, along the Oder and Neisse Rivers, is added, shifting the state 150 miles westwards.
1945	Provisional Government of National Unity is installed.
1947	In forged elections, held under strict police and army control and terror, Communist regime wins 80% of the vote.
1952	New constitution is promulgated.
1953	Stefan Cardinal Wyszynski, Poland's primate, is jailed.
1956	Riots break out in Poznań in June. Gomułka is restored as first secretary in fall.
1970	Bloody riots in Gdańsk bring Gomułka down. Gierek replaces Gomułka.
1979	Pope John Paul II arrives in the first of three visits to Poland.
1980	Unrest sparked by rising prices and falling wages leads to wave of strikes, in particular at the Lenin Shipyard in Gdańsk. Workers form a decentralized independent trade union, Solidarity, led by a 38-year-old electrician, Lech Wałęsa.
1981	As the political and economic crisis deepens, Gen. Wojciech Jaruzelski proclaims martial law. Solidarity is outlawed, thousands of activists are interned, including Wałęsa.
1982	Wałęsa is released from prison and suspends martial law.
1983	Following another visit by Pope John Paul II, the government formally ends martial law and amnesty is granted to political prisoners.
1984	Another general amnesty is declared, and two years later nearly all the political prisoners are set free.
1989	After the previous year's strikes the government is forced to recognize Solidarity and allow it to participate in elections. Solidarity sweeps the polls.
1990	Wałęsa wins the first general presidential election.
1995	Lech Wałęsa loses a close presidential race.
1999	Poland joins NATO.
2004	Poland gains admission into the EU.

Poland, and in 1952 a new constitution was adopted, thus beginning a repressive, STALINIST government with close ties to the USSR Poland's government also sought to abolish the Roman Catholic Church. In 1956, following strikes and riots over food shortages and Soviet control, Władysław GOMUŁKA was elected leader of the United Workers Party. Gomułka eased restrictions on private farming and released Cardinal Stefan WYSZYNSKI, who had been imprisoned in 1953. Strikes again broke out in 1970, and Gomułka was succeeded by Edward GIEREK. Opposition to his government mounted through the decade and peaked in 1979 after the first of three visits by Polish-born pope JOHN PAUL II. In 1980 a strike that started in the Gdańsk shipyards spread to all industries, and the government conceded workers' the right to strike. Lech WAŁĘSA formed the SOLIDARITY (Solidarnoa) union. It sought workers' rights and liberties. In 1981, following a national strike for a five-day work week, Premier Pinkowski was replaced by General Wojciech JARUZELSKI. Martial law was imposed, Solidarity banned and its leaders arrested. The U.S. responded by initiating economic sanctions. In 1982 curfews were eased and further rioting occurred. Lech Wałęsa was released from prison and martial law suspended. Following another conciliatory visit by the pope in 1983, the government granted amnesty to political prisoners, releasing 35,000 of them in 1984 on the 40th anniversary of the People's Republic; the remainder were released in 1986. The U.S. loosened its sanctions, which were lifted in 1987. Martial law ended in 1984, but many restrictions were still in force. Food shortages continued, and opposition to the government grew. Following widespread strikes in 1988, the government was forced to recognize Solidarity and allow it to participate in elections in 1989, when Solidarity-backed candidates won overwhelmingly in parliament. The Polish government, still facing shortages, has announced programs to restructure the economy, including plans to privatize industries. Wałęsa was elected president in 1990 but was defeated in a reelection bid five years later. Poland joined NATO in 1999 and gained admission to the EUROPEAN UNION (EU) in 2004.

Polanski, Roman (1933–) Polish actor and director. Polanski is widely considered one of the most original and disturbing film directors of his generation; both his movies and his personal life have generated much controversy. Born in Paris, Polanski grew up in Kraków, Poland. A survivor of the HOLOCAUST, he later attended the Polish Film School at Lódź (1954). During the late 1950s he wrote, directed or acted in several short films. His first feature, *Knife in the Water* (1962), brought Polanski international notice. He subsequently moved to England, where he directed *Repulsion* (1965) and *Cul de Sac* (1966). His first HOLLYWOOD film was *The Fearless Vampire Killers* (1967), a horror film spoof. It was followed by *Rosemary's Baby* (1968), a suspense thriller about witchcraft in New York City that became a popular hit and is regarded as a classic of its genre. The following year Polanski's wife, actress Sharon Tate, was murdered by Charles MANSON. The sensationalism and publicity surrounding the case drove Polanski to seek refuge in England, where he directed a controversial adaptation of Shakespeare's *Macbeth* (1971). Polanski's *Chinatown* (1974), starring Jack NICHOLSON, was an acclaimed mystery in the FILM NOIR style. *The Tenant* (1976), in which Polanski also acted, was a morbid psychological drama. Shortly thereafter Polanski was arrested in California for statutory rape. While awaiting trial he jumped bail, fled the U.S. and settled in France. His subsequent relationship with actress Nastassia Kinski, whom he directed in *Tess* (1981, an adaptation of Thomas HARDY's *Tess of the D'Urbervilles*) also caused considerable comment. His later films include *Pirates* (1986) and *Frantic* (1988). In 2003 Polanski received an Academy Award in absentia for his work on *The Pianist* (2002).

Police, The U.K. rock group; formed in 1976 by bassist Sting (Gordon Sumner), guitarist Andy Summers and drummer Stewart Copeland. They stirred little interest in the then punk-dominated music scene until all three dyed their hair blond. Their music was more cerebral than that of their peers, with a pronounced THIRD WORLD influence. Their breakthrough album, *Outlandos d'Amour,* included the hit "Can't Stand Losing You." Although they claim to still exist as a group, all have pursued solo careers since the early 1980s. Their last number-one hit as a group was "Every Breath You Take" in 1983. Sting's solo career included a critically dismissed Broadway appearance in *Threepenny Opera* and film work in *Dune* and *The Bride*. He has made many concert appearances on behalf of Amnesty International, as well as ecological causes.

Polisario (Popular Front for the Liberation of Saguía el Hamra and Río de Oro) Liberation group formed in 1973 for the purpose of liberating the Spanish- and later Moroccan-controlled territory of Western Sahara, also called the SAHARAWI REPUBLIC. Established by the indigenous peoples of Western Sahara, Polisario initially operated out of nearby Mauritania as a nomadic insurgent group. However, when in 1975 Spain granted independence to what had been called the Spanish Sahara, MOROCCO claimed the territory and dispatched troops to occupy it. In response, Polisario transferred its operations to western Algeria, to wage a guerrilla war against the Moroccan royal government with the help of its sympathizers in Western Sahara. Between 1975 and 1991, this insurgent conflict continued until both sides concluded a cease-fire in 1991 and permitted the dispatch of a UN peacekeeping force to supervise the truce. The Polisario-Morocco agreement called for an internationally supervised referendum to be held in Western Sahara six months following the establishment of the cease-fire, which would then determine the future status of the region. However, this timetable has yet to be implemented. In July 2003 Polisario officials gave their support to a new UN plan that would offer Western Sahara a limited degree of autonomy from Morocco, during which the UN would oversee preparations for a new referendum giving the region's inhabitants the choice of independence or annexation by Morocco. It remains uncertain whether this plan will be implemented, as both the Moroccan government and more radical elements within Polisario have voiced dissatisfaction with the accord.

political correctness ("pc") A controversial concept, and the term used to describe it, that surfaced in many American universities in the late 1980s and early 1990s. "Political correctness" or "pc" was especially prominent in humanities departments at Duke and Stanford Universities, among other institutions. Faculty members who advocated political correctness generally saw the classroom as a forum for instilling "progressive" or "correct" political ideals in their students. PC advocates criticized traditional courses in Western literature and civilization as biased, and instead favored a "multicultural" approach to history and literature. Political correctness aimed at a larger criticism of Western society, which was viewed as controlled by white males at the expense of women and minorities. On some campuses, faculty members whose courses did not conform to so-called politically correct ideologies were denounced as racist or sexist and were often denied tenure. Critics of political correctness viewed it as a latter-day left-wing version of MC-CARTHYISM. The term was used derisively by those who saw it as an extremist attempt to rewrite history and stifle intellectual debate.

Pollard, Fritz (Frederick Douglas) *(1894–1986)* American athlete and coach. In 1916, after a sensational season as a halfback for Brown University, Pollard became the first black to be named to an all-American college football team. He was the only black head coach of an NFL team until Art Snell was named a head coach in 1989.

Pollock, Jackson *(1912–1956)* American painter. After finishing school in the West, Pollock moved to New York City and enrolled in the Art Students League (1930–33). Pollock was interested in abstract art. His paintings became splotches and splashes and drippings and textures, said by some critics to be thoroughly controlled. His paintings started the art movement that later became known as the "action school." Beginning in 1973 his paintings brought the highest prices ever paid for contemporary art. His *The Search* was sold in 1988 for $4,840,000.

Pol Pot (Saloth Sari) *(1928–1998)* The notorious leader of the Cambodian KHMER ROUGE was born in Kompong Thom Province, the youngest of seven children in a family that could be classified as "rich peasants." He attended a Catholic primary school in Phnom Penh and Norodom Sihanouk High School in Kompong Cham City. In 1949 he received a scholarship for a two-year technician's course at the Ecole Française de Radioelectricité in Paris. There Pol Pot joined a small group of Cambodian students in the "Marxist Circle." He returned to Phnom Penh in 1953 and later joined the Vietnamese-

Khmer UIF cell in the eastern zone. In 1955 he returned to Phnom Penh and became involved with the Khmer People's Revolutionary Party or KPRP. Throughout the 1950s he gained increasing control over party activities in the city. After the murder of party leader Tou Samouth in 1962 (perhaps by the Pol Pot faction), he became acting secretary general of the party. The struggle then returned to the countryside to garner strength for the eventual takeover of the country in April 1975. Pol Pot became prime minister in 1976, and his faction orchestrated policies of execution and forced labor from 1975 to 1979. He retreated in 1979 to the Thai border with an estimated 35,000 remaining Khmer Rouge troops. He and his forces remained the major threat to stability in CAMBODIA until the movement disintegrated, and he died in 1998.

Polya, George *(1887–1985)* American mathematician. As professor emeritus of mathematics at Stanford University, Polya was one of the leading research mathematicians of his time. Among his most important contributions to modern mathematics were the elaboration of the concept of "random walk" in probability theory and the formulation of a crucial theorem in combinational analysis that came to be known as the Polya enumeration theorem. He was also the author of one of the all-time mathematical best sellers, *How to Solve It,* a book that presented practical approaches to effective problem solving.

Pompidou, Georges *(1911–1974)* French political leader and president of FRANCE (1969–74). Originally a teacher, Pompidou served in WORLD WAR II until the fall of France (1940), when he returned to teaching. A member of the RESISTANCE, he joined Charles DE GAULLE's staff in 1944. He became affiliated with the Rothschild bank in 1954, serving as its director. A trusted aide to de Gaulle, he became the principal adviser to the new president of the Fifth Republic in 1958 and was appointed premier in 1962. Pompidou played a strong role in settling the strikes and strife of 1968. However, de Gaulle did not reappoint him as premier in July of that year. After de Gaulle resigned in 1969, Pompidou was elected president.

During his five-year tenure in office, he attempted to deal with France's economic problems by initiating such stern measures as a price freeze and devaluation of the franc. In foreign policy, he drew closer to other European nations and rejected de Gaulle's opposition to Great Britain's entry into the EUROPEAN ECONOMIC COMMUNITY.

Pompidou Center The popular name of the Centre National d'Art et de Culture Georges Pompidou; also known as Beaubourg for the Paris district in which it is located. Originally suggested by President Georges POMPIDOU in 1969 and named in his honor, the structure was completed in 1978. Designed by the Italian-British architectural team of Renzo Piano and Richard Rogers, the building caused a sensation during its first years due to its bold industrial design, which exposes its tubular steel framework and sports enormous, brightly painted utility pipes, brilliant red elevators and escalators in clear plastic tunnels. The center eventually became a Parisian landmark and now houses a museum of modern art, a reference library and research centers for music and industrial design.

Ponge, Francis *(1899–1988)* French poet; considered the last of the original generation of French surrealist poets, he was a precursor of French novelists such as Michel BUTOR and Alain ROBBE-GRILLET. Ponge was known for his "thing-poetry"—lengthy, detailed descriptions of objects, directed toward a restoration of the power and purity of language. His works included *Les parti pris des choses* (The defense of things) and *Le Savon* (Soap), an exhaustive prose poem on the subject of "soap." SARTRE described Ponge's poems as among "the most curious and perhaps the most important of the age." A visiting professor at Columbia University, New York, in 1967, he was a recluse for the last 20 years of his life.

Ponnelle, Jean-Pierre *(1932–1988)* Opera director and designer. In New York Ponnelle's work was generally received unsympathetically, particularly his versions of Wagner's *Flying Dutchman* in 1979 and Massenet's *Manon* in 1986. His productions have been seen in nearly every important opera house in the world, as well as at the BAYREUTH and SALZBURG FESTIVALS.

Ponselle, Rosa (Rosa Ponzillo) *(1897–1981)* American opera singer famous for her broad musical range, impeccable technique and pure, welling voice. A dramatic soprano, she was arguably the greatest interpreter of Verdi heroines in this century. She made her debut at the Metropolitan Opera in New York in 1918, singing Leonora in *La Forza del Destino* opposite her mentor, Enrico CARUSO. The first American-trained singer to star at the Met, she sang 22 roles there until her retirement from the stage in 1937. In addition to such Verdian roles as Leonora, Violetta (*La Traviata*) and the title role in *Aida,* she also was noted for her performances as Bellini's *Norma* and Ponchielli's *Gioconda.* After her retirement, she served as artistic director of the Baltimore Opera and was also a vocal coach.

Pontecorvo, Gillo *(1919–)* Italian-born filmmaker. After working as a foreign correspondent in Paris, Pontecorvo soon demonstrated an interest in filmmaking. In 1956 he released a short-length production called *Giovanna,* which was one of several small vignettes that premiered along with similar pieces in the collaborative film *La rosa dei venti.* The following year, he garnered acclaim for his first full-length feature film, *La grand strada azzura* (1957), for which Pontecorvo received a prize at the Karlovy Vary Festival. In 1960 Pontecorvo was nominated for an Academy Award for Best Foreign Language Film for *Kapo,* a dark drama of life in a World War II concentration camp. In 1966 Pontecorvo released *The Battle of Algiers,* the film for which he is best known. Depicting the urban guerrilla campaign of the National Liberation Front (FLN) for the independence of Algeria from French rule, *Algiers* earned Pontecorvo another Academy Award nomination in 1969 for Best Foreign Language Film, as well as nominations for Best Director and Best Original Screenplay. Following *Algiers,* Pontecorvo shot two additional feature-length films—*Burn!/Queimada!* a 1969 piece starring MARLON BRANDO that proved critical of French 19th-century colonial practices in the Antilles, and *Operation Ogre* (1979), a picture that examined terrorism in Spain during the final months of Francisco Franco's dictatorship. He thereupon abandoned full-length movies to concentrate on producing short feature films throughout the 1980s and 1990s. In 1992 Pontecorvo returned to his documentary roots and filmed *Return to Algiers,* a piece that examined the accomplishments and challenges that had faced the Algerian government following its independence from French rule.

Pontoppidan, Henrik *(1857–1943)* Danish novelist. Pontoppidan's realistic novels depict the social fabric of Denmark in his time and reflect his advocacy of a more democratic society. His three major works are the trilogy *Det Forjaettede Land* (*The Promised Land,* published between 1891 and 1895), the octateuch *Lykke-Per* (*Lucky Peter,* published between 1898 and 1904) and the pentateuch *De Dødes Rige* (*The Kingdom of the Dead,* published between 1912 and 1916). With Karl GJELLERUP, Pontoppidan received the 1917 NOBEL PRIZE in literature. Pontoppidan also published five volumes of memoirs, *Drengeaar* (Boyhood Years, 1933), *Hamskifte* (Sloughing, 1936), *Arv og Goeld* (Inheritance and Debt, 1938), *Familieliv* (Family Life, 1940) and *Undervejs til mig selv* (On the Way to Myself, 1943).

Pool, Ithiel de Sola *(1917–1984)* Communications theorist and political scientist. A professor at the Massachusetts Institute of Technology, Pool was one of the first social scientists to use computer models extensively in research on human behavior. He explored the effects of various modes of communication on society and politics. His book *Candidates, Issues and Strategies* discussed computer simulations of voting behavior used in John F. KENNEDY's 1960 presidential campaign. His *American Business and Public Policy* was considered the standard reference work in the field of social communication. Pool was a fellow of the American Academy of Arts and Sciences.

pop art Term coined in the 1950s by the British critic Lawrence Alloway. It came to define a movement beginning in the late 1950s and flourishing in the '60s, largely in the U.S., that reacted against the sometimes pretentiously serious ABSTRACT EXPRESSIONISM by portraying objects from the everyday world in flat, colorful and impersonal images. Pop artists found their subjects in commercial products such as soup cans and soda bottles, comic strips, advertising art and food. They exalted the surface of things, eschewing the plumbing of artistic depths to celebrate the transitory objects of ordinary life with flashy immediacy. The fusion of high and popular culture that pop art represented had enormous influence on the arts and attitudes of the later 20th century. Among the important figures of the pop art movement are Roy Lichtenstein, Claes OLDENBURG, James Rosenquist and Andy WARHOL.

Popeye The creation of E.C. Segar, Popeye the sailor made his first appearance on January 17, 1929, in the King Features syndicated comic strip *Thimble Theater;* he has been syndicated continuously ever since. Popeye appeared in his first animated cartoon in 1933, and more than 450 of these were made, most of them by Max Fleischer. In both the comic strip and the cartoons, Popeye has only average powers until he eats spinach, which gives him extraordinary strength; he uses his powers mostly to battle his archenemies Brutus (also known as Bluto), the Sea Hag and Alice the Goon. Other notable characters include Olive Oyl, Popeye's girlfriend; Swee'pea, his adoptive son; and Wimpy, the perennial moocher. The live-action motion picture *Popeye* was released in 1980, starring Robin Williams in the title role.

Popov, Dusko *(1912–1981)* Yugoslav-born double agent for Britain during WORLD WAR II, code-named "Tricycle." He passed Nazi secrets to London and gave false information to Berlin. In 1941 he gave an unheeded warning to the U.S. about Japanese plans to bomb the U.S. Navy base at PEARL HARBOR. In 1944 he helped divert German troops from the site of the Allied landing in NORMANDY. The author of a book of memoirs, *Spy, Counter Spy,* he was also thought to be one of the models for Ian FLEMING's fictional spy hero, JAMES BOND.

Popper, Hans *(1903–1988)* Viennese-born pathologist. As a young physician in Austria, Popper conducted pioneering biochemical research. After immigrating to the U.S. in 1938, he was based in Chicago for two decades before moving to New York City. He was known internationally as the founder of hepatology, the study of the liver and its diseases.

Popper, Sir Karl Raimund (1902–1994) Austrian-British philosopher. While a professor of logic and scientific method at the London School of Economics from 1949 to 1969, Popper's insight into the basic procedure of science was fully formulated. His view was that science begins not with observation, but with problems. The problems are then addressed by developing hypotheses, or "conjectures," as Popper called them, which can hold up to repeated attempts to prove them false. Popper's belief, which has found significant support among working scientists, is that it is impossible to select among competing conjectures the one that is "true," but that science consists of ardent attempts at refutation and accepts only those conjectures that survive these attempts.

Popular Front Coalition governments made up of leftist and centrist elements that arose in the mid-1930s. In FRANCE, a Popular Front of socialists, communists and radical socialists led by Léon BLUM governed from 1936 to 1938. Created to preserve the Third Republic against the incursions of FASCISM, the Popular Front enacted a variety of social, labor and economic reforms. It was ultimately overturned by conservatives. In SPAIN, a Popular Front coalition of republicans, socialists, communists and syndicalists won the national elections of 1936. This government formed the republican core during the SPANISH CIVIL WAR (1936–39). A democratic-leftist Popular Front government also led CHILE from 1938 to 1946, instituting many important social reforms.

Porgy and Bess Musical show by American composer George GERSHWIN that blended the idioms of black folk music and the forms of traditional grand opera. Dubose Heyward's novel, Porgy (1925), and the subsequent THEATRE GUILD stage version (1927) told the story of the ill-starred love between the lame Porgy and the faithless Bess, set against the background of Catfish Row (based on Cabbage Row in Charleston, South Carolina). Intrigued by the story's musical possibilities,

composer George Gershwin collaborated with librettist Ira GERSHWIN and Heyward, spending many weeks living and researching the life and music of the blacks on Folly Island, near Charleston. The opera, directed by Rouben MAMOULIAN, premiered at the Theatre Guild's Alvin Theatre on October 10, 1935, with a mostly black cast, including Todd Duncan as Porgy, Anne Brown as Bess and John Bubbles as Sportin' Life. The initial critical reception was mixed. Black composer Duke ELLINGTON deplored Gershwin's "lamp-black Negroisms;" and other critics like Virgil THOMSON attacked its presumed white chauvinism. With the 1942 revival (five years after Gershwin's death) the opera began its real success. In the 1950s it toured Europe, the Near East, the Soviet Union and Latin America. Producer Samuel Goldwyn made a movie version in technicolor in 1959. And since 1970 it has entered the repertoires of many opera companies, including the Metropolitan Opera. In the concert hall arranger Robert Russell Bennett's symphonic suite (composed for conductor Fritz REINER in 1941) has been a popular staple. According to biographer David Ewen, Gershwin did not directly quote Negro melodies but assimilated folk idioms into his own musical expression, claiming to bring this musical tradition for the first time to the legitimate stage. Many blacks today continue to question the validity and the success of that assertion. The lyrics to the show's standards, like "It Ain't Necessarily So," "Summertime," and "I Got Plenty o' Nuttin'," were the results of a close collaboration between Ira Gershwin and Dubose Heyward.

Pork Chop Hill, Battle of Colloquial name for Hill 255, situated on the eastern side of the Iron Triangle along the Yokkokchon River in Korea; site of fighting during the KOREAN WAR. Pork Chop Hill was successfully held by UN forces against attacks from the Chinese army in November 1952 and March and April 1953. On July 6, 1953, Chinese forces attacked again and gained a foothold on the hill, which UN counterattacks on July 7, 8 and 9 failed to dislodge. General Maxwell TAYLOR decided that Pork Chop Hill's tactical value did not justify additional casualties, and on July 10–11, the UN forces evacuated. Two

weeks later, the war ended, and Pork Chop Hill became part of the Demilitarized Zone separating North from South Korea.

pornography and obscenity "Pornography" is sexually explicit written or visual material. "Obscenity" refers to something that is offensive to modesty or decency. The U.S. legal system has devoted considerable attention to defining these terms and determining the extent to which governments can control material with sexually explicit content. On the one hand, the U.S. Constitution's First Amendment unequivocally provides that "no law" may abridge freedom of speech. However, legislatures and the courts have attempted to balance First Amendment rights against majority sensibilities. Generally, U.S. courts upheld state and federal laws banning obscene materials—the courtroom test for obscenity being whether the material tended to deprave and corrupt. By 1957 the Supreme Court had adopted a standard that a work was obscene and not constitutionally protected if an average person using community standards found the dominant theme appealed to the prurient interest. In 1973 the Court refined this test. Material could be banned as obscene only if it was totally without redeeming value, and taken as a whole lacked serious literary, artistic, political or scientific value.

Porsche, Ferdinand (1875–1951) Automotive engineer, designer and manufacturer known for his development of the original VOLKSWAGEN and the sequence of sports cars that carry the Porsche name. Responsible for many automotive designs of the 1920s when he was employed by Daimler-Benz, Porsche established his own firm with his son Ferdinand ("Ferry") Porsche II in Stuttgart, where he worked on the Volkswagen design in the 1930s. The first Porsche car was produced in 1949 by a factory in Austria, with a body designed by Erwin KOMENDA using elements of the regular Volkswagen. It was marketed in 1952 as the Porsche 356 and quickly became a classic, although its bulbous, aerodynamic design was sometimes criticized as clumsy. The Type 911 was introduced in 1964 with a somewhat modified body design. Successive designs for Type 912, the Targa, and the mid-engined 914 built the reputation

of the Porsche as a prestigious status symbol as well as a sports car of outstanding performance.

Port Arthur (Lüshun) City in northeastern CHINA, at the southern end of the Liao-tung Peninsula. In 1898 Russia obtained a lease on the peninsula. Port Arthur subsequently figured prominently in the RUSSO-JAPANESE WAR (1904–05). A Japanese surprise attack on Port Arthur (February 8, 1904) trapped Russia's Pacific fleet here. The Japanese laid siege to Port Arthur and captured it on January 2, 1905. The city remained under Japanese control until the end of WORLD WAR II, when it became the headquarters of a joint Sino-Soviet administration. It was turned over to China 10 years later.

Porter, Cole *(1891–1964)* Celebrated American lyricist and song writer. Porter came from a wealthy Indiana family, studied law at Yale, served in the French Foreign Legion, studied music under Vincent D'INDY at the Schola Cantorum in Paris and, in general, lived the life of a playboy-dilettante. By the late 1920s, he had turned increasingly to show music. Early works, like "You Do Something to Me" (from *Fifty Million Frenchmen*, 1929), "What Is This Thing Called Love?" (from *Wake Up and Dream*, 1929) and "Night and Day" (from *Gay Divorce*, 1932), displayed Porter's trademarks: unexpected chromatics, intricate rhythms and ingeniously naughty lyrics. He wrote the scores to more than 20 shows, including *Anything Goes* (1934) and *Kiss Me Kate* (1948); six motion pictures, including *Born to Dance* (1936) and *The Pirate* (1948); and one television musical, *Aladdin* (1958). Cary GRANT portrayed him in the movie *Night and Day* (1947), which failed to come to terms with the facts of his life and the quirky, mercurial, sometimes hedonistic, aspects of his temperament. A 1937 horseback riding accident left Porter with two crushed legs and damage to his nervous system, necessitating 30 operations over the next 20 years. After a leg was amputated in 1958 he no longer wrote songs, living as a virtual recluse until his death.

Porter, Katherine Anne *(1890–1980)* American novelist and short story writer. Porter's elegantly crafted writing won critical acclaim for more than 40 years. Her literary work, which bore the influence of her Deep South upbringing in Texas and Louisiana, often evoked dark, brooding themes: the sense of the past, the collusion between good and evil and the reality of self-betrayal. Her most famous work was the bestselling 1962 novel *Ship of Fools*, which was made into a film. She won the PULITZER PRIZE and the National Book Award in 1966 for her short fiction *The Collected Stories of Katherine Anne Porter;* among her other works were *Noon Wine, The Old Order, Flowering Judas, Pale Horse, Pale Rider, Maria Concepcion* and *Hacienda.*

Porter, William Sydney See O. HENRY.

Portsmouth, Treaty of Treaty negotiated September 5, 1905, at Portsmouth, New Hampshire, ending the RUSSO-JAPANESE WAR. It was mediated by U.S. president Theodore ROOSEVELT. MANCHURIA was evacuated by both countries and was returned to CHINA. The defeated Russians turned over south SAKHALIN ISLAND and their leases over PORT ARTHUR and the Liaotung Peninsula to JAPAN. Japan superseded RUSSIA as the leading power in KOREA and adjacent areas. President Roosevelt's mediation confirmed the status of the U.S. as a world power.

Portugal Portugal covers an area of 34,308 square miles along the Atlantic coast of the Iberian Peninsula in southwest Europe and includes the semi-autonomous Azores and Madeira

PORTUGAL

1908	King Carlos I is assassinated.
1910	Republic of Portugal declared.
1911	Manuel de Arriagas is elected Portugal's first president.
1916	Germany declares war on Portugal.
1932	António de Oliveira Salazar becomes prime minister and suppresses opposition parties.
1949	Becomes founding member of NATO.
1968	Salazar vacates the premiership and is succeeded by Marcello Caetano.
1974	Leftist army officers seize power in a coup and Antonio de Spínola is named president.
1974–75	Portugal grants independence to its colonies, Guinea-Bissau, Mozambique, Cape Verde, São Tomé and Príncipe and Angola.
1976	In assembly elections General António Ramalho Eanes becomes president and Mário Soares becomes prime minister.
1982	Full civilian government restored.
1986	Soares becomes first civilian president in 60 years, succeeding Eanes; Portugal joins the EC.
1987	Aníbal Cavaco Silva is the first president elected with an overall assembly majority since the 1974 revolution.
1989	Fire destroys the old Chiado district in Lisbon.
1991	Soares is reelected president, and the PSD retains its majority in parliamentary elections.
1995	Cavaco Silva resigns as prime minister; the Socialist Party is installed as a minority government under Prime Minister António Guterres.
1996	Jorge Sampaio, a Socialist, wins the presidency.
1999	Portugal returns Macao to China.
2001	Sampaio is reelected president.
2002	Following general elections, José Manuel Durão Barroso, leader of the Social Democrats, forms a center-right coalition government. The euro enters into circulation as the new currency.
2003	Forest fires destroy vast areas of the country.
2004	Prime Minister Barroso resigns; Pedro Santana Lopes, his successor as leader of the Social Democrats, forms a government.
2005	The Socialists win the general elections. Wildfires sweep across the country and the government asks for outside assistance.

Islands. King Carlos's assassination in 1908 led to instability, insurrection and the declaration of a republic in 1910. Heavy losses during WORLD WAR I brought renewed turmoil, which only stabilized when a popular military coup made General Antonio Carmona president in 1926. Under prime minister Antonio de Oliveira SALAZAR (1932–68) Portugal stayed out of WORLD WAR II, became a founding member of NATO (1949), joined the UNITED NATIONS (1955), witnessed social reforms, and engaged in costly wars to retain its African colonies (see ANGOLAN WAR OF INDEPENDENCE). A bloodless coup in 1974 toppled Salazar's successor, Marcello CAETANO, and brought General António Ramalho Eanes to the presidency. His government recognized the independence of former Portuguese colonies, and restored full civilian government by 1982. In the 1986 election Mário Soares became Portugal's first civilian president in 60 years. From 1996 to 2002 the Socialist Party candidate Jorge Sampaio held the presidency.

Portugal returned Macau, its last overseas territory, to China in 1999. In 2002 Portugal adopted the euro as its national currency. Severe forest fires have plagued the country from 2003 to 2005.

Pospelov, Pyotr N. *(1898–1979)* Soviet propagandist, principal theoretician of the COMMUNIST PARTY of the Soviet Union, and editor of PRAVDA. He was one of the most durable figures in the Kremlin. He survived the Stalinist PURGES of 1936–37, de-Stalinization and KHRUSHCHEV's own downfall.

Post, Wiley *(1899–1935)* American aviator. Post began flying in 1924 by investing money received from insurance for the loss of an eye in an accident. He won the Chicago-Los Angeles Air Derby in 1930 flying the *Winnie Mae*. From his home in Oklahoma City, he served as an aerial navigation instructor and adviser for the U.S. Army. Post set many records in his career. He made the first around-the-world flight between June 23 and July 1, 1931, with Harold Gatty as navigator. He and Gatty wrote about their experience in *Around the World in Eight Days* (1931). Post and his passenger, humorist Will ROGERS, were killed when their plane crashed near Point Barrow, Alaska.

postimpressionism Term coined in 1910 by the British art critic Roger FRY to refer to the work of various French painters who worked from about 1880 to 1910. While differing widely in stylistic approach and technique, the postimpressionist artists were united in their rejection of the aesthetics of Impressionism. Major figures in the group include Cezanne, Gauguin, Toulouse-Lautrec and Van Gogh. The term has also been used to describe the neoimpressionist work of Seurat and Signac.

postmodernism Ill-defined term that refers to the fragmented philosophical and aesthetic influences from the past that continued to influence— often in unexpected and bizarre ways—much of late-20th-century culture. The central idea behind postmodernism is that art and philosophy have, over the past two millennia, already explored all the major creative possibilities open to them. Postmodern cul-

ture, which is generally held to have come to the forefront in the 1950s and '60s, merely reassembles past ideas into old-new juxtapositions that pay homage to those ideas but also place them in an ironic or absurdist light. The artist and philosopher Marcel DUCHAMP anticipated many of the key insights of postmodern aesthetics. Postmodernism has found expression in virtually all the creative arts as well as in architecture and design.

***Potemkin* mutiny** Mutiny that occurred on the Russian battleship *Potemkin* in the Black Sea while anchored off Odessa on June 14, 1905. The mistreated sailors killed the captain and most of the officers, then put the ship out to sea but eventually surrendered. The mutiny and the brutal reprisals that ended the incident are best known as the subject of the classic film *The Battleship Potemkin* (1925) by the pioneering Soviet filmmaker Sergei EISENSTEIN.

Potsdam Conference The last great Allied summit meeting of WORLD WAR II, held from July 17 to August 2, 1945, at Potsdam, Germany. The U.S. delegation was led by President TRUMAN, the USSR by Premier STALIN and the British by Prime Minister CHURCHILL (replaced by his successor, Clement ATTLEE). The conference reaffirmed and clarified agreements already reached at the YALTA CONFERENCE regarding a defeated GERMANY. It stipulated that Germany would not have a

central government but would be administered in four Allied zones: American, British, Russian and French. It decentralized the German economy, agreed upon German disarmament and settled on the punishment of Nazi war criminals. The conference also established a council of foreign ministers to pass on matters of peace settlements and draft peace treaties. The POTSDAM DECLARATION of July 26 also issued an ultimatum to JAPAN, promising destruction of the nation if unconditional surrender was not forthcoming. Disagreements at Potsdam between the Soviets and the Western allies over German reparations, boundaries and unification and over the nature of eastern Europe and the Mediterranean region were portents of the coming COLD WAR.

Potsdam Declaration Ultimatum to Japan issued on July 26, 1945, as a part of the WORLD WAR II POTSDAM CONFERENCE. In it the U.S., Great Britain and China demanded JAPAN's unconditional surrender and, without mentioning the existence of an ATOMIC BOMB, threatened the complete destruction of Japan if the declaration was not acceded to. It also explained Allied intentions in postwar Japan, including the dissolution of the Japanese Empire, the demobilization of the nation's military forces, the prosecution of war criminals, the occupation of the country and the creation of a democratic form of government. Japan did not accept the declaration

Joseph Stalin, Harry Truman and Winston Churchill at the Potsdam Conference (LIBRARY OF CONGRESS, PRINTS AND PHOTOGRAPHS DIVISION)

until the USSR joined the Allies in the Asian war. HIROSHIMA and NAGASAKI were destroyed by U.S. nuclear attacks, and Emperor HIROHITO called for surrender.

Potter, (Helen) Beatrix *(1866–1943)* British illustrator and author. Throughout a lonely childhood, Potter amused herself by sketching nature. Her talent was brought to bear in a series of children's books beginning with *The Tale of Peter Rabbit* (1901), which she had published herself. Her third book, *Squirrel Nutkin* (1903), was professionally published and brought her great success. The delicately illustrated books, which include also *The Tailor of Gloucester* (1902) and *Johnny Town-Mouse* (1918), continue to be enormously popular with children and adults worldwide. Potter kept a journal in an elaborate code, which was finally deciphered and published as *The Journal of Beatrix Potter* in 1964. Her home at Sawrey in the Lake District is open to the public.

Poujadists Followers of Pierre Poujade, founder of a right-wing political movement (Union de Défence des Commerçants et Artisans) violently active in FRANCE between 1954 and 1958. The movement's membership was petit-bourgeois and its ideology antisocialist, anti-intellectual and anti-European. It won 52 seats in the National Assembly in 1956 but declined after Charles DE GAULLE returned to politics and the Fifth Republic was founded.

Poulenc, Francis *(1899–1963)* French composer and pianist. Born in Paris of a well-to-do musical family, he began to study the piano as a small child. Influenced by the style and the aesthetics of Eric SATIE and the poetry of Jean COCTEAU, Poulenc was a member of the postimpressionist musical group Les SIX. His music combines wit, clarity, directness and lyricism. Many of his finest works are intimate piano pieces and songs. From 1936 on he composed sacred music, and in 1944 he began writing operas. Among his best known religious music is the Mass in G (1937). His most celebrated opera is *Dialogue of the Carmelites* (1957). Poulenc also wrote ballet music, concertos, chamber pieces and choral works.

Poulter, Thomas C. *(1897–1978)* American scientist, inventor and explorer. Poulter was second in command on Admiral Richard BYRD's second expedition to the Antarctic (1933–35). He led the expedition that saved Byrd's life after Byrd had spent part of the winter alone. As an inventor, Poulter held more than 75 patents, including ones for antisubmarine devices and for seismic methods of discovering oil. He was later a research consultant for Stanford Research International in California and established its laboratory for the study of biological sonar and its application to the blind.

Pound, Ezra (Loomis) *(1885–1972)* American poet, critic and translator. Born in Hailey, Idaho, Pound was educated at Hamilton College and the University of Pennsylvania, where he met W. C. WILLIAMS and Hilda Doolittle (HD). In 1907 he went to Europe, settling first in England, where he was briefly an informal secretary to YEATS; then in Paris, where he knew Gertrude STEIN and HEMINGWAY; and finally in 1925 in Italy. Pound was a charismatic literary entrepreneur whose grand vision and generous support of major writers such as JOYCE, ELIOT and Marianne MOORE placed him at the forefront of literary MODERNISM. He created both Vorticism and IMAGISM. *A lume spento* (1908), *Personae.* (1909), *Lustra* (1916) and especially *Hugh Selwyn Mauberly* (1920) broke the static mold of GEORGIAN verse

American poet and translator Ezra Pound (LIBRARY OF CONGRESS. PRINTS AND PHOTOGRAPHS DIVISION)

with a voice both shockingly modern and classically serene. In 1925 he began publishing his most important and controversial work, the CANTOS, on which he continued to work until his last years. A scholar of wide, if sometimes sketchy, erudition, Pound drew on Anglo-Saxon, Oriental, French Provençal and Italian Renaissance traditions.

Increasing megalomania led to an obsession with the economic theory of SOCIAL CREDIT and to ANTI-SEMITISM. An admirer of MUSSOLINI and FASCISM, during WORLD WAR II Pound made radio broadcasts for the Fascists in Italy. Indicted for treason in absentia in 1942, he was arrested by U.S. forces toward the end of the war and committed to St. Elizabeth's Hospital in Washington in 1946. In 1949 a violent controversy erupted over his receipt of the BOLLINGEN PRIZE. After his release in 1958, he returned to Italy and entered on a period of bitter, self-enforced silence. To this day the great poet who was also a traitor to his country arouses mixed emotions.

Poveda Burbano, Admiral Alfredo *(1925–1990)* Ecuadoran politician. In 1976 he headed a military junta that seized control of ECUADOR from another military dictator, General Guillermo Rodriguez Lara. The country's last military dictator, his government wrote a constitution in 1978. The government gave up power the following year to elected president Jaime Roldos.

Powell, Adam Clayton *(1908–1972)* Black American congressman and CIVIL RIGHTS activist. The son of a clergyman, the flamboyant Powell was one of the most outspoken and controversial figures in the American Civil Rights movement. He was widely admired for his fiery oratory on behalf of civil rights causes, but many critics considered him a demagogue (see DEMAGOGUES). A Democrat, he represented New York's Harlem district in the House of Representatives from 1945 to 1969. He served as chairman of the House Committee on Education and Labor (1960–67). In 1960 he was involved in a widely publicized lawsuit by a woman he accused of being a "bag woman" for police graft. Thereafter he maintained a home on the island of Bimini in the Bahamas. In 1967 a House committee unseated him on charges of

Congressman and civil rights activist Adam Clayton Powell (LIBRARY OF CONGRESS, PRINTS AND PHOTOGRAPHS DIVISION)

misusing public funds, but he was reelected in a special election. He returned to Congress in 1969 but was fined $25,000 and deprived of his seniority. That year the Supreme Court overturned his expulsion from the House of Representatives. He was defeated for reelection in 1970.

Powell, Anthony (1905–2000) British novelist, essayist and memoirist. With his contemporaries Graham GREENE and Evelyn WAUGH, Powell was one of the most acclaimed and widely read of modern British novelists. He was an influential figure in British letters both as a novelist and by virtue of his work as an editor and literary critic. During the 1930s Powell worked in publishing in London and was briefly a scriptwriter in HOLLYWOOD. During this time he wrote several interesting but minor novels. He served in WORLD WAR II. His magnum opus is the 12-volume novel sequence, *A DANCE TO THE MUSIC OF TIME,* whose individual volumes appeared from the early 1950s through the mid-1970s. In addition, Powell published a four-volume autobiography—*Infants of the Spring* (1976), *Messengers of the Day* (1978), *Faces in My Time* (1980) and *The Strangers All Are Gone* (1982). Conservative in outlook, Powell's writings focus on the transformations in the political and social fabric in Britain from the 1920s to the modern era.

Powell, Colin L. (1937–) American soldier and public official, chairman of the Joint Chiefs of Staff during the PERSIAN GULF WAR. Born in the HARLEM district of New York to parents who had emigrated from Jamaica, Powell was educated at public schools in Harlem and the Bronx. He attended City College, where he was a member of the Reserve Officers Training Corps and was graduated at the top of his ROTC class as a cadet colonel. In 1962 he was sent to VIETNAM, where he saw a tour of duty as a military adviser. Later, while maintaining his military affiliation and rising through the ranks, Powell held a series of sensitive posts in the administrations of Jimmy CARTER and Ronald REAGAN. He was an assistant to Defense Secretary Caspar Weinberger; in 1986 he was appointed deputy national security advisor, becoming national security advisor the following year. In 1988 he was promoted to four-star general and assigned to head the U.S. Army Forces Command. In 1989, he was named chairman of the Joint Chiefs of Staff, thus becoming the first black to hold the highest post in the U.S. military. In this capacity, he came to international prominence as a key adviser to President George H. W. BUSH during the PERSIAN GULF WAR. Powell was named secretary of state by President George W. BUSH. He played a major role in defending the Bush administration's policy toward Iraq prior to the U.S. invasion that toppled the regime of Saddam HUSSEIN in 2003. Following the 2004 presidential election, Powell resigned his post as secretary of state.

Powell, (John) Enoch (1915–1998) British politician. Powell was educated at Trinity College, Cambridge, and served there as a classics don from 1934 to 1938. After serving as a professor of Greek at the University of Sydney, Australia, he joined the army and rose to the rank of brigadier by the end of WORLD WAR II. A member of the CONSERVATIVE PARTY, Powell was elected to the House of Commons in 1950 and subsequently served as parliamentary secretary to the minister of Housing and Local Government in 1955, financial secretary to the Treasury from 1957 to 1958, and minister for health from 1960 to 1963 under Harold MACMILLAN. Powell opposed Britain's entry into the EUROPEAN ECONOMIC COMMUNITY. His highly publicized views, including a call for Britain to curtail nonwhite immigration, caused much controversy. Powell left the Conservative Party in 1974 but returned to Parliament as an Ulster Unionist. He was reelected in 1979 and 1983. Powell, who was also a poet, published *Collected Poems* in 1990.

Powell, Lewis Franklin Jr. (1907–1998) U.S. Supreme Court associate justice. Powell was born in Suffolk, Virginia, and received both his B.A. and his law degree from Washington and Lee University, the latter in 1931. President Richard NIXON appointed Powell to the Supreme Court in 1971, to replace Hugo BLACK. A pragmatist who shunned extreme positions, Powell generally sided with the Court's conservatives on business and criminal law issues and with the liberals on social issues such as ABORTION, civil liberties and separation of church and state. In June 1987 Powell retired from the Court, sparking a furor over who would be his successor. On July 1, President Ronald REAGAN nominated Robert BORK to the Court, but after an acrimonious battle, the Senate refused to confirm Bork. Reagan's second choice, Douglas Ginsburg, withdrew his name from nomination after it was reported that he had experimented with marijuana. Finally, in February 1988, Anthony KENNEDY took Powell's seat on the High Court.

Powers, John A. "Shorty" (1922–1980) American Air Force officer. Powers became widely known in the early 1960s as "the voice of Mission Control" who described the early U.S. spaceflights over radio and television and coined the popular phrase, "everything is A-OK." Because of his close association in the public mind with the MERCURY project astronauts, the public came to regard him as the "eighth astronaut."

Powys, John Cowper (1872–1963) British author. Although he also wrote poetry and essays on a variety of topics, Powys is best known for his idiosyncratic historical novels, which frequently evoke the Dorset countryside where he was raised. His first novel was *Wood and Stone* (1915), but his first major success came with *Wolf Solent* (1929). His best known work is *A Gastonbury Romance* (1932), an ambitious historical novel influenced by myth and legend. He also produced a notable *Autobiography* (1934). Later works include *Porius* (1951) and *The Brazen Head* (1956). There are conflicting critical assessments of Powys's ability as a writer. Powys's two brothers were also men of letters. **Llewelyn Powys** (1884–1939) was an essayist and novelist whose work includes *The Pathetic Fallacy* (1928). **Theodore Francis Powys** (1875–1953) was the author of *Mr. Weston's Good Wine* (1927).

pragmatism See William JAMES.

Prague Spring Term used to characterize a series of economic and political reforms in CZECHOSLOVAKIA, and the period during which they occurred. The Prague Spring developed under the guidance of Alexander DUBČEK, who had been named first secretary of Czechoslovakia's Communist Party on January 5, 1968. It also coincided with the ouster of hard-line communist president Antonin NOVOTNÝ (March 22, 1968), who had long kept Czechoslovakia in the grip of STALINISM. At a conference in Brno (March 16, 1968), Dubček promised the "widest possible democratization" for the country, including the relaxation of censorship. He promised to build "socialism with a human face" and to "bring in new people who can carry out the new policies." The Prague Spring reforms also included greater independence for the government, the courts, trade unions and economic enterprises. On April 5, 1968, the Communist Party leadership adopted a plan of liberal economic reforms. In a speech to the Czechoslovakian parliament on April 24, 1968, Premier Oldrich CERNIK announced that noncommunists would be allowed to participate in the government. That same day, Dubček announced that "we cannot go back and we cannot go halfway," and warned that "moving along unexplored paths . . . requires caution and courage." At the same time, he assured the Soviet Union that Czechoslovakia would remain its ally in the WARSAW PACT. A wave of hope swept through Czechoslovakia. However, the sudden SOVIET INVASION OF CZECHOSLOVAKIA (August 20–21) brought the Prague Spring to an abrupt end. Despite the reimposition of a hard-line communist government, the promises of the Prague Spring remained alive during the next 20 years and were realized in December 1989, when the communists were finally swept out of power.

Prairie School Group of architects who developed an early form of MODERNISM in the American Midwest between 1890 and 1914. The early works of Frank Lloyd WRIGHT (who called his residential designs "Prairie Houses") are the best-known examples of the style, but it also includes the designs of Louis Sullivan and a number of associates and followers of Sullivan and Wright—a body of work with its own distinctive character, quite different from European modernism. Like modernism, the Prairie School is nontraditional and strives for an organic union of strong, simple forms. But unlike orthodox modernism, it makes considerable use of ornament, often based on naturalistic forms suggestive of ART NOUVEAU and earlier Victorian styles. The best known Prairie School figures (aside from Sullivan and Wright) are George G. Elmslie, George W. Maher, Walter Burley Griffin and Marion Mahoney, who was the wife of Griffin.

Pravda The official organ of the Communist Party Central Committee in the former Soviet Union. Founded in opposition to the establishment by the BOLSHEVIKS in 1912, *Pravda* ("truth") had a circulation of about 12 million and was read daily by more than 90 percent of COMMUNIST PARTY members. The paper's value in informing the Soviet public was secondary to its role in shaping the "new Soviet man" and providing the most authoritative Kremlin interpretation of current events. It followed a rigid format from its inception, with reports of worker productivity, official speeches, party proceedings and economic news appearing on the front page, while domestic and international news was found in the back. In the era of GLASNOST, *Pravda* addressed such previously off-limit topics as high-level corruption, the Soviet presence in AFGHANISTAN, the nuclear disaster at CHERNOBYL, drug problems and other social ills, though disinformation continued. The paper was governed by an "Index of Information Not to Be Published in the Open Press," and was censored once before printing and once before distribution (the censor's number appeared at the foot of the back page of every edition). After the disintegration of the USSR in December 1991, *Pravda* became a private leftist publication within the Russian Federation.

Prebisch, Raúl *(1901–1986)* Argentine economist. He helped shape economic development throughout the developing world. In the 1950s he headed the United Nations Economic Commission for Latin America. As director of the UN Conference on Trade and Development in the 1960s, he won important trade preferences for THIRD WORLD countries and helped obtain increased funding for various regional development banks. Most recently he had been an economic adviser to Argentine president Raúl ALFONSÍN.

prefrontal lobotomy See Egas MONIZ.

Prem, Tinsulanonda *(1920–)* Prem was a career military man before serving as prime minister of THAILAND from 1980 to 1988. He was educated at Chulachomklao Royal Military Academy in Bangkok and began his military career as a sublieutenant in 1941. He became the commander of cavalry headquarters in 1968, then assistant commander in chief of the Royal Thai Army in 1977. In 1977 he was appointed minister of the interior and in 1979 minister of defense. Prem began his tenure as prime minister in 1980 and served the longest of any civilian prime minister before he declined to accept a fourth term after general elections in July 1988. He retired from the army before heading the government, thus acting as a civilian, nonpartisan leader. The balance he struck between the political parties and the military enabled him to sustain a fragile democracy throughout his tenure. He thwarted two coup attempts (1981, 1985), thus diluting the military's influence on mainstream politics.

Preminger, Otto *(1906–1986)* Austrian-born movie producer and director. He achieved great success in the U.S. film industry, despite his tempestuous temper and his choosing to work outside the HOLLYWOOD studio system. He emigrated to the U.S. from Vienna in 1935 and achieved a measure of success on Broadway before making his first American film, the murder mystery *Laura* (1944). He challenged the industry's Production Code Office and the Roman Catholic Church when he produced *The Moon Is Blue,* a 1953 adaptation of a mild Broadway sex comedy. The U.S. Supreme Court ultimately ruled that local censorship boards could not block the showing of the film. Other notable Preminger films were *Carmen Jones* (1954), *The Man with the Golden Arm* (1955), *Anatomy of a Murder* (1959), *Exodus* (1962) and *Advise and Consent* (1962).

Prendergast, Maurice *(1859–1924)*

American painter. Born in St. John's, Newfoundland, Canada, he spent his youth in Boston. He traveled to Europe in 1886, studying art in Paris (1891–94) and coming under the influence of such modernist movements as neoimpressionism and symbolism. Throughout his life Prendergast made frequent visits to Europe, traveling to various countries then returning to New York City. He joined with other artists in the formation of the EIGHT in 1908 and was an organizer of the ARMORY SHOW in 1913. Working in oil and watercolor, Prendergast evolved a tapestry-like postimpressionist style that employed lively brushstrokes and rich color in capturing landscapes and figures. He was particularly adept at portraying open-air promenades, as in his *Central Park* (1901) in the collection of the Whitney Museum of American Art, New York City.

Presley, Elvis (Aaron) *(1935–1977)*

American singer, performer and film star. One of the most popular entertainment figures of the 20th century, Presley helped establish ROCK and roll as a dominant musical force. Born in Tupelo, Mississippi, as a child he sang gospel tunes in his neighborhood church. In 1953, while working as a truck driver in Memphis, Tennessee, he recorded two songs for his mother. These recordings led to his discovery by Memphis-based Sun Records, which launched Presley's career as a white singer who could blend country, gospel and black rhythm and blues. "Heartbreak Hotel" (1956) was the first Presley song to reach num-

American rock and roll pioneer Elvis Presley. 1957 (LIBRARY OF CONGRESS. PRINTS AND PHOTOGRAPHS DIVISION)

ber one on the musical charts. Over the next two decades, he recorded numerous hits, including "Don't Be Cruel," "Hound Dog," "Jailhouse Rock," "Love Me Tender" and "Are You Lonesome Tonight." He also starred in over 20 films and in several television specials. The victim of his own spectacular success, Presley was plagued by personal problems, including drug addiction, and he died at age 42. His phenomenal popularity, however, continued after his death.

Pressburger, Emeric *(1902–1988)*

Hungarian-born British screenwriter. His widely acclaimed films made in collaboration with director Michael POWELL included *A Canterbury Tale* (1944), *Black Narcissus* (1947) and their most famous effort, *The Red Shoes* (1948). Pressburger won an ACADEMY AWARD for best original story for *49th Parallel* (1941), considered one of the most effective Allied PROPAGANDA films of WORLD WAR II.

Presser, Jackie *(1926–1988)*

U.S. union leader. Presser was president of the International Brotherhood of Teamsters from 1983 until his death;

his predecessor, Roy WILLIAMS, was convicted of conspiring to bribe a U.S. senator. Presser faced federal charges of using union funds to pay organized-crime figures for work they had not performed. The Justice Department filed suit asking that the union's leaders be replaced by a court-appointed trustee. In 1986, the White House Commission on Organized Crime concluded that neither Williams nor Presser would have become president without the help of Anthony "Fat Tony" Salerno, reputed head of the New York–based Genovese crime family. Salerno was later acquitted on charges of rigging union elections.

Prevert, Jacques *(1900–1977)*

French poet and screenwriter. Prevert was the most popular poet of his time in France. He is noted for his precise use of language, his gruesome images and the use of humor to underscore his social and political ideas. Initially influenced by the surrealists, he was first published in the surrealist monthly *Commerce.* Major poetry collections include the immensely popular *Paroles* (1946), *Lumière d'homme* (1955) and *Imaginaires* (1970). In addition, Prevert wrote many screenplays, such as the acclaimed *Le Crime de Monsieur Lange* (1935) and *Les Enfants du paradis* (1944).

Previn, André (Ludwig Andreas Priwin) *(1929–)* American conductor, pianist and composer. Born in Berlin, he began studying music at the age of six, and by the age of eight he was an accomplished pianist. He and his family fled Hitler's Germany for Paris, where young Previn studied at the Paris Conservatory for a year, and emigrated to the U.S. in 1939, settling in Los Angeles. He studied with Mario CASTELNUOVO-TEDESCO, composed film music, played the piano and conducted a youth orchestra while still a teenager. Previn became a U.S. citizen in 1943. His first celebrity was as a JAZZ pianist, and in 1945 he began a series of popular jazz recordings. He also achieved success as a composer and arranger of film music, winning ACADEMY AWARDS for the arrangements for *Gigi* (1958), *Porgy and Bess* (1959), *Irma La Douce* (1963) and *My Fair Lady* (1964). During the 1960s Previn's interest turned mainly to classical music. He became the permanent conductor of the Houston Symphony Orchestra (1967–69), the London Symphony Orchestra (1969–79), the Pittsburgh Symphony Orchestra (1976–84) and the Los Angeles Philharmonic (1984–89). In 1993 Previn accepted an appointment as the conductor-laureate of the London Symphony Orchestra. His subsequent honors have included a knighthood (KBE) by Queen Elizabeth II (1996) and Kennedy Center Honors in the U.S. (1998) in recognition of his musical accomplishments.

Price, Florence Beatrice Smith *(1888–1953)* Composer. Graduating from the New England Conservatory in 1906, Price taught at Shorter College (1906–10) and at Clark University (1910–12). After further study at Chicago Musical College and the American Conservatory, she won several competitions, including the Wannamaker Prize (1931–32), and in 1933 premiered her *Symphony in E Minor* with the CHICAGO SYMPHONY, the first by a black woman with a major orchestra. Price's works drew on black spirituals and other tunes, avoided jazz and kept in the mainstream of late European romanticism. Her songs were popularized by Marian ANDERSON and others.

Price, (Mary Violet) Leontyne *(1927–)* American singer. Acclaimed for her passionate artistry and the remarkable range of her rich soprano voice, Price first gained recognition for the role of Bess in George GERSHWIN's *PORGY AND BESS*, when it toured the U.S. and Europe in 1952–55. She made her Metropolitan Opera debut as Leonora in Verdi's *Il Trovatore* (1961) and became a leading prima donna of the company until her retirement in 1985. Price was particularly admired for her interpretation of Verdi heroines, especially Aida, and she created the role of Cleopatra in Samuel BARBER's *Antony and Cleopatra,* which opened the new Metropolitan Opera House at Lincoln Center in 1966. In addition, she was the first black woman to sing with La Scala Opera Company in Milan (1959). Following the terrorist attacks of September 11, 2001, Price was one of several performers, including renowned cellist YO-YO MA, who performed at a "Concert of Remembrance" held in Carnegie Hall to honor those who died in the terrorist attacks on New York City and Washington, D.C.

Price, T. Rowe *(1898–1983)* American investment expert. A pioneer in the field of investment counseling, research and analysis, Price was largely responsible for popularizing the "growth stock" concept of investment that advocated making long-term investments in small, well-managed companies. He founded his own investment counseling firm, T. Rowe Price Associates, in 1937. From the early 1950s through the 1960s his name was synonymous with growth stock mutual funds.

Pride, Admiral Alfred Melville *(1897–1988)* American aviator. A pioneer of naval aviation, Pride served on the original crew of the U.S. Navy's first aircraft carrier. During WORLD WAR II he played a major role planning the invasion of OKINAWA and the Japanese home islands (the latter superseded by the dropping of the ATOMIC BOMB on Japan). From 1947 to 1951, he was chief of the navy's bureau of aeronautics.

Priestley, J(ohn) B(oynton) *(1894–1984)* British novelist, dramatist, essayist, broadcaster and critic. "JBP" was considered the last of a line of distinguished "men of letters" in England that extended back through G.K. CHESTERTON to such 19th-century luminaries as Charles Dickens and George Meredith. Priestley was born at Bradford, Yorkshire—a region in which many of his stories are located—and educated at Trinity Hall, Cambridge. His first book was a volume of verse, *The Chapman of Rhymes* (1918), written during his wartime service. After working as a journalist and commentator throughout the 1920s, he achieved his first spectacular success with *The Good Companions* (1929), an enormous novel about a picaresque troupe of traveling performers. He wrote many stage plays and travel books in the next decade, including two brilliant chronicles of travel throughout his own country and the American Southwest—respectively, *English Journey* (1934) and *Midnight on the Desert* (1937). During WORLD WAR II he was a tireless supporter of the Allied cause in his writings and BBC broadcasts and for many years thereafter continued to write works of fiction, cultural history, belles-lettres and philosophy. The image he affected of a rather crusty, pipe-smoking sage celebrating the vanished values of Merrie Olde England is misleading. In truth Priestley was something of a pessimist and a mystic. What he called "the muddle of life" and "the density of evil" haunt his best books such as the tragic *Angel Pavement* (1930) and the grim account of war-torn England, *Black-Out in Gretley* (1942). A dark, bittersweet tang flavors the adventurous *Faraway* (1932) and the nostalgic *Lost Empires* (1965). His preoccupations with precognition, time travel and the supernatural surface in such plays as *I Have Never Been Here Before* (1937). As for his alleged hearty patriotism, it was really qualified by a sense of rootlessness: "I am too restless to develop any loyalty even to a place I really enjoy," he wrote in *Midnight on the Desert.* Elsewhere, he observed that most Englishmen "stagger under their inheritance." And yet he always retained a youthful, wide-eyed wonder about the world around him—his most endearing trait. On his 79th birthday he said he felt like a youth who had been kidnapped off the street and "rushed into a theater and made to don the grey hair, the wrinkles and the other attributes of age, then wheeled on stage. Behind the appearance of age I am the same person, with the same thoughts, as when I was younger."

Prigogine, Ilya *(1917–2003)* Belgian chemist. In 1955 Prigogine produced a seminal work, *Thermodynamics of Irreversible Processes,* in which he argued that a true thermodynamic equilibrium is rarely attained and that a serious limitation in classical thermodynamics is that it is restricted to equilibrium states and reversible processes. Prigogine was most interested in the thermodynamics of nonequilibrium systems, a subject that had been approached somewhat by Lars Onsager. In a radical departure, Prigogine developed the equipment to deal with these states, which he called "dissipative structures." This led to his exploration of such structures in biological processes in 1975. In 1977 he was awarded the NOBEL PRIZE for chemistry for his work in this area.

Prima, Louis *(1911–1978)* American JAZZ trumpeter and bandleader. In 1940 Prima composed the jazz classic *Sing Sing Sing,* which became a standard of Benny GOODMAN. With Keely Smith, his wife and nightclub partner for eight years, he recorded *That Old Black Magic,* which hit the top of the record charts in 1961.

Primakov, Yevgeny *(1929–)* Soviet and Russian politician and government official and Russian prime minister (1998–99). Born in Kiev, Primakov joined the Soviet Communist Party in 1959. He worked for the Soviet daily newspaper PRAVDA throughout the 1950s and 1960s as its Middle East correspondent. In 1989 Primakov was appointed to the Central Committee of the Communist Party, where he helped shape Soviet president MIKHAIL GORBACHEV's policies toward the Eastern European states' bid for full independence from Moscow. In 1991, following the Soviet hard-liners' abortive coup against Gorbachev, the Soviet president appointed him head of the Central Intelligence Service, the foreign intelligence branch of the KGB. When the Soviet Union disintegrated on December 25, 1991, Russian president Boris YELTSIN allowed Primakov to retain that position in the FSB, the Russian successor organization to the KGB. In 1996 Primakov left the Central Intelligence Service when Yeltsin appointed him Russian foreign minister, a post he held for two years.

In 1998, Yeltsin appointed—and the Russian Duma (lower house) approved—Primakov as Russian prime minister. However, his tenure ended in May 1999 when Yeltsin dismissed him for failing to purge his coalition government of members of the Communist Party, which then were masterminding an attempt to impeach the Russian president.

Primo de Rivera, Miguel *(1870–1930)* Spanish general, prime minister of SPAIN (1923–30). A career army officer, Primo de Rivera served in Cuba and the Philippines during the Spanish-American War, just before the turn of the 20th century, and later in Spanish Morocco. He rose to major general (1910) and then lieutenant general (1919), becoming a leading public figure. During a period of political turmoil, King ALFONSO XIII called on Primo to establish a military government (1923). Under the slogan "Country, Religion and Monarchy" Primo suspended the parliament, declared martial law and assumed dictatorial powers. He resigned office in 1930, shortly before his death. His son **José Antonio Primo de Rivera** (1903–36) founded the FALANGE, based on Miguel Primo de Rivera's ideas.

Primrose, William *(1903–1982)* Scottish-born violist. He was a member of the London String Quartet (1935–37), then moved to the U.S. where he joined the NBC Symphony, playing first viola (1937–42). Thereafter he concentrated on a solo career. He taught at several universities and conservatories. Widely considered the greatest violist of his time, Primrose was renowned for his consummate musicianship and sweetness of tone.

Prince, Harold (Hal) *(1928–)* American director and producer. One of America's foremost directors, Prince has directed and/or produced 46 musicals, plays and operas in the U.S. and Britain since he first produced *The Pajama Game* in 1954. He has won 16 Tony Awards for the directing of *Cabaret* (1966), *Sweeney Todd* (1979), *Evita* (1980) and *The Phantom of the Opera* (1987), among others. He has directed and produced several Stephen SONDHEIM musicals, including *A Little Night Music* (1973) and *Pacific Overtures* (1976). He also produced such shows as *Damn Yankees* (1955) and *Fiddler on the Roof* (1964), directed revivals of plays by Eugene O'NEILL and others and served on the National Council for the Arts. In 1994 Prince received the Kennedy Center Honors in recognition of his contributions to American music.

prisoners of war Also known as POWs, they are members of a military

German POWs in a French camp during World War I (LIBRARY OF CONGRESS, PRINTS AND PHOTOGRAPHS DIVISION)

force captured by the enemy during war. Prisoners may be taken by surrender or be captured during battle. Until the 19th century, prisoners of war were considered booty, and many were enslaved, ransomed or killed. However, through humane regulations promulgated in the late 19th and the 20th centuries, POWs are protected from mistreatment by a number of international agreements, most importantly the Hague Conventions and the GENEVA CONVENTIONS. A POW is required only to inform his captors of his name, rank, serial number and birthdate. POWs are entitled to living quarters in safe and inspected camps, to receive adequate food and medical care, to be paid for work and to receive and send mail. These and other rules are regulated and ensured by the international RED CROSS. Despite the elaborate precautions enacted to protect prisoners of war, harsh treatment has been prevalent in many modern conflicts, particularly WORLD WAR II, the KOREAN WAR and the VIETNAM WAR.

Pritchard, Sir John Michael *(1921–1989)* British conductor. Among other posts, he was musical director of the London Philharmonic Orchestra (1962–66) and chief conductor of the BRITISH BROADCASTING CORPORATION (BBC) Symphony Orchestra (1982–89). He specialized in the operas of Mozart and Donizetti.

Pritchett, Sir Victor Sawdon *(1900–1997)* British author and critic. An accomplished novelist and short story writer, Pritchett was probably best known for his literary criticism. He was a newspaper correspondent before achieving recognition as a writer with such works as *Claire Drummer* (1929), *Elopement into Exile* (1932) and *Mr. Beluncle* (1951). His fiction is peopled with eccentric characters; his style is witty and ironic. His critical works include *The Living Novel* (1947) and *The Myth Makers* (1979). He also contributed to the *New Statesman* and the *New York Review of Books* and lectured widely.

Pritikin, Nathan *(1915–1985)* American nutritionist. Self-taught and with no medical credentials, Pritikin developed a diet that he claimed could, together with proper exercise, prevent and even reverse heart disease and other ailments. He developed his diet after having been diagnosed a heart disease victim in 1957. In addition to being low in fat and cholesterol, the diet prohibited salt, sugar, alcohol and caffeine. Pritikin promoted the controversial diet through several best-selling books and at three "longevity centers," which attracted thousands of high-paying clients.

privatization Selling of nationalized industries and other parts of the public sector to private businesses and individuals. Privatization was a hallmark of the THATCHER government in Britain during the 1980s and of France under CHIRAC beginning in 1986.

Prodi, Romano *(1939–)* Italian and European statesman, prime minister of Italy (1996–1998, 2006–) and president of the European Commission (1994–2004). After a distinguished career as a professor of law at the University of Bologna, Prodi entered politics as a progressive member of the Christian Democratic Party. He was appointed minister of industry in 1978 and later served as chairman of the state-owned industrial holding company IRI. Accusations of corruption led to lengthy investigations of his tenure at IRI, but he was acquitted of all charges. He later broke with the Christian Democrats and moved to the left. In 1996 he became prime minister of the first genuinely left-wing coalition to govern Italy since the end of World War II but was overthrown two years later when the Communist Refoundation Party pulled out. After losing office, he served as a very active and influential president to the European Commission from 1999 to 2004. He then returned to Italian politics, forming a center-left coalition opposed to the center-right government of Prime Minister Silvio BERLUSCONI. In elections of April 2006, Prodi's group defeated Berlusconi's group by a such a razor-thin margin that Berlusconi demanded a recount.

Production Code, the Written by Father Daniel Lord, S.J., and adopted by the MPPDA in 1930 as a guideline (HAYS CODE) for the producers of the U.S. motion picture industry, the code controlled the content of U.S. films for more than three decades. Part of the Hays Office (MPPDA) system of self-regulation, the code assumed that movies could "uplift" or "degrade" audiences. Therefore, a basic premise of the code was that films uphold, not question or challenge, the basic values of society. The sanctity of home, marriage and church was to be upheld. Law was not to be belittled or ridiculed. From 1930 to 1933 the code was enforced but not with the severity that industry critics demanded.

In 1934, under pressure from the Catholic LEGION OF DECENCY, a new Production Code Administration was created, and a Catholic censor, Joseph I. Breen, was appointed director by Will Hays. No film could be produced or shown in the U.S. without the approval of Breen and his PCA staff. Studios had to submit scripts to Breen, who rigidly enforced the code. For example, he banned Mae WEST's early films from the screen and so censored her after 1934 that her screen appeal was greatly diminished. Breen demanded that films stress moral values and conservative politics. In U.S. movies adultery was punished, divorce shown as wrong and actresses clothed from head to toe. The code was also used to limit social and political commentary. Breen refused an MGM request to film the Sinclair LEWIS novel *It Can't Happen Here* in 1937 and used his authority to alter films that dealt with sensitive topics like unemployment, housing, racism and drug addiction.

In the late 1940s Breen used the Production Code to fight a new openness in cinema that emerged after the war. He tried to ban *The Bicycle Thief* (1948) because it showed a young boy urinating and contained a scene in a brothel. He refused a PCA seal for Otto PREMINGER's *The Moon Is Blue* because of its cavalier attitude toward sexual relationships. But Breen's dominance was now limited by changing public attitudes, the deregulation of the industry by the federal government, the rise of television and the determination of independent producers to challenge Breen's authority. Breen retired in 1954 and was replaced by his assistant Geoffrey Shurlock. By the late 1960s the industry moved from the self-censorship imposed under the Production Code to an industry rating system—G, for general audiences; M, for mature fans; R, restricted to over 16; and X for adults—that allowed audiences to choose the type of movies they wanted.

Profumo affair Sensational British political scandal. In 1963 it came out that the Conservative war minister John Profumo had been involved with a prostitute, Christine Keeler, who had also associated with a Soviet naval attaché. Profumo initially denied the allegations, but later admitted that he had lied and resigned from the ministry, the Privy Council, and Parliament. Following a government investigation, it was announced that there had been no breech of national security from the affair, but the highly publicized scandal contributed to the CONSERVATIVE PARTY'S defeat in the 1964 elections.

Progressive Conservative Party (Canada) One of the four major Canadian political parties, the Progressive Conservative Party (formerly known as the Conservative Party) dominated in the early years after confederation in 1867. The party advocated strong ties to Britain and a wariness of the U.S. The party also appealed to conservatives in French-speaking Quebec. It became the Progressive Conservative Party when it merged with the Progressive Party, which had broad support in the prairie provinces. World War I created a crisis for the party because French-Canadians objected to conscription. The party never regained its support in Quebec, which has remained a Liberal Party stronghold. Although LIBERAL PARTY prime ministers were in power for most of the latter half of the century, Brian MULRONEY, a PC from Quebec, became prime minister in 1986. Because of the party's minority status in Parliament throughout the 1990s, it merged with the Alliance Party in October 2003 to form the Conservative Party of Canada.

progressive movement Movement that advocated political and social reforms in the UNITED STATES in the early 1900s. The progressive movement was largely a reaction to urban corruption and to abuses by business monopolies. Theodore ROOSEVELT, a Republican and U.S. president from 1901 to 1909, was a leading progressive. In 1912, disap-

pointed with the conservative policies of his successor, William Howard TAFT, Roosevelt unsuccessfully ran for the presidency as candidate of the newly formed, progressive **Bull Moose Party.** Another Progressive Party, centered in the American Midwest and favoring farmers and workers, formed in 1924. Its presidential candidate, the fiery U.S. senator Robert LA FOLLETTE, waged a credible campaign but carried only Wisconsin, his home state.

Prohibition Period between 1919 and 1933 when the manufacture, sale or transport of alcoholic drinks was prohibited in the U.S. Public drunkenness had always been a problem in the U.S., and by 1920 an active temperance movement led by the Anti-Saloon League had succeeded in banning al-

Federal agents destroying liquor barrels during Prohibition (LIBRARY OF CONGRESS, PRINTS AND PHOTOGRAPHS DIVISION)

coholic drinks in a number of states. Following World War I, the movement received a boost when the idea was promoted that drinking alcohol was unpatriotic because many German-Americans were involved in the trade. The Eighteenth Amendment to the U.S. Constitution banned the manufacture and sale of alcoholic drinks, including beer and wine. But bootleggers began to manufacture and distribute illegal alcoholic beverages, which were dispensed in speakeasies. Many otherwise law-abiding citizens simply ignored the ban. Distribution was soon taken over by organized crime figures such as Al CAPONE, and gang warfare broke out. The DEMOCRATIC PARTY platform in the election year of 1932 proposed to repeal the "Great Experiment"; ROOSEVELT won and in 1933 the Twenty-first Amendment made the sale of alcoholic beverages once again legal in most of the U.S.

Prokofiev, Serge (Sergei Sergeyevich Prokofiev) (1891–1953) Soviet composer. Born in the Ukraine, Prokofiev began composing at age five and later studied with Reinhold GLIERE and at the Saint Petersburg Conservatory with Rimsky-Korsakov. A brilliant pianist and conductor, he left the USSR in 1918, shortly after the RUSSIAN REVOLUTION. He toured the world and settled in Paris during the 1920s, only returning permanently to the USSR in 1936. Although he generally enjoyed the approval of the Soviet authorities, in 1948 Prokofiev (along with Dmitri SHOSTAKOVICH and Aram KHACHATURIAN) was accused of "formalism" and personally reprimanded by Joseph STALIN. Prokofiev's early works are innovative and restrained, combining lyricism with dissonance, melodic beauty with abrupt rhythmic effects. His later pieces are more simplified and accessible. All his compositions, however, are very distinctive in style, often treating Russian themes. Among Prokofiev's works are seven symphonies—most notably the First (the *Classical Symphony,* 1916–17) and the Fifth (1944), two violin concertos, five piano concertos, various piano pieces and numerous chamber works. His vocal compositions include the operas *The Gambler* (1915–16), *The Love for Three Oranges* (1921) and *War and Peace* (1953). His dramatic cantata

Alexander Nevsky (1939) was used as the score for Sergei EISENSTEIN's film of the same name. Also a superb composer for the ballet, Prokofiev's works in this genre include *L'enfant Prodigue* (1929), one of several ballets he created for DIAGHILEV's BALLETS RUSSES, and *Romeo and Juliet* (1938). Among his best known works is the symphonic fairy tale *Peter and the Wolf* (1936).

Prokosch, Frederic *(1908–1989)* American author. His best selling first novel, *The Asiatics* (1935), won wide acclaim for its profile of a young American making his way from Beirut, Lebanon, to China. His other works included *The Seven Sisters* (1962), *The Missolonghi Manuscript* (1968) and *Voices* (1983), a memoir of his encounters with such figures as T. S. ELIOT, James JOYCE, and Gertrude STEIN.

propaganda Manipulation of public opinion and behavior in favor of or in opposition to an idea or cause through a number of means, from the use of rhetoric and symbols to written or broadcast messages. The term is generally used in a negative fashion. The word is derived from the Congregatio de propaganda fide (Congregation for the Propagation of the Faith), a Roman Catholic missionary agency established in 1622. With the growth of means for disseminating information after the Industrial Revolution, propaganda assumed a great deal of importance and was an influential part of life in the 20th century. Propaganda differs from education in its deliberately one-sided view of a given issue; only that information is disseminated that will support the propagandists' argument and denigrate the opinions of their opponents. Propaganda was used with considerable success in the BOLSHEVIK movement of the early 20th century, and it is evident in V. I. LENIN's *What Is to Be Done?* (1902), in which he stressed "agitprop," a combination of agitation and propaganda in support of communist revolution. Later in the century propaganda was an important tool of the fascist movements of Adolf HITLER, whose information minister Joseph GOEBBELS was a master propagandist, and of Benito MUSSOLINI. During WORLD WAR II propaganda was an important weapon for both sides of the conflict, and it was extensively used by both the Axis and the Allies, the latter producing material under the auspices of the Office of War Information. In the contemporary era propaganda in printed communications, on the radio and particularly on television has been used for many purposes, from promoting systems of government, to attempting to elect candidates, to selling commercial products through advertising. Moreover, the effectiveness of propaganda campaigns has been increasingly quantified through the use of public opinion surveys. At the same time, a more sophisticated audience seems somewhat better able to distinguish between the efforts of propagandists and those with honestly differing opinions.

protectionism Government economic policy that seeks high tariffs on imported goods in an effort to reduce foreign imports and protect domestic producers and manufacturers. The issue of protectionism has stirred much political debate in the 20th century. Advocates of protectionism (generally supporters of the labor movement) say that protectionist policies protect domestic jobs and help prevent a trade deficit. Opponents say that imposing high tariffs only causes foreign countries to impose similar restrictions on imports, thereby slowing the economy and hurting the very workers the tariffs are meant to help. The HAWLEY-SMOOT TARIFF ACT (1930), enacted at the beginning of the GREAT DEPRESSION, raised U.S. tariffs to their highest levels ever; foreign governments retaliated with similar tariffs, thus damaging world trade and deepening the Depression. In the 1980s some U.S. politicians called for protectionist tariffs to stem the flow of imports from Japan.

Proton booster Soviet "D-Class" launch vehicle, designed to lift heavy loads such as the SALYUT and Mir space stations. It was the first Soviet booster not developed directly from a military rocket. Introduced in July 1965, it is an enlarged version of the smaller "A-class" booster used to launch all three SPUTNIK satellites, as well as VOSTOK, VOSKHOD, SOYUZ, and Progress missions. In the

Allied propaganda poster during World War II told civilians about the Nazi enemy. (LIBRARY OF CONGRESS. PRINTS AND PHOTOGRAPHS DIVISION)

late 1980s the USSR began promoting the Proton launcher for use by the rest of the world as a commercial launch vehicle.

Protopopovs, the Soviet skaters, Lyudmilla Belousova and Oleg Protopopov. This husband and wife ice skating team won two Olympic gold medals for pairs figure skating: at Innsbruck in 1964 and at Grenoble in 1968. Known for their elegant and sophisticated style, the Protopopovs also won several European championships.

Proulx, E. Annie *(1935–)* American author and winner of the Pulitzer Prize and the National Book Award for *The Shipping News* (1994). Born in Norwich, Connecticut, Proulx originally worked as a journalist and authored several "how-to" books before starting to write fictional works in the mid-1980s. In 1988 she published *Heartsongs and Other Stories,* a two-volume collection of short stories. Following the critical success of *Heartsongs,* Proulx began work on three novels— *Postcards* (1992), *The Shipping News* (1993), and *Accordion Crimes* (1996). She has also published *Close Range* (1999), a collection of short stories about the American West, a novella named *Brokeback Mountain* (1998), and *That Old Ace in the Hole* (2002) about life in the southwestern United States. *The Shipping News,* which won the Pulitzer Prize and the National Book Award, was turned into a full-length feature film in 2001. The book and film established Proulx's reputation as one of America's most respected writers of fiction. *Brokeback Mountain* was made into an acclaimed film in 2005.

Proust, Marcel *(1871–1922)* French novelist, story writer and essayist. Proust is generally recognized as the greatest French novelist of the 20th century on the strength of his sequence of seven novels, REMEMBRANCE OF THINGS PAST. Born to a Catholic father and a Jewish mother, Proust suffered from poor health as a child and was a near invalid during his early teens. Nonetheless, he went on to graduate from the Sorbonne and to serve in the French army. In the Parisian society of the 1890s Belle Époque, Proust established a reputation for himself as a dandy. His first volume of stories, *Pleasures and Days* (1896),

won him only a small readership. In the 1900s Proust published a great deal of literary criticism. He was very close to his mother, and her death in 1905 spurred him, the following year, to retire from society and devote himself to literature. Dogged by failing health, Proust devoted the final 15 years of his life to *Remembrance of Things Past,* writing in a cork-lined room to keep out the noises of the Parisian streets.

Prouvé, Jean *(1901–1984)* French designer and architect. Educated in Nancy, Prouvé began executing design commissions in 1918, becoming known for his modernist metal furniture. Associated with LE CORBUSIER in the late 1920s, he was a founder of the Union des Artistes Modernes. He stopped designing in 1950, devoting himself thereafter to architecture. As an architect, he was best known for a series of public buildings in the modern idiom notable for their sophisticated engineering.

Provincetown Players *(1916–1921)* American theatrical ensemble of playwrights and actors. The Provincetown Players were well known for their willingness to premiere socially controversial works by new and experimental playwrights. The most famous figure to emerge from the Provincetown Players milieu was Eugene O'NEILL, whose classic play *Desire Under the Elms* was first produced by an offshoot of the players—the Playwrights' Theatre—in 1924. While the players first appeared at the Wharf Theater in Providence, Rhode Island, the ensemble moved to GREENWICH VILLAGE before resettling in the Provincetown Playhouse in 1918. The Provincetown Players disbanded in 1921.

Provisional Government Government formed by Russia's DUMA in February 1917 in Petrograd upon the collapse of the autocracy. The provisional government promised to form a constitutional assembly and to hold free elections. It abolished the secret police and granted religious freedom. Many of its leaders were of a conservative outlook, although KERENSKY was a moderate socialist. Because of the war effort grave problems, such as redistribution of land and the rights of non-Russian people to self-government, could not be resolved. As a result, dis-

content continued to grow. At the same time as the provisional government, the Soviet of workers' deputies had been established; this had the support of industrial workers and socialists, and in October 1917 they overthrew the Provisional Government.

Prusiner, Stanley *(1942–)* American neurologist and winner of the 1997 Nobel Prize in medicine. Born in Des Moines, Iowa, Prusiner obtained his primary and secondary education in Cincinnati, Ohio, before attending the University of Pennsylvania to study chemistry. While at the University of Pennsylvania, he worked under the guidance of Sidney Wolfson, a member of the university's Department of Surgery, and helped develop a research project that examined the effects of hypothermia on surgery. When Prusiner graduated from the university in 1964, he enrolled in that institution's medical school to continue studying under Wolfson. In 1967 Prusiner obtained an internship with the NATIONAL INSTITUTES OF HEALTH (NIH) that required him to work at the University of California-San Francisco (UCSF), where he studied E. Coli bacteria under the guidance of Earl Stadtman. In 1972 Prusiner began his residency in the university's Department of Nueurology. It was during his residency that Prusiner began to research the causes of a "slow virus" infection termed Creutzfeldt-Jakob disease (CJD) that caused increasing loss of memory and muscular control. Two years later, Prusiner accepted an assistant professorship at UCSF to study CJD through experimentation on mice possessing "scrapie," a disease similar to CJD found in mice and sheep. During Prusiner's research, he found the amino acid sequence responsible for incubating scrapie in mice, which allowed him to discover a similar-acting antibody for possible use in individuals seeking to combat CJD. For his work in the field of medicine, Prusiner won the 1997 Nobel Prize in medicine.

PSFS Building Headquarters of the Philadelphia Savings Fund Society, built in 1932 and generally regarded as the first truly modern skyscraper office building; among the first large buildings in the INTERNATIONAL STYLE to be built in the U.S. It was designed by William LesCaze and George Howe and is remarkable for the consistency and excellence of its overall concept and details. The black granite base contains an austerely geometric banking room with a windowed, rounded corner. Above is a 28-story tower office block with columns exposed along the sides and front, cantilevered forward. A highly successful building, it remains in fine condition and in regular use for its intended purposes.

Public Works Administration (PWA)
U.S. government agency, established in 1933 during the first HUNDRED DAYS of President Franklin D. ROOSEVELT's administration. Part of the NEW DEAL, the PWA was one of the most visible government programs during the GREAT DEPRESSION. As its name suggests, the PWA was responsible for public works. It put thousands of people to work on construction projects throughout the U.S. Numerous public buildings, including many post offices, schools, courthouses and other government facilities were built by the PWA; many of these buildings remained in use toward the end of the century. (See also WORKS PROGRESS ADMINISTRATION.)

Puccini, Giacomo (1858–1924)
Italian composer and one of the most popular operatic composers of the late 19th and early 20th centuries; born in Lucca, Italy, of a distinguished musical family. A precocious musician, Puccini began his musical studies as a child, attending the Istituto Musicale and later studying (1880–83) at the Milan Conservatory. His first opera, the one-act *Le Villi* (1884), met with some success, but it was not until the production of his third work, *Manon Lescaut* (1893), that Puccini became a celebrated and successful composer. His finest works are generally acknowledged to be *La Boheme* (1896), *Tosca* (1900), *Madama Butterfly* (1904) and *Turandot,* which was not quite finished at the composer's death and which premiered at La Scala in 1926. Lesser works include *La Fanciulla del West* (1910) and *Il Trittico* (1918). In his operas, Puccini combined such traditional features of Italian opera as arias and love duets with such Wagnerian innovations as leitmotivs and complex dramatic characterizations. To this mixture he added superb melodies, lush orchestration, exotic settings and erotic tension mingled with sentimentality.

Pudovkin, Vsevelod Illarionovitch (1893–1953)
Soviet filmmaker and theoretician. With colleagues Lev KULESHOV, Sergei EISENSTEIN and Dziga VERTOV, he stood at the center of the great decade of Soviet filmmaking in the 1920s. He was born in Penza and educated in physics and chemistry at Moscow University. In 1920 he entered the State Film School and two years later worked with Kuleshov in the famous "Kuleshov Workshop." Pudovkin's most important films were made in the second half of the decade, *Mat (Mother)* in 1926, *Konyets Sankt-Peterburga (The End of St. Petersburg)* in 1927 and *Potomak Chingis-khan (The Heir to Genghis Khan,* or, *Storm over Asia)* in 1928. Nominally, like Eisenstein's films, they are all concerned with issues of Soviet revolution, but, again like Eisenstein, their chief distinction lies in their applications of film shots to make "the all-inclusive discovery and explanation of the interrelationships of the phenomena of real life." The "linkage" of shots, Pudovkin argued, is the foundation of film art, the building from raw pieces of celluloid a "filmic space and time." The art of film acting, as a consequence, must differ radically from stage technique. The actor must work in brief time-space fragments, becoming a "material" of "equal and undifferentiated value" with other components of cinema, and subject to the same manipulations. Despite these theoretical formulations, however, Pudovkin's films display more compassion, poetic sensibility and interest in individual personalities than do Eisenstein's. After sustaining injuries in a car wreck in 1935, Pudovkin returned to cinema, directing a number of historical films and appearing in others such as Eisenstein's *Ivan Groznyi (Ivan the Terrible)* in 1944. His major theoretical works, *Film Technique* and *Film-Acting* (1926), first appeared in translation in 1933.

Pueblo incident
Capture of the USS *Pueblo,* a navy electronic and radio intelligence-gathering ship, off the eastern coast of NORTH KOREA on January 23, 1968, and its aftermath. The vessel, under Commander Lloyd M. Bucher, was fired on, boarded and seized by ships from the North Korean navy and removed to the port of Wonson. The U.S. demanded release of the ship and its crew together with an apology, maintaining that it had been in international waters at the time of its capture. The North Korean government held the ship and men hostage for 11 months. The U.S. finally acceded to North Korean demands, and in December 1968 it signed an admission of intrusion into North Korean waters, which it disavowed before the signing, and an apology. With this and the promise not to engage in further spying, the ship and crew were released. Afterward, Bucher and others on the *Pueblo* charged that they had been tortured and forced to sign false confessions. The ship's captain gave his version of the events in *Bucher: My Story* (1970).

Puente, Tito (Ernesto Antonio Puente, Jr.) (1923–2000)
American musician, bandleader, composer and producer. A virtuoso timbales player, Puente also played the vibes, sax, piano, bongos and conga. His first band, the Piccadilly Boys, formed in 1947 and soon became the Tito Puente Orchestra. He was a leader of the big band mambo and chachacha styles of the 1950s. As a member or leader of other groups specializing in Latin rhythms, he toured Europe, produced many records and won two Grammy Awards, for *Tito Puente and His Latin Ensemble on Broadway* (1983) and *Mambo Diablo* (1985). His many compositions include the hit "Oye Como Va."

Puerto Rico
The Commonwealth of Puerto Rico is an island covering 3,514 square miles in the Caribbean Sea. The terrain is mostly mountainous, with a coastal plain in the north. The capital is San Juan. American troops invaded the centuries-old Spanish island in May 1898, and in December the island was ceded to the U.S. It became an unincorporated U.S. territory, and U.S. citizenship was granted to Puerto Ricans in 1917. Many islanders, however, wanted greater internal self-government and economic and social reforms, a policy advocated by the Partido Popular Democratico (PPD). The PPD gained a majority in the Senate in elections in 1940, and the first elections to the post of governor in 1947 were won by the PPD's leader, Luis MUÑOZ MARÍN. Puerto Rico was granted a new constitution in 1952 when it became a commonwealth in association with the U.S. Under the PPD administration a program of investment

and industrialization developed the island's economy and improved social conditions. In 1967 a plebiscite produced a majority in favor of commonwealth status, rather than statehood, with only a very small minority in favor of independence.

The PPD remained in power until 1968 when it was defeated by the Partido Nuevo Progresista (PNP), which favors statehood. Luis A. Ferré became governor. In 1972 the PPD was returned to power with Rafael Hernández Colón elected governor. The PNP's candidate for governor, Carlos Romero Barcelo, won in the 1976 elections, but in 1980 the PNP lost its majority in both houses of the Legislative Assembly, although Romero Barcelo retained the governorship. Internal factionalism within the PNP led to divisions in the party over Romero Barcelo's leadership. In 1984 Romero Barcelo was defeated by Hernández Colón for the governorship, arid the PPD maintained its majority in the assembly. Hernández Colón retained the governorship in the election held in November 1988, defeating Baltasar Corrada del Rio of the PNP by a narrow margin. In a 1998 referendum Puerto Ricans again rejected statehood within the U.S. and instead chose to remain a commonwealth. Two years after the referendum, Puerto Rico elected its first female governor, Sila Calderón, of the Popular Democratic Party, for a four-year term. In May 2003 Calderón helped negotiate an end to the U.S. Navy's munitions testing on the offshore island of Vieques. In 2006 the Puerto Rican government ran out of money, forcing the closure of schools and all government agencies.

Pugwash Conferences A series of international conferences begun with the goal of bringing together academics with leading national and international figures in the pursuit of increasing international cooperation and reducing conflict throughout the world. Started in 1957, the first conference was organized by the American philanthropist Cyrus Stephen EATON and the Polish-born British physicist Joseph ROTBLAT. Eaton hoped to use the meeting, held in Pugwash, a small village in Nova Scotia, Canada, to gather scientists from around the world and from both sides in the cold war, and have these individuals discuss the consequences of

the nuclear arms race on humanity. To facilitate similar conversations on issues of equal international concern, Eaton founded the Pugwash Organization—a somewhat decentralized organization that would oversee the scheduling, coordination and financing of these meetings—to select the individuals who would meet independently of their governments to discuss world problems and try to reach a consensus on their solutions. Since its inception, there have been over 275 Pugwash conferences, symposia and workshops held throughout the world, in which over 10,000 men and women have met to discuss issues of international concern. In 1995 the Pugwash Organization received the Nobel Peace Prize for its Conferences on Science and World Affairs that helped to reduce the nuclear arms race and the role of nuclear weapons in international politics.

Puig, Manuel (*1932–1990*) Argentinian novelist. Puig, who was best known for his novel *The Kiss of the Spider Woman* (1979), which was adapted into a highly successful HOLLYWOOD film starring William Hurt and Raul Julia, grew up highly enamored of the film medium that would spread his fame. As a young boy living in a remote region of the Argentine pampas, Puig used films to escape from his culturally narrow environment. After studying philosophy at the University of Buenos Aires, Puig went to Rome in 1955 where he studied film technique. His first novel, *Betrayed by Rita Hayworth* (1971), portrayed the commingling of Hollywood fantasy and the bleak realities of Argentine life. In *The Kiss of the Spider Woman*, two prisoners—one a political radical, the other a homosexual—bide their prison sentence time and reveal their souls through retelling the romantic plots of old movies. Other novels by Puig include *Heartbreak Tango: A Serial* (1973) and *Eternal Curse on the Reader of These Pages* (1985).

Pulitzer Prize American award for journalism, letters and music. The annual Pulitzer Prizes were established in 1915 in the will of the Hungarian-American newspaper publisher Joseph Pulitzer, who also established the Columbia University School of Journalism, which confers the prizes. The

prizes are bestowed on American citizens who distinguish themselves in the field of letters (including history, biography, poetry, drama and fiction), music and journalism (including reporting, photography and criticism). The prizes, originally $1,000, are now $10,000 except for public service in journalism, which is given a gold medal. The first Pulitzer Prizes were awarded in 1917. The Pulitzer Prize is widely regarded as the most prestigious American award in these fields.

punk rock Hard-edged musical style that constitutes a performing subgenre of ROCK and roll. Punk rock first came to attention in both Britain and America in the mid-1970s. The first major punk rock song is generally considered to be "God Save the Queen" (1977) by the British-based group the Sex Pistols, which featured scathingly raw and sneering vocals by lead singer Johnny Rotten and unsophisticated but intensely hard-driving guitar and percussion work. Other major bands that influenced the punk rock style include the Buzzcocks, the Ramones and James White and the Blacks. While punk rock's musical creativity dwindled by the early 1980s, the basic punk rock style continued to hold its popularity with a new generation of rock audiences. Although punk rock subsided as a genre of rock and roll music in the 1990s, it reemerged in the 2000s with groups such as Sum 41 and Simple Plan that have been influenced by the punk rock style.

"Purple Code" See Elizabeth S. FRIEDMAN.

Purser, Sarah (*1848–1943*) Irish painter, designer and stained-glass artist. She studied in Ireland, France and Italy, returning to Dublin in 1878. In addition to creating her own works, she was also an important force in the promotion of native Irish art. In 1924 she founded the Friends of the National Collections of Ireland, and in 1930 she secured from the government sumptuous Dublin quarters to house the Lane Collection and the Modern Art Gallery.

Purvis, Melvin (*1903–1960*) American law enforcement officer. Born in South Carolina, Purvis became a lawyer and joined the FBI in 1927. He was appointed to the FBI's Chicago office in 1932, and for the next three years he presided over the hunt for and apprehension of such public enemy criminals as "Pretty Boy" FLOYD, "Baby Face" NELSON and, most notably, John DILLINGER, whom he and his agents gunned down in 1934. Apparently in conflict with FBI director J. Edgar HOOVER, Purvis resigned from the bureau in 1935. During WORLD WAR II he worked for the U.S. Army War Crimes Office and after the war returned to the practice of law.

Puskas, Ferenc (*1926– *) Hungarian-born soccer player. Puskas was the dominant player on the outstanding Hungarian national team of the early 1950s. A natural goalscorer, Puskas won his first cap at age 18 in August 1945. He was captain of the Hungary team that won the 1952 Olympic gold medal. Puskas's most memorable performance came at Wembley Stadium, England, in 1953 when he scored two goals in Hungary's 6-3 thrashing of England, their first-ever home loss. In a return match in 1964 in Budapest, Hungary won 7-1; Puskas scored two again and established himself as the world's best player. This was the pinnacle of Puskas's career. In the 1954 World Cup in Switzerland, Puskas was injured and Hungary lost to West Germany 3-2 in the final. During the 1956 HUNGARIAN UPRISING, Puskas was touring with his team, Honved, and decided not to return home. He eventually settled in Spain, and joined the European Champions, Real Madrid. He joined forces with the legendary Alfredo di Stefano and led Real to its fifth European Championship in 1960. Puskas played for Spain in the 1962 World Cup and retired in 1966. In 1993 Puskas was allowed to return to Hungary to manage the Hungarian national team in a qualifying match for the World Cup.

Putin, Vladimir (*1952– *) Soviet KGB agent (1975–91), professor of international affairs (1989–91), deputy mayor of St. Petersburg (1994–96), prime minister of Russia (1999), and president of Russia (2000–). Born in Leningrad, Putin attended one of the city's top high schools, where he developed interests in both literature and science, as well as the ambition to join

Russian president Vladimir Putin (NORTH ATLANTIC TREATY ORGANIZATION)

the KGB, the Soviet intelligence agency. In 1970, after being told by a KGB official that the best way to become an agent was to obtain a law degree, Putin enrolled in Leningrad State University's elite law school. Five years later, Putin obtained his law degree and was offered a job by the KGB as a counter-intelligence and later a foreign intelligence agent. In 1985 Putin's superiors, impressed with his work, made him a political intelligence agent in East Germany. In 1990, following the end of communist rule in East Germany, Putin returned to Leningrad (later renamed St. Petersburg) and found work at Leningrad State University as a professor in the International Affairs Department, where he continued to function as a KGB agent. When Putin's good friend and law school mentor Anatoly Sobchak was elected mayor of Saint Petersburg in 1991, he appointed Putin as an aide charged with enticing foreign and domestic firms to invest in the city. By 1994 Putin had done so well in this post that he was chosen as the city's deputy mayor. In 1996 after Sobchak lost his bid for reelection, Putin resigned and soon found work as an aide to Pavel Borodin, the minister of Russia's property administration. Two years later Russian president Boris YELTSIN named Putin as the chief of his Security Council and as the head of the Federal Security Bureau (FSB), the successor organization to the KGB. In August 1999 Yeltsin appointed Putin prime minister following the dismissal of Sergei Stepashin. Four months later, Yeltsin designated Putin as his successor when he resigned from the Russian presidency on December 31. In March 2000 Putin easily won election to the presidency, and was reelected president in 2003.

As president, Putin has sought to enhance Russia's image abroad while consolidating his control of the Russian political system. In particular, Putin continued Russian military efforts to end the separatist insurgency in Chechnya. He refused to negotiate with Chechnyan guerrillas who in October 2002 seized control of a Moscow opera house, instead ordering a special forces strike on the building that killed the terrorists and some of their hostages. Putin has also sought to establish better relations with the states of the EUROPEAN UNION, China, and the U.S., by gaining Russia's admission as a consultative member of NATO, by renewing the strategic partnership between Russia and China and by permitting the U.S. to abrogate the 1972 Anti-Ballistic Missile Treaty.

Pu-yi, Henry (**Aisin-Gioro, Yuan-tong [Hsuan-t'ung]) Emperor**) (*1906–1967*) Last emperor of CHINA (1908–12), who reigned under the name Xuantong (Hsuan-t'ung). Born in Beijing, a grand-nephew of the dowager empress, he succeeded to the throne as a small child. The republican revolution forced his abdication in 1912, and he remained in the Forbidden City under government support and warlord influence until 1924. In 1925 he fled to the Japanese concession in Tientsin, living there until 1931. He became the figurehead (as the Kangde Emperor) of the Japanese puppet state of MANCHUKUO (Manchuria) in 1934. Captured by Soviet troops in 1945, he was imprisoned in Siberia for five years, testifying at the war crimes trial in Tokyo in 1946. Turned over to the People's Republic of China in 1950, he remained in prison until granted amnesty in 1959. After political "reeducation," he became a private citizen in Beijing. His life was the subject of Bernardo BERTOLUCCI's ACADEMY AWARD–winning 1987 film *The Last Emperor.*

PWA See PUBLIC WORKS ADMINISTRATION.

Pyatakov, Grigory L. (*1890–1937*) Politician and leader of the left wing of the Ukrainian Communist Party. In December 1918 Moscow ordered that a concealed Soviet government be set up in Kursk under Pyatakov. Pyatakov accordingly set up a Soviet regime and invaded the UKRAINE with Red troops. In 1937, however, he was tried at the "anti-Soviet Trotskyite Center" trial.

Pyle, Ernie *(1900–1945)* American journalist. Pyle held a variety of newspaper posts in New York and Washington, D.C., during the 1920s and 1930s. In 1935 he become a syndicated columnist and roving reporter. However, his career reached its zenith during WORLD WAR II, when he became perhaps the best-known and most widely read war correspondent. He accompanied American troops on the front lines, covering the war in North Africa, Europe and the Pacific in his regular column. Pyle did not report the course of the war in strategic terms but, rather, chronicled the day-to-day existence of ordinary GIs. He won the 1944 PULITZER PRIZE for his reporting. Pyle was killed by Japanese machine gun fire on April 18, 1945, on the island of Iishima, near OKINAWA.

Pym, Barbara (Mary Crampton) *(1913–1980)* British novelist. Born in Shropshire and educated at Oxford, Pym worked for a time at the International African Institute in London. Her keenly observed satirical novels of provincial English life, including *Excellent Women* (1952), *Less Than Angels* (1955), *Quartet in Autumn* (1977) and *A Few Green Leaves* (1980), are reminiscent of the work of Jane Austen. Pym enjoyed modest success during the 1950s, but in 1961 her publishers dropped her from their list. Her reputation rose again in the late 1970s when Lord David CECIL and Philip LARKIN both cited her as one of the most underrated writers of the 20th century.

Pynchon, Thomas *(1937–)* American novelist. Pynchon is highly reclusive, and few facts concerning the last 30 years of his life are known. In his youth he served in the U.S. Navy, graduated from Cornell University and worked for a brief time as a technical writer for Boeing Aircraft. Since the publication of his acclaimed first novel, *V* (1963), Pynchon has been regarded as one of the most dazzling and difficult fiction writers of modern times. He possesses a detailed knowledge of both literature and modern technology and combines the vocabulary and insights of both fields to create a richly woven verbal tapestry filled with baroque allusions and imagery. Two of his central themes are the elusive nature of paranoia and the pervasive presence of entropic forces in a world that is losing its structured coherence. Pynchon has written only four other novels,—*The Crying of Lot 49* (1966), *Gravity's Rainbow* (1973), which won the National Book Award, *Vineland* (1990) and *Mason & Dixon* (1997)—but his work is meticulously conceived and forms a monumental whole.

Q

Qaddafi, Muammer al- *(1942–)*
Libyan nationalist and revolutionary leader. A bedouin Arab, Qaddafi received a traditional Koranic education, then attended high school, from which he was expelled for nationalist political activity. He subsequently studied history at the University of Benghazi (1962–63), then attended the Libyan Military Academy and the British Royal Signal Corps School at Beaconsfield, England. In 1965 he was commissioned as a signal corps officer in the Royal Libyan Army. He led the 1969 revolution and was promoted by 11 fellow members of the Revolutionary Command Council to be commander in chief, with the rank of colonel. He served as prime minister and defense minister from January 1970 until 1972, when he relinquished the former post. In 1976 he chaired the first General People's Congress (GPC) and was elected general secretary of the GPC secretariat in 1977. His *Green Book* (1976) called for revolutionary Arab socialism. Qaddafi has sought to project himself as the champion of the Arab people but was condemned by the REAGAN administration as a sponsor of international terrorism; the U.S. raid on LIBYA in April 1986 was in retaliation for Qaddafi's previous terrorist actions, as well as a warning to deter him from further terrorism. Following the terrorist attacks on New York City and Washington, D.C., of September 11, 2001, Qaddafi improved his relations with the U.S. and emerged as a voice in the Islamic and Arabic world calling for increasing opposition to terrorist groups such as al-Qaeda. In late 2003, following the overthrow of the Iraqi government of Saddam Hussein by U.S. military forces, Qaddafi announced plans to dismantle Libya's nuclear weapons program and allow international inspections of its weapons sites.

al-Qaeda Meaning "military base" in Arabic, this group was founded in 1988 by Osama BIN LADEN and Muhammad Atef. Originally operating in Peshawar, PAKISTAN, between 1989 and 1991, al-Qaeda served as an umbrella organization in which the various MUJAHIDEEN cooperated in their fight against the Soviet and Soviet-supported forces in AFGHANISTAN. The larger goal of these movements was opposition to non-Islamic governments through any means, including force and terrorist acts. A facet of this larger aim included the expulsion of U.S. forces from SAUDI ARABIA, where they had been stationed since the Gulf War of 1991. From 1991 to 1996, al-Qaeda used its headquarters in Khartoum, SUDAN, to direct the training of its personnel in camps throughout Afghanistan, Pakistan, SOMALIA and KENYA for attacks on a variety of targets. After 1996, it moved its headquarters and principal training camps to Afghanistan, where its leaders established close relations with the TALIBAN, the principal Afghani authority. In its efforts, al-Qaeda repeatedly cooperated with other terrorist organizations, such as the Islamic Jihad in EGYPT (with which it merged in 1998), the Islamic Group, the National Islamic Front in Sudan and HEZBOLLAH in Lebanon (which it has provided with weaponry and access to its training facilities). Additionally, U.S. officials demonstrated financial links between al-Qaeda and several Islamic charities, which served to funnel funds to al-Qaeda operatives. Individuals trained at al-Qaeda bases are believed to have participated in the October 1993 attack on U.S. forces in Somalia that killed 18 army rangers. Other terrorist attacks attributed to al-Qaeda include the August 7, 1998, bombings of the U.S. embassies in Kenya and Tanzania, the attack on the USS *Cole* in October of 2000 and the terrorist assaults on the WORLD TRADE CENTER and the Pentagon on SEPTEMBER 11, 2001.

The international response to al-Qaeda has grown from a wholly U.S. operation to a multinational one. On August 20, 1998, U.S. president Bill CLINTON ordered a CRUISE MISSILE strike on the most extensive al-Qaeda training complex in Afghanistan. By late 2001, in large part because of the attacks on American soil, intelligence cooperation among the nations of France, Britain, Germany, Morocco, and Saudi Arabia resulted in the capture of numerous individuals linked to al-Qaeda. Additionally, a U.S. force entered Afghanistan in a successful effort to remove the Taliban from power and destroy all remaining al-Qaeda bases in that country. However, because of the nebulous nature of al-Qaeda and the wide autonomy allegedly offered to its agents, the capture of its entire hierarchy remained an elusive goal.

Qatar (State of Qater) On the eastern coast of the Arabian Peninsula, the state is comprised of the Qatar Peninsula and several offshore islands; Bahrain lies to the northwest. Qatar came under British influence in 1869, and under a treaty signed in 1916 Britain gained effective control over Qatar's foreign relations, together with responsibility for security and commercial privileges. This protectorate status continued until Qatar gained independence in 1971. In 1972 a palace coup occurred when Shaikh Khalifa ibn Hamad al-Thani ousted his cousin, Shaikh Ahmad. A year before independence, Qatar promulgated a written constitution that provided for a council of ministers and an advisory council. It stipulated that the former was to be appointed by the ruler and that a majority of the advisory council be elected by the general population. To date no elections have been held and, the council of ministers has become little more than a recommendatory authority. In 1995 Sheikh Khalifa was deposed by his son Hamad in a bloodless coup.

The al-Thanis constitute the largest ruling family in the region, and members hold 10 of the 15 cabinet portfolios, including defense, finance and foreign affairs. There are no political parties. Prior to the production of oil in 1949, the population (largely Sunni Muslims) was one of the poorest in the region, with most livelihoods dependent upon fishing and pearling. Petroleum production and export together with the nationalization of both major oil producers, Qatar Petroleum Company and Shell Oil of Qatar, have led to the government providing considerable investment for infrastructural development. Qatar has been a member of the Gulf Cooperation Council since its inception in 1981 and is a member of the Organization of Arab Petroleum Exporting Countries and OPEC. The historic territorial dispute with Bahrain over the Hawar Islands flared up in 1986 when Qatari troops briefly occupied Fasht al-Dibal, a coral reef that was being reclaimed from the sea by Bahrain. It was later destroyed by agreement of both parties. After the 1990 Iraqi invasion of Kuwait, Qatar permitted the stationing of troops from the U.S.-led expeditionary force on its soil, and later supported the U.S.-led liberation of Kuwait code-named OPERATION DESERT STORM. Five years after the end of Desert Storm, an Arabic news network, AL-JAZEERA, was launched in Qatar with heavy funding from the ruling family. The news service became critical of the government of Qatar's decision to permit the U.S. to use its forward bases as the command center for the March 2003 U.S.-led invasion of Iraq code-named Operation Iraqi Freedom. In 2005 Qatar's first written constitution came into effect, providing for some democratic reforms.

Qiao Guanhua (Chaio Kuan Hua, Chiao Kuan-hua) (1908–1983) Chinese communist political leader. During the early 1970s he played a key role in the normalization of relations between the PEOPLE'S REPUBLIC OF CHINA and the U.S. He headed China's first delegation to the UNITED NATIONS. With Henry KISSINGER, Qiao drafted the **Shanghai communiqué** during U.S. president Richard NIXON's 1972 visit to China. He was foreign minister from 1974 until 1976, when he was dismissed following the arrest of the GANG OF FOUR. He then played no public role for several years, but shortly before his

	QATAR
1916	Qatar becomes a British protectorate after a treaty is signed with Sheikh Adbullah al-Thani.
1949	Oil production begins at the onshore Dukhan field in the west.
1971	Qatar declares independence, as the United Kingdom withdraws from the Persian Gulf region.
1972	In a bloodless coup, Emir Sheikh Ahmad bin Ali bin Abdullah al-Thani is overthrown by his cousin and prime minister, Sheikh Khalifa bin Hamad al-Thani.
1981	Qatar joins the Gulf Cooperation Council.
1986	A territorial dispute with Bahrain nearly escalates to war.
1990	Emir agrees to the deployment of Arab and Western forces on Qatar soil following the Iraqi invasion of Kuwait.
1991	Qatar sends ground troops to Saudi Arabia to back the U.S.-led UN forces there during the Persian Gulf War.
1995	Sheikh Khalifa is deposed in a bloodless coup by his son Hamad.
1996	The Arabic news network Al-Jazeera begins operations in Qatar.
2003	Qatar allows the United States military to set up its command center for the military campaign against Iraq.
2005	Qatar's first constitution provides some limited democratic reform.

Qatar

Persian Gulf

BAHRAIN

Ar Ruways
Al Khuwayr

Madinat al Kaban

Al Ghuwayriyah

Adh Dhakhirah

Gulf of Bahrain

Umm as Suwayyah

Hawar Is.
(disputed between Qatar and Bahrain)

Al Jumaliyah

Sumaysimah

Bir Zikrit

Umm Salal Ali

Dukhan

Ash Shahaniyah

Ar Rayyan

Doha

Umm Bab

Al Wukayr

Al Wakrah

Gulf of Salwah

Umm Said

Al Kiranah

SAUDI ARABIA

N

Mazra at Tarina

0   20 miles
0   20 km

© Infobase Publishing

Pascal Jordan, Erwin SCHRODINGER and Louis DE BROGLIE all made important contributions to the field of quantum mechanics; Heisenberg introduced the **uncertainty principle** as a fundamental law of quantum mechanics. This 20th-century branch of science has revolutionized human knowledge of matter and energy.

quark Subatomic particle, believed to be the smallest elementary particle—1,000 times smaller than a proton. Physicists believe that quarks are the basis of protons and neutrons. The existence of quarks was first suggested by Murray GELL-MANN and George Zweig in 1964. The name is taken from a word coined by James JOYCE in *Finnegans Wake* (1939). Quarks can be classified as "charmed" or "strange," among other terms.

Quasimodo, Salvatore (*1901–1968*) Italian poet, critic and translator who won the NOBEL PRIZE for literature in 1959. After completing his studies to become an engineer, Quasimodo joined the Ministry of Public Works in 1928. His first collection, *Acque e terra* (1930, *Waters and Land*), recalled his Sicilian childhood. In 1938 he abandoned his technical trade, and in 1941 he became a professor of literature. Though his early poems showed the influence of symbolism and Hermeticism, over the years his language became simpler and his themes more public and socially committed. Of particular note are *Giorno doppo giorno* (1947, *Day after Day*), *La vita non e sogno* (1949, *Life Is Not Dream*), *La terra impareggiabile* (1958, *The Incomparable Land*) and *Dare e avere* (1966, *To Give and to Have*). He also translated ancient Greek and Latin poetry, Shakespeare, Molière, NERUDA and CUMMINGS.

Quayle, Sir John Anthony (*1913–1989*) British theater, film and television actor. Noted for the wide range of his work—from classical drama to Shakespeare to war movies—he began acting with the Old Vic Company in London but left the theater to enlist in the military in WORLD WAR II. After the war he joined the Shakespeare Memorial Theatre Company (now the ROYAL SHAKESPEARE COMPANY) in Stratford-upon-Avon and served both as an actor

death in 1983 he was appointed adviser to the People's Association for Friendship with Foreign Countries.

Quango (Quasi-Autonomous Non-Governmental Organisation) A body in Britain that has the power to spend public money but is not under direct governmental control.

Quant, Mary (*1934– *) British fashion designer and retailer, a key figure in the rise of British fashion in the 1950s and 1960s. Quant studied art at Goldsmith's College in London, where she met Alexander Greene, who became her partner in 1955. (They were married two years later.) The first Quant shop, Bazaar, opened in London in 1955 on the King's Road; it introduced a modern

youth-oriented concept in display and marketing as well as in the actual garments offered for sale. Quant helped Britain rise to a position of leadership in the fashion world with the introduction of the miniskirt in 1964.

quantum mechanics Branch of physics that deals with matter and energy on an atomic and subatomic level. The quantum theory was first formulated in 1900 by Max PLANCK. According to this theory, energy (light, for example) does not travel in a continuous wave, as was previously thought, but is formed by infinitely small bits ("quanta") pulsing in rapid succession. Albert EINSTEIN (1905), Niels BOHR (1913) and (all in the mid-1920s) Max BORN, Werner HEISENBERG, Paul DIRAC, and as the group's director (1948–56). He also founded the touring Compass group in 1984. Among his best known films were *The Wrong Man* (1957), *The Guns of Navarone* (1961) and *Lawrence of Arabia* (1963). He was nominated for an ACADEMY AWARD in 1970 for his portrayal of Cardinal Wolsey in *Anne of a Thousand Days,* a historical film about Henry VIII and Anne Boleyn. He was knighted in 1985.

Quebec (Québec) Province of eastern CANADA and one of the four founding provinces of the dominion (1867). Although French authority ended in 1763, French culture has remained dominant; in 1974 French was made the sole official language in the province. A group advocating independence arose in the 1960s, but in a referendum in May 1980 Quebec voted against secession. The secession movement revived in the late 1980s. (See also PARTI QUÉBÉCOIS, RENÉ LEVESQUE.)

Quebec Conferences Two talks held in Quebec during WORLD WAR II between U.S. president Franklin D. ROOSEVELT and British prime minister Winston CHURCHILL, with the participation of their military staffs. The first, code-named "Quadrant," was held in August 1943 and involved plans for the NORMANDY landings, Southeast Asia campaigns and the war in Italy. The second, code-named "Octagon" and held in September 1944, concerned the naval war in the Pacific, the Allied advance into Germany, operations in the Philippines and the MORGENTHAU PLAN.

Queen, Ellery (pen name of Frederic Dannay and Manfred B. Lee) Both the author and his celebrated American detective creation, "Queen," was an amateur sleuth, radio-TV-film star, magazine editor, anthologist and chronicler of the history of detective fiction. From *The Roman Hat Mystery* (1929) to *A Fine and Private Place* (1971), his 35 novels and numerous short stories ranged from exercises in pure deduction (*The Chinese Orange Mystery*) to complex psychological dramas (the justly famed "Wrightsville" cases, including *Calamity Town* and *Ten Days Wonder*). Queen himself changed from a snobbish, intellectual dandy to a probing and vulnerable observer of human truths and foibles. He has been portrayed in the movies, radio and television by Lew Ayres, Ralph Bellamy, William Gargan and George Nader. As editor and anthologist, he is without peer. *Ellery Queen's Mystery Magazine* began in 1941 and to date has published the work of virtually every luminary in the field. After the deaths of Lee in 1971 and Dannay a decade later, the magazine continued in other hands. In 1941 Queen published the finest anthology of crime fiction extant, *101 Years' Entertainment: The Great Detective Stories of 1841–1941.*

Queen Mary British-flag OCEAN LINER, considered by many to have been the greatest passenger ship of the 20th century. In 1926 the board of directors of the Cunard Steamship Company ordered a new flagship. The *Queen Mary* was to be the largest, fastest and most glamorous passenger ship in the world. Work on the liner began on December 1, 1930, at the John Brown shipyard at Clydesbank, Scotland. After the project had been delayed for two years because of the GREAT DEPRESSION, the *Queen Mary* was christened and launched on September 26, 1934; further outfitting was required before the ship departed on her maiden voyage from Southampton, England, to New York on May 27, 1936. Her main rival on the transatlantic route was the elegant French liner *NORMANDIE*. Cunard launched a slightly larger sister ship, the *Queen Elizabeth,* in 1938. At the outbreak of WORLD WAR II, the *Queen Mary* was refitted as a troop ship. During the

The Queen Mary *arrives in New York City, 1945.* (LIBRARY OF CONGRESS, PRINTS AND PHOTOGRAPHS DIVISION)

war, she sailed 600,000 miles and carried nearly 900,000 Allied personnel. On one voyage she carried 15,000 soldiers—the largest number of passengers ever carried on any ship. British prime minister Winston CHURCHILL made three secret wartime transatlantic crossings on the *Queen* to attend Allied conferences in North America. Adolf HITLER ordered her sunk, but her top speed of more than 31 knots allowed her to elude enemy U-boats.

The *Queen* returned to transatlantic passenger service in 1947. Competition from passenger jetliners and rising operating costs forced Cunard to withdraw the *Queen Mary* from service in 1967. She was sold to the city of Long Beach, California, where she was permanently berthed and converted into a luxury hotel and museum. The *Queen Mary* weighs 81,237 tons, measures 1,019.5 feet long and had a cruising speed of 28.5 knots per hour. During her heyday, her passengers included many of the most prominent statesmen, authors, musicians, industrialists and film stars of the 20th century. On January 12, 2004, Cunard launched a newer, more modern transatlantic luxury liner, the *Queen Mary II*. With a length of 1,132 feet and a weight of approximately 151,400 gross tons, it has become the world's largest, longest, widest and tallest ocean linear.

Queen Maud Mountains Mountain range in ANTARCTICA south of the Ross Ice Shelf. Discovered in 1911 by Norwegian explorer Roald AMUNDSEN, the range boasts three of the world's great glaciers: Amundsen, Liv and Thorne.

Quemoy incident Quemoy, a Nationalist Chinese–held island six miles off the Red Chinese mainland, was a base for Nationalist raids against the communist mainland from 1953 to 1958. In August–September 1958 it was bombarded and threatened with invasion by the communists. A U.S. fleet moved in with supplies and a guarantee of military assistance.

queremistas (Port., *queremos Getúlio,* "we want Getúlio") Supporters of Getulio Vargas in the 1945 Brazilian presidential election. Vargas was dictator from 1937 to 1945 and from 1951 to 1954, when he committed suicide.

Quick, Armand J. *(1894–1978)* American pathologist. An authority on blood clotting, Quick was considered one of the 20th century's leading specialists on blood diseases. In 1932 he developed the prothrombin time test, also known as the Quick test, which was used to regulate the dosage of blood-thinning drugs and in diagnosing liver diseases.

Quisling, Vidkun *(1887–1945)* Norwegian politician, infamous as a traitor and Nazi collaborator during WORLD WAR II. Graduated from the Norwegian military academy with the highest honors ever awarded up to that time, he was a military attaché in Finland and Russia (1918–21), and later in the 1920s worked with Fridtjof NANSEN on famine relief in the UKRAINE. A fervent anticommunist, he served as NORWAY's minister of defense (1931–33); shortly thereafter, he founded the fascist National Unity (Nasjonal Samling) Party, which failed to win popular support. In the late 1930s he formed close ties with German Nazi leaders. He proclaimed himself prime minister after the German invasion of Norway (1940), and was officially recognized as such by the Germans in 1942. He formally allied Norway with Germany in 1943, but the Norwegian population remained firmly anti-Nazi. After the war he was tried for high treason by a Norwegian tribunal, found guilty and executed. The name "Quisling" has entered the 20th-century vocabulary as an eponym for "traitor."

quiz show scandal Television scandal that revealed in 1959 that many TV quiz shows were actually rigged. During the 1950s, quiz programs had emerged as one of the most popular types of television show. The *$64,000 Question* competed with *Twenty-One* as contestants attempted to turn their knowledge into an instant fortune. The industry's image was tarnished when revelations emerged that many of the big winners were provided with the answers in advance. Producers and sponsors manipulated the shows to boost their ratings and sales. Perhaps the best-known casualty of the scandal was Professor Charles Van Doren of Columbia University, who not only was publicly humiliated but also lost his university post when his complicity in the scheme was exposed. Adding to the air of corruption at the time was the "payola" scandal in which disc jockeys at a number of radio stations were bribed by record companies to promote certain recording artists.

Qumran Village in PALESTINE; on the northwestern shore of the Dead Sea. Qumran, in the WEST BANK region, was part of JORDAN until it was occupied by ISRAEL in 1967. The village was inhabited by a group of religious Jews, probably Essenes, from the second century B.C. until the Romans destroyed it in 68 A.D. In 1947 a shepherd discovered a group of ancient manuscripts in a nearby cave. Archaeologists subsequently uncovered more manuscripts of the same origin. These turned out to have been written by the sect and came to be known as the **Dead Sea Scrolls**—one of the major archaeological finds of the 20th century.

R

Rabbani, Burhanuddin *(1940–)*
Political leader of the United National and Islamic Front for the Salvation of Afghanistan (UNIFSA), also known as the Islamic Council of Mujahideen (ICM). Born in Badakhshan, Rabbani studied at the Kabul religious academy of Darul-uloom-e-Sharia and Kabul University, where he studied Islamic law and theology and joined the faculty in 1963. While in exile in Pakistan for his radical Islamic activities, Rabbani began to utilize his contacts among his former students and within the Jamiat-i-Islami to form a band of MUJAHIDEEN, or Islamic freedom fighters, who mounted an insurgency against the Soviet occupation of Afghanistan that began in 1979.

In 1992 three years after Soviet president Mikhail GORBACHEV had withdrawn Soviet military forces from Afghanistan, the insurgents defeated the remnants of the pro-Soviet government, and established a government in Kabul. Rabbani was elected president and began administering those portions of Afghanistan under government control. Four years later forces loyal to the Taliban, an alliance of Islamic clerics and Mujahideen espousing a form of ISLAMISM, took control of Kabul and forced Rabbani and his government to retreat into the mountainous northwestern regions of Afghanistan. Shortly after its expulsion from Kabul, Rabbani's movement became known as the NORTHERN ALLIANCE, and continued to resist the Taliban's efforts to establish control over all of Afghanistan. The UN continued to recognize Rabbani as the president of Afghanistan until Hamid KARZAI won election as the interim president of Afghanistan following the U.S. invasion of that country that toppled the TALIBAN regime in October 2001. Rabbani, who made a determined but failed bid to assume power after the fall of the Taliban, faded into obscurity.

Rabi, I(sidor) I(saac) *(1898–1988)*
American physicist. Born in Rymanow in the Austro-Hungarian Empire, Rabi immigrated to the U.S. with his family shortly after his birth. He grew up on New York City's Lower East Side and in Brooklyn. Rabi studied electrical engineering, chemistry and physics, receiving his B.S. in chemistry from Cornell University (1919) and his Ph.D. in physics from Columbia (1927). A postgraduate fellowship enabled him to work with Niels BOHR, Werner HEISENBERG, Wolfgang PAULI, Erwin SCHRÖDINGER and Otto Stern in Denmark and Germany in the late 1920s. Rabi was particularly interested in the new field of quantum mechanics, which explained many phenomena not explained by classical physics. He returned to Columbia in 1929 and was associated with the university for the remainder of his career. During World War II he played a major role in the development of RADAR. He received the 1944 NOBEL PRIZE for physics for his discovery and measurement of the radio-frequency spectrum of atomic nuclei whose magnetic spin had been disturbed. This work eventually led to the development of extremely precise atomic clocks and of nuclear magnetic resonance imaging for medical diagnosis. After the war Rabi became an advocate for nuclear arms control. From 1952 to 1956 he was chairman of the general advisory committee to the Atomic Energy Commission. He later headed President EISENHOWER's science advisory council, served on the U.S. delegation to UNESCO and worked for the establishment of an international physics laboratory, CERN, in Geneva.

Rabin, Yitzhak *(1922–1995)* Israeli politician, prime minister (1974–77). Born in Jerusalem, Rabin attended agricultural college (1936–40) before taking part in the Allied invasion of Syria in 1941. He was a member of the HAGANAH and an Israeli Defense Force (IDF) commander in the 1948 war. He was the head of the IDF's Tactical Operations Branch (1950–52) and, after graduating from the British Staff College, served successively as head of the IDF's training department (1954–56), head of the Northern Command (1956–59), deputy chief of staff (1960–64) and chief of staff (1964–68). The IDF's victory in the 1967 war brought him international acclaim, and he left to become ISRAEL's ambassador to Washington in 1968. Upon returning to Israel in 1973 he joined the Labor Party and served as its leader from 1974 to 1977; he was appointed prime minister after its 1974 election victory. He resigned in 1977 after being implicated in a minor infringement of foreign currency regulations, but remained active in politics and was appointed minister of defense by the

Labor-led government of national unity in 1984. He gained immediate popularity by his skillful withdrawal of the IDF from LEBANON, but was criticized by dovish Israelis for continuing his predecessor Ariel SHARON's strong-arm policy against WEST BANK Palestinians. In March 1986 Rabin publicly berated Prime Minister Shimon PERES for advocating unilateral West Bank autonomy. Condemning the proposal as "excessive talk about a concept which nobody can define," he provoked a major crisis within the Labor leadership, which exposed the long rivalry between the two men. Rabin became prime minister following the July 1992 victory of the Labor Party and helped draft the 1993 Oslo Accords with Yasir ARAFAT, which established the PALESTINIAN AUTHORITY (PA) as a quasi-political organization assigned to govern the increasing portions of the West Bank and Gaza Strip. Rabin and Arafat received the Nobel Peace Prize in 1994 for their efforts. On November 4, 1995, Rabin was assassinated by an Israeli student opposed to the accords.

Rachmaninoff, Sergei Vasilyevich
(1873–1943) Russian composer and pianist. From an aristocratic family, Rachmaninoff studied at the Moscow Conservatory (1885–92) and quickly established a career as a virtuoso pianist and composer. Touring Scandinavia during the 1917 RUSSIAN

Russian pianist and composer Sergei Rachmaninoff
(LIBRARY OF CONGRESS, PRINTS AND PHOTOGRAPHS DIVISION)

REVOLUTION, he never returned to his homeland but settled first in Switzerland and then in the United States, where he supported himself by extensive concertizing. One of the greatest pianists of the 20th century, Rachmaninoff also won popular acclaim for his romantic compositions, which are marked by sensuous tonality, rich melody and a melancholic mood. His work includes three symphonies, four piano concertos, the *Rhapsody on a Theme of Paganini* for piano and orchestra, and numerous works for solo piano as well as songs, operas and choral pieces. Rachmaninoff's music has been performed and recorded widely in the West and in Russia.

radar A system for locating a distant object by bouncing radio waves off its surface; the name is an acronym for "*radio detection and ranging.*" Developed independently in several countries during the 1930s, it was first put into practical operation by Sir Robert Watson-Watt. Radar sends electromagnetic wave pulses toward an object by means of a transmitter; the waves reflect off the target and the returning waves are picked up by a receiver, amplified and converted into images displayed on a cathode-ray tube. Usually used to detect aircraft, radar gives information on a target's position, distance, direction, movement and shape. Radar employing long waves was first used in England early in WORLD WAR II. However, these wide beams proved inaccurate and were soon replaced by the accuracy of narrow microwaves produced by a cavity magnetron, a generating device invented (1940) by Sir John T. Randal and Henry A. Boot. By 1940 the British coast bristled with radar installations whose antennae were directed toward enemy countries. Radar was an enormously important defensive and offensive tool for Allied land and naval forces in World War II and was also used by the Germans after 1942 to target antiaircraft guns. Systems were greatly improved and refined after the war. Today, radar continues to be used in many weapons systems and in defensive early warning installations, but is also widely employed in peacetime applications. It is routinely used by commercial airliners and traffic controllers, by weather forecasting systems, in surveying and navigating, and as a

guidance tool for rockets and satellites. Radar technology is also the basis for radio astronomy.

Radek, Karl Bernardovich (Karl Sobelsohn) *(1885–1940?)* Russian author and politician. Born in Poland of Jewish ancestry, he became a journalist and supported the German Social Democratic Party from 1904. He was imprisoned several times, fought in the RUSSIAN REVOLUTION (1917) and tried to organize a communist revolution in Germany (1918–19). He was a member of the presidium of the Communist International (1919–23), but his influence declined when the Comintern proved ineffective. He became head of the Sun Yat-sen Communist University for Chinese students in Moscow (1923–27) until he was expelled from the Communist Party (1927) on a charge of having supported TROTSKY, and was banished to the Urals. He was rehabilitated and wrote for *Izvestiya*. He also helped draft the 1936 constitution. In 1937 he was sentenced to 10 years' imprisonment for treason and is thought to have died in prison.

radio Radio is the transmission of electromagnetic waves from a source to a receiver. In 1901 MARCONI transmitted the letter "S" across the Atlantic; in 1904 John A. Fleming developed the vacuum electron tube; and in 1913 Edwin Armstrong patented the circuit that made long-range reception possible. By 1910 ship-to-shore radio communication was commonplace. The German army first used radio for entertainment during WORLD WAR I. The first commercial station in the U.S., KDKA, was established in Pittsburgh, Pennsylvania, in 1920. During the 1920s the number of radio stations, broadcasts and receivers increased dramatically. A new news and entertainment medium came into being. In 1932 radio transmissions were received from the Milky Way Galaxy. During WORLD WAR II radio technology was used in the development of RADAR. Radio changed every aspect of 20th-century life—industry, science, sports and entertainment.

Radio City Music Hall Theater forming a part of New York City's ROCKEFELLER CENTER complex of office buildings; regarded as one of the major masterpieces of the ART DECO style. The original architects were Reinhard & Hofmeister; Corbett, Harrison & MacMurray; and Hood & Fouilhoux, with the last team responsible for the overall original design of Rockefeller Center (1931–33). The Music Hall is discreetly imbedded within the RKO Building in such a way that it has no clear external identity, except for its corner entrance and marquee; but the interiors, designed with Donald DESKEY in charge of decoration, are a finely preserved showcase of 1930s design. The main auditorium is a vast space seating 6,250, with stage and orchestra pit elaborately equipped with elevators, turntables and other mechanical devices. The lobbies, grand stairway and many lounges and smoking rooms are distinguished examples of Art Deco idiom. The Music Hall has been a popular success and tourist attraction since its opening, as much for its design as for the films and stage shows offered there. The popular Rockettes chorus line has been a fixture at Rockefeller Center for many years.

Radio Station WHA Claimed as the world's oldest, the station was developed in the laboratories of the department of physics of the University of Wisconsin at Madison. When the station started a broadcasting service in 1915, clear broadcasting signals were received as far away as the Great Lakes Naval Station in northern Illinois. In 1922 WHA received a federal license to broadcast and is considered to be the world's oldest continuously operated radio station. When it first went on the air its tubes were hand-blown by local glassmakers and fitted for broadcast by local craftsmen. The station was the first educational radio station and broadcast the first music appreciation program to be sent across the airwaves.

Raft, George (1895–1980) American film actor. He was best known for his portrayal of cool, tough-guy characters in HOLLYWOOD gangster films of the 1930s and '40s. Between 1929 and 1967 he appeared in 105 movies, many of which were low-budget melodramas such as *Scarface, They Drive by Night, Each Dawn I Die* and *Souls at Sea.* In his heyday he was one of Hollywood's

highest-paid stars. However, he turned down the leading roles in *High Sierra, The Maltese Falcon* and *Casablanca*— roles that were subsequently played with great success by Humphrey BOGART, who soon eclipsed Raft as Hollywood's leading romantic tough guy. A frequenter of gambling casinos, Raft was rumored to be involved in organized crime; in 1965 he was convicted of tax evasion.

ragtime Popular American musical form originating in the 19th century; characterized by a syncopated melody set against a rhythmically foursquare bass. Its greatest vogue occurred between 1890 and 1914. Ragtime began in the Midwest, probably the result of improvisations by black pianists and banjo players playing in saloons and sporting houses. It was influenced by dance music, marching band music and ballads combined with African, Caribbean and American rhythms. Sedalia and St. Louis, Missouri, were two important early centers of ragtime. The ragtime written in these cities came to be known as the Missouri style, characterized by lyrical melodies and easy tempos. For years the form was transmitted aurally. The first published rag—"Mississippi Rag" by William H. Krell, a white bandmaster—appeared in 1897. The great popularity of ragtime was partly due to the fact that music in printed form and on piano rolls was widely available. For example, the "Maple Leaf Rag" by Scott JOPLIN, one of the most successful ragtime composers, sold over a million copies shortly after it was published in 1899. Besides Joplin, other composers in the Missouri style were New Jersey–born Joseph E. Lamb (1887–1960) and James Scott (1886–1938), who was based in Kansas City. As the popularity of the form spread, other ragtime styles emerged in other parts of the country. While ragtime was eclipsed by JAZZ about 1914, it enjoyed a revival in the late 1960s and 1970s with the rediscovery of the music of Scott Joplin and other ragtime composers.

Rahman, Sheikh Mujibur (1920–1975) Prime minister of BANGLADESH (1972–75). Leader of the Awami League, he campaigned for the independence of East Bengal from PAKISTAN. Arrested several times and

charged with treason in 1971, he was released upon Indian military intervention against Pakistan (see INDO-PAKISTANI WAR OF 1971). He returned to a hero's welcome on the establishment of the independent republic of Bangladesh at the end of 1971. As prime minister, the problems of creating a socialist state and parliamentary democracy in a desperately poor country proved too much, and Rahman assumed dictatorial powers in 1975. Later that year the army staged a coup, and he was murdered.

Rahman, Tunku Abdul (1903–1990) Malaysian statesman. The son of a sultan, he was educated at Cambridge and became a barrister (lawyer). He entered the Kedah state civil service in 1931 and was a cofounder of the nationalist United Malay National Organization in 1945. Named chief minister of Malaya in 1955, he was elected prime minister of an independent Malaya in 1957 and became prime minister of the newly created Federation of MALAYSIA in 1963. Fiercely anticommunist, he was adept at mediating among the various peoples of Malaysia to create a national consensus. Stresses on the system led to ethnic riots in 1969, and Rahman retired the following year. He later became a revered elder statesman and spoke out against the repressive regime of Prime Minister Mahathir bin Mohamad.

Rahner, Karl (1904–1984) German-born theologian. One of the most prominent Roman Catholic theologians of the 20th century, Rahner played a key role in the reforms of the SECOND VATICAN COUNCIL during the early 1960s. A member of the Jesuit order, he was regarded as progressive on most church issues. He developed a transcendental theological philosophy aimed at lessening the rigidity of the traditional Christian faith. Strongly influenced by the German existentialist philosopher Martin HEIDEGGER, Rahner published more than 4,000 works, including 30 books.

Raid on Entebbe See ENTEBBE, RAID ON.

Raid on Tokyo Bombing raid conducted by U.S. Army planes commanded by James DOOLITTLE on April

18, 1942. It was carried out by 16 B-25 Mitchell bombers launched from the aircraft carrier USS *Hornet*. Although the strike had to be carried on during daytime instead of at night, as originally planned, Doolittle and Admiral William HALSEY decided to go ahead. Thirteen bombers hit Tokyo and three others bombed Nagoya, Osaka and Kobe. Because of the distances involved, none of the planes could reach friendly airfields. One landed in the USSR and the others crash-landed or bailed out over China. In the process five U.S. airmen were killed and eight were captured by the Japanese. While the raid caused little serious physical damage to its targets, it was an enormous propaganda success in the U.S., boosting morale that had been depressed by the Japanese attack on PEARL HARBOR the previous December.

rain forests In the late 20th century, the fate of Earth's rain forests became a matter of grave concern. The human development of rain forest areas in economically depressed THIRD WORLD countries threatens one of Earth's largest, most important natural habitats. The South American rain forests alone may contain half of all living species. Using slash-and-burn methods, settlers are clearing huge areas of forest in a futile effort to make the land suitable for farming; in other areas, indiscriminate logging has taken its toll: In Brazil alone, some 4 million acres of forest vanishes every year. Consequently, thousands of species are being lost, while soil erosion threatens to create new desert. Massive forest fires spew carbon dioxide into the atmosphere, contributing to the GREENHOUSE EFFECT.

Rains, Claude (*1889–1967*) Anglo-American film actor, best known for his portrayals of suave villains. Born in London, Rains began as a child actor at age 11 and moved to the U.S. in 1914, where he was successful on the stage and later in radio. His first film success was as the title character in *The Invisible Man* (1933), adapted from the novel by H. G. WELLS. After his acclaimed portrayal of King John in *The Adventures of Robin Hood* (1938), Rains played a corrupt senator in Frank CAPRA's *Mr. Smith Goes to Washington* (1939) and a roguish Nazi collaborator in CASABLANCA (1942), earning two ACADEMY AWARD nominations. He was nominated twice more for his performances in *Mr. Skeffington* (1944) and in Alfred HITCHCOCK's *Notorious* (1946). He also starred in a remake of *The Phantom of the Opera* (1943) and played supporting roles in *Lawrence of Arabia* (1962) and *The Greatest Story Ever Told* (1965).

Rajk, Lázló (*1909–1949*) Hungarian communist leader. Born near Budapest, he became a communist as a university student and fought from 1936 to 1939 with the International Brigade in the SPANISH CIVIL WAR. Returning to HUNGARY in 1941, he became active in the Communist Party, then an illegal organization. During WORLD WAR II, he resisted German occupation as a member of the underground. After the war he became Hungary's minister of the interior (1946–48) and foreign minister (1948–49). In 1949 he was charged with conspiring with TITO to overthrow the Hungarian government. While the evidence presented was clearly fabricated, he confessed and was hanged. In 1956 the Hungarian government admitted that the conviction had been in error and "rehabilitated" Rajk as a political figure.

Rajneesh, Bhagwan Shree (Chandra Mohan Jain) (*1931–1990*) Indian guru. He began his career in India, where he took the name Bhagwan (god) and preached a combination of free love and Eastern mysticism. He emigrated to the U.S. in 1981 and set up a commune near the tiny town of Antelope, Oregon, outraging local residents. In 1985 he pleaded guilty to violating immigration laws by arranging sham marriages between U.S. followers and foreign disciples. He was deported in 1985 and returned to India in 1986.

Rákosi, Mátyás (*1892–1971*) Hungarian communist leader and prime minister of HUNGARY (1949–53, 1955–56). Active in the communist opposition between the two world wars, Rákosi was sentenced to life imprisonment in 1935. He was released in 1940 to go to Moscow, where he led a committee of Hungarian communists. From 1945 he led the party and the government, presiding over the establishment of a Stalinist regime (see STALINISM). Replaced by the more liberal NAGY in 1953, by 1955 Rákosi had regained control of the party. His repressive methods contributed to the unrest that led to the HUNGARIAN UPRISING OF 1956. In an attempt to appease the Hungarians the USSR persuaded him to resign.

Rakovsky, Khristian Georgyevich (*1873–1938*) Communist leader and diplomat, of Bulgarian origin. Because of his involvement with the socialist movement, Rakovsky was not able to enter Sofia University but studied abroad. In 1900 he was an officer in the Romanian army, but in 1907 he was expelled from Romania. After the communists came to power in Russia, Rakovsky was made a member of the All-Russian Central Executive Committee, and in 1919 of the Central Committee of the Communist Party. The chairman of the council of people's commissars of the Ukraine, he occupied several diplomatic posts, including Soviet ambassador to France (1926–27). He was, however, expelled from the Communist Party in 1927 as a result of his support of TROTSKY. He was readmitted in 1935 and was a departmental head of the People's Commissariat of Health. In 1937 he was dismissed, and in 1938, arrested. He was sentenced to 20 years' imprisonment, and it is believed that he died in a concentration camp.

Ram, Jaglivan (*1908–1986*) Indian politician. The acknowledged leader of INDIA's more than 100 million untouchables, he was born to an untouchable family in Bihar. In 1931 he joined the Congress Party, which under the leadership of Mohandas GANDHI and Jawaharlal NEHRU was the main force behind India's drive to independence. He was a member of nearly every Indian cabinet from that time. He served in the first government as minister of labor and went on to serve twice as minister of agriculture and also as railway minister. From 1970 to 1974 and from 1977 to 1979, he was minister of defense.

Rama IX (Bhumibol Adulyadej) (*1927– *) King Rama IX of the Chikri dynasty is THAILAND's longest-reigning monarch. Crowned May 5, 1950, he spent much of his young life in Switzerland, where he was educated at the École Miremont in Lausanne and the École Nouvelle de la Suisse Romande. He succeeded his elder brother, Ananda Mahidol, on June 9, 1946, after Ananda was found dead in the palace from a gunshot wound. Whether the death was an accident, suicide or murder has never been determined. The king is highly respected not only because of his title but also because of his unending defense of and assistance to Thailand's rural poor. On June 9, 1996, King Rama IX celebrated his golden jubilee as Thai monarch. He is the first Thai king to achieve a reign of this length.

Rambert, Marie (Cyvia Rambam) (*1888–1982*) Ballet dancer, teacher, producer. Born in Poland, Rambert began dancing in Paris. After a season with Serge DIAGHILEV's BALLETS RUSSES, she moved to London where she taught dance and encouraged works by new choreographers. In 1926 she produced Frederick ASHTON's first ballet *A Tragedy of Fashion*. She founded Ballet Rambert in the mid-1930s and spent 30 years producing works by new choreographers and guiding the careers of young dancers. She was knighted in 1962 for her contribution to the development of British ballet.

Ramgoolam, Sir Seewoosagur (*1900–1985*) Mauritian diplomat. Ramgoolam was a physician who became the first prime minister of MAURITIUS after that small Indian Ocean island gained independence from Britain in 1968. He led a succession of coalition governments until his administration was swept out of office in the general election of 1982. He held the largely ceremonial office of governor general until his death.

Ramos, Fidel (*1928– *) Philippine general and secretary of defense; perhaps the most loyal supporter of President AQUINO. Ramos graduated from the U.S. Military Academy at West Point in 1950; he earned a master's degree in civil engineering from the University of Illinois in 1951 and also possesses other military degrees. Ramos ascended through army ranks to become chief of the Philippine constabulary in 1972. He became vice chief of staff of the army in 1981 and chief of staff in 1986. He loyally supported

Aquino against attempted coups and was widely considered an honest and disciplined military man, though not without presidential ambitions. He was appointed secretary of defense in January 1988 after the resignation of Rafael Ileto. In 1990, after Aquino declared that she would not seek reelection, Ramos announced that he would run for the presidency. Ramos won the 1992 presidential election and remained in office until 1998, when he was succeeded by Joseph ESTRADA.

Ramos-Horta, José (*1949– *) East Timorese activist and winner of the Nobel Peace Prize (1996). Born to a Timorese mother and Portuguese father, Horta grew up in Dili, the capital of EAST TIMOR, which was then a Portuguese colony. He was educated in the Catholic mission located in the nearby village of Soibada.

In 1974 he became minister for external affairs and information in the transition government of the future Democratic Republic of East Timor that was assembled by Portugal before its withdrawal from the country in 1975. After the Indonesian invasion of East Timor in December 1975, Horta continued to champion the cause of East Timor's independence and publicized Indonesian abuses of human rights in his country. Horta later served as a mediator between the Indonesian government and the Revolutionary Front for an Independent East Timor (FRETILIN), the indigenous liberation movement within East Timor that he represented before the UN between 1976 and 1989.

In 1992 Horta presented the EUROPEAN UNION (EU) with a multistage plan for East Timorese independence and later urged the British and American governments to suspend military aid to Indonesia. In 1996 Horta and Carlos Felipe Ximenes BELO, a Roman Catholic bishop who championed the East Timor independence movement within the occupied territory, were awarded the Nobel Peace Prize. International pressure obliged the Indonesian government to hold a referendum within East Timor to allow its residents to determine their political future. In September 1999 the UN-supervised referendum resulted in a 78.5 percent vote in favor of independence.

Rampal, Jean-Pierre (*1922–2000*) French flutist. Born in Marseilles, Rampal first studied flute with his father, a professor at the Marseilles Conservatory of Music. He then studied at the Paris Conservatory and in 1945 joined the Paris Opera Orchestra where he was first flutist from 1958 to 1964. In the late 1940s Rampal also began to tour and to make recordings. His records won numerous Grand Prix du Disque awards. He first toured the U.S. in 1958 and returned regularly. He enlarged the flute repertoire by resurrecting forgotten music of the baroque era and also by adapting for flute compositions originally written for other instruments. In the 1990s, he continued to be enormously popular, giving over 150 concerts per year and filling concert halls the world over.

Ramsey, Sir Alfred (*1920–1999*) English soccer player and manager. Ramsey is best known as the mastermind of England's World Cup triumph in 1966. Although his greatest success came as a manager, Ramsey also enjoyed a successful playing career. He was a "polished" right back for Southampton and Tottenham Hotspur, and played 32 times for England. On his retirement, Ramsey joined Ipswich Town as manager and led the team from the obscurity of the second division to the first division championship in 1961–62. Following his success at Ipswich, Ramsey was appointed manager of England. Ramsey's innovative tactics and leadership qualities were well suited to international soccer. He introduced the 4-4-2 formation to English football, and his "wingless wonders" won the World Cup in 1966, defeating West Germany 4-2 in the final. He led England in its unsuccessful defense of the World Cup in 1970 and was dismissed as manager following England's failure to qualify for the 1974 World Cup finals. Ramsey was knighted for his services to soccer.

Ramsey, Arthur Michael (*1904–1988*) British religious leader. Ramsey held the post of archbishop of Canterbury (spiritual head of the Church of England and leader of the worldwide Anglican communion) from 1961 to 1974. A progressive social activist, Ramsey called on Great Britain to do away with nuclear weapons, spoke out against the VIETNAM WAR and opposed curbs on minority immigration into Britain. He also supported abolition of the death penalty and of criminal penalties against homosexuals. In 1966, he met with Pope PAUL VI in Rome in what was the first official visit to a pope by a head of the Anglican Church in 400 years. Upon his retirement in 1974, he was made a life peer and took the title of Lord Ramsey of Canterbury.

Ramu (known as the "Wolf Boy") *(c. 1960s–1985)* In 1976 a wild boy was discovered in the jungle in India, walking on all fours and in the company of three wolves. After examining him, Indian zoologists concluded that he had been raised by wolves. He was placed in a home for paupers run by Mother TERESA, winner of the 1979 NOBEL PRIZE for peace. He learned to bathe and dress himself but never learned to speak. The case gained worldwide attention.

Ranariddh, Prince Norodom *(1944–)* Leader of Cambodian royalist party, FUNCINPEC, and son of Cambodian king NORODOM SIHANOUK. Born in Phnom Penh, Ranariddh first entered politics when he became the representative of his father in Bangkok, Thailand, in 1983, where he sought to restore the royal family to the Cambodian throne after its ouster in a 1970 coup by General Lon Nol. Lon Nol's government was later ousted by the KHMER ROUGE in 1975. In 1991 following the withdrawal of Vietnamese forces from Cambodia and the promise of open and free elections by HUN SEN, the leader of the ruling Cambodian People's Party (CPP), Ranariddh returned to Cambodia to replace his father as the chairman of FUNCINPEC in order to coordinate the party's efforts at winning the elections. In 1993 Ranariddh helped guide FUNCINPEC to victory over the CPP in the Cambodian general elections, which led to the formation of a coalition government between FUNCINPEC and the CPP in which Ranariddh and Hun Sen jointly served as prime minister.

By 1997 relations between Ranariddh's FUNCINPEC and Hun Sen's CPP had deteriorated, and Ranariddh approached several former leaders of the Khmer Rouge, the communist organization that had once ruled Cambodia, in order to obtain their participation in a new coalition government. Hun Sen responded by staging a coup in July 1997 that ousted Ranariddh and sent him into exile. At the end of 1997, Ranariddh returned to Cambodia and resumed his leadership position in the royalist party. In the national elections of July 1998, the CPP won a plurality of votes, but was again forced to join in a coalition government with FUNCINPEC. Although Hun Sen controlled the prime minister's office in this arrangement, Ranariddh's party held several ministerial positions, and Ranariddh himself became the head of the National Assembly.

Rand, Ayn *(1905–1982)* American novelist. Rand was born in Russia and became an American citizen in 1931. Her loathing of the Soviet revolution led her to develop a philosophy of almost rabid capitalism. Her best-selling novels have been greeted with derision on the one hand and various cult followings on the other. Her first major novel was *The Fountainhead* 1943; filmed 1949), which portrayed an iconoclastic architect fighting conventional attitudes. Her best-known novel, *Atlas Shrugged* (1957), presents the archetypical Rand hero, John Galt, an individualist fighting against "nonproductive people" and struggling toward his own ends. *The Virtue of Selfishness: A New Concept of Egoism* (1964) awarded her the status of a leader of the popular intellectual movement "objectivism," and she was in much demand as a lecturer. Other works include *We the Living* (1936) and *The Ayn Rand Lexicon: Objectivism from A to Z* (1984), a posthumous collection of earlier works. She also wrote plays and film scripts.

Randolph, A(sa) Philip *(1889–1979)* American labor leader and CIVIL RIGHTS activist. The son of a Methodist preacher, Randolph moved to New York to study at City College. There he was strongly impressed by the socialist ideas of Eugene V. DEBS. Randolph organized and published the black radical journal *The Messenger;* through this influential vehicle he promoted black causes, including the affiliation of black workers with labor unions. In

American labor and Civil Rights activist A. Philip Randolph (LIBRARY OF CONGRESS, PRINTS AND PHOTOGRAPHS DIVISION)

1925 he created and administered the Brotherhood of Sleeping Car Porters, which became affiliated with the AMERICAN FEDERATION OF LABOR (AFL) in 1936, and he was president of the National Negro Congress in the 1930s. In 1941 he threatened to lead a march on Washington, D.C., to protest the exclusion of blacks from industrial war work, which led to President Franklin D. ROOSEVELT's creation of the Commission on Fair Employment Practices. He was director of the 1963 MARCH ON WASHINGTON that led to increased jobs and civil rights for blacks.

Ranger A precursor to the APOLLO program, which was designed to land men on the moon, the Ranger series of unmanned spacecraft was initiated to relay from the moon's surface information needed for a manned landing. From August 1961 to March 1965, a series of Ranger spacecraft, managed by the JET PROPULSION LABORATORY in Pasadena, California, were launched. *Ranger 7,* one of the most successful, sent back more than 4,000 close-up images of the moon. Unfortunately, of the nine missions launched, only the last three were successful, and the program was replaced by the Lunar Orbiter series in August 1966.

Rank, Otto (Otto Rosenfeld) (*1884–1939*) Austrian psychologist. Rank was born in Vienna and earned a doctorate in philology from the University of Vienna in 1912. He began to study psychoanalysis under Sigmund FREUD in 1905 and went on to serve as Freud's personal secretary. From 1912 to 1924 Rank edited two different psychoanalytic journals and became one of the leading factors behind the growth in influence of psychoanalysis. Rank was the director of the International Psychoanalytic Institute of Vienna from 1919 to 1924. A Jew, he left Austria to escape the Nazis and spent the final years of his life in Paris and New York. His major writings include *Art and Artist* (1907), *The Myth of the Birth of the Hero* (1909) and *The Trauma of Birth* (1924), which Freud regarded as heretical to his own theories due to its emphasis on the birth experience itself as a factor in the creation of neurosis.

Rankin, Jeannette (*1880–1973*) U.S. congresswoman. Rankin initially worked as a seamstress, gaining knowledge of social conditions. After working for woman suffrage on the West Coast in 1910, she led a similar successful campaign in Montana in 1914. In 1916 Rankin became the first woman ever elected to the U.S. House of Representatives. She opposed U.S. entry into WORLD WAR I and WORLD WAR II. She declined to run for reelection in 1942, but continued a private career as an ardent feminist (see FEMINISM). In the 1960s she founded a cooperative homestead for women in Georgia and protested against the VIETNAM WAR.

Ransom, John Crowe (*1888–1974*) American poet and critic. A teacher at Vanderbilt for 23 years, Ransom was the editor and the eldest of the southern poets who contributed to *The Fugitive* from 1922 to 1925. Ransom was a former professor of the group's other leaders, Allen TATE and Robert Penn WARREN. Ransom originated the phrase NEW CRITICISM, a type of literary study closely associated with this group, and encouraged the polemic *I'll Take My Stand* (1930), a statement of agrarian ideals central to the thought of the new southern writers. Later he went to Kenyon College as professor of poetry.

In 1939 he was founder and editor of the *Kenyon Review*. Ransom is best remembered for the poems "Bells for John Whiteside's Daughter" and "Here Lies a Lady."

Rapacki Plan Polish foreign minister Rapacki proposed on February 14, 1958, a ban on the manufacture and deployment of nuclear weapons in Czechoslovakia, Poland and East and West Germany, to be guaranteed by joint NATO-WARSAW PACT inspection. A renewal of the suggestion at the UN on October 2, 1958, met with U.S. and British rejection, as the USSR would retain its conventional weapons superiority.

Rapallo Italian town on the Ligurian Sea, near Genoa. In the **Treaty of Rapallo** (November 12, 1920), Italy and Yugoslavia agreed to establish RIJEKA (Fiume) as a free state, although a protofascist expedition led by Italian poet, adventurer and aviator Gabriele D'ANNUNZIO had seized the city in 1919. In another treaty (between Germany and the USSR, April 16, 1922) Germany became the first government to recognize the Soviet government. This treaty renounced all claims stemming from the war, canceled prewar debts and formalized trade arrangements between the two nations. Among its secret provisions, the treaty allowed Germany to develop (in the USSR) weapons that it was forbidden to have by the Treaty of VERSAILLES.

rap music See HIP-HOP.

Rashid bin Said al Maktum, Sheik (*1914–1990*) Arab diplomat. In 1971, he cofounded the United Arab Emirates, a collection of seven sheikdoms in the PERSIAN GULF. He served as vice president of the UAE, while his brother-in-law Sheik Zayid bin Sultan Al Nuhayyan, ruler of Abu Dhabi, served as president. Previously, the sheikdoms had been ruled separately as the Trucial States under an agreement with Great Britain.

Rasputin, Grigory Yefimovich (*1872–1916*) Siberian peasant who exerted a pernicious influence at the court of Czar NICHOLAS II and on political affairs in RUSSIA in the years leading up to the RUSSIAN REVOLUTION.

Although without education, Rasputin allegedly possessed hypnotic powers, which he did not hesitate to exploit, and claimed to be able to work miracles, preaching that physical contact with him had a healing effect. As a youth Rasputin had been influenced by the Khlysty (Flagellants) sect. In 1903 Rasputin arrived in St. Petersburg as a *starets* (holy man) and as such gained access to the highest circles of society. He exercised virtually unlimited influence on Czarina ALEXANDRA by using hypnotism to stop the hemophiliac czarevich's bleeding. She viewed him as a divine missionary, sent to save the dynasty. The church denounced him as an impostor, and in 1912 he was sent back to Siberia. In 1914 he returned, and by 1915, when the czarina was left in charge of domestic affairs, Rasputin's influence was vast, and many of the more capable ministers were dismissed. He continued his dissolute habits until his assassination by Prince Yusupov in 1916.

Rathbone, Basil (*1892–1967*) Anglo-American actor. Rathbone, who is perhaps best remembered in the U.S. for his portrayals of SHERLOCK HOLMES beginning with *The Hound of the Baskervilles* (1939), was born in South Africa and educated in England. He began his career as a Shakespearean stage actor; his first film in England was *The Fruitful Vine* (1923). Soon thereafter he went to HOLLYWOOD, where he made *Pity the Chorus Girl?* (1924) and other silent films while continuing to act on stage. With the advent of sound, Rathbone, with his cultivated accent, came into his own appearing opposite Norma Shearer in *The Last of Mrs. Cheyney* (1929) and as detective Philo Vance in *The Bishop Murder Case* (1930). Following his role in *David Copperfield* (1935) he settled in Hollywood playing a series of cerebral villains as well as making 14 Sherlock Holmes films. In the 1960s he took on a few unfortunate roles trading on his villainous image, the last of which was *Hillbillys in a Haunted House* (1967). Other important films include *Anna Karenina* (1935), *The Dawn Patrol* (1938) and John FORD's *The Last Hurrah* (1958).

Rathenau, Walter (*1867–1922*) German industrialist, statesman and social theorist. Born in Berlin, the son of Emil

Rathenau (1838–1915), he succeeded his father as president of a vast electrical trust. He organized GERMANY's war economy during WORLD WAR I and, after the war, served as minister of reconstruction (1921) and foreign minister (1922). In the latter office, he worked for reconciliation with the Allies, attempted to comply with reparation obligations and signed the Treaty of RAPALLO with the USSR. An advocate of a moderate decentralized social democracy and a Jew, he was despised by anti-Semitic nationalists. Several of these fanatics assassinated him in Berlin on June 24, 1922. His books include *In Days to Come* and *The New Society* (both 1921).

Rattigan, Sir Terence Mervyn *(1911–1977)* British playwright. Rattigan's early plays, beginning with *French Without Tears* (1936), were popular comedies. With *Winslow Boy* (1946), the story of a father defending his son against an accusation of theft, he established himself as an author of serious drama, a reputation he was to maintain in his subsequent works, such as *The Browning Version;* (1948); *Ross* (1960), which was based on the life of T. E. LAWRENCE; and *Cause Celebre* (1977), which focused on an actual murder trial. In the preface to *Collected Works* (1953), Rattigan introduced "Aunt Edna," an archetypical, middle-brow theatergoer. Many critics—particularly those enamored of "the kitchen sink" dramatists—complained that Rattigan's work was middle brow as well. His popularity was undiminished, and his works continue to be revived.

Ratushinskaya, Irina *(1954–)* Russian poet and dissident; perhaps the last in a long line of distinguished poets who were persecuted under Soviet COMMUNISM during the 20th century. She studied physics at the University of Odessa, where she also began writing poetry and first encountered difficulties with the authorities. After graduation she taught physics and mathematics. In 1980 she and her husband, also a physicist, were denied emigration visas. Arrested for "anti-social" activities in 1982, she was sentenced to seven years of hard labor in the GULAG, to be followed by five years of internal exile. In prison she secretly wrote numerous poems that were circulated in Samizdat. In 1986 PEN organized an international campaign for her release. The Soviet authorities released her on October 9, 1986 (the eve of the Reykjavik Summit), as a goodwill gesture. She and her husband immigrated to Britain, where she continued to write and also lectured about her experiences. Her books include *No, I'm Not Afraid* (1986), *Beyond the Limit* (1987), *Grey Is the Color of Hope* (1988) and *Pencil Letter* (1989).

Rau, Lady Dhanvanthi Rama *(1893–1987)* Indian feminist. A leading advocate of birth control, she was named president of the International Planned Parenthood Federation in 1963. She continued to serve as president emeritus after she resigned the post in 1971. She was the mother of author Santha Rama Rau.

Rauff, Walter Herman Julius *(1907–1984)* Nazi war criminal. An SS colonel, Rauff was accused of supervising the killing of thousands of eastern European JEWS in mobile gas chambers during WORLD WAR II. He was said to have personally designed and directed the "Black Raven" vans in which victims were locked and asphyxiated with exhaust fumes. Possibly 250,000 people died in the vans, which were used before HITLER's death camps were completed (see CONCENTRATION CAMPS, HOLOCAUST). Rauff escaped from a British POW camp in 1946 and settled in Chile in 1958. The Chilean government refused numerous requests to extradite him to stand trial.

Rauschenberg, Robert *(1925–)* American painter. Born in Port Arthur, Texas, he studied at the Kansas City Art Institute, the Académie Julian in Paris, Black Mountain College with Josef ALBERS and New York's Art Students League. He had an important role in various artistic and cultural movements of the mid-century U.S., including HAPPENINGS, POP ART, environmental art and the experimental theater. His most celebrated paintings of the 1950s are his COLLAGE "combines," works that mix a painterly abstraction with everyday objects such as clocks, tires and even stuffed animals. Among the best-known of these are *Gloria* (1956, Cleveland Museum of Art) and *Monogram* (1959, Moderna Museet, Stockholm). His work of the 1960s, such as *Kite* (1963), combines silkscreened images of the popular culture with painted elements, often on large scale. Interested in many facets of the arts and in contemporary technological developments, Rauchenberg has served as a designer for the dancer/choreographer Merce CUNNINGHAM and in 1966 was a cofounder of Experiments in Art and Technology (EAT).

Ravel, Maurice *(1875–1937)* Important French composer who was second only to Claude DEBUSSY in his position as chief architect of modern French music. His *Boléro* (1928) and *Pavane pour une énfante defunte* (*Pavane for a Dead Princess,* 1899) are among the most popular of all modern compositions. He was born in Cibourne in the Basque region of France. At the Paris Conservatory, while less conspicuously radical than his immediate predecessor, Debussy, he nonetheless startled his teachers with his experiments in bold harmonic explorations; and he gained added notoriety through his association with the progressive musical group Apache (which included as members Igor STRAVINSKY and Manuel de FALLA). The range of his compositions was extraordinary. His ballet *Daphnis et Chloé* (1912), arguably his greatest work, was a highlight in the series of BALLETS RUSSES performances from the DIAGHILEV-FOKINE-NIJINSKY triumvirate. The piano works *Jeux d'Eau* (1902) and *Miroirs* (Mirrors, 1905) probably influenced the impressionist cast of Debussy's later piano music. The *Tzigane* (1924) and the *G major Piano Concerto* (1932) outrageously satirize, respectively, gypsy music and American JAZZ; while the weird *La Valse* (1920) virtually destroyed traditional waltz styles. Like Debussy, Ravel revolted against the Wagner hegemony; however, unlike Debussy, Ravel rarely employed the whole-tone scale and hardly ever abandoned tonality. Ravel was the most meticulous of craftsmen and retained a fastidious respect for classical form all his life. As a result, according to critic Virgil THOMSON, "his work presents fewer difficulties of comprehension than that of any other great figure in the modern movement." He was the master of twilight enchantment—the needlepoint sorcery of the *F major Quartet* and the *Ma Mère l'Oye* (1910)—and fantastic humor—the ragtime dialogue between a black Wedgwood teapot and a Chinese cup in *L'Enfant et les Sortileges* (*The Dream of a Naughty Child,* 1925). He died of a brain tumor in 1937, several years after a debilitating automobile accident.

Ravera, Camilla (*1889–1988*) Italian politician; postwar Italy's first woman senator-for-life and one of the founding members of the nation's COMMUNIST PARTY in 1921. A major figure in Italy's WOMEN'S LIBERATION MOVEMENT, Ravera spent five years in prison and eight years in internal exile during the fascist era.

Rawlings, Jerry (*1947– *) Leader of GHANA (June–September 1979 and 1981–2000). In May 1979 Rawlings, then a flight lieutenant in the Ghanaian air force, was arrested for having led an unsuccessful mutiny against his superior officers. However, his popularity with other military officers prompted a large contingent of troops to march on the prison in which Rawlings was held, liberating him. Rawlings orchestrated a coup d'état against the Ghanaian government. After seizing power, Rawlings and his fellow officers formed the Armed Forces Revolutionary Council (AFRC) in June 1979, which declared martial law and ruled Ghana until it could hold national elections toward the end of the month. In September 1979, Rawlings disbanded the AFRC and handed power over to the newly elected president of Ghana, Hilla Limann.

Rawlings later founded the People's National Defense Council (PNDC), a leftist opposition organization. On December 31, 1981, Rawlings staged a successful coup d'état that overthrew Limann and became Ghana's new president. In his efforts to improve the economic and social structure of Ghana, Rawlings sought aid first from the Soviet Union, and later from the INTERNATIONAL MONETARY FUND (IMF), the WORLD BANK, and private investment banks. Despite numerous allegations of human rights abuses by Rawlings, foreign financial institutions invested over $5 billion in Ghana while many of the leftist militants in the PNDC accused Rawlings of deserting his revolutionary ideals.

In 1992 Rawlings handily won election to the presidency, amid allegations of fraud and intimidation. His policies improved economic conditions in Ghana, as foreign investment continued to enter the country, although opponents of Rawlings's policies complained that the influx of foreign capital produced a condition of neoimperialism between Ghana and the foreign sources of its investment capital. Although Rawlings won reelection to the presidency in 1996, he was defeated in 2000 by the NPP presidential candidate, John Agyekum Kufor, and retired from politics.

Rawlings, Marjorie Kinnan (*1896–1953*) American author. A graduate of the University of Wisconsin (1918), Rawlings's early work was as a journalist. All her novels had a southern background, particularly in the backwoods of Florida, except for her final novel, *The Sojourner* (1953), which had a northern setting. In 1938 she wrote *The Yearling,* which won the PULITZER PRIZE in 1939 and has become an American classic. Her other works include *South Moon Under* (1933), *Golden Apples* (1935) and *Cross Creek* (1942).

Ray, Man (*1890–1976*) American painter and photographer. Ray is best known as the only American artist to make a substantial contribution to SURREALISM and to be welcomed into its European circles. Born in Philadelphia, he was raised in New York City and worked there for a time as an advertising illustrator, becoming familiar with graphic art processes. In 1914 he became involved with a circle of American painters including Joseph Stella. In 1915 came a decisive meeting between Ray and Marcel DUCHAMP, who introduced Ray to the aesthetics of DADA. Ray emigrated to Paris in 1921, where he won renown both as a painter and as the inventor of the "Rayogram"—a photographic technique in which objects or persons are positioned so as to cast evocative shadows on light-sensitive paper. For this mechanistic innovation, Ray was dubbed the "machine-poet" by his fellow surrealists. One of his most famous paintings is *L'Etoile de Mer* (1928). *Self-Portrait* (1963) is his autobiography. *Man Ray: Photographs* (1982) is a major collection of his work in that medium.

Rayburn, Samuel Taliaferro (*1882–1961*) American politician. Raised on a Texas farm, Rayburn taught school and became a lawyer in Bonham. Developing an interest in politics, he started his career as a state legislator (1907–12) and became speaker of the Texas house of representatives in 1911. He set a record for tenure when he was elected as a Democrat to the U.S. House of Representatives for 24 consecutive terms (1913–61). Appointed chairman of the Commission on Interest and Foreign Commerce in 1931, he helped design President Franklin ROOSEVELT's NEW DEAL program and coauthored six important laws to support it. Rayburn was Speaker of the House from 1940 to 1947, 1949 to 1953 and 1955 to 1961. He became one of the strongest Speakers in U.S. history. Highly regarded for his integrity and lack of pretension, he was extremely successful in dominating, indirectly, the legislative process and committee assignments through personal relationships with powerful committee chairmen. He was President Harry S. TRUMAN's chief supporter in Congress and one of his closest advisers. Except for civil rights measures, he backed much of Truman's domestic program and eventually supported his foreign policy as well. During the 1950s he worked with the EISENHOWER administration to defeat Republican isolationist measures. Although a supporter of Lyndon JOHNSON for president in 1960, he worked with the KENNEDY administration on much of its initial legislation.

U.S. Representative Sam Rayburn (LIBRARY OF CONGRESS, PRINTS AND PHOTOGRAPHS DIVISION)

RCA Corporation American communications corporation established in 1919. RCA was incorporated in Delaware and later moved to 30 Rockefeller Plaza in New York City. A month after incorporating, it acquired the Marconi Wireless Telegraph Company, a British-dominated company that owned most of the commercial radio communication facilities in the U.S. RCA entered the field of broadcasting in 1926 when it bought WEAF, now WNBC (New York), from AT&T. NBC was incorporated that year, with RCA owning 30% of the stock; Westinghouse Electric Corporation, 20%; and General Electric, 50%. RCA would later own NBC entirely. RCA grew into a giant multinational corporation whose operations extended far beyond broadcasting and included the production of SATELLITES and SEMICONDUCTORS. In 1986, RCA and its subsidiary NBC were acquired by General Electric (GE) for $6.4 billion.

Read, Sir Herbert Edward (1893–1968) British poet and critic. Born in Leeds, Read served in France during WORLD WAR I, the formative event of his life. He was later a professor of fine art. His early poetry collections, such as *Songs of Chaos* (1915) and *Naked Warriors* (1919), showed a strong imagist influence (see IMAGISM). Later poetry, including that in *The End of the War* (1933) and *Collected Poems* (1966), is more esoteric and deemed inaccessible by some. A friend of T. S. ELIOT, Read was an influential figure in the British critical and literary establishment from the 1930s until his death. His critical works include *The True Voice in Feeling* (1953) and *Essays in Literary Criticism* (1969). He also wrote on the arts, notably in *Arts and Industry* (1934) and *Education through Art* (1943), and frequently championed new artistic movements. He recollected the war in such works as *In Retreat* (1925) and his life in the autobiography *The Contrary Experience* (1963). His son, Piers Paul Read (b. 1941), is a novelist.

Reader's Digest American periodical. *Reader's Digest* was conceived by De Witt Wallace, whose marriage to heiress Lila Bell Acheson brought him the backing to begin publishing the magazine in 1922. Its original intent was to present edited versions of articles from other magazines to save readers' time, but as its popularity grew, Wallace adopted the odd practice of paying other magazines to accept stories that he would then edit for use in the *Digest*. It eventually included original material as well. Aimed at the American middle class, the magazine has been criticized for its unintellectual, platitudinous style and subject matter, but by the mid-1950s it had the highest circulation of any magazine in the world. The Reader's Digest, Incorporated empire came to include record clubs, condensed-book clubs and many other assets in addition to the magazine.

Reagan, Ronald Wilson (1911–2004) American actor, politician and 40th president of the U.S. (1981–89). His family moved to Dixon, Illinois, while Ronald was a boy. Following participation in football at Eureka College, he graduated from the Illinois school in 1932. His very successful career as a sportscaster at radio station WHO in Des Moines, Iowa, coupled with his handsome good looks, attracted the attention of HOLLYWOOD, where he had a successful career as a second-rank leading man. His most-remembered movie was *Knute Rockne—All American* (1940). He served in WORLD WAR II as an air force captain.

Ronald Reagan. 40th president of the United States
(LIBRARY OF CONGRESS, PRINTS AND PHOTOGRAPHS DIVISION)

He began a successful administrative career in 1947 as president of the Screen Actors Guild, serving until 1952 and again in 1959. He kept his name before the public in occasional screen roles and on television programs and was a widely heard radio commentator. Changing from a liberal Democrat to a moderate Republican in 1962, he took an interest in politics, beginning with the unsuccessful campaign of Barry GOLDWATER for president in 1964 (the same year in which Reagan made his last screen appearance, in Don SIEGEL's *The Killers*). Two years later, after a meteoric rise in politics, Ronald Reagan was elected governor of CALIFORNIA. Soon to become the most populous state in the union, California provided an important opportunity for an aspiring politician. Reagan was reelected in 1970. His successes in meeting California's budget, reducing the bureaucracy, eliminating the state deficit and reducing social services, were the most noted aspects of his administrations.

Retiring as governor in 1974, he began to put his extraordinary administrative and public relations experience to work in a run for the presidency. He made a strong bid in 1976, but lost the Republican nomination to Gerald FORD. Nominated in 1980, Reagan won a landslide victory over Jimmy CARTER, opposing all the Carter liberal policies and accusing him of gross ineptitude.

Minutes after Reagan was inaugurated, on January 20, 1981, the 52 Americans who had been held hostage in Iran for 444 days were flown to freedom, following an agreement to return a portion of Iran's frozen assets. On March 30, the president was shot in the chest by John Hinckley, Jr., as he walked to his car after an address at the Washington Hilton. On August 5, in one of his boldest strokes, he fired striking air traffic controllers, who had defied his back-to-work order. His dispatch of a task force to lead the invasion of Grenada in 1983 greatly increased his general popularity.

On the domestic front, his administration was dominated by so-called "Reaganomics." This economic program called for substantial tax cuts and reduced spending for domestic programs. With the help of a bipartisan coalition in Congress, he succeeded in programs to cut the budget and reform Social Security. His economic policies and their successes were credited by many economists with reducing inflation, and Reagan remained a firm believer in his economic theories. He also was ever-vigilant in his program to build up the armed forces, which he felt had been dangerously weakened during the Carter administration.

In 1984 Reagan and Vice President George Bush were nominated by the Republicans and won a landslide victory over Walter Mondale. At age 73 Reagan became the oldest person ever to hold the office of president. Surgery in 1985 and 1987 was followed by swift recovery, remarkable for a man of his age.

During most of his first term, Reagan had referred to the Soviet Union as an "evil empire." He was a firm advocate of U.S. support for arming Europe in defense of that empire. However, during his second term, he apparently concluded that his military program had brought the Russian leaders to a change of heart, and the administration began arms control discussions. Reagan's summit meeting with Soviet leader Gorbachev in November 1985 failed to reach general agreement, but the Reagan-Gorbachev meeting in early 1988 resulted in a draft treaty to reduce nuclear arms in Europe. Later that year in Moscow, the two leaders signed the treaty, which was ratified by the appropriate legislatures in each country.

During the early part of his second term, the president received some of the highest popularity ratings in the history of the office—spurred on by low unemployment, a strong economy and low interest rates. He continued to be strong in support of the Central American countries, providing help to El Salvador against the insurgents there and successfully promoting support of the contra rebels in Nicaragua. That support was undercut by the actions of some of his administrators in selling arms to Iran, monies from which sale were diverted to aid for the contras. This contra scandal substantially lessened his national support and international stature, making the balance of his second term a period of uncertain accomplishment. In 1993 it was revealed that Reagan was suffering from Alzheimer's, leading to his retirement and seclusion in his California ranch. Reagan died in June 2004.

Recruit Scandal (Japan) Bribery scandal (1988–89). Recruit Co. (a multicompany conglomerate) made cash available to and sold unlisted, expensive stock in Recruit Cosmos (real estate affiliate) to high-ranking government officials. The stock later traded publicly at much higher rates, creating large profits for officials involved. Prime Minister Takeshita Noboru was implicated and resigned in April 1989. In July 1989, Takeshita's Liberal Democratic Party was defeated for the first time in 34 years and lost its majority in the Diet (parliament).

Red Army Bolshevik army whose task was to protect the Soviet Union from its external enemies. The workers' and peasants' Red Army was formed by Lenin on January 28, 1918, from the workers' militia, the Red Guards. At first consisting of proletarian volunteers, conscription was introduced during the Russian Civil War; at this stage the army was under Trotsky. The Red Army was demobilized at the end of the civil war and the war with Poland, although a core of half a million men was retained. Owing to the party's commitment to war as a means of bringing about revolution, expansion was rapid during the 1920s and 1930s, and in the latter decade ranks were reintroduced and officers' privileges reinstated. At first during World War II the Red Army was fighting mainly a defensive war, but from 1943 the army embarked on offensive operations. Following the war its name was changed to Soviet Army, and it was reorganized along traditional Russian lines. In 1981 there were about 187 divisions, of which some 100 were at combat readiness, with a total force of about 1.8 million.

Red Army Faction Radical wing of the Baader-Meinhof terrorist group.

Red Brigades (Brigate rosse) Leftwing Italian urban terrorist organization, active from the early 1970s into the early 1980s. The Red Brigades waged a violent campaign against the political and business establishment of Italy, using much the same methods as their German counterpart, the Baader-Meinhof Group—bombings, kidnappings and assassinations. Their most infamous act, the kidnapping and murder of former Italian prime minister Aldo Moro in spring 1978, gave rise to public revulsion and tough new antiterrorist measures.

Red Cross See International Committee of the Red Cross; League of Red Cross Societies.

Redding, J. Saunders (1906–1988) U.S. author and historian; one of the founders of the academic discipline of Afro-American studies. In 1949 Redding became one of the first blacks to teach at an Ivy League institution when he was appointed a visiting professor of English at Brown University, his alma mater. In 1970 he became the first black professor on Cornell University's faculty of arts and sciences.

Redding, Otis (1941–1967) American singer. Born in Dawson, Georgia, the son of a Baptist minister, Redding became one of the preeminent male rhythm-and-blues singers of the 1960s. He had his first major success in 1963 with "These Arms of Mine," which he also wrote. In 1967, he was at the height of his career following his performance at the Monterey Pop Festival and his nomination as top male singer by *Melody Maker*. On December 10 of that year, he and four members of his band were killed when their chartered plane crashed into Lake Monona in southern Wisconsin. Early in 1968, Redding's "(Sittin' on) The Dock of the Bay," which he had recorded shortly before the accident, made it to number-one on both the pop and the rhythm-and-blues charts.

Redford, Robert (1937–) American film actor. Born Charles Robert Redford in Santa Monica, California, the handsome blond actor is one of America's authentic superstars. He attended the University of Colorado, quitting to travel and paint. Returning to the U.S. in 1957, he decided on a career as a theatrical scene designer and enrolled in Pratt Institute and the American Academy of Dramatic Arts. He began working as an actor in 1959 and scored his first success in Neil Simon's *Barefoot in the Park* (1963; filmed 1967). Since then he has starred in such film hits as *Butch Cassidy and the Sundance Kid* (1969) and *The Sting* (1973), playing lovable rogues with

Paul NEWMAN as his partner in crime; *The Candidate* (1972), *All the President's Men* (1976) and *The Natural* (1984). Some of his best roles have been under the direction of Sydney Pollack. These include *Jeremiah Johnson* (1972), *The Way We Were* (1973), *The Electric Horseman* (1978) and *Out of Africa* (1985). Redford was also the director of *Ordinary People* (1980) and *The Milagro Beanfield War* (1987). A liberal activist, he has been particularly concerned with environmental issues, purchasing 6,000 acres near Park City, Utah, on which he founded the Sundance Resort and, later, the Sundance Film Festival, Sundance Institute, Sundance Catalog and Sundance television channel. Throughout the 1990s Redford continued to appear in such dramatic films as *Indecent Proposal* (1993), *Up Close and Personal* (1996) and *The Horse Whisperer* (1998), and he directed *The Legend of Bagger Vance* (2000).

Redgrave, Sir Michael Scudamore *(1908–1985)* British actor. One of the leading British actors of his generation, he first made his reputation in the mid-1930s in Shakespearean roles on the London stage. His first film performance, in Alfred HITCHCOCK's *The Lady Vanishes* (1938), made him an overnight movie star. He appeared in 34 other films, the last in 1971. On stage his portrayal of the title character in CHEKHOV's *Uncle Vanya* was considered definitive. Suffering from Parkinson's disease, he made his last appearance in a major theatrical production as a speechless, wheelchair-bound invalid in Simon GRAY's *Close of Play* (1979). Redgrave was the father of two well-known actresses, **Lynn Redgrave** and Vanessa REDGRAVE; his son Colin was also an actor.

Redgrave, Vanessa *(1937–)* British actress. The daughter of distinguished actor Sir Michael REDGRAVE and sister of actress Lynn Redgrave, Vanessa Redgrave was born in London. She studied at the Central School of Speech and Drama in that city and made her stage debut at the Frinton Summer Theatre in July 1957. Although her vocal left-wing politics and public support of the PALESTINE LIBERATION ORGANIZATION have occasionally received more attention than her acting, Redgrave has enjoyed a remarkable career both on the stage and on film. She won the *Evening Standard* Award for Best Actress of the Year on London's West End twice, in 1961 for *The Lady from the Sea* and in 1966 for *The Prime of Miss Jean Brodie*. She was nominated for best actress ACADEMY AWARDS three times, for her performances in *Morgan!*, *The Loves of Isadora* and *Mary, Queen of Scots*. She won an Academy Award for best supporting actress for *Julia*. Redgrave received an Emmy Award for her performance as a lesbian in 1950s America in the Home Box Office production *If These Walls Could Talk* (2000).

Red Guards Term used to describe the radical students and other cadres who carried out MAO ZEDONG's CULTURAL REVOLUTION in CHINA in the late 1960s. The Red Guards disrupted life at all levels and threw the nation into chaos. Brandishing Mao's *Little Red Book* and imbued with a fanatical spirit, they denounced, harassed, arrested, tried and punished those whom they considered enemies of Mao and the revolution. Victims of the Red Guards included educators, intellectuals, artists and writers and Communist Party bureaucrats. Perhaps 400,000 people died at the hands of the Red Guards; many more were imprisoned or forced to work on collective farms as part of their political "reeducation." At the height of the Cultural Revolution, there were an estimated 11 million Red Guards. The guards were disbanded after Mao's death in 1976.

Red Scare Wave of fear of political radicalism that swept the U.S. in the wake of the RUSSIAN REVOLUTION (1917). It culminated in the so-called **Palmer Raids** that occurred during the tenure of Alexander Mitchell Palmer as U.S. attorney general (1919–21). Peaking in 1920, roundups conducted in 33 American cities resulted in the arrests of thousands of citizens and aliens alleged to be "Reds" (communists, socialists, anarchists and other radicals) who were charged with attempting to overthrow the government by force and violence. Several hundred aliens, including Emma Goldman, were subsequently deported.

Redstone, Sumner *(1923–)* CEO of Viacom, Inc. (1987–). While a student at Harvard University, he worked in an intelligence task force designed to crack Japanese diplomatic and military ciphers before graduating with a B.A. in 1944. After graduating from Harvard Law School in 1947, he became a legal secretary for the U.S. court of appeals in San Francisco, while also teaching law at the University of San Francisco. He later became a partner in the Washington, D.C., law firm of Ford, Bergson, Adams, Borkland and Redstone. In 1954 he went to work for National Amusements, Inc., a motion picture distribution house and became president and chief executive officer of the company in 1967 and chairman of the board in 1986. A year later, he orchestrated National Amusements' purchase of a controlling interest in Viacom, a New York City–based entertainment and media corporation, of which Redstone became CEO and chairman of the board. In 1994 Redstone convinced the board of Viacom to purchase Paramount Pictures, renowned for producing such films as the *Star Trek* series and the NATIONAL BROADCASTING CORPORATION (NBC) situation-comedy *FRASIER*. Paramount also owned the national movie, video game, and music rental and sales store Blockbuster. Redstone later convinced Viacom's board to purchase other television and cable networks, such as **MTV**, Nickelodeon, Showtime and Comedy Central. In 1999, the year Viacom purchased Columbia Broadcasting Services (**CBS**), Redstone resigned his position as president of National Amusements, but retained his titles of CEO and chairman of the board of both National Amusements and Viacom, in which he controlled a majority of the voting stock.

Red Shoes, The Classic English film made in 1948 that focuses on the obsessions and ambitions of the ballet world. The film is famous for its romanticism, visual impact, special effects and imaginatively filmed ballet sequences, and had an effect on such major dance films as *An American in Paris* (1951). Based on a Hans Christian Andersen fairy tale, *The Red Shoes* was written and directed by Michael POWELL and Emeric PRESSBURGER, and starred dancers Moira Shearer, Robert HELPMANN and Leonide MASSINE, as well as actors Marius Goring and Anton Walbrook.

Reed, Sir Carol *(1906–1976)* British actor and film director. Reed was among the foremost British directors of his generation. He began his career as a film and theater actor in the 1930s. Reed's featurelength directorial debut came with *Night Train to Munich* (1940), a political thriller. During WORLD WAR II, Reed devoted himself to documentaries on the war effort. Following the war, he directed *Odd Man Out* (1947) and *The Fallen Idol* (1948). Next came his most critically acclaimed film, *The Third Man* (1949). Starring Orson WELLES and Joseph Cotten, and utilizing a brilliant screenplay by Graham GREENE, *The Third Man* masterfully explored postwar despair and intrigue in Vienna. Subsequent films directed by Reed include *The Agony and the Ecstasy* (1965), a treatment of the life of Michelangelo starring Charlton HESTON, and *Oliver!* (1968), a musical that won the ACADEMY AWARD for best picture, while Reed was honored with the award for best director.

Reed, John *(1887–1920)* American journalist who covered the war in eastern Europe, becoming a close friend of LENIN. He was an eyewitness of the 1917 OCTOBER REVOLUTION and wrote his account *Ten Days that Shook the World* (1919). In 1919 he organized the Communist Labor Party in the U.S. and was founder and first editor of the *Voice of Labor.* For a short period he was the Soviet consul in New York. He left the U.S. for Russia, where he died of typhus and was buried in the Kremlin wall. Other works include *The War in Eastern Europe* (1916) and *Red Russia* (1919).

Reed, Stanley *(1884–1980)* U.S. Supreme Court justice (1938–57). Reed was named to the Supreme Court by President Franklin D. ROOSEVELT and wrote more than 300 opinions on a broad range of issues, including social welfare, civil rights and the regulatory powers of the federal government. His decisions often defied prediction. However, he was noted for his support of NEW DEAL legislation and his restrained view of civil liberties. Reed regularly voted to uphold federal economic and social welfare laws and thus helped to legitimize the expansion of government regulatory powers that oc-

curred during the 1930s. Previous to his Court appointment, Reed served as counsel of the Federal Farm Board (1929–32) and as general counsel of the Reconstruction Finance Corporation (1932–35). He was U.S. solicitor general from 1935 until his appointment to the Supreme Court in 1938.

Reed, Walter *(1851–1902)* American army pathologist and bacteriologist. Reed obtained his medical degree from the University of Virginia (1869) before he was 18. He was commissioned in the Army Medical Corps in 1875 and began to specialize in bacteriology. In 1900 he headed a commission to investigate the causes and mode of transmission of an epidemic of yellow fever among American troops in Havana, Cuba. He and other doctors conducted a series of daring experiments using human volunteers. The results of the experiments proved the fever was caused and transmitted by a virus carried by a certain type of mosquito. Shortly before Reed's death, Harvard conferred on him an honorary degree of A.M., and the University of Michigan gave him the degree of LL.D. The Army Medical Center in Washington, D.C., is named in his honor.

regionalism A movement in American painting during the GREAT DEPRESSION of the 1930s that celebrated the sturdy, homespun values and people of the Midwest. It was a timely confluence of many artistic, social and political factors. In reaction to the flood of modern European art on the market, there was a growing desire to support an indigenously American form of art. Anxiety over the depression and growing distrust of urban centers because of the stock market crash (1929) stimulated a yearning for a return to a simpler life closer to the soil. It all began with an exhibition at the Kansas City Art Institute in 1933 by New York art dealer Maynard Walker (a native Kansan). "American Painting Since Whistler" comprised 35 paintings, featuring prominently work by John Stewart Curry, a Kansas commercial illustrator; Grant WOOD, an Iowa painter; and Thomas Hart BENTON, a Missouri mural painter. The December 24, 1934, issue of *Time* magazine picked up on the story, displaying Benton's self-portrait on the cover and a full-

color illustrated article inside, "The U.S. Scene." It was the first time a major American periodical had given so much attention to living artists. It proclaimed Curry, Wood and Benton as the leading painters of the American scene. Nine months later an article by Thomas Craven in *Harper's Monthly,* "Our Art Becomes American: We Draw Up Our Declaration of Independence," confirmed the movement now dubbed "regionalism." The ensuing decade tended to stereotype both the artists and their work. What had originally been a satiric view of midwestern subjects now seemed to soften and mellow. As Tom Benton admitted: "Grant Wood became the typical Iowa small towner, John Curry the typical Kansas farmer, and I just an Ozark hillbilly. We accepted our roles." The movement lost its momentum (if not its public favor) with the transfer of public attention from local to international issues during WORLD WAR II. Wood died of liver cancer in 1942 and Curry of a stroke in 1946. Benton himself barely survived a heart attack in 1952. Attacks on regionalism's supposed "antiartistic" aims and essentially fascist narrowness of ideology in such magazines as *The Magazine of Art* after 1946 further weakened its position in the art world.

Règle du jeu, La *(**The Rules of the Game**)* French film acknowledged as Jean RENOIR's masterpiece and regularly included in *Sight and Sound* magazine's annual poll of the Ten Best Movies of all time. It culminated a great sequence of masterpieces from Renoir's peak phase in the 1930s (including *Le Crime de M. Lange* and *La grande illusion*). The exteriors were shot in the late winter and spring of 1939 in the Château de la Ferté-Saint-Aubin, and the interiors were shot at the Billancourt Studios in Joinville. Although Renoir called his story (freely derived from de Musset and Beaumarchais) a "divertissement," it conveyed so bitter a view of French society that it was censored for its initial release in 1939. (The film was not restored to its original form until 1959.) The story of an outing at a country estate of a disparate group of aristocrats, citizens, and servants is essentially an ensemble piece that, in part, was improvised. It achieves great complexity by its balance of humor and pathos, compassion and satire, artifice and reality. By turns, there are the tender love scenes between the tragic Octave (Renoir himself) and the ambivalent Christine (Nora Gregor); the delicious "vaudevilles" of the amateur theatricals at the estate; and the brutal savagery of the celebrated "rabbit hunt" sequence. This rondelet of love and cruelty was perfectly captured by the mobile camera and deep-space compositions of cinematographer Jean Bachelet. All is flux. Relationships shift, change and realign again. The continual revelation of layered meanings through repeated viewings is exhilarating. A favorite quotation of Renoir's applies: "In nature nothing is created, nothing is lost, everything is transformed."

Rehnquist, William H(ubbs)
(1924–2005) Associate justice, U.S. Supreme Court (1971–86), chief justice (1986–2005). A graduate of Stanford, Harvard and Stanford Law School, early in his career he was a clerk to Supreme Court Justice Robert H. JACKSON. A conservative Republican, he was appointed to the highly visible position of chief legal counsel for the Justice Department under President Richard M. NIXON. He became an eloquent spokesperson for the Nixon administration's positions, some of which were highly controversial. He was nominated to the Supreme Court by President Nixon in 1971; in 1986 President Ronald REAGAN nominated him to fill the vacancy in the chief justice's seat after Warren BURGER's resignation. There was significant opposition to his nomination, although it ultimately proved successful. On the Court, Justice Rehnquist was a consistent conservative, although often in dissent. In later years, a larger conservative block on the Court allowed the Rehnquist Court to issue more conservative rulings, significantly cutting back the rulings issued by the Court during the WARREN and Burger years. In 1998 and 1999 Rehnquist presided over the Senate impeachment of President Bill Clinton. He died in September 2005.

Reich, Wilhelm *(1897–1957)* Austrian psychiatrist. After graduate and postgraduate work at the University of Vienna, Reich trained in psychoanalysis under FREUD. In 1927 he published *The Function of Orgasm,* in which he argued that the release of sexual tension is necessary for personal health. In the late 1920s, Reich became a politically active Marxist. He moved to Berlin in 1930 but was forced to flee Nazi Germany in 1933. He continued his work, now on character structure and political psychology, in Scandinavia before leaving Europe for the U.S. in 1939. In America, Reich conducted his research on "orgone," or sexual energy. He and his colleagues at the Orgone Institute designed an "orgone accumulator," a box that they claimed could cure many diseases, including cancer, by concentrating orgonismic energy from the atmosphere. The government declared Reich's therapy a fraud, and he was sentenced to two years in prison, where he died of a heart attack.

Reichstag fire Fire that destroyed Germany's parliament building on February 27, 1933, a month after Adolf HITLER became chancellor. Blaming the conflagration on communist terrorists, Hitler succeeded in passing legislation that gave him dictatorial powers and suspended civil rights. The police arrested a Dutch worker, Marinus van der Lubbe, along with a number of communist leaders including Georgi DIMITROV. In the subsequent trial, van der Lubbe was found guilty and executed, while the communists were judged to be not guilty. Opponents of the Nazis alleged that the fire had been set by them to ensure the passage of anticommunist laws. However, later evidence suggested that van der Lubbe alone was responsible for the fire.

Reilly, Sidney (Sigmund Rosenbloom)
(1874–1925) Russian-born British secret agent. Reilly, "ace of spies," was a legendary yet shadowy figure who is widely considered to have been the first modern intelligence agent. His activities spanned the first quarter of the 20th century. Of Jewish origin, he emigrated to Britain and offered his services to the foreign office. In the years leading up to WORLD WAR I he was reputedly involved in espionage activities in Germany, where he attempted to obtain secret plans for German battleships. He developed business interests in Russia, which gave him access to high officials. After the RUSSIAN REVOLUTION he worked to keep Russia in the war against Germany. Soon after the BOLSHEVIK (OCTOBER) REVOLUTION he organized a plan to overthrow LENIN and replace the Bolshevik government with a White Russian government headed by himself, but this was thwarted. He spent the next several years working with White Russian emigré organizations in Europe and the U.S. In 1925 he returned to Russia to expose the Trust, a reputed counterrevolutionary group, as an organization controlled by the CHEKA (secret police) designed to funnel funds from the West and lure anti-Bolshevik emigrés back to Russia, where they would be arrested. Reilly himself was arrested by Feliks DZERZHINSKY, head of the Cheka, apparently on the direct orders of STALIN. He was subsequently executed. However, learning of the secret Trust, the suspicious Stalin ordered its members arrested and executed; Dzershinsky himself was a victim of this early purge. Even though he lost his life, Reilly had thus succeeded in his final mission.

The burning of the Reichstag. 1933 (LIBRARY OF CONGRESS, PRINTS AND PHOTOGRAPHS DIVISION)

Reiner, Carl *(1922–)* American comedian, comedy writer and director of television and film. Reiner became a comedy star on Sid CAESAR's Emmy award–winning program *Your Show of Shows* (1950–54, known as *Caesar's Hour* 1954–57) during the "Golden

Age of Television Comedy." Reiner served the show in various roles including sketch writer, straight man and even creating oddball characters with funny accents. On the show, Reiner also teamed up with Mel Brooks to create the classic comedy routine "The Two Thousand Year Old Man," which was made into a successful album. Reiner created another television hit, *The Dick Van Dyke Show* (1961–66), which launched the careers of stars Dick Van Dyke and Mary Tyler Moore; he also costarred in this pioneering "sitcom for adults." In the late 1960s and '70s Reiner's brilliance for comedy continued to flourish, as he shifted his talents to writing, directing or starring in several accomplished films, including *It's a Mad, Mad, Mad, Mad World* (1963), *The Russians Are Coming, the Russians Are Coming* (1966), *The Comic* (1969) and *Oh God* (1977). Several other of his film projects have achieved cult status, such as *Where's Poppa?* (1970) and his fruitful collaborations with comedian Steve Martin, such as *The Jerk* (1979), *Dead Men Don't Wear Plaid* (1982) and *All of Me* (1984). Reiner's son Rob (1945–   ) is also a major Hollywood talent, acting in the hit television show ALL IN THE FAMILY and directing such films as *This Is Spinal Tap* (1984), *Stand By Me* (1986), *The Princess Bride* (1987) and *When Harry Met Sally* (1989). Throughout the 1990s Reiner repeatedly appeared as a county judge on NBC's television series *Law and Order* and *Mad About You*. He played a veteran con artist in the 2001 remake of *Ocean's Eleven* and its sequel, *Ocean's Twelve* (2004).

Reiner, Fritz *(1888–1963)* Hungarian-born orchestra conductor who brought the Chicago Symphony Orchestra to world prominence at mid-century. Reiner was born in Budapest where at age 10 he studied with Béla BARTÓK. Despite family pressure to become a lawyer, he pursued a conducting career, leading the Dresden Court Orchestra from 1914 to 1922 and succeeding Eugène Ysaÿe at the Cincinnati Symphony in the U.S. from 1922 to 1931. He became an American citizen in 1928 and held many posts during the next 25 years—head of the opera and orchestral departments at the Curtis Institute during the 1930s, music director of the Pittsburgh Symphony

Orchestra from 1938 to 1948, conductor of the Metropolitan Opera from 1949 to 1953 and (most significantly) music director of the Chicago Symphony Orchestra during its peak period from 1953 to 1962. Comparisons with Arturo TOSCANINI are inevitable: His baton technique was minimal but legendary in its precision; his mood was irascible and he frequently bullied his players; and he rejected "romantic," effusive interpretations of music in favor of a no-nonsense, objective approach. In addition to his beloved Viennese classics, Reiner was especially renowned for his performances of Bartók, Paul HINDEMITH and Richard STRAUSS.

Reinhardt, Ad(olph) *(1913–1967)* American painter. Born in Buffalo, New York, he studied art history at Columbia University with Meyer SCHAPIRO and at New York University's Institute of Fine Arts. A theorist and teacher, he taught at Brooklyn College from 1947 until his death. His early works are geometric in character and employ strong color contrasts. In the 1950s his work became quieter and tended toward symmetrical monotones. In the 1960s he developed the "black paintings" for which he is best known. These canvases appear totally black at first glance, but further scrutiny reveals a subtle geometry in an extremely close tonal range.

Reinhardt, Max (Max Goldmann) *(1873–1943)* Austrian theatrical director and producer. Reinhardt was one of the most important and influential figures in the development of the modern theater in Europe. He began his theatrical career as an actor (1890–1900), becoming well known for his performances at Berlin's Deutsches Theater. He managed his own theater (1902–05) and took over directorial duties at the Deutsches Theater in 1905. His many productions there set the standard for European experimental theater, and he initiated such practices as including the audience in the production. Reinhardt became known for his spectacularly rich productions, filled with large casts, elaborate costumes and masterful sets. He was just as adept in staging the works of great masters, such as Sophocles, Shakespeare and Goethe, as he was in pro-

ducing and directing works by contemporaries, such as Luigi PIRANDELLO and George Bernard SHAW. In 1919 Reinhardt opened the massive Grosses Schauspielhaus in Berlin, and the following year he initiated the Salzburg Festival, where he staged a yearly production of *Everyman*. Among his greatest successes were GORKY's *The Lower Depths* (1903), *Oedipus Rex* (1910), *The Oresteia* (1919), *Danton's Death* (1920), *A Midsummer Night's Dream* (1934; film, 1935) and *Six Characters in Search of an Author* (1940). The coming of the Nazis caused Reinhardt to flee Germany in 1933. He settled in the U.S., continued his theatrical career on the New York stage and the Hollywood screen and became an American citizen in 1940.

Reisman, David *(1909–2003)* American sociologist. Reisman taught sociology at the University of Chicago from 1946 to 1958. His scholarly book *The Lonely Crowd: A Study of the Changing American Character* (1950), about the trend toward individual isolation and depersonalization, was a bestseller and became a classic of sociology. He taught at Harvard (1958–80) and specialized in the sociology of higher education.

Reitsch, Hanna *(1912–1979)* German flyer. One of the most famous women pilots of the 1930s, Reitsch won many awards for setting altitude and endurance records and during World War II flight-tested the robot-controlled V 1. She piloted what may have been the last German airplane out of besieged Berlin in April 1945 and, as a favorite of Adolf HITLER, is believed to have been one of the last people to see him alive.

relativity, theory of See Albert EINSTEIN.

Relay Two early experimental communications satellites built by RCA for NASA. Both were launched in three-stage Thor-Delta rockets from Cape Canaveral (see CAPE KENNEDY); *Relay 1* blasted off on December 13, 1962, and *Relay 2* was launched on January 21, 1964. Both were designed to transmit either one television channel, 300 one-way voice channels or 12 two-way telephone channels, receiving and retransmitting signals between the

U.S., Europe, Japan and South America. The 170-lb. aluminum satellites were tapered octagons, 33 inches high and 29 inches in diameter at their broad ends. Their 11 watts of power were produced by some 8,200 solar cells on each exterior. *Relay 1* had an orbit with an apogee of 4,612 miles and a perigee of 819 miles with an angle to the equator of 47.5 degrees and a period of 186 minutes. *Relay 2's* orbit had an apogee of 4,606 miles and a perigee of 1,298 miles at an angle of 46 degrees to the equator and a period of 195 minutes. Both operated until their power was shut off, *Relay 1* in February 1965 and *Relay 2* seven months later.

R.E.M. American alternative rock group. Founded in Athens, Georgia, in 1981 by vocalist Michael Stipe, guitarist Peter Buck, bassist Mike Bass, and drummer Bill Berry, R.E.M. began playing in local bars in Georgia and other southeastern states. In May 1982, R.E.M. recorded its first record, *Chronic Town*, through the small independent label I.R.S. Records, followed seven months later by its first full-length record, *Murmur*. While the band experienced some financial success with *Life's Rich Pageant* (1986), which went gold by the end of 1986, R.E.M.'s breakthrough into the genre of popular music came in 1987 with *Document*, which was propelled into the Top 10

Rock band R.E.M., 1991
(PHOTOFEST)

Albums sold that year largely due to its hit single "The One I Love." After signing with the music division of Warner Brothers in 1988, the group recorded its sixth full-length record, *Green* (1988). Three years later R.E.M. released *Out of Time,* the group's first record to reach number one in worldwide sales, with nearly 5 million copies in distribution. While some of R.E.M.'s fans expressed concern that the group's commercial success would lead them away from their alternative rock sound, the band's next album, *Automatic For the People* (1992) represented a return to the introspective songs of R.E.M.'s earlier days. The group maintained its popularity throughout the 1990s with *Monster* (1994) and a world tour that promoted the album. In 1996, the group re-signed with Warner Brothers, and released *New Adventures in Hi-Fi* which contained new songs they had recorded live during their *Monster* tour in 1994. Since 1994, R.E.M. has recorded three albums—*Up* (1998), *Reveal* (2001) and *Around the Sun* (2004).

Remagen Rhine River town in Germany's Rhineland-Palatinate, about 20 miles north of Koblenz. Remagen secured a place in 20th-century history as the location of the Ludendorff Bridge (built during World War I). This was the only Rhine River bridge still standing when the advancing Al-

lies reached the river early in 1945, near the end of WORLD WAR II. After fierce fighting the Allies captured the bridge on March 8, 1945. This victory enabled the Allies to cross the river in force and with heavy equipment, thus numbering the days of HITLER's Reich.

Remarque, Erich Maria *(1898–1970)* German-American author. Most famous for his powerful antiwar novel *All Quiet on the Western Front* (1929), Remarque used the theme of the horrors and chaos of war and its aftermath in all subsequent works. The catalyst for his writing was his stint in the German army during WORLD WAR I. After the war he worked at various jobs including teacher and auto worker. He left Germany in the 1930s when the Nazis rose to power. In 1947 he became an American citizen. Other major novels include *The Road Back* (1931), *Arch of Triumph* (1946), *A Time to Love and a Time to Die* (1954) and *The Night in Lisbon* (1964).

Remembrance of Things Past Seven-volume novel sequence (1913–1927) by French writer Marcel PROUST. *Remembrance of Things Past* stands among the supreme achievements of 20th-century literature. The central theme of the sequence, which was initiated with *Swann's Way* in 1913, is the intricate individual consciousness of time's passing and its implications for human endeavors and for the ultimate event of death. *Remembrance of Things Past* was conceived by Proust when he was 38, and his relatively late arrival to artistic maturity is reflected in the poignancy with which all the characters of the sequence review lives filled with time squandered and opportunities lost. Memory alone—in all its vividness, beauty and anguish—has a restorative power for the human soul. Love and jealousy are seen as inextricably intertwined. On the social scale, *Remembrance of Things Past* depicts the transformation of French society from aristocratic reign to the economic dominance of the untitled bourgeoisie.

Remizov, Alexei Mikhailovich (1877–1957) Writer. Expelled from Moscow University, he spent the next few years at Penza, Ust-Sysolsk and

Vologda. In 1904 he was released from police surveillance and settled in St. Petersburg. He organized the satirical Great and Free House of Apes, of which he was "chancellor," and sent most Russian writers and publishers handwritten charters, stating their position in the house. By World War I Remizov was head of a new school of fiction. His *Mala* and *The Lament for the Ruin of Russia* (1917) convey conditions in Petrograd (St. Petersburg) from 1914 to 1921. His work, however, is extremely varied in style and content. His prose consists of contemporary stories, the best-known of which is *The Story of Ivan Semyonovich Stratilatov* (1909), legends, folk stories, dreams and plays. His verse is less successful. In 1921 Remizov emigrated and settled in Paris.

Remy, Colonel See Gilbert RENAULT.

Renault, Gilbert *(1904–1984)* Renault was one of FRANCE's most decorated heroes of the RESISTANCE against the Germans during WORLD WAR II. Best known by his wartime pseudonym, Colonel Remy, he was the principal organizer of the FREE FRENCH intelligence network, which provided the Allies with valuable information on German troop movements before D-DAY. Renault's autobiography, *Memoirs of a Secret Agent of Free France,* was highly acclaimed when it was published in the U.S. in 1948. He was also a film director and writer.

Renault, Mary (Mary Challans) *(1905–1983)* British novelist. Renault is best known for her popular historical novels, which bring 20th-century insights and knowledge to bear on ancient events, frequently in Greece or Asia Minor. Her novels include *The King Must Die* (1958) and *The Bull from the Sea* (1962), both based on Theseus, legendary king of Athens; *The Persian Boy* (1972), which evokes the reign of Alexander the Great; and *The Friendly Young Ladies* (1985).

Renoir, Jean *(1894–1979)* French director, widely acclaimed as France's greatest filmmaker. Renoir was born in Paris, the second son of Impressionist painter Auguste Renoir. A growing passion for the cinema led to his first directorial effort, *La Fille de l'Eau* (1924).

By the time he filmed his early talkies, *La Chienne* and *Boudu sauve des Eaux* (*Boudu Saved From Drowning,* 1932), he had gained a measure of artistic independence, which he stubbornly fought to maintain the rest of his long career.

His greatest creative period came in the late 1930s with *Le Crime de M. Lange* (*The Crime of M. Lange,* 1936), a drama of collectivism and working-class solidarity (eloquent of Renoir's leftist sympathies with the POPULAR FRONT); *La Grande Illusion* (*The Grand Illusion,* 1937), a drama of relationships in a World War I prison camp; *La Bête humaine* (*The Human Beast,* 1938), a melodrama of trains and murder adapted from Emile Zola; and his masterpiece, *LA RÈGLE DU JEU* (*The Rules of the Game,* 1939), a dark-humored indictment of a world poised on the brink of war. Renoir's war years were spent in HOLLYWOOD where he became an American citizen. His last works included a meditation on the artifices of theater and film, *Le Petit Théâtre de Jean Renoir* (1971), and an autobiography, *Ma Vie et mes films* (*My Life and My Films,* 1974). Before his death in 1979 he received a lifetime achievement ACADEMY AWARD. The range of his achievement makes him difficult to categorize. There is the sparkling humor of the "Arizona Jim" episodes of *M. Lange,* the deeply felt, sensitive, almost documentary observation of nature in *Partie de campagne* (*A Day in the Country,* 1937) and the grim, blunt depiction of the savagery of man in the famous "rabbit hunt" sequence in *The Rules of the Game.* His awesome camera technique was perfectly wedded to his humanistic aims. Andre Bazin hailed Renoir as the spiritual godfather of the so-called French NEW WAVE in the 1950s. His deep-focus frame, moving camera and long takes "permitted everything to be said without chopping the world up into little fragments, that would reveal the hidden meanings in people and things without disturbing the unity natural to them." Ultimately there are no villains and heroes in Renoir's world, no easy labels of praise or blame.

Republican Party American political party founded in 1854; one of the two major political parties in the UNITED STATES. The philosophy of the Republican Party is generally more conservative than that of the DEMOCRATIC PARTY. Republicans tend to support a free rein to business interests, opposing government regulation in the economy and federally funded social programs. They have traditionally been unsupportive of organized labor and of organizations seeking change in society.

The Republican National Committee serves as a coordinator of the national conventions and assists in campaigning and fund-raising, at which, since the 1970s, it has become more effective and organized than its Democratic counterpart.

With the exception of Woodrow WILSON's presidency (1913 to 1921), Republicans controlled the presidency from 1900 to 1932 and dominated both the House and the Senate for most of that time. After Franklin ROOSEVELT's NEW DEAL, the Republican Party went into decline. By 1960 it was in such disarray that some observers predicted its demise.

Following 1969 it began to gain strength. The Republican Party had traditionally been divided between moderates and conservatives, but beginning with Barry GOLDWATER's nomination in 1964, the conservative faction gained party dominance. The party's credibility was damaged during Richard NIXON's administration by the WATERGATE affair, but following the tax revolts of the late 1970s it gained support among those opposed to government spending. Ronald REAGAN's election in 1980 brought renewed vigor to the party, and his support of the Moral Majority brought fundamentalist religious groups, many of which were traditional southern Democrats, to the Republican side. Reagan's personal popularity overshadowed the IRAN-CONTRA SCANDAL, and Republicans prevailed at the 1988 elections when George H. W. BUSH succeeded him. However, despite its successes in retaining the presidency, the Republican Party remained the minority party in both houses of Congress. In the 1990s the Republican Party lost the presidency to Democrat William Jefferson CLINTON in 1992 and 1996, but gained control of both houses of Congress in 1995 and retained it until 2001. In 2001 Republican George W. BUSH was sworn in as president, but the party lost control of the Senate in 2001 due to a poor performance in the 2000 elections and the decision by Republican senator Jim Jeffords of Vermont to become an independent, giving the Democrats a one-member majority in the Senate. However the 2002 elections returned control of the Senate to the Republicans.

Republics, Constituent

The UNION OF SOVIET SOCIALIST REPUBLICS was formed by the union of the Russian Soviet Federated Socialist Republic, the Ukrainian Soviet Socialist Republic, the Belorussian Soviet Socialist Republic and the Transcaucasian Soviet Socialist Republic. The Treaty of Union was adopted by the first Soviet congress of the USSR on December 30, 1922. In May 1925 the Uzbek and Turkmen Autonomous Soviet Socialist Republics and in December 1929 the Tadzhik Autonomous Soviet Socialist Republic were declared constituent members of the USSR, becoming union republics.

At the eighth congress of the Soviets, on December 5, 1936, a new constitution of the USSR was adopted. The Transcaucasian Republic was split into the Armenian Soviet Socialist Republic, the Azerbaijan Soviet Socialist Republic and the Georgian Soviet Socialist Republic, each of which became a constituent republic of the union. At the same time the Kazakh Soviet Socialist Republic and the Kirghiz Soviet Socialist Republic, previously autonomous republics within the Russian Soviet Federated Socialist Republic, were proclaimed constituent republics of the USSR.

In September 1939 Soviet troops occupied eastern Poland as far as the CURZON LINE, which in 1919 had been drawn on ethnographic grounds as the eastern frontier of Poland, and incorporated it into the Ukrainian and Belorussian Soviet Socialist Republics. In February 1951 some districts of the Drogobych Region of the Ukraine and the Lublin Voyevodship of Poland were exchanged.

On March 31, 1940, territory ceded by Finland was joined to that of the autonomous Soviet socialist republic of Karelia to form the Karelo-Finnish Soviet Socialist Republic, which was admitted into the union as the 12th union republic. On July 16, 1956, the Supreme Soviet of the USSR adopted a law altering the status of the Karelo-Finnish Republic from that of a union

(constituent) republic of the USSR to that of an autonomous (Karelian) republic within the Russian Soviet Federated Socialist Republic.

On August 2, 1940, the Moldavian Soviet Socialist Republic was constituted as the 13th union republic. It comprised the former Moldavian Autonomous Soviet Socialist Republic and Bessarabia (the latter ceded by Romania on June 28, 1940), except for the Bessarabia districts of Khotin, Akerman and Ismail, which, together with northern Bukovina, were incorporated in the Ukrainian Soviet Republic. The Soviet-Romanian frontier thus constituted was confirmed by the peace treaty with Romania, signed on February 10, 1947. On June 29, 1945, Ruthenia (Sub-Carpathian Russia) was by treaty with Czechoslovakia absorbed in the Ukrainian Soviet Socialist Republic.

On August 3, 1940, Estonia, Latvia and Lithuania were incorporated in the Soviet Union as the 14th, 15th and 16th union republics. The change in the status of the Karelo-Finnish Republic reduced the number of union republics to 15.

After the defeat of Germany it was agreed by the governments of Great Britain, the U.S. and the USSR (the Potsdam agreement) that part of East Prussia should be ceded to the USSR. The area, which includes the towns of Konigsberg (renamed Kaliningrad), Tilsit (renamed Sovyetsk) and Insterburg (renamed Chernyakhovsk), was joined to the Russian Soviet Federated Socialist Republic by a decree of April 7, 1946.

By the peace treaty with Finland, signed on February 10, 1947, the province of Petsamo (Pechenga), ceded to Finland on October 14, 1920, and March 12, 1946, was returned to the Soviet Union. On September 19, 1955, the Soviet Union renounced its treaty rights to the naval base of Porkkala-Udd and on January 26, 1956, completed the withdrawal of forces from Finnish territory.

In 1945, after the defeat of Japan, the southern half of Sakhalin Island, and the Kuril Islands, were, by agreement with the Allies, incorporated into the USSR. Japan, however, asked for the return of the islands of Etorofu and Kunashiri as not belonging to the Kuril Islands proper. The Soviet government informed Japan on January

27, 1960, that the Habomai Islands and Shikotan would be handed back to Japan on the withdrawal of American troops from Japan. On December 25, 1991, the Union of Soviet Socialist Republics ceased to exist.

Resistance

Movement among citizens of the countries occupied by Germany in WORLD WAR II in opposition to the Nazis. The model for Resistance organization and activity can been said to have been provided by French general Charles DE GAULLE and his followers. According to de Gaulle himself, there were three stages in the development of the Resistance: (1) the establishment of an information network to benefit the Allies; (2) the sabotage of the enemy war machine and rejection of compromise with occupying authority; (3) the organization and training of military forces (in the case of France, the FREE FRENCH) to attack German troops as the Allies advanced and the promotion of a climate hospitable to the restoration of the nation when the enemy was defeated. As the war progressed, individual Resistance groups ranged from small cells to large armies. Organized networks specialized in obtaining military or economic information, providing aid and escape routes for prisoners, maintaining caches of arms, producing propaganda, engaging in sabotage and mounting guerrilla attacks. At the end of the war Resistance groups cooperated closely with the liberating armies in mopping up the retreating German forces. After the war members of the Resistance were swift and often violent in punishing those who had collaborated with the Germans.

Resnais, Alain

(1922–) French film director. Resnais was one of the leading directors of the NOUVELLE VAGUE that dominated the French cinema of the late 1950s and 1960s. He won great acclaim for his very first film, *Night and Fog* (1956), a documentary on the Nazi CONCENTRATION CAMPS. In his later imaginative films, Resnais experimented with flashback and memory to convey the emotional complexity of his characters. These films include *Hiroshima mon Amour* (1959), *Last Year at Marienbad* (1961, screenplay by Alain ROBBE-GRILLET), *Providence* (1977) and *La Vie est un roman* (1982). In 1993 Resnais released the critically acclaimed film *Smoking/No Smoking,* an adaptation of the stage performance of *Intimate Exchanges.* Four years later Resnais premiered *Same Old Song,* a romantic musical film composed of popular music ballads. Both films earned Resnais several French *César* awards, France's version of the American Academy Awards, including Best Film for *Same Old Song* and *Smoking/No Smoking,* and Best Director for *Smoking/No Smoking.*

Resnik, Judith *(1949–1986)* U.S. astronaut, one of seven killed in the explosion of the SPACE SHUTTLE CHALLENGER on January 28, 1986. A research scientist, she held an electrical engineering degree and was also a classical pianist. She became the second American woman in space when she flew on a shuttle mission in 1984.

Respighi, Ottorino *(1879–1936)* Italian composer. Respighi is regarded as a master of orchestration who successfully blended evocative melodies and rich harmonies in his works. In 1900 he became first viola with the Imperial Opera Orchestra in St. Petersburg, Russia, and was greatly influenced by his composition teacher Rimsky-Korsakov. He toured as a concert violinist (1903–08), then taught at the Accademia di Santa Cecilia in Rome from 1913 onward. Respighi's most famous works were two symphonic poems that powerfully evoke the Italian scene: *La fontane di Roma* (1917; *The Fountains of Rome*) and *I pini di Roma* (1924; *The Pines of Rome*). One of his innovations was the insertion of a recording of a singing nightingale in the score of the latter piece.

Réunion Réunion is an island in the Indian Ocean, more than 400 miles east of Madagascar. A French colony until 1946, the 969-square-mile island then became an overseas department of FRANCE, but in practice was not integrated with metropolitan France. From 1959 onward the influential local communist party has campaigned for autonomy for the island. Communists dominate the Anti-Colonialist Front for the Self-Determination of Réunion (FRACPAR, or FRA), formed in 1978. A regional council was elected for the first time in February 1983.

Reuther, Walter *(1907–1970)* American labor union leader. Born in Wheeling, West Virginia, Reuther attended Wayne State University in Detroit. In 1936 he was elected president of the United Automobile Workers (UAW) Local 174 in that city. With his brother Victor, Reuther led the first of the large-scale sit-down strikes, at the Kelsey-Hayes plants in Detroit, and late in 1936 the strike spread to the General Motors plant in Flint, Michigan. In 1937 both GM and Chrysler Motors recognized the UAW as the workers' bargaining agent.

With the end of World War II, Reuther demanded a 30 percent pay raise for GM workers to compensate them for lost overtime and premium pay for war-related work. When the company refused, he led the first major strike of the postwar period, a 113–day walkout of 200,000 GM workers (November 21, 1945–March 13, 1946). This strike helped precipitate strikes in the steel, electrical, meatpacking and other industries, but in the end the workers won an increase of only 18.5 cents an hour. Reuther's aggressive prosecution of the strike won him support among UAW radicals, however, and in 1946 he was elected president of the union. In 1951 he was elected president of the Congress of Industrial Organizations (CIO), and was instrumental in effecting that union's merger with the AMERICAN FEDERATION OF LABOR (AFL) in 1955. In the following years, Reuther was frequently at odds with AFL-CIO chairman George MEANY. In 1968 the UAW withdrew from that organization, claiming that the parent group was moribund and undemocratic. In May 1969 the UAW merged with James HOFFA's International Brotherhood of Teamsters, and the group assumed the name Alliance for Labor Action. On May 9, 1970, Reuther and his wife, May, were killed when their chartered plane crashed in Michigan.

Reverdy, Pierre *(1889–1960)* One of the leading French lyric poets of the 20th century. His powerful and imagistic verse shows the influence of CUBISM, which first emerged as a theory of painting. In the 1910s Reverdy became a leader of a poetic school of cubism that also included fellow French poets Guillaume APOLLINAIRE, Blaise CENDRARS, Jean COCTEAU and Max Jacob. Reverdy also emphasized the need for a "poesie brut," or brutal poetry, that would reject conventional structures and appearances to bring out the true underlying forms of experience. After a brief involvement with SURREALISM in the 1920s, Reverdy chose to follow a life of religious contemplation, retiring to the Abbey of Solesmes in 1926. *La Lucarne Ovale* (1916) and *Plupart du Temps* (1945) are representative volumes of his verse.

Revueltas, José *(1914–1976)* Mexican novelist, story writer, essayist, playwright. Revueltas, who is best known for his prose fiction, was one of the most influential Mexican writers to emerge in the middle decades of the 20th century. A lifelong political activist, he was strongly influenced by Marxism but also drew from the insights of Freudian psychoanalysis and surrealist aesthetics. His most highly regarded novel is *The Stone Knife* (1943), which utilizes cinematic narrative techniques in dealing with the lives of six rural workers attempting to flee from a life-threatening flood. Revueltas also published two noteworthy story collections, *God on Earth* (1944) and *Sleep on Earth* (1960).

Rexroth, Kenneth *(1905–1982)* American poet. Born in South Bend, Indiana, he settled in San Francisco and there, as a cofounder of the San Francisco Poetry Center, with Allen GINSBERG and Lawrence FERLINGHETTI, was associated with the early development of the BEAT GENERATION. An autodidact, he taught himself a number of languages and was devoted to Oriental poetry. His translations include *One Hundred Poems from the Japanese* (1956). His own poetry exhibits an almost Oriental delicacy of image combined with a highly developed Western social conscience. Rexroth's many verse collections include *In What Hour* (1940), *The Phoenix and the Tortoise* (1944), *In Defense of the Earth* (1956) and *New Poems* (1974). He was also the author of a verse play, a number of volumes of essays and *An Autobiographical Novel* (1966).

Reyes, Alfonso *(1889–1959)* Mexican poet, essayist, educator and diplomat; one of the leading Mexican men of letters of the 20th century. Reyes was especially well known for his elegant essays that sought to reconcile and blend the cultures of pre-Columbian and modern-day Mexico. A classicist by temperament, Reyes remained somewhat apart from all literary movements but emerged as a major poet with *Pulse* (1921). In the 1920s and 1930s, Reyes served as the Mexican ambassador to Argentina and Brazil. He also held numerous university teaching positions in his native land. Major collections of his essays include *Criticism and the Roman Mind* (1963) and *Mexico in a Nutshell and Other Essays* (1964).

Reymont, Władysław (Stanislaw Reymont) *(1868–1924)* Polish novelist and essayist. Reymont won the NOBEL PRIZE for literature in 1924 and remains one of the leading Polish novelists of the 20th century, although he is little read by modern-day Western readers. Largely self-educated, he held a wide array of odd jobs in his youth and drew heavily from those experiences in his novels, most of which are written in an intensely realistic style. His magnum opus is the four-volume sequence *The Peasants* (1904–1909), which portrays the struggle of a father and a son who strive to work the land while in conflict over their love for the same woman. Other novels by Reymont include *The Commedienne* (1896) and *The Promised Land* (1899).

Reynaud, Paul *(1878–1966)* French statesman. A lawyer, he was elected to the chamber of deputies in 1919, holding various cabinet posts from 1930 to 1940. He succeeded Edouard DALADIER as premier during WORLD WAR II (1940) and was unsuccessful in attempts to rally France's war efforts. Shortly thereafter he was obliged to surrender leadership to Marshal Henri PÉTAIN, who imprisoned him later that year. Deported to Germany in 1942, he was released in 1945. After the war Reynaud was France's finance minister (1948) and vice premier (1953).

Reynolds v. Sims *(1964)* U.S. Supreme Court decision that established that federal courts can intercede in the drawing of state legislature electoral district boundaries. Although nonwhites were enfranchised, they were largely excluded from elective office by clever drawing of election district boundaries to favor white candidates. Election districts typically differed greatly in population. For many years the federal courts would not allow challenges to electoral district boundaries or reapportionments because the issue was thought to be a political question. In the case *BAKER V. CARR*, the Supreme Court first rejected the hands-off stance, and in *Reynolds* the Supreme Court squarely held that state legislative reapportionment could be challenged in the federal courts. Following this decision, several successful challenges were brought, especially in the South.

Reza Shah Pahlavi (Reza Khan) *(1878–1944)* Shah of IRAN (1925–41); a career army officer and one of the organizers of a 1921 coup d'etat, after which he became war minister and later (1923) prime minister. A strong leader who forged a powerful army, Reza Khan was successful in ousting Russian (1921) and British (1924) forces from their occupation of parts of Persia. Assuming broad powers, he deposed the last ruler of the Qajar dynasty in 1925 and proclaimed himself shah. He moved to modernize Persia, restructuring the government and the armed forces; promoting industrialization; establishing new schools, hospitals, networks of roads and the Trans-Iranian Railroad; and reducing the role of the clergy in government and law. Changing his name, he became the founder of the Pahlavi dynasty. And in 1935 he changed the name of his country—from Persia to the Nazi-endorsed Iran. During World War II his pro-German sympathies prompted the British and Soviet governments to reoccupy Iran; in 1941 he abdicated in favor of his son, MUHAMMAD REZA PAHLAVI. Three years later he died in exile in South Africa.

Rhapsody in Blue Landmark American composition for piano and orchestra that advanced the cause of "popular jazz." Bandleader Paul WHITEMAN and composer George GERSHWIN spent barely a month (from January to February, 1924) preparing an *American Rhapsody* for an announced concert of "Experimental Music" at New York's Aeolian Hall on February 12 of that year. The debut performance of the now-retitled *Rhapsody in Blue* (title suggested by the composer's brother, Ira) featured an orchestration by Ferde GROFE, Gershwin at the piano and Whiteman's modest orchestra. Although the program also featured music by the popular Zez Confrey ("Kitten on the Keys") and Victor HERBERT, the Gershwin contribution stole the show and created a sensation, launching him as a "serious" composer. It was encored at CARNEGIE HALL on April 21, 1924. When the symphonic concert version was prepared in 1926—the one heard today—Grofe again did the orchestration. Although specialists quibble about the music's merits as "concert hall jazz" (just as they also dispute such claims about certain contemporary works by Darius MILHAUD and Aaron COPLAND), there is no questioning the vitality of its eclectic and enduring blend of American vernacular idioms with European classical styles. When the work was performed (by Oscar Levant) in a HOLLYWOOD biopic of Gershwin, *Rhapsody in Blue* (1945), it was inflated into an extravaganza of sound out of all recognition.

Rhee, Syngman *(1875–1965)* President of South Korea (1948–1960). Rhee was in exile in the U.S. from 1912 to 1945, acting as spokesman for Korean independence from Japan. He returned to Korea in 1945 with U.S. support and was elected South Korea's first president following the division of Korea. He was a strong leader in the KOREAN WAR, but his increasingly dictatorial style provoked unrest and riots, which led to his resignation in 1960. He retired in exile to Hawaii.

Rhineland The part of GERMANY west of the Rhine River, centered around Cologne. In general, the Rhineland is taken to include those parts of the German states of North Rhine–Westphalia, Rhineland-Palatinate, Hesse and Baden-Wurttemberg in the Rhine valley. After WORLD WAR I, the region was made a demilitarized zone by the Allies, who did not withdraw until 1930. Defying the terms of the Treaty of VERSAILLES of 1919 and the LOCARNO PACT of 1925, the HITLER government remilitarized the region from 1936 and built the SIEGFRIED LINE, an extensive chain of almost impenetrable fortifications.

Rhine River A principal waterway of Europe that rises in the Swiss Alps and flows for over 800 miles before emptying into the North Sea; contiguous to Austria, Switzerland, Germany, France and the Netherlands. Opened to international navigation in 1868, the victory of the Allies over Germany in WORLD WAR I enabled them to reassert the Rhine as the historic boundary between France and Germany—and to reward France with the left-bank provinces of ALSACE and LORRAINE. Before WORLD WAR II the Rhineland was the site of the German SIEGFRIED and French MAGINOT defensive lines, which played an important part in the early stages of the war. In March 1945 U.S. troops succeeded in crossing the Rhine at REMAGEN. The Rhine is famous in legend and rhyme, but it has lost much of its romantic lustre in modern times. It has suffered considerable pollution as factories along the river have dumped their waste products into the water.

Rhodes Greek island that was the medieval stronghold of the Knights of St. John of Jerusalem. Largest of the Aegean Sea's Dodecanese islands, it was taken by Italy from the Ottoman Turks in 1912 and formally ceded to GREECE in 1947.

Rhodesia (Southern Rhodesia) Now known as ZIMBABWE, this landlocked country of south-central Africa—bordered by Zambia on the north, Mozambique on the east, Botswana on the west and South Africa to the south—bore until 1980 the name of 19th-century capitalist adventurer Cecil Rhodes, who in 1890 led European and South African colonists here under the aegis of his British South Africa Company.

Rhys, Jean (Ella Gwendolwn Rees Williams) *(1890–1979)* British author. Rhys began her career as a chorus girl in London, an experience she would recount in the novel *Voyage in the Dark* (1934). In 1919 she moved to Paris and married her first husband. Her first book was *The Left Bank: Sketches and Studies of Present-Day Bohemian Paris* (1927), to which Ford Maddox FORD wrote the introduction. Her other early works include *Postures* (1928), *After Leaving Mr. Mackenzie*

(1930) and *Good Morning, Midnight* (1939). Rhys returned to England and did not write again until a radio dramatization of *Good Morning, Midnight* brought her back into the public eye. Later works include *Wide Sargasso Sea* (1966), which was set in Dominica where Rhys was born; two short story collections, *Tigers are Better Looking* (1968) and *Sleep it Off, Lady* (1976); and the unfinished autobiography *Smile Please* (1979).

Ribbentrop, Joachim von *(1893–1946)* German foreign minister (1938–45) under the Nazis. A cavalry officer during WORLD WAR I, he was later a wine merchant. He joined the Nazi Party in 1932, becoming chief foreign policy adviser to Adolf HITLER the following year. Ambassador to Great Britain from 1936 to 1938, he returned to Berlin to assume the post of foreign minister. An enthusiastic supporter of the Nazi regime, he helped to cement the Anglo-German naval agreement (1935), was influential in forming the Anglo-Berlin Axis (1936) and played a leading role in securing the NAZI-SOVIET PACT (1939). Indicted at the NUREMBERG TRIALS, he was found guilty of war crimes and hanged.

Rice, Elmer (Elmer Leopold Reizenstein) *(1892–1967)* American playwright. Rice was one of the most prolific American playwrights of the 20th century. At the peak of his fame, in the 1920s and 1930s, he was one of the leading voices in the American theater whose plays always reflected a strong concern for freedom and social justice. *The Adding Machine* (1923), which borrowed techniques from the European school of dramatic EXPRESSIONISM, concerns the plight of a futuristic protagonist, Mr. Zero, who is replaced at his job by a computer. *Street Scene* (1929), which won the PULITZER PRIZE for drama, deals with the pressures of life in a New York tenement. Rice helped to found the Dramatists' Guild in 1937 and also served during that period as a regional director for the Federal Theater Project.

Rich, Adrienne *(1929–)* American poet and feminist theorist. Born in Baltimore, she attended Radcliffe College. At first interested in an elegant precision of verse, as evidenced in her volume *A Change of World* (1951), she

American poet and feminist Adrienne Rich. c. 1977 (LIBRARY OF CONGRESS, PRINTS AND PHOTOGRAPHS DIVISION)

emerged as a poet-activist whose works have mirrored the significant social conflicts of her time and her own growth in relation to them. Her poetry has dealt with movements for black rights, against the war in Vietnam and, most significantly, with the women's movement, for which she is widely considered an articulate spokesperson. Rich mingles the personal and the feminist in poems that define the quality of women's lives in *Diving into the Wreck* (1973), winner of the 1974 National Book Award; *A Wild Patience Has Taken Me This Far* (1981); *The Dream of a Common Language* (1978); *Time's Power* (1989); and other volumes of verse. She is also the author of such essays as *On Lies, Secrets and Silence* (1979) and the powerful and candid study of motherhood, *Of Women Born* (1976). Throughout the 1990s Rich continued to publish collections of her poetry, releasing *An Atlas of the Difficult World* (1991), *Collected Early Poems 1950–1970* (1993) and *Dark Fields of the Republic* (1995). In 1993 she briefly returned to nonfiction with *What Is Found There: Notebooks on Poetry and Politics.* Four years later Rich refused to accept the National Medal for the Arts from President William Jefferson CLINTON, protesting what she denounced as his "cynical politics." Other recent awards include the Academy of American Poets Wallace Stevens Award (1997), the Lannan Foundation Lifetime Achievement Award (1999) and the Bollingen Prize for Poetry (2003).

Rich, Bernard "Buddy" *(1917–1987)* American jazz musician, often hailed as "the world's greatest drummer." He rose from his vaudeville beginnings as Baby Traps to play for the bands of Artie SHAW and Tommy DORSEY before starting his own band after WORLD WAR II. He then toured with trumpeter Harry JAMES. In 1966 he again formed his own band, with which he worked sporadically for the rest of his life. He was known not only for his virtuosic drumming but for his fiery temper and caustic wit.

Richard, Joseph Henri Maurice "Rocket" *(1921–2000)* Canadian hockey player. Known for his flashing eyes and reckless style, the Rocket was one of the most explosive goal scorers of his—or any—era. A perennial all-star at right wing, he was a Montreal Canadien for 19 seasons, and provided much of the firepower for the Canadiens' dynasty. In 1944 he scored 50 goals in 50 games, a feat that has been equaled numerically only in a post-expansion, diluted league. The team won five consecutive Stanley Cups (1956–60), and Richard finished his career with 82 playoff goals. He was named to the Hockey Hall of Fame in 1961.

Richard, Marthe *(1889–1982)* French patriot. During WORLD WAR I she was involved in dangerous espionage work behind German lines. For this she was awarded the Legion of Honor in 1933. During WORLD WAR II she ran an underground network that smuggled downed Allied fliers out of France. A member of the Paris Municipal Council in 1946, she succeeded in passing a law that closed France's bordellos. The law is still known by her name.

Richards, Sir Gordon *(1904–1986)* Britain's dominant jockey for three decades until his retirement in 1954. Richards was champion jockey 26 times and rode more than 4,800 winners, including 14 Classic races. In 1953, he rode his only Epsom Derby winner. He was also knighted that year, the only jockey to receive that honor.

Richards, I(vor) A(rmstrong) *(1893–1979)* British critic and poet. Richards was educated at Magdalene College, Cambridge, where he later became a fellow, and spent several years at Harvard teaching and studying linguistics. Richards was enormously influential on a generation of poets and critics, among them William EMPSON, who was his student at Cambridge, and he is credited with creating a receptive attitude toward MODERNISM. His insistence on careful textual study laid the groundwork for the NEW CRITICISM. Richards's critical works include *Principles of Literary Criticism* (1924), *Science and Poetry* (1926) and the seminal *Practical Criticism: A Study of Literary Judgment* (1929). His poetry was collected in *Internal Colloquies: Poems and Plays* (1972).

Richards, (Isaac) Viv(ian Alexander) *(1952–)* Antiguan cricketer. One of the greatest batsmen in cricket history, Richards is noted for his aggressive approach and masterly improvisation at the crease. Through 1990, he had represented the West Indies a record 121 times, his first selection coming in 1974. During his tenure with the team the West Indies dominated world cricket in both "tests" and "one-day" varieties. Richards scored 7,990 runs (1974–90) in test matches, including 24 centuries, one of which is the fastest of all time (56 balls v. England on April 15, 1986). He was appointed West Indies captain in 1980. Richards's success in "one-day" cricket is unparalleled. He scored the most runs (8,540), the highest individual score (189 v. England on May 31, 1984) and the most catches by a fielder (99). Richards plays for his native Antigua in West Indies domestic cricket; he has also played for Somerset and Glamorgan in England.

Richardson, Dorothy Miller *(1873–1957)* British novelist. While working as a journalist, Richardson became acquainted with H. G. WELLS, who encouraged her to write fiction. *Pointed Roofs* (1919) was the first of a series of autobiographical novels that she called *Pilgrimage;* the last volume was *March Moonlight* (1967), published posthumously. Richardson utilized the technique of STREAM OF CONSCIOUSNESS in her idiosyncratic fiction, which is written from a feminist perspective. Virginia WOOLF was an early champion of Richardson's work, and August Wilson brought about a revival of interest in it in the late 1960s.

Richardson, Sir Ralph David *(1902–1983)* Eminent British stage and film actor. His career spanned more than 60 years. He debuted as Lorenzo in *The Merchant of Venice* in 1921, then acted in modern and Shakespearean roles in provincial theaters before moving to London's West End in 1926. He was highly regarded for his portrayal of Falstaff in parts I and II of Shakespeare's *Henry IV* at London's Old Vic Theatre in the 1940s. From 1944 to 1947 he was joint director of the Old Vic, and in 1947 he was knighted for his efforts to revitalize that theater. Later in his career he received acclaim for his appearances with Sir John GIELGUD in the 1970s in David STOREY's *Home* and Harold PINTER's *No Man's Land;* he was active in the theater until the year of his death. He also made memorable screen appearances in *The Fallen Idol* (1948), *The Heiress* (1949), *Breaking the Sound Barrier* (1952) and *Doctor Zhivago* (1964). Richardson was greatly admired for his distinctive theatrical voice and his ability to combine comic eccentricity with pathos.

Richardson, Tony (Cecil Antonio Richardson) *(1928–1991)* British theatrical and film director. Richardson is one of the few directors to have scored equal successes in his theater and film work. He first came to prominence through his directorial work at the Royal Court Theatre in London in the 1950s, where he staged the premieres of two famous plays by British playwright John OSBORNE, *Look Back in Anger* (1956) and *The Entertainer* (1958), the latter starring Laurence OLIVIER. Richardson also directed an acclaimed production of *The Chairs* (1957) by French playwright Eugene IONESCO. His subsequent theatrical productions—many of which reached Broadway—included *The Seagull* (1964) by Anton CHEKHOV and Shakespeare's *Hamlet* (1969) with Nicol Williamson in the lead role. Richardson created an enduring critical and popular success with his direction of the film *Tom Jones* (1963), based on the bawdy 18th-century novel by Henry Fielding, which starred Albert FINNEY and earned four ACADEMY AWARDS.

Richberg, Donald Randall *(1881–1960)* American public official. Richberg was a Chicago attorney who specialized in railroad and labor legislation.

In 1933 he helped draft the NATIONAL INDUSTRIAL RECOVERY ACT, for which he served as adviser and chief administrator. He was the author of numerous books including *Government and Business Tomorrow* (1943) and *Labor Union Monopoly* (1957).

Richier, Germaine *(1904–1959)* French sculptor. Educated in Montpellier and Paris, she was a student of the sculptor Emile Antoine Bourdelle from 1925 to 1929 and lived in Switzerland from 1939 to 1945. Influenced by her teacher, by the SURREALIST movement as well as by the horrors of WORLD WAR II, she developed a style that employed slender, distorted figures in openwork forms that express the terrors of war and death.

Richler, Mordecai *(1931–2001)* Canadian novelist, critic and screenwriter. Highly regarded by his peers, Richler remained largely unknown to the general public. He began his career as a journalist, first in Canada, then in Paris and London. His first two novels, *The Acrobats* (1954) and *Son of a Smaller Hero* (1955), expressed the feelings of isolation of JEWS in Canada. Perhaps his best-known novel is *The Apprenticeship of Duddy Kravitz* (1959), a coming-of-age novel that is found on the reading lists of many Canadian schools. Richler's acerbic and controversial nonfiction includes *Hunting Tigers under Glass: Essays and Reports* (1969) and *Notes on an Endangered Species and Others* (1974). Other fiction includes *Cocksure* (1968) and *Joshua Then and Now: A Novel* (1980). *Perspectives on Mordecai Richler* appeared in 1986.

Richter, Burton *(1931–)* American physicist. After earning his Ph.D. from the Massachusetts Institute of Technology in 1956, Richter began his work in the physics of subatomic particles at the Stanford Linear Accelerator Center, where he designed the Stanford Positron Electron Accelerating Ring (SPEAR). In 1974, using SPEAR, Richter and his coworkers observed a new elementary particle, which they called "psi." A group of researchers under Samuel Ting at the Brookhaven Laboratory on Long Island simultaneously discovered the same particle, which they labeled "J." (It is now known as the "J/psi.") Richter and Ting shared the 1976 NOBEL PRIZE for physics.

Richter, Curt Paul *(1894–1988)* American psychobiologist credited with originating the idea of the "biological clock." The Johns Hopkins University Medical Institution, where he had been a faculty member, said that Richter had introduced the phrase in a 1927 paper on cyclical internal mechanisms. In other work, Richter demonstrated that human biology was strongly influenced by learned behavior.

Richter, Hans *(1888–1976)* German-American artist. Born in Berlin, he was involved with many of the important avant-garde movements of the early 20th century, including de STIJL, CUBISM, DADA and CONSTRUCTIVISM. In 1918 he and the Swedish painter Viking Eggeling began to create abstract paintings on scrolls, work that eventually led him to the making of abstract films such as *Rhythmus 21* (1921) The rise of Hitler caused him to flee Germany in 1932, when he settled in Switzerland. In 1945 he immigrated to the U.S., where he subsequently taught at City College in New York. Richter is best known for the film *Dreams That Money Can Buy* (1944–47), an experimental work made in collaboration with Marcel DUCHAMP, Max ERNST and Fernand LEGER that explores the fantasy lives of a number of psychiatric patients.

Richter, Karl *(1926–1981)* German conductor, harpsichordist and organist known for his interpretations of the music of Bach. Founder and director of the Munich Bach Chorus and Orchestra, he played a major role in the Bach and Handel revival in the 1950s and 1960s. Although he was not part of the early music/original instruments movements, he helped pave the way with his performances that followed the score without embellishment. He made over 100 recordings, primarily of masterworks of the Baroque period.

Richter, Sviatoslav (Stanislav Teofilovich Richter) *(1914–1997)* Soviet pianist, considered by many to be one of the greatest virtuosos of the latter half of the 20th century. Born near Kiev, Richter was raised in Odessa. He studied at the Moscow Conservatory (1937–44) under Heinrich Neuhaus. In 1940, while still a student, he gave the world premiere of Serge PROKOFIEV's Piano Sonata No. 6, to great acclaim. He was quickly recognized as a major virtuoso

pianist and as a leading interpreter of Prokofiev's piano music. His fame spread to the West, although he did not play outside the IRON CURTAIN until 1960, when he performed in Finland and North America. Richter's playing combined virtuosic technique with lyricism, although his performances were sometimes considered wayward. He received many high honors in the USSR and prizes in the West, and made numerous recordings.

Richter scale A gauge of the magnitude of an earthquake and of the energy released by it; developed in the 1930s by American seismologist Charles F. Richter. During a quake, ground motion is recorded by a seismograph; the readings are then calibrated onto the Richter scale. The numbers on the scale increase geometrically rather than arithmetically. For example, an increase from magnitude 4.0 to 5.0 means that the ground motion of the latter reading is 10 times greater. An earthquake of magnitude 2 is considered the smallest normally felt by human beings. Slight damage begins to occur from an earthquake of 3.5 magnitude, and anything over 5 is considered a serious quake. Contrary to popular assumption, the upper limit of the scale is not 10 but is theoretically infinite. However, the highest reading ever recorded is 8.9, in a quake off the coast of Japan in 1933.

Richthofen, Manfred, Baron von *(1892–1918)* German WORLD WAR I

Baron Manfred von Richthofen, the German World War I flying ace known as the "Red Baron." 1917

aviator. A master of the dogfight, he was credited with shooting down an amazing 80 Allied airplanes from 1916 to 1918. Known as the "Red Baron" for the crimson Fokker triplane he flew, the German ace was killed when his plane was shot down by Allied fire on April 21, 1918. Von Richthofen's sister Frieda was married to the English novelist D. H. LAWRENCE.

Rickenbacker, Edward Vernon "Eddie" *(1890–1973)* American aviator, business executive. At the age of 16, young Rickenbacker was a well-known auto racer, setting several speed records. Volunteering for the American Air Force, he became America's most celebrated aviation ace in WORLD WAR I by destroying 26 German aircraft. He received the Congressional Medal of Honor. Gaining experience as an executive of several commercial airline companies, he became president of Eastern Airlines (1938), which he built into one of the most important airlines in the country. In 1942 he was appointed special representative of the secretary of war to inspect air bases in the Pacific theater of war. His B-17 was shot down while over the Pacific, and Rickenbacker survived on a raft for 22 days; he wrote about this experience in his book *Seven Came Through* (1943).

American flying ace Capt. Edward Rickenbacker. 1919 (LIBRARY OF CONGRESS, PRINTS AND PHOTOGRAPHS DIVISION)

Rickey, Branch (Wesley Branch Rickey) *(1881–1965)* American baseball executive. Rickey had a relatively undistinguished career as a catcher for the St. Louis Browns and the New York Yankees before becoming a coach for the Browns. He was named president of the St. Louis Cardinals organization in 1917, and in 1920 he began a number of farm teams for the Cardinals, a system that became standard in major-league baseball. As general manager for the Brooklyn Dodgers (1942–50), Rickey became famous for ending segregation in big league baseball by hiring Jackie ROBINSON in 1947. General manager for the Pittsburgh Pirates from 1950 to 1955, he was posthumously (1967) voted into the Baseball Hall of Fame.

Rickey, George *(1907–2002)* American sculptor. Born in South Bend, Indiana, he moved to Scotland at the age of six. He studied widely, notably at Oxford, the Academie Andre Lhote in Paris and New York University, and met many of the leading figures of the European modernist movements. Returning to the U.S. in 1930, he became a teacher and concentrated on painting, turning mainly to sculpture in 1950. Rickey was a leading figure in the "kinetic art" movement. His mature work, executed in metal, is CONSTRUCTIVIST in emphasis and employs geometrical forms and blades that move gently in response to air currents. He was especially noted for his large architectural works, such as his commission for the Lincoln Center for the Performing Arts in New York City.

Rickover, Hyman George *(1900–1986)* U.S. admiral; father of the nuclear navy. Born in Makow, Russia (now a part of Poland), Rickover immigrated to the U.S. in 1916 and graduated from the U.S. Naval Academy in 1922. During WORLD WAR II, he served as head of the electrical section of the U.S. Navy's Bureau of Ships. In 1946, he was assigned to the atomic submarine project at Oak Ridge, Tennessee, where he played a crucial role in convincing the navy that nuclear sea power was both feasible and militarily essential. He directed the planning and building of the world's first nuclear-powered ship, the NAUTILUS, which was launched in 1954. Promoted to rear admiral in 1953, vice admiral in 1958 and admiral in 1973, he retired in 1982.

Riddle, Nelson (Nelson Smock Riddle) *(1921–1985)* American bandleader, composer and arranger. Riddle became well known in the 1950s for his song orchestrations for Frank SINATRA. His distinctive arrangements, which borrowed elements from JAZZ and BIG BAND music, were known for their smooth and dusky sound. Among his original compositions was the theme for the 1960s television series *Route 66* and the 1975 Academy Award–winning score for *The Great Gatsby*. In 1983 he collaborated with Linda RONSTADT on the album *What's New?*, which sold more than 3.5 million copies.

Ride, Sally *(1951–)* U.S. astronaut; a much-publicized space traveler when, as the first American woman in space, she made her historic U.S. space shuttle flight aboard STS-7 (June 18–24, 1983). After a second flight aboard U.S. space shuttle mission 41-G (October 5–13, 1984), the publicity-shy Ride moved to the administrative end of NASA and was instrumental in issuing the so-called Ride Report in 1987, which recommended future directions and missions for the space program, including renewed development of lunar flights, an eventual lunar base and manned missions to Mars. Ride retired from NASA in August 1987 to become a research fellow at Stanford University. In 1989 Dr. Ride accepted positions on the faculty of the University of California at San Diego, as well as that university's California Space Institute, in an effort to encourage more female scientists and engineers to consider careers in space-related fields.

Ridgway, Matthew Bunker *(1895–1993)* U.S. Army general. Born in Fort Monroe, Virginia, Ridgway attended West Point, graduating in 1917. In June 1942, Ridgway succeeded General Omar BRADLEY as commander of the 82nd Infantry Division, elements of which engaged in the invasion of Sicily, the attack on Salerno and the invasion of NORMANDY. In August 1944, Ridgway assumed command of the XVIII Airborne Corps, whose troops played an important role in the BATTLE OF THE BULGE. During the KOREAN WAR, Ridgway was appointed commander of the Eighth Army in December 1950, and was credited with revitalizing that force; in the following April he replaced

General Douglas MACARTHUR as commander of the United Nations forces in Korea. In 1953, Ridgway was made chief of staff of the army; he retired in 1955.

Ridley, Sir Harold *(1906–2001)* British ophthalmic surgeon. During WORLD WAR II (1939–45), Ridley became famous for his ability to treat the eye injuries sustained by British pilots in the Royal Air Force (RAF). During his efforts to treat these injuries and ailments, Ridley began to theorize that injured eye lenses could recover more quickly if surgeons implanted a synthetic lens within the eye tissues to prevent the formation of scar tissue and the creation of cataracts. When the war ended, Ridley began a collaboration with John Pike and John Holt, both optometrists, to develop such an artificial lens. By 1949 they had designed a lens made out of transpex and developed a technique for implanting an intra-ocular lens (IOL), a foreign object that prevents the formation of cataracts on eyes. Though initially viewed with serious skepticism by optometrists in Britain and elsewhere, the procedure and the foreign agent became widely accepted by the 1970s. For his contribution to optometry, Ridley was elected to the Royal Society of England as a fellow in 1986. In 2000 Ridley was knighted by Queen Elizabeth II.

Riefenstahl, Leni *(1902–2003)* German movie director and actress. Noted primarily as a director of Nazi PROPAGANDA films, Riefenstahl began her career as an actress in such films as *The Holy Mountain* (1927) and *The White Frenzy* (1931). She formed her own production company in 1932 and directed her first film, *The Blue Light,* that same year. From 1933 to 1938 she directed and produced a number of propaganda films for Adolf HITLER, whom she greatly admired. Her masterpiece, *Triumph of the Will* (1934), is arguably the most powerful propaganda film ever made. *Olympia* (1938), a two-part documentary film of the 1936 Berlin OLYMPICS, is another of her films. Blacklisted by the Allies at the end of WORLD WAR II, she did not work again until 1952 when she directed *Tiefland.* Ironically, in the 1970s and 1980s she won new fame for her photographs of primitive peoples.

Riegel, Byron *(1906–1975)* American biologist and pathologist. Riegel was a pioneer in steroid chemistry. He led the research team that developed the first oral contraceptive. He was considered an authority on vitamin K and drugs related to anticancer and antimalarial agents.

Rietveld, Gerrit Thomas *(1888–1964)* Dutch furniture designer and architect. Born in Utrecht, he was the son of a cabinetmaker, who began designing furniture as a youth and also studied architecture. As a designer, his piece de resistance was his red-blue wooden armchair of 1918, a work that revolutionized furniture design with its angular forms and openwork patterns and that greatly influenced later BAUHAUS designs. From 1919 to 1931 he was a member of de STIJL and contributed a number of articles to its eponymous magazine. His most notable architectural achievement was the 1924 Schroder House in Utrecht, a three-dimensional expression of de Stijl aesthetics that is closely related to the work of Piet MONDRIAN. Rietveld was a founding member of the International Congress of Modern Architecture in 1928 and thereafter continued to work in architecture and furniture design, producing his celebrated zigzag chair in 1934. During the postwar de Stijl revival of the 1950s, he also executed a number of important architectural projects, notably the Otterlo sculpture pavilion (1954).

Rif War of 1919–26 (Abd el-Krim's Revolt) In 1919 the Spanish possessions in northern Morocco were being attacked in two sectors: in the east by the Rif (Riff), Muslim Berber tribes under chieftain ABD EL-KRIM, and in the west by Moroccans under the brigand Ahmed ibn-Muhammad Raisuli. The Spanish high commissioner of Morocco, Damaso Berenguer, achieved success against Raisuli, but General Fernandez Silvestre met disaster at the hands of Abd el-Krim. Silvestre and some 12,000 Spanish troops (out of a total of 20,000) were slain by the Rif at the Battle of Anual on July 21, 1921. This forced Spain's withdrawal from the eastern sector, where Abd el-Krim set up the "Republic of the Rif," with himself as president, and prepared to drive out the French and control all of Morocco.

With a well-equipped force of 20,000 Rif, he moved south and captured many French blockhouses on the way to Fez in 1925. The French and Spanish, putting aside their rivalry in Morocco, formed an alliance to counter Abd el-Krim. Spain's dictator Miguel PRIMO DE RIVERA personally led a large Spanish-French expeditionary force, which landed at Alhucemas Bay on Morocco's Mediterranean coast in September 1925, and began advancing on Abd el-Krim's headquarters, Targuist. From the south a 160,000-man French army led by Marshal Henri P. PETAIN moved rapidly northward, squeezing the fiercely fighting Rif troops into the area north of Taza (1925). Faced with defeat by superior forces, Abd el-Krim surrendered on May 26, 1926; he was exiled to the island of Reunion. At a Paris conference (June 16–July 10, 1926), France and Spain restored the borders of their Moroccan zones, which had been set by a 1912 treaty.

Riggs, Bobby *(1918–1995)* American tennis player and self-proclaimed male chauvinist. While Riggs will remain in the tennis record books for such feats as his 1939 sweep of the Wimbledon singles, doubles and mixed doubles championships, he will be remembered for the challenge he posed to women's tennis in the early 1970s. He claimed that women's tennis was a sham, and that no female player could beat him. His claim seemed to hold up as the first to respond to his challenge, Margaret Court (see Margaret Court SMITH), went down 6–2, 6–1 to the 55-year-old Riggs. Riggs's 1973 match at the Houston Astrodome with the best player in women's tennis, Billie Jean KING, became a publicity extravaganza, televised nationwide to an audience of 50 million. In a triumph for "women's lib," King defeated Riggs 6–4, 6–3, 6–3. In 1995 Riggs died of cancer.

Riis, Jacob *(1849–1914)* Danish-American journalist and social reformer. Born in Ribe, Denmark, he immigrated to the U.S. in 1870. Seven years later he became a police reporter for the *New York Tribune,* working there until 1888, when he joined the staff of the *Evening Sun,* where he was a reporter until 1899. His stories and photographs of the wretched lives faced by immigrants on New York's Lower East Side were extremely important in raising the consciousness of the U.S. and in provoking legislation to improve conditions. He again wrote of these squalid living conditions in his book *How the Other Half Lives* (1890), which was followed by other volumes including *The Children of the Poor* (1892), *Children of the Tenements* (1903) and *Neighbors: Life Stories of the Other Half* (1914). Riis captured the attention of Theodore ROOSEVELT, with whom he founded a New York settlement house, and whom he profiled in *Theodore Roosevelt the Citizen* (1904). His autobiography, *The Making of an American*, was published in 1901.

Rijksmuseum Dutch national museum, located in Amsterdam. An institution of international repute, it originated as the Great Royal Museum founded by Louis Napoleon Bonaparte in 1808, was renamed and moved to the Trippenhuis in 1815 and opened in its present quarters designed by P. J. H. Cuypers in 1885. The museum is famous for its superb collection of 17th-century Dutch paintings by such masters as Frans Hals, Jan Vermeer and Rembrandt. It also has a fine selection of Dutch primitives and landscapes. The Rijksmuseum boasts an excellent collection of European sculpture and is renowned for its drawings and prints, including one of the world's greatest representations of Rembrandt's graphic work.

Rilke, Rainer Maria *(1875–1926)* Czech-born poet, novelist, story writer and essayist. Rilke is the most beloved and critically esteemed German-language poet of the 20th century. Two of his poetical works, the *Duino Elegies* (1922) and the *Sonnets to Orpheus* (1922)—both written while Rilke was living in a small stone tower in Muzot, Switzerland—are regarded as masterpieces both in terms of their lyrical beauty and their spiritual insight.

Rilke was born in Prague in 1875. After an unhappy stint in the military school to which he was sent by his parents, Rilke avoided formal education but steeped himself deeply in all areas of the humanities. His first poems and stories appeared in the 1890s. The novella *The Lay of the Love and Death of Cornet Christoph Rilke* (1899) is a major work of this period. In 1901 he mar-

ried Clara Westhoff. Together with their daughter Ruth, they moved to Paris in 1902, where both husband and wife studied with the sculptor Auguste Rodin. The marriage did not last, and Rilke sought out solitude for the remaining decades of his life. His *New Poems* (1907, 1908) influenced an entire generation of German poets. During WORLD WAR I Rilke briefly served as an office bureaucrat for the German army. In 1919 he moved to Switzerland, where he lived for the remainder of his life. His *Letters to a Young Poet* (1934) remains a popular inspirational work.

Rin-Tin-Tin *(?–1932)* Saved from a World War I trench by American captain Lee Duncan, Rin-Tin-Tin went on to become the preeminent animal star of the silent movie period. Duncan brought the male German shepherd to HOLLYWOOD, and in 1922 the dog appeared in his first feature, *The Man from Hell's River*. Throughout the 1920s, Rin-Tin-Tin was WARNER BROS.' biggest star, and his popularity continued until his death in 1932. Another Rin-Tin-Tin starred in a television series of that title in the 1950s.

Riopelle, Jean-Paul *(1923–2002)* Canadian painter. Born in Montreal, he was Canada's leading abstract painter. Associated with the modernist *automatiste* group in Montreal, he settled in Paris in 1947. There he created a totally nonrepresentational style, painting monumental canvases of mosaiclike strokes executed in vibrant jewellike color. He is known for his oil paintings and for works in such media as ink, pastel and watercolor.

Ripken, Cal, Jr. *(1960–)* American professional baseball player (1978–2001), and holder of the longest streak of consecutive games played in Major League Baseball (MLB) at 2,632. Born in Havre de Grace, Maryland, Ripken joined the Baltimore Orioles in 1978, joined the Orioles' roster in the 1981 season and won the American League (AL) Rookie of the Year Award for his performance that year. By 1983, Ripken led the AL in runs scored (121), hits (211), and doubles (47), appeared in the 1983 All-Star Game and won the AL Most Valuable Player (MVP) Award. Between 1983 and 2001, Ripken was

selected for every All-Star Game, winning the MVP award for that exhibition in 1991 and 2001. During his career, Ripken became best known for his consistent appearance in the Orioles lineup. On September 6, 1995, he broke the record of 2,130 consecutive starts set by Lou Gehrig in the 1939 season. On the baseball field, Ripken was also famous for his near flawless performance as a shortstop: such as during his 1990 season, when he made only three errors in 680 attempts. At the end of the 1991 season, Ripken won another MVP award with a record of a .323 batting average, 34 home runs and 114 runs batted in (RBIs). Although Ripken's defensive performance declined in the mid-1990s, causing him to be shifted from shortstop to third base, he continued to appear in the Orioles' lineup and in All-Star games. On September 20, 1998, Ripken ended his streak of consecutive appearances in the Orioles' lineup when he asked to be benched. Ripken retired at the end of the 2001 season. In addition to his consecutive appearance record, Ripken holds the career record for the number of home runs hit by a shortstop (431).

Ripley, Elmer Horton *(1891–1982)* American basketball star and coach. Ripley was a leading professional player (1908–30) in the early years of the sport. From 1922 to 1953 he coached some of the top college teams, including Yale, Columbia, Notre Dame and Army, bringing Yale the Ivy League championship in the 1932–33 season. He later coached the Harlem Globetrotters (1953–56), the Israeli Olympic team (1956) and the Canadian Olympic team (1960). He was inducted into the Basketball Hall of Fame in 1972.

Rite of Spring, The *(Le Sacre du Printemps)* One of the most famous and (in its day) notorious of all modern ballets. First produced by the BALLETS RUSSES it was a collaboration among some of the greatest figures of the contemporary ballet stage, composer Igor STRAVINSKY, impresario Serge DIAGHILEV and choreographer/dancer Vaslav NIJINSKY. The premiere at the Théâtre des Champs-Elysées in Paris on May 29, 1913, created a veritable riot. Such an uproar arose from an outraged audience that Nijinsky fled to the wings and conductor Pierre MONTEUX could not hear the orchestra. The ballet's "pictures of pagan Russia" began with a series of primitive fertility rites connected with the advent of spring and concluded with a sacrificial ritual in which a chosen virgin literally dances herself to death. It was shocking stuff, all right; but that initial notoriety was amplified by the choreography and music. The movements of the dancers were heavy, lumpy and earth-bound. The Stravinsky music was insistently percussive and dissonant, the rhythms erratic and unpredictable. "The end of the music was greeted by the arrival of gendarmes," Monteux wrote of the premiere. "Stravinsky had disappeared through a window backstage, to wander disconsolately along the streets of Paris." Quickly the music world recovered itself and the ballet was readily accepted in Diaghilev's 1920 version with choreography by Leonide MASSINE. Although there are frequent revivals worldwide, the ballet is best known through the concert suite by Stravinsky. Moviegoers remember it as a sequence in Walt DISNEY's *Fantasia* where the music, rearranged and altered, accompanied the ponderous lumberings of gigantic dinosaurs. It was only an animated cartoon, but Stravinsky purportedly wept. Today *The Rite of Spring* is a staple of the orchestral repertoire, and there are numerous recorded versions, including one conducted by Stravinsky himself.

Ritsos, Yannis (1909–1990) Greek poet. After the defeat of the Greeks by the Turks in the GRECO-TURKISH WAR OF 1921–22, Ritsos's wealthy family suffered financial ruin. His mother and brother died of tuberculosis, and his father and sister became insane. His personal tragedies were intensified by social problems in Greece. Ritsos embraced socialism and looked toward the Soviet Union. In 1936 one of his most famous poems, "Epitaphios," was included in a public book burning by the Metaxas dictatorship. In 1948 he was exiled to a camp in the Greek islands. His books were banned until 1954. After the GREEK COLONELS' coup d'état in 1967 he was again deported; even after his release from the camps, he was kept under house arrest and his works banned until 1972. Ritsos was a prolific writer, and his works have

been translated into dozens of languages. The poems, set to music by Mikis Theodorakis, became an anthem for progressive forces in Greece.

Rivera, Diego (1886–1957) Mexican painter. The foremost modern Mexican muralist was born at Guanajuato and studied with the popular painter José Guadalupe Posada and other Mexican artists. Traveling in Europe from 1907 to 1910 and 1911 to 1921, he was influenced by the work of such Old Masters as Giotto, El Greco and Goya as well as by his friendships with Cézanne and PICASSO. In Europe he also became politicized, deciding that art should be created for the masses and preferably be situated on the walls of public buildings. He returned to Mexico in 1921 to paint the murals about which he had philosophized, exploring the history and social struggles of his native land in bold figurative images. Murals from this period include those in the Ministry of Education in Mexico City and the Agricultural School in Chilpancingo. Visiting Moscow from 1927 to 1928, he was inspired to even greater revolutionary fervor, returning to paint such overtly ideological murals as those at the National Palace (1929–55) and the Palace of Cortes, Cuernavaca (1929–30). His works in the U.S. include frescoes in the San Francisco Stock Exchange (1931), murals of industrial America in the Detroit Institute of Arts and a mural in ROCKEFELLER CENTER, New York City, the latter destroyed by its sponsors because it included a portrait of LENIN. Drawing on archaeological and folk sources, boldly linear and richly colored, Rivera created an indigenous style that has enormously influenced his country's art and gained him an international reputation.

Rivers, Thomas Milton (1888–1962) American virologist. A graduate of Emory College (1909) and Johns Hopkins (1915), Rivers began research in 1918 on a form of pneumonia that accompanied measles. Working with the Rockefeller Institute for Medical Research (1937–55), he performed pioneer viral research on flu, chicken pox and polio and managed the research projects leading to the SALK antipolio vaccines.

RKO Radio Pictures, Inc. One of Hollywood's "Big Five" production/exhibition motion picture studios (along with METRO-GOLDWYN-MAYER, 20TH CENTURY-FOX, PARAMOUNT PICTURES and WARNER BROS.). It was the only major studio born directly out of the TALKING PICTURE revolution. RKO's roots were in the Film Booking Office (FBO) of America, a small production/distribution company whose chief star was Strongheart the Dog. In 1926 Joseph P. KENNEDY acquired FBO and joined forces a year later with David SARNOFF, the president of Radio Corporation of America (RCA). Sarnoff needed a showcase for his new optical sound system, trademarked "Photophone." Theaters controlled by the vaudeville circuit of Keith-Albee-Orpheum were added to the conglomerate in 1928. The giant $300 million corporation was named the Radio-Keith-Orpheum Corporation and the famous radio tower adopted as its logograph. In 1931 David O. SELZNICK became production chief, but after a series of notable releases, including *What Price Hollywood?* (1932), *A Bill of Divorcement* (1932) and *King Kong* (1933), he was replaced by Merian C. Cooper in 1933. Less stable than its competitors, RKO remained in a perpetual state of chaos the rest of its corporate life. A succession of studio heads came and went, including B. B. Kahane, Samuel Briskin, Pandro S. Berman and tycoon Howard HUGHES. The Hughes years sowed the seeds of the studio's downfall with aborted projects, disastrous releases such as *The Conqueror* (1956) and general corporate disarray. Hughes sold the studio to General Teleradio, Inc., in 1955, which in turn released the film library to television. In 1957 Desilu Productions bought the RKO lot for its television production. Despite its checkered history, RKO is remembered for a splendidly diverse output. The ASTAIRE/ROGERS musicals, from *Flying Down to Rio* (1933) to *The Story of Vernon and Irene Castle* (1939), were some of the brightest films of the 1930s. During the WORLD WAR II years a remarkable series of horror films emerged from the Val Lewton unit, including *The Cat People* (1943) and *The Body Snatcher* (1944). The immediate postwar years saw several notable films under the short-lived tutelage of production chief Dore SCHARY—*Crossfire* (1947), *They Live by Night* (1947) and

Out of the Past (1947). A number of important stars and filmmakers built their reputations at the studio—Orson WELLES, George CUKOR, Katharine HEPBURN, composer Max STEINER, Edward Dmytryk, Robert MITCHUM and many others. RKO remains in existence as a corporate entity of General Tire, RKO General Inc. It has abandoned the motion picture field in favor of broadcasting and cable television.

Robbe-Grillet, Alain *(1922–)* French novelist and literary critic. Robbe-Grillet is best known as the foremost theoretician and practitioner of the NOUVEAU ROMAN. His approach to the novel, as outlined in his critical work *For a New Novel: Essays on Fiction* (1963), is to adjure standard dramatic plotting and psychological analysis of character in favor of flat, nonjudgmental depictions of the random events of everyday reality. Life, according to Robbe-Grillet, is neither overtly meaningful nor patently absurd but rather simply is. Novels by Robbe-Grillet include *The Erasers* (1953), *Jealousy* (1957), *In the Labyrinth* (1959) and *Recollections of the Gold Triangle* (1978). His novels influenced the directors of the French cinematic nouvelle vague of the 1960s, especially Alain RESNAIS. Robbe-Grillet wrote the screenplay for Resnais's *Last Year in Marienbad* (1961). In 1996 he wrote and directed the film *The Blue Villa*. He was elected to the Académie Francaise in 2004.

Robbins, Fredrick Chapman *(1916–2003)* American virologist and pediatrician. Having earned his M.D. at Harvard, Robbins practiced at Children's Hospital, Boston, for two years prior to joining the army. During WORLD WAR II he served in the Mediterranean Theater where he was chief of the viral and rickettsial section of the 15th Medical General Laboratory. Joining J. F. ENDERS and T. H. Weller (1948) in research at Children's Hospital, he helped produce polio cultures that led to new vaccines, diagnostic techniques and identification of other viruses. In 1954 he shared the NOBEL PRIZE in physiology and medicine with Enders and Weller for breeding the poliomyelitis virus in tissue culture.

Robbins, Harold *(1916–1997)* American novelist. Robbins is known for his many best-selling novels, which are rife with sex and violence and the conflicts of the wealthy and glamorous. Robbins's first novel, *Never Love a Stranger* (1948), drew on his own experiences as an orphan on the streets of New York and created controversy with its graphic sexuality. Of his many works, perhaps most acclaimed was *A Stone for Danny Fisher* (1951). Other titles include *The Carpetbaggers* (1961), *The Betsy* (1971) and *Piranha* (1986). Several of his books have been adapted into films.

Robbins, Jerome *(1918–1998)* American dancer, choreographer and director. One of the foremost choreographers for the American musical theater and classical ballet, Robbins began his career as a dancer in Broadway musicals (1938–40). He joined the AMERICAN BALLET THEATRE in 1940 and choreographed his first ballet, *Fancy Free,* for that company (1944). His successful adaptation of this ballet to a musical comedy, *On the Town* (with Betty COMDEN and Adolph Green), led to his choreographing the shows *Billion Dollar Baby* (1946) and *High Button Shoes* (1947). During his long association with the NEW YORK CITY BALLET, he was associate artistic director (1949–59) and joint ballet master-in-chief (1983–89), and choreographed such works as *Afternoon of a Fawn* (1953) and *Dances at a Gathering* (1969) for the company. In 1957 he collaborated with Leonard BERNSTEIN to create the landmark musical *West Side Story,* and won two ACADEMY AWARDS for the film version (1962). He also directed and choreographed many other Broadway musicals, including *The King and I* (1951), *Peter Pan* (1954), *Funny Girl* (1964) and *Fiddler on the Roof* (1964), and toured Europe with his own company, Ballets: USA, in 1958 and 1961. On July 29, 1998, Robbins died following complications arising from a massive stroke.

Robbins, Lionel Charles *(1898–1984)* One of the most distinguished British economists of the 20th century. Although initially conservative, he later embraced the liberal theories of John Maynard KEYNES. Robbins served with Keynes on the British delegation to the BRETTON WOODS CONFERENCE that set post-World War II monetary policy. He wrote several books; *An Essay on the Nature and Significance of Economic Science* (1935) was considered the most influential. In the early 1960s he headed a committee on higher education; the **Robbins Report** (1963) had a major effect on expanding the British college and university system. Robbins taught at the London School of Economics (1929–61).

Roberts, Elizabeth Madox *(1881–1941)* American novelist. Born in Perryville, Kentucky, she attended the University of Chicago. She began her literary career as a poet but is remembered primarily for her movingly accurate portraits of life in rural Kentucky told in a language that recalls poetry in its lyricism and rhythmic beauty. Her novels include *The Time of Man* (1923), *Jingling in the Wing* (1928), *The Great Meadow* (1930) and *Black Is My Truelove's Hair* (1938). Roberts also wrote a number of volumes of short stories.

Roberts, Owen J. *(1875–1955)* Associate justice, U.S. Supreme Court (1930–45). An honors graduate of the University of Pennsylvania and its law school, Roberts became an assistant attorney general after a brief time in private law practice. He returned to private practice, building a successful corporate law practice. He interrupted his private career twice, once as a special attorney general in Philadelphia and later in Washington, D.C., investigating the corruption in the Harding administration. Roberts was appointed to the U.S. Supreme Court in 1930 by President Herbert HOOVER and continued to serve throughout Franklin D. ROOSEVELT's administrations. Although a conservative Republican, Roberts wrote a number of groundbreaking opinions, including the opinion in *Cantwell v. Connecticut* (1940) that set aside on First Amendment grounds a Connecticut conviction for preaching in public. In *Wickard v. Filburn* (1942), he expanded federal regulation of interstate commerce by upholding the regulation of grain grown within one state. He dissented in *KOREMATSU V. UNITED STATES*, which upheld the detention of JAPANESE AMERICANS during World War II. After his resignation from the Court in 1945, Roberts became dean of the University of Pennsylvania law school and remained active in public life until his death.

Roberts, Richard *(1911–1980)* American nuclear physicist and microbiologist. Roberts was the principal contributor to the discovery of delayed neutrons, the basis for atomic reactors. His experiments with electronic vacuum tubes aided in the construction of the proximity fuse, a bomb-detonating device that was of important use in WORLD WAR II. As a microbiologist, he discovered the key chemical synthetic processes by which cell duplication occurred.

Robertson, Oscar (*1938– *) American basketball player. In high school, Robertson led his team to a 45-game winning streak. The first college player ever to be named player of the year for three consecutive years, he was drafted in 1960 by the Cincinnati Royal of the National Basketball Association. Before beginning his pro career, he was cocaptain of the U.S. gold medal Olympic team. He remained in Cincinnati for 10 years, where his playmaking as a guard made him an all-star for virtually the entire decade (1961–69), and led the league in assists seven times. Robertson finished his career in Milwaukee and retired with totals of 26,710 points, 9,887 rebounds and 2,931 assists. Robertson's impressive career statistics with the Royal and the Bucks led to his 1980 induction into the Basketball Hall of Fame. In 1996, the 50th anniversary of the establishment of the NBA, Robertson was designated one of the 50 greatest players in the history of that organization.

Robeson, Paul (*1898–1976*) American singer, actor and political activist.

American performer and political activist Paul Robeson (LIBRARY OF CONGRESS, PRINTS AND PHOTOGRAPHS DIVISION)

Born in Princeton, New Jersey, the son of a minister who had been a slave, Robeson began his distinguished career as a scholar-athlete at Rutgers University, then attended Columbia University Law School, graduating in 1923. While practicing law he first became involved in the theater and soon left the legal world to devote himself to acting. Becoming associated with the PROVINCETOWN PLAYERS in 1924, he won acclaim for his performances in a number of plays by Eugene O'NEILL, highlighted by his creation of the title role in *Emperor Jones* (1925; film, 1933). Robeson also used his magnificent bass-baritone voice in concert performances, making his debut in 1925. Performing in Jerome KERN's SHOW BOAT (1928; film, 1936), he created a sensation with his rendition of "Ol' Man River." He was also famous for his interpretations of spirituals and for his performances of songs in over 20 languages. As an actor, he was particularly noted for his performance of the title role in *Othello* (London, 1930; Broadway, 1943–45). Throughout his life Robeson championed leftist causes, calling for uncompromising civil rights and lauding the USSR as a friend to black people. These stands brought him into conflict with the prevailing anticommunism of the late 1940s and 1950s. A controversial figure, Robeson was blacklisted, denied a passport (1950) and brought before the HOUSE UN-AMERICAN ACTIVITIES COMMITTEE (1956). When his passport was renewed in 1958, he left the country, lived in the USSR and Europe, and returned to the U.S. in 1963. His final years were spent in seclusion.

Robinson, Bill ("Bojangles") (*1878–1949*) American dancer. Perhaps the best known tap dancer the U.S. ever produced, he began performing in night clubs and eventually reached the Broadway stage. Moving on to HOLLYWOOD, Robinson made a total of 14 films. Among the most successful were those in which he starred with Shirley TEMPLE, including *The Little Colonel* and *The Littlest Rebel* (both 1935) and *Rebecca of Sunnybrook Farm* (1938). Famed for his grace, showmanship, inventiveness and versatility, as well as for his sheer endurance, Robinson continued dancing well into his mid-60s, becoming the model for several new generations of American tap dancers.

Robinson, Brooks (*1937– *) American baseball player. One of the premier third basemen ever to play the game, Brooks Robinson was an All-Star in 15 of the 23 seasons he played for the Baltimore Orioles. A 16-time Gold Glove, he still holds virtually every fielding record for third basemen, including putouts, assists and fielding percentage. He finished his career with a .263 batting average, finishing over .300 only once, in 1964. That year he was named the American League's most valuable player, with 28 home runs and 118 runs batted in. Robinson retired in 1975 and went on to become an Orioles' broadcaster. He was inducted into the Baseball Hall of Fame in 1983.

Robinson, Edward G. (*1893–1973*) American film actor. Born Emanual Goldenberg in Bucharest, Romania, he emigrated to the U.S. at the age of nine and grew up on New York City's Lower East Side. Attending the American Academy of Dramatic Arts, he began his acting career in 1913. Robinson made his Hollywood mark as the quintessential gangster. His first such role was in a Broadway play, *The Racket* (1927), but he soon made his way to the West Coast. In 1930 he established himself as king of the tough guys with his portrayal of Rico Bandello in *Little Caesar* (1930). Robinson's other movies included *A Slight Case of Murder* (1938), *Double Indemnity* (1944) and *Key Largo* (1948). He also played character roles in such films as the biographical *Dr. Ehrlich's Magic Bullet* (1940) and the psychological drama *The Woman in the Window* (1944). His last part was a supporting role in *Soylent Green* (1973).

Robinson, Edwin Arlington (*1869–1935*) American poet. Born in Head Tide, Maine, and educated at Harvard, he is a major figure in the poetry of the U.S. He was intimately acquainted with the residents of his hometown of Gardner, Maine, eventually transmuting it into the "Tilbury Town" of his early verse. The inhabitants of this small fictional hamlet were the subject of the brief and telling psychological portraits that are Robinson's best-remembered poems. These include "Miniver Cheevy," "Richard Cory" and "Luke Havergal." Virtually unknown at the beginning of his career, he published his first volume of verse, *The Torrent and the Night Before* (1896), at his own expense. A shy, reclusive figure, he moved to New York City in 1899 and lived in some financial difficulty until President Theodore ROOSEVELT, an early admirer, secured him a position at the New York customs house (1905–09). With the publication of *The Man Against the Sky* (1916), he achieved significant critical acclaim and thereafter was able to support himself through writing. Deeply serious and often symbolic, his later volumes include such long narrative poems as *Avon's Harvest* (1921), the PULITZER PRIZE–winning *The Man Who Died Twice* (1924) and *Amaranth* (1934) as well as such lengthy Arthurian tales as *Lancelot* (1920) and *Tristram* (1928), also awarded a Pulitzer Prize.

Robinson, Frank *(1935–)* American baseball player. Frank Robinson began his career in left field with the Cincinnati Reds in 1956. That year he was named to the All-Star team and was rookie of the year. He remained with the Reds for the next 10 seasons, and was named most valuable player a second time before being traded to the Baltimore Orioles. Robinson responded by leading the Orioles to a pennant and a World Series title in 1966, as he took the batting title with a .317 average and 49 home runs. He was traded to the Los Angeles Dodgers in 1970 and to the California Angels the following year, and in 1975 became playing manager of the Cleveland Indians. He retired as a player in 1976 and went on to coach for a number of teams before returning to the Orioles as a coach in 1986. He was named manager of that club in 1988. He was elected to the Hall of Fame in 1982. Robinson left the Orioles in 1991, but returned to baseball in 2002 as manager of the Montreal Expos.

Robinson, Jackie (John Roosevelt Robinson) *(1919–1972)* American baseball player. In the spring of 1947, baseball changed forever when Branch RICKEY signed Jackie Robinson to a Brooklyn Dodgers contract. The first black to play in the Major Leagues, Robinson's competitive drive and personal pride helped carry him through a rookie year filled with taunts and difficulties. Named rookie of the year, he spent 10 more seasons in the Dodger infield. His hitting and base running helped bring the team six league championships and a World Series championship. Robinson's best year,

1949, saw him hit .342 and steal 37 bases, making him the league leader in both categories as well as being named most valuable player. After his retirement in 1956, Robinson devoted himself to political and CIVIL RIGHTS work. He was named to the Baseball Hall of Fame in 1962.

Robinson, Joan (Joan Maurice) *(1903–1983)* British economist. A socialist, Robinson taught at Cambridge University from 1931 to 1971. She collaborated with John Maynard KEYNES, helping him formulate the theory of full employment. She questioned traditional economic assumptions and made significant contributions to theories of international trade and the economics of growth and development.

Robinson, Lennox (Esme Stuart Lennox Robinson) *(1886–1958)* Irish playwright. Robinson is known for his many varied patriotic dramas and comedies depicting Irish life. These include *The Clancy Name* (1911), *Patriots* (1912) and *Church Street* (1955). A friend of W. B. YEATS, Robinson was manager of the ABBEY THEATRE and in 1923 became its director, which he remained until his death. He was coeditor of *The Oxford Book of Irish Verse* (1958) and wrote *The Irish Theatre* (1939) and *Ireland's Abbey Theatre. A History* (1951).

Robinson, Rubye Doris Smith *(1942–1967)* American CIVIL RIGHTS activist. As a sophomore at Spelman College in 1960, she joined a sit-in campaign and helped found the Student Nonviolent Coordinating Committee (SNCC). In 1963 she became administrative assistant to SNCC executive secretary James Forman, and until 1967 served as SNCC's main administrative and logistical planner. By 1964 she had begun advocating black African nationalism and a greater say by women within the SNCC. In 1966 she became the SNCC's executive secretary, supporting the BLACK POWER movement launched in 1966 by James MEREDITH and Stokely CARMICHAEL.

Robinson, Sugar Ray (Walker Smith) *(1920–1989)* Five-time world champion middleweight boxer. Many boxing experts believe that, "pound for pound," he was the best boxer ever. During a career that lasted from 1940

to 1965, he posted a record of 175 wins (with 110 knockouts) and 19 losses (with only one knockout). He was noted for his boxing artistry and his knockout skills. He won the world welterweight championship in 1946 and the middleweight championship in a bout with Jake LaMotta in 1951. Although he lost the middleweight title several times, he regained the crown with fights against Randy Turpin (1951), Carl (Bobo) Olson (1955), Gene Fullmer (1957) and Carmen Basilio (1958). He was elected to the Boxing Hall of Fame in 1967. In his last years he suffered from Alzheimer's disease and diabetes.

Robinson, William (Billy Robinson) *(1884–1916)* Pioneer aviator and aircraft experimenter. Robinson developed one of the first radial air-cooled airplane engines. Receiving permission to fly mail from Des Moines to Chicago, he began the first authorized air mail flight in 1914. When he overshot Chicago, possibly on purpose, he landed in Kentland, Indiana, breaking the nonstop flying distance record, with a flight of 390 miles in four hours and 44 minutes. He lost his life in an attempt to break another aviation record. He had previously reached altitudes of over 14,000 feet, but in attempting to surpass the record of 17,000 feet, he lost control and plummeted to his death.

robot Robots are machines that can be COMPUTER-programmed or guided by remote control to perform a variety of tasks. The word *robot* was coined in 1920 by Czech playwright and novelist Karel CAPEK. Prominent in 20th-century science fiction, robots are often portrayed as ominous mechanical beings that have superhuman strength and minds of their own. In reality, robots bear little resemblance to their fictional counterparts, and they do only what they are programmed to do (although the application of artificial intelligence may allow robots to mimic human behavior). Refined in the late 20th century, robots perform work in settings that would be deadly for humans, such as under the sea or in outer space. Robots have also been used to handle radioactive materials, both routinely and at the damaged THREE MILE ISLAND and CHERNOBYL reactors. Japanese AUTOMOBILE manufacturers were among the first to employ robots to perform high-precision assembly line work. In 2002 Honda Motors unveiled a bipedal walking robot prototype called Asimo. Designed to assist elderly and disabled individuals in daily tasks, and to assume duties too hazardous to humans, the Asimo robot has yet to become available for commercial purchase. Other Japanese firms have produced robots designed to fulfill similar functions, such as Sony's Aibo and R100 Personal Robot in 1999, and Fujitsu's HOAP-1 in 2001.

Robson, Mark *(1913–1978)* Canadian-born film director. Robson first gained prominence in 1949 with *Champion* and *Home of the Brave,* and went on to direct many other films. Oddly, he specialized in two genres that had little in common: war adventure films aimed at male audiences and "soap opera" potboilers geared to predominantly female audiences. In the former category were *The Bridges at Toko-Ri* (1954) and *Von Ryan's Express* (1965), while films in the latter category included *Peyton Place* (1957) and *Valley of the Dolls* (1967). Such movies were box office hits, although they were generally dismissed by critics.

Rochet, Waldeck *(1905–1983)* French communist. As leader of the French Communist Party from 1964 to 1972, he steered the party toward a policy of greater independence from the USSR. He brought about an alliance with socialists and other leftists to support François MITTERRAND in the 1965 presidential election. In 1968 he led the French communists to condemn the SOVIET INVASION OF CZECHOSLOVAKIA.

rock (rock and roll) An original American musical form that saw much of its early development in the South before being modified by influences from other parts of the country and abroad (particularly England). Rock and roll had its origins in the late 1940s as a kind of heavily accented music, with debts to JAZZ, BLUES and popular music played primarily by black musicians. Known as "rhythm and blues" (its politest designation) because of its blues roots, it was also labeled "race" music, and many pop music radio stations throughout the country refused to play it. This con-

tempt was to follow rock and roll well into the 1960s as society sought, vainly and often hysterically, to "stop this trash." Led by the increasingly popular recordings of such performers as Fats DOMINO, Chuck BERRY and "Little Richard" Penniman, rhythm and blues built up an increasingly avid audience among both white and black teenagers.

In 1954, about the time the term *rock and roll* began to appear, a new wave burst upon the public. Elvis PRESLEY made his first recordings in Memphis with Sun Records. A year later, Bill HALEY and the Comets' "Rock Around the Clock" reached the top of the pop charts, and a new era in popular music had begun. These early years, in which the raucous new music vied for popularity with the traditional productions of Eddie Fisher and Doris Day, saw the spectacular rise of Presley with such hits as "Heartbreak Hotel" (1955), "Hound Dog" and "Don't Be Cruel" (both 1956), an appearance on *The Ed Sullivan Show* and a three-picture movie deal.

Rock had taken the country by storm, and much of this early activity was generated in the South. As it grew, it drew upon other existing forms, such as COUNTRY AND WESTERN MUSIC, to produce a hybrid form, "rockabilly," a term derived from "rock" and "hillbilly" to indicate a combination of elements taken from both. Among the best known examples are "That's All Right" (1954) by Presley and "Blue Suede Shoes" by Carl Perkins, another Sun Records singer. Other performers, such as Jerry Lee LEWIS and Charlie Rich, shared a similar background.

Rock and roll music played over British and western European radio stations became equally popular abroad, aided by the success of the film *Rock Around the Clock,* with Bill Haley and Alan Freed, who is generally credited with first applying the term *rock and roll* to the new music. As the 1950s drew to a close the first wave of rock, which had started in the South, was now firmly entrenched throughout the Western world. In the 1960s American-influenced British groups, particularly the BEATLES and the ROLLING STONES, were to return the favor with the "British invasion" that began in 1964. Thereafter, rock was truly an international affair.

Rockefeller, John Davison, Jr. *(1874–1960)* U.S. businessman and

philanthropist; the only son of oil magnate John D. Rockefeller, he took over management of his father's interests in 1911. During their lives, father and son gave over $3 billion to various scientific, cultural and educational institutions. Among his most notable philanthropies were the restoration of Williamsburg, Virginia, the establishment of Rockefeller University and the Rockefeller Foundation as well as the donation of the site for the United Nations headquarters in New York City. He helped plan ROCKEFELLER CENTER, completed in 1939.

Rockefeller, Nelson Aldrich *(1908–1979)* American politician, governor of the state of New York (1958–73) and vice president of the U.S. (1974–77). The grandson of John D. Rockefeller I, the Standard Oil magnate, Rockefeller was born into one of America's wealthiest families. He entered government service in 1940 when he became coordinator of inter-American affairs in the State Department. He was named assistant secretary of state for Latin America in 1944. In the administration of Dwight D. EISENHOWER he was undersecretary of the Department of Health, Education and Welfare from 1953 to 1955, when he became a special assistant to the president for foreign affairs. Rockefeller entered elective politics in 1958, defeating incumbent W. Averell HARRIMAN for the governorship of New York. He served for four successive terms and became a national political

American politician Nelson D. Rockefeller (LIBRARY OF CONGRESS, PRINTS AND PHOTOGRAPHS DIVISION)

figure. As governor, he initiated massive welfare programs. He also started drug rehabilitation programs, reorganized New York's transportation system and constructed lavish public works projects. His handling of an uprising at Attica state prison (1971), in which 42 prisoners and guards were killed, was heavily criticized.

The leader of the liberal wing of the REPUBLICAN PARTY, Rockefeller sought the Republican nomination for president in 1960, 1964 and 1968, but each time was rejected by the party as too liberal. In 1974 Gerald FORD, who had succeeded Richard M. NIXON as president following the WATERGATE SCANDAL, chose Rockefeller as his vice president. As vice president, he headed a special commission (the Rockefeller Commission) that investigated allegations of illegal activities by the CIA. Because of opposition from the conservative wing of the Republican Party, Rockefeller withdrew from consideration as Ford's running mate in the 1976 presidential campaign. He retired to private life at the end of his vice presidential term. Rockefeller's four brothers were also prominent. **John D. Rockefeller III** (1906–78) was a philanthropist; **Laurence Rockefeller** (1910–2004) was a philanthropist and conservationist; **David Rockefeller** (1915–   ) was president and chairman of Chase Manhattan Bank; **Winthrop Rockefeller** (1912–73) served two terms as governor of Arkansas.

Rockefeller Center New York City complex of skyscraper office buildings, admired both as a popular tourist attraction and as an early example of a coherently planned, urban high-rise grouping. Beginning during the GREAT DEPRESSION in 1931, Rockefeller interests bought out all the structures on three entire city blocks in the heart of midtown Manhattan where few large buildings existed. A team of architects developed a coordinated design for a group of 13 large buildings, planning a midblock private street (Rockefeller Plaza), a central garden walk leading to an open sunken plaza and individual skyscraper buildings. The architects were Reinhard & Hofmeister; Corbett, Harrison & MacMurray; Hood & Fouilhoux; and, after World War II, Carson & Lundin. The buildings are of varying height, with the 850-foot RCA building at the center. All have similar external materials, detailing and slab-like forms with setbacks typical of the skyscraper design of the ART DECO era. The project included underground pedestrian shopping areas and truck delivery access, but not the originally intented opera house. There were two large movie theaters (only one, RADIO CITY MUSIC HALL, survives), the radio studios of NBC, many shops and restaurants and some 10 million square feet of office space. Many works of art, sculpture, bas-reliefs and murals are incorporated, including work by a number of leading artists of the 1930s.

Although the architecture of the individual buildings may now seem undistinguished, the coordinated planning of the project and the massing of the group have been greatly admired. Since 1960, Rockefeller Center has been extended, with additional buildings adjacent to it on the north and west (across Sixth Avenue); the newer buildings are of indifferent design quality, though well-related to the concept of the original project. This complex remains a major attraction for visitors to New York and is a continuing example of the value of coordinated architectural planning in contrast to the usual chaos of major urban real estate development. Rockefeller Center was sold to Japanese investors in 1989. When the real estate market began to decline in the early 1990s, the center's Japanese investors, principally Mitsubishi, advocated filing for bankruptcy protection. In 1995, Mitsubishi successfully negotiated the center's management by Rockefeller Center Properties, Inc. (RCPI), which functioned independently of the Rockefeller family. It also signaled an increasing Japanese disengagement from investment in the complex. In 1997 Rockefeller Center was purchased by an investment group led by Tishman Speyer Properties.

Rockne, Knute (1888–1931) Football coach. Rockne excelled in football as a student at Notre Dame University, winning a crucial game with Army in 1913 through the then unused forward pass—a turning point in football strategy. After graduation in 1914, he became a chemistry instructor and assistant football coach at Notre Dame, and head coach in 1918. As head coach for 13 years he led his teams in winning 105 games with only 12 losses and five ties and made Notre Dame a leading football center of the U.S. He revolutionized football theory, stressed offense, developed the precision backfield, called the "Notre Dame shift," perfected line play and other strategy. Among the famous stars he developed were the "Four Horsemen of Notre Dame," the most famous of all backfields. He was noted for his ability to exemplify values and ideals and inculcate qualities of leadership among his "boys." He died tragically in an airplane crash. One of his several books on football was *Coaching, the Way of the Winner.*

Rockwell,   Norman   Perceval (1894–1978) American painter famous for his magazine and book illustrations. Born in a shabby brownstone in New York, Rockwell dropped out of high school at 16 to study art full-time. He preferred the Art Students League to the more prestigious National Academy, which had discouraged his pretensions to be an illustrator. Renting a studio once owned by painter Frederic Remington, he quickly established a reputation for children's subjects in such popular magazines as *St. Nicholas, American Boy* and *Boy's Life.* In later years he worked for LIFE *Look* and *American Artist.* His real ambition, however, was to paint covers for the *Saturday Evening Post*—"the greatest show window in America for an illustrator," he said in his autobiography, *My Adventures As an Illustrator* (1960). From 1916 to 1963 he enjoyed an uninterrupted relationship with the *Post,* painting 322 covers. Here was the Rockwell vision America remembers, an apple-cheeked, ingenuous view of rural life, with barefoot boys and gap-toothed girls, soda-jerks and Boy Scouts, loving grandmas and quaint village characters. "I paint life as I would like it to be," he wrote. "Maybe as I grew up and found that the world wasn't the perfectly pleasant place I had thought it to be, I unconsciously decided that, even if it wasn't an ideal world, it should be and so painted only the ideal aspects of it."

The care and meticulous precision of his work is legendary. Even to those disposed to dismiss his anecdotal, realistic style, his technique and draughtsmanship are impressive. His zeal for "authenticity" led him to use as models his friends and neighbors in the towns of Arlington, Vermont, and Stockbridge, Massachusetts. Perhaps the archetypal image among his *Post* covers is a self-portrait that appeared October 8, 1938: The artist sits with his back to us and scratches his head, puzzling what to make out of the blank canvas before him.

Rodchenko, Aleksandr Mikhailovich *(1891–1956)* Russian painter. Associated with MALEVICH, Rodchenko founded the Russian nonobjectivist movement, an abstract style closely related to his mentor's SUPREMATISM. His best-known painting is probably *Black on Black* (1918; Tretyakov Gallery, Moscow), an artistic answer to Malevich's celebrated *White on White* (1918; Museum of Modern Art, New York City). He is also known for the constructions he created in collaboration with the constructivist Vladimir TATLIN.

Rodeo Classic American ballet. First performed by the Ballet Russe de Monte-Carlo at the Metropolitan Opera in New York on October 16, 1942, it brought together the talents of choreographer Agnes DE MILLE, composer Aaron COPLAND and scenic designer Oliver Smith. Subtitled "The Courting at Burnt Ranch," it is set in the American Southwest and tells the story of the tomboyish Cow Girl in love with the Head Wrangler. She discards her rope and boots for a girlish frock, becomes the belle of the local ball and is eventually carried off by the Champion Roper.

Incidents of riding, roping and a square dance (complete with a "caller") alternate with sentimental episodes. Agnes de Mille appeared as the Cow Girl. "The beauty and genuiness of 'Rodeo' reside precisely in the apparent casualness of its American expression," wrote dance critic George Amberg. The same can be said for Copland's score, a catchy, rambunctious evocation of cowboy tunes and dance rhythms. The ballet is best known today for the orchestral suite Copland wrote in 1945.

Rodgers, Richard *(1902–1979)* Celebrated American composer of Broadway, ballet, the movies and television. Rodgers's shows revolutionized the American musical theater, breaking away from the line of light American musical comedies to establish a more operatic musical drama. Rodgers enjoyed a comfortable boyhood in New York, where he had ample opportunity for musical studies and theatergoing. While at Columbia University, he met the two songwriters with whom his career would be most closely associated, Lorenz HART and Oscar HAMMERSTEIN II. After a few shows of only middling success (*Poor Little Ritz Girl,* 1920), Rodgers and Hart hit their stride with several *Garrick Gaieties* revues and many subsequent successes, from the late 1920s through the early 1940s. These included *A Connecticut Yankee* (1927), *Evergreen* (1930), *Jumbo* (1935), *On Your Toes* (1936), *Babes in Arms* (1937), *The Boys from Syracuse* (1938) and *Pal Joey* (1942). Among Rodgers and Hart's hit songs were "Dancing on the Ceiling," "Little Girl Blue," "My Funny Valentine," "Johnny One Note" and "Bewitched." The two also wrote the film music for *Love Me Tonight* (1933), which featured "Isn't It Romantic," and *Hallelujah, I'm a Bum* (1933).

Rodgers switched partners in 1943, collaborating with Oscar Hammerstein II on *Oklahoma!* It was the first of their many blockbusters, including *Carousel* (1945), with "You'll Never Walk Alone" and "If I Love You"; *South Pacific* (1949), with "Some Enchanted Evening" and "This Nearly Was Mine"; *The King and I* (1951), with "Getting to Know You," "Hello, Young Lovers" and "We Kiss in a Shadow"; and *The Sound of Music* (1959), with "Climb Every Mountain" and "My Favorite Things." After Hammerstein's death in 1960, Rodgers wrote both words and music to *No Strings* (1962). His other compositions include ballet music (the "Slaughter on 10th Avenue" number for *On Your Toes*) and the scores for television's "Victory at Sea" (1952–53) and "Winston Churchill: The Valiant Years" (1960). His autobiography, *Musical Stages,* was published in 1975.

Rodnina, Irina *(1949–)* Soviet skater. Rodnina won three Olympic gold medals in the pairs skating competition, partnered by Aleksei Ulanov at Sapporo in 1970, then by Aleksandr Zaitsev at Innsbruck in 1976 and at Lake Placid in 1980. She also won 10 world championships. She and her partner had a dazzling style full of complicated leaps.

Rodrigo, Joaquin *(1901–1999)* Spanish composer. Although he was blind from childhood, Rodrigo became a gifted composer noted for the use of traditional Spanish rhythms in his works. He became a professor of music history at Madrid University in 1946. His works include the famous *Concierto de Aranjuez* for guitar and orchestra (1940), the *Concierto Andaluz* for four guitars and orchestra (1967) and the *Concierto como un divertimento* for voice and orchestra (1979–81).

Rodzyanko, Michael Vladimirovich *(1859–1924)* Russian president of the DUMA. Having supported the autocracy's suppression of the 1905 Revolution, he unsuccessfully opposed the idea that Czar NICHOLAS II should take command of the army. With Alexander Guchkov he led the Octobrists, a party of right-wing liberals who constituted the majority party in the third and fourth Dumas.

Roehm, Ernst *(1887–1934)* Leader of the Nazi Sturm Abteilung (SA, or storm troopers). Roehm served as a captain in the Germany army in WORLD WAR I. In September 1930, he became chief of staff of the Nazi paramilitary group known as the SA, or "Brownshirts," building the organization into an effective instrument of mass terror. However, tension between Roehm and Hitler rose steadily over the next three years, as Roehm called for the creation of a military state. To appease his more moderate supporters in the army and in the business community, Hitler agreed to destroy the Brownshirts as well as the radical political wing of the Nazi Party. On June 30, 1934, the "Night of the Long Knives," the SS under Heinrich HIMMLER and the special police under Hermann GÖRING murdered an estimated 500 to 1,000 of these elements, as well as others who were deemed enemies of the party. Roehm was shot by SS officers in Stadelheim Prison.

Roerich, Nicholas Konstantin *(1874–1947)* Russian artist. Traveling through his native country (1901–04) and central Asia (1923–28), he became known for his numerous exotic landscapes and figure studies. He was particularly acclaimed for the designs he executed for the MOSCOW ART THEATRE and the DIAGHILEV ballet, notably the stage sets for STRAVINSKY's 1913 RITE OF SPRING. Also an amateur archaeologist, he traveled to the U.S., where New York City's Roerich Museum was established to house his paintings and collection of artifacts.

Roethke, Theodore *(1908–1963)* American poet. Roethke was born in Michigan, where his father was a horticulturist. Roethke's poetry is rich in nature imagery, evoking growth and also the inevitability of decomposition and decay. His first volume of poetry was *Open House* (1941). Other works include *The Lost Son* (1948), *I Am! Says the Lamb* (1961) and the posthumous volumes, *The Far Field* (1964) and *Selected Poems* (1969), an exuberantly sensual collection compiled by his wife, Beatrice. Roethke's work has been likened to that of Blake and was an influence on Sylvia PLATH.

Roe v. Wade *(1973)* U.S. Supreme Court decision legalizing ABORTION in most cases. The case proved extremely controversial because opponents of abortion contended that the Court had, in effect, condoned the murder of the unborn. Although abortion had at one time been a medical decision for doctors, by the 1970s many states had outlawed the practice. The Court held that women have a constitutional right to an abortion; according to the Court's ruling, this right springs from the right to privacy implicit in the Fifth and Fourteenth Amendments. The Court reaffirmed the view that abortion is a medical procedure to be decided upon by a physician and patient. The Court voted 7–2; the majority opinion was written by Justice Harry BLACKMUN. The Court did allow states to regulate abortion during the later stages of pregnancy, however. Abortion continued to be an extremely sensitive political issue through the 1970s and 1980s and into the 1990s, with activists polarized on both sides. (See also WEBSTER V. REPRODUCTIVE SERVICE.)

Rogers, Carl R(ansom) *(1902–1987)* American psychologist. An extremely influential figure in the field, he developed the client-centered approach to psychotherapy. Unlike the standard psychoanalytic approach, this allowed the patient a major say in determining the course of treatment. Rogers was also a founder of **humanistic psychology** and was instrumental in the encounter group movement that emerged in the 1960s. His book *On Becoming a Person* (1961) became a Bible for the human potential movement.

Rogers, Ginger (Virginia Katherine McMath) *(1911–1995)* Actress, comedienne and dancer. Rogers is best remembered for her dancing in 1930s musicals with Fred ASTAIRE. After a brief career as a band singer and some experience on Broadway, Rogers went to HOLLYWOOD. She appeared in such pictures as *Flying Down to Rio* (1933), *Top Hat* (1935) and *Bachelor Mother* (1939). She won an ACADEMY AWARD as best actress in 1940 for *Kitty Foyle*.

Rogers, Roy (Leonard Slye) *(1911–1998)* American singing cowboy and actor. Known as the "King of the Cowboys," Rogers began his career with the Pioneer Trio in grade-B Western movies. His breakthrough role came in 1938 in *Under Western Skies,* and he went on to star, with his horse Trigger, in more than 100 such films. In 1947 he married singer **Dale Evans.** Rogers and Trigger joined Evans and her horse Buttermilk to appear in such films as *Hollywood Canteen* (1944); *Son of Paleface* (1952) was Roy and Trigger's last movie. Roy and Dale starred in a hit 1950s television series whose theme song was "Happy Trails to You." The couple later became involved in charity and religious work.

Rogers, William Penn Adair *(1879–1935)* American humorist. Born in Oolagah, then Indian Territory, now Oklahoma, he grew up on his family's prosperous ranch, worked as a cowboy and began his career as a rodeo entertainer. He was a rider and trick roper in Wild West shows around the world before returning to the U.S. in 1880. Settling in New York City, he began to work in VAUDEVILLE, supplementing his skills at the lariat with down-home banter. From this beginning grew the homespun humor that made Rogers one of America's most beloved entertainers. After working at the ZIEGFELD FOLLIES (1915–17), he moved on to HOLLYWOOD, where he made his first film in 1918. The following year he began a syndicated newspaper column that featured disarmingly simple and insightful analyses of current events. The "cowboy philosopher" continued to dispense his witty brand of rural wisdom in movies, radio shows and books until he and Wiley POST were killed in an airplane crash near Point Barrow, Alaska.

Rohde, Gilbert *(1894–1944)* Pioneering American industrial designer whose career in the 1930s was an important factor in introducing MODERNISM to the U.S. Rohde became familiar with cabinetmaking in his father's shop. He worked as a furniture illustrator for several New York stores before making a trip in 1927 to Paris, where he became familiar with the moderne styles of the 1920s. In 1929 he opened his own design office, working on interiors and producing modern furniture designs at a time when modernism was largely unknown in America. In 1930 he established a relationship with Herman Miller, Inc., that was central to both his career and that furniture company's growth. His designs were clearly modern, although they incorporated decorative elements that now seem to imply ART DECO directions, with much use of exotic wood veneers, glass, mirrors and chrome details. He developed the concepts of modular and sectional furniture and applied the modular idea to office furniture in his Executive Office Group (EOG). Rohde developed various exhibit designs for the NEW YORK WORLD'S FAIR OF 1939. He was briefly the director of the short-lived Design Laboratory School, a project sponsored by the WPA from 1935 until 1938. He was also head of the industrial design program at the New York University School of Architecture from 1939 until 1943.

Rohlfs, Christian *(1849–1938)* German painter. Living at Weimar until 1900, he painted in an impressionist manner and taught for 30 years at the Weimar Art School. Moving to Hagan, he was an instructor at the Folkwang School, where he was influenced by a 1902 exhibition of Van Gogh's works as well as by his friendship with the German expressionist Emil NOLDE. His style altered to a gentle version of EXPRESSION-ISM, and he gradually abandoned oil painting in favor of tempera, watercolor and woodcuts. He is best known for his late paintings, delicately beautiful floral works that he produced while living in Switzerland from 1927 until his death.

Rohmer, Eric *(1920–   )* French film director and critic. Rohmer is a much admired director of subtle, delicate films on questions of everyday morality and the nuances of sexual attraction. He began his career as a writer for CAHIERS DU CINEMA, of which he became the editor after the death of Andre Bazin in 1958. Rohmer was ousted as editor in 1963, as *Cahiers* struggled to balance aesthetics and politics. His feature debut as a director came with *The Sign of the Lion* (1959), an evocation of Paris in August. But his major films—under the group title *Six Moral Tales*—are *La Boulangere de Monceau* (1963), *La Carriere de Suzanne* (1963), *La Collectioneuse* (1966), *My Night At Maud's* (1968), *Claire's Knee* (1970) and *Love in the Afternoon* (1972). In each of these films Rohmer focuses on the telling discrepancies between words and deeds while refraining from making definitive moral judgments on his characters. Rohmer continued to produce films in the 1990s, such as *A Tale of Springtime* (1990) and *Autumn Tale* (1999), and the French Revolutionary drama *The Lady and the Duke* (1999), and into the next decade.

Rohmer, Sax (pen name of Arthur Henry Sarsfield Ward) *(1883–1959)* British author. Although also a playwright and songwriter under his own name, Rohmer is best known as the author of the popular series of adventure books featuring the clever criminal Fu Manchu. These include *The Insidious Dr. Fu Manchu* (1913), *The Mask of Fu Manchu* (1932) and *Emperor Fu Manchu* (1959). In addition to the more than 30 Fu Manchu books, Rohmer also wrote two other detective series featuring Gaston Max and Paul Harley.

Roh Tae Woo *(1932–   )* Elected president of the Republic of KOREA in 1987 and head of the Democratic Justice Party, Roh was educated at the Korean Military Academy and the U.S. Special Warfare School. He fought in the KOREAN WAR and rose in the ranks of the Korean army, becoming com-manding general of the 9th Special Forces Brigade in 1974, commander of the Capital Security Command in 1979 and commander of the Defense Security Command in 1980. He was made a four-star general in 1981 and retired from the army in July of the same year. In 1981 he entered the cabinet as minister of state for national security and foreign affairs. In 1982 he was appointed minister of sports and minister of home affairs. He has held a number of other positions outside the government, including the presidencies of the Seoul Olympic Organizing Committee, the Korean Amateur Sports Association and the Korean Olympic Committee. Roh departed from the presidency in 1993 and was succeeded by Kim Young Sam, the nation's first civilian president. Two years later Roh was arrested on charges of corruption and treason but was pardoned by Kim in 1997.

Rokossovsky, Konstantin Konstantinovich *(1896–1968)* Marshal of the Soviet Union. Of Polish origin, Rokossovsky joined the Red Army in 1919 and became a member of the Bolshevik Party. During WORLD WAR II he was an outstanding Soviet commander. He acted with great heroism at the battles of Moscow (1941–42), STAL-INGRAD (1942–43), Kursk (1943) and in Belorussia and at the battle for Berlin (1944–45). In 1944 he became a marshal and commanded the Soviet forces in Poland. In 1949 he was transferred to the Polish army. He became minister of defense and a member of the Polit-buro of the Polish Communist Party. In 1956 he was dismissed by Wladyslaw GOMULKA and was appointed a deputy minister of defense of the USSR.

Rolland, Romain *(1866–1944)* French novelist and playwright. Rolland is best remembered as a practitioner of the *roman fleuve*, exemplified by his major work, the 10-volume *Jean Cristophe*, which was published between 1905 and 1912 and which follows the family of a musical genius based loosely on Beethoven. Rolland was also interested in music and the theater; his first literary works were play cycles, such as the interrelated *Saint Louis* (1897), *Aert* (1898) and *Le Triomphe de la Raison* (*The Triumph of Reason,* 1899). Largely because of *Jean Cristophe,* Rolland was awarded the NOBEL PRIZE in literature in 1915, in spite of some controversy due to his pacifistic position regarding WORLD WAR I, which he expressed in the essay collection *Au-dessus de la melée* (*Above the Battle,* 1915). Other works include *Michelangelo* (1915), *I Will Not Rest* (1935) and *The Journey Within* (1942).

Rolling Stones British ROCK and roll band, founded in 1963. The Rolling Stones, who are often billed on their concert tours as "The Greatest Rock and Roll Band in the World," have many fans and critics who support that claim. Since their first singles hit, "It's All Over Now" (1964), the Stones have enjoyed phenomenal popularity. The band lineup—which remained remarkably stable through the early 1990s—originally included Mick JAGGER, lead vocalist; Brian Jones, guitar; Keith Richards, guitar and vocals; Ian Stewart, piano; Charlie Watt, drums; and Bill Wyman, bass. In 1969, after the accidental death of Jones, Mick Taylor replaced him on guitar. Taylor was subsequently replaced by Ron Wood in 1974. Jagger and Richards, who have written all of the band's original material since 1965, have both attained the status of international celebrity. Among the many Rolling Stones classic hits are "(I Can't Get No) Satisfaction" (1965), "Ruby Tuesday" (1967), "Let's Spend the Night Together" (1967), "Jumping Jack Flash" (1968), "Honky Tonk Women" (1969), "Brown Sugar" (1971), "It's Only Rock and Roll" (1974) and "Start Me Up" (1981). During the 1980s a feud developed between Jagger and Richards over the kind of music the Stones should produce. Following the Jagger-Richards reunion, the band began recording the tracks to *Steel Wheels* (1989); the year of *Steel Wheels'* release, the Stones were inducted into the Rock and Roll Hall of Fame. After the subsequent *Steel Wheels* tour, the Stones recorded the live album *Flashback* (1991), composed of live tracks from their *Steel Wheels* concerts. When Bill Wyman left the group following the release of *Flashback* and Jagger and Richards again pursued solo projects in the early 1990s, it appeared the Stones might again disband. However Wyman was replaced by Darryl Jones, who helped the band record the critically-acclaimed *Voodoo Lounge* (1994), which won a 1994 Grammy Award for Best Rock Album. The subsequent *Voodoo Lounge* tour proved more successful than *Steel Wheels.* The band

The Rolling Stones (PHOTOFEST)

Romanenko, Yuri *(1944–)* Soviet cosmonaut; one-half of the Romanenko/Grechko *Soyuz 26* (December 10, 1977) mission to the Soviet space station SALYUT. He was also part of the eight-day *Soyuz 38* (September 18, 1980) mission to that station and a long-duration mission to *Mir* in 1987. During their 1977–78 stay aboard *Salyut* 6, Romanenko and Grechko gained international fame by staying in space for a then record-breaking 96 days. The mission has sometimes been referred to as "the flight of the classics," since "Grechko" and "Romanenko" are Ukrainian for "Greek" and "Roman." In 1987, Romanenko set yet another record, 326 days aboard the *Mir* space station; the previous record had been 237 days, set by Leonid Kizim, Vladimir Solovyov and Oleg Atkov aboard *Salyut 7* in 1984. During Romanenko's marathon he went outside the station for several EVAs with fellow cosmonaut Alexander Laveikin, once to clear the docking area for a 27-ton astrophysical module, and a second time to erect a third solar panel for the space station.

Romania The nation of Romania covers an area of 91,675 square miles in southeastern Europe; its name and its Latin-derived language are a mark of its ancient status as a part of the Roman Empire. In 1877 Romanians declared

has since recorded two additional records—the live album *Stripped* (1995) and the studio-recorded *No Security* (1998).

Rölvaag, Ole Edvart *(1876–1931)* Norwegian-born educator and author. Rölvaag is best remembered for *Giants in the Earth* (1927), an epic of early life on the South Dakota prairies. He was educated at St. Olaf College in Northfield, Minnesota, where he later returned to serve as professor and head of the department of Norwegian language and literature. He resigned in August 1931 to write full-time but died only a few months later.

Romaine, Paul (Burton Bleamer) *(1905–1986)* American book dealer. He was a close friend of Ernest HEMINGWAY, whom he met in PARIS in the mid-1920s while both were part of the expatriate American scene there. Targeted for prosecution in 1963 as a seller of the bawdy 18th-century novel *Fanny Hill,* he became the central figure in one of the last major obscenity trials in the U.S. His conviction was later overturned by the Illinois supreme court.

Romains, Jules (pen name of Louis Farigoule) *(1885–1972)* French novelist, dramatist and poet. Romains worked on an epic scale and spent 15 years (1931–46) writing his master-

piece, *Men of Good Will.* One of the longest and most intricate of modern novels, it contained 3 million words and some 400 characters. It spanned 25 years of French history in minute detail. Romains also founded a philosophy called **unanism,** which defined man in the context of his familiar, religious and social groups. He was elected to the French Academy in 1946.

Romania

1919	Gains Transylvania, Bessarabia and southern Dobrudja in post-World War I peace settlement, doubling size of country.
1940–45	During World War II Romania fights first on the German side, then on the side of the Allies.
1947	Democratic parties are purged; King Michael forced to abdicate; Communist People's Republic is declared.
1958	Withdrawal of Soviet troops negotiated.
1967	Nicolae Ceauşescu assumes presidency during which he outlaws birth control to increase population; borrows heavily from West then imposes harsh austerity measures on population to reduce foreign debt.
1988	Ceauşescu announces systemization policy under which 7,000 villages will be demolished and inhabitants resettled in agroindustrial centers.
1989	Anti-government demonstrations begin in city of Timişoara and spread to Bucharest despite authorities' armed efforts to suppress them; Defense Minister Vasile Milea commits suicide rather than obey Ceauşescu order to open fire on demonstrators; Ceauşescu and his wife, Elena, try to flee but are captured and executed after a military tribunal finds them guilty of genocide, corruption and destruction of the economy.
1990	Provisional government president Ion Iliescu brutally suppresses student-led antigovernment rioting when, answering Iliescu's nationally broadcast call, 10,000 miners from Jiu Valley region pour into Bucharest, armed with axe handles and iron bars, occupy the city, beat at random anyone suspected of antigovernment proclivities and wreck the offices of the opposition and only independent, mass-circulation newspaper.
1991	Thousands of ethnic Roma (Gypsies) flee to Germany. Voters approve a new democratic constitution in a referendum.
1992	The Democratic National Salvation Front (DNSF) candidates win a majority of seats in parliament and Nicolae Vacaroui becomes prime minister; Iliescu is reelected president.
1993	Clashes erupt in Translyvania between ethnic Romanians and ethnic Germans and Hungarians.
1996	In parliamentary elections, a coalition of opposition parties, including the Democratic Convention of Romania (DCR) and the Social Democratic Union (SDU) defeats the ruling DNSF Party of Social Democracy of Romania (PSDR; formerly the DNSF); the DCR's Victor Ciorbea becomes prime minister and Emil Constantinescu of the DCR is elected president.
1997	Romania improves relations with Hungary and settles a border dispute over land with Ukraine.
1998	Radu Vasile of the DCR forms a new government coalition; Vasile resigns and Mugur Isarescu, governor of the National Bank, is chosen prime minister.
2000	The PSDR's Iliescu is returned to the office of president; a minority government under Adrian Nastase of the PSDR is formed.
2001	A law returning property nationalized under the communist regime is passed by parliament.
2004	Romania is admitted to NATO. Traian Basescu, centrist alliance leader, is elected president. His ally Carin Tariceanu becomes prime minister.
2005	Romania signs an EU accession treaty; its admission is set for 2008 provided the necessary reforms are implemented.

full independence from the Ottoman Turks, and in 1881 Karl of Hohenzollern-Sigmaringen was crowned King Carol I. Neutral at the outset of WORLD WAR I, Romania fought with the Allies from 1916 and gained Transylvania (from Hungary), Bessarabia (from Russia) and southern Dobrudja (from Bulgaria) under terms of the postwar peace settlement (1920). The Iron Guard, Romania's homegrown fascist movement, dominated a corrupt political establishment in the 1930s. Neutral once again, at the beginning of WORLD WAR II, Romania was forced to restore almost all of its territorial gains to the Soviet Union, Bulgaria and Hungary. King CAROL II abdicated in 1940, and Romania swiftly became an AXIS ally. In August 1944 King Michael declared war on Germany; a postwar peace treaty in 1947 restored all of Transylvania to Romania. Also in 1947, King Michael (1940–47) was forced to abdicate by a radical left-wing government, and the People's Republic was formed. Internal power struggles led to political purges (1948–50) and the establishment of a communist government that nationalized industry and collectivized agriculture. Romania joined the WARSAW PACT, yet maintained its independence from the Soviet Union. Nicolae CEAUŞESCU, who became president in 1967, amassed a huge foreign debt during the 1970s, which led to privation and protests by 1987, when he tried to reduce the debt. His policy of systemization, which involved the destruction of thousands of rural villages and resettlement of the population in agroindustrial centers, brought massive demonstrations in 1989. Ceauşescu attempted to flee but was captured, found guilty of genocide and corruption by a military tribunal and executed on December 25, 1989. A new government has promised reforms and moved toward free elections. In 2001 a law was passed returning property that was nationalized under the Communist regime. Although Romania has not resolved its economic problems inherited from the Ceauşescu era, President Ion Iliescu sought close relations with the U.S. and the EUROPEAN UNION (EU). In 2004, Romania became a member of the NORTH ATLANTIC TREATY ORGANIZATION (NATO). That same year President Iliescu's commission on the Holocaust in Romania released a report detailing the involvement of the Ro-

manian wartime regime in atrocities against Jews and Roma. (See also Gheorghe GHEORGHIU-DEJ.) That same year President Iliescu's commission on the Holocaust in Romania released a report detailing the involvement of the Romanian wartime regime in atrocities against Jews and Roma.

Romanov, Panteleymon Sergeyevich *(1884–1938)* Russian author. While his short sketches give a picture of life during the RUSSIAN CIVIL WAR and the period of the NEW ECONOMIC POLICY, many characters of his novels are recognizable descendants of the 19th-century "superfluous man." His most important novel, *The New Table of Commandments* (1928), however, deals with a Soviet marriage. In 1927 Romanov met with official disapproval and was forbidden to publish, although the ban was later lifted.

Romberg, Sigmund *(1887–1951)* Hungarian-born composer best known for his American operettas. Despite an engineering background in his native Hungary, Romberg found in America more opportunities for composing. From 1914 to 1917 in New York he wrote many knockabout songs for musical revues of the Shubert brothers. However, it was with *Maytime* (1917) and *Blossom Time* (1921) that he discovered his true metier, operetta. Romberg described the form, which had its genesis in the late 19th-century work of Franz Lehár and Gilbert and Sullivan, as "light comedy opera" that "leaned toward the operatic rather than the jazz type." He believed that audiences wanted "a better class of music" than they found in popular musicals. *The Student Prince* (1924), *The Desert Song* (1926) and *New Moon* (1928) had rich musical scores that demanded operatically trained voices. Romberg's rousing choral numbers ("Drinking Song," "The Riff Song" and "Stout-Hearted Men"), lyrical serenades ("Softly, As in a Morning Sunrise") and magnificent duets ("One Alone") brought a classical prestige to the Broadway stage. At least two love songs, "One Flower Grows Alone in Your Garden" (from *The Desert Song*) and "Overhead the Moon Is Beaming" (from *The Student Prince*) achieve a searing intensity quite distinct from anything currently on the American

stage. However, this kind of work was, in the words of a critic, "so many brave St. Georges against the dragonfly, Jazz." Even if operettas would soon be dismissed as old-fashioned, Romberg successfully adapted to a more contemporary kind of musical, *Up in Central Park* (1945), and had his own radio show in the 1940s, "An Evening with Romberg."

Rome, Treaty of Treaty signed on March 25, 1957, by Belgium, France, Italy, Luxembourg, the Netherlands and West Germany that established the EUROPEAN ECONOMIC COMMUNITY (EEC, also known as the Common Market) and the European Atomic Energy Community (EURATOM). The EEC aimed at forming a united European economy by eliminating internal tariffs, setting uniform external tariffs and establishing free movement of people, capital and goods within the member states. EURATOM aimed at integrating the nuclear power efforts of the member countries and creating a commonality of practices and markets in nuclear materials.

Romero, Oscar *(1917–1980)* Roman Catholic archbishop in EL SALVADOR. Following the seizure of power by a military junta in 1979, the highly respected Romero had often spoken out on behalf of human rights and the poor and against extremists of both the right and the left. Above all, he had advocated an end to political violence in the strife-torn nation. On March 24, 1980, Romero was killed by a single bullet while saying Mass in a small chapel in San Salvador. No gunman was identified, but the widespread assumption was that the archbishop had been killed because of his continuing criticism of El Salvador's government. Rioting followed the assassination, in which more than 30 people were killed and another 400 were injured.

Rommel, Erwin *(1891–1944)* German field marshal. Rommel joined the army in 1910, was commissioned an officer in 1912 and served with distinction during WORLD WAR I. He attracted Adolf HITLER's attention between the wars and was made a general in 1939. After commanding an armored division in the attack on France (1940), he was assigned to North Africa, becoming (1941) leader of Germany's crack Afrika

German field marshall Erwin Rommel (LIBRARY OF CONGRESS, PRINTS AND PHOTOGRAPHS DIVISION)

Korps. A skilled and intuitive strategist, he scored a string of successes that earned him a promotion to field marshal and the name "the desert fox." Pushing into Egypt, he was defeated in November, 1942 at the decisive battle of EL ALAMEIN. In 1943 Rommel was appointed a commander in northern France, where he was serving at the time of the Allied invasion at NORMANDY in June 1944. He was severely wounded in a strafing attack the following month. Known to be disillusioned with Hitler's leadership, Rommel was implicated in the plot to overthrow the führer. He was forced to commit suicide by taking poison on October 14, 1944.

Romulo, Carlos Pena (*1899–1985*) Filipino diplomat. One of the signatories of the UNITED NATIONS charter, Romulo was the PHILIPPINES' chief delegate to the UN from 1945 to 1954. As a UN delegate, he was one of the leading champions of the interests of newly independent third world countries. In 1949, he became the first Asian president of the General Assembly. He was a leader at the BANDUNG CONFERENCE of Asian and African nations in 1955. Twice the Philippines' foreign minister, he served in that capacity from 1950 to 1952 and from 1968 to 1984.

Ronchamp Location of, and therefore the usual informal name for, one of LE CORBUSIER's most important works, generally regarded as a key masterpiece of modern architecture—the chapel of Notre-Dame-du-Haut near Belfort in the French Vosges. Built in 1950–55 to replace a structure destroyed during World War II, it marks the architect's abandonment of the strictly geometric forms of his earlier INTERNATIONAL STYLE work in favor of a strongly sculptural, organic, even expressionistic direction. It is a concrete structure, with curving walls and a curved, overhanging, hollow concrete roof, suggesting the shape of an airplane wing or, some say, the form of a traditional nun's hat. The internal space is small but dramatically lit by stained glass windows of Le Corbusier's own design. There is an outdoor chancel for open-air services held for pilgrimage congregations. The site also includes a small hostel to accommodate visitors in simple and austere style.

Ronne, Finn (*1899–1980*) Norwegian-born polar explorer. Ronne accompanied Admiral Richard Evelyn BYRD on Byrd's second Antarctic expedition in 1923. Altogether he took part in 14 major U.S. expeditions, including nine trips to ANTARCTICA. During his career he traveled some 3,600 miles by skis and dog sled, more than anyone else in history, to chart the SOUTH POLE.

Ronstadt, Linda Marie (*1946– *) American singer. Her first hit came in 1967 with the Stone Poneys, singing "Different Drum." Her stylistic range is remarkable, as she has recorded successful albums in such genres as pop-rock, country and big band. Her first solo hit came in 1970 with "Long Long Time." Her most successful year on the rock charts was 1974, with top-five singles "You're No Good" and "When Will I Be Loved." In the 1980s she turned to the works of George GERSHWIN and Irving BERLIN in BIG BAND arrangements by Nelson RIDDLE on the albums *What's New* and *Lush Life*. In 1988, she celebrated her Mexican roots with the Spanish-language album *Canciones de Mi Padre*. Throughout the 1990s, Ronstadt continued to release albums, such as *Dedicated To The One I Love* (1996) and *We Ran* (1998).

Röntgen, Wilhelm Conrad (*1845–1923*) German physicist. After an early education in the Netherlands, then study at the Federal Institute of Technology, Zurich, Röntgen received his doctorate in 1869. He held various university posts, including professor of physics at Würzburg (1888) and professor of physics at Munich (1900). Röntgen researched many branches of physics, including elasticity, the specific heat of gases, capillarity, piezoelectricity and polarized light. He is chiefly remembered for his discovery of X-RAYS, at Würzburg on November 8, 1895. The discovery immediately created tremendous interest. In did not solve the contemporary wave-particle controversy on the nature of radiation, but it stimulated further investigations that led, among other things, to the discovery of radioactivity. It also provided a valuable tool for research into crystal structures and atomic structure, and X-rays were soon applied to medical diagnosis. Unfortunately, it was very much later before their danger to health became understood; both Röntgen and his technician suffered from X-ray poisoning. Although Röntgen was subjected to some bitter attacks and there were attempts to belittle his achievements, his discovery of X-rays earned him several honors, including the first NOBEL PRIZE for physics (1901).

Rooney, Mickey (Joe Yule) (*1922– *) American actor. Rooney is best known for his role as Andy Hardy in the film series about the Hardy family (1937–47) and for the film musicals *Babes in Arms* (1939) and *Strike Up the Band* (1940) in which he starred with Judy GARLAND. He scored his first feature film triumph as Puck in the 1935 film of *A Midsummer Night's Dream*. He made the difficult transition from child to adult roles, earning particular acclaim for his strong character roles in several television specials and for his comic skill in the revue-like musical *Sugar Babies* (all in the 1980s). He won a special ACADEMY AWARD for *Boys' Town* in 1938. In 1990 Rooney briefly appeared in *The Will Rogers Follies,* a musical based on the life of the famous vaudeville comedian, as Clem Rogers, Will's father. On April 5, 2004, Rooney received the John Payne Lifetime Achievement Award in recognition of his work with the armed forces in Europe during World War II.

Roosevelt, Eleanor (*1884–1962*) American humanitarian and first lady.

First Lady and humanitarian Eleanor Roosevelt
(LIBRARY OF CONGRESS, PRINTS AND PHOTOGRAPHS DIVISION)

Born in New York, she was a niece of Theodore ROOSEVELT and married her distant cousin Franklin D. ROOSEVELT in 1905. Although naturally shy, she became active in politics in 1921 when her husband was stricken with polio. As the wife of the governor of New York and, later, of the president, she transformed the role of first lady into a position of visibility and power and became one of the most active and admired women in the U.S. Involving herself in a number of causes, she supported CIVIL RIGHTS for minorities, women's rights, housing and employment reform, international understanding and other causes through speeches, a radio program and a daily newspaper column. During WORLD WAR II she was assistant director of the Office of Civilian Defense (1941–42) and traveled throughout the world to further the Allied cause.

After her husband's death in 1945, she continued her work as a delegate to the UNITED NATIONS (1945–52, 1961–62), as a drafter of the UN Declaration of Human Rights and as chair of the UN Commission on Human Rights (1947–51). Among her autobiographical books are *This Is My Story* (1937), *On My Own* (1958) and *The Autobiography of Eleanor Roosevelt* (1961).

Roosevelt, Franklin Delano (1882–1945) 32nd President of the U.S. (1933–45), he served during an era of crisis, dealing with the complex problems of the GREAT DEPRESSION and leading the nation during WORLD WAR II.

Born at Hyde Park, New York, of an old and distinguished American family, he was educated at Harvard and at Columbia Law School. A lifelong Democrat, he entered politics in 1910 as a New York state senator. In 1912 he fought vigorously against Tammany Hall–supported candidates and for the nomination of Woodrow WILSON, and was awarded the post of assistant secretary of the navy, serving from 1913 to 1920. Roosevelt was the vice presidential candidate on the unsuccessful 1920 ticket of James COX. The following year he was stricken with poliomyelitis. His career apparently over, Roosevelt refused to give up, pursuing a course of rigorous physical therapy and eventually walking with the assistance of leg braces. He supported New York governor Alfred E. SMITH for the presidency in 1924 and 1928. When Smith secured the nomination in 1928, he urged Roosevelt to run for the governor's office. Smith lost, but Roosevelt was victorious. During his four years in Albany, he initiated a number of social reforms that were to serve as a prelude to his legislative program in the White House and assembled the BRAIN TRUST advisers who would counsel him during his presidency. Roosevelt was nominated by the Democrats in 1932 and easily defeated President Herbert HOOVER. He was inaugurated in the midst of a national banking crisis, with some 13 million Americans unemployed.

In his address, he told his audience that "the only thing we have to fear is fear itself," and he immediately began a campaign to deal with the Great Depression during the famous HUNDRED DAYS (March–June 1933), inaugurating programs that entailed the expenditure of vast public funds in the pursuit of economic recovery. Roosevelt's NEW DEAL measures included banking regulation, the abandonment of the gold standard, bank deposit insurance, the passage of the SOCIAL SECURITY ACT and the Wagner Labor Relations Act and the creation of a number of powerful federal agencies whose mandate was to provide relief to suffering Americans and to revivify the American economy, with emphasis on restructuring agricultural, business and labor practices. These agencies included the Federal Emergency Relief Administration, Civil Works Administration, PUBLIC WORKS ADMINISTRATION, WORKS PROGRESS ADMINISTRATION, NATIONAL RECOVERY ADMINISTRATION, AGRICULTURAL

ADJUSTMENT ADMINISTRATION, SECURITIES AND EXCHANGE COMMISSION, Home Owners Loans Corporation, CIVILIAN CONSERVATION CORPS and TENNESSEE VALLEY AUTHORITY. He also initiated the "fireside chats," radio broadcasts in which he informed the public of his intentions and actions. Roosevelt's massive efforts toward curing the ills of the Depression resulted in his overwhelming victory in the 1936 election.

However, opposition to New Deal measures, particularly in the business community, hardened during his second term. When the Supreme Court invalidated a number of New Deal measures, Roosevelt attempted to restructure the Court (1937) but failed. Nonetheless, New Deal programs did much to ameliorate the desperate economic and social situation, and in 1937 Roosevelt secured the passage of new labor legislation that ensured a 40-hour week and minimum wages for many industries. Concentrating on domestic recovery, Roosevelt established a foreign policy that promoted a "good neighbor policy" toward Latin America. His most notable action was probably the recognition of the USSR in 1933. He attempted to maintain American neutrality, but by 1938 he was speaking out strongly against the aggression of Germany and Japan. When World War II broke out in Europe, Roosevelt speeded up a program for national

Franklin Delano Roosevelt, 32nd president of the United States (LIBRARY OF CONGRESS, PRINTS AND PHOTOGRAPHS DIVISION)

armament, seeking to make the U.S. an "arsenal of democracy." Winning an unprecedented third term in 1940, he gradually moved the country toward war. In 1941 LENDLEASE was initiated and the ATLANTIC CHARTER was signed. After the Japanese attack on PEARL HARBOR (December 7, 1941), the U.S. was plunged into the war. Along with Prime Minister Winston CHURCHILL, Roosevelt did much to shape Allied military strategy. With little debate over war policy, Roosevelt was elected to a fourth term in 1944, with Harry S TRUMAN as vice president. As the tide of battle turned in favor of the Allies, Roosevelt participated in a number of international conferences with Churchill, STALIN, CHIANG KAI-SHEK and others, meetings that did much to plan the postwar world. After the YALTA CONFERENCE (February 1945), an exhausted Roosevelt traveled to Warm Springs, Georgia, where he died suddenly on April 12.

Roosevelt, Theodore *(1858–1919)*
Twenty-sixth president of the U.S. (1901–09). A dominant figure in American political life from the turn of the century to the beginning of WORLD WAR I, he was born in New York City of a wealthy and distinguished New York family. Frail in health, he pursued phys-

Theodore Roosevelt. 26th president of the United States (LIBRARY OF CONGRESS. PRINTS AND PHOTOGRAPHS DIVISION)

ical fitness with zeal while cultivating a sharp intellect. He attended Harvard University, graduating in 1880. An independent and progressive Republican, he entered politics as a member of the New York state assembly (1882). The deaths of his mother and his wife in 1884 caused him to retire to a Dakota Territory ranch for two years. Returning to New York City in 1886, he ran unsuccessfully for mayor and became an important figure in the state's Republican Party. At the same time he became known for his writings, including biographies and the historical *Winning of the West* (1889–96). He served as a progressive-minded member of the Civil Service Commission (1889–95) before becoming head of the New York City police board (1895–97) and assistant secretary of the navy (1897–98). At the outbreak of the Spanish-American War (1898), he organized a volunteer cavalry division known as the Rough Riders and won fame for his service in Cuba. Returning to the U.S. as a heroic colonel, he was nominated for governor and won a closely contested race. As governor (1899–1900) he was entirely too progressive to suit Republican boss Thomas Collier Platt, who, in an attempt to rid the state of Roosevelt, engineered a scheme to have him nominated for vice president on the Republican ticket for 1900. Elected, he was spared vice presidential obscurity with the assassination of President MCKINLEY in 1901.

A vivid character, a bluff and powerful speaker, a robust outdoorsman and a spokesman for the ordinary citizen, "T. R." soon became an immensely popular leader. A progressive activist, he took on the abusive power of the large corporations in his "trust-busting" efforts by initiating about 40 lawsuits against the largest of the nation's business monopolies. An ardent conservationist, he also supported land reclamation, irrigation and the expansion of forest reserves. In foreign policy Roosevelt was aggressive and vigorous, particularly in relation to Latin America. He intervened in a Panamanian civil war (1903) and was active in promoting the building of the PANAMA CANAL the following year. His popularity resulted in a landslide victory in the 1904 elections. Highlights of his second term were his mediation of the RUSSO-JAPANESE WAR in 1905, for which he won the 1906 NOBEL PRIZE

for peace, and the passage of the Pure Food and Drug Act of 1906. His handpicked successor, William Howard TAFT, became president in 1909, and Roosevelt retired. However, disputes with the new president drew him back into politics. He was unsuccessful in seeking the 1912 Republican presidential nomination, and subsequently formed a progressive third party (popularly known as the Bull Moose Party). When Roosevelt split the Republican vote, Woodrow WILSON was elected. Roosevelt resumed his Republicanism and remained an important force in the party and the nation until his death.

Root, Elihu *(1845–1937)* American
statesman. Born in Clinton, New York, Root practiced law in New York City and served as U.S. attorney for the southern district of New York from 1883 to 1885. A Republican, he was secretary of war from 1899 to 1904 under Presidents William MCKINLEY and Theodore ROOSEVELT, modernizing the army and, in 1901, founding the Army War College. As Roosevelt's secretary of state (1905–09), he was instrumental in securing improved relations with Latin America and an agreement (1908) with Japan and in negotiating arbitration treaties with various European countries. Root, who declined to run for office, was appointed senator from New York in 1909 and served until 1915. He participated in the Hague Tribunal and played a vital role in negotiating the North Atlantic Coast Fisheries Arbitration of 1910. In 1912 Root was awarded the NOBEL PRIZE for peace in recognition of his efforts to promote world peace. He strongly supported American participation in the LEAGUE OF NATIONS and was a drafter of the constitution for the World Court.

Roots The most-watched dramatic
show in television history. An estimated 100 million viewers (nearly half the population of America) saw the first telecast of the eight episodes in January 1977. Alex HALEY's massive 850-page novel traced his own roots back to 1750 in Gambia, West Africa, with the birth of Kunta Kinte. Subsequent generations of the family were slaves in America from the Revolution through the Civil War. The story ended as Tom, the great-grandson of Kunta,

began a new life in Tennessee. This "miniseries" format "allowed television to achieve the thematic power and narrative sweep ordinarily reserved for film." While there were some isolated incidents of racial unrest following some of the episodes, a survey of the NAACP claimed, in general, that the series stimulated black history awareness and education in schools and colleges. The series garnered an unprecedented 37 Emmy nominations and received 9 Emmys. Alex Haley received a National Book Award and a special PULITZER PRIZE.

Rorem, C. Rufus *(1894–1988)* U.S. economist; his early advocacy of prepaid health care and group medical practice led to the founding of Blue Cross and Blue Shield. Rorem's radical proposals began to be put into practice when he became head of the American Hospital Association in 1937. He was the father of composer Ned Rorem.

Rorschach test One of the best known of all psychological tests, devised by German psychologist Hermann Rorschach. Consisting of a series of abstract inkblot shapes, as well as a separate series of chromatic patterns, it is designed to test the perceptual and analytic tendencies of the test subject. It is administered via the free response of the subject as to what he or she "sees" in the shapes and patterns displayed. Rorschach set forth the research findings on which his test is based in *Psychodiagnostics: A Diagnostics Test Based on Perception* (1942). It is frequently used to this day as a measure of the subconscious contents of the psyche.

Rose, Billy (William Samuel Rosenberg) *(1899–1966)* American producer and lyricist. A showman who produced revues, musicals, Aquacades and expositions, Rose began his career as a lyricist, writing songs for such revues as the *Charlot Revue of 1926*. In 1929 he collaborated with Edward Eliscu and Vincent Youmans on the score for the show *Great Day*, writing lyrics for such songs as "More Than You Know" and "Without a Song." After producing a series of revues on Broadway, he produced the hit shows *Jumbo* (1935) and *Carmen Jones* (1943). The comedienne Fanny BRICE was his first wife.

Rose, Pete *(1942–)* American baseball player and manager. Pete Rose's legacy may be that of the greatest player never named to the Baseball Hall of Fame. Rookie of the year in 1963, Rose led the Cincinnati Reds' "Big Red Machine" to four National League championships and two World Series victories from 1970 to 1976. His aggressive level of play gave him the nickname "Charlie Hustle," and he was as hated in opposing ballparks as he was beloved in his own. He hit close to or over 200 hits a season 12 times and reached the .300 mark in nine consecutive seasons. An outstanding outfielder, his fielding accuracy reached record heights in 1974, with a .992 percentage. During his last season with the Reds, 1978, he had hits in 44 consecutive games, a league record. The following year he joined the Philadelphia Phillies, and the team went on to win the World Series in 1983. After a brief stint in Montreal, he rejoined the Reds as player-manager in 1984. Upon retiring as a player in 1986, Rose stood at the top of the major league all-time hit list, ahead of longtime leader Ty COBB. However, years of rumor about his gambling problems caught up with Rose, and in 1989 baseball commissioner A. Bart GIAMATTI banned Rose from baseball for life for having bet on games, stating that Rose's actions were detrimental to the game of baseball. Rose was subsequently convicted of tax evasion and served a prison term. Although he was declared ineligible for the Baseball Hall of Fame in 1991, Rose's bat remained on display at Cooperstown. Rose formally admitted in January 2004 that he gambled on baseball in an interview with ABC News journalist Charles Gibson.

Rosenberg, Harold *(1906–1978)* American art critic. Born in New York City, during the 1940s and '50s he was one of the chief admirers and theorists of ABSTRACT EXPRESSIONISM and the coiner of the phrase "action painting." The art critic for *New York* magazine and a contributor to many other periodicals, he was known for his intellectually rigorous analyses of contemporary art. Among his books are *The Tradition of the New* (1959), *The Anxious Object* (1966) and *Art on the Edge* (1975).

Rosenberg, Isaac *(1890–1918)* English poet and painter. Born in Bristol, he grew up in London and studied art at the city's Slade School from 1911 to 1914. Establishing some reputation as an artist, he exhibited at the Whitechapel Gallery. Enlisting in the British army in 1915, he fought in WORLD WAR I. His finest poems are considered to be his elegiac verses that describe his wartime experiences. A promising career was cut short when he was killed in battle in France. His *Collected Poems* were published posthumously in 1922.

Rosenberg Trial *(1951)* Sensational U.S. treason trial in which Julius and Ethel Rosenberg were sentenced to death for passing atomic secrets to the Russians. In 1949 the Soviet Union detonated its first atomic bomb, only four years after the first U.S. bomb. U.S. intelligence implicated Julius and Ethel Rosenberg, along with Morton Sobel, as having passed atomic secrets to the Russians.

Although the U.S. and the Soviet Union were still officially postwar allies, the trio were tried for treason in 1951 at the time of the KOREAN WAR and at the height of the anti-left MCCARTHY hysteria. The ensuing treason trial generated daily headlines and resulted in the Rosenbergs being sentenced to death and Sobel to 30 years in prison. The verdict was controversial; many liberals believed the pair innocent or deserving of a much lighter penalty. However, the third volume of Nikita KHRUSCHCHEV's memoirs, published posthumously in 1990, confirmed that Julius Rosenberg had indeed been a Soviet spy and had passed U.S. atomic secrets to the grateful Soviets with the full knowledge of his wife.

Ross, Diana *(1944–)* American singer and actress. Ross began her singing career as the lead performer with a group called "The Supremes." The original Supremes were Jean Terrell, Diana Ross and Florence Ballard. By 1964 the group had received seven gold records in less than two years. It was the first group to have five consecutive records reach the top of the best seller charts. As her fame grew the group's name changed to "Diana Ross and the Supremes." She eventually decided to do solo work and continued her successful career. Ross starred in such motion pictures as *Lady Sings the*

Blues (1972), *Mahogany* (1974) and *The Wiz* (1984). She has been the recipient of a certificate from Vice President Hubert HUMPHREY for her efforts on behalf of President JOHNSON's Youth Opportunity Program, and citations from Mrs. Martin Luther King, Jr., and Reverend Ralph ABERNATHY for contributions to the SOUTHERN CHRISTIAN LEADERSHIP CONFERENCE. Ross won a Grammy award as top female singer in 1972 and was named female entertainer of the year and given the Image award for best actress by the NAACP.

Ross, Harold See NEW YORKER, THE.

Ross, Sinclair *(1908–1996)* Canadian novelist. Born near Prince Albert, Saskatchewan, he was a banker until his retirement in 1968. His reputation rests on his first novel, *As for Me and My House* (1941), a bleak picture of the loneliness of life on the Canadian prairie written in diary form that has become a classic of modern Canadian literature. He wrote three other novels, *The Well, Whir of Gold* and *Sawbones Memorial,* as well as the short story collections. *The Lamp at Noon and Other Stories* (1968) and *The Race and Other Stories.*

Rossellini, Roberto *(1906–1977)* Italian movie director. Rossellini was the first director to draw international attention to the neorealist style of filmmaking. He received international acclaim for his film *Roma, Citta Aperta* (1945). Other important neorealist films were *Paisa* (1947) and *Germania, Anno Zero* (1947). His reputation was enhanced by such films as *Viaggio in Italia* (1952) in which he directed his wife, Ingrid BERGMAN. He has also directed for the theater and television.

Rossi, Aldo *(1931–1997)* Italian postmodern architect and architectural theorist and winner of the Pritzker Architecture Prize (1990). Born in Milan, Italy, Rossi began to study architecture in 1947 when he enrolled at the Milan Polytechnic, a prestigious Italian school devoted to the sciences. After graduating in 1959, he was hired by *Casabella-Continuita,* a Milanese architectural and art magazine. By 1961 he had become editor of *Casabella-Continuita* and began teaching a few classes at his alma mater. In 1966 he published *L'Architettura della citta* (The Architecture of the City), which examined the construction of the city as an organic unit and advocated the use of postmodern designs and concepts. This work established him as a prominent architectural theorist as well as one of the few individuals who articulated a cohesive conception of urban planning.

Rossi is well known for designing and overseeing the construction of a variety of works across the globe. In 1971, he entered his design for the cemetery of San Cataldo in an architectural contest. His sketch won first place and marked Rossi as a pioneering architect for his conceptualization of a cemetery resembling a city for the dead. Shortly after that he began work on Gallaratese, a housing development situated at the edge of Milan. In 1979, he designed the Teatro del Mondo, a floating theater to be used during the Venice Biennale, a year-long prestigious international arts exhibition. For the city of Genoa he designed the Carlo Felice Theatre, which now is home to the National Opera of Italy. Rossi was also commissioned to design structures outside of Italy. In 1987 he completed work on the Toronto Lighthouse Theatre. In the U.S., he is well known for his creation of the Pocono Pines Houses in Pennsylvania, a monumental arch in Galveston, Texas, and the building housing the School of Architecture at the University of Miami. In Japan, he designed the Il Palazzo Hotel and Restaurant Complex in Fukuoka as well as an art gallery in Tokyo. In 1989 Rossi's proposed structure for the German Historical Museum in West Berlin was selected over 200 other entries. In 1990, he was awarded the Pritzker Architecture Prize, the most prestigious award for an architect, for his contributions to the theory and art of architecture. In 1997, shortly after receiving news that his proposed design for a skyscraper in Soho had been chosen, Rossi died in a car crash in New York.

Rostropovich, Mstislav *(1927–)* Russian cellist and conductor. Born in Baku, Azerbaijan, of a musical family, he and his family moved to Moscow in 1931, and he attended the Gnessin Institute and the Moscow Conservatory. There he studied composition under Dimitri SHOSTAKOVICH, who became a close friend and a great influence on his career. He made his professional debut at the age of 13. Winning the World Festival cello competition in Budapest (1949) and the International Competition in Prague (1950), Rostropovich quickly became one of the USSR's most acclaimed soloists. His first appearance outside the USSR was in Florence in 1951, and he soon began an active touring schedule that made him a worldwide reputation for his superb musicianship. He made his first appearance as a conductor in 1961, and he has maintained an active career in conducting. Rostropovich has excelled as a soloist in the entire range of classical cello works, and as a conductor he has stressed such Russian composers as PROKOFIEV and Shostakovich in his repertoire. Essentially apolitical, he incurred the displeasure of Soviet authorities when he sheltered Aleksandr SOLZHENITSYN in his country home in 1970. Under increased musical strictures, he and his wife, the noted soprano Galina VISHNEVSKAYA, and children fled the USSR in 1974. In 1976 he was appointed music director of the National Symphony Orchestra, Washington, D.C., and in 1978 he and his wife were stripped of their Soviet citizenship. They remained as exiles, but with the thawing of the COLD WAR were able to return to the USSR on a musical tour in 1990. Since his participation in a 1991 concert to commemorate the 85th anniversary of Carnegie Hall, Rostropovich has recorded seven albums—*Concerto No. 2 for Cello and Orchestra* (1992), *Trio Sonatas* (1995), *Violin Concertos* (1995), *Lease Breakers* (1996), *Shostakovich: Violin Concerto, Op. 99; Cello Concerto, Op. 107* (1998), *Great Film Music* (1999), and *My First 79 Years* (1999).

Roszak, Theodore *(1907–1981)* Polish-born sculptor best known for his work in welded steel, which often evoked an emotional response through its powerful, sometimes violent images. Roszak was the center of a controversy in 1960 when the eagle he designed for the U.S. embassy in London was pronounced "gaudy" and too big for its sober, subdued surroundings.

Rota, Nino *(1911–1979)* Italian composer best known for his many motion picture scores. A child prodigy in his home town of Milan, Rota composed an oratorio at the age of 11. Later he studied at the Santa Cecilia Academy in Rome and the Curtis Institute in Philadelphia. Although he wrote many orchestral and stage works in his lifetime, including four symphonies and eight operas, his movie scores secured his reputation. He was associated with some of the world's greatest filmmakers, including Luchino VISCONTI (*Il Gattopardo/The Leopard,* 1963), Franco ZEFFIRELLI (*Romeo and Juliet,* 1968) and Francis Ford COPPOLA (the first two *Godfather* films, 1972 and 1974). His long and brilliant association with Federico FELLINI, beginning with *Lo Sceicco bianco* (*The White Sheik,* 1952) and concluding with *Prova d'Orchestra* (*Orchestra Rehearsal,* 1979), produced his most memorable scores. His buoyant, tuneful melodies provide a counterpart to the many parades, circus acts and strutting characters of the Fellini world. Like the painted face of actress Giulietta Masina in pictures like *La Strada* (*The Road,* 1954) and *Le Notti di Cabiria* (*Nights of Cabiria,* 1956), Rota's music holds up the promise of a bright, brittle gaiety; but ultimately, in the words of a Fellini character, it delivers a "very sad song."

Rotblat, Joseph (*1908– *) Polishborn British physicist, founder of the PUGWASH CONFERENCES and winner of the Nobel Peace Prize (1995). Born in Warsaw, Rotblat began to devote his life to the study of physics in graduate school. In 1932, he received his M.A. in physics from the Free University of Poland, followed five years later by his Ph. D. in physics from the Free University. After receiving his doctorate, Rotblat traveled to Britain, where he became the assistant director of the Atom Physics Institute. Two years later, Rotblat began working with the British scientist James CHADWICK to determine the feasibility of constructing an atomic bomb. Rotblat and Chadwick traveled in 1943 to Los Alamos, New Mexico, to work on the top-secret Manhattan Project to produce and test an atomic bomb. In November 1944, when British and American intelligence estimates concluded that Nazi Germany lacked the capability to construct an atomic device, Rotblat left Los Alamos, the only scientist to do so prior to the bomb's use on Hiroshima and Nagasaki.

At the end of World War II, Rotblat was hired as the director of research in nuclear physics at the University of Liverpool, a post he held for the next four years. He also began a crusade against the military uses of atomic power. In 1946 he helped create the Atomic Scientists Association, which sought to dissuade atomic physicists from collaborating in military-oriented research. The following year, he developed the "Atom Train," a traveling exhibition that displayed the possible civilian uses and benefits of atomic energy and criticized its application to military needs. In 1955 he was one of 11 scientists to sign a manifesto drafted by Bertrand RUSSELL and Albert EINSTEIN that asked scientists throughout the world to propose methods of avoiding a nuclear holocaust. To this end, he and American philanthropist Cyrus Eaton founded the first Pugwash Conference in 1957. Named after the small Canadian town in which the first conference was held, it represented an assemblage of prominent scientists and influential individuals opposed to nuclear weaponry and devoted to proposing methods for improving the chances of world peace. Rotblat became the conference's general secretary, a position he has held ever since. In 1958 he helped found the Campaign for Nuclear Disarmament in Great Britain, an independent organization designed to educate the British people about the dangers that the stockpiling of nuclear weapons posed to world peace. For his efforts to promote global disarmament and international stability Rotblat shared the 1995 Nobel Peace Prize with the organization he helped found.

Roth, Philip (*1933– *) American novelist. Roth was raised in an Orthodox Jewish household, and his religious background is reflected in his fiction, which wryly presents the angst of contemporary American life, often controversially. Roth first achieved success with *Good-bye, Columbus* (1959). *Portnoy's Complaint* (1969), perhaps his most notorious book, revealed a man's discussions with his psychiatrist. Roth has also written a series of novels following the life of imaginary novelist Nathan Zuckerman, including *My Life as a Man* (1974), *The Anatomy Lesson* (1983) and *Deception* (1990). Although Roth married his longtime

companion, Claire Bloom, in 1994, the couple separated two years later and were ultimately divorced. Roth received numerous prestigious awards during the 1990s, including the 1993 PEN/Faulkner Award for Fiction for *Operation Shylock* (1993); the 1997 Pulitzer Prize for *American Pastoral* (1997); the 1998 National Medal of Arts; and the 2002 American Academy of Arts and Letters' Gold Medal in Fiction. In 2004 Roth published *The Plot Against America*—an alternate history in which Charles H. Lindbergh wins the presidency at the outset of World War II and leads the U.S. into a Nazi alliance. This book was widely reviewed and received critical acclaim.

Rothermere, Esmond Cecil Harmsworth, Viscount (*1898–1978*) British newspaper publisher. Harmsworth was born into one of Britain's wealthiest and most powerful publishing families. He was the son of Harold Harmsworth (1st Viscount Rothermere, 1868–1940) and the nephew of Alfred Charles William Harmsworth (Lord NORTHCLIFFE). At age 21 Cecil Harmsworth became the youngest person ever elected to the House of Commons. He served in Parliament for 10 years, then entered the publishing business. He later inherited the family business and was publisher of the *Daily Mail* and the *Evening News.* He retired in 1971.

Rothko, Mark (*1903–1970*) American painter. Born in Dvinska, Russia, he emigrated to the U.S. in 1913. He attended Yale University (1921–23) and the Art Students League (1925), where he studied with Max Weber. Subsequently he was heavily influenced by SURREALISM. In the early 1940s he created pale canvases filled with biomorphic forms. By the late 1940s his work had become completely abstract. Perhaps the most lyrical practitioner of ABSTRACT EXPRESSIONISM, he is best known for his large and luminous compositions in which irregular rectangles of color appear to float against a glowing ground. Rothko had a rather mystical approach to his work, viewing his paintings as tools for meditation and expressions of emotion, not as mere formal exercises. He committed suicide on February 25, 1970.

Rothschild, Nathaniel Mayer Victor, third baron *(1910–1990)* A member of the English branch of the famous European banking family, he was a zoologist and business executive. He headed the UNITED KINGDOM's Central Policy Review Staff, known as the Whitehall "think tank," in the early 1970s and later went on to serve as an executive with Royal Dutch Shell. After his former friend Anthony BLUNT was exposed in 1979 as having been the "fourth man" in the BURGESS-MACLEAN-PHILBY Soviet spy ring, Rothschild was also accused of having been a member of the group. He denied the charge, and Prime Minister Margaret THATCHER declared that there was no evidence to support the accusation.

Roth v. United States *(1957)* U.S. Supreme Court decision defining First Amendment protection for obscene material. Roth, convicted of selling and mailing obscene literature in violation of a federal statute, protested that the enforcement of the law violated his First Amendment free speech rights. The Supreme Court held that obscene materials are not protected by the First Amendment.

A divided Court also announced a test to determine if a work was obscene: Would an average person consider that its dominant theme appealed to the prurient interest? Fifteen years later the Court relaxed this test to the following: Would the average person, applying contemporary local standards, find that it appeals to the prurient interest; and, if it depicts in a patently offensive way sexual activity specifically defined by state law, that it lacks any serious redeeming value? Despite this definition, the line between freedom of speech and obscenity remained a point of contention, as demonstrated in the 1989 MAPPLETHORPE controversy and similar cases. (See also PORNOGRAPHY AND OBSCENITY.)

Roussel, Albert *(1869–1937)* French composer. Born in the north of France, he served in the navy before studying (1898–1907) with Vincent d'INDY at the Schola Cantorum, where he became a professor (1902–14). His first compositions, such as the symphonic *Le Poeme de la foret* (1904–06) and the opera-ballet *Padmavati* (1918), were executed in an impressionistic style. Influenced by his study of 18th-century music and by STRAVINSKY, his later works stress a neoclassical approach and are also often touched with Oriental motifs, styles and rhythms. His mature works, notably the last three of his four symphonies and the ballet *Bacchus et Ariane* (1931), exhibit a delicate melodic sense mingled with elegant dissonances. His many other compositions include orchestral pieces, chamber music, choral works and songs.

Rowan, Carl T. *(1925–2000)* American journalist and governmental official. Rowan was born in Tennessee and in 1944 was among the first blacks to receive a navy commission. Following World War II, he attended Oberlin College and the University of Minnesota and in 1950 became a reporter of the *Minneapolis Tribune*. Rowan's books, based on his travels and on reporting assignments, include *South of Freedom* (1952), *The Pitiful and the Proud* (1956) and *Go South to Sorrow* (1957). In 1961, President KENNEDY named Rowan deputy assistant secretary of state for public affairs, and in 1963, ambassador to Finland. In 1964, President JOHNSON appointed him chief of the United States Information Agency (USIA), but Rowan resigned the following year after charges that USIA's VOICE OF AMERICA was biased in favor of the administration. Rowan returned to journalism, producing popular syndicated columns, providing television commentary, contributing to READER'S DIGEST and lecturing.

Rowe, James H. *(1909–1984)* Influential aide to President Franklin D. ROOSEVELT during the 1930s' NEW DEAL era. Rowe was one of the idealistic Harvard-educated lawyers who formed Roosevelt's BRAIN TRUST. He served on scores of federal boards and commissions. He later advised Adlai STEVENSON and Hubert HUMPHREY in their unsuccessful presidential bids and was credited with helping to place Lyndon B. JOHNSON on the ticket as John F. KENNEDY's vice presidential running mate in 1960.

Rowling, J. K. *(1965–)* British author, best known for creating, writing and developing the HARRY POTTER book series. Born in Chipping Sodbury, England, Rowling wanted to become a famous writer since she was six years of age. She cultivated her skills during her primary and secondary education, and, after graduating from the University of Exeter in 1991, Rowling took a job as an English teacher in Portugal. It was during her stay in Portugal that she conceived the basic premise for the *Harry Potter* series—the central figure was a young orphan who is kept ignorant of his magical powers and lineage by spiteful relatives. In 1990, Rowling met and married a Portuguese journalist, Jorge Arantes, with whom she had a daughter in 1993; the marriage ended in divorce later that year. In 1995 Rowling left Portugal and returned to Great Britain, where she began work on what became the first book in the *Harry Potter* series—*Harry Potter and the Philosopher's Stone,* (or *Harry Potter and the Sorcerer's Stone*) published in the U.S. in 1998. The book proved immensely popular in the U.S., Great Britain and 29 non-English speaking markets. It was quickly followed by *Harry Potter and the Chamber of Secrets* (1999), *Harry Potter and the Prisoner of Azkaban* (1999), *Harry Potter and the Goblet of Fire* (2000), and *Harry Potter and the Order of the Phoenix* (2003), and *Harry Potter and the Half-Blood Prince* (2005). Rowling also helped adapt her first three novels to motion pictures. Rowling anticipates writing two additional books in the *Harry Potter* series.

Roy, Maurice Cardinal *(1905–1985)* Roman Catholic primate of Canada (1956–81). Roy was long regarded as a leader of the moderate progressive wing of his church's hierarchy. Named archbishop of his native Quebec in 1947, he was designated a cardinal by Pope PAUL VI in 1965. From 1967 to 1977 he headed two VATICAN agencies, the Council of the Laity and the Pontifical Commission on Justice and Peace.

Royal Ballet Britain's national ballet company. Founded by Ninette de VALOIS and Lilian Baylis in 1931 as the Vic-Wells Ballet, it became Sadler's Wells Ballet in 1940 and the Royal Ballet in 1956. De Valois served as its director until 1963 and was succeeded by Sir Frederic ASHTON (1963–70), Sir Kenneth MACMILLAN (1970–77), Norman Morrice (1977–86), Anthony DOWELL (1986–2001), Ross Stretton (2001–02) and Monica Mason (from 2002). Internationally acclaimed, the company has its own school and a home theater at Covent Garden Opera House and balances classical tradition with original choreography. *The Sleeping Beauty* (first mounted in 1946) has become its signature work. Other famous ballets presented by the company include Ashton's *Symphonic Variations* and *The Dream,* and Macmillan's *Romeo and Juliet* and *Manon.* Dancers associated with the company include Dame Margot FONTEYN, Rudolph NUREYEV, Antoinette Sibley and Anthony Dowell.

Royal Danish Ballet One of the oldest ballet companies in the world (established 1748), the Royal Danish Ballet was dominated during the 19th century by August Bournonville, who created a series of ballets that form the Danish classical repertory and established the excellence of Danish male dancing. The company declined after Bournonville's death but experienced a second flowering under the direction of Harald Lander (1932–51). Lander gave the company an international repertoire and gained it international recognition. The directors that followed Lander have struggled to maintain the Bournonville ballets and style while developing a contemporary repertory. Outstanding 20th-century Royal Danish dancers include Margot Lander, Borge Ralov, Henning Kronstam, Erik BRUHN, Peter MARTINS and Peter Schaufuss.

Royal National Theatre A theater complex in London consisting of three theaters, performance and exhibition space, restaurants, and shops that was established in 1962 with Sir Laurence OLIVIER as director of its board. Subsequent directors are Peter HALL, Richard Eyre and David Aukin. The idea for the theater was a long time in being realized. In 1907 the Shakespeare Memorial National Theatre Committee was established. In 1944 a site on the South Bank of the Thames was found, and in 1976 the Lyttelton, Olivier and Cottesloe theaters began to open. "Royal" was added to the name in 1988. The repertory company presents both traditional and modern, experimental drama.

Royal Shakespeare Company A British theater company established in

1960 under the direction of Peter HALL. The company achieved success in 1963 with its production of the The *Wars of the Roses* cycle of Shakespeare's works, but it presents the works of other traditional and modern playwrights as well. The company, which has had many eminent theatrical personalities among it ranks, has performed in Stratford and London as well as touring internationally. In the 1980s the company went to Broadway with an adaptation of Dicken's *Nicholas Nickleby,* Hugo's *Les Miserables* and an unfortunate presentation of Stephen KING'S *Carrie.*

Royce, Josiah *(1855–1916)* American philosopher. Born in Grass Valley, California, Royce studied at the University of California and received his doctorate from Johns Hopkins University in 1870. Royce taught at the University of California until 1882, when he joined the faculty of Harvard, where he taught for the rest of his life. Royce was the foremost American idealist of his day. He combined idealism and nationalism in a peculiarly American way, taking into consideration both history and science and stressing action as well as thought. He posited an absolute God, an all-knowing cosmic purpose, in an absolute self, an absolute mind and an absolute community, which deserves humanity's loyalty. Royce saw mankind as a part of the logos and thus able to know reality beyond itself. His ideas were very influential in the religious and ethical thought of his era. Among his books are *The World and the Individual* (1900–01), *The Philosophy of Loyalty* (1908) and *Modern Idealism* (1919).

Ruanda-Urundi A colonial territory in central Africa that was formerly known as Belgian East Africa but has now been divided into the independent states of RWANDA and BURUNDI; the capital was at Usumbura (now Bujumbura). The area became part of German East Africa in the early 20th century. In 1916, during WORLD WAR I, it was taken by BELGIUM. In 1924 the LEAGUE OF NATIONS assigned the territory to Belgium as a mandate. In 1946 Ruanda-Urundi was made a trust territory of the UNITED NATIONS. The two nations of Rwanda and Burundi were created when the territory was granted independence on July 1, 1962.

Rubin, Jerry *(1938–1994)* American political activist. Rubin became involved in the Vietnam ANTIWAR MOVEMENT in Berkeley, California, in 1964. He was very adept at organizing and gaining media attention for antiwar rallies. In 1968 Rubin's Yippie (Youth International) Party demonstrated during the Democratic National Convention in Chicago; Rubin and others were arrested. Media coverage of confrontations between the police and the demonstrators overshadowed the convention. (See also CHICAGO 7 TRIAL.)

Rubinstein, Arthur *(1887–1982)* Legendary Polish concert pianist; one of the most popular pianists of the 20th century, during his lifetime his fame was equaled only by that of Vladimir HOROWITZ, whose style and personality were very different. Born in Lodz (in Russian Poland), as a young man Rubinstein spent much time in Paris and Berlin and toured widely in Europe and North and South America. Although a prodigy, Rubinstein did not gain acceptance as a great pianist until the 1930s. He was one of the first pianists to take advantage of the new medium of electronic recording, and during his long career he recorded virtually his entire repertoire. His interpretations of the music of Chopin are regarded as definitive; his performances of Beethoven and Brahms, among other composers, were exceptional. Stylistically, Rubinstein's playing was remarkable for its effortless lyricism and lack of romantic affectation,

Concert pianist Arthur Rubinstein (LIBRARY OF CONGRESS, PRINTS AND PHOTOGRAPHS DIVISION)

yet also for its great warmth, subtlety and expressiveness; in many ways, he was the first truly modern pianist. He gave concerts until the age of 90.

Ruby, Jack (Jacob Rubinstein) *(1911–1967)* American nightclub operator, assassin of Lee Harvey OSWALD. Ruby was a shadowy figure in Dallas, Texas, a feature of local nightlife with reputed connections to organized crime. Allegedly a great admirer of President John F. KENNEDY, he shot the president's alleged killer on November 24, 1963, as Oswald was being escorted to an armored truck in the basement of the Dallas municipal building. Ruby has often been accused of implication in one of any number of assassination plots. However, he steadfastly denied this as well as any previous connection with Oswald. Convicted of murder, Ruby died in prison while awaiting retrial on appeal.

Rudel, Hans Ulrich *(1916–1982)* German bomber pilot during WORLD WAR II. Rudel was one of the most decorated German soldiers of the war. He flew 2,500 missions in a Stuka dive-bomber, mostly on the Russian front (see WORLD WAR II ON THE RUSSIAN FRONT). He was credited with destroying 519 tanks, 150 gun emplacements and 800 combat vehicles. He continued to espouse Nazi doctrines for many years after the war.

Rudolph, Wilma *(1940–1994)* American athlete. Born into a poor family in St. Bethlehem, Tennessee, Rudolph was stricken with a childhood illness that left one leg crippled. With physical therapy, she made a full recovery, and at age 16 she had secured a place on the 1956 U.S. Olympic track team, where she was a member of the bronze-medal-winning relay team. In the 1960 Olympics, Rudolph won three gold medals—in the 100 meters, the 200 meters and again in the relay—earning her the nickname "the Black Gazelle." Rudolph set three records in 1961, for the 60- and 220-yard dashes and for the 400-meter relay. That year she was named the Associated Press female athlete of the year and was awarded the Sullivan Memorial Trophy by the AAU as outstanding amateur athlete of 1961. In later years,

Rudolph became a coach and teacher and was active in youth charities.

Ruffian *(1972–1975)* Thoroughbred racehorse. The greatest filly of her time, Ruffian seemed destined to become one of the greatest racehorses of all time. The winner of five straight races as a two-year-old, she was named the champion filly of 1974. In 1975, the big black filly reeled off five more wins, including New York's triple distaff crown. The bringing together of Ruffian and that year's leading colt, Foolish Pleasure, in a match race at Belmont generated enormous interest. While the two horses were head-to-head, Ruffian stumbled. Her right foreleg was broken, and her gallant attempt to keep running damaged the leg irreparably. Attempts were made to save her, but the filly thrashed about and caused herself further damage. Ruffian was put down and is buried in the infield at Belmont.

Ruffing, Charles "Red" *(1904–1986)* U.S. athlete. His baseball career spanned 22 seasons ending in 1947. Considered the best-hitting pitcher of his era, he spent 15 seasons with the New York Yankees. His lifetime regular season record was 273 victories and 225 defeats, with four consecutive 20-win seasons. His career batting average of .269 included eight seasons over .300. He was elected to the Baseball Hall of Fame in 1967.

Ruggles, Carl *(1876–1971)* American composer. Born in Marion, Massachusetts, he attended Harvard University. Like his friend Charles IVES, Ruggles was an American original who rejected traditional musical forms. A conductor of small orchestral and chamber groups and a teacher at the University of Florida at Miami (1937–46), he was careful and self-critical, creating a comparatively small oeuvre. Dense and vigorous, his complexly atonal compositions include works for the piano and voice as well as chamber music and orchestral pieces. Among his better-known works are the orchestral *Men and Mountains* (1924), the tone poem *Sun-Treader* (1932) and the piano piece *Evocations* (1934–43).

Ruhr German river that flows westward into the Rhine at Duisburg. The

name Ruhr often also refers to the valley itself, GERMANY's industrial heartland. The Ruhr valley includes such centers of industry as Bochum, Dortmund, Duisburg and Essen. Huge coal and steel empires were developed here by the Krupp and Thyssen families during the 19th century. From 1923 to 1925 the Ruhr was occupied by Belgian and French forces during a dispute over Germany's postwar reparations payments. Adolf HITLER used the French occupation as an excuse to rise against the WEIMAR REPUBLIC in his unsuccessful BEER HALL PUTSCH of 1923. The Ruhr was the primary center of Germany's war production during WORLD WAR II. As such, it was heavily bombed by the Allies; the cities of the region suffered great damage. After the war, the Ruhr remained under the control of the Allies until 1954, when it was turned over to WEST GERMANY.

Rule, Elton Hoert *(1916–1990)* American executive. Rule was president of ABC (American Broadcasting Company) from 1973 to 1983. His pioneering use of mini-series, made-for-TV movies and Monday Night Football helped the once-ailing company become the dominant U.S. television network in the 1970s.

Rumor, Mariano *(1915–1990)* Italian politician. A Christian Democrat, Rumor held the post of premier five times between 1968 and 1974. He served during turbulent times in ITALY and had to contend with economic crises, student protests, labor unrest and terrorism from extremists of both the left and the right. In 1976 he was investigated for possible involvement in the LOCKHEED SCANDAL. The U.S. aircraft maker had admitted bribing Italian officials to help ease negotiations over a large airplane contract. Rumor denied the charges and was narrowly exonerated by parliament.

Rumsfeld, Donald *(1932–)* U.S. secretary of defense (1975–77, and 2001–2006). Born in Chicago, Rumsfeld began his political career in 1962 when he was elected to the U.S. House of Representatives from Illinois. In 1969 he became the head of the Office of Economic Opportunity in the administration of Richard NIXON. After Nixon's reelection in 1972, Rumsfeld was appointed U.S.

ambassador to NATO and briefly served as a member of President Gerald Ford's "transition team" before becoming the country's youngest secretary of defense in 1975.

When the Ford administration ended in January 1977, Rumsfeld served in several high positions in private industry until being named secretary of defense by President BUSH in 2001.

As secretary of defense, Rumsfeld focused on reforming the U.S. armed forces to deal with post–cold war threats to the U.S. He was instrumental in persuading President Bush to withdraw from the 1972 Anti-Ballistic Missile Treaty and actively promoted a NATIONAL MISSILE DEFENSE system. After the terrorist attacks of SEPTEMBER 11, 2001, Rumsfeld was a staunch advocate of military action to topple the Taliban regime in AFGHANISTAN. He also successfully argued for the overthrow of Iraq's Saddam HUSSEIN, and masterminded "Operation Iraqi Freedom" that achieved that result in March 2003. Rumsfeld, Vice President Dick Cheney and Deputy Secretary of Defense Paul Wolfowitz (the three principal proponents of overthrowing the Hussein regime because it possessed weapons of mass destruction) came under sharp criticism in the aftermath of the war in Iraq when no weapons of mass destruction were found. Rumsfeld resigned after Republicans were soundly defeated in the 2006 elections.

Runcie, Robert *(1921–2000)* Archbishop of Canterbury (1979–90) and spiritual leader of the Anglican Church. Runcie was known for his outspoken liberal political views, which sometimes clashed with the policies of Tory prime minister Margaret THATCHER. In particular, Runcie called for a less strictly materialistic approach to economic issues and the plight of the poor. Runcie parted company with his predecessor, Archbishop Donald COGGAN, by insisting that the ordination of women as priests was a reform for which the Anglican Church was not yet ready. Prior to his election as archbishop, Runcie had been bishop of St. Albans and a professor of theology at Cambridge University.

Rundstedt, Karl Rudolf Gerd von *(1875–1953)* German military commander during WORLD WAR II. Rundstedt led the BLITZKRIEG in Poland (1939), the French campaign in 1940 and the Russian campaign in 1941. He was supreme commander in the west from 1942 to 1945. Rundstedt led the German counteroffensive, known as the Battle of the BULGE, in 1944. The British held him as a possible war criminal after Germany's defeat, but he was released in 1949 because of poor health. (See also Battle of FRANCE; WORLD WAR II ON THE EASTERN FRONT; WORLD WAR II ON THE WESTERN FRONT.)

Runyon, Damon *(1884–1946)* American author. Runyon began his career as a sports writer and brought the immediacy of reporting to his colorful fiction, which painted a racy picture of New York's underworld during the 1920s and '30s. His short stories, such as "Guys and Dolls" (1931), have been collected into such works as *The Damon Runyon Omnibus* (1944) and *The Best of Damon Runyon* (1966), and many of them have been adapted into plays and films.

Ruschi, Augusto *(1916–1986)* Brazilian naturalist. His work included cataloging 80% of known species of Brazilian hummingbirds. He became a hero in his country for defending a nature preserve against deforestation and encroaching coffee farms. His death from cirrhosis of the liver came less than six months after his widely publicized announcement that Amazonian Indian treatments had cured him of progressive liver failure, which he said had come from handling poisonous toads. At least one British medical specialist had attributed Ruschi's condition not to toads but to the cumulative effect of treatment with antimalarial agents.

Rushdie, Salman *(1947–)* British novelist. A Muslim, Rushdie was born in Bombay, India. His family emigrated to Pakistan in 1964, and he was educated at King's College, Cambridge. He remained in England, initially to pursue a career as an actor. Rushdie's first novel, *Grimus* (1975), did not impress readers or critics. He established his reputation with *Midnight's Children* (1981), which won the Booker Prize, among other awards. Rushdie's fiction is associated with MAGIC REALISM and is rich in Muslim imagery. Rushdie received a peculiar notoriety with the publication of *The Satanic Verses* (1988). A critically acclaimed story of the struggle between good and evil, the book contains two chapters, "Mahound" and "Return to Jahiliya," that many Muslims deem to be a blasphemous and obscene mockery of the origins of Islam. On February 14, 1989, the Ayatollah KHOMEINI pronounced a death sentence on Rushdie, urging Muslims to execute not only him but the publishers of the book. A day later an aide to Khomeini offered a million-dollar reward for Rushdie's death, and he was forced into hiding. Many bookstores, fearful of attack, stopped selling the book, and his publishers were hesitant about releasing a paperback edition, causing much outcry about freedom of speech and censorship. The book was banned in several countries, among them Pakistan, India and Egypt, and violent protests in these countries caused several deaths. Rushdie attempted to appease his critics with the essay "In Good Faith" (1990) and issued an apology in which he reaffirmed his respect for Islam. While in hiding, Rushdie published *Haroun and the Sea of Stories* (1990). Rushdie continued to publish novels, including *The Moors Last Sight* (1995), *The Ground Beneath Her Feet* (1999) and *Fury* (2001). In September 1998 the Iranian government began to show signs of moderation when it announced that it would not enforce its earlier *fatwa* regarding Rushdie, and would no longer encourage other individuals or organizations to implement it.

Rushworth, Robert *(1924–1993)* U.S. military flier and test pilot who made more flights in the X-15 rocket plane than any other pilot. During one of his 34 flights, on June 27, 1963, Rushworth reached an altitude of 55 miles (285,000 feet), earning astronaut status by the air force definition. Over the course of his career he flew 50 different aircraft, logging more than 6,500 hours of flying time. Rushworth started out in 1943 as a U.S. Army enlisted man. He trained as an aviation cadet and became a pilot in 1944, after which he flew combat missions in China, Burma and India. He left the military in 1946 to get a degree in mechanical engineering, but by February 1951 he was back in the air force, earned an M.S. in aeronautical engineering in

1954 and became a test pilot. From 1957 to 1966 he flew experimental aircraft and rocket planes at Edwards Air Force Base, earning a Distinguished Flying Cross for a tricky landing of the X-15. In 1996 he went back to combat duty, this time in VIETNAM. On returning to the states in 1969, he served as commander of several test centers.

Rusk, Dean (David Dean Rusk) *(1909—1994)* U.S. secretary of state (1961–69). After teaching political science in the 1930s and serving in World War II, Rusk followed his mentor George C. MARSHALL into the State Department. He was named assistant secretary of state for Far Eastern affairs in 1950 and, under Dean ACHESON, played an important role in the formulation of policy during the KOREAN WAR. In 1952 Rusk left the State Department to become head of the Rockefeller Foundation. President John F. KENNEDY appointed him secretary of state in 1961, and he retained that post under President Lyndon B. JOHNSON. Rusk advocated worldwide economic cooperation and military opposition to communist expansion, becoming a prominent apologist (with Robert McNAMARA) for the escalation of the VIETNAM WAR. In 1970 he became a professor of international law at the University of Georgia.

Rusk, Howard Archibald *(1901–1989)* American physician, a pioneer in the science of medical rehabilitation. His interest in rehabilitation began while he was in charge of the Army Air Force Convalescent Training Program in WORLD WAR II. During the war he helped develop programs to rehabilitate soldiers using both physical and psychological means. Many of his techniques became part of standard medical practice around the world. Rusk received numerous awards, including three Albert Lasker Awards, the Distinguished Service Medal and the French Legion of Honor. The Howard A. Rusk Institute of Rehabilitative Medicine was named for him. He was also a president and chairman of the World Rehabilitation Fund, which he founded in 1955.

Ruska, Ernst *(1906–1988)* German electrical engineer credited with the development of the ELECTRON MICRO-SCOPE in 1931. Ruska received belated recognition for that achievement when he shared the NOBEL PRIZE for physics in 1986.

Russell, Bertrand A(rthur William), (third earl Russell) *(1872–1970)* British philosopher, mathematician and social critic. Russell, who won the NOBEL PRIZE for literature in 1950, was one of the most influential and widely read philosophers of the 20th century. He was born into an aristocratic British family and educated at Cambridge University, but for most of his life Russell advocated political and social beliefs—such as pacifism and left-wing economic reforms—that went contrary to his class and background. Russell's first great work, completed in collaboration with Alfred North WHITEHEAD, was the three-volume *Principia Mathematica* (1910–13), which asserted that mathematics was essentially an extension of philosophical logic. In 1916, during WORLD WAR I, Russell was dismissed from the faculty of Cambridge University for his pacifist beliefs. In the final decades of his life, Russell was active in the antinuclear weapons movement. His major works included *Why I Am Not a Christian* (1927), *Marriage and*

Influential mathematician. philosopher and activist Bertrand Russell (LIBRARY OF CONGRESS. PRINTS AND PHOTOGRAPHS DIVISION)

Morals (1929) and *The History of Western Philosophy* (1945).

Russell, Bill (William Fenton Russell) *(1934–   )* American basketball player. Russell is generally acknowledged to be the greatest basketball player of all time, and was so voted by the Professional Basketball Writers Association. After leading his college team at the University of San Francisco to two championships, he was drafted by the Boston Celtics and remained with them for his entire career (1956–1969). At center, Russell was named most valuable player five times, and the team won 11 championships. During the last three years of that span, Russell also coached the team to two championships and was the first black coach in league history. His totals as a player included 21,620 rebounds and 14,522 points. He went on to coach the Seattle Supersonics (1973–1979). He was named to the Basketball Hall of Fame in 1974. In 1980 Russell was named the greatest player in NBA history by the Professional Basketball Writer's Association of America.

Russia Former European-Asian empire, supplanted and expanded by the UNION OF SOVIET SOCIALIST REPUBLICS. After the dissolution of the USSR in December 1991, the newly independent Russian Federation inherited the Soviet seat in the United Nations General Assembly and Security Council. The name was also applied to the USSR's RUSSIAN SOVIET FEDERATED SOCIALIST REPUBLIC. At the turn of the century, under Czar NICHOLAS II, the Russian Empire stretched from the German and Austro-Hungarian borders in the west to the Pacific Ocean on the east, including the vast but sparsely populated north Asian territory of SIBERIA. Much of present-day Poland was under Russian control. In 1894 Russia had entered into an alliance with France and an arrangement with Great Britain; this alliance was formalized as the TRIPLE ALLIANCE in 1907. Meanwhile, the construction of the Trans-Siberian Railroad between 1891 and 1905 opened Siberia and the Far East to exploitation and settlement. Russian and Japanese competition over Manchuria and KOREA led to the RUSSO-JAPANESE WAR of 1904–05, in which Russia was soundly defeated. This de-

feat pointed up the glaring weaknesses of the Russian military, political and economic system and helped to bring about the RUSSIAN REVOLUTION OF 1905. The czar was forced to grant a constitution and establish a parliament (the DUMA), but factional squabbling and the czarist government's stubborn reluctance to go beyond cosmetic changes doomed the system to failure.

In August, 1914, Russia was drawn into WORLD WAR I, ostensibly as a defender of Slavic peoples in the Balkans and elsewhere. However, the nation was as ill-prepared for this war—if not more so—than it had been for the war with Japan. Russia's advantage in manpower was offset by the nation's inability to properly arm, feed and train its soldiers. Moreover, much of the leadership was incompetent. The Russian army suffered catastrophic defeats at the hands of Germany and Austria-Hungary. Mass discontent in the ranks, fueled by the bitter conditions of warfare and by resentment against the aristocratic officer corps and the apparently

callous czarist government, led to desertion and to the spread of revolutionary propaganda. On the home front, food shortages developed. Revolution broke out in February 1917, and Nicholas abdicated on March 15 (see FEBRUARY REVOLUTION.) A provisional government was organized; in May it admitted socialists and in July made Alexander F. KERENSKY its head. Historians speculate that had this government made peace with Germany, it might have survived and guided Russia on a democratic path. However, it insisted on carrying on the unpopular war, while economic conditions continued to deteriorate. The disciplined, well-organized BOLSHEVIKS, under V. I. LENIN and Leon TROTSKY, staged a coup in late October (Old Style calendar; early November, New Style), and the Kerensky government collapsed (see OCTOBER REVOLUTION). The Bolsheviks consolidated their control of the government and reached a peace agreement with Germany in the treaty of BREST-LITOVSK. In 1918 the czar and

his family were executed. Despite opposition from various anti-Bolshevik forces (see WHITES), including Western troops, the Bolsheviks prevailed, eventually bringing Russia under their authority (see RUSSIAN CIVIL WAR) and establishing the COMMUNIST PARTY as the sole power in the new Union of Soviet Socialist Republics. Following Russia's independence from the USSR in December 1991, it was governed by President Boris YELTSIN (1991–99) and Vladimir PUTIN (2000–), who was reelected president in 2004. With the end of the cold war Russia and the United States announced a new agreement in 2002 to cut their nuclear arsenals. That same year Russia joined in a special partnership with NATO to help fight terrorism. Russia has had to deal with a recent surge in domestic terrorism, such as when Chechen rebels held 800 people hostage in a Moscow movie theater in 2002 and again in 2004 when they seized a school full of children in Belsan. Putin's government was embarrassed but survived a confidence

RUSSIA	
1904–05	The Russo-Japanese War is caused by Russian expansion into Manchuria.
1905	A revolution, though suppressed, forces the czar to accept a parliament (Duma) with limited powers.
1914	Russo-Austrian rivalry in the Balkans is a major cause of the outbreak of World War I; Russia fights in alliance with France and Britain.
1917	As a result of the Russian Revolution, the czar abdicates and a provisional government is established; the Bolsheviks seize power under Vladimir Lenin.
1918	The Treaty of Brest-Litovsk ends the war with Germany; the former czar is murdered; the Russian Empire collapses; Finland, Poland, and the Baltic States secede.
1918–22	A civil war is waged between the Red Army, led by Leon Trotsky, and White Russian forces, with foreign support; the Red Army is ultimately victorious; control is regained over Ukraine, Caucasus, and Central Asia.
1922	The former Russian Empire is renamed the Union of Soviet Socialist Republics.
1991	The Soviet Union breaks apart as republics declare their independence; Boris Yeltsin, leader of the reform movement, is elected president of Russia June 12. Yeltsin bans Russian Communist Party; Commonwealth of Independent States (CIS) created as a means to maintain ties between states of the former Soviet Union.
1996	Yeltsin is reelected president.
1998	Russian troops enter Chechnya to put down independence move.
1999	A severe economic crisis strikes the Russian economy.
2000	Vladimir Putin is elected president.
2001	Closer cooperation between Russia and the West as Putin expresses support for U.S. and its military campaign against the Taliban and al-Qaeda.
2002	Russia and the U.S. agree to cut their nuclear arsenals from over 6,000 missiles each to about 2,000 each by 2012. NATO-Russia Council established in which Russia and NATO will have an equal role in decision making to fight terrorism and other security threats. Chechen rebels seize a Moscow theater, most of the rebels and about 120 hostages are killed when Russian troops storm the building.
2004	Putin wins a landslide election for a second term as president. More than 330 killed, many of them children, when government forces storm a school occupied by rebels in North Ossetia. Putin blames international terrorists with links to Chechen separatists.
2005	The government survives a no-confidence vote in the Duma called by communist and nationalist opposition over its benefits and pension reforms, which had sparked widespread protests.

vote in 2005 called by the opposition parties over pension reform.

Russian Civil War of 1918–21 In 1918, several months after the popularly elected Russian assembly was disbanded as a counterrevolutionary body (see OCTOBER REVOLUTION), civil war broke out between the ruling BOLSHEVIKS (or communists) and the anti-Bolshevik WHITES. It was triggered by a clash between Czech troops (in transit through Siberia) and the Bolsheviks, whose punishment of the Czechs provoked the Czechs to raid Siberian villages. Taking advantage of the situation, the Whites began battling the Bolsheviks' newly formed Red Army and successfully took almost all of Siberia. During the struggle, Czar NICHOLAS II and his entire family were murdered at Ekaterinburg (Sverdlovsk) in July 1918. A month later, British, French, Japanese and American troops, in support of the Whites, landed at Vladivostok on the Sea of Japan, while British and American forces disembarked at Archangel on the Arctic's White Sea and helped a new provisional government to establish itself there. Through these foreign efforts, Bolshevik rule was eliminated east of the Ural Mountains.

However, the Red Army under Leon TROTSKY waged fierce battles and ultimately defeated three White armies from the Caucasus, Baltic and Siberian areas. The Czechs withdrew, but the other foreign powers continued to furnish troops and supplies to fight the communists. Terrorism and assassinations increased on both sides, and communist distrust of non-Bolsheviks was hardened. After peace negotiations failed, a White army advanced toward Moscow, reaching Orel, about 200 miles to the south, and another White force came within 10 miles of Petrograd (Leningrad). But the Red Army turned them back and won a victory at Novorossisk on the Black Sea. After the western Siberian city of Omsk, headquarters of the anticommunist forces of Admiral Alexander V. KOLCHAK, fell to the Reds in November 1919, and the foreign forces withdrew from the war, the Whites were gradually crushed as they fought in hostile territory. The bloody civil war, which also saw the KRONSTADT REBELLION, ended with the communists firmly in control of the government and the country (including Siberia) by 1921. (See also DENIKIN; FINNISH WAR OF INDEPENDENCE; RUSSO-POLISH WAR OF 1919–20; WRANGEL.)

Russian Revolution *(1917)* The revolution of March and November (Old Style February and October) 1917 that overthrew the Russian monarchy and established the world's first communist state. It began with the FEBRUARY REVOLUTION, when riots over shortages of bread and coal in Petrograd (formerly St. Petersburg) led to the establishment of the Petrograd Soviet of workers' and soldiers' deputies, dominated by the MENSHEVIKS and Social Revolutionaries, and of a provisional government of DUMA deputies, which forced NICHOLAS II to abdicate. The failure of the provisional government, under Prince George LVOV and then KERENSKY, to end Russia's participation in WORLD WAR I and to deal with food shortages led to the de-

mand of the BOLSHEVIKS under LENIN for "all power to the Soviets." The Bolsheviks, who had gained a majority in the Soviet by September, staged the OCTOBER (or Bolshevik) REVOLUTION, seizing power and establishing the Soviet of people's commissars. The new government made peace with Germany in early 1918 but almost immediately faced opposition at home. In the subsequent CIVIL WAR (1918–21) the Red Army was ultimately victorious against the anticommunist WHITES but with the loss of some 100,000 lives. In addition, some 2 million Russians emigrated.

Russian Revolution of 1905 An insurrection in RUSSIA. It was an expression of the widespread discontent that foreshadowed the RUSSIAN REVOLUTION of 1917. It began on BLOODY SUNDAY, January 22, 1905, when a group of striking workers, led by Father GAPON, marched peacefully to the Winter Palace in St. Petersburg only to be met by gunfire. The massacre precipitated nationwide strikes, uprisings and mutinies (including the mutiny on the cruiser *Potemkin*). By October Russia was gripped by a general strike, which with the establishment of the St. Petersburg Soviet (workers' council) dominated by the MENSHEVIKS, including TROTSKY, forced Emperor NICHOLAS II to promise a constitutional government (see DUMA). The revolution was substantially crushed by the end of December.

Russian Social Democratic Labor Party Founded in 1898 as the Social Democratic Labor Party, the party consisted of orthodox Marxists, revisionists and trade unionists. Although the party split into BOLSHEVIKS and MENSHEVIKS at the second party congress in 1903, it was later formally reunited, but both factions continued to exist. In 1919 the Bolsheviks no longer used the name Russian Social Democratic Party, but the Mensheviks opted to retain it.

Russian Soviet Federated Socialist Republic (RSFSR) The largest of the 15 republics of the former UNION OF SOVIET SOCIALIST REPUBLICS (USSR). With such cities as Moscow (the capital of the RSFSR as well as of the USSR) and LENINGRAD, it was the political, social, economic and cultural nerve center of the Soviet Union. Stretching some

5,000 miles from eastern Europe and the Baltic Sea across northern Asia (SIBERIA) to the Pacific Ocean, it contained more than half the population of the Soviet Union and more than three-quarters of its land. The BOLSHEVIKS established the RSFSR in January 1918. In 1922 the RSFSR was formally united with the UKRAINE, Belorussia and Transcaucasia to form the Union of Soviet Socialist Republics. By virtue of its plentiful natural resources and its location in the heartland of the old Russian Empire, the RSFSR became highly industrialized during the 20th century. In the late 1980s, with various ethnic groups throughout the USSR demanding autonomy, the Russian republic became the center of a resurgent Russian nationalism. Communist maverick politician Boris YELTSIN was elected president of the republic and challenged the authority of the central Soviet government. When the USSR ceased to exist in December 1991, the Russian Federation became an independent state with Yeltsin as its president.

Russo-Finnish War of 1939–40 On the outbreak of WORLD WAR II, Soviet Russia demanded FINLAND lease a naval base on the Hanko Peninsula, demilitarize its Mannerheim Line fortifications and cede several islands. Finland refused and about 1 million Soviet troops invaded. From November 30, 1939, to March 12, 1940, 300,000 Finnish troops and international volunteers held off the Soviets, using the Finnish winter to advantage. At Suomussalmi the Finns nearly annihilated two Soviet divisions. They were unable to halt the incessant Soviet assaults, however. Aided by heavy artillery and air bombardments, the Soviets breached the Mannerheim Line in February 1940. The Finns sued for peace when the Soviets pushed on toward Vyborg on March 12, 1940, ceding the Karelian isthmus and Vyborg (Viipuri). In June 1941 the Finns joined the German invasion of the USSR.

Russo-Japanese War War (1904–05) arising from the conflict of Russian and Japanese aspirations in Asia. RUSSIA refused to withdraw from MANCHURIA, despite having agreed to do so in 1902, and also wished to gain concessions in KOREA. Alexander Bezobrazov's timber company began work on the Korean side of the Yalu River, and in 1904 the Russian fleet was attacked by the Japanese at PORT ARTHUR. In May 1905 the Japanese virtually destroyed Russia's Baltic fleet at Tsushima. Britain's proposal of American mediation was accepted. At the peace conference, presided over by Theodore ROOSEVELT, in Portsmouth, New Hampshire, Russia ceded Port Arthur, the southern line of the Chinese Eastern Railway and the southern half of Sakhalin Island to JAPAN.

Russo-Persian War of 1911 After the Persian Revolution of 1906–09, Russia sent troops to Kazvin in northern Persia to protect its interests there, in violation of the Anglo-Russian agreement of 1907. William Morgan Shuster, an American serving as Persian treasurer, clashed with Russia, which supported an attempted coup by the former shah and demanded Shuster's removal; the parliament refused. The Russians committed atrocities in Tabriz, took over Azerbaijan and advanced on Tehran. Persia's regent governing for the minor Ahmed Shah enacted a coup, closed down the assembly and accepted Russia's demand.

Russo-Polish War of 1919–20 As German troops withdrew from POLAND after WORLD WAR I, Russian Bolshevik troops advanced westward. Polish forces under General Józef PIŁSUDSKI pushed the Russian forces back into UKRAINE. The Allies approved an eastern Polish border within Russia, but Piłsudski, seeking to seize the Ukraine, allied with anti-Bolshevik Ukrainians under Simon PETLYURA, capturing Kiev on April 25–May 7, 1920. A Soviet counterattack drove the Poles out, and Soviet troops were threatening Warsaw by August. With aid from the French under General Maxime WEYGAND, Polish armies defeated Soviet troops under Mikhail Tukacheveski in September 1920 along the Niemen River. An armistice ended fighting on October 12, 1920, and by the Treaty of Riga (March 18, 1921) Poland's territorial claims eastward were accepted by the Russian government.

Rustin, Bayard (*1910–1987*) American civil rights leader. He was one of the foremost theorists and practitioners of the CIVIL RIGHTS MOVEMENT. A close advisor to the Reverend Martin Luther KING, Jr., since the 1950s, Rustin was a principal organizer of the 1963 Washington, D.C., march and rally at which King delivered his "I have a dream" speech (see MARCH ON WASHINGTON, 1963). A socialist, pacifist and Quaker, he remained a lifelong believer in nonviolent protest. He favored a coalition approach to achieving social change, involving alliances with labor, white liberals, Jews and other minorities, an approach often criticized by other black leaders. Rustin, who was openly gay, urged black leaders to adopt a more active role in the fight against AIDS (acquired immune deficiency syndrome).

Ruth, George Herman "Babe" (*1895–1948*) American baseball player. The greatest home run hitter of his time, Ruth discovered baseball while at St. Mary's Industrial School in Baltimore. After gaining experience with a local minor league team, he signed with the Baltimore Orioles and was later sold to the Boston Red Sox as a pitcher. He pitched 29-2/3 scoreless World Series innings for them, and had a 94–46 overall record, but by 1918 he had been shifted to the outfield so that he could hit every day. Sold to the New York Yankees in 1920 for $125,000, Ruth began the 14 seasons of home run hitting that established him as the "Sultan of Swat." He broke the home run record in three consecutive seasons (1919–21), hit 60 home runs in 154 games in 1927, led the American League in home runs for 12 seasons and hit 50 or more home runs in four seasons—all records. His career total of 714 home runs was the

New York Yankees baseball legend Babe Ruth
(LIBRARY OF CONGRESS, PRINTS AND PHOTOGRAPHS DIVISION)

record until it was surpassed by Hank AARON in 1974 and Barry Bonds in 2006. Less well known is the fact that Ruth set a lifetime record of 2,056 bases on balls. Somewhat notorious for his rowdy nightlife, Ruth was fined for misconduct several times, and after his retirement in 1935 he failed to attract the job of team manager that he desired. He became the second player to be elected to the Baseball Hall of Fame (1936).

Rutherford, Ernest (*1871–1937*) New Zealand-born British physicist. One of the century's most influential scientists, Rutherford revolutionized our understanding of atomic physics. Born near Nelson, New Zealand, he received his B.A. from Canterbury College, in Christchurch, in 1892, his M.A. the following year and a B.S. in 1894. Rutherford next entered Cambridge University as a research student for J. J. Thomson at the prestigious Cavendish Laboratory and assisted in the research that led to Thomson's discovery of the electron. From 1898 to 1907, Rutherford taught at McGill University in Montreal, where he performed landmark experiments in radioactivity, including those marking the discovery of alpha and beta particles. In 1907, Rutherford accepted a post at Manchester University in England. The following year he was awarded the NOBEL PRIZE for chemistry. In 1911 he presented a new model of the atom, still generally accepted, that called for a mass of positively charged particles in the center with negatively charged electrons orbiting about the periphery. Rutherford moved in 1919 to Cambridge University, where he headed the Cavendish Laboratory until his death. He headed the Royal Society from 1925 to 1930, and he was elevated to the peerage in 1931.

Rutledge, Wiley Blount (*1894–1949*) Associate justice, U.S. Supreme Court (1943–49). A graduate of the University of Wisconsin, Rutledge graduated from the University of Colorado Law School after his education had been interrupted by tuberculosis and financial difficulties. After a brief time in private practice he became a law professor. Rutledge was appointed by President Franklin D. ROOSEVELT to the U.S. Court of Appeals for the District of Columbia and was elevated to the U.S. Supreme Court in 1943. His career on the Court was cut short when he died unexpectedly in 1949.

Rutskoi, Alexander (1947–) Soviet and Russian major-general and politician. During the Soviet military involvement in AFGHANISTAN (1979–89), Rutskoi served between 1985 and 1986 as a regimental commander in the occupation forces counterinsurgency operations against the various bands of MUJAHIDEEN, or Islamic militants that opposed the pre-Soviet government and its Soviet military protectors. In 1990 he also entered politics, becoming a People's Deputy (legislator) in the Russian Soviet Federated Socialist Republic (RSFSR), as well as a member of the USSR's Supreme Soviet (the national parliament). He became a strong supporter of fellow Russian nationalist Boris YELTSIN and leader of the Communists for Democracy Movement. In early 1991 the Communist Party expelled Rutskoi prompting him to transform his marginal faction into a major social-democratic party.

After his election as vice president of the RSFSR, where he became a supporter of Yeltsin's efforts to increase the republic's autonomy within the tottering Soviet Union. During the August 1991 coup against Soviet president Mikhail GORBACHEV, Rutskoi joined Yeltsin in resisting the decrees of new president, Gennady YANAEV, which forced the cabal to crumble within a few days. When the Soviet Union disintegrated on December 25, 1991, Rutskoi became the vice president of Russia.

After Yeltsin dissolved the Duma in September 1993, the Duma remained in session and announced Yeltsin's removal as president and Rutskoi's designation as acting president. In the next month troops loyal to Yeltsin shelled the parliament building, captured the rebel forces, and arrested Rutskoi. Although ordered to stand trial for treason, Rutskoi was pardoned by Yeltsin in February 1994.

Rwanda German colony (1885–1914), Belgian mandate and administered

RWANDA	
1916	The region is occupied by Belgium during World War I.
1923	Belgium is granted a League of Nations mandate to administer Ruanda-Urundi; Belgium rules indirectly through Tutsi chiefs.
1959	Inter-ethnic warfare is fought between the Hutu and the Tutsi, forcing the mwami (king) Kigeri V into exile.
1961	A republic is proclaimed after the mwami is deposed.
1962	Rwanda becomes independent, with Grégoire Kayibanda, leader of Parmehutu, as president.
1973	As a fresh wave of Hutu-Tutsi conflict threatens to engulf the country, Kayibanda is toppled in a swift bloodless coup led by Major General Juvenal Habyarimana; the constitution of 1962 is partially suspended, and the national assembly is dissolved.
1975	Habyarimana launches the National Revolutionary Movement of Development (MRND) as the sole political party.
1983	Habyarimana is reelected to another term as president.
1988	Habyarimana is reelected president.
1990	Between 5,000 and 10,000 rebel Tutsi invade Rwanda from neighboring Uganda.
1994	Habyarimana and the Burundian president are killed aboard an airplane shot down over Kigali. Extremist Hutu militia and Rwanda military begin systematic massacre of the Tutsis. An estimated 600,000 to 1 million Rwandans are killed in the civil war. A cease-fire is declared in July.
1995	The UN establishes a tribunal to investigate the Hutu-Tutsis massacre.
1996	Rwandan troops invade and attack Hutu militia-dominated camps in Zaire in order to drive home the refugees.
1997	More than 300 Tutsis are killed in a refugee camp as ethnic conflict continues.
2000	President Pasteur Bizimungu, a Hutu, resigns in March and Major General Paul Kagame, a Tutsi, is sworn in as the fifth president of Rwanda.
2003	Voters back a new constitution designed to prevent another genocide.

Rwanda

UGANDA

DEMOCRATIC REPUBLIC OF THE CONGO

Kidaho
Lake Burera
Kirambo
Ruhengeri
Lake Ruhondo
Gisenyi
Nyarutovu
Kabaya
Rushashi
Murambi
Ngororero
Kiyumba
Kigali
Kanombe
Gitarama
Kibuye
Gishyita
Birambo
Rwamatamu
Kaduha
Kanazi
Rwesero
Nyabisindu
Karaba
Gikongoro
Cyangugu
Bugumya
Butare
Bugarama
Kibingo

Lake Kivu
Nyauarungu R.
Ngarama
Lake Rwanye
Biumba
Lake Hago
Lake Muhazi
Lake Ihema
Rwamagana
Lake Nasho
Lake Mugesera
Lake Lweru
Kibungo
Kirehe
Rusumo
Lake Tshohoha
Lake Rweru
Lake Sake
Kagera R.

Kagera R.

TANZANIA

DEMOCRATIC REPUBLIC OF THE CONGO

BURUNDI

N

0   25 miles
0   25 km

© Infobase Publishing

---

territory (1914–62), and African independent nation (1962–   ). In the 19th century Germany gained control of the African territories known as Ruanda and Urundi, uniting them under the administrative entity called German East Africa. At the end of the war, the Treaty of Versailles deprived Germany of all of its African colonies, transferring them to the custody of the newly created League of Nations, with Belgium administering it as a mandate.

When Germany invaded Belgium in 1940 during the Second WORLD WAR (1939–45), Belgian control of Rwanda was greatly weakened. This push toward independence coincided with a sharp increase in conflict between Hutu and Tutsi over the persistence of the *ubuhake* system, a traditional feudal relationship whereby the Hutu had served as indentured servants of the Tutsi. By 1959, this ethnic conflict within Rwanda resulted in an undeclared civil war between the two peoples, forcing the Tutsi king and some 200,000 of his kin to flee to UGANDA. Profiting from the Tutsi em-

igration, the Hutus declared Rwanda an independent republic in January 1961. In the September 1961 national elections, the Hutu-dominated Parmehutu Party handily won control of the new national assembly, which passed a measure prohibiting the return of the Tutsi monarch. Under increasing pressure from the UN, Belgium recognized the independence of this republic in July 1962 under the leadership of Grégoire Kayibanda, the leader of the Parmehutu Party, which upon independence was renamed the Democratic Republican Movement (MDR).

In 1973 Kayibanda was overthrown by his defense minister, General Juvénal Habyarimana, who disbanded the national assembly and the MDR to consolidate his power. In 1975 Habyarimana founded the National Revolutionary Movement of Development (NRMD), the successor to the MDR that dominated the constitutional convention summoned by Habyarimana to write a new constitution. In 1983 and 1988 Habayarimana ran unopposed as the

NRMD's candidate. In 1990, two years after his second election, renewed fighting began between the Hutu-dominated government and the Rwandan Patriotic Front (RPF), a collection of Tutsi forces operating from neighboring Uganda.

In April 1994 a plane carrying Habyarimana and Cyprien Ntaryamira, the president of neighboring Burundi, was shot down, killing both men. The NRMD and Rwandan military blamed the RPF for the action, and instigated a wave of mass murder against Rwanda's remaining Tutsi population, which in turn prompted reprisals by the RPF against Hutu in the areas it controlled. A 2,500-strong French force sent to restore order to Rwanda failed to stop the assaults of the RPF and NRMD. More than 600,000 people (mainly Tutsi) were killed in the violence in Rwanda by the end of 1994.

By July 1994 both sides agreed to implement a cease-fire and serve under the transitional government of the moderate Hutu Pasteur Bizimungu allowing Hutu and Tutsi refugees to begin to return to Rwanda. Later that year, the UN established the International **Criminal Tribunal for Rwanda** (ICTR), which later served as a model organization for the International Criminal Tribunal for Yugoslavia. However, many Hutus believed to have been responsible for instigating genocide against Tutsis remained in refugee camps in Zaire. In October 1996, several months after the UN had inaugurated the ICTR in Tanzania, the Rwandan government responded to reports of increasing paramilitary activity in these camps by backing an attack on them by nearby Tutsi forces. The following year, survivors of these Hutu camps conducted reprisals of their own on Tutsi regions. In 2000, following the resignation of Bizimungu, vice president and minister of defense Paul KAGAME, himself a Tutsi, became the new president of Rwanda and sought to bring peace to his devastated country. A new constitution that bans the incitement of ethnic hatred was put into effect in 2003.

Ryan, (Lynn) Nolan (1947–   ) American baseball player. Known as "The Myth" during his four years with the New York Mets, his early years were plagued by lack of control and blister problems. In the worst deal in Met history (if not in baseball history), Ryan (along with two other players) was traded to the California Angels for Jim Fregosi in 1971. In California, he began to achieve mastery over his astonishing fastball, and became the first righthander since Bob Feller to strike out 300 batters in a season. He signed with the Houston Astros in 1979, and later remained in his native Texas as he signed with the Rangers in 1988. Clocked at over 100 miles per hour, Ryan is baseball's all-time strikeout leader with over 5,000–1,000 more than the second-highest total, held by Steve Carlton. Ryan pitched his sixth no-hitter in 1990, at the age of 43. That year he also reached the milestone of 300 wins. An astute businessman, Ryan owns a bank, a town and several ranches throughout Texas, but continued to play—and best—players half his age. He pitched an astonishing seventh no-hitter in May 1991. By the time of Ryan's retirement in 1993, the pitcher had set a league record in all-time strikeouts (5,714), and finished with a career record of 324-292. Ryan was elected to the Baseball Hall of Fame in 1999.

Rykov, Alexei Ivanovich *(1881–1938)* Russian member of the militant wing of the Social Democratic Labor Party and of its Bolshevik faction. Rykov worked as an underground agent in RUSSIA but broke with LENIN in 1910 to become leader of the "party-minded BOLSHEVIKS," a subfaction that was more tolerant toward the MENSHEVIKS. After the OCTOBER REVOLUTION in 1917 he advocated a coalition government of all socialists parties. Chairman of the supreme council of national economy in 1918–20 and 1923–24, in 1921–24 he was deputy chairman of the council of people's commissars, and later chairman. A member of the Politburo, he became a leading member of the RIGHT OPPOSITION. He was executed following the last show trial of the GREAT PURGE.

Ryskind, Morris ("Morrie") *(1895–1985)* American comedy writer. Ryskind collaborated with playwright George S. KAUFMAN on a series of MARX BROTHERS stage and screen hits, including *Cocanuts, Animal Crackers* and *A Night at the Opera.* He share the 1932 PULITZER PRIZE for drama with Kaufman for the musical *Of Thee I Sing.* A socialist in his youth, he later became a staunch anticommunist. In 1947, he testified before the HOUSE COMMITTEE ON UN-AMERICAN ACTIVITIES on communist infiltration of the Screenwriters Guild. He went on to become a member of the JOHN BIRCH SOCIETY and to write a politically conservative column for the *Los Angeles Times* from 1960 to 1971.

Ryun, James ("Jim") Ronald *(1947–)* American track and field star. Ryun was born in Wichita, Kansas, and was the first athlete to break the four-minute mile while still in high school. Although he held many world records during the 1960s and in 1966 was named sportsman of the year by *Sports Illustrated,* he never won an Olympic medal. A fall during the 1968 Olympics ended his chance for a medal. After retiring as an active competitor, Ryun founded the Jim Ryun Distance Running Camps to help develop young runners, and was active in philanthropic causes. In 1996 Ryun was elected to the House of Representatives as a Republican from Kansas. (See also OLYMPIC GAMES.)

S

Saarinen, Eero *(1910–1961)* Finnish-born American architect whose varied and imaginative work in both furniture design and architecture was a significant part of the design scene in the 1950s. The son of famous Finnish architect Eliel SAARINEN, who relocated in the U.S. in 1923, Eero Saarinen grew up at Cranbrook Academy where his father was a principal teacher. He planned to become a sculptor and studied in Paris from 1930 to 1931, but returned to study architecture at Yale. He graduated in 1934 and worked briefly for Norman BEL GEDDES before returning to Cranbrook. Saarinen worked there with Charles EAMES and won two first prizes with him in the 1940 Organic Design in Home Furnishing competition, organized by the MUSEUM OF MODERN ART in New York. As an architect, Saarinen began in partnership with his father in 1936 and often worked with Robert F. Swanson as associate or partner (from 1944 to 1947). In 1939 Saarinen, Swanson, and Saarinen won a national competition for a never-built Smithsonian Gallery of Art for Washington, D.C. A number of distinguished schools, a 1942 church in Columbus, Indiana, and the music shed at Tanglewood, Massachusetts, were among the projects completed before the death of the elder Saarinen.

Thereafter, Eero carried on the practice in his name alone, with Joseph Lacy, John Dinkeloo and Kevin Roche as partners. The General Motors Technical Center (1948–56) at Warren, Michigan, is designed in a severe INTERNATIONAL STYLE. In later work, Saarinen took pride in developing a unique design direction for each project, never adopting a personal style to be applied to every project. Nevertheless, all his buildings share a quality that might be described as sincerity, a directness and simplicity along with a certain poetic sensibility. Important works in a sculptural vocabulary include MIT's Kresge auditorium (a huge spherical triangle touching the ground at only three points) and a cylindrical, brick chapel (1953–55) in Cambridge, Massachusetts, as well as the Yale Hockey Rink (1953–59) in New Haven and the TWA passenger terminal (1956–62) at Kennedy Airport in New York. More restrained are the CBS tower (1965) in New York and the John Deere office building (1965) in Moline, Illinois, which were both completed after Saarinen's death. One of his last designs, the main building of northern Virginia's Dulles International Airport (completed 1963) combines the restrained and the sculptural directions in his work with a vast, curving, cable-suspended roof hanging between sloping concrete supports.

Saarinen, Eliel *(1873–1950)* Leading architect of the national Romantic movement in Finland who built a second career in a more modernist direction after relocating in the U.S. in 1923. Born in Rantasalmi, Finland, Saarinen was trained at the Helsinki Polytechnic. His early work was done in partnership with Herman Gesselius and Armas Lindgren, themselves leaders in Finnish architecture of the early 20th century. Their offices and houses in Hvittrask are fine examples of the Romantic style at its best. Saarinen alone was responsible for the executed design of the Helsinki Railway Station (1910–14), a building that brought him international fame. His second-prize design in the 1922 competition for the Chicago Tribune Building received critical acclaim and led to his coming to the United States. He became associated with Cranbrook Academy in 1925, designed its buildings and taught architecture there, eventually becoming its president (1932–46). Frequently, he designed interiors, furniture, lighting fixtures and other decorative elements for his buildings, working in a vocabulary that combined MODERNISM, a craft orientation and a decorative style relating to the ART DECO work of the 1930s. He practiced alone and then in partnership with his son Eero SAARINEN, producing a number of distinguished buildings, such as a 1942 church in Columbus, Indiana, and the shed at Tanglewood, Massachusetts, which combined the rigors of INTERNATIONAL STYLE modernism with a delicacy and charm that stemmed from the Scandinavian Romantic movement of his early career.

Saarland Small German state between the French frontier and the German state of Rheinland-Pfalz; drained by the Saar River, its capital is Saarbrücken. The Saar became the 10th state of the Federal Republic of Germany (WEST GERMANY) in 1957. After

GERMANY's defeat in WORLD WAR I, the Treaty of VERSAILLES (1919) assigned the Saarland's coal mines to France for 15 years. The region was returned to Germany's Third Reich in 1935. After HITLER claimed France's Lorraine in 1940, he combined the two regions under the name Westmark. Heavy fighting between the Allies and Germans took place along the Saar River in December 1944. The Saarland fell within the French occupation zone after the war.

Saba, Umberto *(1883–1957)* Italian poet. Born in Trieste under the Austro-Hungarian Empire, Saba was trained as a clerk and primarily self-educated. His first verses appeared in 1911 and 1912. Saba was a close friend of Italo SVEVO, who shared his profound interest in Freud. Due to his Jewish heritage, during WORLD WAR II he was forced to close the small antiquarian bookshop that supported him to live in exile in France and Italy, where he was sheltered by Eugene MONTALE, among others. The definitive 1961 edition of his *Canzoniere (Songbook)* comprised three volumes, corresponding to the poems of his youth, maturity and old age. A lyric autobiography, it was continually revised over the years. *Storia e cronistoria del Canzoniere* (1948, *History and Chronicle of the Songbook*) is a systematic self-criticism of his own poetry.

Sabin, Albert Bruce *(1906–1993)* Polish-American microbiologist. Born in Bialystok, Russia (now Poland), Sabin immigrated to the U.S. with his family in 1921 and was naturalized in 1930. He attended New York University, receiving an M.D. in 1931. Becoming a medical researcher, he was on the staff of the Rockefeller Institute before becoming a member of the college of medicine at the University of Cincinnati in 1939. He was appointed research professor of pediatrics there in 1946. Sabin is known for his development of an oral live-virus vaccine against poliomyelitis. Mass field tested in 1959, the vaccine has now largely replaced the earlier killed-virus vaccine developed by Jonas SALK. It gives a stronger and longer-lasting immunity than the earlier vaccine and protects against both paralysis and infection. Sabin concentrated on cancer research in his later work.

Sabra and Shatila massacre *(September 16, 1982)* Following the PLO evacuation of BEIRUT, Lebanese Christian militiamen attacked the Sabra and Shatila refugee camps in West Beirut and killed hundreds of the inhabitants. ISRAEL came under international criticism for the attacks because the Christian militia were considered its allies, and Israeli complicity was suspected. Israel itself conducted an investigation into the atrocities, which led to the resignation of several Israeli military officers who had been stationed in the region. Israeli defense minister Ariel SHARON was also forced to resign.

Sacco and Vanzetti case Long, controversial U.S. criminal case in which two Italian-born American anarchists were convicted of murder and executed after lengthy, well-publicized legal appeals and international protests about the conduct of the trial. In May 1920 Nicola Sacco and Bartolomeo Vanzetti were arrested and charged with the armed robbery and murder of two employees of a shoe factory in South Braintree, Massachusetts. The evidence at trial was not substantial, and the trial judge made a number of prejudicial rulings at the trial, in which they were convicted and sentenced to the electric chair. Alarmed at the possible miscarriage of justice extensive appeals were taken, and the pair received support and publicity among liberals and immigrants in the U.S. At the time the U.S. was caught up in a hysterical anti-Red campaign led by Attorney General Palmer, who had presidential ambitions. Critics charged that the pair were convicted without evidence merely because they were avowed anarchists. The case also received considerable attention in the U.K. and in Europe. The legal appeals lasted six years, and in a highly unusual move the governor of Massachusetts appointed a commission headed by the president of Harvard University to review the judicial process. The commission sustained the trial verdict, though it criticized the conduct of the trial judge. Despite protests and street demonstrations Sacco and Vanzetti were executed in August 1927. The execution provoked more demonstrations both within the U.S. and abroad.

Sachs, Nelly (Leonie) *(1891–1971)* German-born Jewish poet. As a young girl, Sachs began corresponding with the novelist Selma Lagerlöf, who was later instrumental in helping Sachs and her mother flee Nazi GERMANY in 1940. Although Sachs had written traditional, romantic poetry as a young woman, she is best known for work written after she escaped to Sweden. These collections include *In den Wohnungen des Todes* (In the habitations of death, 1946) *Und Niemand weiss weiter* (And no one knows how to go on, 1957) and *Flucht und Verwandlung* (Flight and transformation, 1959). Her poems recall the horrors of the HOLOCAUST and the suffering of the Jewish people, often with mystic imagery. Sachs also wrote the plays *Eli: Ein Mysterienspiel vom Leiden Israels* (*Eli: A Mystery Play of the Sufferings of Israel*, 1951) and *Zeichen im Sand* (*Marks in the Sand* 1962), among others. Sachs shared the 1966 NOBEL PRIZE in literature with S. Y. AGNON.

Sachsenhausen Village in eastern Germany's state of Brandenburg, about five miles north of Berlin. It was infamous as the site of a Nazi CONCENTRATION CAMP, established during the 1930s. In April 1945, as the Soviet army advanced toward BERLIN, the German authorities evacuated the camp and forced its 40,000 inmates— many near death—to march out of the path of the Soviet juggernaut.

Sackville-West, Vita (Victoria Mary) *(1892–1962)* British poet and novelist. Sackville-West portrayed her childhood home in Kent in *Knole and the Sackvilles* (1922) and in her best-known novel, *The Edwardians* (1930). Her poetry includes *The Land* (1926), which won the Hawthornden Prize, and *Collected Poems* (1933). Sackville-West met Virginia WOOLF in 1922. The two became lovers, and the relationship was the inspiration for Woolf's *Orlando* (1928). Sackville-West's lifestyle and unconventional relationship with her husband, Nigel Nicolson, whom she married in 1913, have been much written about—notably by their son, Nigel Nicolson, in *Portrait of a Marriage* (1973).

Sadat, (Mohammed) Anwar el- *(1918–1981)* President of EGYPT (1970–81). The son of a poor government clerk and his half-Sudanese wife, Sadat was one of 13 children. He received his earliest education from an Islamic cleric and earned a lifetime reputation for piety. He graduated (1938) from the Royal Military Academy, which had previously been reserved for the aristocracy. During WORLD WAR II he was imprisoned by the British for opposing their policy in Egypt. He later joined the FREE OFFICERS movement and took part in the coup against King FAROUK led by Gamal Abdel NASSER. He subsequently held a variety of posts leading to the vice presidency (1969) and succeeded to the presidency on Nasser's death (1970). During Nasser's rule, Sadat had been widely regarded as a weak figure and was dismissed by some critics as "Nasser's poodle." Many thought he would be merely an interim president, but he quickly consolidated his power. In 1972 he reversed Nasser's policy of close ties to the USSR and expelled the Soviet military advisers from Egypt. Like Nasser, he initially took a hard line against ISRAEL. He coordinated the Arab surprise attacks on Israel in October 1973, which resulted in a disastrous defeat for Egypt (see ARAB-ISRAELI WAR OF 1973). With the intercession of U.S. secretary of state Henry KISSINGER's SHUTTLE DIPLOMACY, he agreed to terms for a disengagement with Israel in January 1974. Efforts for a more comprehensive peace made only limited progress until 1977, when Sadat boldly followed up Israeli hints and made a sudden surprise visit to JERUSALEM to meet with Israeli premier Menachem BEGIN and address the Knesset. This action initiated the peace process that led to the CAMP DAVID ACCORDS of 1978, sponsored by U.S. president CARTER. For his role in establishing peace with Israel, Sadat shared the 1978 NOBEL PRIZE for peace with Begin. But while Sadat won enormous respect in the U.S. and other Western nations, many Arabs denounced him as a traitor to the Arab cause. The peace with Israel, the erratic pace of economic progress and the Westernization of some segments of Egyptian society were accompanied by increasing Islamic fundamentalist unrest. Sadat responded with a widespread crackdown on Muslim extremists in September 1981. On October 6, while he was reviewing a military parade in Cairo, a small band of commandos in the parade dismounted from their truck and fired into the reviewing stand, killing Sadat and several other officials. Sadat was regarded as a complex man, a humble autocrat of unusual flexibility, whose unquestioned dignity and undeniable warmth made him a formidable politician and world statesman.

Sadler, Barry *(1941–1989)* American singer-songwriter. While serving as a U.S. Special Forces medic in VIETNAM during the VIETNAM WAR, he wrote and recorded "The Ballad of the Green Berets." This tribute to the special forces became the number-one song in the U.S. for five weeks in 1966. In 1988, while training anticommunist Nicaraguan CONTRA guerrillas in Guatemala, he was shot in the head and paralyzed. He subsequently died as a result of wounds.

Sagan, Carl *(1934–1996)* One of the best-known astronomers in America, Sagan did much in his many television appearances to put astronomy and the space program before the American people. He received his Ph.D. at the University of Chicago in 1960 and in 1968 became associate professor of astronomy and director for planetary studies at Cornell University. Although Sagan's primary interests were planetary surfaces and atmospheres, an area in which he did much respected scientific work, he also did pioneering studies in the possibilities of extraterrestrial life. A vocal and untiring advocate of both the romantic and popular sides of science, Sagan is the author of many popular books, including two outside the field of astronomy, *The Dragons of Eden* and *Broca's Brain.*

Sagan, Françoise (Francoise Quoirez) *(1935–2004)* French novelist, playwright and screenwriter. Sagan made a sensation with her first novel, *Bonjour tristesse (Hello, Sadness,* 1954; filmed 1958). Written when she was 18, the novel was critically acclaimed as well as a *succès de scandale* for its dispassionate tone and depiction of a young woman breaking up her father's affair. Her second novel, *Un certain sourire (A Certain Smile,* 1956; filmed 1958), enjoyed similar success, but her subsequent fiction was never as successful or admired. Later works included *Incidental Music; Stories* (1983) *Avec mon meilleur souvenir* (1984) and *Un Chagrin de passage* (1994). Sagan also wrote plays and screenplays of her own novels as well as those of others.

Sagdeyev, Roald *(1933–)* Soviet scientist. As head of Russia's Institute for Space Research (IKI) Sagdeyev is credited with breathing new life into the Soviet space program in the early 1970s. Under his direction the program not only became more open but also realized such spectacular successes as the *Venera 9* and *10* projects to Venus and the Vega mission to Halley's Comet.

Sahrawi Arab Democractic Republic (SADR) Essentially a government-in-exile, the SADR lays claim to—but does not actually control—the western half of WESTERN SAHARA. In February 1976 Spain terminated its colonial rule of the region (then called Saguía el Hamra and Río de Oro), and granted the territory its independence. After Spain's complete withdrawal, Mauritania and Morocco both announced their annexation of the territory. Morocco's declaration had been foreshadowed for several months by the appearance of Moroccan military forces and political administrators in Western Sahara, which occurred with the tacit acceptance of the Spanish colonial authorities. Before the end of Spanish rule, Mauritania had served as the base of operations for POLISARIO (Popular Front for the Liberation of Saguía el Hamra and Río de Oro), a political-military organization dedicated to the independence of the Western Sahara. However, this alliance quickly fractured when it became evident that Mauritania—which had also dispatched forces to Western Sahara—did not intend to hand power over to Polisario but instead sought to annex those parts of the country it controlled. As a result Polisario transferred its base of operations to Algeria in 1976, established a government-in-exile, which claimed the legitimate right to rule the Saharawi Arab Democratic Republic and waged a guerrilla campaign against both Morocco and Mauritania. In 1979 Mauritanian forces withdrew from the regions they controlled and were replaced by Moroccan forces. In 1991 both Polisario and Morocco agreed to a

UN-sponsored truce. Although a UN peacekeeping force was permitted to enter the country with the consent of the warring parties, the referendum in the Western Sahara, which was supposed to occur six months following the implementation of the cease-fire in 1991, has yet to occur, and the fate of the SADR remains uncertain.

Sahel Region of Africa south of the Sahara, with the savannas to the south. The nations of MALI, NIGER, CHAD and SUDAN fall largely within the Sahel. The Sahel was the site of much human misery during the latter half of the 20th century. In the late 1960s, a prolonged drought devastated local agriculture and brought severe famine to the region.

Sahl, Mort (1927–) Born in Montreal but raised in Los Angeles, California, Sahl was one of the most influential stand-up comedians of the 1950s and '60s. After working at an Alaskan air force base and graduating from the University of Southern California in 1950, Sahl began to perform stand-up in San Francisco. In contrast to the "normal Vegas comic," Sahl developed a unique style that used a casual, free-form technique, which included stream of consciousness, ad-libs, political commentary and his trademark prop—a rolled up newspaper. Labeled a "Will Rogers with fangs," Sahl mercilessly remarked about presidents (Eisenhower, Nixon and Kennedy), politicians (McCarthy) and virtually anyone else in the public eye. In the 1970s Sahl focused his attention on writing for television and film, performing with less regularity. In 1988 he had a brief but successful one-man show on Broadway. Today Sahl is acknowledged as the leading influence on comedians Lenny BRUCE, Woody ALLEN and countless others.

Said, Edward (1935–2003) Palestinian-born scholar and political activist. Said was born in 1935 in Jerusalem, the capital of the British Mandate of Palestine administered under the auspices of the LEAGUE OF NATIONS. Following the 1947 partition of Palestine, Said's family left to live with relatives in Cairo, Egypt. After receiving a B.A. from Princeton University in 1957 and a Ph.D. from Harvard University in 1964, Said taught

Political commentator and professor Edward Said. 1980 (SOPHIE BASSOULS/CORBIS SYGMA)

comparative literature at Columbia University. He initially developed a reputation as a literary scholar with the publication of *Joseph Conrad and the Fiction of Autobiography* (1966), a work that identified fictional elements within Conrad's letters and autobiographical elements within Conrad's fiction. Said's increasing interest in what he regarded as the persistence of Western imperialist influences in the Arab world, led Said to found the new field of postcolonial studies, which united several academic disciplines. Said began to develop his new theoretical stance in *Orientalism* (1978), which examined the evolving image in the West of Arab civilization and Islam. Said's later works, such as *The Question of Palestine* (1979) and *Covering Islam* (1981), continued his efforts to examine Western stereotypes of the Arab and Islamic world and the Palestinian people's struggle for self-determination. In 1991 he resigned from the Palestinian National Council in protest against the emerging Palestinian-Israeli peace process that culminated in the 1993 Oslo Accords. Said insisted that the only just and effective path to peace in the Middle East would be an international campaign of sanctions and diplomatic pressure against Israel, modeled on the international campaign mounted against South Africa to force it to terminate the system of APARTHEID. Said favored the creation of a single secular state in Palestine in which Arabs and Jews would enjoy

equal rights of citizenship, again citing the precedent of the solution reached in South Africa between African National Congress leader Nelson MANDELA and National Party leader F. W. DE KLERK. In October 3, 2003, Said died after a 12-year struggle with leukemia.

Saigon (Ho Chi Minh City) Former capital city of the former South VIETNAM; on the right bank of the Saigon River, north of the Mekong River delta. Originally a settlement of the Khmer people, its history dates back many centuries. It was the capital of French INDOCHINA from 1887 to 1902. As a result of long French settlement in the 19th and 20th centuries, Saigon's architecture is more European than Asian. After the French withdrawal, Saigon became the capital of the new nation of South Vietnam in 1954. During the VIETNAM WAR it served as the command headquarters for U.S. forces in the country. It was infiltrated and attacked by the VIET CONG during the TET OFFENSIVE (1968). When the North Vietnamese broke through South Vietnamese lines in April 1975, panic struck Saigon as thousands of Vietnamese attempted to flee the city. The U.S. organized a hasty evacuation for U.S. personnel and as many endangered South Vietnamese (those who had worked closely with the U.S.) as it could accommodate. The city fell to the communists on April 30, 1975. The victorious North Vietnamese renamed Saigon after the venerated communist leader, HO CHI MINH.

St. Denis, Ruth (Ruth Dennis) (1879–1968) American dancer, choreographer and teacher. A founder of the American modern dance movement, St. Denis achieved fame as a choreographer/dancer with her work *Radha* in 1906. After successful solo dance tours of Europe (1906–09) and America (1909–10), she teamed with and married Ted SHAWN (1914). They founded Denishawn School and Dance Troupe (1915) where such great dancer/choreographers as Martha GRAHAM got their start. She also founded the dance department at Adelphi College (1938), appeared at the JACOB'S PILLOW DANCE FESTIVAL (1949–55) and gave lecture/dance performances throughout the country. Among her famous choreographic works, many of which are based on Eastern religions and cultures, are *Cobras, Nautch* and *Incense.*

Saint-Exupéry, Antoine de *(1900–1943)* French aviator, novelist, travel writer and children's book author. Saint-Exupéry was educated at a Jesuit college in Le Mans and at the College of Saint Jean in Fribourg. He served in the French air force from 1921 to 1923 and flew in Morocco. Saint-Exupéry remained in North Africa as a pilot for the Air Mail Service, which experience formed the basis for his first book, *Courrier Sud* (1929). He next moved to Argentina, where he headed an air mail service there. His writing career was established with the international success of his novel *Night Flight* (1931), which dealt with the tragic death of a mail pilot. Saint-Exupéry attempted to set a time record for a flight from Paris to Saigon but crashed in the Arabian desert; the story of his survival is recounted in *Wind, Sand and Stars* (1939). *The Little Prince* (1943) is his classic children's story. He died in 1943 while serving as a reconnaissance pilot over North Africa for the American forces during WORLD WAR II.

St. Jacques, Raymond (James Arthur Johnson) *(1930–1990)* American actor. He helped lower racial barriers for other black actors with his performances in numerous films and television shows. His films include *Black Like Me* (1964), *The Pawnbroker* (1965), *The Green Berets* (1968) and *Cotton Comes to Harlem* (1970). He also appeared on the TV western series *Rawhide* in the 1960s and in the miniseries *Roots* (1977).

Saint Jean de Maurienne Agreement A secret agreement reached in April 1917 by representatives of the British, French, Italian and Russian governments regarding post–World War I territorial arrangements. It promised to give Italy a part of Turkey, but was never implemented. In 1918 the BOLSHEVIK government of Russia revealed the understanding, leading to Greek and Turkish distrust of Italy.

Saint Kitts and Nevis Located at the northern end of the Leeward Islands chain of the West Indies, the federation comprises St. Kitts (formerly known as St. Christopher [6.5 square

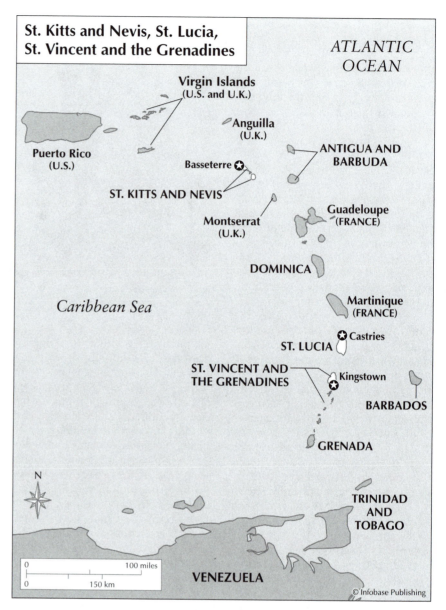

St. Kitts and Nevis, St. Lucia, St. Vincent and the Grenadines

miles]) and Nevis (36 square miles). The two islands are divided by a 2-mile-wide sea strait known as the Narrows. Both islands are volcanic in origin and are dominated by mountains that rise to 3,793 feet (at Mount Misery on St. Kitts) and 3,232 feet on Nevis. Over 75% of the population of 40,000 live on St. Kitts. The British joined Anguilla administratively to the other two islands in 1816. Universal suffrage was granted in 1951, and in 1967 the territory attained full internal self-government. Robert Bradshaw, leader of the ruling Labour Party, became premier. In 1967 Anguilla declared itself independent of St. Kitts. British troops intervened in 1969, and in 1971 the island reverted to being a

British dependent territory; it was formally separated from St. Kitts–Nevis in 1980.

Bradshaw died in May 1978 and was succeeded by Paul Southwell, who also died a year later. New premier Lee Moore called elections for February 1980, but the Labour Party lost and was replaced by a coalition of the People's Action Movement (PAM) and the Nevis Reformation Party (NRP), which sought greater autonomy for Nevis. Dr. Kennedy Simmonds of the PAM became premier and then prime minister on the attainment of full independence from Britain on September 19, 1983. The PAM-NRP coalition remained in power after winning general elections in 1984 and 1989, in spite of the PAM

SAINT KITTS AND NEVIS

1871–1956	The islands become part of the Leeward Islands Federation.
1951	Universal adult suffrage is granted.
1958–62	The islands become part of the Federation of the West Indies.
1967	St. Kitts, Nevis and Anguilla achieve internal self-government within the Commonwealth, with Robert Bradshaw, Labour Party leader, as prime minister.
1971	Anguilla returns to British dependency status after rebelling against domination by St. Kitts.
1980	The People's Action Movement (PAM) and the Nevis Reformation Party (NRP) centrist coalition government, led by Kennedy Simmonds, are formed after an inconclusive general election.
1983	The nation's first constitution proclaims the Federation of Saint Christopher and Nevis; Saint Christopher and Nevis becomes a member of the Commonwealth.
1984	In House of Assembly elections, the ruling coalition of the PAM and the NRP is returned to power with a decisive victory.
1988	The country is officially renamed the Federation of Saint Kitts and Nevis.
1989	The ruling PAM-NRP coalition returns to power after losing one seat in House of Assembly elections.
1998	A popular referendum proposing the secession of Nevis fails to gain the required two-thirds majority, leaving the federation intact.
2005	Due to unprofitability the government decides to shut down the islands' sugar industry.

achieving a clear majority of seats in the national assembly. A separatist movement in Nevis failed as a result of a 1998 referendum that fell far short of the two-thirds majority vote required for independence.

St. Laurent, Louis Stephen *(1882–1973)* Canadian political leader, prime minister of CANADA (1948–57). Born in Compton, Quebec, St. Laurent attended Laval University and was a well-known corporate lawyer before entering political life in 1941. He was minister of justice, attorney general and minister of external affairs (the latter post, 1946–48) during the administration of MacKenzie KING. In 1948 he succeeded King in the post of LIBERAL PARTY leader and became prime minister in November of that year. While St. Laurent was in office, Canada assumed a larger role on the world stage, Newfoundland became a province (1949), the Old Age Security Act was enacted (1951) and the ST. LAWRENCE SEAWAY was agreed upon and partially constructed. As the country swung to the Conservatives, the Liberals failed to

obtain a majority in the 1957 election, and St. Laurent was succeeded as prime minister by John G. DIEFENBAKER. He retired as party head in 1958 and returned to his law practice.

Saint Laurent, Yves *(1936–)* French fashion designer sometimes regarded as the "king of fashion" for his enormous success based on design that is practical, charming or pretty while still expressive of haute couture style. Saint Laurent was an art student in Paris when, at the age of 17, he won a fashion sketch contest staged by the International Wool Secretariat. At 19 he was employed by Christian DIOR, becoming head designer for that house on Dior's death in 1958. With the support of an American financial backer, he opened his own firm in 1962, established his ready-to-wear line, Rive Gauche, in 1966 and added men's wear design in 1974. His work is known for its practical qualities, along with a certain glamour and occasional exotic touches based on oriental art and

gypsy and African motifs. His name and YSL initials have became a recognized brand name, licensed with vast commercial success to cosmetics, linens, perfumes (including the popular Opium and Y), sweaters and other products. Saint Laurent was honored with a retrospective exhibit of his work in 1983 at the Costume Institute of the Metropolitan Museum of Art in New York. In 1996 Saint Laurent made two critical professional decisions: to broadcast his haute couture fashion show on the Internet and to cease production of large fashion shows for his pret-à-porter line. On June 2, 1999, the Council of Fashion Designers of America honored Saint Laurent with its Lifetime Achievement Award. Five months later, Gucci purchased the Saint Laurent line for $1 billion. He announced his retirement in 2002.

Saint-Laurent-sur-Mer Town on the bay of the Seine River, eight miles northwest of Bayeux. For two weeks in June 1944 it was the busiest harbor in Europe, courtesy of the Allied invaders of NORMANDY in WORLD WAR II. A large artificial harbor, towed by the invasion fleet from England, was later greatly damaged by a severe gale—but not until it had successfully landed a great deal of ordnance, artillery and heavy-duty war matériel.

St. Lawrence Seaway International waterway along a part of the boundary between the U.S. and Canada; a link between the Great Lakes and the Atlantic Ocean, the seaway is comprised of a system of locks, dams and canals on the St. Lawrence River and channels that connect the river with the Great Lakes. Measuring 2,342 miles in length, it was opened in 1959. The seaway allows large ocean-going ships passage to such inland cities as the U.S.'s Buffalo, Chicago, Detroit and Milwaukee, and Canada's Montreal, Hamilton, Thunder Bay and Toronto. It accommodates vessels up to 730 feet long, with a cargo capacity of up to 28,000 tons. Of great commercial importance, the seaway handles annual traffic of approximately 50 million short tons (45 million metric tons). It also provides for hydroelectric facilities.

Saint Louis Symphony Founded in 1880, the symphony of St. Louis, Missouri, has the distinction of being the second-oldest in the United States. Among its distinguished conductors was Rudolph Ganz, one of America's most noted music educators, who was also a distinguished composer. In St. Louis, Ganz introduced concerts for children. TIME magazine, in its annual evaluation for 1988, described the St. Louis Symphony as second only to the CHICAGO SYMPHONY in musical quality. This distinction has come about mainly through the efforts of its current conductor, Leonard Slatkin, who is also known as a masterful advocate of contemporary American classical composers.

Saint Lucia Saint Lucia, the second largest island in the Windward group of the West Indies (see map on page 1086), is situated in the East Caribbean 24 miles south of Martinique and 20 miles north of Saint Vincent. Ownership of the island alternated between Britain and France many times before it was finally ceded to Britain in 1814.

SAINT LUCIA

1871–1960	St. Lucia joins the Windward Islands Federation.
1951	Universal adult suffrage is granted.
1967	St. Lucia acquires internal self-government as a West Indies associated state.
1979	St. Lucia becomes an independent member of the Commonwealth, with John Compton as prime minister. In general elections, the St. Lucia Labour Party (SLP) wins an upset victory; Allan Louisy is named prime minister.
1981	Prime Minister Louisy is forced to resign.
1982	John Compton takes office as prime minister.
1987	John Compton is reelected prime minister.
1997	Kenny D. Anthony is elected prime minister, ending 15 years of government leadership by Compton and the UWP.
2004	Prime Minster Anthony announces that he will run again in the next election.

Universal suffrage was introduced in 1951 and full internal autonomy in 1967. Elections in 1974 were won by the ruling United Workers' Party (UWP), led by John Compton; it campaigned for full independence, which was attained on February 22, 1979.The UWP was defeated in elections held shortly afterward by the St. Lucia Labour Party (SLP), led by Allan Louisy. In May 1981 Louisy was forced to resign, leading to the collapse of the SLP government in January 1982 amid strikes and demonstrations. Fresh elections were won overwhelmingly by the UWP, and Compton returned as prime minister. In elections held in 1987 the UWP was returned to power, but with a majority of only one seat over the SLP. Compton called a new election for later the same month, hoping to obtain a more decisive mandate, but the distribution of seats remained the same. In 1997 Anthony and his SLP coalition registered the largest victory in the nation's history by defeating Compton and the UWP. In 2004 Anthony announced that he would seek a third term in the next general election.

Saint Malo Conference A December 4, 1998, meeting between British prime minister Tony BLAIR and French president Jacques CHIRAC. Blair and Chirac met in the resort town of Saint Malo on the French side of the English Channel to evaluate proposed efforts by the EUROPEAN UNION (EU) to form a multinational military force capable of being dispatched as a peace-keeping force to troubled regions within Europe and the world. Since the formation of the European Community, Britain had steadfastly resisted all French efforts to create a European organization outside NATO. After conferring for several days, both Blair and Chirac issued a joint statement that advocated a common European Security and Defense Policy (ESDP), which would commit all EU member states to the same foreign policy toward regions like KOSOVO, in which Serbian president Slobodan MILOŠEVIĆ was seeking to expel all ethnic Albanians. The ESDP also gave its assent to earlier French efforts to form an EU-wide rapid reaction force (see WESTERN EUROPEAN UNION) for deployment within Europe and even suggested that such a force could be dispatched abroad to protect the EU's interests throughout the world.

Saint Martin (Sint Maarten) One of the Leeward Islands, in the West Indies east of Puerto Rico, divided between the Dutch and the French. Dutch Sint Maarten is in the south of the island; it is associated with the NETHERLANDS ANTILLES. The French section is associated with GAUDELOUPE. Marigot is the capital of the French Saint-Martin, while Dutch-speaking Philipsburg is the chief town of Sint Maarten. A popular tourist destination, the island is visited by many cruise ships.

St. Petersburg City in the northwest USSR, on the Gulf of Finland. Commonly called "the Venice of the North," St. Petersburg occupies both banks near the mouth of the Neva River as well as numerous small islands in the Neva. Built at the beginning of the 18th century under Czar Peter the Great as Russia's "window on the West," the city entered the 20th century as the capital of imperial RUSSIA. The unsuccessful RUSSIAN REVOLUTION OF 1905 against the rule of Czar NICHOLAS II broke out here. After Russia entered WORLD WAR I against Germany, the city's name was Russified; Petersburg became Petrograd (1914). The city figured prominently in the RUSSIAN REVOLUTION of 1917; V. I. LENIN arrived here from Finland to direct the BOLSHEVIKS, who deposed the KERENSKY government at the Winter Palace. With the Bolsheviks in control, the capital was transferred to Moscow (1918). After Lenin's death (1924) Petrograd was renamed Leningrad.

Within a few months after the German invasion of the USSR began (June 22, 1941), HITLER's forces had reached Leningrad and virtually surrounded it. Thus began the SIEGE OF LENINGRAD. At least one million people died in Leningrad during the siege, which lasted for 872 days. The city was subsequently largely restored. Among the city's many architectural and cultural treasures are the Winter Palace, the Hermitage Museum, and the Academy of Arts. Leningrad has always been noted for its literary heritage; in the 20th century it was home to poets Anna AKHMATOVA, Joseph BRODSKY and Osip MANDELSTAM, as well as composer Dmitry SHOSTAKOVICH. After the breakup of the Soviet Union, the city was renamed St. Petersburg.

Saint-Pierre See MARTINIQUE.

Saint Pierre and Miquelon St. Pierre and Miquelon—93 miles square—are islands in the North Atlantic Ocean that are a relic of France's once-mighty New World empire. The terrain is mostly barren rock; the capital is St. Pierre. The first permanent settlement was established in 1604. The importance of France's last possessions in North America is that they allowed the French to exploit the rich fishing grounds of Newfoundland. Fishing for cod allowed the islands to prosper until the introduction of factory ships, and frozen fish facilities reduced the importance of the islands' harbors. Saint Pierre and Miquelon, off the coast of Canada's Newfoundland, became an overseas territory of France in 1946 and in 1976 was made a department, against the wishes of many of the islanders. General strikes and unrest over departmental status intensified during the late 1970s and early 1980s. In 1976 Canada declared a 200-mile economic interest zone around its shores, prompting the French to declare a similar zone around Saint Pierre, although the Canadians recognized only a 12-mile limit. In 1987 it was agreed to take the dispute to the International Court of Justice. However, in October negotiations over future fishing quotas broke down, and French vessels were banned from Canadian waters. In April 1988 several fishermen and island politicians were arrested by Canadian authorities for fishing in Canadian waters. The total population of the islands is 6,300. Although the islands' economy had been steadily declining because of disputes between Canada and St. Pierre over fishing rights, a 1992 arbitration panel designated an economic zone of more than 12,000 square kilometers as the exclusive domain of the island territory. The French government hoped that this economic ruling, along with a projected increase in tourism and indications of substantial oil reserves beneath the sea floor of this economic zone, would improve the quality of life in St. Pierre and Miquelon.

St. Valentine's Day Massacre Sensational gangland execution that occurred in a Chicago garage on St. Valentine's Day, 1929. Dressed in police uniforms, gunmen in the employ of Al CAPONE machine-gunned seven men connected with the gang of George "Bugs" Moran. It was one of the most vicious and violent crimes of a vicious and violent era. The massacre was thought to have been perpetrated in reprisal for a whiskey hijacking, and it effectively wiped out an important Capone rival.

Saint Vincent and the Grenadines The Windward Islands nation of St. Vincent and the Grenadines lies in the east Caribbean, 93 miles west of Barbados; it has a total area of 150 square miles, most of it being the chief island (see map, page 1086), St. Vincent. Universal suffrage was introduced in 1951 and full internal self-government in 1969. Elections in 1972 resulted in the People's Political Party (PPP) and the St. Vincent Labour Party (SVLP) each winning six seats in the House of Assembly. The balance of power was held by an independent, James Mitchell, who joined the PPP to form a government with himself as premier. Mitchell's government collapsed in 1974 and was replaced after elections by a coalition of the PPP and SVLP, whose leader, Milton Cato, led the country to full independence from Britain on October 27, 1979. Discontent at the government's record and failure to improve the economy led to its defeat in 1984 by the New Democratic Party (NDP), founded by Mitchell. Mitchell became prime minister and strengthened the NDP's position by polling 71 percent of the vote and winning all 15 seats in the house of assembly in elections in May 1989. In 1994 and 1998 Mitchell and the NDP again won reelection at the polls, but their victories came from steadily declining majorities. Mitchell's resignation and replacement in 2000 by Arniham Eustace preceded a rash of antigovernment uprisings in response to the NDP's effort to increase retirement pensions for parliamentary delegates. In response, the government moved up national elections from 2003 to 2001, and in 2001 ULP leader Ralph Gonsalves was elected prime

SAINT VINCENT AND THE GRENADINES

1951	Universal adult suffrage is granted.
1958–62	The islands become part of the West Indies Federation.
1969	The islands achieve internal self-government.
1979	St. Vincent and the Granadines becomes fully independent as a special member of the Commonwealth. In House of Assembly elections Prime Minister Milton Cato's St. Vincent Labour Party wins 11 of 13 seats.
1984	In general elections the New Democratic Party, led by James F. Mitchell, wins nine of 13 House of Assembly seats, while the St. Vincent Labour Party wins only four. Cato steps down, and James F. Mitchell takes office as prime minister.
1989	The New Democratic Party takes all elective seats in the House of Assembly. James Mitchell retains the prime ministership.
1994	The New Democratic Party, holds onto 12 seats in the house, and Mitchell is again selected as prime minister.
1998	The New Democratic Party, headed by James Mitchell, narrowly wins a fourth term.
2000	Mitchell resigns and is succeeded by his finance minister, Arniham Eustace.
2001	The St. Vincent Labour Party wins 12 seats in the House of Assembly and Ralph Gonsalves becomes prime minister.
2005	Prime Minister Gonsalves and his Unity Labor Party win a second term in office.

minister. In 2005 Gonsalves and his Unity Labor Party won a second term.

Saipan Volcanic island in the MARIANAS of the western Pacific; under U.S. control, a part of the UN-established Trust Territory of the Pacific Islands. A Spanish possession from 1565 to 1899 and German from 1899 to 1914, in 1920 the 47-square-mile island was mandated to JAPAN with the other Marianas by the LEAGUE OF NATIONS. Its air base was a prime U.S. target in WORLD WAR II. The strategic surprise of the American invasion in June 1944 caught the Japanese unprepared (and also lured the Japanese Combined Fleet out of Philippine waters). The lessons learned by Japan's doomed garrison were put to use in the later defense of IWO JIMA and OKINAWA—to the misfortune of the Americans. Total American casualties on Saipan were over 14,000, while 24,000 Japanese were killed or committed suicide—and only 1,780 were taken prisoner (more than half of them Korean). The U.S. used Saipan as a base for attacking the Japanese mainland.

Sakdal Uprising (1935) Sakdal, meaning "accuse" in Tagalog, a major Philippine language, signified the anger of the landless peasants in central Luzon. Many joined the Sakdal movement led by Benigno Ramos calling for lower taxes, land reform and independence. As a party, the Sakdals drew many votes in the 1934 Philippine elections. On May 2, 1935, armed Sakdals seized government buildings in 14 towns in Luzon. Government troops quickly suppressed the rebellion, Ramos escaped to Japan, and the party was declared illegal.

Sakhalin Long, narrow island off the Pacific coast of Russia; separated from the Soviet mainland by the Tatar Strait, Sakhalin's eastern shores are bordered by the Sea of Okhotsk. North of the Japanese main island of Hokkaido, it was colonized by both Russia and Japan in the 18th and 19th centuries. The population became mostly Russian after 1875. Sakhalin was a penal colony for common criminals as well as a place of exile for political opponents of the czarist government; the noted Russian

author Anton CHEKHOV visited Sakhalin and wrote about the conditions there. Sakhalin also served as a center of Russian commercial interests in the Far East. Following its defeat in the RUSSO-JAPANESE WAR, Russia ceded the southern part of Sakhalin to Japan. This territory was returned to the USSR after WORLD WAR II.

Sakharov, Andrei Dmitrievich (1921–1989) Soviet nuclear physicist, dissident and human rights activist. Possibly the most brilliant nuclear physicist of the 20th century, Sakharov played a key role in the Soviet development of the HYDROGEN BOMB in the late 1940s and the '50s. As such, he held a leading position in the Soviet scientific community. However, he eventually became alarmed by the threat of radioactive contamination from nuclear testing and the threat of nuclear war. Increasingly opposed to the Soviet government's policies, he spoke out against human rights abuses and other failures of the Soviet system. Following the international publication of an article titled "Thoughts on

Progress, Peaceful Co-Existence and Intellectual Freedom" (1968), he was shunned by the Soviet establishment. He received the 1975 NOBEL PRIZE for peace for his efforts on behalf of human rights. After he criticized the Soviet invasion of Afghanistan, he and his wife, Yelena Bonner, were exiled to the closed city of Gorky in 1980. There they were frequently harassed by the KGB and were forbidden to communicate with other dissidents and with Westerners. In 1987 they were released on the order of Soviet leader Mikhail GORBACHEV. In the new atmosphere of GLASNOST, Sakharov was hailed by many for his courage and his moral stance, although hard-liners reviled him. He continued to press for political, social and economic change. In April 1989 he was elected to the new Congress of People's Deputies, where he led a reform group. He died of a heart attack on December 14, just after taking part in an important debate in the congress.

Saki (Hector Hugh Munro) *(1870–1916)* British author of macabre and wryly amusing short stories. He was born in Akyab, Burma, the son of an inspector-general for the Burma police. After a boyhood in English boarding schools, later police service in Burma and travel through the Balkans as a London press correspondent, his satiric columns and short stories began appearing under the pen name "Saki" (the name of the cupbearer in *The Rubaiyat of Omar Khayyam*) in the *Westminster Gazette* and *Morning Post*. Volumes of the stories were *Reginald* (1904), *Reginald in Russia* (1910), *The Chronicles of Clovis* (1911), *Beasts and Super-Beasts* (1914) and two posthumous works, *The Toys of Peace* (1923) and *The Square Egg* (1924). These are stories that, in the words of a Saki character, "are true enough to be interesting and not true enough to be tiresome." They depict a familiar world of overstuffed drawing rooms, gossipy garden parties, amateur theatricals, lonely railway carriages and exclusive club rooms—invaded by fierce society matrons, foppish young men, inveterate liars and murderous animals. No sentiment whatever can exist in these savage conditions. Only predators survive—those who, like the great ferret "Sredni Vashtar," lay "special stress on the fierce, impatient side of things." There are the wolves of "The Interlopers," the were-beasts of "Gabriel-Ernest" and "Music on the Hill," the wicked "romancers" of "The Open Window" and "A Defensive Diamond," and the witches of "The Peace of Mowsle Barton." Were vicious struggles for survival ever portrayed more grimly—yet more comically—than in "The Strategist?" It is, ultimately, a fatalistic vision. "After all," says Reginald, one of Saki's bright young men, "life teems with things that have no earthly reason." Was there, then, a terrible symmetry (or inevitability) about the sniper's bullet that killed Munro on November 14, 1916, while serving in the trenches with the Royal Fusiliers?

Salam, Abdus *(1926–1996)* Pakistani physicist. Salam helped establish the International Center for Theoretical Physics in Trieste, to assist physicists from developing countries. His own work concerned the behavior and properties of elementary particles, for which he received the 1979 NOBEL PRIZE for physics, in conjunction with Sheldon Glashow and Steven WEINBERG. Through independent work, these three physicists each contributed to a theory that explained weak and electromagnetic interactions, including the phenomenon of neutral currents and their strengths. This "theory" was first confirmed in 1973 at the European Organization for Nuclear Research.

Salam al-Khalidi, Anbara *(1897–1986)* Lebanese author. A translator and pioneer campaigner for Arab women's rights, in 1927 she became the first Arab woman in greater SYRIA to unveil her face in public. This act necessitated her retirement into private life for a time. In 1929 she married Ahmad Samih al-Khalidi, who at that time was the foremost Arab education official in PALESTINE. The couple collaborated on historical and educational studies. Her books included the first translations into Arabic of Homer's *Odyssey* and Virgil's *Aeneid*.

Salan, Raoul *(1899–1984)* French soldier and rebel leader. A WORLD WAR II veteran, General Salan was one of FRANCE's most decorated soldiers. During the war, he serviced in the FREE FRENCH forces in FRENCH WEST AFRICA. He was later with the French army in INDOCHINA (1945–53). However, Salan is remembered as the man who twice brought France to the brink of civil war during the ALGERIAN WAR OF 1954–62. He was senior French officer in Algiers (1956), and in 1958 became commander in chief of the French forces in ALGERIA. His defiance of civilian authority over the Algerian issue in 1958 helped General Charles DE GAULLE topple the Fourth Republic and come to power as the first president of the French Fifth Republic. However, Salan soon disagreed with de Gaulle over France's Algerian policy. In 1960, Salan formed the O.A.S. (Organisation de L'Armée Secrète, or Secret Army Organization) and waged a terrorist campaign to try to kill de Gaulle and prevent Algerian independence. Captured in 1962 and sentenced to life imprisonment, he received amnesty with other plotters in 1968 and was fully pardoned and reinstated in the army in 1982 by President François MITTERRAND.

Salazar, Antonio de Oliveira *(1889–1970)* Portuguese statesmen and dictator (1932–68). Born in a village near Lisbon, he was educated at a seminary, studied law at Coimbra University and became a professor of economics there. He served briefly in the chamber of deputies in 1921 and as finance minister in 1926. Recalled to office in 1928 by General Antonio de Carmona, he assumed complete control of Portuguese finances and soon was able to deal with the nation's chronic economic crises. Becoming premier in 1932, he assumed dictatorial powers. The following year he promulgated a new constitution that governed under fascist-like corporate principles (see FASCISM). He suppressed all dissent and maintained a large army and a vigilant secret police. His foreign policy sought ties with Spain, Great Britain and the U.S. During WORLD WAR II he kept Portugal neutral while maintaining cordial relations with the Allies. He instituted a series of domestic reforms after the war. His latter years were largely spent in a vain attempt to suppress rebellion in Portugal's African colonies. He was succeeded as premier by Marcello CAETANO in 1968 while in a coma following a stroke. Government officials never told him that he had been replaced, fearing that the news might kill him, but kept up a charade of meeting with him as if he were still in power. Salazar continued to live in the chief of state's official residence until his death.

Salinas de Gortari, Carlos *(1944–)* Mexican politician and president of Mexico (1988–94). Born in Mexico City, Salinas received his B.A. from the National Autonomous University of Mexico in 1969 and his Ph.D. in political economy and government in 1978 from Harvard University. While serving as director of financial planning, in the mid-1980s, Salinas renegotiated the Mexican national debt, particularly with American creditors, and sharply reduced government expenditures in an effort to solve Mexico's severe financial crisis caused by the decline in oil prices.

When he succeeded Miguel de la Madrid as president of Mexico in 1988, the pursuit of free trade became one of Salinas's primary aims. Along with an effort to sell off Mexico's numerous nationalized industries, Salinas negotiated with U.S. president George H. W. Bush and Canadian prime minister Brian Mulroney for the development of a free-trade zone throughout North America. By 1991 the three leaders had developed a rough outline for what became the North American Free Trade Agreement (NAFTA), which was signed by the three leaders in December 1992 and ratified by their parliaments in 1993; the first stage of the proposed free-trade zone went into effect in January 1994.

In November 1994 Salinas was succeeded by PRI candidate Ernesto Zedillo Ponce de Léon, who pledged to continue Salinas's policy of free trade and controlled devaluation of the peso to encourage foreign and domestic investment in Mexico's manufacturing industries. Instead of the dynamic economic upswing that Salinas envisioned with the creation of NAFTA and his currency devaluation schemes, the Mexican economy was soon beset by an uncontrollable decline of the peso, which deterred the investment of further foreign capital in the Mexican economy. In 1995 Salinas's elder brother, Raúl, was arrested on charges of tax evasion, fraud and involvement in the 1994 assassination of a prominent politician. Shortly thereafter Carlos Salinas and his family left Mexico to live in exile in Switzerland.

Salinger, Jerome David *(1916–)* American novelist and short story writer. Salinger, who in the 1950s and '60s was widely read by American youths and attained a virtual cult status, has earnestly sought seclusion from the public eye. Hence relatively little in known about his life. Salinger was raised in New York City and educated at various schools including a military academy, much like Holden Caulfield, the protagonist of CATCHER IN THE RYE (1951), his most famous novel. Salinger served in the American infantry during WORLD WAR II and was decorated for bravery. In the decade following the war, Salinger's stories appeared frequently in *The New Yorker* magazine. Many of them concerned members of the fictional Glass family, all of whom were brilliant and extraordinarily sensitive to the everyday horrors of modern life. Salinger's other major works are *Nine Stories* (1953), *Franny and Zooey* (1961) and, in tandem, *Raise High the Roof Beam, Carpenters and Seymour: An Introduction* (1963).

Salisbury See HARARE.

Salk, Jonas (Jonas Edward Salk) *(1914–1995)* American microbiologist. Born in New York City, Salk received his M.D. from New York University Medical School in 1939. He researched the influenza virus at the University of Michigan, becoming an assistant professor of epidemiology there in 1946. In 1947 he moved to the University of Pittsburgh, where he was appointed professor of bacteriology in 1949. There he began work on the vaccine for poliomyelitis that would be the first such vaccine proved effective against the disease and that would make him a national hero in the U.S. His formulation, a formaldehyde-killed vaccine, was extensively field tested in 1953 and 1954. It was used throughout the world until it was largely supplanted by Albert SABIN's live-virus vaccine in 1960. In 1963 he became director of the Salk Institute for Biological Studies at the University of California, San Diego. His later researches concentrated on the search for an AIDS vaccine.

SALT The SALT (Strategic Arms Limitation Talks) I Treaty, signed May 26, 1972, by the U.S. and the Soviet Union, was the first agreement by those nations to limit their offensive nuclear weapons. As such, it was a highlight of DÉTENTE. The pact prohibited either country from building any new ICBM or submarine-based missile launchers for a period of five years. The SALT II Treaty, signed on June 18, 1979, further limited the number and type of offensive nuclear weapons the two countries were allowed to keep in their arsenal.

Salt March Two-hundred-mile march (1930) by Mohandas K. GANDHI and his followers to the sea to make salt from seawater, in defiance of a British ban on the Indian manufacture of salt. As part of his nonviolent campaign to achieve Indian self-sufficiency, Gandhi challenged the monopoly and the salt tax. Setting out on March 12, he reached the sea and made salt on April 5. He was arrested on May 4. Anti-British rioting followed later that month in Bombay and elsewhere.

Salyut The name given to the first seven Soviet space stations. The name means "salute" and honors Soviet cosmonaut Yuri GAGARIN, the first human in space. The first Salyut was launched April 19, 1971. *Salyut 7*, launched April 19, 1982, was "retired" though still orbiting when the *MIR* space station was launched in 1986.

Salzburg Festival Annual summer music festival held since 1920 in the town of Mozart's birth; suspended during World War II. Mozart festivals given in Salzburg from 1877 to 1910 attracted worldwide attention, especially when soprano Lilli Lehmann performed (1905–10). Richard STRAUSS Max REINHARDT, Hugo von HOFMANNSTHAL and Franz Schalk founded the expanded festival in 1920. From 1957 until his death in 1989, Herbert von KARAJAN served as artistic director. Many of the great musicians of the world have appeared at the festival, including conductor Arturo TOSCANINI, composer-conductor Richard Strauss, and singers Marilyn Horne and Frederica VON STADE. The scope of the festival has broadened to include works by composers other than Mozart, such as Benjamin BRITTEN and Samuel BARBER.

Samaroff, Olga (Olga Hickenlooper) *(1882–1948)* American concert pianist and teacher. Samaroff (a name she adopted because it sounded more European than her own maiden name) made her concert debut in 1905, appearing with the New York Philharmonic at CARNEGIE HALL. She appeared with all the major American orchestras and was once married to conductor Leopold STOKOWSKI. She taught piano at the Juilliard Graduate School of Music from 1925 until her death.

Sambre River The Sambre River rises in France's Aisne department and flows northeastward to join the Meuse River at Namur in Belgium. In the 20th century it was the site of an important British victory in November 1918, as WORLD WAR I was drawing to a close.

Samil Independence Movement *(1919–1920)* JAPAN annexed KOREA against its will in 1910, and after WORLD WAR I Koreans argued unsuccessfully at the Paris Conference for their right of self-determination. On March 1, 1919, cultural and religious leaders signed a "Proclamation of Independence" in SEOUL, the capital. The independence movement spread rapidly, and in the following year over 1,500 peaceful demonstrations involving about 2 million people were held throughout the country. Japanese police and military harshly suppressed the demonstrators, killing or wounding 23,000, arresting 47,000 and imprisoning 5,000. The Japanese carried out minor reforms, permitting limited self-governance. Today, March 1 commemorates the demonstrators' patriotism in both South and North Korea.

samizdat Term coined by Soviet dissenters for the system of preparing and circulating writings, usually in typescript form, so as to avoid official censorship. Though this phenomenon appeared on a large scale in the late 1950s during the period of DESTALINIZATION, the word itself dates from the mid-1960s. It is a parody of the official acronym Gosizdat (State Publishing House) and means "self-publishing" or "do-it-yourself publishing." In *samizdat*, materials were circulated on the chain-letter principle. Typescript copies of the original text were passed on to trusted colleagues who in turn made further copies and handed them on to their friends to do likewise.

The authors and distributors of *samizdat* often operated under conditions of great difficulty and risked arrest and imprisonment in the event of discovery. Two articles of Soviet law specifically prescribed terms of imprisonment for citizens who sought to express their opinions in ways disapproved of by the authorities. Article 190–1 of the Russian Soviet Federated Socialist Republic Criminal Code, "dissemination of fabrications known to be false which defame the Soviet state and social system," and Article 70 of the same code, "anti-Soviet agitation and propaganda," carried maximum penalties of three and 12 years' imprisonment respectively.

Samizdat became a permanent feature of Soviet life in the post-Stalin period. It provided an alternative, unofficial and uncontrolled channel of communication. *Samizdat* provided a forum for opinions, as well as a source of information on political, national, religious and literary themes that could not find expression in the official press and publishing. It was not limited to the larger Russian cities but was also well developed in some of the non-Russian republics of the Soviet Union, particularly in Lithuania and Ukraine. A striking feature of *samizdat* was the wide range and volume of its material. The range of subjects varied from petitions, protests and statements to complete novels, e.g., PASTERNAK's *DOCTOR ZHIVAGO*, and lengthy historical works, e.g., SOLZHENITSYN's *THE GULAG ARCHIPELAGO*. Perhaps the most outstanding achievement of *samizdat* was the appearance between 1968 and 1980 of over 50 issues of the journal *A Chronicle of Current Events*, the mouthpiece of the human rights movement in the USSR. The *Chronicle* reported on human rights violations throughout the Soviet Union and was noted for its objectivity and accuracy.

The practice of circulating uncensored material privately has a long tradition in Russia. It can be traced as far back as the 1820s when the poet Pushkin, the playwright Alexander Sergeyevich Griboyedov and others are known to have privately distributed manuscripts of works disapproved of by the censors. The practice flourished in the second half of the 19th century as various revolutionary groups, and later political parties and national movements, emerged. It continued after the Bolshevik seizure of power in October 1917, and the creation of a new system of censorship. By the mid-1930s, however, the practice was effectively stamped out everywhere except in the labor camps, and it did not begin to reappear until after STALIN's death in 1953.

Samoa, American American Samoa is a group of five volcanic islands and two coral atolls in the South Pacific Ocean that cover a total of 77 square miles; the capital is Pago Pago. In 1872 the Americans, in their search for a strategic harbor for their navy, gained exclusive rights from the high chief of the Polynesian inhabitants to use the harbor of Pago Pago on Tutuila, the main island in the eastern group. Rivalries among Germany, Britain and the U.S. eventually led to a convention between them, whereby the U.S. acquired Eastern Samoa. The territory, which became known as American Samao in 1911, was administered by the U.S. Navy from 1900 to 1951, after which the U.S. Department of the Interior took over. American Samoa remains an unincorporated territory of the U.S.; its people are U.S. nationals, but not citizens. The 1960 constitution, combining traditional practices with the needs of a modern state, gives American Samoans self-government, with certain powers reserved to the U.S. secretary of the interior. A nonvoting delegate is elected to the U.S. House of Representatives. In 1978 Peter Tali Coleman became the first popularly elected governor; he was succeeded in 1984 by A. P. Lutali. A revised constitution, drawn up in 1986, excludes commoners and women from voting but has yet to be ratified by the U.S. Congress.

Samoa (Independent State of Samoa; formerly Western Samoa) Located in the southwestern Pacific Ocean, approximately 1,600 miles northeast of New Zealand (see map on page 957), Samoa is composed of two main islands (Upolu and Savai'i) and a number of smaller islands, and has a total land area of 1,093 square miles. New Zealand annexed Western Samoa, as Samoa was known before independence, in 1914 and administered it

(1920–62) on behalf of the LEAGUE OF NATIONS and the UNITED NATIONS. A constitution was drafted and independence achieved in 1962. The island state became a full member of the British Commonwealth in 1970 and joined the UN in 1976. In 1997 the archipelago formally changed its name to Samoa. The following year the federal government increased media censorship. In 2002 Samoa and New Zealand began to reconcile their differences following a formal apology by New Zealand for its colonial-era treatment of Samoan citizens. In February 2004 Australia announced it was giving a $7 million grant to fund Samoan training of its security forces.

Samsonov, Alexander Vasilyevich *(1859–1914)* Russian general. Samsonov commanded the army that invaded East Prussia in August 1914 and was defeated by Generals LUDENDORFF and von HINDENBURG at the battle of Tannenberg; two Russian corps were destroyed and three others were reduced to half their size in one of the most decisive Allied defeats of WORLD WAR I. Samsonov committed suicide.

Sandburg, Carl *(1878–1967)* American poet and biographer. A major American poet, he was born in Galesburg, Illinois, the son of Swedish immigrants. A laborer by the age of 13, he fought in the Spanish-American War

American poet Carl Sandburg. 1955 (NEW YORK WORLD-TELEGRAM AND *THE SUN* NEWSPAPER COLLECTION, LIBRARY OF CONGRESS, PRINTS AND PHOTOGRAPHS DIVISION)

and returned to his hometown to attend a local college. Graduating in 1902, he traveled across the U.S., worked on various newspapers and published his first poetry in 1904. Secretary to Milwaukee's socialist mayor from 1910 to 1912, he settled in Chicago in 1913, writing for a number of newspapers until the late 1920s. Little attention was paid to his poems until 1914, when they began to appear in Chicago's *Poetry* magazine. His reputation was established with the publication of *Chicago Poems* (1916) and was augmented by his next volume, the PULITZER PRIZE–winning *Cornhuskers* (1918). Sandburg's other books of verse include *Smoke and Steel* (1920), *Good Morning, America* (1928), *The People, Yes* (1936), *Complete Poems* (1950, PULITZER PRIZE, rev. ed. 1970) and the posthumous *Breathing Tokens* (1978). Writing with profound concern for the American experience and the American worker in unrhymed Whitmanesque free verse, his simple and vigorous language transformed ordinary life into a poetry that has influenced the course of American verse. Deeply interested in the history of the U.S., Sandburg was the author of an epic six-volume biography of Abraham Lincoln (1926–39). He also wrote a novel, *Remembrance Rock* (1948); a collection of folk songs, *The American Songbag* (1927); children's tales that include *Rootabaga Stories* (1922); and the autobiographical *Always the Young Strangers* (1953).

Sandino, Augusto César *(1893–1934)* Legendary Nicaraguan rebel and patriot. Opposed to the military government that deposed an elected civilian government in a 1925 coup, Sandino led rebel forces in the NICARAGUAN CIVIL WAR OF 1925–33. Sandino demanded that U.S. marines who had been sent to NICARAGUA be withdrawn unconditionally. Sandino stopped fighting in 1933, after the U.S. forces left Nicaragua, and was pardoned by the newly elected government. However, the following year he was murdered in Managua by members of the national guard, which had opposed Sandino's forces in the war. In the 1970s his name was taken by the rebels who opposed the rule of SOMOZA; they called themselves the **Sandinistas.** (See also Daniel ORTEGA SAAVEDRA.)

San Francisco earthquake Disastrous earthquake that struck the city of San Francisco at 5:13 A.M. on April 18, 1906. It resulted from a violent movement of the San Andreas Fault. The quake, which measured 8.3 on the RICHTER SCALE, lasted less than a minute. It toppled structures throughout the city, cracked gas and water mains and caused widespread destruction. Even more devastating was the three-day-long fire that, sparked by the quake, almost completely razed San Francisco.

Sanger, Frederick *(1918–)* British biochemist. Sanger was awarded his Ph.D. in 1943 from Cambridge University, where he worked throughout his career. In 1955, he established the amino-acid structure of insulin, which had earlier been isolated by F. G. BANTING and C. H. Best. This discovery, which led to the synthesis of artificial insulin, won Sanger his first NOBEL PRIZE in chemistry in 1958. In 1977 Sanger and his group used original techniques to map the complete DNA of the virus Phi X 174. For this revolutionary research, which led to the creation of genetic material in the laboratory, Sanger was awarded his second Nobel Prize in chemistry, which he shared with Walter Gilbert and Paul Berg.

Sanger, Margaret (Margaret Higgins) *(1883–1966)* American social reformer and a pioneer of the birth control movement in the U.S. Born in Corning, New York, Sanger studied nursing and was a pupil of Havelock ELLIS. As a public-health nurse, she was a witness to the terrible problems created, on the one hand, by overly large families, and on the other, by botched abortions. Convinced of the necessity of family planning, she began a campaign of education and in 1914 founded the National Birth Control League. In 1915 she was arrested for sending informational material on birth control through the mails. The following year she opened a birth control clinic in Brooklyn and was again arrested. Gradually winning over both the public and the legal system, Sanger organized birth control conferences, was founder-president of the National Committee on Federal Legislation for Birth Control from 1923 to 1937 and became the first president of the International Planned Parenthood Foundation in 1953. Her autobiography was published in 1938.

San Marino, Republic of San Marino is a landlocked republic on the slopes of Monte Titano in east-central Italy, 12 miles west of the Adriatic Sea. The world's smallest republic, it has a total area of 24 square miles and is divided into nine castles or districts. San Marino claims to be the world's oldest republic. San Marino volunteers fought for ITALY in WORLD WAR I and from 1923 the republic came under the domination of MUSSOLINI's fascist regime. In WORLD WAR II, San Marino followed Italy in declaring war on Britain (1940) but abolished the fascist system and declared its neutrality shortly before Italy's surrender (September 1943). A year later San Marino declared war on Germany after German forces entered its territory and captured its 300-man army. The postwar party structure reflected Italy's. A Communist/Socialist (PCS/PSS) coalition (1945–57) was followed (1957–73) by one between the Christian Democrats (PDCS) and the Independent Social Democrats (PSDIS). By virtue of its economic union with Italy, San Marino became an integral part of the European Communities in the 1950s. Women obtained the vote in 1960 and became eligible for election in 1973. In June 1986, the Christian Democrats and the Communists, as the two largest parties, formed a grand coalition, which was returned to power in the May 1988 elections. In 1992 San Marino joined the United Nations (UN). In 2002 San Marino, a banking haven, signed a treaty with the OECD agreeing to help combat tax evasion.

San Roman, José Alfredo Perez (*1931–1989*) Cuban-American co-commander of the U.S.-trained Cuban exile force that failed in its attempt to invade CUBA at the BAY OF PIGS in April 1961. San Roman was taken prisoner together with 1,100 of his men; they were freed 20 months later, after the U.S. supplied Cuba with $53 million in food and medical supplies. After returning to the U.S. he served in the U.S. Army and worked as a truck driver. He committed suicide.

Santana Afro-Latin rock music group in the U.S. Created in 1966, the group originally consisted of electric guitarist Carlos Santana, keyboard player and vocalist Gregg Rolie, drummer Michael Shrieve, with David Brown, Marcus Malone and Mike Carabello providing occasional musical support. However, over 40 years, the sole consistent member has been the electric guitarist, Carlos Santana, from which it draws its name. Santana quickly became known for its fusion of jazz, synthetic, and Latin music. The groups performance at the WOODSTOCK festival (1969), where they played "Soul Sacrifice," and introduced music fans all over the U.S. to what the band originally called "Cubano rock." Immediately following Woodstock, Columbia Records signed Santana to a marketing deal, and the group soon produced *Santana, Abraxas,* and *Santana III.* Although the group remained popular, and its songs—such as "Samba Pa Ti," "Everybody's Everything," "Jingo" and "Evil Ways"—did well in the U.S. and U.K., Carlos Santana regularly played independently of his band, recording separate soul-inspired albums.

In 1981 Carlos Santana changed the direction of his band, centering its sound around jazz with *Zebop!* (1981), which had tracks that featured Willie Nelson and Booker T. Jones. Four years later he released *Beyond Appearances* (1985) and embarked on a nationwide promotional tour with artist Bob Dylan. In 1986 he returned to his Latin roots and developed the soundtrack to the film *La Bamba,* inspired by Richie Valens's brief career. He continued to work on individual projects throughout the 1980s and the early 1990s, recording the album *Freedom* (1987) with Buddy Miles and creating what became a legendary guitar solo on John Lee Hooker's album *The Healer* (1989).

In 1999 Santana released *Supernatural,* his most successful album, which won him nine Grammy Awards in 2000.

Santayana, George (*1863–1952*) Spanish-born American philosopher and literary critic. Santayana, who taught at Harvard from 1889 to 1912 before spending the remainder of his long life in a secluded Italian villa, was acclaimed as one of the great literary stylists of his age. Indeed, the beauty of

his writing came to supersede the influence of Santayana's eclectic philosophy, which was an unsystematized blend of skepticism, Epicureanism and Platonic humanism. Santayana was at his best as an appreciator of the arts, and *The Sense of Beauty* (1896) remains a major work in the field of aesthetics. His five-volume magnum opus, *The Life of Reason: Phases of Human Progress* (1905–06), studies creative evolution within human civilizations. Metaphysical works by Santayana include *Skepticism and Animal Faith* (1923) and the four-volume *The Realms of Being* (1927–40). A novel, *The Last Puritan* (1936), was a surprising bestseller. The three-volume *Persons and Places* (1944–53) was Santayana's autobiography.

Santmyer, Helen Hooven (*1895–1986*) American author. Her mammoth novel, *And Ladies of the Club,* about life in a small midwestern town, turned her into a celebrity at age 88. The book shot up the best seller lists after being published commercially in 1984 (Ohio State University Press had brought out a limited edition in 1982). She had worked on the book for more than 50 years while working as an English professor, college dean and librarian.

Sanusi Revolt of 1915–17 The Sanyusiyah brotherhood, Sufist and puritanical Muslims, established themselves in eastern LIBYA, fighting against French expansionism in the Sahara and Italian colonization in Libya. They attacked British forces in the Egyptian desert during WORLD WAR I, and in November 1915 the British needed reinforcements to stop them. A British offensive in February–March 1916 drove them to the Suva Oasis. In 1917 the British pushed them back to Libya, where they antagonized the Italians. Sanusis gained control of Libya after WORLD WAR II, when their leader became IDRIS I. Idris reigned until deposed in 1969 by Muammer EL-QADDAFI.

São Tomé and Príncipe Two main islands, São Tomé and Príncipe, and the rocky islets of Caroco, Pedras, Tinhosas and Rolas, make up this democratic republic situated in the Bight of Biafra, off the coast of West Africa. Cocoa was introduced by the Portuguese in the 19th century, but production declined after 1905, when an

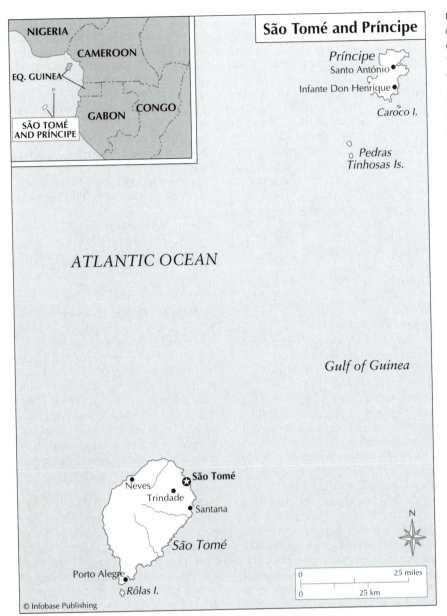

São Tomé and Príncipe

NIGERIA
CAMEROON
EQ. GUINEA
GABON   CONGO
SÃO TOMÉ AND PRÍNCIPE

ATLANTIC OCEAN

Príncipe
Santo António
Infante Don Henrique
Caroco I.

Pedras
Tinhosas Is.

Gulf of Guinea

São Tomé
Neves
Trindade
Santana

São Tomé

Porto Alegre
Rôlas I.

© Infobase Publishing

0   25 miles
0   25 km

N

the party regained power in national elections three years later, and President Trovoada survived a bloodless military coup in 1995 and was re-elected a year later. In 2001 Fredique de Menezes was elected president, only to survive a coup attempt by military in 2003. In 2005 São Tomé signed oil exploration and production agreement with international oil firms.

Saragat, Giuseppe *(1898–1988)* Italian politician. A prominent figure in the history of Italian socialism, Saragat was president of ITALY from 1964 to 1971. A staunch anticommunist, he tried to keep the Socialist Party, then led by Pietro NENNI, from strengthening its ties to the communists. In 1947, he broke with Nenni and founded his own party, the Socialist Party of Italian Workers, which later became the Social Democratic Party. Before his election to the presidency, he served as foreign minister in the center-left administration headed by Christian Democrat Aldo MORO.

Saramago, José *(1922–)* Portuguese writer and winner of the 1998 Nobel Prize in literature. Born on the outskirts of Lisbon, Portugal, he published his first novel, *Terra do Pecado (Country of Sin)* in 1947. Following its release, Saramago stopped producing works of fiction and instead immersed himself in advancing journalism and political activism in opposition to the Portuguese dictator António DE OLIVERIA SALAZAR. Following the overthrow of Salazar's successor, Marcello CAETANO, in a 1974 prodemocracy coup, Saramago resumed his writing of fiction. In 1982 he achieved critical acclaim with the 18th-century romance *Memorial do convento* (titled *Baltasar and Bilmunda* in the 1987 English translation). Two years later, he released *O ano da morte de Ricardo Reis (The Year of the Death of Ricardo Reis)*, a work set in 1930s Portugal during the earlier years of Salazar's rule. Saramago's 1991 novel, *Oevangelho Segundo Jesus Cristo (The Gospel According to Jesus Christ)*, generated great controversy among Christian circles for its willingness to question traditional beliefs about the details of Christ's life. In 1998 Saramago was awarded the Nobel Prize in literature in recognition of his skillful use of literature to expose Portugal's fascist past,

international boycott was imposed over the conditions of virtual slavery suffered by plantation laborers. In 1960 a nationalist liberation group was set up, which reorganized itself in 1972 as the Movimento de Libertacão de São Tomé e Príncipe (MLSTP), under the leadership of Dr. Manuel Pinto da Costa. After the armed forces' coup in Portugal in April 1974, the MLSTP was recognized as the sole representative group. When independence was achieved on July 12, 1975, da Costa became the first president. In 1978 a coup attempt by foreign mercenaries was suppressed. In late 1984 President da Costa proclaimed the islands to be nonaligned; in 1985, the

ministers of foreign affairs and planning, supporters of cooperation with the Soviet Union, were dismissed. Major constitutional changes were announced in October 1987, providing for the election by universal suffrage of the president and the national people's assembly. In March 1988 an invading force of 46 armed men unsuccessfully attempted to seize police headquarters near the capital, on Sao Tome. During their trial, which began in July 1989, the would-be invaders, among them Cape Verdeans and Angolans, admitted that they had been trained in South Africa. In 1991 the first multiparty elections resulted in the departure of the MLSTP-PSD from power. However,

SÃO TOMÉ AND PRÍNCIPE

1960	The first political party is formed, the forerunner of the socialist-nationalist Movement for the Liberation of São Tomé and Príncipe (MLSTP).
1974	A military coup in Portugal leads to strikes, demonstrations, and an army mutiny in São Tomé; thousands of Portuguese settlers flee the country.
1975	São Tomé and Príncipe achieves full independence, with Manuel Pinto da Costa as president. The popular assembly approves new constitution.
1978	The government puts down a coup by former health minister Carlos Da Graca.
1984	Da Costa declares São Tomé and Príncipe to be nonaligned.
1987	The MLSTP central committee announces major constitutional changes, providing for the direct election of the president and the legislature.
1988	Coup attemp fails.
1991	The ruling MLSTP is defeated in multiparty legislative elections.
1995	President Trovoada remains in power despite a bloodless military coup.
1996	President Trovoada is reelected to a second term in July.
2001	Fredique de Menezes, leader of the centrist Independent Democratic Action Party, is elected president.
2003	Military coup takes place while President de Menezes is in Nigeria. Upon his return he is able to strike a deal with the junta and stay in power.
2005	São Tomé, along with Nigeria, signs its first offshore oil deals with international oil firms.

Academy Award–winning actress and political activist Susan Sarandon, 1990 (PHOTOFEST)

and to imaginatively reconstruct historical eras and events.

Sarandon, Susan (*1946– *) American film actress and winner of the Academy Award for Best Actress (1996). In 1968, Sarandon landed her first starring role in the film *Joe* (1970). However, she did not develop a popular following until the cult success of *The Rocky Horror Picture Show* (1975). Although in 1980 she received her first Academy Award nomination for her performance in *Atlantic City,* her films did not begin to achieve commercial success until she appeared in *Bull Durham* (1988). In this comedy, she starred opposite Kevin Costner and Tim Robbins as a fan of a minor league baseball team who uses her sexuality to improve the players' (Costner, Robbins) performance. The film also introduced her to Robbins, who has been her companion since that film. In 1991 Sarandon experienced critical and commercial success in the feminist film *Thelma & Louise,* in which she starred with Geena Davis as two women fleeing arrest after committing vigilante justice against a rapist.

Sarandon has also been known for her political activism in favor of liberal causes. Her work in *Dead Man Walking,* in which she portrayed a nun who visits a convicted murderer scheduled for execution, won her an Academy Award for Best Actress in 1996. In 2003 she and Robbins were among many Hollywood film and television stars who openly criticized President George W. BUSH's decision to invade Iraq in "Operation Iraqi Freedom."

Sarawak Malaysian state on the northwestern side of the island of BORNEO. A British protectorate from 1888, it was occupied by Japan in WORLD WAR II. After the war it was ceded to the UNITED KINGDOM as a Crown colony (1946). Sarawak was a center of anti-Malaysian rebellions prior to the formation of MALAYSIA in 1963. Kuching (formerly called Sarawak) is its capital.

Sarazen, Gene (**Eugene Saraceni**) (*1902–1999*) American golfer. Sarazen was one of the leading players of golf's first golden age, in the 1920s and 1930s. In 1922, he won the U.S. Open and PGA tournaments. He went on to win the PGA title twice more, along with an additional U.S. Open title and a British Open. In 1935, he won the Masters Tournament in a memorable playoff with Craig Wood. Sarazen represented the United States on six Ryder Cup teams.

Sargent, John Singer *(1856–1925)* American painter. Born in Florence, Italy, of American parents, he was raised in Europe and educated in Italy, France and Germany. He studied with Carolus-Duran in Paris, traveled widely and made his first journey to the U.S. in 1876. He first exhibited his work in the Salon of 1878. By the time he moved to London in 1884, he had already established a reputation as a virtuoso portraitist. He remained in London for most of his life, portraying fashionable society figures with a remarkably painterly bravado. The style and elegance of his portraits were enhanced by his amazing facility for capturing textures with his sweeping brushstrokes. Among his best-known portraits are *Mme. X* (Metropolitan Museum of Art, New York City) and *Isabella Stewart Gardner* (Gardner Museum, Boston). Spending a good deal of his time in the U.S. in the 1890s, he was commissioned to paint a mural series, *The History of Religion,* for the Boston Public Library, a project he finally completed in 1916. At the beginning of his career and after 1910, Sargent also produced a number of superb watercolor landscapes done in a highly personal impressionistic style.

Sarkis, Elias *(1924–1985)* Lebanese lawyer and diplomat. Sarkis served as presidential chief of staff from 1958 to 1966, and governor of the Central Bank from 1968 to 1976. He held the office of president of LEBANON from 1976 to 1982. A Maronite Christian, he was unable to stem fighting among that country's religious factions. He left office at the end of his six-year term and settled in FRANCE.

Sarnoff, David *(1891–1971)* American businessman, pioneer of the broadcasting industry. Born in Uzlian, Russia, he immigrated to the U.S. with his family in 1900, settling in New York City. He worked as a cablegram messenger boy and, after teaching himself Morse code, became a telegraph operator for the Marconi Wireless Telegraph Co. while also attending Pratt Institute. He first received public notice for broadcasting the first news of the sinking of the SS TITANIC in 1912. Four years later Sarnoff outlined to the Marconi management his idea for a radio receiver. When the Radio Corporation of America (RCA) absorbed Marconi in 1921, Sarnoff became RCA's general manager. The company soon began to manufacture radios on a mass basis. In order to increase the market for these receivers, RCA, under Sarnoff's direction, organized (1926) the first successful commercial radio network in the U.S., the National Broadcasting Company (NBC). He became RCA's president in 1930 and chairman of the board in 1947. Sarnoff was also a leader in the development of American television. He set up an experimental station in 1928 and 12 years later launched a commercial channel. A brigadier general during WORLD WAR II, he was communications consultant to General Dwight D. EISENHOWER. He retired as chief executive officer of RCA in 1966 and was succeeded by his son, Robert W. Sarnoff, but he remained board chairman until his death.

Saroyan, William *(1908–1981)* American novelist, playwright and songwriter. Raised in an Armenian-American community in Fresno, California, he moved to San Francisco during the GREAT DEPRESSION of the 1930s and quickly established his reputation as a prolific writer with an ascerbic wit. Famed for the rapid pace of his writing, he was also possessed of a rapid-fire temper that caused him to break with HOLLYWOOD over the production of his novel *The Human Comedy* (1943) and to refuse the 1939 PULITZER PRIZE for his play *The Time of Your Life* because he resented "wealth patronizing art." In addition to his novels, plays and songs, Saroyan's output also included more than 400 short stories. A romantic nonconformist, he called the Associated Press five days before his death to leave a posthumous statement: "Everybody has got to die, but I have always believed an exception would be made in my case. Now what?"

Sarraute, Nathalie (**Nathalie Tcherniak**) *(1900–1999)* Russian-born French novelist and literary critic. Sarraute commenced her literary career relatively late in life, having worked as an attorney through her late 30s. But she became one of the pioneers of the NOUVEAU ROMAN (new novel) literary movement in France. Her first published work, *Tropisms* (1938), a collection of short sketches, rejected the traditional literary conventions of plot and moral analysis, instead focusing on the small, instinctual life responses—tropisms—of her characters that revealed their true, unconsciously motivated life. Subsequent novels by Sarraute, written in a similar vein, include *The Planetarium* (1959), *The Golden Fruits* (1963), *Do You Hear Them?* (1972) and *Fools Say* (1976). *The Age of Suspicion* (1956) is a collection of her critical essays, while *Childhood* (1984) is a partial autobiography.

Sartre, Jean-Paul *(1905–1980)* French philosopher, novelist, playwright and literary critic. Sartre, who was awarded the NOBEL PRIZE in literature in 1964 but declined it in protest of the values of bourgeois capitalist society, was perhaps the most influential French writer of the 20th century. His first major work was the novel *Nausea* (1938), in which the existential nothingness of daily existence was vividly portrayed. In 1943 came BEING AND NOTHINGNESS, Sartre's major philosophical work. His play *No Exit* (1944) explores the manipulative fears and greed that cause unhappiness in human relationships. After the war, Sartre produced a series of novels, notably *The Age of Reason* (1945), that probed the dilemmas of French life during the Nazi occupation. *Questions of Method* (1957) and *Critique of Dialectical Reason* (1960) sought to blend Marxism and EXISTENTIALISM, to the widespread displeasure of both camps. Sartre composed a number of major critical studies, including *Baudelaire* (1947) and *Saint Genet* (1952) (on Jean GENET). Sartre was the longtime lover and companion of Simone DE BEAUVOIR and was also, in the 1940s, closely linked to fellow existentialist Albert CAMUS.

Sassoon, Siegfried *(1886–1967)* British poet and pacifist. Although he had written earlier poetry, Sassoon's first major works were written during WORLD WAR I, in which he served as a lieutenant on the Western Front. Shocked by the savagery and the enormous casualties of the war, he produced poetry with a desolate air that railed against complacent patriotism. Sassoon encouraged the work of Wilfred OWEN, whom he met while both were recuperating in Scotland in 1917. Published in *Counter-attack*

(1918), Sassoon's verse was not immediately popular with a public still entrenched in wartime nationalism and enamored of the GEORGIAN poets. His work began to receive acclaim in the 1920s, when *Satirical Poems* (1926) appeared; collections of his works were published in 1947 and 1961. He also wrote the acclaimed, semiautobiographical novels *Memoirs of a Fox-Hunting Man* (1928), *Memoirs of an Infantry Officer* (1930) and *Sherston's Progress* (1936), which were later collected into *The Complete Memoirs of George Sherston* (1937); and the autobiographies *The Old Century and Seven More Years* (1938), *The Weald of Youth* (1942) and *Siegfried's Journey* (1945). His diaries were published in 1981 and 1983, edited by R. Hart-Davis.

Satanic Verses, The See Salman RUSHDIE.

satellite The first artificial Earth satellite, SPUTNIK I (launched by the USSR on October 4, 1957), has been followed by hundreds of other Soviet, U.S., European and Asian satellites. By the early 1960s, satellites such as TELSTAR and RELAY had begun to revolutionize global communications. Placed in geostationary orbits, they relay telephone, radio or television signals from one part of Earth to another. The INTELSAT (international satellite network), founded in the 1970s, provides international telecommunications service. Weather satellites have made reliable forecasting possible and can track weather patterns over a period of time. LANDSAT satellites provide photographs that help scientists to understand the effects of various types of land use on Earth's fragile ecosystem. Both the U.S. and Soviet Union (and later, Russia) used reconnaissance or "spy" satellites.

satellite television The transmission of cable television channels to individuals, educational institutions or businesses possessing satellite dishes linked to communications satellites in stationary orbit around the Earth. The transmission of the signal occurs in two stages. First, a ground-based radio tower transmits the programs offered by the various television stations to the geosynchronous orbiting satellites at various radio frequencies. These satellites then broadcast these frequencies to the various subscribing satellite dishes within their scope. To prevent the theft or "piracy" of these satellite signals by individuals with a satellite dish who do not subscribe to the satellite service, the frequency is coded or "scrambled" by the communications satellite in such a fashion that it can be "descrambled" only by individuals possessing the proper software. During the 1980s, satellite television lagged behind cable services as the preferred means of acquiring cable television, in large part because the available communications satellite technology could not offer its subscribers the same number of television and cable channels that a land-based cable television company could through coaxial and later fiber-optic cables. However, this changed with the development of direct-broadcast satellites (DBS) in 1990. Unlike its larger and more limited predecessors, companies with DBS in orbit could offer their subscribers as many as 200 television and cable networks. Additionally, DBS technology reduced the size requirement of the receptor satellite dish, making the technology and the service more accessible to consumers with a limited amount of space in which to erect such a receptor system. In the U.S., DirecTV is one such example of a satellite provider with DBS technology.

Satie, Erik *(1866–1925)* Parisian composer who, with DEBUSSY and RAVEL, was one of the chief architects of modern French music. Born and raised in Honfleur, in the Calvados region of France, he learned early to thumb his nose at the excesses of post-Wagnerism and the pretentiousness of Impressionism. It was his firm conviction, recounts Virgil THOMSON, "that the only healthy thing music can do in our century is to stop being impressive." Forsaking the Paris Conservatory after only one year, the 20-year-old youth lived in virtual poverty, working as a pianist in Montmartre cafes, where he wrote musical polemic in a small newspaper and forged an important friendship with Claude Debussy. Satie's characteristic blend of pop tunes, unusual harmonies, austere textures, sardonic humor and bizarre titles marked early piano works like the *Gymnopédies* (1888), the *Gnossiennes* (1890) and the *Pièces en forme de poire* (1903) for critical abuse as well as the praise of Debussy and Ravel. At the age of 40 he returned to musical studies at the Schola Cantorum and subsequently produced his most important works: the collaboration with PICASSO, COCTEAU and DIAGHILEV of the landmark cubist ballet PARADE (1917); the setting for voice and orchestra of Plato's dialogues, *Socrate* (1918); and experiments in film music—*Musique d'ameublement* or "furniture music," per Satie—for *Relâche* (1924). Before his death from cirrhosis of the liver in 1925, he had been adopted as a mentor by the young composers of LES SIX. An inspection of his reclusive quarters after his death revealed dozens of shiny blue suits, an out-of-tune piano, hundreds of umbrellas and an inscription on the wall, "This house is haunted by the devil." (See also CUBISM.)

Sato, Eisaku *(1901–1975)* Prime minister of Japan. After graduating from Tokyo University in 1924, Sato held a number of government positions before being elected to the house of Representatives (the lower house of the Diet, or parliament) in 1949. In 1953, he was made secretary-general of the Liberal Democratic Party. From 1958 to 1964, Sato held a number of cabinet posts, before succeeding Ikeda Hayato as party leader and prime minister in November of that year. Sato remained in office until July 1972, making him the longest-serving premier in the nation's history. During his tenure, Japan became a major economic power, and relations with Southeast Asia and the U.S. were strengthened. In 1974 Sato won the NOBEL PRIZE for peace for his antinuclear stance.

Saturday Evening Post American weekly periodical begun in 1821. The *Post* was established as a Saturday magazine of miscellany with no illustrations. By 1897 it faced bankruptcy but was purchased by Cyrus H. K. Curtis who installed George Horace Lorimer as editor. The magazine, which was written to appeal to a middlebrow audience, became famous for its romantic fiction, mysteries, western serials and illustrations of archetypal American life by Norman ROCKWELL. By the 1920s, the magazine was a success. Contributors included Agatha CHRISTIE. J. P.

MARQUAND, William FAULKNER, Ben HECHT, Stephen Vincent BENET, Dorothy THOMPSON and Will ROGERS. Despite that eclectic group of writers, the magazine's policy was Republican, conservative and isolationist. In 1962, the *Post* began to lose money, and it was shut down in 1969. It was later revived as a nine-times-a-year publication and achieved a circulation of 467,000, but never regained the immense popularity of its heyday.

Saturday Night Live Late-night American comedy/variety series. It premiered on NBC on October 11, 1975. Producer Lorne Michaels and the original cast—Chevy Chase, Jane Curtin, John Belushi, Dan Aykroyd, Gilda Radner, Garret Morris and Bill Murray (who joined the show in 1977)—concocted a "live," weekly 90 minutes of topical satire, slapstick comedy and music. In a sense, it became the *LAUGH-IN* of the 1970s, taking the irreverent pulse of its day. A "second generation" of comics took over after 1980, including Eddie Murphy, Billy Crystal, Martin Short and Randy Quaid. Later series regulars included Dana Carvey, Jon Lovitz and Dennis Miller. Some things have always been a part of the format over the years, such as the use of unlikely guest hosts each week. The revival of *SNL*'s popularity came in 2000 when Michaels discovered a bevy of new stars, such as Chris Katan, Will Ferrell, Tracy Morgan, Jimmy Fallon, Maya Rudolph, Amy Poehler and Cheri Oteri, who quickly developed into veteran performers and created recurring characters.

Saudi Arabia Saudi Arabia is located on the Arabian Peninsula of southwestern Asia and covers an area of 829,790 square miles. In 1902 Abd al-Aziz IBN SAUD began a 30-year campaign during which he conquered all of present-day Saudi Arabia and established the Kingdom of Saudi Arabia in 1932. In 1938 oil was discovered and production began under the U.S. controlled Aramco (Arabian American Oil Company), bringing great prosperity to Saudi Arabia. King Saud died in 1953 and his son Ibn Abdul Aziz al-Saud took his place as king. In 1960 Saudi Arabia was one of the founding members of the Organization of Petroleum Exporting Countries (OPEC). King

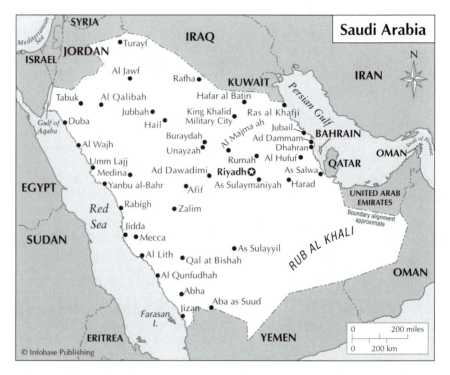

Saud was overthrown in 1964 and replaced by Prince Faisal. The country has been a dominant force in Middle East politics, supporting the monarchists during the civil war in North Yemen (1962–67), supporting IRAQ in the IRAN-IRAQ WAR and attempting to mediate a peace in LEBANON (1980s). In 1975 King Faisal was assassinated, and his brother became King Khaled, although the real power was held by another brother, Fahd, who eventually became king in 1982. Fanatic fundamentalists occupied the Great Mosque at Mecca in 1979 but were removed in bloody fighting. In 1980 a Shia Muslim revolt was quelled and reforms initiated. In 1982 King Khalid died and was succeeded by Prince Fahd. During the 1987 haj to Mecca there were violent clashes between Iranian pilgrims and Saudi forces. After Iraq's invasion of KUWAIT (1990), King Fahd asked for U.S. help to defend his country against Iraqi aggression (see PERSIAN GULF WAR). Saudi Arabia became the base of operations for the successful UNITED NATIONS–backed action against Iraq (August 1990–February 1991). In 1993 King Fahd created a Consultative Council of 60 members to advise him. In 1996 King Fahd suffered a major stroke and his half brother and heir, Crown Prince ABDULLAH, became

the de facto ruler of the kingdom. After the terrorist attacks on New York City and Washington, D.C., of September 11, 2001, Saudi Arabia came under increasing international criticism for its tolerance toward Islamic militants such as the Saudi-born Osama BIN LADEN, and other advocates of radical ISLAMISM. In response King Fahd in December 2001 denounced terrorism as incompatible with Islam and called for its eradication, while the Saudi government increased its efforts to work with U.S. intelligence officials against terrorist groups such as AL-QAEDA. Despite these promises, terrorist activities continue in Saudi Arabia. Since 2001 there have been several deadly attacks, several on Western targets and some claimed by al-Qaeda. Saudi security forces have cracked down hard on these militants, which has given rise to complaints about excessive force. Despite Saudi Arabia's efforts in 2002 to ban the use of torture, some human rights advocates say abuses still exist. Saudi Arabia is also making small steps to a more representative government. In 2003 King Fahd allowed the Consultative Council to submit legislation without his permission, and in 2005 the first nationwide municipal elections were held, though women were still not allowed to vote.

SAUDIA ARABIA

1902	Ibn Saud organizes a Bedouin revolt and regains Riyadh.
1932	Hejaz and Nejd are renamed the United Kingdom of Saudi Arabia.
1938	Oil is discovered and production begins under Aramco.
1940s	Commercial exploitation of oil begins, bringing great prosperity.
1953	King Saud dies; his son Ibn Abdul Aziz al-Saud succeeds him as king.
1960	Saudi Arabia becomes a founding member of Organization of Petroleum Exporting Countries (OPEC).
1964	Kind Saud is deposed and replaced as king by Faisal.
1975	King Faisal is assassinated; Crown Prince Khalid succeeds him as king, and Prince Fahd is named crown prince.
1979	Members of a fanatical fundamentalist Muslim sect known as the Safiyeen Salfiyeen take over the Grand Mosque at Mecca.
1980	Saudia Arabia experiences wide-scale riots in Shia Muslim areas.
1982	King Khalid dies; he is succeeded as monarch by Prince Fahd.
1987	More than 400 die when Iranian Shiite pilgrims clash with Saudi police.
1990	As secular Iraq overruns monarchist Kuwait, Saudis allow build-up of massive U.S.-led force on Saudi soil; Western troops segregated from Saudi citizens; King Fahd holds Arab members of coalition in line with anti-Iraq policy.
1991	Saudi troops take part in assault on Iraq; first modern military operation; joins new regional alignment with Egypt, Syria and U.S.
1993	A Consultative Council (Majlis al-Shura) is established following a proposal by King Fahd. It consists of a chairman and 60 members chosen by the king. Saudi Arabia is divided into 13 administrative divisions.
1995	King Fahd suffers a stroke; Crown Prince Abdullah becomes the interim head of state.
1996	King Fahd resumes control of state affairs. A bomb explodes at a U.S. military compound near Dhahran, killing 19 and wounding over 300.
2001	Fifteen of the 19 hijackers involved in the September 11 attacks in New York City and Washington, D.C., are Saudi citizens. King Fahd calls for the eradication of terrorism.
2002	A revised criminal code bans torture but human rights campaigners say violations continue.
2003	Suicide bombers kill 35 people at housing compounds for Westerners in Riyadh. Rallies in Riyadh call for reforms. The king grants wider powers to the Consultative Council, enabling it to propose legislation without his permission.
2004	A car bomb at security forces headquarters in Riyadh kills four and wounds 148. An al-Qaeda linked group claims responsibility. An attack on the U.S. consulate at Jeddah leaves five staff and 14 attackers dead.
2005	First ever nationwide municipal elections are held. Women are not allowed to vote. King Fahd dies (April). He is succeeded By his half brother, former crown prince Abdullah.

Sauguet, Henri (1901–1989) French composer. His simple but elegant works made him one of France's most important composers of the 1920s. He wrote the music for 14 ballets, eight theatrical productions and 35 films as well as numerous vocal and instrumental works, including the opera *La Chartreuse de Parme*.

Savage, Michael Joseph (1872–1940) Prime minister of NEW ZEALAND (1935–40). Born in Australia, he became a gold miner and labor leader. In 1907 he immigrated to New Zealand, where he continued his union activities and in 1933 became a founding member of the LABOUR PARTY. Holding the post of Labour's parliamentary leader from 1933, he formed New Zealand's first Labour government after the party's victory in the 1935 elections. He was reelected in 1938. During his terms in office, Savage instituted various social and educational reforms, enacted social security legislation and helped to revive a flagging economy. A popular leader, he died in office.

Savak Iranian secret police under the shah, dispersed after the Islamic IRANIAN REVOLUTION OF 1979. Many former Savak members were murdered by the people in revenge for crimes of torture and murder.

Savary, Alain (1918–1988) French politician. During WORLD WAR II Savary was in the French RESISTANCE and was a leader in the government formed just after Liberation. He was a member of the National Assembly and held ministerial posts under Charles DE GAULLE and in other governments. A prominent socialist, he was secretary general of that party from 1969 to 1971. Savary served as education minister from 1981 until he was forced to resign in 1984 after a lengthy public uproar over his proposals to reform the country's private school system.

Savimbi, Jonas (1934–2002) Angolan military and political leader. Savimbi studied at universities in Lisbon and Lausanne before returning to ANGOLA. There he joined Holden Roberto's fledgling nationalist movement. In 1962 he was involved in the evolution of this group into the National Front for the Liberation of Angola (FNLA). After conflicts with Roberto, he left the FNLA and formed his own group, the National Union for Total Independence of Angola (UNITA), in 1966. In the ANGOLAN CIVIL WAR that began in 1975, Savimbi was defeated in his quest to control Angola by Agostinho NETO's Popular Movement for the Liberation of Angola (MPLA). Continuing his struggle throughout the 1970s and '80s, he was supported with political and material aid from South Africa and Western countries including the U.S. In 1990 there were allegations that Savimbi's forces had slaughtered elephants in Africa in order to raise money by selling their tusks. At the same time, the rebels and the government were engaged in negotiations aimed at bringing about a peaceful solution to the civil war. Savimbi agreed to the 1994 LUSAKA ACCORDS, which called for free national elections for an Angolan government. However, he withdrew from the accords later that year and seized Congolese territory to continue his rebellion against the MPLA. UNITA continued to wage guerrilla war against the government until Savimbi was killed by government forces in 2002.

savings & loan scandal During the 1980s, the administration of President Ronald REAGAN adopted deregulation of industry as a national priority. Financial institutions were largely deregulated, and both banks and savings and loan associations became far more aggressive in offering attractive returns to savers—and in accepting far more risky loans. When many borrowers defaulted and real estate values plummeted in the Southwest and elsewhere a number of savings and loan institutions failed. The problem was so severe that the federal program for insuring savings and loans—the FSLIC—was nearly insolvent and had to be merged into the FDIC. Investigations of the scandal uncovered many sharp operators, and also favoritism and systematically lax regulation of the S&Ls. The scandal also resulted in the so-called Keating Five investigation of five U.S. senators who were accused of improperly using their influence over regulators on behalf of Charles Keating, an S&L executive. (See also KEATING FIVE SCANDAL.)

Savitskaya, Svetlana (1948–) Soviet cosmonaut. The second Soviet woman to fly in space, Savitskaya and fellow cosmonauts Leonid Popov and Alexandr Serebrov flew the *Soyuz T-7* mission (August 19, 1982) to link up with the Soviet space station SALYUT 7. During her second flight aboard a SOYUZ spacecraft, the *Soyuz T-12* (July 17, 1984), she became the second woman in space, performing 3.5 hours of extravehicular activity (EVA). In 1993 Savitskaya retired from her duties as a cosmonaut. In 1999 she was elected to the Russian Duma (the lower national legislature).

Sawchuk, Terrance Gordon "Terry" (1929–1970) Canadian hockey player. A Calder Trophy winner as National Hockey League rookie of the year with the Detroit Red Wings in 1950, Sawchuk was one of the most enigmatic of that enigmatic breed, goaltenders. A quiet, intense man who played most of his career in the pre-mask era, his face was a road map of scars and lacerations. His goals against average stayed below 2.00 during his first five years in the league. He won the Vezina Trophy four times as the league's best goalie, and led the Toronto Maple Leafs to an upset Stanley Cup victory in 1967. His astounding 103rd shutout came with the New York Rangers, the last stop on what had become a peripatetic career. Sawchuk died that off-season during a shoving match with a teammate. He entered the Hockey Hall of Fame in 1971.

Saw Maung (1928–1997) burmese general; began his military career after 1945, rising through the ranks to become head of the Southwest Command in the early 1980s. Saw Maung became minister of defense in 1988 and led the September 1988 army coup. He subsequently became head of the Myanmar (see BURMA) government.

Sayers, Dorothy L(eigh) (1893–1957) British novelist, essayist, medieval scholar and anthologist. She is best known for her stories about the amateur detective Lord Peter Wimsey. In the words of historian Howard Haycroft, she held "preeminence as one of the most brilliant and prescient artists the genre has yet produced." The daughter of a clergyman-schoolmaster, Sayers grew up in the fen country of East Anglia (the location of her most famous Wimsey novel, *The Nine Tailors*, 1934). After taking top honors in medieval literature in Somerville College, Oxford, she taught at Hull High School for Girls and worked for an advertising agency in London. Her detective stories about the eccentric Lord Wimsey and his independent-minded Harriet Vane, Miss Climpson (leader of a group of female detectives) and Montague Egg (a traveling salesman) were acclaimed and secured her a modest independence. Her translations of Dante in the 1950s were hailed in academic circles. Publicly flamboyant, privately secretive, her fiction alone reveals her inner loneliness. Her alter ego, the spinster Miss Climpson, who appears in several Wimsey stories, is resourceful, formidable—but essentially alone. "I'd never been treated as a woman," Sayers confided once, "only as a kind of literary freak . . . I loathe being deferred to." (Her illegitimate son, Anthony, remained a carefully kept secret all her life.) She never relaxed her high standards in detective fiction. In the initiation ritual she wrote for London's Detective Club, of which she became a member in 1919, she made prospective members swear that they "play fair" with their readers; otherwise, she admonished, "May your Pages swarm with Misprints and your Sales continually Diminish. Amen."

Sazonov, Sergei Dmitriyevich *(1861–1927)* Russian diplomat and statesman. Sazonov started working for the foreign ministry in 1883 and in 1910 was appointed foreign minister. He attempted to ease relations with Germany, but relations with Great Britain deteriorated. He eventually forced the Germans to relinquish command of Turkish troops in Constantinople. After the assassination of Archduke FRANZ FERDINAND, Sazonov pressured the czar to agree to complete mobilization. He was dismissed in 1916 as a result of his view that an autonomous POLAND should be created. In 1917 he was appointed ambassador to London and then acted as foreign minister for Admiral A. V. KOLCHAK.

Scalia, Antonin *(1936–)* Associate justice, U.S. Supreme Court (1986–present). A graduate of Georgetown University and Harvard Law School, Scalia practiced with a large Cleveland law firm before becoming a law professor at the University of Virginia. He worked in the NIXON administration, eventually becoming head of the White House office of legal counsel. He returned to teach at the University of Chicago Law School where he became known as a leading conservative legal scholar. President Ronald REAGAN appointed Scalia to the U.S. court of appeals for the District of Columbia, whose judges at the time were known as being extremely liberal. In 1986 President Reagan appointed Scalia to the Supreme Court. On the Court Scalia helped forge a solid conservative majority that rejected the judicial activism of the prior 50 years. He indicated his fundamental opposition to ABORTION in a separate majority opinion in *WEBSTER V. REPRODUCTIVE SERVICES* (1989). Scalia was noted for his careful legal scholarship. Throughout the 1990s and early 21st century Scalia anchored a conservative faction of the Court, which included Chief Justice Rehnquist and Justice Clarence Thomas.

Scandinavia Historic region in northern Europe, consisting of DENMARK, NORWAY and SWEDEN. Strictly speaking, FINLAND is not part of the region, although it is often considered to be so because of its geographic proximity to these other nations. ICELAND too is sometimes referred to as part of it because Iceland's people are of Scandinavian descent. Norway and Sweden occupy the Scandinavian Peninsula. After almost a century, the union of Norway and Sweden was ended peacefully in 1905, and in 1918 Iceland gained independence from Denmark. Germany seized Denmark and Norway by force (April 1940) during WORLD WAR II, while Sweden remained neutral; Finland was dominated by the USSR. Iceland's union with Denmark ended entirely in 1944. The Scandinavian nations are known for having pioneered the modern WELFARE STATE.

Scapa Flow Sea basin surrounded by the Orkney Islands (principally Main-

land and Hoy), off the north coast of Scotland. During both World Wars, Scapa Flow was the site of an important British naval base. The British naval vessel *Vanguard* was torpedoed here in 1917. In October 1939, in the opening days of WORLD WAR II, the *Royal Oak* was sunk by a German U-boat, causing a temporary closing of the base. On June 21, 1919, the bottom of Scapa Flow turned into a naval museum when the officers and crew of the interned German High Seas Fleet opened the underwater valves of their ships and sent them to Davy Jones's Locker. The Scapa Flow naval base was closed permanently in 1956.

Scargill, Arthur *(1938–)* British union leader. Scargill, a miner from Yorkshire, became president of the National Union of Mineworkers (NUM) in 1981. A radical Marxist, he aroused much controversy, and even the LABOUR PARTY, traditionally friendly to unions, sought to distance itself from his rhetoric. Scargill led the NUM through the year-long coal miners strike of 1984–85, in which the union was ultimately unsuccessful. The strikers hoped to persuade the state-owned British Coal Board to abandon its plans to cut back in workers and close old mines; after the strike some 70,000 workers were laid off and 67 mines closed. Some NUM members opposed to Scargill's extremism broke from the NUM and formed the Union of Democratic Mineworkers. Scargill's tenure as leader of the NUM ended in 2000. In 2006 he became leader of the Socialist Labour Party.

Schacht, Hjalmar (Horace Greeley) *(1877–1970)* German financier. A successful banker, Schacht became commissioner of currency of the WEIMAR REPUBLIC in 1923. In this post he managed to stabilize GERMANY's currency and put an end to the enormous inflation that had plagued the nation. He simultaneously served as president of the Reichsbank (1923–30), Germany's leading financial institution, before resigning because of his opposition to Germany's continuing reparation payments. At the beginning of the Nazi era, Schacht continued to serve the German government, again becoming president of the Reichsbank in 1933 and helping to finance Germany's rearmament. In

1934 he was also appointed minister of economics, but resigned the position in 1937 after a series of disagreements with Hermann GOERING. Opposing Adolf HITLER's enormous rearmament program as inflationary, Schacht was removed from the Reichsbank in 1939. Increasingly opposed to Nazi policy, he was accused of involvement in the plot to assassinate Hitler and jailed in 1944. Tried for war crimes at NUREMBERG in 1946, he was acquitted and went on to hold various posts in German finance. Schacht wrote an autobiography, *Confessions of the Old Wizard* (1953, tr. 1956).

Schaeffer, Rev. Francis August (*1912–1984*) Evangelical theologian and leading scholar of fundamentalist Protestantism. Ordained as a Presbyterian, Schaeffer and his wife in 1955 founded *l'Abri* (*The Shelter*), a chalet and spiritual center in the Swiss Alps. Schaeffer attracted thousands of students and intellectuals by teaching a reasoned rather than an emotional approach to religion. *L'Abri*, eventually expanded to six countries, including the U.S. Schaeffer's 23 philosophical books included the 1976 bestseller, *How Should We Then Live?*

Schaffner, Franklin (Franklin James Schaffner) (*1920–1989*) American stage, television and film director. In the 1950s and early '60s he directed many major television productions, including "Person to Person" with Edward R. MURROW. He also directed the successful Broadway adaptation of Allan DRURY's *Advise and Consent* (1960). As a film director, he specialized in large-scale historical dramas and adaptations of popular novels. He received a total of 28 ACADEMY AWARD nominations for such films as *Planet of the Apes* (1968), *Nicholas and Alexandra* (1971), *Papillon* (1973) and *The Boys from Brazil* (1978). His 1970 film *Patton* won a total of seven Academy Awards, including best picture and best director.

Schapiro, Meyer (*1904–1996*) American art historian. Born in Lithuania, he immigrated to the U.S. at the age of three, grew up in New York City and attended Columbia University, receiving a Ph.D. and teaching there from 1928. A partisan of modernist movements from the 1930s and an important critic of contemporary art, he was one of the most influential of all American art historians. In addition to social, psychological and aesthetic analyses of 19th- and 20th-century art, Schapiro also did significant research in early Christian and medieval art. He is known for such essays as "The Nature of Abstract Art" (1937) and "Leonardo and Freud" (1956), as well as many books, including studies of Van Gogh (1950) and Cézanne (1952).

Schary, Dore (*1905–1980*) HOLLYWOOD film writer and movie producer, playwright and political activist. Failing as a playwright and actor on Broadway in the 1930s, Schary set out for Hollywood. His fortunes rose after he won an ACADEMY AWARD for the original story of *Boys Town* (1938). He was briefly production chief at RKO, where he specialized in socially conscious movies including *Crossfire* (1947), an exposé of ANTI-SEMITISM in the U.S., and *The Boy with Green Hair* (1948), an antiwar film. As production chief at METRO-GOLDWYN-MAYER (1948–56) he continued his two-pronged policy of presenting entertainment vehicles and "message" films, balancing musicals such as the classic *An American in Paris* (1951) and *Seven Brides for Seven Brothers* (1954) with serious dramas such as *The Blackboard Jungle* (1955), a realistic treatment of urban juvenile delinquency. In 1956 he wrote his finest play, *Sunrise at Campobello*, about Franklin D. ROOSEVELT; four years later he adapted it for the screen. A lifelong political activist, during the 1950s Schary fought McCARTHYISM and the blacklist in Hollywood. He produced or oversaw the production of some 250 movies and wrote more than 40 screenplays.

Schaufuss, Peter (*1950–   *) Danish dancer and ballet director. Schaufuss joined the Royal Danish Ballet in 1965, then became, successively, a principal dancer with the NEW YORK CITY BALLET (1974–77) and the National Ballet of Canada (1977–83). He has also been a guest artist with several other dance companies, and is especially noted for his productions of August Bournonville's *La Sylphide* (London Festival Ballet, 1979) and *Napoli* (National Ballet of Canada, 1981). He won the silver medal at the Moscow Ballet Competition in 1973. Since 1984 he has been artistic director of the London Festival Ballet. Schaufuss left Berlin's Deutsch Oper Ballet in 1994 to serve as the artistic director of the Royal Danish Ballet. Three years later he founded his own touring company, the Peter Schaufuss Ballet, the first independent Danish ballet company to tour internationally. In 2003 Schaufuss received the United Exhibits Group's inaugural award designed to commemorate a Danish citizen who had achieved international renown. By 2004 Schaufuss's group had staged over 300 performances throughout the world, including *The King,* a ballet based on the life of Elvis Presley.

Schecter Poultry v. U.S. (*1935*) Unanimous U.S. Supreme Court decision holding that segments of the NEW DEAL's NATIONAL INDUSTRIAL RECOVERY ACT (NRA) were unconstitutional. A cornerstone of President Franklin D. ROOSEVELT's New Deal program, the NRA sought to regulate competition within ailing industries by setting up "fair competition" codes. The Court held the act impermissibly regulated activities that were not within Congress's power and also gave the president too much power in designing the codes. The case marked the first salvo in the conservative Supreme Court's opposition to FDR's New Deal program.

Scheidemann, Philipp (*1865–1939*) German official. Elected to the Reichstag in 1903, Scheidemann proclaimed the WEIMAR REPUBLIC in 1918. He served as chancellor of the new republic for five months before resigning in protest of the punitive TREATY OF VERSAILLES that ended World War I. Scheidemann held other elected positions before fleeing the Nazis in 1933. (See also NAZISM.)

Schenck v. United States (*1919*) U.S. Supreme Court decision that defined the limits of free speech. The famous opinion, written by Justice Oliver Wendell HOLMES, upheld enforcement of the Espionage Act of 1917 against an attack on the statute as a violation of the First Amendment's protection of free speech. Holmes announced that the concept of free speech was not absolute and that words were not protected when they created a clear and present danger. The opinion contains

Holmes's famous admonition that the First Amendment would not protect a man who falsely shouts "fire!" in a theater and thereby causes a panic.

Scherchen, Hermann (*1891–1966*) German conductor. Scherchen was one of the most ardent and influential interpreters of modern classical music. He was a special champion of the composers of the Viennese expressionist school—Alban BERG, Arnold SCHOENBERG and Anton WEBERN—and frequently conducted premieres of their works. Scherchen began his career as a violist with the Berlin Philharmonic from 1907 to 1910. But he soon turned to full-time conducting, being named in 1928 musical director of the Konigsberg Philharmonic Orchestra. With the rise of the Nazis, Scherchen fled Germany in 1933. He spent most of his remaining years in Switzerland, where he was active not only as a conductor but also as a teacher and as a pioneer in the development of electronic-acoustical music.

Schiele, Egon (*1890–1918*) Austrian painter. An expressionist, he was strongly influenced by Gustav KLIMT. Like Klimt, he took the erotic for much of his subject matter, was often criticized for his works and even jailed for obscenity in 1912. Filled with a lonely, haunted angst, his figures are defined by a jagged and delicate linearity and often vibrant colors. While much of his work is highly sexual in nature and reflects a deep interest in Freudian psychology, it conveys more of a sense of anxiety than of sensuality. He was also a talented portraitist and is noted for his almost frighteningly direct self-portraits. He and KOKOSCHKA were the leaders of Austrian EXPRESSIONISM, and his promising career was cut short by his death in the influenza epidemic of 1918.

Schindler, Alma (*1879–1964*) Pianist, memoirist and wife, successively, of Gustav MAHLER, Walter GROPIUS and Franz WERFEL. Schindler was one of the leading female figures in fin de siecle Vienna. The daughter of painter Anton Schindler, she was highly trained in piano and musical composition. During her marriage to Mahler, she exercised a considerable influence on his compositions; Mahler composed the so-called "Alma theme" in the opening movement of his Sixth Symphony as her musical portrait. She published a selection of Mahler's letters (1924) and later wrote a memoir (1940) of him. After Mahler's death in 1911, Schindler was married to Gropius and Werfel.

Schindler's List 1993 motion picture. Based on Thomas Keneally's 1982 novel *Schindler's Ark*, *Schindler's List* describes the adult life of Oskar Schindler, a German munitions factory owner who established a plant outside of Krakow, Poland, that employed and housed many Jewish workers who otherwise would have been sent to the nearby concentration camp at Plaszów. However, in 1944 when the Wehrmacht (the German army) began to retreat from Warsaw in the face of numerically superior Soviet forces, the Nazi authorities in Warsaw decided to transport all Jews in Plaszów and Schindler's factory to Auschwitz for their execution. To prevent this, Schindler (played by Liam Neeson) convinced the Nazi leadership to permit the transfer of Schindler's factory to Czechoslovakia, where it would continue to feed the German war effort. After the Nazis approved his request, Schindler prepared a list of over 1,000 employees (nearly all Jewish) he wanted to accompany him to Czechoslovakia. The picture's director, Steven Spielberg, chose to film *Schindler's List* almost entirely in black-and-white, which he thought would heighten the sense of severity surrounding the picture, despite concerns that this move might compromise its commercial success. These predictions were proven wrong when *Schindler's List* was a hit at the box office, and it won seven Academy Awards in 1993 for Best Picture, Best Director, Best Adapted Screenplay, Best Art Direction, Best Cinematography, Best Film Editing and Best Original Music Score.

Schirra, Walter (*1923– *) U.S. astronaut; a veteran of the APOLLO program, Schirra has also flown MERCURY and GEMINI spacecraft. As pilot of the *Mercury-Atlas 8* (October 3, 1962) during the early days of the American space program, Schirra's six-orbit nine hour and 13 minute spaceflight helped pave the way for the next U.S. step into space, the Gemini program. On the two-man *Gemini-Titan 6-A* mission (December 15–16, 1965), Schirra and Thomas STAFFORD added a light-hearted note by reporting the sighting of a UFO resembling Santa Claus, and they concluded their report with Schirra giving an off-key rendition of "Jingle Bells." The *Apollo 7* mission (October 11–22 1968) was conducted in a more serious vein. In the course of 11 days in space, Schirra and astronauts Donn Eisele and Walter Cunningham had the unenviable job of proving the controversial Apollo spacecraft qualified for flight after the tragic launchpad fire that killed Gus GRISSOM, Roger CHAFFEE and Edward WHITE on January 27, 1967.

Schlabrendorff, Fabian von (*1907–1980*) German army officer involved in plots against Adolf HITLER during WORLD WAR II. In 1943 von Schlabrendorff smuggled a bomb disguised as a case of brandy aboard Hitler's plane, but the bomb failed to explode. The following year, with Count Claus von Stauffenberg, he took part in the famous failed assassination attempt on Hitler on July 20, 1944. Von Schlabrendorff was arrested, tortured by the GESTAPO and spent the remainder of the war in a CONCENTRATION CAMP. After the war he was a lawyer and judge in West Germany.

Schlemmer, Oskar (*1888–1943*) German painter. Born in Stuttgart, he studied there with Adolf Hoelzel. He became acquainted with avant-garde art in Berlin, soon developing a personal style of modernism that emphasized geometrically streamlined and machine-like human figures. He was an influential teacher at the BAUHAUS from 1921 to 1929, heading the sculpture and theater departments. At this time he also concentrated on stage design and is particularly noted for his *Triadic Ballet* (1922) with music by Paul HINDEMITH. As a sculptor, he created constructivist-like reliefs in mortar and wire. An art teacher in Berlin from 1932 to 1933, he was dismissed by the Nazis, and spent his last years as a manual laborer.

Schlesinger, Arthur M., Jr. (*1917– *) American historian and winner of the Pulitzer Prize (1946 and 1966) and the National Book Award (1966 and 1979). Born in Columbus, Ohio, Schlesinger attended Harvard University, where his father taught history. After graduating from Harvard summa cum laude with a B.A. in history in 1938, Schlesinger enrolled in the graduate school in the Harvard Society of Fellows from which he graduated in 1943. During World War II (1939–45), he served in the Office of Strategic Services (OSS), the forerunner of the Central Intelligence Agency (CIA). At the end of the war, Schlesinger returned to Harvard, where he was appointed associate professor of history. The same year he released *The Age of Jackson,* for which he received his first Pulitzer Prize. In 1952 and 1956, Schlesinger split his time between lecturing at Harvard and working on the campaign staff of presidential candidate Adlai Stevenson. Four years later Schlesinger again divided his duties between academia and presidential politics, although this time he became an aide to Massachusetts senator John F. KENNEDY. After Kennedy's election, Schlesinger became a speech writer and adviser to the president. He resigned from that position in 1964 shortly after Kennedy's assassination. In 1966 Schlesinger accepted the Albert Schweitzer Chair in the Humanities at the City University of New York (CUNY), where he served until retiring in 1994. He also published *A Thousand Days: John F. Kennedy in the White House* in 1966, for which he received his second Pulitzer Prize and his first National Book Award. Additional books by Schlesinger include the multivolume *The Age of Roosevelt* (1957), *The Imperial Presidency* (1973), *Robert Kennedy and His Times* (1973, for which he received his second National Book Award), *The Cycles of American History* (1986) and *The Disuniting of America* (1991).

Schlieffen Plan Master plan for GERMANY's strategy in WORLD WAR I prepared by Field Marshal Alfred, Count von Schlieffen, chief of the German general staff from 1891 to 1905. The plan assumed a two-front war that could be won by swiftly defeating France and then attacking Russia with the full force of the German military machine. It required Germany to engage in a bold flanking movement through Belgium into France. In a modified and somewhat weakened form, prepared by Schlieffen's successor, H. J. L. von Moltke, the plan was attempted at the outbreak of WORLD WAR I in 1914. It was unsuccessful due to France's delaying defense, Russia's military might, Germany's lack of organization and other factors. The concept of the lightning strike embodied in the Schlieffen Plan was later used by the Nazis in their blitzkriegs at the beginning of WORLD WAR II.

Schlumberger, Jean *(1907–1987)* French designer. One of the foremost jewelry designers of the 20th century, he achieved international renown through his association with Tiffany & Co. in New York City. His clients included some of the world's most glamorous women. In 1957 he set the legendary Tiffany diamond, the largest canary diamond in the world.

Schmeling, Max(imilian) *(1905–2005)* German boxer. Schmeling was the first European in the 20th century to win the heavyweight championship of the world. He began his career as European light-heavyweight champion and German heavyweight champion, came to the U.S. in 1928 and took the world championship two years later. His most memorable fights are his 12-round knockout of Joe LOUIS in 1936, and Louis's return of the favor, in 1938. Schmeling left the U.S. after Nazi boosterism made him unpopular. He later renounced NAZISM and returned to boxing. He retired after World War II, in 1948, with a record of 55–15, with 38 knockouts.

Schmidt, Helmut *(1918–)* Chancellor of WEST GERMANY (1974–82). An economist, Schmidt joined the German Social Democratic Party (SDP) in 1946 and was elected to the Bundestag in 1953. In 1965 he became chairman of the SDP and was later minister of defense (1969–72) and of finance (1972–74) in the cabinet of Willy BRANDT. He succeeded Brandt as chancellor in 1974 and was reelected in 1976 and 1980. Schmidt followed a pragmatic course, distancing himself from Brandt's OSTPOLITIK policy and favoring closer ties with the Western alliance.

Schmidt, Mike *(1949–)* U.S. baseball player. Schmidt was considered by many to be the greatest ever at third base; in his best year, 1980, he had 48 homers, 121 runs batted in and a .286 average. That season he was named the National League's most valuable player, an honor he won three times, as well as the World Series most valuable player. His career total of 548 home runs in 18 seasons ranked seventh on the career list, and he won the Gold Glove award for fielding 10 times. He retired from the Philadelphia Phillies in 1989, with career statistics of 1,595 runs batted in, 2,234 hits, 1,883 strikeouts and 1,506 runs. In 1995 Schmidt was elected to the Baseball Hall of Fame with 96.52 percent of the ballots cast.

Schmidt-Rottluff, Karl *(1884–1976)* German painter. Born in Saxony, he studied architecture in Dresden, where he met the artists HECKEL and KIRCHNER and, with them in 1905, cofounded the expressionist group DIE BRÜCKE. His vigorously rhythmic and emotionally dramatic oils, often landscapes or portraits, are composed of simple forms executed in blocks of intense, flat colors. He is also noted for his many extremely powerful woodcuts. Schmidt-Rottluff settled in Berlin in 1911, was forbidden to paint by the Nazis and became a professor of art in postwar East Berlin.

Schmitt, Harrison *(1935–)* U.S. astronaut and the first scientist to walk on the moon. Schmitt flew on the *Apollo 17* (December 7–19, 1972) lunar landing mission, the last of the APOLLO series. A geologist, he spent three days on the lunar surface with astronaut Eugene CERNAN while command module pilot Ronald Evans orbited above. The mission, which made extensive use of the Lunar Rover, was one of the most scientifically successful of the Apollo series. Schmitt resigned from NASA in 1975 and in 1976 was elected to the U.S. Senate from the state of New Mexico. Schmitt retired from the Senate in 1982 after completing his six-year term.

Schnabel, Artur *(1882–1951)* Austrian-Polish born pianist and composer best known for his authoritative interpretations of the music of Schubert and Beethoven. Schnabel studied with Leschetizky in Vienna and in the 1920s and 1930s became one of the foremost performers and teachers in Berlin. His cycles of the complete Beethoven piano sonatas were legendary. He repudiated the romantic virtuoso piano tradition of the day. According to one of his students, pianist Claude Frank, "Schnabel thought of himself as a musician rather than a pianist. He was completely at the service of the music itself. He made you forget the notes—and there were many wrong ones in his performances—and listen to the music." Pianist-commentator Abram Chasins remarked that "Schnabel could be so careless about technical details that a performance or a recording would sound more like a 'priva rista' reading than a prepared execution. . . . [Yet] his art was a fighting faith. He was perpetually vigilant against attempts to serve expediency or compromise." Schnabel himself said, "I am a simple musician." But he said it with the air of an emperor. Schnabel singlehandedly resurrected the piano sonatas of Franz Schubert, which had been all but forgotten. He also helped restore the sonatas and concertos of Mozart to the standard repertoire.

Schneider, Alan (Abram Leopoldovich) (1917–1984) Russian-born American stage director. Schneider was considered one of the most important directors in contemporary theater. In his 40-year career, he was closely associated with the works of Samuel BECKETT, Edward ALBEE, Harold PINTER and Bertolt BRECHT. He directed the American premiere of Beckett's WAITING FOR GODOT (1956). Schneider won a Tony Award for his 1962 Broadway production of Who's Afraid of Virginia Woolf?

Schneiderman, Rose (1882–1972) Polish-born American labor leader. In the early 1900s she organized the Women's Trade Union League. She served as the league's president for many years. During the GREAT DEPRESSION of the 1930s she was a member of President Franklin D. ROOSEVELT'S BRAIN TRUST. She was later secretary of the New York State Labor Department.

Schnitzler, Arthur (1862–1931) Austrian playwright and novelist. The son of a prominent Viennese Jewish doctor, he was trained as a physician and practiced medicine during the earlier part of his career. A sophisticated observer of fin-de-siècle society in Vienna, he gained fame for the sparkling wit, ironic vision and psychological in-

sight he brought to bear in lively portrayals of the many sides of love and human sexuality. His first recognition came with the play Anatol (1893, tr. 1911), an episodic account of a playboy's erotic adventures. His other dramas include Liebelei (1895, tr. 1907), Reigen (1900, tr. Merry-Go-Round, 1953), an erotic romp that became a successful French film as La Ronde in 1950, and Der einsame Weg (1903, tr. The Lonely Way, 1915). Schnitzler dealt with the theme of ANTI-SEMITISM in his play Professor Bernhardi (1912, tr. 1927) and focused on various social problems of his day in other works. He also wrote a number of novels, including the autobiographical The Road to the Open (1908, trans. 1923), and short stories, such as None but the Brave (1901, tr. 1926).

Schoenberg, Arnold (1874–1951) Viennese-born composer, leader of the New Viennese School, whose innovations in atonality and nontonal serial techniques profoundly influenced modern music in the 20th century. He studied with Alexander Zemlinsky in Vienna. His first major works, while solidly within the Wagnerian, late romantic tradition, stretched tonal ambiguity almost to the breaking point—Verklaerte Nacht (Transfigured Night, 1899) and Pelleas und Melisande (1905). The public hostility that had greeted these works turned to outright brawls and riots with the premieres in London, Berlin and Vienna of later works that finally broke with tonality, the chilling Pierrot Lunaire and the landmark Five Pieces for Orchestra (both in 1912). Schoenberg worked to bring order and discipline to this free tonality with the dodecaphonic system, a jaw-breaking word designating compositions based on a series of notes, or "row," containing all the 12 chromatic tones in a succession chosen by the composer. "Ich fuehle Luft von anderem Planeten," prophetically sang the soprano voice introduced at the end of the Second String Quartet (1908)—"I feel air from another planet." By the time the Third String Quartet was premiered in 1927, nothing like this music had been heard before. However, during the later years of Schoenberg's American residence—he left Germany in 1933 out of distaste for the Nazi regime—he maintained

what Leonard BERNSTEIN called "a rocky romance with tonality." Works such as The Ode to Napoleon (1942) flirted with tonal systems, while the numerous late transcriptions of Strauss and Brahms were quite traditional tonal works. Schoenberg himself admitted that "the longing to return to the older style was always vigorous in me." (And we recall that the last piece in Pierrot Lunaire yearned for the "alter Duft aus Maerchenzeit"—the "ancient fragrance of once-upon-a-time.") Disciples Anton von WEBERN and Alban BERG carried on his torch, and most subsequent composers have had to grapple with his influence. Some, like Igor STRAVINSKY, ultimately accepted it, and others, like Bernstein, finally rejected it.

Schröder, Gerhard (1944–) German politician, member of the German Social Democratic Party (SPD) and German chancellor (1998–2005). After graduating from the University of Göttingen in 1976, Schröder became the president of the Young Socialists League Jusos, which brought him to the attention of the Social Democratic Party (SPD)'s leadership. In 1980 he was elected a Socialist member of the Bundestag, the lower house of the German parliament. After his election as minister-president of Lower Saxony in 1990, his popularity throughout the country grew. Schröder's management of Lower Saxony proved so popular that the SPD won more sizable majorities in 1994 and 1998. Throughout the 1990s, Schröder's career also benefited from growing dissatisfaction with the performance of the Christian Democratic Union (CDU), the conservative German political party led by Chancellor Helmut KOHL.

In 1998, the SPD defeated the CDU in the national elections, winning on a platform proposing moderate social, economic and political reforms that Schröder had helped to formulate. The SPD formed a government coalition with the Green Party, a government with Schröder as chancellor and Green Party leader Joschka Fischer as foreign minister.

As chancellor, Schröder attempted to alleviate the high unemployment rate that has continually plagued Germany since its reunification through a reduction in the tax rates for German families in lower income tax brackets. He also sought to reduce Germany's dependence on nuclear energy because of the environmental risks posed by the waste products of nuclear power plants.

In foreign policy, Schröder sought to improve relations with the other members of the EUROPEAN UNION (EU). He promoted closer collaboration among the EU member states, as that organization moved toward full economic and greater political and military integration. Schröder developed particularly close relations with French president Jacques CHIRAC and supported the French project for the creation of a EU "Rapid Reaction Force." Schröder also ensured Germany's participation in the KOSOVO WAR, a conflict in which NORTH ATLANTIC TREATY ORGANIZATION (NATO) forces used air strikes to force SERBIA to halt its persecution of Albanian Muslims residing in the Kosovo district of Serbia. However, he joined with Chirac in leading European opposition to U.S. President George W. Bush's campaign to overthrow the Iraqi regime of Saddam HUSSEIN, denouncing U.S. unilateralism during his successful 2002 reelection campaign. He also openly criticized treatment of "enemy combatants" imprisoned at the U.S. naval base at Guantánamo Bay, Cuba. In 2005 Schröder stepped down as chancellor after his party fared poorly in nationwide elections and was forced to become junior partners in a "grand coalition" with the Christian Democratic Party. After leaving politics Schröder was criticized for taking a top job in a Russian-led consortium building a gas pipeline to western Europe.

Schrödinger, Erwin (*1887–1961*) Austrian physicist. Schrödinger was educated in Vienna at both the gymnasium and the university, where he obtained his doctorate in 1910. After serving as an artillery officer in World War I, he taught at various German-speaking universities before he succeeded Max PLANCK as professor of physics at the University of Berlin in 1927. In 1933 Schrödinger's bitter opposition to the Nazis drove him into his first period of exile, which he spent in Oxford, England. Homesick, he allowed himself in 1936 to be tempted by the University of Graz in Austria, but, after the ANSCHLUSS in 1938, he found himself once more under a Nazi government, which this time was determined to arrest him. Schrödinger had no alternative but to flee. Fortunately, the prime minister of Ireland, Eamon DE VALERA, himself a mathematician, was keen to attract Schrödinger to a newly established Institute of Advanced Studies in Dublin. Working there from 1939 Schrödinger gave seminars that attracted many eminent foreign physicists (as well as the frequent presence of de Valera) until his retirement in 1956, when he returned to Austria.

Starting from the work of Louis DE BROGLIE, Schrödinger in 1925–26 developed wave mechanics, one of the several varieties of quantum theory that emerged in the mid-1920s. He was deeply dissatisfied with the early quantum theory of the atom developed by Niels BOHR, and complained of the apparently arbitrary nature of a good many of the quantum rules. Schrödinger took the radical step of eliminating the particle altogether and substituting for it waves alone. His first step was to derive an equation to describe the behavior of an electron orbiting an atomic nucleus. Schrödinger eventually succeeded in establishing his famous wave equation, which when applied to the hydrogen atom yielded all the results of Bohr and de Broglie. It was for this work that he shared the 1933 NOBEL PRIZE in physics with Paul DIRAC. Despite the considerable predictive success of wave mechanics, there remained problems for Schrödinger, when the probabilistic interpretation of Max Born soon developed into a new orthodoxy. Schrödinger found such a view totally unacceptable, joining those other founders of quantum theory, EINSTEIN and de Broglie, in an unrelenting opposition to indeterminism entering physics.

In 1944 Schrödinger published his *What is Life?,* one of the seminal books of the period. It influenced many talented young physicists who, disillusioned by the bombing of HIROSHIMA, wanted no part of atomic physics. Schrödinger solved their problem by revealing a discipline—free from military applications—that was significant and, perhaps just as important, largely unexplored. He argued that the gene was not built like a crystal but that it was rather what he termed an "aperiodic solid." He went on to talk of the possibility of a "code" and observed that "with the molecular picture of the gene it is no longer inconceivable that the miniature code should precisely correspond with a highly complicated and specific plan of development." Such passages, written with more insight than that contained in most contemporary biochemical works, inspired a generation of scientists to explore and decipher such a code.

Schultz, "Dutch" (**Arthur Flegenheimer**) (*1902–1935*) American gangster. Born in the Bronx, New York, Schultz was a minor criminal until the mid-1920s, when he organized a gang and strong-armed his way into the control of the Bronx beer trade. He quickly enlarged his operations to include the Harlem numbers racket. An erratic, savage and miserly mobster, he was quick to have his opposition gunned down and acquired a reputation for violence beyond even the usual gangland standards. After his gunmen's murder of Vincent "Mad Dog" Coll in 1932, Schultz reigned supreme in New York City crime under the protection of Tammany Hall boss Jimmy Hines. When special prosecutor Thomas E. DEWEY began to investigate organized crime in 1935, Schultz argued that he should be killed. Syndicate mobsters disagreed and hired assassins from MURDER, INC. to do away with the Dutchman. Ambushed in Newark, New Jersey, he lingered for two days before succumbing.

Schuman, William (*1910–1992*) American composer, educator and administrator. Born in New York, Schuman studied composition with Charles Haubiel and attended the Teacher's College at Columbia University. He earned a B.A. in 1935 and an M.A. in 1937. He taught at Sarah Lawrence College from 1935 to 1945. His work *American Festival Overture* was performed by the Boston Symphony in 1939. This led to performances in Boston of his Third and Fifth Symphonies, with Schuman conducting. His Fourth Symphony was performed in Cleveland in 1942. In 1945 Schuman became president of the Juilliard School of Music in New York. He left Juilliard in 1962 to become president of the Lincoln Center for the Performing Arts, a post he held until 1969. In recognition of his contributions to the musical life of the U.S. Schuman was the recipient of Kennedy Center Honors in 1989.

Schumann, Elisabeth *(1885–1952)* German-American singer. A soprano, Schumann was known equally for her work in the opera house and on the concert stage. Born in Merseburg, Thuringia, Germany, she debuted with the Hamburg Opera in 1909 and sang with that company for a decade, enjoying special success in her Mozart roles. Schumann made her Metropolitan debut in 1914, as Sophie in *Der Rosenkavalier* (probably her most famous role) by Richard STRAUSS. She performed for two decades for Strauss at the Vienna State Opera, also enjoying triumphs during this period at the SALZBURG FESTIVAL (1922–35), the Zurich Mozart Festival (1917) and Covent Garden (1924). During these years, she also made guest appearances throughout Europe and in South America. In 1938, Schumann moved to the U.S. with her husband, Karl Alwin, and their son, Gerd; that year she joined the faculty of the Curtis Institute of Music in Philadelphia, where she taught for the rest of her life. In 1944 she became an American citizen. She died in New York City on April 23, 1952.

Schumann-Heink, Ernestine *(1861–1936)* Austrian-American opera singer. A contralto, Schumann-Heink made her operatic debut on October 13, 1878, as Azucena in the Dresden Opera's production of *Il Trovatore*. In the years before World War I, she sang at the Hamburg Municipal Opera, Berlin's Kroll Opera, Covent Garden in London, the BAYREUTH FESTIVAL and the Metropolitan Opera in New York. In 1903–04, Schumann-Heink made a triumphal concert tour of the U.S., and in 1905 she became an American citizen. After her "farewell" tour in 1926, she appeared mostly in concerts and on the radio, also appearing in the 1935 film *Here's to Romance*. She died in Hollywood on November 17, 1936.

Schuschnigg, Kurt von *(1897–1977)* Austrian political leader. A nationalist and supporter of the Hapsburg restoration, Schuschnigg served as AUSTRIA's minister of justice from 1932 to 1934 and its minister of education from 1933 to 1934. After the as-

sassination of Engelbert DOLLFUSS in 1934, Schuschnigg became chancellor, heading a semifascist regime. When Adolf HITLER demanded absorption of Austria through ANSCHLUSS, Schuschnigg countered with a call for an Austrian plebiscite. His struggle against Hitler was successful until 1938, when he was forced to resign and was replaced by Nazi Arthur SEYSS-INQUART. Schuschnigg was arrested after the Germans entered Austria in March 1938 and imprisoned until 1945. He testified for the prosecution at the NUREMBERG TRIALS (1946) and was subsequently a professor in the U.S. (1947–67).

Schwartz, Delmore *(1913–1966)* American poet. Schwartz is perhaps best known for the ambitious poetic work *Genesis, Book I* (1943), which explores the experience of an American of Russian-Jewish descent living in New York City. *Vaudeville for a Princess* (1950) is a later collection of poetry and prose. Schwartz also wrote the short story collection *The World Is a Wedding* (1948), which revolves around middle-class Jewish life. Schwartz taught at Harvard University from 1940 until 1947. He served as editor of *PARTISAN REVIEW* and became poetry editor of the *NEW REPUBLIC* in 1955, serving also as an occasional film critic for them. His later years were spent in obscurity. He was the model for the fictional title character in Saul BELLOW's *Humbolt's Gift*.

Schwarzkopf, Elisabeth *(1915–2006)* German opera singer. Schwarzkopf began her opera career as a coloratura in such roles as Zerbinetta in *Ariadne auf Naxos* at the Charlottenburg Opera in Berlin but became a lyric soprano after World War II, gaining fame for her roles in the operas of Mozart and Richard STRAUSS. She made her American debut in 1955 with the San Francisco Opera. One of her most distinguished roles, the Marschallin in *Der Rosenkavalier*, was preserved in a famous recording and film of the production with conductor Herbert von KARAJAN at the Salzburg Festival in 1960. She was also renowned for her Lieder singing, giving recitals and making recordings of the art songs of Gustav MAHLER and Franz Schubert, among others. In 1953 she married her second husband, record producer **Walter Legge**, director of EMI and founder of London's Phil-

harmonia Orchestra. She had given master classes in opera and Lieder singing around the world since 1976. In 1992 Schwarzkopf was named a Dame Commander of the Order of the British Empire.

Schwarzkopf, H. Norman *(1934–)* American general who led the allied coalition forces against IRAQ during the PERSIAN GULF WAR (1990–91). Born in Trenton, New Jersey, Schwarzkopf was the son of the chief investigator of the LINDBERG KIDNAPPING CASE. He grew up in New Jersey and in Tehran, IRAN, where President Franklin D. ROOSEVELT had sent his father to advise the shah. The younger Schwarzkopf consequently developed a life-long interest in the Middle East. He graduated from the U.S. Military Academy at West Point in 1956 and later earned a master's degree in guided missile engineering from the University of Southern California. He served two tours of duty in the VIETNAM WAR and was twice wounded. In 1983 he commanded the U.S. invasion of GRENADA. That year he was also assigned to develop contingency plans for the U.S. military in the event of a crisis in the PERSIAN GULF region. In 1988 he became head of the Central Command, responsible for U.S. military forces in the Middle East, Africa and the Persian Gulf. When IRAQ invaded KUWAIT in August 1990, Schwarzkopf commanded the U.S. forces ordered to SAUDI ARABIA by U.S. president George H. W. BUSH in **Operation Desert Shield.** He was made supreme commander of all the coalition forces in the region. With the chairman of the Joint Chiefs of Staff, General Colin POWELL, and other military leaders, Schwarzkopf devised a plan of attack to drive the Iraqis from Kuwait with a minimum of allied casualties. He directed **Operation Desert Storm,** which began on January 17, 1991 (local time) with an air bombardment of Iraq that lasted six weeks. The ground phase of the war was launched on February 24, 1991; Schwarzkopf's forces liberated Kuwait in less than a week. Known affectionately to his troops as "Stormin' Norman," Schwarzkopf gained great respect for his expressed concern not only about the success of the allied mission but about the safety of his troops and of Iraqi civilians. After his return from the Middle East, Schwarzkopf retired from the U.S. Army (1992) and became an occasional television commentator on military affairs.

Schweitzer, Albert *(1875–1965)*
German theologian, philosopher, musicologist, organ player, doctor and humanitarian. Schweitzer, who won the NOBEL PRIZE for peace in 1952, became a world-famous figure in his later years as a result of his dedicated work as a doctor and Christian missionary at a hospital that he constructed and administered in Lambaréné in French Equatorial Africa (now the nation of Gabon). Schweitzer turned to the study of medicine only in 1905, having already established himself both as a theologian of note and as a scholar and virtuoso interpreter of the organ works of Johann Sebastian Bach. Schweitzer, who earned doctoral degrees in both philosophy and theology, wrote *The Quest for the Historical Jesus* (1906) in defense of a faith-oriented approach to Jesus that rejected historical evidence as a criterion of belief. His *J. S. Bach* (1908) remains a major musicological work that asserted for the first time the importance of pictorial imagination in Bach's compositions. A commitment to serve humanity led Schweitzer to give up his comfortable role as a scholar at the University of Strasbourg and to move to Africa in 1913, where he spent most of his remaining years. An absolute reverence for life became the hallmark of Schweitzer's philosophy. *My Life and Thought* (1933) is his autobiography, while *The Light Within Us* (1959) is representative of his later writings.

Schwitters, Kurt *(1887–1948)*
German artist best known for his work in collage, a technique he developed into an important modern abstract art form. Schwitters was trained in conventional painting at the Dresden Academy and began his career painting traditional portraits. His inclinations toward the DADA movement suffered a setback when he was refused membership in the 1918 Club Dada in Berlin. He developed his own, similar direction with the name *Merz* and began to create his *Merzbilder,* "trash pictures," made by pasting together bits of paper and other miscellaneous items, often picked up from the street. He also constructed *Merzbau,* abstract conglomerations of scrap materials that reached room size, anticipating the "environments" created by some conceptual artists of the 1980s. With the rise of NAZISM in the 1930s, Schwitters was forced to relocate, first in Norway and then in England. His work has had a continuing influence in the development of modern art and design, with a particularly strong impact on graphic design, where collage techniques have been used in such commercial work as advertising layout.

Sciascia, Leonardo *(1921–1989)*
Italian novelist. Sciascia's first work to appear in English, *Le parrocchie di Regalpetra* (1956, translated as *Salt in the Wound*) was a book of essays depicting an imaginary town in Sicily. Its portrayals of Italian politics and the Mafia established themes to which Sciascia would often return. His novels, which have been described as intelligent suspense stories, include *Mafia Vendetta* (1963), *Candido, or A Dream Dreamed in Sicily* (1979) and *La sentenza memorabile* (1982).

Scientology
Quasi-religious movement founded by pulp writer L. Ron HUBBARD in 1952. Hubbard, who became extremely wealthy (and reclusive) after the success of his legally established Church of Scientology, began as a writer for the now-vanished pulp fiction magazines, selling stories in every genre, from westerns to detective, but garnering most of his fame in the science fiction field. It was the leading monthly *Astounding* that first published Hubbard's articles on dianetics—a theory of allegedly "clear" mental health through the elimination of repressed past traumas—that formed the fundamental basis of Scientology. Scientology extracts a great deal of money from its ardent followers, and the practices of the Church of Scientology have been closely investigated in Great Britain and Canada, among other countries.

Scobee, Francis Richard "Dick" *(1939–1986)*
American astronaut who was the commander of the space shuttle *CHALLENGER* when it exploded on January 28, 1986. A combat pilot in the U.S. Air Force in the VIETNAM WAR, he logged more than 6,500 hours of flights in 45 types of aircraft. He served on a shuttle crew in 1984.

Scofield, John *(1951–)*
American electric guitarist. Scofield typifies the younger group of virtuosic post-bop, jazz musicians whose musical roots range from BEBOP and the MODAL JAZZ of John COLTRANE to ROCK and roll and rhythm and blues. Initially influenced by the urban blues guitar styles of B. B. King, Albert King and Chuck BERRY, Scofield broadened his horizons through studies at the Berklee School of Music in Boston (along with the University of North Texas in Denton, at the top of the new breed of jazz schools that began appearing after World War II). Engagements with mainstream artists such as baritone saxophonist Gerry Mulligan and trumpeter Chet Baker led to work with the jazz-rock fusion groups of drummer Billy Cobham and keyboardist George Duke. A stint in the early 1980s with jazz legend Miles DAVIS propelled Scofield to international fame. Since the mid-1980s, Scofield has toured and recorded mostly under his own name. Stylistically, like such fellow modern jazz guitarists as John Abercrombie and Pat Metheny, Scofield has evolved a highly personal and galvanizing style forged from virtuosic alloys of post-bebop harmonics, blues, rock and even country.

Scopes Trial
Infamous landmark judicial case that took place in 1925. In March of that year, the Tennessee legislature passed a statute that prohibited

Physician, humanitarian and winner of the Nobel Peace Prize, Albert Schweitzer, 1955 (NEW YORK WORLD-TELEGRAM AND *THE SUN* NEWSPAPER COLLECTION, LIBRARY OF CONGRESS, PRINTS AND PHOTOGRAPHS DIVISION)

public schools from teaching theories of evolution that differed from accepted biblical accounts. In July, John Scopes, a Dayton physics teacher, was put on trial for defying the statute by presenting Darwin's theory of evolution in his classroom. The American Civil Liberties Union came out in Scopes's defense and obtained the services of a distinguished lawyer, Clarence DARROW, to argue Scopes's case. Populist and perennial presidential candidate William Jennings BRYAN argued for the prosecution. The trial was dramatic, drawing international attention. Although Darrow insisted the statute was a violation of the separation of church and state, Scopes was convicted. He was later released by the state supreme court on a technicality.

Scorsese, Martin *(1942–   )* American film director. Scorsese is one of the major American film directors of the modern era. His films often deal with the dark side of American culture—its obsessions with violence and status—but Scorsese has also displayed an elegaic and even a comic sensibility. Educated at New York University film school, Scorsese scored his first critical success with *Mean Streets* (1973), a drama set in his native Little Italy district in New York City. The film helped make actor Robert DE NIRO a star. Scorsese and De Niro have collaborated several times since in films including *Taxi Driver* (1976), a chilling study of urban alienation and violence; *Raging Bull* (1979), the story of boxer Jake La Motta; and *Goodfellas* (1990), a look at life within organized crime. *The Last Waltz* (1978) is a documentary of the final rock concert by The BAND. *After Hours* (1985) is an absurdist comedy about New York night life. *The Last Temptation of Christ* (1988), based on the novel by Nikos KAZANTZAKIS, drew the ire of religious fundamentalists for its recognition of the human, sensual side of Christ's being. Scorsese continued to direct films throughout the 1990s, producing such pieces as the 19th-century adaptation of an Edith Wharton novel, *The Age of Innocence* (1993), the mafia drama *Casino* (1995), the Tibetan spiritual film *Kundun* (1997), the 19th-century urban tale *Gangs of New York* (2002), and the Howard Hughes biopic *The Aviator* (2005).

Scott, Charles S., Sr. *(1932–1989)* American CIVIL RIGHTS attorney. In 1951 he helped lead the fight to integrate public schools by bringing a lawsuit against the Topeka, Kansas, school board on behalf of a black elementary school student, Linda Brown. The case eventually went to the Supreme Court as BROWN V. BOARD OF EDUCATION. The court's 1954 decision in favor of Brown produced the landmark ruling that declared racial segregation in public schools unconstitutional.

Scott, Francis Reginald *(1899–1985)* Canadian politician, lawyer and poet. In the 1920s he was one of Canada's leading modernist poets (see MODERNISM). In the 1930s he helped found the Cooperative Commonwealth Federation, a democratic socialist party; he later served as its national chairman (1942–50). He was an authority on Canadian constitutional law. In the 1950s he was a member of legal teams that argued and won three landmark cases before Canada's Supreme Court. He served as dean of McGill University's school of law (1961–64). During his career he published several volumes of poetry. His *Collected Poems* (1981) won the prestigious Governor General Award.

Scott, Hazel *(1920–1981)* American pianist and singer, born in Trinidad. She was best known as an outstanding JAZZ performer but was equally outstanding as a BLUES and classical musician. A child prodigy, she enrolled in New York's Juilliard School of Music at age eight. She later starred in clubs, on Broadway and in films, including *The George Gershwin Story*. In 1945 she married U.S. representative Adam Clayton POWELL, Jr.; they divorced in 1960. She often performed in support of various CIVIL RIGHTS groups. On one occasion, she appeared before the HOUSE UN-AMERICAN ACTIVITIES COMMITTEE (HUAC) to defend her Civil Rights activities.

Scott, Robert Falcon *(1868–1912)* British explorer and naval officer. Scott is remembered as the leader of one of the most tragically ill-fated expeditions in the history of geographic exploration. He first explored the Antarctic region in the early 1900s as a member of a Royal Navy expedition. In 1910, he became

British explorer Robert Falcon Scott (LIBRARY OF CONGRESS, PRINTS AND PHOTOGRAPHS DIVISION)

the leader of a second expedition that had as its primary goal becoming the first to reach the SOUTH POLE. After lengthy preparations and grueling effort, the Scott expedition reached the Pole on January 17, 1912—only to find a flag planted there on December 14, 1911, by a Norwegian expedition led by Roald AMUNDSEN. Fierce blizzards led to the death of all members of the Scott expedition in March 1912, as they were attempting to return to civilization. Scott's diaries of the expedition, found on his person, were published in 1913. The British film *Scott of the Antarctic* (1948) dramatized the story of this expedition. Scott has long been revered as a model of quiet English self-sacrifice, but later research has suggested that he was motivated largely by vanity, was ill-prepared for his trek to the Pole and needlessly endangered the lives of his companions.

Scotto, Renata *(1934–   )* Italian coloratura soprano. Born in Savona, Scotto studied at the Verdi Conservatory in Milan and made her debut there in 1954 as Violetta in *La Traviata*. Roles at La Scala (Milan), Covent Garden (London) and the Vienna State Opera followed. Scotto made her U.S. debut in 1960 as Mimi in *La Bohème* at the Chicago Lyric Opera. In 1965 she debuted at the Metropolitan Opera in New York performing Cio-Cio-San in *Madama Butterfly*. During the next decade Scotto played leading coloratura roles at opera houses around the world. She specialized in the Italian bel canto repertoire and was known for the agility of her high register and elegant phrasing of legato passages. She also appeared in Metropolitan Opera telecasts and has recorded extensively.

Scottsboro case Notable legal case that established that under U.S. law persons facing the death penalty have a constitutional right to counsel, time to prepare for trial and a right to a fair jury. The case involved a series of trials. Lasting six years, it gained international attention and helped focus attention on the legal inequality of blacks and whites in the American South.

In 1931 nine young blacks (subsequently known as the "**Scottsboro Boys**") were tried in state court in Scottsboro, Alabama, on charges that they raped two white women in a freight car. The accused were given an attorney only at the last minute, and the initial trial was held only six days after their arrest. The nine were tried and convicted by an all-white jury. (Blacks were excluded from juries throughout the South at the time.) The Scottsboro Boys were all either sentenced to death or to 75 to 99 years of jail for the conviction. However, the convictions were appealed to the U.S. Supreme Court, which twice reversed the trial court's convictions because of procedural errors at trial. After a retrial, five of the accused were dismissed as defendants. Four others were paroled in the 1940s, long after one of the women had admitted that no rapes had occurred. The last surviving defendant, Clarence Willie Norris, was officially pardoned by the state of Alabama in 1976. The Scottsboro cases established a constitutional right to an attorney in a capital case and the right to an integrated jury.

Scoville, Herbert "Pete," Jr. *(1915–1985)* American military expert. A physical chemist by training, from 1948 to 1955 he worked on the development of nuclear weapons as technical director of the Defense Department's Armed Forces Special Weapons Project. From 1955 to 1963 he served as deputy director for research and technology in the CENTRAL INTELLIGENCE AGENCY (CIA). While holding that post he became convinced of the need to control nuclear weapons. After leaving the CIA, he

served for six years as assistant director of the Arms Control and Disarmament Agency, his final government position. From 1969 on, he campaigned tirelessly for arms control through books, articles, lectures and frequent appearances on Capitol Hill.

Scriabin, Alexander Nikolayevich *(1872–1915)* Composer of piano and orchestral music. In 1888 he entered the Moscow Conservatory, and from 1898 to 1903 he taught there. He married pianist Vera Isakovich in 1897. From 1900 on, he was interested in mystical philosophy, and the end of his First Symphony was designed to be a glorification of art as religion. Theosophical ideas inspired his *Le Divin Poème* (1905) and *Poème de l'estase* (1908). He eventually viewed himself as a messiah who would reunite Russia with the Spirit. He devised a "liturgical act," which made use of poetry, dancing, colors and scents, as well as music, in an attempt to induce a "supreme final ecstasy." His music became progressively more idiosyncratic.

Scribner's American monthly magazine from 1887 to 1939. Established by Charles Scribner's Sons, the New York publishing house, *Scribner's* was a celebrated literary magazine presenting fiction, poetry, biography, varied essays and criticism. Its contributors included Henry JAMES, Stephen Crane, Edith WHARTON, Jacob A. RIIS, S. S. Van Dine, Ernest HEMINGWAY, Thomas WOLFE, F. Scott FITZGERALD, Clarence DARROW, Lewis MUMFORD and Edmund WILSON. It was illustrated by N. C. WYETH and Maxfield PARRISH, among others, and its cover was designed by Stanford White. Its circulation reached a peak of 200,000 in 1910, but it went into decline shortly thereafter. An attempt to appeal to a broader audience in the early 1930s was unsuccessful, and by 1936 its circulation had dropped to 40,000. In 1937 *Scribner's* was sold to Harlan Logan Associates, but after two years of financial struggle the magazine was discontinued.

SDS See STUDENTS FOR A DEMOCRATIC SOCIETY.

Seabiscuit *(1933–1947)* American race horse. Purchased in 1936 for $7,500, the ill-tempered, half-crippled

Seabiscuit went on to become the leading money winner of his time. A come-from-behind winner, he seemed to toy with his adversaries in the stretch, letting them smell victory before snatching it away again. He was ridden primarily by the oft-injured Johnny Pollard and the legendary George Woolf. Pollard was aboard for the horse's legendary match race victory over the great War Admiral at Pimlico. Seabiscuit twice lost the Santa Anita Handicap by inches, but in 1940, in the final race of his career, he won it and became the greatest money-winner of the time.

Seaborg, Glenn Theodore *(1912–1999)* American chemist. In 1939 Seaborg became an instructor at the University of California at Berkeley. During WORLD WAR II he went to Chicago as one of the principal figures in the development of the ATOMIC BOMB in its initial phases, at the University of CHICAGO. Returning to Berkeley he became chancellor of the university in 1958. In 1961 President John F. KENNEDY asked him to serve as head of the Atomic Energy Commission, a post he retained until 1971. Seaborg was the first scientist to head the AEC. He represented the U.S. at atomic and other scientific conferences and served on numerous scientific and educational boards. Upon leaving the AEC, he returned to the University of California at Berkeley. He shared the 1951 NOBEL PRIZE for chemistry. He was the discoverer of nine elements, a unique achievement for which he received the Enrico Fermi Award in 1959.

Seale, Bobby *(1937–)* American black activist. Born in Dallas, Texas, he studied at Merritt College in Oakland, California, where he met Huey NEWTON. The two founded the BLACK PANTHERS in 1966, with Seale as chairman. Active in the ANTI-WAR MOVEMENT, he was indicted in 1969 as one of the "Chicago Eight" for his participation in demonstrations at the 1968 Democratic convention. A mistrial was later declared and charges were dropped. In the early 1970s Seale led the Panthers away from armed struggle and toward self-help programs. In 1973 he ran for mayor of Oakland, losing but receiving a very respectable vote total. He left the party shortly after the election. His autobiography, *A Lonely Rage,* was published in 1978.

Seanad Éireann Irish senate, consisting of 49 members elected by the universities and panels of candidates representing Irish society and 11 nominated by the TAOISEACH. Elections must take place within 90 days of the dissolution of the DÁIL ÉIREANN.

search-and-destroy An operational term used in the VIETNAM WAR. It was adopted by the MACV (U.S. Military Assistance Command Vietnam) in 1964 to describe operations designed to find, fix in place and destroy enemy forces and their base areas and supply caches. Originally intended to delineate one of the basic missions performed by South Vietnamese military forces, the term became widely used by U.S. forces later in the war. Public repugnance toward the brutality implied by the term in addition to vivid media accounts of destruction of Vietnamese villages helped undermine support for the war.

Searle, Ronald *(1920–)* English cartoonist. Educated at the Cambridge School of Art, he was a Japanese PRISONER OF WAR during WORLD WAR II. He is well known for witty drawings, executed in a delicately linear style, that have appeared in such periodicals as *The NEW YORKER* and *Punch.* He has also been involved in films, as the creator of the mischievous female students of St. Trinian's School who became the subjects of several English comedies and as the designer of animation sequences for *Those Magnificent Men in Their Flying Machines* (1965) and *Scrooge* (1970). His cartoons have been included in such collections as *Forty Drawings* (1946), *Searle's Cats* (1968) and *Searle's Zoodiac* (1977). During the 1990s Searle issued a collection of St. Trinian's drawings in *The Best of St. Trinian's* (1993) and continued to contribute drawings to magazines such as *The New Yorker.*

Sears, Roebuck & Company American department store and mail-order chain. It began in 1886 as a watch-selling sideline of Minnesota-born railroad worker Richard Warren Sears. The business prospered, and he soon started the R. W. Sears Watch Company. Sears moved from Minneapolis to Chicago in 1887 and was joined by Indiana-born Alvah Curtis Roebuck. The company produced its first mail-order catalog, a 32-page affair, in 1891. Two years later the company name was changed to Sears, Roebuck & Company. By 1920 the company's sales volume had grown to $245 million. Offering an almost incredible range of goods, often to rural Americans whose opportunity for shopping was severely limited, the catalog supplied necessities and luxuries to millions of Americans and became one of the country's greatest retailing success stories. While it has undergone many changes, the Sears stores and catalog survived and prospered into the final decade of the 20th century.

SEATO (South East Asia Treaty Organization) Conceived by Secretary of State John Foster DULLES as a kind of Southeast Asian NATO, SEATO was founded in 1954. It included the U.S., Britain, France, Australia, New Zealand, Pakistan, Thailand and the Philippines. A separate protocol extended SEATO's protection to the nonmember states South Vietnam, Laos and Cambodia. For the U.S. the purpose of SEATO was to provide a framework for building stable states to contain communist expansion. While Australia, New Zealand, Thailand and the Philippines assisted U.S. efforts in South Vietnam by dispatching combat forces, other SEATO nations did not share American concerns. Because of these major political differences, SEATO was relatively ineffective and was disbanded in 1977.

Seattle Slew *(1974–2002)* American thoroughbred racehorse. Purchased at public auction for only $17,500 in 1977, Seattle Slew went on to become the first Triple Crown winner since SECRETARIAT. The son of Bold Reasoning was the first horse in racing history to head into the three races undefeated. The heavy favorite going into the Kentucky Derby, his lackluster performance while winning led to criticism of both the horse and his rider, Jean Cruguet. They went on, however, to win the Preakness in the second-fastest time ever and the Belmont in masterful fashion. By the time of his death in 2002, Seattle Slew had sired 102 stakes winners.

Seaver, Tom *(1944–)* American professional baseball player. Born in Fresno, California, Seaver began pitching for the New York Mets in 1967. In 1969 his pitching record of 25 wins and 7 losses helped guide the Mets to the World Series and secured for him the NL's Cy Young Award for the best pitcher in the league that year. He later won the award in 1973 and 1975. On April 22, 1970, Seaver set a Major League record when he struck out 10 consecutive San Diego Padre batters. While playing for the Chicago White Sox, Seaver became the 17th pitcher to win 300 games in 1985. His final impressive statistics were 311 wins, a .603 winning percentage, a 2.86 career earned run average (ERA) and 3,272 strikeouts. Seaver was inducted into the Baseball Hall of Fame in 1992.

Seberg, Jean *(1939–1979)* American film actress. Born in Marshalltown, Iowa, she had her first role as the star of Otto PREMINGER's *St. Joan* (1957) and was later seen in *Bonjour Tristesse* (1958). The crop-haired actress became famous for her performance as an American gamine in Jean-Luc GODARD's new wave classic *Breathless* (1959). Her later films included *The Five-Day Lover* (1960) and *Lilith* (1964). Hounded for her radical political views, the actress settled in Europe. Often-married (once to author Romain Gary) and psychologically troubled, she committed suicide at age 40.

second front Allied invasion of the European mainland requested by Joseph STALIN in 1941 to take the enormous pressure of German attack off the USSR. The U.S. was involved in the Pacific war, and European attention was focused on the African campaign. Early in 1942 requests for a second front were widespread in Europe and the U.S. However, coordination of efforts, sufficient planning for such a large enterprise and naval difficulties prevented the Allies from acting until a second front was finally agreed upon at the QUEBEC CONFERENCE of August 1943. It was accomplished on June 6, 1944, with the NORMANDY landing.

Second or Great Boer War The discovery of gold in 1886 drew the British to the Transvaal, exacerbating British-Boer tensions and leading finally to declaration of war against Great Britain by the Transvaal and the Orange Free State in October 1899. Boer forces scored initial successes, seizing Kimberly, Mafeking and Ladysmith. In 1900 heavy British reinforcements under Field Marshal Lord Frederick Roberts and General Lord Horatio Kitchener turned the tide, seizing BLOEMFONTEIN, capital of Orange Free State, on March 13, 1900, and occupying the country. The British invaded Transvaal, captured JOHANNESBURG and Pretoria in May–June 1900 and crushed battlefield resistance. The British annexed the Boer states, but it took Lord Kitchener two years of bitter fighting and repression to quell guerrillas led by Jan SMUTS, Louis BOTHA and Christaan de Wet. By the Treaty of Vereeniging (May 31, 1902) British sovereignty was recognized by the Boers in exchange for an indemnity and other concessions.

Second Vatican Council See VATICAN II.

Secretariat (1970–1989) Thoroughbred racehorse, affectionately known as "Big Red" and widely considered "the horse of the century." The Kentucky-bred son of Bold Ruler and Somethingroyal, in 1973 he became the first horse since 1948 to win American racing's Triple Crown. In doing so, he set two track records that still stood at the time of his death. The chestnut colt ran the 1-1/4-mile Kentucky Derby at Churchill Downs in 1:59 2/5 minutes and ran the 1-1/2 Belmont Stakes in 2:24 minutes. The latter record, which produced a spectacular 31-length win, was more than two seconds faster than any other winning Belmont time. Secretariat won 16 victories in 21 career starts and earned $1,316,808 before being retired to stud after his three-year-old season. He sired more than 40 stakes winners. He was put down by lethal injection at Claiborne Farm in Paris, Kentucky, suffering from laminitis, a degenerative hoof disease.

secret police, Soviet From 1917 to 1922 the Soviet security service was known as the CHEKA (All-Russian Extraordinary Commission for Combating Counter-Revolution and Sabotage). This was reorganized as the GPU (State Political Administration) in 1922 and as the OGPU (United State Political Administration) in 1923. In 1934 the OGPU was succeeded by the NKVD (People's Commissariat for Internal Affairs), in 1943 by the NKGB (People's Commissariat for State Security), in 1946 by the MGB (Ministry for State Security) and in 1953 by the MVD (Ministry of Internal Affairs). From 1954 the Secret Police was known as the KGB (Committee for State Security).

The secret police directed its energies against the church, private traders, KULAKS, the intelligentsia and any who disagreed with the regime. It became a particularly sinister and powerful tool under YEZHOV during the GREAT PURGE in which 8 to 10 million people perished. The KGB also was responsible for foreign espionage.

Securities and Exchange Commission (SEC) The Securities and Exchange Commission was established by Congress in 1934 to oversee enforcement of the federal securities laws that were passed in 1933 and 1934. Congress concluded that a major cause of the stock market crash of 1929 and the Depression was a lack of regulation in the securities markets. Headed by Joseph P. Kennedy (father of John F. KENNEDY) and later by William O. DOUGLAS, who was to become a Supreme Court justice, the SEC quickly became the federal government's preeminent regulatory agency.

The SEC has responsibility for requiring public disclosure of facts and financial data by firms issuing securities and also by companies whose shares are publicly traded. The SEC regulates the stock exchanges as well as the activities of stock brokers, dealers and investment advisers, investigates and prosecutes securities fraud and also oversees takeovers and proxies. The SEC has been especially vigorous in prosecuting "insider trading"—the misuse of inside information by those with access to confidential corporate information.

Seeckt, Hans von (1866–1936) German general. Born of a military family in Schleswig, he was commissioned in 1885 and joined the general staff at the century's end. During WORLD WAR I, he commanded German forces in Poland, Turkey and the Balkans. After the war, as the head of the army (Reichswehr) from 1919 to 1926, he was effective in circumventing restrictions placed on the German military by the TREATY OF VERSAILLES. Training troops outside the formal army, which was limited to 100,000 men, and secretly acquiring forbidden weaponry, von Seeckt rebuilt the German army into a formidable fighting force. From 1930 to 1932, he was a member of the Reichstag, and he ended his military career as a military adviser to CHIANG KAI-SHEK in China from 1934 to 1935.

Seefried, Irmgard (1919–1988) German-born Austrian soprano; best known for her interpretations of operas by Wolfgang Amadeus Mozart. Although Seefried spent most of her career with the Vienna State Opera, she also performed as a recital and concert singer. Critics praised the clarity of her voice and the warmth of her interpretations.

Seeger, Alan (1888–1916) American writer, known mainly for his WORLD WAR I poem "Rendezvous" and for his own death in the war. Born in New York, he lived in Mexico as a child and later went to Harvard. In 1912 he went to Paris, where he led a bohemian life. He joined the French Foreign Legion at the outbreak of World War I, and his war poetry became enormously popular because of its heroic and patriotic sentiment. Seeger and his entire unit were mowed down by German machine guns at the battle of the SOMME on July 4, 1916. Reported in American newspapers, his death helped stir American public opinion against Germany and toward involvement in the war at a time when the U.S. was officially neutral. "Rendezvous," containing the line "I have a rendezvous with death," was memorized by a generation of American schoolchildren.

Seeger, Charles L. (1886–1979) American musicologist. Seeger introduced and taught the first U.S. course in musicology (1912–19) at the University of California at Berkeley. He was the father of folksinger Pete SEEGER.

Seeger, Pete (1919–) American folk music composer, guitarist and vo-

calist. Seeger is one of the most important figures in 20th-century American folk music. He has been a performer and composer since the 1930s, when he developed an enduring friendship with fellow folk musician and social activist Woody GUTHRIE. Seeger, who served in the U.S. military during World War II, in 1955 declined to answer questions on communist activities before the House Committee on Un-American Activities. He was convicted for contempt—a conviction that was overturned in 1962. Among Seeger's major folk compositions are "If I Had A Hammer," "Where Have All the Flowers Gone?," "Kisses Sweeter Than Wine," "I'll Sing Me A Love Song" and "The Happy Whistler." He was also a co-lyricist of the protest anthem "We Shall Overcome." In the 1950s, Seeger was a member of the popular folk group the Weavers, which enjoyed such hits as "Goodnight, Irene" and "On Top of Old Smoky."

See It Now Innovative television program of the 1950s, the prototype for the modern television news documentary. Coproducers Edward R. MURROW and Fred W. Friendly adapted the format of their successful weekly radio show, *Hear It Now*—a "magazine of the air"—into a half-hour television series that premiered on CBS on Sunday afternoon, November 18, 1951. It went into a prime-time slot, 6:30 P.M., for the 1952–53 season; thereafter, until its demise in July 1958, it was irregularly scheduled (provoking Gilbert Seldes to quip that it should be called "See It Now and Then"). The technology was new; program number one demonstrated the capabilities of the newly developed transcontinental coaxial cable and microwave networks (which meant that Murrow could "cue" the Atlantic and Pacific Oceans on two different monitor screens). Coverage included visits with troops in Korea, natural disasters like floods and interviews with personages like Winston CHURCHILL and Arnold TOYNBEE. And there were forays into what Murrow called "the hard, unyielding realities of the world in which we live": the Milo Radulovich program (1954) discussed nuclear energy and the atomic bomb; and the Joseph MCCARTHY segment (1954) openly attacked his anticommunist "witch-hunts." Although programs like

this cost CBS the support of sponsors like Alcoa, a far greater threat proved to be a new kind of prime-time program that soon would push *See It Now* off the air. It must have been with a chill of impending doom that Murrow watched the premiere on the night of June 7, 1955, of the first of the big-time game shows, *The $64,000 Question.*

Seferis, George (*1900–1971*) Greek poet and diplomat. Seferis, who won the NOBEL PRIZE in literature in 1963, is one of the greatest figures in Greek literature of the 20th century. His verse, which frequently deals with classical themes, was markedly influenced by MODERNISM, and most particularly by the poetic styles of T. S. ELIOT and of Serferis's countryman Constantine CAVAFY. Seferis was a career diplomat who served in numerous posts, including ambassador to London from 1947 to 1962. Seferis first won fame as a poet with the publication of *Mythistorema* (1935), the poems of which treat the intertwining of history and myth.

Segal, George (*1924–2000*) American sculptor. Born in New York City, he attended New York University and Rutgers. His first one-man show was held in New York in 1956. One of the "New Realists" of the early 1960s, Segal is best known for life-sized cast-plaster figures of ordinary people frozen in everyday moments, often with props such as window- or door-frames. Displaying an unusual sense of immediacy, some of his works remain in the rough plaster while others are cast in bronze and often finished in a white patina resembling the original plaster. Typical works are *Bus Driver* (1961, Museum of Modern Art, New York City) and *Restaurant Window* (1967, Walraff-Richartz Museum, Cologne). Many of his later bronzes are designed for site-specific architectural installation; among these are *Commuters* at the Port Authority Bus Terminal, New York City, and *Gay Liberation,* created for a park in Greenwich Village, New York City. In 1999 Segal received a National Medal of Arts from the National Endowment for the Arts.

Segovia, Andrés (*1893–1987*) Spanish classical guitarist. Over the course of an eight-decade career, he came to be regarded as the most important performer

and teacher in the history of the guitar. In the early 1900s he more or less invented classical guitar technique on his own. Later, through transcription of early contrapuntal music, he showed the possibilities of the guitar as a concert instrument and was largely responsible for the 20th-century resurgence of interest in the instrument. The repertory for the guitar was greatly expanded by the music of composers inspired by Segovia's virtuosity. He continued to fill concert halls worldwide when he was well past his 90th birthday.

segregation Separation of the races by law and custom. It can be seen in one of its most extreme manifestations in South Africa's APARTHEID. In the U.S., segregation of blacks from other Americans had its genesis in slavery. It was codified after the Civil War by the restrictive Black Codes. By the beginning of the 20th century, segregation of African Americans was entrenched in American society, written into law in the southern states and often a matter of established practice in the rest of the country. The beginning of the century also marked the beginning of many organized efforts to secure CIVIL RIGHTS for black Americans and to reverse segregation. Through the efforts of W. E. B. DU BOIS and others, the NATIONAL ASSOCIATION FOR THE ADVANCEMENT OF COLORED PEOPLE (NAACP) was formed in 1909, and this organization has been in the forefront of the fight against segregation ever since. The thrust toward ending segregation, particularly the legal sort found in the South, gathered momentum in the 1930s. By the beginning of World War II President ROOSEVELT ordered an end to segregation in defense plants; the Fair Employment Practices Act (1947) barred discrimination in hiring based on race or national origin and President TRUMAN forbade (1948) segregation in the military. Perhaps the most important milestone in the integration struggle during the 20th century was the decision in the 1954 Supreme Court case *BROWN V. BOARD OF EDUCATION,* in which the Court ruled against segregation in the public schools. Further inroads were achieved in the 1960s, a decade that saw unprecedented violence and struggle in the fight against segregation and for Civil Rights, with the passage of the CIVIL

RIGHTS ACT OF 1964, the VOTING RIGHTS ACT OF 1965 and the Fair Housing Act (1968). While the Civil Rights struggles of the 1960s subsided, issues regarding segregation and integration, whether de jure or de facto, continued to be important in the closing decades of the 20th century.

Seifert, Jaroslav *(1901–1986)* Czechoslovakian poet. Seifert was a prolific poet whose style underwent several changes during a lengthy writing career that began in earnest in the 1920s. His earliest volumes, such as *City in Tears* (1921) and *All Love* (1923), reflected both Seifert's enthusiasm for the RUSSIAN REVOLUTION of 1917 and the experimental poetics of Dadaism and SURREALISM. But by 1929 Seifert had rejected the Stalinist turn of Soviet communism. In the 1930s his poems became more direct and lyrical, with less linguistic experimentation. *Eight Days* (1937) is representative of this period. The Nazi conquest of CZECHOSLOVAKIA led to censorship, but Seifert continued to write poems that expressed the anguish of his conquered homeland, as in *The Stone Bridge* (1944) and *Helmet of Clay* (1945). In the decades following WORLD WAR II, Seifert continued to write while adding his voice to those who protested the Soviet rule of Czechoslovakia. In 1956 he wrote of the impact of Soviet censorship: "If a writer is silent, he is lying." In 1969 Seifert became president of the Czechoslovakian Writers Union but resigned shortly thereafter in protest of Soviet restrictions on artistic freedom. His later volumes include *The Casting of Bells* (1967) and *An Umbrella from Picadilly* (1979). Seifert's work was virtually unknown in the West until he won the NOBEL PRIZE for literature in 1984. (See also DADA.)

Seine River French river that flows through PARIS. It rises in the Plateau de Langres of France's Côte d'Or department and flows for 482 miles, emptying into the English Channel near LE HAVRE. After the Germans under General von Kluck advanced past the MARNE and toward Paris at the beginning of WORLD WAR I, the Allies hastily threw up a defensive line along the Seine east of Paris. Von Kluck had orig-

inally planned to encircle the city, but the Allied action foiled this plan.

Seinfeld A situation comedy, or "sitcom," that appeared on NBC from 1990 to 1998. Created by Jerry Seinfeld (who played himself in the title role) and Larry David, *Seinfeld* largely revolved around the New York City life of Jerry Seinfeld, a stand-up comedian trying to develop and market a sitcom based upon his life. Plot developments also revolved around members of Seinfeld's on-screen family as well as his friends, such as boyhood buddy George Costanza (played by Jason Alexander), ex-girlfriend Elaine Benis (played by Julia-Louis Dreyfus) and bizarre neighbor Cosmo Kramer (played by Michael Richards). Popularly described as "a show about nothing," the series became well known for its blurring of the line between reality and fiction, as Seinfeld and David often incorporated events within Seinfeld's real life into the plot developments on the television show, and Seinfeld opened many episodes with excerpts from his stand-up comedy routines that were related to the episodes' story line. It also introduced phrases such as "yada, yada, yada" and "re-gifting" into the American slang vocabulary and converted a small but growing group of Americans to the celebration of the completely secular winter holiday "Festivus." During its eight seasons, *Seinfeld* won an Emmy award for Outstanding Comedy Series and four Emmy Awards for its cast members— one for Julia-Louis Dreyfus and three for Michael Richards. Although the series ended in 1998, *Seinfeld* continued to remain popular through its syndication on multiple networks. In 2002, when the television magazine *TV Guide* released its rankings of the "50 Greatest Shows of All Time," it placed *Seinfeld* at the top of its list.

Selfridge, Harry Gordon *(1864–1947)* American-born merchant. Selfridge became a partner in the Marshall Field Company and manager of its retail store in CHICAGO before selling out his interest in 1904. With several partners he bought the firm of Schlesinger and Mayer and changed the name to H. G. Selfridge and Company. This store was sold to Carson, Pirie, Scott

and Company of Chicago in August of 1904. Selfridge traveled to London in 1906 and organized Selfridge and Company Ltd., wholesale and retail merchants, and built one of the largest stores in Europe. He became a naturalized British citizen on June 1, 1937.

Sellers, Peter *(1925–1980)* British actor. Sellers became one of the leading comedic actors in films through his rare combined mastery of physical comedy, verbal delivery and outlandish disguise. He first came to prominence in the 1950s in a series of British-made comedies including *The Ladykillers* (1955) and *The Mouse That Roared* (1959). Sellers appeared in multiple roles in *Dr. Strangelove: Or, How I Learned to Stop Worrying and Love the Bomb* (1964), the classic black comedy by Stanley KUBRICK. In the 1960s and '70s, Sellers made a highly popular series of films in which he portrayed the bumbling French gendarme Inspector Clouseau; these included *A Shot in the Dark* (1964) and *The Pink Panther Strikes Again* (1976). One of Seller's most acclaimed roles was in *Being There* (1980) as Chance, the near-idiot gardener for a wealthy Washington mansion whose sole interest is television and who becomes, by a series of flukish events, an influential political and media figure.

Selma Industrial city and county seat of Dallas County, Alabama; on the Alabama River, some 50 miles west of Montgomery. In 1965 Selma was the scene of important CIVIL RIGHTS demonstrations led by Dr. Martin Luther KING, Jr. King had gone to Selma at the beginning of the year to organize a black voter registration drive. Many demonstrators, including King, were arrested as the local authorities attempted to bar blacks from registering. The KU KLUX KLAN also opposed the Civil Rights movement and tried to intimidate the organizers with violence. King planned a march from Selma to Montgomery to call national attention to the Civil Rights movement. On March 7 state troopers broke up a march, using tear gas, night sticks and whips on the marchers. One protester, Rev. James Reeb of Boston, died two days later from injuries. President Lyndon B. JOHNSON condemned the brutality, and there was a national outcry. A second march was turned back by police, but a third attempt was successful. After reaching Birmingham on March 25, King told his followers that Selma had become "a shining moment in the conscience of man. If the worst in American life lurked in the dark streets, the best of American instincts arose passionately from across the nation to overcome it." The events that occurred in Selma helped persuade Congress to pass the VOTING RIGHTS ACT OF 1965.

Selye, Hans *(1907–1982)* Austrian-born endocrinologist who established a clear link between stress and illness. In 1932 he immigrated to Canada, where he founded and directed the International Institute of Stress in Montreal. He conducted numerous studies on the physiological effects of stress. He reported his findings in some 33 books and 1,600 articles.

Selznick, David O. *(1902–1965)* America motion picture producer, best known for GONE WITH THE WIND. Selznick was the son of Lewis J. Selznick, a pioneer film producer of the 1910s and 1920s; his elder brother Myron was one of the top talent agents in HOLLYWOOD. David began his own career as an assistant story editor at MGM in 1926, working for his father's former partner, Louis B. MAYER, whose daughter he married. He then moved to Paramount, where he became an associate producer, and to new studio RKO, where he was named vice president in charge of production and was responsible for *King Kong* (1933), among other films. Selznick returned to MGM in 1933, replacing an ailing Irving THALBERG as the studio's production chief; he produced some of MGM's glossiest blockbusters, including *Dinner at Eight* (1933), *David Copperfield* (1935) and *A Tale of Two Cities* (1935).

In 1936 he formed his own independent company, Selznick International, and perfected his "hands on" policy of filmmaking, overseeing through his famous memos every detail of a picture. Whether he made a satiric melodrama (*A Star Is Born,* 1937), a Civil War romance (*Gone With the Wind,* 1939), wartime homefront epic (*Since You Went Away,* 1944) or su-

percharged western (*Duel in the Sun,* 1946), his priorities were the same: "Our mission is to discover the nature of the demand and meet it as best we can." A persistent wooer of talent, he lured Alfred HITCHCOCK to Hollywood and produced four of his pictures, including *Rebecca* (1940) and *Notorious* (1946). He courted actress Phyllis Isley, signed her to a contract, changed her name to Jennifer Jones, married her and got her an ACADEMY AWARD for his *Song of Bernadette* (1943). The great American public proved fickle in the end and generally stayed away from his last picture, *A Farewell to Arms* (1957).

semiconductors Semiconductors are materials that have some electrical conducting properties but also some resisting properties. Silicon is the most widely used semiconductor. Semiconductors have myriad and important applications in modern electronics and communications technology. They are essential components in COMPUTERS. (See also SUPERCONDUCTORS; TRANSISTOR.)

semiotics The study of signs—broadly defined as any agreed-upon set of signifiers, from written letters to hand signals to visual symbols—as products of human culture and as means of communication. Semiotics emerged as a major field of intellectual endeavor in the 20th century, although past thinkers including Saint Augustine and John Locke had written on the subject of signs and their meaning. Pioneering writers on semiotics in the 20th century include the American philosopher Charles Peirce and the Swiss linguistics theorist Ferdinand de Saussure. Saussure stressed the terms *signifier* (the form of the sign) and *signified* (the idea expressed), while Peirce drew attention to the "interpretant," a new sign created by the interaction of the first two. Semiotics has been applied to literary criticism as a means of highlighting the role of fixed language rules in literary creation. The French critic Roland BARTHES was particularly influential in this area by his emphasis on the creative role of the reader in comprehending the text. Semiotics has often been linked to STRUCTURALISM as an intellectual method, in that both seek out structures that govern diverse individual expression.

Sen, Amartya *(1933–)* Indian-born British economist and winner of the 1998 Nobel Prize in economics. Born in Santiniketan, India, Sen demonstrated a talent for higher math at the Presidency College in Calcutta, from which he graduated with a B.A. in economics with a minor in mathematics in 1953. Upon graduation, he traveled to the United Kingdom and enrolled at Trinity College, Cambridge, receiving a second B.A. in economics in 1955, followed by a Ph.D. in 1959. As a professor of economics, Sen has lectured and taught at a variety of universities, such as the Jadaypur University in Calcutta, Cambridge University, the London School of Economics, Oxford University, Cornell University, Harvard University, University of California at Berkeley, Stanford University and the Massachusetts Institute of Technology. Since 1998 he has been a professor at Trinity College, Cambridge. In 1970 Sen published *Collective Choice and Social Welfare,* an economic text that sought to offer a new index system for societal wealth and poverty, as well as to evaluate the means by which individual wills and rights merge to form a collective decision. The book also advocated new methods of distributing this wealth throughout societies. It was because of the contributions this text made to the field of economics and human welfare that Sen was awarded the Nobel Prize in economics in 1998.

Sendak, Maurice *(1928–)* American children's book illustrator and writer. Born in Brooklyn, he is known for unsentimental books that convey the world of childhood with all of its angers and terrors. A brilliant draftsman, he has worked in a number of styles, from the broad grotesques of *Where the Wild Things Are* (1963), winner of the 1964 Caldecott Medal, to the delicately linear black-and-white drawings of *Higglety Pigglety Pop!* (1967). Both these books were written and illustrated by Sendak, as were such works as *The Nutshell Library* (1962), *In the Night Kitchen* (1970) and *Outside Over There* (1981). In addition, he has illustrated such books as Isaac Bashevis SINGER's *Zlateh the Goat and Other Stories* (1966) and *The Juniper Tree and Other Tales from Grimm* (1973). A fascination with the theater has led him to write the libretto and design the sets for an opera version of *Where the Wild Things Are* and the musical version of *Really Rosie* as well as to create the costumes and sets for new productions of Mozart's *The Magic Flute* and JANACEK's *The Cunning Little Vixen*. Sendak published two books during the 1990s—*I Saw Esau* (1992) and *We Are All in the Dumps with Jack and Guy* (1993). He also provided the illustrations for Arthur Yorink's *The Miami Giant* (1993). He received the 1996 National Medal of Arts from President William Jefferson CLINTON in recognition of his contributions to children's literature and illustrations.

Sendic, Raúl *(1924–1989)* Uruguayan revolutionary. He was the founder of the leftist Uruguayan guerrilla group known as the Tupamaros; the group, formed in 1962, was one of the first leftist insurgency movements in Latin America. Its activities ranged from robbery on behalf of the poor to kidnappings, assassinations and bombings. Two of the group's most notorious actions were the 1971 kidnapping of the British ambassador and the 1970 kidnapping and murder of a U.S. adviser. This latter case formed the basis of the COSTA-GAVRAS film *State of Siege*. Sendic served more than 13 years in prison and was one of the last political prisoners released following URUGUAY's return to civilian rule in 1985. On his release, he reorganized the Tupamaros as a political party.

Senegal Senegal occupies an area of 75,729 square miles on the west coast of Africa; it is bordered by Mauritania, Mali and Guinea and totally surrounds Gambia. At the beginning of the century, Senegal was part of the Federation of FRENCH WEST AFRICA. Briefly incorporated into the independent Mali Federation, the country seceded and declared the independent Republic of Senegal in 1960, with Léopold SENGHOR as the first president (1960–81). In 1968 the French aided Senghor in controlling growing student and labor unrest, which stemmed from a worsening economy. His successor, Abdou Diouf (1983–2001), has had to deal with increasing economic and social problems as well as a secessionist movement by the prosperous province of Casamance. In 1991 Senegal signed a peace treaty with Gambia in an effort

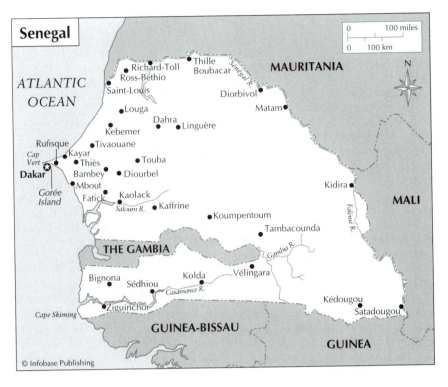

to contain the success of the separatists in the Casamance region. However, the rebels continued to wage their guerrilla campaign against the government until they signed a peace accord with newly elected president Abdoulaye Wade in 2001. Although fissures immediately emerged within the separatists, an um-

	SENEGAL
1960	(June 20) Becomes independent from France as part of the Mali Federation; (Aug. 20) secedes from the federation and becomes the Republic of Senegal with Léopold Senghor as president.
1963	(Mar. 7) New constitution created strengthening Senghor's political power.
1966	Legally recognized opposition parties no longer exist.
1973	Catastrophic drought strikes Sahel.
1975	All political prisoners are released.
1976	New constitution allows for up to three opposition parties.
1981	(January) Senghor retires and names Abdou Diouf as president.
1988	Diouf elected president for the second time.
2000	Diouf is defeated by opposition leader Abdoulage Wade.
2004	The Casamance rebels and the government sign a peace agreement.

brella separatist organization named the Casamance Movement of the Democratic Forces (MFDC) reaffirmed the separatists' commitment to pacifism in a 2003 statement. In 2004 the MFDC and the government signed a pact to end the secessionist struggle.

Senghor, Léopold Sedar *(1906–2001)* African statesman and poet, president of SENEGAL (1960–80). Senghor was a leading figure in the movement for African independence in the 1950s and 1960s, and is also internationally regarded as a literary figure. He was educated in Dakar and Paris, where he studied philosophy and pursued an academic career in the 1930s. He turned to politics after World War II and was elected as a deputy for Senegal in the French Constituent Assembly. Senghor subsequently helped to frame the constitution giving each French West African territory its own assembly and more deputies in the French parliament. He served as a deputy himself until 1958. Originally a member of the French Socialist Party, he left it in 1948 to start his own party, the Bloc Démocratique Sénégalaise. This party evolved into the Union Progressiste Sénégalaise (UPS). Senghor was minister-councillor for cultural affairs, education and justice in the French government in 1959–60. In 1959 he became president of the federal assembly of the Mali Federation of Senegal and Sudan; after the federation split in 1960, he became president of the Republic of Senegal. He was reelected in 1963, 1968, 1973 and 1978. Retiring in 1980, he was succeeded by his prime minister, Abdou Diouf. In addition to his political career, Senghor pursued an active literary career and philosophical interests as a poet and theorist of NEGRITUDE and African socialism.

Sennett, Mack (Michael Sinnott) *(1880–1960)* Celebrated American motion picture producer, best known for his *Keystone Comedies*. Born to working-class Irish immigrants in Quebec, he shifted from common laborer to stage actor when he began working in New York burlesque. As "Mack Sennett" he appeared in and wrote many BIOGRAPH movie shorts in 1910–11 for D. W. GRIFFITH. For his own new production company, Keystone, he gathered together associates from his Biograph days—Ford Sterling, Fred Mace and Mabel Normand—and developed new stars, like Roscoe "Fatty" Arbuckle, Chester Conklin, Mack Swain and Charles CHAPLIN to make the frenetic, hyper-kinetic slapstick comedies that made his reputation. By the time Keystone was absorbed into the Triangle Film Corporation in 1915, Sennett was supervising bigger-budget, two-reel comedies that depended less and less on slapstick. After Triangle foundered in 1918, Sennett spent the next 20 years dabbling in features, Harry LANGDON comedies and sound shorts for W. C. FIELDS and Bing CROSBY (1932). In 1936 he received a special ACADEMY AWARD for his comic contributions to film. Broke and embittered near the end of his life, Sennett could still write in his autobiography, *King of Comedy* (1954): "I believe I have associated intimately with more fools than any man living, a blessing for which I thank God."

September 11, 2001 The day of the most deadly attack on U.S. soil. At approximately 8:45 A.M. EST, a hijacked plane flying from Boston's Logan International Airport crashed into one of the two towers of the WORLD TRADE CENTER in New York City, creating a life and death situation within those two structures and nearby buildings. Emergency rescue crews from the New York Police Department (NYPD), the Fire Department of New York (FDNY) and the Port Authority Police Department (PAPD) were immediately dispatched to aid in the recovery of survivors. Fifteen minutes later, a second hijacked plane, also from Logan Airport, crashed into the second tower of the World Trade Center. By noon both towers had collapsed—probably due to structural deficiencies in fire proofing—spilling debris throughout the New York financial district and entombing those emergency workers and building occupants still inside the two structures. In Washington, D.C., a third hijacked airplane crashed into the walls of the Pentagon before scrambled F-16 fighters could shoot it down. A fourth hijacked plane, United Flight 93, was traveling over rural Pennsylvania when passengers—after discerning from cellular telephone conversations with family members and others what had taken place in New York City—decided to storm the cockpit and attempt to wrest control of the plane from the terrorists, lest their plane serve as another piloted missile. Although they failed to regain control of the aircraft, and the plane crashed into a Pennsylvania field, these passengers prevented the plane's use as a fourth vehicle of destruction. By the end of the day, 2,749 Americans and foreigners had died in New York City, Washington, D.C. and rural Pennsylvania as a result of these attacks.

In the aftermath of September 11, U.S. intelligence agencies sought to determine the individuals or organizations responsible for planning and executing the seizure and use of these four aircraft. They soon concurred that the Afghanistan-based terrorist group AL-QAEDA had trained 19 of its members to fly large passenger aircraft and arranged for their travel on the four airplanes used for the attacks. Once aboard they seized control of the aircraft by taking passengers hostage with box-cutter knives and gaining access to the cockpit, where they killed the pilots, and (aside from United Flight 93) flew the planes into their targets. In response to these attacks, U.S. president George W. BUSH declared a "War on Terror" against al Qaeda, its leader Osama BIN LADEN and its host government, the TALIBAN of AFGHANISTAN (which was overthrown by U.S. military forces in October 2001). In response to the September 11 attacks, the Bush administration established a Department of Homeland Security and persuaded Congress to pass the Patriot Act, with the goal of preventing circumstances that could lead to another attack on U.S. territory.

Serbia Former kingdom in the Balkans region; subsequently the largest and most influential of the six constituent republics that formed YUGOSLAVIA. After centuries of domination by the Ottoman Turks, the Serbs forced them out of most of their ancestral lands in 1829. Thereafter, the Karageorge (or Karageorgević [Karadjordjvic]) and Obrenović families fought each other for control of the government. In 1903 King Alexander was assassinated, ending the Obrenović line of succession. Peter I, a member of the Karageòrge family, ascended the throne. He strengthened the parliament and revived Serbia's economy. Peter I and Serbia guided the formation of the Balkan League, an alliance of MONTENEGRO, BULGARIA and GREECE designed to offset the power of AUSTRIA-HUNGARY and the waning OTTOMAN EMPIRE. With Russian assistance the league defeated Turkey in 1912 in the First BALKAN WAR. However, Serbia turned against its former ally Bulgaria in 1913, in the Second Balkan War. When Crown Prince FRANZ FERDINAND, heir to the Austro-Hungarian throne, was assassinated by a Serbian nationalist at SARAJEVO (June 28, 1914), the empire slapped Serbia with an ultimatum that led to the start of WORLD WAR I. Serbia was occupied by the Central Powers in November 1915. Following the end of the war in 1918, Serbia became part of the Kingdom of the Serbs, Croats and Slovenes, renamed Yugoslavia in 1929. From 1941 to 1945, during WORLD WAR II, Serbia was a puppet state of Nazi GERMANY. King PETER II, last of the Karageorges, spent the war in exile and lost his throne when Yugoslavia became a republic on November 29, 1945. Despite Yugoslav leader TITO's efforts to balance power evenly among the six Yugoslav republics, Serbia remained politically dominant. Anti-Serbian demonstrations and moves for greater autonomy by the other republics threatened to break up Yugoslavia. Led by Slobodan MILOŠEVIĆ, Serbia remained at the forefront of military efforts to prevent the secession of the Yugoslav provinces of CROATIA (1991–92), MACEDONIA (1991), BOSNIA AND HERZEGOVINA (1992–95) and the Serbian region of KOSOVO (1998–99), from declaring their independence. MILOŠOVIĆ was ousted from office in October 2000 and was arrested the following year. In 1992, following the earlier secession of Croatia and Slovenia and the outbreak of civil war over Bosnia's declaration of independence, Serbia and Montenegro formed a new political entity known as the Federal Republic of Yugoslavia. In 2003 a restructured Serbia and Montenegro became official as a new constitution was approved. The Serbian Radical Party gained the most votes in parliamentary elections that year.

Serbia and Montenengro

The only former constituent republics of the former YUGOSLAVIA to remain in the Yugoslav Federation, SERBIA and MONTENEGRO (see entries) merged to form the Federal Republic of Yugoslavia in 1992, renamed Serbia and Montenegro

in 2003. The states maintain a joint defense but have separate capitals (Belgrade and Podgorica), economies and currencies. In a referendum on May 21, 2006, Montenegro voters, by a narrow margin, elected to end their country's union with Serbia.

Sergio, Lisa *(1905–1989)* Pioneer radio broadcaster in Benito MUSSOLINI's Italy who immigrated to the U.S. and became a commentator on American radio. During her years on Italian radio, she sang and translated Mussolini's speeches into English and French until she was fired in 1937 for making changes in PROPAGANDA commentary. Faced with arrest, she escaped to the U.S. and became a dedicated antifascist. (See also FASCISM.)

serial music General term frequently applied to the various nontonal systems employed by Arnold SCHOENBERG and his followers to replace Western traditions of tonal music. After the turn of the century, composers like Gustav MAHLER, Igor STRAVINSKY and Bela BÁRTÓK pushed tonal ambiguity almost to the point of no return, to what Leonard BERNSTEIN later called "the tonal crisis." Schoenberg, whose *PIERROT LUNAIRE* (1912) had achieved complete atonality, devised systems to impose order upon the 12 equal tones of the chromatic scale. His theory of the "twelve-tone row," or dodecaphonic system, consisted of a preconceived constellation of 12 tones where no single tone could be repeated until all 11 others had sounded. Schoen-

SERBIA/SERBIA AND MONTENEGRO

1912–13	During the Balkan Wars, Serbia expands its territory at the expense of Turkey and Bulgaria.
1914	Austrian archduke Franz Ferdinand is assassinated by a Serbian national. This incident sparks World War I.
1915	Serbia is occupied by the Central Powers.
1918	Serbia joins Croatia and Slovenia, formerly under Austrian Habsburg control, to form the Kingdom of Serbs, Croats, and Slovenes.
1929	The new name of Yugoslavia ("Land of the Southern Slavs") is adopted.
1934	Alexander I is assassinated by a Macedonian with Croatian terrorist links; his young son Peter II succeeds, with Paul, his uncle, as regent; Nazi Germany and Fascist Italy increase their influence.
1941	Following a coup by pro-Allied air force officers, Nazi Germany invades. Peter II flees to England.
1945	Josip Broz (Marshal Tito) leads the Partisans to victory against the Axis powers. Yugoslavia becomes a republic.
1946	Serbia holds the most political power of the six Yugoslav republics.
1953	Tito becomes president of Yugoslavia, a post he holds for the next 27 years.
1980	Tito dies and executive power is transferred to a collective presidency.
1989	Serbia, under President Slobodan Milošević, proclaims a new constitution for Yugoslavia and suspends the autonomy of Vojvodina and Kosovo.
1991	Slovenia votes for secession in the first free multiparty elections in Yugoslavia and declares independence; Croatia, Bosnia-Herzegovina, and Macedonia also proclaim independence. War erupts in Croatia between Serbs, backed by the Yugoslav military, and Croats.
1992	Civil war opens in Bosnia-Herzegovina among ethnic Serbs, ethnic Croats, and Bosnian Muslims. Serbia and Montenegro, the remaining states of Yugoslavia, consolidate as the Federal Republic of Yugoslavia (FRY) and adopt a new constitution. Milošević is reelected as president of Serbia.
1995	The presidents of Bosnia-Herzegovina, Croatia and Serbia sign a peace accord in Dayton, Ohio, ending the war in Bosnia-Herzegovina; the resettlement of 650,000 Serb refugees from Croatia to Kosovo increases racial tensions in this ethnically Albanian region.
1998	The Albanian separatist group Kosovo Liberation Army (KLA) attempts to unify Kosovo with Albania; violence escalates as Serbian police attempt to regain regional control.
1999	The Yugoslav army and Serbia's police forces pursue ethnic Albanian rebels in Kosovo, forcing hundreds of thousands of Albanians to flee; after 78 days of massive air strikes by NATO, Serbian and Yugoslav forces withdraw from Kosovo.
2000	Slobodan Milošević is ousted in a national election.
2001	Milošević surrenders to security forces after an armed standoff. He is eventually transferred to The Hague to face accusations of war crimes.
2002	In March Serbia and Montenegro reach a EU-negotiated agreement to abolish the Federal Republic of Yugoslavia and replace it with a loose union to be called Serbia and Montenegro.
2003	In February, a new constitution is adopted and the name of the remnant of the former Yugoslavia is changed to Serbia and Montenegro.
2006	Hearings begin at The Hague in the International Court of Justice dealing with Serbian war crimes. Milošević dies in prison at The Hague, five years after being extradited to stand trial for war crimes. In a referendum on May 21, Montenegrans decide to sever their country's union with Serbia.

berg's ideas were carried to extremes by his disciple Anton von WEBERN. In works like the *Orchestral Variations* he devised a 12-tone *color* system in which no given instrument could play two successive notes until the other instruments had made their appearance. He abandoned the essentials of harmony and counterpoint completely and replaced the row with multiple possible sequences so the music could not be reduced to any given sequence of 12 notes. Webern, in turn, influenced post–World War II composers like Pierre BOULEZ and Karlheinz Stockhausen who went on to develop concepts like the "technique of groups"—the serial treatment of entire sections of sonorous material. Other developments included experimentation by John CAGE in electronically produced music and in the chance accumulations of notes and noise.

Serkin, Rudolf *(1903–1991)* Austrian-American concert pianist. Born in Bohemia, Serkin made his first public appearance at age five, and at nine he went to Vienna to study piano. At the age of 12, he debuted as a soloist with the Vienna Symphony Orchestra, and from 1919 to 1920 he studied composition with Arnold SCHOENBERG. After meeting Adolf Busch (later his father-in-law), he lived with the violinist and his family in Berlin and performed with him in a series of memorable joint recitals and in ensembles with other musicians. Serkin made his U.S. debut in a sonata recital with Busch in 1933, and first appeared as a soloist here three years later. After the outbreak of World War II in Europe, Serkin and his family immigrated to the U.S. He became a member of the faculty at Philadelphia's Curtis Institute of Music, serving as its director from 1968 to 1975. In 1949 he cofounded Vermont's Marlboro School of Music and acted as director of the summer Marlboro Music Festival. Serkin's repertoire centered on the music of Mozart, Beethoven, Schubert, Mendelssohn, Schumann and Brahms. He was known for his strong technique and his poetic, subtly nuanced interpretations.

Serling, Rod See THE TWILIGHT ZONE.

Service, Robert William *(1874–1958)* Canadian poet. Service is best remembered for his ballads such as "The Shooting of Dan McGrew," which were inspired by the rough frontier life he observed during the gold rush to the Yukon in 1895. Service's collections include *Songs of a Sourdough* (1907), *Rhymes of a Rolling Stone* (1912) and the autobiographical *Ploughman of the Moon* (1945) and *Harper of Heaven* (1948).

Sesame Street Live-action American children's television show broadcast on the Public Broadcasting System (PBS) network. In the late 1960s, nationally renowned puppeteer Jim HENSON was hired by Children's Television Workshop (CTW) founder Joan Ganz Cooney to help create an educational children's show that would feature life-sized puppet characters interacting with human actors and actresses. Cooney believed that the presence of smaller, more approachable and more entertaining puppet characters (later termed "Muppets") would encourage preschool and kindergarten age children to observe their actions carefully and therefore absorb the Muppets' lessons on such skills as the letters of the alphabet, the use of numbers and appropriate behavior. In 1969 Cooney and Henson's hour-long program premiered. Entitled *Sesame Street*, it was taped in studios in New York City and originally focused on the interaction between human characters such as Bob, Gordon and Susan (neighborhood residents on the fictional Sesame Street) and Mr. Hooper (the local grocery store owner), as well as several Muppet characters voiced by Henson and Frank Oz. These characters were Kermit the Frog; Bert, Ernie, and the Cookie Monster; Big Bird and Grover; and Oscar the Grouch. Along with the story lines that resulted from interaction among these characters, *Sesame Street* would contain animated or live-action short pieces that taught children lessons about numbers, letters and certain products used by children.

Since its creation, *Sesame Street* has been honored with numerous Daytime Emmy Awards, including the Emmy Award for Outstanding Pre-School Series. To keep its programs relevant, *Sesame Street*'s producers constantly changed the content of its programming, introduced new Muppet and human characters and developed story lines to explain issues facing children. For instance, to show its audience that

there was no shame in having an imaginary friend, Sesame Street introduced a new Muppet in the 1970s. Named Mr. Snuffleupagus, he became the best friend of Big Bird, but would disappear before anyone other than Big Bird could see him. In a similar effort to show children the benefits of a multicultural society, the ethnic makeup of *Sesame Street*'s actors and actresses was diverse, including a Jewish-American (Mr. Hooper), several African Americans (the husband-and-wife couple Gordon and Susan Robinson, as well as Mr. Hooper's assistant, David) and Hispanic Americans (Luis, the repairman, and Maria). In 1982, following the death of Will Lee, the actor who played Mr. Hooper, *Sesame Street* chose to have his character die and dedicated an entire episode to showing the effects of Hooper's death and Big Bird's understanding of its meaning.

Some innovations in the program have met with great controversy. In 2002 *Sesame Street* provoked ire from conservative critics when it announced that it would introduce Kami, an HIV-positive character, into the South African version of the U.S. show, *Takalani Sesame*. Some conservative organizations claimed that segments devoted to the new Muppet would make it appear as if there was little danger to having HIV or AIDS. In response, *Sesame Street* producers insisted the addition would only serve to assure children who had HIV/AIDS or who knew someone with the disease that their troubles were shared by others, and to offer advice on how to cope with this development.

Sessions, Roger *(1896–1985)* American composer. Considered one of the foremost American composers of the 20th century, he was known for the uncompromising rigor of his musical thinking. Early in his career he composed complex neoclassical scores influenced by Igor STRAVINSKY. Later, after befriending Arnold SCHOENBERG, he adopted 12-tone or SERIAL MUSIC style that Schoenberg had pioneered. Among Sessions's works were nine symphonies, a violin concerto, a piano concerto, two operas and a concerto for orchestra for which he won the 1982 PULITZER PRIZE for music. A noted theoretician and teacher, Sessions taught at Princeton University (1953–65), the University of

California at Berkeley and the Juilliard School of Music. Many of his students went on to become well-known composers.

Seton, Anya (*1916–1990*) U.S. author. She was a best-selling author of historical and biographical novels. Among her most popular works were *Dragonwyck,* which was made into a 1946 film starring Vincent Price, and *Foxfire,* made into a 1955 film starring Jane Russell.

Seuss, Dr. (Theodor Seuss Geisel) (*1904–1991*) American children's book author and illustrator Dr. Theodor Seuss Geisel, known to the world as Dr. Seuss, was born in Springfield, Massachusetts. He wrote over 50 delightfully nonsensical tales including works that have become children's classics, such as *Horton Hears a Who* (1954), *The Cat in the Hat* and *How the Grinch Stole Christmas* (both 1957). His words and rhymes are intended to help preschoolers to recognize and pronounce syllables, and his bold and fanciful cartoon illustrations are designed to enchant. He was also a cartoonist, using the pen name Theo Le Seig for these works. Seuss-related projects continued despite the author's death in 1991, including two live action screen adaptations of his books—*How the Grinch Stole Christmas* (2000) and *The Cat in the Hat* (2003)—and *Seusssical the Musical,* an off-Broadway musical that involved several well-known Seuss characters such as the Cat in the Hat, Horton the Elephant and Gertrude McFuzz in an effort to restore order to the Jungle of Nool.

Sevareid, Eric (*1912–1992*) American journalist. Sevareid began his career as a reporter for the *Minneapolis Journal* and later worked for the Paris edition of the *New York Herald-Tribune.* In 1939, he was summoned to London by Edward R. MURROW and asked to join CBS News. Sevareid was the last reporter to broadcast from Paris before the German occupation in 1940. In his long association with CBS News, Sevareid covered every presidential election from 1948 to 1976 and a variety of beats in the United States and abroad. In 1964, he began appearing on the *CBS Evening News,* for which he continued to serve as a consultant following his retirement in 1977.

Severini, Gino (*1883–1966*) Italian painter. He was educated in Rome, where he met modernist artists such as Giacomo BALLA and Umberto Boccioni, and settled in Paris in 1906. During his years in France he formed close ties with members of the Parisian avant-garde and associated himself with CUBISM. He was in France in 1910 when he signed the Futurist manifesto. Becoming associated with FUTURISM and strongly influenced by Seurat and neoimpressionism, Severini embraced the Futurist aesthetic of motion, while adding to it a uniquely delicate touch and decorative approach. His happy, sequin-spattered canvas *Hieroglyph of the Bal Tabarin* (1912; Museum of Modern Art, New York City), which was exhibited in the first exhibition of Futurist work held in Paris in 1912, is a characteristic example of his work.

Sèvres, Treaty of Post–WORLD WAR I treaty that led to the dissolution of the OTTOMAN EMPIRE. Signed on August 10, 1920, in a suburb of Paris, the treaty dismissed all of TURKEY's territorial claims in Arab Asia and North Africa; the Ottomans were also forced to grant independence to Armenia and autonomy to Kurdistan. GREECE was given territory in Thrace, the Aegean and the Anatolian west coast, and was given the administration of Smyrna for five years. Turkish nationalists rejected the treaty, and it was superceded by the Treaty of LAUSANNE in July 1923.

Sexton, Anne (Anne Harvey Sexton) (*1928–1974*) American poet. The poems of Sexton's first books, *To Bedlam and Part Way Back* (1960) and *All My Pretty Ones* (1962), were begun as therapy after a nervous breakdown led to her hospitalization. She was influenced by Robert LOWELL, whose workshop in poetry she attended with Sylvia PLATH and Maxine Kumin, to break the academic and formal constraints common to American poetry in the 1950s. Her poems are notable for their fresh and startling imagery and their unconventional, often FEMINIST as well as personal, themes. *Live or Die* won a PULITZER PRIZE in 1966. After her divorce in 1974, her writing became more religious and despairing, and she committed suicide. *The Death Notebooks* (1974), *The Awful Rowing Towards*

God (1975) and *45 Mercy Street* (1976) were published posthumously.

Seychelles Located in the Indian Ocean, almost a thousand miles northeast of Madagascar, the Republic of Seychelles consists of 115 islands and islets dispersed over 250,900 square miles of ocean, with a total land area of 175 square miles. The Seychelles became a British Crown colony in 1903. The political influence of plantation owners was unchallenged until the emergence of nationalist parties in the 1960s. James Mancham's Seychelles Democratic Party was by 1974 seeking independence. Mancham formed a coalition government in 1975 with his more radical rival, France-Albert René of the Seychelles People's United Party, leading the country to independence (June 28, 1976)—with Mancham as executive president and René as prime minister.

René, increasingly critical of Mancham's international jet-set image, overthrew him in June 1977. He launched a social reform program and sought to diversify from excessive dependence on tourism. René's party, retitled the Seychelles People's Progressive Front, became the sole party under the June 1979 constitution. Mancham was accused by René of backing unsuccessful coup attempts involving mercenaries (April 1978, November 1979, November 1981). The last of these, launched from South Africa, led to the trial and imprisonment there of its organizer, Colonel "Mad Mike" Hoare. Tanzanian troops supported the René regime and suppressed a mutiny in August 1982. In 1984, exiled opponents formed a Seychelles National Movement, whose president, Gerald Horeau, was assassinated at his London home (November 30, 1985). In 1991 René announced that nongovernment parties would be allowed to run in national elections. René and his Seychelles Progressive People's Front proceeded to inaugurate the newly devised constitution of 1993 by winning the constitution's first national elections, followed by victories in 1998, 2001 and 2002. In 2004 René stepped down and was replaced by former vice president James Michel.

Seyss-Inquart, Arthur (*1892–1946*) Austrian political leader. A Nazi, Seyss-Inquart was appointed chancellor of

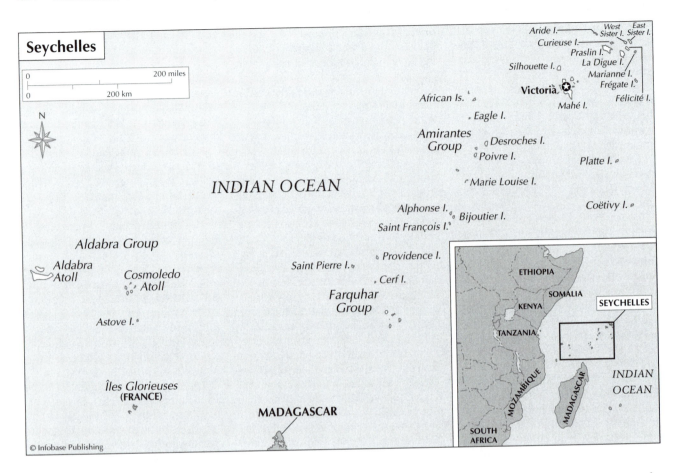

Seychelles

0 ——— 200 miles
0 ——— 200 km

N

Aride I. — West Sister I. East Sister I.
Curieuse I.
Praslin I.
Silhouette I.   La Digue I.
Marianne I.
Victoria
Frégate I.
Félicité I.
African Is.
Mahé I.

Eagle I.

Amirantes Group
Desroches I.
Poivre I.
Platte I.
Marie Louise I.

INDIAN OCEAN
Coëtivy I.
Alphonse I.
Bijoutier I.
Saint François I.

Aldabra Group
Providence I.
Aldabra Atoll
Saint Pierre I.
Cosmoledo Atoll
Cerf I.
Farquhar Group
Astove I.

Îles Glorieuses (FRANCE)

MADAGASCAR

© Infobase Publishing

ETHIOPIA
SOMALIA
KENYA
SEYCHELLES
TANZANIA
MOZAMBIQUE
SOUTH AFRICA
MADAGASCAR
INDIAN OCEAN

AUSTRIA in March 1938 after the Germans forced the dismissal of Kurt von SCHUSCHNIGG. A few days after German troops entered the country, only hours after Seyss-Inquart's appointment, ANSCHLUSS was proclaimed and he became Austria's governor. A year later he was named deputy governor-general of occupied POLAND. Seyss-Inquart was appointed to the post of German high commissioner of the occupied NETHERLANDS in 1940, and he proved relentless in his hunt for Dutch JEWS, thousands of whom were deported and sent to Nazi CONCENTRATION CAMPS. In 1945 he was arrested by Allied troops. Sentenced to death by the NUREMBERG WAR CRIMES TRIALS, he was hanged in 1946.

Shackleton, Sir Ernest Henry

(1874–1922) English explorer, innovative and persistent and endowed with outstanding leadership qualities. Shackleton made full use of technological advances and media coverage during his polar expeditions. After several years in the merchant marine, he joined Captain Robert Falcon SCOTT's 1901 Antarctic expedition. Leading his own expedition to ANTARCTICA in 1907, he discovered the Beardmore Glacier, crossed the Polar Plateau to within 97 miles of the South Pole and took the first motion pictures of Antarctica. In addition, some of his group reached the South Magnetic Pole. His 1914 expedition to cross the Antarctic continent failed when his ship was crushed by the ice, a misfortune that allowed Shackleton to etch his name forever into the annals of personal heroism. He led his entire party almost 200 miles across the ice, then with a few companions crossed almost 800 miles of rugged seas, crossed the craggy island of South Georgia to a whaling station and eventually managed to rescue every last member of his expedition. Shackleton died during his last journey to explore the islands of the sub-Antarctic.

Shaeffer, W. A.

(1867–1946) Inventor, manufacturer. As a jewelry store operator in Fort Madison, Iowa, Shaeffer toyed with the idea of a better writing instrument. He devised a means of pulling ink into a rubber container in the handle of a pen, using a lever and suction. This ink was then delivered in a continuous flow to the pen point. This relatively simple 1912 invention revolutionized writing and resulted in the founding of the Shaeffer pen manufacturing factory. The pens have carried the Shaeffer name around the world. The business, one of the largest of its kind, has been continued by three generations of Shaeffers, who have managed to keep pace with modern developments in writing instruments of all kinds. The company is known for profit sharing and other employee considerations. (See also Ladislao BIRO.)

Shaffer, Peter Levin

(1926–) British playwright. With the production of his first play, *Five Finger Exercise* (1958), Shaffer was cited as the most promising British playwright of that year. He maintained his reputation with *The Private Ear* and *The Public Eye*, a joint production in 1962, and *Black Comedy* (1965). Perhaps his best known plays are *Equus* (1973; filmed 1977), a psychological drama examining the relationship between a repressed psychiatrist and his patient; and *Amadeus* (1979; filmed 1987), a study of the nature of creativity in the conflicts between the composers

	SEYCHELLES
1903	Seychelles becomes a British Crown colony, separate from Mauritius.
1963–64	The first political parties are formed.
1976	Following the London Constitutional Conference, the Seychelles is granted independence as a republic within the Commonwealth, with James R. Mancham as president.
1977	President Mancham is ousted in a coup led by Prime Minister France Albert René, who assumes the presidency.
1979	René enacts a new constitution, turning Sechelles into a one-party state.
1981	South African mercenaries attempt an unsuccessful coup.
1982	Mutiny by the army is foiled.
1984	In the presidential election, sole candidate France Albert René is reelected.
1985	Opposition leader Gerald Horeau is assassinated in London.
1991	Constitutional changes legalize the formation of additional political parties.
1993	A new constitution is adopted. René is elected as president against two opponents.
1998	René is reelected.
2001	René is reelected president, receiving 54.2% of the vote.
2004	René steps down; replaced by former vice president James Michel.

Mozart and Salieri. Other works include *The Royal Hunt of the Sun* (1964) and *Lettuce and Lovage* (1988). Shaffer's twin brother, Anthony, is also a playwright whose works include *Sleuth* (1970) and *Murderer* (1975).

Shahn, Ben *(1898–1969)* American artist. Born in Lithuania, this important social realist immigrated to the U.S. in 1906. He worked as a lithographer until 1930, becoming known for a series of paintings and drawings executed from 1931 to 1932 that express his outrage over the SACCO-VANZETTI CASE. One of the best known of these is *The Passion of Sacco and Vanzetti* in the collection of New York City's Whitney Museum of American Art. Shahn's concerns were overwhelmingly political and social, his approach liberal and humanistic. His keen graphic sense led him to create many notable posters and to use the mural as a medium, working with Diego RIVERA on murals at Radio City in 1933 and creating murals at the Bronx Post Office, New York City, from 1938 to 1939. Taking an interest in photography, he produced memorable images of the poverty of rural America while working for the Farm Security Administration from 1933 to 1938. Deeply affected by World War II, in the 1940s he created a moving series of paintings dealing with war-torn Europe. While remaining figurative, his last works tend to be less political and deal with subjects in a more abstract manner.

Shalamov, Varlam *(1907–1982)* Russian writer and poet. Shalamov was arrested in 1937 for declaring that Ivan BUNIN, an expatriate writer and Nobel laureate, was a classic of Russian literature. For this crime he spent 17 years in the Kolyma labor camps in eastern Siberia (see GULAG). He recounted his experiences in *Kolyma Notes,* autobiographical short stories, which found their way to the West. In the 1970s Shalamov was forced to denounce the publication of his own works abroad.

Shamir, Yitzhak *(1915–   )* Prime minister of ISRAEL (1983–84, 1986–92). Shamir immigrated to Palestine in 1935 and studied law in Jerusalem. He joined the Irgun in 1937 but left it for Lehi (the STERN GANG) in 1940 and became part of that group's leading triumvirate after Stern's assassination in 1942. Shamir was twice exiled by the mandate authorities but escaped and returned to Israel in 1948. He spent most of the next 17 years abroad as a senior Mossad operative. In 1965 he became a businessman and in 1970 joined his old Irgun rival Menachem BEGIN's Herut Party. Shamir was elected to the Knesset in 1973 and served as its speaker from 1977 to 1980, a period during which he campaigned against the CAMP DAVID agreements on the grounds that they gave too much to Egypt in exchange for too little. He served as foreign minister for three years from 1980 and took over as prime minister after Begin's resignation in 1983. He failed to lead the Likud to victory in the 1984 elections, but managed to form a coalition with Labor, which had won a narrow majority. The agreement provided for a handing over of the premiership to him halfway through the government's term in office, which occurred in October 1986. The taciturn premier, a strong supporter, on security grounds, of the Greater Israel movement, announced upon taking office that he saw as his main task "the consolidation of the Jewish presence in all parts of the Land." In 1991 Shamir participated in the Madrid peace talks with representatives of Arab states and the Palestinians. He was defeated in the elections of 1992 and was replaced as prime minister by Yetzhak RABIN of the Labor Party. Shamir resigned as the head of Likud the following year and retired from public service.

Shankar, Ravi (*1920–   *) Indian sitar player-composer. Shankar might have spent his career in relative obscurity as a lecturer at the University of California, had not BEATLE George Harrison sought him out as a sitar instructor for the song "Norwegian Wood." Rock quickly embraced the sitar's haunting and exotic sound during the late 1960s, but almost as quickly the instrument became associated with rock's idea of mysticism—which had drug-related overtones. Shankar then returned to the relatively obscure life of the sitar virtuoso. He recorded *The Sounds of India* and *The Genius of Ravi Shankar,* as well as *Live at Monterey* (1967). In 2003 Shankar received the prestigious ISPA Distinguished Artist Award.

Shankar, Uday (*1902–1977*) Indian dancer, choreographer and teacher. A leading Hindu dancer, Shankar combined classical Indian dance with a modern dance idiom and captured the attention of Western audiences with his charismatic, often erotic performances. The brother of musician Ravi SHANKAR, he initially worked with his father as a painter and producer in the theater. He devoted himself to dance after staging and dancing in Anna PAVLOVA's ballet *Radha-Krishna* (1924). He toured Europe and the U.S. with Pavlova (1924–28), then returned to India and formed his own company with which he frequently toured in Europe, the U.S. and India. Backed by British and American funding, he established the Uday Shankar Indian Culture Center to research, film and teach classical dance and music (1938). Though closed during WORLD WAR II, the center reopened in 1965.

SHAPE (Supreme Headquarters, Allied Powers in Europe) NATO headquarters in Brussels.

Shapley, Harlow (*1885–1972*) American astronomer. Shapley was born in Nashville, Missouri, and earned his Ph.D. in astronomy from Princeton in 1913. In 1921, he left the Mount Wilson Observatory in California to become head of the Harvard College Observatory, where he worked until 1952. By 1920, Shapley had determined the size and structure of the Milky Way Galaxy as well as the approximate position of our solar system within it; for this he received the nickname "the modern Copernicus." Under Shapley's leadership, the Harvard Observatory became a leading center of astronomical study and the site of important research on galaxies, binary stars and related phenomena.

sharia A body of Islamic law used by religious and political leaders in some Islamic countries to define appropriate and inappropriate behavior by their citizens. Meaning "the way" in Arabic, sharia is based on three sources: the commandments for daily life laid down in the Koran (the Islamic holy book); the Sunnah, a standardized collection of sermons, platitudes, psalms and statements by Muhammad, the prophet and founder of Islam; and *ijma,* an agreement among Islamic scholars and communities past and present about a particular issue of daily life and morals. If these three sources of sharia do not offer an explicit ruling on a particular action, then Islamic clerics and judges employ a fourth technique, known as *qiyas,* in which they closely read the Koran and the Sunnah and search for parallels between the action in their own time and the one described during the time of Muhammad and the other prophets. When they find an appropriate past parallel or situation analogous to the contemporary issue, they concur and devise a new law, which then becomes part of the *ijma.*

While sharia covers a variety of activities of daily life, it also acknowledges a clear distinction between violations of Islamic law, which are punishable by temporal powers, and those punishable only by Allah (the Arabic word for God). For instance, only human actions proscribed under sharia that are considered violations of what is *wajib,* or "obligatory," and those actions that sharia defines as expressly *haram,* or "prohibited," can be punished by followers of Islam. Additionally, sharia is not consistent throughout the Islamic world. During the past formulation of *ijma* and *qiyas* by Islamic scholars and clerics, divergent opinions have on occasion emerged, leading to the creation of an independent body of Islamic laws derived from communal consensus and interpretation of the Koran and Sunnah. As a result of such divisions, a fundamentally conservative interpretation of sharia, founded on a literal reading of the Koran and the Sunnah, has emerged and led to a very strict set of new laws codified in *ijma* and *qiyas*. In the post–cold war era, efforts by Islamic fundamentalists to apply these conservative interpretations of sharia in several Arab states have caused concern in the Western world. The U.S. government in particular has strongly opposed the emergence of Islamic theocracies ruled by a strict interpretation of the sharia, such as the TALIBAN regime in AFGHANISTAN, regarding such societies as breeding grounds for anti-Western terrorism.

Sharon, Ariel (*1928–   *) Israeli politician, minister of agriculture (1977–81), minister of defense (1981–83) and prime minister (2001–06). Born in the town of Kefar Malal in what was then the British mandate of PALESTINE, Sharon fought in the ARAB-ISRAELI WAR of 1948–49. As a general in the Israeli Defense Forces (IDF) he participated in military actions in the Suez campaign (1956), the SIX-DAY WAR (1967) and the YOM KIPPUR WAR (1973).

In 1974 he was elected to the Israeli Knesset (parliament) as a member of the Labor Party. Three years later, he left the Labor party and became a Knesset candidate of the right-wing LIKUD Party, which won a parliamentary majority in the 1977 elections and formed a government under Prime Minister Menachem BEGIN. Sharon was appointed minister of agriculture and spent the next four years promoting the establishment of government-financed Israeli settlements in the West Bank and Gaza Strip, two territories occupied by Israel after the 1967 war that were inhabited predominantly by Palestinian Arabs.

As minister of defense in 1982, Sharon ordered Israeli forces to advance into LEBANON, where the PALESTINE LIBERATION ORGANIZATION (PLO) was directing terrorist attacks against northern Israel. Sharon was reprimanded by an Israeli investigatory commission for being "indirectly responsible" for the murder of several hundred Palestinian refugees by Christian militias in Beirut and was removed from his position as defense minister. As minister of infrastructure between 1996 and 1998, Sharon increased the number of Israeli settlements in the West Bank and Gaza Strip that had begun under his earlier tenure in office. After serving as foreign minister in a Likud government in 1998–99, Sharon replaced Benjamin NETANYAHU as head of Likud after the Labor Party took power.

In September 2000 Sharon paid a visit to the TEMPLE MOUNT, an important holy shrine in both the Jewish and Islamic faiths. His visit resulted in violent street demonstrations by Palestinian youths and some Palestinian Authority (PA) security forces, which led to a new outbreak of Palestinian-led terrorist attacks against Israeli citizens (see INTIFADA II) and a new wave of reprisals against Palestinians in the West Bank and Gaza. As the violence continued into October, Labor prime minister Ehud BARAK called new elections and was defeated by Sharon. As prime minister Sharon used the IDF repeatedly to confine PA president Yasir ARAFAT to his compound. He also demonstrated a willingness to negotiate a settlement with PA authorities after the death of Arafat in 2004 and the accession of Mahmoud Abbas as head of the PA. In 2005 Sharon withdrew all Jewish settlements and IDF forces from the Gaza Strip and then, when Likud members criticized his conciliatory policy toward the Palestinians, he resigned from Likud and formed a new centrist party called Kadima (Forward) that was committed to a negotiated settlement with the PA. In 2006 Sharon suffered a severe cerebral hemorrhage and lapsed into a coma. His duties were assumed by acting prime minister Ehud Olmert, his longtime collaborator who had joined him in Kadima.

Sharp, George G. (*1874–1960*) English-born American naval architect; founder of the still-active firm of George G. Sharp, Inc., which has been responsible for the design of more than 1,500 ships, including a number of outstandingly innovative designs. Sharp was educated in Scotland and came to the U.S. in 1902. He worked for a number of shipbuilding organizations in positions of increasing importance until 1916, when he was appointed chief surveyor of the American Bureau of Shipping. In 1920 he founded his own firm in New York. The 1939 Panama Line passenger ships *Ancon, Cristobal* and *Panama* were notable for their innovative design, for their striking appearance and for their interiors (with decorative design by the office of Raymond LOEWY), which used only fireproof materials throughout. The Sharp firm was also responsible for many wartime designs. In the 1950s and 1960s, Sharp developed the first cellular containerships and the first roll-on/roll-off (RO) ships, which greatly improved the efficiency of cargo loading and unloading operations; both types are now in general use worldwide. The first nuclear-powered merchant ship, the NS *Savannah,* a ship of handsomely streamlined form that was eventually converted to an ocean research vessel, was designed by the Sharp firm. The firm continues to be a leading designer of merchant and naval ships for both U.S. and foreign clients.

Sharpton, Al(bert Charles), Jr. (*1954– *) African-American Pentecostal minister, civil rights activist, and political candidate. Born in Brooklyn, New York, Sharpton was ordained as a Pentecostal minister at the age of 10. In 1971, Reverend Sharpton founded the National Youth Movement to increase community assistance for underprivileged youths and against involvement with local drug lords, distributors and users.

In 1986, Sharpton organized protests in Howard Beach, New York, following the death of an African American who was attempting to escape a white mob. In 1987 he became one of three advisers to Tawana Brawley, an African-American teenager who alleged (falsely) that six Wappingers Falls, New York, police officers had raped and sodomized her before leaving her for dead. He also helped organize African-American protests after the 1991 Brooklyn death of a young black child hit by a Hasidic Jewish driver in a traffic accident. Sharpton led a protest campaign in 2000 after the acquittal of NYPD officers involved in the death of immigrant Amadou Diallo.

In addition to his career as a civil rights advocate, Sharpton has also repeatedly run for political office. In 1992 and 1994 he made unsuccessful bids for a U.S. Senate seat, for the mayoralty of New York City in 1997, and for the Democratic presidential nomination in 2004.

Sharpeville massacre Shootings that occurred in Sharpeville, South Africa, a black township near Johannesburg, on March 21, 1960. An estimated 20,000 unarmed demonstrators, organized by the Pan-Africanist Congress, were protesting the pass laws, APARTHEID legislation that required black South Africans to carry passbooks at all times, when police opened fire. About 70 protestors were killed and another 190 were wounded. The Sharpeville massacre remains one of the most violent single incidents in the struggle against apartheid.

Shastri, Lal Bahadur (*1904–1966*) Indian statesman, prime minister (1964–66). Born in Benares, Shastri joined Mohandas K. Gandhi's CONGRESS PARTY in 1920, and participated in numerous nonviolent protests, for which he was imprisoned on several occasions. He was elected to the central legislature in 1952, serving as minister of railways until 1956, as minister of commerce and industry (1957–61) and as minister of home affairs (1951–63). He succeeded the ailing Jawaharlal Nehru as prime minister in 1964. After the INDO-PAKISTANI WAR OF 1965, Shastri met with President AYUB KHAN and signed a peace agreement. However, he suffered a heart attack and died the following day.

Shaw, Artie (Arthur Arshawsky) (*1910–2004*) American JAZZ clarinetist and big band leader. Shaw became one of the most popular big band leaders of the late 1930s and early 1940s. Born in New Jersey, he worked for numerous bands in the 1920s and early 1930s as a clarinet sideman. His perfect clarinet technique, featuring a catchy, swinging style, made Shaw a highly popular performer. In 1937, he formed his own big band and enjoyed numerous hits through 1942, including "Begin the Beguine," "Star Dust" and "Moonglow." Shaw served in the United

States Navy during WORLD WAR II and led an overseas service big band. He gave up performing in 1955 and turned to theatrical and film production in the 1960s. His eight wives included Hollywood actresses Lana Turner and Ava Gardner.

Shaw, George Bernard (*1856–1950*) Anglo-Irish playwright and critic. A leading figure in 20th-century theater, Shaw was born in Dublin and moved to London in 1876 where he began to write and to educate himself at the British Museum. He wrote five unsuccessful novels, which include *Cashel Byron's Profession* (1886) and *An Unsocial Socialist* (1887), and ghosted articles of musical criticism, later writing under his own name for such publications such as *Dramatic Review, The World* and *The Star*. His criticism was later collected into *Shaw's Music* (1981, three volumes). He became a drama critic for *The Saturday Review* in 1895, and in his opinionated, controversial articles he championed Ibsen. These articles were collected in *Our Theatres in the Nineties* (1932, three volumes). A vegetarian who eschewed alcohol and tobacco, Shaw was also a socialist and a member of the FABIAN SOCIETY. While serving on its executive committee from 1885 to 1911, Shaw trained himself in public speaking and gave lectures on its behalf as well as contributing to and editing *Fabian Essays in Socialism* (1889). Shaw's first play, *Widower's Houses* (1892) as well as several subsequent ones, including *Arms and the Man* (1893) and *Mrs. Warren's Profession* (1899), were not well received initially. It was not until *John Bull's Other Island* (1904) that he achieved critical and popular success. Shaw's plays, carried largely by dialogue, presented contemporary moral dilemmas with characteristic "Shavian" wit. Shaw was an extremely prolific writer, and his many important works include *Man and Superman* (1903); *Major Barbara* (1905, filmed 1941); *Pygmalion* (1913), which evidences his interest in language and was adapted into the successful musical *My Fair Lady* (1956); *Heartbreak House* (1920); and *Buoyant Billions* (1948). Shaw was awarded the NOBEL PRIZE for literature in 1925. Other works include *The Intelligent Woman's Guide to Socialism and Capitalism* (1928) and *Everybody's Political What's What* (1944). Shaw married Charlotte Payne-Townshend in 1898 and remained with her until her death in 1943, although it was evidently only a companionable marriage of convenience, and he was occasionally linked with other women.

Shaw, Irwin (*1913–1984*) American popular novelist. Shaw first won acclaim for his play *Bury the Dead* (1936); his short stories of the 1930s and 1940s also won critical praise, and his World War II novel *The Young Lions* (1948) found a wide readership. Thereafter he was known as a bestselling novelist. His later books include *Rich Man, Poor Man* (1970), which was made into a television miniseries, and *Evening in Byzantium* (1973).

Shawn, Edwin Myers "Ted" (*1891–1972*) American modern dancer. Originally a divinity student, Shawn was introduced to the study of dance as therapy after an illness. In 1914, he met and married Ruth ST. DENIS, also a dancer, and together they founded the Denishawn School in Los Angeles in 1915 and later moved the school to New York City. The couple ended their personal and professional association in 1930. In 1941 he founded the JACOB'S PILLOW DANCE FESTIVAL near Lee, Massachusetts, as a summer residence/theater for his dancers and developed it into an internationally important dance center.

Shcharansky, Anatoly (*1948– *) Soviet mathematician and dissident. A leading Jewish dissident during the 1970s, Shcharansky was convicted in 1978 of espionage, treason and "anti-Soviet agitation." His case attracted much attention in the West, mobilizing human rights advocates. His supporters maintained that the charges were brought because he was an outspoken critic of Soviet policy toward Jews. He was released as part of a Soviet-American swap of alleged spies in 1986. Shcharansky immigrated to Israel, where he changed his name to Nathan Sharansky. He became active in Israeli politics, representing the interests of Russian immigrants. Sharansky has since served in the governments of three successive Israeli prime ministers—Benjamin NETANYAHU, Ehud BARAK, and Ariel SHARON—as minister of industry and trade; interior; and construction, respectively.

Shcherbitsky, Vladimir Vasilievich (*1918–1990*) Soviet politician. Known as a hard-liner, Shcherbitsky had been a member of the POLITBURO since the days of Leonid I. BREZHNEV. As long-time chief of the Ukrainian Communist Party, he was accused of suppressing information about the radiation damage from the CHERNOBYL nuclear power plant accident in the Ukraine in 1986. He was ousted from both posts in September 1989 as part of a shake-up orchestrated by Soviet leader Mikhail GORBACHEV.

Sheed, Francis Joseph (*1897–1981*) Anglo-American Roman Catholic lay theologian, writer, lecturer and publisher. Sheed founded the English publishing company Sheed & Ward in 1926 and later opened a New York branch. He published the works of major British philosophers, historians and church apologists. His best-known book, *Theology and Sanity,* became a standard theological text. He was the father of the American novelist Wilfred Sheed.

Sheeler, Charles (*1883–1965*) American painter. Born in Philadelphia, Sheeler attended that city's School of Industrial Art and the Pennsylvania Academy of the Fine Arts, studying under

Playwright and critic George Bernard Shaw
(LIBRARY OF CONGRESS, PRINTS AND PHOTOGRAPHS DIVISION)

William Merritt Chase. He traveled to Europe with his teacher and was influenced by the vivid color of FAUVISM. His early work was exhibited in the 1913 ARMORY SHOW. Sheeler is best known for paintings produced after World War I, executed in a kind of cool American CUBISM, with sleek, streamlined, volumetric shapes and subjects drawn from architecture and machinery, as well as land- and seascape. Also a skilled photographer, his style is thought to be partially derived from his immaculately photographed barns, towers and Shaker furnishings. The clean abstraction of the work of Sheeler and his contemporary Charles Demuth has been termed "precisionism" by art historians. Among his characteristic paintings are *American Landscape* (1930, Museum of Modern Art, New York City) and *California Industrial* (1957).

Sheen, Archbishop Fulton J(ohn) *(1895–1979)* American Roman Catholic clergyman, radio and television evangelist and author. In his heyday Sheen was one of the best-known church figures in the United States. He became the first regular preacher over national radio in the 1930s on *The Catholic Hour.* He later conducted the popular 1950s television series *Life Is Worth Living.* He wrote more than 60 books and pamphlets, taught philosophy at Catholic University and served as bishop of Rochester, New York, for three years before his retirement in 1969. A traditionalist, he was famous for his attacks on communism and Freudian psychoanalysis. He also espoused causes of social justice.

Shehu, Mehmet *(1913–1981)* Premier of ALBANIA (1954–81). A hard-line communist, Shehu was the closest aide of Albanian communist leader Enver HOXHA. He survived many purges and was known for his fiery temper. His death was reportedly a suicide.

Shelepin, Alexander Nikolayevich *(1918–1994)* Communist official. Having studied in Moscow, Shelepin joined the party in 1940 and worked in the Komsomol apparatus; in 1958 he was appointed first secretary of its central committee and became a member of the party central committee. He was chairman of the committee of state security

(KGB) from 1958 to 1961. He was removed from the leadership, and thus eliminated as a potential opponent to BREZHNEV, in 1975.

Shelley, Norman *(1903–1980)* British radio actor. In 1940 during the BATTLE OF BRITAIN in WORLD WAR II, Shelley was enlisted by the British government to deliver a radio broadcast version of Winston CHURCHILL's famous "We Shall Never Surrender" speech. Churchill had made the speech to Parliament, but it was not recorded. Shelley imitated Churchill's voice with such uncanny accuracy that his recording helped rally the all-but-defeated nation against Germany and stirred American public opinion. The use of Shelley remained one of the war's best-kept secrets and was not disclosed until 1979.

Shelley v. Kramer *(1948)* U.S. Supreme Court decision outlawing private, racially restrictive covenants. During the first half of the century it was common for real estate deeds to bar the sale of the property to black Americans or members of other minority groups. Although the law forbade racial discrimination, private agreements upheld it. In 1948 the Supreme Court held that while the states did not have the power to ban such private agreements, the Fourteenth Amendment barred the states from permitting their court systems to enforce these racially restrictive covenants. By its decision the Court made these covenants unenforceable.

Shen Congwen (Shen Yuehuan) *(1902–1988)* Chinese novelist; one of the most widely anthologized modern writers in English-language collections of Chinese literature. His works produced a vivid picture of life in the Chinese countryside during the chaotic warlord era of the 1920s and 1930s. *Long River,* regarded by many critics as his finest novel, appeared in 1943. In the ensuing decade, he became a victim of politics, being denounced by communists and GUOMINDANG (KUOMINTANG) supporters alike. His books were banned in Taiwan, while mainland publishing houses burned his books and destroyed the printing plates. It was not until 1978 that the Chinese government began reissuing his works, although in very limited editions.

Shepard, Alan *(1923–1998)* U.S. astronaut. On May 5, 1961, Shepard became the first American in space when he took a 15.5 minute suborbital flight for 304 miles reaching an altitude of 116 miles before landing in the Atlantic. The flight was short and sweet and effective. America had its first man in space. Shepard later recounted that the flight happened so fast that he managed only a 30-second glimpse out of the spacecraft's small window. Shepard got a better view of space 10 years later, when as commander of *APOLLO 14* (January 31–February 9, 1971) he spent two days on the surface of the moon. The only one of the original MERCURY astronauts to fly to the moon, Shepard was born in East Derry, New Hampshire, the son of a career army officer. Although his father had attended West Point, Shepard earned his B.S. from the United States Naval Academy in 1944. After service in World War II he attended the U.S. Navy Test Pilot School at Patuxent River in 1950, serving as an instructor from 1951 to 1953. After retiring from NASA and the navy in 1974, Shepard entered the private sector. In 1971 he served as a delegate to the 26th UN General Assembly.

Shepard, Sam *(1943–)* American playwright and film actor. Shepard first burst into theatrical prominence in the 1960s when he wrote a series of striking one-act plays—*Cowboys* (1964), *Rock Garden* (1964), *Chicago* (1965) and *Icarus' Mother* (1965)—that dealt movingly with the decline of the free-roaming American West and the advent of technology. *Rock Garden* was subsequently incorporated into the Kenneth Tynan Broadway hit *Oh, Calcutta!* Shepard moved on to full-length plays including *La Turista* (1966), *Operation Sidewinder* (1970), *The Tooth of Crime* (1972), *The Curse of the Starving Class* (1977), the PULITZER PRIZE winning *Buried Child* (1978), *Seduced* (1979), *True West* (1980), *Fool For Love* (1983) and *A Life of the Mind* (1986). He has also won acclaim as a film actor through his dramatic roles in *The Right Stuff* (1983) and *Country* (1984), in which he costarred with his wife, Jessica Lange. In 1986 Shepard was elected to The American Academy of Arts and Letters.

Shepherd, General Lemuel Cornick, Jr. *(1896–1990)* U.S. military leader. He was a decorated veteran of World War I, World War II and the Korean War. In 1945, he led the last land battle of World War II, defeating Japanese troops on the island of OKINAWA. Commandant of the U.S. Marine Corps from 1952 to 1955, he was the first head of the marines to serve as a member of the Joint Chiefs of Staff.

Sheppard case Sensational pair of murder trials during the 1950s and 1960s involving Cleveland surgeon Sam Sheppard, who was accused of murdering his wife. After Marilyn Sheppard was found dead in her suburban Cleveland home her husband was arrested for her murder. Sam Sheppard, who confessed during the trial to having an extramarital affair, alleged that he had been knocked unconscious by his wife's assailant. The murder trial attracted wide attention, especially in Cleveland, where emotions were inflamed by the local press. Sheppard was convicted and was sentenced to life in prison in 1954. Sheppard's supporters continued their efforts on his behalf, and he gained a new trial in 1966 after the U.S. Supreme Court threw out the first conviction because of the trial's carnival atmosphere. Sheppard was ultimately acquitted, but his life deteriorated. After a divorce and a medical malpractice suit he briefly became a professional wrestler before his death in 1970.

Sheriff, Robert Cedric *(1896–1975)* British playwright and novelist. Sherriff was a gifted and entertaining writer who enjoyed long-term success with the British public both through his fiction and his plays. He first made his mark with his play *Journey's End* (1928), an incisive portrayal of life in the trenches during WORLD WAR I. Sherriff continues to be best remembered for his plays, which include *Badger's Green* (1930), *Home at Seven* (1950), *The White Carnation* (1953), *The Long Sunset* (1955) and *The Telescope* (1957).

Sherwood, Bobby *(1914–1981)* American JAZZ trumpeter, band leader, composer and musical arranger of the BIG BAND era. In the 1930s Sherwood was an arranger and conductor for the radio shows of Bing CROSBY and Eddie Cantor. He also worked for Hollywood film studios, writing musical arrangements for stars such as Fred ASTAIRE, Judy GARLAND, Jeanette MacDonald and Nelson Eddy. As a trumpeter, he played with important jazz figures including Artie SHAW, Zoot SIMS and Stan GETZ.

Sherwood, Robert Emmet *(1896–1955)* American playwright. Born in New Rochelle, New York, Sherwood attended Harvard, becoming a magazine writer, a film critic from 1920 to 1928 and an editor at *Life* from 1924 to 1928. He achieved success with his first play, the comedy *The Road to Rome* (1927), but became best known for dramas such as *The Petrified Forest* (1935), *Idiot's Delight* (1936), *Abe Lincoln in Illinois* (1938) and *There Shall Be No Night* (1941), the last three of which all won PULITZER PRIZES. During WORLD WAR II, Sherwood served with the Office of War Information and was a speech writer for Franklin D. ROOSEVELT. He wrote of the president and his adviser Harry HOPKINS in the biographical *Roosevelt and Hopkins* (1948), another Pulitzer Prize winner. Also active in films, Sherwood was the recipient of an ACADEMY AWARD for his moving script *The Best Years of Our Lives* (1946).

Shevardnadze, Eduard *(1928–)* Soviet foreign minister. Shevardnadze joined the COMMUNIST PARTY OF THE USSR as a young man and began to advance in the party bureaucracy in his native Georgia, holding the posts of minister of internal affairs and secretary general there. In 1976, he was appointed to the central committee of the national party and in 1978 was named to the Politburo. In July 1985 he was named Soviet foreign minister. Over the next five years, Shevardnadze played an important role in drafting foreign policy, in improving Soviet relations with China and Japan and in conducting arms control negotiations with the U.S. In addition, he worked doggedly but unsuccessfully to find a negotiated settlement of the war in Afghanistan. On December 20, 1990, Shevardnadze abruptly resigned as foreign minister, saying he believed the Soviet Union to be on the verge of succumbing to a right-wing dictatorship. Following the breakup of the USSR in December 1991, Shevardnadze returned to Georgia, where he served as chairman of the new national parliament and acting head of state (1992–95), and president of Georgia (1995–2003). During his 11 years in power, Shevardnadze became known for his pro-Western stances on international security issues, such as the Russian effort to suppress the separatist movement in CHECHNYA. Following parliamentary elections on November 2, 2003, which international observers and opposition leaders denounced as fraudulent, Shevardnadze announced his resignation on November 23, 2003, after a meeting with opposition leaders.

Shikanai, Nobutaka *(1911–1990)* Japanese media entrepreneur. He built the Fujisankei Communications Group into JAPAN's largest media and entertainment conglomerate before turning it over to his son-in-law in 1989. He often generated controversy with his right-wing views, and with such actions as paying former U.S. president Ronald REAGAN and his wife Nancy $2 million to visit Japan in 1989. He was also a collector of modern art who built one of the most famous museums in Japan.

Shiki, Masaoka (Masaoka Tsunenori) *(1867–1902)* Japanese poet, essayist, critic. Shiki abandoned his studies at Tokyo Imperial University for a career as a journalist. Although he contracted tuberculosis, he continued to work as a war correspondent during the Sino-Japanese War of 1894–95. Thereafter, he was bedridden and in continual pain. Shiki is known as a reformer of the traditional forms of Japanese poetry, the haiku and the tanka, and as the best haiku writer of modern times. He introduced colloquial speech and contemporary subjects to the tradition. He published several influential studies, including *The Essence of the Haiku* (1895) and *Buson: The Haiku Poet*. The latter served to popularize the work of the 18th-century poet and painter Buson. Shiki's collected works comprise 22 volumes.

Shimazaki Toson *(1872–1943)* Japanese writer. Shimazaki began his literary career as a poet, but achieved greatest recognition as a novelist and was an extremely influential figure in 20th-century Japanese fiction. His classic work *Hakai* (1906, trans. *The Broken Commandment,* 1974) is a work of profound social concern that is considered Japan's first naturalistic novel. His later fiction is largely autobiographical in character.

Shin Bet Israeli security service.

Shingo, Shigeo *(1900–1990)* Japanese industrial management specialist. While with the Toyota Motor Co., he and Taiichi OHNO developed the "just-in-time" manufacturing system, whereby inventories were kept deliberately low to reduce costs and increase flexibility. He was also credited with promoting the "poka yoka" system of mistake-proofing, which provided feedback to managers to help them identify production problems.

Shining Path (Sendero Luminoso) Terrorist organization in Peru. Founded in the 1960s by a left-wing college professor named Abimael Guzmán, the Shining Path took up arms against the Peruvian government in 1980 in the name of Maoist revolution. The organization exploited the resentments of Peru's impoverished indigenous peoples against the landed oligarchy that had long held the economic and political reigns of power. It often cooperated with another left-wing terrorist group, Tupac Amaru (named after an 18th-century opponent of Spanish colonial rule). In the early 1990s it staged attacks on government buildings, assassinated government officials, and engaged in indiscriminate bombings in populated areas. To raise funds for its cause, the Shining Path kidnapped wealthy people for ransom, robbed banks, and engaged in drug trafficking. As a result of the Shining Path's terrorist campaign, more than 30,000 people died and countless were injured. In 1992 President Alberto Fujimori cracked down on the movement by unconstitutional means: He disbanded the congress and courts as obstacles to his counterinsurgency drive and proceeded to wage a pitiless campaign against the guerrilla movement. In 1992 Guzmán was arrested and jailed (after convictions by military courts) along with thousands of other suspects. Though Fujimori's crackdown resulted in a sharp decline in terrorist activity, many innocent people

were imprisoned, and opposition to his authoritarian rule grew. After Fujimori went into exile in Japan, the Peruvian courts struck down the antiterrorist laws under which he had operated and ordered retrials in civilian courts to determine the innocent and the guilty. In recent years Shining Path has dwindled to what experts estimate to be only a few hundred dedicated members who operate in remote rural areas.

Shinn, Everett *(1873–1953)* American painter. Born in Woodstown, New Jersey, Shinn attended the Pennsylvania Academy of the Fine Arts. Settling in New York City, he became the youngest member of the realist group known as The EIGHT. Unlike other Ashcan School figures who tended to paint grim urban scenes, Shinn gravitated toward bustling panoramas of contemporary street life and theatrical tableaus painted in a vivid, impressionist-influenced style. His exuberant theater scenes include *London Hippodrome* (1902, Art Institute of Chicago) and *London Music Hall* (Metropolitan Museum of Art, New York City). Shinn is also known for his lively murals and magazine illustrations.

Shinwell, Emanuel, Lord *(1884–1986)* British politician. A combative veteran of Britain's trades union movement, Shinwell became a leading LABOUR PARTY politician and held three successive cabinet posts as minister of fuel and power, war secretary and minister of defense in the government headed by Prime Minister Clement ATTLEE. After serving for many years in the House of Commons, Shinwell gave up his seat in 1970 and entered the House of Lords as a life peer. He became disillusioned with Labour's leftward drift in the 1970s and from 1982 sat in the Lords as an independent. His 100th birthday, in October 1984, was celebrated in grand style by the House of Lords, and he became the first centenarian to address either house of Parliament.

Shipov, Dimitri Nikolayevich *(1851–1920)* Liberal politician. Chairman of the Moscow Zemstvo, Shipov organized unofficial congresses of zemstvo representatives in the 1890s and 1900s. In 1905 he was one of the founders and 10 leaders of the OCTOBRIST Party, and in

the following year, a leader of the party of peaceful renovation.

Shirer, William L. *(1904–1993)* American journalist and author. Shirer began working for the Paris edition of the NEW YORK HERALD-TRIBUNE and later served in Paris as correspondent for the *Chicago Tribune.* In 1937, he was hired by William R. MURROW for CBS, where he worked as a commentator until 1947. Shirer reported on the ANSCHLUSS and the German army's invasion of France. He was also a columnist for the *New York Herald-Tribune* from 1942 to 1948. Shirer is the author of the acclaimed *Berlin Diary* (1941) and *The Rise and Fall of the Third Reich* (1960), which won a National Book Award.

Shklovsky, Iosif Samuilovich *(1916–1985)* Soviet astrophysicist. Widely known for his speculations on alien life, Shklovsky led the USSR's search for extraterrestrial intelligence. As a theoretical researcher, he was the first scientist to propose an explanation for the strange light emanating from the Crab Nebula.

Shlonsky, Abraham *(1900–1973)* Israeli poet and translator. Born in Russia, Shlonsky moved to Palestine in 1921, becoming one of the leading modernist poets writing in the Hebrew language. Shlonsky is also known as an editor and as a sensitive translator, rendering the work of European masters such as Shakespeare and Pushkin into Hebrew.

Shockley, William Bradford *(1910–1989)* American physicist known for his invention of the TRANSISTOR and for his controversial theories on blacks. In 1956 Shockley shared the NOBEL PRIZE for physics with John BARDEEN and Walter H. BRATTAIN for the work they did at Bell Laboratories on the invention of the transistor. In the 1950s the device revolutionized all forms of electronics, from high technology to consumer goods, by allowing the development of faster, better, smaller and cheaper products. In the 1970s, however, Shockley began to alienate his colleagues and anger the public with his assertions that blacks were genetically inferior to whites and should be encouraged to volunteer for sterilization.

He sued the *Atlanta Constitution* after a 1980 column in the newspaper compared his suggestion to Nazi experiments in GENETIC ENGINEERING. He eventually won his case, but was awarded only $1 in damages. At the time of his death, Shockley was professor emeritus of electrical engineering at Stanford University.

Shoemaker, Willie (1931–2003)

William Lee Shoemaker—better known as "Willie," "Bill" and "The Shoe"—is widely considered the greatest jockey in the history of American racing. Twenty-five ounces at birth, the diminutive Shoemaker never topped 95 pounds, but he had a legendary ability to guide thoroughbred racehorses across the finish line in first place without needing to use a forceful whip hand. He rode the first of his 8,833 winners in 1949, and his last in 1990, winning $123 million in purses. In those 41 years, he won the Kentucky Derby four times, the Preakness twice and the Belmont five times. At the age of 54, he became the oldest rider ever to win the Derby. Perhaps his most famous Derby ride was the one he lost in 1957; riding Gallant Man to seeming victory, Shoemaker misjudged the Churchill Downs finish line and began to rein in his mount with 1/16 of a mile remaining in the race. In 1990, Shoemaker retired to pursue a career as a trainer. An automobile accident in 1991 left him paralyzed. Shoemaker retired as a trainer that same year.

Sholokhov, Mikhail Alexandrovich

(1905–1984) Soviet author. Born in a small Cossack village in the Don region, Sholokhov was educated in Moscow and worked as a teacher, clerk and journalist. In 1920 he started to publish sketches and joined several literary circles. The start of his literary career was boosted by Alexander Serafimovich's help. In 1926 Sholokhov is thought to have begun his famous trilogy, *Tales of the Don,* although it has been alleged that he did not in fact write it. *The Quiet Don* was published in 1926–40, *And Quiet Flows the Don* in 1934 and *The Don Flows to the Sea* in 1940. A member of the Communist Party from 1931, he was elected to the Soviet Academy of Sciences, and later to the central committee of the Soviet Union. From 1946 he served as a deputy to the Supreme Soviet. He was awarded the NOBEL PRIZE for literature in 1965. He later launched an attack on Andrei SINYAVSKY. (See also SOCIALIST REALISM.)

Shostakovich, Dmitri Dmitrievich

(1906–1975) Dmitri Shostakovich is widely regarded as the most significant Soviet composer of the 20th century. A graduate of the Petrograd (St. Petersburg) Conservatory (1926), Shostakovich first won attention with his graduation piece, the First Symphony (1926). His career subsequently mirrored the tumultuous history of the USSR and the dilemma of an artist torn between serving the dictates of a mass ideology and his own personal vision. Shostakovich alternately found himself acclaimed as a great "people's artist" and denounced for straying from the dictates of the Communist Party. The quality of his music often reflects its political content: His "public" works tend to be trite and bombastic, while his more personal music is often searing and intense. His Second and Third Symphonies, celebrating events in Soviet history, were well received, but his 4th was banned because of its originality, as was his opera *Lady MacBeth of Mtensk* (1934). His official reputation was restored with the stirring Fifth Symphony (1937), among the most popular of his 15 symphonies. His Seventh ("Leningrad"), composed during the World War II SIEGE OF LENINGRAD, was acclaimed as a portrayal of that city's beleaguered defenders. However, his Eighth Symphony (1943) was attacked by ZHDANOV at the 1948 Communist Party

Russian composer Dmitri Shostakovich (LIBRARY OF CONGRESS, PRINTS AND PHOTOGRAPHS DIVISION)

Congress, and STALIN himself accused Shostakovich (along with PROKOFIEV and KHACHATURIAN) of "formalism." Likewise, his Thirteenth Symphony ("Babi Yar," 1962), a choral setting of poems by Yevtushenko, was criticized by KHRUSHCHEV and banned because of its implications of Soviet ANTI-SEMITISM. Among his most enduring works are the Tenth Symphony (1953) and Eighth String Quartet (1962). His son **Maksim Shostakovich** was a noted conductor who emigrated to the West.

Show Boat

Classic Broadway musical show, one of the landmarks of the modern stage. Novelist Edna FERBER had never seen a show boat (or the Mississippi River, for that matter) when she began the story in 1924. It recounted the adventures of the show boat *Cotton Blossom,* and a gallery of diverse characters, including the comic Cap'n Andy, the lovely Magnolia, the dashing gambler Gaylord Ravenal, the black ship's hand, Joe (originally "Jo") and the tragic mulatto Julie. The Broadway musical adaptation by composer Jerome KERN, librettist Oscar. HAMMERSTEIN II and producer Florenz Ziegfeld made theater history at its premiere at the Ziegfeld Theater in New York, December 27, 1927. Contrasting with the typically light and fluffy musical show of the day, *Show Boat* had controversial subject matter—miscegenation, alcoholism and desertion—and an unusually tight integration of song and story. "Old Man River," "Make Believe," and "Can't Help Lovin' That Man" became standards. Actress Helen Morgan was an overnight success as Julie, and revivals in 1929 and 1932, respectively, made stars of Irene DUNNE as Magnolia and Paul ROBESON as Joe. There have been three movie versions, two for Universal in 1929 and 1936, and one for MGM in 1951. However, according to the show's historian, Miles Kreuger, it was not until an EMI/Angel recording in 1989 that the original version was restored. "Many songs were cut over the years," Kreuger says, "as were most of the racial (some would say racist) vernacular common to the time period depicted in the story. Unlike other classics, *Oklahoma!* and *Carousel,* for example, there has been no 'original' version extant until now." While the model for Ferber's show boat, the *James Adams Floating Theatre,* sank in 1928, happily the musical show, freshly refurbished, continues to sail on.

Shriver, Sargent (Robert Sargent Shriver) *(1915–)*

American public official. Born in Westminster, Maryland, Shriver attended Yale University, graduating from its law school in 1941. He served in WORLD WAR II and was a magazine editor before becoming a business associate of Joseph P. KENNEDY, whose daughter, Eunice, he later married. Business manager for his brother-in-law John F. KENNEDY's presidential campaign, Shriver became the first director of the PEACE CORPS (1961–66). He also held the office of director of the Office of Economic Opportunity under President Lyndon B. JOHNSON from 1964 to 1968. He was ambassador to France from 1968 to 1970. After vice-presidential nominee Thomas EAGLETON withdrew from the campaign in 1972, Shriver became George MCGOVERN's running mate in his unsuccessful bid for the presidency. From 1990 to 2003 Shriver served as chairman of the board of the Special Olympics. Throughout his tenure Shriver continued to receive awards and commendations in recognition of his civic contributions, such as the 1994 Presidential Medal of Freedom from U.S. president William Jefferson CLINTON and the Distinguished American Award from the John F. Kennedy Library and Foundation. After his retirement from the Special Olympics in 2003, his son-in-law, California governor Arnold Schwarzenegger, reappointed Shriver to the State Park and Recreation Commission, a post Shriver had held previously since 2001.

Shukairy, Ahmed *(1907–1980)*

First head of the PALESTINE LIBERATION ORGANIZATION (PLO). Shukairy worked in the ARAB LEAGUE (1951–57) and served as SAUDI ARABIA's ambassador to the UNITED NATIONS (1957–62). A leading hard-line opponent of Arab peace with ISRAEL, he was elected head of the PLO when it was created in 1964. He held the post until after the disastrous Arab losses to Israel in the SIX-DAY WAR (1967).

Shula, Don *(1930–)*

American professional football player (1951–57) and coach (1963–96). Shula graduated from John Carroll University in Cleveland, Ohio, where he played offensive running back in 1951. Shula began his career as a professional player in the National Football League (NFL) when he was signed by the Cleveland Browns and became a defensive cornerback. After a brief career with Cleveland, the Baltimore Colts and the Washington Redskins, Shula retired from the NFL in 1957 to seek a coaching position in college football.

In 1958 he was hired as an assistant coach for one year by the University of Virginia. After a similar one-year stint at the University of Kentucky, Shula served as defensive coordinator for the Detroit Lions of the NFL for three seasons. In 1963 he was named head coach of the Baltimore Colts, becoming the youngest man to hold that position in the NFL. During his seven years as the Colts' head coach (1963–69), Shula won an impressive 72.8% of his games (with a win-loss-tie record of 73–26–4). With acclaimed veteran quarterback Johnny Unitas calling the plays, Shula led the Colts to four postseason appearances, including two berths in the NFL Championship Game in 1964 (renamed the Super Bowl in 1967) and 1968. Shula left Baltimore at the end of the 1969 season to become head coach of the Miami Dolphins, a post he occupied until his retirement. At Miami Shula helped found one of the most dominant dynasties in NFL history, reaching the Super Bowl five times (1971–73, 1982, and 1984), and winning it twice (1972 and 1973). In 1972 his Miami Dolphins became the only NFL team ever to win all its regular season and postseason games. On November 14, 1993, Shula won his 325th professional game as a head coach, surpassing George Halas's record for the most career wins. In 1996 after finishing his 26th season at Miami, Shula retired from coaching with a career regular season record of 328 wins, 156 losses and 6 ties. In 1997 Shula was unanimously voted in and inducted into the Pro Football Hall of Fame.

shuttle diplomacy

Mediation between conflicting parties that involves constant travel by a representative from one antagonist to the other in order to achieve a settlement. Alternatively, the representative may be a third party, as was the case with Henry KISSINGER and Philip Habib on behalf of the U.S. in attempting to mediate in the Arab-Israeli conflict.

Finnish composer Jean Sibelius

Sibelius, Jean (Julius Christian Jean Sibelius) *(1865–1957)*

Finnish composer. Born in Tavastehus, Sibelius abandoned the study of law for music. He was educated at the conservatories of Helsinki, Berlin and Vienna. His early compositions reflect the influence of late-romantic German composers and of Tchaikovsky. Many of these works, including *En Saga* (1892), *The Swan of Tuonela* (1893), *Finladia* (1900) and the First (1899) and Second Symphonies (1902) employ Finnish folk music or embody national themes. Coinciding with the rise of Finnish nationalism, these compositions came to be regarded as anthems of the Finnish resistance to Russian rule; they established Sibelius as FINLAND's leading composer and one of its foremost citizens. In 1897 the Finnish government awarded Sibelius a lifetime grant that allowed him to devote his time to composing. Sibelius's output includes seven symphonies, a violin concerto (1903), tone poems, chamber works and music for theater. His later symphonies, with their austere textures and mysterious sense of foreboding, rank among the most original musical accomplishments of the 20th century. Sibelius gave up composing after his tone poem *Tapiola* (1926) and spent the remaining 30 years of his life at his country home (Jarvenpaa) as an international but secluded celebrity. For many years, musicians and audiences speculated about an "eighth symphony" that Sibelius was supposedly composing, but this work never materialized. A 1935 poll identified Sibelius as American audiences' favorite composer; later, his reputation went into decline, except in Finland and Britain. Sibelius is now widely regarded as one of the most significant symphonic composers of the 20th century.

Siberia Geographically a part of Asia, politically most of Siberia belongs to Russia. This northern third of Asia, from the Ural Mountains to the Pacific Ocean, saw little settlement by Russians until construction of the Trans-Siberian Railroad (1891–1905). An autonomous government, formed in 1918 after the RUSSIAN REVOLUTION OF 1917, was overthrown by the counterrevolutionary Admiral KOLCHAK. With the aid of an Allied Expeditionary Force, Kolchak's WHITES held Siberia until 1920, when it came decisively under communist control. During WORLD WAR II entire industrial plants were moved from European Russia to Siberia to escape capture and destruction by the invading Germans. Siberia had long been a dreaded place of political exile and imprisonment—first under the czars and subsequently under the communists. During the rule of STALIN, Siberian labor camps were swelled with prisoners numbering into the millions—many of whom did not survive to return to their homes.

Sidra Crisis, Gulf of On August 19, 1981, a pair of U.S. Navy F-14 jet fighters downed two Libyan SU-22s in the Mediterranean Sea over the Gulf of Sidra, about 60 miles from the Libyan coast. Libya claimed that part of the Gulf of Sidra as its territory, and Libyan leader QADDAFI had proclaimed a "line of death" protecting the area. The U.S. considered the area international waters. The confrontation occurred in the final hours of a two-day U.S. Navy military exercise in the Mediterranean and in the northern part of the Gulf of Sidra.

Siegfried Line German defense system in the west, running from the Swiss border to Kleve in North Rhine–Westphalia, opposite the Netherlands. Set up by Nazi Germany in the 1930s, it was named after the hero of Wagner's

Ring Cycle—reflecting Adolf HITLER'S devotion to Wagner, Teutonic legend and the dream of greater German glory. The Siegfried Line ran more or less parallel to the Rhine River and, in its southern reaches, faced France's MAGINOT LINE. It was not breached by the Allies until the last months of WORLD WAR II. A popular British wartime song scoffed at this much-vaunted symbol of German military might, promising that the Allies would "hang out our washing on the Siegfried Line."

Sienkiewicz, Henryk (1846–1916) Polish novelist, short-story writer and essayist. A prolific writer, Sienkiewicz had a strong Polish and Roman Catholic outlook on life. He was highly regarded during his lifetime, and received the NOBEL PRIZE for literature in 1905. Today he is mainly remembered for his historical novel *Quo Vadis?* (1896) and for a trilogy of novels about 17th-century Poland.

Siepi, Cesare (1923–) Italian bass. Born in Milan, Siepi won a national vocal competition at 18 and made his operatic debut in 1941. During World War II, he escaped conscription into the German army by fleeing to Switzerland. He returned to Italy in 1945 and began singing at La Scala when the Milan opera house reopened in 1946; he made his Metropolitan Opera debut in 1950. Spending over two decades at the Metropolitan, Siepi became one of the company's principal bassos and was particularly noted for his performances of the title roles in *Don Giovanni, The Marriage of Figaro* and *Boris Godunov*, as well as Mephistopheles in *Faust*. After his concert debut in Verdi's *Requiem* (1951), he also made numerous appearances in recital.

Sierra Club American-based environmentalist and preservationist group (1892–). Formed on May 28, 1892, the Sierra Club was named after the

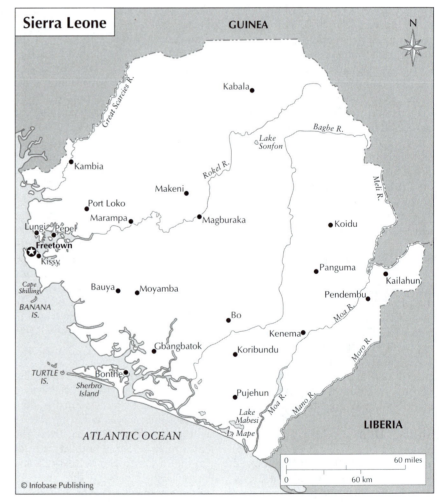

Sierra Nevada Mountains, where one of the club's founding members and its inaugural president, John Muir, led public outings in an effort to make Americans more aware of the need to conserve the country's natural resources. In particular Muir wanted the group to promote recreational visits by the American public to Yosemite National Park (established in 1890) because he and other founding members believed that the natural beauty of Yosemite would convert Americans to the Sierra Club's preservationist cause. Since its creation, the Sierra Club has sought to preserve and occasionally extend federally protected lands. Throughout its earlier years, the club focused its efforts on preserving regions in the western U.S., such as its 1907 effort to prevent the erection of a dam in the Hetch Hetchy Valley in Yosemite Park. In 1916, after repeated efforts, the Sierra Club helped convince Congress to establish the National Park Service, which was charged with managing areas like Yosemite. In 1964 the club helped persuade Congress to pass the Wilderness Act, which gave the federal government the authority to protect national wildlife lands from encroachment.

In 1970, Sierra Club members launched a similar lobbying effort that helped create the Environmental Protection Agency (EPA). By 2003 the Sierra Club's membership had increased to 700,000.

In addition to petitioning Congress to prevent the placement of mechanical works—such as dams—in wildlife areas, the Sierra Club repeatedly lobbied state and federal lawmakers to prevent industries from gaining access to natural resources located on protected lands. In 1991 it successfully lobbied Congress to defeat the Johnston-Wallop Act, which would have opened the Alaskan Arctic National Wildlife Refuge to exploitation by oil and natural gas companies. In 2001, the Sierra Club launched a similar effort when President George W. BUSH announced that he would seek congressional approval for allowing natural gas and oil extraction from Alaska in an effort to reduce dependence on foreign energy sources.

Sierra Leone Sierra Leone, bordered by Guinea and Liberia, covers an area of 27,692 square miles on the West African coast. Originally a British Crown colony, it was granted independence in 1961 and became a republic within the COMMONWEALTH in 1971. Economic problems and rioting led President Siaka Stevens (1971–85) to declare a state of emergency in 1977 and again in 1981. A new constitution providing for a one-party state was approved in 1978. Economic instability continued to plague the country during the presidency of General Joseph Momoh (1985–1992), and an economic state of emergency was imposed in 1987 after strikes by public employees. In 1991 an eight-year civil war began when the Revolutionary United Front (RUF) began a guerrilla campaign against the government. The conflict ended as the result of a 1999 peace accord in which RUF leaders were promised government positions and exemptions from war crimes trials. However, UN forces sent in to enforce the July agreement came under fire in April 2000, and several UN peacekeepers were taken hostage by various rebel groups. By May 2001 the UN, with the aid of a British-trained Sierra Leone army, began disarming rebels according to the 1999 peace agreement. Eleven months later, the UN began

SIERRA LEONE	
1961	Sierra Leone becomes an independent country within the Commonwealth of Nations.
1971	Under the new constitution, Sierra Leone becomes a republic within the Commonwealth, with Siaka Stevens as president.
1978	Constitutional referendum approves new constitution allowing for only one political party.
1985	President Stevens steps down and nominates General Joseph Saidu Momoh as his successor; Momoh is installed as president.
1987	Momoh declares state of economic emergency after strikes by public employees.
1991	Civil war is waged by the Revolutionary United Front against the government.
1999	The Lomé Peace Accord, between the rebel AFRC (Armed Forces Revolutionary Council) and the government, is signed in July.
2000	Several hundred UN peacekeeping troops taken hostage by the rebels.
2001	UN forces begin disarming the rebels.
2002	First elections since the end of the civil war are held on May 14. Kabbah is elected president by a landslide.
2004	UN-backed war crimes tribunal opens.
2005	The last UN peacekeeping troops leave Sierra Leone.

withdrawing its forces. After the creation of a new constitution and national elections in May 2002, Ahmad Tejan Kabbah and his Sierra Leone People's Party emerged as the dominant political force in the nation. Under Kabbah's leadership, Sierra Leone has cooperated with the June 2004 UN-led war crimes trials of senior military officials in the nation's long and bloody civil war.

Signoret, Simone (Simone Kaminker) *(1921–1985)* One of France's most renowned actresses, over the course of a career that spanned four decades, Signoret won the 1960 ACADEMY AWARD for best actress for the film *Room at the Top*. She gave other notable performances in such films as *Diabolique, Ship of Fools* and *Madame Rosa*. She married actor-singer Yves MONTAND in 1951. Their left-wing political activities prevented them from entering the U.S. during the 1950s. During the last decade of her life, she also published several books, the last of which, *Adieu, Voldia,* was a best seller.

Sikkim Tiny Himalayan country tucked between China to the north, Nepal to the west and India to the south. Officially a Buddhist state, it was a British protectorate until the partition of British INDIA in 1947. A treaty made it an Indian protectorate; in 1975 Sikkim's ruler was pressured into accepting a constitution that reduced his power and made Sikkim an associated state of India.

Sikorski, Władysław *(1881–1943)* Polish general and statesman. Born in Galicia, Sikorski studied engineering at the Universities of Cracow and Lvov. He fought in WORLD WAR I, and in the postwar period held a number of cabinet posts (1922 to 1925). Distrusted by Premier PIŁSUDSKI for his democratic sympathies, he was retired from the army in 1926 and dismissed from public service two years later. After Germany's conquest of Poland in 1939, Sikorski escaped to France, became premier of the Polish government in exile and organized an army that, under his command, fought on the side of the Allies during WORLD WAR II. In 1941 he restored Poland's diplomatic relations with the USSR, but broke them off again after the KATYN massacre. He was killed in an airplane crash at Gibralter while on a trip to inspect Polish forces in the Mediterranean.

Sikorsky, Igor Ivanovich *(1889–1972)* Russian-American engineer. Sikorsky was born in Kiev and emigrated to the U.S. in 1919. In 1913 he had produced the Bolsche, the first multi-engined airplane. He is best remembered for his design and production of single-rotor helicopters, which he began producing in the U.S. in 1940.

silent film A general term designating the years of cinema history before the advent of the TALKING PICTURE—from the first experiments in photography and projection in the mid-1890s to the adoption of mechanically synchronized sound by the industry after 1927. The descriptive terms used for the medium during these years tell a "rags to riches" story, as the sneering epithets of "flickers" and "galloping tintypes" were replaced by more stuffy terms, like "photoplay."

In many important ways the silent film period developed and consolidated the practices and effects used in modern cinema. By 1915, with the epoch-marking appearance of D. W. GRIFFITH's *The BIRTH OF A NATION,* the movies were making the transition from a hand-me-down orphan of the theater—slavishly imitating the business practices and entertainment formulas of the popular stage and vaudeville (the exhibition house circuits, the "star system," the wholesale takeover of the most popular stories and plays)—to an autonomous and powerful industry, boasting of huge, vertically integrated studios and theater chains, internationally known performers like Charles CHAPLIN and Mary PICKFORD and a growing critical acceptance in newspapers and magazines. With the last great silent pictures, like *Napoleon* (Abel GANCE, 1927), *The Passion of Joan of Arc* (Carl DREYER, 1928), *The General Line* (Sergei EISENSTEIN, 1929) and *The Crowd* (King VIDOR, 1928), the film medium had fully matured. Not only were technical processes familiar today already being exploited—color, 3-D, wide screen, experiments in synchronized sound, hand-held cameras and telephoto lenses, artificial lighting, etc.—but also the aesthetic foundations of image and montage were being formulated by poets and thinkers like Vachel LINDSAY and Hugo Munsterberg in America, Louis Delluc in France and Lev KULESHOV in Russia.

But, as historian Kevin Brownlow has observed, the silent film was not merely a prologue to the modern sound film; rather, it was a medium with its own unique identity. Without dialogue and with limited use of intertitles as a substitute and for commentary, the burden of storytelling and characterization had to be borne by gesture, pantomine, movement and sophisticated pictorial effect devices (split-screen, dissolve, superimposition, etc.). Further, before the standardization after 1928 of a 24-frame-per-second film speed (necessary for the new, synchronized-sound systems of motor-driven cameras and projectors), cinematographers captured the action by hand-cranking their cameras, varying from 12 to 28 frames per second. This flexibility, says Brownlow, "allowed the cameraman to slow down or speed up the action during shooting, sometimes *within the shot*." The results are seen, most typically, in the slapstick "fast motion" chases of the Keystone Kops and the surreal "slow motion" dream sequences of René CLAIR and Abel Gance.

Each country made its own contribution to the silent film. By 1905 France, Great Britain and America were making popular documentary and narrative films, seen in the work of the LUMIÈRE BROTHERS and Georges MELIES, Cecil HEPWORTH and Edwin S. Porter. Denmark and Italy led the field by 1913 in elaborate spectacles and costume pictures. America dominated world markets during World War I with the ambitious productions of Griffith and the star vehicles of Chaplin and Pickford. In the 1920s Germany and Russia achieved their own golden ages with the expressionist drama of Fritz LANG and the revolutionary masterpieces of Eisenstein and PUDOVKIN. And in France René Clair and Abel Gance made movies in the SURREALISM and DADA modes.

The term *silent film* is misleading, since from the very beginning most motion pictures—including animation, newsreels and short subjects—had some kind of sound/musical component. Mood-inducing music was performed during the filming; "live" actors frequently spoke their lines from positions behind the screen during projections; adapted and original scores were written for most of the pictures; and musicians—ranging from pianists to full symphony orchestras—accompanied performances with scores specially composed for a given program. Most countries experimented with mechanically synchronized sound.

Tragically, sporadic and careless restoration of silent films has left us little of their original beauty and power. Some commentators, forced back upon their recollections, envelop the period with hazy nostalgia and false romanticism. Others, viewing today's oft-duplicated prints struck from deteriorating negatives projected at the wrong speeds (and sans music), encounter only shadows of shadows, gesticulating images mutely pleading for our attention. The reality in both instances was far different, concludes Brownlow: "The silent film was not only a vigorous popular art, it was a universal language—Esperanto for the eyes."

Silesia A region of east-central Europe now divided among GERMANY, POLAND and the CZECH REPUBLIC. A Prussian province until WORLD WAR I, most of Silesia was given to the new nation of Poland after the war. Nazi Germany took it back during WORLD WAR II, until the Red Army rolled through in 1945. The POTSDAM CONFERENCE of 1945 confirmed Polish sovereignty over most of Silesia, but post-war Polish-German tensions saw a major exodus of Silesia's German-speaking peoples to the west. In 1972 West Germany renounced all claims to Silesia. The region contains considerable coal and iron deposits.

Silkin, John (John Ernest Silkin) (1923–1987) British LABOUR PARTY politician. As a member of Parliament, Silkin represented Deptford in southeast London from 1963 until his death in 1987. Silkin was chief government whip from 1966 to 1969. Between 1969 and 1979, he served as minister of public buildings and works, minis-

ter of planning and local government and minister of agriculture.

Silkin, Lord (Samuel Charles Silkin) (1918–1988) British attorney general from 1974 to 1979 during the WILSON and CALLAGHAN governments. Silkin was a LABOUR PARTY member of Parliament for many years. In 1975 he advised the Wilson government to attempt to halt the publication of the *Crossman Diaries* by the *Sunday Times*. He also declined to prosecute post office workers threatening to boycott mail destined for SOUTH AFRICA. He refused to allow a private prosecution of what would have been an illegal strike, a position that was ultimately vindicated.

Silkwood, Karen (1946–1974) American nuclear safety advocate. A laboratory technician at the Kerr-McGee Corporation plutonium plant in Cimarron, Oklahoma, Silkwood began investigating safety practices and regulations at the plant and became an active labor organizer. In November 1974, Silkwood discovered she had been contaminated by radiation whose source was plutonium found in her apartment. She was killed in an automobile accident on November 13, 1974, while on her way to meet with a reporter from *The New York Times* and a union official to present her allegations of safety violations. Many felt that the plutonium had been planted in her apartment to intimidate her and that Kerr-McGee may have been responsible for her death. In 1979 a federal jury in Oklahoma City awarded $10.5 million in damages to her estate, ruling that her contamination had resulted from Kerr-McGee's negligence. Silkwood's death and the subsequent lawsuit galvanized labor and environmental groups, and gave rise to a growing antinuclear movement. The film *Silkwood* (1983) dramatized her story.

Sillanpaa, Frans Emil (1888–1967) Finnish novelist. Sillanpaa's first major novel was *Mark Heritage* (1919), which reflected his impressions of the 1918 Finnish Civil War. He is best remembered for the acclaimed *The Maid Silja* (1931). Sillanpaa was editor of *Panu*, a literary journal, and wrote many short stories and novels about Finnish life.

He was awarded the NOBEL PRIZE in literature in 1939.

Sillitoe, Alan (1928–) British author. Sillitoe began writing with the encouragement of Robert GRAVES, whom Sillitoe met while traveling in Majorca with American poet Ruth Fainlight, whom he later married. Sallitoe's first volume of poetry was *Without Beer or Bread* (1957); his first novel was *Saturday Night and Sunday Morning* (1958, filmed 1960). With its provincial setting, the novel drew comparisons to the work of the ANGRY YOUNG MEN, although Sillitoe's hero was firmly rooted in the working class, not rising above it. The acclaimed title story in the collection *The Loneliness of the Long Distance Runner* (1959, filmed 1962) tells the story of a rebellious Borstal boy. Other works include the novels *Her Victory* (1982) and *Out of the Whirlpool* (1987) and the poetry collections *Storm and Other Poems* (1974) and *Barbarians and Other Poems* (1974). Sillitoe has also written plays and screenplays. Throughout the 1990s Sillitoe continued to produce works such as the first volume of his autobiography, *Life without Armour* (1995), as well as works of fiction such as *The Broken Chariot* (1998), *The German Numbers Woman* (1999), *Birthday* (2001), which was the sequel to *Saturday Night and Sunday Morning,* and *A Man of His Time* (2004).

Sills, Beverly (Belle Miriam Silverman) (1929–) American opera singer. Sills is one of the most popular opera personalities and one of the great coloratura sopranos, especially noted for her bel canto singing and her acting ability. She made her debut in 1947 with the Philadelphia Civic Opera. She has been most closely associated with the New York City Opera, making her debut with that company as Rosalinde in *Die Fledermaus* in 1955. Her 1966 performance as Cleopatra in Handel's *Giulio Cesare* made her a superstar. Already acclaimed as a great diva, she finally debuted in opera houses worldwide after 1967, and made her Metropolitan Opera debut in 1975. Among her most famous roles are Lucia in *Lucia di Lammermoor,* the three British queens in the Donizetti operas (*Roberto Devereux, Maria Stuarda, Anna Bolena,*) and all three soprano roles in

Les Contes d'Hoffmann. In 1980 she retired from singing and became director of the New York City Opera (until 1989), revitalizing the repertory and reviving classic Broadway musicals. In addition she had made recordings, appeared on television specials and served on the council of the National Endowment for the Arts. Sills ended her self-imposed retirement in 1994 when she accepted the chair of the Lincoln Center for the Performing Arts, a position she held for eight years. In 2002 Sills left Lincoln Center to become chair of the Metropolitan Opera. She announced her resignation from that position in 2005.

Silone, Ignazio *(1900–1978)* Italian novelist, essayist and autobiographer. Silone is one of the major figures in Italian literature of the 20th century. His major novels, written in a powerfully realistic style, reflect Silone's strong commitment to social justice. Orphaned at an early age, Silone was raised in poverty and early on was drawn to Communist Party politics. In the 1920s and '30s, after MUSSOLINI rose to power, Silone was forced to live in exile from Italy, spending time in Russia and Switzerland. In 1931, due to the repressions of STALINISM, Silone left the Communist Party and moved toward a broader humanism that reflected ultimate spiritual values without taking on religious beliefs. Silone became internationally famous in the 1930s through the success of his novels *Fontamara* (1933), which portrayed the impact of fascist rule on an Italian village, and *Bread and Wine* (1937). *Emergency Exit* (1965) is a collection of autobiographical essays.

Silvers, Phil (Phil Silversmith) *(1912–1985)* American comic actor. Silvers was best known for his role as the conniving Sgt. Ernie Bilko in one of the most popular television shows of the 1950s, *The Phil Silvers Show* (originally *You'll Never Get Rich*). The show ran from 1955 to 1959 and continues to appear in syndication. He also appeared in a number of films and Broadway shows. In 1972 Silvers made his last Broadway appearance in a revival of the musical *A Funny Thing Happened on the Way to the Forum,* for which he won a Tony Award. The show's run was cut short after he suffered a stroke;

thereafter, his career was limited mostly to guest appearances.

Simenon, Georges *(1903–1989)* Belgian novelist. Simenon was best known as the creator of Paris police detective Inspector Maigret. An extremely prolific author, he wrote each of his books in a matter of days. Altogether he turned out 84 Maigret mysteries, 136 other novels, more than 1,000 articles and short stories and 200 pseudonymous novellas early in his career. According to his American publisher, during his lifetime more than 600 million copies of his books were sold around the world in 47 languages. His non-Maigret novels, many of which won critical praise, were generally psychological dreams that ended in tragedy.

Simler, George B. *(1921–1972)* American air force officer. In 1965 in the early stages of America's involvement in the VIETNAM WAR, Simler was director of all American air flight missions in Southeast Asia. He subsequently held that authority over all American air missions throughout the world (1967–69). In 1970 he was appointed head of the Air Force Air Training Command. At the time of his death in a jet crash in Texas, he held the rank of lieutenant general.

Simon, Carly *(1945–   )* American singer-songwriter. As a singer terrified of live performance, Carly Simon's success has rested solely on her recorded performances. Her first major success came in 1971 with the top-10 "That's the Way I've Always Heard It Should Be." Her second album, *Anticipation,* solidified her position as one of the leading solo artists of the 1970s and provided the number-one hit "You're So Vain." Her marriage to folk-rock performer James Taylor coincided with a leveling off in her career, although they scored a hit with the duet "Mockingbird." After their marriage ended, Simon had a string of successes with songs she wrote for films, including "Nobody Does It Better," written for the James Bond film *The Spy Who Loved Me,* "Let the River Run" for *Working Girl* and "Coming Around Again" for *Heartburn.* Although diagnosed with breast cancer in 1997, Simon continued her

recording career with albums such as *The Bedroom Tapes* (2000).

Simon, Claude *(1913–2005)* French novelist. Simon, who won the NOBEL PRIZE for literature in 1985, first won international acclaim in the 1950s as a leading practitioner of the NOUVEAU ROMAN, which deemphasized traditional plot and characterization in favor of direct portrayals of existential reality. Simon, who as a youth studied painting and was greatly influenced by the aesthetic theories of painter Raoul DUFY, emphasized that he approached writing with an emphasis on artistic composition of language. His major novels include *The Wind* (1957), *The Flanders Road* (1961), *The Battle of Pharsalus* (1969), *Triptych* (1973) and *Georgics* (1981). Simon served in the French RESISTANCE during WORLD WAR II.

Simon, Sir John Allsebrook (first Viscount Simon) *(1873–1954)* British barrister and statesman. Born in Manchester, Simon studied at Oxford and became a barrister in 1899. He was elected to Parliament as a Liberal in 1906, serving until 1918, and again from 1922 to 1931. He was solicitor general from 1910 to 1913, attorney general from 1913 to 1914 and home secretary from 1915 to 1916, resigning over his opposition to WORLD WAR I conscription. He fought in France from 1917 to 1918. Simon took part in the LABRADOR boundary settlement in 1926, and from 1927 to 1930 he was chairman of the commission on Indian affairs that issued the SIMON REPORT. He returned to the Ramsay MACDONALD cabinet as foreign secretary (1931 to 1935), and later was home secretary (1935 to 1937) and chancellor of the exchequer (1937 to 1940). One of the strongest supporters of the APPEASEMENT policy toward Germany, in 1935 he became the first British cabinet member to visit Adolf HITLER.

Simon, Neil (Neil Martin Simon) *(1927–   )* American playwright and screenplay writer. Simon is one of the most popular comedic writers in the history of show business. The author of over 20 hit Broadway plays, Simon has also become a major force in HOLLYWOOD through his film adaptations of his plays as well as his original screenplays. Simon began his career in the

1950s as a comedy writer for numerous television shows including *Caesar's Hour* and *The Phil Silvers Show*. He scored his first Broadway success with *Come Blow Your Horn* (1961), then followed with many more plays that he adapted into films such as *Barefoot in the Park* (1967), *The Odd Couple* (1968), *Plaza Suite* (1971), *Last of the Red Hot Lovers* (1972), *The Prisoner of Second Avenue* (1975), *The Sunshine Boys* (1975), *Chapter Two* (1979), *Brighton Beach Memoirs* (1986) and *Biloxi Blues* (1988). The latter three constitute an autobiographical trilogy by Simon that blends his comic touch with serious dramatic shadings. Original screenplays by Simon include *Max Dugan Returns* (1983) and *The Slugger's Wife* (1985). He won the 1991 PULITZER PRIZE for his play *Lost in Yonkers*.

Simon and Garfunkel *(1957–1970)* American folk and rock music singing duo. Paul Simon and Art Garfunkel first performed together in 1957 as "Tom and Jerry" at fraternity parties and other unglamorous venues. But in the mid-1960s, they emerged as major stars. Simon was far and away the major musical force in the duo, writing the songs, performing on guitar and handling the bulk of the lead vocals. Their major hits included "The Sounds of Silence" (1966), "Homeward Bound" (1966), "I Am a Rock" (1966), "Scarborough Fair" (1968), "Mrs. Robinson" (1968, which became hugely famous through its use in the Mike NICHOLS film *The Graduate*) and "Bridge Over Troubled Water" (1970). In 1970, Simon broke off the partnership with Garfunkel to pursue a highly successful solo career that has included the acclaimed albums *Graceland* (1987) and *The Rhythm of the Saints* (1990). The duo has reunited off and on since then including at the Grammy Awards in 2003 when they were presented a Lifetime Achievement Award.

Simon Report Report issued in 1930 by the Indian Statutory Commission, which met from 1927 to 1930 under the chairmanship of Sir John SIMON. It was critical of then-current governmental systems, recommended indirect election to a central Indian legislature and urged more responsible government. Its recommendations were strengthened in London meetings of 1931 to 1932, which supported the establishment of an Indian Federation. Many of the criticisms embodied in the report were addressed in the India Act of 1935.

Simplon Pass In southwestern Switzerland, an alpine pass running from Brig in Switzerland to Iselle in Italy. Its roadway, constructed by Napoleon I, fell into disuse after the completion in 1906 of one of the engineering marvels of the century, the **Simplon Railway Tunnel**. The 13-mile-long tunnel was the longest in the world until the construction of the ENGLISH CHANNEL TUNNEL, completed in 1994.

Simpson, Louis (Louis Aston Marantz Simpson) *(1923–)* American poet. Simpson was born in Jamaica but was educated and later taught in the U.S. Simpson's first collection, *The Arrivistes: Poems, 1910–1949* (1949), was praised for its portrayal of contemporary themes and ideas in traditional poetic forms. Beginning with *A Dream of Governors* (1959), he began to experiment more with the structure of his poetry and its imagery. Other works include *At the End of the Open Road* (1963), poems; *North of Jamaica* (1972), an autobiography; and *A Revolution in Taste: Studies of Dylan Thomas, Allen Ginsberg, Sylvia Plath and Robert Lowell* (1978). Simpson was awarded the PULITZER PRIZE for poetry in 1964. Simpson published his memoir, *The King My Father's Wreck*, in 1995.

Simpson, Orenthal James *(1947–)* American football player. The dominant college running back of the late 1960s, Simpson led the University of Southern California Trojans to a Rose Bowl victory in 1968. That same year, he ran for a record 1,309 yards and was awarded the Heisman Trophy. Choosing to play with the Buffalo Bills of the American Football League, he gave the league an added dose of credibility, bringing it one step closer to parity with the older National Football League. In 1973, he rushed for a record-breaking 2,003 yards. His record of 23 touchdowns in a single season has stood for more than 15 years. His lifetime total is 11,236 yards rushing over 11 seasons. After retiring from the game, Simpson became a commercial spokesman, actor and sports commentator. In June 1994 Simpson was arrested for the alleged murder of ex-wife Nicole Brown Simpson and her friend Ronald Goldman. Although acquitted in October 1995 (see O. J. SIMPSON MURDER TRIAL), a civil court ruled in 1997 that Simpson was responsible for their deaths and ordered him to pay $8.5 million in damages to the families of both victims.

Simpson, Wallis Warfield See Duchess of WINDSOR.

Simpsons, The Animated situation comedy series created by cartoonist Matt Groening (1954–). Premiering in 1987 as a weekly segment on *The Tracy Ullman Show* on the newly created Fox television network, it developed such a following that Fox offered to give *The Simpsons* its own half-hour time slot. When *The Simpsons* appeared as an independent program in 1989, it quickly proved appealing to critics and popular audiences. One of the show's characters, Bart Simpson (voiced by Nancy Cartwright), soon developed a massive following among children and adolescents for his irreverent comments, and soon T-shirts with Bart Simpson quotes, such as "Don't Have a Cow, Man" and "Ay Carumba!" appeared in stores. The series also led to the creation of a new, category for the Emmy Awards—Best Animated Series—which *The Simpsons* won in 1990, 1991, 1995, 1997, 1998 and 2001. Julie Kavner and Cartwright also each won an Emmy Award for their voice-over performance work in 1992. Along with its regular characters, *The Simpsons* featured guest appearances by celebrities such as Mel Gibson, John Madden, Julia-Louis Dreyfus, Darryl Strawberry, and Kelsey Grammer, who appeared either as themselves or as specific characters, such as Grammer's recurring "Sideshow Bob." The series also became a source of controversy because of Bart's repeated flaunting of his status of an "underachiever" and for its portrayal of a dysfunctional family, drawing criticism in 1992 from both U.S. president George H. W. BUSH and his wife, first lady Barbara Bush.

Sims, John Haley "Zoot" *(1925–1985)* Jazz saxophonist. A leading jazz performer, Sims's career spanned more than 40 years from the 1940s into the '80s. At first he was associated with the BIG BANDS of Benny GOODMAN, Woody HERMAN, and Stan KENTON. From the mid-1950s on he worked primarily as a freelancer, appearing in clubs and festivals all over the world. He made more than 40 recordings as a featured performer.

Sinai Peninsula Triangular-shaped peninsula in northeastern EGYPT between the Gulf of Suez on the west and the Gulf of Aqaba on the east. The region is primarily desert. At the beginning of the 20th century it was under the control of the khedive of Egypt, who owed nominal authority to the Ottoman sultan but was under British influence. The Sinai was a battlefield during the ARAB-ISRAELI WARS of 1956 and 1973 as well as the SIX DAY WAR of 1967; during these wars, it was contested by ISRAEL and Egypt. In 1974 UN troops stood between the Egyptian-occupied east bank of the Gulf of Suez and Israeli armies. In accordance with the CAMP DAVID agreements of 1978, all Israeli forces had gradually withdrawn by 1982. (See also CAMP DAVID TALKS.)

Sinatra, Frank (Francis Albert Sinatra) (*1915–1998*) American JAZZ and popular music singer and film actor. Sinatra, whose nicknames included "The Voice" and "The Chairman of the Board," was one of the greatest show business stars of the 20th century. As a vocalist, he is ranked as one of the finest jazz and pop stylists ever and is especially noted for his impeccable phrasing and his ability to "swing" a tune. Born in Hoboken, N.J., Sinatra began his career as a vocalist in the 1930s. He achieved stardom after joining the Harry JAMES band in 1939, and in 1940 he moved to the Tommy DORSEY big band. By 1942, Sinatra was the adored favorite of his young, female "bobby-soxer" fans. Among his many hit songs from the 1940s to the present are "Come Rain or Come Shine," "I'll Never Smile Again," "In the Wee Small Hours," "I've Got You Under My Skin," "The Lady Is a Tramp," "Strangers in the night," "New York, New York," "My Way" and "There Are Such Things." Sinatra also enjoyed a long and successful film career that in-

cluded musicals such as *On the Town* (1949) and *Guys and Dolls* (1955) and dramatic films such as *From Here to Eternity* (1953)—for which he won an ACADEMY AWARD for best supporting actor—*Some Came Running* (1958) and *The Detective* (1968). Although his voice deteriorated somewhat through the years, Sinatra remained active through his 75th birthday, and the passage of time only confirmed his classic status.

Sinclair, Upton Beall (*1878–1968*) American author. An ardent socialist with unfulfilled political ambitions, Sinclair gained fame when he turned from the dime novels he wrote to pay his way through college to the composition of a Chicago stockyard exposé, *The Jungle* (1906). The book was an enormous popular success, brought about reform of the labor conditions Sinclair abhorred and enabled him to establish and support the socialist commune Helicon Home Colony in Englewood, New Jersey. Never concerned with aesthetic matters of the literary craft, Sinclair wrote journalistic novels intended to expose and correct particular social inequities. His other works include *The Moneychangers* (1908), *King Coal* (1917), *Boston* (1928), which was about the SACCO-VANZETTI case and *Plays of Protest* (1912). His *Dragon's Teeth* (1942) won a PULITZER PRIZE in 1943.

Singapore Singapore, at the southern tip of Southeast Asia's Malay Peninsula, consists of the main island of Singapore and 57 smaller islands. Connected to the mainland by a causeway, the republic covers a total land area of 239 square miles. Under British rule from 1867, the strategically important island became a successful free port. Britain constructed naval bases on Singapore after World War I. Nevertheless, in WORLD WAR II Singapore's sea-oriented defenses were overcome by a carefully planned overland attack down the Malay Peninsula, and the country was occupied by Japan in 1942. With the restoration of British control in 1945, Singapore became a Crown colony, then a self-governing state in 1959. A state within the Federation of Malaysia from 1963 to 1965, Singapore gained independence as a republic within the Commonwealth in 1965. LEE KUAN YEW served as prime minister from 1959 to 1990, guiding the country to increased economic prosperity while countering opposition demands for more political freedom. In 1993 Singapore held its first presidential elections. Despite its economic strength, Singapore suffered a severe recession during the Asian financial crisis of the late 1990s. The nation quickly recovered, however, and became the first Asian nation to sign a free-trade deal with the United States in 2003. But while its business

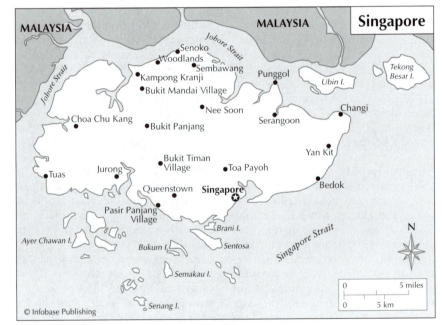

SINGAPORE

1867	The Straits Settlements become a Crown colony of the British Empire.
1922	Singapore is chosen as the principal British military base in Far East.
1942	Japan captures Singapore, taking 70,000 British and Australian prisoners.
1945	British rule is restored after Japan is defeated.
1946	Singapore becomes a separate Crown colony.
1959	Singapore promulgates its first constitution and becomes a self-governing state of the British Commonwealth.
1963	Singapore amends its constitution to join with Sarawak, North Borneo (later called Sabah) and the Federation of Malaysia to form Malaysia.
1965	Singapore leaves Malaysia to form its own republic.
1990	Prime Minister Lee resigns after holding office since 1959.
1993	Singapore hold its first presidential election.
1998	Singapore succumbs to the Asian financial crisis but begins a recovery toward year-end.
2003	First Asian nation to sign a free-trade deal with the United States.
2005	An Australian man convicted of drug smuggling is executed, despite high-level protest from other countries.

policies may be liberal, its legal system is considered harsh by many. In 2005 an Australian man convicted of smuggling drugs was executed for his crime.

Singer, Isaac Bashevis (1904–1991) Yiddish author. Singer immigrated to New York from Poland in 1935 and began his career as a journalist for the *Jewish Daily Forward,* a Yiddish language periodical that published his early short stories. His first novel published in English was *The Family Moskat* (1950). Singer's fanciful novels and short stories detail the lives of Polish Jews in various periods of history as well as the present and examine the role of the Jewish faith in their lives. Other works include the novels *The Magician*

of Lublin (1960), *Shosha* (1978) and *Enemies: A Love Story,* and the short story collections *A Friend of Kafka* (1970) and *The Death of Methuselah and Other Stories* (1988). Singer received the NOBEL PRIZE in literature in 1978.

Sinkiang See XINJIANG.

Sinn Féin (Ir., "ourselves alone") Irish nationalist movement founded by Arthur Griffiths in 1902, originally with the aim of securing independence from Britain. Griffiths was succeeded by more militant leaders, including James CONNOLLY and Padraig PEARSE, who organized the 1916 EASTER RISING in Dublin. In the latter half of the century, and especially after the outbreak of sectarian strife in

NORTHERN IRELAND in 1968, Sinn Féin was influential as the political wing of the IRISH REPUBLICAN ARMY (IRA). Sinn Féin participated in the 1998 Good Friday Agreement, which established a joint Catholic and Protestant government for Northern Ireland. However, its refusal to disarm led Ulster unionist David TRIMBLE to leave the government and led British prime minister Tony BLAIR to suspend the agreement in October 2002.

Sino-Japanese War of 1937–45 In the 1930s Japan had extended its influence into China north of the Great Wall. In July 1937 shots exchanged at the Marco Polo Bridge north of Beijing (Peking) soon escalated into an undeclared war. Japanese bombers attacked northern cities; its fleet attacked Shanghai. The capital, Nanjing (Nanking), fell in December 1937; Hangzhou (Hangchow) became the new capital. Canton and Hangzhou were captured in 1938, and the capital moved to Chongqing (Chungking). The Japanese controlled all the coastal ports, railroads and major cities of China by 1938. By 1941, with the U.S. in the war, the Allies flew supplies to Chongqing "over the hump" of the Himalayas. With a new air force, aided by the U.S., the Chinese bombed Japanese strongholds, while in the north, Communist guerrillas harassed the Japanese occupation. The Japanese failed to occupy the Chinese countryside or to establish a successful puppet government. Russia entered the war on August 8, 1945, soon liberating Manchuria. By Japan's surrender, September 2, 1945, many coastal areas had been retaken by Chinese forces.

Sino-Soviet Treaty of 1945 Agreement signed by China and the USSR. The treaty's key terms included the USSR's promise of aid to the national government, Soviet recognition of Chinese sovereignty in Manchuria, Chinese recognition of an independent Outer Mongolia (if a plebiscite showed that this independence had popular support), China's agreement to open-port status for the city of Dairen and its granting to the USSR of a free lease to half of the city's port facilities. This treaty was largely an expansion and a clarification of various agreements reached at the YALTA CONFERENCE, in which China had not been a participant.

Sinyavsky, Andrei Donatevich
(1925–1997) Soviet author. Sinyavsky, while a literary critic at the Gorki Institute of World Literature in Moscow, first began attracting attention in the West with the publication of the essay "On Socialist Realism" in the French magazine *L'Esprit* in 1959. The essay assailed the notion of art as an instrument of propaganda. It was first published unsigned, but later reprints appeared under the pseudonym **Abram Tertz.** His first works of fiction to appear in the West were *The Trial Begins* (1960), a black comedy originally published as *Sud Idyot* and *Sad Idzie* (1959), *Fantasticheskie Povesti* (1961; *Fantastic Stories,* 1963), and *The Makepeace Experiment* (1964), published originally as *Lyubivom*. In 1965 Sinyavsky, along with author Yuli DANIEL, was arrested for his pseudonymous writings. In 1966 they were brought to trial and charged with writing anti-Soviet propaganda. Sinyavsky was sentenced to seven years in a labor camp. The case caused a worldwide uproar, as it was the first time that a writer had been held criminally responsible for the possible interpretations of a work of literature. Many authors from around the world pled Sinyavsky's cause to Soviet Premier KOSYGIN, yet he remained in prison where he began writing what would become *A Voice from the Chorus* (1976; originally *Golos iz khora,* 1973). In 1973 Sinyavsky was allowed to immigrate to Paris where he had been offered a position at the Sorbonne. His later works include the novel *Goodnight!* (1989).

Sirica, John Joseph *(1904–1992)* Federal district court judge who gained national prominence during the WATERGATE scandal. Sirica graduated from Georgetown University Law School, having worked his way through school as a boxing coach. He worked as a U.S. attorney in Washington, D.C., and later entered private practice. Politically active, he was appointed to the federal bench by President Dwight D. EISENHOWER. An able judge, he was known as "Maximum John" because of his often harsh sentences. In 1972 Sirica was thrown into the spotlight when as chief judge of the district court he presided over the trial of seven operatives of President Richard M. NIXON's reelection committee who had broken into Democratic headquarters at the Watergate apartment complex. In a highly publicized trial the judge aggressively asked questions from the bench and after their convictions he sentenced the defendants provisionally on the condition that they cooperate with investigators. The defendants did in fact cooperate, which implicated others including U.S. Attorney General John Mitchell, who along with President Nixon was ultimately forced to resign.

Sirk, Douglas (Detlef Sierck) *(1900–1987)* German-born film director. Sirk was known for his HOLLYWOOD melodramas, including *Magnificent Obsession* (1954) and *Written on the Wind* (1956). After finishing *Imitation of Life* (1959) he left Hollywood and returned to Europe, where he resumed a career in the theater. His films eventually developed a cult following, especially in Europe.

SIS See M16.

Sisson, C(harles) H(ubert) *(1914–2003)* English poet, essayist and translator. Born in Bristol and educated at the Universities of Bristol (1934), Berlin and Freiburg (1934–35) and the Sorbonne (1935–36), Sisson enjoyed a long career as a civil servant. He published no poetry until well into middle age, declaring that "one should speak, whether in prose or verse, because one has something to say, and not otherwise." Much of his work is politically critical and satirical, though he also wrote on religious and moral themes. His piercing wit and mordant tone are the greatest pleasures of his verse; in that vein he described his work as "no more than an ironic contribution to a hopeless situation." His poetry includes *The London Zoo* (1961), *Numbers* (1965), *Metamorphoses* (1968) and *Anchises* (1976). His *Collected Poems* appeared in 1984. Sisson translated Horace, Catullus, Dante and Heine.

Sister Carrie Published in 1900, the 20th century's first masterpiece of unflinching realism and now regarded as a landmark in the development of the modern American novel. The story of its writing and hostile reception has become the stuff of literary legend. Theodore DREISER was a struggling young journalist in New York at the turn of the century when he first devised the story of Carrie Meeber, an 18-year-old Chicago factory worker who is seduced and taken to New York by her lover, a thief named Hurstwood. Dreiser knew both the milieu and the characters well. The first he derived from his reportorial assignments in the squalid Bowery, the great hotels and the glittering Broadway theaters. The latter he drew from the experiences of his sister, Emma, who had eloped to New York with her lover, a married man who had stolen money from a Chicago saloon. The bulky manuscript was accepted by Doubleday, Page & Co. but, presumably due to its sensational subject matter and scrupulous detail, its subsequent circulation and sale was restricted to barely 650 copies. Dreiser, bruised and depressed by its hostile critical reception, went into a decline that lasted almost seven years. The real reputation of the book begins with its second publication in 1907 by the new firm of B. W. Dodge. Measured against the occasionally forced tone of Stephen Crane and the melodramatic excess of Frank Norris, *Sister Carrie* remains an astonishing achievement. The contrasting fortunes of Hurstwood and Carrie create powerful, oscillating rhythms built upon relentlessly moving events. Two such different fates, seemingly delicately balanced and intertwined, are actually forged together in likeness of cold steel. They are victims of the urban flux, writes Dreiser, to "the blare of sound, a roar of life, a vast array of human lives." The novel was adapted in 1952 into a tepid screen version starring Jennifer Jones and Laurence OLIVIER.

Sitwells, The Notable English literary family comprised of **Dame Edith Sitwell** (1887–1964) and her brothers **Sir Osbert Sitwell** (1892–1969) and **Sir Sacheverell Sitwell** (1897–1988). Dame Edith began writing poetry at an early age, and shared with her brother Osbert a scathing contempt for the GEORGIAN poets. They were advocates of MODERNISM, and from 1916 to 1921 edited the periodical *Wheels*. Dame Edith's first volume of poetry was *The Mother and Other Poems* (1915), and her subsequent works and theatrical personality made her a well-known literary figure. Her only novel, *I Live under a Black Sun* (1937), was not a success, but her war-inspired poetry, which includes *Street Songs* (1942) and *The Shadow of Cain* (1947), were highly acclaimed. Her poem "Masquerade" provided the text to William WALTON's musical piece of the same name.

Sitzkrieg See PHONY WAR.

Six, Les Group of six young French composers who, just after World War I, united in opposition to the IMPRESSIONISM of composers such as Claude DEBUSSY and Maurice RAVEL. Inspired by the writings of Jean COCTEAU and the compositions and musical philosophy of Erik SATIE, Les Six included Georges AURIC, Louis Durey, Arthur HONEGGER, Darius Milhaud, Francis POULENC and Germaine Tailleferre.

Six Counties The counties of NORTHERN IRELAND: Antrim, Armagh, Down, Fermanagh, Londonderry and Tyrone. With Cavan, Donegal and Monaghan, they originally formed the province of Ulster, but in 1923 these three were made part of the Dominion of IRELAND, while the other six remained part of the UNITED KINGDOM.

Six-Day War *(1967)* In May 1967 EGYPT's president Gamal Abdel NASSER (1918–70) demanded (and obtained) the removal of a United Nations emergency force (UNEF) from Egyptian territory. Shortly afterward, Nasser ordered a shipping blockade of the Strait of Tiran, effectively closing the Israeli port of Elat on the Gulf of Aqaba. By this time Syrian, Egyptian and Israeli forces had mobilized along their respective borders, along which guerrilla raids had taken place frequently since the end of the ARAB-ISRAELI WAR OF 1956. Suddenly, on June 5, 1967, Israeli warplanes attacked and bombed two dozen Arab airfields, destroying more than 400 Egyptian, Syrian and Jordanian planes on the ground. Israeli land forces invaded the SINAI PENINSULA, JERUSALEM's Old City, JORDAN's WEST BANK, the GAZA STRIP and the GOLAN HEIGHTS and occupied these area when the war ended with a UN-sponsored cease-fire on June 10, 1967. (See also ARAB-ISRAELI WAR OF 1973.)

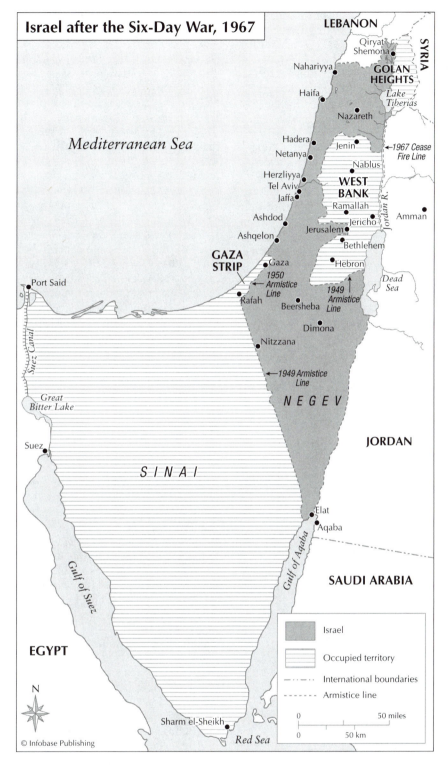

Israel after the Six-Day War, 1967

60 Minutes American documentary television series begun in 1969. CBS's *60 Minutes* introduced the "news magazine" format, in which a mixture of hard and soft news stories are presented in discrete segments. *60 Minutes* focuses on controversy and the exposing of corruption in government and business. The show's news team has included Mike Wallace, Morley Safer, Henry Reasoner, Dan Rather and Diane Sawyer. Since its inception, *60 Minutes* has been enormously popular and is seen by upwards of 23 million people a week.

Skardon, William James "Jim" *(1904–1987)* British counterespionage agent. Skardon gained a reputation as one of M15's most formidable interrogators. He was involved in almost all the important spy cases of his time, but probably achieved his greatest success with the interrogation that drew a confession from the atom spy Klaus FUCHS in 1950.

Skidmore, Owings & Merrill American architectural firm founded in 1936 by Louis Skidmore, Nathaniel Owings and John O. Merrill. Skidmore and Owings were chief design consultants on the 1933 Chicago Exposition, and one of the most influential forces in post–World War II architecture. The firm is known for its skyscrapers in the INTERNATIONAL STYLE. Its "glass box" designs became the standard pattern for office buildings throughout the 1950s and 1960s, beginning with Lever House in New York (1952). Other notable buildings by Skidmore, Owings & Merrill include the U.S. Air Force Academy in Colorado Springs (1954–62) and the John Hancock Center (1970) and Sears Tower (1974) in Chicago.

Skinner, B(urrhus) F(rederic) (1904–1990) U.S. psychologist. He was a pioneer in the field of behaviorism, seeking to explain even complex human behavior as a series of conditioned responses to outside stimuli. He created the so-called Skinner box, an enclosed experimental environment for laboratory animals. Among his books were *Walden Two* (1948) and *Beyond Freedom and Dignity* (1971).

Skylab U.S. space station; in service for two years, it was manned by three teams of astronauts in 1973 and 1974. Unmanned for the following five years, it crashed to Earth in 1979.

Slánský trial Trial on charges of treason of Rudolf Slánský, vice premier of CZECHOSLOVAKIA and Communist Party secretary, and 13 other party officials. The show trial, held from November 17 to 30, 1952, with fabricated evidence and heavily anti-Semitic overtones, resulted in the conviction and hanging of 11 of the accused, including Slánský. It was the greatest communist purge outside the USSR and coincided with a period of enor-

mous ANTI-SEMITISM by Joseph STALIN inside the USSR.

Slayton, Donald "Deke" (1924–1993) One of the original seven MERCURY astronauts selected in 1959, Deke Slayton was grounded by a heart problem and did not have a chance to fly until his APOLLO-SOYUZ Test Project flight, July 15–24, 1975. During that well-publicized flight, a joint mission and link-up in space between the U.S. and USSR, Slayton and fellow astronauts Thomas STAFFORD and Vance Brand docked with a Soviet Soyuz spacecraft and spent two days sharing quarters and conducting experiments with Russian cosmonauts Alexei LEONOV and Valery Kubasov. After unlinking and spending five more days in space alone, the Apollo spacecraft accidentally filled with deadly exhaust gas on its return splashdown. Slayton's lungs were severely burned, and the three-man Apollo crew came near to losing their lives. Apollo-Soyuz was Slayton's only spaceflight, but during it he logged a total of nearly nine days in space.

Slim, William Joseph (1891–1970) British field marshal. In Burma during World War II, Slim commanded Britain's "forgotten army" of British and Indian troops, who swept the Japanese from the Indian frontier in one of the most arduous campaigns of modern warfare. Slim was knighted in 1944 and served as chief of the British Imperial Staff from 1948 to 1952. From 1953 to 1960, he was governor-general of Australia.

Sloan, Alfred Pritchard, Jr. (1875–1966) President of General Motors Corporation. Sloan was born in New Haven, Connecticut, but grew up largely in Brooklyn, New York. He received an engineering degree from the Massachusetts Institute of Technology in 1895. Sloan was president of the Hyatt Roller Bearing Company from 1898 to 1916, when he sold it to William Durant, founder of GM. Sloan was president of the resulting GM subsidiary, United Motors Corporation, until 1919, when that company was dissolved and he was named a vice president and director of GM. In 1923, Sloan succeeded as president of GM

Pierre S. du Pont, who had himself succeeded Durant in 1920. During his presidency, which extended until 1937, Sloan, in his methodical, unostentatious way, drastically reorganized GM and guided it to undisputed first place among auto manufacturers worldwide. He served as chairman of the board of GM until 1956, when he retired. The term "Sloanism" refers to GM's policy, under Sloan, of offering a diversity of products to the consuming public, as opposed to Henry FORD's policy of offering a single, mass-produced model.

Sloan, John (1871–1951) American painter. Born in Lock Haven, Pennsylvania, Sloan studied at the Pennsylvania Academy of the Fine Arts with Robert HENRI. He became an illustrator, working in Philadelphia on the *Inquirer* and the *Press* and continued to create newspaper illustrations after he moved to New York City in 1904. A member of The EIGHT, he was an early social realist who excelled in portrayals of the crowded streets of New York City. A social and artistic activist, he was art director of the radical magazine *The Masses* from 1912 to 1914 and a founder and president of the Society of Independent Artists from 1918 to 1944. He was also an influential teacher at New York City's Art Students League, his long tenure lasting from 1916 to 1937. Characteristic paintings include *McSorley's Bar* (Detroit Institute of Arts) and *Wake of the Ferry* (Phillips Collection, Washington, D.C.). Sloan was also a skilled etcher, whose graphic subject matter—mainly street scenes and nudes—are also typical of his paintings.

Slovakia Along with the CZECH REPUBLIC, one of two countries that formerly made up the state of CZECHOSLOVAKIA that achieved independence from the AUSTRO-HUNGARIAN EMPIRE at the end of WORLD WAR I. After being severed from Bohemia and Moravia (populated mainly by Czechs) and established as a puppet state of Nazi GERMANY from 1939 to 1945, Slovakia rejoined its former partner at the end of WORLD WAR II. In June of 1992 Czechoslovak national elections gave control of the national parliament to the Movement for a Democratic Slovakia (HZDS), a Slovak party led by Vladimir Mečiar, and the

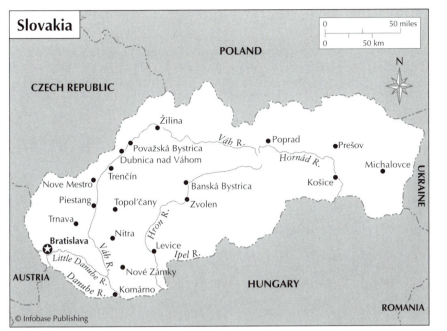

Slovakia

vealed that a majority of citizens in both republics favored the preservation of Czechoslovakia, the CDP and the HZDS both pushed bills through the parliaments prescribing the partition of the country on December 31, 1992. The day following the breakup of Czechoslovakia, the independent states of Slovakia and the Czech Republic came into existence, with their respective capitals of Bratislava and Prague.

As the first prime minister of Slovakia, Mečiar scheduled national elections in February 1993, and slowed down the privatization of state-owned industries that had begun with the collapse of communism in 1989. While his party did well in national elections, retaining its majority in the Slovak parliament and winning the first presidential elections, a rivalry emerged between Mečiar and the new Slovak president, Michal Kováč. By March 1994 Kováč had forced Mečiar's complete withdrawal from national politics, and formed a coalition government overseen by Jozef Moravčik, the leader of the Democratic Union of Slovakia Party. Moravčik soon set about reversing

Civic Democratic Party (CDP), a conservative Czech party headed by Václav Klaus. Each leader became prime minister of Czechoslovakia's Czech and Slovak respective republics. A month after the national elections, Mečiar supported a declaration of sovereignty by the Slovakian parliament, which gave Slovakia the power to nullify any law passed by the national Czechoslovak legislature. Although surveys of the country's population re-

SLOVAKIA	
1918	The Austro-Hungarian Empire is dismembered; Slovaks join Czechs to form the independent state of Czechoslovakia.
1939	Germany annexes Czechoslovakia and severs Slovakia from Bohemia and Moravia.
1945	Soviet troops enter Prague. Slovakia is reunited with the rest of Czechoslovakia.
1992	A leftist government comes to power in Slovakia; Czechoslovakia dissolves into two nations, the Czech Republic and Slovakia, in the so-called Velvet Divorce; a new constitution is established.
1993	Parliament elects Michal Kováč of the Movement for a Democratic Slovakia (MDS) president. Vladimir Mečiar, also of the MDS, is prime minister in coalition government.
1994	New coalition led by Jozef Moravčik of the Democratic Union of Slovakia is formed following a no-confidence vote in Mečiar government.
1998	In elections, HZDS gains most seats, but a coalition government is formed that is led by SDK. Constitution is changed to allow for direct presidential elections.
1999	Rudolf Schuster wins the country's first direct presidential elections.
2002	Mikulas Dzurinda wins second term as premier in a center-right coalition government.
2004	Slovakia joins NATO and the EU.

Mečiar's attempt to slow down the privatization of state industries and to reduce discrimination against Slovakia's Hungarian minority. However, by October 1994 Mečiar had regained control of the HZDS and helped the party win 35% of the vote in the fall elections. A month later, Mečiar formed a coalition government with the leftist Association of Slovak Workers and the ultranationalist Slovak National Party and resumed the office of prime minister. He immediately halted any additional sales of government industries and began to strengthen the state's control over radio and television media resources.

In May 1995 Mečiar renewed his power struggle with Kováč by supporting a nonbinding vote of no confidence in the parliament and orchestrating the termination of Kováč's authority over the Slovak armed forces. Although Kováč finished out his term in office in 1998, his failure to win reelection, and the inability of any presidential candidate to gain a parliamentary majority, gave increasing power to Mečiar's government. However, this advantage was short-lived, as several opposition parties led by Mikuláš Dzurinda organized a new parliamentary coalition in October 1998 that deposed Mečiar and led to his resignation from parliament and as the head of the HZDS. Dzurinda's coalition soon amended the Slovak constitution to provide for the direct election of the president. The coalition's candidate, Rudolf Schuster, won the first such election in May 1999. In 2002 Dzurinda's coalition retained its hold on power, and the HZDS remained the most prominent force in Slovakian politics. Schuster and Dzurinda pledged to deal with Slovakia's persistently high unemployment rate, which reached 20% in 2003. To improve the economy, both Schuster and Dzurinda campaigned for Slovakia's membership in the EUROPEAN UNION, which received popular approval in a May 2003 referendum. In 2004 Slovakia joined NATO and the EU.

Slovenia Possession of Austro-Hungarian Empire (c. 1335–1918), Yugoslav territory (1918–41), Italian possession (1941–45), province of communist Yugoslavia (1945–91), and independent state (1991–). Until the end of WORLD WAR I (1914–18), the province of Slovenia spent the first part

of the 20th century as a territory under the AUSTRO-Hungarian Empire. As the imperial authority began to collapse during the war, Slovenian nationalists began to assert their demands for independence from Habsburg rule. At the PARIS PEACE CONFERENCE of 1919, Slovenian delegates participated in the successful campaign for the creation of an independent kingdom of southern Slavs called the Kingdom of the Serbs, Croats and Slovenes, which was renamed the Kingdom of Yugoslavia in 1929. During WORLD WAR II (1939–45) when GERMANY invaded YUGOSLAVIA in 1941 to support the Italian military campaign in Greece, Slovenia was placed under Italian control until Italy's defeat in 1945. However, as Allied guerrilla and military forces liberated Yugoslavia, Slovenian nationalists chased out most of the territory's ethnic Italians and confiscated their possessions. In the territorial settlements after WORLD WAR II, Slovenia was increased in size by adding Slovenian-inhabited territory along the Adriatic Sea. It was also reunited with Yugoslavia, which was headed by Communist partisan leader Josip Broz, known later as Marshal TITO. While Slovenia functioned as an autonomous region under communist Yugoslavia, Slovenian nationalists grew increasingly dissatisfied with the multiethnic country's continuing political dominance by the Serbs.

In April 1990 Slovenian leaders, inspired by Soviet president Mikhail GORBACHEV's policy of GLASNOST, or "openness," arranged for the province's first free and open multiparty elections. When the ballots were counted, the nationalist Slovenian parties had obtained a majority of seats in the provincial parliament, and a Slovenian nationalist, Milan Kučan, was elected Slovenia's first president. Following a 90 percent vote in favor of secession from Yugoslavia in December 1990, Slovenia and CROATIA both declared their independence six months later. The Serbian-dominated government responded by dispatching Yugoslav People's Army (JNA) forces to overthrow the governments of both newly independent nations. In the ensuing 10-day battle, the hastily formed Slovenian troops blunted the JNA ad-

SLOVENIA

1918	On the collapse of the Habsburg Empire, Slovenia unites with Serbia, Croatia and Montenegro to form the Kingdom of Serbs, Croats and Slovenes, under the Serbian Karageorgević dynasty.
1929	The kingdom becomes known as Yugoslavia.
1941–45	The region is occupied by Nazi Germany and Italy during World War II.
1945	Josip Broz, known later as Marshal Tito, becomes premier and defense minister of liberated Yugoslavia; the process of collectivization begins with restrictions on land ownership.
1953	Tito is elected president of Yugoslavia.
1980	Tito dies.
1990	Slovenia and Croatia hold first multiparty elections in more than 50 years and elect Milan Kučan as their first president; in a referendum, the Slovenian people vote for independence.
1991	After a brief war, Slovenia gains its independence from Yugoslavia; a new constitution is adopted.
1992	Slovenia is recognized by the EU; Slovenia becomes a member of the UN; the first free elections for parliament are held. Kučan is relected president.
1995	EU and Slovenia begin negotiations on EU membership; Slovenia reaches an agreement with Italy regarding compensation for property confiscated from Italians who fled Slovenia after World War II.
1997	President Milan Kučan is elected to a third term; EU opens full membership talks with Slovenia.
2002	Prime Minister Drnovšek beats Kučan for the presidency.
2004	Slovenia joins NATO and the EU.

vance and expelled the Yugoslav Army from Slovenian territory. By January 1992 Slovenia had been formally recognized as an independent state by all the members of the EUROPEAN UNION (EU), and then by the U.S. in April. In December 1992 Kučan won reelection with 64 percent of the popular vote, and began working with the Liberal Democracy of Slovenia (LDS), a moderately liberal party that had advocated Slovenia's inclusion in the EU and the NORTH ATLANTIC TREATY ORGANIZATION (NATO). The LDS won the largest representation in the parliament and formed a governing coalition. Both President Kučan and the new Slovenian prime minister, LDS leader Janez Drnovšek, worked to resolve this country's border disputes with ITALY and CROATIA, to arrange for joint Croatian-Slovenian control over the formerly Yugoslav nuclear facilities at Krško and to award compensation for descendants of those Italians whose property was seized in 1945. These measures im-

proved relations with Italy and Croatia and helped ease Slovenia's path toward admission to the EU, which it achieved in December 1997. Slovenia's inclusion in the EU helped the LDS retain its parliamentary leadership in the November 1996 elections, and Kučan won reelection as Slovenian president the following year. In 2002 Kučan failed to retain his office and was succeeded by Drnovšek, who presided over Slovenia's accession to the EU and NATO in 2004.

Slovik, Eddie *(1921–1945)* American army private executed for desertion (January 31, 1945) during WORLD WAR II—the first such execution since 1864. In 1944, assigned to an infantry regiment and shipped overseas, Slovik deserted, returning the next day with a written vow to do so again. The army had been plagued with some 40,000 desertions in Europe during the war. Many other deserters had been convicted, but their death sentences had been commuted. It was felt that the

army intended to make an example of Slovik, whose past criminal record may have influenced their choice. It failed as a deterrent, largely because the army kept the execution secret; even Slovik's wife was unaware of the cause of his death until 1953 when the documentation was declassified. The public was informed in 1954 when journalist William Bradford HUIE published *The Execution of Private Slovik*. In 1977 Slovik's widow appealed for a reversal of his conviction, maintaining that he had been unfairly singled out, and she petitioned for a $70,000 payment plus interest on his National Service Life Insurance policy. Her appeal was rejected by the secretary of the army, and the case was referred to the Justice Department. In 1987 Slovik's remains were exhumed from a war criminals' grave in France and reburied in Detroit.

Smalley, Richard E. *(1943–2005)* American chemist and winner of the Nobel Prize in chemistry (1996). Born in Akron, Ohio, Smalley received a B.S. in chemistry from the University of Michigan in 1965 and his Ph.D. in chemistry from Princeton University in 1973. Upon receiving his doctorate, he worked at the University of Chicago as a research associate until 1976, when he joined Rice University's chemistry department. In the early 1980s Smalley and his Rice colleague Robert F. Curl began to investigate the physical composition of atomic clusters of semiconductors, such as silicon. He developed a laser device that would vaporize these elements and compounds, and then examined the way in which they vaporized to determine the precise physical structure of the compound.

By 1985 Smalley and Curl had investigated the application of their device to the reproduction of thin chains of carbon compounds that fellow Rice chemist Harold Kroto had discovered lying deep within interstellar space. As all three scientists began to collaborate on determining the chemical structure of these compounds, they identified a new physical configuration for carbon. Unlike the other carbon configurations that existed on Earth, such as graphite and diamond, this new arrangement consisted of 60 carbon atoms bonded together in a structure that resembled a soccer ball. Curl, Kroto and Smalley later named this configuration buckminsterfullerene, since the physical layout of this compound bore a resemblance to some of the geodesic domes designed by R. BUCKMINSTER FULLER, an American architect. In 1990 their collective production of buckminsterfullerene was confirmed in a separate laboratory experiment. Six years later, Curl, Kroto and Smalley won the Nobel Prize in chemistry for their discovery.

Smersh (*Smert' Shpionam* [Death to Spies]) Acronym for a division of the Soviet security organ that eliminated real, suspected or potential opponents to the Soviet government. Most of its targets had lived for a while outside the control of the Soviet regime during World War II as civilian deportees, refugees or prisoners of war. Smersh favored large-scale arrests, executions or deportation.

Smith, Alfred E(manuel) "Al" (*1873–1944*) American political leader. Born into a poor immigrant family on

American politician Alfred E. Smith (LIBRARY OF CONGRESS, PRINTS AND PHOTOGRAPHS DIVISION)

New York City's Lower East Side, Smith became active in Democratic city politics and was elected to the New York state assembly (1904–15). In 1913 he became Speaker of the assembly, and in 1918 he was elected governor of New York. He was defeated in his bid for reelection in 1922, but was returned to office in 1924, and again in 1926. Smith proved a popular, reformist governor, and in 1928, with the assistance of Franklin D. ROOSEVELT, he became the first Roman Catholic candidate for president, but was defeated by Herbert HOOVER. Smith retired to private life, becoming president of the company that built and operated the EMPIRE STATE BUILDING as well as editor of *New Outlook* magazine (1932–34). His memoirs, entitled *Up to Now*, were published in 1929.

Smith, Bessie (*1898–1937*) American singer. Called the "Empress of the Blues," Smith was a famous black singer who made 150 recordings during her career. A student of sorts of the first great female blues singer, "Ma" Rainey, Smith rapidly developed a style of her own and came to be regarded as one of the greatest blues singers of her time. She sang with such famous instrumentalists as Benny GOODMAN, Fletcher Henderson and Louis ARMSTRONG. Some of her most famous recordings include "Jailhouse Blues" and "Cold in Hand Blues." Smith was

seriously injured in an automobile accident in 1937, and it is said that she died of her injuries because a nearby hospital refused to care for her because of her race.

Smith, Gerald L. K. (*1898–1976*) American clergyman, editor and lecturer. Born in Pardeeville, Wisconsin, Smith came of a long line of fundamentalist preachers and became the minister of a Shreveport, Louisiana, church in 1928. In the 1930s Smith turned his considerable oratorical skills to the support of Huey LONG. After Long's assassination in 1935, Smith's views became increasingly fanatical and right-wing. An opponent of the labor movement and of President Franklin D. ROOSEVELT's NEW DEAL, he was a supporter of the pro-Nazi and anti-Semitic views of Father Charles COUGHLIN and a booster of what he called "true Americanism." In 1937 he founded the **Committee of One Million** to oppose communism, and five years later he established the right-wing monthly *The Cross and the Flag*, which he edited. In 1947 he established the Christian Nationalist Crusade, an organization that he headed until his death. (See also DEMAGOGUES.)

Smith, Holland McTyeire (*1882–1967*) U.S. Marines officer. He earned the nickname "Howlin' Mad" as a general in the marines. He pioneered methods of amphibious warfare, and commanded forces in the Gilbert, Marshall and Marianas Islands campaigns during WORLD WAR II. Smith was commander of the Fleet Marine Force in the Pacific from 1944 to 1945.

Smith, Ian (*1919– *) Prime minister of RHODESIA (1964–78). Smith first came to prominence during WORLD WAR II as a SPITFIRE fighter pilot in the BATTLE OF BRITAIN. A member of the Southern Rhodesia legislature from 1948 to 1953, he was a member of the federal parliament from 1953 to 1962, founder of the Rhodesian Front Party in 1962 and prime minister from 1964 to 1978. He declared independence for Southern Rhodesia unilaterally in 1965 (see UDI). After unsuccessful talks with British prime minister Harold WILSON aboard HMS *Tiger* in 1966 and HMS *Fearless* in 1968, Smith declared Rhodesia a republic in 1970. Forced by guerrilla war and external pressures to negotiate an internal settlement, he sought agreement with black moderates led by Bishop Abel MUZOREWA, forming a joint black and white government in 1978. Smith became minister without portfolio in the Zimbabwe-Rhodesia government under Muzorewa in 1979 and came to London for talks that finally settled the Rhodesia crisis. He returned as one of the white members of the first parliament of independent ZIMBABWE following the election won by Robert MUGABE, but was suspended from parliament in 1987.

Smith, James H., Jr. *(1909–1982)* American WORLD WAR II bomber pilot and assistant secretary of the navy (1953–56). In a highly publicized incident in 1953, Smith reinstated a navy official who had been accused of having communist leanings. Smith thus became one of the first officials of the EISENHOWER administration to resist MCCARTHYISM. He later headed the U.S. foreign aid program as chairman of the International Cooperation Administration (1957–59).

Smith, Kate *(1909–1986)* American singer. Smith's stirring rendition of Irving BERLIN's song "God Bless America" made her a symbol of U.S. patriotism. She acquired the rights to the song from Berlin, and her lusty rendition turned the song into a second national anthem during WORLD WAR II, when she traveled thousands of miles to entertain service people and sell war bonds. Her theme "When the Moon Comes over the Mountain," was one of 3,000 songs she recorded. She experienced a curious resurgence of popularity in the early 1970s when hockey's Philadelphia Flyers began to win whenever they substituted her recording of "God Bless America" for the national anthem. She even sang in person before several critical games, as the team went on to win two championships.

Smith, Lillian *(1897–1966)* American author and Civil Rights activist. She cofounded *The North Georgia Review* in 1936. As *South Today* it became the first white-run southern journal to publish the work of blacks. Her novels include *Strange Fruit* (1944) and *Killers of the Dream* (1949), which condemned racism. Her *One Hour* exposed

the McCarthy hysteria of the 1950s (see MCCARTHYISM), while *Our Faces, Our Worlds,* (1964) celebrated the CIVIL RIGHTS MOVEMENT. A friend of Dr. Martin Luther KING, Jr., Smith was also on the executive board of the CONGRESS OF RACIAL EQUALITY (CORE).

Smith, Maggie *(1934–)* British actress. An outstanding actress of both stage and screen, she has performed with the Old Vic Company, the National Theatre and the Stratford (Ontario) Festival, as well as in numerous West End and Broadway plays. In Britain she has won four best actress awards, including one for *Hedda Gabler* (1970) and one for *Virginia* (1981), while in the U.S. she won the 1990 Tony Award for *Lettice and Lovage.* Her many films include Oscar-winning performances in *The Prime of Miss Jean Brodie* and *California Suite.* She has also won many other acting awards and was made a Dame Commander of the Order of the British Empire (D.B.E.) in 1989. In 2001 Smith appeared as Professor Minerva McGonagall in *Harry Potter and the Sorcerer's Stone.* She reprised the role in *Harry Potter and the Chamber of Secrets* (2002) and *Harry Potter and the Prisoner of Azkaban* (2004).

Smith Court, Margaret *(1942–)* Australian tennis player. The rangy Smith was known for her strong serve and ground strokes, which helped her win seven consecutive Australian championships (1960–1966). At the peak of her career she won the French and U.S. Opens (1962) and Wimbledon (1963). In recent years, Smith has been outspoken in her political views, decrying the presence of lesbians on the professional tour. She was ordained and in 1991 founded Margaret Court Ministries.

Smith, Michael J. *(1945–1986)* American astronaut who was the pilot of the space shuttle *CHALLENGER* when it exploded on January 28, 1986. A U.S. Navy officer, Smith served as a combat pilot in the VIETNAM WAR and was decorated.

Smith, Stevie (Florence Margaret Smith) *(1902–1971)* British poet and novelist. Smiths's poetry, which includes the collections *A Good Time Was*

Had by All (1937), *Not Waving but Drowning* (1957) and *Scorpion* (1972), became increasingly popular after her retirement as a secretary in 1953, when she began giving poetry readings in her home in London. Her work, while on the surface witty and droll, carries an underlying sense of isolation and an obsession with death. She would often illustrate her poems with idiosyncratic *faux-naif* drawings, many of which can be found in *Some Are More Human than Others* (1958) and *Me Again: The Uncollected Writings of Stevie Smith, Illustrated by Herself* (1981). Smith was awarded the Chomondeley Award in 1966 and the Queen's Gold Medal for Poetry in 1969. She also wrote three novels, *Novel on Yellow Paper* (1936), *Over the Frontier* (1938) and *The Holiday* (1949). *Stevie,* an acclaimed film based on her life and starring Glenda JACKSON, was released in 1981.

Smith, Walter Wellesley "Red" *(1905–1982)* American sportswriter. Smith's impeccable and distinctive style combined with an integrity and wide-ranging knowledge that extended far beyond the sports arena gained him thousands of devoted readers and the respect of his peers. He began his career as a society news reporter in 1927, but soon switched to covering sports for the *St. Louis Star* (1928–36) and later the *Philadelphia Record* (1936–45). Moving to New York, he wrote for the *Herald Tribune* (1945–66) and also started a column that by 1972 was syndicated in 500 U.S. and foreign newspapers. In 1976 he won a PULITZER PRIZE for Distinguished Commentary. During his last 10 years he was the chief staff sportswriter of *The New York Times* and was considered the dean of American sportswriters.

Smith, William French *(1917– 1990)* U.S. attorney general. From the 1960s he was a friend and legal adviser to Ronald REAGAN. As president, Reagan appointed him attorney general in 1981, a post he held until 1985. During his tenure as head of the Justice Department, he presided over a shift to a more conservative agenda that included stronger attacks on organized crime and illegal drugs. Some critics saw a weaker enforcement of Civil Rights and antitrust laws during Smith's tenure.

Smith Act *(1940)* Controversial federal law prohibiting advocacy of the forcible or violent overthrow of the American government. Passed during the early days of World War II and before the U.S. entered the conflict, it was aimed at conspiracies by wartime subversives against the government. In later years it was used against leftists and suspected communists. The act was challenged in the case of *DENNIS V. UNITED STATES* (1951) as a violation of the First Amendment's protection of free speech. The Supreme Court upheld the statute, reasoning that a conspiracy to advocate the overthrow of the government would create a peril even if no action is imminent.

Smith and Dale American VAUDE-VILLE comedy team comprised of Joe Smith (1884–1981, born Joe Sultzer) and Charlie Dale (1881–1971, born Charles Marks). The two comedians started their partnership in 1898, playing in vaudeville theaters and Bowery saloons in New York. They went on to win wide acclaim for classic comedy sketches such as *Hungarian Rhapsody, Dr. Kronkheit, The New School Teacher* and *Venetian Knights*. In the early 1930s they starred in several HOLLYWOOD films. They remained active into the 1960s, appearing in nightclubs and on television. Smith and Dale helped establish the pattern of the deadpan straightman and his antic sidekick, a pattern followed by such later comedy teams as ABBOTT AND COSTELLO, Bob HOPE and Bing CROSBY, and Jerry LEWIS and Dean Martin. Smith and Dale were the models for the two aging vaudeville comedians in Neil SIMON's play *The Sunshine Boys* (1972, filmed 1975).

Smuts, Jan (Jan Christiaan Smuts) *(1870–1950)* South African soldier and statesman. Born in the Cape Colony, he was educated at Victoria College, Stellenbosch, and Cambridge. Smuts became a lawyer (1895) and was appointed state attorney in 1898. During the BOER WAR, he headed Boer commando forces in the Cape Colony (1901–02). Convinced of the necessity of Anglo-Boer cooperation, he and Louis BOTHA cofounded the moderate Het Volk Party in 1905. In 1910 Smuts played a leading role in the establishment of the Union of SOUTH AFRICA; he served as its minister of the interior

and mines (1910–12), finance (1912–13) and defense (1910–19). In 1916 he commanded Allied forces in their campaign against the Germans in East Africa. He served in the British war cabinet from 1917 to 1918 and represented South Africa at the VERSAILLES peace conference of 1919. A confirmed internationalist, Smuts was instrumental in creating the LEAGUE OF NATIONS. Returning to South Africa, he succeeded Botha as prime minister in 1919, serving until 1924. He was minister of justice under Gen. James Hertzog (1933–39) and again became prime minister upon the outbreak of WORLD WAR II. Declaring war on Germany, he sent economic aid to Great Britain, and his forces fought in a number of campaigns in Africa and Italy.

After the war, he was South Africa's representative at the 1945 conference that drafted the UNITED NATIONS charter. Smuts's moderating views on racial segregation were at variance with the prevailing views of white South Africans and largely accounted for his defeat by the National Party in the 1948 general elections. A man of great intellectual accomplishment, Smuts was also an evolutionary theorist, a botanist and a philosopher. He was noted for his powerful and thoughtful speeches and was the author of a number of books. The seven-volume *Selections from the Smuts Papers* was published between 1966 and 1973.

Smyslovsky, Boris *(1897–1988)* White Russian general. Smyslovsky commanded the First Russian National Army in the ranks of the German Wehrmacht during WORLD WAR II. His unit was the first Russian force to fight with HITLER against STALIN after the German invasion of the USSR in 1941. A member of the Russian Imperial Guard before the Bolsheviks seized power in 1917, Smyslovsky believed only the NAZIS were capable of defeating the Soviets and restoring the old regime. After the war he acquired Argentine citizenship under an assumed name.

Smyth, Henry *(1898–1986)* American physicist. During WORLD WAR II, while at Princeton University, Smyth's involvement in ATOM BOMB research led him to write the U.S. government's of-

ficial report on the development of the bomb, *Atomic Energy for Military Purposes*. The **Smyth Report**, as it was known, was published in 1945, shortly after the atomic bombings of HIROSHIMA and NAGASAKI. He was on the U.S. Atomic Energy Commission from 1949 to 1954, and from 1961 to 1970 was U.S. representative to the International Atomic Energy Agency.

Snead, Samuel Jackson *(1912–2002)* U.S. golfer. "Slammin' Sam" Snead was one of the dominant golfers of the first half of the 20th century. Although he is credited with 135 victories, he never won the U.S. Open, finishing second several times. A four-time winner of the Vardon Trophy, awarded by the PGA for the lowest average score in its events, he won the Masters Championship in 1949, 1952 and 1954 and the Professional Golfers' Association championship in 1942, 1949 and 1951.

Snedden, Sir Billy (Billy Mackle Snedden) *(1926–1987)* Australian politician. A leader of Australia's LIBERAL PARTY, Snedden held a number of senior posts after entering the federal house of representatives in 1955. During that tenure, he served as attorney general (1963–66), leader of the house (1966–70), minister of labor (1969–71) and treasurer (1971–72). He was Liberal Party leader in opposition from 1972 to 1975 and was speaker of the house for seven years until retiring in 1983.

Sneh, Moshe *(1909–1972)* Israeli communist politician. Sneh was commander-in-chief of HAGANAH, the underground guerrilla movement formed to gain Israel's independence. Sneh was later a member of the Knesset and a leader of Israel's small Communist Party. He broke with the Kremlin after the Soviets gave aid to the Arabs during the SIX DAY WAR of 1967.

Snider, Duke (Edwin Donald Snider) *(1926–)* American baseball player. Duke Snider is acknowledged as one of the three great center fielders in New York during the 1950s, along with Willie MAYS and Mickey MANTLE. Snider's play for the legendary Brooklyn Dodgers made him the dominant home run hitter of the 1950s. A graceful fielder with a strong arm, he was named a National League All-Star six times. The only man to hit four home runs in two World Series, he appeared in six fall classics with the Dodgers. He went with the team when they moved to Los Angeles in 1958, although the configuration of that park was not complementary to his style as a hitter. He was signed by the Mets in 1963, and spent his last season, 1964, with the Giants. He was named to the Hall of Fame in 1980 and wrote a best-selling autobiography in 1988.

Snoop Doggy Dogg (Calvin Broadus)

(1972–) American rap artist. Born Calvin Broadus in Long Beach, California, Snoop first appeared on the national rap or HIP-HOP music scene in 1991. The following year, Snoop signed with Death Row Records and collaborated with producer Dr. Dre on 'Nuthin But a G Thang.' This album became among the top selling, and the title track one of the most requested songs in the pop music world. Charges of participating in the drive-by murder of Phillip Woldermariam in Southern California actually enhanced Snoop's message among the rap audience as an artist who still lived the lifestyle of the urban gang member, or "gangsta." During the trial, Snoop continued to record singles for his first independent album, Doggystyle. More than 7 million copies of the album were sold worldwide. However, it elicited criticisms for misogynistic lyrics. In February 1996 Snoop was acquitted fully in the death of Woldermariam. In August 1998, he brought out Da Game Is To Be Sold, Not To Be Told. As his success as a rap artist declined, Dogg followed in the footsteps of his onetime collaborator, Dr. Dre, and became an executive producer of rap albums.

Snow, C(harles) P(ercy) (Baron Snow of Leicester) (1905–1980)

British novelist, essayist and physicist. Snow was a brilliant and versatile figure, earning a degree in physics at Cambridge University and working in scientific circles, at the same time establishing himself as one of the leading British novelists of his generation. His major literary work was the eleven-volume novelistic series, Strangers and Brothers, that appeared between 1940 and 1970 and chronicled the values and failings of the British intelligentsia and of the middle class. Snow, who held government advisory posts during both WORLD WAR II and the 1960s LABOUR PARTY era, was knighted in 1957 and became a member of the House of Lords. His most controversial work, the essay The Two Cultures and the Scientific Revolution (1960), decried the growing gap in knowledge and sympathy between the artistic and scientific communities.

Snow White and the Seven Dwarfs

The first full-length animated feature film and a milestone in the career of Walt DISNEY. He always had been fascinated with the Brothers Grimm story (he had seen a live-action Marguerite Clark film in Kansas City in 1915 during his boyhood) and in 1934 began planning an animated version. Dissatisfied with the cost inefficiency of producing only short cartoons (and aware these brief formats allowed little time for character development), he defied all the nay-sayers and proposed a feature-length project. It took four years. All the studio's technical resources were lavished on the picture: the newly developed multiplane camera added three-dimensional illusion, "rotoscoping" photographed live-action actors and transferred the images to drawings and unusually vivid color, music, and pacing imparted a freezing horror to the scenes with the Wicked Queen. "Character animation, as we called it, came into its own here," recalled veteran Disney animator Frank Thomas. "We were each assigned a particular character and a handful of particular situations. We had to become our drawings, just like an actor becomes his part. We acted them out, learned our lines, and made faces into our mirrors." As a result, dwarfs like "Dopey," "Grumpy" and "Doc" have become a part of the modern cultural vernacular. Songs like "Whistle While You Work," "One Song" and "Some Day My Prince Will Come," by Frank Churchill and Leigh Harline, have become standards. And the picture, after its unprecedented five weeks at the RADIO CITY MUSIC HALL (December 1937–January 1938), won a "Special" Oscar accompanied by seven miniature Oscars (see ACADEMY AWARDS). The box office success saved the Disney studios from financial ruin and spawned a host of imitations from rival studios, including the spoof "Coal Black and de Sebbin Dwarfs" from WARNER BROS. (which, for obvious reasons, is seldom seen today). However, not everyone joins in the acclaim. Because of the horror sequences the picture was banned in Great Britain. And fairy tale authority Bruno BETTELHEIM deplored such "ill-considered additions to fairy tale" as Disney's differentiation of each dwarf, which made it difficult to grasp "the story's deeper meaning." He may have a point, since few today can remember all seven dwarfs.

Soames, Baron (Arthur Christopher John Soames) (1920–1987)

British diplomat. A military hero during WORLD WAR II, in the early 1950s Lord Soames served as parliamentary secretary to his father-in-law, Sir Winston CHURCHILL. He held office under five subsequent conservative prime ministers. From 1968 to 1972, as ambassador to FRANCE, he played a key role in ensuring Great Britain's entry into the EUROPEAN COMMUNITY. His four-month stint as governor of RHODESIA in the period leading up to that colony's independence from Great Britain and emergence as the country of ZIMBABWE in 1980 was regarded as his greatest achievement.

Sobers, Gary (Sir Garfield St. Aubrun Sobers) (1936–)

Barbadan cricketer. Widely regarded as cricket's best all-rounder, Sobers excelled as both a batsman and bowler. In 93 test matches for the West Indies, Sobers scored 8,032 runs and bagged 235 wickets. His most notable achievement was his innings of 365 not out, the highest score in test cricket, which Sobers scored for the West Indies v. Pakistan in Kingston, Jamaica, on February 27–March 1, 1958. Sobers set another cricket milestone on August 31, 1968, when he became the first batsman to score the maximum 36 runs off a six-ball over, playing for Nottinghamshire v. Glamorgan in the English County Championship. Sobers began his test career in 1954 and first captained the West Indies in 1965. Overall Sobers captained the West Indies 39 times and played 39 tests, 1954–74. His career totals in test and first-class cricket were 28,315 runs and 1,043 wickets. A fine fielder, Sobers recorded 109 catches in test cricket. Following his retirement,

Sobers was knighted for his services to cricket. In 1998 the government of Barbados declared Sobers one of its national heroes.

Sobhuza II *(1899–1982)* King of SWAZILAND (1900–82). Sobhuza became king at the age of one and was the longest-reigning monarch of any country in the 20th century. Known to his people as "the Lion," he seized absolute power after Swaziland gained independence from Britain in 1969. He encouraged foreign investment and kept peace with neighboring SOUTH AFRICA and MOZAMBIQUE.

Sobibor Nazi CONCENTRATION CAMP in German-occupied Soviet territory (now within Poland) during WORLD WAR II. In June 1941 HITLER authorized the execution of all communists and Jews caught behind German lines. Sobibor was created in April 1942 to exterminate Jews captured during the German advance into Russia. At its peak the camp was capable of liquidating up to 20,000 victims per day. The only successful mass escape from a concentration camp occurred at Sobibor.

Sobukwe, Robert Mangaliso *(1924–1978)* South African black nationalist leader. Sobukwe founded and led the banned Pan African Congress. He was an advocate of passive resistance. He was imprisoned for three years in connection with the 1960 SHARPEVILLE MASSACRE, in which police opened fire on him and other blacks protesting the use of identity cards. After his three-year jail term expired, he was held an additional six years under a special amendment to the Suppression of Communism Act that later became known as the "Sobukwe Clause." After his release from prison he was put under a five-year banning order that was renewed in 1974.

social credit A political movement that advocated a redistribution of wealth by increasing workers' purchasing power. The movement originated with Clifford Hugh Douglas, a Scot who theorized that national income could be increased by increasing worker purchasing power, this by socializing the banking system (to ease credit) and by the payment of national dividends to workers. The workers' in-creased purchasing power would stimulate production, which would in turn increase the money supply. Social credit theories gained some support during the GREAT DEPRESSION of the 1930s but never became national policy in any country.

Social Democratic Party (SDP) British political party founded in 1981 by the so-called gang of four—David OWEN, Shirley WILLIAMS, Roy JENKINS and William RODGERS. These four leading moderates in the LABOUR PARTY objected to the leftward turn the Labour Party had taken, and saw the SDP as an alternative for disillusioned Labour supporters. The SDP's stance was a moderate, reformist social democratic one. In 1981 it formed an alliance with the LIBERAL PARTY. Although the party enjoyed some success in by-elections and showed significant support in opinion polls, its candidates failed to make substantial headway in the general elections of 1983 and 1987. In 1988 the SDP was dissolved, its members merging with the Liberal Party to form the **Liberal Democratic Party.**

Socialist International See INTERNATIONAL.

Socialist Realism The "basic method" of art and literature. Although works of Socialist Realism existed prior to 1930, in 1934 the doctrine was officially adopted at the first all-union congress of Soviet writers. Accordingly, art should be the truthful, historically concrete presentation of reality in its revolutionary development and must also assist with the ideological remaking and education of writers in the spirit of socialism. Thus all art was constrained by the duty to base it on Marxist-Leninist philosophy.

Socialist Revolutionaries Political party founded in 1902 by the leaders of revolutionary populism. It was led by Viktor Chernov and Nicholas Avksentev. It demanded socialization of the land, a federal state structure and self-determination for non-Russian peoples. One section of the party, the Left Socialist Revolutionaries, having supported the Bolsheviks in 1917, played a part in the Bolshevik government until the Treaty of BREST-LITOVSK of 1918. In 1922 the Bolsheviks suppressed the party.

Social Security Act of 1935 Landmark U.S. law that created a universal safety net for working Americans by establishing old age pensions, unemployment insurance and survivor and disability benefits. Prior to 1935 the federal government was not involved in the social welfare area. The lack of programs was especially acute during the GREAT DEPRESSION of the 1930s when millions were out of work and many of the aged had lost their savings in bank failures and the stock market crash. The Social Security Act contained help for three groups: the aged, the unemployed and women and children. The act provided old age pensions for those who had worked and contributed; unemployment compensation benefits, administered by the states; and increased health services for the needy. The system was to be funded through both employee and employer contributions. The program was administered by the Social Security Administration, which would also oversee the later MEDICARE program, providing hospitalization of senior citizens.

Söderblom, Nathan *(1866–1931)* Swedish Lutheran clergyman and theologian. Söderblom, who won the NOBEL PRIZE for peace in 1930, is best remembered for his ardent devotion to the cause of ecumenism. His greatest achievement was the organizing of the Universal Christian Conference on Life and Work in Stockholm in 1925. The success of this conference led ultimately to the creation, in 1948, of the WORLD COUNCIL OF CHURCHES. Söderblom, who taught for many years at the University of Uppsala, was a popular teacher who sparked a renewed interest in Christianity amongst the youths of his native land. His writings include *Christian Fellowship* (1923) and *The Church and Peace* (1929).

Solal, Martial *(1927–)* Algerian-born French jazz pianist and winner of the Jazzpar Award (1999). When he was seven, Solal began to study the piano with his mother, an opera singer in Algiers, the capital of the French territory of ALGERIA. By the time he was an adult, he had become greatly influenced by jazz musicians, such as "Fats" WALLER,

Bud Powell and Earl "Fatha" HINES and began playing accompaniment to jazz pieces in Algiers before moving to Paris, France in 1950. It was in Paris that he earned the attention of prominent French and American jazz musicians, such as Don Byas, Miles DAVIS, Lucky Thompson and Sidney Bechet. Along with his own recordings and his collaborations with artists such as Lee Konitz, Hampton Hawes, John Lewis and Stéphane GRAPPELLI, Solal also composed more than 20 motion picture soundtracks and scores, starting with the JEAN-LUC GODARD film *Breathless* (1959). In 1999 Solal became the first resident of a non–English-speaking country to win the Jazzpar award, given to a jazz artist in recognition of his or her contributions to the world of jazz music.

Solana, Javier (Francisco Javier Solana Madariaga) *(1942–)* Spanish professor, politician, secretary-general of the NORTH ATLANTIC TREATY ORGANIZATION (NATO) (1995–99), High Representative of the Common Foreign and Security Policy (CFSP) agency and secretary-general of the Council of the EUROPEAN UNION (EU) (1999–). Born in Madrid, Spain, Solana studied and taught physics. He was elected to the Spanish parliament in 1977 as a member of Spain's Socialist Party, and he remained there until 1995. Solana held a variety of ministerial posts in Socialist governments, including minister for foreign affairs (1992–95).

As secretary-general of NATO, Solana supervised the organization's Implementation Force (IFOR), a yearlong peace-keeping force dispatched to Bosnia as part of the 1995 DAYTON ACCORDS. Solana arranged for a prolonged NATO peacekeeping presence in Bosnia through the replacement of IFOR with a new Stabilization Force (SFOR). In 1997 Solana coordinated efforts by NATO to incorporate Russia into the alliance with the status of a "partner," which would permit Russia to occupy a consultative position in the formulation of NATO policy. This new relationship with a former NATO foe, termed the Founding Act, served as the template for a similar arrangement with Ukraine two months later and has led to the inclusion of 28 such partner countries within NATO's decision-making apparatus. In October 1999 Solana resigned as secretary-general of NATO and became High Representative of the new CFSP and Secretary General of the Council of the EU. In 2004 he was designated as the EU's first minister of foreign affairs. In those positions he has represented the EU in negotiations with various countries and organizations. He was one of the prime architects of the "Road Map for Peace" for the Middle East, along with representatives of the UN, the U.S. and Russia.

Solidarity (Solidarność) Polish trade union. Unofficial strikes by workers in POLAND's coalfields and shipyards in the summer of 1980 forced the government to permit the formation of independent trade unions. Solidarity was officially formed on September 22, 1980, by Lech WAŁĘSA, an electrician at the Lenin Shipyard in Gdańsk, POLAND. In the following months, the union's membership swelled and, together with the Catholic Church, Solidarity became a potent force against communism in Poland, claiming 10 million members. On December 12, 1981, Solidarity called for a national referendum on free elections. The following day Prime Minister JARUZELSKI declared martial law, banned Solidarity and arrested its leaders. However, Solidarity continued to operate underground, with many members showing open but peaceful defiance of the government. Solidarity was re-legalized in April 1989. In free elections in June 1989, Solidarity members won many seats in the new national assembly. In August, 1989, journalist Tadeusz MAZOWIECKI was elected prime minister of Poland. However, many Solidary supporters were dissatisfied with the pace of change and with deteriorating economic conditions, and the movement split into two factions. Mazowiecki led the intellectual wing, while Wałęsa was favored by rank-and-file workers. After his defeat in a three-way election for the presidency of Poland in 1990, Mazowiecki threw his support to Wałęsa, who was subsequently elected.

Solomon (Solomon Cutner) *(1902–1988)* British pianist; known by his first name alone, he created a stir as a child prodigy from his first appearances. Solomon went on to a major career as a mature concert artist whose technical gifts were matched by his intellectual understanding of his repertory. In his later years he focused particularly on Mozart, Beethoven, Schumann and Brahms. His career was cut short in the late 1950s after he suffered a stroke.

Solomon Islands Scattered over 249,000 nautical square miles of the southwestern Pacific Ocean between New Guinea and Vanuatu, the Solomon Islands archipelago consists of several hundred islands with a total land area of 10,980 square miles (see map on page 957). However, the country's social and economic problems continued to worsen until finally in 2003 the government called on Australia to send peacekeeping troops to restore law and order. The six main islands are GUADALCANAL, Malaita, New Georgia, San Cristóbal (now known as Makira), Santa Isabel and Choiseul. The larger islands are typified by densely forested mountain ranges with deep river valleys, ringed by narrow coastal plains, supporting the bulk of the population, and coral reefs. Most of the outer islands are small, evolving coral atolls. The abuses of labor recruiters led Britain in 1893 to establish a protectorate over the southern Solomons; in 1900 Britain acquired the northern Solomons from Germany. Commercial development began early in the 20th century with the development of the copra industry on a large scale, until a fall in prices in the 1920s. During WORLD WAR II the Japanese occupied the main islands from 1942 to 1943, until Allied forces drove them out after fierce fighting. Antigovernment movements, notably Marching Rule, emerged in the postwar period. But after their decline and a lessening of the political tension that had hampered development and administration, there was a gradual increase in the establishment of local government councils. In 1976 self-government was introduced, and "Solomon Islands" was officially adopted in place of "British Solomon Islands Protectorate." The country became independent on July 7, 1978, as a constitutional monarchy within the Commonwealth, with the governor-general as the British monarch's representative. A cyclone caused widespread destruction in 1986. In a scandal over the allocation of cyclone-damage aid, Prime Minister Sir Peter Kenilorea re-

SOLOMON ISLANDS

1900	A unified British Solomon Islands Protectorate is formed and placed under the jurisdiction of the Western Pacific High Commission (WPHC), which has its headquarters in the Fiji Islands.
1942–43	The islands are occupied by Japan. They are the site of fierce fighting during World War II, especially on Guadalcanal, which is recaptured by U.S. forces, with the loss of 21,000 Japanese soldiers and 5,000 U.S. troops.
1943–50	The Marching Rule (Ma'asina Ruru) cargo cult populist movement develops on Malaita island, campaigning for self-rule.
1976	The islands become fully self-governing.
1978	The Solomon Islands becomes an independent state within the Commonwealth.
1986	A cyclone causes widespread damage; Prime Minister Kenilorea resigns amid a scandal over disaster aid; Ezekial Alebua becomes prime minister.
1989	Solomon Mamaloni regains the office of prime minister.
1997	Bartholomew Ulufa'alu becomes prime minister as a head of a coalition government.
2001	In February the Mauru peace agreement brokered by Australia is signed by Marau Eagle Force.
2002	Social and economic problems get worse, with the government unable to pay wages.
2003	With the country on the brink of anarchy, the government asks Australia and New Zealand to send a peacekeeping force. The force is sent and order is restored.

signed in late 1986 and was succeeded by Ezekiel Alebua, a colleague from the ruling Solomon Islands United Party. The Alebua government was decisively defeated at a general election in February 1989 and was replaced by a government led by Solomon Mamaloni, the leader of the People's Alliance Party. While the government of Bartholomew Ulufa'alu battled an insurgent campaign from the Malaitan Eagle Force (MEF) from 1998 to 2000, it agreed to a peace settlement that involved peace-keeping troops from Australia to patrol the MEF's disarmament. However, the country's social and economic problems continued to worsen until finally in 2003 the government called on Australia to send peacekeeping troops to restore law and order.

Solomon R. Guggenheim Museum

Located in New York City, one of the most important museums in the U.S. specializing in the collection and display of modern art. Founded in 1939 as the Museum of Non-objective Art, the importance and visibility of the institution were vastly enhanced when it moved into its present building, a major late work of Frank Lloyd WRIGHT. This building, completed in 1959, is a unique and striking design in reinforced concrete, having as its main exhibit space a spiral ramp wound around a skylit central space that runs the full height of the building. Wright died before the building was completed so that some details may not be quite as he intended. Although the architecture is often criticized as so strong as to over-power the works exhibited there, the museum is still one of Wright's masterpieces as well as one of the most exciting New York City buildings. The museum later required more space, and considerable controversy developed over the Gwathmey, Siegel & Associates' addition.

Solow, Robert M. (1924–) American economist, professor and recipient

Architect Frank Lloyd Wright, Baroness Hilla Rebay and Solomon R. Guggenheim with a model of the Solomon R. Guggenheim museum. 1947 (NEW YORK WORLD-TELEGRAM AND THE SUN NEWSPAPER COLLECTION, LIBRARY OF CONGRESS, PRINTS AND PHOTOGRAPHS DIVISION)

of the Nobel Prize in economics (1987). Born in Brooklyn, New York, Solow received his B.A. (1947) and Ph.D. (1951) in economics from Harvard University. In 1950 he joined the economics faculty at the Massachusetts Institute of Technology, where he has remained for the rest of his academic career. In 1961 Solow worked for President John F. KENNEDY's Council of Economic Advisors, where he helped formulate the president's economic policies.

Solow helped transform the manner in which economists account for economic growth and wage adjustments. In his paper "A Contribution to the Theory of Growth," he contended that full employment of the labor market in a given country could be achieved by adjustments in the hourly wage paid to employees. In another paper he wrote in 1957, called "Technical Change and the Aggregate Production Function," Solow examined economic growth in industrial countries. He argued that the most dynamic and unaccounted for sources of this growth were technological advances in production and distribution, which led to the technology-driven aspects of economic growth that came to be known as the "Solow residual." As a result of Solow's article, governments such as SOUTH KOREA began to invest heavily in improving their nations' educational systems in the hopes of being able to maximize economic growth produced by the Solow residual. In 1987 Solow won the Nobel Prize in economics for his contributions to the understanding of the technological factors causing economic growth.

Solti, Sir George (1912–1997)

Hungarian-British conductor. Born in Budapest, Solti studied piano with Béla BARTÓK, Zoltán KODÁLY and Ernst VON DOHNANYI at the Liszt Academy, graduating in 1930. He entered the music profession as an opera coach. In 1936 he assisted Arturo TOSCANINI at the SALZBURG FESTIVAL and in 1938 made his conducting debut at the Budapest State Opera. After spending World War II in Switzerland, Solti was appointed director of the Munich State Opera (1946–52) by the American military government. He subsequently served as director of the Frankfurt Opera (1952–61), the Royal Opera at Covent Garden (1961–71) and the

Chicago Symphony Orchestra (1971–90), among other posts. He became a British subject and was knighted in 1972. Solti became widely known in the late 1950s, when he began recording the complete *Ring* cycle of Richard Wagner. This widely hailed set established high sonic and technical standards for the new medium of stereophonic recording, and it is still considered one of the most impressive opera recordings ever made. Likewise, some critics considered the Chicago Symphony under Solti to be the finest orchestra in the world. Solti is known for the intensity, brilliance and precision of his performances, which emphasize the dramatic rather than the lyrical aspects of the music. He was most effective leading large-scale symphonic and operatic works and championed such 20th-century composers as Bartok, Gustav MAHLER, Richard STRAUSS, Igor STRAVINSKY and Arnold SCHOENBERG. Solti made numerous recordings and won more Grammy Awards than any other classical musician.

Solzhenitsyn, Alexander Isayevich

(1918–) Russian dissident novelist, memoirist and historian who chronicled the horrors of STALINISM in several important books. Solzhenitsyn has been regarded as the conscience of the Soviet Union in the 20th century. He studied mathematics and physics at Rostov University, as well as obtaining a degree in literature. During World War II Solzhenitsyn served in the Red Army as a gunner and artillery officer at the front, for which he was decorated. In February 1945 he was arrested in Konigsberg by SMERSH on the grounds that he had criticized STALIN; he then spent eight years in labor camps. Released in 1953, Solzhenitsyn spent three years in internal exile. During this time he suffered from stomach cancer but recovered after treatment. He subsequently taught in a secondary school in Ryazan. In 1962, with KHRUSHCHEV's approval, he was permitted to publish *One Day in the Life of Ivan Denisovich*, an account of life in the Soviet GULAG, in the journal *Novy Mir*. This work established his reputation. However, in 1968 he was attacked in the *Literaturnaya Gazeta*. He won the NOBEL PRIZE for literature in 1970, but was expelled from the writers' union that same year and arrested and de-

ported in 1974, following the publication in Europe of the first volume of the GULAG ARCHIPELAGO. Solzhenitsyn eventually settled in Vermont. As well as denouncing Soviet communism, Solzhenitsyn has also been highly critical of Western materialism. In the late 1980s, the GORBACHEV government announced that Solzhenitsyn was free to return to the USSR, but he refused this invitation. In 1990 Solzhenitsyn also refused a literary prize for the *Gulag Archipelago* offered by the Russian Republic, saying that "the phenomenon of the Gulag has not been overcome either legally or morally. . . . This book is about the suffering of millions and I cannot reap an honor from it." Solzhenitsyn's other works include *Cancer Ward* (1968), *The First Circle* (1968), *August 1914* (1971, tr. 1972) *The Oak and the Calf* (1975, tr. 1980) and *From Under the Rubble*. After the breakup of the Soviet Union in 1991, Solzhenitsyn returned to Russia in 1994. Three years later, he was inducted into the Russian Academy of Sciences. In 2000 he attempted to use his national prestige to encourage new Russian president Vladimir PUTIN to enact a series of political, economic and social reforms that Solzhenitsyn hoped would return Russia to a more traditional, paternalistic society. Since returning to his homeland, Solzhenitsyn has published *The Russian Question* (1995), *Indivisible Allies* (1997) and *Two Hundred Years Together* (2003), the latter work generating controversy because of its portrayal of the important role Russian Jews played in the Bolshevik Revolution and the early years of the SOVIET UNION.

Somalia (Somali Democratic Republic)

Somalia, located on the Horn of Africa, covers an area of 246,136 square miles. Northern Somalia became a British protectorate in 1885; southern Somalia became an Italian protectorate in 1889, then a UNITED NATIONS trusteeship in 1950. Northern and southern Somalia were unified when full independence was gained in 1960, but ethnic rivalries erupted. President Shermakhe was assassinated in 1969, and the subsequent military coup brought Major General Mohammed Siyad Barre to power. In 1964 and 1977 Somalia went to war with its biggest neighbor, ETHIOPIA, over claims

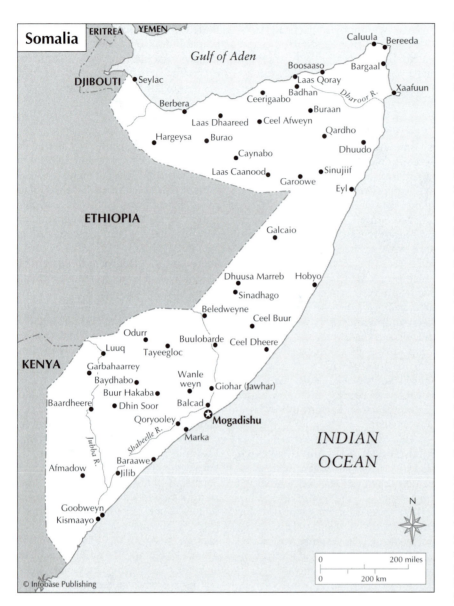

Somalia

ERITREA
YEMEN
Gulf of Aden

DJIBOUTI • Seylac
• Berbera
Hargeysa • Burao
• Laas Dhaareed • Ceel Afweyn
• Caynabo
• Laas Caanood
• Garoowe
Caluula • Bereeda
Boosaaso Bargaal
Laas Qoray
Badhan • Xaafuun
Ceerigaabo
Buraan
Qardho
Dhuudo
Sinujiif
Eyl

Dharoor R.

ETHIOPIA

KENYA

Galcaio

Dhuusa Marreb Hobyo
• Sinadhago
Beledweyne
Ceel Buur
Odurr
Buulobarde Ceel Dheere
• Luuq Tayeegloc
Garbahaarrey
Baydhabo • Wanle weyn
Buur Hakaba • Giohar (Jawhar)
Baardheere • Dhin Soor Balcad
Qoryooley ✪ Mogadishu
Marka

INDIAN
OCEAN

Shabeelle R.
Jubba R.

Afmadow
Baraawe
Jilib

Goobweyn
Kismaayo

N

0   200 miles
0   200 km

© Infobase Publishing

to the Ogaden region—resulting in a defeat in 1978 that led Barre to shift allegiances from the Soviet Union to the United States. Opposition groups carried on a guerrilla war from bases in Ethiopia until 1987, when they occupied northern Somalia and a full-scale civil war erupted. The rebels captured the capital and overthrew the government early in 1991, but the political situation remained uncertain. In 1991 opposition elements ousted Barre, leaving Somalia controlled by warlords such as Mohammad Farrah AIDEED, whom President William Jefferson CLINTON unsuccessfully attempted to oust with U.S. forces in 1993. By 1995 UN peacekeepers abandoned a three-year unsuccessful effort in Somalia to restore order and establish a conduit for dissemination of humanitarian aid throughout the country. While the 1996 death of Aideed failed to bring an end to Somalia's internal chaos, a 1997 Cairo conference of rival warlords sought to lay the groundwork for a broad coalition government.

But the various factions have not succeeded in establishing a central government with effective authority throughout the country. Northern clans declared an independent Republic of Somaliland, which includes the administrative regions of Awdal, Woqooyi, Galbeed, Togdheer, Sanaag and Sool. Since 1998 an autonomous state called Puntland has operated in the regions of Bari and Nugaal and northern Mudug. A Transitional National Government created in neighboring Djibouti in 2000 failed to acquire legitimacy, and a Transitional Federal Government established in 2004 has been unable to move to the capital of Mogadishu.

Somerville and Ross Collective pen name of Irish authors Edith Onone Somerville (1858–1949) and Violet Florence Martin (1862–1915). Somerville and Ross were second cousins who first met in 1886 and subsequently began collaborating on writing fiction. Their combined voice was seamless, and their fiction, while reflecting their Protestant Ascendancy backgrounds, humorously chides their social class. Much of their work, such as *The Real Charlotte* (1894), depicts the decline of the Big House. They are perhaps best remembered for the popular stories *Some Experiences of an Irish R. M.* (1899), which was successfully adapted for television by the BBC in the 1980s. After Martin's death in 1915, Somerville, who claimed to be in communication with her, continued writing less successfully as Somerville and Ross, though *The Big House of Inver* (1925) is notable in its depiction of the decline of a social institution.

Somme, Battles of the Two important WORLD WAR I battles that were fought near the Somme River in northwest France. The First Battle of the Somme took place from June 24 to November 13, 1916. It pitted the forces of the British Fourth Army and the French Sixth Army against an entrenched German force along the Somme. It was intended to dislodge the highly fortified Germans from their positions and to relieve pressure on the French at VERDUN. Following weeklong artillery fire, the Allies attacked on July 1, led by the British under Field Marshal Sir Douglas HAIG. Terrible casualties were taken by the British, who suffered 60,000 casualties and 19,000 dead on the first day alone, and who lost over 400,000 men (the French lost almost 200,000) during the 20 weeks of successive attacks. The cost to Germany too was catastrophic, with casualties amounting to about 600,000. The battle proved indecisive, with the German positions only slightly changed but the objectives at Verdun largely achieved. However, the enormous losses sustained by Germany at the Somme and at Verdun

---

SOMALIA

1948	Ethiopia regains Ogaden region from Somalia.
1960	Britain and Italy each grant independence to their Somali territories, which reunify to form a republic.
1964	War with Ethiopia for Ogaden region; first national elections.
1969	Major General Mohammed Siyad Barre comes to power in military coup; adopts policy of "scientific socialism," governing through a Revolutionary Council of 25.
1981	Somali National Movement (SNM) is formed in opposition to Barre regime and, with other rebel groups, undertakes guerrilla war against the government from bases in Ethiopia.
1988	Fighting over Ogaden region ends when Ethiopia and Somalia sign peace agreement.
1990	Siyad Barre's bodyguards kill 65 at soccer match, shooting into crowd that booed and threw stones as Barre made pre-game speech; in the continuing civil war, rebels approach capital and Barre is forced to flee his palace.
1991	Siyad Barre is overthrown.
1993	U.S. forces fail to oust warlord Muhammad Aideed.
1995	United Nations peacekeepers withdraw from the country.
1996	Aideed dies, but chaos and factional strife continues.
2000	Transitional National Government established in neighboring Djibouti.
2004	Transitional Federal Government created, but fails to establish legitimacy.

---

have been considered the beginning of the end of the German cause. The Second Battle of the Somme took place from March 21 to April 5, 1918. In an attempt to inflict a decisive defeat on the Allies before the arrival of U.S. forces, German troops under General Erich LUDENDORFF attacked along a 60-mile front. Early German successes against the British (again under Haig) and the French were reversed when French reserves under general Ferdinand FOCH counterattacked. This battle also took a terrible toll, with the Allies and the Germans each suffering almost 250,000 casualties.

Somoza Debayle, Anastasio (1925–1980) President of NICARAGUA (1967–72, 1974–79). The Somoza family controlled Nicaragua for 45 years; Anastasio Somoza was the last of the Somozas to hold office. His imposition of martial law in 1972, suppression of opponents and violations of human rights led the U.S. to abandon its support for Somoza, despite the risk of a takeover by left-wing Sandinista guerrillas. Somoza fled the country in 1979 as Sandinista troops marched on the capital. He was assassinated in 1980.

sonar System used to locate underwater objects by means of echoing sound waves; an acronym for "sound navigation and ranging." It was first developed by Allied scientists during WORLD WAR I as a device for locating submarines and icebergs. In essence, sonar is the same system used by marine animals, notably porpoises, to locate their prey. The sonar device generates pulses of underwater sound waves through a transmitter. When an echo from a submerged object or the bottom of a body of water returns it is picked up by a hydrophone receiver, passed through an amplifier and, converted into electrical impulses, displayed. This display may be in the form of a stylus writing on a strip of moving paper, may be shown on a cathode-ray tube or may be broadcast as sound through a loudspeaker. The time elapsed between the sending of the sound and the return of its echo indicates the depth of the object or ocean floor. Sonar is used for the detection of submarines and for communication between submarines; also employed by commercial and sport fishermen as a locator for schools of fish and in marine seismology, archaeology and exploration.

Sondheim, Stephen (1930–) American composer and lyricist. An outstanding composer and lyricist of the American musical, Sondheim first gained recognition as a lyricist for *West Side Story* (1957). Among successful musicals for which he wrote both music and lyrics are *Company* (1970), *Follies* (1971), *A Little Night Music* (1973) and *Sweeney Todd* (1979), each of which won a Tony Award. He is known for the operatic nature of his scores and for his experimentation, such as in the Kabuki-like *Pacific Overtures* (1976); *Sunday in the Park with George* (1984), inspired by Georges Seurat paintings; and *Into the Woods* (1987), based on fairy tales. In the 1990s and 2000s Sondheim has produced four new musicals for

Broadway—*Assassins* (1991); *Passion* (1994), based on the book by James Lapine; *Saturday Night* (1997), which he originally wrote in 1954; and *Bounce* (2003). He has also continued to receive awards in recognition of his contributions to the American music scene, such as the 1985 Pulitzer Prize for drama for *Sunday in the Park with George* and the 1993 Kennedy Center Honors.

Song Meiling (Sung Meiling, Soong Mei-ling) *(1897–2003)* Song Meiling was a member of the wealthy and influential Song (Sung or Soong) family in Shanghai. She was trained in sociology at Wellesley College in the U.S. and was married to CHIANG KAI-SHEK (Jiang Jieshi) from 1927 until his death in 1975. Her son Chiang Ching-kuo (Jiang Qingguo;1910–88) succeeded his father as head of the KUOMINTANG (Guomindang) Party. Although she held few official posts, she served as her husband's adviser and became internationally known while traveling widely to seek support for the Kuomintang cause. In 1988 she joined other conservative mainlanders in an unsuccessful attempt to block Li Denghui (LEE TENG-HUI's) confirmation as head of the Kuomintang. Song lived in the U.S. from 1975 until her death.

Song Qingling (Sung Qingling, Soong Ching-ling) *(1892–1981)* Chinese stateswoman and a leading figure in the People's Republic of CHINA, often called the "conscience of China." Educated in the U.S. (1908–13), shortly after her return to China (1913) Song (Sung or Soong) succeeded her older sister as the secretary of the nationalist revolutionary leader SUN YAT-SEN. She married Sun (1914) while they were in temporary exile in Japan. After Sun's death (1925), she was critical of the policies of his successor, CHIANG KAI-SHEK (Jiang Jieshi). In 1927 she resigned from the KUOMINTANG (Guomindang), which Sun had established, and spent two years in the USSR. Thereafter she lived quietly in Shanghai, moving to HONG KONG (1937) after war broke out with JAPAN. She returned to Shanghai at the end of the war (1945). Although she supported the communists under MAO ZEDONG (Mao Tse-tung), she was not herself a member of the Communist Party. After 1949 she served in a number of high posts in the People's Republic of

China and was held in high esteem by the Chinese. A month before her death she was named honorary chairman of China, the nation's highest tribute.

Sonneborn, Rudolf Goldschmid *(1898–1986)* American industrialist and Zionist leader. Sonneborn developed a small family business into a flourishing concern dealing with petroleum specialty products. Active on behalf of the Jewish community in PALESTINE from as early as the end of World War I, he did much to assist Jewish refugees in Europe during WORLD WAR II. After the creation of Israel in 1948, he was in the forefront of campaigns that raised hundreds of millions of dollars for the new state.

Son of Sam killings Series of eight attacks in New York City from July 1976 to August 1977, in which six young persons were killed and another seven were wounded. For more than a year, New York City was terrorized by the pseudonymous killer, who signed himself "Son of Sam" in letters to newspapers and who claimed that "Sam" was forcing him to commit the crimes. The shootings, which ranged over the Bronx, Queens and Brooklyn and which were all committed with a .44-caliber pistol, were mostly directed at young women or at couples parked in cars. Finally, on August 10, 1977, a 25-year-old mailman and former auxiliary policeman named David Berkowitz was apprehended. He pleaded guilty and was sentenced to 30 years in prison, the harshest penalty allowed under law.

Sontag, Susan *(1933–2004)* American intellectual, critic, essayist, novelist, short story writer and filmmaker. Sontag studied at Berkeley, Chicago, Harvard and Oxford and was at various times a lecturer in English, philosophy, and religion. She is probably best known for *Against Interpretation* (1966), which argued that the proper response to art is intuitive not intellectual. *Trip to Hanoi* (1968) voiced her opposition to the VIETNAM WAR. *Styles of Radical Will* (1969) explored ways of altering one's consciousness for aesthetic purposes. Other works include *On Photography* (1977), *Illness as Metaphor* (1978) and *Under the Sign of Saturn* (1980). In *AIDS and Its Metaphors* she explored the ef-

fects of AIDS on social thought. Neither her experimental films nor her novels—*The Benefactor* (1963), *Death Kit* (1967), *The Volcano Lover* (1992)—were as successful as her criticism. Sontag's influential essays appeared regularly in leading cultural periodicals, and she was widely esteemed as an intellectual leader in matters of aesthetic taste and moral judgment. In 2000 Sontag received the National Book Award for her fourth and final novel, *In America* (2000).

Sony Japanese manufacturer of consumer electronic products, known for its high standards of both technical quality and design. The firm was founded immediately after World War II as TTK (an abbreviation of the Japanese for Tokyo Telecommunications Engineering) by Masaru Ibuka and Akio Morita. In 1955 the firm marketed the first transistor radio, the TR-55, under the Sony brand name, beginning a flow of miniaturized electronic products. The 1959 portable television, TV5-303, made TV compact and convenient. The Trinitron color TV tube of 1968 introduced a new level of color picture quality and began a sequence of TV products of good design quality that have become internationally known. The 1979 Walkman cassette tape recorder introduced the pocketable hi-fi music system. Although Sony designers remain anonymous, the quality of Sony design has been a major factor in the success of the firm's products.

In 1980 Sony began to develop more expensive high-technology product lines. It marketed a word-processing system for the English-speaking business and consumer markets, the "Series 35." By 1982 it had developed its own computer, the SMC-70, which was one of several machines similar to the PERSONAL COMPUTER (PC) developed by IBM (INTERNATIONAL BUSINESS MACHINES). Sony was the first electronics firm to design the smaller and more durable 3.5-inch floppy disks and disk drives (1982) and the then-high-resolution graphics computer display monitor (1983). In 1992 Sony became well known for its portable compact disc (CD) music players, which soon replaced the Sony Walkman as the preferred method of listening to recorded music. In 1995 Sony introduced the first flat-panel television display system. Unlike previous television sets, which had curved screens so as to allow viewers to see the same picture from different angles, the flat-panel set—named the "Plasmatron"—accomplished the same effect without the curved surface. This new television set design became the foundation for later advances made by Sony and other television makers into the high-definition television (HDTV) market.

Sony also developed a powerful presence in the entertainment industry. In 1968, it joined with the COLUMBIA BROADCASTING SERVICES (CBS) to found CBS/Sony Records, Inc., which in 1978 created the important subsidiary Epic Records. By 1988, Sony had bought out CBS's share in their joint venture. In 1989 Sony purchased another CBS-related company, Columbia Pictures. By 1993 Sony also began forays into the emerging computer games industry when it founded Sony Computer Entertainment (SCE). In 1994 SCE released the Sony Playstation, a console system designed to interface with television sets. In addition to licensing computer game manufacturers to develop versions of their product for the Playstation, SCE also began to develop its own line of computer games. In 2000 Sony introduced the Sony Playstation 2, which led to the production of more graphically intense computer games and enabled SCE to compete with the Nintendo and Microsoft computer game systems released that year.

Soong Ching-ling See SONG QINGLING.

Soong Mei-ling See SONG MELING.

Sopranos, The A cable-television drama series developed for broadcast on the Home Box Office cable network in 1999 by David Chase. *The Sopranos* focus on the New Jersey–based Soprano Mafia family, headed by Tony Soprano (James Gandolfini). The series also followed Soprano's developing relationship with his psychologist, Dr. Jennifer Melfi (Lorraine Bracco), and the growing rift between Soprano and his wife, Carmella (Edie Falco), and two children, Meadow (Jamie-Lynn DiScala) and A. J. (Robert Iler). *The Sopranos* became well known for its ability to retain viewers in its Sunday evening time slot, despite being avail-

able to the smaller cable audience and possessing a dark and violent story line. A formidable force at awards shows, the program garnered 12 Emmy Awards, including three Outstanding Lead Actor Awards in a Drama Series for James Gandolfini and three Outstanding Lead Actress Awards in a Drama Series for Edie Falco.

Sopwith, Sir Thomas Octave Murdoch *(1888–1989)* British aircraft designer. A pioneer in the field of aircraft design, Sopwith was best known for his WORLD WAR I Sopwith Camel fighter plane. The Sopwith Camel was considered the most maneuverable of all World War I aircraft and shot down more enemy aircraft than any other Allied plane. Canadian flying ace Captain Roy Brown was piloting a Sopwith Camel when in 1917 he shot down Germany's best-known fighter pilot, Baron Manfred VON RICHTHOFEN, the "Red Baron." Although Sopwith was forced to liquidate his original aviation company after the war's end, he later helped found Hawker Aircraft Co., which produced the world's first vertical-take-off-and-landing aircraft, the Hawker Harrier jump jet.

Souers, William Sidney *(1892–1973)* American naval officer and intelligence officer. Souers spent WORLD WAR II in naval intelligence in the U.S., attaining the rank of rear admiral (1943) and the post of deputy chief of naval intelligence (1944). After the war President TRUMAN appointed him director of the new Central Intelligence Group (1946), the forerunner of the CENTRAL INTELLIGENCE AGENCY (CIA). Souers was subsequently first executive secretary of the National Security Council (1947–50) and an adviser to Truman during the Korean War.

Soupault, Philippe *(1897–1990)* French writer and poet. Soupault was one of the founders of the surrealist movement in the early 1920s (see SURREALISM). Together with André BRETON and Louis ARAGON, he founded the review *Litterature,* which became a major vehicle for young intellectuals of the day. With Breton he wrote *Les Champs magnétiques* (Magnetic fields), a collection of poems that was considered to be the first surrealist text.

Souphanouvoung *(1909–1995)* Prince of LAOS. Born into the Lao royal family, Souphanouvoung became president of the Lao People's Democratic Republic in 1975. The prince always enjoyed national prominence because of his royal blood. He received his higher education in Paris and joined an Indochinese engineering corps in Vietnam upon his return. He began his revolutionary activities in 1944, was a member of the Lao Issara government that fled to Thailand after World War II and became chairman of the Lao Resistance Front in 1950. Souphanouvoung was the chief spokesman for the PL and its chief negotiator with the RLG for over two decades. In 1962 he was named deputy prime minister in the second coalition government. After the 1975 takeover he held the president's post until late 1986 when he fell ill and resigned. His actual political power within the Pathet Lao was often a subject of debate. Some considered him a figurehead, manipulated by the Vietnamese and their chosen Lao leaders because of his name and traditional status. However, his picture hung next to that of KAYSONE PHOMVIHAM, cabinet chairman, in all public areas in Vientiane.

Soustelle, Jacques-Émile *(1912–1990)* French diplomat and anthropologist. While serving as governor-general of ALGERIA in the mid-1950s, he became convinced that the colony should remain French. This conviction clashed with Gen. Charles de GAULLE's 1959 decision to grant Algeria independence, and Soustelle quit the government. In 1962 he joined a secret army that conducted a campaign of assassination and sabotage in an effort to keep Algeria French. He was charged with "attempts against the state," and fled the country. In 1968, after a general amnesty was declared, he returned to devote himself to politics and the study of pre-Colombian culture. He was named to the Académie Française in 1983.

Souter, David *(1939–)* Associate justice, U.S. Supreme Court (1990–). A graduate of Harvard University and Harvard Law School and a Rhodes Scholar at Oxford University, David Souter spent the majority of his legal career in public service. After a brief time in private practice he became an assistant deputy attorney general in his native New Hampshire, rising to become the state attorney general in 1976. Two years later he became a state judge and was soon appointed to the supreme court of New Hampshire. In 1990, Souter was named to the U.S. Court of Appeals for the First Circuit. Two months later he was President George BUSH's surprise choice to fill the Supreme Court seat left vacant by the resignation of William BRENNAN. During his confirmation hearings, Souter avoided giving his personal views on particular controversial issues, including ABORTION; conservatives hoped that he would prove to be the deciding vote necessary to overturn *ROE V. WADE.* Souter wrote the 1994 unanimous Court opinion for *Campbell v. Acuff-Rose Music,* which permitted parodies of existing works without the original artist's permission.

South Africa (Republic of South Africa) Located at the southernmost

point of the African continent, South Africa occupies an area of 476,094 square miles. In 1910 the Union of South Africa was established as a dominion under the British Crown. After World War II, it sought independence from Britain and became a republic in 1961. Legislation to preserve white supremacy led to introduction of the policy of APARTHEID in 1948. The apartheid policy created 10 homelands to preserve the identity of various African ethnic groups, but the homelands had no rights or power. Opposition to apartheid was led by the AFRICAN NATIONAL CONGRESS (ANC) headed by Nelson MANDELA, who was imprisoned in 1963 for committing sabotage. Stringent measures were taken and discriminatory laws passed to keep the South African blacks powerless. Uprisings in 1976, the death of black leader Steven BIKO in 1977 and the violent repression of riots in 1984 and 1985

brought international condemnation and the imposition of trade sanctions (1986–87) by several Western countries. Archbishop Desmond TUTU emerged as a leader against apartheid. President P. W. BOTHA introduced some reforms during his tenure (1983–89), and his successor, F. W. DE KLERK, moved toward negotiations with black leaders, releasing Mandela in 1990 and lifting restrictions on the ANC and other antiapartheid groups. After de Klerk abolished the last vestiges of apartheid, an interim constitution in 1993 established a democratically elected national assembly. In the country's first multiracial elections in April 1994, the ANC won a decisive majority. Mandela became president. He pursued a conciliatory policy toward the white minority, encouraging it to remain in the country. In 1999 he was succeeded by Thabo MBECKI. Mbecki and the ANC stayed in power when

	SOUTH AFRICA
1910	Cape Colony, Natal, Transvaal and Orange Free State form the Union of South Africa.
1948	A policy of apartheid ("separateness") is adopted.
1961	South Africa becomes a republic and leaves the Commonwealth.
1963	Nelson Mandela is jailed for life.
1976	Violent racial riots erupt in the black township of Soweto and are put down after much bloodshed.
1984	New constitution adopts state presidential form of government; Pieter W. Botha is elected first state president under the new constitution; Bishop Desmond Tutu is awarded the Nobel Peace Prize.
1985	Botha announces limited reform of apartheid, including repeal of the Mixed Marriage Act and the Immorality Act, and amendment of the Prohibition of Political Interference Act. Continued racial violence forces the government to ban press and television coverage of antiapartheid demonstrations. United States announces limited sanctions against South Africa.
1989	F. W. de Klerk is elected NP leader and state president.
1990	Nelson Mandela is released from prison.
1992	A referendum by white voters overwhelmingly approves the government's plan to remove apartheid.
1994	Country holds its first inclusive multiracial elections. Mandela becomes president.
1999	Thabo Mbeki replaces Nelson Mandela as head of the ANC and is elected president of South Africa.
2003	The government approves a major program to treat HIV/AIDS.
2004	The ANC and Thabo Mbecki win the elections.

South Africa

ZIMBABWE

BOTSWANA

NAMIBIA

MOZAMBIQUE

Messina
Louis Trichardt
Phalaborwa
Pietersburg
Matlabas R.
Olifants R.
Nelspruit
Mmabatho
Pretoria
Middelburg
Johannesburg
Mafikeng
Krugersdorp
Witbank
Boksburg
SWAZILAND
Carletonville
Soweto Germiston
Springs
Kuruman
Vereeniging
Vryheid
Ulundi
Upington
Newcastle
Alexander Bay
Hartz R.
Vaal R.
Welkom
Kroonstad
Dundee
Richard's Bay
Postmasburg
Virginia
Ladysmith
Port Nolloth
Orange R.
Kimberley
Pietermaritzburg
Kleinsee
Springbok
Bloemfontein
LESOTHO
Prieska
Riet R.
Durban

ATLANTIC OCEAN

De Aar

St. Helena Bay

Umtata

INDIAN OCEAN

Queenstown

Graaf Reinet
Mdant Sane
Bisho

Wellington
Uitenhage
East London
Cape Town
Worcester
Paarl
Port Elizabeth
Cape of Good Hope
Algoa Bay
Vals Bay
Mossel Bay
Cape Agulhas

N

© Infobase Publishing

0   200 miles
0   200 km

Note: Pretoria is the administrative capital.
Cape Town is the legislative capital.

they won the 2004 elections. In the face of an AIDS epidemic, the government has approved programs in hope of controlling the spread of the disease.

South Arabia, Federation of Federation formed by 1963 merger of Britain's colony of ADEN with its protectorate, the Federated Emirates of the South. The federation collapsed and British forces withdrew in 1967, after which Aden and South Arabia merged to form the independent South Yemen, now part of YEMEN.

South East Asia Treaty Organization See SEATO.

Southern Christian Leadership Conference (SCLC) American Civil Rights organization. Founded in 1957 by Martin Luther KING, Jr., it was headed by him until his assassination in 1968. Its aims are to achieve equal rights for blacks through nonviolent protest and to sponsor community development. From its beginning, the leadership has largely been made up of black Protestant clergymen. It first gained wide attention for its 1963 campaign to desegregate public facilities in Birmingham, Alabama. The SCLC is

perhaps best known for organizing the massive 1963 MARCH ON WASHINGTON, which mobilized some 250,000 Americans in the CIVIL RIGHTS cause. Its voters' rights campaigns were highlighted by the 1965 conflict between demonstrators and police in Selma, Alabama, which brought world attention to the plight of blacks in the South. The organization was headed by Rev. Ralph ABERNATHY from 1968 to 1977, but its influence, prestige and membership dwindled after Dr. King's death. Its headquarters are in Atlanta, Georgia.

Southern Rhodesia See ZIMBABWE.

South Pole At 90 degrees south latitude and 0 degrees longitude, this is the south end of the Earth's axis, on the continent of ANTARCTICA. In 1909 the British explorer Sir Ernest SHACKLETON came within 97 miles of the Pole. On December 14, 1911, it was reached for the first time by an overland expedition led by Norwegian explorer Roald AMUNDSEN; the expedition of British explorer Robert F. SCOTT, which arrived over a month later, perished on its return journey. On November 29, 1929, Americans Richard E. BYRD and Bernt Balchen were the first to fly over the

pole. Scientific exploration continued throughout the century. A 1958 COMMONWEALTH expedition led by Vivian FUCHS was the first to cross Antarctica by land via the South Pole. In 1990 an international team led by American adventurer Will Stegner traversed the Pole by dogsled.

Souvanna Phouma, Prince (1901–1984) Laotian political leader. Souvanna served as prime minister of LAOS intermittently from 1951 to 1975, when Marxist PATHET LAO rebels took power and established the Lao People's Democratic Republic. A neutralist, he attempted to establish a coalition government incorporating pro-Western elements and the communist insurgents, who were led by his half-brother, Prince SOUPHANOUVOUNG. Souvanna also served as ambassador to France (1958–60).

Soviet Far East See FAR EASTERN REPUBLIC.

Soviet Union See UNION OF SOVIET SOCIALIST REPUBLICS.

Soweto uprising In June 1976 a group of students staged a march through the black township of Soweto (outside Johannesburg, SOUTH AFRICA) to protest the government's Bantu education program. Police opened fire, killing several marchers, and unarmed students retaliated by throwing bottles and stones. The official count at week's end was 176 killed, 1,139 wounded and 1,298 detained. The protest spread. A march of 20,000 to 40,000 produced more deaths. The uprising galvanized black political activity and led to the Black Consciousness Movement and other organizations.

Soyinka, Wole (1934–) Nigerian dramatist, novelist and poet. Born in Abeokuta, the son of a well-to-do Yoruba couple, Soyinka attended University College, Ibadan, and Leeds University. As a student he wrote his first two important plays, *The Swamp Dwellers* and *The Lion and the Jewel,* both of which examine the conflict between tradition and change in contemporary Africa. Returning to Nigeria in 1960, he wrote a number of plays including *The Trials of Brother Jero.* Soyinka's first novel, *The Interpreters* (1965), explores the lives of Europeanized Nigerians.

Accused of conspiring with Ibo rebels during the BIAFRA rebellion, he was imprisoned (1967–69), an experience he movingly described in *The Man Died* (1972). Soyinka's other plays include *The Bacchae, Death and the King's Horseman* and *Opera Wonyosi,* an adaptation of BRECHT's *Three-penny Opera.* He is the author of poetry including *A Shuttle in the Crypt* (1972) and of the autobiography *Ake: The Years of Childhood* (1981). In 1986 Soyinka became the first African to be awarded the NOBEL PRIZE in literature.

Soyuz A Soviet spacecraft originally designed to carry three cosmonauts. First used in 1967, the first mission ended in the deaths of its three cosmonauts. Its name, meaning "union," indicates its main mission, to provide transportation to and from a space station, where it could dock during missions aboard the station. The descendants of this spacecraft, the Soyuz TM series, were still being flown in the late 1980s. Soyuz capsules were repeatedly used to supply the *Mir Space Station* until that satellite's disintegration in March 2001.

Spaak, Paul-Henri *(1899–1972)* Belgian statesman and political leader. A major figure in international affairs of the post–WORLD WAR II period, Spaak helped write the charter of the UNITED NATIONS and served as first president of the General Assembly (1946). He was regarded as one of the founders of the EUROPEAN ECONOMIC COMMUNITY (EEC). He helped create the NORTH ATLANTIC TREATY ORGANIZATION (NATO) and was its secretary-general from 1957 to 1961. Spaak served in 17 Belgian governments, including six stints as foreign minister. He also held presidential posts in the EUROPEAN COAL AND STEEL COMMUNITY, the Council of Europe and the ORGANIZATION FOR EUROPEAN ECONOMIC COOPERATION.

Spaatz, Carl *(1891–1974)* U.S. military officer. After Pearl Harbor Spaatz served as chief of the Air Force Combat Command and in 1942 became head of the U.S. Eighth Air Force. He led the Allied Northwest African Air Forces and the Mediterranean Allied Air Forces in 1943. Spaatz commanded the U.S. Strategic Air Force in Europe during 1944–45. In that post he secured air superiority over Germany by concentrating attacks on vital industrial targets. In 1945–46 Spaatz commanded the U.S. Strategic Air Force in the Pacific.

space medicine Sometimes referred to as "bioastronautics," space medicine has been classified as a separate medical field since the early 1960s. Every aspect of the physical and psychological conditions encountered in spaceflight is studied by the specialists at the Aerospace Medical Center, San Antonio, Texas. Sophisticated tests, examinations and training are provided for astronauts and are designed to meet all conditions and problems that might be encountered in space. These include human reactions to acceleration forces, cosmic rays and weightlessness. Instruments-carrying astronauts have recorded their brain waves, respiration and blood pressure along with other data needed to prepare for future flights into space. Specialists in space medicine have developed personal life-support systems, which provide astronauts with food, oxygen and water so that they may perform "space walks" outside the safety of the space capsule. Among future problems confronting space medicine specialists are management of illness in space and ways of providing the necessary exercise and entertainment needed for mental health on long voyages through space.

space shuttle American spacecraft. Unlike the manned spacecraft used in previous U.S. space programs (MERCURY, GEMINI and APOLLO) administered by NASA, the space shuttle can land on a runway and can be reused on subsequent missions into space. The shuttle's roomy cabin can accommodate up to eight astronauts, and a large payload bay enables the shuttle to carry satellites into space. The space shuttle program was intended not only for space exploration and for conducting space experiments, but it was also conceived partly as a commercial enterprise: private communications companies would pay NASA to carry their telecommunications satellites into space aboard the shuttle. Some of the shuttle missions have also been secret military missions, presumably involving testing of components for the STRATEGIC DEFENSE INITIATIVE program.

The first shuttle, *Columbia,* was launched into space with two astronauts on April 12, 1981, and returned to Earth on April 14. Over the next four and a half years, another 23 successful missions were carried out aboard NASA's four space shuttles (*Challenger, Discovery* and *Atlantis* having joined *Columbia* in the program). However, the scheduled 25th flight of the shuttle program ended in tragedy when the *Challenger* exploded moments after launch on January 28, 1986; the seven crew members were killed (see CHALLENGER DISASTER). The remaining shuttles were grounded and there was an investigation into the disaster. The shuttle program resumed on September 29, 1988, when the *Discovery* was launched into orbit. Apart from the *Challenger* disaster, the space shuttle program has been plagued by numerous delays, mounting costs, and an inability to deliver on expectations. The program continued into the 1990s, but some members of Congress and many people in the space business began to question the wisdom of using manned spacecraft to do what unmanned craft can do perhaps more safely, cheaply and efficiently. NASA suspended its shuttle launches immediately after the disintegration of the Space Shuttle *Columbia* upon reentry in February 2003. The problem that caused the *Columbia* disaster also unexpectedly recurred during the launch of *Discovery* in 2005. As a result NASA decided to again postpone flights until additional modifications could be made.

Spaggiari, Albert *(?–1989)* French bank robber. Spaggiari masterminded the 1976 robbery of the Société Générale Bank in Nice, France, that became known as "the heist of the century." Together with a gang of 20 associates, he tunneled into the bank and made off with about $9 million in cash, gold and jewelry. He was caught and jailed but escaped from a magistrate's office in March 1977. Thereafter, he evaded the authorities and lived in an undisclosed location. He died of lung cancer; his body was found at his mother's house in Hyères, France.

Spahn, Warren *(1921–2003)* American baseball player. Arguably the best lefthanded pitcher of all time, Spahn led the Braves for 18 years. He earned immortality in the jingle "Spahn and Sain and pray for rain," referring to the fact that the Braves had only two reliable pitchers. He won 20 games 12 times and was an All Star 14 times. He moved with the Braves from Boston to Milwaukee and led the team to the pennant in 1957, when he was 36, and won a World Series game, as the Braves defeated the Yankees. He threw his first no-hitter in 1960 at age 39 and followed with another at the age of 40. He was sold to the Mets in 1964 and finished his major league career with the Giants in 1965. He continued to pitch in the minor leagues until he retired in 1967. He was named to the Hall of Fame in 1973.

Spain Spain occupies an area of 194,846 square miles and shares the Iberian Peninsula of southwestern Europe with Portugal; it includes the Canary and Balearic Islands (in the Atlantic Ocean and Mediterranean Sea) and the municipalities of Ceuta and Melilla on the North African coast of Morocco. After the dictatorship of General Primo DE RIVERA (1923–30) and the abdication of King ALFONSO XIII in 1931, Spain had a brief period as a republic (1931–36) before General Francisco FRANCO exported a military rebellion from Spanish Morocco to Spain. The resulting SPANISH CIVIL WAR (1936–39) galvanized international support—for either the socialist government or Franco's profascist forces. When Barcelona and Madrid surrendered in 1939, Franco became dictator (1939–75). Spain remained neutral during WORLD WAR II in spite of Axis pressure for Franco to support the Germans and the Italians, who had materially aided his cause in the civil war. Conflict with Britain over Spanish claims to GIBRALTAR led to the closing of the Spain-Gibraltar border in 1969; it was reopened in 1985, after the two countries agreed to discuss Gibraltar's sovereignty (see GIBRALTAR DISPUTE). The 1973 assassination of the prime minister by militant Basque separatists brought several executions in 1975, resulting in international condemnation of the Franco government. Upon Franco's death (1975) his chosen successor, Juan CARLOS, became king and introduced a new constitution, declaring Spain a democratic, parliamentary monarchy. Spain joined NATO in 1982

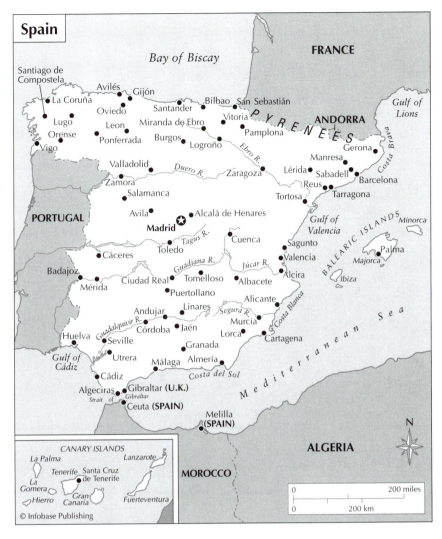

but voted to remain outside the military structure (1986) and to reduce U.S. forces in Spain (present since 1953). The government continued to face terrorism from the Basque separatist movement. In 1996 the conservative José María AZNAR replaced Socialist Felipe González as prime minister. In 2003 Spain joined the U.S.-led coalition that invaded Iraq and deposed its leader, Saddam Hussein. In the following year Aznar retired, and his party was ousted from power after a terrorist attack organized by a radical Islamic group tied to AL-QAEDA killed 191 Spaniards on a commuter railroad. Gay marriage was legalized in 2005. In 2006 ETA declared a truce in its terrorist campaign against the Spanish government.

Spandau Prison Built as a fortress in the 16th century, in the 20th century Spandau gained notoriety as the prison

in which Nazi war criminals were incarcerated after the NUREMBERG TRIALS of 1945–46. Located in Berlin, Spandau was administered by France, the United Kingdom, the U.S. and the USSR, the four powers that had occupied and divided GERMANY after that country's defeat in WORLD WAR II. With the death in 1987 of Hitler crony Rudolf HESS, the last Nazi inmate, Spandau was razed.

Spanel, Abram Nathaniel (1901–1985) American businessman. In 1932 Spanel founded the International Laytex Corp., which would later be known as the International Playtex Corp. He was one of the first industrialists to install air conditioning for his workers and to provide them with such benefits as paid health and life insurance. For nearly four decades, he disseminated his liberal views through paid editorial advertisements in dozens

SPAIN

1923	Imposition of military dictatorship by General Primo de Rivera.
1931	King Alfonso abdicates in favor of the Second Republic, which introduces universal adult suffrage.
1933	Right-wing Falangist Party founded.
1936	Jose Calvo Sotelo, leader of the fascist National Bloc, is assassinated, causing military intervention; Francisco Franco is named head of state; Spanish civil war commences.
1937	Aerial bombardment of Guernica by German planes marks the first-ever use of massive civilian bombing for military ends.
1939	(March) Nationalists are victorious and Franco establishes himself as dictator, with Nazi sympathies.
1953	U.S. military bases allowed in Spain with the signing of the Pact of Madrid.
1969	Franco closes the border with Gibraltar.
1973	(Dec. 20) Basque separatist kills Prime Minister Admiral Luis Carrero Blanco in a Madrid bomb explosion.
1975	(Nov. 20) Franco dies; Juan Carlos ascends to the throne.
1976	(July 20) Adolfo Suárez González becomes prime minister; National Movement is disbanded and political parties and trade unions are legalized.
1978	(December) New constitution approved declaring Spain to be a democratic parliamentary monarchy.
1979	Basque country and Catalonia become autonomous communities.
1981	(Feb. 23) Attempted coup by members of the Civil Guards is foiled by the intervention of King Juan Carlos.
1982	(May) Becomes 16th member of NATO; Socialist Party leader Felipe González Márquez is elected prime minister.
1989	González Márquez is elected to a second term.
1992	Barcelona Olympic Games and Expo '92 boost the Spanish economy.
1993	González Márquez is reelected prime minister to a third term.
1996	The conservative Popular Party wins national elections with José María Aznar as prime minister; the terrorist group ETA refuses to meet the government's demand for a permanent cease-fire.
2000	Aznar and his Popular Party are reelected.
2002	Spain replaces the peseta with the euro; the radical Basque separatist party Batasuna is suspended for three years because of its suspected links to ETA.
2003	The ban on Batasuna is imposed indefinitely.
2004	Explosions in rush-hour trains in Madrid kill 191 persons; An Islamic group with links to al-Queda is later blamed; Socialists under José Luis Rodríguez Zapatero win the general election in defiance of earlier polls.
2005	Car bombs explode in Madrid, injuring about 40. ETA is suspected to be behind the attacks; voters approve the EU constitution in a referendum; gay marriage is legalized.
2006	ETA declares a truce, renouncing its terrorist campaign against the government.

of newspapers. He retired as Playtex's chairman in 1972. A prolific inventor, he held more than 2,000 patents.

Spanish civil war (1936–1939)

Military revolt against the unstable socialist Republican government of SPAIN. The Nationalists, as the rebels were called, were led by General Francisco FRANCO. All Europe took sides in this ideological struggle between democracy and tyranny, freedom and FASCISM. Nazi GERMANY and fascist ITALY supplied bombers and land forces to the Nationalists, and the Soviet Union and the International Brigades—volunteers from Europe and the United States—supplied and fought with the Republicans. During 1936 the Basques and Catalans, and much of the east and north, held out against Franco's forces. On March 5, 1939, the Republican government flew to exile in France, and later that month Madrid was captured by the Nationalists. There were over half a million casualties in this civil war.

Spanish Sahara

On the Atlantic coast of northwestern Africa, this former Spanish colony became an overseas province of Spain in 1958. It was granted independence in 1976. (See also SAHARAWI ARAB DEMOCRATIC REPUBLIC, WESTERN SAHARA.)

Spark, Muriel (1918–2006)

British novelist and story writer. Born and educated in Edinburgh, Scotland, Spark spent several years in Africa, the setting for many of her early short stories. Returning to Britain, she edited the Poetry Society's *Poetry Review* (1947–49). After winning the *Observer* fiction competition in 1951, she devoted herself to her writing. Her books, including *Memento Mori* (1959), *The Prime of Miss Jean Brodie* (1961, filmed 1969), *Loitering with Intent* (1981) and *A Far Cry from Kensington* (1988), are spare, witty and elegant, often tinged with surrealism, and reflect her concerns as a convert to Catholicism. Spark has also written poems and plays. In her later years she lived in Italy. Throughout the 1990s Spark continued to publish works such as her two novels, *Symposium* (1990) and *Reality and Dream* (1996); *The Young Man Who Discovered the Secret of Life and Other Stories* (1999), a collection of short works; and her autobiography, *Curriculum Vitae* (1992). In 1993 she was made a dame of the British Empire.

Sparkman, John J(ackson) (1899–1985)

American politician. A Democrat from Alabama, Sparkman served in the U.S. House of Representatives for 10 years before winning a special election to the Senate in 1946. He supported the creation of the TENNESSEE VALLEY AUTHORITY, President Franklin D. ROOSEVELT's NEW DEAL programs, and President Harry S TRUMAN's FAIR DEAL proposals. However, he opposed most Civil Rights legislation. Sparkman was Adlai E. STEVENSON's vice presidential running mate in the 1952 presidential election. Sparkman remained influential in the Senate until his retirement in 1979, chairing the important Senate Foreign Relations Committee as well as an earlier committee on banking, housing and urban affairs.

Sparkman & Stephens

U.S. firm of naval architects noted for the design of sailing yachts. The company was established in New York in 1928 by Olin and Roderick STEPHENS and Drake Sparkman. With Olin Stephens as its leading designer until his retirement in 1979, the firm designed many cruising and racing yachts, including a series of America's Cup winners. *Freedom,* a 135-foot luxury yacht built in Italy in 1986 with an all-aluminum hull, is a fine example of the work of the firm. Sparkman & Stephens designs have set a high standard in both performance and aesthetics for modern sailing craft.

Spartacists

Also known as the Spartacus Party, an organization of radical German socialists. Drawing its name from the leader of a Roman slave revolt, the group was founded in 1916 under the leadership of Karl Liebknecht and Rosa LUXEMBURG. They advocated a classical Marxist dictatorship of the proletariat, opposing the government of WILHELM II and, after the emperor's fall in 1918, the moderate socialist government that followed. They were active propagandists, occasionally engaging in acts of terrorism. The Spartacists became the new German Communist Party after a 1918–19 meeting. They organized a revolt and a general strike in Berlin early in 1919. It was quickly put down by military action, and both Liebknecht and Luxemburg were arrested and killed.

Spassky, Boris (1937–)

Russian journalist and chess player, he studied at the Leningrad State University faculty of journalism and worked as a trainer at the Leningrad section of the voluntary sport society. Spassky has played in numerous international chess tournaments; in 1956 he was the USSR grand master, the international grand master and world chess student champion. He was world champion from 1969 to 1972. Spassky lost his title to American chess prodigy **Bobby Fisher.** In 1992 Spassky again played and lost to Fisher in a rematch of the 1972 championship tournament.

Speaker, Tris(tram) (1888–1958)

American baseball star. Considered one of baseball's all-around greats, especially in defense, Speaker began his professional career as an outfielder with the Boston Red Sox (1907–15), continuing with the Cleveland Indians (1916–26), then with Washington in 1927 and Philadelphia in 1928. His lifetime batting average was .344. He was elected to baseball's Hall of Fame in 1937.

Special Air Services (SAS)

Elite commando and antiterrorist unit in the British army. The Special Air Services evolved out of the World War II LONG-RANGE DESERT PATROL GROUP established by David STIRLING. Operating in tight secrecy during the 1980s, the SAS was involved in hostage crises, seiges and raids on terrorist headquarters. In their most daring action on May 5, 1980, the SAS stormed the Iranian embassy in London, which had been taken over by terrorists, and rescued hostages held there. Members of the group took part in an 1987 ambush in NORTHERN IRELAND in which eight members of an IRA bombing squad were killed. The SAS was also responsible for the controversial killing in Gibraltar (March 6, 1988) of three unarmed IRA agents who were apparently planning to plant a bomb to kill British soldiers in the colony. Critics charged that the SAS operated as if it were above the law and said that the terrorists could have been arrested rather than shot. The group's motto is "Who Dares Wins."

special theory of relativity

See Albert EINSTEIN.

Speer, Albert *(1905–1981)* German architect and administrator who served as minister of armaments and war production in the government of Adolf HITLER during WORLD WAR II. As a young architect in BERLIN, Speer joined the NAZI Party in 1931. He was one of the few people to gain Hitler's complete confidence—possibly because Hitler himself had been an aspiring architect and regarded the young Speer as a son. Hitler appointed Speer his chief state architect. In this capacity, Speer undertook several massive building projects, designing the stadium where the NUREMBERG RALLIES were later held as well as the new chancellery building. In 1942, as the war began to turn against Germany, Speer was appointed minister of armaments and war production. Despite a shortage of labor, equipment and material, Speer actually managed to increase industrial output. After Hitler's suicide he served as economics minister in the short-lived interim government established (May 1945) by Admiral DOENITZ. In the NUREMBERG TRIALS (1946) Speer was charged with having used millions of people, including PRISONERS OF WAR, in forced labor. He pleaded guilty—the only important Nazi leader to do so. Sentenced to 20 years' imprisonment, he served his full term in SPANDAU PRISON. After his release in 1966 he wrote three controversial books describing his experiences as Hitler's trusted confidante and his time in prison. In the first of these (*Inside the Third Reich,* 1970), he described his growing disillusionment with Hitler and disclosed his abortive attempt near the end of the war to assassinate the führer. Readers sympathetic to Speer held him up as an example of how an intelligent and well-meaning person can be seduced by power. To his critics, however, Speer was merely a self-serving and manipulative opportunist whose war crimes were inexcusable.

Spelling, Aaron *(1923–2006)* American television producer. Born in Dallas, Texas, Spelling acquired his reputation as a producer by designing such popular programs as *Starsky and Hutch, S.W.A.T., Charlie's Angels, Family* and *Dynasty.* His success with these popular television shows prompted Spelling to found his own entertainment company, Spelling Entertainment Group, Inc., in the early 1990s. With this company Spelling began working with the Fox Broadcasting Corporation's new television network, for which he designed the popular evening soap operas *Beverly Hills 90210* and *Melrose Place.* In 1996 Spelling began working with the WB, a new television network launched by the Warner Bros. Studios. For the WB, Spelling developed several shows, the most successful of which have been *7th Heaven* and *Charmed.*

Spellman, Francis Joseph *(1889–1967)* Roman Catholic cardinal and archbishop of New York. Spellman was the most visible and powerful Catholic clergyman in America from the 1940s through the 1960s. Ordained as a priest in 1916, he became archbishop of New York in 1939 and was elected to the college of cardinals in 1946. Highly conservative politically, Spellman was an outspoken supporter of Senator Joseph MCCARTHY, even after the latter's condemnation by the United States Senate in 1954. Spellman was also an ardent supporter of the Vietnam War, a stance that brought him into conflict with his superior, Pope PAUL VI.

Spence, Sir Basil *(1907–1976)* British architect. Spence remains best known for his designing of the rebuilt Coventry Cathedral—a design that was commissioned in 1951 and completed in 1962. Spence retained the steeple of the original cathedral as the only major vertical ascent in his design, which included much creative integration of older sections of the cathedral as well as modern touches such as sawtooth-styled side walls. Spence first came to prominence in the 1930s as a designer of large country houses in Scotland. In the final decades of his life, Spence and his architectural firm specialized in university site projects and also designed the chancellery of the British embassy in Rome (1971).

Spencer, Sir Stanley *(1891–1959)* English painter. Spencer is one of the major figures in 20th-century British painting. His canvasses, which often deal with spiritual themes, have been compared—in terms of their simplicity and luminosity—to the pictorial works of William Blake. Spencer studied art in the Slade School in London and was an official war artist for the British government in both WORLD WAR I and WORLD WAR II. His most famous painting is *The Resurrection: Cookham* (1924), which utilizes his native village as the setting for the resurrection of Christ. In the 1930s, Spencer earned the ire of the British public for a series of erotically explicit canvasses. His younger brother Gilbert was also a painter.

Spender, Sir Stephen (Stephen Harold Spender) *(1909–1995)* British poet, editor, literary journalist, critic and translator. While a student at Oxford, Spender came under the influence of AUDEN. In 1930 he accompanied ISHERWOOD to Germany; *Poems* appeared in 1933. Spender was the most politically active member of the Thirties Generation, and his writings reflected his belief in the coming of a new world order. *Forward from Liberalism* (1937) argued for COMMUNISM as a means of defeating FASCISM in Europe. In 1939–41 he served as editor, with Cyril CONNOLLY, of *Horizon;* from 1953–67 he was an editor of *Encounter.* After World War II he published little poetry, and overall his reputation as an intellectual overshadowed his poetry. In 1962 he was made a CBE (commander, Order of the British Empire).

Spengler, Oswald *(1880–1936)* German historian and philosopher. Spengler was one of the most influential historians of the 20th century. He achieved international recognition and a wide readership upon the publication in two volumes of his magnum opus, THE DECLINE OF THE WEST (1918, 1922). Spengler taught at numerous German universities. Despite his aversion to the Nazi movement, Spengler was falsely hailed as a precursor of Nazi philosophy by Josef GOEBBELS.

Spielberg, Steven *(1947–)* American filmmaker. Spielberg began making short films in 8mm at age 10 and by the age of 16 had made *Firelight,* a prototype of the later *Close Encounters of the Third Kind* (1977). After haunting the precincts of UNIVERSAL Studios he won the support of a producer to make a 20-minute short, *Amblin,* whose success got him a contract to direct episodes for the television series *Colombo* and *Night Gallery.* His television movie *Duel* (1971) was shot in only 16 days and was hailed by critic Pauline Kael as "one of the most phenomenal debut films in the history of the movies." Spielberg's major films are distinguished by a staggering camera technique and uncanny ability to cut on action. The early works are essentially chase films: the Texas police chase of Goldie Hawn in *Sugarland Express* (1974); the stalking of a small boat by a great white shark in *Jaws* (1975). And everybody chases everybody in the three *Indiana Jones* films. In such later works as *The Color Purple* (1985) and *Empire of the Sun* (1987) Spielberg shows more attention to integrating character and relationships into the action. As a producer, he has had a magic touch with successes like the three *Back to the Future* pictures, *Poltergeist* (1982) and THE TWILIGHT ZONE (1983), his tribute to the classic television series (for which he directed the "Kick the Can" segment). The riotous *Who Framed Roger Rabbit?* (1988), produced by Spielberg in association with Walt Disney Studios, combined live actors with animated characters. Although justly renowned for such virtuoso sequences as the toys running amok in E.T. and the jitterbug dance in *1941*, Spielberg can also deliver effective, quiet moments—like the chilling "shark monologue" of Robert Shaw in *Jaws* and the whimsical "trick-or-treat" scene in E.T. In 1993 Spielberg received an Academy Award for Best Director for his work on *Schindler's List* (1992). His many successful cinematic productions since then include *Saving Private Ryan* (1998), *Memoirs of a Geisha* (2005), and *Munich* (2005).

Spillane, Mickey (Frank Morrison) *(1918–2006)* American writer. Spillane began his career while still in college, as a contributor to pulp magazines. He went on to redefine the detective genre with his hard-boiled heroes Mike Hammer and Tiger Mann. Sexist, sadistic and crude, the books found an audience around the world. His works include the best-selling *I, the Jury* (1947), *My Gun Is Quick* (1950) and *Kiss Me Deadly* (1952). In later years, Spillane became something of a personality and star of award-winning beer commercials.

Spitfire Famous single-engine propeller fighter plane designed by Reginald MITCHELL in the 1930s and used by the Royal Air Force (RAF) to defend the UNITED KINGDOM during the BATTLE OF BRITAIN in WORLD WAR II.

Spitsbergen Large island and archipelago north of the Arctic Circle and 360 miles north of NORWAY; officially became a part of Norway on August 14, 1925. Arctic explorers like NOBILE and BYRD used Spitsbergen as a jumping-off point for many of their expeditions.

Spitz, Mark Andrew *(1950–)* U.S. swimmer. Arguably the greatest swimmer of all time, Spitz set 35 world records. A dedicated swimmer from a young age, early in his career he was frequently booed by his own teammates for his conceit. He won five gold medals in the 1967 Pan American Games and made a respectable showing in the 1968 Olympic Games, with two gold team medals and individual medals for second and third. He perfected his style while on the team at Indiana University and led that team to four national championships from 1969 to 1972. In the 1972 Olympic Games, he won an astonishing seven gold medals. In the late 1980s, he began preparing for an Olympic comeback. However, in 1991 he failed to qualify for the U.S. Olympic team and subsequently retired from competitive swimming.

Spock, Benjamin (Benjamin McLaine Spock) *(1903–1998)* American pediatrician, psychiatrist and antiwar activist; studied medicine at Yale and Columbia in the 1930s and served as a U.S. Navy psychiatrist during World War II. Spock achieved nationwide fame with the publication of his immensely influential *The Common Sense Book of Baby and Child Care* (1946), which has since been republished in numerous editions and stands as the all-time best-selling book by an American author. In the 1960s, Spock became national cochairman of the Committee for a Sane Nuclear Policy (SANE) and actively opposed the VIETNAM WAR. In 1968, Spock and other defendants were charged with conspiracy to aid and abet draft evaders. After a highly publicized trial, the case against Spock was ultimately dismissed. In 1972, Spock ran for president as the candidate of the pacifist People's Party. Spock's autobiography is

Spock on Spock: A Memoir of Growing Up with the Century (1989).

Spoleto Festivals (Italy and USA) The Festival of Two Worlds in Spoleto, Italy, was founded by composer Gian Carlo MENOTTI in 1958. One of the most comprehensive international arts festivals, it is held annually from late June to mid-July and presents all types of music, ballet, theater, art exhibitions and poetry readings. The festival has gained a reputation for providing a venue for new talent, such as composer Nino ROTA, who premiered his opera *Napoli Milonaria* there. In 1977 Menotti founded the Second World festival—Spoleto Festival USA—in Charleston, South Carolina. Held annually from late May to early June, this international festival is also devoted to all the arts. Performers who have appeared there include vocalist Johanna Meier, conductor Clayton Westerman and the Dance Theater of Harlem.

Spratly Islands A group of more than 600 small islands and small formations such as coral reefs and sand bars located in the South China Sea. In 1933 the Spratly Islands were claimed and administered by FRANCE as an extension of its colony in Indochina. During WORLD WAR II (1939–45), the islands were seized and governed by JAPAN as part of its Greater East Asia Co-Prosperity Sphere. At the end of the war, control over the Spratly Islands was awarded to the Nationalist Chinese government headed by CHIANG KAI-SHEK, which established a military garrison on the largest of the islands, Itu Aba. Following the overthrow of the Chinese Nationalist regime in 1949 by MAO ZEDONG's Chinese Communist forces, and the Nationalists' relocation to the island of Taiwan, other nations later claimed sovereignty over the Spratly Islands. In addition to the two Chinese governments, BRUNEI, MALAYSIA, the PHILIPPINES and VIETNAM established small military garrisons on some of the islands in the chain. CHINA has constantly refused to submit the matter to arbitration through the UN. As is the case with the PARACEL ISLANDS, which lie north-northeast of the Spratly chain, the conflicting claims over the Spratly Islands stems from the substantial oil and natural gas resources that geological surveys have suggested lie beneath the islands and their territorial waters. The attempts to control these potentially valuable resources has led to sporadic conflicts between the garrisons, such as a clash between Chinese and Vietnamese forces in 1988.

Springer, Axel *(1912–1985)* West German publisher. Springer headed Axel Springer Verlag, one of western Europe's biggest publishing empires. The group's flagship newspapers were the conservative *Die Welt* and *Bild Zeitung,* a sensational tabloid with the largest circulation in western Europe. The company also published magazines and books and in the mid-1980s began to branch out into television. Known for his strong opposition to communism and left-wing terrorism, Springer was a strong proponent of German reunification and an outspoken friend of Israel.

Springsteen, Bruce *(1949–)* American rock-and-roll singer, composer, guitarist and band leader. Springsteen is one of the most passionate and popular performers in the history of ROCK and roll. Raised in New Jersey, he played in bar bands in his home state and in New York City before being signed to a contract by Columbia Records producer John HAMMOND in 1972. Springsteen's first album, *Greetings from Asbury Park, New Jersey* (1973), earned him critical comparisons to Bob DYLAN but was not a great commercial success. With the album *Born To Run* (1975), Springsteen found a wide audience for himself and his now consolidated back-up group, the E Street Band, featuring guitarist Steve Van Zandt and saxophonist Clarence Clemons. Springsteen has been a steady hit-maker ever since, with albums including *The River* (1980), *Nebraska* (1982), *Born in the U.S.A.* (1985) and *Tunnel of Love* (1989). In 1989 Springsteen finally broke with the E Street Band. In 2001 he reunited with the E Street Band to record *The Rising* (2002), an album inspired by American experiences following the terrorist attacks of SEPTEMBER 11, 2001.

Sputnik First artificial satellite, launched by the Soviet Union. The Soviet news agency Tass astounded the world by announcing on October 5, 1957, that the USSR had successfully launched "the first artificial earth satellite" on the previous day. *Sputnik,* whose Russian name means "something that is traveling with a traveler" (the traveler in this case being the Earth), was a 23-inch aluminum sphere weighing 184 pounds and fitted with four steel antennae emitting continuous radio signals on two frequencies over the next 21 days. It traveled at approximately 18,000 miles per hour in its orbit about 560 miles above the Earth's surface.

Despite the satellite's minute size, *Sputnik*'s effects were far reaching. The launching deeply wounded Western pride, especially since *Sputnik* was nine times heavier and orbited twice as high as the Vanguard Project satellite then under development in the U.S. It also resulted in an unprecedented emphasis on science in education and defense, as American policy makers sought to regain technological superiority over the Soviet Union. In reaction to the *Sputnik* launching, President EISENHOWER signed into law in July 1958 legislation for the creation of a National Space and Aeronautics Agency, thereby joining the "space race" that culminated with the American landing of a human on the Moon in July 1969.

The Soviet Union followed up the success of *Sputnik 1* with the launching of the 1,121-pound *Sputnik 2,* containing a small dog, on November 3, 1957; the dog, named LAIKA, survived in space for ten days, proving that living organisms could survive in that environment. (See also EXPLORER.)

Spycatcher **affair** See Peter WRIGHT.

Square Deal President Theodore ROOSEVELT's personal political philosophy that later became the platform of the Progressive Party. Roosevelt stood for American citizenship and patriotism, family values, hard work and material success and also Christian brotherhood. TR first used the phrase *square deal* during a tour of the West, and it almost immediately became a popular expression.

Srebrenica A town in the AUSTRO-HUNGARIAN EMPIRE (1908–18), the Kingdom of Yugoslavia (1918–41), Hungary (1941–45), the communist republic of Yugoslavia (1945–92), and the republic of BOSNIA AND HERZEGOVINA (1995–). In 1908 the Austro-Hungarian Empire annexed the territory of Bosnia and Herzegovina, which included the town of Srebrenica. At the end of World War I (1914–18), all of Bosnia including Srebrenica was incorporated into the newly created Kingdom of Serbs, Croats, and Slovenes (later renamed YUGOSLAVIA in 1929). It remained under Yugoslav control until 1941, when Yugoslavia was invaded by German forces seeking to rescue Italian troops retreating from Italy's disastrous invasion into GREECE during WORLD WAR II. Shortly after this invasion, Yugoslavia was divided among ITALY, GERMANY, and HUNGARY, with the Srebrenica region being awarded to Hungary. At the end of the war, Srebrenica was returned to Yugoslav control under the leadership of the communist resistance leader Josip TITO.

Following the example of Slovenia and Croatia, both of which had seceded from Yugoslavia in 1991, Bosnian authorities organized a regional referendum that was held in 1992 to determine whether the province would seek independence. Ethnic Serbs within Bosnia and Herzegovina, some of whom lived near Srebrenica, refused to participate in the vote because they did not want to fall under the jurisdiction of a new government controlled by non-Serbs. When 97% of Bosnia voted for independence, a civil war began between Serbian-controlled Yugoslavia and the infant Bosnian state. As that conflict escalated, allegations emerged that Serbian military and paramilitary forces had adopted a policy of "ethnic cleansing" in those parts of Bosnia they controlled. The UN responded by declaring six regions within Bosnia as "safe areas," in which Bosnian refugees could congregate without fear of attack. However, Serbian forces seized Srebrenica in July 1995 and murdered more than 7,000 Bosnian Muslims from the town and outlying districts and conducted a brutal campaign of rape and plunder. Following the signing of the December 1995 DAYTON ACCORDS, the prosecution of Serbian military, paramilitary and political officials for these crimes fell under the authority of the International War Crimes Tribunal for Yugoslavia (ICTY).

Sri Lanka (Democratic Socialist Republic of Sri Lanka) Sri Lanka—

SRI LANKA

1948	Independence; newly formed state under United National Party (UNP) strips 800,000 Tamil plantation workers (of Indian origin) of citizenship and suffrage rights.
1954	Sri Lankan Freedom Party (SLFP) demands Sinhala be made country's sole official language and its united front organization—Mahajana Eksath Peramuna (MEP)—wins majority in National Assembly; proclamation of Sinhala as official language met with wave of Tamil civil disobedience; violent anti-Tamil pogroms follow.
1972	Ceylon renamed Sri Lanka.
1983	State of emergency declared in response to mounting security threats posed by Tamil guerrillas fighting for a separate state—Eelam—in the north and east of island.
1987	Unable to overcome militant Tamil groups, most importantly the Liberation Tigers of Tamil Eelam (LTTE), the Sri Lankan government allows Indian forces to enter the north and east regions of the country to disarm and quell rebels.
1990	After protracted dispute over formula for withdrawal of Indian troops policing Tamil areas, India finally withdraws; hundreds die in ethnic violence as civil war continues.
1993	President Ranasinghe Premadasa is assassinated (May 1); Chandrika Kumaratunga is elected president.
1994	The 17-year-old rule of the United National Party ends with victory for the People's Alliance.
1998	Fighting continues between government forces and Tamil rebels.
1999	Norway offers to mediate Sri Lanka–Tamil Tiger peace talks; Chandrika Kumaratunga is reelected president.
2000	People's Alliance wins parliamentary elections by a narrow margin; violence continues between the government and the Tamil Tigers.
2001	Parliament is suspended hours before a no-confidence vote by President Kumaratunga; the United National Party wins a narrow victory in parliamentary elections.
2002	The government and the Tamil Tigers sign a permanent cease-fire agreement, paving the way for talks; decommissioning of weapons begins as peace talks in Norway lead to government and rebels agreeing to share power.
2003	Tamil Tigers say that they are being marginalized and suspend talks; floods leave more than 200 dead and 4,000 homeless.
2004	Early general elections and the party of President Kumaratunga, the People's Alliance, wins 105 to 225 parliamentary seats, just short of a majority; Mahinda Rajapalese is sworn in as prime minister; tsunami waves in December kill more than 30,000 in coastal communities.
2005	A state of emergency is proclaimed after Foreign Minister Lakshman Kadirgamar is assassinated.
2006	Tamil Tigers and government renew commitment to 2000 cease-fire.

one large island and several smaller islets collectively called Adam's Bridge—is located off the southeast coast of the Indian subcontinent and covers a total land area of 25,325 square miles. Originally called Ceylon, the island country was ruled by Britain until achieving independence in 1948.

Sri Lanka's history has been dominated by conflicts between the Hindu Tamils of the north and the Buddhist Sinhalese of the south. The Tamil minority suffered repression during the 1950s, while riots in 1977 left many dead. Ceylon changed its name to Sri Lanka and became a republic in 1972.

A state of emergency has existed since 1983 because of Tamil guerrillas fighting to force creation of a separate Tamil state. With the agreement of the Sri Lankan government, INDIA sent forces into Tamil territory to subdue the rebellion in 1987, withdrawing in 1990. In 1993 the separatist group Liberation

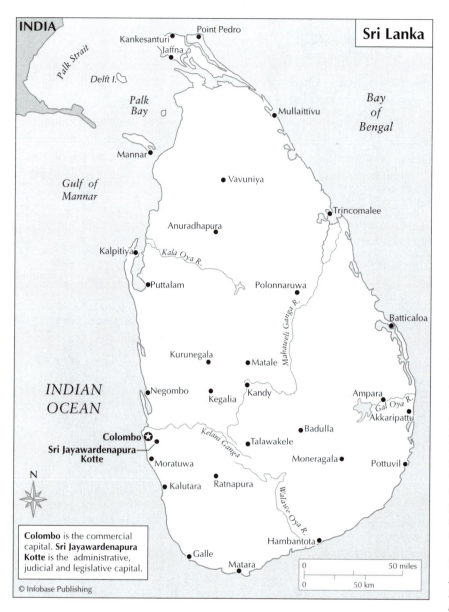

INDIA

Point Pedro
Kankesanturi
Jaffna
Palk Strait
Delft I.
Palk Bay
Sri Lanka
Mullaittivu
Bay of Bengal
Mannar
Gulf of Mannar
Vavuniya
Trincomalee
Anuradhapura
Kalpitiya
Kala Oya R.
Puttalam
Polonnaruwa
Mahaweli Ganga R.
Batticaloa
Kurunegala
Matale
INDIAN OCEAN
Negombo
Kegalia
Kandy
Ampara
Gal Oya R.
Akkaripattu
Colombo
Sri Jayawardenapura Kotte
Kelani Ganga
Badulla
Talawakele
Moratuwa
Moneragala
Pottuvil
N
Kalutara
Ratnapura
Walawe Oya R.
Hambantota
Galle
Matara

Colombo is the commercial capital. **Sri Jayawardenapura Kotte** is the administrative, judicial and legislative capital.

0   50 miles
0   50 km

© Infobase Publishing

Tigers of Tamil Eelam (LTTE) assassinated President Premadasa, igniting a civil war that lasted until a 2002 peace accord that offered autonomy to the Tamil region. In December 2004 a major earthquake struck the Indian Ocean, creating a tsunami that killed more than 30,000 Sri Lankans. In 2006 the Tamil Tigers and the government renewed their commitment to the 2000 cease-fire in the face of increasing rebel violence.

SS (Schutzstaffel) Elite military corps of the NAZI Party. The SS was created in 1925 through the merger of Hitler's shock troops, the Stosstuppe, and a right-wing guard organization called the Stabswache. At first a small

group that protected Nazi leaders and defended the party against attack, it was vastly enlarged and turned into a rigorously disciplined force under the leadership of Heinrich HIMMLER, who became its head in 1929. Under Himmler, membership in the SS grew to 50,000, and they adopted the infamous uniforms with their runic double-"S," death's head insignias and black shirts. In 1934 the SS destroyed Ernst ROEHM's Storm Troops (Sturm Abteilung, or SA) in the bloody "NIGHT OF THE LONG KNIVES." After this purge, the SS became Germany's major police force, and by 1939 the country was divided into various SS areas, each under the direction of an SS officer-police chief. As WORLD WAR II progressed,

the SS became increasingly powerful, with the extermination of the Jews and other "enemies of the Reich," the supervision of imported forced laborers and the running of CONCENTRATION CAMPS all under SS control. In addition, the SS had special units known as the Waffen SS within the regular German military forces. Noted for their reckless bravery and ruthless brutality, at the height of the war they numbered 38 divisions with some 900,000 men.

Stafford, Jean (1915–1979) American novelist and short story writer. Raised in Colorado, Stafford later lived in Boston. She won a PULITZER PRIZE (1970) for her *Collected Stories*. She was the first wife (1940–48) of the poet Robert LOWELL.

Stafford, Thomas (1930–) U.S. astronaut. The soft-spoken Stafford, nicknamed "Mumbles" by his fellow astronauts, made four spaceflights between 1965 and 1975. His missions included copiloting *Gemini 6-A* (December 15–16, 1965) with Walter Schirra; commanding *Gemini 9-A* (June 3–6, 1966) with Eugene Cernan; commanding *Apollo 10* (May 18–26, 1969) with Cernan and John Young; and commanding the American participants in the APOLLO-SOYUZ link-up mission (July 15–24, 1975). He logged over 21 days in space.

Stagg, Amos Alonzo (1862–1965) American football's "Grand Old Man." Stagg coached football at the University of CHICAGO for 41 years. After he retired from the Chicago post at the age of 70, he coached at the College of the Pacific from 1933 to 1946 and at Susquehanna University from 1947 to 1952. Stagg developed many new football techniques, including the tackling dummy. He became even more famous as the oldest active coach in the United States and as the coach with the greatest number of coaching seasons.

Stalin, Joseph Vissarionovich (Dzhugashvili) (1879–1953) Dictator of the USSR and leader of the world communist movement. Along with his near-contemporary Adolf HITLER, Stalin stands as one of the most ruthless and destructive figures of the 20th century. During his rule, Stalin's reach extended into virtually every aspect of life in the Soviet Union, and millions of Soviet citizens perished as a result of Stalin's decrees. The son of a Georgian shoemaker, he was expelled from the Tbilisi Theological Seminary in 1898 as a result of his interest in the revolutionary movement. He then joined the Russian Social Democratic Party and, in 1903 its BOLSHEVIK faction. Having worked in the underground movement in Transcaucasia, he was made part of the Bolshevik central committee by LENIN and ZINOVIEV. Banished to Petrograd after the February Revolution of 1917, Stalin edited the party's newspaper, *Pravda*. Stalin served as commissar for nationalities and commissar for worker-peasant inspection (1919–23) and became a very close collaborator of Lenin. During the CIVIL WAR he served as a commissar for nationalities.

In 1922 he was appointed secretary-general of the central committee, although Lenin, nurturing misgivings about Stalin's suitability for this position, was planning to remove him from it. Lenin's death prevented this, and Stalin's political career continued unchecked. Together with Zinoviev and KAMENEV he defeated TROTSKY, and then with BUKHARIN and RYKOV's help he defeated Zinoviev and Kamenev in the struggle for power. MOLOTOV, VOROSHILOV, Kaganovich, Ordzhonikidze and KIROV then helped him to defeat Bukharin and Rykov's RIGHT OPPOSITION. From 1929 to 1934 he ruled with them, assuming the position of leader until they opposed him. This provided the catalyst for abandoning collective leadership and for instigating the GREAT PURGE. With Stalin as official head of government in 1940 and chairman of the state defense committee, a reign of terror ensued.

Stalin's refusal to believe numerous intelligence reports of an impending German invasion in 1941 gave Hitler's armies a toll-free ticket that led them to the outskirts of Moscow and ensured a long and bitter war. Generalissimo during WORLD WAR II, he outwitted CHURCHILL and ROOSEVELT. He became increasingly obsessed with problems of security. He was jealous, anti-Semitic, chauvinistic and xenophobic, while demanding to be treated as a virtual demigod by all. He died in 1953, just as he was launching another purge. (See also DOCTORS' PLOT.)

Stalingrad, siege of *(1942–1943)* In May and June of 1942 German tanks, divebombers and other forces were approaching the lower Volga River and the Caucasus. Having crossed the Don River, they reached the outskirts of Stalingrad and besieged the city. By mid-November 1942, the British victory at EL ALAMEIN and the Allied pursuit of the defeated Germans resulted in no more reinforcements for the German army near Stalingrad. Fresh Russian reinforcements were brought in, and on November 20 Yeremenko broke the enemy line. The Russians launched a great thrust from the north, and Marshal von Manstein was forced to retreat. The encircled Germans under General von Paulus surrendered on February 2, 1943, having sustained a loss of 200,000 men. (See also WORLD WAR II ON THE RUSSIAN FRONT.)

Stalinism Name given to Stalin's political theorizing and rule of the USSR, the eastern European bloc countries and the world communist movement. Based on Marxism, Leninism and national Bolshevism, STALIN with the help of MOLOTOV, ZHDANOV and VYSHINSKY added such doctrines and ideas as the existence of the state under full communism, SOCIALIST REALISM in the arts, the concept of building socialism in one country, the people's great love for the Communist Party, their unanimous support of Stalin and the security organs to eliminate "misguided" dissenters. CONCENTRATION CAMPS were much in use, especially during Stalin's GREAT PURGE. Some aspects of Stalinism became obsolete, particularly after KHRUSHCHEV's secret report to the 20th Party Congress; others, such as the role of the Communist Party, remained. Forms of Stalinism were practiced by commu-

German troops invading the Soviet Union (LIBRARY OF CONGRESS, PRINTS AND PHOTOGRAPHS DIVISION)

nist leaders in several eastern bloc countries, including Enver HOXHA of ALBANIA and Nicolae CEAUSESCU of ROMANIA.

Stambolisky, Alexander *(1879–1923)* Bulgarian political leader. Born into a well-to-do peasant family, Stambolisky studied agriculture in Germany and became a leader of the Agrarian Party. Leading the opposition to Czar FERDINAND, he was imprisoned during World War I for his opposition to Bulgaria's entry into the war as an ally of Germany. After his release he served as president of a short-lived republic (1918). When BORIS III succeeded Ferdinand, Stambolisky became premier (1919), and by the following year he had become the virtual dictator of Bulgaria. Hostile to both liberal and communist doctrine, he instituted a peasant dictatorship and embarked on a campaign of agrarian reform. He was assassinated in a 1923 coup by right-wing forces who opposed his associations with Yugoslavia.

Stanislavsky, Konstantin Sergeyevich *(1865–1938)* Russian director, actor, teacher. One of the great theorists of 20th-century theater, Stanislavsky influenced theater worldwide with his emphasis on a realistic acting style and naturalism in scenic design. In the U.S. his theories on acting led to the development of method acting. Initially an actor, he became cofounder of the Society of Literature and Art in 1888, then cofounder of the Moscow Art Theater in 1898. He achieved his first success as a director in 1891 with a production of Leo Tolstoy's *The Fruits of Enlightenment*. His greatest triumphs were as director of the plays of CHEKHOV. His influence outside Russia came primarily as a result of his books, including *An Actor Prepares* (1926) and *Building a Character,* and the teachers trained by him.

Stanwyck, Barbara **(Ruby Stevens)** *(1907–1990)* American actress. Stanwyck appeared in more than 80 films, playing a variety of strong-minded, warmhearted women. They included classic films such as *Stella Dallas* (1937), *The Lady Eve* (1941), *Double Indemnity* (1944) and *Sorry, Wrong Number* (1948). At the height of her film career, in 1944, the Bureau of Internal Revenue listed her $400,000 salary as the highest of any woman in the U.S. One of the first films stars to make the transition to television, she portrayed Victoria Barkley, in the *Big Valley* western series from 1965 to 1969, and won three Emmy Awards for her work. Although she never won any of the four Academy Awards for which she had been nominated, she was given an honorary ACADEMY AWARD in 1982.

***Stardust* Spacecraft** An American spacecraft launched on February 7, 1999 aboard a Delta 2 rocket from Cape Canaveral Air Station in Florida with the goal of becoming the first mission sponsored by the National Aeronautics and Space Administration (NASA) to return space particles from beyond the Earth-Moon orbit. After a seven-year journey, the Stardust successfully landed on a desert in Utah on January 15, 2006. It contained interstellar dust as well as material that had been captured from the comet Wild 2, which the spacecraft had encountered in the course of its 2.9 billion mile round-trip flight.

Stargell, Willie (Wilver Dornell Stargell) *(1940–2001)* American baseball player. A member of the Pittsburgh Pirates for 20 years, Stargell began a string of 13 consecutive home run seasons in 1964. A seven-time All Star, his best season came in 1979 as he led the Pirates to World Series victory, batting .400, with three home runs. He shared regular season National League Most Valuable Player honors (the oldest player to earn the title), but stood alone as League Championship Series MVP and World Series MVP. A fearsome power hitter, he was responsible for the only two blasts ever to sail completely out of Dodger Stadium. He was named to the Hall of Fame in 1988.

Stark, Harold R. *(1880–1972)* American admiral. Stark was chief of naval operations in the Pacific at the time of the Japanese attack on PEARL HARBOR (December 7, 1941). He was relieved of his command and made commander of U.S. forces in European waters.

Starker, Janos *(1924–   )* Hungarian-American cellist. Born in Budapest, Starker began playing the cello at the age of seven, later studying at the Franz Liszt Academy. After service in World War II, he was named (1945) principal cellist of the Budapest Philharmonic and the Budapest Opera Orchestra. He left Hungary the following year, touring throughout Europe, and immigrated to the U.S. in 1948. There he became first cellist for the Dallas Symphony (1948–49), the Metropolitan Opera Orchestra (1949–53) and the Chicago Symphony (1953–58). In 1958 he left orchestral playing in order to concentrate on his career as a soloist, and he also became a professor of music at Indiana University. Starker made his New York debut in 1960, and has since appeared throughout the world, averaging some 80 concerts a year. Known for his tonal richness and fine musicianship, he has largely concentrated on the works of Bach, Beethoven and Brahms and has performed a good deal of modern music. In 1998 Starker received a Grammy Award for Best Instrumental Solo Performance for his recordings of Bach suites for unaccompanied cello.

START (Strategic Arms Reduction Talks) Long-term negotiations between the UNITED STATES and the UNION OF SOVIET SOCIALIST REPUBLICS concerning nuclear armaments, bombers, ballistic missiles and space weapons (see STRATEGIC DEFENSE INITIATIVE). The fourth round of START was held in GENEVA, Switzerland, in 1986. Although Mikhail GORBACHEV's proposal for a worldwide ban on all nuclear weapons by the year 2000 was rejected, by 1991 much progress had been made toward arms reduction. The START Treaty was signed by Soviet president Mikhail GORBACHEV and U.S. president George H. W. BUSH in 1991. A second treaty (START II) was signed in 1993 by Bush and Russian President Boris YELTSIN.

Star Wars Popular name (often with derisive connotations) for the STRATEGIC DEFENSE INITIATIVE (SDI) proposed by U.S. President Ronald REAGAN in 1983; the name is derived from a popular 1977 science fiction film of the same title.

Stassen, Harold Edward *(1907–2001)* Former Minnesota governor, candidate for the Republican nomination for president in 1948, 1952 and 1964. Continuing, as late as 1988, to announce his candidacy for the top post—without much hope of selection—he became known as the "perennial candidate." Stassen was an attorney in Dakota County before being elected governor of Minnesota in 1938. He was reelected twice and resigned early in this third term to serve in the navy. While governor, Stassen gained national attention by supporting a labor law that provided a "cooling-off" period before striking. After service in WORLD WAR II Stassen was a delegate to the conference in San Francisco that founded the UNITED NATIONS. He was appointed president of the University of Pennsylvania in 1948. He served until 1953 when he resigned to serve as a mutual security administrator and then as a foreign operations administrator, controlling American aid to many countries. Stassen attempted to win the nomination for governor of Pennsylvania in 1958, but lost. In 1987, at the age of 80, Stassen again announced his intention to run for the presidency in 1988 but made little headway beyond the announcement.

states' rights A doctrine whereby the states claimed all powers not reserved by the U.S. Constitution for the federal government. The assertion of this doctrine caused many clashes between the states and the federal government, culminating in the Civil War of 1861–65. The states based their claim on the Tenth Amendment, which states, "The powers not delegated to the United States by the Constitution, nor prohibited by it to the States, are reserved to the States respectively, or to the people."

The defeat of the Confederacy effectively crushed the doctrine of states' rights, although it resurfaced in the 20th century during the period of desegregation in the 1950s and 1960s. State governors such as Orval E. FAUBUS of Arkansas and George C. WALLACE of Alabama made states' rights statements, and southern state legislatures passed a number of laws to try to circumvent federal desegregation policies. During this period federal troops were called out several times to assist the desegregation process. Although over 200 years the U.S. government has effectively consolidated its power, it is unlikely that the concept of states' rights will ever completely disappear.

Statute of Westminster British statute adopted in 1931 delineating the status of dominions. Responding to resolutions of the Imperial Conferences of 1926 and 1930 brought about by stirrings of independence in the Commonwealth, the Statute of Westminster decreed that dominions were "autonomous communities . . . united by a common allegiance to the Crown, and freely associated as members of the British COMMONWEALTH OF NATIONS."

Stauffenberg, Count Claus Schenk von (1907–1944) German aristocrat and military officer. A staff officer in WORLD WAR II, Stauffenberg was wounded in battle and considered a genuine war hero. Disillusioned with Adolf HITLER's leadership as Germany's situation in the war became desperate, Stauffenberg took the leading role in the July 20, 1944, attempt to assassinate the führer. After the bomb he had planted failed to kill Hitler, Stauffenberg himself was executed by German soldiers.

Stavisky affair French financial scandal of 1933–34. In December 1933 the financier Serge Alexandre Stavisky was found to have been issuing worthless bonds for the municipal pawnshop of Bayonne. He fled to Chamonix, where he committed suicide in January 1934. After his death it was widely alleged that he had been protected by corrupt and influential officials, and the premier, Camille Chautemps, was forced to resign. Rightist groups such as the ACTION FRANÇAISE continued to agitate, alleging that Stavisky had been murdered in a government cover-up. Bloody rioting broke out in Paris in February 1934, toppling the government of Edouard DALADIER, followed by a general strike. The threatened Third Republic was saved by the formation of a coalition by Gaston Doumergue (1863–1937). However, the scandal had the effect of bringing the republic and the parliamentary form of government itself into lasting disrepute and of fostering right-wing ideology in France.

Stead, Christina Ellen (1902–1983) Australian novelist. Born and educated in Australia, Stead moved to London in 1928 and later traveled and lived in Europe and America with the American political economist William J. Blake, whom she eventually married. She returned to Australia permanently in 1974. Stead's first work was the collection of gothic stories The Salzburg Tales (1934), but it is for the acclaimed novel The Man Who Loved Children (1940), a sardonic portrait of an American family, that she is best known. Other novels include House of All Nations (1938), Dark Places in the Heart (1966, published in Britain as Cotter's England, 1967) and Miss Herbert (The Suburban Wife, 1976). Her fiction reflects her left-wing and feminist viewpoints, as well as her abhorrence of the tyranny of egotism.

Stealth Term used to describe military aircraft (both fighters and bombers) designed so that they are virtually undetectable by enemy RADAR. The U.S. military began developing Stealth technology in the 1970s, during the CARTER administration. The Stealth program was top secret, and the first Stealth aircraft—the B-2 bomber, designed and manufactured by Northrop—was not seen by the public until 1988. Stealth aircraft saw their first wartime use during the PERSIAN GULF WAR (1991), in which U.S. Air Force flew 40 Lockheed F-117A Stealth fighterbombers in combat without a single loss.

Steber, Eleanor (1914–1990) American singer. An outstanding soprano with the Metropolitan Opera (Met) during the 1940s and 1950s, Steber also gave recitals in the U.S. and Europe and appeared at the major European music festivals. She made her Met debut as Sophie in Der Rosenkavalier in 1940, and became particularly noted for her roles in such Mozart operas as The Marriage of Figaro and The Magic Flute. She also starred in revivals of the musicals Where's Charley? and The Sound of Music (1966–67) at Lincoln Center for the Performing Arts, and conducted master voice classes at the Juilliard School of Music, among other schools.

Steel, David (Martin Scott) (1938–) British politician. Steel, a Scot, entered Parliament in 1965 as a Liberal representing Roxburgh, Scotland. He succeeded Jeremy THORPE as LIBERAL PARTY leader in 1976. Steel formed an agreement with the Labour government in 1977 and 1978 (the "Lib-Lab Pact"), and an alliance with the SOCIAL DEMOCRATIC PARTY (SDP) in 1983. He was strongly in favor of his party's decision to merge with the SDP (1987), and stepped down in 1988 to allow new leadership for the new party. Steel was made a Life Peer in 1997, and in 1999 he became an active member of the Scottish Parliament created by British prime minister Tony Blair.

Steeleye Span British folk-rock group formed in 1968; members were Tim Hart, guitar and dulcimer, Ashley Hutchings, bass, Maddy Prior and Gay Woods, vocals and Terry Woods, guitar, mandolin and vocals. The band's pedigree was similar to that of other successful folk-rock groups of the time, including FAIRPORT CONVENTION. Steeleye Span achieved a high level of commercial success for a folk-oriented group, even as their personnel shifted with virtually every album. Their best-selling albums came in the mid-'70s, and included Below the Salt, Parcel of Rogues and Now We Are Six.

Steffens, Joseph Lincoln (1866–1936) American journalist and autobiographer. Steffens was one of the most influential American journalists in the first three decades of the 20th century. He first came to national prominence in the 1900s as a leading investigative reporter of the type labeled—in a speech by a displeased President Theodore ROOSEVELT—"muckrakers." Steffens, while writing for the New York Post and other publications in the 1900s, focused on political corruption in American cities. He published three influential books on this theme: The Shame of the Cities (1904), The Struggle for Self-Government (1906) and The Upbuilders (1909). In the 1910s and 1920s, Steffens traveled widely and worked as a foreign correspondent. Late in life he wrote his Autobiography (1931), which is still regarded as an American classic in that genre.

Steichen, Edward (1879–1973) American photographer, one of the American pioneers of photography practiced as a conscious art form. An early associate of photographer Alfred STIEGLITZ, Steichen was also the brother-in-law of poet Carl SANDBURG. In the

Photographer Edward Steichen positions himself for a shot during World War II. 1943. (LIBRARY OF CONGRESS, PRINTS AND PHOTOGRAPHS DIVISION)

1900s, Steichen contributed celebrity photographic portraits—such as tycoon J. P. Morgan—to various periodicals. In the 1920s and 1930s, he broadened his focus to include fashion photography for *Vogue* and *Vanity Fair*. From 1947 to 1962, he served as director of the department of photography of the New York-based Museum of Modern Art. It was there in 1955 that Steichen organized the famous photographic exhibit *The Family of Man* (also published in book form).

Stein, Gertrude *(1874–1946)* American author and patron of the arts. Born in Pennsylvania and educated at Radcliffe, Stein studied under William JAMES and George SANTAYANA. In 1902 she moved to Paris, where she began collecting the works of young artists. She established an artistic and literary salon at her home in the rue de Fleurus, where artists Pablo PICASSO, Henri MATISSE and Juan GRIS and writers Ernest HEMINGWAY, Sherwood ANDERSON and Ford

Maddox FORD among others frequently gathered during the 1920s and '30s. In 1907 she met Alice B. Toklas, who became her life-long companion and secretary. Stein later wrote *The Autobiography of Alice B. Toklas* (1933), Stein's own memoirs written as if by Toklas herself. Stein's first novel, which she wrote during the period when she sat for Picasso's portrait of her, was *Three Lives* (1907). Other works include *The Making of Americans* (1945), an attempt at the history of her family; *Tender Buttons* (1914), a poetic work in her repetitive, STREAM-OF-CONSCIOUSNESS style; *Wars I Have Seen* (1945), a description of occupied Paris during WORLD WAR II; and a play, *Four Saints in Three Acts*. Though remembered almost as much for who she was as for what she wrote, Stein was an important innovator in the use of language and a major practitioner of literary MODERNISM. She coined the famous phrase "the lost generation."

Steinbeck, John (John Ernst Steinbeck) *(1902–1968)* American novelist, story writer, playwright, essayist and screenplay writer. Steinbeck, who won the NOBEL PRIZE for literature in 1962, was a prolific, versatile and moving writer. He is best remembered for *The Grapes of Wrath* (1939), a novel widely considered to be a 20th-century classic. Set largely in the Oklahoma dustbowl during the GREAT DEPRESSION of the 1930s, *The Grapes of Wrath* recounts the efforts of the impoverished Joad family to move to California in hopes of a better life. Steinbeck studied at Stanford University, though he dropped out before earning a degree. His first novel was *Cup of Gold* (1929), but he first earned acclaim with *Tortilla Flat* (1935), set in the hills above Monterey, California, a region Steinbeck also described in *Cannery Row* (1945). *Of Mice and Men* (1937), a novel about the sad lives of two migrant workers, one of whom is mentally retarded, was successfully adapted for the Broadway stage by Steinbeck in collaboration with George S. KAUFMAN. Steinbeck dealt with nature and ecology in *Sea of Cortez: A Leisurely Journal of Travel and Research* (1941). The novel *East of Eden* (1954) and the nonfiction *Travels With Charlie in Search of America* (1962) are the most famous of Steinbeck's later works.

Steinberg, William *(1899–1978)* German-American conductor. Born in

Cologne, Steinberg was a musical prodigy on the violin and piano and made his first appearance as a conductor at 13. After studies at Cologne University, he became (1920) the assistant to Otto KLEMPERER. He conducted the German Theater, Prague (1925–29) and the Frankfurt Opera Orchestra (1929–33) before being forced out by the Nazis. In 1934 he assembled a group of other Jewish musicians into the Jewish Culture League and performed for Jewish audiences for the next two years. Leaving Germany in 1936, he fled to Palestine, where he assembled, trained and conducted the Palestine Symphony Orchestra (now the Israel Philharmonic). In 1937 Steinberg took the post of assistant to Arturo TOSCANINI at the NBC Symphony, and he became a U.S. citizen in 1944. He served as music director of the Buffalo Symphony Orchestra from 1945 to 1952 and of the Pittsburgh Symphony from 1952 to 1976, developing it into one of the country's most noted orchestras. Steinberg was known for his intensely precise musical interpretations and the pure beauty of his sound.

Steindler, Arthur *(1878–1959)* Austrian-born surgical pioneer, one of a pioneer team of medical men who made the medical center of the University of Iowa known worldwide for its excellence. Dr. Steindler became one of the world's most distinguished orthopedic specialists. He was responsible for the development of many of the techniques used universally today, including methods of bone care, treatment, straightening, grafting, lengthening and other orthopedic practices.

Steinem, Gloria *(1934–)* American feminist and magazine editor. Educated at Smith College, Steinem began her journalism career in the 1960s as a freelance writer for several New York-based magazines, including *Esquire*, *Vogue* and *New York*, for which she wrote a liberal political column, *The City Politic*, that first brought her national attention. By the late 1960s, Steinem was focusing on FEMINISM as her key political interest. In 1971, she was a founding member—along with Bella Abzug, Shirley Chisholm and Betty FRIEDAN—of the National Women's Political Caucus. That same year, Steinem was a key force behind the establish-

Journalist and feminist Gloria Steinem, photographed by Warren K. Leffler. 1972 (U.S. News and World Report Magazine Collection, Library of Congress, Prints and Photographs Division)

ment of the Women's Action Alliance. In 1972 Steinem became editor of *Ms.* magazine, a major national feminist journal for which she has continued to edit and write. She has also become active as a patron and sponsor of feminist-inspired artistic, cultural and political events. In 1993 Steinem released *Moving Beyond Words,* a collection of her essays. (See also WOMEN'S MOVEMENTS.)

Steiner, Max *(1888–1971)* The dean of American film composers; his music for *Gone with the Wind* (1939) remains the most familiar of all movie scores. Born in Vienna, Austria, to a prosperous family (his father managed the prestigious Theater an der Wien), Steiner studied composition and orchestration with Felix WEINGARTNER and Gustav MAHLER at the Imperial Academy of Music. His interests in musical theater drew him to London, Paris and finally New York in 1914. After 15 years orchestrating and conducting Broadway shows for Victor HERBERT, Jerome KERN and George GERSHWIN, he went to HOLLYWOOD in 1929 to adapt Ziegfeld's *Rio Rita* to the screen. At RKO, in addition to arranging such musicals as the Fred ASTAIRE–Ginger ROGERS series, he composed his first important film scores for *Bird of Paradise* (1932) and *King Kong*

(1933). His most productive period was at WARNER BROTHERS, where he averaged eight scores a year (150 films in all), including many of the Humphrey BOGART, Errol FLYNN and Bette DAVIS vehicles. He won ACADEMY AWARDS for his music for *The Informer* (1935), *Now, Voyager* (1943) and *Since You Went Away* (1944). *Casablanca* demonstrates his use of classical techniques, including permutations upon a designated main theme ("As Time Goes By"), the assigning of leitmotifs to characters and situations, the use of "descriptive" and mood-enhancing music to complement the story and a superb sensitivity for string writing. Steiner biographer Tony Thomas: "It was Steiner more than any other composer who pioneered the use of original composition as background scoring for films."

Steinmetz, Charles *(1865–1923)* German-American electrical engineer. In 1889, Steinmetz immigrated to the U.S. From 1893 to 1923, he worked for the General Electric Company in Schenectady, New York; beginning in 1902 he also taught at Union College in that city. Steinmetz explained the power loss resulting from magnetic resistance and demonstrated that alternating current could partially compensate for that loss, thereby hastening the commercial use of alternating current. Although Steinmetz's reputation rests primarily on his theoretical work, he was also awarded 200 patents.

Stella, Frank *(1936–   )* American painter. Born in Malden, Massachusetts. Stella studied at Princeton University and became a prominent figure in the New York art world during the 1960s. His early 1960s work mainly consisted of large minimal black paintings of angular "pinstripes" that contrasted strongly with abstract expressionist work in their measured formalism and pictorial restraint. Later in the decade, he produced polychrome striped works in metallic pigments, often on shaped canvases. Later, his style moved into shaped works with complicated curvilinear forms that jut into space and richly colored and patterned surfaces. Stella continued to accept commissions throughout the 1990s, such as his murals for the Princess of Wales Theater in Toronto.

Stengel, Charles Dillon "Casey" "The Old Professor" *(1889–1975)* American baseball player and manager. Casey Stengel was one of the most colorful characters in the history of baseball. His wit perhaps obscured the fact that he was one of the greatest managers ever. Stengel played outfield from 1912 to 1925, much of that time with the Brooklyn Dodgers. He went on to manage that team from 1934 to 1936 and later several other teams. It was not until 1949 that he joined the New York Yankees, an association that would become legend. He managed the team to five consecutive World Series championships. In 1960 he was fired by the Yankees but returned to baseball two years later with the New York Mets. The team owed much of its reputation as New York's Amazin's to Stengel's verbal dexterity. A fast-talking master of the nonsequitor, he was able to deflect interest from the team's utter fecklessness to its loopy charm. He retired in 1965 and was named to the Hall of Fame a year later. Stengel died during the league championships in 1975. His funeral was delayed one week—until an off-day—so that all of baseball could attend.

Stenmark, Ingemar *(1956–   )* Swedish skier. A slalom and giant slalom specialist, Stenmark became a folk hero in Sweden for his come-from-behind performances on the slopes. First overall in the World Cup from 1976 to 1978, he was first in the giant slalom six times in the late 1970s and early 1980s, and first in slalom from 1975 to 1981 and again in 1983. World champion in giant slalom and slalom in 1978 and slalom in 1982, he is best remembered for his 1980 OLYMPIC performances at Lake Placid. Both the slalom and giant slalom were vintage Stenmark, as he turned in cautious first runs and thrilling, seemingly reckless runs in the second round, and took the gold medal in both events. He was not permitted to take part in the 1984 games as a result of his turning "professional."

Stephens, Olin J. *(1908–   )* U.S. naval architect best known for the design of sailing yachts, including a number of highly successful racing craft. Stephens designed his first 6-meter racing yacht, *Thalia*, in 1926, after only one term at MIT. In 1928 he established the firm of SPARKMAN & STEPHENS with his brother Roderick and Drake Sparkman as partners. *Dorade,* a yawl of 1930, established a new standard for sailing yachts, with successes in a Bermuda race and a transatlantic race shortly after it was built. In 1937, Harold S. Vanderbilt asked Stephens to work with Starling Burgess on the design of the America's Cup yacht, *Ranger,* built with a steel hull. A succession of winning America's Cup racers followed, including *Columbia; Constellation; Courageous; Freedom,* a 1980 winner; and *Intrepid* (often viewed as Stephens's greatest design). *Finisterre* of 1955, a 39-foot centerboard design, established a modern standard for yachts designed for equal success in racing and extended cruising. Stephens retired in 1979, but the firm remains active.

Stephenson, Sir William S. *(1896–1989)* Canadian-born millionaire, industrialist and spy master. After the outbreak of WORLD WAR II, Prime Minister Winston CHURCHILL sent Stephenson to the U.S., where he served as a link between Churchill and President Franklin ROOSEVELT. Stephenson helped organize the U.S. wartime intelligence operation, the Office of Strategic Services (OSS), a forerunner of the CIA. His wartime adventures were related in the 1979 best seller *A Man Called Intrepid.*

Stepinac, Aloysius *(1898–1960)* Yugoslavian prelate. Stepinac was appointed archbishop of Zagreb in 1937. He served in the Croatian state council during World War II, in a government established by the nationalistic terrorists known as the USTASE. After the war he was convicted of collaboration and imprisoned until 1951, when he was ordered to remain in his native city of Krasic. Marshal TITO opposed Stepinac, while the Vatican treated him as a persecuted figure and elevated him to cardinal in 1953. This disagreement over Stepinac was an important factor in the gulf between the Yugoslavian government and the Roman Catholic Church.

Steptoe, Patrick Christopher *(1913–1988)* British obstetrician-gynecologist. With Cambridge University physiologist Robert Edwards, Steptoe pioneered the first in vitro ("test-tube") fertilization procedure. In 1978,

he delivered the world's first TEST-TUBE BABY by cesarean section in northern England.

Sterba, Richard *(1898–1989)* American psychoanalyst. He touched off a major international musicological controversy with the 1945 publication of *Beethoven and His Nephew: A Psychoanalytic Study of their Relationship* (1945), written with his wife, Editha. The book argued that Beethoven had been a repressed homosexual whose inner conflicts had resulted in sadistic attempts to control his nephew, Karl. Although their theory was later at least partially discredited, the Sterbas were widely acknowledged to have helped lay the groundwork for the later popular school of musical psychobiography.

Stern, Curt *(1902–1981)* German-born geneticist. After receiving his doctorate in zoology from the University of Berlin (1923), Stern spent two years as a postdoctoral fellow at Columbia University in New York. There he worked with a group of scientists who virtually developed the modern science of genetics, discovering many of the fundamental rules of heredity. He returned to Berlin in 1928, but fled to America when Adolf HITLER came to power (1933). During WORLD WAR II he worked on the MANHATTAN PROJECT that developed the ATOMIC BOMB, and pioneered the study of the effects of radiation on living organisms. He was an adviser to the Atomic Energy Commission when it was formed in 1945. He taught at the University of California, BERKELEY (1947–70) and wrote *The Principles of Human Genetics* (1949), which remained a standard textbook for two decades.

Stern, Isaac *(1920–2001)* American violinist. Born in the USSR, as an infant Stern came to the U.S. with his family and settled in San Francisco. He entered the San Francisco Conservatory at 10 and made his debut as a soloist with the San Francisco Symphony the following year and his New York debut at Town Hall in 1937. After this he began a series of brilliant worldwide tours, and by the early 1940s he was acclaimed as one of the world's master violinists. Noted for his exquisite tone and superb musicianship, he performed as a soloist with every major or-

chestra and at every important music festival. He also became known for his many chamber music performances, particularly with the Istomen-Stern-Rose Trio, which he cofounded. His repertoire was extensive, including not only classic violin pieces but 20th-century music as well. He premiered works by composers such as Paul HINDEMITH, William Schuman and Leonard BERNSTEIN. Stern maintained close musical ties with Israel, where he often performed, and was an officer of the America-Israel Cultural Foundation and a cofounder of the Israeli Music Center. Stern was also closely associated with CARNEGIE HALL in New York City. When the hall was threatened with demolition in the late 1950s, Stern organized a movement to save it. He subsequently served as president of the Carnegie Hall Corporation and was a leading figure in numerous events connected to Carnegie Hall.

Sternberg, Josef von (Josef Sternberg) *(1894–1969)* Austrian-born Jewish film director. Von Sternberg is primarily remembered for his richly textured films of the 1930s that starred Marlene DIETRICH. The aristocratic "von" of his name was added on as a show business touch during von Sternberg's early years in HOLLYWOOD, during which he worked as an assistant director. Von Sternberg made his directorial debut with *The Salvation Hunters* (1925), then followed up with a series of gangster films including *Underworld* (1927) and *Thunderbolt* (1929). But he won international fame with *The Blue Angel* (1930), in which von Sternberg introduced Dietrich to cinema audiences in the seductive role of Lola Lola, for which she is best remembered. Several more films with Dietrich followed—*Morocco* (1930), *Dishonored* (1931), *Shanghai Express* (1932), *Blonde Venus* (1932), *The Scarlet Empress* (1934) and *The Devil Is a Woman* (1935). Each film featured innovative backlighting and glamorous costuming, but von Sternberg's preference for atmosphere over plot led to his commercial decline. His last film was *Anatahan* (1953).

Stern Gang (Lohamei Herut Yisrael, Fighters for the Freedom of Israel) Jewish guerrilla group founded by Avraham STERN. It operated in

PALESTINE in the mid-1940s and was responsible for the assassination of Count Folke BERNADOTTE, the United Nations mediator in Palestine in 1948.

Stettinius, Edward R. *(1900–1949)* U.S. government official. Born into a prominent New York City family, Stettinius went to work in Washington as a lobbyist for General Motors. In 1938, he was named chairman of the board of U.S. Steel, but in 1939 he resigned that post and in 1940 joined the National Defense Advisory Commission, the first of a number of government appointments over the next few years. In 1944, President Franklin D. ROOSEVELT appointed Stettinius secretary of state, and in 1945, the new president, Harry S TRUMAN, named him first U.S. ambassador to the UNITED NATIONS. Stettinius resigned in 1946 after a disagreement with then-secretary of state James BYRNES. He died of a heart condition three years later.

Stevens, George *(1904–1975)* Prestigious American motion picture director. A native Californian, Stevens traveled as a youngster in his parents' touring theater company. He worked as a cameraman in the 1920s and photographed many LAUREL AND HARDY comedy shorts, including the classic *Big Business* (1928). After serving an apprenticeship directing comedy shorts for RKO and UNIVERSAL, he debuted as a director of "A" films with the delightful *Alice Adams* (1935), starring Katharine HEPBURN. After several top-notch genre pieces, including the ASTAIRE-ROGERS musical *Swing Time* (1936) and the swashbuckling adventure *Gunga Din* (1939), he served in WORLD WAR II as a lieutenant colonel in the Army Signal Corps. His film unit covered, among other events, the liberation of the DACHAU inmates. He entered his most successful decade in the 1950s with several big-budget epics, including *A Place in the Sun* (a 1951 adaptation of DREISER's *An American Tragedy*), the classic western *Shane* (1953), the "modern" western *Giant* (1956) and the epic *The Greatest Story Ever Told* (1965). Increasingly, Stevens's drive for perfection, outsized budgets and interminable running times strangled the life out of his films. As historian Andrew Sarris concludes: "All in all, his little movies have outlasted his big ones."

Stevens, John Paul, III *(1920–)* Associate justice, U.S. Supreme Court (1975–). A native of Chicago and a graduate of the University of Chicago and Northwestern Law School, Stevens served as a law clerk to Justice Wiley RUTLEDGE after law school. After practicing antitrust law in Chicago, Stevens was appointed to the U.S. court of appeals for the seventh circuit by President Richard M. NIXON in 1970. In 1975 President Gerald FORD appointed Stevens to the U.S. Supreme Court. Although he has been termed a moderate judge, a more apt description might be a maverick with no ideological agenda. However, he proved a staunch defender of both CIVIL RIGHTS and civil liberties, often providing the decisive fifth vote in close decisions. With the addition of David SOUTER (1990), Clarence Thomas (1991), Ruth Ginsburg (1993) and Steven Breyer (1994) to the Supreme Court, Stevens, Ginsburg and Breyer have generally become associated with the "liberal" faction of that judicial body.

Stevens, Risë (Risë Steenberg) *(1913–)* American singer. An acclaimed mezzo-soprano, she performed at major opera houses worldwide, in movies and on network radio programs. She made her debut at the Prague Opera in the title role of *Mignon* in 1936, and made her Metropolitan Opera debut in the same role in 1938. In 1945 she appeared as *Carmen*, which became her most famous role. She also starred in the film version of the operetta *The Chocolate Soldier* (1941) and in a revival of the musical *The King and I* at Lincoln Center for the Performing Arts (1964). From 1975 to 1978 she served as president of Mannes College of Music.

Stevens, Robert Ten Broeck *(1899–1983)* American secretary of the army (1953 to 1955). Heir to the textile firm of J.P. Stevens and Co., he entered the family business after serving in WORLD WAR I. During the GREAT DEPRESSION he served on the NATIONAL RECOVERY ADMINISTRATION (NRA) and was director of the Federal Reserve Bank of New York (1934–53). During WORLD WAR II he was director of purchases in the office of the quartermaster general. Following the election of Dwight D. EISENHOWER as president, Stevens, a Republican, was appointed secretary of the army. He became famous for his televised confrontations with Senator Joseph MCCARTHY during the ARMY-MCCARTHY SENATE HEARINGS in 1954. During the hearings, he denied McCarthy's allegations of communist infiltration in the army and condemned the senator's tactics. Stevens's firm stand was the beginning of McCarthy's downfall. Stevens resigned from his post for personal reasons (1955) and returned to business.

Stevens, Siaka (Siaka Probyn Stevens) *(1905–1988)* Sierra Leone politician. Stevens led the West African nation of SIERRA LEONE for 17 years, first as prime minister and then as president. Stevens became prime minister in 1968 after a military coup and assumed the presidency in 1971. He retired from the presidency in 1985, becoming one of only a few black African leaders to give up power voluntarily.

Stevens, Wallace *(1879–1955)* American poet and essayist. Stevens is regarded as one of the greatest English-language poets of the 20th century, although his literary career was relatively slow in unfolding, and he won real fame late in life. Born in Reading, Pennsylvania, and educated at Harvard University, Stevens wrote his earliest poems for the *Advocate*, an undergraduate journal. He subsequently pursued a legal and business career and ultimately became a vice president with the Hartford Accident and Indemnity Company. He published his first volume of poems, *Harmonium* (1923), at age 44. His later volumes include *The Man with the Blue Guitar* (1937), *Transports of Summer* (1947), *The Auroras of Autumn* (1950), *Collected Poems* (1954) and *Opus Posthumous* (1957). One of the most original figures in 20th-century American letters, Stevens is neither a popular nor an easy poet. Although his work includes elements of symbolism and SURREALISM, he cannot be placed in any literary school. His poems rarely deal with subjects in the "real world," but are usually meditations on the imaginative intellect. They are marked by recurring and startling images, unexpected turns of thought and a highly musical and formal diction. *The Necessary Angel* (1951) is a volume of literary essays. Stevens won the BOLLINGEN PRIZE for poetry in 1950 and the PULITZER PRIZE in 1955.

Stevenson, Adlai Ewing, II *(1900–1965)* American statesman. After studies at Princeton and Harvard, Stevenson received his law degree from Northwestern University. His first public office was in the AGRICULTURAL ADJUSTMENT ADMINISTRATION from 1933 to 1934. During WORLD WAR II he was a special counsel to Secretary of the Navy Frank Knox. After the war, Stevenson was an alternate delegate to the UNITED NATIONS. In 1948 he was elected governor of his home state, Illinois, on a reform Democratic ticket—with the largest plurality in the state's history to that point. He is credited with spearheading 78 "clean-up" measures. In 1952 he was drafted as the Democratic candidate for president, despite the fact that he refused to campaign for the nomination. However, as the nominee he did campaign vigorously, in a manner said to have been "marked by eloquent speeches whose wit and civility were often memorable." He was defeated then and again in 1956 by Dwight D. EISENHOWER. In that campaign he was hampered by what some

Ambassador and presidential candidate Adlai Stevenson (LIBRARY OF CONGRESS, PRINTS AND PHOTOGRAPHS DIVISION)

considered his overly intellectual approach to national issues, as contrasted to Eisenhower's more homey touch. Stevenson served as one of the U.S.'s most notable ambassadors to the United Nations, from 1961 until his death.

Steward, Julian Haynes *(1902–1972)* American anthropologist. Steward received his Ph.D. at the University of California (1929) and went on to teach at numerous universities around the country. He was a noted expert on cultural evolution in the United States and worked at the Smithsonian Institution. While there, in the Bureau of American Ethnology, he edited the seven-volume *Handbook of South American Indians* (1946–59). Some of his other works include *Area Research, Theory and Practice* (1950) and *Theory of Culture Change* (1955).

Stewart, Jackie (John Young Stewart) *(1939–)* Scottish auto racing driver. Stewart began his career in 1954 as a garage mechanic, working his way up to racing mechanic and then driver in 1961. He was named to the British national motor team in 1965, and in 1969 won the South American, Spanish, Dutch, French, British and Italian championships. Awarded the Order of the British Empire in 1972, Stewart retired in 1973, after the death of a teammate, with a total of 27 Grand Prix championships. He went on to a career as a racing commentator. In 2001 the race car driver was knighted by Queen ELIZABETH II.

Stewart, James *(1908–1997)* American film and theater actor. Stewart, one of the most popular actors in HOLLYWOOD history, enjoyed a lengthy career and the adoration of fans and critics alike. After graduation from Princeton University, he joined the University Players, a theater ensemble that also included Henry FONDA. Stewart moved to Hollywood in the 1930s and emerged as a leading man with a gift for light comedy in films such as *You Can't Take It With You* (1938) and *Mr. Smith Goes to Washington* (1939), both directed by Frank CAPRA. He won a best actor Oscar for *The Philadelphia Story* (1940). During World War II Stewart served in the Army Air Force as a bomber pilot. He returned to Hollywood, reuniting with

director Capra in *It's A Wonderful Life* (1946), a box-office dog in its day but now considered a movie classic. In the 1950s and 1960s, Stewart shifted to tougher roles in such westerns as *Winchester 73* (1950) and *Bend of the River* (1952). He also starred in the Alfred HITCHCOCK thrillers *Rear Window* (1954), *The Man Who Knew Too Much* (1956) and *Vertigo* (1958). *Harvey* (1950) demonstrated once again his talent for light comedy. In recent decades, Stewart made only brief and infrequent film appearances, as in *The Shootist* (1976) and *The Big Sleep* (1978).

Stewart, Potter *(1915–1985)* American jurist. During his tenure as a Supreme Court Justice (1958–81). Stewart often provided the pivotal swing vote. During his first 11 years on the court, he often dissented from many of the liberal rulings under Chief Justice Earl WARREN. Afterward, he came to occupy the decisive center of the more conservative court under Chief Justice Warren E. BURGER.

Stickley, Gustav *(1857–1942)* American designer and furniture maker. In 1898 Stickley founded a furniture company in Eastwood, New York, to produce his designs, which were inspired by the English Arts and Crafts movement. Also known as "Mission style," Stickley's simple oak pieces became widely popular. In 1901, he began publication of *The Craftsman* magazine to promote his design concepts as well as his progressive social ideas. Stickley's company declared bankruptcy in 1915, but his work continued to exert a strong influence on other early 20th-century architects and designers, including Frank Lloyd WRIGHT.

Stieglitz, Alfred *(1864–1946)* American photographer and editor widely regarded as the father of modern photography. Born in Hoboken, New Jersey, and educated in mechanical engineering and photochemistry in Karlsruhe and Berlin, Stieglitz returned to New York in 1890 and founded the influential journal *Camera Work*, the most important organ of the PHOTO-SECESSION movement. He promoted modern art in America, establishing in New York an exhibition space for advanced American and European art called "291" (after its Fifth Avenue address). Between 1908 and 1917 he presented important shows of photographers and painters—members of the Photo-Secession and modern painters such as MATISSE, PICASSO and BRANCUSI. After World War I Stieglitz continued to support the work of native artists, particularly of his wife, Georgia O'KEEFFE. Concludes historian William Innes Homer, "Stieglitz elevated American photography to a respected international position, performing his task so well that the American School became preeminent the world over."

Stiglitz, Joseph E. *(1943–)* American economist, economic adviser to U.S. president William Jefferson CLINTON (1993–97), chief economic adviser to the International Bank for Reconstruction and Development (WORLD BANK) (1997–99) and recipient of the Nobel Prize in economics (2001). Born in Gary, Indiana, Stiglitz received his B.A. in economics from Amherst College in 1965 and his Ph.D. in economics from the Massachusetts Institute of Technology in 1967. He joined the economics department at Yale University, where he was awarded tenure in 1970. By 1979 he had been awarded the John Bates Clark Award by the American Economic Association in recognition of his contributions to the field of economics while still under 40 years of age. Stiglitz gained a reputation as an expert on monetary policy and an advocate of improving a nation's information and education infrastructure to maximize economic growth. In 1993 he was selected to be the chairman of President Clinton's Council of Economic Advisers. He remained in that post until 1997, when he accepted an appointment at the World Bank as its chief economist and senior vice president. In 2001 he resigned his positions at the World Bank and accepted a professorship in economics at Columbia University. Later that year Stiglitz was awarded the Nobel Prize for economics in recognition of his emphasis on the importance of information for economic growth.

Stijl, de ("the style") Dutch art movement of a severe nonfigurative character, also known as neoplasticism. It was formally initiated along with a journal of the same name in 1917 by a group of artists, architects and poets. Led by Dutch artists Theo van DOESBURG and Piet MONDRIAN, the movement stressed the elimination of all ornamental flourishes in favor of strict geometric compositions and the use of primary colors, black and white. This austere doctrine and the images it produced had worldwide influence, and the movement continued until 1931 (the magazine closed in 1928). It proved especially applicable to architecture, where it was important in the work of J. J. P. Oud, Gerrit RIETVELD, Walter GROPIUS and the BAUHAUS movement in general. Its strong, clean lines and pure color also influenced a wide range of visual expression, from posters to packaging and advertising.

Still, Clifford *(1904–1980)* American painter. Still was one of the founders of the artistic school of ABSTRACT EXPRESSIONISM that came to prominence in America in the 1940s and '50s. He was known for his fiercely independent and uncompromising views on artistic matters and the need for American painters to develop a unique style that was free of European tradition. Born in North Dakota, Still was educated in Washington state and taught at the California School of Fine Art (now the San Francisco Art Institute) from 1941 to 1949. In 1950 he moved to New York City, where the abstract expressionist movement began to flourish. Despite his own prominence, Still was highly critical of artists who sought to become self-conscious leaders of artistic movements.

Still, William Grant *(1895–1978)* American composer, arranger and conductor. Still was best known for his *Afro-American Symphony* (1931). He studied with the French composer Edgar VARESE. In 1936 he became the first black to conduct a major U.S. orchestra when he led the Los Angeles Philharmonic at the Hollywood Bowl. Still also arranged JAZZ scores for W. C. HANDY and Paul WHITEMAN, and provided musical arrangements for films, radio, television and the stage.

Stilwell, Joseph Warren *(1883–1946)* American general. Born in Palatka, Florida, Stilwell attended West Point and was commissioned in the army in 1904. He served in World War I and spent three tours of duty in CHINA during a period of 13 years. With the outbreak of the war, Stilwell was again posted in China, where in 1942 he was named chief of staff to General CHIANG KAI-SHEK and commander of American forces in the China-Burma-India theater of battle. He was defeated in Burma and retreated to India late in May 1942. There he regrouped his forces and struggled to retake Burma, a task that was eventually accomplished in 1945. In the meantime, however, Stilwell's frequent clashes with Chiang, whom he constantly criticized, had provoked his 1944 recall to the U.S. The outspoken general, popularly referred to as "Vinegar Joe," spent the rest of the war commanding American forces on OKINAWA.

Stimson, Henry Lewis *(1867–1950)* American statesman. Born in New York City, Stimson attended Yale University and Harvard Law School and became a successful Wall Street lawyer. After failing as the Republican gubernatorial candidate in 1910, he became (1911–13) President TAFT's secretary of war and served in World War I. He was governor-general of the Philippines from 1928 to 1929 and was recalled to be Herbert HOOVER's secretary of state (1929–33). In this post he pressed for disarmament as chairman of the U.S. delegation to the London Naval Conference (1930–31) and the Geneva Disarmament Conference (1932). Opposing the Japanese invasion of Manchuria (1932), he refused to recognize their puppet regime in a treaty policy known as the Stimson Doctrine. He was appointed secretary of war a second time by President Franklin D. ROOSEVELT, serving from 1940 to 1945. An energetic and effective secretary, he organized U.S. armed forces, advocated an Allied invasion across the English Channel, advised the president on nuclear affairs and was an important voice in the debate over dropping the ATOMIC BOMB on Japan. His autobiography, *On Active Service in Peace and War,* was published in 1948.

Sting *(1951–)* Popular British musician. Born Gordon Sumner in Wallsend, England, Sting joined with Stewart Copeland and Andy Summers as the lead singer and bass player for the rock band The Police in 1976. Sting began to develop a solo career in 1982 when he released the single "Spread A Little Happiness" from the soundtrack of the film *Brimstone and Treacle* (1982), in which he also appeared. In 1985 The Police disbanded, and Sting formed his own touring band, The Blue Turtles, which included famed New York City jazz saxophonist Branford Marsalis. Working in a recording studio in Jamaica, the group recorded its first album, *The Dream of the Blue Turtles* (1985), and Sting performed several of the album's songs, such as "Fortress Around Your Heart," at the 1985 Live Aid rock concert. In 1991 Sting released *The Soul Cages,* his third solo album, in which several of his songs represented his efforts to reconcile himself to the recent deaths of his parents. In 1993 Sting released *Ten Summoner's Tales,* which proved commercially and critically popular. His *Brand New Day* (1999) produced several popular singles in the U.S. and abroad, such as "Brand New Day" and "Desert Rose." *Brand New Day* won two awards for Sting at the 2000 Grammy ceremonies for Best Pop Album and Best Male Pop Performance. In 2003 Queen ELIZABETH II named Sting a commander of the British Empire (CBE) in recognition of his contributions to the music industry and to humanitarian causes around the world.

Stirling, Sir (Archibald) David *(1915–1990)* British commando, founder of the Long-Range Desert Patrol Group and the SPECIAL AIR SERVICES. During WORLD WAR II IN NORTH AFRICA, Colonel Stirling formed the Long-Range Desert Patrol Group and led them in daring raids behind enemy lines. Stirling was so successful that the Germans dubbed him "the Phantom Major." Captured by the Germans, he escaped, was recaptured and spent the remainder of the war in Colditz Castle, Germany's top-security prisoner-of-war camp. For his exploits Stirling was decorated for bravery. After the war Stirling left the army and went to Rhodesia. He founded the Capricorn Africa Society, a group that promoted racial harmony. He later directed Watchguard International, Ltd., a security firm that trained and advised security units for Arab and African countries. Stirling was knighted by Queen ELIZABETH II in 1990.

Stitt, Sonny *(1924–1982)* American alto saxophonist. Stitt was one of the most prolific recording artists in JAZZ history, Stitt's musical style was often compared to that of Charlie "Bird" PARKER. A week before Parker's death in 1955, Parker reportedly told Stitt, "Man, I'm handing you the keys to the kingdom."

Stockhausen, Karlheinz *(1928–)* German composer and music theorist. Stockhausen studied at the University of Cologne and was a composition student of Frank Martin in Cologne (1950–51) and of Olivier MESSIAEN and Darius MILHAUD in Paris (1951–53). An innovative avant-gardist, he met and collaborated with Pierre BOULEZ and worked with the tape-recorded and variously altered sounds of "music concrete." Stockhausen has been associated with various modern musical idioms, including the 12-tone system and serial, electronic and aleatory music, in which performer improvisation is encouraged. His compositions have often been termed difficult, exploiting as they do dissonant and percussive effects as well as experiments with tone, volume and duration. Among his works are *Gruppen* (1955–59), *Klavierstuck XI* (1956), *Telemusik* (1966) and *Sirius* (1975–76). Stockhausen continued to record throughout the 1990s, orchestrating such pieces as *Tuesday from Light* (1993), *Friday from Light* (1995) and *Wednesday from Light* (1996).

stock market crash of 1929 Disastrous collapse of stock prices on the U.S.'s national stock exchanges, signaling the start of the GREAT DEPRESSION of the 1930s. For many years, the value of American corporate stock had climbed as the economy expanded. Speculators often bought stock on margin—borrowing their broker's money to buy the stock in anticipation of quick profits and a quick return of the borrowed money. For various reasons, the decade-long market boom collapsed in little more than a week (October 24–29). The value of thousands of stocks plummeted as panicked sellers dumped their stocks; by December 1, 1929, New York Stock Exchange shares had lost an estimated $26 billion from their highest value on September 3. The crash disillusioned many business leaders, and the economy started on a severe and painful economic contraction that lasted nearly a decade.

stock market crash of 1987 Collapse of stock prices that was similar to the STOCK MARKET CRASH OF 1929 but whose consequences were less severe. In 1987, the U.S. stock market had been through an almost unprecedented seven-year "bull market." The bubble burst on October 19, 1987, when prices on the New York Stock Exchange plunged over 508 points, almost a 23 percent drop in value. The London and Tokyo stock exchanges experienced similar crashes during the same week. Interestingly, the 1987 crash was more severe than the 1929 crash from both an absolute and percentage view. However, the market rebounded later in the year, and the recession in 1990–91 seemed only indirectly related to the 1987 crash.

Stockwell, General Sir Hugh *(1903–1986)* British military officer. Stockwell commanded Britain's land forces in the 1956 Anglo-French invasion of the Suez Canal Zone (see SUEZ CRISIS). After that campaign, he was military secretary to the secretary of state for war from 1957 to 1959 and deputy supreme commander of NORTH ATLANTIC TREATY ORGANIZATION (NATO) forces in Europe from 1960 to 1964.

Stoica, Chivu *(1908–1975)* Premier of ROMANIA (1955–61). A communist revolutionary, while in his mid-20s Stoica was sentenced to 15 years' hard labor for his role in a railway strike (1933). He was released after the communists gained power in 1944, and later became a member of the ruling Politburo in communist Romania. He was dismissed from the Central Committee and the presidium by Nicolae CEAUSESCU in 1969.

Stokowski, Leopold *(1882–1977)* Flamboyant American conductor of Polish and Irish descent. Stokowski brought the Philadelphia Orchestra to world prominence between 1912 and 1936. He was born in London and studied composition at Oxford with Charles Stanford. His first major post was in America with the Cincinnati Symphony Orchestra from 1909 to 1912. After his stint with the Philadelphia Orchestra he organized the All-American Youth Orchestra in 1939 and toured South America. His numerous subsequent associations included posi-

Conductor Leopold Stokowski. 1944 (LIBRARY OF CONGRESS, PRINTS AND PHOTOGRAPHS DIVISION)

tions with the Hollywood Bowl in 1945, co–music director (with Dmitri Mitropoulos) of the New York Philharmonic from 1945 to 1950 and founder in 1962 of the American Symphony in New York. With Arturo TOSCANINI and Serge KOUSSEVITZKY, Stokowski was the most famous American conductor of his time. He personified the public image of the artist, keeping the spotlight on his aureole of fluffy white hair and long, white fingers (he scorned the baton), and keeping his colorful private life in the newspaper headlines. He appeared in the movies—as himself, of course—most notably costarring with Deanna Durbin in *100 Men and a Girl* (1937) and with Mickey Mouse in *FANTASIA* (1940). An inveterate tinkerer, he experimented with innovative microphonic techniques. Critic Virgil THOMSON summed up the intellectual establishment's contempt for "Stokie," accusing him of "distorted interpretations" and "lapses of musical taste"—references to his notorious orchestral transcriptions of Bach organ works and his "retouchings" of other scores. However, his services to new music were significant. He conducted the American premieres of Gustav MAHLER's Second and Eighth Symphonies, Igor STRAVINSKY's *LE SACRE DU PRINTEMPS,* Alban BERG's *WOZZECK* and Charles IVES's Fourth Symphony. "There are millions who find solace in music," this showman/charlatan/genius wrote, without batting an eye, in *Music for All of Us* (1943). "It opens

for them the sun-batched gates of inspiration." He remained active well into his 80s.

Stolypin, Peter Arkadyevich

(1862–1911) Russian statesman. As a liberal conservative, he failed to win the approval of either the extreme right or the radicals. From 1906 Stolypin was minister of the interior and chairman of the council of ministers. While firmly suppressing the 1905 Revolution, he wished to carry out liberal reforms. Under his agrarian reforms of 1906–11, peasants were permitted to leave village communities, settle in separate farms, buy land and encouraged to settle in less populated areas. In 1907 Stolypin altered the electoral system by imperial decree. He was assassinated by a Socialist Revolutionary terrorist in 1911.

Stone, Edward Durell *(1902–1978)* American architect. Stone's first successes were the interior of the RADIO CITY MUSIC HALL and the MUSEUM OF MODERN ART (with Philip L. Goodwin) in New York. Among his best-known designs were the U.S. embassy in New Delhi, India, the General Motors Building and the Huntington Hartford Gallery in New York, the State University of New York campus in Albany and the John F. Kennedy Center for the Performing Arts in Washington, D.C.

Stone, Harlan Fiske *(1872–1946)* Associate justice, U.S. Supreme Court (1925–41); chief justice (1941–46). A native of New Hampshire and a graduate of Amherst and Columbia University Law School, Stone served as U.S. attorney general (1924–25) under President Calvin COOLIDGE (who was one class behind him at Amherst). As attorney general, Stone helped restore integrity in the federal government during the investigation of the TEAPOT DOME SCANDAL of the HARDING administration. After only a year, Coolidge named Stone to the Supreme Court. President Franklin D. ROOSEVELT later nominated him as chief justice on the retirement of Charles Evans HUGHES. Stone was a supporter of "judicial restraint," deferring to congressional intent. Although a conservative, he voted to uphold NEW DEAL legislation passed by Congress. Stone served for 22 years and died on the bench.

Stone, Irving (Irving Tennenbaum) *(1903–1989)* American author. Stone pioneered and specialized in the genre known as the biographical novel. Many of his heavily researched, voluminous works in that genre became best sellers, beginning with the first, *Lust for Life* (1934), based on the life of Dutch painter Vincent van Gogh. Perhaps the best known of his biographical novels is *The Agony and the Ecstasy* (1961), based on the life of Michelangelo.

Stone, I(sidore) F(einstein) *(1907–1989)* American journalist and author. A liberal iconoclast, Stone published the muckraking newsletter *I.F. Stone's Weekly* from 1953 through 1968. He used the newsletter as a vehicle to attack MCCARTHYISM, racism, the nuclear arms race and American involvement in the VIETNAM WAR. Although his principal sources of information were newspapers and official documents such as the records of congressional debates and obscure committee hearings, he thoroughly combed them and, in the process, uncovered several major instances of government wrongdoing. He was among the first to challenge the factual basis of the Gulf of TONKIN Incident (1964) that led to escalated U.S. involvement in Vietnam. When he was in his 70s he learned classical Greek in order to do research for a best-selling book, *The Trial of Socrates* (1988), in which he criticized Socrates for preaching against Athenian democracy.

Journalist I. F. Stone. 1983 (LIBRARY OF CONGRESS, PRINTS AND PHOTOGRAPHS DIVISION)

Stone, Marshall Harvey (*1903–1989*) American mathematician. Stone's eminent and influential work integrated diverse areas of abstract mathematics, including analysis, algebra and topology. As chairman of the mathematics department at the University of Chicago (1945–52), he helped make the department one of the foremost in the U.S. He was also an emeritus professor at the University of Massachusetts. In 1983 he received the National Medal of Science.

Stoneham, Horace Charles (*1904–1990*) American sports entrepreneur. As owner of the New York—later San Francisco—Giants from 1936 to 1976, Stoneham was one of the last of the old-time baseball owners who were involved in every aspect of the business. He took over as president of the team following the death of his father, Charles A. Stoneham, and steered the team to four pennants and one world championship in New York. When attendance at the Polo Grounds dwindled, he moved the team to California in 1958. The Giants won one more pennant under Stoneham's ownership in 1962.

Stoppard, Tom (Tomáš Straussler) (*1937– *) Czechoslovakian-born British playwright. Stoppard is regarded by many critics as the most gifted comic playwright to have emerged in Britain in the postwar era. He first won acclaim with *Rosencrantz and Guildenstern Are Dead* (1966), which borrowed from the techniques of THEATER OF THE ABSURD in presenting the confusion of two minor characters from Shakespeare's *Hamlet* as they view the tangled goings on in Hamlet's family. *Jumpers* (1972) parodied the linguistic tangles of modern philosophy. *Every Good Boy Deserves Favor* (1977) was a sharply satiric look at political oppression in Eastern Europe. Other plays by Stoppard include *The Real Thing* (1982) and *Hapgood* (1988). He also wrote the screenplay for the film adaptation of John LE CARRE's *The Russia House* (1990). He was knighted in 1997, and in 1999 Stoppard received an Academy Award for Best Screenplay for his work on *Shakespeare in Love* (1999).

Storey, David Malcolm (*1933– *) British novelist and playwright. Storey's first novel, *The Sporting Life* (1960), reflected his experiences as a professional rugby player, which he later recalled in the play *The Changing Room* (1971). Much of his early fiction reflects the influence of D. H. LAWRENCE. As a playwright Storey established himself with *In Celebration* (1969), in which the educated sons of a miner return home and face their feelings of discontent and alienation there. Storey is the son of a miner in Wakefield. His other varied plays include *The Contractor* (1970), *Home* (1970) and *Mother's Day* (1976). His later novels include *Pasmore* (1972) and *Saville* (1976), which won the Booker Prize that year. Storey's works often evoke the isolation and insecurity incurred by class mobility. Storey remained active throughout the 1990s and into the 21st century. In 1992 he produced the play *Stages,* which premiered at the Royal National Theatre. He also published three novels: *A Serious Man* (1998), which chronicled the life of a successful artist enduring a personal crisis; *As It Happened* (2002), which depicted the life of a fictional academic; and *Thin-Ice Skater* (2004), which examined the lives of two half-brothers.

Stout, Rex (Todhunter) (*1896–1975*) American mystery novelist. Born in Noblesville. Indiana, Stout moved to New York City and became the founder-director of the Vanguard Press. During a long career that began in the pulp magazines of the 1910s, Stout created over 70 detective novels, 46 of them featuring the chubby and sedentary gourmet sleuth Nero Wolfe. These books include *Fer-de-Lance* (1934), his first mystery tale, *Too Many Cooks* (1938), *If Death Ever Slept* (1957), *Royal Flush* (1965) and *Three Aces* (1971).

Stout, William Bushnell (*1880–1956*) American aeronautical engineer. Stout sold the Stout Metal Aircraft Company to FORD MOTOR COMPANY in 1925, but remained as a vice president and general manager during the development of the FORD TRIMOTOR transport plane from a single-engine transport. Stout founded Stout Air Services in 1926, the first company in the U.S. to provide passenger service exclusively. The airline flew between Detroit and Grand Rapids, Michigan. With the development of the Trimotor, Stout moved the airline from Detroit to Cleveland in 1927 and added a Detroit to Chicago route. Stout opened the Stout Engineering Labs in 1929 for research and development in aeronautics. His company developed and built the all-metal Sky Car, a new type of airplane for private owner use, and, under contract to the Pullman Car and Manufacturing Company, developed a high-speed Railplane. Stout's last major invention was a fiberglass automobile with its engine in the rear.

Strachey, (Evelyn) John (*1901–1963*) British official and author. After graduating from Oxford, where he was active in socialist politics, Strachey was elected a Labour member of Parliament in 1929. He resigned in 1931 but was elected again in 1945, and he served in the chamber until his death, holding a variety of cabinet posts. Strachey was known as a prominent theoretician of the Labour cause, and he published many books on politics, including *The Coming Struggle for Power* (1932), *The Nature of the Capitalist Crisis* (1935), *The End of Empire* and *On the Prevention of War* (1962).

Strachey, Lytton (*1880–1932*) British biographer and critic. Born to a prominent army family, Strachey was educated at Trinity College, Cambridge, where he met Virginia WOOLF and others with whom he would later associate in the BLOOMSBURY GROUP. Strachey's first work is the vibrant *Landmarks in French Literature* (1912). With *Eminent Victorians* (1918), which consisted of biographical essays on Florence Nightingale, Cardinal Manning, General Charles George Gordon and Dr. Thomas Arnold, Strachey achieved fame and notoriety, for he incorporated satire, psychological analysis and telling anecdotes. The book marked a turning point in the history of biography. Subsequent works include *Queen Victoria* (1921), which some regard as his masterwork, and the popular *Elizabeth and Essex: A Tragic History* (1928), which some critics deemed salacious and facetiously called Strachey's only work of fiction.

Strand, Paul (*1890–1976*) American photographer, member of the PHOTO-SECESSION and documentary filmmaker. His was an objective vision of "unadorned" nature. In the words of mentor Alfred STIEGLITZ, "His work is brutally direct and devoid of flim-flam." He was born in New York in 1890. The gift of a Brownie camera at age 12 confirmed his photographic ambitions, and soon he was studying with Lewis HINE and Stieglitz. His exhibition at Stieglitz's "291" gallery in 1916 (and subsequent notice in the important journal *Camera-Work*) brought something new to American photography. The views of city streets and people were candid and fresh. The face of a blind beggar expressed all the crushing forces of urban poverty. A white picket fence starkly outlined against grey buildings had all the affirmative power of beauty located in a despairing world, Strand spent much of his time in the 1920s and 1930s working with cinematography. He shot location footage for HOLLYWOOD studios and made some of the first movie documentaries in America, including the classic *Manhattan* (1921), a view of the abstract designs of the city; *The Wave* (1936), a record of fishermen's strike in the Bay of Vera Cruz; and (with collaborators Ralph Steiner and Pare Lorenz) *The Plow That Broke the Plains* (1936), a document of agricultural problems in Depression America made for the federal Resettlement Administration. Committed to the social problems of his times, he formed his own documentary company, Frontier Films, from 1937 to 1942. However, a growing distaste for postwar MCCARTHYISM led him to leave the country in 1950 and relocate in Paris, where he returned to still photography. He stubbornly insisted that the artist maintain "a real respect for the thing in front of him"—a credo as spare and moving as the images he produced.

Strang, William (Lord Strang, from 1954) *(1893–1978)* British diplomat. Strang accompanied Prime Minister Neville CHAMBERLAIN on his visits to HITLER prior to WORLD WAR II (see MUNICH PACT). During the war, he was Britain's representative on the European Advisory Commission, which planned the terms of Germany's surrender. Later he was permanent undersecretary of state for four years (1949–53) until his retirement.

Strasberg, Lee *(1901–1982)* American teacher of "method" acting. Born in Austria-Hungary, Strasberg emigrated to the U.S. at an early age and studied acting with two disciples of Konstantin STANISLAVSKY. He joined the Theater Guild in 1924 as an actor and stage manager. In 1948 he became artistic director of the new New York Actors Studio, remaining active in that role until his death. At the Actors Studio, Strasberg exerted a major influence on American theater, teaching student actors such as Marlon BRANDO, Marilyn MONROE, Robert DE NIRO, Ellen BURSTYN, Joanne Woodward, Paul NEWMAN, Jack NICHOLSON and Dustin HOFFMAN.

Stratas, Teresa (Anastasia Strataki) *(1938–)* Canadian-born opera singer known for her intense characterizations. An acclaimed singing actress in opera since the late 1950s, Stratas was born in Toronto to a Greek immigrant family. She made her debut as Mimi in PUCCINI's *La Boheme* in 1958 with the Toronto Opera. She made her Metropolitan Opera debut in a small role in *Manon* (1959), but achieved prominence in 1961 when she replaced the lead soprano in a performance of *Turnadot*. Other outstanding roles include Marguerite in *Faust,* Violetta in *La Traviata* and Sardula in the U.S. premiere of Gian Carlo MENOTTI's *The Last Savage.* In addition, she has starred in several movies, including *Eugene Onegin* and *Otello.*

Strategic Air Command (SAC) Long-range bomber and missile force of the United States Air Force. Headquartered at Offutt Air Force Base in Omaha, Nebraska, SAC has been called the "headquarters of the nation's peace-keeping force" since its founding in 1946. SAC's combat-ready air forces, including an estimated 1,300 jet bombers and tanker airplanes (1990), can be mobilized within seconds of a warning. Bombers can be dispatched within 15 minutes. An airborne command plane, one of several in the air at all times, would be able to direct attacks if the ground command post was destroyed. In 1992 President George H. W. BUSH terminated the command group as part of his effort to restructure U.S. defense commitments with the end of the cold war.

Strategic Arms Limitation Treaties See SALT.

Strategic Defense Initiative (SDI) Controversial U.S. anti-missile defense system. Nicknamed "Star Wars," the Strategic Defense Initiative was launched by U.S. president Ronald REAGAN on March 23, 1983, when he announced plans to build a land- and space-based defensive shield against enemy ballistic missiles. The proposed system would use such high technology as lasers, microwave devices, particle beams and projectile beams to destroy missiles high above the Earth. Proponents of the system view it as a historic breakthrough that could make nuclear weapons themselves obsolete. Critics of SDI argue that it is a violation of the 1972 Anti-Ballistic Missile Treaty between the Soviet Union and the United States, that it would create a dangerous new arms races and that it is in any event technologically unfeasible. Despite President George H. W. BUSH's support for SDI, development of the program lost some momentum during his administration. Funding for the program was cut substantially, and the initial plan to use laser systems was largely abandoned in favor of less expensive, more promising space-based interceptors called "Brilliant Pebbles," small orbiting rockets that would use impact rather than explosive force to destroy the missiles. During the Clinton administration (1993–2001) plans to implement the program were put on hold. But after the election of President George W. BUSH in 2000, technologies developed under SDI were incorporated into Bush's plan for a NATIONAL MISSILE DEFENSE system.

Strater, Henry *(1896–1987)* American realist painter. Strater was part of the Lost Generation of Americans with artistic aspirations who converged on Paris after WORLD WAR I. There he associated with future literary giants such as the poet Ezra POUND and novelists F. Scott FITZGERALD and Ernest HEMINGWAY. He illustrated Pound's CANTOS and was the basis of a character in Fitzgerald's novel *This Side of Paradise.*

Strauss, Franz Josef *(1915–1988)* West German politician; premier of the West German state of BAVARIA and one of the leading politicians of post-1945 WEST GERMANY. After the defeat of Nazi Germany Strauss cofounded the conservative Christian Social Union, which he later led for 25 years. He played a major role as the architect of West German rearmament while defense minister from 1956 to 1962. He was forced to resign in 1962 after he pressed treason charges against *Der Spiegel* magazine for printing an article critical of the German military. He was finance minister from 1966 to 1969 and became one of the most eager pursuers of trade and contacts with EAST GERMANY, the USSR and other communist countries.

Strauss, Lewis Lictenstein *(1896–1974)* American statesman. An advocate of the development of the HYDROGEN BOMB, he served on the Atomic Energy Commission from 1946 to 1950 and later was its chairman (1953–58). Strauss was appointed secretary of commerce by President Dwight EISENHOWER in November 1958, but the Senate refused to confirm the nomination in June 1959.

Strauss, Richard *(1864–1949)* German composer and conductor; one of the towering musical figures of the 20th century. An outstanding composer of opera and orchestral works, he had achieved recognition as a composer by age 18. From 1885 to 1924 he served as conductor for various European orchestras, including the Munich Opera and the Vienna State Opera. A series of successful symphonic poems, including *Macbeth* (1886–88) and *Don Quixote* (1886–97), led to the staging of the major one-act operas *Salome* (1905) and *Elektra* (1909). His successful collaboration with poet and librettist Hugo von HOFMANNSTHAL produced several full-length operas including *Der Rosenkavalier* (1911) and *Ariadne auf Naxos* (1912). *Der Rosenkavalier,* in which he pays homage to Mozart—the Mozart of *The Marriage of Figaro*—is generally regarded as his masterpiece and is widely considered one of the greatest operas of the 20th century. Strauss was also a founder of the SALZBURG FESTIVAL (1920).

Strauss's activities during the Nazi era have been a matter of controversy. He was initially willing to go along with NAZISM, but later fell out of favor with the Nazi leadership because of his collaborations with the Jewish writers von Hofmannsthal and Stefan ZWEIG and because of his antiwar attitudes. He was officially "denazified" by a court in 1948. A final burst of creative genius during his later years produced such works as the one-act opera *Capriccio* (1942), the orchestral piece *Metamorphosen* (1945) and the haunting *Four Last Songs*. Despite dissonant passages in many of his works, especially his later operas, Strauss never abandoned tonality; his music, influenced by Richard Wagner, has been described as both romantic and post-romantic.

Stravinsky, Igor Fedorovich *(1882–1971)* Russian-born composer whose influence upon the course of modern music has been lasting and profound. Stravinsky was born in Oranienbaum near St. Petersburg. Despite his avowed interest in music, he was forced by his father into law studies and had to continue his music studies in private. Gaining the influence of composer Nikolai Rimsky-Korsakov, he presented his first works in a private concert in 1907. Ballet impresario Sergei DIAGHILEV heard his *Feu d'Artifice* (*Fireworks*) two years later and promptly commissioned new works for his BALLETS RUSSES. *L'Oiseau de Feu* (*The Firebird,* 1910), *Petrouchka* (1911) and the notorious *Le Sacre du Printemps* (THE RITE OF SPRING, 1913) created a sensation and subsequently have become cornerstones in the modern ballet repertoire. The percussive, dissonant "neo-primitivism" and Russian nationalism of these works, including *Le Chant du Rossignol* (*The Song of the Nightingale,* 1917) and *Les Noces* (*The Wedding,* 1917), were gradually replaced after 1919 by a more spare, neoclassical style.

Russian composer Igor Stravinsky (LIBRARY OF CONGRESS, PRINTS AND PHOTOGRAPHS DIVISION)

L'Histoire du Soldat (*The Soldier's Tale,* 1918), for example, was severely scored for only seven instruments, three performers and a narrator and was full of contrapuntal techniques. *Pulcinella* (1920) was derived from the music of the 18th-century composer Pergolesi. This style continued later in America (where after 1939 he remained as a citizen) in *The Symphony in Three Movements* (1946), the ballet *Orpheus* (1948) and the opera *The Rake's Progress* (1951). However, at the age of 70 Stravinsky embarked upon the last phase of his career. A ballet, *Agon* (1957), and an opera, *Noah and the Flood* (1962), embraced the dodecaphonic and serial techniques derived from Arnold SCHOENBERG. Stravinsky's last years were full of international honors, a recording project for Columbia Records and the tireless efforts on his behalf by his protege, Robert Craft. "Stravinsky tried to keep musical progress on the move," said Leonard BERNSTEIN, "by driving tonal and structural ambiguities on and on to a point of no return." New techniques of "polytonalities" and asymmetrical rhythmic patterns freshly stimulated the ear like, in Bernstein's words, "an ascerbic, needling cold shower." Sometimes criticized as cold, emotionless and detached, Stravinsky was nonetheless wholly devoted to his art. Perhaps he may be compared to the puppet Petrouchka in the ballet of that name—a bundle of sticks and rags that concealed a passionate human heart.

streamlining Widely used term for design work in which concepts of aerodynamics are applied to generate forms based on forms first developed for aircraft. For example, a bulletlike nose and a tapering tail were found to improve the flight characteristics of dirigibles and were later introduced in the design of airplanes. As these forms became visible in the 1930s, many industrial designers began to use them for strictly visual appeal. At first, streamlining was most often applied to moving vehicles, such as locomotives, whole trains, automobiles and ships. As streamlined forms became equated with newness and functional excellence, they were adopted for less logical objects—furniture, office machines, toasters and even, in a famous design by the firm of Raymond LOEWY, a pencil sharpener. As a design theme of the 1930s and early

1940s, streamlining has acquired a certain quality of nostalgia, bringing it to recent popularity, even (or perhaps especially) in its more absurd applications—the clocks, toasters and radios now regarded as collectible.

stream of consciousness Literary technique that came into special prominence in the 20th century. The term *stream of consciousness* refers to the attempt by fiction writers to capture the sense of a character's interior world by directly depicting the thoughts, feelings and sensory impressions of that character. The writer, in using this technique, steadfastly avoids all authorial comments of an exterior or omniscient nature. The most famous practitioner of the stream-of-consciousness technique is James JOYCE, who explored its possibilities fully in *ULYSSES* (1922) and *Finnegans Wake*. Other pioneering stream-of-consciousness works include *To the Lighthouse* (1925) by Virginia WOOLF, *The Sound and the Fury* (1929) by William FAULKNER, and *UNDER THE VOLCANO* (1947) by Malcolm LOWRY. The stream-of-consciousness technique was subsequently practiced widely by other fiction writers.

Streep, Meryl (*1949–*) American motion picture actress celebrated for the diversity of her many roles. Performing was always a part of Streep's life, from opera training and high school theatrics to a major in drama at Yale and performances at the Yale Repertory Theater. After winning a Tony Award for her role in a revival of Tennessee WILLIAMS's *27 Wagons Full of Cotton* (while serving a stint in the 1976 New York Shakespeare Festival), she began her movie career in *Julia* (1977). A political pundit in *The Seduction of Joe Tynan* (1979), a lesbian in Woody Allen's *Manhattan* (1979), the doomed Karen SILKWOOD in *Silkwood* (1983), the novelist Isak DINESEN in *Out of Africa* (1987) and an accused murderess, Lindy Chamberlain, in *Cry in the Dark* (1988)—this succession of highly varied roles has displayed her almost chameleonlike ability to get into a character. She has had ACADEMY AWARD nominations for almost every film, winning the best actress award for *Kramer vs. Kramer* (1979) and *Sophie's Choice* (1985).

In the first half of the 1990s, Streep performed in only four motion pictures—the comedies *Defending Your Life* (1991) and *Death Becomes Her* (1992) and the dramas *The House of Spirits* (1993) and *The River Wild* (1994)—none of which proved as financially or critically successful as her earlier work. Her role in the highly acclaimed *The Bridges of Madison County* (1995) reversed this trend. It proved a box-office success and won Streep another Academy Award nomination for her portrayal of an Italian-American wife who begins an affair with a traveling photographer played by Clint EASTWOOD. Streep later received additional nominations for her appearances in the romantic comedy *One True Thing* (1998) and the drama *Music Of The Heart* (1999). In 2003, Streep received her 13th Academy Award nomination for her role in *Adaptation* (2002) and overtook Katharine HEPBURN as the actress with the most Academy Award nominations.

Streisand, Barbra (*1942–*) American singer and actress. Streisand first achieved success in the Broadway play *I Can Get It for You Wholesale* in 1963. She was nominated for a Tony for her performance and costarred with actor Eliot Gould, who became her first husband. Her career mushroomed: Streisand won a Grammy for her first album, an Emmy for her first television special, and tied with Katharine HEPBURN for an ACADEMY AWARD for her first film, *Funny Girl* (1968). Other films include a remake of the film *A Star Is Born* (1976), for which she cowrote and recorded the ACADEMY AWARD–winning song, "Evergreen"; *Yentl* (1983), which she also cowrote, produced and directed and *Nuts* (1987). In the 1990s Streisand starred in, directed and produced two motion pictures: *The Prince of Tides* (1991) and *The Mirror Has Two Faces* (1996), and served as executive producer of several television films. In 2004 she appeared in the feature film *Meet the Fockers*.

Stresa Conferences Two historic conferences held in the northern Italian resort town of Stresa during the 1930s. The first, held from September 5–20, 1932, was a meeting concerning European economic cooperation that included representatives from 15 countries. The second, from April 11–14, 1935, was a conference held by the prime ministers, foreign ministers and staffs of France, Great Britain and Italy.

Convened to solidify the three old Allies' opposition to HITLER's rearming of Germany in contravention of the TREATY OF VERSAILLES, it was the last pre–World WAR II meeting at which Italy was still in the Allied camp.

Stresemann, Gustav (*1878–1929*) German statesman. Born in Berlin, Stresemann received a doctorate in economics in 1900 and was a founder (1902) and director of the League of German Industrialists. He entered political life in 1907 as the youngest member of the Reichstag. An ardent nationalist and supporter of the German monarchy in World War I, he moderated his views after his nation's defeat. He felt that Germany's best chance of regaining its national status in Europe was to accept the harsh and unpopular terms of the Treaty of Versailles. As chancellor (1923) and foreign minister (1923–29), he did his best to mitigate these crushing terms and to bring Germany back as a respected member of the community of nations. He succeeded in evacuating the French from the industrial RUHR in 1924 and assented to two significant reparations agreements, the DAWES PLAN (1924) and the YOUNG PLAN (1929). Stresemann was a prime architect of the LOCARNO PACT (1925) and in 1926 was successful in securing Germany's admittance to the LEAGUE OF NATIONS as a great power. A signatory of the Kellogg-Briand Pact (1928), he and his French counterpart, Aristide BRIAND, were awarded the 1926 Nobel Peace Prize.

Strindberg, August (**Johann August Strindberg**) (*1849–1912*) Swedish playwright, novelist and essayist. Although Strindberg explored many writing genres, it is as a dramatist of exceptional vision and emotional power that he is best remembered. In his earliest plays he was strongly influenced by the social realism of Norwegian playwright Henrik Ibsen. But Strindberg soon moved on to concentrate on the psychic depths of his characters, who were often locked into unhappy marriages. Strindberg employed poetic language and a stark sensual realism that anticipated the expressionist movement in the European drama of the 1920s (see EXPRESSIONISM). Strindberg's best-known plays include *The Father* (1887), *Miss Julie* (1889), *Till Damascus* (1900), *A*

Dream Play (1905), *The Storm* (1907) and *The Ghost Sonata* (1908).

Stritch, Samuel Alphonsus *(1887–1958)* Catholic cardinal. Ordained a Roman Catholic priest in 1910, he served in many official positions in Tennessee, Ohio and Illinois before being named a cardinal in 1946. As head of the diocese of Chicago, the largest in the country, he became increasingly influential. He was the first American ever to be appointed to the Roman Curia, the principal governing body of the Roman Catholic Church. Shortly before his death, he was appointed head of all Catholic mission work.

Stroessner, Alfredo *(1912–2006)* Dictator of Paraguay. The son of a German immigrant to Paraguay, Stroessner became a general in the army, then assumed power in a coup in 1954. After a one-party election, he was elected president that year. Reelected in seven successive ballots widely considered to be rigged, Stroessner controlled the country for the next 35 years, making him the longest-ruling head of state in the Western Hemisphere. During his tenure, Paraguay became a notorious haven for international fugitives, and his regime was widely criticized for violations of human rights and suppression of political dissent. In 1989 Stroessner was ousted in a coup by General Andrés Rodríguez, the second-ranking officer in the Paraguayan armed forces.

Stroheim, Erich von *(1885–1957)* Austrian-born film director, actor, screenplay writer and set designer. Von Stroheim is one of the legendary figures of the cinema. He is remembered both as the archetypal Prussian officer in numerous films from the 1910s to the 1950s (one 1918 film advertisement billed him as "The Man You Love To Hate") and as one of the most gifted and extravagant directors of the silent film era of the 1920s. After a brief tour of active duty in the Austrian army during World War I, von Stroheim immigrated to America and found work in HOLLYWOOD as an actor and as an assistant director under D. W. GRIFFITH. Von Stroheim made his own directorial debut with *Blind Husbands* (1918) and went on to make a series of sexually sophisticated films including *Foolish Wives* (1921) and *Merry-Go-Round* (1922).

His films were commercially successful, but von Stroheim earned the ire of Hollywood producers for his chronically over-budget productions. His critical masterpiece is the epic-length *Greed* (1924), which was never released as von Stroheim edited it but remains a cinematic landmark for its breathtaking vision, notably a climactic scene shot in Death Valley. When the silent era ended, von Stroheim could no longer find work as a director, though he continued to act in numerous films including *Sunset Boulevard* (1950).

Strömgren, Bengt *(1907–1987)* Swedish-born astronomer. Strömgren grew up in Denmark and pursued his scientific career there and in the U.S. In 1940 he succeeded his father in the directorship of the Royal Copenhagen Observatory. He later directed the University of Chicago's Yerkes Observatory in Wisconsin. He gained international recognition for his research and theories on stellar matter and interstellar space.

structuralism Diverse school of thought that has influenced anthropology, linguistics, literary criticism and philosophy. The two essential premises of structuralism are (1) that social and aesthetic phenomena do not have inherent meaning but rather can be sensibly defined only as parts of larger governing systems; and (2) that the true meaning of these phenomena can be revealed only when these larger systems are recognized and understood. Structuralism is related in approach to SEMIOTICS, the study of meaningful signs within systems. Major figures in the development of structuralism include the linguist Ferdinand de Saussure, the anthropologist Claude LÉVI-STRAUSS and the literary critic Roland BARTHES. De Saussure utilized structuralism to probe the underlying structures of all languages, whereas Lévi-Strauss applied it to explain ritual beliefs in alternative cultures and Barthes drew from it to place literary works within the dominant cultural forces of their time. (See also DECONSTRUCTION.)

Struve, Peter Bernardovich *(1870–1944)* Economist and sociologist. Of German origin, Struve was one of the main theorists of Marxism in Russia in the 1890s. In 1898, he drafted the Social Democratic Labor Party's manifesto, but then changed allegiance and became leader of the Liberal Constitutional movement. In 1905 he joined the Constitutional Democratic Party and was an important member of the Vekhi movement.

Students for a Democratic Society Radical left-wing student organization, formed in the U.S. in the mid-1960s. Active in the ANTIWAR MOVEMENT, the SDS urged resistance to the draft and a redistribution of political power. In April 1968 the SDS organized the student takeover of campus buildings at Columbia University and in August of that year led demonstrations at the Democratic National Convention in Chicago. Critics of the SDS charged that its members sought to disrupt society rather than make it more democratic. Among prominent SDS leaders were Mark Rudd and Tom Hayden.

Sturges, Preston *(Edmund Preston Biden)* *(1898–1959)* American screenwriter and director known for his screwball and romantic comedies in the 1940s. Sturges worked unsuccessfully as an inventor, composer and cosmetics salesman before gaining success as a playwright with the hit Broadway comedy *Strictly Dishonorable* (1929). After his other theater productions received only lukewarm receptions, Sturges turned to HOLLYWOOD screenwriting. He scripted more than a dozen successful films, including *The Power and the Glory* (1933) and *Thirty-Day Princess* (1933). In 1940 he was given the opportunity to direct his original script *The Great McGinty* (originally titled *Down Went McGinty*). The film was a critical and commercial success, and Sturges went on to win the ACADEMY AWARD for best screenplay. Given free reign as writer-director, Sturges followed with a string of sparkling comedies—*Christmas in July* (1940), *The Lady Eve* (1940), *Sullivan's Travels* (1941), *The Palm Beach Story* (1942), *The Miracle of Morgan's Creek* (1942) and *Hail the Conquering Hero* (1943)—that featured his personal blend of slapstick, biting satire and clever dialogue. However, these successes were followed after the mid-40s with a succession of flops, apart from the comedy *Unfaithfully Yours* (1948).

His repeated efforts to return to film and the theater failed, and Sturges died an alcoholic. In the 1980s and '90s, Sturges's films have enjoyed revivals and received new critical and popular attention.

Sturgis, Russell (1836–1909) American architect, critic and author. One of the first to recognize and promote the work of architect Frank Lloyd WRIGHT, Sturgis was a graduate of the Free Academy (now City College) of New York. He designed many buildings, including the Mechanics Bank of Albany, N.Y., Flower Hospital in New York City, and a Yale University chapel. In the early 1900s he wrote and edited books about architecture, art history and art appreciation.

Sturmer, Boris Vladimirovich (1848–1917) Prime minister of RUSSIA. A previous master of ceremonies at court, Sturmer was appointed prime minister in 1916. He was also in charge of the ministry of foreign affairs. A puppet of RASPUTIN, he was not liked and was dismissed from the Duma on November 23, 1916.

Stuttgart Exhibition (1927) Also known as the Weissenhofsiedlung, an architectural exhibition commissioned by the Deutsche Werkbund, a group of German artists and industrialists. It marked an early milestone in the career of the architect Ludwig MIES VAN DER ROHE, who prepared the plan for the exhibition, selected architects to design over 30 buildings and himself created an important block of housing for the show. Other architects involved in the project included Walter GROPIUS, LE CORBUSIER, Peter BEHRENS and J. J. P. Oud. This exposition was an important event in the establishment of modern architecture as a viable style.

Styron, William (1925–2006) American novelist and winner of the Pulitzer Prize for literature (1968). Born in Newport News, Virginia, Styron graduated with a B.A. from Duke University in 1947. After moving to New York, he found work as an assistant editor for a publishing house and began to write his first novel, *Lie Down in Darkness,* which was published to great acclaim in 1951, and left his editing position to work full time as a writer. Two years later, he published the short novel *The Long March,* which described the life of a pair of marines in a military training facility—or "boot camp"—and may have been influenced by his own service during World War II. By 1960 he had written and published his third novel, *Set This House on Fire,* which described the problems besetting a group of American expatriates in Europe.

While Styron won critical acclaim for his first three books, it was his fourth work, *The Confessions of Nat Turner* (1968), that brought him national and international fame. A fictionalized account of an unsuccessful 1831 slave revolt in the southern U.S., *Confessions* earned Styron a Pulitzer Prize in 1968 and lavish tributes from literary critics. *Sophie's Choice* (1979), which described the life and loves of a Holocaust survivor in New York, was equally well received by reviewers and the public.

Along with his experiences in the southern U.S. and in the marines, Styron found inspiration for his literary work in his struggle with mental illness. In 1985 he realized that he was suffering from depression and began psychotherapy and antidepressant medication to cope with his mental illness. Five years later, he published *Darkness Visible: A Memoir of Madness,* which provided a personal insight into his battle against depression. Some critics have also claimed that his book *A Tidewater Morning: Three Tales from Youth* (1993)—which revealed many sorrowful moments of Styron's childhood—represented a second attempt to achieve a literary catharsis from the inner demons that tormented him.

submarine After a century of tinkering, the submarine had come into practical use by the early 1900s. France, Britain and the U.S. all had submarines, but Germany was the first to see the craft's potential as a naval weapon. At the outbreak of WORLD WAR I, Germany had twice as many long-range submarines as Britain. These slow-moving, diesel-powered vessels had to surface regularly, but battery-powered electric motors allowed them to operate underwater and sink Allied ships with their torpedoes. German submarines were effective against Allied shipping in the North Atlantic in WORLD WAR II, while U.S. submarines struck at Japanese supply lines in the Pacific. Submarine technology made its greatest leap with the introduction of the nuclear-powered submarine in the 1950s (see NAUTILUS). Nuclear submarines could remain at sea for months without refueling and could stay submerged for days. With high-tech equipment and such weapons as the nuclear-armed Polaris and Poseidon missiles, they were a formidable strategic resource. With the end of the cold war in 1991, submarine construction decreased, and only the Seawolf and the Virginia class submarines have been developed in the U.S.

Sudan Located south of Egypt and north and west of Ethiopia, Africa's largest country covers an area of 967,243 square miles. Once known as the Anglo-Egyptian Sudan, the vast country was controlled from Egypt by the UNITED KINGDOM from 1898 to 1956, when independence was granted. Conflict between the economically undeveloped Christian south and the dominant Muslim north erupted into civil war in 1956. Colonel Joafar el Nemery, who came to power in 1969 in a

German submarine (LIBRARY OF CONGRESS, PRINTS AND PHOTOGRAPHS DIVISION)

Sudan

bloodless coup, brought a temporary end to the war by granting limited autonomy to the Christian south in 1972. However, his introduction of Islamic law in 1983 rekindled the rebellion and led to his overthrow in 1985. A state of emergency was declared in 1987, and the army took control in 1989. Attempts by former U.S. president Jimmy CARTER to mediate a peace broke down, and the Christian south continued to push for secession. In 1998 U.S. president William Jefferson CLINTON alleged that a pharmaceutical plant located in Khartoum was producing chemical weapons and ordered a U.S. cruise missile strike on the plant's grounds. No evidence was found that the plant was producing chemical weapons. The Muslim government in the north continued to wage a ruthless campaign to suppress the Christian and anamist secessionists in the south until 2005, when the government and the southern rebels signed a peace agreement. In the meantime, an insurrection against the government in the western region of Darfur led to brutal repression by government forces. In 2006 the Sudan government and the main rebel faction in Darfur signed a peace accord, yet smaller rebel groups have rejected the deal. An estimated 2 million people have fled the fighting, causing a major humanitarian crisis, and violence continues.

	SUDAN
1898	Anglo-Egyptian force defeats Islamic Mahdist uprising after long struggle.
1925	British develop cotton plantations and irrigation.
1936	ASHQIPA nationalist party formed.
1955	Black non-Islamic troops in south rebel against northern Islamic commanders; form Anya Nya—"snake venom"—movement.
1956	British grant independence in the midst of civil war and economic decay.
1958	General Abboud takes power.
1965	Elections held; el-Mahdi of People's Party elected.
1966	Cotton price drops; economy in ruins.
1969	Colonel Nemery takes power, forms one-party government; civil war continues.
1972	Addis Ababa Agreement; temporary stop to civil war.

1983	Nemery introduces traditional Koranic law (sharia); south rebels again under U.S.-educated Colonel Garang.
1984	Drought leads to widespread starvation.
1985	Food riots in Khartoum; Nemery deposed by troops.
1986	Elections; el-Mahdi returns from exile to win; civil war intensifies.
1989	Coup by General al-Bashir; Jimmy Carter leads unsuccessful talks with rebels; locusts damage food crops; freak rains ending drought destroy mud houses, leave 1 million homeless in Khartoum; U.S. airlifts food.
1990	Government and rebels stop food shipments, create "man-made famine" to reduce each other's supporters.
1991	U.S. closes embassy due to Bashir pro-Iraq stance; Bashir agrees to UN food airlift; sharia is imposed in northern Sudan.
1993	The Government Revolutionary Command Council, in power since the 1989 coup, dissolves itself after appointing al-Bashir president.
1996	The first elections since the 1989 coup are held, but political parties are banned.
1997	The U.S. imposes sanctions against Sudan, claiming Khartoum supports international terrorism.
1998	A new constitution is adopted; widespread famine occurs; the U.S. launches a cruise-missile attack against an alleged chemical weapons factory in Sudan following attacks on U.S. embassies in Uganda and Kenya.
1999	The government allows registration of political associations, ending a 10-year ban.
2000	Presidential and legislative elections are boycotted by the main opposition parties.
2001	The government accepts a Libyan/Egyptian initiative to end the civil war that calls for reforms and a conference of national reconciliation; U.S. imposes sanctions due to Sudan's record of humans rights violations and alleged support of terrorism.
2002	The southern rebel organization SPLA and the government sign a peace agreement providing for a six-month renewable cease-fire in the central Nuba Mountains.
2003	Rebels in the western region of Darfur rise against the government.
2005	Government and southern rebels sign a peace agreement, including a permanent cease-fire and an accord on power and wealth sharing; a UN report affirms that the government and the military are engaging in systematic abuse of human rights in Darfur; international donors pledge $4.5 billion in aid to help southern Sudan recover from the civil war; deadly clashes in Khartoum between southern and northern Sudanese following the death in an air crash of the former southern rebel leader John Garang, who had been the country's first vice president.

Sudan People's Liberation Army (SPLA)

A military force created in 1983 in Sudan by Lieutenant Colonel John GARANG. Garang, an officer in the Sudan People's Armed Forces (SPAF), was ordered to enter Bor, a town in the largely Christian southern region of the country and suppress an estimated 500 government troops who had mutinied after receiving orders to relocate to the predominantly Islamic region in the north. A Christian himself, Garang joined the rebels on his arrival and encouraged nearby garrisons to join in the mutiny. He promptly announced the formation of the SPLA to overthrow the Muslim-dominated government in Khartoum.

By the mid-1990s, the SPLA had acquired control of much of SUDAN. Garang and his SPLA cohorts repeatedly refused to negotiate with the Khartoum government and instead took steps to establish their domain as an independent state. They received assistance from the U.S., which in 1996 funneled an estimated $20 million in "nonlethal" military aid to the SPLA and a similar organization, the Sudanese Liberation Army. The U.S. justified this assistance because of the Sudanese government's alleged support for international terrorism. In

1997 groups of officers left the SPLA and formed the South Sudan Independence Movement/Army (SSIM/A). This new organization joined with several of the smaller southern organizations in signing a peace accord with the northern government. Garang announced in 1998 the SPLA would enter into negotiations with the representatives from Khartoum. After many years of fruitless peace talks, a peace agreement was signed in January 2005 which ended the fighting and led to the formation of a coalition government with Garang as vice president. After serving for only a few weeks, Garang was killed in a helicopter crash.

Sudetenland Region in central Europe, currently within the Czech Republic. Although the population of the Sudetenland included many German-speaking people, the region was assigned to Czechoslovakia when that nation was formed in 1918. In the 1930s, German chancellor Adolf HITLER claimed the Sudetenland as German territory and demanded that Czechoslovakia turn it over to the Nazi reich. Hitler's demand provoked an international crisis, complicated by pro-Nazi demonstrations in the Sudetenland itself. Italian dictator MUSSOLINI arranged a conference in Munich at which Germany, Italy, France and the United Kingdom discussed the fate of the Sudetenland (1938). In the MUNICH PACT, France and the U.K. turned the Sudetenland over to Germany in return for Hitler's pledge that he would not seek any more territory. Czechoslovakia was effectively partitioned. The following year (1939) Hitler went back on his word as German troops occupied PRAGUE and much of the rest of Czechoslovakia. After the war, Czechoslovakia expelled over 3 million German-speaking inhabitants from the region.

Sue, Louis (*1875–1968*) French architect and designer, a prominent figure in the ART DECO design of the 1920s and 1930s. Sue was trained as a painter in Paris and also became active as an architect after 1905. He visited Austria in 1910, becoming aware of SECESSION design of the period. In 1912 he set up his own studio in Paris, designing textiles, furniture and ceramics. In 1919 he was a partner (with Andre Mare) in establishing the Compagnie des Arts Français, devoted to the production of design based somewhat on neoclassical origins, in opposition to the emerging MODERNISM of the time. The firm exhibited at the 1925 Paris Exhibition and designed various Paris shops before achieving special note with its interiors of the French liner *Ile-de-France* in 1928. Sue also designed the Deauville suite on the liner *NORMANDIE* of 1935. His interior design was featured in the 1937 Paris Exhibition pavilion of the Société des Artistes-Décorateurs. His 1938 interiors for the Paris house of Helena Rubinstein mixed Art Deco modernism with African art and antiques in a lavish fashion that was somewhat surrealistic in effect. Sue retired in 1953.

Suez Canal Major ship canal across the Isthmus of Suez in northeastern EGYPT. Along with the PANAMA CANAL, it is one of the most important artificial waterways in the world. More than 100 miles long, the Suez Canal connects the Mediterranean Sea with the Gulf of Suez and the Red Sea and, eventually, the Indian Ocean. The canal thus allows ships traveling between Europe and Indian Ocean ports (as well as ports on the PERSIAN GULF) to avoid the lengthy route around Africa in favor of a quicker and more direct route.

Constructed by the French between 1859 and 1869, the Suez Canal was opened in 1869. The 1888 Convention of Constantinople declared the canal to be a neutral facility operated by the Suez Canal Company. The canal remained open throughout WORLD WAR I and WORLD WAR II; during both wars, it was controlled by the Allies and used for Allied shipping. In 1956 it was nationalized by Egyptian president Gamal Abdel NASSER, provoking the SUEZ CRISIS as the UNITED KINGDOM and FRANCE attempted to seize the canal militarily (see ARAB-ISRAELI WAR OF 1956). The canal remained closed for several months, reopening in April 1957 under Egyptian control. During the SIX-DAY WAR (1967) and the ARAB-ISRAELI WAR OF 1973, the Suez Canal was in the war zone as ISRAEL battled Egypt for control of the region. Several ships were sunk or trapped in the canal. The canal did not reopen until 1975.

Suez Crisis Following the Egyptian nationalization of the strategically im-portant SUEZ CANAL on July 26, 1956, Britain, FRANCE and ISRAEL secretly agreed for Israel to attack Egypt through Sinai, while Britain and France occupied the Canal Zone on the pretext of separating the combatants. Israel attacked on October 29. Britain and France began air attacks on Egyptian air force bases on October 31 and landed paratroops at Port Said and Port Fuaz at the mouth of the canal on November 5. These actions provoked intense domestic and international criticism of the two nations. The U.S. refusal to support Britain and France forced a cease-fire on November 6 and the deployment of a United Nations Emergency Force. The Suez Crisis confirmed Britain's decline internationally and pushed NASSER closer to the USSR. British prime minister Anthony EDEN resigned in disgrace two months later.

Suharto (*1921– *) President of INDONESIA (1968–1998). Born in a village near Yogyakarta, central Java, Suharto underwent basic military training at cadet schools in the early 1940s. He served in several companies and regiments during the war of independence against the Dutch from 1945 to 1949. During the 1950s and first half of the 1960s Suharto rose through the army command, attaining the rank of major general. He assumed leadership of the army in the immediate aftermath of the September 30, 1965, attempted coup and was raised to the rank of general in July 1966. With the removal of SUKARNO from power in March 1967, Suharto was appointed acting president. He was inaugurated as president on March 27, 1968, and was reelected to that position in 1973, 1978, 1983 and 1988. Essentially unchallenged, he dominated Indonesian political life throughout that period. Suharto resigned as president in 1998 in response to riots and protests over the country's economic crises. In 2000 Suharto was placed under house arrest for corruption during his regime, however doctors declared him unfit to stand trial for reasons of declining health, and in 2006 Indonesian prosecutors closed the case on the grounds of Suharto's ill health.

Sukarno (*1901–1970*) Indonesian statesman, first president of the republic of Indonesia (1945 to 1966). Born in eastern Java, Sukarno was educated at Dutch schools and studied engineering. As a student he was active in a club that resisted cooperation with the Dutch colonial powers. By 1928 the club had become the Indonesian Nationalist Party, and Sukarno had emerged as its leader. During the 1930s the young firebrand was jailed and exiled a number of times. He cooperated with the occupying Japanese forces during World War II, simultaneously working with the independence movement. At the end of the war in 1945, he declared the nation independent and proclaimed himself president. Following a neutralist policy, he hosted the Afro-Asian BANDUNG CONFERENCE in 1955. Becoming increasingly authoritarian, the following year he announced a "guided democracy." In 1959 he dissolved the parliament, and in 1963 he proclaimed himself president for life. His foreign policy took an increasingly procommunist tack, and he was implicated in a communist plot against the Indonesian military in 1965. A military counterattack by General SUHARTO eventually resulted in Sukarno's forced retirement in 1966.

Sullivan, Ed *(1902–1974)* American newspaper columnist and television variety show host. Sullivan was one of the best-known celebrities of his era, through both his Broadway beat column, *Little Old New York,* for the New York *Daily News,* and his high visibility as host of the *Ed Sullivan Show* on the CBS television network. The show ran from 1948 to 1971 and featured early television appearances by Elvis PRESLEY and the BEATLES, among other stars. Sullivan, who first joined the *Daily News* in 1932, was the delight of comic impressionists, who enjoyed miming his stiff, hunched posture and his trademark line—"really big show."

Sullivan, Louis (Louis Henry Sullivan) *(1856–1924)* American architect. Widely considered the first architectural modernist in the U.S., Sullivan was born in Boston and studied briefly at the Massachusetts Institute of Technology and at the Ecole des Beaux-Arts, Paris. He is best known for his adage "form follows function," the idea that the outward form of a structure should express its utilitarian function. This dic-

tum forms the philosophical cornerstone of the modernist movement in architecture. Sullivan is noted for his designs of early skyscrapers in which an architectonic and functionalist modernism is embellished by gorgeously organic decorative ornament. Settling in Chicago in 1879, he joined the firm of Dankmar Adler and in 1881 became a partner. There he produced such important designs as the Auditorium Building (Chicago, 1886–89), the Wainwright Building (St. Louis, 1890), the Stock Exchange Building (Chicago, 1893–94) and the Guaranty (now Prudential) Building (Buffalo, 1894–95). Sullivan ended his partnership with Adler in 1895. He produced his last major building, the Schlesinger-Meyer department store (now Carson Pirie Scott), Chicago, from 1899 to 1904.

Going against the tide of the then fashionable neoclassicism, he found it increasingly difficult to obtain clients and concentrated his efforts on less important projects, located mainly in medium-sized midwestern cities. There he created a beautiful series of small banks, notably the National Farmers' Bank (Owatonna, Minnesota, 1907–08) and the Merchants' National Bank (Grinnell, Iowa, 1914). Sullivan was the most influential figure in the development of modern architecture in the U.S. He envisioned a thoroughly American design in the democratic tradition, one that employed the materials of contemporary technology in an organic way and that expressed a profound connection with nature. His architectural philosophy was enunciated in such books as *Kindergarten Chats* (1918) and *Autobiography of an Idea* (1924) and was brought to fruition later in the 20th century by a number of disciples and pupils, notably Frank Lloyd WRIGHT.

Sully-Prudhomme, René *(1839–1907)* Essentially a 19th-century figure, the French philosophical poet Sully-Prudhomme received the first NOBEL PRIZE for literature in 1901. The Swedish Academy awarded the prize in recognition of his "excellent merit as an author, and especially of the high idealism, artistic perfection, as well as the unusual combination of qualities of the heart and genius to which his work bears witness." His work is now largely forgotten, but his name is memorial-

ized by the Sully-Prudhomme Prize that he established for young French poets with his Nobel Prize money.

Summersby, Kay (Kay Summersby Morgan) *(1909–1975)* Confidential secretary, driver and confidante to General Dwight D. EISENHOWER during WORLD WAR II. Summersby was a member of the British Women's Auxiliary Corps and met Eisenhower in England while he was Supreme Commander, Allied Forces in Europe. Their relationship was a closely guarded secret throughout the war. In 1973 it was rumored that Eisenhower at one time wished to divorce his wife, Mamie Dowd Eisenhower, and marry Summersby, but Summersby denied this. Nonetheless, this footnote in history remained a subject of speculation in the popular press and in books through the 1970s and the 1980s and was the subject of a 1978 television movie.

Summerskill, Edith Clara *(1901–1980)* British feminist, social reformer and physician. A member of the LABOUR PARTY, Summerskill was an MP from 1938 to 1961, and briefly chaired the party (1954–55). Among the feminist causes she successfully championed were equal financial status for married women, the right of a married woman to keep her maiden name and the availability of painless childbirth methods. She also campaigned to improve health care. She developed her own general practice among the London poor and was largely responsible for the founding of the Socialist Medical Association. This, in turn, helped bring about the NATIONAL HEALTH SERVICE (NHS) after World War II.

Sunay, Cevdet *(1899–1982)* President of TURKEY (1966–73). Sunay played a key role in maintaining a parliamentary democracy when strife between military and political leaders forced the resignation of Premier Suleyman DEMIREL's government in 1971.

Sunday, Billy (William Ashley) *(1863–1935)* American evangelist and prohibitionist. Sunday, a minister of the Chicago Presbytery, ordained April 15, 1903, is said to have preached to more people than any other man in Christian history before the age of mass communication. He is further given credit for being the single greatest factor in causing the decline of the saloon in the United States. Between 1904 and 1907 Sunday received from 1,000 to 5,000 converts per month. He galvanized evangelistic meetings in major cities across the country, during which he was known to jump over the pulpit, tear his hair and occasionally roll on the floor, while still delivering sermons with sincere warmth. Sunday began life in the Midwest as a very successful professional baseball player from 1883 to 1890 with Chicago, Pittsburgh and Philadelphia teams and is credited with developing the bunt.

Sun Ra (Herman "Sonny" Blound) *(1914–1993)* American keyboardist-composer-band leader. Sun Ra exemplifies what might be called free-form, postmodern jazz. Achieving early prominence as a pianist-arranger with big band leader Fletcher HENDERSON in the late 1940s, Sun Ra moved to Chicago where his Myth-Science or Solar Arkestra became a key part of that city's thriving avant-garde music scene. By the 1960s, his eclectic approach had consolidated; like much of the period's new music, there were juxtapositions of old and new, with traditional big band and Dixieland elements mixing freely with various electronic effects and open-ended improvisations. Sun Ra also incorporated mixed media strategies by utilizing modern dance as well as slide and light shows; exotic costuming and musical motifs loosely derived from Egyptian and astronomical sources added yet another dimension to his concert and club appearances, which some bracketed as PERFORMANCE ART. In spite of having little sustained work, Sun Ra kept the Solar Arkestra together by dint of his charismatic personality and vision. Though his greatest influence was on the European avant-garde, Sun Ra was significant as an emblem of the idiosyncratic fusions of musical, theatrical and literary sources characterizing so much of what is described under the rubric of contemporary "postmodern art."

Sun Yat-sen (Sun Wen, Sun Yixian, Sun I-hsien) *(1867–1925)* Chinese revolutionary leader. The father of the Chinese republic was born in Guangdong (Kwangtung) Province. The son of fairly well-to-do peasants, he attended a church school in Honolulu (1879–82) and was strongly influenced by Christianity. He studied medicine in Canton and Hong Kong, where he practiced for a short time. Devoted to the overthrow of the Qing (Ch'ing) dynasty, Sun fled CHINA in 1895 after a failed revolt. He toured the world, picking up the support of expatriate Chinese and studying contemporary Western social and political theories. In 1905, in Japan, he founded the Tongmenghui (T'ungmeng hue; Alliance Society), a revolutionary league. Two years later he issued a manifesto containing the first published version of his Three Principles of the People (Sanminzhuyi; San-min chu-i). These cornerstones of his political ideology were nationalism, democracy and the livelihood of the people. When revolution broke out in China in 1911, Sun was elected provisional president of the newly formed Chinese Republic. Within months he resigned in favor of YUAN SHIHKAI, who was able to stabilize the republic through his political power. As Yuan's imperial ambitions surfaced, Sun's associate Sung Chiao-jen organized a rival party, the Guomindang (KUOMINTANG), and Sun became its leader. In 1913 he led an unsuccessful revolt against Yuan and fled to Japan. Returning to China in 1917, he became president of a rival government in Canton in 1921. In 1924 he began a policy of cooperation with the communists and received aid from the USSR in hopes of attaining full national authority and uniting the country. Two years after his death the communists and the Kuomintang split, each claiming to be Sun's true political heir. Today, Sun Yat-sen is a revered national hero in China, and his tomb in Nanjing is a national shrine.

Sun Yefang *(1907–1983)* Chinese economist. Sun Yefang's advocacy of economic incentives and price mechanisms in the People's Republic of CHINA under MAO ZEDONG led to his imprisonment at the beginning of the CULTURAL REVOLUTION (1966). However, following the death of Mao and the arrest of the GANG OF FOUR, his ideas won official acceptance and helped form the basis of DENG XIAOPING's economic modernization program.

superconductors Superconductors are materials that conduct electricity without any resistance. There are no known naturally existing superconductors; in most materials, superconductivity can occur only at extremely low temperatures. The basic principles of superconductivity were discovered by American physicists John BARDEEN, Leon N. COOPER and John Robert Schrieffer, who shared the 1972 NOBEL PRIZE in physics for their work. Superconductors have important applications in electromagnetics and, potentially, in sophisticated electronic circuitry.

Superman The first and most influential comic book hero made his first appearance in 1938, in DC Comics' *Action Comics #1*. The creation of Jerry Siegel and Joe Shuster, Superman was a native of the doomed planet Krypton who had been sent to Earth as an infant and raised in the midwestern town of Smallville by foster parents Jonathan and Martha Kent. As an adult, "Clark Kent" moves to the nearby city of Metropolis, where he becomes a reporter on the *Daily Planet,* working alongside colleagues Perry White, Jimmy Olsen and Lois Lane. In his hidden life as a crime-fighting superhero, Superman fights the forces of evil, utilizing the extraordinary powers he enjoys on Earth, including flying, X-ray vision and super strength. He is impervious to bullets and is susceptible only to kryptonite, a piece of Krypton that has survived the planet's explosion. Besides comic books, Superman has performed his feats in novels, on radio, in movie serials, in animated cartoons, on television and in feature-length motion pictures.

supply-side economics An economic theory stressing the importance of the aggregate supply of goods and services in influencing prices and employment in the economy. Supply-side economics was a reaction to Keynesian economics, which focused attention on the demand side. Supply-side theories were applied to the U.S. economy by President Ronald REAGAN, who radically lowered taxes with the goal of increasing savings and investment without an increase in inflation. Proponents of the supply-side theory used the **Laffer curve** to theorize that tax cuts could pay for themselves by increasing incentives and production, which would generate additional tax revenues. Although liberals and many Democrats attacked the tax cut as a boon to the wealthy, supporters argued that the **"trickle down"**

effect of the tax cut would benefit the entire economy.

Suppression of Communism Act
(1950) South African legislation banning the Communist Party, defining all persons advocating political, industrial, social or economic change as "Communists." The justice minister was empowered to impose banning orders on individuals, limiting their rights to publish, speak or meet others and effectively providing for house arrest.

suprematism Abstract art movement of an extreme geometrical character that was created by the Russian painter Kasimir MALEVICH in 1913. At first it was built solely on the square, while later its elements increased to encompass the square, circle, triangle and cross, all flatly painted on pure canvas. It was important in the USSR until 1921, when the government turned against abstract art movements. The austere concepts of suprematism were largely spread by the BAUHAUS publication (1927) of the German translation of its manifesto, Malevich's *Non-Objective World*, and the movement was an important influence on the development of European modernism. Perhaps the best-known suprematist work is Malevich's *White on White* in the collection of the Museum of Modern Art, New York City.

Supremes, the See Diana ROSS.

Suriname Suriname covers an area of 63,022 square miles on the Atlantic

coast of northeastern South America. A Dutch possession since 1677, the former Dutch Guiana became an equal member of the "Tripartite Kingdom" of the NETHERLANDS in 1954. Coalition governments, formed among political parties that had developed around racial identity, governed the country between 1958 and 1969. Full independence was granted in 1975. A military coup in 1980 brought Desi Bouterse to power. He dissolved the

SURINAME	
1954	Dutch Guiana becomes self-governing.
1975	Dutch Guiana achieves independence as Republic of Suriname.
1980	Army chief of staff Desi Bouterse overthrows government.
1982	Army tortures and kills 15 opposition leaders; Netherlands cuts off aid in response.
1986	Surinamese Liberation Army starts guerrilla war in name of restoring constitutional rule.
1987	New constitution approved; civilian government restored.
1991	New civilian government organized; Ronald Venetiaan first elected president since the 1980 coup.
1998	Widespread strikes against Wijdenbosch's trade and exchange rate policies; calls for the president's resignation.
2004	UN establishes tribunal to mediate the border dispute with Guyana.

legislature and dismissed the president. Subsequent power struggles between political and military groups resulted in strikes and demonstrations and the killing of several prominent citizens. A new constitution was introduced in 1987, and a gradual transition to democracy is underway. In 1991 Ronald Venetiaan became the first president elected to head a civilian government since the 1980 coup. The country faced an economic downturn in the 1990s, with widespread strikes in 1998. In 2004 the UN set up a tribunal to resolve the maritime border dispute with Guyana.

surrealism Movement in art and literature that attempted to liberate artistic expression from convention and reason. Founded in Paris in 1924 by Andre BRETON, whose *Manifeste du surrealisme* (Manifesto of Surrealism) was published that year, surrealism built on the foundation laid by such post-World War I movements as CUBISM, FUTURISM and DADA. However, it replaced the revolutionary nihilism of Dada with a more positive philosophy that attempted to rejuvenate aesthetic expression. As a literary movement, surrealism is concerned more with creating novel combinations of words than in the literal meanings of those words. In literature, surrealism appeared principally in France, where its adherents included Louis ARAGON, Robert DESNOS, Paul ELUARD, Henri Michaux, Benjamin Peret, Jacques PREVERT and Philippe Soupault, as well as the filmmaker Jean COCTEAU. In Britain, poet Dylan THOMAS was strongly influenced by the surrealists, and in America the work of E. E. CUMMINGS and William Carlos WILLIAMS also shows elements of surrealism. In the visual arts, the influence of surrealism was more widely felt, becoming dominant in the 1920s and '30s. Artists such as Salvador DALI, Max ERNST, René MAGRITTE, Joan MIRÓ, Andre MASSON and Yves TANGUY embraced surrealism, and their works demonstrated the fantastic imagery, dream-like symbols, incongruous juxta-positions and spontaneity characteristic of the movement. Although surrealism managed to survive World War II, it never regained the prominence it enjoyed in the prewar years.

Surveyor Following the RANGER and Lunar Orbiter series, the Surveyor program launched seven exploratory probes to the Moon between May 1966 and January 1968. Beginning with *Surveyor 1,* five of the probes succeeded in making the soft landings on the surface of the Moon that would be essential to the future manned APOLLO missions. They sent back valuable geological, scientific and engineering data, including over 10,000 photographs from one mission alone. In another first, *Surveyor 6* succeeded in lifting off from the Moon's surface and moving 10 feet to a new location.

Susskind, David Howard (1920–1987) American television, motion picture and theater producer. Susskind was one of America's earliest and best-known TV talk show hosts. He set up his own production company in 1952, and by the late 1950s was producing more live television than the three U.S. networks combined. Over the years his productions won numerous awards. Susskind took to the airwaves himself as an interviewer in 1958 with *Open End,* a late-night New York City talk show without set time limits. In 1976 *Open End* became *The David Susskind Show,* a two-hour program eventually carried by 100 stations; it remained on the air until 1986. Susskind continued to focus on serious issues—although in a combative manner that was not universally admired—long after other talk shows had veered to entertainment.

Sutherland, George (1862–1942) Associate justice, U.S. Supreme Court (1922–38). Born in Britain, Sutherland graduated from Brigham Young University and attended the University of Michigan Law School for one year before starting to practice law in Utah. After serving as a state senator he was elected to the U.S. House of Representatives and then to the Senate in 1904. In the Senate Sutherland proved a reactionary, opposing the passage of both the Clayton Antitrust Act and the Federal Trade Commission Act. His own REPUBLICAN PARTY failed to put him up for reelection in 1916. Sutherland stayed in Washington and helped Warren G. HARDING in his successful presidential campaign. Sutherland was rewarded with several government posts, and in 1922 Harding appointed him to the Supreme Court. Sutherland was predictably conservative on the Court, opposing much of President Franklin D. ROOSEVELT's NEW DEAL legislation during the 1930s. He retired in 1938 after Roosevelt's unsuccessful COURT-PACKING ATTEMPT.

Sutherland, Graham Vivian (1903–1980) British painter. Sutherland gained fame in the 1930s as a landscape painter; his landscapes reflected both a sense of romanticism and aspects of SURREALISM. During WORLD WAR II he was commissioned to record scenes of wartime Britain. The result was a body of powerful work depicting the violence and destruction of the war. After the war, he gained new acclaim as a portrait painter. His notable works of this period included portraits of Somerset MAUGHAM, Helena Rubenstein and Lord BEAVERBROOK. Sutherland became embroiled in controversy when Sir Winston CHURCHILL publicly criticized Sutherland's 1955 portrait of him.

Sutherland, Joan (1926–) Australian opera singer. Acclaimed for her large, beautiful voice and her bel canto singing, Sutherland is one of the outstanding coloratura sopranos of the second half of the 20th century. Originally trained as a Wagnerian soprano, she became a coloratura under the guidance of her husband, conductor **Richard Bonynge.** She made her London debut at Covent Garden in 1952, but it was her electrifying performance as Lucia in Franco Zeffrelli's production of *Lucia di Lammermoor* in 1959 that made her famous. In 1960 she made her American debut with the Dallas Opera in Handel's *Alcina,* another role for which she is known. Other famous roles include Marie in *The Daughter of the Regiment,* Donna Anna in *Don Giovanni* and the title role in *Norma.* In addition, she has made several critically acclaimed recordings, performed on television, and appeared at the Glyndebourne and Edinburgh Festivals. Her partnership with the Italian tenor Luciano PAVAROTTI was legendary. Sutherland was made a dame of the British Empire in 1979 and retired from the operatic stage in 1990.

Sutton, Willie ("the actor") (1901–1980) American bank robber and prison escape artist of the 1930s and 1940s. Sutton was noted for his meticulously planned bank robberies, which he often pulled off while wearing ingenious disguises. His criminal career spanned 35 years, ending in 1952; he estimated that he robbed close to $2 million. He spent more than half his life behind bars.

Sverdlov, Yakov Mikhailovich
(1885–1919) Russian politician. He joined the Social Democratic Labor Party in 1901 and from 1902 to 1917 acted as a professional revolutionary for the BOLSHEVIKS. In 1913 he was made part of the Central Committee. Following the February Revolution Sverdlov was the chief organizer of the party and became chairman of the All-Russian Central Executive Committee of the Soviets. He was a close collaborator of LENIN.

Svevo, Italo (Ettore Schmitz)
(1861–1928) Italian novelist. Svevo, who has become recognized as one of the leading Italian novelists of the 20th century, owes his present renown largely to the championing of his work by James JOYCE. In the 1910s the expatriate Joyce served as an English tutor to Svevo, who was unhappily devoting himself to a business career. Two previous novels by Svevo—*A Life* (1892) and *As a Man Grows Older* (1898)—had received negative reviews, and Svevo had concluded that he was not destined to write. But with Joyce's encouragement, Svevo produced his most famous work, *Confessions of Zeno* (1923), an intricate comic novel revolving around the central protagonist's attempts to quit smoking. The novel, which was among the first works of literature to make major use of Freudian psychoanalytical themes, received international acclaim. *Further Confessions of Zeno* (1969) appeared posthumously.

Svoboda, Ludvik *(1895–1979)* President of CZECHOSLOVAKIA (1968–75). A career army officer, Svoboda became a hero of WORLD WAR II by forming and leading a Czech unit within the Soviet army. He did not emerge onto the political scene until 1968. During the PRAGUE SPRING of that year he was chosen to replace Antonin NOVOTNÝ as president of Czechoslovakia. As a war hero, he had credibility both with the reformers (led by Alexander DUBČEK) and with the Soviets and hardliners. During the SOVIET INVASION OF CZECHOSLOVAKIA soon thereafter, he went to Moscow to negotiate with Soviet leaders. Svoboda was the only political figure of the Prague Spring to survive the postinvasion purges of the Czechoslovak Communist Party, in which some 400,000 Czechs lost their party membership. Svoboda was reelected president in 1973 but resigned due to illness two years later and was replaced by Communist Party secretary Gustav HUSÁK.

Swanson, Gloria (Gloria Josephine May Svensson or Swenson) *(1899–1983)* Legendary American film star of the 1920s. Swanson began her film career in the 1910s, but achieved real stardom in a series of SILENT FILMS for Cecil B. DE MILLE. A highly publicized series of marriages and divorces in the late 1920s, the near-bankruptcy incurred by the unfinished *Queen Kelly* (1928) and the difficulties of the transition to sound led to her retirement from the screen in the mid-1930s. A comeback in Billy WILDER's *Sunset Boulevard* (1950) brought her one of her greatest roles, the neurotic fading movie star Norma Desmond. Her later years were spent promoting cosmetics and health foods. Swanson appeared in over 60 movies as well as in numerous television programs and some stage plays. She was reportedly the first actress to make over $1 million a year. Small of stature, she nonetheless imparted a grand presence on the screen. "I am big," says her character in *Sunset Boulevard,* "it's the pictures that got small."

SWAPO (South-West Africa People's Organization) Founded in 1960 by Sam Nujoma and Herman Toivo Ja Toivo. In 1920 NAMIBIA was mandated by the LEAGUE OF NATIONS to South AFRICA, which later attempted to integrate it into its other territories. In 1966 SWAPO began mounting guerrilla actions against South African military units, following a United Nations resolution revoking South Africa's mandate. In 1971 the United Nations recognized SWAPO as "sole authentic representative of the people of Namibia." SWAPO was excluded from the independence negotiations and process in the 1970s, and a National Assembly and Council of Ministers were instituted by South Africa. Conflict between South Africa and SWAPO continued through the 1980s. In 1989 SWAPO won 57.3 percent of the vote in UN-supervised elections to determine the future of Africa's last colony. SWAPO retained its political control over Namibia with the reelection of both SWAPO parliamentary candidates and NUJOMA in 1994 and 1999.

Swart, Charles *(1893–1982)* First president of the Republic of SOUTH AFRICA (1961 to 1967). Before South Africa withdrew from the British Commonwealth, Swart served as minister of justice (1948–59) and governor general (1959–61). He helped draft a number of the nation's APARTHEID laws.

Swaziland (Umbuso Weswatini)
The landlocked kingdom of Swaziland in southern Africa, less than 100 miles from the Indian Ocean, covers a total area of 6,702 square miles. Britain assumed sovereignty in 1894, and in 1903 the governor of the Transvaal was empowered to administer Swaziland. In 1906 those powers were transferred to a high commissioner for Basutoland, Bechuanaland and Swaziland. Limited self-government was granted in 1963. The British resisted South African pressure for incorporation within SOUTH AFRICA, and the Imbokodvo (Grindstone) National Movement, formed by King SOBHUZA II, won all 24 seats in the House of Assembly in 1967, as a kingdom was proclaimed under British protection. Full independence was achieved on September 6, 1968. Swaziland maintained close links with South Africa in the 1970s and joined the South African Customs Union; the Swazi government signed a secret nonaggression pact with South Africa in February 1982 and expelled several AFRICAN NATIONAL CONGRESS members. Nevertheless, the South Africans launched a raid in June 1986 on the Swazi capital of Mbabane, killing three ANC members. In 1973 and 1977 King Sobhuza II dismissed parliament and abolished the constitution, only to replace it with a new one two years later. Sobhuza II died in August 1982 and was succeeded by his teenage son, Prince Makhosetive. A power struggle ensued between the traditionalists and the modernists, which continued through the 1980s. Makhosetive was crowned as Mswati III on April 25,

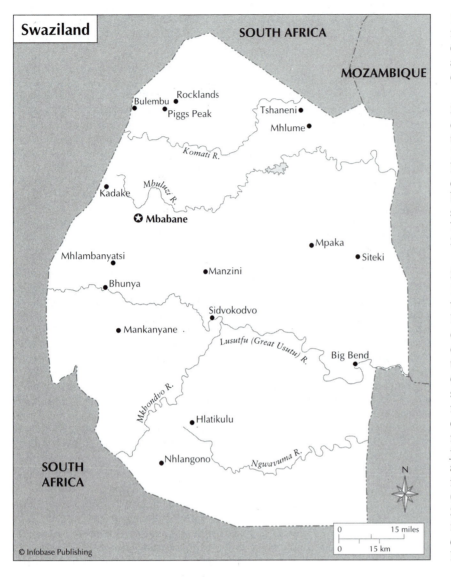

Swaziland

SOUTH AFRICA

MOZAMBIQUE

Bulembu • Rocklands
• Piggs Peak
Tshaneni •
Mhlume •

Komati R.

Kadake •
Mbuluzi R.

✪ Mbabane

• Mpaka
• Siteki

Mhlambanyatsi •
• Manzini

Bhunya •

Sidvokodvo •

• Mankanyane

Lusutfu (Great Usutu) R.
Big Bend •

Mkhondvo R.

• Hlatikulu

SOUTH
AFRICA

• Nhlangono
Ngwavuma R.

N

| 0 | | 15 miles |
| 0 | | 15 km |

© Infobase Publishing

1986. In 2004 the Swaziland government issued an international appeal for economic, humanitarian and medical aid to stem an increasing famine and check the spread of HIV/AIDS.

Sweatt, Heman (*1913–1982*) African American whose lawsuit against the state of Texas led to a landmark 1950 Supreme Court decision challenging the doctrine of "separate but equal" education for blacks. Sweatt brought suit after being denied admission to the all-white University of Texas Law School in 1946. The Supreme Court ordered him admitted.

Sweden Sweden covers an area of 172,786 square miles on the Scandinavian Peninsula of northern Europe. Neutral during both World Wars, Sweden was criticized by the Allied powers during those wars for its continued trade with Germany. The Social Democratic Party, which dominated successive governments from 1932 to 1976, made Sweden one of the most affluent countries in the world, as well as the most advanced WELFARE STATE. Sweden joined the UNITED NATIONS as a non-aligned country and became a founding member of the Nordic Council (1953) and EFTA (1959). In 1975 Sweden initiated a constitutional reform that limited the monarchy to ceremonial functions. Prime Minister Olof Palme was murdered in 1986; the gov-

SWAZILAND	
1903	Following the South African War, Swaziland becomes a special British protectorate, or High Commission territory, against South Africa's wishes.
1963	Limited self-government is granted.
1968	Swaziland gains independence following successful talks in London.
1973	King Sobhuza II declares constitution unworkable and voids it.
1977	The parliamentary system is abolished and replaced by traditional tribal communities.
1982	King Sobhuza dies.
1986	Prince Makhosetive is installed as King Mswati III.
2001	The king forbids men from having sex with teenage girls for the next five years to help stem the AIDS crisis.
2004	Prime minister declares a humanitarian crisis after three years of little rainfall. The UN reports that Swaziland has the world's highest rate of HIV infection.

Sweden

Norwegian Sea

NORWAY

DENMARK

FINLAND

ESTONIA

LATVIA

LITHUANIA

© Infobase Publishing

| 0 | | 200 miles |
| 0 | | 200 km |

ernments formed by his successor, Ingvar Carlsson, have been plagued by political scandals and economic problems. Following a narrowly supported 1994 referendum, Sweden joined the EUROPEAN UNION (EU) in 1995.

Swing Era, the The Swing Era, extending from the early 1930s to the late 1940s, was named for the type of popular music associated with the period. "Swing" music was played by instrumental ensembles typically ranging from 12 to 16 musicians, a repertory based largely on tunes from Tin Pan Alley, Broadway shows and Hollywood movies, and a subtly insinuated pulse where all four beats of the measure were given approximately equal weight. Growing out of the New Orleans– and Chicago-styled jazz groups of the "Roaring Twenties," these larger instrumental units typically included four to five saxophones (usually "doubling" on clarinet), three to four trombones and four to five trumpets; the rhythm section, by the mid-1930s, included piano, guitar (replacing banjo), string bass (replacing tuba) and drums. It was a period of virtuoso soloists (trumpeters Harry JAMES and Roy Eldridge, for example) and "star" leaders both black (Fletcher HENDERSON, Duke ELLINGTON, Count BASIE) and white (Benny GOODMAN, Glenn MILLER, Woody HERMAN, Stan KENTON). Popularized by new media such as network radio and the sound film, Swing Era big bands kept America dancing during the GREAT

SWEDEN	
1919	Universal adult suffrage introduced.
1932	Social Democrats under Per Albin Hansson take power.
1949	The Riksdag passes the new Freedom of the Press Act.
1969	Olof Palme becomes prime minister.
1973	Carl XVI Gustav succeeds his grandfather Gustav VI.
1975	Implementation of constitutional measures that reduce the monarch to ceremonial functions and create a unicameral Riksdag with a three-year term.
1986	Palme is shot dead on a Stockholm street and is succeeded as prime minister by Ingvar Carlsson.

(Table continues)

DEPRESSION of the 1930s and the war years of the 1940s. In the mid-1940s, Swing bands began to fade due to war-inflated traveling expenses and the public's growing affection for crooners like Frank SINATRA. Today, the big band sound resounds on "oldies" radio broadcasts and in traveling "ghost" bands playing the repertoires of such Swing Era favorites as Miller, Herman and Ellington. Big bands have also become important training grounds for nurturing young improvisers in the burgeoning jazz education movement.

Switzerland (Swiss Confederation)
Situated in central Europe, the landlocked Alpine country of Switzerland covers an area of 15,939 square miles. One of the most prosperous and politically stable countries in the world, Switzerland has become a center for international banking. After declaring its neutrality in 1815, the country reaffirmed its nonbelligerent status during both World Wars, playing a humanitarian role through the work of the International Red Cross (founded in Geneva in 1864). Switzerland maintains observer status at the UNITED NATIONS, participating in many UN agencies, and was a founding member of EFTA (1959). Restrictions on foreign workers and alien residents were imposed after the 1967 and 1971 elections, which brought increased power to radical right-wing groups demanding such curbs. Women were given the right to vote in federal elections in 1971. Following a narrowly supported referendum in 2002, Switzerland joined the

United Nations, but voted in 2003 not to adopt the euro as its currency.

Symington, Stuart (William Stuart Symington) *(1901–1988)* American politician, Democratic senator from Missouri (1953–76). Symington entered government service in 1945 when President Harry S TRUMAN appointed him chairman of the Surplus Property Administration. When the air force was formed in 1947, he was named its first secretary. During the ARMY-MCCARTHY HEARINGS in 1954, he emerged as a strong opponent of Sen. Joseph R. MC-CARTHY. In 1956 and 1960 he ran unsuccessfully for the Democratic presidential nomination. Although he had long supported a strong U.S. military force, in the 1960s he became increasingly critical of military spending and the U.S. presence in VIETNAM. He retired from the Senate in 1976.

Syndicate, the New York–based organization of theatrical producers and businessmen who at the turn of the century controlled the American popular stage. As a result of the Panic of 1893, the theater establishment, like

SWITZERLAND

1901	Albert Einstein becomes citizen.
1920	First session of League of Nations meets in Geneva.
1971	Women gain right to vote in national elections; constitutional article accepted on protection of environment.
1984	Elizabeth Kopp is first woman member of Federal Council.
1986	Thirty tons of toxic wastes released into Rhine in fire at Sandoz company warehouse in Basel; spill considered worst environmental disaster in Europe in decade; voters reject Swiss membership in UN.
1990	Outlaws money-laundering; tightens immigration laws, including banning seekers of political asylum from working for first three months of stay.
1992	Switzerland becomes a member of the International Monetary Fund and the World Bank.
1995	The Swiss Banking Association, under pressure from Jewish groups, agrees to look for unclaimed bank accounts belonging to victims of the Holocaust.
1998	The Swiss Banking Association agrees to pay $1.25 billion directly to Holocaust survivors.
1999	The first female and first Jewish president, Ruth Dreifuss, takes office; in national elections, the right-wing People's Party places second.
2002	In a referendum, a narrow majority votes in favor of joining the United Nations.
2003	The People's Party becomes the largest party in the National Council after winning almost 28 percent in national elections.
2004	Voters approve using stem cells from human embryos in research.
2005	Power failures bring trains to a halt in the most serious breakdown in Swiss rail history; a referendum vote approves opening the job market to workers from the 10 newest EU members.

other businesses, was on the verge of economic collapse and crippling unemployment. As had happened with the forming monopolies in oil, tobacco and rubber, the theaters formed their own trust. This so-called Syndicate dominated the artistic and business practices of the stage from 1896 to 1915, growing from just 33 theaters to thousands of houses and hundreds of traveling companies nationwide. This was the age of the touring show. The Syndicate brought badly needed order to theater construction, traveling-circuit management and play production. It centralized control of the star system, exploiting the talents of such contemporary luminaries as Maude ADAMS, Henry Irving and De Wolfe Hopper, and encouraged such blockbuster productions as *Ben Hur* (1899) and the ZIEGFELD FOLLIES. Of the six organizing

producers—Sam Nixon, Fred Zimmerman, Al Hayman, Marc Klaw, Abe Erlanger and Charles Frohman—only Frohman was directly involved in theatrical production. Klaw was the legal brains behind the operations, and Erlanger provided the business acumen. The relative merits of the Syndicate continue to be debated. On the positive side, it increased employment and standardized house conditions. It toughened copyright protections against the infringing new medium, the motion picture. It introduced business operations of binding contracts and promotions that are in use today. It invested heavily in theatrical real estate and construction. On the other hand, it enforced a monopoly over producers and players, blackballing such recalcitrants as actress Minnie Maddern Fiske and producer David BELASCO. Priorities in

box-office draw encouraged a standard in artistic mediocrity that resisted experiment and change. After 1905 the Syndicate faced formidable competition from the new Shubert organization of theater houses. After the 1915 death of Charles Frohman, the Syndicate declined and gradually lost control to its rival. Meanwhile, the Little Theater movement encouraged the local control of theater houses and play production.

Synge, (Edmund) John Millington
(1871–1909) Irish playwright. Following his education at Trinity College, Dublin, Synge traveled to Paris, where he lived the bohemian life of a struggling and impoverished writer. There in 1896 he was befriended by the poet W. B. YEATS. Yeats urged him to abandon Paris and go to the Aran islands off the west coast of Ireland. Synge did so,

spending his summers there between 1898 and 1902, and was transformed into a major artist. He subsequently wrote six remarkable plays imbued with a deep sympathy for the Irish peasantry and the rhythms of natural Irish speech. In 1906, with Yeats and Lady Augusta GREGORY, he became a director of the ABBEY THEATRE, where most of his work was first performed. His plays include *In the Shadow of the Glen* (1903), *Riders to the Sea* (1904, adapted as an opera by Ralph VAUGHAN WILLIAMS, 1937) and *The Tinker's Wedding* (1908). His masterpiece was *THE PLAYBOY OF THE WESTERN WORLD* (1907), which caused riots when it was first performed at the Abbey. Synge suffered from Hodgkin's disease and was unable to complete his last play, *Deirdre of the Sorrows* (1910). While they aroused controversy, Synge's ironic, realistic and poetic plays enormously influenced subsequent Irish theater.

Syria (Syrian Arab Republic) Syria is located on the Mediterranean Sea in the Middle East and covers an area of 71,480 square miles. Ruled from Constantinople by the Ottoman Turks until the collapse of the OTTOMAN EMPIRE at the end of WORLD WAR I, Syria became a French mandate of the LEAGUE OF NATIONS in 1920. Nationalist sentiments led to riots and strikes until the country gained independence in 1946. After several coups in the 1950s and early 1960s political control was seized by the BA'ATH PARTY (Arab Socialist Renaissance Party) in 1963. Ba'ath military leader Hafiz al-ASSAD seized power in 1970. Uprisings led by Sunni Islamic fundamentalists challenged Assad's rule from 1976 to 1982. In 1976 Syria intervened in the LEBANESE CIVIL WAR and mounted a major military operation in 1987 to end the fighting in BEIRUT. Syria's anti-Israel stance and sponsorship of radical Palestinian factions created tensions with the United States. Syria has been widely condemned for its human rights abuses and identified as a sponsor of international terrorism. However, Syria supported the UNITED NATIONS sanctions against IRAQ for its invasion of KUWAIT (1990) and joined the United States and other countries in the successful war to oust Iraq (August 1990–February 1991). Assad died in 2000 and was succeeded in the presidency by his son Bashar al-Assad. After the furor caused by the assassination of anti-Syrian Lebanese politician in 2005 (in which Syrian officials were implicated) Syria withdrew all of its military forces from Lebanon.

Szabo, Gabor *(1941–1982)* Hungarian guitarist. A freedom fighter, Szabo fled Hungary after the Soviet Union crushed the HUNGARIAN UPRISING (1956) and settled in the U.S. He wrote moody pieces that blended American JAZZ and ROCK and roll rhythms with melodies from Hungary, India and South America. His virtuosity and distinctive melodic style strongly influenced American jazz artists.

Szell, George *(1897–1970)* Hungarian-born orchestra conductor who at midcentury brought the Cleveland Symphony Orchestra to world prominence. Szell was regarded as one of the finest technicians in the post-TOSCANINI era of conducting. He was born in Budapest and trained in Vienna, conducting his first concert at age 16. After studying with Max Reger in Leipzig and with the encouragement of Richard STRAUSS, he succeeded Otto KLEMPERER at the Strasbourg Municipal Theatre in 1917. Other posts included conducting at Darmstadt (1921–1924), Duesseldorf (1922–1924), Berlin (1924–1929) and Prague (1927–1937). During a visit to the U.S. in 1939 World War II broke out and he decided to stay, becoming a citizen in 1946. He became principal conductor of the New York Metropolitan Opera from 1942 to 1946 and that year went to the Cleveland Symphony Orchestra, where he remained until his death. His tenure with the orchestra made it one of the greatest ensembles in the world. Like Arturo Toscanini and Fritz REINER, Szell stressed absolute fidelity to the score. Scorning showmanship and "romantic" interpretation, he demanded clear articulation and a perfect balance among sections. "It is perfectly legitimate to prefer the hectic, the arhythmic, the untidy," he said, "but to my mind great artistry is not disorderliness." His great series of recordings for CBS-Epic attest to his sensitivity for the works of Haydn, Mozart and Beethoven, although he performed relatively little the French, Russian and modern repertoire. In particular there were notable cycles of Schumann symphonies, the Beethoven piano concertos (especially with pianist Leon Fleischer) and works by William WALTON and Antonin Dvorak.

Szent-Györgyi, Albert *(1893–1986)* Hungarian-born biochemist. Szent-Györgyi won the 1937 NOBEL PRIZE in

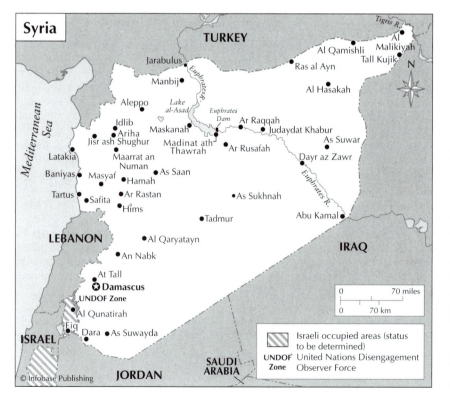

SYRIA

1918	British-Arab force drives Turks from Damascus; Prince Faisal calls for Syrian nation.
1920	Treaty of San Remo; League of Nations mandates Syria to France; agitation for independence begins.
1926	Lebanon separated from Syria and made independent.
1936	General strike against French rule.
1941	British and Free French defeat Vichy French at Damascus.
1946	French grant independence; Shukri al-Kuwatly is first president.
1948	Syria defeated in attack on Israel.
1949	Military coup.
1957	Election of Ba'ath Party—pan-Arab, secular socialist movement.
1958	Syria forms United Arab Republic with Egypt.
1962	Nasser seeks Egypt-Syria merger; anti-Nasser coup in Damascus; UAR dissolved.
1963	Anti-Nasser wing of Ba'athists takes power.
1967	Golan Heights lost to Israel in Six-Day War; relations with U.S. broken.
1970	Moderate Ba'athists under Assad take power.
1973	Attacks Israel; fought to standstill.
1976	Troops occupy Lebanon; assert traditional ties with Syria.
1977	Sadat visits Israel; Assad breaks ties.
1979	Violence between Sunni Moslems and minority Alewite sect—now powerful through Assad's membership.
1980	Assad supports Iran in war on Iraq; nearly joins war.
1982	Sunni fundamentalist uprising crushed.
1985	Abu Nidal conducts international terror campaign from Damascus.
1989	Soviet aid declines.
1990	Syrian troops participate in Beirut peace arrangements; Assad calls for "Holy War" against Israel; joins U.S.-led force opposing Iraqi occupation of Kuwait.
1991	Assad hints at recognition for Israel; joins U.S.-led regional defense plan with Egypt and Saudis.
1994	Syria offers to normalize relations with Israel in exchange for the Golan Heights.
2000	President Hafez al-Assad dies and is succeeded by his son, Bashar.
2001	Pope John Paul II pays a historic visit; Syrian troops depart Beirut and move to other parts of Lebanon following Lebanese and international criticism of their presence in the country; pro-reformists detained, crushing hopes for a relaxation of the authoritarian regime.
2002	U.S. officials include Syria on a list of states that make up an "axis of evil."
2004	U.S. imposes economic sanctions on Syria over what it terms Syria's support for terrorism and its failure to stop militants from entering Iraq; UN Security Council resolution calls for all foreign forces to pull out of Lebanon.
2005	Syria announces that all of its forces have left Lebanon; high Syrian government officials are accused of complicity in the assassination of the anti-Syrian Lebanese politician Rafik Hariri.

medicine or physiology for his isolation of vitamin C. Although he remained in Hungary during World War II, he spent much of the war in hiding because of his anti-Nazi activities. He came to the U.S. in 1947 and assumed the post of director of research at the Institute of Muscle Research. In 1954 he won an Albert Lasker Award for his research on heart muscle contraction. He received a number of grants for cancer research, but his "bioelectronic" theory of cancer did not gain wide acceptance.

Szeryng, Henryk *(1918–1988)* Polish-born violinist; a leading exponent of the Romantic school of violin playing. While serving with the Polish government-in-exile during WORLD WAR II he had occasion to go to Mexico, where he decided to settle. He became a Mexican citizen in 1949, later traveling on a diplomatic passport as Mexico's cultural and goodwill ambassador.

Szigeti, Joseph *(1892–1972)* Hungarian-American violinist. Born in Budapest, Szigeti was the child prodigy of a violin teacher. He studied with Jeno Hubay and made his professional debut at the age of 11. He performed widely in Germany and made his first tour of Europe in 1912. A superb musician, he was skilled in the classical repertoire and became known for his performances of work by contemporary composers, many of whom, including BÁRTÓK, BLOCH, BUSONI and PROKOFIEV, wrote works especially for him. He made his American debut with the Philadelphia Orchestra in 1925. Szigeti and his wife fled Europe after the fall of France. They settled in California, and he became an American citizen in 1951.

In the U.S. he was particularly known for his radio concerts and for his many recordings. His autobiography, *With Strings Attached,* was published in 1947.

Szilard, Leo *(1898–1964)* Hungarian-American physicist. Szilard was born in Budapest and received his doctorate from the University of Berlin in 1922. In 1934, while working in London, he discovered the principle of the nuclear chain reaction, and in 1939, he confirmed the feasibility of using uranium to generate a nuclear reaction. Having immigrated to the U.S. in 1938, the following year Szilard persuaded Albert EINSTEIN to write a letter to President Franklin D. ROOSEVELT, urging him to authorize development of an ATOMIC BOMB. Roosevelt agreed, and the Manhattan Project was begun. In 1942, while working on the bomb, Szilard and Enrico FERMI created the first self-sustaining nuclear reactor. One of the first to recognize the potential of atomic energy, Szilard later regretted his work on the Manhattan Project, and he became one of the first advocates of nuclear disarmament. After the war, Szilard changed the focus of his research to molecular biology.

Szold, Henrietta *(1860–1945)* Zionist and educator. Szold pioneered the landmark Baltimore School for Immigrant Workers (1891) and was editor of the Jewish Publication Society of America (1892–1916). In 1912 she was the founder of Hadassah, the world's largest Zionist movement. The first woman elected a World Zionist executive, she directed Youth Aliyah Bureau (1933–45), the world movement to rescue young European Jewish children from the Nazis, and strove for Arab-Jewish cooperation through common social programs. (See also JEWS; ZIONISM.)

Szymborska, Wisława *(1923–)* Polish poet and winner of the Nobel Prize for literature (1996). Born near Poznań, Szymborska and her family moved to Cracow in 1931, where she enrolled to study Polish literature and sociology at Jagellonian University in 1945. While at Jagellonian, she published several poems describing Poland's traumatic experience during WORLD WAR II (1939–45). She initially praised the postwar communist government of Poland for its improvements of the quality of life in her published collections of poetry, *Dlatego zyjemy* (*That's Why We're Alive*) (1952) and *Pytania zadawane sobie* (*Questions for Oneself*) (1954). However, after the de-Stalinization campaign initiated by Soviet premier Nikita KRUSHCHEV in February 1956, Szymborska repudiated her earlier works as propaganda produced under the stress of living under the Stalinist regime. The following year she published her third collection, *Wolanie do Yeti* (*Calling Out to the Yeti*), which represented Joseph STALIN as the incarnation of the Yeti, or Abominable Snowman, and condemned him for the manner in which he abused this metaphoric strength. She also used her poetry to remind communist Poland of its glorious national heritage and culture, as in her fourth collection of poems, *Sol* (*Salt,* 1962). In recognition of her incisive criticism of communist repression through poetry and her effort to promote national pride in order to preserve a Polish identity independent of Soviet domination, Szymborska was awarded the Nobel Prize for literature in 1996.

T

Taepo Dong missile launch On August 31, 1998, North KOREA announced to the world that it had successfully launched a Taepo Dong 1 rocket, which had soared into the atmosphere traveling eastward over the Sea of Japan and the Japanese islands. It eventually fell into the Pacific Ocean, an estimated 950 miles from its launch site and approximately 300 miles east of the Japanese island of Honshu. Although U.S. officials remarked that the rocket had failed to place a satellite into orbit around the Earth, many observers speculated that the launch was meant to convey North Korea's capability of developing a missile that could reach the territory of its adversaries, such as South KOREA, JAPAN and even the U.S. In the 2000 presidential election, Republican candidate George W. BUSH repeatedly warned of the danger represented by this missile, and pledged that the development of a NATIONAL MISSILE DEFENSE system would become a top priority if he were elected president. Since the Taepo Dong's brief voyage, the North Korean government has repeatedly hinted that if Washington wants it to halt development of these missiles (which might be sold to other states such as Pakistan), the U.S. would have to pay North Korea at least $500 million a year to compensate it for the loss in revenue from rocket sales.

Taft, Robert Alphonso (*1889–1953*) U.S. senator, son of President William Howard TAFT. Robert Taft practiced law in Ohio and served in the state legislature. He was elected to the U.S. Senate in 1938. A foe of big government, he opposed F. D. ROOSEVELT on a number of his programs and became the leader of the conservative Republicans. His influence in Congress was so great that he blocked many of President Harry S. TRUMAN's FAIR DEAL measures, turning Truman into an unforgiving foe. Although he was an isolationist before WORLD WAR II, Taft favored the UNITED NATIONS. He was coauthor of the TAFT-HARTLEY ACT, regulating labor practices—considered his principal legislative accomplishment. Taft opposed U.S. entry into the NORTH ATLANTIC TREATY ORGANIZATION (NATO). He considered the Truman administration to be soft on communism and supported the early investigations of Senator Joseph McCARTHY concerning communist infiltration into government. Taft was so thoroughly in tune with his party's line that he became known as "Mr. Republican." He unsuccessfully sought the Republican nomination for president in 1940 and in 1948.

In 1952 he was considered to be the most likely Republican nominee for the office. However, the candidacy of Dwight D. EISENHOWER brought on a long struggle with Taft supporters that almost split the party. After losing the nomination of 1952 to Eisenhower, he loyally supported the Republican ticket. Taft became the majority leader in the Senate and worked closely as an Eisenhower adviser. Some authorities consider Robert Taft to have been one of the most influential senators in U.S. history.

Taft, William Howard (*1857–1930*) Twenty-seventh president of the UNITED STATES and 10th chief justice of the U.S. Supreme Court. Upon graduation from Yale in 1878, Taft attended Cincinnati Law School and took a law degree in 1880. He began the practice of law in Cincinnati and almost immediately took an active part in local Republican politics, holding several minor public offices before being appointed to serve on the superior court of Ohio (1887–90). In 1890 his selection by President Benjamin Harrison as U.S. solicitor general brought him into national political prominence.

Beginning in 1892, he was presiding judge of the sixth federal circuit court of appeals and spent eight years on that bench. He gained a reputation as serving conservatively but effectively in the post. Although considered antilabor, his decisions were based on what he thought were the proper limits of labor actions, and he opposed such practices as secondary boycotts and violence.

In 1900, as president of the U.S. commission to the PHILIPPINES, he began at once to organize an efficient civilian government there, continuing his effective administration when he became the first U.S. governor of the Philippines. He was particularly successful in improving relations between the Philippine people and the United States. In 1904 President Theodore

William Howard Taft, 27th president of the United States and chief justice of the Supreme Court (LIBRARY OF CONGRESS, PRINTS AND PHOTOGRAPHS DIVISION)

ROOSEVELT appointed Taft secretary of war, and they became close friends, with Taft as one of the president's most cherished advisers. He was a prime mover in the organization of the PANAMA CANAL construction.

Personally chosen by Roosevelt as his successor, Taft had little difficulty in the election of 1908. The parcel post system, the postal savings bank and the Department of Labor were among the innovations of his administration. Principal accomplishments were a trade agreement with Canada and arbitration treaties with France and Britain. However, the Senate failed to ratify any of these. His antitrust actions were more numerous than Roosevelt's, but failed to attract much attention. Increasingly attuned to the conservative wing of the REPUBLICAN PARTY, he approved the Payne-Aldrich Tariff Act of 1909, which made few concessions to tariff reduction, because Taft felt it was the best politically possible act. But this angered the Progressive Republicans, and his growing conservatism led him to fall out of favor with Theodore Roosevelt. Roosevelt fought Taft for the Republican presidential nomination in 1912. Failing to get the nod, which went to Taft, Roosevelt organized his own Progressive Party (popularly called the Bull Moose Party) and ran for president. The Republican Party was split, and the Democrats won one

of the closest elections in American history. Taft retired to private life, teaching law at Yale University.

In 1921 he was appointed to the post of chief justice of the Supreme Court by President Warren G. HARDING. He made substantial contributions to the administrative procedures of the Court, inaugurating methods that managed to eliminate the backlog of cases on the docket. In 1925 he was instrumental in the passage of the Judges' Act. This permitted the courts more discrimination in accepting cases.

One of his important opinions came in *BAILEY V. DREXEL FURNITURE CO.* (1922), in which he concurred with the majority that Congress had exceeded its authority to the extent of a loss of state sovereignty. In *Adkins v. Children's Hospital* (1923), he demonstrated his more liberal side, upholding a women's minimum wage law in the District of Columbia. His majority opinion in *Myers v. United States* (1926) clarified and extended the power of the president to remove executive officeholders. Taft resigned as chief justice early in 1930 due to poor health and died a month later. William Howard Taft is the only person in U.S. history to have served as both president and chief justice.

Taft-Hartley Act (Labor-Management Relations Act) *(1947)* Congressional act, sponsored by Senator Robert A. TAFT and Representative Fred A. Hartley. The Taft-Hartley Act regulates organized union activity. In 1935 Congress passed the NATIONAL LABOR RELATIONS ACT (NLRA), also known as the Wagner Act, which recognized the right of workers to bargain collectively through unions and also established the National Labor Relations Board to investigate "unfair labor practices" by employers. After World War II, a rash of major strikes turned both public and congressional opinion against organized labor. The result was the Taft-Hartley Act whose passage was vigorously opposed by the union movement. The Taft-Hartley Act, passed by Congress over President Harry S TRUMAN's veto, amended the NLRA by defining as prohibited such "union unfair labor practices" as the closed shop, which requires union membership as a precondition of employment, secondary boycotts of an

employer's suppliers or customers and jurisdictional strikes. The Landrum-Griffin Act (1959) imposed additional restrictions on union activities.

Tagore, Sir Rabindranath *(1861–1941)* Indian poet, story writer, philosopher, playwright, educator and statesman. Tagore, who won the NOBEL PRIZE for literature in 1913, was the greatest literary figure to have emerged from the Indian subcontinent in the 20th century. His prolific output included over 100 volumes of poetry, some 50 dramas, 40 works of fiction and numerous spiritual and philosophical studies emphasizing the age old wisdom of his native land. Tagore was born in Calcutta, the son of a wealthy Brahmin. In 1878 he went to study law in England, but then gave up his studies to return to India to write and to devote himself to the growing nationalist movement there. *Gitanjali* (1912), a volume of poems, won him international acclaim, and Tagore subsequently made lecture tours of both England and the U.S. In 1915 Tagore was knighted but surrendered the title to protest the British suppression of the Punjab riots. *Sadhana: The Realization of Life* (1914) is Tagore's best-known philosophical work.

Taiwan (Republic of China) Taiwan—comprised of the island of Taiwan (also known as Formosa), the P'eng-hu Lien-tao Islands and the islands of Lau Hsu, Lu Tao, Quemoy, Matsu and a few small islets—is located off the southeast coast of CHINA and covers a total land area of 13,965 square miles. Ruled by JAPAN from 1895 to 1945, Taiwan reverted to China after Japan's defeat in WORLD WAR II. Rebellion against Chinese rule was brutally suppressed in 1947. After communists occupied China's mainland in 1949, Generalissimo CHIANG KAI-SHEK (Jiang Jieshi) brought his defeated Nationalist KUOMINTANG forces to Taiwan. He established the Republic of China, which was officially recognized by the United States as the only legal Chinese government (1951). The Taiwan government represented China in the UNITED NATIONS until the People's Republic of China was given that right in 1971, thereby excluding Taiwan from the world body. Chiang Kai-shek's son, Chiang Ching-Kuo (Jiang Qinqguo),

Taiwan

CHINA

Tung-yin
Tao
Liang Tao
Pei-kan-t'ang Tao
Ma-tsu Tao
Pai ch'uan Liek Tao

East China Sea

P'eng-chia Yu

Tan-shui
Taipei
Chi-lung
T'ao-yuan   Pan-ch'iao
Wu-ch'iu Yu
Hsinchu   Ilan
Nei-wan
Su-ao
Miao-li
Feng-yuan
T'ai-chung
Chang-hua   Hua-lien
Chung-hsing Hsin-ts'un
Tou-liu   Ch'e-ch'eng
Chia-i
Hsin-ying
Ch'ih-shang
Ch'eng-kung-chen
T'ainan

Chin-men
Quemoy
Hsiao-chin-men Tao

Taiwan Strait

PESCADORES
(PENGHU)   Ma-kung
Pa-chao Yu   P'eng-Hu Tao
Ch'i-mei Yu

Pescadores Channel

T'aitung
P'ingtung
Kao-hsiung   Feng-shan
Fang-liao
Liu-ch'iu Yu   Ta-wu

Lu Tao

N

South China Sea

Heng-ch'un
Lan Yu

Luzon Strait

© Infobase Publishing

0   50 miles
0   50 km

---

became president in 1978 (reelected in 1984) and proceeded to open informal relations with the People's Republic in 1987–88. Along with Japan, HONG KONG and South KOREA, Taiwan has become a major force in international trade; consumer electronics products manufactured in Taiwan are exported to the U.S. and other countries. Kuomintang control ended with the 2000 election of Democratic Progressive Party presidential candidate Ch'en Shui-pien (Chen Shui-bian). President Ch'en survived an assassination attempt on the eve of his reelection in 2004. Tension between China and Taiwan still run high, with Taiwan condemning a new Chinese law in 2005 that would give China the right to invade if Taiwan declares independence.

Tajikistan Territory in Central Asia under Russian (1876–1917) and Soviet (1921–91) control, before becoming an independent republic (1991–). By 1876 the territory of modern-day Tajikistan had come under the control of the Russian Empire. After the first Russian Revolution of 1917, the TAJIK inhabitants of the region enjoyed a brief period of independence. However, the Bolshevik forces that seized control of Russia in November 1917 fought and eventually subdued small Tajik rebel bands to gain control of parts of Central Asia.

By 1921 the Bolshevik state had incorporated the Tajik region, along with KYRGYZSTAN, UZBEKISTAN and parts of TURKMENISTAN and KAZAKHSTAN, as the new Turkistan Autonomous Soviet Socialist Republic (ASSR), which in 1922 was one of several regions incorporated into the UNION OF SOVIET SOCIALIST REPUBLICS (USSR). In theory the Tajik region obtained greater autonomy through its 1924 designation as the Tajik ASSR (a component of the Uzbek Soviet Socialist Republic) and its 1929 advancement to independent SSR status. However, only members of the Russian controlled Tajikistan Communist Party could hold positions in government, thereby ensuring Moscow's total control of all governmental activities in Tajikistan.

The Russian domination of the republic increased under the rule of Joseph STALIN, who in the 1930s purged the Tajikistan Communist Party of all indigenous leaders in order to assure the party's unwavering allegiance to his rule. Stalin also forced the region's small farms into collectivization and began efforts to develop the SSR's vast aluminum reserves by establishing a mine and refinery at the city of Tursunzoda.

At the end of Soviet leader Mikhail GORBACHEV's policy of GLASNOST, or "openness," during the second half of the 1980s, Tajik leaders succeeded in winning the designation of the Tajik language as the official language of the republic. The legislature of the Tajik SSR, the Tajik Supreme Soviet, announced in August 1990 that the republic was sovereign and did not recognize the laws emanating from the USSR. In November the Tajik Supreme Soviet elected the head of the Tajikistan Communist Party, Qahhor Mahkamov, as the president of the republic.

Although Mahkamov was initially popular among some Tajik nationalist circles, his support for the abortive coup against Gorbachev in August 1991 led to his resignation that month. The following month, the Tajik SSR joined the other SSRs in declaring its full independence from Moscow and became the independent Republic of Tajikistan. In November 1991 Rahmon Nabiyev became the country's first popularly elected president. Despite its newfound political liberty, Tajik leaders sought to retain political and economic links with its former fellow SSRs, and joined the COMMONWEALTH OF INDEPENDENT STATES (CIS), a confederation of SSRs formed on December 8, 1991, to ensure political, economic and military cooperation among some of the newly independent republics of the former Soviet Union.

	TAIWAN
1945	After Japan's defeat Taiwan reverts back to China.
1947	(February) Taiwanese revolt against Chinese Nationalist rule is crushed.
1949	The Nationalist Kuomintang forces flee to Taiwan and establish the Republic of China under Chiang Kai-shek; Chiang establishes martial law and bans other political parties.
1951	(January) U.S. announces that it will recognize only Taiwan as the legal representative of China.
1971	UN General Assembly votes to unseat Taiwan and replace it with the People's Republic of China.
1975	Chiang Kai-shek dies and his son, General Chiang Ching-kuo, succeeds him.
1979	(January 1) U.S. announces its recognition of the People's Republic of China and that it is terminating its mutual defense treaty with Taiwan; (April) U.S. passes an act providing for Taiwan security in absence of diplomatic relations.
1986	(September) The Democratic Progress Party is formed in contravention of martial law.
1987	(July) Chiang announces the replacement of martial law by a new national security law.
1988	(January) Chiang Ching-kuo dies and is succeeded by Lee Teng-hui, his vice president—the first native Taiwanese to be appointed head of state.
1989	(December) In national elections the Nationalist Kuomintang Party suffers its first electoral defeat to the Democratic Progress Party.
1990	(March) Amid protest, President Lee, the only official candidate, is reelected for a six-year term by the National Assembly.
1991	Lee Teng-hui declares an end to the civil war with the People's Republic of China; the Kuomintang Party (KMT) wins a landslide victory in elections to parliament.
1996	Lee Teng-hui is elected president in the first democratic election for the office.
2000	The KMT candidate is defeated in a presidential election; Democratic Progressive Party presidential candidate Chen Shui-bian is elected.
2001	Taiwan test fires Patriot antimissile defense system bought from the U.S., as mainland China carries out military exercises simulating an invasion of the island; the 50-year ban on trade and investment with the PRC is lifted; the KMT Party loses its parliamentary majority for the first time.
2002	Taiwan officially enters the World Trade Organization, a few weeks after the PRC.
2004	President Ch'en Shui-pien wins a second term by a narrow vote following an apparent assassination attempt on the eve of the vote.
2005	Taiwan condemns a new Chinese law giving Beijing the legal right to use force should Taipei declare formal independence; Nationalist (KMT) Party leader Lien Chan (Lian Zhan) visits the PRC for the first meeting between Nationalist and Communist leaders since 1949; a constitutional reform allows amendments to be put to a referendum; the PRC protests that it will make it easier for activists to promote independence.

Antigovernment protests erupted in Dushanbe in March 1992. Tajik troops opened fire on a group of demonstrators and a civil war followed. In September 1992 the opposition, led by the Islamic Rebirth Party and the Democratic Party of Tajikistan, captured President Rakhman Nabiyev and forced him to resign. However, the Supreme Soviet, dominated by the Tajikistan Communist Party, abolished the office of president and made its leader, Imomali Rahmonov, the de facto leader of Tajikistan. In December 1992 troops loyal to Rahmonov expelled opposition forces of the

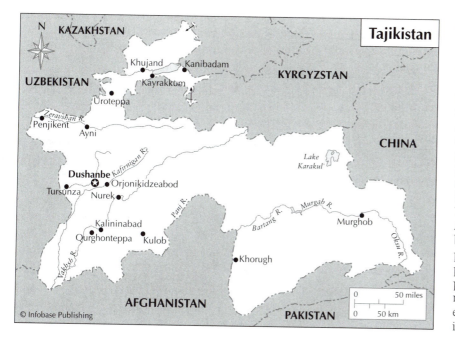

Tajikistan

Popular Democratic Army (PDA) from their base in Dushanbe to AFGHANISTAN and instituted a wave of repression in the country. Rahmonov eventually persuaded CIS member states to help bring peace to the region by dispatching a multinational peace keeping force to the Afghanistan-Tajikistan border in December 1993. In September 1994 these peace talks between Rahmonov and opposition leaders resulted in a cease-fire, and a month later a UN peacekeeping force replaced the CIS contingent in Tajikistan. In 1997 Rahmonov and Said Abdullo Nuri, the leader of the combined Islamic Tajik groups, agreed to a peace accord that permitted banned opposition parties to reenter Tajikistan politics and guaranteed these parties nearly a third of all high-ranking government appointments. But a low-intensity conflict continued between the

TAJIKISTAN

1921	Tajikistan becomes part of the Turkestan Soviet Socialist Autonomous Republic.
1924	The Tajik Autonomous Soviet Socialist Republic is formed.
1929	Tajikistan becomes a constituent republic of the Soviet Union.
1930	The collectivization of agriculture is completed despite widespread resistance.
1989	Tajik is declared official language.
1991	President Kakhar Makhamov is forced to resign after supporting failed anti-Gorbachev coup in Moscow. Independence is declared. Tajikistan joins the Commonwealth of Independent States. Rakhman Nabiyev is elected president.
1992	Violent demonstrations by Islamic and prodemocracy groups force Nabiyev to resign. Civil war between pro-Nabiyev and anti-Nabiyev forces claims 20,000 lives. Imomali Rahmonov, a pro-Nabiyev communist, takes over the government as president.
1993	Government forces regain most of the western part of the country. CIS forces are drafted to patrol border with Afghanistan, the base of the Islamic rebel forces.
1994	Cease-fire ends the civil war.
1997	Four-stage peace plan is signed.
1998	Rahmonov announces a general amnesty to opposition leaders in exile; rebels are crushed in the north.
1999	Rahmonov is reelected in an election that is widely criticized for fraud.
2003	A referendum gives Rahmonov the ability to run again for two more seven-year terms as president.
2005	The ruling party wins an overwhelming victory. International observers report possible voting fraud.

government and radical Islamic groups. A referendum in 2003 allowed President Rahmonov two consecutive seven-year terms, and the ruling party won the 2005 elections by a significant margin. Both votes were criticized as being fraudulent.

Tajiks The dominant ethnic group in TAJIKISTAN. Composing approximately 65 percent of the state's population, the Tajiks are descendents of Indo-European tribes. The Uzbeks, the second most populous ethnic group within Tajikistan, are of Turkic heritage. Tajiks and Uzbeks both practice the Sunni branch of Islam. During the period of Soviet rule (1921–91), Soviet officials attempted to reduce the Tajiks' cultural identity through encouraging increased immigration of Russian peoples to Tajikistan and by suppressing the Tajik language.

Since obtaining their independence from the Soviet Union in September 1991, Tajiks have generally split into three ideological camps. The first camp is composed of individuals who espouse a form of reactionary and authoritarian neocommunism, and have been led by such men as Qahhor Mahkamov, who was Tajikistan's president in 1990 and 1991, and Imomali Rahmonov, who has led the country since September 1992. The second faction consists of those Tajiks who seek the establishment of a Western-style democracy in their country. The third contains those espousing the establishment of a version of ISLAMISM and seeks to ensure that SHARIA—or Islamic law—becomes the law of the land. In the civil war that raged from 1992 to 1998, the Russian government began to express concerns that some of the more extreme Islamists, represented by such groups as the United Tajik Opposition (UTO), were receiving support from the Islamic fundamentalist group the TALIBAN that had seized power in Afghanistan in 1996.

Takeshita, Noboru (*1924–2000*) Prime minister of Japan from late 1987 until his resignation in mid-1989, Takeshita came from the affluent family of a sake brewer in the Shimane prefecture, near the Sea of Japan. He attended Waseda University in Tokyo and in 1944 took a course in KAMIKAZE pilot training; before he finished it, the war was over. In 1951 he was elected to a seat in the local assembly and in 1958 became an LDP member of the national house of representatives. Known since his youth for an ability to compromise, Takeshita began to move up in the party hierarchy and held a number of government posts. He was Eisaku Sato's chief cabinet secretary in 1971, and twice he served as minister of finance (1979–80, 1982–86). In July 1986 Takeshita became secretary-general of the LDP, and a year later he formed his own faction, which superseded the Tanaka faction. In October 1987 he was elected the 12th president of the LDP, and in November 1987 he became Japan's 17th postwar prime minister.

Tal, Mikhail Nakhemyevich (*1936–1992*) Soviet chess player. Born in Latvia, he won his first Soviet chess championship in 1957, winning it again in 1958, 1967, 1972, 1974 and 1978. In 1960 he defeated BOTVINNIK to become world chess champion, the youngest man to hold the title (Gary KASPAROV broke the record 25 years later). Despite ill health brought on by kidney problems, Tal won a reputation for his quickness, confidence, love of complexity and crushing, aggressive game.

Talaat, Mehmed (*1874–1921*) Turkish statesman. Born in Salonika (now Thessaloniki, Greece), Talaat worked as the chief clerk at the Salonika post office. There he formed the "Society [later Committee] of Union and Progress" together with other opponents of the reactionary regime of Sultan ABDUL HAMID II. This society soon recruited army officers who led the YOUNG TURK rebellion in 1908. Always favoring nationalism over liberalism, Talaat, with the army generals ENVER BEY and Ahmed DJEMAL, dominated Turkish politics until Turkey's defeat in WORLD WAR I (1918). He also served as the interior minister during World War I.

Taliban An Islamist movement that ruled AFGHANISTAN from 1996 to 2001. Created in the early 1990s in the southwestern Afghan city of KANDAHAR by Mullah Mohammad OMAR, an Islamic cleric, the Taliban inserted itself into the Afghani civil war of 1992–96. The young religious zealots of the Taliban vowed that once they gained control of the country, they would restore peace through a strict enforcement of SHARIA, or Islamic law. Omar and his associates reportedly received moral and financial support from several Pakistan-based MADRASSAS, or Islamic schools, that espoused ISLAMISM. In 1994 the Taliban began to consolidate its hold on the Kandahar province and gained many admirers among the dominant PASHTUN ethnic group in Afghanistan. By September 1995 it had achieved control over the northwestern province of Herat, and began to expand into the interior of the country. In September 1996 Taliban military units entered the Afghan capital of Kabul, where they toppled the government of President Burhanuddin RABBANI. Rabbani and his defense minister, Ahmed Shah MASOOD, regrouped in the northeast corner of the country and formed the NORTHERN ALLIANCE—a coalition of anti-Taliban forces. The governments of PAKISTAN, SAUDI ARABIA and the UNITED ARAB EMIRATES promptly recognized the Taliban as the official government of Afghanistan. By 1998 the Taliban had gained control of 90 percent of the country.

Once in power, the Taliban fulfilled its pledge to make sharia the law of the land. Women were required to wear a burka, a garment that completely covered them from view, and were severely restricted in their ability to move freely in public. Men were forbidden to shave their beards, and were required to dress according to the dictates of the Taliban's version of sharia. The application of sharia even extended to inanimate objects, as evidenced by the Taliban's destruction of two 1,500-year-old Buddha statues, located in Bamiyan province 150 miles from Kabul in March 2001. The Taliban also developed a close relationship with the Islamic terrorist group AL-QAEDA. The Taliban permitted this group to establish camps in rural eastern Afghanistan to train Muslim men for holy war against the West. In 1998 after determining that al-Qaeda was behind two terrorist bombings of U.S. embassies in KENYA and TANZANIA, U.S. ships in the Persian Gulf launched several cruise missiles against these al-Qaeda facilities. Three years later U.S. Intelligence confirmed that al-Qaeda militants had planned and executed the terrorist attacks on the United States on SEPTEMBER 11, 2001. U.S. president George W.

BUSH demanded that Mullah Omar and the Taliban hand over all al-Qaeda leaders, in particular the head of the group, Osama BIN LADEN, for trial in the U.S. When the Taliban refused to surrender and expel all al-Qaeda officials, U.S. forces invaded Afghanistan and removed the Taliban from power in October 2001. Although some Taliban and al-Qaeda leaders were killed or captured, both Mullah Omar and Osama bin Laden escaped and went into hiding along the Afghanistan-Pakistan border.

Taliesin Frank Lloyd WRIGHT home near Spring Green, Wisconsin; designed by him to follow the contour of a hill. It was built of brown stucco and limestone, quarried nearby. Wright called it "an example of the use of native materials and the play of space relations, the long stretches of low ceilings extending outside over and beyond the windows, related in direction to some feature in the landscape." In later years the structure gave its name to and became a part of Wright's larger activities through his foundation and his Taliesin Fellowships for architectural apprentices.

talking pictures Generic label applied in the late 1920s to motion pictures with synchronized sound. Although there had been many earlier experiments in synchronizing sound to moving images—by recording sound either on cylinders (Edison's "Kinetophone") or on the film strip (Lee DE FOREST's "Phonofilm")—it was not until the introduction in 1926 of the WARNER BROS. "Vitaphone" process, a sound-on-disc method developed in association with Western Electric, that the "talkie" revolution really began. *Don Juan,* a John BARRYMORE swashbuckler with a synchronized sound background score, attracted only mild attention when it premiered in August 1926. But on October 6, 1927, Al JOLSON's *The Jazz Singer,* featuring a synchronized score and a handful of talking sequences, created a sensation. Within the next few months another Jolson vehicle, *The Singing Fool,* and the "all-talking" feature *The Lights of New York* convinced everybody that sound was no mere novelty but the next, inevitable step in the evolution of the industry.

Virtually overnight, every studio in America and abroad scrambled to retool their operations. Significantly, Warners was the only major studio to use the sound-on-disc system. Although the recorded sound quality was exceptionally good, there were problems. "We couldn't record loud sounds, for example," recalled Warners sound engineer Bernard Brown. "Our valve-springs would stick together and give us overload. Synchronization between projector and phonograph in the theaters was very tricky. And it was difficult to edit sound in wax."

Meanwhile, the other major studios in America and abroad considered several sound-on-film options. William FOX, Warner's most powerful rival, opted for a sound-on-film process called "Movietone," which derived from pioneering photoelectric technology by inventors Lee de Forest and Theodore Case. Like other sound-on-film systems, it recorded sound patterns on the edge of the film strip, scanned them during projection through a light-sensitive photoelectric cell and converted them into electric impulses—which were transformed back into sound waves and amplified with loudspeakers. Movietone was introduced throughout 1927–29 with a pioneering program of sound newsreels (such as a document of the LINDBERGH flight), numerous short musical subjects and its first all-talking feature, *In Old Arizona.* A new studio, RKO, was formed in 1929 to take advantage of RCA's "Photophone." In Europe, a German system, "Tobis-Klangfilm," became widely used.

Between 1928 and 1930 a smothering sea change swept over the motion picture. "King Mike," as the new technology was called, brought the once fluid and dramatic SILENT FILM to a grinding halt. Film crews buried themselves alive in stuffy, insulated sound studios. Noisy cameras (and their operators) disappeared into soundproof booths. Actors (newly imported from the Broadway stage) froze into static tableaux near the all-important fixed microphones. Dialogue seemed to die in this airless void. Some formerly successful superstars, like John Gilbert, failed in the new medium—a problem not of vocal quality but of distorting microphones. The mere novelty of sound quickly palled.

Not surprisingly, the talkies stirred up heated debate among artists, critics and viewers. While H. G. WELLS hailed them as the "art form of the future," G. B. SHAW sniffed that they were merely a regression to the theatrical past. Critic George Jean Nathan was merely gloomy, pronouncing the new talkies "cold corpses." But French filmmaker Rene CLAIR, for whom sound "had driven poetry off the screen," was also one of the handful of directors to demonstrate the real possibilities of sound-image combinations. His *Sous les Toits de Paris* (*Under the Roofs of Paris,* 1929) showed how sound could be recorded and mixed separately from the image montage.

In America that same year more breakthroughs came in the use of boom mikes, blimped cameras and multiple-channel sound mixing in early talkies like Victor Fleming's *The Virginian* and Rouben MAMOULIAN's *Applause.* And in an important 1928 manifesto Russian theoreticians Sergei EISENSTEIN and Vsevelod PUDOVKIN published their principles of asynchronous sound, describing the potentials of sound-image counterpoint. In practice and in theory, the talkies were here to stay.

Tallchief, Maria (*1925– *) American ballerina. Of American Indian descent, Tallchief danced with the Ballet Russe de Monte Carlo (1942–47), then with Ballet Society and NEW YORK CITY BALLET (1948–65). She was married to George BALANCHINE (1946–52) and became most closely identified with his ballets, creating roles in such works as *Firebird* (1948) and *Allegro brillante* (1956). As the principal ballerina, she was regarded as the most technically brilliant American-born ballerina of her time. She also appeared as a guest artist with other dance companies, and founded the Chicago City Ballet in 1981. Tallchief has continued to receive awards in recognition of her contribution to American ballet, including the Kennedy Center Honors in 1996 and the National Medal of the Arts awarded by the National Endowment for the Arts in 1999.

Talvela, Martti (Olava) (*1935–1989*) Finnish operatic bass. Talvela was considered one of the greatest interpreters of the title role in Modest Mussorgsky's *Boris Godunov*. The physically imposing Talvela appeared frequently at the Metropolitan Opera in New York City and at the Bayreuth Festival in Germany. He was elected director of the Finnish National Opera shortly before his death from a heart attack.

Tamayo-Mendez, Arnaldo (*1942– *) Cuban cosmonaut-researcher aboard *Soyuz 38* (September 1980). With fellow cosmonaut Yuri Romanenko, he spent eight days in space, seven of them linked with the Soviet *Salyut 6* space station and cosmonauts Leonid Popov and Valery Ryumin. Tamayo-Mendez was the first black and the first Hispanic to fly in space.

Tambo, Oliver (*1917–1993*) South African antiapartheid leader and head of the African National Congress (ANC) from 1967. Born in South Africa and educated at the University of Fort Hare, Cape Province, Tambo's political involvement in the protest against Apartheid began in 1944, when he and Nelson Mandela helped to found the ANC Youth League. In a legal partnership with Mandela from 1951 to 1960, Tambo was banned from attending ANC meetings from 1954 to 1956, when he was arrested on treason charges. The charges were dropped in 1957, and Tambo became deputy president of the ANC the following year. Tambo was again banned from attending meetings in 1959, went into exile in London in 1960 and was later based in Zambia. With Mandela's incarceration in 1964, Tambo became the foremost spokesman for the ANC, accepting no compromises in his demands for unambiguous majority rule in South Africa. Although the ANC formed alliances with the South Africa Communist Party, Tambo himself was not a member of the Communist Party. In December 1990, partially disabled from a stroke he suffered the year before, Tambo was allowed to return to South Africa. Tambo on several occasions addressed the United Nations, which referred to him as "the legitimate representative of South African people." His speeches and articles were collected in *Oliver Tambo Speaks: Preparing for Power* (1988). In 1993, two years after returning to South Africa, Tambo died from a stroke.

Tanaka, Kakuei (*1918–1993*) Prime minister of Japan. Tanaka became wealthy in his own construction company before being elected to the house of representatives (the lower house of the Diet, or parliament) in 1947. In 1972, after holding several cabinet and party posts, he was named president of the ruling Liberal Democratic Party (LDP) and prime minister of the nation. Two years later, Tanaka was forced to resign from office after being accused of accepting approximately $2 million in bribes from the Lockheed Corporation in exchange for arranging the purchase of that company's planes for All Nippon Airways. In 1976, despite his indictment on the charges, Tanaka and his codefendants were reelected to the Diet; throughout his long trial the ex-premier remained one of the most powerful politicians in Japan, leading the largest faction within the LDP. Convicted in 1983, he was sentenced to four years in prison and fined $2 million. In 1985 Tanaka suffered a stroke, and in 1989 he announced his retirement from the Diet. In December 1993 Tanaka died of pneumonia.

Tandy, Jessica (*1909–1994*) British-born American stage and film actress. Tandy enjoyed a long and distinguished stage career, the highlight of which was her Broadway triumph as Blanche du Bois in the premiere of *A Streetcar Named Desire* (1947) by Tennessee Williams. In later years she enjoyed equal success in films with acclaimed roles in *Cocoon* (1985) and, most notably, *Driving Miss Daisy* (1989), for which she won an Academy Award as Best Actress. Tandy made her stage debut in London in 1927 and her Broadway debut in 1930. She starred in stage productions in both countries over the following decades. With her second husband, actor Hume Cronyn, she appeared in several plays, including *A Day By The Sea* (1955) by N. C. Hunter and *Three Sisters* (1963) by Anton Chekhov. With roles in *Fried Green Tomatoes* (1991), *Used People* (1992), and *Nobody's Fool* (1994), Tandy continued to appear in films until her death from ovarian cancer.

Tanganyika Former colony in East Africa; it now comprises the mainland portion of the nation of Tanzania. From 1891 until World War I Tanganyika was a German protectorate within German East Africa. British forces gained control of the area during the war; after the war the League of Nations assigned it to the United Kingdom as a mandate. Tanganyika gained full independence in 1961, and in 1964 merged with Zanzibar to form Tanzania.

Tanguy, Yves (*1900–1955*) French painter. Born in Paris, Tanguy spent his early years as a merchant seaman. A friend of Jaques Prevert, he was immersed in the artistic milieu of early 20th-century Paris, but he did not begin to paint until the day in 1923 when he saw a painting by Giorgio de Chirico in a gallery window. Self-taught, Tanguy went on to create a dreamlike personal vision, and in 1925 he joined the newly formed surrealist group (see Surrealism, Dada). His characteristic paintings are delicately tonal imaginary landscapes of indefinite space and mist in which strange biomorphic forms bend and float. Tanguy moved to the U.S. in 1939, settling in Connecticut (1942) and becoming a U.S. citizen in 1948.

tank Armored military vehicle, armed with a large shell-firing gun and machine guns; propelled on steel treads. Barbed wire and the machine gun gave the defense the advantage in World War I trench warfare. Cavalry, which in previous wars had been used for swift offensive thrusts, was rendered obsolete. The tank, the first offensive weapon capable of breaking through trench defenses, first saw action in September 1916 in the battle of the Somme. The tank came into its own with the German Blitzkrieg in World War II. German field marshal Erwin Rommel and U.S. general George S. Patton were brilliant exponents of tank warfare. The greatest tank battle in history occurred in 1943 at Kursk in the USSR, where the Soviets decisively defeated the Germans. Tanks have been used in virtually every major war since World War II, and have proved especially effective when used with air support in quick-moving desert warfare, as in the Six-Day War (1967) and the Persian Gulf War (1991).

Tan-Zam Railway Chinese-aided project of the mid-1960s to provide landlocked ZAMBIA with a rail route to the sea through TANZANIA, avoiding dependence on the white regime in RHODESIA during the period of UDI.

Tanzania (United Republic of Tanzania) On the east coast of Africa just south of the equator, Tanzania covers an area of 364,805 square miles that includes the island territories of Zanzibar, Pemba and Matia. Formerly known as **Tanganyika**, the country was a German colony from 1884 until the end of WORLD WAR I, when it became a British mandate under the LEAGUE OF NATIONS. After World War II, Tanganyika was designated a UNITED NATIONS Trust Territory under British control, until achieving independence in 1961. The island of Zanzibar united with Tanganyika in 1964 to form the United Republic of Tanzania. Under the leadership of its first president, Dr. Julius NYERERE (1962–85), Tanzania supported the liberation movements of other countries in southern Africa and repulsed an invasion by UGANDA in 1978, maintaining armed forces in that country until 1981. After Nyerere's resignation in 1985, his successor, Ali Hassan Mwinyi, attempted to raise productivity and attract foreign investment and loans by dismantling government control of the economy. This policy continued under Benjamin

	TANZANIA
1961	Gains independence under Prime Minister Julius Nyerere; Louis Leakey finds oldest human bones.
1962	Nyerere elected first president of Republic of Tanganyika by overwhelming majority of population.
1964	Sultan of Zanzibar deposed and republic proclaimed; Zanzibar Act of Union with Tanganyika formally creates Tanzania.
1978	Uganda President Idi Amin's forces invade Tanzania; Tanzania pushes back Ugandan forces and, in turn, invades Uganda, remaining until Amin regime overthrown.
1980	Nyerere is reelected president (from which post he will retire in 1985); Zanzibar granted new constitution under which it will elect own president.
1983	Human Resources Deployment Act authorizes government to round up vagrants, unemployed people, and resettle them forcibly in productive sectors.
1989	Bans trade in ivory.
1990	Julius Nyerere steps down as chairman of the CCM party to be succeeded by Mwinyi.
1992	Opposition parties are legalized.
1993	Regional parliaments for Zanzibar and mainland Tanzania are created.
1994	Tutsi-Hutu violence in Rwanda leads to about 700,000 refugees fleeing to Tanzania.
1995	The ruling CCM party wins 214 seats in the assembly in multiparty elections; CCM's Benjamin Mkapa is elected president.
1998	Julius Nyerere dies.
2000	President Mkapa is reelected.
2001	Disturbances break out in Zanzibar, and the ruling CCM party in Tanzania and the Civic United Front, the main opposition party in Zanzibar, agree to form a joint committee to restore calm.
2002	Tanzania's worst train disaster with nearly 300 killed when a passenger train rolls into a freight train at high speed.
2004	The presidents of Tanzania, Uganda and Kenya sign an accord at Arusha to establish a customs union, which is meant to boost trade.
2005	Prime Minister Jakaya Kikwete is elected president.

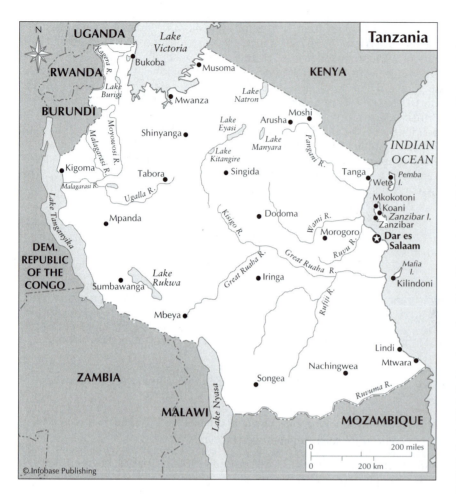

Mkapa, who was elected president in 1995. In 2003 nearly 300 people were killed in Tanzania's worst train disaster. Prime Minister Jakaya Kikwete won the 2005 presidential election, succeeding Mkapa.

Taoiseach Official title of the prime minister of IRELAND.

Tarbell, Ida *(1857–1944)* American journalist and biographer. Tarbell won renown in the 1900s as one of a group of socially conscious investigative reporters who became known—after a speech by President Theodore ROOSEVELT that bitterly attacked their alleged negative methods—as "muckrakers." Tarbell's chief work was a two-volume exposé on the monopolistic tactics of John D. Rockefeller and fellow oil industry magnates, *The History of the Standard Oil Company* (1904). By the 1920s, Tarbell had mellowed in her attitudes toward American business, and she wrote admiring biographies of entrepreneurs Elbert H. Gary (1925) and Owen Young (1932).

Tardieu, Jean *(1903–1995)* French playwright, poet and art critic. Tardieu was an influential force in both French theater and poetry for much of the 20th century. Raised in an artistic family, Tardieu studied at the Sorbonne in Paris. Although he wrote plays early on, Tardieu first achieved literary success with his poems. Volumes such as *The Hidden River* (1933), *Accents* (1939) and *Petrified Days 1942–1944* (1947–48) were marked by strong, pulsing rhythms and striking imagery that showed the influence of SURREALISM. During WORLD WAR II, Tardieu served in the French RESISTANCE. After the war he returned to playwriting. Tardieu's plays are generally short and resemble poetic monologues or dialogues rather than full-scale dramas. His spare language, black humor and absurdist themes have led critics to see Tardieu as an influence on the THEATER OF THE ABSURD. *Chamber Theater 1* (1955) and *Theater II: Plays for Acting* (1960) contain the best of his theatrical works. *About Painting That is Abstract* (1960) is his best-known work of art criticism.

Tarkenton, Fran(cis Asbury) *(1940–)* American football player. By the time he retired in 1978, Tarkenton held virtually every passing record in professional football. As quarterback for the University of Georgia, he led his team to an Orange Bowl in his senior year. He began his professional career with the Minnesota Vikings and completed 17 of 23 passes in his first start. A few years later, in 1967, he was benched in a coaching dispute and was traded to the New York Giants. Tarkenton led the Giants for five years and then returned to Minnesota for the final six years of his career. Over his career he gained 47,003 yards and completed 3,686 passes. He has gone on to a career in motivational speaking.

Tarkington, (Newton) Booth *(1869–1946)* Novelist and dramatist. Tarkington is best remembered for *Seventeen* (1916), portraying the joys and problems of adolescence. He also presented a cross-section of life in his hometown of Indianapolis in such works as the 1918 PULITZER PRIZE–winner *The Magnificent Ambersons* (1918). His best work is considered to be *Alice Adams* (1921), which brought him a second Pulitzer in 1921. Among his other honors were the gold medal of the National Institute of Arts and Sciences and the Theodore Roosevelt Memorial medal. He served in the Indiana house of representatives from 1902 to 1903.

Tarzan of the Apes The 20th century's best-known version of the "noble savage" myth, Tarzan may be rivaled only by SHERLOCK HOLMES and PETER PAN as modern literature's most popular and recognizable figure. The first four books in Edgar Rice BURROUGHS's 24-volume series—*Tarzan of the Apes, The Return of Tarzan, The Beasts of Tarzan* and *The Son of Tarzan* (published in hard cover between 1914 and 1917)—tell most of the story: A baby is born to an English couple stranded in Africa. After their deaths he is raised by a female ape, Kala, and becomes a great chief in the ape tribe. Upon learning of his human ancestry, he journeys to England, France and America in search of both a bride and an aristocratic title. Finally, he returns to his African estates in "Waziri Country" as an English nobleman with his wife and son. The character, known variously as "Tarzan" ("white-skin" in the ape tongue), "John Clayton" and "Lord Greystoke" by the English, and simply as "M. Jean C. Tarzan" by the French, first appeared in the pages of *The All-Story Magazine* (October 1912). Until Burroughs's death in 1950, scarcely a year passed without a new, ever more bizarre Tarzan adventure. Through two world wars he battled Germans, Japanese and communists. He discovered many lost races, hunted bizarre animals and even penetrated the Earth's core. Once, he auditioned—and was turned down—for the role of "Tarzan" in a HOLLYWOOD movie (*Tarzan and the Lion Man,* 1933). Burroughs chafed as the character assumed an independent life in the movies, radio, newspaper cartoon strips and elsewhere. The complex, intelligent man who had a good deal to love and hate about both civilization and the jungle was being reduced to an illiterate, barely articulate lout in a loin cloth. (However, Burroughs admitted that some of the early Johnny Weissmuller pictures for MGM, especially *Tarzan and His Mate* [1934] were rattling good adventures—and indeed they were.) Meanwhile, the growing suspicion that Tarzan was indeed a real person has been "confirmed" by author Philip Jose Farmer's biography *Tarzan Alive* (1972). Burroughs, more ambivalent on this point, simply wrote in 1927 that Tarzan "is an interesting experiment in the mental laboratory we call imagination."

Tashkent Agreement Temporarily successful mediation (January 1966) by Soviet premier KOSYGIN between prime ministers SHASTRI of INDIA and AYUB KHAN of PAKISTAN over the KASHMIR dispute, following armed conflict between the two states in 1965. (See also INDO-PAKISTANI WAR OF 1965).

TASS (Telegraphic Agency of the Soviet Union) The official Soviet news agency, founded in 1925. The agency dealt with news both at home and abroad. It was attached to the council of ministers, and its work was carefully controlled by the propaganda department. After the disintegration of the Soviet Union in 1991, TASS was renamed ITAR-TASS and became the national news agency of the Russian Federation.

Tate, Allen (*1899–1979*) American poet, critic and teacher. A graduate of Vanderbilt University in Tennessee (1922), he was associated with John Crowe RANSOM and Robert Penn WARREN. He helped found and edit the journal *The Fugitive* (1922–25) and was later editor of the influential *Sewanee Review.* With Ransom, he helped establish the NEW CRITICISM. He was president of the National Institute of Arts and Letters in 1968 and received its National Medal for Literature in 1976. His best-known poem, "Ode to the Confederate Dead," is widely considered a minor masterpiece.

Tati, Jacques (Jacques Tatischeff) (*1908–1982*) French actor, director and screenwriter. Tati is considered a comic master of the French cinema. As an actor he was best known as Monsieur Hulot, the bungling character he played in his 1953 film *Mr. Hulot's Holiday.* His film *Mon Oncle* won the 1958 ACADEMY AWARD for best foreign film. Tati once said that his films were meant to proclaim "the survival of the individual in a world that is more and more dehumanized."

Tatlin, Vladimir (*1885–1953*) Artist and founder of CONSTRUCTIVISM. After an unhappy childhood, at the age of 18 Tatlin ran away to become a sailor and traveled to Egypt. This had a profound influence on his art. After studying at the Penza School of Art and at the Moscow College of Painting, Sculpture, and Architecture, Tatlin worked as a free-lance painter, and sent works to the Union of Russian Artists and the Union of Youth exhibitions. He later contributed works to the KNAVE OF DIAMONDS (1913). In the same year, he journeyed to Berlin with some Ukrainian singers and played the accordion with them at the Russian Exhibition of Folk Art. With the proceeds, he went to Paris and visited Picasso. From 1913 to 1914, Tatlin began to explore the possibility of "painting relief" and became known as the founder of constructivism.

Tatum, Art (*1909–1956*) American jazz pianist. Tatum was one of the transcendent influences in the history of jazz. His technical accomplishments were unexcelled; his authority over the entire range of the keyboard, the delicate lightness of touch and capacity to spin out endless variations on the standard repertory of popular Broadway, Hollywood and Tin Pan Alley tunes made him the envy of his peers. He also was able to incorporate elements from the other great jazz pianists of his day—Thomas "Fats" WALLER, Earl "Fatha" HINES and Teddy WILSON—without substantially altering his virtuosic and swinging lyricism. Having established his reputation in an essentially solo context, in 1943 Tatum, influenced by the successful piano trio of Nat "King" COLE, formed his own trio with bassist Slam Stewart and guitarist Tiny Grimes (later replaced by Everett Barksdale); the trio format is the one that gave rise to perhaps his greatest improvisatory flights, though his extensive solo recordings for impresario Norman Granz in the 1950s are also of import. Tatum has been an important influence for such varied modern jazz stylists as Bud Powell, Lennie Tristano and Herbie HANCOCK.

Tauber, Richard (*1892–1948*) Austrian tenor. Born in Linz, Tauber studied at the Hoch Conservatory in Frankurt. Beginning his musical career as a conductor, he made his singing debut in Chemnitz, Germany, in 1913 as Tamino in *The Magic Flute.* A popular *bel canto* tenor, he appeared throughout Europe and made his American debut in 1931. Tauber was noted for his operatic roles, particularly in works by Mozart, for his masterful lieder interpretations and for his performances in various operettas, many of them by his friend the Austrian composer Franz LEHAR. He became famous for his role as Prince Sou-Chong in Lehar's *Das Land des Lachelns* (*The Land of Smiles*). Tauber fled Austria in 1938, settling in London and becoming a British subject in 1940. Today he is also remembered as the personification of Viennese elegance and charm.

Taussig, Helen Brooke (*1899–1986*) American physician. She is recognized as the founder of pediatric cardiology. In the 1940s, she and Dr. Alfred Blalock developed the successful "blue baby" operations, a surgical procedure that eventually saved the lives of thousands of children born with congenital heart defects. In 1959, she became the first woman to be made a full professor at the Johns Hopkins Medical School. In the early 1960s she played a key role in preventing the repetition in the U.S. of an epidemic of major birth defects in Europe among babies born to women who had taken the tranquilizer thalidomide. In 1965, she became the first woman to be elected president of the American Heart Association.

Taylor, A(lan) J(ohn) P(ercival)
(1906–1990) British historian. His most controversial book was *The Origins of the Second World War* (1961), in which he argued that HITLER had not been solely responsible for WORLD WAR II but had merely taken advantage of opportunities. He was the author of 29 books, including *The Struggle for Mastery in Europe, 1848–1918* and *English History, 1914–45* for the Oxford History of England series. He was well known as a columnist for the *Sunday Express.* Although he taught at Oxford for 25 years, he was never made a professor.

Taylor, Billy
(1921–) American jazz pianist and educator. As a prime exponent of the post-bebop modern piano style, Taylor (since 1952) has most often displayed his supple keyboard skills at the helm of various editions of the Billy Taylor Trio. As an educator committed to spreading the gospel of jazz, Taylor helped establish the model Jazzmobile program, which since 1965 has taken the sounds of jazz to New York City's inner-city youth. As a broadcaster, Taylor achieved fame as leader of an 11-piece jazz band for television's *David Frost Show* (1969–72); in 1981, he began hosting jazz features for CBS's *Sunday Morning* with Charles Kuralt. In 1975 Taylor earned a D.Mus.Ed. from the University of Massachusetts-Amherst; his *jazz Piano: History and Development* (1982), a standard text, is informed by scholarly precision and a wealth of experience going back to his days as house pianist at New York's fabled Birdland, where the young Taylor backed such jazz luminaries as Charlie PARKER, Dizzy GILLESPIE and Roy Eldridge. The pianist's efforts on behalf of "America's classical music" have made Taylor jazzdom's most visible and effective spokesman, both as a panelist for the National Endowment for the Arts and as a keynote speaker for the International Association of Jazz Educators.

Taylor, Charles
(1948–) President of LIBERIA (1997–2003). Born to an Americo-Liberian (a descendent of freed American slaves) and a member of the indigenous Gola people, Taylor received a B.A. from Bentley College in the United States. He returned to Liberia in 1980, just before President William Tolbert was assassinated during a military coup organized by Samuel K. Doe, a sergeant in the Liberian army. Doe appointed Taylor the head of the General Services Agency, where he oversaw government purchases. In May 1983 accusations that Taylor used his position to steal over $900,000 from the government's accounts prompted him to leave Liberia and seek refuge in the U.S. A year later a Boston court ordered his arrest and imprisonment while state and federal officials considered the Liberian government's extradition request. In September 1985 Taylor escaped from the prison, fled the U.S., and remained incognito for the next four years.

In December 1989 Taylor reappeared in Liberia at the head of a guerrilla band called the National Patriotic Front of Liberia (NPFL). Operating 100 miles from the Liberian capital, Monrovia, Taylor openly called for the overthrow of Doe's government. Strengthened by an influx of volunteers, the NPFL conducted hit-and-run attacks against Doe's forces. By 1990 the NPFL had seized control of the country and captured and executed Doe. The split between Taylor and a rival led to a five-year civil war that only ended with a UN-brokered peace settlement that organized presidential elections in 1997. Taylor handily won those elections with over three quarters of the popular vote and was sworn in as the new president of Liberia. As president, he came under increasing international condemnation for his willingness to sell munitions and weapons in exchange for diamonds to rebel forces in the bordering state of SIERRA LEONE. His willingness to aid these rebels, despite their brutal mutilation of civilians in Sierra Leone, led a UN war crimes tribunal to indict him in 2003. When anti-Taylor riots within Liberia intensified, Taylor accepted the offer of asylum in Nigeria and left the presidency, allegedly taking with him more than $3 million in government funds. Early in 2006 the Nigerian government turned him over to the UN war crimes tribunal for prosecution.

Taylor, Elizabeth (Elizabeth Cole)
(1912–1975) British novelist. Taylor worked as a governess and a librarian before her marriage in 1934. With her first novel, *At Mrs. Lippincote's* (1945), she established her reputation as a shrewd observer of the British middle class. Her other acclaimed novels, which include *A Wreath of Roses* (1950), *In a Summer Season* (1961), *Mrs. Palfrey at the Claremont* (1972) and the posthumously published *Blaming* (1976), portray the inward lives and longings behind her characters' facades. Taylor's short story collections include *Hester Lilly* (1954), *A Dedicated Man* (1965) and *The Devastating Boys* (1972).

Taylor, Elizabeth
(1932–) American film actress. Born in London to American parents, Taylor and her family settled in Los Angeles just before the outbreak of World War II. She had her first screen role at the age of 10 and became a star after her performance in *National Velvet* (1944). The violet-eyed beauty has played a wide variety of roles during her long career. Her most notable motion pictures include *Father of the Bride* (1950), *A Place in the Sun* (1951), *Giant* (1956), *Cat on a Hot Tin Roof* (1958) and *Butterfield 8* (1960, ACADEMY AWARD). A favorite of gossip columnists, Taylor is as celebrated for her private life as for her movie roles. She has been married seven times, twice to Richard BURTON, with whom she costarred in two of her most memorable films, *Cleopatra* (1963) and *Who's Afraid of Virginia Woolf* (1966, Academy Award). In the latter part of her career, she has worked mainly in the theater and in television. In recognition of her charitable endeavors, particularly her fundraising activities to combat AIDS, she was made a dame of the British Empire in 1999 and was awarded the Presidential Citizens Medal (2001) and Britannia Award for Artistic Excellence in International Entertainment (2005).

Taylor, Glen Hearst
(1904–1984) American politician. Taylor was U.S. senator from Idaho (1945–51) and vice presidential candidate on Henry

A. WALLACE's Progressive Party ticket (1948). Taylor first gained attention for his colorful show business act as "The Singing Cowboy" in the 1920s and 1930s. Elected to the Senate as a Democrat, he supported liberal domestic legislation and CIVIL RIGHTS and opposed big business and the TAFT-HARTLEY ACT. He also opposed President Harry S TRUMAN's foreign policy, especially Truman's policy toward the USSR. He denounced the TRUMAN DOCTRINE, the MARSHALL PLAN and the NORTH ATLANTIC TREATY ORGANIZATION and demanded an end to the COLD WAR. During the election of 1948, conservatives and liberals alike portrayed both Taylor and Wallace as dupes of the communists. Taylor's 1950 Senate reelection bid was defeated when he lost Idaho's Democratic primary. Taylor subsequently retired from politics and entered private business.

Taylor, Maxwell Davenport *(1901–1987)* Military officer. A 1922 graduate of the U.S. Military Academy at West Point, New York, he helped organize the first army airborne division, the 82nd, in the early years of WORLD WAR II. He was cited for bravery when he chose to cross enemy lines at great personal risk just 24 hours before the Allied invasion of Italy (1943) to discuss with Italian leaders the possible seizure of Roman airfields. He also led the 101st Airborne Division in assaults on Normandy and the Netherlands. In 1953 he served as commanding general of the 8th army and directed the UNITED NATIONS forces in KOREA; in 1955 was appointed army chief of staff; in 1962, chairman of the Joints Chiefs of Staff; and in 1964, U.S. ambassador to SOUTH VIETNAM. Urging President Lyndon B. JOHNSON to increase U.S. participation in the war with North Vietnam, he was one of the most important factors in expanding that unpopular conflict.

Taylor, Paul *(1930–)* American dancer, choreographer and company director. Taylor has performed with various modern dance companies, including those of Merce CUNNINGHAM (1953–54) and Martha GRAHAM (1955–61), creating roles in many of the latter's works, such as *Clytemnestra*

(1958) and *Embattled Garden* (1958). Since 1954 he has directed his own company, which has performed throughout the world. A major figure in modern dance in America, Taylor creates works characterized by a classical orientation, use of humor and often touches of the macabre. Some of the best-known of his over 50 works include *Three Epitaphs* (1956), *Aureole* (1962) and *Esplanade* (1975). He has received many awards including best choreographer at the Paris Dance Festival (1962) and L'Ordre des Arts et des Lettres (1984).

Taylor, Robert (Spangler Arlington Brugh) *(1911–1969)* American film actor. Born in Nebraska, Taylor studied at Pomona College in Southern California. His first screen appearance was in 1934, and he attained stardom after playing the lead in *Magnificent Obsession* (1935). Known mainly for his handsome profile but a versatile actor as well, Taylor starred in such vehicles as *His Brother's Wife* (1936), *Camille* (1937), *Yank at Oxford* (1938), *Waterloo Bridge* (1940), *Bataan* (1943) and *Quo Vadis* (1951).

Taylor, Telford *(1908–1998)* American attorney and author. After working in Franklin ROOSEVELT's administration, Taylor entered the army during World War II. Promoted to brigadier general, he was chief U.S. prosecutor during the NUREMBERG TRIALS of Nazi war criminals. After the war, Taylor taught law at Columbia University and Cardozo law schools and published a number of books, including *Nuremberg and Vietnam* (1970), in which he criticized U.S. policy in Southeast Asia; *Courts of Terror,* about Soviet Jews; and *Munich: The Price of Peace,* about the APPEASEMENT of HITLER.

Teagarden, Jack *(1905–1964)* Jazz trombonist, vocalist and big band arranger. Teagarden is renowned as one of the greatest JAZZ trombonists of all time. His trademark full-toned sound showed a marked BLUES influence. Teagarden began his career in the 1920s working as a sideman for numerous bands throughout the Southwest. He moved to New York in the late 1920s and began recording with various bands. In 1939, he formed his own big band, which had as its theme song

"I Gotta Right to Sing the Blues," a tune that Teagarden also recorded with the Benny GOODMAN big band. From 1947 to 1951, Teagarden toured with the Louis ARMSTRONG All-Stars. He remained active as a band leader and sideman until his death.

Teague, Walter Dorwin, Sr. *(1883–1960)* American industrial designer, one of the leaders in the development of the profession in the 1920s and the 1930s. Teague was a student at the Art Students League of New York before starting work as a professional illustrator. In 1927 his name was given to an Eastman KODAK representative as a possible source of some sketches for a name camera. Teague insisted on a far more thorough study of the project, leading to a long-standing relationship with Kodak and the launching of his own design firm. In his 1940 book, *Design This Day,* he outlined his philosophy relating traditional aesthetic theory to the concepts of MODERNISM as he had encountered it in Europe on a 1926 visit. Early work of the Teague office often combined a touch of ART DECO decorative form with straightforward functionalism. The famous Kodak Baby Brownie camera of 1935 was a simple molded box of black plastic (then a new material), but its rounded corners and parallel ribbing made it modernistic, to the delight of purchasers who made it an immense commercial success. Later designs for Kodak included the tiny Bantam Special (1936), a gleaming, streamlined miniature camera in black and polished aluminum, and the 620 Special, a larger roll film camera incorporating both a coupled range finder and a coupled exposure meter, a remarkable innovation in 1939. Work for other clients eventually included New Haven Railroad passenger cars, NEW YORK WORLD'S FAIR exhibits for Ford and U.S. Steel and a very visible standard service station design for Texaco. Teague came to be regarded as one of the four leaders of the industrial design profession along with Norman BEL GEDDES, Henry DREYFUSS and Raymond LOEWY. In 1944 he became the first president of the Society of Industrial Designers.

Teapot Dome Scandal In 1922, during the administration of President

Warren G. HARDING, Secretary of the Interior Albert FALL leased naval oil reserve lands at Teapot Dome, Wyoming, to oil producers Harry Sinclair and E. L. Doheny, without competitive bidding and after accepting loans of hundreds of thousands of dollars. Fall resigned in 1923 and joined Sinclair Oil. Indicted after a Senate investigation, in 1929 he was convicted of taking a bribe and imprisoned (1931–32). The event cast a continuing shadow on the memory of the Harding administration.

Teasdale, Sara (*1884–1933*) American poet. Excessively sheltered early in life by her parents, Teasdale published, while traveling with a chaperone, *Sonnets to Dues and Other Poems* (1907) and *Helen of Troy and Other Poems* (1911). These brought her some critical attention, and following her marriage in 1914 she broke away from her family to lead a more daring, although never entirely happy, life as a poet. She received the 1918 PULITZER PRIZE for *Love Songs* (1917), and she published several other collections before taking her own life.

Teatro Grottesco (Theater of the Grotesque) Italian theater movement. The Teatro Grottesco emerged during WORLD WAR I in an effort to lead Italian theater away from the grand rhetoric and unquestioning nationalism of then dominant Italian playwright Gabriele D'ANNUNZIO. The name *Teatro*

American poet Sara Teasdale. 1932 (LIBRARY OF CONGRESS, PRINTS AND PHOTOGRAPHS DIVISION)

Grottesco came from the subtitle of a 1916 play, *The Mask and the Face,* by the Italian playwright Chiarelli. Plays staged by the Teatro Grottesco questioned societal values and surface appearances. A leading playwright of the movement was Rosso di San Secondo.

Tebaldi, Renata (*1922–2004*) Italian opera singer. Tebaldi was regarded as an outstanding lyric and spinto soprano during the height of her career in the 1940s and 1950s. She gained national attention in Italy when she sang at a concert organized by Arturo TOSCANINI for the reopening of La Scala in 1946. In 1950 she made her La Scala opera debut in *Aida,* viewed as one of her finest roles. She sang in opera houses worldwide and made many excellent recordings before her retirement in the early 1970s. Other famous roles included Mimi in PUCCINI's *La Bohème,* Desdemona in *Otello* and the title roles in *Tosca* and *Madama Butterfly.* Tebaldi's famous rivalry with soprano Maria CALLAS was largely the creation of the press.

techno music A form of music that derives mainly from electronically synthesized sounds and percussion, techno initially emerged in the 1980s in Detroit, Michigan. Initially, techno soundtracks were played mostly at dance clubs and rave clubs, as well as on the *Midnight Funk Association,* a late-night music program broadcast on the Detroit radio station WJLB. Though it is unclear when the term *techno* was developed to describe the genre, the 1988 Virgin Records release of *Techno! The New Dance Sound of Detroit* marked the first time that a major recording label had identified the new branch of popular music. Techno has since proved popular in European and American markets and dance clubs, generating such number one singles as "Blue" by the band Eifel 66.

Tedder, Arthur William (first baron Tedder of Glenguin) (*1890–1967*) British air marshal. A career military man, Tedder fought in the infantry and the Royal Air Force (RAF) during WORLD WAR I. As chief of the British air forces in the Middle East from 1941 to 1943, he was instrumental in driving German forces out of Tunisia. Tedder was appointed commander in chief of Britain's Mediterranean Air Command in

1943. From 1943 to 1945 he was deputy commander of all the Allied invasion forces, giving valuable air support to the NORMANDY invasion and subsequent advances. The much-decorated strategist was raised to the peerage in 1946. In the postwar years he served as air chief of staff (1946–50) and became chancellor of Cambridge University in 1950. His memoirs, *With Prejudice,* were published in 1966.

Teheran Conference WORLD WAR II meeting held in Tehran (Teheran), Iran, from November 28 to December 1, 1943, by U.S. president Franklin Delano ROOSEVELT, British prime minister Winston CHURCHILL and Soviet premier Joseph STALIN and their staffs. The conference strengthened three-power ties and featured strategy talks regarding the conduct of the war in Europe, including plans for the Allied invasion of FRANCE. During the conference, Stalin again pledged to fight against JAPAN after the end of the conflict with GERMANY. The powers also agreed to guarantee an independent IRAN.

Teilhard de Chardin, Pierre (*1881–1955*) French Catholic theologian and paleontologist; one of the most unique thinkers among 20th-century theologians. After being ordained a Jesuit priest in 1911, Teilhard went on to earn a doctorate in paleontology from the Sorbonne. After a brief teaching stint at the Institut Catholique in Paris in the mid-1920s, he was ordered by his Jesuit superiors—who mistrusted his attempts to reconcile evolutionary theory and traditional theology—to refrain from teaching in France and to restrict himself to scientific writings only. Teilhard obeyed these restrictions, spending the bulk of his remaining years in China and there participating in the discovery of the paleontological remains of Peking Man. His influential theological works, such as *The Phenomenon of Man* (1955), were all published posthumously. In them, Teilhard expresses optimism for the survival of the human species and argues for regarding the planet Earth as worthy of holy reverence.

television Electronic communications medium that has had a profound effect on life in the 20th century. The first television system was patented by

Paul Nipkow in Germany in 1884. The first workable television set was produced by Scottish inventor John Logie BAIRD in 1926. In the U.S. General Electric began television tests that same year and in 1928 produced the first television play, *The Queen's Messenger*. During the 1930s great technological advances occurred: In the U.S. the RCA CORPORATION spent millions on research; a crude television service was developed in Germany; and in Great Britain a camera tube known as Emitron was developed. In 1937 the BBC produced the first outside broadcast—the coronation procession of GEORGE VI. NBC began experimental broadcasts in 1931 and in 1939 broadcast the opening of the NEW YORK WORLD'S FAIR. NBC was granted the first commercial television license in the U.S. in 1941. World War II interrupted the development of commercial television. In 1950 9 percent of U.S. households had a television; by 1960 87 percent owned a TV. Correspondingly, attendance at movies declined, RADIO lost listeners and libraries reported a drop in book circulation. The first communications SATELLITE, TELSTAR, was sent into orbit in 1962, allowing millions around the globe to witness the funeral of John F. KENNEDY via live TV and satellite in 1963. The ability of television to bring news, sports and entertainment events live to a worldwide audience has made the world in the 20th century a "global village." At the start of the 21st century, high-definition television (HDTV) and digital video recording devices such as TiVo supplanted satellite transmission at the vanguard of television technology, while cable companies such as Comcast began developing digital cable networks in order to keep pace with the proliferation of TV-based media now available to consumers.

Teller, Edward *(1908–2003)* Hungarian-American physicist. After completing his doctorate in physical chemistry at the University of Leipzig in 1930, Teller studied with Neils BOHR, the distinguished Danish physicist. He left Germany when the Nazis came to power and became an American citizen in 1941. During WORLD WAR II Teller worked on the MANHATTAN PROJECT, which developed the atomic bomb, and from 1949 to 1951

he was an assistant director of the science laboratory at Los Alamos, N.M. During the 1950s he taught physics at the University of California. In 1954 he became an associate director of the Atomic Energy Commission's Lawrence Livermore Laboratory in Livermore, California.

During the 1950s Teller became a leading scientific spokesman for the maintenance of U.S. atomic weapons superiority. He believed that American supremacy was the only means of countering what he viewed as an aggressive Soviet arms policy. Described by *Newsweek* as "the principal architect of the H-bomb," Teller was a leading advocate of that weapon's development. In the 1954 AEC security hearings, he testified against granting J. Robert OPPENHEIMER a security clearance, claiming that Oppenheimer's opposition to the H-bomb project had delayed its development. Teller opposed the three-year moratorium on atomic testing that ended in September 1961 when the USSR resumed atmospheric explosions, and he favored the renewed U.S. testing, which began later that month. Calling nuclear test ban negotiations "dangerous," he said they "have helped the Soviets" and "have impeded our own testing."

During the August 1963 Senate hearings on the NUCLEAR TEST BAN TREATY, Teller was the most influential scientist to testify against ratification. His principal objection was to the ban's prohibition of atmospheric tests, which were necessary for the further development of antiballistic missiles (ABMs). Teller feared that the Soviets had a lead in ABM production and that the treaty might enable them to increase that lead. Warning that current detection techniques would be ineffective for policing the agreement, Teller also believed that the treaty would inhibit the military's ability to respond in case of war since it stipulated that atomic weapons could be used only three months after repudiation of the agreement. Teller's views were rejected by Gen. Maxwell TAYLOR, Glenn SEABORG and other military and government officials who testified in support of the treaty. President KENNEDY rebutted many of Teller's objections in a news conference in late August and signed the treaty in October. In addition to his call for atomic

superiority, Teller believed that the threat of international communism required an aggressive American stance in other areas.

Telstar First privately owned communications satellite to orbit the Earth, it was built by the American Telephone & Telegraph Co. and its Bell Telephone Laboratories and blasted into orbit on July 10, 1962. A 170-pound, 34.25-inch-diameter sphere, it was launched from CAPE CANAVERAL by NASA in the nose of a three-stage booster rocket. Its orbit had an apogee of 5,636 miles, a perigee of 593 miles at an angle of 44.8° to the equator, with a period of 158 minutes. *Telstar I* had one transponder to receive and retransmit signals and was powered by over 3,500 solar cells on the outer part of the sphere and nickel-cadmium batteries in its interior. It ceased to operate on February 21, 1963, and was followed by *Telstar II*, which was launched later in 1963 and rendered inoperable in May 1965. Both *Telstar* satellites were capable of processing six telephone calls or one television channel. The first *Telstar* transmitted the first transatlantic TV broadcast, and the second transmitted the first such color-TV program. Both *Telstars* gathered important information on the effects of radiation on satellite communications.

Temin, Howard Martin *(1934–1994)* American molecular biologist. Temin's years of research into the two classes of viruses, those with DNA and those with RNA genes, led to his discovery in 1970 of the enzyme known variously as reverse transcriptase or RNA-directed DNA polymerase, which he deduced was capable of producing a sequence of viral replication outside of the Central Dogma of molecular biology, as it was then known. This reaction was also discovered independently by David BALTIMORE. For this, Temin and Baltimore shared the 1975 NOBEL PRIZE for physiology or medicine, along with Renato DULBECCO.

Temple, Shirley *(1928–)* American actress and diplomat. Born in Santa Monica, California, Shirley Temple became the most popular child star in HOLLYWOOD history. Her earliest work was in one-reel comedy shorts in 1931. Signed to a TWENTIETH CENTURY-

FOX contract after her role in the feature-length *Stand Up and Cheer* (1934), she quickly became the studio's biggest star. A talented singer, dancer and actress with blond ringlets, a sparkling smile and irresistible dimples, she cheered Depression-era audiences in such films as *Little Miss Marker* (1934), *The Little Colonel* (1935), *Captain January* (1936, in which she sang her trademark "On the Good Ship, Lollipop"), *Wee Willie Winkie* (1937) and *Rebecca of Sunnybrook Farm* (1938). She made several films in the 1940s, including *Since You Went Away* (1944), but could never recapture her earlier superstar status; Temple retired from the movies after *A Kiss for Corliss* (1949). As Shirley Temple Black (she married businessman Charles Black in 1950), she became active in Republican politics. She served as a delegate to the United Nations in 1969, was American ambassador to Ghana from 1974 to 1976 and was U.S. chief of protocol in 1976. Her autobiography, *Child Star,* was published in 1988; in 1989 she was named U.S. ambassador to Czechoslovakia. In 1998 Temple was one of the recipients of the Kennedy Center Honors.

Temple, William *(1881–1941)* British theologian and archbishop of Canterbury. Temple, whose father, Frederick Temple, also served as archbishop of Canterbury (1896–1902), was a highly influential figure in the religious life of Britain. Educated in philosophy at Oxford University, Temple was named bishop of Manchester (1921–29) and archbishop of York (1929–42) before becoming archbishop of Canterbury in the final years of his life (1942–44). As a Christian socialist with a widely respected pulpit, he helped attain greater respectability for the British LABOUR PARTY. In addition, his theological works, such as *Nature, Man and God* (1934) and *Christianity and the Social Order* (1942), were influential in bringing a broader, international ecumenism to the Anglican Church.

Ten Boom, Corrie *(1892–1983)* Dutch writer and religious activist. During WORLD WAR II Ten Boom and her family sheltered JEWS from the NAZIS in the NETHERLANDS. The Ten

Booms were credited with saving more than 700 Jews from German CONCENTRATION CAMPS; she herself was finally arrested and sent to a concentration camp. Her wartime experiences formed the basis for her coauthored best-selling book, *The Hiding Place* (1974), and a movie of the same name produced in association with the American evangelist Billy GRAHAM.

Tennessee Valley Authority (TVA) Independent federal agency established to control flooding, develop and promote navigation and produce electrical power along the course of the Tennessee River and its tributaries. First proposed in the 1920s as a solution to the problem of what to do with the wartime Muscle Shoals project in Alabama, it was redrafted and set up by President Franklin D. ROOSEVELT in 1933. Construction of the first project, Norris Dam on the Clinch River near Knoxville, was begun in the fall of that year. Unique among federal agencies because its headquarters are in the region instead of in Washington, D.C., it has jurisdiction over a drainage area of nearly 41,000 sq. mi., including parts of Tennessee, Kentucky, Virginia, North Carolina, Georgia, Alabama and Mississippi. An early model for other river development plans, the TVA system operates 32 major dams, 21 of them constructed by the TVA and the remainder purchased from, or operated for, private companies. The production and sale of electric power was highly criticized by privately owned power companies who charged that the TVA was exempt from taxation and not obligated to make a profit.

In 1960 the TVA was allowed to issue up to $750 million in bonds for its proposed power capacity increase in lieu of having to apply to Congress for appropriations. Along with dominating the economic life of the Tennessee Valley as far as power production (109.8 billion kilowatts were generated in 1974) and river traffic, the system has also been responsible for the establishment of recreational facilities and the control of malaria in the region, and has been involved in numerous land and wildlife conservation programs (1.5 million acres of land reforested by 1975).

Teresa, Mother (Agnes Gonxha Bojaxhiu) *(1910–1997)* Roman Catholic nun and missionary. Born in Skopje (then within the Ottoman Empire, now in Macedonia) of Albanian parents, Mother Teresa joined the Sisters of Loreto in 1922, studied English in Dublin and embarked for CALCUTTA, India, in 1929. There she taught high school until 1948 and became fluent in Bengali and Hindi. In 1946 she received "a call within a call" to leave the convent and "help the poor, while living among them." Two years later she received permission from the archbishop of Calcutta and began her work outside the convent, adopting a white sari for her habit and becoming an Indian citizen. In 1950 she started a new order, the Missionaries of Charity, whose vows included giving free service to the poorest of the poor. She established a home for the dying in 1954 and soon after founded an orphanage for abandoned children. Beginning in 1965 she opened centers, hospitals, schools and orphanages in many countries. In 1979 Mother Teresa was awarded the NOBEL PRIZE for peace. In 1990 she resigned temporarily as superior general of her order because of ill health, but resumed her activities soon thereafter. The Missionaries of Charity now numbers hundreds of sisters of many nationalities working throughout the world, and Mother Teresa is

Catholic nun and founder of the Missionaries of Charity Mother Teresa. 1979 (HULTON-DEUTSCH COLLECTION/CORBIS)

considered a model of selfless devotion to her fellow human beings.

Tereshkova, Valentina *(1937–)*

Soviet cosmonaut and the first woman to fly in space. Tereshkova, an accomplished parachutist, faced her mission with little training and considerable courage. On June 16, 1963, her tiny VOSTOK 6 capsule was lifted into orbit to the great roar of its boosters. There she spent three days circling the Earth, completing 48 orbits. In one mission she outshone all six American MERCURY astronauts who had flown up to that time, and her call sign "Chaika" ("Seagull") caught the imaginations of women everywhere whose vision encompassed more than traditional homemaking and motherhood. She made television broadcasts from space and kept in constant radio contact with Valery BYKOVSKY, who was flying *Vostok 5* at the same time. The American space program did not put a woman in space until June 18, 1983, a decision that brought criticism and charges of sexism. Ironically, the Soviets included only one other woman in their space program, Svetlana SAVITSKAYA, 1982 and 1984. In 2000 Tereshkova was presented with the Greatest Women Achiever of the Century award by the International Women of the Year Association.

Terkel, Louis "Studs" *(1912–)*

American journalist and writer. Born in New York City, Studs Terkel has been a sportswriter, actor, playwright and newspaper reporter. A superb interviewer, he is particularly noted for his oral histories of important eras in 20th-century America, including *Hard Times: An Oral History of the Great Depression in America* (1970) and *The Good War: An Oral History of World War II* (1986). Among Terkel's other books are *Division Street, America* (1966) and *Working People Talk About What They Do All Day and How They Feel About What They Do* (1974). A lively, street-smart, voluble man, he has become a familiar feature in the popular media, moderating his own radio and television shows and participating in numerous televised documentaries such as PBS's *The Civil War* (1990). Terkel received several awards commemorating his contributions to American

media, including the National Medal of Humanities (1997) and the Presidential National Humanities Medal (1999). Terkel's later publications include *Race: How Blacks and Whites Think and Feel About the American Obsession* (1992), *Coming of Age: The Story of Our Century by Those Who've Lived It* (1995) and *Will the Circle Be Unbroken: Reflections on Death, Rebirth, and Hunger for a Faith* (2001).

Terry, Luther Leonidas *(1911–1985)*

American physician. As surgeon general of the U.S. from 1961 to 1965, Terry was responsible for the historic government report linking cigarette smoking to lung cancer and other diseases. Upon its release in 1964, the report bolstered antismoking efforts throughout the world. In 1965, at Terry's urging, Congress introduced the requirement that cigarette packages carry a health warning. Six years later he helped obtain a ban on cigarette ads on radio and television.

Terry-Thomas (Terry Thomas Hoar Stevens) *(1911–1990)*

British comedian and actor. Terry-Thomas specialized in playing slightly demented English dandies and cards, first winning fame in Britain in the television series *How Do You View?* in the 1950s. His gap-toothed grin, mustache, cigarette-holder and upper-class accent became his trademarks. He later moved to HOLLYWOOD and starred in films such as *It's a Mad, Mad, Mad, Mad World* (1963), *Those Magnificent Men in Their Flying Machines* (1965) and *How to Murder Your Wife* (1965).

Tertz, Abram See Andrei SINYAVSKY.

Test Ban Treaty See NUCLEAR TEST BAN TREATY.

"test-tube babies" See IN VITRO FERTILIZATION.

Tetley, Glen *(1926–)*

American dancer and choreographer. Tetley has danced with a number of ballet and contemporary dance companies, including those of Hanya Holm (1946–51), Martha GRAHAM (1958) and AMERICAN BALLET THEATRE (1960). In 1962 he choreographed his first dances, most notably *Pierrot Lunaire,* for his own

group. Then in 1964 he joined the Netherlands Dance Theatre as dancer/choreographer, eventually becoming its artistic adviser (until 1970). He succeeded John CRANKO as director of the Stuttgart Ballet in 1974, creating one of his most popular ballets, *Voluntaries,* for that company in honor of Cranko. He resigned the directorship in 1976 and continued to work as a freelance choreographer until becoming the artistic adviser for the National Ballet of Canada in 1987. Tetley continued to direct and choreograph ballets throughout the 1990s, including *Dialogues* (1991), which premiered at the Kennedy Center, *Oracle* (1994), for the National Ballet of Canada and the sextet *Amores* (1997), a tribute to the ballerina Darcey Bussell.

Tet Offensive

"Tet" is a traditionally celebrated Vietnamese holiday. It had been customary during the VIETNAM WAR to observe a cease-fire during the Tet holidays, and 1968 was no exception; in fact the NATIONAL LIBERATION FRONT (North Vietnam's front organization for the VIET CONG) had publicly called for scrupulous observance of the Tet cease-fire. While intelligence reports had been received that the North Vietnamese Army (NVA) and Viet Cong might take advantage of the holiday to launch an attack, there was no feeling that a major offensive was imminent. On January 30, 1968, the Tet holiday began, but shortly after midnight several cities were attacked and by noon on January 30 all U.S. units were placed on maximum alert. At 3:00 A.M. on January 31 the North Vietnamese and Viet Cong launched what has become known as the Tet Offensive. Simultaneous attacks were made on Hue and other major cities, towns and military bases throughout Vietnam. One assault team got within the walls of the U.S. embassy in Saigon before they were destroyed. Television footage of this attack received widespread attention in the U.S. Initial media reports stated that U.S. and South Vietnamese Army forces had been surprised and defeated.

But it was not the U.S. that was defeated on the battlefield. It was the North Vietnamese army and especially the Viet Cong. Their "general offensive and general uprising" had been a tactical disaster. Not only had their military forces been resoundingly defeated, but their ideological illusion that the South Vietnamese people would flock to their banner during the "general uprising" proved false. From Tet 1968 on, the NVA realized it would not be able to attain its political objective with guerrilla forces, and increasingly the war became an affair for the regular forces of the NVA. But if the U.S. had won tactically, it suffered a fatal strategic blow. False expectations had been raised at home that the war was virtually won. Public opinion had turned against the war in October 1967, and the events of Tet confirmed that disenchantment. The Tet Offensive cost the government and the military the confidence of the American people. Not only did the American public turn further against the war, but the commander-in-chief, President Johnson, seemed psychologically defeated by the Tet Offensive. Challenged within his own party for renomination and with public support slipping away, he thereafter publicly announced that he would not seek reelection. Although the war continued for another seven years, the war for the support of the American people was lost on January 30, 1968. From that point on, the problem was not how to win the war but how to disengage.

Texaco Star Theater Popular variety show in the early years of American television. During its peak years on NBC—from June 8, 1948, to the end of the 1951 season—it became a national obsession as millions clustered around any available set on Tuesday evening to watch the clownish Milton BERLE ("Uncle Miltie") and his burlesque antics. Relying on his vaudeville experience, Berle helped launch the standard television variety formula. "I suggested to the powers at Texaco a show in which I would serve as host," he writes in his autobiography, "do some of my routines and introduce guest stars, who would do their specialities, and then I would mix it up with them for some comedy." The show originated live from Studio 6B in the RCA Building at Rockefeller Center in New York City. Four men dressed in Texaco uniforms stepped in front of a curtain, singing "Oh, we're the men of Texaco/We work from Maine to Mexico," after which

Berle emerged in an outlandish costume (a pilgrim, a caveman, frequently a woman) and presided over a divine kind of madness—taking pratfalls with the acrobats, singing silly duets with guests like Elvis PRESLEY and dodging hundreds of thrown pies and squirting seltzer bottles. A Nielsen rating in late 1950 revealed that a little over 60 percent of TV-equipped homes were tuned in to the show, and historian Arthur Wertheim credits a 1950–51 boom in the sale of TV sets to the show's incredible popularity. As early as 1952 the format began to change, Berle's aggressive persona was softened and ratings began to drop. In the mid-1950s Berle was replaced as host by a succession of entertainers, like Jimmy DURANTE and Donald O'Connor. The show finally succumbed in the mid-1960s, a victim of changes in audience tastes.

Texas School Book Depository
See Lee Harvey OSWALD.

Tey, Josephine (Elizabeth Mackintosh) *(1896–1952)* Scottish playwright and novelist. Tey is perhaps best known for her series of mystery novels featuring Scotland Yard Inspector Alan Grant. These books include *Ms. Pym Disposes* (1946) and *The Singing Sands* (1952). *A Shilling for Candles* (1936) inspired Alfred HITCHCOCK's 1937 film *Young and Innocent*. Under the pseudonym Gordon Daviot, Tey was also a successful playwright. Her plays include *Richard of Bordeaux* (1933, produced in 1932), *The Laughing Woman* (1934) and *The Little Dry Thorn* (1953, produced in 1947).

Teyte, Dame Maggie (Margaret Tate) *(1888–1976)* English soprano. Born in Wolverhampton, Teyte studied at the Royal College of Music in London and privately in Paris. She made her debut at a Mozart festival in Paris in 1905. From 1908 to 1910, she appeared with the Opéra Comique, Paris, where she became renowned for the role of Mélisande in *Pelléas and Mélisande*. She made her debut in London in 1909 and in the U.S. in 1911, was a member of the Boston Opera Company (1915–17) and made extensive tours of the U.S. Beginning in 1932, she became one of the BBC's principal radio artists. During World War II, she sang for Allied troops and

in Myra HESS's National Gallery concerts in London. Teyte became well known for her recordings of French songs and performed in U.S. tours during the 1940s. Her final operatic performance took place in 1951, and her last U.S. tour in 1954. In 1957 Teyte was made a chevalier of the Legion of Honor by France and a dame of the British Empire by England.

TGV (Train à Grande Vitesse)
French high-speed train—the fastest scheduled passenger train in the world. The TGV was inaugurated on September 27, 1981, on the Paris-Lyons route, making the run in two hours. The electric-powered TGV cruises at 160 miles per hour on specially welded rails. The soundproofed train includes 10 passengers cars, with 386 seats. In the first two months of operation, TGVs carried 1 million passengers—an average of 13,000 per day. TGVs have since been added to the Paris-Marseilles and the Paris-Bordeaux runs. Previously, the fastest train was Japan's Bullet Train, at 130 miles per hour. In 1990 the TGV established a world record speed of 320 miles per hour.

Thailand
Thailand, wedged between BURMA, LAOS and CAMBODIA, is a part of the Indochina Peninsula in Southeast Asia and covers an area of 198,404 square miles. Known as Siam until 1939, the country was ruled as an absolute monarchy until a bloodless coup in 1932 established a constitutional monarchy. Under Prime Minister Phibun Songkhram (1939–44), Thailand pursued an anti-Western policy and collaborated with the Japanese invasion of the country in 1941. Phibun was overthrown in 1944 but regained control in 1948. From the 1950s to the early 1970s the military held power. In 1971 the military government collapsed in the face of social problems, protests and the withdrawal of the king's support. The new democratic government failed, and the military took control again in 1977. By 1979 Thailand was embroiled in problems associated with VIETNAM's occupation of Cambodia. A bloodless coup in 1991 deposed another civilian prime minister and returned Thailand to military rule. Following the rapid devaluation of the

THAILAND

1910	Death of King Chulalangkorn after 42-year reign; Siam is the last uncolonized state in Southeast Asia.
1932	Westernized Siamese revolt to form constitutional monarchy, but military under Colonel Phahon emerges with power.
1939	Marshal Phibun, admirer of Hitler, stages anti-Western, anti-Chinese campaign; "Thailand" adopted as name.
1941	Phibun collaborates with Japanese takeover.
1944	Japanese collapse; civilian government set up.
1946	King Ananda dies mysteriously.
1948	Business leaders fear communist threat; Phibun regains power.
1957	Marshal Sarit imposes dictatorship.
1963	New constitution; buildup of U.S. bases adds to prosperity; builds tourism.
1969	Limited parliamentary elections.
1973	Massive student demonstrations lead to democratically elected government, which begins leftist programs and seeks ties with China, Vietnam.
1976	Military reasserts control.
1977	Campaign to stimulate foreign investment.
1979	Flood of refugees from Kampuchea.
1983	Amnesty for outlawed communists.
1988	Peaceful change of governments through free elections.
1991	The government of Prime Minister Chatichai is ousted by the military in a bloodless coup; U.S. stops aid.
1992	Parliamentary elections that are believed manipulated by the military are held; a five-party civilian coalition under Chuan Leekpai of the Democratic Party takes over.
1995	Banharn Silpa-archa of the Thai Nation Party becomes prime minister.
1996	A new constitution is drafted.
1997	The baht collapses, spawning an economic crisis throughout the Pacific Rim; the IMF and U.S. furnish loans.
2001	The populist Thai Love Thai Party under Thaksin Shinawatra, who becomes prime minister, wins legislative elections.
2003	Campaign to eliminate drugs leads to more than 1,000 suspects being killed, the government blames criminal gangs while civil rights groups say the killings were encouraged by the authorities.
2004	A massive earthquake in the Indian Ocean creates a tsunami that strikes western Thailand, killing over 5,000 people.
2005	Prime Minister Thaksin Shinawatra begins a second term after his party wins a landslide election.
2006	Prime Minister Thaksin Shinawatra is ousted in a bloodless military coup.

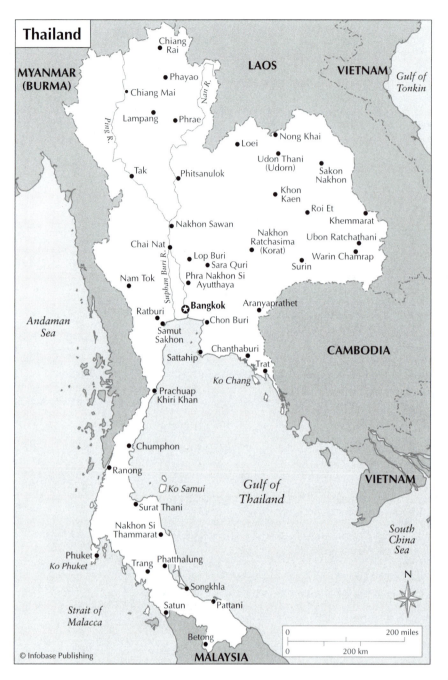

Thailand

MYANMAR (BURMA)

LAOS

VIETNAM

Gulf of Tonkin

Chiang Rai

Phayao

Chiang Mai

Lampang

Phrae

Nan R.

Ping R.

Loei

Nong Khai

Udon Thani (Udorn)

Sakon Nakhon

Tak

Phitsanulok

Khon Kaen

Roi Et

Khemmarat

Nakhon Sawan

Ubon Ratchathani

Chai Nat

Nakhon Ratchasima (Korat)

Suphan Buri R.

Lop Buri

Sara Quri

Warin Chamrap

Surin

Nam Tok

Phra Nakhon Si Ayutthaya

Ratburi

Bangkok

Aranyaprathet

Andaman Sea

Chon Buri

Samut Sakhon

Chanthaburi

Sattahip

Trat

Ko Chang

CAMBODIA

Prachuap Khiri Khan

Gulf of Thailand

VIETNAM

Chumphon

Ranong

Ko Samui

South China Sea

Surat Thani

N

Nakhon Si Thammarat

Phuket

Ko Phuket

Trang

Phatthalung

Songkhla

Strait of Malacca

Satun

Pattani

Betong

MALAYSIA

0   200 miles

0   200 km

© Infobase Publishing

bhat in 1997, the INTERNATIONAL MONETARY FUND (IMF) intervened to stabilize the country's finances and reduce the disruptive influence of the Thai currency's problems on the other economies of Southeast Asia. Thailand fully recovered from the 1997–98 financial crises within a few years and became one of Asia's most impressive economic performers in the early years of the 21st century.

In January 2001 the first general elections were held under the reformist 1997 constitution. The populist Thai

Love Thai Party became the first party in Thailand's history to secure a simple majority in parliament. In December 2004 a magnitude 9.0 earthquake in the Indian Ocean caused a massive tsunami that washed over western Thailand, including the resort areas near Phuket. Five thousand people were killed, about one-fourth of whom were foreigners. In 2005 Prime Minister Thaksin Shinawatra was elected to a second term but was forced to step down in 2006 due to allegations of corruption and was ousted in a September coup.

Thalberg, Irving G. *(1899–1936)* Legendary American motion picture producer; credited by biographer Bob Thomas not only for inventing the big-studio system that kept American movies supreme throughout the world, but also for his "unceasing pursuit of quality." The Brooklyn-born son of German parents suffered rheumatic fever throughout his childhood and never finished high school. From 1918 to 1923 he worked for film mogul Carl LAEMMLE, rising from private secretary to production head of UNIVERSAL PICTURES in Los Angeles. The fresh-faced "Boy Wonder" was precocious, tough and an astute judge of story material. From 1924 until his death in 1936 he supervised production at MGM under the management of Louis B. MAYER, helping to shape the studio into the most successful operation in the film industry. Obsessed with filmmaking at all levels, closer to home he guided the career of his wife, actress Norma Shearer, to five ACADEMY AWARD nominations (she won once, in 1930). His personally supervised prestige projects included the von STROHEIM–directed *Greed* (1924), the epic *Ben Hur* (1927), the GARBO-Gilbert vehicle *Flesh and the Devil* (1927), the maritime epic *Mutiny on the Bounty* (1935), the oversized *Romeo and Juliet* (1936) and the adaptation of Pearl BUCK's *The Good Earth* (released posthumously in 1937).

Although some of his power was curtailed when he was replaced as production chief in 1933 by David O. SELZNICK, Thalberg retained to the end his own independent production unit. He initiated the "sneak preview" concept. He subjected scripts to endless rewrites, employing such notable writers as F. Scott FITZGERALD. And some of his projects ran against the glossy MGM grain—the horrific but poignant *Freaks* (1933) and the zany MARX BROTHERS film *A Night at the Opera* (1935). Although he worked in the most visible business in the world, he jealously guarded his own privacy, refusing to use his name on a film's credits. ("I want to make it perfectly clear that my name should be on nothing," he once said, "not even my parking space.") However, anonymity was not to be. His name is inscribed on the "Irving G. Thalberg Memorial Award," bestowed occasionally since 1937 by special vote of the academy. He was the model for the characters of "Miles Calman" and "Monroe Stahr" in Fitzgerald's *Crazy Sunday* and the unfinished novel *The Last Tycoon* (1940).

thalidomide A drug used as a sedative to induce sleep and to prevent nausea in pregnancy, and widely marketed in Europe from 1957 to 1961. In 1962 it was found to cause defects in developing fetuses leading to severe malformations at birth. Its use was particularly widespread in West Germany and Great Britain, where it was given official approval. The most severe of the birth defects was phocomelia, the development of short and often useless hands and feet. Before it was removed from the market in 1962, the drug had deformed or killed between 8,000 and 10,000 babies in 20 countries. The drug was never officially approved in the U.S., but had been distributed in sample form and given to many American women.

Tharp, Twyla *(1941–)* American dancer and choreographer. A graduate of Barnard College, Tharp studied dance with Merce CUNNINGHAM and Alwin Nikolais, among others, and debuted with the Paul TAYLOR Dance Company in 1963. In 1965 she formed her own company and began to choreograph works for other companies as well as for her own. Her works are a blend of popular dance forms (jazz, social dance) and formal ballet technique, and she often uses popular music by composers such as Fats WALLER and the BEACH BOYS for her dances. Her best known works include *Eight Jelly Rolls* (1971), *Deuce Coupe* (1976) and *Push Comes to Shove* (1976), which she created especially for Mikhail BARYSHNIKOV and AMERICAN BALLET THEATRE (ABT). She also choreographed and directed the Broadway musical *Singin' in the Rain* (1985). She has disbanded her company, and has since become affiliated with ABT. In 1992 Tharp received a MacArthur Fellowship to aid her work in ballet and modern dance choreography. In 2003 she had a Broadway success as choreographer of *Movin' Out,* a show set to music by Billy Joel. She won a 2003 Tony Award for choreography for the this show.

Thatcher, Margaret Hilda (Margaret Hilda Roberts, Baroness Thatcher of Kesteven) *(1925–)* British politician, CONSERVATIVE PARTY leader and prime minister of the UNITED KINGDOM (1979–90). The daughter of a Grantham, Lincolnshire, grocer, Thatcher was educated as a research chemist at Somerville College, Oxford, but subsequently pursued a career in politics. Elected to Parliament (1959) as a Conservative, she gained wide attention as minister for education (1970–74) in the cabinet of Edward HEATH when she abolished free milk for schoolchildren. In 1975 she ousted Heath in an acrimonious contest for party leadership. Four years later she won a landslide victory (May 3, 1979) over James CALLAGHAN and became the first woman prime minister in British history. She was reelected in 1983 following the British victory in the FALKLANDS WAR, and again in 1987. In 1988 she became the longest-serving prime minister in the 20th century. A staunch supporter of the free market, Thatcher undertook an ambitious plan to revitalize Britain's economy and curtail the WELFARE STATE. Pursuing strict monetarist policies and dominating both her own cabinet and Parliament, she cut public spending, sold off unprofitable nationalized industries to private investors and curbed the power of the trade unions (see also NATIONALIZATION, PRIVATIZATION). She also cut personal income tax rates significantly, but more than doubled Britain's value-added tax (VAT). Her measures resulted in a rise in the standard of living for many Britons; however, high unemployment, recurring inflation and social unrest in the inner cities persisted, and her confrontation with the coal miner's union (1984–85) caused much bitterness. In her foreign policy Thatcher was nationalistic and anticommunist but pragmatic. She was the first Western leader to meet with Soviet leader Mikhail GORBACHEV and to recognize his significance. Often critical of the EUROPEAN ECONOMIC COMMUNITY (EEC), Thatcher enjoyed warm relations with U.S. president Ronald REAGAN. Thatcher's introduction of a flat-rate "community charge" or poll tax to replace local property taxes ("rates") proved highly unpopular and provoked riots in 1990. Her government suffered another setback in October 1990 when Thatcher publicly denounced a plan for the monetary integration of Europe, which all other EEC nations—and many Conservatives—supported. Sir Geoffrey HOWE, a longtime Thatcher supporter and senior Conservative official, resigned from the cabinet, sparking a revolt by back-bench MPs who felt that Thatcher no longer represented the majority of the party. After failing to defeat MP Michael HESELTINE in a party leadership vote, Thatcher announced her resignation (November 1990). She was succeeded as party leader and prime minister by her chancellor of the exchequer and protégé, John MAJOR. Thatcher was subsequently awarded the Order of Merit by Queen ELIZABETH II. Thatcher was elevated to the peerage, as Baroness Thatcher of Kesteven, in 1992, which entitled her to a seat in the House of Lords. Following several minor strokes, Thatcher retired from the House in 2001. She now heads the Thatcher Foundation. One of the most important if most controversial political figures of her time, Thatcher exerted immense influence on the course of Britain in the 1980s, on general notions of government, politics and economics and on the Western Alliance.

Thaw case Sensational 1906 murder trial of playboy millionaire Harry K. Thaw, who shot prominent architect Stanford White in the roof garden restaurant of the old Madison Square Garden in New York. White had a reputation for seducing young women, including the 16-year-old Evelyn Nesbit. Thaw, known as a lecherous womanizer, was later married to Nesbit, who was a popular actress on Broadway. He regularly beat his young wife, and during one of these episodes, Nesbit revealed to him details of her earlier relationship with White. Some time later, while the couple was attending a musical at the Garden's roof restaurant, Thaw spotted White, calmly walked up to him and shot him dead in front of a startled crowd. In the ensuing, highly publicized murder trial, the defense portrayed White as a deviant who seduced young girls after having them pose on the red velvet swing in his hideaway. Although the first trial resulted in a hung jury, a second jury found Thaw insane. After being committed to a mental hospital he was temporarily released. However, he was recommitted after horsewhipping a teenage male sexual partner.

Thaw was released years later and died in 1947.

Theater of the Absurd

A style of playwrighting that became dominant in Europe after World War II and flourished worldwide throughout the 1950s and 1960s. Major playwrights who have been grouped under the "Absurd" rubric include Samuel BECKETT, Friedrich DURRENMATT, Jean GENET, Eugène IONESCO, Luigi PIRANDELLO and Tom STOPPARD. Theater of the Absurd is noted for its acceptance of the existential viewpoint that life has no meaning beyond what each individual arbitrarily applies to it (see EXISTENTIALISM). It holds that all laws and societal mores are relative and favors comic situations in which characters are mocked for their shallow ideals and hypocrisies and lauded when they show the simple courage to live according to their own inner dictates. Dramatic pathos arises from the sense of despair all must ultimately face when absolute truths are found lacking. As to stage presentation, the conventions of realism are usually flouted by spare, stylized set designs that emphasize a sense of alienation between the individual and the environment.

Theater of the Grotesque

See TEATRO GROTTESCO.

Theatre Guild

American production company. The Theatre Guild was formed in New York in 1919, originally based in the Garrick Theatre, moving to its own Guild Theatre in 1925. The guild distinguished itself producing innovative American and foreign drama. Important early productions include George Bernard SHAW's *Heartbreak House* (1920), Henrik Ibsen's *Peer Gynt* (1923) and Elmer RICE's *The Adding Machine* (1923). The Guild also presented the musical *Oklahoma!* (1943). Guild actors include Helen HAYES, Alfred LUNT and Lynne FONTANNE and Alla Nazimona. The Theatre Guild was incorporated into the American National Theatre and Academy in 1950.

Theiner, Georg

(1927–1985) Czech writer; editor of the *Index on Censorship* issued by Writers and Scholars International. Born in Prague, he fled to Britain following the Nazi invasion of CZECHO-SLOVAKIA. Theiner returned after the war, working for the official Czech news agency. He lost his job in 1948 when he refused to join the Communist Party. His dissent eventually landed him in a forced labor camp in the Siberian coal fields until 1953. Following the Soviet invasion of Czechoslovakia in 1968, he returned to London where he spent the rest of his life.

Theosophy

Group of occult, mystical and spiritualist teachings. While the general term has long referred to theories on the divinely inspired structure of the universe, in modern usage it means the teachings of the Theosophical Society founded in New York in 1875. The society's principal leader at that time was Helena Petrovna Blavatsky, a Russian-born charlatan with remarkable imaginative and analytical powers who wrote massive theoretical tomes, including the multivolume *The Secret Doctrine* (1888), which became a mainstay text of the Theosophical movement. While Blavatsky was ultimately shown to have used false mechanisms to create so-called spiritual effects—such as sudden letters from secret Himalayan Masters—the influence of her teachings has endured. Theosophy is a highly eclectic blend of Eastern Brahmanism and Buddhism with Western spiritualism and occult traditions such as astral travel. In the 20th century, the Theosophical Society endured many schisms and divisions. One Theosophical sect, the Star in the East, held forth Jidda KRISHNAMURTI as world savior during the 1920s. But in 1929, Krishnamurti dissolved the sect and renounced his savior role, going on to become a highly influential philosopher and thinker.

Thibaud, Jacques

(1880–1953) French violinist. Born in Bordeaux, Thibaud studied violin at the Paris Conservatory (1894–96). He made his concert debut in Paris in 1898, and debuted in the U.S. in 1903. He fought with distinction in WORLD WAR I, returning to the concert stage after the war to tour virtually every major city in the world. He was noted for his work as a guest artist and for his chamber music performances, particularly in trios with Pablo CASALS and Alfred CORTOT. Acclaimed for his interpretations of Mozart and the composers of the French school, Thibaud was an exponent of the classic French violin technique, emphasizing stylistic elegance over bravura performance. A member of the RESISTANCE movement during WORLD WAR II, he remained active as a performer during and after the war. He was killed in an airplane crash en route to a concert in Indochina.

Thieu, Nguyen Van

(1923–2001) Vietnamese general and politician, president of South Vietnam (1967–75). Commissioned in the infantry, he distinguished himself in action against the VIET MINH. When the South Vietnamese army was established in 1959, Thieu was appointed commander of its 21st Infantry Division. He also served as commandant of the National Military Academy. After graduating from the U.S. Command and General Staff College at Fort Leavenworth, Kansas, in 1947, Colonel Thieu commanded the South Vietnamese army First Infantry Division from 1960 to 1962, when he was appointed to command the Fifth Infantry Division near Saigon. During the coup that overthrew President Ngo Dinh DIEM in November 1963, Colonel Thieu led one of his regiments in an attack on the barracks of the presidential bodyguard. Promoted to brigadier general, Thieu was appointed commander of IV Corps. To end the near anarchy that followed the assassination of President Diem, General Thieu took part in a coup by Air Vice Marshal Nguyen Cao Ky in December 1964. A civilian government was installed, and Thieu, now a major general, became part of a 25-man Armed Forces Council. In June 1965 another coup resulted in a 10-man military National Leadership Committee, which elected General Thieu chairman and chief of state and Air Marshal Ky premier. When elections were held in 1967 the situation was reversed. Thieu was elected president and Ky vice president. Ky chose not to run against Thieu in 1971, and Thieu was reelected to the presidency, although charges of a rigged election surfaced.

Pressured by the United States to agree to the PARIS PEACE ACCORD in 1973, which left the North Vietnamese army (NVA) in control of large segments of the country, President Thieu's position was further undermined when the U.S. Congress cut promised military aid and especially when, after an open NVA attack on Binh Long Province in November 1974, President FORD failed to honor U.S. guarantees to uphold the terms of the Paris Accords. With four NVA corps closing in on Saigon and all hope of outside assistance gone, President Thieu resigned and on April 25, 1975, flew to Taiwan. He later resided in Great Britain and in the United States.

Third International See COMINTERN.

Third World Term in use in the second half of the 20th century; refers to former colonies, now independent. "First World" nations are the industrialized, democratic Western countries, such as the U.S., Canada, Britain and France. The "Second World" consisted of communist nations behind the IRON CURTAIN. Third World nations are mainly in Africa, Asia and Latin America.

Thomas, Charles Allen (1900–1982) American physical chemist. During WORLD WAR II Thomas was part of the MANHATTAN PROJECT team that developed the ATOMIC BOMB. He later served on a panel recommending international control of atomic power for peaceful purposes. He was president (1950–60) and board chairman (1960–65) of the giant Monsanto Chemical Corp. He also served as president and board chairman of the American Chemical Society and was a founding member of the American Academy of Engineering.

Thomas, D(onald) M(ichael) (1935–) British novelist and poet. Thomas was educated at Oxford and learned Russian while training for the British Foreign Service. His extensive knowledge of Russian literature has been a major influence on his own creative work. As a poet Thomas has published several volumes of original verse including *Two Voices* (1968), *Logan Stone* (1971), *Love and Other Deaths* (1975), *The Honeymoon Voyage* (1978), *Dreaming in Bronze* (1981) and *Selected Poems* (1983). He has also translated the verse of the renowned 20th-century Russian poet Anna AKHMATOVA. But Thomas has earned his primary fame as a novelist whose best-known work, *The White Hotel* (1981), features an in-

tensely realized Russian milieu. Other novels by Thomas include *The Flute Player* (1979), which is dedicated to the spirits of persecuted Russian poets including Akhmatova and Boris PASTERNAK, as well as *Birthstone* (1980) and *Ararat* (1983). Thomas continued to publish throughout the 1990s, releasing novels such as *Lying Together* (1990), *Flying in to Love* (1992), *Pictures at an Exhibition* (1993), *Eating Pavlova* (1994) and *Lady with a Laptop* (1996) and the biography *Alexander Solzhenitsyn: A Century in His Life* (1998).

Thomas, Dylan (1914–1953) Welsh poet and story writer. Thomas is one of the legendary figures of 20th-century English poetry. Not only was he an exceptionally gifted lyric poet, but he also possessed a melodic voice that made him a great favorite both on BRITISH BROADCASTING CORPORATION radio programs and on poetry reading tours in Great Britain and the U.S. Thomas was born in the Welsh seaport town of Swansea. He received little formal education but described himself as being deeply steeped as a child in both Welsh folklore and the Bible. After working at a variety of odd jobs, including hack journalism, he achieved early fame as a lyric prodigy in the 1930s. *The Map of Love* (1939) is a representative selection of his early poems and prose. Thomas's writing style bears traces of romanticism, symbolism and SURREALISM, but is wholly idiosyncratic. In the 1940s and 1950s, Thomas became a highly public figure due to his radio work and readings. With his Irish wife, Caitlin, he lived in the Welsh fishing village of Laugharne; they had three children. But Thomas drove himself to an early death through alcohol, collapsing at the age of 39 during a reading tour in New York City. Thomas's larger-than-life public image has tended to obscure the true value of his work, and critics are divided over his ultimate significance. *Portrait of the Artist as a Young Dog* (1940) and *Adventures in the Skin Trade* (1955) contain the best of his stories. His *Collected Poems* (1960) has remained a perennial favorite.

Thomas, Edward (1878–1917) British poet and prose writer. Of Welsh parentage, Thomas was educated at St. Paul's School, London, and at Lincoln

College, Oxford. Sensitive and moody, he made a meagre living as a freelance writer and reviewer for various journals and newspapers. His evocative essays on the pre–World War I English countryside capture a now-vanished way of life. In 1913 he met Robert FROST, who was then living in England. Thomas was the first major critic to recognize Frost's importance. Frost, in turn, encouraged Thomas to write poetry himself. In the remaining few years of his life Thomas wrote 140 poems, many of which rank among the finest English poems of the 20th century; only six were published during his lifetime. At age 37, Thomas enlisted in the British army ("the Artists' Rifles") in WORLD WAR I and was killed in action during the battle of ARRAS, April 9, 1917. Although his work is not widely known outside the British Isles, it has greatly influenced many later British and Irish writers, including Philip LARKIN and Seamus HEANEY.

Thomas, Lowell (Jackson) (1892–1981) American broadcaster, author and world traveler. As a foreign correspondent during WORLD WAR I, he met the British soldier T. E. LAWRENCE and accompanied him on several missions. Thomas's subsequent book, *With Lawrence in Arabia* (1924), was a highly romanticized account of Lawrence's exploits; it made both Thomas and Lawrence world famous—and also embarrassed Lawrence. Thomas's career as a radio news broadcaster spanned nearly half a century from 1930 to 1976. During this period, his voice was one of the most familiar in America. He was not an intellectual or a tough investigative reporter; his easy-going accounts of the day's events, he acknowledged, were not intended to "destroy the digestive system of the American people." His radio career was paralleled by several others. Millions of Americans got their first glimpse of foreign lands through his colorful travelogues. He made trips to regions in Alaska, Africa, India and other parts of the world that few Westerners had visited at the time. His explorations resulted in dozens of books, newsreels, slide shows and television programs that made Thomas wealthy.

Thomas, Norman (Norman Mattoon Thomas) (1884–1968) American socialist leader. Born in Marion,

Ohio, Thomas attended Princeton University and Union Theological Seminary. After his graduation in 1911 he became pastor of the East Harlem Presbyterian Church, New York, and did social work in this poverty-stricken area of the city. He became a pacifist and was a founder (1917) of the organization that became the AMERICAN CIVIL LIBERTIES UNION. In 1918 Thomas joined the Socialist Party and ceased his religious activities. He ran unsuccessfully for governor of New York in 1924 and 1938 and as mayor of New York in 1925 and 1929. At the death of Eugene V. DEBS in 1926, Thomas assumed the leadership of the Socialist Party. Subsequently, he continued his quixotic attempts to achieve electoral office, running for the presidency every four years from 1928 to 1948. An opponent of both fascism and communism, he opposed American entry into World War II and subsequent Soviet expansionism. In the postwar world, he advocated controlled international disarmament and in 1957 was a cofounder of the Committee for a Sane Nuclear Policy. During the 1950s, he was an outspoken opponent of McCARTHYISM, and in the 1960s he strongly denounced the VIETNAM WAR. Throughout his career, Thomas acted as conscience and gadfly, criticizing America's social inequities and its two major political parties. Among his books are *Socialism of Our Time* (1929), *The Test of Freedom* (1954) and *Socialism Reexamined* (1963).

Thomas, William *(1863–1947)* American sociologist. After graduating from the University of Tennessee in 1884, Thomas taught English there and at Oberlin College. From 1894 to 1918 he taught sociology at the University of Chicago. He spent the rest of his life researching and writing and produced important theories dealing with man's relationship with his environment. He divided man's behavior into four areas that became his well-known "four wishes" theory. His published works include *Source Book of Social Origins* (1909), *The Unadjusted Girl* (1923) and *The Polish Peasant in Europe and America* (1918–19).

Thomaz, Americo *(1894–1987)* Portuguese politician. After a career as an admiral and naval minister, in 1958

Thomaz became PORTUGAL's president in elections that were widely regarded as rigged by the dictator and prime minister Antonio SALAZAR. "Reelected" twice, Thomaz was ousted as president in an almost bloodless left-wing coup in 1974.

Thompson, Daley *(1958–   )* British decathlete. Between 1978 and 1987, Thompson won every decathlon he completed; his string was broken when he placed ninth at the World Track and Field Championships that year. Thompson was only the second man in history (after Bob Mathias) to win two Olympic gold medals in the event (in 1980 and 1984). In 1983 he won the world championship, and in 1986 he won his third straight Commonwealth decathlon as well as the decathlon at the European Track and Field Championships. In 1992 Thompson retired from professional athletic competitions.

Thompson, Dorothy *(1894–1961)* American foreign correspondent, newspaper columnist and radio commentator. Thompson, who enjoyed her greatest influence and readership in the 1930s, was one of the leading journalistic voices against HITLER and Nazi ANTI-SEMITISM. She strongly urged an interventionist position for the United States in the late 1930s, when an isolationist stance toward Europe was favored by the bulk of public opinion. British prime minister Winston CHURCHILL lauded Thompson for her efforts in obtaining American military and economic aid for Great Britain during WORLD WAR II. Thompson, who attended Syracuse University, began her journalistic career in the 1920s and married American novelist Sinclair LEWIS in 1928 (they divorced in 1942). Her thrice-weekly column was featured in the *New York Herald-Tribune* from 1936 to 1941 and syndicated nationally through 1958.

Thompson, Hunter *(1939–2005)* American journalist and political essayist. Thompson emerged in the 1960s as one of the leading practitioners of the NEW JOURNALISM, a style of reportage that emphasized subjective opinion and personal involvement in the story being reported upon. Thompson, to whom the adjective

"gonzo" (meaning crazed or outlandish) is frequently applied, was the most controversial of the New Journalists because of the vituperative extremes of his style and the anarchistic flavor of his political viewpoints. Many of his journalistic pieces first appeared in *Rolling Stone*. His major books include *Hell's Angels* (1966), *Fear and Loathing in Las Vegas, A Savage Journey to the Heart of the American Dream* (1972) and *Fear and Loathing: On the Campaign Trail '72* (1973). Thompson continued as a prolific journalist, although his influence declined with the shift in political mood from the 1960s to the 1990s. He was caricatured as "Uncle Duke" in the Garry Trudeau comic strip *Doonesbury*. Thompson continued to publish best-selling works, including *Screwjack* (1991); volumes III and IV of the Gonzo Papers, *Songs of the Doomed* (1990) and *Better Than Sex* (1994); volume I of the *Fear and Loathing Letters*; *The Proud Highway*; *Letters from a Desperate Southern Gentleman* (1997); and *The Kingdom of Fear: Loathsome Secrets of a Star-Crossed Child in the Final Days of the American Century* (2003). He committed suicide at his home near Aspen, Colorado, in 2005.

Thompson, Joe *(1887–1980)* American model sculptor whose clay works helped revolutionize automobile design. Thompson was among the first craftsmen in the industry to work extensively with clay in transforming sketches into three-dimensional automobile designs. He went on to create the first models for the Model A FORD, the Pontiac, the Opel and the LINCOLN-ZEPHYR.

Thompson, Mickey *(1928–1988)* American auto racer. Thompson became famous in the 1950s as the "Speed King," when he set the first of his nearly 500 speed and endurance records. In 1960, driving a four-engine streamlined car across Utah's Bonneville Salt Flats, he became the first person to go 400 miles per hour on land. In later years, he became a racing promoter.

Thomson, Sir Joseph John *(1856–1940)* British physicist and head of Oxford's Cavendish Laboratory; best known for his research on cathode rays. His discovery of the electron in 1897 revolutionized physics. He also initiated the research that led F. W. ASTON to develop the mass spectrograph, which identifies a substance's chemical components by separating ions according to mass and charge. Thomson won the 1906 NOBEL PRIZE for physics for his work on the conduction of electricity through gases.

Thomson, Roy Herbert (first baron of Fleet) *(1894–1978)* British newspaper publisher. Born in Canada, Thomson bought a small radio station in 1931 and a weekly newspaper in 1933. After building a chain of radio stations and newspapers in Canada, he emigrated to Britain in 1953. There he continued to expand his holdings and acquired the prestigious *Sunday Times* (1962) and *London Times* (1967). His empire included 285 publications as well as radio and TV stations on four continents.

Thomson, Virgil Garnett *(1896–1989)* Prominent American composer and influential music critic. The polarities of Thomson's life and work were marked by two cities, Paris and Kansas City. They were the only places he "felt at home," he said; and they inspired, on the one hand, Thomson's wit and elegance, and, on the other, his homespun simplicity and common sense. He was born in Kansas City, Missouri, where as a boy he played the organ at Calvary Baptist Church services. After a brief stint in WORLD WAR I in the Military Aviation Corps, he relocated to Harvard and later to Paris, where he began lifelong friendships with sometime collaborators Pablo PICASSO, Jean COCTEAU, Ernest HEMINGWAY and Gertrude STEIN (with the latter he wrote two operas, *Four Saints in Three Acts*, 1928, first performed in 1934; and *The Mother of Us All,* 1947). Back in New York in the mid-1930s Thomson wrote the score for the Orson WELLES/Negro Theater Project adaption of *Macbeth* (1936). For filmmaker Pare Lorentz he wrote the scores for two important documentary films about American land reclamation projects, *The Plow That Broke the Plains* (1936) and *The River* (1937). In 1938 Thomson's ballet, *The Filling Station,* became the first successful ballet on American themes and the first performed by American dancers. In these and many other works Thomson fused

modern harmonic practices with American folk music idioms like cowboy songs, Cajun tunes and jazz. The Baptist hymn, particularly "How Firm a Foundation, Ye Saints of the Lord," appears everywhere in his work and is the basis for one of his finest orchestral works, *Symphony on a Hymn Tune* (1928, premiered in 1945).

Meanwhile, he was beginning a career as a music critic. In the fall of 1940 he succeeded Lawrence Gilman as music critic of the *New York Herald Tribune* where, until his retirement in 1954, he was a powerful, outspoken—frequently astringent—champion of new music. (See his anthologies of collected criticism, *The Musical Scene* [1946] and *Music Right and Left* [1951].) His later years were full of honors: the French Legion of Honor; the PULITZER PRIZE (for his musical score to Robert FLAHERTY'S *The Louisiana Story* [1949]); and the National Medal of the Arts, among others. Sporadically he left his New York Chelsea Hotel residence to visit his favorite cities, Paris and Kansas City. To the last he remained tough and uncompromising about his art and his criticism. "I don't get into feuds with artists or composers," he said during one of his last interviews. "I get into feuds with management. I'm an artist. I defend the artist." He died in his sleep in New York City on September 30, 1989.

Thornton, Charles B. "Tex" *(1913–1981)* American business executive. Thornton won fame during WORLD WAR II as the inventor of a "statistical control" system to monitor the military's global resources. He then went on to apply his organizational and management skills in the civilian world as one of the so-called Whiz Kids who reorganized the ailing FORD Motor Company in the mid-1940s. In 1953 he acquired a small microwave tube company and turned it into the huge conglomerate **Litton Industries.** He remained chairman and chief executive officer until his death. As head of Litton he devised the modern concept of conglomerates, buying small, prosperous companies that did not lead in their fields, thus avoiding violation of monopoly laws.

Thorpe, James Francis "Jim" *(1888–1953)* American athlete. Great-grandson of the American Indian chief

Black Hawk, Thorpe started his athletic career at the Carlisle Indian Industrial School, Pennsylvania, where he played on the football team from 1908 to 1912. Thorpe was voted All-American in 1908, 1911 and 1912. He participated in the 1912 OLYMPIC GAMES in Stockholm, Sweden. He played professional baseball with the New York Giants in 1913, 1914 and from 1917 to 1919. In 1920 he became the first president of the American Professional Football Association. In 1932 he was voted the greatest football player of the first half of the 20th century.

Thorpe, Jeremy *(1929–)* British politician. Thorpe was leader of the LIBERAL PARTY from 1967 to 1976, when a former male model claimed to have had sexual relations with him and Thorpe was forced to step down. In 1978 he was arrested for conspiracy to murder the model. Although he was later acquitted, the THORPE TRIAL brought an end to his political career. Thorpe was succeeded by Jo Grimond as leader of the Liberal Party.

Thorpe trial In 1978, Jeremy THORPE, a former leader of the British LIBERAL PARTY, was arrested for conspiring to murder a former male model, Norman Scott. Scott had created a political scandal for Thorpe in 1976 by claiming to have had sexual relations with him. The murder plot was first revealed in 1977 when a former airline pilot, Andrew Newton, told a reporter that he had been paid to kill Scott by a Liberal Party fund-raiser. Newton claimed he had lost his nerve and shot Scott's dog instead. Arrested along with Thorpe were David Holmes, a former deputy treasurer of the Liberal Party, and two businessmen, George Deakin and John le Mesurier. All were acquitted following a trial in 1979, although Thorpe's political career was effectively ended.

Thousand Days, War of a *(1899–1903)* Bitter political struggles between liberals and conservatives disrupted COLOMBIA, and when Manuel Sanclemente (1820–1902) was elected president by the conservatives in 1898, wrangling within the Conservative Party emboldened the liberals to revolt in 1899. Vice President José Manuel Marroquín (1827–1908), a conservative, ousted Sanclemente on July 31,

1900, and became president. Three years of violent clashes between armed liberals and conservatives dragged Colombia into economic ruin. Marroquín's troops finally suppressed the liberal rebels, restoring order in June 1903, after an estimated 100,000 Colombians had been killed. Later that year, PANAMA, with U.S. help, successfully established its independence from Colombia.

Three Mile Island accident Critical, nonfatal accident at the Three Mile Island nuclear power plant, on the Susquehanna River, near Harrisburg, Pennsylvania, U.S.A. On the morning of March 28, 1979, a malfunction in the primary and emergency core cooling systems of the plant's no. 2 reactor resulted in the formation of a giant hydrogen gas bubble in the reactor vessel. The level of the cooling water surrounding the uranium fuel rods in the reactor fell, exposing the tops of the rods and causing intense heat. Authorities feared that a "meltdown" of the uranium fuel core could occur; such a meltdown would release lethal radioactivity over a wide area and cause many deaths and long-term contamination. There was also the possibility that the gas bubble might explode. Nuclear engineers worked to cool the uranium fuel core and finally managed to shut down the reactor on April 27. During the accident, the plant released radioactive gases, and the governor advised pregnant women and preschool children within a five-mile radius of the plant to leave the area. The mishap was later investigated by a presidential commission, which urged fundamental changes in the way reactors were built, operated and regulated. The commission's report acknowledged that the Three Mile Island accident was "the most severe accident in U.S. commercial nuclear power operating history." The Three Mile Island accident focused worldwide attention on the possible dangers of nuclear power, and led to mass demonstrations against nuclear power, although officials continued to assert that nuclear power was safe. Amazingly, the accident occurred only two weeks after the release of a controversial movie, *The China Syndrome,* about a meltdown at a nuclear power plant. (See also CHERNOBYL DISASTER; WINDSCALE ACCIDENT.)

Threepenny Opera, The **(*Die Dreigroschenoper*)** German musical play by Bertolt BRECHT featuring songs by Kurt WEILL. From the time of its debut performance in Berlin in 1928, *The Threepenny Opera* has stood as a classic work of the 20th-century theater. It was Brecht's first major success as a playwright and features his unique blend of black humor and incisive social commentary. It also went against the long tradition of musical theater as comedic or light in tone, with Weill's fiercely dramatic score highlighting Brecht's social message. The basic plot of *The Threepenny Opera* concerns the marriage, criminal conviction and ultimate pardon of "Macheath," a robber who reflects the greed and opportunism that mirrors society as a whole. The play warns that good persons find it difficult to hold out against the enticements of a corrupt society—a prescient view, given the rise of the NAZIS in GERMANY four years after the play's opening.

Three Stooges, the Perhaps the century's most violent practitioners of slapstick comedy, the Stooges began in vaudeville with three members: mop-haired Moe Howard (born Moses Horwitz, 1897–1975), his greasy-haired brother Shemp (born Samuel Horwitz, 1895–1955) and Ted Healy (born Charles Earnest Nash, 1896–1937). Before the trio began to make films, changes took place: Shemp was replaced by his heavyset, bald brother Curly (born Jerome Horwitz, 1903–1952); Healy left due to differences with the other members; and in stepped frizzy-haired comedian Larry Fine (born Louis Feinberg, 1902–

1975). With these three members—Larry, Moe and Curly—the boys wreaked havoc on the movie screen in more than 200 short comedies and a handful of B-movies from 1933 to 1965, including *Pop Goes the Easel* (1935), *Dutiful But Dumb* (1941), *Hold That Lion* (1947) and *Spooks* (1953). While the boys maintained an enormous popularity throughout their careers (particularly among younger audiences), their wild, often abusive antics—eye-poking, face slapping, fists in the belly, vocal yowls—offended many and amused few critics. When Curly suffered a stroke in 1946, brother Shemp—who had worked successfully solo in films—returned to the Stooges until his death in 1955. Joe Besser (1907–1988) then joined the group for a period. In the late 1960s and early '70s ex-burlesque comic Joe DeRita (born Joseph Wardell, 1909–) performed sporadically with Moe and Larry, but the Stooges officially disbanded when Larry died in 1975.

Thresher On April 10, 1963, the nuclear powered U.S. Navy SUBMARINE USS *Thresher* sank during deep diving tests in the North Atlantic. The entire crew of 126 men was killed—the worst submarine disaster in U.S. history. It was presumed that a piping system failure had caused the engine room to flood. There were fears that the ship's nuclear reactor could leak and contaminate the ocean, but Vice Admiral Hyman RICKOVER assured the public that there was "no radioactive hazard." The *Thresher* had been commissioned in 1961 and was the first of its class of nuclear submarines.

The Three Stooges (left to right): Moe Howard, Curly Howard and Larry Fine, 1938 (NEW YORK WORLD-TELEGRAM AND THE SUN NEWSPAPER COLLECTION, LIBRARY OF CONGRESS, PRINTS AND PHOTOGRAPHS DIVISION)

Thurber, James *(1894–1961)* American humorist, cartoonist and playwright, considered one of America's greatest humorists since Mark Twain. Thurber regarded his boyhood in Columbus, Ohio, as the prime source for all his later ideas and attitudes. The colorful characters in his family were the models for his comic essays and stories collected in *My Life and Hard Times* (1933) and *My World and Welcome to It* (1942). The strong-minded female relatives, particularly, seem to have left him with a permanent distrust—albeit an affectionate one—of women; and an injury to one eye (which was subsequently removed) reinforced his solitary ways and wry, detached manner. He moved to New York in the mid-1920s where he began a persistent assault on that edifice of sophisticated humor, *The New Yorker* magazine. He placed some essays in 1927 and soon was working on the popular column, "The Talk of the Town." With office mate humorist E. B. WHITE, he collaborated on his first successful book, *Is Sex Necessary?* (1929), providing also a number of highly idiosyncratic cartoons (described by White as depicting "the daily severity of life's mystery"). The Thurber world was full of implausible animals, affectionate dogs, harried husbands, ferocious wives and an almost surreal humor. For the rest of his life, Thurber would be identified with *The New Yorker* essays and drawings. Among his other works are two plays, *The Male Animal* (1940) and *A Thurber Carnival* (1960); and several collections of relatively serious fantasies like *Fables for Our Time* (1939). He began to lose the sight in his one remaining eye in 1940. "The imagination doesn't go blind," he wrote. "When I write now . . . I am not handicapped by vision." If he had a personal credo, it was best expressed in the foreword to his last book, *Lanterns and Lances* (1960): " . . . Let us not look back in anger, or forward in fear, but around in awareness."

Tiananmen Square massacre Violent military crackdown on June 3–4, 1989, on students and workers in the DEMOCRACY MOVEMENT that occurred in the huge Tiananmen Square in the center of Beijing, People's Republic of CHINA. The violence came two weeks after the government declared martial law and warned the students to call off their protests. Tensions had been in-creasing for several days before the massacre. On June 1, Chinese authorities banned all press coverage, photographs and videotapes of any demonstrations in the city or of army troops enforcing martial law. The following day, June 2, the official Communist Party newspaper announced that army troops had taken up positions at "10 key points" in and around the capital. That evening, more than 100,000 people turned out for a rally in support of the students. Shortly after midnight on June 3, between 2,000 and 10,000 unarmed soldiers headed toward Tiananmen Square in an effort to remove the students; however, they were blocked by students and workers and retreated. On the afternoon of June 3, police and troops began to fire tear gas and beat protestors in various parts of the city. Around midnight, dozens of tanks and armored personnel carriers and armed soldiers launched a direct assault on the protesters. Accounts of the crackdown varied; Western observers estimated that as many as 5,000 civilians were killed and 10,000 injured; the Chinese government reported that very few had been killed or injured. After the massacre, troops cordoned off the square to prevent any further protests. During the following weeks, Chinese authorities arrested hundreds of prodemocracy activists in Beijing and throughout the nation. Communist PROPAGANDA portrayed the Tiananmen Square massacre as a heroic action by the army to save China from turmoil; prodemocracy activists and many foreign governments condemned the event as wanton slaughter. In 1991 the Chinese government reiterated that it had been justified in using force to restore order, and warned that it would do so again in similar circumstances.

Tibbett, Lawrence Mervil *(1896–1960)* American opera singer and actor who was one of the foremost stars of the Metropolitan Opera between 1925 and 1950. Tibbett was a leader in the movement to popularize opera in radio, movies and television. Born in Bakersfield, California, as "Tibbet" (he added the final "t" later), he first pursued an acting career with Tyrone Power, Sr.'s Shakespearean company. After a stint in the navy during World War I he began a singing career and, contrary to prevail-ing traditions in operatic singing, chose to study in New York rather than abroad. His sensational performance at the Met as a last-minute replacement in the role of "Ford" in Verdi's *Falstaff* in 1925 became the stuff of opera legend. It launched a busy career that embraced 52 roles and 644 performances until his retirement in 1950. Today, he is most remembered for his Verdi roles, like Amonasro in *Aida,* Iago in *Otello* and the title roles in *Rigoletto* and *Simon Boccanegra* (the latter generally considered his finest achievement). In modern opera he created the roles of Brutus Jones in Louis Gruenberg's adaptation of Eugene O'NEILL'S *The Emperor Jones* in 1933 and Eadgar in Deems Taylor's *The King's Henchman* in 1927.

His flamboyant style and charismatic personality was ideally suited to HOLLYWOOD, where he was the first major opera star to make feature-length TALKING PICTURES, most of them operetta-derived projects like *The Rogue Song* (1930) and *The New Moon* (1930). His best film, *Metropolitan* (1935), was a knowing wink at the pretensions and absurdities of grand opera. "Too much opera is still trying to make the people adapt themselves to it," he was fond of saying, "instead of adapting itself to them." In his efforts to take music to as many people as possible, he worked indefatigably in live radio and television. He fought tirelessly for the rights of performing artists, forming the American Guild of Musical Artists, Inc. (AGMA) in 1936 and serving as its president until 1953. He died from injuries sustained in an auto accident.

Tibet (Xiang Autonomous Region) Located in southwestern China, Tibet covers an area of 463,300 square miles. A distinct ethnic and linguistic group from the Chinese, the Tibetans struggled for autonomy during the 20th century. Britain unsuccessfully attempted to exert influence in 1904, after Francis Younghusband led an expedition to the region. Tibet declared its independence in 1911, but Communist China reasserted Chinese suzerainty over Tibet in 1950, promising internal autonomy but actually threatening Tibetan culture when troops invaded and established a new government. An anti-Chinese revolt in 1959 led to the flight of the 14th Dalai Lama (the religious and political leader of Tibet) to India, and a period of violent repression followed. In 1965 China assimilated Tibet as an autonomous region. Further uprisings occurred in 1987, 1988 and 1989. By the 21st century, an increasing Chinese population in Tibet produced a wide socioeconomic gap between native Tibetans and Chinese entrepreneurs and government employees, as was the case in the Xinjiang-Uighur Autonomous Region (XUAR).

***Tiger* Talks** A meeting, December 2–4, 1966, on the Royal Navy cruiser HMS *Tiger* off Gibraltar between British prime minister Harold WILSON and Rhodesian prime minister Ian SMITH to reach a settlement of RHODESIA's Unilateral Declaration of Independence (see also UDI). The talks failed as did further ones on HMS *Fearless* in October 1968 through Smith's refusal to accept unimpeded progress toward black majority rule.

Tikhomirov, N. I. *(1860–1930)* Russian rocket pioneer. As early as 1894, Tikhomirov had started experiments that would become the first practical research in Russian rocketry. By 1912 he had presented his plans for development of a liquid-propellant rocket to the minister of the Russian navy, and he continued to submit proposals over the coming years. The uneasy political climate following the RUSSIAN REVOLUTION left his work all but unnoticed, until finally, in 1919, he caught the attention of officials, having made a direct appeal to LENIN in May of that year. Two years later, the Revolutionary Military Council set up a research laboratory for the study of rocket propulsion. With his assistant, V. A. Artemiev, Tikhomirov's lab officially opened on March 1, 1921, in Moscow. The lab concentrated on solid-fuel propellants and performed tests between 1923 and 1925, moving to Leningrad in 1925. By 1928, Tikhomirov's laboratory had become the GDL (Gas Dynamics Laboratory), with an official affiliation with the Soviet Military Research Council. The work of the GDL that ensued became the foundation from which today's Russian rocketry was to develop.

Tikhomirov, Vasily *(1876–1956)* Dance teacher. He was a pupil of Paul Gerdt and became a teacher at the BOLSHOI school of ballet in 1896. He taught many leading dancers and was considered one of the best teachers of his time.

Tikhonov, Nicholas Semyonovich *(1896–1979)* Russian poet. He was influenced at various stages in his career by Nicholas GUMILEV, Vladimir MAYAKOVSKY and Boris PASTERNAK. He became chairman of the Writers' Union in 1944, but he was removed by Andrei ZHDANOV in 1946 and replaced by Alexander FADEYEV. He received the Order of Lenin and the Stalin Prize for his work and in the 1950s was one of those who instigated a critical campaign against Pasternak. His first publications, two collections of poems, were *The Horde* (1922) and *Meade* (1923).

Tikhonravov, Mikhail K. *(1900–1974)* Russian rocket pioneer. Designer of the first hybrid, solid-liquid-propellant rocket, Tikhonravov saw his concept take off in a successful test, GIRD 09, on August 17, 1933. The rocket was built by a team that included Sergei KOROLEV, who was to become unquestionably the greatest figure in Soviet rocket design. During its test, GIRD 09 reached a height of 1,312 feet, and the event was recorded with fervor: " . . . starting with this moment Soviet rockets must fly over the Union of Republics . . . rockets must conquer space!"

Tilden, Bill (William Tatem Tilden II) *(1893–1953)* American tennis player. During his career, Tilden dominated the game of tennis as no one had before. In 1920, he became the first American ever to win Britain's Wimbledon championship, a title he won three times. He won the American National Turf Court Championship seven times, and was ranked number one in the world from 1920 to 1929. He was a dramatic and flamboyant player, who abhorred the snobbery inherent in the game at the time, and helped broaden tennis's appeal beyond the country club set. He turned professional in 1931 and gave exhibition matches. Tilden was arrested for contributing to the delinquency of male minors twice before he died, impoverished, in 1953.

Tillich, Paul *(1886–1965)* German-born theologian and philosopher. Tillich was one of the leading theological figures of 20th-century EXISTENTIALISM. After ordination into the Evangelical Lutheran Church, he served as a chaplain for German forces during WORLD WAR I. During the Weimar Republic of the 1920s, he was active as a religious socialist. In 1933 Tillich fled the NAZI regime to come to the United States, where he taught at Harvard University and the University of Chicago, among other institutions, and was highly influential in shaping academic disciplines for the study of religion. His major works include the three-volume *Systematic Theology* (1951–1963) and *The Courage to Be* (1952).

Tillstrom, Burr *(1917–1985)* American puppeteer. Tillstrom created *Kukla, Fran and Ollie,* one of the most popular U.S. TV shows of the 1950s. The show, which featured a cast of puppets known as the Kuklapolitan Players, ran live for more than 10 years. It was hosted by singer-actress Fran ALLISON, who was the only human member of the cast. Tillstrom, who was never seen on the show, did all the puppets' voices. From 1971 to 1979 he, Allison and the puppets hosted the CBS Children's Film Festival.

Time American periodical. *Time,* a weekly news magazine, was founded in 1923 by Henry LUCE and his former college friend Briton Hadden, who died in 1929. *Time,* which they had originally intended to call *Fact,* began by culling news from *The New York Times,* but became enormously successful and soon had news bureaus worldwide. It became known for its annual "Man of the Year" issue, and it also featured articles on the arts and society, many of which have evolved into separate publications such as *People* magazine. The magazine is the flagship of the huge Time-Life, Incorporated publishing empire. *Time* magazine and its subdivisions, such as Time-Life Books, are owned by Time-Warner.

Timoshenko, Semyon Konstantinovich *(1895–1970)* Marshal of the Soviet Union. Of Ukrainian origin, Timoshenko commanded a division in Semyon BUDENNY's first cavalry army during the RUSSIAN CIVIL WAR and commanded RED ARMY units during the 1939–40 war with Finland. In

1940 he was appointed commissar for defense and was responsible for the introduction of stricter army regulations. His work as commander on the Western Front following the German invasion of the Soviet Union was not particularly successful. He later commanded a number of military districts and retired in 1960.

Tinbergen, Nikolaas (1907–1988)
British zoologist. After gaining a Ph.D. in zoology (1932) at Leiden University, Tinbergen taught there until 1949, becoming a professor of experimental biology. He then joined Oxford University, where he helped to originate the Animal Behaviour Research Group, within the department of zoology, becoming first reader (1962) and then professor of animal behavior (1966). Like Konrad Lorenz, Tinbergen exercised considerable influence in establishing the comparatively new science of ethology. His work (like Lorenz's) emphasizes the importance of field observations of animals under natural conditions, though amplified by laboratory experiment designed to trigger responses under controlled conditions. His studies embrace both vertebrate and invertebrate animals, from arctic foxes, seals, sticklebacks and sea birds to digger wasps, butterflies and snails—investigating such topics as animal camouflage and warning colors, and social, courtship and mating behavior. One of Tinbergen's most important theses was his belief that a study of aggression in animals could lead to a greater understanding of such behavior in man and perhaps provide some means of modifying it and its effects. His work in relating ethology to the human condition led to his being awarded, jointly with Lorenz and Karl von Frisch, the NOBEL PRIZE for physiology and medicine in 1973. His most influential publication, *The Study of Instinct* (1951), presents a summary of the work of ethologists in the first half of the 20th century.

Tiomkin, Dimitri (1899–1979)
Russian-born composer of motion picture scores. Tiomkin studied composition at the St. Petersburg Conservatory of Music and later in Berlin under Alexander GLAZUNOV and Ferrucio BUSONI; he performed in cinema theaters and music halls as a pop pianist and arranger. In 1928 he gave the European premiere of GERSHWIN's *Concerto in F* in Paris. After moving to HOLLYWOOD he composed his first original film score for *Resurrection* (1931). When an accident to his right hand cut short a concert career, he turned exclusively to film composing. His long association with director Frank CAPRA began in 1937 with *Lost Horizon* and subsequently included *Mr. Smith Goes to Washington* (1939), *Meet John Doe* (1941) and *It's a Wonderful Life* (1946). His ACADEMY-AWARD–winning scores for *The High and the Mighty* (1954), *The Old Man and the Sea* (1958) and *High Noon* (1951) only begin to suggest his amazing range. There was the simplicity of *High Noon*'s folksy ballad, "Do Not Forsake Me, Oh My Darling"; the inflated drive of his "big" scores for *Duel in the Sun* (1946) and *The Alamo* (1960); the weird, horrific effects of *The Thing* (1951); and several suspenseful scores for Alfred HITCHCOCK (including *Shadow of a Doubt,* 1943, and *Dial M for Murder,* 1954). His autobiography, *Please Don't Hate Me,* appeared in 1960. Although the quality of Tiomkin's scores varied from project to project, he remained faithful to the classical traditions in which he was trained. Accepting his Oscar in 1955 for *The High and the Mighty,* he said: "I would like to thank Beethoven, Brahms, Wagner, Strauss, Rimsky-Korsakov."

Tippett, Sir Michael Kemp (1905–1998)
British composer and music critic. Tippett, one of the best known British composers of the 20th century, was strongly influenced by the modernist composing techniques of Igor STRAVINSKY. Educated at the Royal College of Music in London, Tippett went on to compose popular works that included *Concerto for Double String Orchestra* (1939) and the antifascist oratorio *A Child of Our Time* (1943), which reflected Tippett's pacifist views as a conscientious objector during WORLD WAR II. Later works by Tippett include *The Mid-summer Marriage* (1952) and *The Mask of Time* (1984). His musical writings include *Moving into Aquarius* (1959) and *Music of the Angels* (1980).

TIROS
Acronym for Television and Infrared Observation Satellite, the name given to each of 10 weather satellites that were launched by NASA between April 1, 1960, and July 1, 1965. Using television cameras, sun-angle and horizon scanners, infrared sensors, tape recorders and radios, they examined and recorded the Earth's cloud cover, storms and other weather phenomena. Constructed of aluminum and stainless steel, the 270-lb. cylindrical satellites were 19" high and 42" in diameter and were powered by exterior solar cells and interior nickel-cadmium batteries.

Tirpitz, Alfred von (1849–1930)
German admiral. Born in Küstrin (now Kostrzyn, Poland), he joined the Prussian navy as a cadet in 1865. He soon became an expert in torpedoes and from 1871 on supervised the development of this newly invented weapon for the German navy. Appointed German naval minister in 1897, he began to build a major fleet of battleships, a program that was a source of constant antagonism to Great Britain. He was named grand admiral in 1911. At the outbreak of WORLD WAR I, Tirpitz encouraged the building of a German submarine fleet and supported unrestricted submarine warfare. Frustrated in his efforts to implement this submarine policy, he resigned in 1916. His wartime memoirs were published in 1919. Tirpitz later organized a right-wing nationalistic political party and was a deputy to the Reichstag from 1924 to 1928.

Tiso, Josef (1887–1947)
Slovak political leader. Born near Bratislava, he was ordained a priest in 1910. A Slovak nationalist, Tiso was instrumental in building the Slovak People's Party, a separatist political group. He served as minister of health (1927–29) in the Czechoslovakian coalition government. Tiso succeeded to the leadership of the People's Party in 1938 and that year became premier of the autonomous Slovak Republic created under the provisions of the MUNICH PACT. He proclaimed an independent republic of SLOVAKIA with himself as president in 1939, accepting the status of a German protectorate later that year and siding with the Axis powers during WORLD WAR II. After the war, he went into hiding in Austria, where he was arrested in 1945. Tried as a war criminal, he was found guilty, sentenced to death and hanged on April 18, 1947.

Titanic British OCEAN LINER that, in one of the most famous disasters of the 20th century, struck an iceberg and sank on April 14–15, 1912. On its maiden voyage from Southampton to New York, the liner, which was the largest (900 feet long, 11 decks high) and most luxurious ship afloat and had been called unsinkable, collided with an iceberg in the North Atlantic. Of the over 2,200 aboard some 1,500 were killed. Contributing to the terrible loss of life was the fact that the lifeboats carried by the liner were insufficient to hold all those aboard and that a nearby ship, the *California,* did not respond to the *Titanic*'s SOS call. Later inquiries found that the ship had been traveling much too fast for the icy conditions, which were unusual that far south, and thus was unable to avoid the collision.

Titanic, discovery of the In September 1985 scientists from the Woods Hole Oceanographic Institute in Massachusetts located the wreckage of the legendary ocean liner TITANIC, which sank in 1912. The ship rested 12,500 feet beneath the surface of the Atlantic Ocean, about 500 miles south of Newfoundland. On July 13, 1986, these scientists, led by Robert D. Ballard, explored the *Titanic* from the *Atlantis II* research ship. Their three-man *Alvin* submarine allowed them to roam the liner and its surroundings for a total of 33 hours over 11 dives, ending July 24, 1986. Close viewing was made possible by the *Jason Jr.,* a robot camera that was able to enter the *Titanic* and explore below decks. The camera was tethered to the *Alvin* by a cable and operated from the submarine by remote control. The expedition took 57,000 photographs and 140 videotapes. The wreck of the *Titanic* was found to be broken into two sections and badly rusted. But many goods from the ship were still intact and were well preserved. No human remains were found. The most remarkable discovery was that contrary to expectations, there was no long gash along the ship's side. Ballard said it seemed that the *Titanic* had not been torn open by the iceberg with which it collided, but instead had ground against it. The ship's steel plates had probably buckled, forcing their rivets to pop and opening seams that allowed the ship to flood.

Tito, Marshal (Josip Broz) *(1892–1980)* Yugoslav political leader, president of YUGOSLAVIA (1953–80). Born Josip Broz near the Croatia-Slovenia border, he served with the Austrian infantry in WORLD WAR I and was captured by the Russians in 1915. Escaping in 1917, he joined the BOLSHEVIK revolutionaries at Petrograd and subsequently fought with them during the RUSSIAN CIVIL WAR (1918–21). He returned to Croatia in 1920, becoming a metal worker in Zagreb and a prominent trade union leader. Broz joined the illegal Yugoslav Communist Party, adopting the code name "Tito." Captured by the police in 1928, he was jailed from 1929 to 1934. A member of the politburo from 1934, he was assigned the task of revivifying Yugoslavia's Communist Party. After GERMANY invaded Yugoslavia in 1941, Tito became a leader of the PARTISANS in their resistance to NAZI occupation. With support of the Allies, who repudiated rival resistance leader Draza MIHAILOVIC, Tito was appointed the official head of a new Yugoslav federal government in 1945.

Virtual dictator of the nation, Tito was elected head of a communist-led National Liberation Front government later in 1945, and he quickly proclaimed Yugoslavia a republic and forced the abdication of King PETER II. An advocate of Yugoslav independence, Tito broke with the USSR in 1948 and led his nation in a non–Soviet bloc communist regime. Maintaining his status as a nonaligned country, he established friendly relations with Eastern European states and was usually on cordial terms with Western powers and other nonaligned countries as well. While he achieved a measure of reconciliation with the Soviets in 1955, he was by no means an apologist for all of their policies, and he condemned the armed Russian interventions in HUNGARY (1956) and CZECHOSLOVAKIA (1968). On the home front, he worked toward increased participation in government by the workers and greater economic decentralization. Elected president of Yugoslavia in 1953, he became president for life in 1974 and served in that office until his death in 1980.

Tjader, Cal *(1925–1982)* American JAZZ vibraphonist and percussionist. Tjader was known for his light touch and his original style of Latin-influenced music. He was a prolific performer. After starting his own sextet in the mid-1950s, he turned out albums at breakneck speed. He won a Grammy in 1981 for "La Onda Va Bien."

Toast of the Town, The American television's most famous variety show. Every Sunday night, from June 20, 1948, to June 6, 1971, The Toast of The Town (renamed *The Ed Sullivan Show* in 1955) brought to American homes the strangest mix of jugglers, rock stars, classical artists and theater and film luminaries this side of the June Taylor Dancers. SULLIVAN, a columnist for the *New York Daily News,* brought together a typically eclectic group of guests for the first program: the comedy team of Martin and Lewis, concert pianist Eugene LIST and theater showmen RODGERS and HAMMERSTEIN. No matter that critics complained of the weird blend of talent and Sullivan's awkward presence; or that nightclub comics wickedly lampooned his stiff, peculiar mannerisms and strangled voice—the show worked. And worked. And worked. It was even the affectionate butt of the 1960 Broadway musical, *Bye Bye Birdie,* which contained a hushed and reverential choral number—"Ed Sullivan." To play Sullivan was to make headlines; and many luminaries made their television debuts here—Charles LAUGHTON, Bob HOPE, the BEATLES and Walt DISNEY. In a peculiar quirk of fate a full-hour edition was devoted to Disney on February 8, 1953. A year later Disney began his own television hour on ABC in competition with Sullivan. Eventually Disney surpassed his rival as the longest-running prime-time network show in history. That's show business.

Tobin, James *(1918–2002)* American economist and recipient of the Nobel Prize in economics (1981). Tobin received a B.A. in economics from Harvard University in 1939, and an M.A. from the same institution in 1940. In the early stages of America's participation in WORLD WAR II (1939–45), Tobin worked in the Office of Price Administration (OPA), one of the new government agencies established by U.S. president Franklin D. ROOSEVELT. In 1942 Tobin left the OPA to serve in the naval reserve as an officer on the destroyer USS *Kearney.* At the end of the war, Tobin returned to Harvard, where he received his Ph.D. in 1947. Three years later, he was hired to teach economics at Yale University, where he obtained tenure in 1957 and remained on the faculty until his death in 2002. In 1961 Tobin was appointed a member of U.S. president John F. KENNEDY's Council of Economic Advisors, where he served with Robert M. SOLOW until 1962.

As an economist, Tobin became known for his staunch advocacy of the economic policies of John Maynard KEYNES, such as active state intervention in the economy to prevent the beginning of a recession. To this end, Tobin championed a bold plan for taxation by the UNITED NATIONS (UN) of investment within the foreign currency market, so as to discourage investments that would not increase a nation's economic productivity or provide additional jobs for people across the world. It was also Tobin's hope that the UN would use the revenue it gathered for humanitarian purposes, and to fund long-term loans to developing companies. However, it was for his portfolio selection theory, which explained why investors in the stock market should diversify their investment holdings in order to minimize risk, that won Tobin the Nobel Prize in 1981. On March 11, 2002, Tobin died in New Haven, Connecticut.

Toftoy, Holger N. *(1902–1967)* U.S. military officer. As chief of technical intelligence for U.S. Army ordnance in Europe, Toftoy was responsible for OPERATION PAPERCLIP, which brought Wernher von BRAUN and approximately 129 German scientists and engineers to the United States after WORLD WAR II. Known as "Mr. Missile," Toftoy was continuously on the scene in the early development of guided missiles, including the Redstone missile, which was one of the pioneering rockets used in the U.S. space program. He served for four years as commanding general of Redstone Arsenal in Huntsville, Alabama (1954–58) prior to his retirement in 1960.

Togo Togo, wedged between Ghana and Benin, covers an area of 21,921 square miles on the Gulf of Guinea in western Africa. Part of the German colony of Togoland from 1894 to 1914, the country became a LEAGUE OF NATIONS mandate known as French Togoland in 1922, then a UNITED NATIONS Trust Territory in 1946. In 1956 French Togoland became an autonomous republic within the FRENCH COMMUNITY; in 1960 it became completely independent. The assassination of the first president, Sylvanus Olympio, during a

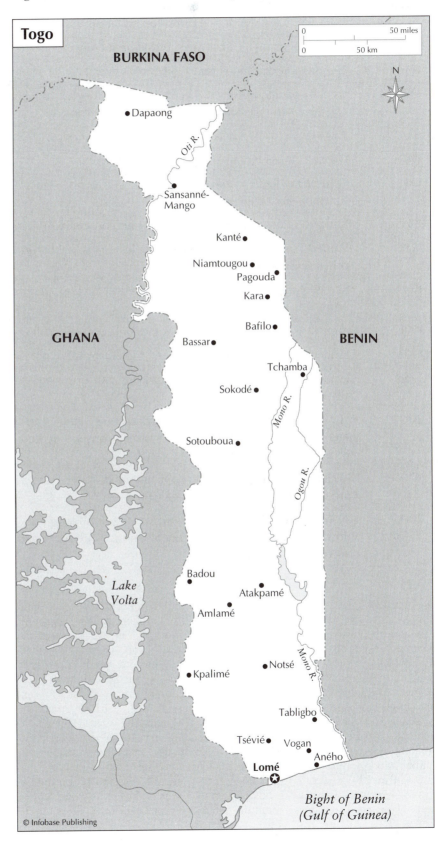

Togo

1884–1914	Togoland is a German protectorate until captured by Anglo-French forces; cocoa and cotton plantations are developed using forced labor.
1922	The region is divided between Britain and France under a League of Nations mandate.
1946	The division continues under a UN trusteeship.
1956	French Togoland votes to become an autonomous republic within the French union. The new Togolese Republic achieves internal self-government.
1960	The Republic of Togo becomes a sovereign nation, with Sylvanus Olympio as president.
1963	Olympio is assassinated by military insurgents.
1967	General Eyadema assumes supreme power as president; the constitution and the National Assembly are suspended.
1972	National referendum approves indefinite continuation of the Eyadema regime.
1980	Eyadema proclaims Third Republic under a new constitution and has himself elected for another seven-year term.
1985	Series of terrorist bombings in Lomé. After a coup attempt French troops come to the government's assistance.
1991	After strikes and demonstrations Eyadema agrees to share power.
1993	Eyadema dissolves the government. Violent protests for democratic reforms ensue.
1998	Eyadema is once again elected president, but observers from the UN and the United States say the vote was fraudulent.
2000	The UN and the Organization of African Unity launch an inquiry into allegations made by Amnesty International that Togo's armed forces executed hundreds of people during the run-up to the 1998 presidential election.
2001	An international commission concludes that there were systematic human-rights violations after the presidential election of 1998.
2005	Eyadema dies after 38 years in power. His son Faure takes power but is forced to stand down due to international condemnation. Faure agrees to hold elections, which he wins amid accusations of voting fraud.

---

coup in 1963 led to another coup, which brought General Etienne Eyadema to power in 1967. Terrorist attacks in 1985–86, which implicated the involvement of neighboring countries, brought French and Zairean troops to the aid of Togo. International allegations of mistreatment of political prisoners, coupled with internal discontent, pressured Eyadema to initiate some reforms. Although Eyadema admitted opposition forces into the government in 1991 and agreed to abide by a new constitution in 1992, he dissolved the coalition government in

1993 and has repeatedly been censured for human rights violations. During the 1998 presidential elections, widespread reports of extrajudicial executions led to pressure from AMNESTY INTERNATIONAL and other human rights groups for an investigation. A joint commission of inquiry organized by the UN and the ORGANIZATION OF AFRICAN UNITY (OAU) released a report in 2001 concluding that "systematic violations of human rights" had occurred during the election and proposing periodic visits to the country by a United Nations rapporteur to monitor the in-

vestigation carried out by the Togo government and to protect witnesses to the inquiry. Gnassingbé Eyadema died in early 2005 after 38 years in power. The military's immediate but short-lived installation of his son, Faure Gnassingbé, as president provoked widespread international condemnation. Mr Faure stood down and called elections which he won two months later. The opposition said the vote was rigged.

Tojo, Hideki (*1884–1948*) Japanese general, political leader and prime minister of wartime JAPAN (1941–44). Born in Tokyo, Tojo attended Japan's military college and was military attaché to GERMANY after WORLD WAR I. The leader of Japan's militarist party from 1931 and a leading advocate of armed Japanese expansionism, he became war minister in 1940 and was instrumental in forging his nation's alliances with Germany and ITALY. Becoming prime minister in 1941, Tojo authorized the attack on the U.S. fleet at PEARL HARBOR and urged his country's offensive thrusts throughout Asia. He remained Japan's wartime leader until repeated defeats forced him to resign in 1944. After the war, Tojo was arrested (1945) as a war criminal, tried before a military tribunal, found guilty and hanged.

Tokyo Rose *(1916–2006)* Japanese-American propaganda broadcaster. Iva Ikuko Toguri d'Aquino was born in Los Angeles of Japanese parents. Visiting Japan when WORLD WAR II broke out, she was stranded in Tokyo. In 1942 she began work at the Domei news agency, soon moving to Radio Tokyo. There she became one of 13 women announcers whose task it was to try to demoralize American troops stationed in the Pacific. Broadcasting music and chat that urged the men to surrender or return home, the seductive-voiced announcer was nicknamed "Tokyo Rose" by her GI listeners. Returning to the U.S. in 1948, she was convicted of treason the following year, but claimed she had been forced to make the broadcasts. Released from prison in 1956, she was formally pardoned by President Gerald FORD in 1977, and her U.S. citizenship was restored.

Tolkien, J(ohn) R(onald) R(euel) *(1892–1973)* English fantasy novelist and literary scholar. Tolkien is ranked by many critics and readers as the greatest fantasy writer of the 20th century. His most famous work is THE LORD OF THE RINGS trilogy, comprised of the three novels *The Fellowship of the Ring* (1954), *The Two Towers* (1954) and *The Return of the King* (1955). Tolkien, who was educated at Oxford University, also taught at that university for many years and wrote noteworthy scholarly studies of medieval English literature, such as *A Middle English Vocabulary* (1922). He was also good friends with fellow scholars and writers C. S. LEWIS and Charles Williams, both of whom also wrote in the fantasy vein. Tolkien described his *The Silmarillion* (1977) as an attempt to create a mythology for his native England.

Toller, Ernst *(1893–1939)* German playwright and poet. Toller was a leading figure in the expressionist school of German drama, as well as a vivid and fiercely political poet. He is best remembered for his plays, which combined intense emotionality with leftist political didacticism. Two of his early plays, *The Inner Change* (1919) and *Masses and Man* (1920), led to Toller being imprisoned as a communist. Subsequent plays by Toller focused on the themes of working class revolt and individual struggle and martyrdom. These include *The Machine Wreckers* (1922), *Hoppla!* (1927), *Draw the Fires!* (1930) and *The Blind Goddess* (1932).

Tolstoy, Count Aleksey Nikolayevich *(1883–1945)* Russian novelist, playwright and NATIONAL BOLSHEVIK. He rose to fame as a NEOREALIST before the 1917 revolution, and supported the WHITES during the CIVIL WAR. He emigrated, but as a member of the Change of Landmarks organization, Tolstoy returned to Russia. At first, as a FELLOW TRAVELER, he was regarded with suspicion, but by the mid-1930s, he was regarded as a loyal Stalinist and did much to create the STALIN cult. He is also remembered for his trilogy on the intelligentsia between 1914 and 1921, *The Road to Calvary* (1920–41).

Tombaugh, Clyde William *(1906–1997)* American astronomer who discovered the planet Pluto. Raised on a Kansas farm, Tombaugh developed an early interest in astronomy. As a teenager, he studied Mars and Jupiter through homemade telescopes and sent drawings of his observations to the Lowell Observatory in Arizona. The observatory hired him to photograph the then-unknown planet that lay beyond Neptune. On February 18, 1930, at age 24, Tombaugh discovered the planet, Pluto—the first planetary discovery since 1846. Tombaugh received the Jackson-Gwilt Medal and Gift of the Royal Astronomical Society of Great Britain in 1931. During his long career he constructed 10 reflecting telescopes and made several thousand visual and photographic observations through the large Lowell telescope. He was also a professor at New Mexico State University, where he taught astronomy, geology and meteorology. He continued to lecture into his 80s.

Tonga The Kingdom of Tonga consists of an archipelago of some 172 islands (36 permanently inhabited) in the southwest Pacific, 404 miles east of FIJI and 1,863 miles northeast of Sydney, Australia; total area is 289 square miles (see map on page 957). In 1900 Tonga signed a Treaty of Friendship and Protection with Britain in order to ward off German advances; under the treaty, Tongan foreign policy was conducted through a British consul. King George Tupou II died in 1918 and was succeeded by his daughter, Queen Salote Tupou III. During WORLD WAR II she placed Tonga's resources at the disposal of the Allies. On the queen's death in 1965 her son, Prince Tungi, became King Taufa'ahau Tupou IV. Tonga and Britain signed a new Treaty of Friendship in 1958; complete independence from Britain came in 1970, when Tonga also joined the COMMONWEALTH. Although the 1987 general election indicated areas of discontent, overall political power has remained with the king's appointees and the nobility, who together constitute a permanent majority within the legislature. The king's 70th birthday in July 1988 was marked by official celebrations. Elections in February 1990 resulted in several prominent prodemocracy commoners entering the legislature. Despite vigorous efforts throughout the 1990s by opposition groups, such as the Tonga People's Party, to create a liberal constitution for the country, Tonga remained solidly under the control of the monarchy, which brought the country into the UNITED NATIONS (UN) in 1999. A tentative step toward reform was taken in early 2005 when elected officials were appointed to the cabinet for the first time. Previously, all cabinet members had been handpicked by the king from outside parliament, but demands for change have became stronger. A public sector strike in 2005, marked by major street protests,

	TONGA
1900	The Friendship ("Protectorate") Treaty is signed between King George Tupou II and Britain, establishing British control over defense and foreign affairs but leaving internal political affairs under Tongan control.
1918	Queen Salote Tupou III ascends the throne.
1965	Taufa'ahau Tupou IV becomes king.
1970	Tonga becomes a fully independent nation within the Commonwealth.
1987	Elections of people's representatives to Legislative Assembly are dominated by newcomers, who are severe critics of the government.
1990	In general elections, Akilisi Pohiva and his reformist supporters win six of the nine seats reserved for people's representatives in the legislature.
1992	Critics of Tonga's monarchial government organize a prodemocracy convention, which the monarchy boycotts.
1994	The prodemocracy movement founds the People's Party, Tonga's first political party.
1999	Tonga is granted membership in the UN.
2005	Elected officials enter the parliament for the first time. Thousands march on the capital demanding democratic reform.
2006	The first nonroyal prime minister is elected.

expanded into a campaign for political reform.

Tonight Show, The Popular American late-night television talk/variety show, which since 1954 has shaped the nighttime viewing habits of several generations of viewers. The prototype was the short-lived "Broadway Open House," which appeared at 11:00 P.M. on weeknights from 1950 to 1951 on the NBC network. Sylvester "Pat" Weaver, NBC programming chief, brought in newcomer Steve ALLEN, and the show, retitled the *Tonight* show premiered on September 27, 1954. Allen's relaxed manner, talent for ad-libbing and sketch comedy and quick eye for young talent—which would include bandleader Skitch Henderson and singers Steve Lawrence, Eydie Gorme and Andy Williams—immediately established the format that would survive generally unchanged to this day. After Allen left to do his own show in 1956 successors included Jack Lescoulie (*America after Dark*, 1957) and Jack Paar (*The Jack Paar Show*, 1957–62). Then on October 2, 1962, the calm and unflappable Johnny CARSON took over and the show was re-

named *The Tonight Show Starring Johnny Carson*. Characters and sketches like "Carnack the Magnificent" (who first appeared in 1964) and "The Mighty Carson Art Players" (which first appeared in 1966) quickly became a part of the national vernacular. In May 1972 the show moved permanently from New York City to Burbank, California. In May 1992 Carson retired from *The Tonight Show,* and was succeeded by Jay Leno. The early episodes of the original *Tonight* show have been lost. A man in charge of the NBC storage facility emptied out all the kinescopes of the shows and burned them in the late 1950s.

Tonkin Gulf Resolution On August 2, 1964, the U.S. destroyer *Maddox*—on patrol in international waters in the Gulf of Tonkin off the coast of North VIETNAM—was attacked by North Vietnamese torpedo boats. The attack was repulsed. On August 4 the *Maddox,* joined by the destroyer *Turner Joy,* again reported an attack by North Vietnamese torpedo boats. Using these incidents as a *casus bellum,* President JOHNSON asked Congress for a resolution empowering him to "take all nec-

essary measures to repel an armed attack against the forces of the U.S. and to prevent further aggression." On August 7 the so-called Gulf of Tonkin Resolution (officially the Southeast Asia Resolution) passed the Senate by a vote of 88 to 2 and the House by a unanimous voice vote of 416 to 0. Some have claimed that Congress was misled by the Gulf of Tonkin Resolution and did not intend to grant the president a de facto declaration of war. On March 1, 1966, long after the bombing of North Vietnam had begun and American ground combat forces had been committed to battle, Senator Wayne Morse introduced an amendment to repeal this resolution. This amendment was defeated in the Senate by a vote of 92 to 5. On August 18, 1967, President Johnson repudiated the Gulf of Tonkin Resolution as the legal basis for the war in VIETNAM and fell back on his authority granted by Article II of the Constitution as commander in chief of the armed forces. (See also VIETNAM WAR.)

Tooker, George (*1920–*) American painter. Born in Brooklyn, New York, Tooker studied at Harvard and the Art Students League. An American SURREALIST, the artist takes for his subject the anonymity and unease of contemporary urban life. Immaculately realistic and preternaturally still, often painted in egg tempera, his works portray round-headed, flat-faced, almond-eyed figures in enigmatic and vaguely threatening situations. Among his characteristic paintings are *The Table*, *The Subway* (Whitney Museum, New York City) and *Mirror II* (Addison Gallery, Andover, Massachusetts).

Torre, Joe *(1940–)* American professional baseball player (1960–77) and manager of the New York Yankees (1995–). Born in Brooklyn, New York, Torre played as a catcher for the Milwaukee (and later Atlanta) Braves from 1960 to 1969, when he was traded to the St. Louis Cardinals. He won the National League's Most Valuable Player Award in 1971 for leading the league with a .363 batting average and 137 runs-batted-in (RBIs). At the end of the 1974 season the Cardinals traded Torre to the New York Mets. The Mets released him from his contract halfway through the 1977 season, and Torre then announced his retirement.

During his last year as a player, Torre also served as the Mets' manager, but was fired from that position in 1981 after five consecutive losing seasons. Hired to manage the Atlanta Braves, Torre led them to the National League Atlantic Division pennant in 1982. However, after failing to duplicate that success in 1983 and 1984, when the Braves finished second and third in their divisions, respectively, Torre was fired at the end of the 1984 season. In 1990 Torre succeeded Whitey Herzog as manager of the Saint Louis Cardinals and served in that capacity for five years. He succeeded Buck Showalter as manager of the New York Yankees in November 1995. It was as a Yankee that Torre recorded his greatest managerial successes. His team compiled a record of 786 wins and 506 losses, won eight American League pennants, and won the World Series in 1996, 1998, 1999, and 2000.

Torrijos, Omar Herrera *(1929–1981)* Panamanian military and political leader. A career officer, Torrijos had attained the rank of lieutenant colonel by 1968, when he and Colonel Boris Martinez led the coup that toppled PANAMA's president Arnulfo ARIAS MADRID. The following year Torrijos was responsible for sending Martinez into exile; he took control of Panama, at the same time elevating himself to brigadier general. Panama's de facto leader from 1969, he was officially named chief of state in 1972. Torrijos became a strong and often repressive leader. He instituted a number of reforms in his country's economy, taking land from Panama's powerful oligarchy and distributing it to the hitherto landless, and in its social practices, by such innovations as birth control education. An advocate of Panama's right to the PANAMA CANAL, he negotiated with U.S. president Jimmy CARTER and was responsible for the 1978 canal treaties. In 1978 he resigned as president, but retained control over the country as head of the National Guard until his death in a plane crash on July 31, 1981.

Torvill and Dean British ice dancers. **Jayne Torvill** (1957–), a former insurance clerk, and **Christopher Dean** (1958–), a former policeman, were granted £14,000 by the Nottingham City Council to help with their training. They repaid that loan by going on to become the greatest ice dancing team in the history of the sport. At the Helsinki World Championships in 1983 they posted their first unbroken string of 6.0s for artistic impression, scoring 5.9s for technical merit. In 1984 at the Sarajevo Winter OLYMPICS, their stunning interpretation of RAVEL's *Bolero* pushed the limits of the sport, for which they received 12 6.0s of a possible 18. The team went on to their fourth world championship, followed by a career as professional skaters.

Toscanini, Arturo *(1867–1957)* Italian-born opera and symphonic conductor. During his 68-year career, Toscanini was the most famous conductor in the world. Born in Parma, Italy, he graduated from the Parma Conservatory in 1885 as a cellist. His conducting career began during a South American tour with an orchestra; as a last-minute replacement, he conducted *Aida* from memory. Many appointments followed: principal conductor at La Scala, Milan, for 16 years; conductor of the New York Philharmonic-Symphony Orchestra for seven years; and leader of the NBC Symphony for 17 seasons. He conducted at many world premieres, including PUCCINI's *La Bohème* (1896), *La Fanciulla del West* (*The Girl of the Golden West*) (1910), *Turandot* (1926) and Pietro Mascagni's *Pagliacci* (1892). With the NBC Symphony, formed in 1937 by David SARNOFF, president of the Radio Corporation of America (RCA), he reached millions of people by radio and through numerous studio recordings. No greater testament to his abilities as an opera conductor can be found than the fact that he was the preeminent Verdi conductor in Italy and the preeminent WAGNER conductor in Germany. However, his fierce opposition to FASCISM and NAZISM led him to refuse to appear in both countries during WORLD WAR II. Although small in stature, his intense eyes, expressive hands and phenomenal musical memory placed him in absolute control of any orchestra. He was the embodiment (and the subsequent public image) of the "superstar" musician, although he said he rejected personal interpretations in favor of absolute fidelity to the score.

totalitarianism Type of government in which the state controls all aspects of its citizens' lives. Totalitarianism is not an ideology, but rather a means for assuring that an ideology, such as COMMUNISM, can achieve its ends without opposition. A peculiarly 20th-century development, it allows no scope for private life; the individual exists only to serve the state. Totalitarian governments attempt to control all forms of thought through relentless PROPAGANDA. Even the discoveries and conclusions of science will appear to underwrite the ideology of the party or state. The USSR under STALIN, Cambodia under POL POT and the KHMER ROUGE and Nazi Germany are prime examples of totalitarian regimes. George ORWELL's novel *1984* paints a chilling portrait of a totalitarian society, while *The Origins of Totalitarianism* by German philosopher Hannah ARENDT provides a perceptive analysis of totalitarianism. Despite the crushing power of totalitarian regimes, with their omnipresent secret police and the immense human suffering that they have caused, 20th-century history suggests that such systems collapse through their own internal weaknesses.

Tourette, La Convent (monastery) at Eveux near Lyons in France designed (1957–60) by LE CORBUSIER, one of his most distinguished works in the post–World War II style often called NEW BRUTALISM. Forming a hollow square, the building is made up of a church on one side and a U-shaped group of monastic buildings around a central courtyard. Le Corbusier is said to have studied the medieval Cistercian monastery of Le Thoronet, making it a basis for the utter simplicity and austerity of his design, which relies entirely on the geometry of its proportions (based on Le Corbusier's modular system) to achieve a sense of extraordinary beauty and serenity in a structure of rough concrete ("*beton brut*"). The monks of the monastery have now relocated in accord with changing ideas of their religious duties, and the building has become a study and research center.

Townes, Charles Hard (*1915– *) American physicist. A graduate of Furman University (1935) and California Institute of Technology (1939), he worked during WORLD WAR II with RADAR and microwave spectroscopy. He taught physics at Columbia University (1948–59), where he wrote a paper on maser and LASER power in 1958. He was vice president and director of research of the Institute of Defense Analysis (1959) and joined the University of California staff in 1967. He shared the NOBEL PRIZE for physics (1964) with Russians Nikolai Busov and Alexander Prochorov for work in quantum electronics and oscillators and amplifiers, leading to maser and laser technology.

Townsend, Francis Everett (*1867–1960*) American physician. While practicing medicine in Southern California during the Depression, Townsend formulated a scheme for a national retirement pension. Called the "Townsend Plan," it would have provided $200 per month to retirees over the age of 60 who would agree to spend the money the month it was received; the funds were to be raised by a 2 percent sales tax on business transactions. The Townsend Plan gained millions of advocates, but it was obviated by the SOCIAL SECURITY ACT OF 1935.

Toynbee, Arnold J(oseph) (*1889–1975*) British historian. Toynbee was one of the most influential historians of the 20th century. His magnum opus was the 12-volume *A Study of History* (1934–61), in which Toynbee examined the entire course of recorded world history and concluded that each and every dominant civilization was subject to an all but inevitable cycle of triumphant early struggle, vigorous growth and stagnant decline. Educated at Oxford University, Toynbee was a member of British Intelligence during WORLD WAR I and attended the postwar Paris peace conference. He taught for many years at the University of London. *Experiences* (1969) is his autobiography.

Toyota JAPAN's largest AUTOMOBILE manufacturer, and the second-largest in the world. Founded in 1933, in the mid-1950s it revolutionized manufacturing with the **just-in-time** system. Toyota sales were mainly domestic until the early 1970s, when the Arab OIL EMBARGO and the soaring cost of gasoline caused many Americans to turn to smaller, more fuel-efficient cars. Toyota now exports more than half the cars it makes in Japan and also operates assembly plants in several foreign countries, including the U.S.

Tracy, Spencer (*1900–1967*) American film and theater actor. Tracy is one of the legendary figures of American film, a craggy leading man who won over audiences and critics by virtue of his remarkable acting ability. Tracy began his acting career on the stage in the 1920s, scoring a Broadway hit as a prisoner on death row in *The Last Mile* (1929). He moved on to HOLLYWOOD where he continued to be typecast as a gangster until his dramatic breakthrough in the film *The Power and the Glory* (1933). Tracy won his first best actor ACADEMY AWARD for his role in *Captains Courageous* (1937) and his second for his portrayal of Father Flanagan in *Boys Town* (1938). In the 1940s and 1950s he was teamed with Katharine HEPBURN (with whom he carried on an enduring off-screen romance) in a number of films, including *Woman of the Year* (1942), *State of the Union* (1948), *Adam's Rib* (1949) and *Pat and Mike* (1952). He also gave notable performances in *The Old Man and the Sea* (1958), *Inherit the Wind* (1960) and *Judgment at Nuremberg* (1961). Tracy was reunited with Hepburn in his last film, *Guess Who's Coming to Dinner* (1967).

Trades Union Congress (TUC) Federation of about 160 British trade unions, founded in 1968. The TUC's basic function is to coordinate union action by annual conferences of union representatives where matters of common concern are discussed. As an umbrella organization, the TUC is somewhat analogous to the AFL-CIO in the U.S.

Trakl, Georg (*1887–1914*) Austrian poet. Trakl is one of the most intense and visionary poets of the 20th century. While most of his verse was published only posthumously, Trakl was recognized in his own lifetime by luminaries such as the philosopher Ludwig WITTGENSTEIN, who gave the poet a substantial sum of money to support his writing. Wittgenstein observed that Trakl's poems possessed "the tone of a man of real genius." Born in Salzburg, Trakl trained as a chemist but soon turned to poetry as his true vocation. During his short tragic lifetime, he abused drugs and alcohol and suffered from incestuous longings for his sister. Drafted by the Austrian army at the start of WORLD WAR I, he committed suicide in a military hospital in Cracow, Poland. Trakl's poems have been frequently translated into English. *Selected Poems* (1968), edited by the British poet Christopher Middleton, contains a good bilingual sampling of Trakl's verse.

transistor Miniature device that permits a very small signal (in the form of electrical current) in one circuit to control a relatively large current in another circuit. Invented in 1947 by John BARDEEN, Walter H. BRATTAIN and William SHOCKLEY at Bell Laboratories in New Jersey, the transistor revolutionized the electronics industry. Further research and work on transistors and transistor theory led to astonishing breakthroughs in the field of superconductivity. Technological advances have made it possible to install millions of transistors on a single **silicon chip** (also known as a microchip). The transistor has had an immense effect on everyday life. It replaced bulky vacuum tubes and made possible the development of a myriad of products taken for granted in the early 21st century, ranging from the transistor radio to the home computer. The cheap cost of the transistor has also made these products available to a mass market of consumers. Communications satellites, modern telephone equipment, videocassette cameras and recorders—all would be impossible without the transistor.

Trans-Jordan See JORDAN.

Trans-Siberian Railway Railway, running from Chelyabinsk in the Urals to Vladivostok on the Pacific, constructed between 1891 and 1915. It is 4,388 miles long and is the world's longest railway. Its construction greatly aided Russian colonization of SIBERIA and the Far East.

Trapp, Baroness Maria von (Maria Augusta Kutschera) *(1905–1987)* Austrian singer. She was the guiding force behind a family of singers who became known throughout the world when their story was told in the play and film *The Sound of Music*. The family's tale of flight from Austria in 1938 to avoid complicity with Nazi rule was transformed, in 1965, into one of Hollywood's greatest success stories. Julie Andrews portrayed Baroness von Trapp in the film.

Traubel, Helen *(1903–1972)* American opera singer. One of the great Wagnerian sopranos of her time, Traubel made her concert debut in 1924 with the St. Louis Symphony. In 1937 she sang the only female role in the world premiere of Walter Damrosch's opera *The Man Without a Country.* She made her debut as a member of the New York Metropolitan Opera as Sieglinde in *Die Walküre* in 1939. During her 14 years with the Met, Traubel's most famous roles were Isolde in *Tristan und Isolde* and Brunnhilde in *Die Walküre*. From 1953 she gave concerts, appeared in nightclubs and on television and in two films and also authored a mystery set at the Met.

Traven, B. (pen name of Ret Marut, Otto Feige or Traven Torsvan?) B. Traven is one of the most mysterious figures in 20th-century literature; his exact identity and place and date of birth are still subject to much doubt. Some investigators believe that B. Tra-

ven was the pen name of Otto Feige, a German who traveled widely and worked variously as a manual laborer, an actor and the editor of an anarchist journal. He was also rumored to be the illegitimate son of Kaiser Wilhelm I. Traven's widow announced in 1990 that he had been Ret Marut, a leftwing revolutionary in Germany during WORLD WAR I; he may have been born in Chicago. Sometime between 1914 and 1924 Traven arrived in Mexico, where he lived for the bulk of his remaining years. His novels and stories were written in German and first published in Germany in the 1920s. They have since been translated into more than 30 languages and sold more than 25 million copies, and are now required reading in Mexican schools. Traven wrote about serious issues of social justice, cruelty and greed while employing a taut, suspenseful style. His most notable books include *The Death Ship* (1926), *The Treasure of the Sierra Madre* (1927, made into a classic film by director John HUSTON in 1948) *Stories By The Man Nobody Knows* (1961) and *The Night Visitor* (1966).

Treblinka Nazi CONCENTRATION CAMP. In June 1941, Hitler proposed the FINAL SOLUTION in his attempt to destroy people he considered "non-aryan." In June 1942 Treblinka was established in central Poland as an extermination/death camp. Many of its victims were JEWS from the Warsaw ghetto. At its peak as many as 25,000 were killed daily—over 870,000 in all. One survivor later testified, "Treblinka has no beginning and no end, whoever was in Treblinka will never get out of it."

Trend, Lord (Burke St. John) *(1914–1987)* British civil servant. Trend was secretary of the cabinet (1963–73) during the governments of British prime ministers Harold MACMILLAN and Harold WILSON. After a 50-year career in civil service, he was made a life peer upon his retirement in 1974. In 1974–75 he undertook an inquiry to determine whether Sir Roger Hollis, former director general of MI5, the counterintelligence unit of the British intelligence service, was a Soviet spy.

Trepper, Leopold *(1904–1982)* Polish-born anti-fascist. As leader of

the so-called Red Orchestra network in NAZI Europe, Trepper was one of the most successful spymasters of WORLD WAR II. The network was largely responsible for supplying intelligence that helped the Soviets defeat Hitler's forces at STALINGRAD (1942–43). Later arrested by the GESTAPO, Trepper escaped and became active in the RESISTANCE. However, on his return to the USSR in 1945 he was arrested by the Soviets on charges of having collaborated with the Germans—a common fate for many Russians and Poles in similar circumstances. Repatriated to Poland under house arrest after STALIN's death in 1955, he was allowed to emigrate to Israel in 1973 after a worldwide campaign for his release.

Tretyakov, Sergei Mikhailovich *(1892–1939)* Soviet author and journalist. Tretyakov's poetry includes the collection *Iron Pause* (1919), but it was as a playwright that he achieved fame. His grotesque anticolonial *Road China* (1926) was widely successful. He proclaimed the death of fiction and a new empirical writing that would be the true expression of Marxist-Leninist materialism and suggested the creation of literary workshops. He was arrested and executed during the Purges as an alleged Chinese spy.

Trevelyan, George M(acaulay) *(1876–1962)* English historian. Trevelyan was one of the most widely read and influential English historians of his generation. His approach was marked by a deeply humanistic belief in political and societal progress. Educated at Harrow and at Trinity College, Cambridge, Trevelyan served as Regius Professor of Modern History at Cambridge (1927–40) and as master of Trinity College (1940–51). While Trevelyan wrote numerous volumes on English history from the Elizabethan period to the modern era, he remains best known for his three-volume *History of England* (1926).

Trevelyan, John *(1904–1986)* British film censor. As secretary of the British Board of Film Censors from 1958 to 1971, Trevelyan became as well-known a figure in Britain as any nonacting member of the film industry. Though opposed to censorship in principle, he argued that safeguards for children were needed by society.

Trevino, Lee Buck *(1939–)* U.S. golfer. Although his personality sometimes overshadowed his achievements, the charismatic Trevino was one of the leading golfers of the 1970s. He won two U.S. Opens, the second in a memorable 1971 playoff with Jack NICKLAUS, two PGA championships and two British Opens. He represented the United States on six Ryder Cup teams and five World Cup teams. After 27 tour victories, he went on to combine play on the Senior Tour with a career as a broadcaster.

Trevor, William (William Trevor Cox) *(1928–)* Anglo-Irish novelist and short story writer. Trevor is notable for his poignant, closely drawn fiction that focuses on Ireland. His first, *A Standard of Behavior* (1958) was well received, but he achieved greater recognition with *The Old Boys* (1964), which he would later adapt into a play. While his work is often sad, Trevor is able to infuse it with an ironic wit. For example, one of his finest novels, *Mrs. Eckdorf at O'Neill's Hotel* (1973), borrows from the absurd vision of Flann O'BRIEN and the realism and sympathy of James JOYCE. His many short story collections include *The Day We Got Drunk on Cake, and Other Stories* (1967), *Angels at the Ritz and Other Stories* (1975) and *Family Sins and Other Stories* (1990). Other novels are *Other People's Worlds* (1980), *The Silence in the Garden* (1988) and *Death in Summer* (1998). Trevor has also written plays and adapted his fiction for British television.

Trevor-Roper, Hugh Redwald (Baron Dacre of Glanton) *(1914–2003)* British historian. Trevor-Roper attended Oxford, where he was Regius Professor of Modern History from 1957 to 1980. Also involved in contemporary affairs, he was director of the *Times* newspapers from 1974. He was created a baron in 1979. Trevor-Roper was a prolific writer with enormous range. His books include *Archbishop Laud* (1940), *The Last Days of Hitler* (1947), *The Gentry, 1540–1640* (1953), *The Rise of Christian Europe* (1966), *Renaissance Essays* (1985) and *Catholics, Anglicans and Puritans* (1987).

Trial, The Classic novel (1937) by Czechoslovakian author Franz KAFKA.

The Trial stands as one of the paradigmatic novels of the 20th century. Its basic plot concerns the travails and anguish of one Joseph K., who is summoned to appear before a tribunal at a vague future date for an unspecified offense. While Joseph K. regards himself, at first, as innocent, his own underlying sense of guilt and of spiritual confusion lead him, in essence, to inwardly try the merits of his own soul while continuing to yearn for outward official absolution. Numerous critics have interpreted *The Trial* as a masterful parable on the absurdly tangled relationship between government bureaucracy and individual citizens, as well as a commentary on the absence of a clearly revealed moral or spiritual law for humankind. A film version of the novel was directed by Orson WELLES in 1962. (See also THE CASTLE.)

Triangle Shirtwaist fire Deadly fire that occurred in a women's clothing workshop in a loft building in New York City on March 25, 1911. Blocked exits and inadequate fire escapes caused many to be trapped inside the burning building and resulted in the death of 146 workers, mainly young Jewish and Italian women, many of them poor immigrants. The fire drew the public's attention to the terrible conditions in America's urban sweatshops. This aroused consciousness ultimately resulted in legislation that improved fire, health and sanitary regulations and upgraded factory working conditions.

"trickle-down" theory See SUPPLY-SIDE ECONOMICS.

Triennale Design exhibition held every three years at Milan, Italy. The first Milan Triennale was held in 1933, showing the work of many of Europe's pioneer modern designers, including Walter GROPIUS, LE CORBUSIER, Adolf LOOS and Ludwig MIES VAN DER ROHE. The sequence of exhibitions was interrupted during World War II, but resumed in 1947 and continues as a showcase of modern, mostly Italian, design achievements.

Trifonov, Yuri Valentinovich *(1925–1981)* Soviet novelist. Trifonov was best known for works that explored the Stalinist era and the moral conflicts of Moscow intellectuals (see also STALIN, STALINISM). His first novel, *Students* (1950), won a Stalin Prize, but his later

books were more original. Although he was not among the more outspoken dissident writers, he wrote with great allusive artistry that tested the limits of Soviet censorship. Among his major literary works were *The Old Man* (1984), *The Exchange* (1978), *Taking Stock* (1978) and *The Long Goodbye* (1978).

Trilling, Lionel *(1905–1975)* American literary critic, novelist and educator. Trilling was one of the most influential literary critics of his generation. Educated at Columbia University, he taught at that institution for over four decades. His first book, *Matthew Arnold* (1939), was an intensive study of the 19th-century English critic who strongly influenced Trilling as to the importance of culture as a formative aspect of personality. *The Middle of the Journey* (1947), Trilling's only novel, concerns a one-time political liberal who finds that all political ideologies have begun to fail him. *The Opposing Self* (1955) is a collection of essays on the importance of an ongoing struggle between self and society. Trilling's later works include *Sincerity and Authenticity* (1972) and *Mind in the Modern World* (1973).

Trimble, David (Baron Trimble of Lisnagarvey) *(1944–)* Leader of the Ulster Unionist political party in Northern Ireland and winner of the Nobel Peace Prize (1998). After practicing law and lecturing on law for Queen's University, Trimble joined the Vanguard Progressive Unionist Party, which staunchly advocated continued union with Great Britain and championed the cause of Ulster's Protestants. When the Vanguard Unionists disintegrated in 1978, Trimble joined the more moderate Ulster Unionist Party and was promptly elected party secretary.

In 1990 Trimble was elected to the British Parliament representing the Upper Bann region of Northern Ireland, and in 1995 became head of the Ulster Unionist Party. He signed the 1998 Good Friday Agreement, which established a joint power-sharing arrangement between Irish nationalists and Unionists in an executive authority and parliament called the Northern Ireland Assembly. Trimble then became the prime minister of this government. For this political breakthrough Trimble and John HUME, (Social Democratic and Labour Party [SDLP] leader and

Irish nationalist leader) were awarded the Nobel Peace Prize in 1998.

Trimble's willingness to negotiate with the Irish nationalists, including SINN FÉIN, the political wing of the IRISH REPUBLICAN ARMY (IRA), led to a Unionist backlash against him. As he came under increasing criticism within his own party, Trimble denounced the IRA for failing to complete its total disarmament by June 2001, as required by the Good Friday Agreement, and resigned the following month. In October 2001 the IRA agreed to resume the process of disarmament, and Trimble attempted to return to the Northern Ireland government. But he was prevented from doing so by dissenters in his own party, and by British prime minister Tony BLAIR's decision to disband the parliament and authority in 2002. In 2006, however, it was announced that Trimble would take a seat in the House of Lords, as Baron Trimble of Lisnagarvey, a life peerage.

Trinidad and Tobago Southernmost of the Caribbean islands, Trinidad is seven miles north of Venezuela and covers an area of 1,863 square miles; Tobago (116 sq. mi.) is 20 miles northeast of Trinidad. British

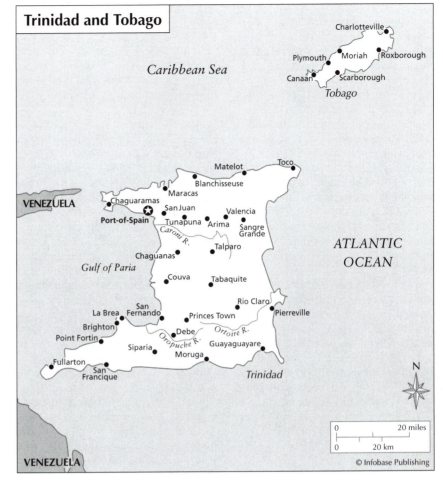

TRINIDAD AND TOBAGO	
1889	Trinidad and Tobago are amalgamated as a British colony.
1958–62	Trinidad and Tobago becomes part of the West Indies Federation.
1962	Following the breakup of the West Indies Federation, Trinidad and Tobago is granted independence.
1976	Trinidad and Tobago adopts a republican constitution.
1980	The country experiences a rash of firebombings, arsons and political shootings.
1990	Members of a Muslim sect stage a coup attempt; the rebels surrender the following day.
1992	The Muslim militants are granted amnesty by the government.
1993	Economic growth is spurred by the discovery of large supplies of natural gas.
2001	Early general elections yield an unprecedented tie in which the governing party and the main opposition party win 18 seats each.
2002	Another parliamentary election is held that ends the deadlock.
2003	The state-owned sugar company shuts down with a loss of 8,000 jobs.
2005	At least 10,000 march in protest against the soaring rate of violent crime.

possessions since 1787 and 1814, respectively, Trinidad and Tobago were linked together in 1888. They became part of the Federation of the West Indies in 1958 and achieved full independence in 1962. In 1976 the Republic of Trinidad and Tobago was formed and joined the COMMONWEALTH OF NATIONS. Since the 1980s various opposition political groups have jockeyed for power. These political struggles continued into the 1990s, and were highlighted by a series of parliamentary ties in 2001 and 2002. In October 2002 Patrick Manning's People's National Movement broke the tie in delegates by obtaining a narrow majority.

Triple Alliance Alliance among GERMANY, the AUSTRO-HUNGARIAN EMPIRE and ITALY in the years leading up to WORLD WAR I. These nations pledged to help defend one another if any one of them was attacked. The formation of the Triple Alliance stirred distrust among other European nations; Britain, France and Russia formed the TRIPLE ENTENTE in response. During World War I Italy fought against her former allies.

Triple Entente Alliance among the UNITED KINGDOM, FRANCE and RUSSIA that made these nations partners in WORLD WAR I. The Triple Entente was formed in response to the perceived threat posed by the TRIPLE ALLIANCE. In 1904 Britain and France formed the ENTENTE CORDIALE. Three years later, Britain and Russia signed the ANGLO-RUSSIAN CONVENTION.

Trippe, Juan Terry (1899–1981) American airline pioneer. In 1927 Trippe founded PAN AMERICAN WORLD AIRWAYS, which he headed for the next 41 years. An aggressive entrepreneur, he seized every opportunity to extend international airline service, eventually expanding Pan Am's original 90-mile route into a worldwide network connecting the U.S. with 85 countries. Under his leadership Pan Am established a number of firsts in air passenger transportation. He established the first international airmail service (1927), the first scheduled service between the U.S. and Asia (1935) and the first scheduled service between U.S. and Europe (1939). Trippe's success made long-distance air travel an everyday reality and also spelled the end of the era of the great OCEAN LINERS. Ironically, in the decade after Trippe's death, Pan Am experienced serious financial difficulties, and the airline's existence was in jeopardy.

Tropic of Cancer Autobiographical novel published in 1934 by American writer Henry MILLER. *Tropic of Cancer,* which is today widely regarded as a classic work of 20th-century American literature, drew a great deal of controversy in the first three decades after its publication. The book initially appeared in PARIS in 1934. Miller, an expatriate American living in the French capital during the worldwide GREAT DEPRESSION, wrote an uninhibited and joyous account of his bohemian life and appetites. Those appetites included great books and art, fine wines, the observation of Parisan street life and frequent sex with all manner of women. It was Miller's frank accounts of sexual pleasure that led to *Tropic of Cancer* being banned in numerous countries, including the U.S. In 1964 the U.S. Supreme Court ruled that *Tropic of Cancer* was a significant work of artistic expression and hence not obscene.

Trotsky, Leon (Lev Davidovich Bronshtein) (1879–1940) Soviet politician. Trotsky joined the Social Democrats in 1896. He was banished to SIBERIA but escaped and became a member of Iskra. When the party split in 1903, he became a MENSHEVIK, prophesying that Leninist theory would result in a one-man dictatorship. He was again banished as a result of his role in the 1905 Revolution, when he held the position of chairman of the St. Petersburg Soviet. While trying to reunite the factions of the Russian Social Democrats, he led the internationalist wing of the Mensheviks during WORLD WAR I. Expelled from FRANCE as a result of his pacifist propaganda, Trotsky settled in the United States. Back in Russia following the February REVOLUTION, Trotsky became a BOLSHEVIK and the chief supporter of LENIN, and played a leading role in organizing and carrying out the OCTOBER REVOLUTION. Trotsky was head of the St. Petersburg Soviet and its military revolutionary committee, com-

Russian revolutionary Leon Trotsky (LIBRARY OF CONGRESS, PRINTS AND PHOTOGRAPHS DIVISION)

missar for foreign affairs (1917–18), commissar for war (1918–25), leader of the RED ARMY during the RUSSIAN CIVIL WAR, and from 1919 to 1927 was a member of the Politburo. A frequent opponent of STALIN, Trotsky was expelled from the party in 1927. The "combined opposition" of Trotsky, Grigory ZINOVIEV and Lev KAMENEV was unsuccessful, and in 1929 he was expelled from the Soviet Union. He was accused of espionage during the GREAT PURGE and was murdered in Mexico City by Soviet agents. In 1930 he wrote *My Life: An Attempt at an Autobiography.*

Trudeau, Garry (1948–) American cartoonist. Trudeau attended Yale University, where he edited the campus humor magazine and published a cartoon strip in the school's *Daily News.* In 1970, he created for the Universal Press Syndicate the topical cartoon strip *Doonesbury,* which lampoons public figures and satirizes contemporary American life. The strip, which won a wide readership, is syndicated in about 500 newspapers and collected into several paperback books. In 1975 Trudeau was awarded the PULITZER PRIZE. By 2004 *Doonesbury* had increased its exposure and appeared in almost 1,400 daily and Sunday newspapers around the world.

Trudeau, Pierre Elliott (1919–2000) Canadian prime minister. Born in Montreal, Trudeau studied at the

University of Montreal, Harvard, the École des Sciences Politiques (Paris) and the London School of Economics. He worked as a labor and civil rights lawyer and taught law at the University of Montreal before being elected a Liberal member of the Canadian parliament government of Lester Pearson. Trudeau became prime minister in 1968, a post he held until 1979 and then from 1980 to 1984. As prime minister, Trudeau successfully opposed Quebec separation, and in 1981 he gained approval of the new Canadian constitution. In the international arena, Trudeau supported arms reductions and argued for enhanced participation of developing nations in the world economy.

Truesdell, Karl, Jr. (*1882–1955*) American air force general. Truesdell led the first U.S. Air Force daylight bombing raid on BERLIN in WORLD WAR II. He also led the mission that dropped supplies to Polish patriots fighting against the NAZIS in the streets of Warsaw in 1944. He retired with the rank of major general.

Truffaut, François (*1932–1984*) French film director and critic, a leader (with Jean-Luc GODARD, Claude CHABROL and Jacques Rivette) of the NOUVELLE VAGUE of the late 1950s. From the circumstances of his lonely childhood—neglect at home, time in a reform school, a prison sentence for deserting the army—he retreated into the dream world of the movies. An association with the most important critic of the day, André Bazin (who became his unofficial adopted father), led to a staff position as film critic on *CAHIERS DU CINEMA*. He soon achieved notoriety as one of the fiercest polemicists in a small circle of young contributors, including Godard. Like them he had a love-hate relationship with the HOLLYWOOD cinema—detesting its commercial priorities but admiring its formulas and energies. More importantly, cinema for Truffaut was a "first-person" medium, like a confession or an intimate diary; and through the alter-ego of "Antoine Doinel" (played by actor Jean-Pierre Léaud), Truffaut enacted in film after film all the pain, uncertain joys and sexual arousals of his own life. In *Les Quatre Cents Coups* (*The 400 Blows,* 1959), Doinel runs away from home and is put in a reform school. In successive films—*L'Amour à Vingt Ans* (*Love at Twenty,* 1962), *Baisers volés* (*Stolen Kisses,* 1968) and *Domicile conjugal* (*Bed and Board,* 1970)—Doinel endures first love, rejection and eventual courtship and marriage. In other films Truffaut indulges his affection for American genres, like the gangster film (*Tirez sur le pianiste/Shoot the Piano Player,* 1960), the thriller (*La Mariée était en Noir/The Bride Wore Black,* 1968) and science fiction (*Fahrenheit 451,* 1966).

Many critics regard the ACADEMY AWARD–winning *La Nuit americaine* (*Day for Night,* 1973), the story of a filmmaker, as Truffaut's most telling achievement; others find his most touching personal statement in *La Chambre verte* (*The Green Room,* 1978), where he appears as a man who preserves in photographs the memory of the dead. It invites us to remember the words of the narrator in an earlier film, *Les Mistons* (*Mischief-Makers,* 1957): "Some moments are so precious we become slaves to them." The frozen moments of the celluloid film strip both bound—and liberated—Truffaut.

Trujillo, Rafael (Rafael Molina Trujillo) (*1891–1961*) Dominican political leader, president of the DOMINICAN REPUBLIC (1930–38, 1942–52). A career military man, Trujillo joined the army in 1919 and was trained in a country occupied by U.S. Marines; he rose to the rank of general in 1927, three years after American forces left his country. He led a coup against President Horacio Vasquez in 1930, ran unopposed for the presidency and was elected later that year. In the years that followed, Trujillo ruled the nation as dictator, even when he was officially out of office. He was a wily and ruthless ruler, wielding terror to repress any opposition to his government. Trujillo was in a constant state of difficulty with neighboring Caribbean states, and he was eventually censured by the ORGANIZATION OF AMERICAN STATES. He was assassinated by army officers on May 30, 1961.

Truly, Richard (*1937– *) U.S. astronaut; logged over eight days in space during his two U.S. SPACE SHUTTLE missions, STS-2 (November 12–14, 1981) and STS-8 (August 30–September 5, 1983). STS-8 was the first U.S. Space Shuttle mission to be launched and to land at night. Truly succeeded James FLETCHER (in his second term) as administrator of NASA in April 1989, after serving as associate administrator for space transportation systems since February 1986. After leaving NASA in 1992, Truly served as director of the Georgia Tech Research Institute from 1992 to 1997.

Truman, Harry S. (*1884–1972*) Senator from Missouri and 33rd president of the UNITED STATES. Following graduation from public school in Independence, Harry Truman went to work on his father's farm and pursued a series of odd-job occupations. During WORLD WAR I he served in the Meuse-Argonne theater, and after the armistice he returned to Missouri to open a haberdashery business that proved unsuccessful. Truman never received a formal college education and used this fact to garner the support of the common man, but he did attend Kansas City School of Law from 1923 to 1925.

Truman began his political career as an adherent of the Democratic Party machine of Kansas City's Thomas J. PENDERGAST but without acquiring any of the unsavory reputation of the machine. After serving in local offices and judgeships, he was elected to the U.S. Senate in 1923 and reelected in 1940. As senator, he established a national reputation, heading a committee formed

Harry S. Truman, 33rd president of the United States (LIBRARY OF CONGRESS, PRINTS AND PHOTOGRAPHS DIVISION)

to investigate defense department contracts awarded to private industry.

Picked by President Franklin D. ROOSEVELT to be his running mate in the 1944 election, Truman became president when Roosevelt died on April 12, 1945. His immediate concern was to end WORLD WAR II in the Pacific, which he managed by authorizing the world's first ATOMIC BOMB drops (1945) on the Japanese cities of HIROSHIMA and NAGASAKI. Despite most predictions, he was reelected to a full term by defeating Thomas E. DEWEY in 1948.

During his two terms, Truman continued the domestic policies of Roosevelt, but his most important achievements were in foreign policy. At first an advocate of cooperation with Russia, he then formulated the TRUMAN DOCTRINE (May 15, 1947) to protect GREECE and TURKEY from communist domination. With UNITED NATIONS approval he sent U.S. military forces to protect SOUTH KOREA from invasion by communist NORTH KOREA. The first U.S. ground troops arrived there on June 1, 1950. One of his most controversial acts was the removal of General Douglas MACARTHUR (April 11, 1951) from his Far Eastern command, because Truman contended that MacArthur had failed to heed a presidential directive. This raised a great furor among MacArthur's many supporters. Truman also established the MARSHALL PLAN to assist European recovery from World War II, beginning April 2, 1948. On September 25, 1949, the president signed the NATO pact, forming the NORTH ATLANTIC TREATY ORGANIZATION for the defense of North Atlantic countries.

In domestic matters, he proposed the far-reaching reforms that he called the FAIR DEAL. Some of his proposals were intended to complete Roosevelt NEW DEAL programs. The Fair Deal called for measures dealing with civil rights, improvement of schools nationwide and assistance for the disadvantaged and the elderly. The Fair Deal was blocked by conservatives of both parties, and Truman failed to overcome this obstacle. However, much of the Truman plan for the Fair Deal was carried out during the Lyndon Baines JOHNSON period. Although eligible for a second full term, Truman chose to retire in 1952 to his home in Independence.

Truman Doctrine Policy promulgated by President Harry S. TRUMAN in 1947. It began with Truman's request of March 1947 for massive military and economic aid to GREECE and TURKEY. Aimed at containing the spread of international communism, the doctrine provided for assistance to countries resisting "attempted subjugation by armed minorities or by outside pressures" and clearly spelled out an American COLD WAR ideology that would prevail for over four decades.

Trump, Donald (1946–) American entrepreneur known for his brash deal-making and glitzy lifestyle during the 1980s, when he amassed a giant real estate empire. His company built the elaborate Trump Tower skyscraper in New York City and casino-hotels in ATLANTIC CITY, New Jersey. In 1989 Trump financed the purchase of the bankrupt Eastern Airlines shuttle with junk bonds through the investment firm Drexel Burnham Lambert. In 1990 his empire suddenly began to collapse. The Trump Shuttle and the newly opened Taj Mahal hotel lost millions. Unable to make his debt payments, Trump was forced into near bankruptcy. However, Trump consolidated his business holdings, and remains one of the most prominent real estate and casino moguls in the U.S. In 2003 he starred in *The Apprentice,* a new reality show, on which contestants tried to win a top position in one of Trump's companies.

Tsander, Fridrikh (1887–1933) Among Russia's foremost early rocket pioneers, Tsander began working on liquid-propelled rocket engines in the 1920s. Static tests of his rockets—the OR-1 powered by gasoline and air and the OR-2 propelled by gasoline and oxygen—had begun by the 1930s. He also pioneered the idea of a space station, along with several of his contemporaries, including K. E. TSIOLKOVSKY, Y. V. Kondratyuk, Hermann OBERTH, Walter Hohmann, Guido von Pirquet and Hermann NOORDUNG. Tsander's book, *Problems of Flight by Means of Reactive Devices* (or, *Problems of Jet Propulsion*), published in 1934, made a significant contribution in that field. In November 1933, the same year Tsander died, the first fully liquid-propelled Soviet rocket, GIRD X, was suc-

cessfully tested. It was powered by Tsander's OR-2 engine.

Ts'ao K'un (Cao Kun) (1862–1938) Chinese military and political figure, president of the Republic of CHINA (1923–24). Ts'ao was a soldier in Korea and Manchuria during the SINO-JAPANESE WAR (1894–95), rising to the rank of division commander. When revolution broke out in China in 1911, his division was sent as a peacekeeping force to Peking by his mentor Yuan Shih-k'ai (YUAN SHIKAI). After Yuan's death in 1916, his supporters split, and Ts'ao eventually headed the Chihl (Jihli) Clique, which bested the Anhwei Clique in 1920. After defeating the Manchurian warlord Chang Tso-Lin (Zhang Zuokin) in 1922, Ts'ao attempted to unify China, and served as its president for two years. He was forced to resign by the warlord Feng Yuhsiang (Feng Yuxiang).

Tsatsos, Constantine (1899–1987) Greek scholar and politician. An author and law professor, Tsatsos combined academic activity with politics for much of his life. He held several cabinet posts in liberal governments in the 1950s and 1960s. He became president after the collapse of the 1967–74 military dictatorship and the December 1974 referendum that abolished the Greek monarchy. From 1975 to 1980 he served as the first elected president of the republic of GREECE.

Tshombe, Moise (Moise Kapenda Tshombe) (1919–1969) Congolese political leader. Born in the BELGIAN CONGO, Tshombe was educated at an American mission school. A businessman, he served on the Provincial Council of Katanga (now Shaba) Province from 1951 to 1953. In 1959 he founded the CONAKAT (Confédération des Associations Tribales du Katanga), a Belgian-supported political party advocating an independent but loosely federated Congo. In 1960 he attended the Brussels Congo Conference, where he pressed the CONAKAT program, which was rejected later that year when the Congo became independent as a centralized republic. After independence, Tshombe, the provincial president, led the mineral-rich Katanga's secession from the republic, thus creating the Congo Crisis. For the next two and a half years he and his army of Katangese and white mercenaries fought for Katangan independence. During this period the controversial Tshombe was implicated in the murder (1961) of Patrice LUMUMBA. In 1963 Tshombe's forces were defeated by troops of the central government supported by UN forces. He fled to Spain but returned in 1964 when President Joseph KASAVUBU named him prime minister in a reconciliation government. The following year, he was dismissed from the office, and in 1966 he was accused of treason. Again going into exile, he was sentenced to death in absentia in 1967. Later that year he was kidnapped and brought to Algeria, where he died under house arrest two years later.

Tsiolkovsky, Konstantin (*1857–1935*) Pioneer Russian space theorist, sometimes called "the grandfather of the space age." Tsiolkovsky is seen by many as the prophet of today's modern space programs, both Soviet and American. Born to a poor family, he was a self-educated schoolteacher who had been practically deaf from childhood. Taking an early interest in the problems of space and spaceflight, he wrote a remarkable series of technical papers and articles dealing with all aspects of his subject from astronautics to space suits and colonization of the solar system, including the problems of building and operating future space stations. "The Earth is the cradle of mankind, but mankind cannot stay in the cradle forever," Tsiolkovsky once wrote. In a fitting tribute the inscription on his gravesite reads "Mankind will not remain tied to the Earth forever." Well-informed opinion is that the Soviet government planned to launch their first artificial satellite, *SPUTNIK,* on the hundredth anniversary of Tsiolkovsky's birth, but delays put off the launch by several days.

Tsiranana, Philibert (*1910–1978*) President of MADAGASCAR (1959–72). He was appointed head of a provisional government in 1958. He became the country's first elected president in 1959 and declared the island's full independence from French colonial rule in 1960. He was reelected twice, but in 1972 was deposed in a bloodless military coup.

Tsunami disaster (*2004*) A huge wave caused by an undersea earthquake in the Indian Ocean off the western coast of northern Sumatra, Indonesia, on December 26, 2004 (local time). The earthquake, the second-largest ever recorded by a seismograph, sent 100-foot waves that devastated the shores of Indonesia, Malaysia, Sri Lanka, southern India, Thailand and other countries. More than 250,000 people were killed by the tsunami, making it the deadliest in recorded history, and millions were left homeless and without jobs due to the destruction of property and businesses near the shores hit by the wave. Governments and charities donated billions of U.S. dollars to aid the victims of one of the worst humanitarian disasters in history.

Tsvetaeva, Marina (*1892–1941*) Russian poet. Regarded as one of the major Russian poets of the 20th century, Tsvetaeva was born the daughter of a Moscow University professor. By the age of 18 she had won acclaim for her poetic gifts; *Evening Album* (1910) was her first book. She married Sergei Efron in 1912. During the RUSSIAN CIVIL WAR he joined the White Army, and they were separated for five years, throughout which she endured grinding poverty. In 1922 she followed Efron into exile in Prague, then to Paris from 1925 to 1939. Tragedy shadowed much of her life. One daughter died of starvation in 1919, and another was sent to the labor camps. Her husband, after operating as a Soviet agent abroad, was arrested and executed when they returned to the USSR in 1939. Tsvetaeva hanged herself in 1941 in the provincial town of Yelabuga.

Tuan, Pham (*1947–   *) The first Asian in space, the Vietnamese Pham Tuan served as cosmonaut-researcher, with Viktor Gorbatko, aboard the Soviet *Soyuz* 37 (July 1980), spending eight days in space as *Soyuz* linked up with the SALYUT space station and its occupants Leonid POPOV and Valery Ryumin.

Tuchman, Barbara (Barbara Wertheim Tuchman) (*1912–1989*) American historian whose best-selling books focused on war and the lives of men involved in war. Tuchman became well known in 1962 with the publication of *The Guns of August,* a classic study of the events leading up to WORLD WAR I. The book won Tuchman her first PULITZER PRIZE the following year. Her second Pulitzer Prize was won for the biography of U.S. general Joseph STILWELL, *Stillwell and the American Experience in China, 1911–1945* (1971). Among her other best-selling works were *A Distant Mirror: The Calamitous Fourteenth Century* (1978), *The March of Folly: From Troy to Vietnam* (1984) and *The First Salute* (1988). Although professional historians occasionally found fault with her accuracy on minor facts, she was universally praised for her lucid style and dramatic narrative ability.

Tucker, Preston Thomas (*1903–1956*) Flamboyant but unsuccessful American automobile designer and manufacturer. Following an early career as an auto salesman and a manufacturer of war materiel, Tucker founded a company to produce his own automobile. However, after the car's highly publicized premiere in Chicago on June 19, 1947, the firm collapsed due to financial and management problems; only 51 of the autos were produced. Tucker filed for bankruptcy in 1949 and was subsequently indicted on, but acquitted of, mail fraud and securities violations. He died of cancer on December 26, 1956.

Tucker, Richard (*1913–1975*) American opera singer. Noted for his large, rich voice, Tucker was an outstanding tenor of the 1950s and 1960s. In 1945 he made his debut at the New York Metropolitan Opera as Enzo in *La Gioconda.* International recognition came with his performance as Radames in *Aida* in 1949. Specializing in the Italian and, to a lesser degree, the French repertories, Tucker excelled as Alfredo in *La Traviata* and Manrico in *Il Trovatore,* among other roles.

Tudjman, Franjo (*1922–1999*) Croatian politician and president of CROATIA (1990–99). Born in Veliko, in the Croatian province of YUGOSLAVIA, Tudjman began his involvement in politics in 1940, when he joined a national student movement demanding democratic reforms within Yugoslavia's monarchical regime. After the 1941 German invasion of Yugoslavia during WORLD WAR II (1939–45), Tudjman supported the resistance movement that sought to liberate Yugoslavia. At the end of the war, Tudjman entered military service in the regime of Yugoslav communist leader Marshal Tito, rising to the rank of general in the Yugoslav People's Army by 1960. In 1961 Tudjman resigned his commission and moved to Zagreb, where he served in the Croatian provincial parliament from 1965 to 1969 while lecturing on history at the University of Zagreb.

During the second half of the 1980s he founded and directed the Croatian Democratic Union (HDZ), a political party that championed the independence of Croatia and the rights of Croats residing in Bosnia-Herzegovina. When Yugoslavia permitted the first free multiparty elections in the constituent republics, the HDZ won control of the Croatian parliament, and Tudjman was elected its president and reelected in 1992 and 1997. In 1991, Yugoslavia began to disintegrate into its constituent provinces of Croatia, SLOVENIA, BOSNIA and HERZEGOVINA, MACEDONIA, MONTENEGRO, and SERBIA. When the Serbian-dominated Yugoslav government sought to halt this development, Tudjman declared Croatia's independence on July 25, 1991. The Yugoslav National Army (JNA) and its affiliated paramilitary forces immediately invaded Croatia, launching the Yugoslav Civil War (1991–95). However, Croatian counteroffensives had completely expelled JNA forces from its territory by 1995, and Tudjman forced Yugoslav president Slobodan MILOŠEVIĆ to recognize Croatia's independence in the 1995 DAYTON ACCORDS. At the Dayton conference, Tudjman came under criticism for his own expulsion of Bosnians within Croatia. On December 11, 1999, following hospitalization due to his battle with cancer, Tudjman died in Zagreb.

Tudor, Antony (William Cook) (1909–1987) British-born choreographer. Tudor revolutionized ballet through the introduction of psychologically revealing gestures reflecting the influence of Freudian thought. He created his first ballet in London in 1931 and five years later produced his early masterpiece *Jardin aux Lilas* (*Lilac Garden*). In 1939 he came to the U.S. at the invitation of the AMERICAN BALLET THEATER and was closely associated

with that company for much of the rest of his career. Perhaps the most popular of his works was *Pillar of Fire* (1942), which catapulted American dancer Nora Kaye to stardom. Other notable Tudor ballets were his personal favorite, *Dark Elegies* (1937), *Undertow* (1945) and *Echoing of Trumpets*.

Tugendhat House Major early work of Ludwig MIES VAN DER ROHE built in Brno, Czech Republic, in 1930. In it, the space concepts first demonstrated in the BARCELONA PAVILION are introduced in a large and luxurious residence. The main living space of the house is an open area, not divided into conventional rooms, but partially divided by screen walls of rich materials.

The outside walls are of floor-to-ceiling glass, arranged to retract into the basement so as to leave the house entirely open to the out-of-doors. Structural support is provided by slim steel columns encased in chromium. Bedrooms and service spaces are of more conventional design. A number of special furniture designs were developed for the house, some of them once more in production. The Tugendhat House, widely known through publication, became an influential classic of the INTERNATIONAL STYLE.

Tugwell, Rexford Guy (1895–1979) American economist and government official, a member of President Franklin D. ROOSEVELT's BRAIN TRUST. Tugwell be-

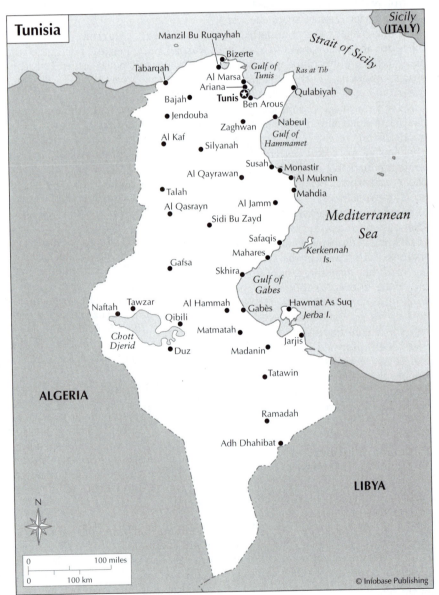

came undersecretary of agriculture in 1934, and later headed the Rural Resettlement Administration (1935–36). He was one of Roosevelt's top advisers on NEW DEAL programs, including tax reform, relief and public works. During WORLD WAR II he was governor of Puerto Rico. A strong believer in national economic planning, he was considered a brilliant and controversial figure.

Tukhachevsky, Michael Nikolayevich *(1893–1937)* Marshal of the Soviet Union. Of a noble family, Tukhachevsky served as an officer in WORLD WAR I, but in 1918 he joined the BOLSHEVIKS and the RED ARMY. He was commander in 1918–19 and was commander of all the Red forces in the Caucasus in 1920. In 1921 he was commander of the government forces against the KRONSTADT REBELLION. He was head of the military academy, commander of the western and Leningrad military districts and the Red Army's chief of staff (1925–28). Deputy commissar for military and naval affairs in 1931, in 1935 Tukhachevsky was appointed one of the first five marshals. He was accused of leading a military conspiracy and was tried and shot during the GREAT PURGE. His reputation was rehabilitated in 1958.

Tung, C(hao) Y(ung) *(1911–1982)* Chinese shipping magnate. Born in mainland China, Tung fled to Hong Kong in 1949 during the Communist takeover (see also CHINESE CIVIL WAR OF 1945–49). He founded his own shipping empire, the C. Y. Tung Group, building it into the second-largest independent merchant fleet in the world, with about 150 ships totaling some 11 million deadweight tons.

Tunisia Tunisia covers an area of 63,153 square miles on the Mediterranean coast of North Africa. A French protectorate from 1883 to 1956, Tunisia was occupied by the Axis powers during WORLD WAR II, until liberated by British and American forces in 1943. Independence from FRANCE was granted in 1956, with the leader of the nationalist movement, Habib BOURGUIBA, becoming president. Elected president for life in 1974, he established a government that survived labor unrest in 1968 and 1978 and rioting in 1984, as well as a coup attempt in 1980. He was deposed in 1987 in a bloodless coup. Disputes with Algeria and Libya were resolved in 1983 and 1987, respectively. In 1999 Tunisia held its first multiparty presidential elections, in which President Ben Ali was reelected to the position he has held since 1989. In 2004 Ben Ali was again elected president.

Tunner, William H. *(1906–1983)* U.S. Air Force general who directed the BERLIN AIRLIFT in 1948–49. During his military career, he was considered the leading authority on airlifts. A veteran of WORLD WAR II, during the 1950s he served as commander of U.S. air forces in Europe and deputy chief of staff for operations (1957) and was named commander of the Military Air Transport Service in 1958.

TUNISIA	
1881	Tunisia becomes a French protectorate, with the bey (governor) retaining local power.
1942–43	Tunisia is briefly occupied by Germany during World War II.
1956	France grants full independence on March 20. Habib Bourguiba is appointed prime minister. Tunisia joins the United Nations.
1957	The bey of Tunis is deposed. Republic of Tunisia is proclaimed, with Bourguiba as its first president.
1959	Constitution of the republic is promulgated. National elections are held.
1968	Students riot against U.S. and U.K. embassies.
1974	National elections are held; Bourguiba is elected president for life and given enlarged powers.
1978	UGTT-led general strike erupts into violent riots, the worst in the nation's history, in which more than 46 are killed.
1984	Bread riots break out following steep hike in food prices; Bourguiba rescinds price increases.
1987	Bourguiba declared unfit to govern, and Ben Ali sworn in as president.
1989	Ben Ali is reelected president.
1994	Radical Islamic groups threaten the political stability of Tunisia. Ben Ali is reelected president.
1999	Ben Ali is reelected president.
2004	Ben Ali wins a fourth term in office.

Tunney, Gene (James Joseph Tunney) *(1898–1978)* American boxer. As a U.S. Marine stationed in Paris, Tunney won his first championship, that of the American Expeditionary Forces. After the war, he turned to professional boxing and won the light heavyweight title in 1922. A skillful rather than overpowering fighter, he moved up through the heavyweight ranks and won a chance at that title in 1926. Tunney faced Jack DEMPSEY, whom he completely outboxed before a crowd of more than 130,000. The duo met again in 1927, where Tunney won a much-debated decision in 10 rounds. Tunney fought only once more and then retired with his heavyweight crown intact. A popular public figure, he married an heiress and went on to a successful business career.

Tupamaros Marxist urban guerrillas in URUGUAY, about 1,000 in number, including many professional men. They were effective in creating unrest before 1972 when police and right-wing paramilitary groups carried out actions against them. Since then they have been relatively inactive. In 1999 leaders of the guerrilla group emerged to support liberal presidential candidate Tabore Vazquez in his unsuccessful campaign.

Tupper, Earl S. *(1907–1983)* American businessman who in 1942 created **Tupperware**, an elaborate line of plastic food and drink containers that revolutionized the American kitchen and led to the acceptance of plastics in the household. Tupperware was manufactured by the Tupperware Corporation and was originally sold primarily at "Tupperware parties," neighborhood gatherings where the products' uses were demonstrated. The company claimed that an average of 75,000 such parties took place daily around the world. In 1958 Tupper sold the company to the Rexall Drug Co. for $9 million, but the products continued to bear his name. More than $800,000 worth of Tupperware was sold in 1982, the year before Tupper's death.

Turing, Alan (Alan Mathison Turing) *(1912–1954)* British mathematician. Turing studied at Cambridge University, where he gained a fellowship in 1935. From 1936 to 1938 he worked at Princeton. He was at the National Physical Laboratory from 1945 to 1948 and subsequently became reader in mathematics at Manchester University.

His most important work consisted in giving a precise mathematical characterization of the intuitive concept of computability. Turing developed a precise formal characterization of an idealized computer—the Turing machine—and equated the formal notion of effective decidability with computability by such a machine. Turing was thus able to show that a number of important mathematical problems could have no effective decision procedure. In 1937 he showed the undecidability of first-order predicate calculus and in 1950 that of the word problem for semigroups with cancellation.

He was able to put his theoretical work on computability into practice during his time at the National Physical Laboratory when the ACE computer was built under his supervision, and later when he became assistant director of the Manchester automatic digital machine.

Turing had the misfortune to be a homosexual at a time when this was still a criminal offense in England. He committed suicide as a direct result of a prosecution for alleged indecency.

Turkey Situated partly in southeastern Europe and partly in western Asia, Turkey covers an area of 300,868 square miles—a lot less than it covered at the beginning of the 20th century. The OTTOMAN EMPIRE, decrepit heir of

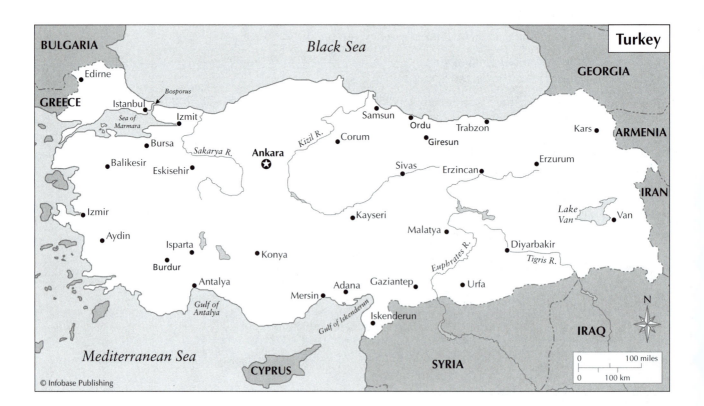

TURKEY

1908	Young Turks force sultan to restore constitutional rule and convene a parliament.
1911	War with Italy results in loss of Libya.
1920	Turkey accepts loss of Arab territories in the Middle East with the signing of the Treaty of Sevres.
1922	(October) Sultan Mohammed VI is deposed and the sultanate abolished.
1923	(October 29) A Turkish republic is declared with Ankara as its capital and Atatürk as president.
1952	Turkey joins NATO.
1971	(March) Süleyman Demirel is forced from the premiership by the army and martial law is imposed.
1974	(July) Turkey invades northern Cyprus, creating an ongoing crisis with Greece.
1982	(November) New constitution reaffirms Turkey's democratic, secular and parliamentary identity.
1987	(March) Martial law lifted except in the four Kurdish provinces.
1989	(October) Turgut Özal is elected president.
1991	Hundreds of thousands of Iraqi Kurds fleeing from Saddam Hussein attempt to cross into Turkey; the True Path Party led by Süleyman Demirel replaces the Motherland Party as the largest party in parliamentary elections.
1992	Kurdish separatist violence mounts.
1993	Demirel becomes president, and Tansu Çiller, the new leader of the True Path Party, becomes Turkey's first female prime minister.
1996	The Motherland and True Path Parties form a coalition that fails; True Path forms a coalition with the Welfare Party, an Islamic party, and Necmettin Erbakan becomes the first Islamist leader to rule the country.
1997	The military compels Erbakan to step down; Yilmaz is named prime minister; the European Union rejects Turkey's application for membership.
1999	Abdullah Öcalan, leader of the Kurdistan Workers' Party, is captured; an earthquake strikes western Turkey, killing at least 15,000 and injuring about 30,000.
2000	Öcalan calls for a cease-fire and Kurdish rebels renounce violence and announce they will seek their goals through democratic means.
2001	The Constitutional Court bans the main opposition party, the pro-Islamic Virtue Party; its members form a new party called Saadet; parliamentary reforms outlaw capital punishment and allow broadcasts in Kurdish.
2002	Islamist-based Justice and Development Party (AK) wins a landslide election; deputy leader Abdullah Gul is appointed prime minister; women are granted full legal equality with men.
2003	AK leader Recep Tayyib Erdogan wins a parliamentary seat and Gul resigns as prime minister, replaced by Erdogan; laws ease restrictions on freedom of speech, grant additional Kurdish language rights and reduce the role of the military in government; two car bombs explode near Istanbul's main synagogue, killing 25; suicide bombings at the British consulate and a British bank kill 28.
2005	The new lira currency is introduced; a bomb attack on a passenger train kills six; the government blames Kurdish rebels; negotiations begin on European Union membership.

an empire that had once stretched from the Plains of Hungary to the Gulf of Aden, was dominated from 1908 to 1920 by reformers known as the YOUNG TURKS, who aligned Turkey with the Central Powers during WORLD WAR I. The Central Powers lost the war, and Turkey lost the few remnants of its once-glorious empire. In the GRECO-TURKISH WAR OF 1921–22, Turks resisted Allied occupation by the Greek army, decisively defeated the Greeks at the Sakarya River and drove them 250 miles westward, into the Aegean Sea, slaughtering Greeks by the thousands at Smyrna. Sultan Mohammed VI was deposed in 1922 and the sultanate abolished. The Turkish Republic was declared in 1923, and Mustapha Kemal (later surnamed ATATÜRK), hero of Turkey's victory on the GALLIPOLI PENINSULA in 1915, became the first president (1923–38). The capital was moved from Constantinople to ANKARA; in 1924 a new constitution abolished the caliphate and made Turkey a secular state.

Neutral during most of WORLD WAR II, Turkey finally declared war on Germany and Japan in 1945. Turkey joined NATO in 1952. Political instability during the 1950s and 1960s culminated in the imposition of martial law in 1971. Turkey's invasion of northern CYPRUS in 1974 created a crisis with Greece that remains unresolved (see CYPRIOT WAR OF 1974). In 1980 the military under General Kenan EVREN seized power after several years of ineffective coalition governments, a worsening economy and intense violence. A new constitution was approved in 1982, with Evren acting as head of state until 1989. Turkey and its president, Turgut ÖZAL, supported UNITED NATIONS sanctions against Iraq for its invasion of Kuwait in 1990 and supported the multinational military intervention to expel Iraqi forces from Kuwait the following year. In 2002 the Islamic-based Justice and Development Party dominated national elections. However, the party's leaders, including Prime Ministers Abdullah Gul (2002–03) and Recep Tayyip Erdogan (2003–   ) pledged to abide by Turkey's secular constitution. Turkey became a strong ally of the United States in the war on terrorism launched by U.S. president George W. BUSH in 2001. However, the Turkish parliament voted to prohibit U.S. military forces from using Turkish territory to invade northern Iraq as part of the campaign to overthrow Iraqi president Saddam Hussein in the spring of 2003. In 2005 negotiations got under way for Turkey's application for admission to the European Union (EU), though apposition to Turkish membership in several EU countries ensured that those talks would be long and arduous.

Turkish War of Independence

Movement of 1919–23 led by Mustapha Kemal (later called ATATURK) to prevent the Allied powers from dismembering the Turkish heartland of the OTTOMAN EMPIRE after World War I. When Sultan Mohammed VI refused to resist the Allies, Kemal, a prominent Turkish general, led his forces from Asiatic Turkey against both the sultan and the Allies. By 1920 Kemal had forced the government in Constantinople (now Istanbul) to refuse territorial concessions. The Allies occupied Constantinople, and Kemal declared an independent government to be established in Ankara. In 1922 Kemal's forces occupied Constantinople and moved toward establishing a republic. The war ended with Greece's defeat in the GREEK-TURKISH WAR (1921–22). At the Conference of Lausanne (1923) Turkey's present boundaries were drawn, and the sultanate and caliphate were abolished.

Turkmenistan Central Asian territory under Russian (1884–1917), Soviet (1921–91) and independent rule (1991–   ). As Russian military forces sought to expand into Central Asia during the 1860s and 1870s, they encountered notable resistance from the Turkmen people in what is today Turkmenistan. In 1877 Russian military forces had established several outposts on the Turkmen's periphery and began a conflict designed to bring the territory under Russian control. The Turkmens rebelled when Czar Nicholas II of Russia attempted in 1916 to draft large numbers of them for service in WORLD WAR I (1914–18). Led by the Yomud tribe, the Turkmen rebellion forced the czar to deploy a sizable contingent of his army to quell the revolt by the end of the year.

After the revolution of November (O.S.: October) 1917 the BOLSHEVIKS launched a campaign to bring all Russian territory firmly under their control. In April 1918 the Red Army gained control of Turkmenistan and included it in the Turkistan Autonomous Soviet Socialist Republic (ASSR) comprising the modern day countries of KYRGYZSTAN, UZBEKISTAN, TAJIKISTAN and segments of Turkmenistan and KAZAKHSTAN.

By 1920 the Reds had regained full control of Turkmenistan after crushing an independence movement that had been supported by British troops during World War I. In 1924, two years after the establishment of the

TURKMENISTAN

1869–81	Turkmenistan falls under the control of czarist Russia
1916	The Turkmen revolt violently against Russian rule.
1920	Turkmenistan is brought back under Russian control following an invasion by the Soviet Red Army.
1922	The region is part of the Turkestan Soviet Socialist Autonomous Republic.
1924	Turkmenistan becomes a constituent republic of the Soviet Union.
1920s and 1930s	Sporadic armed resistance and popular uprisings in response to Soviet program of agricultural collectivization.
1985	Saparmurad Niyazov becomes Communist Party leader.
1991	Turkmenistan declares independence under Niyazov; later joins the Commonwealth of Independent States.
1992	New constitution is promulgated.
1999	Parliament votes Niyazov president for life.
2000	Niyazov announces that he will step down by 2010, after reaching the age of 70.
2004	Only candidates in favor of President Niyazov run in parliamentary elections, which are criticized by foreign governments as a sham.

UNION OF SOVIET SOCIALIST REPUBLICS (USSR), the Soviet government dissolved the Turkistan ASSR and established several Soviet Socialist Republics (SSRs) along ethnic lines, under the federal structure of the USSR. One such SSR was the Turkmen SSR.

The subjugation of the Turkmen increased dramatically with the accession of JOSEPH STALIN as the absolute ruler of the USSR. In 1928, Stalin proclaimed his first Five Year Plan, a detailed list of expected industrial and agricultural projects to be implemented throughout the USSR. In the case of the Turkmen SSR, this plan mandated the end to the largely nomadic pastoral life of the Turkmen people; henceforth, the arable land would be devoted solely to the production of commodities such as cotton, grown on Stalin's collective farms. During the 1930s Soviet officials arrested, exiled and executed Turkmen nationalists who were deemed subversive elements within the USSR.

After Soviet leader Mikhail Gorbachev introduced his political policy of GLASNOST ("openness"), which allowed for the formation of nongovernmental groups within the USSR,

prominent Turkmen intellectuals formed in 1989 the eclectic organization Agzybirik, which celebrated Turkmen history and cultural identity. The Turkmen Communist Party, headed since 1985 by Saparmurad Niyazov, was forced to grant several concessions to Turkmen nationalists. These included the recognition of the Turkmen language as an official language of the republic in May 1990; the declaration in August 1990 that the Turkmen SSR's laws superseded those of the USSR; and the creation of the new office of president, to which Niyazov was elected by popular vote in October 1990.

In October 1991 two months after an abortive coup against Gorbachev, the Turkmen parliament issued a declaration of independence from the USSR, and adopted the name Republic of Turkmenistan. The Turkmen Communist Party also changed its name to the Democratic Party of Turkmenistan (DPT). However, Turkmenistan sought to retain political, economic and military connections to its former fellow SSRs, and in December 1991 joined the newly created COMMONWEALTH OF INDEPENDENT STATES (CIS). As a member of

the CIS, Turkmenistan has sought to preserve good relations with the Russian Federation, permitting ethnic Russians inside Turkmenistan to possess dual citizenship and approving the stationing of Russian troops along Turkmenistan's border with AFGHANISTAN.

Turkmenistan's political life since independence has been dominated by Niyazov. In 1994 he organized a referendum that extended his presidential term until 2002 and in that year handily won reelection. He has additionally benefited from the dominance that the DPT has exercised in the parliament; since 1994 the parliament has been dominated by the DPT, the only legally recognized party in Turkmenistan. Under Niyazov and the DPT, civil liberties in Turkmenistan have been severely restricted; freedom of the press was not guaranteed under the 1992 constitution; and the major television and radio media outlets have remained under government control. In 2000 Niyazov announced he would step down by 2010. Parliamentary elections were held in 2004 but were criticized by foreign diplomats as a sham because no opposition candidates ran.

Turks and Caicos Islands The Turks and Caicos Islands are a group of 30 islands (eight of which are inhabited) in the Atlantic Ocean, just north of the island of Hispaniola; the capital is Grand Turk. In 1873 the islands became a dependency of Jamaica, some 400 miles to the southwest, and remained so until 1959, when they received their own governor. On Jamaica's independence from Britain in August 1962, the islands again became a British Crown colony. The Turks and Caicos received their own governor again in 1972 and greater internal autonomy in 1976. In 1980 the ruling proindependence People's Democratic Movement (PDM) agreed with the British government that independence would be achieved if the PDM won the 1980 general election. The PDM lost the election to the Progressive National Party (PNP), which supported continued dependent status. The leader of the PNP, Norman Saunders, became chief minister. In 1985 Saunders and two of his associates were arrested and convicted in the U.S. on drug charges. The PNP maintained itself in power by winning the by-elections held as a result, but on July 24, 1986, the governor dissolved the government and replaced it with an advisory council after a report found that Chief Minister Nathaniel Francis, two other ministers and two PDM members of the legislative council were unfit to hold office. A constitutional commission was created to suggest possible revisions to the constitution and electoral process. A general election under the provisions of the new constitution, with voting in multi-member constituencies, was held on March 3, 1988. It was won convincingly by the PDM, whose leader, Oswald Skippings, became prime minister. Despite the greater autonomy possessed by the islands since 1988, they have remained dependencies of Great Britain.

Turner, Dame Eva (1892–1990) British opera singer. She was one of the first British divas to achieve international fame. Noted for a dramatic soprano voice of extraordinary range and power, she was best known for her performances in the title role of Puccini's *Turandot*. After her retirement in 1949, she became a teacher at the University of Oklahoma and at the Royal Academy of Music in London.

Turner, Frederick Jackson (1861–1932) American historian. Born in Portage, Wisconsin, Turner taught at the University of Wisconsin from 1885 to 1910 and at Harvard from 1910 to 1924. Although not a prolific writer, Turner had a major influence on American historical writing. In 1893 he delivered an address, "The Significance of the Frontier in American History," that brilliantly outlined the effect of the frontier on American democracy. Turner emphasized the importance of abundant, free land in reinforcing democratic beliefs and saw the close of the frontier as a turning point in American political history.

Turner, Joseph Vernon "Big Joe" (1911–1985) American singer. A Kansas City BLUES "shouter," Turner was widely known as the "Boss of the Blues." He was perhaps the most recorded and imitated blues singer in U.S. history, and was the first to perform and popularize such seminal rock and roll songs as "Shake, Rattle and Roll" and "Corrina, Corrina."

Turner, Ted (Robert E. Turner III) (1938–) American entrepreneur. Turner began working in his father's advertising business in Georgia in 1960. After his father shot himself over business losses in 1963, Turner brought the firm out of debt and made a success of it. He became known for his cable television empire and also as the winner of the 1977 America's Cup and owner of the Atlanta Braves baseball team and Atlanta Hawks basketball team. He began by buying small television stations and making their programming available nationwide by satellite. In 1980 he launched Cable News Network (CNN), which was enormously successful and by 1990 was available and watched worldwide. Turner Broadcasting Inc. later began expanding its media holdings. Turner formed alliances with the networks: ABC became involved with Turner's ESPN sports channel in 1987, and CBS and Turner negotiated an alliance for joint presentation of the 1992 and 1994 Winter Olympics in 1990, although his threatened takeover of CBS in 1985 had caused serious management problems for the network. He acquired the rights to 1,000 Columbia films in 1989 and also bought MGM-United Artists film company that year.

Turner also aroused controversy in 1990 when he announced that his cable station, TBS, would present *Abortion for Survival*, a program advocating the right to abortion. In 1996 TBS merged with Time Warner Inc. Turner headed the new company's cable division. In 1997 Turner pledged $1 billion to the UN. Time Warner merged with AOL in 2001, and Turner remained as vice chairman. He resigned this post in 2003 but sought reelection as director of Time Warner's board in 2006.

Turner, Thomas Wyatt (1877–1978) American CIVIL RIGHTS pioneer and educator. Turner founded the Federation of Colored Catholics and was a charter member of the NATIONAL ASSOCIATION FOR THE ADVANCEMENT OF COLORED PEOPLE. A friend of Booker T. WASHINGTON, he taught biology at Tuskegee Institute in 1901. He was a professor for 10 years at Howard University and for over 20 years at the Hampton Institute.

Tutsi and Hutu massacres (1994) In April 1994 the Rwandan president, JUVÉNAL HABYARIMANA, a member of RWANDA's Hutu ethnic group and leader of the National Revolutionary Movement of Development (NRMD), and Cyprien Ntaryamira, the president of the neighboring state of Burundi, died when the airplane both leaders were flying in was shot down by a surface-to-air missile. Immediately following Habyarimana's death, radical leaders of the NRMD and within the greater Hutu community charged that the Rwandan Patriotic Front (RPF), an insurgent movement headquartered in Uganda and dominated by Tutsis (the other major ethnic group in Rwanda), was responsible for orchestrating the assassination. Extremist Hutu militants immediately began a massacre of Tutsis within Rwanda in revenge for Habyarimana's death. These murders in turn provoked equally violent responses from members of the RPF as well as other armed Tutsis. In an effort to avoid full-scale genocide within Rwanda, millions of Tutsis, Hutus and humanitarian aid workers for NON-GOVERNMENTAL ORGANIZATIONS (NGOs) fled the country, while the International Red Cross organized a series of refugee camps in neighboring countries. By the end of May 1994, when the RPF had captured the capital city of Kigali and expelled the more extreme elements of the NRMD, the Red Cross estimated that over 800,000 Hutus and Tutsis had been murdered within the brief period of a few months, with several million remaining homeless in the makeshift refugee camps in neighboring countries. Despite the brutality exhibited by both sides, the UNITED NATIONS and Western nations such as the U.S. and FRANCE did not dispatch a peacekeeping force to the country. In response to the international outrage at the extent of the genocide within Rwanda, the UN established an International Criminal Tribunal for Rwanda (ICTR). Based in northern TANZANIA, the ICTR won its first conviction in September 1998, when it found NRMD mayor Jean-Paul Akayesu guilty of genocide. In 1999, the ICTR served as the model for The Hague–based International Criminal Tribunal for Yugoslavia (ICTY).

Tutu, Desmond *(1931–)* South African Anglican archbishop. Tutu, who won the NOBEL PRIZE for peace in 1984, was one of the leading black spokespersons for a nonviolent end to APARTHEID. Tutu is a strong advocate of black unity and of the policies of the AFRICAN NATIONAL CONGRESS. Because of his status as the spiritual leader of the Anglican Church in SOUTH AFRICA, he is also a voice that can be heard by the white minority of that country. Born in South Africa, Tutu attended King's College, London. In 1976 he was named bishop of Lesotho, South Africa. In 1978 he became secretary-general of the South African Council of Churches, an ecumenical group that was a key force against apartheid. Tutu was an outspoken opponent of the Afrikaner-dominated National Party and was subjected to much government harassment before the abolition of apartheid.

Tuvalu Covering a total land area of 9.2 square miles, the nine atolls formerly known as the Ellice Islands lie in the west central Pacific, 652 miles north of Fiji and 2,496 miles northeast of Sydney, Australia. The coral chain is 360 miles long. Britain annexed the islands in 1892 and formed the Gilbert and Ellice Islands Protectorate; in 1916 these became a Crown colony. In 1942, during WORLD WAR II, American forces

occupied the Ellice Islands to counter the advance of the Japanese, who had invaded the Gilberts. The period from 1963 to 1977 saw steady constitutional development toward the present system of government in Tuvalu. In 1974 the Ellice Islanders voted in a referendum to separate from the Micronesian Gilbertese. Tuvalu achieved independence on October 1, 1978, as a constitutional monarchy within the COMMONWEALTH, with the governor general as the queen's representative. In March 1984 Tuvalu established diplomatic relations with Kiribati, and in 1987 the Tuvalu Trust Fund was set up by Britain, New Zealand, Australia and South Korea to provide development aid. Dr. Tomasi Puapua, who became prime minister following the general election of 1981, was re-elected in 1985. In 2000 Tuvalu was admitted to the UN.

Tuve, Merle A. *(1901–1982)* American physicist. He was educated at the University of Minnesota (B.S., 1922) and Johns Hopkins University (Ph.D., 1926) and taught mainly at the Carnegie Institute in Washington, D.C. (1926–42, 1946–66). His discoveries opened the door for the development of RADAR and nuclear energy. His studies in atomic structure led to his confirmation (1933) of the existence of the neutron. His observation that shortpulse radio waves reflected off the upper atmosphere was the theoretical basis for the development of radar. During WORLD WAR II he worked for the U.S. Office of Scientific Research and Development; here he oversaw the development of the **proximity fuse,** a device that set off artillery or anti-aircraft shells as they neared their target. The proximity fuse also stopped the German buzz bomb attacks on Britain.

20th Century–Fox (Twentieth Century Fox Film Corporation) One of the Hollywood "Big Five" production/exhibition motion picture studios (along with METRO-GOLDWYN-MAYER, WARNER BROS., RKO and PARAMOUNT). It was formed in 1935, a merger between an established studio fallen on hard times, the Fox Film Corp., and a new studio, Twentieth Century. The origins of the Fox Film Corp. go back to the nickelodeon days when entrepreneur

William Fox formed the Greater New York Film Rental Company to distribute motion pictures. In 1915 he moved the operation to Los Angeles and changed the name to the Fox Film Corp. By the late 1920s, Fox had acquired numerous theaters, produced successful features with top stars and directors and made important experiments with synchronized sound. However, he ran afoul of government antitrust actions and was forced out of the company in 1930. Meanwhile, Darryl F. ZANUCK, a successful production chief at Warner Bros., was growing dissatisfied with his relationship with Jack Warner. He resigned in 1933 and with former United Artists executive Joseph Schenck formed Twentieth Century Pictures. The next two years saw releases like *The Affairs of Cellini* (1934), *The House of Rothschild* (1935) and *Les Miserables* (1935). After the merger with Fox in 1935, Zanuck assumed complete control. For the next 20 years a diverse roster of stars, filmmakers and pictures were developed. Little Shirley TEMPLE, the most famous child star of her day, virtually kept the studio afloat in the 1935–39 period, with hits like *Captain January* (1936) and *Wee Willie Winkie* (1937). Director John FORD was in his prime, scoring with *Drums Along the Mohawk* (1939), *The Grapes of Wrath* (1940), *Young Mr. Lincoln* (1940) and many others. Some of the greatest of all Technicolor musicals from the 1940s exploited the so-called Fox Blondes, Betty Grable, June Haver and Alice Faye (Marilyn Monroe came along in the 1950s). Outside of Warner Bros., the studio developed the most important series of "social consciousness" films in the 1940s with pictures like *Wilson* (1943), *Gentleman's Agreement* (1947) and *The Snake Pit* (1947). In 1956 Zanuck left the company. After the debacle of *Cleopatra* (1961), he returned as chairman of the board with son Richard as Hollywood production chief. Although some smash successes followed, like *The Sound of Music* (1965) and the first *Star Wars* film in 1977, both Zanucks were eventually forced out. Since 1985 Australian magnate Rupert MURDOCH has been the studio's owner. Ironically, in 1989 the studio's moviemaking division assumed the name of William Fox's original silent-era studio, the Fox Film Corp.

20th Party Congress Meeting of the Communist Party of the Soviet Union held in February 1956; presided over by Premier Nikita KHRUSHCHEV and attended by Soviet party members and representatives of other national parties. During the meeting, the first since the death of Joseph STALIN (1953), Khrushchev gave a secret speech in which he denounced Stalin for his destructive and dictatorial policies and in which he condemned the "cult of personality" that had grown up around the former Soviet strongman. This speech was made public several months later. At the same conference, Khrushchev also announced that war with capitalist forces was no longer inevitable, and he pressed for "peaceful coexistence" between the world's two ideological camps. The conference was important in easing COLD WAR tensions and in providing the USSR with the philosophical revisions necessary for eventual reform.

Twenty-one Demands A number of demands presented by JAPAN to CHINA in 1915 by which Japan attempted to make China a virtual protectorate. Declaring war against GERMANY in August 1914, Japan made its participation in WORLD WAR I a pretext for invading Kiaochow, Germany's leased territory in Shantung Province. Japan then presented its Twenty-one Demands to president YUAN SHIH-K'AI, threatening war if they were not met. Divided into five groups, the demands stipulated that Japan would assume Germany's role in Shantung; that it would have special commercial and colonial rights in Manchuria and Mongolia; that Japan would have exclusive coal-mining privileges in China; that China would exclude further coastal development to any power but Japan; and that Japan would serve as adviser in China's political, military, commercial and financial affairs. The demands were intended to realize Japan's imperialistic aims in China and to undermine the influences of Russia and Great Britain. They were presented in secret, but were leaked to the American minister in Beijing and soon became known worldwide. Ultimately, the demand for control over every aspect of Chinese life was dropped, but China was forced to accede to other provisions of the ultimatum. The demands provoked enormous suspicion and resentment of Japan by

the Chinese public, ultimately providing impetus for the MAY FOURTH MOVEMENT and for the whole national unification movement.

Twilight Zone, The Television's most famous anthology series of fantasy and science fiction. Prestigious playwright Rod Serling (*Patterns, Requiem for a Heavyweight*) had written a time travel fantasy called "Time Element" for the *Desilu Playhouse* in 1958. Enthusiastic response led to a pilot for a weekly CBS series to be called *The Twilight Zone*. Serling, who thought he invented the term, found out later that it had been in common use among air force pilots to describe a lack of visibility of the horizon. Serling wrote the first story, "Where Is Everybody?" and narrated and hosted the show, which premiered on October 2, 1959. He remained with the program, narrating and furnishing many of the scripts, until the series' demise in September 1965. The half-hour format predominated, except for the fourth season, when shows were expanded to an hour. Everything about the series became famous: Serling's beetle-browed appearance and stentorian narration ("You're travelling through another dimension"); the oscillating monotony of the musical theme (written by Marius Constant); and the weird characters arrayed against the ordinary world—"the witches and the warlocks, the elves and the gnomes, the odd ones and the not-quite-right ones," as Serling described them. Original stories and scripts came from some of Serling's favorite writers: Richard Matheson, Charles Beaumont, Ray BRADBURY, Jerome Bixby and Jerry Sohl. And prestigious directors worked here, like Jacques Tourneur, Norman Z. McLeod, John Brahm and Richard Donner. Pound for pound, there were more memorable moments than in any television series this side of Owl Creek Bridge: the transformation of an old man into the Devil in "The Howling Man"; the creature on the airplane wing in "Nightmare at 20,000 Feet"; the slapstick homage to the legendary Buster KEATON in "Once Upon a Time"; the switcheroo ending of "To Serve Man." And everybody remembers the meek little bookworm (Burgess Meredith) in "Time Enough at Last"; he plans to catch up on his reading after the Bomb has destroyed the world—until he breaks his glasses.

Twining, Nathan F. (*1897–1982*) U.S. Air Force officer. During WORLD WAR II Twining commanded allied aerial campaigns in Europe and in the South Pacific and won several decorations. Later, during the COLD WAR, he played an important role in the development of U.S. nuclear air weapons and the supersonic missiles and jets designed to deliver them. He was air force chief of staff (1953–57) and chairman of the joint chiefs of staff (1957–60) during the EISENHOWER administration.

Twomey, Seamus (*1919–1989*) One of the Irish founders of the Provisional branch of the IRISH REPUBLICAN ARMY (IRA), which was set up in the wake of renewed sectarian strife in NORTHERN IRELAND in 1969. Twomey was arrested in the Irish Republic in 1973, later escaped by helicopter from a Dublin prison but was recaptured in 1977 and sentenced to a five-year prison term.

Tynan, Kenneth (*1920–1980*) British theater critic, playwright and essayist. Tynan was a highly influential force in theater and in popular culture during his lifetime. In addition to his writings, he expressed his forceful and controversial views in frequent radio and television appearances. Tynan first came to prominence in the 1950s as a drama critic for the *London Observer* who championed the new realism of British drama. He went on to serve for 10 years as the literary manager of Britain's National Theater and to author an erotic musical, *Oh Calcutta*, that began a lengthy Broadway run in the 1960s. Tynan's reviews and profiles of theatrical and Hollywood figures appeared frequently in *The New Yorker.*

Typhoid Mary (*1868–1938*) Name given to Irish immigrant Mary Mallon, who was probably the first known carrier of the typhoid fever bacillus in the U.S. Infected by a bout of the disease, she knowingly spread it by working as a cook in New York City-area homes and institutions. During 1906–07 she is thought to have been involved in at least 25 cases of the highly infectious disease. Identified and detained in a city hospital, she refused treatment and was released in 1910. In 1915, after an outbreak of typhoid fever at New York's Sloane Hospital, she was found to have worked in its kitchen. Arrested and hospitalized, she continued to refuse treatment. She eventually became a laboratory technician and was confined to the grounds of the hospital, where she died.

Tyson, Michael Gerard *(1966–)* American boxer. "Iron Mike" Tyson rose from his background as a street fighter in Brooklyn to the heavyweight championship of the world. Discovered while in reform school by noted trainer Cus D'Amato, he went on to an amateur record of 24–3 before turning professional in 1985. The following year, Tyson became the youngest heavyweight champion in history. A devastating puncher, he defended his title successfully for three years, amassing a professional record of 37–0 before being upset by underdog Buster Douglas in 1990. Tyson's career has been marked by scandal, including erratic behavior and a well-publicized divorce from actress Robin Givens. In February 1992 Tyson was convicted of raping Desiree Washington and was sentenced to jail until 1995. Although he regained the WBC and WBA belts titles in 1996, he lost both to Evander Holyfield later that year. In 1997 Tyson bit off part of Holyfield's ear during a WBA heavyweight fight in Las Vegas and then spit out a mouthful of his opponent's ear, declaring "I'm an animal in the ring."

Tyuratam The Soviet spacecraft launch site, on the broad, flat steppes of Central Asia, about 200 miles from the town of Baikonur (the name often used by the Soviets for the launch site).

Tzara, Tristan *(Sami Rosenstock)* *(1896–1953)* Romanian-born poet, aesthetic theorist and playwright. Tzara is not widely read, but he remains one of the most influential thinkers of the 20th century by virtue of his seminal role in the founding of the DADA movement in Zurich, Switzerland, in 1916. According to fellow Dadaist Hans ARP, it was Tzara himself who coined the word *dada*. In any event, it was Tzara who wrote its first Manifestoes and became its leader in attacking the accepted conventions of bourgeois culture and the pretensions of human reason. Tzara, born into a Jewish family, published his first poems in Romanian in 1912. Shortly thereafter, he switched to French as his literary language. Tzara moved to Zurich in 1915 and then to Paris in 1919. There he became involved with SURREALISM and ultimately clashed with its leader, André BRETON. Tzara's major works include *Twenty-five Poems* (1918) and the play *The Gas Operated Heart* (1923).

U

Udaltsova, Nadezhda *(1886–1961)* Painter and one of the chief representatives of the Cubist school in RUSSIA. Udaltsova studied with Lyubov Popova at Arseneva's gymnasium (1907–10), and they then took a studio together in Moscow. They went to PARIS in 1912, but Udaltsova returned to Russia in 1914. One of her best-known paintings is *At the Piano.*

Uganda (Republic of Uganda) Located on the equator in East Africa, Uganda is a landlocked country covering an area of 91,111 square miles—a protectorate of the British Empire from 1895 until granted independence in 1962. Resistance to Prime Minister Milton OBOTE's leftist policies and suspension of the constitution resulted in Idi AMIN and the army seizing power in 1971. During Amin's eight-year rule thousands of Ugandans were killed, foreigners were expelled and the economy collapsed. Uganda was accused of collusion with terrorists when passengers from a highjacked Air France plane were held hostage at Entebbe Airport until Israeli commandos rescued them (see raid on ENTEBBE). In 1979 Amin was overthrown, and in 1980 Obote was elected president. Opposition from the National Resistance Army (NRA) led by Yoweri Museveni resulted in intense guerrilla warfare and tremendous loss of life. The NRA gained control of most of Uganda by 1986, and Museveni became president, forming a coalition government. The Museveni government has brought some stability to the country in spite of continued resistance in some areas and an attempted coup in 1988. At the same time, AIDS has spread through a large percentage of the population, causing a major health crisis in the country. Museveni retained leadership of Uganda through several elections, including one in 1996, the first time that Ugandans could directly vote for a presidential candidate. In 1997 Museveni dispatched troops to participate in a multinational campaign to depose President Mobutu Sese Seko of Zaire. The following year, Ugandan and

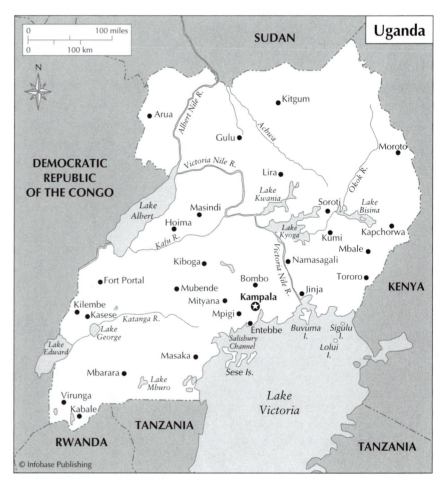

1256

UGANDA

1962	Becomes independent member of Commonwealth with Milton Obote as prime minister.
1966	Obote suspends constitution, declares himself executive president.
1971	Obote is overthrown in military coup led by Major General Idi Amin; suspension of Political Activities Decree abolishes all constitutional rights; Armed Forces (Power of Arrest) Decree places the armed forces above the law; Detention (Presumption of Time Limit) Decree grants army wide powers of detention without trial and the power to shoot on sight; an estimated 300,000 Ugandans are killed over the next eight years.
1973	Foreign businesses are expropriated without compensation and distributed among the military and police.
1979	Amin overthrown by Ugandan exiles with help of Tanzanian army; after year of political chaos, Obote returns to power; opposition leader Yoweri Museveni forms National Resistance Army (NRA) and starts guerrilla war against Obote; civilian casualties from government anti-guerrilla activity exceed those of Amin's rule.
1985	Obote overthrown in tribal coup that brings General Tito Okello to power; Okello unable to defeat NRA, which occupies Kampala and takes control of country by next year.
1986	Yoweri Museveni sworn in as president and creates National Resistance Council government, which includes 68 ministers with broad range of political interests; rival political parties banned.
1990	Led by Major General Fred Rwigyema, who fought in NRA with President Museveni, a rebel army of refugee Rwandan Tutsi tribesmen, many of whom had been in Ugandan army, invade Rwanda in attempt to seize government that is dominated by rival Hutu tribe; Ugandan government condemns attack and declares no prior knowledge of invasion.
1993	Museveni revokes the power of traditional tribal rulers in an effort to centralize and modernize government.
1994	Two rebel groups, the Ugandan National Democratic Alliance and the Ugandan Federal Army, sign cease-fire agreements with the government.
1995	A new constitution is adopted; the ruling military council is replaced with an elected legislative assembly and a popularly elected president.
1996	Museveni wins the presidential elections in a landslide victory; legislative elections are held for the new National Assembly.
1997	Local elections are held for the first time in decades and they occur without violence; troops sent to Zaire to help depose President Mobutu Sese Seko.
1998	Museveni purges the armed forces after an alleged assassination plot is uncovered; Uganda sends troops into the Democratic Republic of the Congo to support rebels fighting to overthrow Laurent Kabila.
2000	Allied Democratic Forces carry out guerrilla warfare in an effort to overthrow Museveni's government; a national referendum votes in favor of continuing the no-party system of government.
2001	East African Community (EAC) is inaugurated in Arusha, Tanzania, calling for a common East African passport and flag and economic and monetary integration; the members are Uganda, Tanzania and Kenya.

(Table continues)

2002	Sudan and Uganda sign an agreement to contain a Ugandan rebel group, Lord's Resistance Army (LRA), active along the border; the LRA seeks to govern Uganda along the lines of the biblical Ten Commandments; a peace agreement is signed with the Uganda National Rescue Front rebels, following more than five years of negotiations.
2004	The government and the LRA rebels hold first face-to-face talks, but they reach an impasse.
2005	Parliament approves a constitutional amendment ending presidential term limits; voters in a referendum support a return to multiparty politics.

Rwandan troops returned to Zaire (renamed the Democratic Republic of the Congo) to fight the forces of the country's new president, Laurent KABILA. In 2001, he defeated opposition candidate Kizza Besigye, gaining 69 percent of the vote. Despite his electoral success, Museveni failed to eliminate all violent opposition to his regime. In March 2002 he began working with SUDAN to eliminate the theocratic insurgency of "prophet" Joseph Kony. In 2004 the government and the LRA rebels held peace talks but could not reach an agreement. Parliament approved a constitutional amendment in 2005 that would void presidential term limits.

Uighurs An ancient Islamic and Turkic people dispersed throughout the modern-day states of KAZAKHSTAN, KYR-GYZSTAN TURKMENISTAN and UZBEKISTAN and in the province of XINJIANG (Sinkiang) in the northwestern part of the People's Republic of China (PRC). In 1943 and 1944 Uighur militants organized insurrections against Chinese rule, but they were eventually repressed by the military forces of the Chinese leader CHIANG KAI-SHEK. The Uighurs remained a problem after the establishment of the PRC in 1949. Numerous nationalist bands staged guerrilla insurrections against Chinese rule. In an effort to placate the nationalist sentiment within Uighur-dominated territory, MAO ZEDONG established the Xinjiang-Uighur Autonomous Region (XUAR) on October 1, 1955, which theoretically granted the Uighur people substantial autonomy in their regional affairs. This soon proved illusory, as the PRC continued to exercise complete control over the province, preventing any nongovernment-controlled institutions, such as mosques and Islamic schools, to operate, and ensuring that the Han Chinese ethnic minority within the XUAR enjoyed a higher standard of living than the Uighurs.

The victory of MUJAHIDEEN (Islamic freedom fighters) against the Soviet military occupation forces in Afghanistan in 1989, followed by the independence of the predominantly Muslim Soviet republics of Kazakhstan, Kyrgyzstan, Turkmenistan and Uzbekistan in 1991, emboldened Uighur nationalists to try to duplicate the success of their Islamic brethren in these Central Asian states. They began to recruit followers for a long insurgent campaign and kidnapped and assassinated officials within their regional communist parties who were loyal to Beijing. In 1997 Uighur nationalists orchestrated a terrorist bombing campaign throughout China that included explosions within Beijing. PRC officials responded by intensifying the campaign to suppress Uighur culture and religion; this campaign led to the arrest of thousands of Uighurs suspected of supporting this independence movement. The Chinese government also coordinated strategy with the governments of Kazakhstan and Kyrgyzstan, which faced similar Uighur secessionist movements within their borders.

Following a bomb explosion in a Chinese shopping center in the XUAR in October 2001, the PRC announced an intensification of the campaign to suppress Uighur terrorism. The PRC declared that foreign-based "terrorist" organizations in the XUAR, such as the East Turkestan Islamic Movement and the Home of East Turkestan Youth, were linked to Islamic terrorist leaders such as Osama BIN LADEN. Beijing claimed that its repressive policies were analogous to the U.S.-led "War on Terror" against the TALIBAN and AL-QAEDA following the terrorist attacks of SEPTEMBER 11, 2001. In December 2003 the Chinese Ministry for National Security issued a list of individuals and organizations accused of terrorist attacks against Chinese officials, property and citizens—all of which were members of the Uighur community.

Ukraine Nation in eastern Europe, formerly a part of the Soviet Union, contiguous with the Ukrainian Soviet Socialist Republic (established 1922). The inhabitants, the Ukrainians, are a Slavic people. Throughout much of its long history, the Ukraine has been dominated by either Poland or Russia. It entered the 20th century as part of the Russian Empire under Czar NICHOLAS II. In 1918, the Ukraine declared independence from Russia and formed its own government. During the ensuing RUSSIAN CIVIL WAR, the Ukraine was fought over by the Red Army of the BOLSHEVIKS and the anti-Bolshevik WHITES and was also claimed by POLAND, while the Ukrainians vainly attempted to maintain their independence. With their victory in the civil war, the Bolsheviks incorporated the Ukraine into the new UNION OF SOVIET SOCIALIST REPUBLICS in 1922, although Ukrainian nationalism was not subdued. During the reign of Joseph STALIN, the Ukraine suffered from a disastrous famine caused largely by Stalin's policy of forced collectivization of the Ukrainian farms and his confiscation of Ukrainian grain for export. When GERMANY invaded the Soviet Union during WORLD WAR II, the Ukrainians at first welcomed the Germans as liberators. However, the Nazis regarded them not as potential allies against Stalin but as an inferior race fit only for slavery, and the

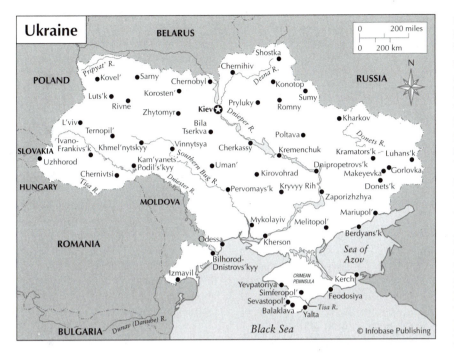

Ukraine

BELARUS · POLAND · RUSSIA · SLOVAKIA · HUNGARY · ROMANIA · MOLDOVA · BULGARIA · Black Sea · Sea of Azov

© Infobase Publishing

brutal German occupation caused much death and suffering. In the mid-1980s the region again suffered, this time from radioactive contamination resulting from the CHERNOBYL DISASTER. Ukraine's road to renewed independence began in 1991. On August 24, 1991, only a day after the failure of a

coup against Gorbachev, the Ukrainian Supreme Soviet declared the republic's independence. Although Gorbachev took steps to persuade Ukrainian leaders to change their position, a December referendum resulted in a 90 percent vote in favor of independence, and in the election of Leonid Kravchuk as the first president of Ukraine. Although desiring independence from the USSR, Ukrainian politicians sought to preserve links with former fellow Soviet Socialist Republics (SSRs), such as BELARUS and RUSSIA. On December 8, 1991, Ukraine helped form the COMMONWEALTH OF INDEPENDENT STATES (CIS), a loose confederation of former SSRs that sought to retain political, economic and military ties with each other. However, the relationship between Ukraine and Russia was immediately hampered by both nations' claim to inherit the Soviet Black Sea Fleet, by an independence movement on the Crimean Peninsula sponsored by ethnic Russians and by Ukrainian efforts to retain the nuclear weapons of the USSR based on Ukrainian soil. Kravchuk resolved the

	UKRAINE
1917	A revolutionary parliament (the Rada), proclaims Ukrainian autonomy within a federal Russia.
1918	Ukraine declares full independence.
1922	The Ukrainian Soviet Socialist Republic (Ukrainian SSR) becomes part of the Union of Soviet Socialist Republics (USSR).
1932–33	Enforced collectivization of agriculture causes another catastrophic famine, with more than 7.5 million deaths.
1941–44	Germany occupies Ukraine; many Ukrainians collaborate; millions of Ukrainians and Ukrainian Jews are enslaved and exterminated by the Nazis.
1986	A major environmental disaster is caused by the explosion of a nuclear reactor at Chernobyl, north of Kiev.
1991	The Soviet Union dissolves, and Ukraine enters into the Commonwealth of Independent States, with Leonid Kravchuk as president.
1992	Ukraine agrees to eliminate all of its nuclear weapons within seven years.
1994	Leonid Kuchma is elected president.
1997	Ukraine and Russia agree on the division of the Black Sea Fleet, with the Ukraine keeping about one-fifth of the fleet.
1999	Kuchma is reelected president.
2004	In what becomes known as the Orange Revolution, citizens take to the streets to protest the results of the presidential election; the government overturns the results, and a new election goes to the opposition candidate.

nuclear issue when he agreed to transfer the weapons to Russia in 1992. Ukraine also encountered serious economic problems as Kravchuk attempted to transform the centrally planned economy into a free market system, a process that led to tremendous economic crises. As a result of this economic decline, Kravchuk suffered a narrow defeat in the 1994 presidential elections, and was replaced by Leonid Kuchma, who resumed his predecessor's free-market reforms and improved economic and political relations with Russia under the CIS.

Although Kuchma strove to improve Ukrainian-Russian relations through the CIS, Ukraine also sought closer relations with Europe. In 1993 it obtained a limited membership in the NORTH ATLANTIC TREATY ORGANIZATION (NATO) under that organization's PARTNERSHIP FOR PEACE program. In May 1997 Russian and Ukrainian leaders resolved the dispute over possession of the Black Sea Fleet; it provided for the Russian government to purchase 80 percent of the fleet from Ukraine, and for a 20-year Russian lease on the Crimean port of Sevastopol, where the fleet would remain stationed.

In economic matters Kuchma's efforts at reform were not successful. Repeated conflicts with the Ukrainian parliament impeded his promised free-market reforms, after which his own economic advisers convinced Kuchma that a more gradual economic transition was in order. By 1999 the economy began to show signs of a recovery, which helped Kuchma win election to a second five-year term. In late 2004 a peaceful mass protest (often referred to as the "Orange Revolution") forced the government to overturn a rigged presidential election and allow an internationally monitored election that brought to power a reformist government under President Viktor Yushchenko.

Ulam, Stanislaw Marcin (1909–1984) Polish-born mathematician. Considered one of the greatest figures in 20th-century mathematics, Ulam was a key figure in the development of the HYDROGEN BOMB. In 1935 Ulam joined the Institute for Advanced Study in Princeton, New Jersey, at the invitation of mathematician John von NEUMANN. In 1943 he was recruited to work on the MANHATTAN PROJECT in Los Alamos, New Mexico, where he remained until 1967. With physicist Edward TELLER he devised the "Teller-Ulam" solution, which made the H-bomb possible. Ulam served as professor and chairman of the mathematics department at the University of Colorado. His books include *Adventures of a Mathematician.*

Ulanova, Galina Sergeyevna (1910–1998) Prima ballerina. She made her debut in 1928 at the Kirov Theater, Leningrad, in *Les Sylphides.* Her dancing represented a survival of the best of the prerevolutionary Russian school. She was taught by Agrippina VAGANOVA, who was in turn taught by Nicholas Legat; her parents were dancers at the Imperial Theater in St. Petersburg, the Maryinsky. Although comparatively unknown outside the Soviet Union until her visit to London in 1956, she established herself as one of the world's greatest dancers. In addition to her stage performances, she appeared in the films *Giselle* (1957) and *Romeo and Juliet* (1954). On retiring in 1963, she joined the Bolshoi Theater as ballet mistress.

Ulbricht, Walter (1893–1973) East German political leader. Born in Leipzig, Ulbricht was a Social Democrat and trade unionist through World War I but joined the German Communist Party on its founding in 1918 and remained a lifelong Marxist. He was a member of the Reichstag from 1928 to 1933, fleeing HITLER to settle in Moscow in 1933. Ulbricht returned to GERMANY with conquering Russian troops in 1945, becoming deputy premier of the newly created German Democratic Republic in 1949 and secretary general of the Socialist Unity Party (successor to the Communist Party) in 1950. As the autocratic leader of EAST GERMANY, he molded his nation into a strict Stalinist state and helped to make it the world's eighth-ranked economic power. Opposed to the policies of West Germany and angered by the exodus of East Germans to the West, Ulbricht was responsible for the 1961 construction of the BERLIN WALL. He gave up his post as party secretary to Erich HONECKER in 1971 but remained in the figurehead position of chairman of the Council of State until his death.

Ultra Code name for the material gained from Britain's successful effort to break the codes produced by Germany's **Enigma** cipher machine during WORLD WAR II. The first Enigma machine was produced by Germany in 1926, and it was modified in 1937. The most important characteristic of the machine was that codes produced by it could not be deciphered without the use of another Enigma device. With Polish help, England and France were able to reconstruct Enigma, and by 1939 two replicas of the machine were in Allied hands. In 1940 cryptanalysts (including mathematician Alan TURING) working for the British War Office at Bletchley Park, England, broke Germany's Enigma cipher. From then on the Allies were able to eavesdrop on virtually all of Germany's most important coded messages and get vital German intelligence. Information obtained included data on the activity and location of German U-boats that enabled the Allies to sink about 30 enemy SUBMARINES, as well as vital intelligence on the Italian campaign, the Mediterranean and Middle East theaters and the activities of ROMMEL's Afrika Korps.

Ulysses (1922) Classic novel by the Irish writer James JOYCE. *Ulysses* is perhaps the single most acclaimed novel of the 20th century. Since its independent publication in Paris in 1922 by the bookseller Sylvia BEACH, who believed in *Ulysses* as a work of genius while commercial publishers shied away from its experimental language and sexual frankness, the novel has earned the highest praise from each successive generation of writers and literary critics. The basic plot concerns the strangely intertwined wanderings of two men, the young artist Stephen Dedalus and the cuckolded husband Leopold Bloom, through a June day and night in Dublin. Each chapter of the novel derives thematic inspiration from episodes of the *Odyssey* by the Greek epic poet Homer, and Bloom and Dedalus bear a resemblance to Odysseus and his son Telemachus. *Ulysses* was the first major work to make use of the STREAM OF CONSCIOUSNESS technique—precise linguistic rendering of the random thought flows and fantasies of its individual characters. While *Ulysses* was at first banned in the U.S. for obscenity, a famous 1933 ruling by federal judge John M. Woolsey stirringly affirmed its literary greatness.

Underwood, Oscar Wilder *(1862–1929)* American politician. A member from Alabama of the U.S. HOUSE OF REPRESENTATIVES (1897–1915) and Senate (1915–27), Underwood was a strong supporter of President Woodrow WILSON's foreign policies. He was a contender for the presidential nomination in 1912, and in 1913 wrote the Underwood Tariff Act, which severely reduced tariff rates until it was nullified by WORLD WAR II.

Undset, Sigrid *(1882–1949)* Norwegian novelist. Undset was the daughter of a noted archaeologist and antiquarian whose interests would later influence her work. Her first works were *Fru Marta Oulie* (1907, *Mrs. Marta Oulie*), the short story collection *Den lykkelige alder* (1908, *The Happiest Years*) and *Fortellingen om Viga-Ljot og Vigdis* (1909, translated as *Gunnar's Daughter*). It was with *Jenny: Roman* (1911, *Jenny: A Novel*) that she first achieved acclaim. The novel is a roman a clef portraying her affair with an older married man, Anders Castus Svarstad, whom she would later marry. Undset is most celebrated for the medieval fiction she wrote later in life. This includes the trilogy *Kristin Lavransdatter,* which consists of the novels *Kransen* (1920, translated in the U.K. as *The Garland* and in the U.S. as *The Bridal Wreath*), *Husfrue* (1922) translated as *The Mistress of Husaby* and *Korset* (1922, *The Cross*). This was followed by the related novels *Olav Audunsson i Hestviken* (1925, *The Master of Hestviken*) and *Olav Audunsson og hans born* (1927, *Olav Audunsson and His Children*), which were published as a tetralogy in English consisting of *The Axe, The Snake Pit, In the Wilderness* and *The Son Avenger,* referred to as a whole as *The Master of Hestviken.* Undset was awarded the NOBEL PRIZE for literature in 1928.

Ungaretti, Giuseppe *(1888–1970)* Italian poet and essayist. Ungaretti was born of Italian emigrants living in Alexandria, Egypt. He was educated in Egypt but left in 1912 to study law at the Sorbonne in Paris. While in Paris Ungaretti became active in artistic circles, forming friendships with the poet Guillaume APOLLINAIRE and the cubist painters Georges BRAQUE and Pablo PICASSO, as well as with members of the Italian futurist circle (see FUTURISM).

Ungaretti fought in the Italian infantry during WORLD WAR I, during which time he published his first book of poems, *Il Porto Sepolto* (1916). In the 1920s, Ungaretti was for a time a supporter of Benito MUSSOLINI. In 1936 Ungaretti became professor of Italian literature at the University of São Paolo, Brazil. His international reputation as a poet was consolidated with a series of volumes he published late in his life—*Poesie disperse* (1945), *Il Dolore* (1947), *Un Grido e Paesaggi* (1952) and *Vita d'un Uomo* (1969), which contained his collected poems.

unidentified flying object Also known as a UFO—an airborne object whose appearance or behavior cannot be readily identified or explained. Anecdotal evidence suggests that the people of the ancient world saw "flying objects" they could not identify. Modern sightings began in the U.S. in 1878 and continued during 1896–97. In the 20th century, UFOs were reported by flyers in World War II and by citizens of Scandinavia and, to a lesser degree, other European countries in 1946. UFOs came to wide public attention after June 24, 1947, when Kenneth Arnold, an American pilot flying over the Cascade Mountains in the state of Washington sighted nine shining and weaving disks that, he said, moved "like a saucer skipping across water." From this description came the popular term *flying saucer.* As interest mounted, so did the other reported sightings, some by ordinary citizens, some by trained military observers. Since then UFO sightings have reoccurred in clusters, peaking in southern Europe in 1954, in New Guinea in 1958, in the Soviet Union in 1967 and in the U.S. in 1947, 1952, 1957, 1965–67 and 1973. Most sightings have eventually been explained as such things as weather balloons, planets, fireballs and other meteorological phenomena, the sun's rays bouncing off airplanes and even mass hysteria and outright hoax. A U.S. Air Force investigation, Project Blue Book, which studied UFO reports from 1948–69, concluded that the "objects" posed no threat to national security and that no evidence could be found for any extraterrestrial origin for them. The report notwithstanding, people continue to see objects in the sky that they cannot identify, and some 10 percent of all

those objects seem to remain a 20th-century mystery.

Union of South Africa Name of the southernmost nation in Africa from 1910 until 1961, when it became the Republic of South Africa. (See also SOUTH AFRICA.)

Union of Soviet Socialist Republics (USSR) The Union of Soviet Socialist Republics was, for most of the 20th century, the largest country in the world: it covered a total area of 8,647,172 square miles, nearly 1/6th of the total global land surface, and extended east-west across northern Eurasia for nearly 6,210 miles from the Pacific Ocean to the Baltic Sea, and for nearly 3,105 miles north-south at its widest point. The USSR consisted of 15 Union (constituent) Republics, occupying (with a few exceptions) the area that before 1918 was imperial RUSSIA. The RUSSIAN REVOLUTION of 1917 forced the abdication of Czar NICHOLAS II and installed a provisional government (see FEBRUARY REVOLUTION) to rule Russia; the subsequent OCTOBER REVOLUTION brought a Marxist (Bolshevik) government to power, led by V. I. LENIN, which sought to eliminate all vestiges of the old regime and to radically transform Russian society. In the course of the 20th century, this transformation brought about periods of intense human suffering but also made the USSR into a world superpower.

The BOLSHEVIKS renamed Russia the Russian Soviet Federated Socialist Republic in 1918 (with Moscow reinstated as the capital), and in December 1922 this became part of the Union of Soviet Socialist Republics following the consolidation of Soviet power in the UKRAINE, Transcaucasia and Central Asia. The Bolshevik Party became the Russian Communist Party (Bolsheviks) in 1918, the All-Union Communist Party (Bolsheviks) in 1925, and the COMMUNIST PARTY OF THE SOVIET UNION (CPSU) in 1952.

During the RUSSIAN CIVIL WAR the Bolsheviks pursued a policy of WAR COMMUNISM, involving highly centralized economic administration, conscription of all private and public wealth and manpower, a ban on private trade and forcible requisitioning of grain and other foodstuffs from the peasantry. "War communism" gradually alienated the regime from the workers

Union of Soviet Socialist Republics

1917	Lenin and Bolsheviks seize power in October Revolution.
1918–21	Russian Civil War and period of War Communism.
1924	Death of Lenin.
1925–29	Stalin consolidates his power, expels key opponents from the Communist Party.
1928	Stalin launches first five-year plan for rapid industrialization.
1929	Trotsky forced into exile; Stalin begins campaign against the Kulaks.
1934	Assassination of Sergei Kirov.
1936–38	Stalin's Great Purge; millions executed or imprisoned.
1939	Soviet Foreign Minister Molotov and German Foreign Minister von Ribbentrop sign German-Soviet Nonaggression Pact.
1940	USSR annexes Latvia, Lithuania, Estonia.
1941	Germany invades the Soviet Union in World War II.
1941–44	Siege of Leningrad.
1942	Soviets stop Germans at battle of Stalingrad.
1943	Soviets defeat Germans in massive tank battle at Kursk.
1945	Soviets drive Germans out of eastern Europe, occupy several eastern European nations, including Poland, Czechoslovakia, Hungary; (April) Soviet troops link up with Americans on the Elbe River; (April–May) Soviets enter Berlin; end of World War II in Europe.
1948–49	Soviets close off West Berlin, precipitating Berlin Crisis; Allies respond with Berlin Airlift.
1953	Death of Stalin.
1955	Formation of Warsaw Pact, military alliance of communist eastern bloc nations under USSR.
1956	Khrushchev condemns Stalin for "cult of personality" at 20th Party Congress; Soviets and Warsaw Pact troops invade Hungary to put down anticommunist uprising.
1957	(October 4) USSR becomes first nation to put artificial satellite into orbit with launch of *Sputnik 1*; (November 3) Soviets launch the dog Laika into Earth orbit aboard *Sputnik 2*—first Earth creature in space.
1958	Boris Pasternak forced to repudiate Nobel Prize in literature.
1959	Soviet *Lunik 3* spacecraft passes behind the moon, sends back first pictures of moon's far side.
1961	(April 12) Soviet cosmonaut Yuri Gagarin becomes first human in space, making single Earth orbit aboard *Vostok 1*.
1962	(October) Cuban missile crisis—USSR and U.S. on brink of nuclear war before USSR backs down and removes ballistic missiles from Cuba.
1963	Nuclear Test Ban Treaty among the U.S., USSR and Britain.
1964	Khrushchev removed from office, replaced by Brezhnev and Kosygin.
1968	(April) Soviet invasion of Czechoslovakia ends Prague Spring reforms; Brezhnev Doctrine signals that the USSR will not tolerate deviation from hard-line communism among the Warsaw Pact nations.

1974	Novelist–historian Alexander Solzhenitsyn expelled from USSR after publication of *The Gulag Archipelago.*
1975	Soviet Soyuz spacecraft links up with U.S. Apollo spacecraft, first joint U.S.–USSR space venture.
1979	Brezhnev signs SALT II agreement with U.S. President Carter; Soviet invasion of Afghanistan.
1980	U.S. boycotts summer Olympic Games in Moscow in protest of Afghanistan invasion.
1982	(November) Brezhnev dies; succeeded by Yuri Andropov.
1984	(February) Andropov dies; succeeded by Konstantin Chernenko.
1985	(March) Chernenko dies; succeeded by Mikhail Gorbachev; beginning of glasnost and perestroika reforms.
1986	(April) Chernobyl nuclear power plant disaster.
1990–91	Gorbachev's economic reforms in trouble; secessionist movements in Lithuania, Georgia and elsewhere threaten to break apart the USSR; Boris Yeltsin calls for Gorbachev's resignation; USSR supports UN and U.S. action against Iraq; Warsaw Pact dissolved after eastern European nations oust communist governments and restore democracy.
1991	Attempted coup against Gorbachev fails (August); the USSR is dissolved (December 25) as republics declare their independence; Gorbachev resigns and Boris Yeltsin, the leader of the reform movement, is elected president; Yeltsin bans Communist Party; Commonwealth of Independent States (CIS) is created as a vehicle to maintain ties among states of the former Soviet Union.

and peasants and prompted manifestations of discontent culminating in the KRONSTADT REBELLION, a mutiny in March 1921 at the Kronstadt naval garrison near Petrograd. Shortly afterward, recognizing the need to recoup popular support for the regime as well as to restore the war-ravaged industrial base, Lenin announced the NEW ECONOMIC POLICY (NEP). Originally limited to replacing forcible requisitioning of peasants' produce with a tax-in-kind on surpluses, the NEP became a general retreat from principles of a socially owned economy toward what Lenin termed "state capitalism," combining state ownership of the "commanding heights" of the economy (heavy industry, public utilities and the financial system) with a free market and private ownership of small-scale industry and agriculture. When Lenin died in January 1924, the party leadership was split into four factions led by Leon TROTSKY; Joseph STALIN; Grigory ZINOVIEV and Lev KAMENEV; and Nikolai BUKHARIN, Alexei RYKOV and Mikhail Tomsky. Zinoviev and Kamenev allied with Stalin to ensure that Trotsky did not succeed Lenin as leader, and were instrumental in convincing the party central committee to ignore Lenin's recommendation (made shortly before his death) that Stalin should be ousted as party general secretary (an office he had assumed in 1922) because he was accumulating unlimited authority. However, fear of Stalin's growing power prompted Zinoviev and Kamenev to break with him in 1925, and in the following year they allied with Trotsky, while Stalin allied with Bukharin's group. Stalin's opponents were expelled from the party in 1927;

UNION OF SOVIET SOCIALIST REPUBLICS: LEADERS

1917–1924	V.I. Lenin
1924–1927	Collective leadership, with Joseph Stalin as central figure
1927–1953	Joseph Stalin
1953	Interim government led by Georgi Malenkov, Vyacheslav Molotov, Lavrenti Beria, Nikita Khrushchev
1953–1964	Nikita Khrushchev
1964–1982	Leonid Brezhnev, with Alexei Kosygin initially as joint leader
1982–1984	Yuri Andropov
1984–1985	Konstantin Chernenko
1985–1991	Mikhail Gorbachev

Zinoviev and Kamenev were subsequently readmitted, but Trotsky was forced into exile in 1929. Economic policy was a key issue in the factional struggle: Trotsky advocated accelerated industrialization, financed at the peasants' expense, whereas Bukharin favored conciliation of the peasantry. In this he was supported initially by Stalin, but once the Left opposition was defeated in 1927 Stalin turned against the Right opposition and in 1929 secured the expulsion of Bukharin, Rykov and Tomsky from the politburo. At the beginning of 1928 Stalin launched a policy of rapid industrialization under the first five-year plan, signaling the end of the NEP. Meanwhile, in the countryside a growing crisis over the withholding of grain supplies by the KULAKS (well-off peasant farmers who were generally hostile to government agricultural policy) prompted a government terror campaign in 1929–30, during which the kulaks were liquidated. These measures met with fierce resistance and caused massive disruption to agriculture, leading to widespread famine in 1932–33. During the 17th Party Congress in January 1934 there were suggestions that Stalin should be replaced by Sergei KIROV (the party leader in Leningrad). In December 1934 Kirov was assassinated (probably on Stalin's orders), and his death was made the pretext for a reign of terror that reached its height in 1936–38 (see GREAT PURGE). An estimated half a million people were executed and millions more were imprisoned (mostly without trial) in forced labor camps, while at show trials Stalin's former opponents in the party leadership (including Zinoviev, Kamenev, Bukharin and Rykov) were condemned to death after making obviously false confessions of treason and terrorism. Trotsky was also sentenced to death in absentia and was murdered by a Soviet agent in Mexico in 1940. Severe political repressions lasted until Stalin's death in March 1953.

Unsuccessful Soviet attempts to form an alliance with Great Britain and France were followed by the signing in August 1939 of a nonaggression pact with Nazi Germany (see GERMAN-SOVIET NONAGGRESSION PACT). On June 22, 1941, Germany violated the pact and invaded the Soviet Union, capturing vast territories and inflicting massive human and material damage in the European part of the country. The German armies were finally expelled in 1944 after a struggle in which about 20 million Soviet citizens lost their lives (see WORLD WAR II ON THE RUSSIAN FRONT). Soviet troops went on to liberate the nations of Eastern Europe, where Soviet-backed communist regimes took power; in 1955 the WARSAW PACT created a formal military alliance of the Soviet Union and these nations (except YUGOSLAVIA, which had broken with the Soviet Union in 1948). Meanwhile the wartime alliance with Great Britain, France and the U.S. was supplanted by the COLD WAR of mutual suspicion, hostility and a contest to achieve military supremacy.

On his death in 1953, Stalin was succeeded by a triumvirate comprising Georgi MALENKOV (Stalin's successor as prime minister and party leader), Vyacheslav MOLOTOV (the foreign minister) and Lavrenti BERIA (the notorious head of the SECRET POLICE). However, after little more than a week Malenkov was forced to relinquish the party leadership to Nikita KHRUSHCHEV, while Beria was expelled from the party in July 1953 and was later executed for treason. At the 20TH PARTY CONGRESS in February 1956, Khrushchev launched a bitter attack on Stalin's dictatorship and cult of personality. Later that year the USSR sent troops into HUNGARY to crush the HUNGARIAN UPRISING. In the following year Malenkov, Molotov and Lazar KAGANOVICH attempted to depose Khrushchev, whereupon they were expelled from the party central committee (see ANTI-PARTY GROUP CRISIS). By the early 1960s Khrushchev's erratic domestic policies (including unworkable overhauls of regional administration and economic planning) and his unpredictable conduct of international relations (see CUBAN MISSILE CRISIS) were arousing strong opposition. In October 1964 his critics in the leadership engineered his replacement as party first secretary (later general secretary) by Leonid BREZHNEV, under whom Khrushchev's comparatively liberal policies were largely reversed and a limited degree of STALINISM was reimposed. After the Soviet invasion of CZECHOSLOVAKIA in 1968, the so-called BREZHNEV DOCTRINE enunciated the right of the Soviet Union to intervene in socialist countries where socialism was threatened; this doctrine was put into practice when Soviet troops entered AFGHANISTAN in 1979. Upon his death in November 1982, Brezhnev was succeeded by Yuri ANDROPOV both as party general secretary and president of the presidium of the Supreme Soviet (ceremonial head of state). Andropov introduced cautious economic reforms and a major anticorruption campaign, and began to remove leading officials associated with Brezhnev, but he fell seriously ill after less than a year in office and died in February 1984. He was succeeded in both posts by Konstantin CHERNENKO, a conservative former Brezhnev protege. In the 13 months until Chernenko's death in March 1985, Andropov's limited reforms were continued, albeit at a more cautious pace and without any major new initiatives.

Mikhail GORBACHEV (at 54 the youngest member of the party politburo) was elected by the party central committee as Chernenko's successor on March 11, 1985. Formerly an Andropov protégé, he immediately resumed the campaign to remove "Brezhnevite" officials and to root out corruption, leading to a massive turnover in the government and party leadership. Complaining that the economy had been stagnating since the 1970s, he announced a policy of complete PERESTROIKA ("restructuring"), to involve technical innovation, more efficient use of labor and materials and managerial autonomy; subsequent initiatives introduced limited private enterprise, including private farming, and a reduction in central planning. However, by the end of 1990 this had failed significantly to improve economic performance. Perestroika in the economy was accomplished in the political and cultural spheres by the policy of GLASNOST ("openness"). Glasnost led to a freer press, official willingness to acknowledge unwelcome developments, a frequently damning reappraisal of Soviet history and greater tolerance of individual expression: by the end of 1988 virtually all political prisoners had been freed. However, the loosening of fetters on Soviet political life led to the unleashing of pent-up ethnic tensions. In February 1988 a dispute flared between Armenians and Azerbaijanis. Massive demonstrations and strikes gripped Armenia and Azerbaijan intermittently throughout 1988–89. During 1989 intercommunal violence and nationalist unrest erupted in other southern republics, notably Uzbekistan and Georgia. Also in 1988–89 Estonia, Latvia and Lithuania witnessed a coalescence of the goals of unofficial nationalist agitation with official initiatives for greater autonomy: in all three republics the authorities permitted the establishment in October 1988 of independent movements that combined support for Gorbachev's reforms with radical autonomy programs and proposals for political pluralism, while the official initiatives featured unilateral declarations of the republics' "sovereignty" and open condemnation of their 1940 annexation by the Soviet Union.

Soviet foreign policy also changed under Gorbachev as he began a global diplomatic offensive. Four summit meetings between Gorbachev and U.S. president Ronald Reagan culminated in December 1987 in the signing of the Treaty on Intermediate Nuclear Forces, providing for the elimination over a three-year period of all intermediate-range land-based nuclear weapons held by the Soviet Union and the U.S. Soviet troops were withdrawn in full from Afghanistan by February 1989.

In accordance with constitutional amendments passed on December 1, 1988, elections were held in early 1989 for a new supreme representative body, the 2,250-member Congress of People's Deputies. When the congress convened on May 25, 1989, it overwhelmingly elected Gorbachev to a new executive presidency. The work of the congress and of a restyled Supreme Soviet, notably the freedom and contentiousness of debate, demonstrated a radical change in the conduct of Soviet politics. However, with increasing ethnic unrest, calls for greater economic reforms and new challenges to Gorbachev's authority (notably by popular communist reform politician Boris Yeltsin), Gorbachev seemed to retreat from his earlier emphasis on glasnost and perestroika and side with hard-line elements in the politburo. When Gorbachev demanded stronger powers, his foreign secretary, Edvard Shevardnadze (a leading figure in the reform wing of the party and widely respected in the West) resigned in protest. Early in 1991, in moves reminiscent of the earlier crackdowns on Hungary and Czechoslovakia, the USSR used force to quell independence movements in Lithuania and Es-

tonia. Soviet Georgia declared independence from the USSR in April 1991, and a wave of strikes swept the republic. On December 25, after a failed coup by hard-liners against Gorbachev, he announced the dissolution of the USSR and resigned as president.

UNITA (National Union for the Total Independence of Angola) A group fighting alongside the MPLA and FNLA between 1961 and 1975 to achieve Angolan independence (see Angolan War of Independence). Following independence in 1975, MPLA and UNITA set up rival governments. In the subsequent Angolan Civil War, the South African–backed UNITA (led by Jonas Savimbi) and FNLA were defeated. In the late 1980s UNITA forces still controlled some areas of southern Angola. In 1989 there was evidence that UNITA forces had slaughtered thousands of elephants, using their ivory tusks to finance a continuation of the war. In the 1990s UNITA signed the Bicesse Accords (1991) and Lusaka Accords (1994) with the ruling MPLA, which called for an end to the Angolan Civil War. However, UNITA withdrew from both agreements and continued its military campaign against the government until government forces killed Savimbi in 2002.

Unitas, John Constantine (1933–2003) American football player. During a college career with a mediocre team, his personal numbers as quarterback were good enough for him to be drafted by the Pittsburgh Steelers. Let go by that team, Unitas turned to semi-pro ball until he was offered a slot on the roster of the Baltimore Colts in 1956. The following year, he was named the NFL's most valuable player. In 1958 he led the Colts to the league championship over the New York Giants. He finished his career with the San Diego Chargers, holding most passing records, including most consecutive games throwing for a touchdown, 47.

United Arab Emirates A federation of seven emirates located along the east-central coast of the Arabian Peninsula; total area of 32,270 square miles. Until 1971 the emirates were British protectorates and were called the Trucial States. With independence in that year Abu Dhabi, Dubai, Sharjah, Ajman, Umn al-Qaiwain and Fugairah formed the United Arab Emirates. Ras al-Khaimah joined the federation in 1972. Territorial disputes with Saudi Arabia and Iran, with the latter country entering into armed conflict with Ras al-Khaimah for a period, were settled

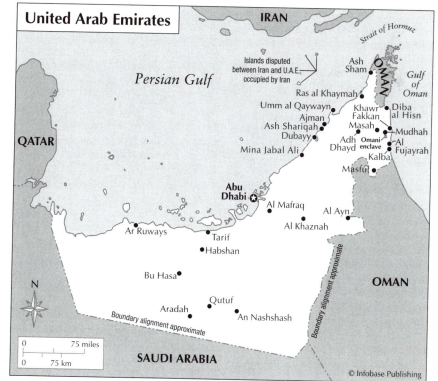

UNITED ARAB EMIRATES	
1971	United Kingdom withdraws its forces from the Persian Gulf region and ends treaty obligations with the Trucial States; six of the Trucial States—Abu Dhabi, Dubai, Sharjah, Ajman, Umm al-Qaywayn, and Fujairah—federate themselves as a sovereign and independent nation. Provisional constitution of UAE is promulgated.
1972	Ras al-Khaimah joins UAE.
1974	Accord is reached with Saudi Arabia over border disputes relating to the Buraimi Oasis; diplomatic relations are established with Saudi Arabia.
1991	The UAE sends ground troops to the 28-nation allied coalition in the Persian Gulf War.
2001	The government orders financial institutions to freeze the assets of 62 individuals and organizations suspected by the US of funding terrorist organizations.
2005	The UAE announces it will hold elections for half the seats in the Federal National Council; the other half is to be appointed by the rulers.

by 1974. The petroleum-rich sheikdoms of Abu Dhabi and Dubai have political predominance, causing some tensions with the other emirates. In November 2001 the government began cooperating with U.S. president George W. Bush's "War on Terror" when it ordered its banks to freeze all assets belonging to a list of 62 people and groups allegedly connected to the terrorist group AL-QAEDA that was responsible for the terrorist attacks of SEPTEMBER 11, 2001. In 2005 the UAE announced it would hold its first elections for seats in the Federal National Council.

United Artists One of Hollywood's "Little Three" motion picture companies (along with COLUMBIA PICTURES and UNIVERSAL PICTURES). Founded in 1919 by four of the greatest names in the movies—Mary PICKFORD, Douglas FAIRBANKS, Sr., Charles CHAPLIN and D. W. GRIFFITH—United Artists was the first company in which motion picture performers acquired complete autonomy over their work. As heads of their own respective production companies, they controlled all artistic, financial and promotional activities. They insisted each picture be sold and promoted individually, not as part of a package of films, which was the standard practice at the time. Some of the best-known work of each member came from the first decade of the studio. Fairbanks turned exclusively to costume epics like *The Mark of*

Zorro (1920) and *Robin Hood* (1923). Chaplin discontinued short comedies and turned to features like *The Gold Rush* (1925) and *The Circus* (1927). Mary Pickford turned from the "little girl" roles of *Pollyanna* (1920) to more mature roles in *Dorothy Vernon of Haddon Hall* (1925) and *The Taming of the Shrew* (1929). And Griffith, before his departure in 1924, made two of his most successful films, *Way Down East* (1920) and *Orphans of the Storm* (1922). In 1925 Joseph Schenck became the board chairman, and an influx of new talent began releasing through the studio—Buster KEATON, Gloria SWANSON, and William S. Hart. A chain of theaters was organized in 1926, the United Artists Theatre Circuit, Inc., which gave the company guaranteed screenings. In the 1930s the company became increasingly a packager for the films of independent producers, Walter Wanger and David O. SELZNICK and, in London, Alexander KORDA. After some difficult times in the 1940s the studio went through a series of reorganizations. Then in retirement, Chaplin and Pickford sold off their stock in 1950. A syndicate took over until 1967 when TransAmerican Corporation bought the company. A merger with METRO-GOLDWYN-MAYER began in 1981. And five years later the conglomerate's film library was purchased for television by entrepreneur Ted TURNER. Notable films from the 1950 to 1990 period include *The African Queen* (1952), *High Noon* (1952), *Some Like It Hot* (1959),

the James Bond films of the 1960s and *Rain Man* (1988).

United Kingdom The death of Queen Victoria (January 22, 1901) and the accession of EDWARD VII ended an era in which Britain had projected self-confidence both at home and abroad. The foundation of the Labour Movement (February 27, 1900) signaled that a new force, the urban proletariat, would be demanding a voice in Parliament. The budget was strained by foreign wars. The BOER WAR (1899–1902) in SOUTH AFRICA was controversial for the British use of mass internment in CONCENTRATION CAMPS to cut off the Boer soldiers from their support among the Afrikaner population.

As the LABOUR PARTY's strength grew at the polls, the Liberal government of Prime Minister Henry CAMPBELL-BANNERMAN introduced the first old-age pensions in 1908, unemployment insurance and labor exchanges in 1909, medical and limited unemployment insurance in 1911 and a limited working week in the same year, and a minimum wage for coal-miners in 1912. In 1905, after a bill to allow women the vote was defeated in Parliament, suffragettes were imprisoned for assaulting police. It was not until the Representation of People Act in 1917 that wives over 30 could vote—as well as all men over 21. In 1918 Parliament allowed for women MPs.

United Kingdom

ATLANTIC OCEAN

SCOTLAND

North Sea

NORTHERN IRELAND

REPUBLIC OF IRELAND

Irish Sea

WALES

ENGLAND

London

English Channel

Channel Islands

© Infobase Publishing

Shetland Islands
Lerwick

Orkney Islands
Thurso
John o'Groats
Stornoway
Outer Hebrides
Inner Hebrides
Inverness
Aberdeen
Perth
Dundee
Firth of Forth
Glasgow
Edinburgh
Londonderry
Omagh
Lisburn
Belfast
Isle of Man
Douglas
Newcastle upon Tyne
Carlisle
Sunderland
Middlesbrough
Blackpool
Leeds
York
Kingston upon Hull
Preston
Bradford
Manchester
Holyhead
Liverpool
Sheffield
Grimsby
Chester
Stoke-on-Trent
Nottingham
Shrewsbury
Leicester
Norwich
Aberystwyth
Birmingham
Coventry
Cambridge
Ipswich
Northampton
Fishguard
Oxford
Felixstowe
Swansea
Cardiff
Bristol
Reading
Canterbury
Bristol Channel
Bath
Winchester
Dover
Salisbury
Hastings
Exeter
Southampton
Brighton
Bournemouth
Portsmouth
Eastbourne
Plymouth
Torquay
Isle of Wight
Penzance
Isles of Scilly
Alderney
Guernsey
Sark
Jersey
Severn
Thames

N

0   100 miles
0   100 km

The Liberal Herbert ASQUITH, who succeeded Campbell-Bannerman as prime minister in 1908, attacked the power of the House of Lords. Asquith emerged in 1910 with a Liberal government dependent on Labour and Irish Nationalist support. The House of Lords accepted (by passing the Parliament Act in August 1911) strict limitations on its power to hold up the passage of legislation.

British governments began to accept the idea of Irish HOME RULE but faced a dilemma over Ulster, a largely Protestant province (see IRELAND; NORTHERN IRELAND). A Home Rule Bill was amended to exclude Ulster; it became law in September 1913. With world war impending, the government shelved the Irish issue. When Germany invaded Belgium, Britain declared war in response (August 4, 1914). An all-party coalition government was formed under Asquith (May 1915), who was succeeded by David LLOYD GEORGE in December 1916. Parliament voted for conscription in January 1916. WORLD WAR I proved to be an exercise in futility and despair. Although Britain and its allies ultimately won the war, the human cost was staggering. Some 750,000 British troops died, along with 200,000 other soldiers from the BRITISH EMPIRE, a third of them Indian. The war cost Britain US $35 billion—more than any nation except Germany.

Lloyd George's postwar coalition faced a rising unemployment that reached 2.2 million by June 1921. The unemployment benefit was increased, and food and coal rationing was reintroduced. During the 1920s Britain faced a challenge in INDIA (where GANDHI launched massive campaigns of passive resistance); particularly volatile was the Middle East, where Britain and France had been awarded LEAGUE OF NATIONS mandates. The imperial conference of 1926 agreed that CANADA, AUSTRALIA, NEW ZEALAND, South Africa and NEWFOUNDLAND would be self-governing dominions, equal in status to Britain. In Ireland, the Free State compromise offered to the south in December 1921 extricated Britain from its attempt to sustain rule by martial law.

The wartime coalition ended when the CONSERVATIVE PARTY won the election of November 1922, and Labour, under Ramsay MACDONALD, became the official opposition. Prime Minister Andrew Bonar LAW was followed (May 1923) by Stanley BALDWIN, who lost an election (November 1923) over his pro-tariff policy. The first Labour government, with Liberal support, lasted just one year. Britain's first GENERAL STRIKE (May 3–12, 1926) rekindled class animosities. Ramsay MacDonald's second minority Labour government (June 1929–August 1931) maintained fiscal conservatism despite the international GREAT DEPRESSION. Unemployment topped 2,000,000. MacDonald backed draconian spending cuts, losing the support of his own party but surviving in 1931 as prime minister of an all-party NATIONAL GOVERNMENT. The austerity measures precipitated nationwide strikes and hunger marches. Faced with belligerent NAZISM in Germany and FASCISM in Italy, the government reversed its policy of cutting arms spending in November 1933. Stanley Baldwin led the Conservatives to a huge general election victory in November 1935, but his new government faced public outrage at appeasement of Italy over Abyssinia (see ITALO-ETHIOPIAN WAR OF 1935–36).

1936 began with the death of King GEORGE V and ended with a constitutional crisis that saw the abdication (December 11, 1936) of his successor, EDWARD VIII, compelled to step down because he intended to marry divorcee Wallis Simpson (see Duchess of WINDSOR). In May 1937 GEORGE VI was crowned king, and Neville CHAMBERLAIN succeeded Baldwin as prime minister. The House of Commons in April 1938

United Kingdom

1899–1902	Boer War.
1900	Labour Party formed.
1901	Death of Queen Victoria.
1909	Liberal government introduces unemployment insurance.
1911	Reformation of the House of Lords.
1914–18	Nearly 1 million soldiers from the United Kingdom and British Empire killed in World War I; over 2 million wounded.
1916	(April) Easter Rebellion in Ireland put down by British troops.
1926	First nationwide general strike in Britain.
1936	Death of King George V; abdication crisis; Edward VIII gives up the throne to marry Wallis Warfield Simpson.
1938	Neville Chamberlain signs Munich Pact with Adolf Hitler, proclaims "peace in our time."
1939–45	World War II.
1940	(May 10) Winston Churchill becomes prime minister, pledges to fight until Nazi Germany is defeated; (May–June) 340,000 British troops evacuated from Dunkirk, France, as Germans advance; Royal Air Force (RAF) wins strategic victory over German Luftwaffe in Battle of Britain.
1945	Clement Attlee's Labour government begins to institute "Welfare State" and nationalize key industries.
1947	India granted independence.
1948	National Health Service begins operation.
1956	Suez Crisis—United Kingdom and France intervene in Arab-Israeli War, rebuffed by United States; Prime Minister Eden resigns.
1963	Profumo scandal leads to resignation of Prime Minister Harold Macmillan.
1969	British troops sent to Northern Ireland to restore order between Catholic and Protestant communities.
1972	Britain joins European Economic Community.
1978–79	"Winter of Discontent"—widespread labor strikes lead to defeat of Callaghan's Labour government in general election (May 3, 1979); Margaret Thatcher becomes Britain's first woman prime minister, initiates radical conservative policies.
1981	Four leading politicians leave Labour Party to found moderate Social Democratic Party.
1982	Argentina seizes Falkland Islands; British convoy sails to Falklands, defeats Argentinians.
1983	Prime Minister Thatcher reelected.
1984	IRA bombs Brighton hotel in attempt to kill Thatcher and cabinet members.
1985	Britain and Ireland sign Anglo-Irish Accord ("Hillsborough Agreement") as framework for solution to Northern Ireland problem.
1987	Liberal Party and Social Democratic Party merge, forming Liberal Democrats; Thatcher wins reelection.
1990	Unpopular community charge (poll tax) replaces local rates (property taxes) in England and

	Wales, leading to protests and rioting; Thatcher forced to resign over European issue; British forces sent to Saudi Arabia as part of UN coalition against Saddam Hussein.
1991	British air and ground forces participate in Operation Desert Storm to oust Iran from Kuwait in Persian Gulf War.
1994	The "Chunnel" begins direct transportation between the United Kingdom and France by means of a tunnel under the English Channel.
1997	The Labour Party wins a landslide general election and Tony Blair becomes prime minister; Hong Kong reverts to Chinese rule.
1998	Scotland and Wales are granted limited self-government; Good Friday Peace Accords commence a truce in Northern Ireland and call for creation of a regional assembly.
1999	The House of Lords is reformed.
2001	The Labour Party wins another landslide general election and Blair wins a second term as prime minister.
2003	The United Kingdom joins the U.S.-led military campaign against Iraq (March).
2004	The Iraq Survey Group concludes that Iraq did not possess weapons of mass destruction before the U.S.-led invasion; Blair admits flaws in prewar intelligence but stands by the action taken.
2005	A controversial terrorism bill is passed after extensive debate, including the longest sitting ever of the House of Lords; the bill calls for effective house arrest of suspects; the Labour Party under Blair wins a third term, although with a much reduced majority (May); 52 people are killed and about 700 injured in four suicide bomb attacks on London's transport system (July); the Irish Republican Army formally announces an end to its armed campaign.

approved a deal with France to defend CZECHOSLOVAKIA against a threatened German invasion. Chamberlain, however, clung to the belief that APPEASEMENT would avert war, and described as "peace in our time" his MUNICH PACT with HITLER (September 30, 1938), allowing Germany to take over the SUDETENLAND. When Hitler broke his promise by invading the rest of Czechoslovakia within six months, Britain formed a military pact with Poland and France (April 1939) and introduced conscription. When Germany and the USSR signed a surprise nonaggression pact in August, Britain began evacuating children from the cities. Germany invaded Poland on September 1, and Britain entered WORLD WAR II on September 3.

Britain introduced food rationing, censorship and an Emergency Powers Act, banning strikes and commandeering goods. After failing to halt Germany's invasion of NORWAY, Chamberlain resigned in May 1940. Winston S. CHURCHILL became prime minister at the head of an all-party coalition government, offering "nothing but blood, toil,

tears and sweat." After the evacuation of DUNKIRK, Britain stood alone against German aerial bombing of London, Coventry and other major cities. The RAF won what became known as the BATTLE OF BRITAIN, but the raids continued. By mid-1941 bombs were falling at a rate of up to 100,000 a night, and in two months 20,000 Londoners died. Women joined war work (compulsory for all in 1943). In 1944 German v-1 buzz-bombs began falling on England, but by then the tide had turned. In North Africa, General MONTGOMERY's Eighth Army had ended ROMMEL's German advance at EL ALAMEIN (see NORTH AFRICAN CAMPAIGN). The U.S. entered the war on the Allied side in December 1941, having already leased bases and lent arms to Britain; they had cemented their "special relationship" with the ATLANTIC CHARTER in August 1941. Britain became a virtual armed camp for Allied troops, preparing for the June 1944 invasion of Germany's FORTRESS EUROPE. The war cost half a million lives from Britain and the empire and Commonwealth.

Churchill called the first election since 1935, which he lost to Clement ATTLEE's Labour Party in a landslide victory (July 5, 1945). By 1946 the new Parliament had voted to nationalize the Bank of England, railways, ports, road haulage, civil aviation, coal, electricity, gas, atomic energy and finally steel. The NATIONAL HEALTH SERVICE (NHS) opened, along with National Insurance offices, in July 1948. The 1940s also saw Britain grant independence to India/Pakistan.

Pauperized by the war and the loss of its merchant fleet, in 1946 Britain accepted a 936-million-pound loan from the U.S., and reintroduced wartime rationing, some of which continued until the early 1950s. Britain was also helped by the U.S. MARSHALL PLAN. Britain began lifting manufacturing restrictions in 1948 but devalued the pound by 30 percent in September 1949. In October 1951 Churchill and the Tories returned to power, and in February 1952 King George VI died and was succeeded by his elder daughter, Queen ELIZABETH II. That same month Churchill revealed that Britain

UNITED KINGDOM: PRIME MINISTERS

1895–1902	Robert Gascoyne-Cecil, Lord Salisbury (Conservative)
1902–1905	Arthur James Balfour (Conservative)
1905–1908	Henry Campbell-Bannerman (Liberal)
1908–1916	Herbert Asquith (Liberal; wartime coalition 1915–16)
1916–1922	David Lloyd George (Liberal; wartime coalition 1916–18)
1922–1923	Andrew Bonar Law (Conservative)
1923–1924	Stanley Baldwin (Conservative)
1924	Ramsay MacDonald (Labour; coalition with Liberals)
1924–1929	Stanley Baldwin (Conservative)
1929–1935	Ramsay MacDonald (Labour; national coalition 1931–35)
1935–1937	Stanley Baldwin (Conservative; national coalition 1935)
1937–1940	Neville Chamberlain (Conservative)
1940–1945	Winston Churchill (Conservative; wartime coalition)
1945–1951	Clement Attlee (Labour)
1951–1955	Winston Churchill (Conservative)
1955–1957	Anthony Eden (Conservative)
1957–1963	Harold Macmillan (Conservative)
1963–1964	Alec Douglas-Home (Conservative)
1964–1970	Harold Wilson (Labour)
1970–1974	Edward Heath (Conservative)
1974–1976	Harold Wilson (Labour)
1976–1979	James Callaghan (Labour)
1979–1990	Margaret Thatcher (Conservative)
1990–1997	John Major (Conservative)
1997–	Tony Blair (Labour)

had the atom bomb. British troops enforced a defense pact and SUEZ CANAL agreement in 1952 and flew into KENYA in response to MAU MAU unrest.

Churchill handed over the leadership in April 1955 to Sir Anthony EDEN, who won a snap election. In 1956 Chancellor Harold MACMILLAN launched the tightest credit squeeze since 1931 to stifle inflation. When Nasser nationalized the Suez Canal in July 1956, Britain froze its Egyptian assets and arranged for a joint Anglo-French force to bombard Suez while Israel attacked from the north—but had to withdraw under U.S. pressure and the threat of a run on sterling (see SUEZ CRISIS). Eden resigned and handed the premiership to Macmillan in January 1957. Macmillan emphasized the U.K.-U.S. special relationship, accepting U.S. nuclear missiles in Britain. He introduced cheaper home loans and luxury taxes and opened the first motorway (1958). Overseas, he welcomed peaceful independence for Malaya (see MALAYSIA) but sent troops to quell unrest in CYPRUS and JORDAN. Macmillan promised independence to NIGERIA and Cyprus, and in February 1960 he delivered his WIND OF CHANGE speech, heralding a decade of decolonization on the African continent. Macmillan favored membership in a EUROPEAN FREE TRADE ASSOCIATION and continued preferential trade with the British COMMONWEALTH; in 1961 Britain applied to join the EUROPEAN ECONOMIC COMMUNITY, but France's President DE GAULLE vetoed the idea of British membership on special terms.

The government passed a stricter Commonwealth Immigrants Act in July 1962 to stem immigration from the Caribbean and Indian subcontinent. Following the PROFUMO AFFAIR, Macmillan resigned in favor of Sir Alec DOUGLAS-HOME. Labour under Harold WILSON narrowly won the general election in October 1964. Committed to a national economic plan, Wilson faced immediate crises; he raised income tax, set an import tax and borrowed more than a billion pounds. Labour greatly increased its majority in the 1966 election, and a huge majority of MPs supported Wilson's new application for EEC membership, but de Gaulle dismissed it (May 16, 1967). After an influx of East African Asians with British passports in 1968, Enoch POWELL's "rivers of blood" speech (April 21, 1968) condemned immigration. In August 1969, British troops were sent to Northern Ireland to restore order after sectarian rioting broke out between Catholics and Protestants.

The Conservatives under Edward HEATH were elected in June 1970. After a year of Heath's leadership, strikes were at their highest level since 1926, with 8.8 million working days lost. In 1971 the first British soldier died in Northern Ireland. The new radical "provisional" wing of the IRA started a terror campaign against British troops. IRA members were interned and all marches banned. The IRA began a series of bombings in Britain itself. Conversion to decimal currency (February 15, 1971) came amid rising unemployment and inflation. Britain joined the EEC (January 22, 1972) after getting special terms for certain Commonwealth products. After the IRA bombed a British Army base at Aldershot, England, Heath imposed direct rule on Ulster (March–April 1972). In November 1973 new Arab oil price increases forced petrol rationing. An election, called for March 1974, returned Harold Wilson to office. He conceded to almost all the demands of striking miners. As 1974 ended, inflation stood at 26 percent; a budget raised the VAT and initiated defense spending cuts. In February 1975 Margaret THATCHER ousted Heath as Tory leader, becoming the first woman to head a British political party. A North Sea oil pipeline came into operation. By March 1977 Labour needed Liberal support to stave off a no-confidence vote and formed the so-called "Lib-Lab Pact." The social contract between unions and government collapsed as unions condemned the incomes policy and sought higher wage deals. Fresh strikes hit Britain in the winter of discontent of early 1979. A general election in May 1979 was won by the Tories with a majority of 43 seats.

New Prime Minister Thatcher vowed to take a tougher line with the IRA after the assassination of Lord MOUNTBATTEN (August 27, 1979). RHODESIA's 14 years of unilaterally declared independence ended in the Lancaster House peace deal signed in London (December 21, 1979). The stationing of American CRUISE MISSILES in Britain prompted the biggest nuclear disarmament protests in 20 years. Oil price rises fueled inflation, and, by squeezing the money supply, Thatcher caused industrial retrenchment. By August 1980 2 million were out of work. Thatcher outlined her PRIVATIZATION policy: selling off nationalized industries, starting with British Aerospace and proceeding over the next decade with British Gas, Electricity, British Telecommunications, British Steel and the water boards. A new share-owning democracy would at one stroke break class barriers and boost government revenue. In January 1981, four senior politicians resigned from the Labour Party and started the SOCIAL DEMOCRATIC PARTY, which subsequently formed an electoral alliance with the Liberal Party. In Ulster in May 1981 there were riots in Belfast in protest of the death by hunger strike of IRA member Bobby Sands. But most eyes were fixed on the wedding of Prince CHARLES to Lady Diana Spencer (July 29, 1981).

By January 1982 unemployment topped 3 million. The government recovered its popularity with the British

St. Paul's Cathedral in London (LIBRARY OF CONGRESS, PRINTS AND PHOTOGRAPHS DIVISION)

victory in the FALKLAND ISLANDS WAR. On June 10, 1983, the electorate returned Thatcher with a 144-seat majority. A bitter one-year miners' strike (March 1984–March 1985) saw half the pits shut down, police clashing with pickets and union funds sequestrated by the courts. In October 1984 an IRA bomb intended to kill the whole cabinet exploded in a Brighton hotel (see BRIGHTON BOMBING). In May 1985 two football disasters, the Bradford fire (over 40 dead) and the Heysel stadium rampage in Brussels, Belgium (38 dead), shocked the nation. The November 1985 Anglo-Irish accord gave Eire a role in Northern Ireland (see HILLSBOROUGH ACCORD).

The Anglo-French ENGLISH CHANNEL TUNNEL got the go-ahead in 1986. In June 1987 the Tories were elected for a third time, and the SDP-Liberal Alliance broke down in failure; the SDP and Liberals subsequently merged as the Liberal Democrats. In 1988 the trade deficit deepened while house prices soared. An airliner (PAN AM 103) crashed over Lockerbie in Scotland on December 21, the victim of international terrorism. During 1990 protests, sometimes violent, occurred throughout England in response to the introduction of a controversial "community charge" or poll tax to fund local government. In autumn 1990, Mrs. Thatcher was forced to resign after disagreements with her cabinet over the proposed European Monetary Union (see EUROPEAN MONETARY SYSTEM); she claimed that the new European integration scheduled for 1992 could threaten parliamentary sovereignty. Thatcher was replaced by Chancellor

of the Exchequer John MAJOR. Britain strongly supported the allied coalition in the PERSIAN GULF WAR, and British forces played a significant role in the fighting. In 1997 the Labour Party won a landslide victory, and Tony BLAIR replaced Major in 10 Downing Street. After his election, Blair sought to reform the House of Lords and improve the British economy. In 2002–03 he defied British public opinion by strongly supporting U.S. president George W. BUSH's campaign to invade IRAQ and overthrow the government of Saddam HUSSEIN. Britain remained outside the European Monetary Union that went into effect in 1999 with the introduction of the euro. But Blair sought to serve as a bridge between the United States and the EU by maintaining good relations with both. After winning a third term in 2005, Blair announced that he would not stand for reelection when his term expired.

United Nations (UN) International organization formed after WORLD WAR II as a successor to the largely discredited LEAGUE OF NATIONS. It was officially founded on October 24, 1945, when the UN charter was ratified by its 51 original members meeting in San Francisco. In general, the organization aims at the elimination of war and the promotion of international cooperation, human rights and freedom. By 2002 the UN had 191 member states. The principal organizational components of the United Nations are six: the Security Council, General Assembly, Economic and Social Council, Trusteeship Council, International Court of Justice and Secretariat. In addition, there are a number of specialized agencies that deal with a multitude of social, economic and political issues.

All the principal organs of the UN have their headquarters in New York, with the exception of the International Court, which is situated in The Hague. The Security Council has a membership of 15: the permanent "Big Five" (China, France, U.K., USSR, U.S.) and 10 others chosen by the General Assembly for two-year terms. The Security Council has the main responsibility for maintaining international peace through its recommendations and actions that include economic sanctions and military efforts. Important decisions require a nine-vote majority, and vetoes by the Big Five are permitted. The General Assembly is made up of all UN member states and is the organization's main deliberative body. It can make recommendations but cannot compel any actions. Important decisions require a two-thirds majority. The Economic and Social Council has 54 members, elected to three-year terms by the General Assembly. It deals with economic and social questions and reports to the assembly and other organs. The council also coordinates specialized agencies and initiates activities relating to such issues as trade, human rights, population control, the status of women and social welfare.

The Trusteeship Council oversees non-self-governing territories that were previously governed under League of Nations mandates and others formed since then. It includes representatives of the administering states, representatives from the Security Council and other elected members. The International Court of Justice, which superseded the World Court, consists of 15 judges selected by the General Assembly and Security Council who serve nine-year terms. The court renders judgments on disputes between member nations but has only a limited jurisdiction. It also issues advisory opinions. The Secretariat is the UN's administrative body; with a large staff, it is headed by a secretary-general. These have been: Trygve LIE (1945–53), Dag HAMMARSKJÖLD (1953–61), U THANT (1961–72), Kurt WALDHEIM (1972–81), Javier PEREZ DE CUELLAR, (1982–92), Boutros Boutros GHALI (1992–97), and Kofi ANNAN (1997–). The Secretariat's varied work includes studying and reporting on international trends in politics and economics, mediating international disputes, administering UN peacekeeping activities, organizing conferences, compiling statistics and bringing appropriate international situations to the attention of the UN's many specialized agencies. These agencies include the Food and Agriculture Organization, General Agreement on Tariffs and Trades, International Atomic Energy Agency, International Development Association, International Monetary Fund and WORLD HEALTH ORGANIZATION. Among the UN's many other agencies are the UNITED NATION'S CHILDREN'S FUND (UNICEF), the Confer-

ence on Trade and Development and the High Commission for Refugees.

Early hopes for international accord were largely shattered by the coming of the COLD WAR, which split the international community and the UN into two warring camps and rendered many of the organization's efforts ineffective. With the waning of the Cold War and the increase in the UN's THIRD WORLD membership, the balance of power in the organization has also tended to shift away from the U.S. and the USSR, which dominated the organization's first decades. Although the end of the cold war in 1991 appeared to promise a strong role for the UN in world affairs, the deep division in the Security Council during the buildup to the U.S.-led invasion of IRAQ in 2003 damaged the reputation and influence of the organization. Scandals involving allegations of sexual harassment by a high UN official and financial improprieties concerning the UN-administered Oil For Food program in Iraq also prompted criticism of the organization.

United Nations Children's Fund (UNICEF) Children's relief arm of the UNITED NATIONS. The United Nations Children's Fund was originally established in 1946 as the United Nations International Children's Emergency Fund by the UN General Assembly to aid the approximately 20 million European children suffering in the aftermath of WORLD WAR II. Under its first executive director, the American Maurice Pate, UNICEF spent some $112 million distributing clothing, food and medical care and rebuilding food production and distribution facilities. In 1950 UNICEF began to turn its attention toward long-term programs for children's welfare in developing countries as well, and in 1953 was reorganized and renamed, though the well-known acronym was maintained. It has continued to provide nutritional, medical and educational materials to children and their mothers worldwide. In 1990 UNICEF organized a World Summit for Children in New York City, which sought to establish international goals for minimum children's health, nutrition and education needs. UNICEF is funded by voluntary contributions, mostly from member nations. Additional funds come from charitable organizations and the sale of UNICEF holiday cards. UNICEF has its head-

quarters in the UN complex in New York City and some 30 regional offices in Europe, North and South American, Asia and Africa.

United Nations Educational, Scientific and Cultural Organization (UNESCO) UNESCO was established by the United Nations General Assembly in 1946 to promote cultural contact and understanding between member countries and to encourage scientific and educational collaboration among them. Due to a perceived anti-Western bias, the U.S. withdrew from UNESCO in 1984. The BUSH administration upheld the U.S. withdrawal in 1990, citing UNESCO's poor management and refusal to defend freedom of the press. In 1998 UNESCO was responsible for developing the UN-endorsed Universal Declaration on the Human Genome and Human Rights, which sought to establish international guidelines about developments in genetic engineering (see CLONES AND CLONING). UNESCO is headquartered in Paris, FRANCE.

United Nations Relief and Rehabilitation Administration (UNRRA) The United Nations Relief and Rehabilitation Administration was formed in 1943, during WORLD WAR II, when the term "United Nations" referred to the anti-Axis Allies. It was established to assist in reconstruction and rehabilitating refugees at the end of the war. Between 1943 and 1949, UNRRA spent approximately 600 million pounds on relief work worldwide, three-quarters of which funding came from the U.S. Following the implementation of the MARSHALL PLAN, UNRRA's diversified programs were taken up by other specialized agencies, such as UNICEF, the WORLD HEALTH ORGANIZATION and OXFAM, and it was dissolved in 1949.

United Press International (UPI) American news agency; formed in 1958 by the merger of the United Press, begun in 1907, and International News Service, founded in 1909. In 1907, E. W. Scripps established United Press by merging the Scripps-McRae Press Association, Scripps News Association and Publishers' Press Association. Unlike AP, its competition, UPI was a profit-making service that anyone could buy. In its early days, telegraphers transcribed Morse code coming

over the wire on typewriters. UP established many foreign bureaus, and by 1914 some 200 newspapers subscribed to the service. In 1982, the E. W. Scripps Co. sold UPI to the Media News Corporation of Nashville, Tennessee. UPI had almost 6,500 subscribers worldwide, and its staff of over 10,000 in 235 news bureaus transmitted about 4.5 million words of copy a day. UPI suffered continual economic difficulties throughout the 1990s, and went to the brink of bankruptcy before being purchased by News World Communications Inc. in May 2000.

United States of America By the end of the 19th century, the U.S. had become a leading economic power. The Spanish-American War of 1898 catapulted the U.S. out of its isolationism and into European-dominated international affairs. The war left it a major power in the Caribbean and in the Pacific, with the acquisition of Puerto Rico, Guam and the Philippines and effective control of the island of Cuba. America's expansion outside the continental U.S. continued with the opening of the PANAMA CANAL in 1914 and the purchase of the Danish Virgin Islands in 1916. During the same period, the U.S. formulated its Open Door policy toward China, which was designed to force Europeans to accept American businessmen on an equal footing.

When WORLD WAR I broke out in Europe in 1914, the vast majority of Americans were in favor of staying neutral. President Woodrow WILSON reflected these sentiments and spent the first three years of the war trying to mediate between Britain and Germany and keep America out of the war. But the German decision in January 1917 to launch an all-out submarine attack against neutral shipping led to the U.S. entering the war on the Allied side. The infusion of 1,250,000 American soldiers was an important factor in defeating the German Western Offensive that began in March 1918, after which Germany was forced to accept an armistice. At the subsequent PARIS PEACE CONFERENCE, Wilson dominated the negotiations with his FOURTEEN POINTS. The idealism of Wilson's position was undermined by the Allies' desire to exact vengeance upon their defeated enemies and by the failure of the U.S. Senate to ratify the treaty (and so join the LEAGUE OF NATIONS).

The immediate postwar years saw a short depression, but by 1925 the economy was booming. Throughout the 1920s industrial production increased by 50 percent. The growth was stimulated by the laissez-faire economic policies of the administrations of Presidents Warren HARDING (1921–23) and Calvin COOLIDGE (1923–29). But this unbridled growth also encouraged rampant speculation, and in October 1929 the New York stock market collapsed (see STOCK MARKET CRASH OF 1929; GREAT DEPRESSION). Republican President HOOVER attempted some remedial action but was hampered by his commitment to laissez-faire economics. In 1932, Democrat Franklin D. ROOSEVELT, who promised a NEW DEAL of unprecedented government intervention to bring the U.S. out of the Depression, was elected president. In his first HUNDRED DAYS in office, Roosevelt sent Congress bills that created the TENNESSEE VALLEY AUTHORITY, unemployment relief, banking reforms, an agricultural recovery program, federal supervision of investment securities and that prevented the foreclosure of mortgages on private homes. This legislation was later followed by the SOCIAL SECURITY ACT and the Fair Labor Standards Act, which established a minimum wage. The New Deal did much to alleviate the personal hardships of the Depression but failed to correct the structural weaknesses that had created it and were eventually to be eliminated only by the outbreak of WORLD WAR II in Europe.

Renewed hostilities between Britain and Germany forced Britain to turn again to the U.S. for capital and defense material, which was made available on generous terms under the LEND-LEASE Act (1941). The U.S. entered the war on December 7, 1941, after the Japanese bombed the U.S. Pacific fleet at PEARL HARBOR. The U.S. played a much larger role in World War II than it had in World War I. An estimated 16 million men and women went into uniform. They fought in North Africa, Western Europe, Asia and the Pacific. Factory output doubled, with the result that the U.S. produced 196,400 aeroplanes, 6,500 naval vessels and 86,300 tanks. World War II also saw the American development of the ATOMIC BOMB, which would come to dominate international relations in the postwar period.

Roosevelt died on April 12, 1945, and was succeeded by Vice President Harry S TRUMAN, who ordered the dropping of atomic bombs on HIROSHIMA and NAGASAKI to end the war in the Pacific. The relationship between the Western Allies and the Soviet Union had been deteriorating; efforts to find common ground, such as the YALTA CONFERENCE (1945), were only partially

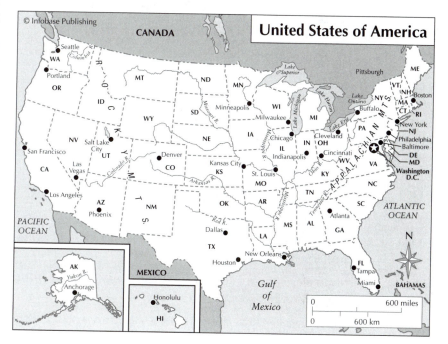

UNITED STATES

1901	McKinley assassinated; Cuba made U.S. protectorate.
1905	Theodore Roosevelt makes first trip outside U.S. by a sitting president—to Panama Canal Zone.
1908	Ford Motor Co. builds first Model T.
1914	Wilson proclaims neutrality in Europe; Marines enter Veracruz, Mexico.
1915	First transcontinental phone call.
1917	War declared on Germany.
1918	Battle of the Meuse-Argonne; Wilson issues 14 points for world peace; armistice signed.
1919	Prohibition ratified.
1920	Harding defeats Cox; *Main Street* by Sinclair Lewis published.
1923	Teapot Dome scandal begins to unfold.
1929	Stock market crash begins Great Depression.
1932	Franklin D. Roosevelt elected to first of four terms.
1933	Prohibition repealed; Roosevelt sets up New Deal programs for economic recovery.
1936	Boulder Dam completed; auto workers gain power through sit-down strikes.
1938	Self-propelled combine introduced; leads to massive grain harvests.
1940	Lend-Lease program sends war materiel to Britain; first peacetime draft.
1941	Pearl Harbor attacked; war declared on Axis powers; war industries boost economy.
1942	Battle of Midway turns tide of war in Pacific.
1944	D-day; invasion of Normandy signals coming defeat for Germany.
1945	Atomic bombs used against Japan; Axis powers surrender; Roosevelt dies and is succeeded by Truman.
1948	Marshall Plan and Berlin Airlift aid postwar Europe.
1949	NATO founded to confront Soviets.
1950	U.S. troops oppose North Korean invasion of South Korea; Senator Joseph McCarthy begins investigation of communists in government.
1952	Eisenhower elected.
1953	Armistice in Korea; Julius and Ethel Rosenberg executed as Soviet spies.
1954	First private nuclear power plant begins construction; Elvis Presley records "Don't Be Cruel."
1960	Kennedy elected; U-2 spy plane shot down over USSR.
1962	Nation faces nuclear war in Cuban missile crisis; John Glenn orbits Earth.
1963	Kennedy assassinated; Johnson assumes presidency.
1964	Gulf of Tonkin Resolution passed; Vietnam buildup begins; Civil Rights Act passed; Martin Luther King, Jr., wins Nobel Peace Prize.
1968	Nixon elected; riots destroy inner cities after Martin Luther King, Jr., assassinated; Robert F. Kennedy assassinated.
1969	*Apollo 11* makes first Moon landing; Woodstock music festival celebrates the "counterculture."

1970	Student protesters killed by troops at Jackson State and Kent State.
1972	Nixon reelected in landslide; visits China; Watergate break-in.
1973	Vice President Agnew indicted; oil prices skyrocket.
1974	Nixon resigns to avoid impeachment; Patty Hearst kidnapped by Symbionese Liberation Army.
1975	Fall of Saigon ends Vietnam War.
1976	Jimmy Carter upsets Gerald Ford in presidential election.
1978	Carter mediates Camp David accords between Israel and Egypt.
1981	American hostages in Tehran released minutes after Reagan inaugurated.
1983	Two hundred forty-one marines killed in Lebanon bombing; AIDS epidemic sweeps nation; invasion of Grenada.
1987	Congressional hearings on sale of arms to Iran and illegal aid to contra rebels; "Just Say No" campaign against drugs.
1988	George H. W. Bush elected; power of Soviet Union reduced by internal disorder.
1990	Massive scandal in savings and loan industry unfolds; Michael Milken imprisoned for illegal stock trading; Bush gives ultimatum to Iraqi invaders of Kuwait; begins huge troop buildup.
1991	U.S.-led forces invade Iraq; create new balance of power in Middle East.
1993	William Jefferson Clinton begins two terms as president
1994	The Republican Party wins control of both houses of Congress.
1996	Federal spending remains within budgeted projections for the first time since 1969; William Jefferson Clinton wins reelection.
1998	An independent council charges that Clinton lied under oath; voting along party lines, Congress impeaches Clinton, making him the first elected president in U.S. history to be impeached; he is acquitted by the Senate.
2000	The economy enjoys the longest uninterrupted expansion in U.S. history (February); in one of the narrowest elections in U.S. history, the Supreme Court decides in favor of Republican George W. Bush over Democrat Albert Gore, who wins a plurality of votes nationwide.
2001	Four passenger airplanes are hijacked and crashed into the World Trade Center in New York City, the Pentagon in Washington, D.C., and into a field in Pennsylvania; 3,025 are killed in the attacks; U.S. leads massive campaign that ousts the Taliban regime in Afghanistan and seeks to locate Osama bin Laden, believed hiding in Afghanistan and who is suspected of masterminding the September 11 attacks (October); the PATRIOT Act gives the government greater powers to fight terrorism (October); energy conglomerate Enron is declared bankrupt (December).
2002	The Department of Homeland Security is created; the space shuttle *Challenger* breaks up while reentering the atmosphere; all seven astronauts aboard are killed.
2003	A U.S.-led coalition attacks Iraq and topples the regime of Saddam Hussein (March).
2004	U.S. abuses of Iraqi prisoners bring worldwide condemnation (May); former president Ronald Reagan dies (June); a Senate report says that the U.S. went to war in Iraq on "flawed information" (July); George W. Bush wins a second term (November 4).
2005	Hundreds are killed when Hurricane Katrina sweeps through the Gulf coast states; much of New Orleans is submerged (September).

successful. Disputes broke out in Eastern Europe and in Korea over the political complexion of governments to be installed in the liberated territories. This antipathy developed into the COLD WAR as the U.S. and the Soviet Union each sought to prevent the other from extending its influence. The MARSHALL PLAN revitalized Western European economies with American aid. The 1949 formation of the NORTH ATLANTIC TREATY ORGANIZATION (NATO) committed the U.S. to the defense of Western Europe and eventually led to over 300,000 American troops being permanently based in Europe.

In Asia, the Chinese communists led by MAO ZEDONG drove CHIANG KAI-SHEK off the mainland of China to the island of Taiwan, where he established a government-in-exile. On the advice of his diplomats, President Truman refused to throw full American military support behind Chiang. This led to later accusations that Truman and various American diplomats had "lost" China.

In the charged anticommunist atmosphere of the late 1940s and early 1950s, Americans were prepared to believe that the success of the Chinese communists was part of a global strategy orchestrated by the Soviet Union with the aid of disloyal Americans. The loss of China also encouraged Truman and successive presidents to take an increasingly interventionist line in Asian affairs. This led to the KOREAN WAR (1950–53), support for the French in their Indochina War (1946–54) and, finally, the VIETNAM WAR (1964–75). In Europe, some of the major cold war crises were the Berlin Blockade of 1948 and the Berlin crises of 1953 and 1961, the year of the erection of the BERLIN WALL. Fear of the Soviet Union spilled over into domestic politics with the rise of demagogic senator Joseph MC-CARTHY. In September 1949, the Soviet Union exploded its first atomic bomb. The U.S. responded with the development of the HYDROGEN BOMB, which the USSR quickly matched. The two countries then competed in developing the quantity and quality of nuclear weapons and delivery systems as well as increasingly expensive conventional forces.

Truman was succeeded by Republican Dwight D. EISENHOWER (1953–61), who adopted a laissez-faire policy toward the economy. Government intervention increased under the successive Democratic administrations of John F. KENNEDY (1961–63) and Lyndon B. JOHNSON (1963–69). By the time of the Johnson administration, the economy was beginning to feel the strain of heavy defense expenditures and expanded social spending. Another source of concern was the lack of CIVIL RIGHTS for American blacks. In 1954, the U.S. Supreme Court ruled that racial segregation in public schools was unconstitutional. The black community embarked on a campaign of civil disobedience to secure its constitutional rights. The civil disobedience erupted into race riots in the 1960s and eventually led to passage of the CIVIL RIGHTS ACT (1964). But the deep-seated prejudices of some white Americans were underscored by the assassination of Martin Luther KING Jr. in April 1968.

Throughout the first 20 years of the postwar period, the U.S. based its claim to world leadership on a superior New World morality. President Kennedy's assassination in November 1963 shocked the world and to some extent marked the end of these illusions. The death of Kennedy was quickly followed by the VIETNAM WAR, which seriously split American society (see ANTIWAR MOVEMENT). In 1964 Congress passed the TONKIN GULF RESOLUTION authorizing the president to take whatever steps were necessary to prosecute the war, which the U.S. had been supporting in a limited capacity. Over 541,000 U.S. troops saw combat. Under President NIXON, the troops were gradually withdrawn. Although it was the South Vietnamese who lost Saigon and the war in 1975, official casualty figures revealed that 46,079 Americans had earlier been killed and 303,640 wounded. Public opposition to the war was fueled by reports of atrocities such as the MY LAI MASSACRE of Vietnamese civilians (1969).

In 1972 the Democratic Party's Washington, D.C., campaign headquarters was burgled by a team hired by the campaign committee of President Nixon. The subsequent investigation led to the WATERGATE scandal and Nixon's resignation in August 1974. While Nixon's handling of Watergate was deemed reprehensible, his foreign policy marked America's coming of age as a superpower. Under the direction of Henry KISSINGER, the U.S. adopted a realpolitik approach to foreign affairs.

Nixon paid a historic visit to China (1972) and developed a working relationship with the Soviet Union, which became known as detente. Diplomatic relations with China were eventually established in 1979. At the same time, suspicion grew of U.S. covert involvement in attempts to destabilize or overthrow left-wing regimes, notably in CHILE and in ANGOLA. Part of the reason for improved relations with the communist bloc was a more complex, multipolar system of conflicting national aspirations. U.S. dominance of the world's economy was challenged by the growing power of the EUROPEAN ECONOMIC COMMUNITY and Japan, and the emerging nations of Asia and Africa were establishing governments and pursuing policies that failed to fit into the capitalist-versus-communist formula. Nixon was succeeded by Vice President Gerald FORD (1974–77), who retained Kissinger as secretary of state and maintained his predecessor's foreign and domestic policies. In 1976 Jimmy CARTER was elected president. Carter offered a fresh face and unblemished past to an American electorate seeking a politician untainted by Vietnam or the discredited Washington power circles. Although he scored a notable foreign-policy success with the conclusion of the U.S.-sponsored Egyptian-Israeli CAMP DAVID agreement (1978), he was humiliated by the seizure of American hostages in Tehran in 1979 (see IRAN HOSTAGE CRISIS).

In 1980, former film actor Ronald REAGAN was elected president. For many Americans, Reagan and his policies typified basic national values that predated the Roosevelt years. On domestic issues, he stressed the importance of family, thrift and industriousness. In foreign affairs, he took a tough anti-Soviet position and backed this up with increased defense spending. Reagan secured public support for these policies with a relaxed manner and a series of televised homespun homilies that struck a basic chord with the American public. Toward the end of his term, the administration held summit meetings between Reagan and Mikhail GORBACHEV at Geneva (1985), Reykjavík (1986) and Washington (1987). Congress had become unwilling to fund Reagan's proxy crusade against NICARAGUA's left-wing Sandinista government. The upshot was the uncovering of what became known as the IRAN-CONTRA SCANDAL (November 1986), implicating several National Security

UNITED STATES: PRESIDENTS

1897–1901	William McKinley (Republican)
1901–1909	Theodore Roosevelt (Republican)
1909–1913	William Howard Taft (Republican)
1913–1921	Woodrow Wilson (Democrat)
1921–1923	Warren G. Harding (Republican)
1923–1929	Calvin Coolidge (Republican)
1929–1933	Herbert Hoover (Republican)
1933–1945	Franklin D. Roosevelt (Democrat)
1945–1953	Harry S. Truman (Democrat)
1953–1961	Dwight D. Eisenhower (Republican)
1961–1963	John F. Kennedy (Democrat)
1963–1969	Lyndon Baines Johnson (Democrat)
1969–1974	Richard M. Nixon (Republican)
1974–1977	Gerald R. Ford (Republican)
1977–1981	James Earl Carter (Democrat)
1981–1989	Ronald Reagan (Republican)
1989–1993	George H. W. Bush (Republican)
1993–2001	William Jefferson Clinton (Democrat)
2001–	George W. Bush (Republican)

Agency officials. Less convoluted was U.S. hostility toward LIBYA, whose leader, Col. QADAFFI, the administration held responsible for supporting acts of terrorism in the Middle East.

Reagan was succeeded by Vice President George H. W. BUSH, who defeated Democratic contender Michael DUKAKIS in the 1988 elections. Bush was faced with the continuing American budget deficit, international financial instability and the lack of a clear response to the wave of liberalization within communist regimes. After IRAQ invaded KUWAIT (August 2, 1990), Bush sent several hundred thousand U.S. troops to protect Saudi Arabia in Operation Desert Shield. He mobilized world opinion and persuaded the UN to support joint international action to drive Iraq from Kuwait. American forces launched Operation Desert Storm, the largest U.S. military operation since the Vietnam War, on January 16, 1991, bombing numerous military tar-

gets in Iraq. A wave of patriotism swept the U.S.; Iraq was handily defeated in February. However, the U.S. recession continued, and other international problems followed in the wake of the war. The continued recession hurt Bush's popularity, and he lost the 1992 election to Democrat William Jefferson CLINTON. During his eight years in office, Clinton presided over a booming economy helped by a technology-driven rise in stock prices and an influx of cheap consumer goods from developing countries. In 2000 Republican candidate George W. BUSH narrowly defeated Democratic candidate Al GORE (see FLORIDA BALLOT CONTROVERSY). As president, Bush responded to the terrorist attacks of SEPTEMBER 11, 2001, by ordering the invasion of AFGHANISTAN in October 2001. Free elections were held in both Afghanistan and Iraq, burnishing the reputation of the U.S. as the champion of democracy throughout the world.

But American casualties caused by the continuation of the insurgency against the American occupation in Iraq, together with scandals involving torture in U.S. detention facilities in Iraq and elsewhere, led to public disillusionment with Bush's activist foreign policy. After failing to obtain the approval of the UN Security Council, he ordered the invasion of IRAQ by a U.S.-led coalition that toppled the regime of Saddam HUSSEIN in 2003. In 2005 Hurricane Katrina battered the Gulf coast states, also causing the levees protecting the city of New Orleans to fail, resulting in massive flooding and hundreds of deaths.

United States v. Butler (*1936*) U.S. Supreme Court decision ruling that the New Deal's AGRICULTURAL ADJUSTMENT ACT was unconstitutional. President Franklin D. ROOSEVELT's NEW DEAL program attempted to have the federal government regulate agriculture through a system of subsidies and production quotas. Farmers would be paid subsidies if they reduced their production—with the goal of stabilizing production and commodity prices. The farm subsidies were to be financed out of a tax on food processors.

The Supreme Court struck down the act as unconstitutional because the federal government had no power to regulate agriculture, a purely local activity. Additionally, the Court reasoned that the tax was unlawful because its purpose was regulation rather than revenue-raising. The decision was a major blow to the New Deal program. The Supreme Court later reversed itself and upheld federal price supports and regulation of agriculture, even when the farm products were raised and sold within one state.

United States v. Curtiss-Wright Export Corp. (*1936*) U.S. Supreme Court decision granting the president almost unlimited power in the field of foreign affairs. Congress had granted the president the right to embargo arms shipments to countries at war in South America. The statute was attacked as an illegal delegation of congressional power to the president. However, the Supreme Court upheld the delegation, holding that Congress had the power to vest a great deal of power in the president to conduct the nation's foreign affairs.

United States v. Darby (1941) U.S. Supreme Court decision outlawing the sale of goods produced by child labor. In 1918 the Supreme Court had struck down an earlier law that attempted to ban child labor, reasoning that manufacturing was not "commerce" and was outside the scope of Congress's regulatory authority. In 1937 Congress again attempted to discourage child labor by passing the Fair Labor Standards Act, which severely limited the use of child labor in factories and also established a federal minimum wage and the 40-hour work week. Although the law was challenged, the Supreme Court upheld both the wage and hour provisions and the ban on the sale of products manufactured by child labor. The act was an important milestone in employee rights.

United States v. Nixon (1974) Unanimous U.S. Supreme Court decision holding that President Richard M. Nixon could not claim an executive privilege to protect tape recordings of conversations made in the White House. During the 1972 election, in which Nixon was reelected president, the DEMOCRATIC PARTY headquarters at the WATERGATE Apartments was burglarized. When the president and his staff later tried to hide the details of the burglary, the entire administration was rocked, and the president was forced to resign.

During the scandal it was revealed that Nixon had taped his White House conversations, and he refused to comply with a subpoena to turn these over to investigators, claiming they were protected by an executive privilege similar to an attorney-client privilege. The Court rejected the contention that any privilege protected the president's conversations with his aides and ordered the tapes to be turned over.

UNIVAC Acronym for *Universal Automatic Computer*—a COMPUTER invented by J. Presper Eckert and John Mauchley in 1951; it was the successor to their ENIAC. While more advanced than the ENIAC, UNIVAC was still huge, bulky and slow by the standards of the late 20th century. It was the first computer to be used commercially, and its first customer was the U.S. Census Bureau. On election night in 1952, UNIVAC became the first computer ever used to tally votes.

Universal Pictures One of HOLLYWOOD's "Little Three" production companies (along with UNITED ARTISTS and COLUMBIA PICTURES). Its formative years were presided over by the formidable Carl LAEMMLE. Having established by 1909 one of the largest film exchanges in America, he turned to production that same year in defiance of the monopoly, the Motion Pictures Patents Company, and established his own Independent Motion Picture Company. In 1912 he combined it with several other companies to form "The Universal" (a name he allegedly borrowed from the sign on a Universal Pipe Fittings truck). Three years later he opened the largest motion picture production facility in the world, Universal City, located in the San Fernando Valley. It remains the oldest continuously operating studio in America. The silent era was marked by the emerging talents of director John FORD, production chief Irving THALBERG and actor Lon CHANEY. Future studio chief at Columbia Harry COHN got his start as one of Laemmle's secretaries. With the TALKING PICTURE revolution, Carl Laemmle, Jr., was appointed head of production and several prestige pictures appeared, including *ALL QUIET ON THE WESTERN FRONT* (1929) and *SHOW BOAT* (1936). He also initiated one of the studio's most famous series of pictures, their horror films, including *Dracula* (1931), *FRANKENSTEIN* (1931) and *The Invisible Man* (1933). However, by the mid-1930s the studio was on the verge of financial collapse, and after Carl, Jr., was replaced by a series of other producers, the roster of releases reverted to the low-budget. These included the popular Deanna Durbin musicals and, later in the 1940s, the Basil RATHBONE SHERLOCK HOLMES movies and the ABBOTT AND COSTELLO comedies. In 1946 Universal merged with International Pictures. Decca Records bought the company in 1952 and subsequently was absorbed in 1962 by MCA, the former talent agency. By now, their movie output had been upgraded, ranging from a glossy series of Doris Day vehicles to blockbusters like *Airport* (1970), *The Sting* (1973), *Jaws* (1975) and E.T. (1982). In 1964 the Universal City Tours began. In 1989 Universal opened a second studio in Florida. In September 2001 Vivendi concluded a deal to sell Universal Pictures to GENERAL ELECTRIC (GE), which would unite the film company with its NBC network to form

NBC Universal. As part of the conditions of that deal, Vivendi has retained a 20% interest in the new GE division.

University of California v. Bakke See BAKKE CASE.

Unknown Soldier Name given to an unidentified member of the armed forces who has died in the service of his or her country. Since the end of WORLD WAR I, a number of nations have memorialized their unidentified war dead with a tomb in which a symbolic one of their number is buried. In the U.S., a soldier who had been killed in France was buried in a temporary crypt at Arlington National Cemetery on Armistice Day, November 11, 1921. Exactly 11 years later, the completed Tomb of the Unknown Soldier was dedicated. On Memorial Day of 1958, the memorial came to include the unidentified dead of other wars when the remains of a soldier from WORLD WAR II and another from the KOREAN WAR were also buried in the tomb, which was officially renamed the Tomb of the Unknowns. An unknown soldier from the VIETNAM WAR was interred in the crypt on Memorial Day in 1984. The tomb is provided with a military honor guard at all times, and services are held there each Memorial Day. Other such memorials are located under the Arc de Triomphe in Paris; in Westminster Abbey in London; in front of the Victor Emmanuel monument in Rome; and at the base of the Colonnade of the Congress in Brussels.

UNMOVIC (United Nations Monitoring, Inspection and Verification Commission) Immediately after the end of the PERSIAN GULF WAR (January to March 1991), the UN created the UNITED NATIONS SPECIAL COMMISSION (UNSCOM), an international arms inspection agency to ensure that Iraq would destroy all of its weapons of mass destruction (WMD), which it defined as nuclear, biological or chemical weapons and missiles with a range of more than 150 kilometers. Between 1991 and 1998 Iraq president Saddam HUSSEIN repeatedly argued that the U.S. CENTRAL INTELLIGENCE AGENCY (CIA) had infiltrated its agents within UNSCOM and was using the authority granted the commission to commit espionage against the Iraqi government. He therefore denied UNSCOM agents access to some Iraqi weapons facilities and eventually expelled the weapons inspectors in 1998. In response the UN Security Council passed Resolution 1284 on December 17, 1999, which created UNMOVIC to resume UNSCOM's earlier mission. UN secretary-general Kofi ANNAN appointed Swedish scientist Dr. Hans Blix to head UNMOVIC and also selected 16 other individuals—including scientists weapons specialists and engineers—to assist Blix in his efforts. As with UNSCOM, UNMOVIC's activities were funded from a UN-imposed levy on Iraqi oil exports. UNMOVIC agents entered Iraq in November 2002 and began to conduct inspections of Iraq's weapons facilities.

Although UNMOVIC's repeated inspections did force Hussein to destroy several missiles that possessed flight ranges in excess of 150 km, Blix could not affirm that his agency had examined all Iraqi facilities suspected of producing WMDs and requested sufficient time to do so. In 2003 U.S. president George W. Bush decided to short-circuit the process set in motion by UNMOVIC and use U.S. military force to overthrow Hussein before he could employ the WMDs that U.S. intelligence believed the Iraqi dictator still possessed. Ultimately, WMDs were not discovered in Iraq.

UNPROFOR (United Nations Protective Forces) A UN-sponsored multinational force designed to assure safe havens during the Yugoslav Civil War (1991–95). UNPROFOR was initially created in early 1992 within the newly independent republic of Croatia to create three UN Protected Areas (UNPAs) within CROATIA in which all residents would be protected from military or paramilitary assault. As the initial conflict between Croatia and the Yugoslav government intensified, and as BOSNIA AND HERZEGOVINA also declared its independence from YUGOSLAVIA, UNPROFOR extended its duties to allow passage of civilians into UNPAs in Croatia and Bosnia, serve as the border patrol force between warring states, administer the airport of Sarajevo, ensure in conjunction with NATO forces that demilitarized and "no-fly" zones were not violated by any party in the civil war and ensure the delivery of humanitarian aid overseen by the International Red Cross. When Bosnian and Croat forces accepted a

cease-fire in February 1994, UNPROFOR was charged with monitoring the adherence of both sides to the agreement, as it did with the Yugoslav-Croatian cease-fire accord of March 1994. On March 31, 1995, the UN Security Council ended UNPROFOR's existence and replaced it with three separate yet interrelated peace-keeping forces to administer the situation in the former Yugoslavia.

UNSCOM (United Nations Special Commission) Established on April 3, 1991, following the end of the Persian Gulf War (January to March 1991). UNSCOM was designed to ensure the elimination of all Iraqi-possessed weapons of mass destruction (WMDs), or nuclear, biological or chemical weapons and missiles with a range greater than 150 kilometers. Overseen by the executive chairman of UNSCOM, Swedish ambassador to the UN Rolf Ekéus, the commission contained 20 other individuals from nations such as the U.S., Russia, France, Indonesia, Japan and Nigeria, and was financed by funds coming from Iraq and contributions from UN member nations. On July 1, 1997, Ekéus was replaced by Australian UNSCOM member Richard Butler, who supervised the agency's investigations of Iraq until June 30, 1999. Following Butler's departure as executive chairman, UN secretary-general Kofi ANNAN did not appoint a successor, instead preferring to allow UNSCOM's deputy executive chairman, Charles Duelfer of the U.S., to administer the commission until it was replaced on December 17, 1999, by the UNITED NATIONS MONITORING, VERIFICATION AND INSPECTION COMMISSION (UNMOVIC). Annan and the Security Council chose to replace UNSCOM with UNMOVIC because Iraqi president Saddam HUSSEIN had repeatedly denied UNSCOM access to several alleged WMD-related sites on the grounds that officials working for the U.S. CENTRAL INTELLIGENCE AGENCY (CIA) had obtained positions at UNSCOM, and IAEA inspectors had allegedly used these positions to spy on non-WMD related matters of Iraqi national security.

Untermeyer, Louis *(1885–1977)* American poet and editor. While working in a New York City jewelry company, Untermeyer began writing at night, publishing his first volume of

poetry in 1911. He left his job to write full time in 1923, and he produced some 20 collections of traditional poetry, two novels and many volumes of criticism. His varied works include *This Singing World* (1926), *Blue Rhine, Black Forest: A Hand and Day-Book* (1930) and *A Treasury of Laughter* (1946). He is best known in his capacity as an editor, and his many anthologies include *Modern American Poetry* (first edition, 1919), *Modern British Poetry* (1920) and *A Treasury of Great Poems, English and American* (1942). Untermeyer was English poetry consultant to the Library of Congress from 1961 to 1963 and wrote two volumes of autobiography, *From Another World* (1939) and *Bygones* (1965).

Updike, John (Hoyer) *(1932–)* American author. Updike, who was born in Pennsylvania and educated at Harvard University, published his early short stories in THE NEW YORKER, where he served as staff writer from 1955 to 1957. He is best known for his fictional tetralogy, *Rabbit, Run* (1960), *Rabbit, Redux* (1971), *Rabbit Is Rich* (1981), which won the 1982 PULITZER PRIZE for fiction, and *Rabbit at Rest* (1990), which follows the life of Harry Angstrom through four decades of sexual and social upheaval. Updike's fiction generally presents middle-class Americans, whom he depicts as self-obsessed and materialistic, diverting and sedating themselves with marital infidelity and alcohol. Other fiction includes the novels *Couples* (1968), *The Witches of Eastwick* (1984) *Roger's Version* (1988), *Seek My Face* (2002), *Villages* (2004) and the short story collections *Pigeon Feathers and other stories* (1962) and *Problems and Other Stories* (1979). In 1991 Updike received a second Pulitzer Prize for *Rabbit at Rest*. In 2003 Updike was awarded the National Medal for the Humanities.

Upper Volta See BURKINA FASO.

Urban League American CIVIL RIGHTS organization; its full name is the National Urban League. Founded in 1910, its aims are the end of racial discrimination and the increase of economic status and political power for blacks and other racial minorities in the U.S. Under the direction of Whitney YOUNG (1961–71), the League broadened its programs and adopted a more aggressive approach to problems, while maintaining a basically moderate and nonviolent stance. Beginning in 1968, it shifted from mainly social service work to grass-roots organizing in the ghetto. Led by Vernon Jordan since 1972, it has focused on such aspects of urban poverty as police relations, welfare, tenants' rights and employment. With headquarters in New York City, it had a membership of some 50,000 in the early 1990s.

urban renewal American movement aimed at eliminating inadequate housing and business properties in city areas and replacing them with improved facilities. Urban renewal began with the slum clearance projects of the 1930s and was a particular priority in the 1950s, due to the Housing Acts of 1949 and 1954. These provided federal funds to cities earmarked for the destruction of slums in the inner cities and for new construction. Cities purchased blighted areas, cleared the land by demolishing the old buildings and resold the tracts to developers. These developers were to submit competitive bids and follow city plans for redevelopment, whether for private or public housing, institutions or commercial use. In the course of urban renewal, many cities used the power of eminent domain, forcing the sale of private property to the government. During the 1950s, more than 2,000 of these projects were initiated, and many successes achieved. Urban renewal has produced housing as well as such public facilities as parks, schools, hospitals and museums, and cities such as Chicago, New York City, St. Louis and San Francisco have profited from such projects. Their main drawback, however, has been the displacement of families caused by the destruction of their homes and the lack of sufficient new lower- and middle-income housing to fill their needs. Urban renewal efforts were revived by President Jimmy CARTER in the late 1970s in a program that attempted to deal with urban recovery. In the 1980s, however, the federal government sharply curtailed its housing efforts, and urban renewal was left to city and state governments, many of which lacked the funds to pursue the task with vigor.

Urey, Harold C(layton) (1893–1981) American chemist. Born in Walkerton, Indiana, he attended Montana State University (B.S., 1917), the University of California, Berkeley (Ph.D., 1923) and the Institute for Theoretical Physics at the University of Copenhagen, where he studied under Niels BOHR. He taught chemistry at Johns Hopkins University from 1924 to 1929 before joining the faculty at Columbia University, where he taught until 1945. In 1931 he was successful in isolating deuterium (heavy hydrogen), a landmark discovery that earned him the NOBEL PRIZE for chemistry in 1934. Urey later did research on a diffusion process for separating uranium isotopes and on heavy water, work that he continued in the wartime MANHATTAN PROJECT that produced the ATOM BOMB. After the war, Urey was a professor at the University of Chicago (1945–58) and later served as a professor-at-large at the University of California. He was also involved in a campaign to warn the public about the dangers posed by atomic energy. Urey later worked in geochemistry and astrophysics on the nature of climate change and the origins of life on Earth.

Urrutia, Manuel Lleo (1901–1981) Cuban political leader. A judge, he became the first president of revolutionary CUBA when Fidel CASTRO overthrew the government of Fulgencio BATISTA in 1959. Six months later, however, he denounced COMMUNISM and was forced to resign his largely symbolic post. He then spent four years of house arrest and asylum in the Venezuelan and Mexican embassies in Havana. In 1963 he was granted a safe-conduct pass to the U.S., where he published a book criticizing Castro's Cuba as a "Red hell." Settling in Florida, he headed a league of 22 anti-Castro exile groups known as the Democratic Revolutionary Alliance, which condoned violence directed at government authorities in Cuba. (See also BAY OF PIGS.)

Uruguay (Eastern Republic of Uruguay) Uruguay covers an area of

© Infobase Publishing

URUGUAY	
1903	After a period of military rule, José Batlle y Ordóñez, a progressive from the center-left Colorado Party, becomes president. As president from 1903 to 1907 and from 1911 to 1915, he gives women the franchise and creates an advanced welfare state as a successful ranching economy develops.
1933	A coup is launched, followed by period of military dictatorship.
1947	Vice President Luis Batlle y Barres becomes president.
1967	Tupamaros launch their insurgency.
1973	The military seizes power and suspends the constitution and all political activity.
1984	Agreement is reached on the basic law governing restoration of civilian rule.
1985	Presidential elections are held and all political prisoners are released; censorship is lifted.
1989	Lacalle Herrera elected president.
2000	A special commission launches an investigation to try to find out what happened to the 160 people who disappeared during the years of military dictatorship in the 1970s and 1980s.
2004	Tabaré Vázquez, head of the left-wing Frente Amplio coalition party, is elected president.

68,021 square miles on the Atlantic coast of eastern South America. Political and economic problems created during the 19th century were alleviated during the presidency of José Batlle y Ordóñez (1903–07; 1911–15), who promoted economic growth and class harmony. His successors chose a different course, which led to a coup in 1933, followed by a period of prosperity and stability under Luis Batlle Berres (1947–56). The late 1950s and 1960s brought severe economic problems and political repression, which led to the brutal suppression of Tupamaros guerrilla groups in 1971–72 and the military seizure of power in 1973. Mass emigration and the continuing economic and social crises brought a return to democracy in 1984. In 1989 the elections resulted in Luis Alberto Lacalle Herrera becoming president. In 2000 the Uruguayan government launched a special commission dedicated to determining the fate of 160 individuals declared missing during the nation's military rule of the 1970s and 1980s. In 2004 left-wing politician Tabaré Vázquez was elected president, winning at the head of the Frente Amplio (Broad Front) coalition party.

Uruguayan Revolution of 1933
URUGUAY suffered from depression in 1931 when Gabriel Terra (1873–1942)

of the liberal Colorado Party was elected president. Facing opposition from radicals and conservatives and checked by the national council of administration, Terra dissolved both council and congress March 30, 1933, and abolished the constitution. A new constitution promulgated in 1934 concentrated power in the presidency and provided proportional representation in the cabinet and senate. Reelected, Terra ruled dictatorially, suppressed a small revolt (1935) and restricted freedom of press and speech, but Uruguay's economy improved. In 1938 Terra was succeeded by his brother-in-law General Alfredo Baldomir (1884–1948) in a fairly free election. Baldomir restored democratic government.

USSR See UNION OF SOVIET SOCIALIST REPUBLICS.

Ustaše Name of a secret Croatian terrorist group formed in 1929 by nationalist Ante Pavelić (1889–1959); originally, a term applied to Croatian rebel bands. Operating during the 1930s from bases in HUNGARY, AUSTRIA and ITALY, the Ustaše fought the Yugoslav monarchy and was implicated in the murder of King ALEXANDER in 1934. In collaboration with German and Italian forces, it established an independent Croatian government in

1941 and was responsible for the slaughter of many Serbians. After the war, Pavelić fled to SPAIN and ARGENTINA, but his movement lived on as an anticommunist Croatian separatist group. As such, it carried out assassinations and bombings in SWEDEN, WEST GERMANY and AUSTRALIA during the 1960s and 1970s.

Ustinov, Dimitri Fedorovich *(1908–1984)* Soviet party official. Ustinov joined the COMMUNIST PARTY of the Soviet Union in 1927. In 1934 he graduated from the Institute of Military Mechanical Engineering and worked as a fitter and machine operator. From 1934 until 1941, Ustinov was USSR people's commissar. He climbed up the ranks of party posts, being made a member of the Central Committee in 1952. He was the USSR minister of the defense industry (1953–57), chairman of the USSR supreme economic council (1963–65) and a member of the Presidium and Politburo central committee. From 1976 Ustinov was minister of defense, general of the army and marshal of the Soviet army.

Ustinov, Peter (Peter Alexander Ustinov) *(1921–2004)* English film and theater actor, playwright, director. Ustinov was one of the more versatile talents in show business, having scored successes both on the stage and in films, as well as through his writings. He began his career on the London stage in the 1930s, and in the 1940s his first plays were produced, including *House of Regrets* (1942) and *The Banbury Nose* (1944). From the 1950s, Ustinov was active as a film actor, with notable roles in *Beat the Devil* (1954), *Lola Montez* (1955), *Spartacus* (1960), *Topkapi* (1964), for which he won an Oscar as best supporting actor, and as Agatha CHRISTIE's Hercule Poirot in several films based on the fictional detective's exploits. His later plays included *Romanoff and Juliet* (1956) and *Beethoven's Tenth* (1983).

U Thant *(1909–1974)* Burmese diplomat. Educated at University College, Rangoon, he was a teacher and headmaster before entering the diplomatic service in 1948. He served in the Burmese ministry of information from 1949 to 1957, becoming Burma's permanent representative to the UNITED NATIONS in 1957. After the death of Dag HAMMARSKJOLD in 1961, Thant was named acting secretary-general and was elected to the post the following year, serving until his retirement in 1971. During his early years in office, Thant helped to resolve the CUBAN MISSILE CRISIS (1962), the civil wars in the CONGO (1963) and CYPRUS (1964) and the INDO-PAKISTANI WAR (1965). Later crises proved more difficult to end, and Thant struggled with the VIETNAM WAR, the SIX-DAY WAR of 1967 (which he helped to mediate) and the 1971 Indo-Pakistan War. Thant helped to steer the UN toward a greater role in the economic, social and political development of THIRD WORLD nations and was influential in the organization's decision to recognize the People's Republic of CHINA in 1971.

Utley, Freda *(1898–1978)* British-born author, lecturer and journalist. Utley began her career as a correspondent for the *Manchester Guardian* (1926–28). From 1930 to 1936 she served as a senior scientific worker at Moscow's Institute of World Economy and Politics, part of the ACADEMY OF SCIENCES OF THE USSR She was subsequently a war correspondent in CHINA, covering the SINO-JAPANESE WAR. She emigrated to the U.S. in 1939 after her husband's arrest and death in a Soviet prison camp. Utley became a U.S. citi-

zen in 1950. She testified at the McCarthy hearings on communist influence over U.S. Far Eastern policy in the early 1950s. (See also Joseph MCCARTHY.)

U2 Irish rock band. Formed in 1978 Dublin by vocalist Bono (born Paul David Hewson), guitarist The Edge (born David Evans), bass player Adam Clayton and drummer Larry Mullen. In 1979 U2 released its first single, "Out of Control," which became the top single in Ireland that year. Its first album, *Boy,* released in 1981, received many positive reviews, and with the help of a promotional international tour the band's album sales and fan base began to grow. U2's second album, *October* (1982), showcased the political activism that would later become associated with the band, and in particular Bono: it contained the single "New Year's Day," which expressed optimism about the future of the SOLIDARITY movement in Poland, and "Sunday Bloody Sunday," which decried the violent situation in Northern Ireland.

U2 increased its involvement in humanitarian causes, performing at Live Aid, helping to orchestrate the Ireland-based concert Self-Aid and lending their musical talents to the anti-apartheid song "Sun City." U2's fifth album, *The Joshua Tree* (1987), proved to be its most successful release, reaching the number one spot on both the British and American album charts. Its follow-up release, *Rattle And Hum* (1988), had the odd effect of generat-

ing sales of 14 million copies worldwide, while being panned by critics for its content and for the band's documentary by the same name that sought to make an icon out of Bono.

Though U2's albums since *Joshua Tree* have declined in their social message, Bono has repeatedly used his stardom to advocate such causes as the peace process in Northern Ireland, an end to nuclear testing and debt relief for impoverished developing countries. After making public the singles "The Sweetest Thing" (1988) and "The Ground Beneath Her Feet" (2000, written by Salman Rushdie) U2 released the album *All That You Can't Leave Behind* (2000), containing the top-ten single "Beautiful Day," which won three Grammy Awards, including Song Of The Year, in 2001. In 2005 the band released the album *How to Dismantle an Atomic Bomb,* and Bono and Bill and Melinda Gates, were named "Persons of the Year" for their philanthropy and humanitarian activities.

U-2 Incident *(1960)* Downing of an American Lockheed U-2, a high-altitude photographic reconnaissance airplane, by a Soviet surface-to-air missile over Sverdlovsk, Russia, on May 1, 1960. Days later, at a summit meeting between U.S. President EISENHOWER and USSR Chairman KHRUSHCHEV in Paris, the Soviet leader demanded an apology for the incident. The U.S. at first denied any spying activities but—confronted with the wrecked plane and the admissions of the pilot, Fran-

Influential Irish rock band U2 (PHOTOFEST)

cis Gary Powers—was forced to admit to its spy overflights. After the incident, a major embarrassment to U.S. intelligence, U-2 flights over the USSR ceased. Powers was returned to the U.S. in an exchange for Soviet spy Rudolf Abel in February 1962.

Uzbekistan Central Asian territory under Russian (1876–1917), Soviet (1921–91) and independent rule (1991–). In the 1850s, the Russian Empire began a military campaign against the Central Asian khanate of Quqon, which controlled the modern-day state of Uzbekistan, and annexed the khanate in 1876. In the following decades religious tensions emerged between the expanding numbers of Russian immigrants (who practiced the Russian Orthodox faith) and the predominantly Islamic indigenous popu-

UZBEKISTAN	
1917	Following the Bolshevik revolution in Russia, the Tashkent soviet ("people's council") is established, which deposes the emir of Bukhara and the other khans in 1920.
1921	The region becomes part of the Turkestan Soviet Socialist Autonomous Republic.
1924	Uzbekistan becomes a constituent republic of the USSR
1930s	Era of Soviet agricultural collectivization; the local Communist Party conducts Stalinist purges.
1959–82	The Uzbekistan republic achieves a degree of de facto autonomy; corruption and nepotism flourish.
1991	As Soviet Union breaks up, independent Republic of Uzbekistan is proclaimed; Communist Party reorganizes itself as People's Democratic Party of Uzbekistan (PDPU), and its leader, Islam Karimov, is elected president.
1992	Regime clamps down on opposition parties and independent press.
1995	Referendum approves extension of Karimov's term to 2000.
1997	Crackdown on so-called Wahhabi sect in Namangan leads to hundreds of arrests.
1999	Explosions rip through downtown Tashkent, killing around 15.
2000	Karimov wins reelection in vote near-universally denounced as undemocratic; regime executes six men found guilty in Tashkent bombings.
2001	Leaders of Russia, China, Kazakhstan, Kyrgyzstan, Tajikistan and Uzbekistan launch the Shanghai Cooperation Organization (SCO) to fight militancy and to promote trade investments. Uzbekistan joins the international fight against terrorism and allows the United States to use its airbases for its action in Afghanistan.
2002	The United States earmarks $100 million in aid for Uzbekistan for its support of the U.S.-led campaign in Afghanistan. In a referendum, Karimov wins support for extending the presidential term from five to seven years.
2004	Violence from Islamic militants increases; suicide bombers target the U.S. and Israeli embassies in Tashkent.

lation. In 1916 efforts by Czar NICHOLAS II to conscript Uzbeks into work battalions for service in WORLD WAR I (1914–18) incited a general insurrection in the territory. As with the regions of TAJIKISTAN and TURKMENISTAN, that was quickly and brutally suppressed by Russian military forces.

In March 1917, the end of the czarist government appeared to offer the peoples of Central Asia a chance for independence, but after the Bolshevik Revolution of November 1917, the Red Army began to reassert control of Uzbekistan, incorporating part of it into the Turkestan Autonomous Soviet Socialist Republic (ASSR).

In 1924, three years after the creation of the UNION OF SOVIET SOCIALIST REPUBLICS (USSR), the Uzbek Soviet Socialist Republic (SSR) was created out of a union of other Soviet republics with Uzbek territory in the Turkestan ASSR; in 1929 the Uzbek SSR lost part of its territory to the Tajik SSR, which until then had been an ASSR under Uzbek control. The majority of the population was alienated by the Communists' repeated efforts to repress the Islamic religion through the closure of mosques and MADRASSAS (Islamic schools). This increasingly centralized control accelerated in 1928 with the beginning of Soviet leader Joseph STALIN's first Five-Year Plan, which required that all small farms within the Uzbek SSR be amalgamated into several state-run farms devoted to producing commodities needed by the Soviet market. During the 1930s, Stalin purged the Uzbek Communist Party through arrest and execution and ruthlessly suppressed the practice of Islam.

During the period of glasnost, or "openness," instituted by Soviet leader Mikhail GORBACHEV (1985–91), Uzbeks were allowed to form associations independent of the government, and mosques and madrassas began to operate openly. This led to a resurgence of pride in Uzbek language, literature and culture, as well as the formation of political associations. In 1990 the People's Democratic Party (PDP) replaced the defunct Communist Party, and PDP leader Islam Karimov was chosen as the new president of the Uzbek SSR.

After the failed coup against Gorbachev in August 1991, the Uzbek Supreme Soviet declared its independence from the USSR. However, it sought to preserve constructive ties with its former fellow SSRs, and in December 1991 joined the newly created COMMONWEALTH OF INDEPENDENT STATES (CIS), a confederation of former SSRs that sought to preserve positive political, economic and military ties among the newly created nations. December 1991 also marked the first national elections of the new republic, renamed Uzbekistan. Karimov and his PDP received a substantial majority of the vote and retained their dominance in the executive and legislative branches of government. In 1992 the government banned all opposition parties, and legislative and presidential elections in 1999 and 2000 were marred by widespread fraud. Karimov has repeatedly justified such authoritarian methods on the grounds that opposition forces represent an outgrowth of **Islamism,** a political-religious movement that seeks to make SHARIA (Islamic law) the law of Uzbekistan, much as the like-minded TALIBAN did in AFGHANISTAN. In January 1995 Karimov did make some concessions to democratic reformers when he proclaimed that the government would permit the formation of political groupings within the Uzbek parliament. This led to the immediate emergence of the Justice Social Democratic Party and the National Revival Democratic Party.

Karimov justified his authoritarian rule as necessary to combat the forces of radical Islam in the country. His warnings about the threat of Islamic terrorism gained some credence following a series of terrorist bombings in 1999 in the capital of Tashkent. As a result, Uzbekistan helped to form the Shanghai Cooperation Organization (SCO), a multinational group—including CHINA, KAZAKHSTAN, KYRGYZSTAN, RUSSIA and TAJIKISTAN—dedicated to combating religious and ethnic militancy. In October 2001 Karimov's government permitted the U.S. to station troops in Uzbekistan as part of U.S. president George W. BUSH's military campaign against the Taliban regime in Afghanistan and AL-QAEDA. Since then Bush has repeatedly increased the level of U.S. aid offered to Uzbekistan, despite mounting allegations of political repression and government mismanagement of the nation's natural gas reserves and cotton crop. Violence from Islamic militant continues to increase. In 2004 suicide bomb attacked the U.S. and Israeli embassies in Tashkent.

V

Vaganova, Agrippina *(1879–1951)* Russian ballerina and teacher. She published *Fundamentals of the Classic Dance* (1934) and was an influential teacher who stressed that technique is grounded in developing bodily strength, balance and coordination. Her pupils included Natalya DUDIN-SKAYA and Galina ULANOVA.

Vakhtangov, Yevgeny Bagrationovich *(1833–1927)* Russian actor and director. He was a pupil of Konstantin STANISLAVSKY. VAKHTANGOV joined the MOSCOW ART THEATER in 1911 as an actor and producer in its First Studio, and in his own Third Studio from 1920. In 1926 the Third Studio was renamed the Vakhtangov Theater. He experimented with the concept of the modern mystery play.

Valachi, Joseph M. *(1903–1971)* American gangster. A minor member of the American MAFIA, he was a soldier in the New York ranks of Salvatore Maranzano and "Lucky" LUCIANO until sentenced to prison on a narcotics charge in 1959. After murdering a fellow prisoner, he turned informer and became one of the few members of the criminal organization to break its code of silence. Valachi was a main witness in the widely televised Senate investigation of organized crime that took place in September–October, 1963, describing in detail the murderous inner workings of the New York Mafia. His testimony was supplemented by his memoirs, *The Valachi Papers*, published in 1969.

A protected inmate, Valachi died in prison of natural causes.

Valentine, Kid Thomas *(1896–1987)* American jazz musician. A jazz trumpeter and long-time leader of the Preservation Hall dance band, he was a legend among New Orleans jazz musicians. Known just as Kid Thomas, he and his band members played all over the world.

Valentino, Rudolph (Rodolfo di Valentino d'Antonguolla) *(1895–1926)* Italian-born silent film actor; a legendary figure from the silent film era of the 1920s. As a romantic lead, Valentino became the exotic symbol of male sexual allure for millions of women around the world. While critics dismissed him as an actor, his dark looks and flamboyant style made him a box-office star. Valentino emigrated from ITALY to America as a young man and worked as an exhibition dancer on the New York club scene before moving to Hollywood in 1918. His major film successes were *The Four Horsemen of the Apocalypse* (1921), *The Sheik* (1921), *Blood and Sand* (1922), *The Eagle* (1925) and *The Son of the Sheik* (1926). At the height of his fame he died of a perforated ulcer.

Valeriano, Napoleon D. *(1917–1975)* Philippine military leader and specialist in international affairs. Valeriano resisted the Japanese invasion of the PHILIPPINES early in WORLD WAR II IN THE PACIFIC and survived the BATAAN death march. In the late 1940s and early 1950s he helped suppress the Hukbalahap Rebellion. A strong supporter of U.S.-Philippines cooperation, he held the rank of colonel in both the Philippine and U.S. armies.

Valéry, Paul *(1871–1945)* French poet and essayist. Valéry is one of the most unique and esteemed figures in 20th-century French literature. In one sense, he was the last great representative of the 19th-century poetic school of symbolism. Valéry was an ardent disciple of symbolist poet Stephane Mallarmé, and Valéry's own poems—most notably his verse masterpiece *La Jeune Parque* (1917)—show the influence of Mallarmé's oblique imagery and precisely toned language. But Valéry was also a modernist in terms of his fascination with the nature of consciousness itself. In essays such as *Introduction to the Method of Leonardo da Vinci* (1894), Valéry explored the means by which the human mind perceived the world and sought to attain self-knowledge. Valéry also wrote frequently on aesthetic subjects such as painting, architecture and the dance. He was elected to the French Academy in 1927 and to the chair of poetry at the Collège de France in 1937.

Valium Trade name for diazepam, a tranquilizer and sedative hypnotic drug. In the late 20th century, Valium was one of the most widely prescribed drugs in the Western world. It is used to relieve anxiety and stress. It also is prescribed in treating recovering alcoholics. Patients who take diazepam can develop physical and psychological dependence and may come to rely on the drug as a cure-all.

Vallee, Rudy (Hubert Prior Vallee) *(1901–1986)* American singer. A singing idol of the late 1920s and '30s, he personified the term "crooner," and foreshadowed such entertainers as Frank SINATRA in his ability to generate mass hysteria among female fans. His show business career took off in 1928 at the Heigh Ho Club in New York City. The club was the inspiration for his "heigh-ho, everybody" greeting, as well as for his singing through a megaphone to amplify his nasal voice. In 1929, he made his first film, *The Vagabond Lover,* and went on to make many more over the next two decades. He enjoyed a resurgence in the 1960s for his Broadway portrayal of a tycoon in *How to Succeed in Business Without Really Trying.*

Vallejo, Cesar (Abraham) *(1892–1938)* Peruvian poet. Vallejo grew up in a poor mestizo family but nonetheless attended university (1913–17), studying literature and law. His first book, *Los heraldos negros* (1918), was virtually ignored. *Trilce* (1922) included more radical, experimental poetry, some of it written in prison where he was detained unjustly for inciting to riot. Embittered by the repressive regime in PERU, he left for PARIS in 1923; except for trips to RUSSIA in 1928, 1929 and 1931 and to SPAIN in 1936 and 1937, he remained there till his death. He joined the Communist Party in 1931. His ultramodern, emotionally powerful poems represent a cry for justice in a world of suffering and chaos. *Poemas humanos* (1939) and *Espana, aparta de mi este caliz* (1940) were published posthumously by his wife.

Valois, Ninette de (Edris Stannus) *(1898–2001)* Irish-born British dancer, choreographer and ballet director. One of the pioneers of British ballet, Valois first gained notice as a *demi-caractère* dancer, primarily with Serge DIAGHILEV's BALLETS RUSSES (1923–25). She founded the Academy of Choreographic Art in London in 1926, then established the Vic-Wells Ballet (with Lilian Baylis) in 1931 and served as its director until 1963, guiding the company through its transformation into the SADLER'S WELLS BALLET and finally the ROYAL BALLET (1956). She was an adviser to the Royal Ballet School and became a Life Governor in 1971. Recipient of many awards, including dame commander of the British Empire (D.B.E.) in 1951, she retired at age 73. Her many choreographic works include *Job* (1931) and *Checkmate* (1937).

Van Allen, James Alfred *(1914–2006)* American physicist. Van Allen's intensive work in terrestrial magnetism and applied physics was instrumental in the experiments launched in 1958 by America's first satellite—EXPLORER I—which measured cosmic rays and other energy particles. The discovery of unexpectedly high radiation levels in certain regions of the Earth's atmosphere contradicted the observations cited five months earlier by the Russians' first satellite, *SPUTNIK I,* and led to further space exploration. Subsequent breakthroughs included locating where the Earth's magnetic field traps high-speed charged particles. These zones were christened Van Allen belts, in honor of the man whose entire life's work has greatly advanced our knowledge of the cosmos.

Vance-Owen Plan A peace plan proposed in 1992 by former U.S. secretary of state Cyrus Vance and British statesman and EUROPEAN UNION representative Lord DAVID OWEN. The Vance-Owen Plan sought to end the continuing civil war between the newly proclaimed republic of BOSNIA AND HERZEGOVINA and the Serbian-dominated government of Yugoslavia. To end the conflict, Vance and Owen proposed the division of Bosnia into 10 ethnically homogenous provinces, each of which would possess substantial autonomy overseen by a federal government with limited powers. The plan was designed to assure the sizable Bosnian Serb minority that it would not come under the domination of the Bosnian Muslim majority. Although the Vance-Owen Plan won the support of the Bosnian Croat and Bosnian Muslim populations, Bosnian Serb leaders rejected it in 1993 on the grounds that the territorial provisions of the plan did not take into account their victories on the battlefield. In November 1995 the civil war in Bosnia was brought to an end when the Croat, Serbian and Bosnian heads of state signed the DAYTON ACCORDS.

Van Damm, Sheila *(1922–1987)* British race car driver; the top British woman in auto racing during the 1950s. In 1960, Van Damm inherited the Windmill Theater from her father, who had kept it open at the height of the Blitz in September 1940. Forced to close it in 1964, Van Damm retired afterward.

Vandenberg, Arthur Hendrick *(1884–1951)* U.S. senator. Vandenberg was born in Grand Rapids, Michigan. He was editor and publisher of the *Grand Rapids Herald* from 1906 to 1928 when he was appointed to the U.S. Senate. An influential Republican who became president pro tem in 1947, he served in the upper house until his death. Vandenberg opposed most NEW DEAL legislation. Prior to WORLD WAR II he was an isolationist, but in the postwar period, he became a leading proponent of bipartisan support for President Harry S TRUMAN's foreign policy. Vandenberg served as chairman of the Senate Committee on Foreign Affairs (1946–51) and was instrumental in securing Senate approval of the MARSHALL PLAN and the NORTH ATLANTIC TREATY ORGANIZATION. He served as a delegate to the UN Conference on International Organization in San Francisco (1945) and to the Paris Peace Conference in 1947.

Vandergrift, Alexander Archer *(1887–1973)* U.S. Marine Corps officer. Vandergrift commanded the First Marine Division in the capture of GUADALCANAL (1942), which was the first full-scale U.S. offensive against the Japanese during World War II. Promoted that year to major general, he held the island against repeated attempts to retake it. Vandergrift also commanded the First Marine Amphibious Corps at the Bougainville Invasion (1943). He was appointed the 18th commandant of the Marine Corps in 1944.

Vander Meer, Johnny *(1914–1997)* Known as "Double No-Hit" Johnny, Vander Meer spent his professional baseball career in Ohio, first as a pitcher with the Cincinnati Reds from 1937 to 1950. He gained his greatest fame as the only pitcher in the history of professional baseball to hurl two consecutive no-hitters, first against the Boston Braves and second against the Brooklyn Dodgers. After his career in Cincinnati, he went to Cleveland in 1951.

Van Deventer, Mills *(1862–1942)* Associate justice, U.S. Supreme Court (1910–37). A graduate of DePauw University and the University of Cincinnati Law School, Van Deventer practiced law with his father in Marion, Indiana, but soon moved to Wyoming Territory, where he briefly served as territory chief justice. Active in Republican politics, he was brought to Washington, D.C., as an assistant attorney general. President Theodore ROOSEVELT appointed him a judge of the U.S. Court of Appeals for the Eighth Circuit in 1903. President William Howard TAFT appointed Van Deventer to the Supreme Court in 1910. He proved a conservative on the bench, generally opposed to government regulation of business.

Van Druten, John (*1901–1957*) British-born playwright and novelist. Van Druten remains best known for his play I AM A CAMERA (1951), which was adapted from *Goodbye to Berlin*, a collection of sketches and stories on 1930s BERLIN by Christopher ISHERWOOD. *I Am A Camera* later became the basis for the hit musical CABARET (1966). Van Druten immigrated to the U.S. after the banning of his early play *Young Woodley* (1925) in Britain due to its controversial handling of the theme of adolescence. In the U.S., Van Druten earned a reputation as an adroit writer of light comedies, most notably *Bell, Book and Candle* (1950).

Vanguard The U.S. Naval Research Laboratories had already begun Project Vanguard to design a rocket capable of launching satellites into space when the Soviets launched their SPUTNIK satellite in October 1957. On December 6, 1957, at CAPE CANAVERAL, a Vanguard rocket bearing a 6-inch satellite was ignited and exploded a few seconds later. A second Vanguard broke up in flight in February 1958. At last, in March 1958, the three-pound *Vanguard 1* soared into space, equipped with a radio transmitter that would continue to send signals for nearly six years. Between December 1957 and September 1959, 11 Vanguard launch attempts were made, with only three successes.

Van Heusen, Jimmy (Edward Chester Babcock) (*1913–1990*) American composer. Along with his lyricist partners Johnny Burke and Sammy CAHN, he wrote such popular songs as "Moonlight Becomes You" and "My Kind of Town." Many of his biggest hits were performed by Frank SINATRA, who recorded 76 Van Heusen songs, and Bing CROSBY. Four of his songs—"Swingin' On a Star" from the film *Going My Way* (1944), "All the Way" from *The Joker is Wild* (1957), "High Hopes" from *A Hole in the Head* (1959) and "Call Me Irresponsible" from *Papa's Delicate Condition* (1963)—won ACADEMY AWARDS. He was one of 10 songwriters inducted into the Songwriters Hall of Fame when it was founded in 1971.

Van Niel, Cornelius Bernardus (*1897–1985*) Dutch-born microbiologist. In the 1930s Van Niel became the first scientist to explain the chemical basis for photosynthesis. He arrived at the correct formula while working with bacteria; in the 1940s, his formula was shown to be correct for green plants as well. For many years he taught at Stanford University's Hopkins Marine Station in Southern California.

Vanuatu Located in the South Pacific Ocean, 621 miles west of Fiji and 249 miles northeast of New Caledonia, the Vanuatu archipelago has a total area of

VANUATU	
1906	The islands are jointly administered by France and Britain as the Condominium of the New Hebrides.
1980	Vanuatu becomes an independent republic as the Anglo-French condominium is terminated. Jimmy Stevens, backed by an American right-wing organization known as the Phoenix Foundation, leads a secessionist uprising on Espiritu Santo and proclaims an independent republic; the revolt is suppressed with the help of British, French, and Papua New Guinean troops.
1983	In elections to parliament, the Vanuaaku Party gains 24 seats under Walter Lini as Prime Minister.
1987	Lini is reelected prime minister in November. Parliamentary seats are increased to 46.
1988	Barak Tame Sope is charged with instigating serious rioting in Vila, resulting in one death and several injuries. Sope is dismissed from the Council of Ministers. He and four others resign from the VP and are dismissed from parliament. Eighteen UMP members boycott three successive parliamentary sittings and are expelled form parliament. Sokomanu dissolves parliament and installs Sope as interim prime minister. Sokomanu and Sope are arrested, charged with treason, convicted, and sentenced to prison.
1989	Fred Timakata is named president.
1996	President Jean-Marie Leye and former deputy prime minister Barak Sope are briefly abducted by the Vanuatu Mobile Force as part of a long-standing pay dispute with the government.
2002	Barak Sope is sentenced to three years for abuse of office as a prime minister.
2005	Thousands of people are evacuated as Mount Manaro, an active volcano on Ambae, begins to spew ash and steam.

5,697 square miles. (See map on p. 957.) It consists of 13 large islands and 70 islets. Joint British and French rule of the islands was formalized in 1906. On July 30, 1980, the islands achieved independence as the Republic of Vanuatu, which became a member of the COMMONWEALTH. In September 1980 a secession movement in Espiritu Santo, the largest island, was put down with help from PAPUA NEW GUINEA. In 1983 Vanuatu became a member of the Non-Aligned Movement, and the ruling left-wing Vanuaaku Party, under the leadership of Prime Minister Walter Lini, was returned to government. The party won a further election in November 1987 but was subject to increasing internal dissension as Barak Sope attempted to wrest the leadership from Lini. Following Sope's expulsion from the Vanuaaku Party, his uncle, George Sokomanu—the country's president—tried to dismiss Lini's agreement and swear in Sope as prime minister. Both Sope and Sokomanu were imprisoned for mutiny, although the latter was later released on appeal. In 1989 Fred Timakata, a former member of Lini's cabinet, was elected president of Vanuatu. Vanuatu continued to experience political and financial instability throughout the 1990s and into the early 21st century. In 1996 President Jean-Marie Leye and former deputy prime minister Barak Sope were abducted (and later released) by the country's Vanuatu Mobile Force to resolve that organization's payment dispute with the government. Six years later Sope was convicted of financial crimes and was sentenced to three years of imprisonment. In 2005 thousands had to be evacuated when an active volcano began to spew ash and steam.

Vare, Glenna Collett *(1903–1989)* American golfer. She was a pioneer of women's golf in the U.S. She won six national women's titles between the years 1922 and 1935 and was named a charter member of the Women's Golf Hall of Fame in 1950. The Vare Trophy, given annually by the Ladies Professional Golfers Association (LPGA) to the player with the lowest average on the tour, was named for her.

Varese, Edgar (Edgard Varese) *(1883–1965)* American composer. An experimentalist whose music often elicited controversy, Varese exerted considerable influence on the development of modern music with his concept of "organized sound." He spent his early career in Paris and Berlin among the avant-garde artists. In 1915 he came to the U.S.; then in 1922 he and Carlos Salzedo cofounded the International Composers' Guild. Many of his compositions use electronic devices and taped sounds. His most important works include *Deserts* (1954) and *Ionisation* (1931).

Vargas Llosa, Mario *(1936–   )* Peruvian novelist, intellectual and political figure. Vargas Llosa attended military school and university in Lima and obtained a doctorate in Madrid (1958); thereafter he lived in Paris until 1966. He has also resided in London, Barcelona and the U.S. He first achieved renown and notoriety with *La ciudad y los perros* (1963; tr. 1966 as *The Time of the Hero*). A thousand copies of the book, which described his military school experience, were burned on the school's patio. Subsequent novels include *La casa verde* (1966; tr. 1968 as *The Green House*), *Conversacion en la catedral* (1969; tr. 1975 as *The Conversation in the Cathedral*), *Pantaleon y las visitadoros* (1973; tr. 1978 as *Captain Pantoja and the Special Service*), *La tia Julia y el escribidor* (1977; tr. 1982 as *Aunt Julia and the Scriptwriter*), *La Guerra del fin del Mondo* (1981; tr. 1984 as *The War of the End of the World*) and *Historia de Mayta* (1985; tr. 1986 as *The Real Life of Alejandro Mayta*). He has also written studies of GARCÍA MÁRQUEZ (1971) and Flaubert (1975). A one-time leftist and supporter of communist CUBA, Vargas Llosa later changed his views, becoming an advocate of democracy who vigorously opposes tyrannies of the right or left. In 1990 he ran unsuccessfully for the office of president of PERU. Vargas Llosa continued to publish works throughout the 1990s, including *A Fish in the Water* (1993), which narrated his experiences during the 1990 presidential campaign.

Vasiliev and Maximova Soviet dancers, Vladimir Victorovich Vasiliev (1940–   ) and Yekaterina Sergeyevna Maximova (1934–   ). This husband and wife have forged a popular partnership, appearing together in such ballets as *Sleeping Beauty* and *Spartacus* to much acclaim. In 1964 each won a gold medal at the International Ballet Competition in Varna, Italy. As stars of the BOLSHOI BALLET they have gained an international reputation, Vasiliev for his virtuosity and dynamic stage presence and Maximova for her beautiful technique. Individually, he has excelled in such ballets as *Ivan the Terrible* (1975) while his wife is admired for her roles in *The Stone Flower* and *Don Quixote*.

Vatican (State of the Vatican City) The ecclesiastical state of Vatican City, seat of the Holy See, lies within Rome, ITALY, on the western bank of the Tiber. Its total area of 0.17 square mile makes it the world's smallest state. In the 19th century, the Papal States were incorporated by force into the emerging Italian state, culminating in the seizure of Rome in 1870 by King Victor Emmanuel II. In protest, successive popes refused to leave the Vatican until February 1929, when Pope PIUS XI and MUSSOLINI concluded the Lateran Treaties, which recognized the Holy See's sovereignty in Vatican City and incorporated a concordat by which Catholicism became Italy's state religion. During WORLD WAR II Pope PIUS XII incurred much international criticism by adhering to a strict neutrality. In the postwar era, the Vatican combined its spiritual role with active diplomacy as a neutral sovereign state, signing the Final Act of the Conference on Security and Cooperation in Europe (1975) and establishing diplomatic relations with over 100 countries, including Britain (1982) and the U.S. (1984). In 1978 Cardinal Karol Wojtyla of Poland became, as Pope JOHN PAUL II, the first non-Italian pontiff since the 16th century. He undertook an unprecedented number of papal visits abroad and survived two assassination attempts, one in Rome in 1981 and another in Portugal a year later.

The privileged status of the Catholic Church in Italy was ended under a revised concordat signed in February 1984. In a major reorganization of Vatican administration, the pope delegated most of his temporal duties to Secretary of State Cardinal Agostino Casaroli, amid concern over the alleged involvement of the Vatican Bank in the 1982 fraudulent bankruptcy of Milan's Banco Ambrosiano. Ambrosiano's collapse was precipitated by the death of its chairman, Roberto Calvi, who was found hanging beneath Blackfriars Bridge in London on June 18, 1982. Calvi's death was first found to be suicide; at a second inquest in June 1983 an open verdict was returned; in February 1989 a Milan court ruled that his death had been murder. Under a financial settlement agreed upon in May 1984 the Vatican Bank agreed to pay 109 creditor banks $250 million of the $406 million it owed following the liquidation of Banco Ambrosiano. In the later years of his papacy, John Paul II attempted to improve relations between the Catholic Church and the world's Jewish community. In 1993 the Vatican established formal relations with Israel. Seven years later he traveled to Israel and issued a public apology for all sins committed by Catholics since the church's founding, which some interpreted as an appeal for forgiveness for the historical record of Catholic anti-Semitism. John Paul II also attempted to use his influence to promote a peaceful settlement between Israel and the Palestinians. In 2005 Pope John Paul II died and was succeeded by the former cardinal Joseph Ratzinger of Germany who took the name Pope BENEDICT XVI.

Vatican II *(1962–1963)* Council summoned by Pope JOHN XXIII to promulgate reforms within the Roman Catholic Church. Proceedings began on October 11, 1962, in the presence of over 8,000 Catholic bishops and observers from Anglican and Orthodox churches. The 16 decrees that emerged encouraged greater tolerance toward non-Catholic Christians and provided for the use of the vernacular rather than Latin in Catholic liturgy. Vatican II was a watershed in the history of the Catholic Church in the 20th century, with far-reaching consequences for Catholics and non-Catholics alike. Many of the council's decrees continued to stir controversy decades after they were issued. Traditionalists have argued that the council contradicted many of the long-accepted practices and beliefs of the church, while liberals have complained that the reforms did not go far enough in making the church responsive to the contemporary world.

vaudeville A term used to describe popular variety entertainment in the U.S. during the early part of the 20th century. Similar to the music halls in Britain, a vaudeville program contained a dozen or so variety acts: singers and comedy sketches; dance, magic and animal acts; and even swimmers and acrobats. Many well-known performers—BURNS AND ALLEN, Bob HOPE, Jimmy DURANTE, the MARX BROTHERS, Eddie CANTOR, Al JOLSON, Jack BENNY and many more—got their start in show business on the vaudeville stage. Vaudeville was at its peak during the 1910s and early 1920s. During the 1920s the popularity of SILENT FILM and RADIO soared, causing vaudeville's decline.

Vaughan, Harry Hawkins *(1893–1981)* American military officer and aide to Harry S TRUMAN. He served with fellow Missourian Truman during WORLD WAR I and earned a number of decorations as an artillery captain in France. He also established a long-lasting friendship with the future president. He worked for Truman's Senate reelection campaign (1939–40). After service in Australia in WORLD WAR II, he became Vice President Truman's military aide (1944), remaining in that position throughout Truman's vice presidency and presidency. A plain-spoken individualist like his mentor, Vaughan's remarks often caused controversy, and he was reprimanded by the Senate (1949) for misuse of influence.

Vaughan, Sarah (Sarah Lois Vaughan) *(1924–1990)* American jazz vocalist. Vaughan was noted for the remarkable three-octave range of her voice and her mastery of such vocal techniques as vibrato, vocal leaps, skat singing and improvisation. Her career spanned nearly 50 years, beginning in the 1940s, and included such popular recordings as "Make Yourself Comfortable" (1954), "Mr. Wonderful" (1956) and "Broken-Hearted Melody" (1959). Although she began by singing be-bop with such performers as Dizzy GILLESPIE, Charlie PARKER and Billy ECKSTINE, she later branched out into pop music as well. She remained a popular performer throughout her career, and appeared at nightclubs, jazz festivals and with symphony orchestras until shortly before her death.

Vaughan, Stevie (Stephen Ray) *(1954–1990)* American musician. He was one of the U.S.'s top blues and rock guitar players. Together with his band, Double Trouble, he won the 1984 Grammy for best traditional blues recording for "Texas Flood." In 1989 he won the Grammy for best contemporary blues recording for "In Step." He performed with such rock artists as David BOWIE, Joe Cocker and Eric CLAPTON. The younger brother of guitarist Jimmie Vaughan, he died in a helicopter crash while touring with Clapton.

Vaughan Williams, Ralph *(1872–1958)* British composer. A prolific composer whose work spans more than half of the 20th century, Vaughan Williams is best known for his nine symphonies, the *Fantasia on a Theme by Thomas Tallis* (1910), *The Lark Ascending* (1920, for orchestra and violin solo) and his setting of the traditional folksong *Greensleeves* (1929). He also composed operas, ballet music, film scores and songs. He studied with Sir Charles Stanford and Hubert Parry at the Royal College of Music in London, as well as with Max Bruch in Berlin and Maurice RAVEL in Paris. However, the major influences on his style were English folk song and the polyphonic English church music of the 16th century. Slow to mature as a composer, he did not complete his First Symphony (*A Sea Symphony*, a massive choral work set to poems by Walt Whitman) until 1910. Although he occasionally experimented with dissonance (notably in the Fourth Symphony, 1931–34), his music is generally evocative and melodically and harmonically rich. Other important compositions include the Second Symphony (*A London Symphony*, 1913), the Fifth Symphony (1943), *Five Variants on Dives and Lazarus* (1939) and *The Pilgrim's Progress* (1951). His second wife was the poet Ursula Wood.

Vavilov, Nicholas Ivanovich *(1887–1943)* Russian botanist and chemist. He held many important posts, including that of director of the All-Union Institute of Plant Breeding (1924–40), and enjoyed an international reputation as one of the greatest contributors to the study of botanical populations. Although he had supported some of the experiments of Trofim D. LYSENKO, he opposed many of the latter's more outrageous scientific claims. As a result he was arrested (1940) and died in a concentration camp. After the death of STALIN his reputation was rehabilitated.

Veblen, Thorstein B. *(1857–1929)* American economist. Veblen is considered one of the most creative thinkers in American economic history. He studied at Carleton College and took a Ph.D. in philosophy from Yale in 1884, but could not find a teaching place and so returned home to farm work. Eventually he was accepted at the University of CHICAGO to teach political economy (1892–1906). His scholarly and satiric book *The Theory of the Leisure Class* (1899) attacked false values and social waste and brought him almost instant fame. He advocated a planned economic society in which scientists and engineers would play a significant role. His ideas were so controversial that he was forced to leave the university and spent many years at other schools.

V-E Day Victory in Europe—May 8, 1945. On this day, Germany's unconditional surrender (signed the day before) was ratified, ending WORLD WAR II IN EUROPE.

Veeck, Bill *(1914–1986)* American sports executive. During his various stints as the owner of three major league baseball teams, the Cleveland Indians, the St. Louis Browns and the Chicago White Sox, he became known as the "Barnum of Baseball." He installed the first exploding scoreboard, invented season tickets and bat days and introduced the practice of printing players' names on the back of their uniforms. In 1951, he perpetrated one of the most memorable stunts in baseball when he sent a midget to bat. More than a brilliant promoter, he twice led unimpressive teams to pennants in a short time, the Indians in 1948 and the White Sox in 1959. In 1948, he signed the first black player to play in the American League, Larry Doby. Veeck was named to the Baseball Hall of Fame in 1991.

Velasco Ibarra, José María *(1893–1979)* President of ECUADOR (1934–35; 1944–47; 1952–56; 1960–61; 1968–72). One of Ecuador's leading politicians, Velasco was elected president five times but completed only one term

(1952–56). Each of his other four terms ended when he was overthrown by the military.

Velcro The Swiss inventor Georges de Mestral was reportedly inspired to create Velcro after wondering why burrs stuck to his trousers. He discovered that the burrs were made up of thousands of tiny hooks, and he went on to develop Velcro (a combination of "velvet" and "crochet," the French word for hook). Its strips of tiny loops and tiny nylon hooks made it suitable for use in everything from clothing to spacecraft and artificial hearts.

Velikovsky, Immanuel *(1895–1979)* Russian-born psychoanalyst, astronomer-theorist and author. Velikovsky was known mainly for his unorthodox theories of cosmic evolution. A controversial and iconoclastic figure, in his writings he combined a vast knowledge of biblical and mythological lore with Freudian psychology. In his book *Worlds in Collision* (1950), he claimed that a comet had collided with the Earth in 1500 B.C., causing tumultuous changes on the planet. While many readers considered Velikovsky a great visionary, his ideas

never won acceptance from the scientific establishment.

Venezuela (Republic of Venezuela) Venezuela covers an area of 352,051 square miles on the Caribbean Sea coast of northern South America, stretching to mountainous inlands and the northern edge of the Amazon Basin. Dictator Juan Vicente GÓMEZ ruled the country from 1908 to 1935. In the 1920s oil was discovered, changing the country's economy from predominantly agricultural to industrial. Subsequent social change led to the formation of opposition groups among students, intellectuals and labor unions, which demanded an end to dictatorship and repression. Under the leadership of Romulo BETANCOURT (1945–48, 1958–63) a new constitution was created and economic and social reforms enacted. The corrupt military government of Marcos Pérez, which seized power in 1948 and had U.S. support, was ousted in 1958, and Betancourt returned as president. After 1963 the presidency changed hands several times amid growing economic problems and student and union demonstrations. President Carlos Andréz Pérez was elected

VENEZUELA

1908	Juan Vicente Gómez seizes power and becomes a virtual dictator.
1920s	Oil is discovered.
1935	General Eleazar López Contreras becomes president on Gómez's death and initiates political and economic reform.
1945	Romulo Betancourt elected president, begins constitutional reforms.
1948	Marcos Pérez overthrows Betancourt and begins dictatorial rule.
1958	Pérez overthrown by military; Betancourt returns to office.
1960	Venezuela takes the lead in forming OPEC.
1976	All foreign mining companies are nationalized.
1988	(December) Running as a populist, Carlos Andrés Pérez wins the 1988 presidential elections.
1992	Junior military officers mount an unsuccessful coup (February); President Pérez forms a government of national unity; a second coup attempt takes place (November).
1993	Pérez resigns a year ahead of schedule amid new charges of corruption; Rafael Caldera wins presidential election (December).
1994	Banco Latino collapses, launching a chain of bank failures, and a state bailout is necessitated.
1998	Hugo Chávez wins the presidency on an antiestablishment platform, promising to institute a major restructuring of Venezuelan society.
1999	Chávez sponsors a referendum that approves creation of a constituent assembly to draft a new constitution; draft constitution is completed and approved in December referendum; oil prices drop leading to a major economic contraction; heavy rains cause massive landslides in December that kill around 30,000 people in coastal areas north of Caracas.
2000	New constitution comes into effect establishing a strong presidency and a unicameral legislature; Chávez is reelected with a strong legislative majority.
2002	Chávez is forced to resign by military high command rebels; he returns to office after the collapse of the interim government (April).
2004	President Chávez wins a referendum in which voters approve he should serve out his remaining two and one half years in office.
2005	Chávez signs a decree on land reform designed to eliminate large estates.

in 1988, but the economic recession and social unrest continued. After leading an abortive coup attempt in 1992, Hugo CHÁVEZ was elected president of Venezuela in 1998, and, save for a three-day ouster in April 2002, has remained in power. Chávez's administration alienated large sections of the population as a result of a drastic decline in the value of the bolivar, the national currency, in 2002. The country was beset with economic woes in the same year following a strike in the oil industry, followed by a nine-week general strike. Despite growing calls for his resignation, Chávez announced he would remain in office following an August 2004 referendum in which a majority of Venezuelans voted to allow him to serve out the remaining two and a half years in his term. He proceeded to enact sweeping land reforms and used the increased earnings from oil exports to finance social welfare programs. Chávez's vocal criticism of U.S. foreign policy and friendship with Fidel Castro generated strong criticism from the Bush administrations in Washington.

Venizelos, Eleutherios (Elefthérios Venizélos) *(1864–1936)* Greek statesman, six-time premier between 1910 and 1933. Born on Crete, he played an important part in the 1897 revolt against the Turks. In 1905, he announced the union of GREECE and Crete, a goal that was not to be achieved until 1913. In 1909 he went to Greece at the behest of the Military League, which was pressing for political reforms. Becoming premier in 1910, he led Greece during the BALKAN WARS (1912–13) and greatly increased the nation's territory. He was a strong proponent of the Allied cause in WORLD WAR I, causing conflicts with the pro-German king CONSTANTINE I, who forced his resignation in 1915. Elected premier again that year, he was again forced from office by the king. He formed a provisional government at Salonika the following year and after the king was compelled to step down became premier again in 1917 and brought Greece into the war on the Allied side. Venizelos lost the elections in 1920, and Constantine was restored. After the defeat of TURKEY and Constantine's abdication (1922), Venizelos served briefly as premier in 1924 and retired from office. An elder statesman, he won the elections in 1928, was forced to resign by royalist pressure and the trials of economic depression in 1932 and was premier again for a short period in 1933. Fearing that the monarchy would be reinstated, he was involved in the unsuccessful armed insurrection of 1935 and forced into exile in Paris, where he died the following year.

Venter, J. Craig (1946–) American biologist. Born in Salt Lake City, Utah, Venter originally sought a career as a professional swimmer. However, in 1966 he was drafted into the army and sent to Danang, South Vietnam, where he served as a medical corpsman. On returning to the U.S. after the completion of his military service, Venter enrolled at the University of California-San Diego (UCSD), where he graduated in 1972 with a B.S. in biochemistry. Three years later Venter obtained his Ph.D. from UCSD in physics and pharmacology. In 1984 Venter began working for the National Institute of Neurological Disorders and Strokes, a division of the NATIONAL INSTITUTES OF HEALTH (NIH). In 1990 while investigating neurological disorders, he developed a technique called expressed sequence tags (ESTs) for determining the sequence of genes in human, animal, plant and microbe cells.

In 1992 Venter left the NIH to help found the Institute for Genomic Research (TIGR), a nonprofit organization dedicated to additional understanding and sequencing of the genomes of plants and animals. After six years of serving as the president of TIGR, Venter collaborated with the biopharmacolog-

ical firm Perkin-Elmer to create Celera Genomics, with the goal of making that institution the leader in producing information on human, plant, animal and microbial genomes for use in developing new medicines. By June 2000 after several years of collaboration with Dr. Francis Collins of the NIH's Human Genome Project, Celera announced it had completed a multiyear project on the human genome and published the sequencing of its 3.12 million base pairs in the February 16, 2001, edition of *Science* magazine. In May 2002 Venter formed three nonprofit organizations under TIGR to examine the moral and societal implications of developments within genetic sciences.

Venturi, Robert (1925–) American architect and recipient of the Pritzker Architecture Prize (1991). Born in Philadelphia, Pennsylvania, Venturi attended Princeton University, where he received his B.A. summa cum laude in 1947 and his Masters of Fine Arts (M.F.A.) in 1950. Venturi traveled to Rome in 1954 as the recipient of the American Academy of Rome's Prize Fellow, and remained there until 1956, when he returned to the U.S. to begin a career as a lecturer at American architectural schools such as Yale, Princeton, Harvard, UCLA and Rice, as well as the American Academy in Rome. As a lecturer, author and academic, Venturi began to champion the creation and preservation of a complex urban architectural collage, even if at times this resulted in the nearby placement of contrasting architectural styles, or even if these styles emerged within a single building. Venturi also developed practical experience as an architect, working in the offices of Milwaukee architect Eero SAARINEN (for whom he helped design the Milwaukee County War Memorial Center), and Philadelphia architects Louis I. KAHN and Oscar STONOROV. In 1958 Venturi founded his own practice, which by 1967 had been expanded into Venturi, Scott Brown & Associates with architects John Rausch, and Venturi's wife, Denise Scott Brown.

As a professional architect, Venturi's first independent design came in 1964 when he drafted the plans for his mother's house in the Philadelphia suburb of Chestnut Hill. Since then, Venturi has helped design a variety of buildings, such as the Redy Creek

Emergency Service Headquarters (a fire station for Disney World, Florida, finished in 1995), the Seattle Art Museum (1990), the Salisbury Wing of the National Gallery in London (1991), the Philadelphia Orchestra Hall (1980) and the Museum für Kunsthandwerk in Frankfurt, Germany (1980). In 1991 in recognition of his contribution to the field of architecture through his lectures, his designs, and his theoretical books such as *Complexity and Contradiction in Architecture* (1966), Venturi was awarded the Pritzker Prize, the highest international award for architecture.

Verdun, Battle of (1916) Verdun, the major French fortress on the Meuse River, became the object of a German offensive in February 1916, during WORLD WAR I. After a heavy artillery bombardment, German troops advanced and captured several of the smaller forts surrounding Verdun. French forces counterattacked and stopped the German drive. The battle raged on for months. Areas were taken and retaken by both sides; there were strong attacks and counterattacks. "They shall not pass" became the cry of French resistance, and indeed Verdun did stand resolute against relentless German shelling. By August 1916, the Germans realized they could not capture the fortress and ceased their attacks. About a million Frenchmen lost their lives in this struggle, which was one of the most destructive of the war.

Verey, Rosemary (1918–2001) British horticulturist. Although never receiving any formal education in the art of horticulture, Verey began to take an avid interest in gardening following her husband's acquisition of his family's estate, Barnsley. After repeated visits and lessons from the Verey family gardener, Charlie Hall, Verey began a 20-year transformation of the estate grounds through the planting of herbs, trees and even the creation of a new species of rose, the Sweetheart Rose. As tourists, horticulture admirers and photographers observed and praised her designs, her neighbor, Avilda Lees-Miller, approached her and suggested that both women collaborate in the composition of *The Englishwoman's Garden* (1980), a book designed to offer suggestions to the novice horticulturalist. The book became an international bestseller, and Verey began to receive commissions to design a variety of private and public gardens in Great Britain and the U.S. By the time of her death in 2001, her dossier included the cottage garden at Highgrove, an estate of CHARLES, PRINCE OF WALES; an herb garden for Princess Michael of Kent and a white-themed garden for Sir Elton JOHN. In 1996 Verey received the Order of the British Empire (OBE) for her contribution to horticulture, as well as her designs at Highgrove. The following year, she received the Royal Horticultural Society's Victorian Medal of Honor, the highest honor awarded by that society.

Vernadsky, Vladimir Ivanovich
(1863–1945) Russian geochemist and mineralogist. He was considered a founder of geochemistry. Although he was active in the ZEMSTVA movement and opposed the BOLSHEVIKS, he returned to his work after the Civil War and was founder of the biogeochemical laboratory of the Academy of Sciences in Leningrad, becoming its director in 1928.

Versailles, Treaty of
Several treaties negotiated and signed at the French palace of Versailles. In the 20th century, the term applies to the treaty of 1919, the most important of the five peace treaties that officially ended WORLD WAR I because it fixed the terms of the peace with GERMANY. The Treaty of Versailles was the result of negotiations at the lengthy and often rancorous PARIS PEACE CONFERENCE. It was signed on June 28, 1919, by the defeated Germany on one side and the victorious FRANCE, ITALY, UNITED KINGDOM and UNITED STATES on the other. The treaty forced Germany to admit war guilt and placed stringent limitations on its ability to rearm. Largely through the insistence of the French, Germany was obliged to pay heavy war reparations. It was also compelled to give up certain territories. The most significant of these were: the restoration of Alsace and Lorraine to France, the awarding of much of Prussia to Poland and the creation of Danzig as a free city. The treaty largely rejected President WILSON'S FOURTEEN POINTS but did establish the LEAGUE OF NATIONS. It placed Germany's colonies under League mandates, forced Germany to accept French administration of the Saar and demanded plebiscites that gave the residents of territories previously held by the Central Powers the right of self-determination. While Germany protested that the treaty was overly severe, the nation had no choice but to sign it, and the Treaty of Versailles became effective in January 1920. The treaty's harsh terms are often cited as a contributing cause for the rise of NAZISM in post–World War I Germany.

Vertov, Dziga
(1896–1954) Russian filmmaker and theoretician, father of the Russian newsreel and documentary film. He was born Denis Kaufman in Russian-held Poland. During the early years of World War I he studied medicine and psychology; but soon his interest in FUTURISM and its preoccupation with machines and technology led him to poetry and the adoption of a new name, "Dziga Vertov" (which means "turning," or "revolving"). With the Bolshevik seizure of power in October 1917 he became editor of the newsreel *Film Weekly.* To his editing bench in Moscow came raw film actualities from across RUSSIA. His assembled film strips went by "agit-train" to villages and soldiers at the fronts with information and propaganda about the "revolutionary struggles." After the war, he continued to champion the documentary film at the expense of the fiction, HOLLYWOOD-style, film, which he called "a scabby substitute" for life. His monthly newsreel, *Kino-Pravda (Film-Truth)* appeared from 1922–25; and his studio, Kultkino, produced information films after 1925. Numerous pamphlets and manifestoes hailed the "Kino-Eye," or "Camera-Eye," as the new means to "decipher in a new way a world unknown to you," to assemble and record actualities ("life facts") into new cinematic structures ("film things"). His masterpiece, *Cheloveks Kinoapparatom (Man with a Movie Camera,* 1929) was a free-wheeling kaleidoscope of special effects and actualities—life in Moscow captured and reassembled by the camera eye and film editor. But, like his colleagues PUDOVKIN, KULESHOV and EISENSTEIN, such experiments ran Vertov afoul of the STALIN regime. After two sound films, *Entusiazm,* (*Enthusiasm,* 1931) and *Tri Pesni O Leninye* (*Three Songs of Lenin,* 1934) Vertov fell out of favor and spent the remainder of his life editing newsreels. A revival of interest in his work came in the 1960s, a decade after his death.

Verwoerd, Hendrik Frensch
(1901–1966) South African politician and prime minister (1958–66). Born in Holland, he was brought to SOUTH AFRICA as a baby by his missionary parents. He was educated in GERMANY and at Stellenbosch University, where he taught psychology and sociology from 1927–37. In 1928 he became editor of the Afrikaans nationalist newspaper *Die Transvaaler,* following an editorial policy of opposition to the nation's entry into WORLD WAR II, to Jan SMUTS and to black Africans, Jews and the British. After becoming a senator in 1948, he held a number of positions in the nationalist government, notably minister of native affairs (1950–58). In 1958, he became the leader of the National Party and prime minister. He was a harsh proponent of white supremacy and racial separation, upholding APARTHEID and aiding in the establishment of "Bantu homelands." Instrumental in making South Africa a republic in 1961, he severed the nation's ties with the British Commonwealth. He was stabbed to death by a fanatic parliamentary messenger during a session of parliament in 1966.

Vesely, Artem (Nicholas Ivanovich Kochkurov)
(1899–1939) Russian novelist. He wrote several novels about the revolution, including *The Fiery Rivers* (1942), *Land of My Birth* (1926) and *Russia Washed with Blood* (1929–31). His historical novel about Yermak, a 17th-century adventurer and conqueror of Siberia, *The Sporting Volga,* was published in 1933. He was detained in 1939 in the GREAT PURGE, and nothing was heard of him again.

Vichy, France
Government that controlled unoccupied France and its colonies for much of WORLD WAR II after the German invasion in 1940. Authorized by a vote of the French National Assembly meeting in the resort town of Vichy in July 1940 and headed by Premier Henri-Philippe PÉTAIN, it succeeded France's Third Republic. A new constitution was promulgated that established a corporate state, and a new

government controlled by right-wing politicians and stressing the virtues of order and authority was put in place. The Vichy regime collaborated with the Nazis to a greater or lesser extent during its existence depending on who held the real power in the government, with collaboration strong under Pierre LAVAL and strongest under Admiral Jean Francois DARLAN. After German troops entered unoccupied France in November 1942, the Vichy regime lost virtually all of its real autonomy and increasingly became a tool of Germany. The regime fled to Germany as the Allies advanced and ceased to exist on German surrender in 1945.

Vickers, Jon(athan Steward) (1926–) Canadian singer. An internationally acclaimed dramatic tenor, Vickers made his opera debut in *Rigoletto* at the Toronto Opera Festival in 1952. From 1957 to 1960 he sang with the opera at Covent Garden and first performed one of his most celebrated roles, Aeneas in *Les Troyens*. He debuted at the New York Metropolitan Opera in 1960 as Canio in *I Pagliacci*. His most famous roles include the title role in *Peter Grimes*, Samson in *Samson and Delilah* and the title role in *Parsifal*. In addition, he appeared in the film versions of *Carmen, Otello* and *I Pagliacci*.

Victor Emmanuel III (1869–1947) King of ITALY (1900–46). The son of Humbert I, Victor Emmanuel married Princess Helena of Montenegro in 1896 and succeeded to the throne upon the assassination of his father. At first a proponent of neutrality, he entered WORLD WAR I on the Allied side in 1915. Unable to cope with the postwar turmoil in Italian politics, in 1922 he invited Benito MUSSOLINI to become premier and thus brought the Fascists to power (see FASCISM). During the Fascist era, Victor Emmanuel gained the titles of Emperor of Ethiopia (1936) and King of Albania (1936), but he was virtually a figurehead throughout his reign. After the Fascist grand council withdrew support from Mussolini in 1943, the king dismissed the premier, had him arrested and replaced him with Pietro BADOGLIO. When Italy surrendered to the Allies seven weeks later, Germany occupied Rome, and Victor Emmanuel fled to Brindisi. In 1946, the unpopular monarch abdicated in favor of his son, Humbert II. A

year later, Victor Emmanuel died in exile in EGYPT.

Vidal, Gore (Eugene Luther Vidal) (1925–) American writer. An eclectic writer who has produced novels, plays, poetry, song lyrics and critical essays, Vidal usually focuses on social, political and historical themes in his works. His first novel, *Williwaw* (1946), was a critical and popular success, but his 1968 novel *Myra Breckinridge* stirred controversy because of its transsexual main character. Vidal is best known for his television plays *Visit to a Small Planet* (1955) and *The Best Man* (1960), which were later adapted to film and the stage, and for his historical fiction, including *Burr* (1973) and *Lincoln* (1984). He has also written two science fiction novels, *Messiah* (1954) and *Kalki* (1978). Collections of his political essays include *The Second American Revolution* (1982). In the 1990s Vidal appeared in two motion pictures, *Bob Roberts* (1992) and *Gattaca* (1997).

Vidor, King (1894–1982) American film director. Vidor began working in HOLLYWOOD in the 1920s, setting out to make films about the lives of ordinary people at a time when he thought movies were overacted and bore little resemblance to the real world. He directed the classic silent films *The Big Parade* (1925) and *The Crowd* (1928) for METRO-GOLDWYN-MAYER, and went on to direct some 50 films over the next 30 years. Many of his early sound films challenged Hollywood notions of movies as commercial, escapist entertainment. Notable among his early sound films are *Hallelujah* (1929), with an all-black cast; *The Champ* (1931) and the erotic *Bird of Paradise* (1932). Vidor nearly went broke when he used his own money to write, direct and produce *Our Daily Bread* (1934), about farm life during the Great Depression. Other Vidor films include *Stella Dallas* (1937), *The Citadel* (1938) and *The Fountainhead* (1949), an adaptation of Ayn RAND's novel. His adaptation of Tolstoy's *War and Peace* (1955) featured a fine performance by Henry FONDA, among others, but failed to capture the historical vitality and complexity of the novel. Perhaps his best and most popular later film was the epic western *Duel in the Sun* (1946). He retired from movie-making after *Solomon and Sheba* (1959).

Viet Cong Viet Cong was a derogatory term for Vietnamese communists in South VIETNAM during the VIETNAM WAR. At the end of the war between the French and the VIET MINH (1946–54) 90,000 Viet Minh troops in what was to become South Vietnam were to be repatriated to the north. But the Viet Minh left behind an estimated 5,000 to 10,000 soldiers as a fifth column in the south. Instructed by Hanoi to lie low until 1959, they were then activated by the North Vietnamese Politburo to begin a guerrilla war in the south in an attempt to subvert and overthrow the standing government. Viet Cong forces included "main force" units organized into companies and battalions (and later into regiments and divisions) and after 1964 reinforced by North Vietnamese regular army units. There was also what was called the Viet Cong infrastructure, or VCI, which consisted of a party secretary, a finance and supply unit and information and cultural, social welfare, and proselytizing sections to gain recruits both from the civilian population and the South Vietnamese military. SEARCH-AND-DESTROY operations by both U.S. and South Vietnamese units were designed to neutralize the Viet Cong and North Vietnamese army main force units while clear-and-hold operations, and after 1968 the Phoenix program, were designed to root out the VCI with interdependent operations. The Viet Cong were effectively destroyed by the TET OFFENSIVE of 1968, when believing their propaganda that such an attack would provoke a "general uprising," the Viet Cong led an assault on cities throughout South Vietnam. Thereafter the Viet Cong remnants were cadred and controlled by North Vietnamese regulars.

Viet Minh (contraction of "Vietnam Doc Lap Dong Minh," League for Vietnamese Independence) The Viet Minh was founded at the Eighth Plenum of the Indochina Communist Party in 1941. It was the overall title of the Vietnamese—nationalists as well as communists—who fought the French from 1946 to 1954.

Vietnam (The Socialist Republic of Vietnam) Vietnam is a part of the Indochina Peninsula on the coast of Southeast Asia and comprises an area of 127,210 square miles. At the beginning of the 20th century Vietnam was under French control, but covert nationalist organizations proliferated, including the Indochina Communist Party, founded by Ho Chi Minh in 1930. During World War II Japan occupied the country. After the war the Democratic Republic of Vietnam was formed with Ho as president, but the Potsdam Agreement (1945) temporarily divided the country into the Chinese-occupied north, which recognized Ho's government, and the British-occupied south, which did not. The French seized Saigon, then bombed Haiphong in 1946, starting a war with Ho's communist regime. The French surrendered in 1954, and Vietnam remained divided, with Ho's government in the north and the U.S.-supported regime of Ngo Dinh Diem in the south. Diem's oppressive rule led to the formation of the National Liberation Front (Viet Cong) and his overthrow in 1963. The military regime of General Nguyen Van Thieu came to power in the south in 1965.

U.S. involvement in the Vietnam War escalated when U.S. patrol boats were attacked in the Gulf of Tonkin in 1964 (see Tonkin Gulf Resolution). The southern-based Viet Cong joined the war against the U.S. Peace negotiations began in 1969 among all warring groups; the final Paris Peace Accord was signed in 1973. The Saigon regime fell in 1975, and the country was reunified as the Socialist Republic of Vietnam in 1976, with Pham Van Dong as premier. Vietnam invaded Cambodia in 1978, overthrowing a murderous Khmer Rouge regime that had been killing its own people by the hundreds of thousands and making border raids into Vietnam. From the mid-1980s the government of Nguyen Van Linh focused on rebuilding the country's economy. In 1994 the U.S. lifted its trade embargo and restored diplomatic relations in 1995. Relations have thawed to the extent that in 2000 President William J. Clinton visited Vietnam, and in 2005 Prime Minister Phan Van Khai became the first Vietnamese leader to visit the U.S. since the Vietnam War.

Vietnamese Civil War of 1955–65

With American military advisory assistance, Premier Ngo Dinh Diem of South Vietnam (proclaimed an independent republic after the French Indochina War of 1946–54) gained control of the army and used it to fight three rebellious, well-equipped religious groups (the Binh Xuyen, Hoa Hao and Caodaist sects). In 1955, Binh Xuyen rebels in Saigon (Ho Chi Minh City), South Vietnam's capital, battled government troops until being driven out of the city; the rebels' continued harassment forced Diem to attack them at Can Tho and Vinh Long and in the Seven Mountains. When Diem refused to hold general elections in 1956 as promised, North Vietnam directed Viet Cong rebels to begin a campaign of guerrilla warfare and terrorism to overthrow South Vietnam's regime. Diem suppressed a military revolt against him (1960), but his U.S.-trained army proved generally ineffective against the tactics of the Viet Cong, who established the National Front for the Liberation of South Vietnam. U.S. military aid increased in an effort to wipe out the Viet Cong; South

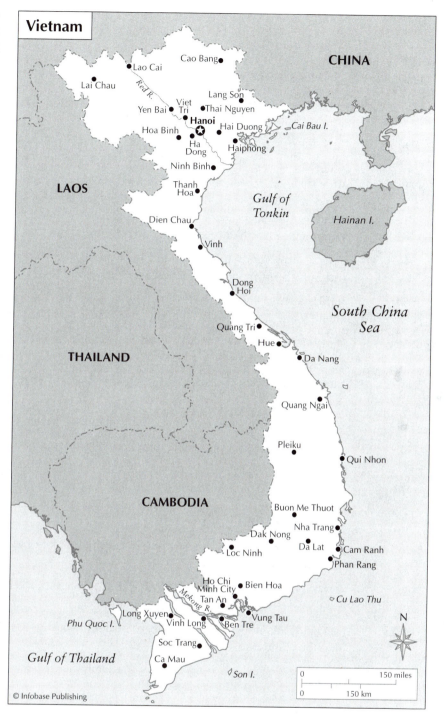

VIETNAM

1930   Ho Chi Minh founds Indochinese Community Party; nationalist uprising in Tonkin, followed by a communist-led peasant revolt.

1940   Japanese forces occupy Vietnam in World War II.

1941   Ho establishes Viet Minh as alliance of communist and nationalist interests; Viet Minh carries on guerrilla resistance to Japanese with some assistance from U.S. military.

1945   After Japanese surrender, Viet Minh takes over Hanoi and Saigon; Emperor Bao Dai abdicates; Democratic Republic of Vietnam (DRV) declared with Ho as president and Hanoi as capital; Potsdam agreement, concluded among U.S., Britain and Soviet Union, temporarily divides Vietnam into north zone, occupied by Chinese, and south zone, occupied by British troops.

1946   Compromise signed by French and Vietnamese governments recognizing DRV as "free state" within French Union; repeated clashes follow and finally French navy bombards Haiphong.

1954   French forces capitulate following 56-day siege of French stronghold, Dien Bien Phu, by Viet Minh forces; Geneva Cease-fire Agreement provisionally partitions country along 17th parallel.

1955   French forces leave country; in south Ngo Dinh Diem becomes chief of state in popular referendum, replacing Emperor Bao Dai; Republic of Vietnam (RVN) proclaimed with capital at Saigon.

1960   National Liberation Front (NLF), South Vietnamese guerrillas supported by Hanoi, launch insurrection.

1961   U.S. and RVN sign treaty of amity; U.S. military presence in country increases 10-fold.

1963   Military junta led by General Duong Van Minh assassinates Diem in coup, allegedly with U.S. cooperation.

1964   U.S. destroyer *Maddox* attacked in Tonkin Gulf by Hanoi torpedo boats; U.S. Congress passes Tonkin Gulf Resolution sanctioning use of U.S. armed forces in Vietnam; 185,000 U.S. troops land by year end.

1965   U.S. President Lyndon Johnson orders continuous bombing raids on North Vietnam below 20th parallel.

1967   In national elections, army chief of staff Nguyen Van Thieu is elected president with Ky as vice president.

1968   NLF and DRV launch Tet offensive, attacking Saigon and 30 provincial capitals; Johnson orders bombing halt.

1969   President Richard Nixon announces Vietnamization policy under which U.S. begins phased pull-out of troops; Ho Chi Minh dies.

1972   U.S. resumes intensive bombing of the north.

1973   Paris Peace Agreement ending U.S. involvement in the Vietnam War is signed by Secretary of State Henry Kissinger and NLF representative Le Duc Tho; last U.S. forces leave Vietnam.

1975   NLF sweeps across south to Saigon; General Duong Van Minh announces unconditional surrender of the Republic of Vietnam.

1976   Vietnam's reunification officially proclaimed under the name Socialist Republic of Vietnam.

1979   In support of Kampuchean National United Front for National Salvation fighting Pol Pot's Khmer Rouge regime, Vietnamese troops overrun Cambodia, seize Phnom Penh, oust Pol Pot government.

1989	Vietnam continues scheduled withdrawal of troops from Cambodia and participates in peace negotiations among the rival interests dividing Cambodia.
1991	Vietnam agrees to resolve cases of American soldiers missing since the Vietnam War.
1995	United States restores diplomatic relations with Vietnam.
2000	U.S. president William Jefferson Clinton visits Vietnam; U.S. and Vietnam sign a trade agreement.
2001	The Communist Party chooses Nong Duc Manh as its new leader.
2002	The Communist Party orders the seizure and destruction of unauthorized books by regime critics; President Tran Duc Luong is reappointed to a second term by the National Assembly, which reappoints Prime Minister Phan Van Khai to a second five-year term.
2005	Prime Minister Phan Van Khai meets U.S. president George W. Bush in the first visit to the U.S. by a Vietnamese leader since the end of the Vietnam War.

Vietnam's "strategic hamlet program" was started in 1962 to resettle peasants in towns defended against the Viet Cong. The Diem government's harassment of opposing Buddhist priests led to riots and self-immolations. On November 1–2, 1963, a military coup toppled the South Vietnamese government; Diem was killed, and a military-controlled provisional regime was established. A period of political instability ensued, with South Vietnam trying to strengthen its anticommunist military effort. By 1965, the Armed Forces Council, headed by Generals Nguyen Cao KY and Nguyen Van THIEU, was run-

ning the country. (See also VIETNAM WAR.)

Vietnamese Uprisings of 1930–31

Failure to gain concessions from the French led the Vietnamese to form revolutionary organizations; the Viet Nam Quoc Dan Dang (VNQDD), led by Nguyen Thai Hoc (1904–30), hoped to achieve an independent democratic government. A planned military uprising began February 9–10, 1930, when native troops at Yen Bai garrison in Tonkin (north Vietnam) mutinied, killing the French officers. The French crushed the uprising before it could spread, and Hoc

and other leaders were beheaded. Afterward many VNQDD members joined the Indochina Communist Party (ICP) formed in 1930 by Nguyen That Thanh, later known as HO CHI MINH (1890–1969). The ICP fomented uprisings in Tonkin and central Vietnam which were harshly suppressed by the French, but the disturbances continued, gaining in vehemence.

Vietnam Veterans Memorial

The Vietnam Veterans Memorial in Washington, D.C., was the dream of Vietnam veteran Jan Skruggs, whose Vietnam Veterans Memorial Fund collected $7 million and conducted a design contest for the memorial. It was won by a 21-year-old architecture student at Yale, Maya Ying Lin, in 1981. Her design consisted of a 594-foot chevron-shaped wall of polished black granite cut into a hillside, with the names of servicemen and servicewomen killed or missing in Vietnam engraved into the surface. Dedicated in 1982, the memorial was the object of some controversy because many veterans felt that its stark modernistic design failed to properly commemorate the sacrifice of the men and women who fought and died in Vietnam. In an effort to accommodate those who felt this way, a more traditional statue of four fighting men was placed near the wall. That statue, by sculptor Frederick E. Hart, was dedicated on Memorial Day, 1984. The wall, the most visited memorial in Washington

American soldier injured by a Vietcong booby trap (LIBRARY OF CONGRESS, PRINTS AND PHOTOGRAPHS DIVISION)

in 1984, now contains the names of 58,022 service members who died or are missing in action in Vietnam.

Vietnam War *(1956–1975)* The country of VIETNAM had been divided at the 17th parallel into the Republic of Vietnam (South Vietnam) and the Democratic Republic of Vietnam (North Vietnam) after the FRENCH INDOCHINA WAR OF 1946–54. In 1956, a civil war broke out between the communist government of the north, supported by the VIET MINH, and the nominally democratic, U.S.-backed government of the south. At first the fighting was mainly bloody guerrilla warfare carried out by Viet Minh soldiers—the so-called VIET CONG—who had returned to their homes in the south and fought there against the Army of the Republic of Vietnam (ARVN). The U.S. provided military advisers to the ARVN and in 1961 authorized them to fight with the South Vietnamese units they were training.

On August 23, 1964, North Vietnamese patrol boats reportedly attacked two U.S. destroyers in the Gulf of TONKIN. U.S. president Lyndon B. JOHNSON was given congressional authorization to repel any armed attack, and U.S. warplanes began bombing raids over North Vietnam. American troops were sent to South Vietnam to participate as allies of the South Vietnamese. North Vietnamese army units marched continuously down the HO CHI MINH TRAIL in Cambodia to fight alongside the Viet Cong. In an attempt to clear the countryside, U.S. forces and the ARVN initiated the tactics called "SEARCH AND DESTROY," "free fire zones" and "pacification." They also regularly bombed military and civilian targets in the north and supply dumps in Cambodia.

At the end of January 1968, the communist-formed NATIONAL LIBERATION FFRONT (NLF) and the Viet Cong launched their great TET OFFENSIVE against 36 provincial cities and wreaked wide destruction in South Vietnam before they withdrew with heavy losses. Their fighting ability, however, amazed the world. Meanwhile, protests and demonstrations occurred frequently in the U.S. against this undeclared war. At that time, 1968–69, about 500,000 American troops were in Vietnam. In July 1968, the U.S. announced a new policy of "Vietnamization," in which the South Vietnamese themselves would gradually do all the fighting. In May of the next year, U.S. Army units began to leave, but air support units remained. In 1972, the communist forces of the NLF crossed the demilitarized zone (DMZ) around the 17th parallel and seized a northern South Vietnamese province. The U.S. retaliated by mining the harbors of Haiphong and other North Vietnamese ports. When the peace talks between the U.S. and North Vietnam, which had been going on sporadically since 1968, broke down entirely in December 1972, U.S. president Richard M. NIXON ordered 11 days of intensive "Christmas bombing" of North Vietnamese cities. Later, talks resumed and led to a cease-fire agreement among the U.S., Viet Cong and North and South Vietnam on January 27, 1973.

But the fighting continued as before, with both sides accusing the other of violations. In 1974, the ARVN began withdrawing troops from distant outposts, and the NLF seized several provincial capitals. The long-expected communist offensive started in January 1975; NLF forces gained control of Vietnam's central highlands. When the South Vietnamese government decided to evacuate its northern cities of Quang Tri and Hue, its collapse and defeat were in sight. Southern coastal cities were abandoned, civilians and army troops took flight and the remaining U.S. personnel escaped from the country by sea and air. On April 30, 1975, South Vietnam surrendered unconditionally to the communists, who occupied its capital, SAIGON (Ho Chi Minh City), without a fight. North and South Vietnam were formally united as the Socialist Republic of Vietnam on July 2, 1976.

Villa, Francisco "Pancho" *(Doroteo Arango Arámbula) (1878?–1923)* Mexican rebel leader. One of the larger-than-life figures of the early 20th century, Pancho Villa was considered a patriot and hero by his followers and a bandit by his enemies. Of peasant origin, he became involved in Mexican national politics when he joined Francisco Madero in the MEXICAN CIVIL WAR OF 1911 and helped overthrow dictator Porfirio DÍAZ. He was also a leading figure in the MEXICAN REVOLT OF 1914–15. He incurred the wrath of the U.S. government when his forces crossed the border and raided the town of Columbus, New Mexico, in 1916 (see VILLA'S RAIDS). For all his involvement in contemporary Mexican affairs, Villa never held any official position. He withdrew from public life in 1920 and was assassinated in 1923.

Villa-Lobos, Hector *(1887–1959)* Brazilian composer. A champion of Brazilian nationalism, Villa-Lobos was one of the most original and prolific composers of the 20th century. He wrote over 1,300 compositions, including several ballets, operas, oratorios, symphonies and string quartets. He re-created the melodies and rhythms of folk songs and Indian songs in his works, developing an eclectic compositional technique. His most important works include the 15 *Chords* (composed 1920–29) with their

Mexican rebel leader Pancho Villa (third from right) became a national hero for his role in Mexico's political struggles. (LIBRARY OF CONGRESS. PRINTS AND PHOTOGRAPHS DIVISION)

vigorous dance rhythms, and the nine suites, *Bachianas Brasileiras* (composed 1932–44). In 1932 he became director of music education in Brazil, introducing bold new approaches that emphasized native resources. He established the Brazilian Academy of Music in Rio de Janeiro in 1945.

Villa's Raids *(1916–1917)* The 1911 overthrow of Mexico's dictator-president Porfirio DÍAZ (1830–1915), set off a struggle for power. Francisco Pancho VILLA (1878?–1923), with American support, was winning until 1915 when Alvaro Obregon (1880–1928) defeated him, elevating Venustiano Carranza (1859–1920), Villa's enemy, as Mexico's chief. The U.S. recognized Carranza. In response, Villa's forces attacked Americans in Mexico, and raided across the border in Columbus, New Mexico, March 9, 1916, killing about a dozen. U.S. president Woodrow WILSON (1859–1924) ordered General John J. PERSHING (1860–1948) on a punitive expedition in pursuit of Villa in Mexico. Pershing withdrew after 11 months, unable to capture Villa. The invasion so angered Mexicans that Villa became a national hero, despite leading rebels until 1920.

Villella, Edward *(1936–)* American dancer and company director, primarily responsible for changing the image of the male ballet dancer through his athletic prowess and virility in performance. Villella danced with the NEW YORK CITY BALLET (1957–78), quickly becoming one of the company's stars and creating roles in such ballets as BALANCHINE's *A Midsummer Night's Dream* (1962). His most famous role was as Balanchine's *Prodigal Son*. After retiring from performing, Villella served as artistic coordinator of the Eglevsky Ballet (1979–84), director of Ballet Oklahoma (1983–85) and founder-director of the Miami City Ballet (1986–present).

Villepin, Dominique-Marie-François-René-Galouzeau de *(1953–)* French diplomat and statesman. Born in Rabat, Morocco, while it was still a French protectorate, Villepin received a diploma from the Institut d'Études Politiques de Paris and graduated from the École Nationale d'Administration in 1980. From 1980 to 1995 he held a variety of posts in the French foreign ministry and French embassies in Washington and New Delhi. When Jacques Chirac became president of France in 1995 he selected Villepin as secretary-general of the president's office. From 2002 to 2004 Villepin served as foreign minister and achieved notoriety because of his diplomatic maneuvering and eloquent speeches in the UN Security Council in opposition to the U.S.'s plans to invade Iraq. In 2004 he became minister of the interior and was named prime minister by Chirac in the following year. He is regarded by many observers as Chirac's protégé and a likely candidate for the presidency at the expiration of Chirac's term in office in 2007. But mass street demonstrations by young French people and their allies in the trade union movement against a Villepin-sponsored employment law caused a sharp drop in his popularity.

Vilna Dispute Conflict between POLAND and LITHUANIA over the city of Vilna, Lithuania's medieval capital. Beginning in 1918, the city was claimed by Poland. It was seized by Polish forces in October 1920 and was incorporated into Poland in 1922. The dispute over the nationality of the city prevented relations between Poland and Lithuania in the period between the two world wars. Vilna was returned to Lithuania by the USSR in October 1939. Under its Lithuanian name, Vilnius, it is now the capital of Lithuania.

Vincent, Francis T. "Fay" *(1938–)* American lawyer, business executive and commissioner of baseball. When Bart GIAMATTI became baseball commissioner in 1989 he chose his friend Fay Vincent as deputy commissioner. Unanimously elected as commissioner following Giamatti's sudden death later that year, Vincent was thrust into the public limelight. The soft-spoken attorney quickly won the respect of citizens, fans and players for his sensitive handling of the 1989 World Series after the deadly 1989 San Francisco earthquake. In July 1990 he took firm action to remove George Steinbrenner as principal owner of the New York Yankees. Before entering baseball, Vincent served as director of the Securities and Exchange Commission's (SEC) Division of Corporation Finance and as chief executive of COLUMBIA PICTURES. In 1992, after receiving a vote of no confidence from the owners of Major League Baseball franchises, Vincent resigned as commissioner.

Vinson, Carl *(1883–1981)* American politician. A Democrat from Georgia, he served in the U.S. House of Representatives for a record 50 years (1914–65). For 14 of those years (1950–64) he was chairman of the powerful House Armed Services Committee; before that, he headed the Naval Affairs Committee (1931–47) and was largely responsible for building up the U.S. Navy during WORLD WAR II. Known as the "Swamp Fox" for his mastery of parliamentary procedure and virtually unchallenged rule over military matters, he was considered a potential secretary of defense in 1950. He ended all speculation about his possible appointment to that post by saying "Shucks, I'd rather go on running the Pentagon from up here." His major role in strengthening the nation's defense was saluted in 1980 when a new nuclear aircraft carrier was named in his honor—the first U.S. Navy warship to be named after a person still living.

Vinson, Fred(erick Moore) *(1890–1953)* American politician, public servant and chief justice of the Supreme Court (1946–53). A graduate of Centre College and its law school in Kentucky, Vinson was a successful local businessman and lawyer before his election to Congress in 1924. He became a member of the Ways and Means Committee, which initiates tax legislation, and a prominent supporter of President Franklin D. ROOSEVELT's NEW DEAL. In 1938 Roosevelt appointed him to the U.S. court of appeals for the District of Columbia. Five years later, Vinson undertook a new career as Roosevelt's director of the Office of Economic Stabilization. In 1945 he briefly headed the Office of War Mobilization and Reconversion. Shortly after Roosevelt's death (1945), President Harry S. TRUMAN named Vinson secretary of the treasury. Vinson quickly became one of Truman's closest and most trusted advisers. In 1946 Truman appointed him chief justice of the Supreme Court. On the Court, the pragmatic Vinson continued to work closely with Truman.

He supported increased governmental regulation and executive power. He dissented in the case of *Youngstown Sheet and Tube Co. v. Sawyer* (1952), in which the majority decided that President Truman had exceeded his authority in seizing steel mills to prevent a steel strike. He wrote several significant opinions in racial discrimination cases and cautiously extended CIVIL RIGHTS for blacks. Truman unsuccessfully tried to persuade Vinson to enter the 1952 presidential race. He died unexpectedly in 1953 while still on the Court, and was succeeded by California governor Earl WARREN.

Virgin Islands, British The British Virgin Islands are on the northwestern edge of the Caribbean and cover a total area of 58 square miles; the capital is Road Town. Between 1872 and 1956 they were administered as part of the Federal Colony of the Leeward Islands. A new constitution granting greater internal self-government was introduced in 1977. Elections in 1975 had the Virgin Islands Party (VIP) and the United Party (UP) each winning three seats. An independent member, former chief minister Willard Wheatley, held the balance of power. He formed a government with the VIP, with himself as chief minister. In 1979 Wheatley's deputy H. Lavitty Stoutt was able to secure enough support after elections in that year to become chief minister. Another tied election result in 1983 allowed the one independent member, Cyril Romney, to form a government with the UP, with Romney as chief minister. In 1986 Romney faced allegations over illegal conduct, and he called an early general election rather than face a vote of "no confidence." In the elections, the VIP won a majority of the seats, and Stoutt returned to power as chief minister. Tourism is the mainstay of the economy, although a series of powerful hurricanes in the 1990s damaged the islands' infrastructure and economy.

Virgin Islands, United States The U.S. Virgin Islands are on the northwestern edge of the Caribbean and cover a total area of 136 square miles; the capital is Charlotte Amalie. The terrain is mostly hilly or rugged and mountainous. Denmark, which had

held the islands since the 17th century, sold them to the U.S. in 1916 for $25,000,000, and they were transferred to U.S. military administration in 1917. U.S. citizenship was granted in 1927. In 1931 a civil administration replaced control by the Navy Department, and the islands came under the control of the Department of the Interior. Revisions of the Organic Act in 1954, which created an elected senate, prompted the development of political parties, the principal parties being affiliates of the U.S. Republican and Democratic Parties. The Virgin Islands were given the right to elect their own governor in 1968, and the first election in 1970 was won by Melvin Evans of the Republicans. In 1974 Cyril King, the leader of a breakaway faction of the Democratic Party known as the Independent Citizen's Movement, was elected governor. King died in 1978 and was succeeded by his deputy, Juan Luis, who was reelected in 1982. The elections in 1986 were won convincingly by the Democrats, and Alexander Farrelly became governor. A referendum on a constitution giving greater autonomy to the islands failed to achieve a sufficient majority in favor when it was held in November 1981.

Virgin Land Campaign In 1953, Soviet Premier KHRUSHCHEV ordered the reclamation of virgin and waste land in Central Asia. Within three years nearly 90 million acres (36.4 million hectares) had been cultivated in Kazakhstan, Siberia and the southern Urals. The aim was self-sufficiency in cereals. After the initial stage of the campaign, intensive rather than extensive cultivation was practiced. The campaign was interpreted by some as an attempt to russify minor nationalities.

Visconti, Luchino (Count di Madrone) (*1906–1976*) Italian stage and film director. Visconti won international fame both for his directorial work in the theater and for his controversial films that often focused on the decadent state of European culture and politics. He began his career as a stage director in Paris, then moved to the Teatro Eliseo in Rome, where he presented an innovative repertoire of modern classic plays by Anton CHEKHOV, Jean COCTEAU and Tennessee WILLIAMS,

among others. Visconti took up film directing in the postwar era and became renowned for his lush visual style and settings that highlighted the moral decay of his characters. Among his best-known films are *The Leopard* (1963), *The Damned* (1969) and *Death in Venice* (1971), an adaptation of the famous novella by Thomas MANN.

Vishnevskaya, Galina (*1926– *) Russian soprano. Born in Leningrad (St. Petersburg), Vishnevskaya spent her childhood in Kronstadt where she began her singing career during World War II. Returning to Leningrad in 1943, she received vocal training and became a member of the Leningrad Light Opera Company. She joined the Bolshoi Opera in 1952, rising steadily to stardom in such roles as Cio-Cio-San in *Madama Butterfly,* Violetta in *La Traviata,* Mimi in *La Boheme, Tosca* and *Aida.* In 1955, while at the Prague Festival, she met the Soviet cellist Mstislav ROSTROPOVICH, and days later the two were married. From 1955 to 1960 she made appearances throughout Europe, making her debut in the U.S. in 1960. Starring in *Aida* in 1961, Vishnevskaya became the first Soviet prima donna to appear with the Metropolitan Opera. After she and her husband sheltered Aleksandr SOLZHENITSYN in 1970, both musicians fell from favor with the Soviet authorities, and their musical activities were severely curtailed. In 1974 they left the USSR, and in 1978 they were stripped of Soviet citizenship. Dividing her time among London, Paris, New York and Washington, Vishnevskaya has since made numerous appearances in the U.S. and Europe. In 2002 Vishnevskaya received the Puccini Prize for her renditions of such Puccini works as *Tosca, Turandot,* and *La Bohème.*

Vishnevsky, Vsevolod (*1900–1951*) Soviet novelist and playwright. He was basically a propagandist, and in the screenplay *The Unforgettable Year 1919* (1949) he flatters STALIN by the sheer exaggeration of his involvement in the CIVIL WAR. His plays included *Trial of the Kronstadt Mutineers* (1921) and *The Optimistic Tragedy* (1932).

Vishniac, Roman (*1897–1990*) Russian-born biologist and photographer. His best-known works were the series of photographs he had taken of Jewish life in eastern Europe in the 1930s. The photographs depicted the lives of ordinary JEWS in GERMANY, POLAND, LITHUANIA, LATVIA, HUNGARY, ROMANIA and CZECHOSLOVAKIA on the eve of the HOLOCAUST. He later concentrated on scientific microphotography, and emigrated to the U.S. in 1940. He became a professor at Pratt Institute and Yeshiva University.

Vitria, Emmanuel *(1920–1987)* French transplant recipient. He lived a record 18 years with a transplanted heart. He became the world's longest surviving heart transplant patient in 1977 upon the death of a U.S. woman who had been operated on one month earlier than he had been. After his transplant, he ignored medical advice and continued to smoke, drink and eat rich foods, apparently with little ill effect.

Vize, Vladimir Yulyevich *(1888–1954)* Russian geographer and explorer. He was part of the team led by G. Y. Sedov that attempted to reach the NORTH POLE (1912–14). He helped organize the North Polar Drift Expedition in 1937, and between 1910 and 1937 he participated in 14 Arctic expeditions.

V-J Day Victory in JAPAN—August 14, 1945. On this day, Emperor HIROHITO formally announced Japan's surrender to the Allies, ending WORLD WAR II.

Vlasov, Andrei Andreyevich *(1900–1946)* Russian general and leader of the anticommunist movement among Soviet PRISONERS OF WAR during WORLD WAR II in Germany. He enlisted in the Red Army in 1919 and played a prominent part in the defense of Kiev and Moscow (1941–42). After capturing him in 1942, German officers persuaded him to assist with the Russian anticommunist movement. He was chairman of the Committee for the Liberation of the Peoples of Russia in 1944. He surrendered to the Americans in 1945 and was returned to the Soviets, who executed him.

Vodopyanov, Mikhail V. *(1900–1980)* Soviet flier and Artic adventurer. He gained prominence in the mid-1930s when he pioneered new polar air routes and took part in the rescue of a marooned scientific expedition along the north coast of Siberia. He is believed to have been the first person to land a plane at the NORTH POLE.

Voice of America (VOA) Radio broadcasting arm of the International Communication Agency. Established in 1942, the VOA began broadcasting in English to Germany during WORLD WAR II. It now broadcasts radio programming in English and 44 other languages for overseas audiences. Its intent is to promote the American viewpoint worldwide, and its programming includes news, analysis of events from Washington, feature programs and music. Its traditional function as an organ of propaganda has aroused controversy and endangered the integrity of its news programming. Despite the end of the COLD WAR, the Voice of America remained active throughout the world, providing an American-based news source through radio, satellite television and the INTERNET in 44 languages. Its Web site offers one of the largest collections of audio and video Web casts available online.

Voinovich, Vladimir *(1932–)* Exiled Russian writer who lives in Paris. After serving in the Soviet army in Poland, Voinovich worked as a carpenter and started to write. In 1963 he published *I Want to Be Honest* in *Novy Mir.* In 1966 he signed a letter defending Yuri DANIEL and Andrei SINYAVSKY and in 1968 signed one protesting the arrest of Alexander GINZBERG and Yuri Galakovsk. In 1973 Voinovich refused to attack Andrei SAKHAROV, although pressure was put on him to do so. In 1974 he was expelled from the Writer's Union and in 1980 went into exile. His satirical novel *The Life and Extraordinary Adventures of Private Ivan Chonkin* has won him much support abroad as well as in Russia, among those who have managed to read it in Samizdat. After the collapse of the Soviet Union Voinovich's Russian citizenship was restored in 1990. He has won many awards, including the Sakharov Award in 2002.

Volkov, Vladislav *(1935–1971)* Soviet cosmonaut, flight engineer aboard the ill-fated *Soyuz 11* flight that initially met with enormous success, including an unprecedented 23-day stay aboard a space station. Headed for home, as the crew jettisoned the docking module a pressure equalization valve blew open prematurely. Volkov and fellow cosmonauts Georgy DOBROVOLKSY and Viktor PATSAYEV were not wearing pressurized suits, and all three died instantly.

Volkswagen German automobile manufacturer; in German the word means "people's car," a name given to an automobile design proposal of Ferdinand PORSCHE in 1933. The encouragement of the HITLER regime led to actual production beginning in 1936. The body design for the rear-engined car was developed by Erwin KOMENDA. In time it became widely popular and was sold in vast numbers worldwide after World War II. The design is regarded as either ugly or as a model of simple functionalism. In English the name "beetle" or "bug" came to describe its rounded, streamlined shape. As increasing prosperity made the original VW seem too spartan in quality and as concerns developed about its safety record, Volkswagen turned to development of a replacement design, with front wheel drive and more comfort. The resulting car, variously named Golf, Polo and Rabbit in different versions and markets, has largely taken the place of the original VW.

Voloshin, Maximilian Alexandrovich *(1877–1931)* Russian symbolist poet. Born in southern Russia, he traveled extensively in Central Asia and around the Mediterranean. He also lived in Paris, studying painting there. Voloshin's poetry reflects the influence that Catholic mysticism, the occult, the Aegean and ancient Greek culture had on him. He wrote a series of historical poems on the subject of the destiny of Russia, as a result of the Revolution, in which he developed the concept of a "Holy Russia." He felt that a country of Christian mysticism was being oppressed by the state.

V-1 and V-2 rockets Rockets developed by Germany and used as flying bombs during WORLD WAR II. The **V-1** was basically a winged airplane with an automatic pilot. Also known as the **buzz bomb,** it was the first of Germany's *Vergeltungs-waffen* (vengeance weapons), so named because they were used to retaliate against Allied air attacks. First proposed in 1939, it made its maiden flight two years later. The V-1 was powered by gasoline and driven by a pulse-jet engine; it measured about 25 feet long, weighed five tons and contained some 1,000 pounds of explosives. Maximum altitude was 3,000 feet, range, under 200 miles, speed, 400 mph. Upon reaching its target, it was directed into a steep dive, its engines cut and its warhead electrically detonated upon contact with the ground. It arrived with a whine and then an abrupt silence, during which those attacked had only seconds to seek shelter. Because the V-1 could not be directed with any precision to a specific target but fell at random within a general area, it had limited military usefulness; rather, it was a terror weapon, designed to demoralize Britain's civilian population. More than 8,000 V-1s were used to bomb London in attacks launched near Calais, France, beginning in 1944.

The much more advanced V-2 was developed from 1938 to 1942 at PEENE-MUNDE, Germany, under the direction of Wernher VON BRAUN. It, too, had a liquid-propelled jet engine; however, the fuel was methyl alcohol, and it carried its own liquid oxygen, which was used as a combustion booster. This feature enabled the V-2 to cruise at oxygen-depleted high altitudes. The cigar-shaped rocket was 45 feet long and 66 inches in diameter; it weighed 13 tons, with a one-ton warhead, and its range was over 200 miles. The V-2 was fired vertically to an altitude of some 15–18 miles. It then went into an inclined trajectory, guided by graphite flaps controlled by a preset gyroscope and directed by radio. Its maximum speed was some 3,600 mph. The V-2 was successfully test-launched for the first time in October 1942. From September 6, 1944, to March 27, 1945, over 4,000 V-2 rockets were launched against London, Antwerp and other targets. The V-2 was the precursor of many modern intercontinental ballistic missiles and spacecraft; several of the project's engineers were brought to the U.S. after the war and became leading figures in the U.S. space program. (See also OPERATION PAPERCLIP.)

Vonnegut, Kurt, Jr. (1922–) American author. Although his works were generally ignored by mainstream critics until the publication of his novel Cat's Cradle (1963), Vonnegut is now regarded as a master of contemporary fiction. His dominant themes of the dehumanizing effects of technology, the need for kindness and the struggle of man against a hostile universe are presented in a style that blends irony, satire, fantasy, the tragicomic and a colloquial speech that contains many coined words. His first novel, Player Piano, was published in 1952. In 1969 he published his best-known work, Slaughter-house Five, which re-creates his experiences as a prisoner of war in Dresden during the Allied firebombing in WORLD WAR II. Other major works include the novels Breakfast of Champions (1973) and Slapstick (1976), the play Happy Birthday, Wanda June (1970), the story collection Welcome to the Monkey House (1968), Hocus Pocus (1990) and Timequake (1997). He has also taught at several schools, including Harvard University.

Von Stade, Frederica (1945–) American singer. An outstanding mezzo-soprano, she gained international renown as Cherubino in The Marriage of Figaro. She made her Metropolitan Opera debut in a small role in The Magic Flute in 1970 and her European debut as Cherubino at the Royal Theater at Versailles in 1973. She has performed at the Glyndebourne and Salzburg Festivals and with opera companies throughout the world. Her many roles include Rosina in The Barber of Seville and Melisande in Pelleas and Melisande. In 1998 von Stade performed Richard Danielpour's Elegies, a work based on her father's experiences in World War II (1939–45).

Voroshilov, Kliment Efremovich (1881–1969) Soviet military and political leader, and a close friend of STALIN. He joined the Bolsheviks in 1903, organized the workers of Lugansk in the 1905 revolution and was subsequently deported. After returning to RUSSIA in 1917, Voroshilov earned an outstanding military reputation as a Red Army commander during the Civil War. He was a member of the central committee of the Communist Party and entered the Politburo in 1926. Following Stalin's death in 1953, he was appointed chairman of the Presidium of the Supreme Soviet. In 1960, however, he was dropped from the Presid-

ium and in 1961 was expelled from the central committee; he was later restored to full membership. (See also REVOLUTION OF 1905.)

Vorster, B(althazar) J(ohannes) "John" (1915–1983) Prime minister of SOUTH AFRICA (1966–78). He was interned during World War II because of his pro-Nazi sympathies. A member of South Africa's Nationalist Party, he was elected to the South African parliament in 1953. In the early 1960s he served as minister of justice and police. During this time he created a repressive security apparatus, banned multiracial organizations, arrested thousands who opposed APARTHEID and crushed South Africa's Communist Party. As prime minister, he staunchly upheld apartheid. Implementing a program conceived by his predecessor, Hendrik VERWOERD, Vorster established nominally independent "homelands" or mini-states for the nation's blacks; in reality, these states, which occupied the poorest land, were economically and politically dependent on South Africa. Toward the end of his tenure as prime minister, Vorster eased some discriminatory policies, opening more theaters, hotels and parks to blacks and allowing racially mixed sports competitions. In 1978 he stepped down because of ill health, accepting the ceremonial post of president. However, he resigned the presidency in 1979 after a government report concluded that he had been involved in the so-called **Muldergate Scandal**, the illegal state funding of a multi-million-dollar propaganda program while he was prime minister.

Voskhod A modified Soviet VOSTOK spacecraft, used for two manned missions in 1964–65. Its name means "ascent."

Vostok The first manned Soviet spacecraft. Its name means "east." (See also Yuri GAGARIN.)

Voting Rights Acts of 1965 Landmark U.S. CIVIL RIGHTS legislation that enforced voting rights for blacks throughout the U.S. Although the post–Civil War Fifteenth Amendment to the Constitution and three 20th-century Civil Rights laws guaranteed equal political rights to blacks, this promise remained largely unfulfilled for nearly 100 years after the war. Various devices, including poll taxes, literacy tests and outright harassment and intimidation, were used to prevent blacks from voting. The Voting Rights Act was passed to eliminate these injustices. The act basically gave the federal government the power to supervise local registration procedures and elections wherever voting participation was below 50 percent. In practice, the law applied only in the South, where blacks were being systematically excluded. Under the law local voting laws would be valid only on federal court approval. Federal law would control voter requirements, and stiff fines were imposed for violation of the act. Once the federal government became involved, universal suffrage became more than an empty promise.

Voyager 1 Voyager 1 was actually the second-launched of the two ambitious U.S. Voyager space probes. However, it was designated 1 because its path enabled it to reach its destination before VOYAGER 2. Launched September 5, 1977, it was designed to fly past the largest planets of the solar system, Jupiter and Saturn, as well as the outer planets, Uranus and Neptune. It passed Jupiter in March 1979 and reached Saturn more than a year and a half later, in November 1980, sending back the first close-up pictures of those giants. In 1998 *Voyager 1* surpassed the distance record set by NASA's *Pioneer 10* space probe. In November 2003 *Voyager 1* approached the boundary of the solar system, placing it 8.4 billion miles from the Earth.

Voyager 2 The U.S. *Voyager 2* spacecraft, launched on August 20, 1977, passed within 3,000 miles of the planet Neptune August 24–25, 1989. The fly-by produced a multitude of striking images and startling discoveries about the distant planet, climaxing a 12-year interplanetary mission. The mission earlier also yielded revelations about Jupiter, Saturn and Uranus. The mission's success dramatically exceeded the initial expectations of its planners. Covering four of the five outer planets of the solar system, it was the most far-ranging exploration of the planets since the space age began with the launch of *SPUTNIK* in 1957. With the completion of the mission, only Pluto, the outermost planet, remained unexplored by spacecraft. The mission was directed by scientists at NASA's JET PROPULSION LABORATORY in Pasadena, California. The mission's chief project scientist since 1972, Edward C. Stone, called it "a journey of a lifetime."

Voznesensky, Andrei A. *(1933–)* Russian poet. After studying architecture Voznesensky embarked on a full-time career as poet. His first work was published in 1958, and he has traveled abroad on reading tours, which have included several visits to the U.S. He enjoyed the approval of the regime apart from a short time in 1963. His first book, *Mosaica* (1960), consists mostly of lyrical poems; later collections of his work, such as *The Triangular Pear* (1962), show greater subtlety and irony.

Vreeland, Diana (Dalziel) *(1903?– 1989)* Legendary fashion arbiter and editor. She was editor of *Harper's Bazaar* (1939–62) and of *Vogue* (1962–71). Under her editorship, the magazines chronicled the most extreme examples of glamour and the newest fashions. She was fired as editor of *Vogue* in 1971 for promoting fashions that were considered too avant-garde to be marketable. In 1973 she began a new career mounting historical fashion exhibits for the Metropolitan Museum of Art's Costume Institute.

Vyborg, Battle of See FINNISH WAR OF INDEPENDENCE.

Vyborg Manifesto About 180 deputies met in Vyborg to protest the dissolution of the first DUMA by NICHOLAS II in July 1906. The largest majority were Kadets, and the manifesto urged the people not to pay taxes or undertake military service when conscripted. The plan failed, and the deputies were arrested, given three months' imprisonment and, probably more important for Russia, deprived of their right to stand for election to the second Duma.

Vyshinsky, Andrei Yanuaryevich *(1883–1954)* Soviet lawyer and politician. He became public prosecutor in 1931 and was soon notorious for the rancor and vindictiveness with which he conducted state trials, notably in the Metropolitan-Vickers trial (1933) and the GREAT PURGES of 1936–37. After 1940 he became active in foreign affairs and was MOLOTOV's successor as foreign minister (1949–53), having been deputy minister (1940–49). As a delegate to the UNITED NATIONS he often attacked Western policies with the same venom that he had shown in the Soviet courts.

W

Wafd (Arab., "delegation") Main nationalist party of interwar EGYPT. It was discredited by wartime cooperation with the British, and considered corrupt by NASSER and SADAT. Following its 1950 election victory, FREE OFFICERS encouraged civil unrest, and Wafd was dismissed by King FAROUK before he himself was deposed in 1952. Wafd and all other Egyptian parties were dissolved in 1953.

Wagner, John Peter "Honus" ("The Flying Dutchman") *(1874– 1955)* American baseball player. Wagner spent 56 years with the Pittsburgh organization, the first 17 years (1900–17) as a player, the remainder as a coach. One of the greatest shortstops of all time, his long arms and huge hands added to his legendary fielding skill. Over the course of his career, he played every position except catcher. He led the league in hitting eight times and topped the .300 mark 17 times. A Honus Wagner baseball card is now worth over $100,000, or 10 times more than Wagner was ever paid in any year of his career. He was named to the Hall of Fame in 1936.

Wahabbism A fundamentalist sect of Sunni Islam. Founded in the 18th century by Muhammad ibn Abd al Wahab, Wahabbism promotes the purification of Islam and Islamic society by eradicating foreign and heretical influences and the adoption of a conservative and literal interpretation of SHARIA, or Islamic law. Wahabbism found its greatest support in the Nejd, a region on the western part of the Arabian Peninsula, where its clergy provided the House of Saud with material and moral support in its successful campaign to take control of much of the Arabian Peninsula and establish in 1932 the Kingdom of SAUDI ARABIA. In turn, the Saudi royal family promised that once it had obtained control of the holy pilgrimage cities of Mecca and Medina, which had been controlled for centuries by the Hashemite dynasty, it would purify the city of all non-Muslim elements, ensure both towns' total devotion to practitioners of Islam and maintain the strictest possible interpretation of sharia as the law of the land. Since defeating the Hashemites in 1926, the Saudi dynasty has honored that promise.

In the latter half of the 20th century, Wahabbism came under increasing criticism from secular states for its devotion to ISLAMISM, a literal application of the Koran, the Islamic holy book, to all facets of life. During the rule of Egyptian president Gamel Abdel NASSER, Wahabbi clerics provided financial support to the like-minded Egyptian Muslim Brotherhood, which sought to undermine Nasser's efforts to reduce the presence of sharia in Egyptian society. Following the start of the AFGHAN CIVIL WAR (1979–89), many Saudis espousing Wahabbism, such as Osama BIN LADEN, traveled to Afghanistan to form bands of Islamic freedom fighters known as MUJAHIDEEN, where they helped defeat the Soviet occupation and overthrow the pro-Soviet government in Kabul. Saudi Wahabbi clerics and congregation members were also suspected of assisting the independence movement of the predominantly Islamic Yugoslav provinces of BOSNIA AND HERZEGOVINA (1992–95) and KOSOVO (1995). After the terrorist attacks on the U.S. of SEPTEMBER 11, 2001, Saudi Arabian officials have come under increasing pressure from the U.S. to curtail extremist Wahabbi clerics within their country, who have called for the total expulsion of American military forces and business interests from Saudi territory. Wahabbi militants were suspected of masterminding terrorist attacks at three American housing compounds in the Saudi capital of Riyadh on May 12, 2003. While Saudi ministers have promised to crack down on those involved in these attacks, they have declined to condemn Wahabbism, claiming that only a fringe element has espoused terrorist methods.

Wailers, The See Bob MARLEY.

Wainwright, Jonathan Mayhew *(1883–1953)* American general who commanded the U.S. and Filipino forces on BATAAN and CORREGIDOR after General MACARTHUR was ordered to leave in March 1942. Outnumbered and desperately short of supplies, Wainwright's forces held out until May 6, 1942, when they surrendered to the Japanese. Wainwright was mistreated as a PRISONER OF WAR for more than three years. He was freed after the liberation of the Philippines and was present on the battleship USS *MISSOURI* when the Japanese formally surrendered to General MacArthur in Tokyo Harbor. Wainwright was awarded the Congressional Medal of Honor.

Waite, Terry *(1940–)* Lay official of the Church of England. In the 1980s, as a special representative of Archbishop of Canterbury Robert RUN-CIE, Waite held a number of meetings with terrorists in LEBANON to win the release of several Western hostages. On January 20, 1987, Waite disappeared in Beirut and was taken hostage himself. He was released from captivity in 1991.

Waiting for Godot *(1952)* Two-act play by Irish-born author Samuel BECKETT; perhaps the classic work of the school of playwriting known as THEATER OF THE ABSURD. Written by Beckett in 1952, *Waiting for Godot* received its first public performance in 1953 and has since become a standard part of the theater repertoire around the world. The plot concerns two down and out men, Vladimir and Estragon, failed suicides who are waiting in vain for a man named Godot—whose identity and purpose are never clarified—to meet them as agreed upon. Vladimir and Estragon display an oddly British music-hall style of humor as they bide their time on the roadside. Passing them by are two strange vagabonds, Pozzo and Lucky, who in act one behave as ring-master and slave but find their roles reversed in act two, when a blinded Pozzo is now led along by Lucky. Interpretations of *Waiting for Godot* abound, ranging from a depiction of existential nihilism to a modernist religious parable on the nature of faith.

Wake Island Atoll in the central Pacific, between Hawaii and Guam; Japanese outpost during WORLD WAR II. Japanese forces overran Wake's small garrison of U.S. Marines on December 23, 1941; the island was retaken by U.S. forces in September 1945.

Waksman, Selman Abraham *(1888–1973)* Ukranian-American microbiologist. Waksman immigrated to the U.S. in 1910 and received his Ph.D. from the University of California at Berkeley in 1918. For the next four decades, he taught at Rutgers, where he had done his undergraduate work.

In 1939 Waksman began a systematic search among soil microbes for germ-destroying compounds he called "antibiotics." In 1943 he isolated the antibiotic streptomycin from the mold *Streptomyces griseus* and discovered that it was successful in treating a type of tuberculosis as well as other diseases. In 1952 he was awarded the NOBEL PRIZE for physiology or medicine for this work.

Walcott, Derek *(1930–)* West Indian poet and playwright, widely considered one of the finest English-language poets of his generation. Born in St. Lucia of English and black West Indian parentage, Walcott was educated at St. Mary's College (class of 1953), St. Lucia, and the University of the West Indies, where he taught comparative literature. He began his writing career in Trinidad as a book reviewer, art critic and playwright, and in 1959 he founded the Trinidad Theater Workshop. His first work, *Twenty-five Poems*, was published in 1948. He has since written more than 20 volumes of poetry and plays, combining lush imagery and Caribbean dialect with traditional English literary forms. Selections from his nine books of poetry, including the entire text of his autobiographical *Another Life,* are gathered in his *Collected Poems 1948–1984* (1986); his plays are collected in *Dreams on Monkey Mountain and Other Plays* (1970). Later work includes *The Arkansas Testament* (1987) and *Omeros* (1990), a Homerian epic embedded in the history and contemporary rhythm of Caribbean life. Walcott has taught at various universities in the U.S., including Harvard and Boston University. In 1981 he was awarded a MacArthur Fellowship. Walcott won the 1992 Nobel Prize in literature and the Queen's Medal for Poetry in 1998. Since *The Arkansas Testament*, Walcott has published three new poetry collections—*Omeros* (1990), *The Bounty* (1997) and *Tiepolo's Hound* (2000).

Waldheim, Kurt *(1918–)* Austrian diplomat and president (1986–92). Waldheim entered the Austrian diplomatic service immediately after World War II. He was Austria's foreign minister from 1968 to 1970 and was an unsuccessful presidential candidate in 1971. He succeeded U THANT as

secretary-general of the UNITED NATIONS in 1971. Regional conflicts and mutual suspicion between the power blocs hampered Waldheim's efforts, especially in the Middle East, while he lacked any practical means of overcoming the procrastinating tactics of the South Africans over NAMIBIA. He retired from the UN in 1982. In 1986 Waldheim was elected president of Austria amid controversy surrounding his alleged Nazi activities during World War II. He was subsequently barred from entering the U.S. on a state visit. In 1992 Waldheim chose not to run for reelection as Austria's president.

Walesa, Lech *(1943–)* Polish labor leader and statesman, president of POLAND. (1990–95). Born in a village near Warsaw, the son of a carpenter, Walesa attended a state vocational school and became an electrician. After military service, he began work (1967) in the Lenin Shipyard at Gdańsk. There he became a shop steward and was active in the movement to promote workers' rights. In 1976, after joining protests against the economic policies of Edward GIEREK, Walesa was fired from his shipyard post. Supporting himself with odd jobs, he became more active in Poland's labor movement, and in 1979 signed a charter demanding independent trade unions and the right to strike. When strikers seized the Lenin Shipyard in 1980, Walesa was reinstated and became head of a strike coordinating committee. Later that year he was named chairman of the newly approved SOLIDARITY union and soon became known for his moderate and even-handed approach, his ability to win concessions from the government and his willingness to compromise with authorities in order to solidify union gains. When Prime Minister Wojciech JARUZELSKI imposed martial law and outlawed Solidarity in December 1981, Walesa and other union leaders were imprisoned. He was released after nearly a year of solitary confinement. For his activities on behalf of Poland's workers, Walesa was awarded the 1983 Nobel Peace Prize, and he was widely hailed as a national hero. Throughout the 1980s Walesa trod a careful path but continued to press the government for reforms, often in direct dialogue with communist leaders. By the late 1980s, Wałesa had achieved many of his goals, including the re-legalizatiion of Solidarity and the promise of free elections. In the 1990 presidential elections, Wałesa defeated Premier Tadeusz MAZOWIECKI, a Solidarity intellectual, but was forced into a runoff with expatriate businessman Stanisław Tyminski, whom he bested in a landslide. Wałeşa remained president until Solidarity's defeat in the 1995 elections, after which he retired from public life.

Walker, Alice *(1944–)* Black American writer. Born in Georgia and educated at Sarah Lawrence College, Walker is a prolific writer of fiction, essays and poetry. Walker's work is marked by a keen interest in African-American history and culture and a strong spiritual sensibility. She is perhaps best known for her novel *The Color Purple.* The book was a great commercial success and was made into a film, but was also controversial for its use of dialect, which some critics thought stereotypical, and its negative portrayal of black men. It was adapted as a musical play in 2005. Walker is the author of several other novels (including *Meridian,* about the CIVIL RIGHTS struggle of the 1950s and '60s) poetry collections (including *Goodnight, Willie Lee* and *Ill See You in the Morning*), volumes of short stories and essays, *By the Light of My Father's Smile: A Novel,* and a biography of Langston HUGHES for children. Walker founded a small publishing house as well. She is also the editor of an anthology of work by Zora Neale HURSTON, and is largely responsible for a renewed interest in Hurston, an important figure in the HARLEM RENAISSANCE. In 1983 Walker received the Pulitzer Prize for *The Color Purple* (1982). Walker has since continued to produce anthologies, essays, memoirs and novels, including *Horses Make a Landscape Look More Beautiful* (1984), *Living by the Word: Selected Writings, 1973–1977* (1988), *To Hell with Dying* (1988), *The Temple of My Familiar* (1989), *Possessing the Secret of Joy* (1993), *By the Light of My Father's Smile: A Novel* (1999), *Absolute Trust in the Goodness of the Earth; New Poems* (2003) and *The Third Life of Grange Copeland* (2003).

Walker, James "Jimmy" *(1881–1946)* Mayor of NEW YORK CITY (1925–32). Dubbed "Beau James" by the tabloid press because of his sartorial splendor, Jimmy Walker was a handsome and popular mayor known to frequent fashionable night-spots during the prosperous 1920s. Walker was known for his quick wit; in a debate over a censorship law while he was in the state legislature, Walker commented that he had never seen a girl ruined by a book. Walker, the son of Irish immigrants, was a loyal member of Tammany Hall—the New York Democratic club—served in the state legislature for 16 years and was ultimately rewarded with the mayoralty. He had previously worked for 10 years as a songwriter on New York's Tin Pan Alley. Walker's luck ran out shortly after the STOCK MARKET CRASH OF 1929. Although previous city administrations had been characterized by graft and corruption, the level of wrongdoing escalated under Walker and was ultimately exposed in a series of public investigations. One commissioner explained that his ill-gotten gains appeared magically in a tin box under his mattress. Walker resigned in 1932 and fled to Europe to seek his girlfriend, Betty Compton, whom he later married. He was succeeded by the reform mayor Fiorello LAGUARDIA.

Walker, Joseph *(1921–1966)* U.S. test pilot. Between March 1960 and August 1963, Walker made 25 flights in the X-15 experimental rocket plane at Edwards Air Force Base. He set world record in both speed and altitude, taking the feisty plane to 4,104 miles per hour and to an altitude, on August 22, 1963, of almost 67 miles (354,300 feet). Walker made two X-15 flights to altitudes higher than 62 miles, which is the International Aeronautical Federation (FAI) standard for qualifying spaceflights. He died in a mid-air crash.

Wall, Max (Maxwell George Lorimer) *(1908–1990)* British comedian, best known for his music hall performances in the 1920s and 1930s. Wall's most famous creation was the character Professor Wallofski. The character's bizarre walk was said to have inspired John Cleese of MONTY PYTHON'S FLYING CIRCUS. Wall won renewed popularity

late in life in the late 1960s, appearing in a number of serious theater works, including Samuel BECKETT'S *WAITING FOR GODOT* and *Krapp's Last Tape.*

Wallace, George Corley *(1919–1998)* American politician. Born into a lower-middle-class family in Clio, Alabama, Wallace earned a law degree from the University of Alabama (1942), served in World War II and was later a circuit court judge (1953–59). He began his political career as a Democrat and a committed segregationist. Elected governor in 1962, during his first inaugural speech he vowed that he would fight for "segregation now, segregation tomorrow, and segregation forever." He gained national attention in 1963 when, defying a desegregation order from President John F. KENNEDY, he stood in a doorway of the University of Alabama to block the admission of two black students; he yielded after the state National Guard was federalized. He also opposed the integration of local schools, but again backed down after receiving a federal court order.

In 1965 he tried to prevent Martin Luther KING, Jr.'s, march from SELMA to MONTGOMERY. Capitalizing on disaffection with both major parties and stressing STATES' RIGHTS, populist views and a hawkish position on the VIETNAM WAR (see HAWKS), Wallace campaigned for the U.S. presidency as an independent in 1968; he won 45 electoral votes and nearly 10 million popular votes. While

Alabama governor George Wallace (LIBRARY OF CONGRESS. PRINTS AND PHOTOGRAPHS DIVISION)

campaigning for the Democratic presidential nomination in 1972, he was shot and partially paralyzed. During the late 1970s and the 1980s, Wallace reversed many of his earlier positions on race relations and gained new credibility among black voters. Wallace served longer than any other governor of Alabama (1963–67, 1971–75, 1975–79, 1983–87); he was also the behind-the-scenes power while his first wife, Lurleen Wallace, was governor (1967–71). (See also CIVIL RIGHTS MOVEMENT.)

Wallace, Henry A(gard) *(1888–1965)* American politician, presidential candidate and vice president (1941–45). Born and raised in Iowa, Wallace was the son of a noted agriculturist who served as U.S. secretary of agriculture in the administration of President Warren G. HARDING. Wallace himself soon earned his own reputation as an agricultural expert and a champion of farmers. During the 1920s he changed his party affiliation from Republican to Democrat. Chosen as secretary of agriculture by President Franklin D. ROOSEVELT in 1933, Wallace helped shape the active federal farm policy under the NEW DEAL. Most notably, he reorganized the Department of Agriculture and helped draft the Agricultural Adjustment Act of 1933. He also spoke out in support of labor reform, CIVIL RIGHTS and welfare legislation. Roosevelt chose Wallace as his vice presidential running mate in 1940. Wallace served one term as vice president, but proved too liberal for many in the party, and Roosevelt was persuaded to replace him with Harry S TRUMAN as his running mate in 1944. Named secretary of commerce by Roosevelt, Wallace continued to serve in that post under Truman, but became increasingly critical of Truman's anticommunist foreign policy. Wallace took a naive view of Joseph STALIN's repressive domestic and expansive foreign policies, and pushed for U.S. cooperation with the USSR. Forced to resign in September 1946, Wallace continued to attack Truman's foreign policy, criticizing not only U.S. intervention in GREECE but also the MARSHALL PLAN. In 1948 Wallace and the Progressive Citizens of America (PCA), which included many Communist Party members, launched a third-party presidential campaign. Al-

U.S. vice president Henry A. Wallace (LIBRARY OF CONGRESS, PRINTS AND PHOTOGRAPHS DIVISION)

though at first a credible candidate, Wallace soon lost support from liberals because of his refusal to repudiate Communists within the PCA. He won 1.2 million votes in the election but failed to carry any states. Although he continued to make controversial statements, Wallace's political influence declined thereafter.

Wallace, Irving *(1916–1990)* American author. His books were frequently panned by the critics, but they were read by millions of people. His 16 novels and 17 nonfiction works were reported to have sold a total of more than 120 million copies around the world. Among these were *The Chapman Report* (1960), *The Prize* (1962) and *The Fan Club* (1974). With his son, David Wallechinsky, he wrote *The People's Almanac* (1975) and *The Book of Lists* (1977).

Wallenberg, Raoul *(1912–19?)* Swedish diplomat. Posted as an envoy to Hungary in 1944, Wallenberg is credited with rescuing some 20,000 Hungarian JEWS from the Nazi HOLOCAUST. He used a number of methods to secure their escape, often issuing them Swedish passports. He disappeared into the Soviet sector in 1945. It is known that he was arrested, and the USSR reported his death in 1947. However, a number of reliable witnesses have reported seeing him after

that date, alive in Soviet prison camps. Wallenberg was awarded an honorary American citizenship in 1981.

Wallenstein, Alfred *(1898–1983)* American conductor and cellist, believed to be the first native-born American ever to conduct a major symphony orchestra. He was principal cellist with the Chicago Symphony Orchestra and the New York Philharmonic before becoming music director of the Los Angeles Philharmonic from 1943 to 1956. As music director of WOR radio in New York City from 1935 to 1945, he also pioneered the programming of classical music on radio.

Waller, Thomas "Fats" *(1904–1943)* During the 1920s and 1930s, Thomas "Fats" Waller won enormous success as a songwriter, entertainment "personality" and gifted jazz pianist. His unique keyboard style was marked by a strong rhythmic pulse, springhtly right-hand improvisations and strong left-hand harmonic underpinnings reconfigured from the "stride" tradition that Waller had learned as a youth in his native New York City from stride piano greats Russell Brooks and James P. Johnson. His lithe virtuosity was further refined through piano studies with Leopold Godowsky. In 1922, Waller made his first solo recordings; greater recognition came with his effervescent accompaniments for BLUES singers Bessie SMITH and Alberta Hunter. Waller gained widespread prominence as a radio personality where his satiric reframings of popular songs made his

Entertainer and jazz pianist Fats Waller (LIBRARY OF CONGRESS, PRINTS AND PHOTOGRAPHS DIVISION)

singing and pianistic talents nationally known. However, Waller is best remembered as the composer of such ingenious and witty songs as "Ain't Misbehavin'," "Honeysuckle Rose,' "Squeeze Me," "Jitterbug Waltz" and "Keepin' Out of Mischief Now," all standards in the repertory of the American popular song; many of these were written for such successful and pioneering all-black Broadway shows as *Keep Shufflin'* (1928) and *Hot Chocolates* (1929). Waller also is credited as being the first keyboardist to successfully exploit the jazz possibilities of the pipe organ and electric Hammond organ.

Wallis, Sir Barnes Neville *(1887–1979)* British aircraft designer who invented the "bouncing bombs" used to destroy German dams along the RUHR River in WORLD WAR II. Wallis's invention and the bombing mission were the subjects of a postwar book and film, *The Dam Busters* (1954). Working for Vickers, he also designed the World War II Wellington bomber. As chief of aeronautical research for the British Aircraft Corporation (1945–71), he designed the first successful swing-wing airplane. Wallis was knighted in 1968.

Wallis, Hal B. *(1899–1986)* American film producer. From his early career with WARNER BROS. through his later days as an independent, he was associated with some of HOLLYWOOD's best-known films, including *Little Caesar* (1930), *The Maltese Falcon* (1941), *Casablanca* (1942), *Come Back, Little Sheba* (1952) *and True Grit* (1969). He was credited with the discovery of many actors, including Burt LANCASTER and Kirk DOUGLAS. He helped make stars out of an array of others, including Edward G. ROBINSON, Humphrey BOGART and Bette DAVIS. *Rooster Cogburn* (1975) was his last film.

Wallis and Futuna Islands The Wallis and Futuna Islands are volcanic islands in the South Pacific Ocean, north of New Zealand and northeast of New Caledonia. They cover a total area of 106 square miles; the capital is Mata-Utu. The Wallis and Futuna Islands were first settled over 2,000 years ago. Dutch navigators arrived at Futuna in 1616. Wallis takes its name from the English sea captain who was the first European to land there in 1767. In 1886 Wallis became a French protectorate, Futuna following in 1887. The islands assumed the official status of a colony of France in 1924. During WORLD WAR II Wallis was an important American military base, and the runway at Hihifo remains of strategic value to the French.

Wall Street Journal, The American newspaper founded in 1889. Established by Charles H. Dow and Edward D. Jones, *The Wall Street Journal* is now owned and published by Dow Jones & Co. The *Journal* has a circulation of approximately 2,000,000 daily, the largest of any American paper, and is published in four regional editions. Its main emphasis is business, financial and economic news, but it also contains general news and features. Its editorial policy is conservative, supporting a free market economy and corporate America.

Wal-Mart U.S.-based global chain of retail stores. In 1962 Sam Walton, the corporation's founder, opened the first Wal-Mart in Rogers, Arkansas. The store offered a variety of household and sporting goods, clothing, electronic devices, food items, toys and entertainment items. By purchasing large quantities from these items' producers, Wal-Mart was able to reduce wholesale purchasing costs and sell these items at retail prices substantially lower than local grocery and convenience stores. Although it was originally only a regional department store powerhouse, Wal-Mart developed a national purchasing, supply and retail network by the 1990s, when it began to compete effectively with other national retail stores like Kmart and Target, as well as regional retail stores like Ames and Ann & Hope. In 1998 Wal-Mart announced its plans to test-market a series of "Super-Centers" that would contain not only the retail items found in regular Wal-Mart stores, but also groceries and an in-house pharmacy, deli, bakery and seafood section. Along with its regular stores and Super-Centers, Wal-Mart also owns Sam's Club, a chain of warehouse-style stores that sell items in bulk to the club's paying members.

As Wal-Mart began to expand its network of stores, local businesses in small towns near the site of projected Wal-Mart stores began to band together, in organizations such as Sprawl-Busters, and organize boycotts of Wal-Mart stores. These organizations argued that while the national chain offered products at lower prices, it paid its employees the minimum hourly wage and would divert profits from the community to Wal-Mart's corporate accounts. The chain has also drawn increasing criticism for its opposition to the unionization of its employees, as was indicated by Wal-Mart's decision to terminate its meat-cutting operations for its Super-Centers following the decision by the meat-cutting employees of one superstore to form a union.

Walpole, Sir Hugh Seymour *(1884–1941)* British novelist. Born in New Zealand, Walpole was raised and educated in Great Britain. His first successful novel was his third, *Perrin and Mr. Traill* (1911), which reflected his brief experiences as a schoolmaster. *The Dark Forest* (1916) drew on his experiences in the Russian Red Cross during World War I, and also dealt with homosexuality. A friend of Virginia WOOLF, Walpole admired literary MODERNISM and worried that his own popular fiction was too traditional. Other works include *Jeremy* (1919), *The Cathedral* (1922) and a series of historical novels beginning with *Rogue Herris* (1930), which are set in the Lake District where Walpole lived. Walpole was unattractively portrayed as Alroy Dear in Somerset MAUGHAM's *Cakes and Ale* (1930) Walpole was knighted in 1937.

Walser, Robert *(1878–1956)* Swiss novelist and poet. Walser was a haunting and evocative literary visionary whose German language stories and novels were greatly admired by contemporaries, including Hermann HESSE and Franz KAFKA. Born in Biel, in central Switzerland, Walser left school at age 14 and worked at a series of odd jobs to support both his fondness for lengthy walking tours and his nascent writing. His first poems and stories appeared in 1898, and Walser continued to write in those genres over the next three decades. The best-known of his eight novels, only four of which survive, is *Jakob von Gunten* (1908). Walser's writings were never commercially successful, and he endured fierce poverty. In 1929, he committed himself to the Waldau Sanatorium near Berne, Switzerland, where he was diagnosed as schizophrenic. After an involuntary transfer in 1933 to a sanitorium in eastern Switzerland, Walser never wrote again. He died on Christmas Day, 1956, while taking a walk on the sanitorium grounds. His *Selected Stories* (1982) appeared in English with a foreword by Susan Sontag.

Walsh, Raoul *(1887–1980)* American film director. In a career that spanned nearly 50 years, he directed more than 100 films. His movies, characterized by swift-paced action, included adventure dramas, gangster films and westerns. He won early acclaim for such silent films as *The Thief of Bagdad* (1924), *What Price Glory?* (1926) and *Sadie Thompson* (1928). However, he achieved his best work directing Errol FLYNN, Humphrey BOGART, and James CAGNEY in the 1940s. Among his films of this period were *The Roaring Twenties* (1939), *They Drive By Night* (1940), *Strawberry Blonde* (1941), *High Sierra* (1941), *Objective Burma* (1945) and *White Heat* (1949).

Walter, Bruno **(Bruno Schlesinger)** *(1876–1962)* German-born orchestra and opera conductor. Walter was born in Berlin. Although trained as a piano prodigy, he was inspired by Hans von Bulow to become a conductor. At age 17 he had his first engagement with the Cologne Opera. A year later, in 1894, he met the man who was so profoundly to affect his life and music, the composer Gustav MAHLER. After a succession of appointments in Breslau (1896), Pressburgh (1897) and Berlin (1900), he was invited by Mahler to work as his assistant at the Vienna Court Opera, where he remained until 1913. After Mahler's death he gave the premieres of *Das Lied von der Erde* in Munich in 1911 and of the Ninth Symphony in 1910. An indefatigable traveller, Walter toured the U.S. several times, performed throughout Europe and Russia and distinguished himself at Covent Garden in London for a cycle of Mozart operas. In 1933 he fell victim to ANTI-SEMITISM and was forced to abandon his post at the Leipzig Gewandhaus Orchestra (where he was succeeded by Richard STRAUSS). During the war years he led many American

orchestras in the standard Austrian-German repertoire, and, of course, he continued to champion the music of Mahler. Many of his last recordings were made with the Columbia Symphony Orchestra, a magnificent ensemble culled from the Hollywood studios and the Los Angeles Philharmonic. Music was, for Walter, a religious experience. The musician was its high priest. The conductor, he wrote in his autobiographies, *Theme and Variations* (1947) and *Of Music and Music Making* (1957), must be able to fulfill the "spiritual demands of the works he performs." Music, he insisted, was witness to man's "divinely creative and ruling character." Like MONTEUX and TOSCANINI, he conducted until well into his 80s.

Walters, Barbara *(1931–)* American journalist. Walters established herself during her 12-year stint as cohost of NBC's *Today* television show, where she was noted for her personal interviewing technique. In 1976, she became the first woman to coanchor a network news show and the highest-paid newscaster in television, with a $1-million-a-year contract. Walters shared the anchor spot on the *ABC Evening News* with Harry Reasoner, but the two failed to get along, and Walters was criticized for having no hard news experience. Both were removed from the show within a year. Walters went on to cohost the news magazine *20/20* and to do celebrity interviews. In 2004 it was announced that Walters would relinquish her coanchor duties on *20/20*. She later co-created and produced *The View*, a talk show on which she also appears.

Walton, Sir William Turner *(1902–1983)* One of the major British composers of the 20th century, Walton wrote orchestral music, ballets, film scores and operas as well as coronation marches for King GEORGE VI and Queen ELIZABETH II. He achieved fame in 1923 with the first performance of his *Facade,* musical parodies accompanying satirical poems by Edith SITWELL. Among his other compositions are the Viola Concerto (1929), *Belshazzar's Feast* (1931), the Violin Concerto (1939) and the scores for Laurence OLIVIER's film classics *Henry V* (1945) and *Richard III* (1955).

Wang, An *(1920–1990)* Chinese-born physicist, computer engineer and

entrepreneur. Wang emigrated to the U.S. in 1945, and three years later invented the computer memory core, which was the most common device used for storing computer data before the invention of the microchip. In 1951 he founded Wang Laboratories, which went on to become one of the world's largest producers of office word-processing systems. The company experienced a slump in the late 1980s, and posted a loss of some $400 million in 1989. In response, Wang sold off some of the company's assets and eased out his son, who had been named president in 1986, in favor of an outsider.

Wang Ching-wei (Wang Jingwei) *(1883–1944)* Chinese nationalist leader. While still a student, he became a friend and disciple of SUN YAT-SEN. After an attempt on the life of the Chinese regent in 1910, he was sentenced to life imprisonment, but was released with the outbreak of revolution in 1912. He subsequently studied in France, returned to China in 1917 and became a leader of the left wing of the KUOMINTANG and an opponent of CHIANG KAI-SHEK. He was China's premier from 1932–35. Opposed to the policies of Chiang, wary of the Communists and convinced of the futility of war with Japan, Wang served as head of a Japanese puppet government in Nanking (Nanjing) throughout World War II, from 1940 until his death.

Wang Hongwen See GANG OF FOUR.

Wankel, Felix *(1902–1988)* German inventor. Wankel developed the Wankel rotary engine in a private workshop in the period between the two world wars. His invention required fewer moving parts than a conventional engine and produced more power in less space with less noise and vibration. The first Wankel-powered car did not appear until 1964, and only the Mazda Motor Corporation of Japan adopted the design for many of its models. The Wankel engine's perceived fuel inefficiency caused it to lose popularity following the 1973 oil crisis.

War Admiral *(1934–1959)* Thoroughbred racehorse. Undefeated as a three-year-old, this son of MAN O'WAR captured the Triple Crown in 1937 and was named Horse of the Year. He went on to win the Jockey Club Gold Cup in 1938, but his most notable race was one he lost in 1939. War Admiral's 1-1/8 mile match race against Sea Biscuit at Pimlico is regarded as one of the greatest races of all time, the horses and jockeys dueling every stride of the way, with Sea Biscuit the eventual winner by three lengths in the record time of 1:56:6. War Admiral retired after his four-year-old season to a successful stud career.

war communism Name given to the Bolshevik government's social and economic policies of 1918–21. In order to support the BOLSHEVIKS in the RUSSIAN CIVIL WAR fully, and to build communism in general, war communism was characterized by the nationalization of industry and trade, wages in kind for workers and enforced labor service. These measures were unpopular, and in 1921 there occurred several uprisings. War communism was replaced by the NEW ECONOMIC POLICY in 1921.

Ward, Dame Barbara Mary (Baroness Jackson of Lodsworth) *(1914–1981)* British economist, journalist and author. Ward was foreign editor of the *Economist* during World War II, as well as a popular public speaker and radio personality. In the postwar years she was a strong advocate of foreign aid to underdeveloped nations. While serving on UNITED NATIONS and VATICAN special commissions, she urged the transfer of wealth from rich to poor nations. Her belief in the interdependence of nations extended to world environmental policies.

Warhol, Andy (Andrew Warhola) *(1927–1987)* American artist, film maker and celebrity, the best-known figure to emerge from the POP ART movement of the 1960s. He won fame early in the 1960s with his images of Campbell's soup cans. Later works included images of Marilyn MONROE and other celebrities. His New York City art studio, "the Factory," was a legendary hangout for artists and social dropouts, whose lives he portrayed in his unconventional films. A constant presence on the New York social scene, he remained elusive as he went about photographing and tape-recording celebrities for his *Interview* magazine. Warhol had a flair for attracting publicity and for coming up with memorable quotes, such as "In the future, everybody will be famous for 15 minutes."

Warner, Jack L. *(1892–1978)* American film producer. Jack Warner was the youngest of the four brothers who founded WARNER BROTHERS Studios in 1923. He was production director, president or chairman of the board for over 50 years. A pioneer in talking pictures, he produced over 5,000 movies. These included several with dog-star RIN-TIN-TIN in the 1920s, the gangster cycle's *Little Caesar* and *Public Enemy,* as well as the Bushy BERKELEY musicals in the 1930s, and *Casablanca, The Treasure of the Sierra Madre, My Fair Lady* and *Bonnie and Clyde.*

Warner Bros. One of HOLLYWOOD's "Big Five" production/exhibition motion picture studios (along with METRO-GOLDWYN-MAYER, 20TH CENTURY-FOX, RKO, and PARAMOUNT) and the only one operated by a family. Harry, Albert, Sam and Jack Warner were the sons of a Polish immigrant who had come to American in the early 1880s by cattleboat. After dabbling in various nickelodeon projects, the brothers moved to Los Angeles and in 1918 produced their first important feature film, *My Four Years in Germany.* The studio moved into high gear in the 1920s with its most popular stars John BARRYMORE and the legendary canine, RIN-TIN-TIN. An important acquisition came in 1925 when the brothers bought the Vitagraph Company, a Brooklyn-based studio from the early days of the silent film. Experiments began in 1926 with Western Electric to develop a sound-on-disc synchronized-sound system for TALKING PICTURES. Numerous sound short films and features like *Don Juan* (1926) and *The Jazz Singer* (1927) stimulated industry-wide the talkie revolution. The four brothers at this time had the following responsibilities: Sam was the technological experimenter, but he died before *The Jazz Singer* realized his dreams. Jack oversaw all production at the Burbank studio, Albert was in charge of overseas distribution and Harry acted as president from his New York office. An energetic policy of theater acquisition was consolidated in 1929 with the purchase of the First National chain. More than most stu-

dios, Warner Bros. in the 1930s established its own "look" and style, largely due to its efficient factory system and the supervision until 1933 of all production by Darryl F. ZANUCK. "Social consciousness" films and contemporary dramas included gangster films like *The Public Enemy* (1930) and *Little Caesar* (1930); problem dramas like *Five-Star Final* (1931) and *I Am a Fugitive from a Chain Gang* (1932); biographies like *The Story of Louis Pasteur* (1936); and musicals like *42nd Street* (1932) and *Gold Diggers of 1933.* Directors known for their fast, lean style included Mervyn LeRoy and William Wellman. Stars famous for their fast-talking, cynical manner included James CAGNEY, Edward G. ROBINSON and Bette DAVIS. The bizarre hallucinations of musical wizard Busby BERKELEY revolutionized the art of the form. Apart from the Walt DISNEY studio, no other Hollywood studio contributed more to the World War II effort than Warners'. First to release an anti-Nazi film, *Confessions of a Nazi Spy* (1939), the studio went on to make numerous short subjects, documentaries and features promoting the Allies (*Casablanca,* 1943; *Air Force,* 1943; *Mission to Moscow,* 1944; etc.). In 1956, after divesting itself of its theaters due to antitrust government activities, the studio sold rights to its films to Associated Artists, which in turn sold them to UNITED ARTISTS. In 1967 Jack, by now the only brother left in the business, sold out to Seven Arts, and two years later the company was renamed Warner Communications. Time, Inc., merged with Warner in 1989 to form Time-Warner, Inc., which now supervises film production.

"War of the Worlds" broadcast *(October 30, 1938)* Famous radio broadcast that inadvertently convinced millions of American citizens that a Martian invasion had occurred. The CBS *Mercury Theatre of the Air,* produced by John HOUSEMAN and Orson WELLES, performed on a Sunday night its adaptation of H. G. WELLS's science fiction novel *The War of the Worlds.* Although an announcer periodically stressed that listeners were hearing a dramatization, the excellence of the performances (notably Welles himself as an eyewitness broadcaster of the Martian landings in New Jersey) coupled with a realistic and cleverly constructed script created panic across the United States. An estimated 4 million listeners believed that the invasion had occurred. Reactions included heart attacks and attempted suicides. CBS and Welles ultimately apologized, while the FCC took steps to see that such an incident could not recur. Social scientists still ponder why the broadcast was so widely believed, attributing public credulity in part to the atmosphere of crisis—HITLER and the GREAT DEPRESSION—that dominated the news in the late 1930s.

War On Drugs A domestic and international conflict waged by the U.S. federal government in an effort to end the flow of illegal narcotics (such as cocaine, heroin, marijuana and ecstasy) into U.S. territory. In 1970 President Richard M. NIXON signed the 1970 Comprehensive Drug Abuse Prevention and Control Act into law. A year later, as the federal government continued its campaign against the drug trade, Nixon announced the beginning of a "War on Drugs" waged by federal law enforcement agencies that would end the cultivation, distribution and use of these toxic substances. By 1973 Nixon created the Drug Enforcement Agency (DEA), the chief federal agency for coordinating the fight against drug smuggling and trafficking by federal, state and local law enforcement agents. While Nixon's measures were continued under his immediate successors, Presidents Gerald FORD and Jimmy CARTER, they were intensified under President Ronald Reagan, who enacted the 1986 Anti-Drug Abuse Act, a federal law requiring longer prison sentences for both possession and distribution of narcotics. Reagan's wife Nancy joined the campaign by helping to establish the "Just Say No" movement with Soleil Moon Frye, the child television actress who played the title role on the evening situation-comedy *Punky Brewster.*

During the administrations of George H. W. BUSH, William Jefferson CLINTON and George W. BUSH, the DEA has continued to operate in conjunction with law enforcement agencies at all levels of government. Private organizations have also gotten involved and with some federal funds have begun and sustained a multimedia campaign

to make children and adults aware of the dangers of drug use and to encourage parents to remain heavily involved in adolescents' lives as a means of deterring their children from using drugs. The U.S. had also begun to send military forces abroad to work in conjunction with governments, such as that of COLOMBIA, to seize illegal drugs that are cultivated and refined abroad for shipment to the U.S. The U.S. also provides military training so that such foreign governments can improve their own capability to seize drug related facilities run by such extra-governmental organizations as the **F.A.R.C.** and the **Medellín Cartel.**

Warren, Earl (*1891–1974*) American politician, chief justice of the U.S. Supreme Court (1953–69). A judicial activist, Warren was leader of the influential "Warren Court" of the 1950s and 1960s that issued many landmark CIVIL RIGHTS and individual liberties cases. A graduate of the University of California, the Republican Warren was elected state attorney general and gained a reputation as a crime fighter. He capitalized on this reputation and was elected governor of California, a post he held from 1942 until his appointment to the Supreme Court (1953). At the time in California, a candidate could enter any party's primary elections; Warren was so popular that he once won both the Republican and Democratic primaries for attorney general and then repeated the feat as governor. In 1948 he was the unsuccessful candidate for vice president on the Republican ticket with Thomas DEWEY. Although he sought the Republican presidential nomination in 1952, he withdrew and endorsed Dwight D. EISENHOWER.

After the death of Chief Justice Fred VINSON, President Eisenhower nominated Warren as chief justice. Eisenhower later reportedly called Warren's appointment "the biggest damn-fool mistake I ever made." Although Warren was a Republican and, at least during his early years in office, a conservative governor, he proved a liberal once on the high court. The Warren majority was known as an activist Court and established many landmark decisions. Warren himself wrote many of the opinions, including *BROWN V. BOARD OF EDUCATION* (school

Chief Justice Earl Warren (LIBRARY OF CONGRESS. PRINTS AND PHOTOGRAPHS DIVISION)

desegregation), *MIRANDA V. ARIZONA* (right against self-incrimination) and *Cooper v. Aaron.* This case, heard by itself in a highly unusual special summer session, refused to grant further delays for school desegregation in LITTLE ROCK, Arkansas, after the *Brown* decision. Warren also headed the WARREN COMMISSION that investigated the assassination of President John F. KENNEDY. He retired from the Court in 1969.

Warren remains perhaps the most controversial chief justice of the 20th century. Libertarians continue to regard him as a champion of civil liberties, while conservatives charge that the Warren Court overstepped the proper role of the judiciary and favored the rights of criminals at the expense of law enforcement officials.

Warren, Robert Penn (*1905–1989*) American author. One of the most versatile American men of letters of the 20th century, Warren was a poet, novelist, teacher and critic. He won the PULITZER PRIZE three times—in 1946 for his novel *ALL THE KING'S MEN,* the tale of a populist southern politician (inspired by Huey LONG) who becomes corrupted by power; in 1957 for *Promises; Poems, 1954–1956;* and in 1978 for *Now and Then: Poems 1976–1978.* Warren was also the first poet laureate of the U.S. from 1986–88. His other honors include the National Medal for Literature in 1970 and the Presidential Medal of Freedom in 1980. Besides his achievements in fiction and poetry, Warren was coauthor (with Cleanth BROOKS) of two seminal works of literary criticism, *Understanding Poetry* (1938) and *Understanding Fiction* (1943), which helped introduce the NEW CRITICISM into American colleges.

Warren was born in Guthrie, Kentucky, and attended Vanderbilt University, graduating in 1925. He pursued graduate studies at Berkeley, Yale and Oxford, where he was a Rhodes Scholar. He taught at Louisiana State University in the 1930s (where he edited *The Southern Review*), at the University of Minnesota in the 1940s and at Yale from 1950 until retirement.

Warren Commission Government investigation of the 1963 assassination of President John F. KENNEDY. The events surrounding the assassination had aroused suspicion. Lee Harvey OSWALD, the alleged assassin, had been shot while in police custody by Jack RUBY. Although he appeared to have acted alone, Oswald had a Russian wife, and many suspected a conspiracy. Some suggested Russia or Cuba was to blame, while others pointed a finger at organized crime. The matter was investigated by a commission headed by Supreme Court chief justice Earl WARREN. Other members of the eight-member panel were Representative Gerald FORD, who later became president, two senators and former CIA chief Allen DULLES. After a massive investigation the commission concluded that Oswald had acted alone. Critics refused to believe that the assassination was not the result of a conspiracy, and the Warren Commission report remains controversial.

Warsaw Pact A military alliance, formally known as the Warsaw Treaty Organization (WTO); established on May 14, 1955, as a Soviet-bloc counterpart to the NORTH ATLANTIC TREATY ORGANIZATION (NATO). Formed a week after a remilitarized WEST GERMANY entered NATO, it included ALBANIA, BULGARIA, CZECHOSLOVAKIA, EAST GERMANY, HUNGARY, POLAND, ROMANIA and the USSR. It provided for a unified military command headquartered in Moscow, with Soviet or Soviet-trained divisions stationed in

member nations to provide a common defense in case of attack on any one or more of the signatories. Albania formally withdrew from the pact in 1968. The one action in which Warsaw Pact nations collaborated was the armed occupation of Czechoslovakia that destroyed the democracy movement of 1968. Following the fall of communist governments in Eastern Europe in 1989–90 and the reunification of GERMANY in October 1990, the Warsaw Pact effectively unravelled. It was formally dissolved on July 1, 1991.

Warsaw Uprising (*August–October 1944*) Revolt against Nazi occupation forces in Warsaw by the Polish underground, a resistance group known as the Home Army and commanded by General Count Tadeusz Komorowski (1895–1966). As Germany's fortunes were on the wane and the Soviet army reached the Vistula, underground forces attempted to take the Polish capital from the Germans. During the first four days of August, the Home Army was successful in gaining control of over half of the city. However, oncoming Soviet troops halted for resupply, and the Polish forces soon ran short of food and ammunition. Although some supplies were flown in by Allied airmen, it was not enough to sustain the Poles. SS reinforcements coupled with German troops in Warsaw quelled the rebellion in fierce fighting, and, after a futile Soviet assault in September, the Home Army was forced to capitulate in October. In reprisal for the uprising, the Germans razed much of the city.

Washington, Booker T. (*1856–1915*) American educator, the preeminent African-American figure of his time. Born a slave on a Virginia farm, he was freed at the age of nine and from 1872 to 1875 was enrolled at Hampton Institute. After teaching for some years, in 1881 Washington became head of the Tuskegee Normal and Industrial Institute, in Alabama, which he built into a major institution for black students. In 1895, he delivered his famous Atlanta Exposition Address, arguing "In all things that are purely social we can be as separate as the fingers, yet one as the hand in mutual progress." While he then quickly became the black spokesman most acceptable to whites, other black leaders, most notably W. E. B. DUBOIS, rejected his segregationist position and railed against Jim Crow laws and other forms of discrimination. Washington wrote four books about his experiences, most notably *Up From Slavery*, published to much acclaim in 1901 and translated into over 15 languages. Washington was tireless in his efforts to find northern patrons for Tuskegee (receiving more than $600,000 worth of bonds from Andrew Carnegie) and was invited to the White House by President Theodore ROOSEVELT in 1901.

Washington Conference Held from November 21, 1921, to February 6, 1922, this post-World War I conference was intended to provide for naval disarmament and to ease tensions in the Far East. Convened in Washington, D.C., it was attended by representatives of BELGIUM, CHINA, FRANCE, the UNITED KINGDOM, ITALY, JAPAN, the NETHERLANDS, PORTUGAL and the U.S. Three main

Civilians being taken prisoner during the destruction of the Warsaw Ghetto, 1943 (LIBRARY OF CONGRESS, PRINTS AND PHOTOGRAPHS DIVISION)

treaties resulted. In the Four Power Treaty of December 1921, the U.K., France, Japan and the U.S. agreed to respect one another's Pacific possessions. These nations plus Italy were signatories of the Five Power Naval Armaments Treaty of February 1922, which provided for a 10-year moratorium on the building of warships and established a ratio controlling the number of such ships each could maintain. In another agreement, China's independence was collectively guaranteed, and Japan was pledged to return Shantung to China. The Washington Conference treaties remained in effect until the mid-1930s.

Washington Post, The American newspaper established in 1877. Founded as a Democratic paper, the *Post* was acquired by John R. McLean in 1905. The paper went into receivership after the stock market crash and was bought by Eugene Meyer in 1933. Meyer rejuvenated the *Post* and in 1948 transferred his voting stock to his daughter and son-in-law, Katharine and Philip GRAHAM. When Philip committed suicide in 1963, Katharine Graham became president, and she and her sons continued to oversee the paper and its holdings. One of the most influential newspapers in the nation, the *Post* championed civil liberties and civil rights in the postwar years and supported the United Nations. It was assailed for its attack on McCARTHYISM in the 1950s. In 1954, the *Post* acquired and absorbed its competition, the *Washington Times-Herald,* and in 1961 it acquired NEWSWEEK magazine. The next year it set up the Los Angeles Times-Washington Post News Service.

Graham hired Benjamin C. BRADLEE as managing editor in 1965; three years later he became executive editor. The *Post,* which had already aroused the enmity of the NIXON administration for its criticism of Vice President Spiro AGNEW, broke the story of WATERGATE, to which Bradlee had assigned reporters Bob WOODWARD and Carl BERNSTEIN. In 1973, the paper received a PULITZER PRIZE for its investigation of Watergate. The paper continues to be noted for its investigative reporting and maintains its standing as the nation's leading political paper. The Washington Post Company's holdings include additional newspapers, magazines and four television stations,

Bradlee retired in 1991. In 1993 Katherine Graham resigned as chief executive officer of the *Post.*

Wasserman, August von (1866–1925) German bacteriologist. Wasserman was educated at the Universities of Erlangen, Vienna, Munich and Strasbourg, where he graduated in 1888. From 1890 he worked under Robert Koch at the Institute for Infectious Diseases in Berlin, becoming head of the department of therapeutics and serum research in 1907. In 1913 he moved to the Kaiser Wilhelm Institute, where he served as director of experimental therapeutics until his death. Wasserman is best remembered for the **Wasserman test**, which he introduced in 1906 for the diagnosis of syphilis. The test is still widely used as a diagnostic tool.

Waste Land, The (1922) Written by T. S. ELIOT while he was recovering from a nervous breakdown in 1921–22, this long poem in five sections is generally regarded as the most important works of Eliot's early period. Using a complex structure and symbolism inspired in part by the mythic archetypes of Jessie L. Weston's *From Ritual to Romance* and Sir James Frazer's *The Golden Bough, The Waste Land* contrasts the sterility of modern life to the richness of traditional spiritual and mythological forces. In a remarkable collaboration, the original text (over 1,000 lines) was radically altered and condensed by Ezra POUND to produce a more concentrated and ambiguous work of just over 400 lines. Many readers and critics were initially baffled by the poem's juxtaposition of topical images and colloquial language with obscure literary allusions. However, it was soon widely recognized as a revelation of modern sensibility. The publication of *The Waste Land* is often considered the birth of literary MODERNISM.

Wat, Aleksander (1900–1967) Polish poet and intellectual. Jewish by birth, Wat was involved in various European intellectual movements in the 1920, Including DADA and FUTURISM. During this time he lived in Warsaw, Berlin and Paris, associating with some of the leading modernist writers of the time (see MODERNISM). In 1929 he became editor of an influential Polish

Communist journal. However, after HITLER and STALIN partitioned POLAND in 1939, Wat was arrested by the Soviets on charges of being a Trotskyite, Zionist and agent of the VATICAN. He spent WORLD WAR II in various Soviet prisons and converted to Christianity in 1941. He returned to Poland in 1946. Although he remained out of official favor because he refused to adhere to the doctrine of SOCIALIST REALISM, he continued to write. A writer of wide culture, although little known outside intellectual circles, Wat was one of the leading European thinkers of his generation.

Watergate The name given to a series of scandals in the administration of President Richard M. NIXON leading to Nixon's resignation on August 9, 1974. Watergate refers to the burglarizing of the Democratic Party national headquarters in Washington, D.C., on June 17, 1972. Five men arrested in the break-in and two of their accomplices were tried and convicted. James McCord, one of the convicted burglars, charged that there had been a cover-up of the burglary. In the wake of the McCord accusation and the investigative reporting of Carl Bernstein and Bob WOODWARD of *The WASHINGTON POST*, a special Senate committee chaired by Senator Sam ERVIN (Democrat-North Carolina) held nationally televised hearings into the Watergate affair in the spring and summer of 1973. Former White House counsel John DEAN charged that the Watergate break-in was approved by Attorney General John MITCHELL and that White House aides H. R. "Bob" Haldeman and John Ehrlichman were involved in the cover-up. In May 1973, then attorney general Elliot Richardson appointed Archibald COX as a special prosecutor to investigate the entire "Watergate affair." Cox began to uncover evidence of improper conduct in the Nixon reelection committee and illegal wiretapping by the administration. In July 1973, it became known that presidential conversations in the White House had been taped since 1971. In October 1973, when Cox tried to obtain these tapes from the president, Nixon fired him. This touched off calls for Nixon's impeachment from the press and from some in government. The House Judiciary Committee began an impeachment inquiry, which ended in the adoption of three articles of impeachment against Nixon in July 1974. On August 5, 1974, Nixon released the transcripts of three of the recorded conversations that Special Prosecutor Leon JAWORSKI (whom Nixon had appointed to replace Cox) had sought from him. Nixon admitted that he had known about the Watergate cover-up shortly after the burglary had occurred and that he had tried to stop the Federal Bureau of Investigation's inquiry into the break-in. On August 9, 1974, Nixon resigned, and Vice President Gerald R. FORD was sworn in as president. The next month, Ford pardoned Nixon for any crimes he might have committed as president; however, Mitchell, Haldeman, Ehrlichman and Dean were among those who were convicted for their part in the Watergate scandals.

Watkins v. United States (1957) U.S. Supreme Court McCarthy-era decision involving the power of congressional investigations. A congressional committee, the HOUSE UN-AMERICAN ACTIVITIES COMMITTEE, questioned a union leader about his membership in and relations with the U.S. Communist Party. When he refused to implicate others, he was prosecuted for contempt and convicted. On appeal he protested that the committee's questioning constituted a fishing expedition with no particular goal. The Supreme Court held that the investigating committee had exceeded its power and the defendant had the right to refuse to answer questions that were not relevant to its investigation. The decision was controversial at the time because anticommunist sentiment was still strong in the U.S.

Watson, James Dewey (1928–) American biochemist. In 1951 Watson began to pursue in earnest the structure of DNA, at the Cavendish Laboratory in Cambridge, England. By 1953 he and Francis CRICK published *General Implications of the Structure of Deoxyribonucleic Acid,* which showed how genetic information can be expressed in the form of a chemical code. For this work, Watson and Crick shared the 1962 NOBEL PRIZE for physiology or medicine with Maurice Wilkins. He continued to study the genetic code at the California Institute of Technology and later at Harvard. He concentrated

on cancer research at the Cold Springs Harbor Laboratory in New York, where he became director in 1968. Also in 1968, he published his controversial account of the discovery of the structure of DNA, *The Double Helix.* From 1988 to 1992 Watson was appointed the head of the Human Genome Project. In 2004 he became the chancellor of the Cold Springs Harbor Laboratory.

Watson, John Broadus (1878–1958) American psychologist and advertising agent. A graduate of Furman University (1900), Watson promoted a comprehensive understanding of behaviorist theory, thus altering the course of U.S. psychological thinking by focusing on observed responses to external stimuli rather than introspective analysis. He was president of the American Psychological Association (1915), a noted educator and the author of several influential works, including *Behaviorism* (1925).

Watson, Tom (1949–) American golfer. The first player to earn a half-million dollars in a single year, he was the first to win the PGA championship six times. The dominant player of the 1970s and early 1980s, he won five British Opens, two Masters titles and one U.S. Open. He has represented the United States on the Ryder Cup team four times. In 1999 Watson began playing on the Senior PGA tour.

Watts riots (August 11–16, 1965) The attempted arrest of a drunk driver in Los Angeles's predominantly black Watts district flared into six days of rioting, looting, arson and sniping by an estimated 7,000 to 10,000 blacks. The National Guard was called out. Thirty-five people were killed, 864 treated in hospital for injuries and 4,170 arrested. The riots were later ascribed to poverty, unemployment, racism and general disrespect for law and order.

Waugh, Evelyn (Arthur St. John Evelyn Waugh) (1903–1966) British novelist. An indifferent student at Hertford College, Oxford, Waugh became a schoolmaster, and his experiences as such inspired the acclaimed and enormously popular *Decline and Fall* (1928), his first novel. Waugh's subsequent witty and intelligent social satires, such as *Vile Bodies* (1930) and *A Handful of*

Dust (1934), chronicled the cynical "Bright Young Things" of the 1920s and 1930s. Waugh was also an inspired journalist and travel writer. After a short-lived marriage in the late 1920s, he was received into the Catholic Church. In 1937 he married Laura Herbert, a cousin of his first wife. Waugh served in the Royal Marines during World War II. There is a profound sense of desolation and regret for the vanished prewar world in *Brideshead Revisited* (1945), perhaps his best-known novel. Other works include the wartime trilogy consisting of *Men at Arms* (1952), *Officers and Gentlemen* (1955) and *Unconditional Surrender* (1961). His *Diaries* were published in 1976. Waugh was a champion of "high Tory" values and has been much criticized for snobbery. Waugh's brother, **Alex Waugh** (1898–1981), was also a novelist and noted travel author whose works include *The Loom of Youth* (1917), and Waugh's son, **Auberon Waugh,** was a journalist.

Wavell, Archibald Percival (first earl Wavell) (1883–1950) British soldier and colonial administrator. Born and educated at Winchester and a graduate of Sandhurst, he entered the military as an officer in the Black Watch regiment in 1901. His early service was in the BOER WAR and in India. During WORLD WAR I, he served in Belgium and on ALLENBY's staff in Palestine. He returned there as head of the British forces, assigned to deal with the Arab-Jewish conflicts of 1937–39. During WORLD WAR II, he was appointed commander in chief of the Middle East (1939), defeated the Italians in North Africa (1940–41) but was routed by German forces late in 1941. Exchanging commands with General AUCHINLECK, he commanded British troops in India in 1941 and in Southeast Asia in 1942. Hit by losses to the Japanese in Singapore and Burma, the Asian command was abolished, and Wavell again assumed command in India. In 1943, he became the Indian viceroy and governor general and was made a field marshall. Thereafter, until his resignation in 1947, Wavell attempted to prepare India for independence and to ease the tensions between Hindus and Muslims.

Wayne, John (Marion Michael Morrison) (1907–1979) American film star. An actor of limited range,

Wayne nonetheless transcended his limitations to become a cultural icon, a larger-than-life figure who represented American rugged individualism. In a 50-year career he appeared in more than 200 films, nearly half of which were westerns. His films grossed over $800 million, and he was among the top-10 box office stars for a record 25 consecutive years. Wayne began acting in HOLLYWOOD in 1928, appearing mainly in low-budget action films and serials that brought him little popular or critical attention. He made his breakthrough in the 1939 classic western *Stagecoach*, directed by his friend John FORD; Wayne went on to star in 14 pictures by Ford, notably *She Wore a Yellow Ribbon* (1949), *The Quiet Man* (1952) and *The Searchers* (1956).

Nicknamed "the Duke," Wayne was idolized by moviegoers, especially during the 1940s, 1950s and early 1960s. He projected an image of brave, rugged, sincere and sometimes stubborn masculinity. Best known for his portrayal of the quintessential hero of the American West, Wayne also made his mark in war movies, in which he usually portrayed what many believed was the ideal U.S. Army, Navy or Marine Corps officer. Among his best WORLD WAR II movies were *They Were Expendable* (1945) and *Sands of Iwo Jima* (1949). In his later years, Wayne's screen persona was transferred to the realm of politics. He became a prominent spokesman for conservative causes, and his support of America's involvement in the VIETNAM WAR led many to dismiss him as a simpleminded patriot. Many of his films of this time were critical failures, although he gave fine performances in *True Grit* (1969), for which he won his only ACADEMY AWARD, and *The Shootist* (1976), his last movie.

Weathermen Radical left-wing group whose aim was to overthrow the American political system. The group's name was drawn from the lyrics of songwriter Bob DYLAN. The membership was drawn from a well-educated social strata. The Weathermen committed specific and well-planned acts of violence, including bombings, robberies and murders in the U.S. in the 1970s. (See also SDS.)

Weather Report Jazz-rock ensemble cofounded in 1970 by keyboardist Joe Zawinul and saxophonist Wayne Shorter. Weather Report epitomized and influenced the artistic evolution and popular success of the FUSION approach, where freewheeling improvisations float above ostinato-like ROCK, funk and Latin rhythmic patterns. In contrast to the various BEBOP-oriented styles from the 1950s and 1960s, which emphasized virtuosic soloing, jazz-rock fusion exploited popular dance rhythms (like the swing bands of the 1930s and 1940s) and collective improvisation (similar in concept to the Dixieland tradition of New Orleans). Weather Report also capitalized on the availability of a new generation of electronic instruments and processors, unlike the jazz "mainstream," which did not swerve from its devotion to acoustic instruments. The band appealed to a wide and largely youthful audience that had grown up with rock and roll; in the process, it brought notoriety to its two leaders, Zawinul and Shorter, as well to such prominent musicians of the 1970s and 1980s as electric bassist Jaco Pastorius and drummer Peter Erskine. The band's greatest hit was "Birdland" (1976). The group broke up in 1985.

Weaver, Robert Clifton (1907–1997) American statesman. The great-grandson of a slave, Weaver put himself through Harvard by working as an electrician. He received a B.S. in economics (1929), an M.A. two years later and a Ph.D. in 1934, after which he took a position with the Department of the Interior. Under President Franklin ROOSEVELT he was an adviser on housing and unemployment, moving into war mobilization in the 1940s. Weaver was president of the NATIONAL ASSOCIATION FOR THE ADVANCEMENT OF COLORED PEOPLE, and in 1961 he was appointed by President John KENNEDY to run the Housing and Home Finance Agency. In 1966 President Lyndon JOHNSON recommended him to head the newly formed Department of Housing and Urban Development.

Weavers, The American folk music quartet founded in 1949 by Pete SEEGER, Ronnie Gilbert, Lee Hays and Fred Hellerman. Influenced by Woody GUTHRIE, the group helped spark the folk music boom of the 1950s. The members had left-wing backgrounds and specialized in union songs and songs of social protest. In the 1950s, they were investigated by anticommunist groups and the HOUSE UN-AMERICAN ACTIVITIES COMMITTEE (HUAC) and were blacklisted for a time. Their songs included "If I Had a Hammer" and "Where Have All the Flowers Gone?" After the Weavers officially disbanded in 1963, the members went their separate ways but occasionally regrouped to give reunion concerts.

Webb, Chick (William Webb) (1909–1939) American jazz drummer and big band leader. Webb was an accomplished jazz drummer of great verve and timing, best remembered as the leader of one of the preeminent JAZZ big bands of the 1920s and 1930s. Among the featured vocalists who performed with the Webb big band was Ella FITZGERALD, who joined the band in 1935 and sang one of the band's biggest hits, "A-Tisket A-Tasket" (1938). Webb was a cocomposer of numerous jazz and pop songs, including "Stompin' at the Savoy," "Lonesome Moments," "Holiday in Harlem," "You Showed Me The Way" and "Heart of Mine." Webb died prematurely due to tuberculosis of the spine.

Webb, Clifton (Webb Parmalee Hollenbeck) (1891–1966) American stage and film actor. Webb, who began his acting career as a teenager, enjoyed a long and successful career in which he triumphed both on Broadway and in Hollywood. From the 1910s through the 1930s, Webb starred in numerous Broadway musicals—most notably *Listen Lester* (1919) and *Sunny* (1925)—in which his singing and dancing talents were featured. From the mid-1940s through the 1950s, Webb shifted his focus to Hollywood, where he became a successful character actor who specialized in dignified upper-class roles. His best-known films are *Laura* (1944), *Sitting Pretty* (1948) and *Titanic* (1953).

Webb, James E. (1906–1992) NASA's second administrator, from February 1961 until October 1968. During his tenure, the MERCURY, GEMINI and APOLLO programs were developed.

Webb, Sidney and Beatrice British authors and social reformers, Sidney

James Webb (1859–1947) and (Martha) Beatrice Webb (nee Potter, 1858–1943). The Webbs, who were married in 1892, were committed socialists. Before their marriage, Beatrice, who came from a wealthy family, had written *The Co-operative Movement in Great Britain* (1891). Sidney Webb had been a civil servant, but turned to politics as a member of the London Country Council in 1892. Both helped found the Fabian Society in 1884 and the London School of Economics in 1895. They sat on many Royal Commissions, for one of which Beatrice wrote a minority report in 1909 which influenced the Poor Law, and they were active in the trade union movement. In 1913, they were instrumental in starting *The New Statesman,* a weekly socialist paper. Following World War I, Sidney sat on the executive committee of the LABOUR PARTY, and in 1922 was elected to Parliament. In 1924 and from 1929 to 1931, he held various ministerial posts in the Labour government. The Webb's works of social history include *The History of Trade Unionism* (1894), the ten-volume *English Local Government* (1906–1929), *The Decay of Capitalist Civilization* (1921) and *Soviet Communism* (1935). Beatrice's diaries provided the fodder for her works, *My Apprenticeship* (1926) and *Our Partnership* (1948).

Weber, Max *(1864–1920)* German social scientist. Weber studied at a number of German universities and later taught at the Universities of Freiburg, Munich and Heidelberg. His interests and writings in the social sciences were wide ranging and extremely influential. A founder of modern sociology, he sought to create systematized concepts of the social sciences, and was the author of the influential volume *Methodology of the Social Sciences* (1922, tr. 1949). He rejected the idea that any one factor determines social dynamics and stressed a multi-faceted understanding of society. Deeply interested in religion and its impact on society, he developed an analysis that linked the self-denying asceticism of Calvinism with the genesis of capitalism in *The Protestant Ethic and the Spirit of Capitalism* (1904–05, tr. 1930). Prefiguring much of later sociological thought, Weber was deft in his analysis of politics and class, and he stressed

the importance of the development of bureaucracy in the economic and political life of Western society. Among his other books are *General Economic History* (1924, tr. 1927) and *Economy and Society* (4th ed. 1956, tr. 1968).

Weber, Max *(1881–1961)* American painter. Born in Russia, Weber and his family immigrated to the U.S. in 1891 and settled in Brooklyn, New York. He attended Pratt Institute (1898–1900) and traveled abroad in 1905, studying in Paris with Arthur Dow and Jean Paul Laurens and traveling throughout Europe. Weber became thoroughly familiar with the tenets of European modernism and also became personally acquainted with many of the European avant garde painters of the era. Returning to New York in 1909, his own work first reflected the brilliant coloristic experiments of FAUVISM, then the spatial innovations of CUBISM and later the swirling movement of FUTURISM. One of the best-known of his cubist paintings is the lively and colorful *Chinese Restaurant* (Whitney Museum, New York City). Weber's post-1917 work tends to be more figurative and to deal often with specifically Jewish subject matter. The social concerns of the 1930s are reflected in his works of that period, while his post–World War II paintings are increasingly linear and range from the abstract to the figurative.

Webern, Anton von *(1883–1945)* Viennese composer and influential disciple of the modern 12-tone techniques of Arnold SCHOENBERG. He was born in Vienna and with colleagues and friend Alban BERG studied with Schoenberg from 1904 to 1910. His first works, like the *Passacaglia for Orchestra* (1908), clung to tonal implications; while later works, beginning with the song cycles on texts by Stefan GEORGE (1909) and the *Six Pieces for Orchestra* (1910) experiment with atonality. Adopting some of the so-called "12-tone" techniques pioneered by Schoenberg—basing compositions on the rigorous use of patterns of the 12 chromatic intervals—he composed the important *Symphony* (1928) and the *Variations for Orchestra* (1940). During this time Webern made a living conducting in Vienna, generously filling his programs with the music of his idols—Brahms,

Wagner, MAHLER and—of course—Arnold Schoenberg. There are striking distinctions that may distinguish Webern's music from that of his colleagues. He was noted for the clear—even simple—textures of his polyphony and instrumentation. Without compromising the modernity of his work, he achieved a direct and immediate response from his listeners that makes his work increasingly popular today. And, above all, he strove for an amazing brevity and conciseness to many of his pieces. He is the great aphorist of the serial composers (the fourth of the *Five Pieces for Orchestra,* 1913, requires only 19 seconds for performance). Describing this aspect of the work, Schoenberg said: "Each glance may be extended to a poem, each sigh to a novel." Webern's death came suddenly in 1945 while staying with his daughter in Mittersill, Austria. Unaware of a curfew imposed on all Austrians by the occupying American forces, he was shot while taking a stroll.

Webster v. Reproductive Health Services *(1989)* U.S. Supreme Court case regarding ABORTION. The case involved a Missouri law prohibiting abortions in public hospitals and clinics, barring the use of public funds to inform women of or counsel women to have abortions and requiring doctors to test to determine whether a fetus 19 weeks old was viable. The law was challenged as unconstitutional by those in favor of legal abortions. Missouri officials were joined by the REAGAN administration asking the court to rule in favor of the Missouri law and to overturn *ROE V. WADE,* the controversial 1973 decision allowing abortions. The *Webster* case was highly charged politically. On July 3, 1989, the Court ruled to uphold the Missouri law by a 5 to 4 decision. However, it did not overturn *Roe v. Wade.* The majority opinion was written by Chief Justice William REHNQUIST and joined by justices Byron R. WHITE and Anthony M. KENNEDY. Justice Antonin SCALIA voted with the majority but strongly criticized his colleagues for not overturning *Roe* outright. Justice Sandra Day O'CONNOR also voted with the majority but asserted that the case did not necessitate a new ruling on *Roe.* Justice Harry A. BLACKMUN, the author of *Roe. v. Wade,* wrote a critical dissent. He was joined by Justices William J. BRENNAN, Jr. and Thurgood MARSHALL. A separate dissent was presented by Justice John Paul STEVENS. Essentially, the decision neither reaffirmed nor overturned *Roe v. Wade,* but turned the issue back to the individual states until a more decisive test case could be brought before the Court. Thus, abortion again became a major issue in state and local politics and was the focus of the 1989 elections throughout the U.S.

Wedemeyer, Albert Coady *(1897–1989)* U.S. Army general who helped plan the grand Allied strategy for winning WORLD WAR II. Toward the end of the war he served as U.S. commander in China.

Wegener, Alfred Lothar *(1880–1930)* German meteorologist and geologist. Wegener distinguished himself with his 1915 hypothesis of continental drift, published as *Origin of Continents and Oceans.* His proposal—that the continents were once contiguous—at first was met with outrage. To support his premise, Wegener used four main arguments, which in part were corroborated in 1929 by Arthur Holmes, who was able to account for the continental movement as suggested by Wegener. Advances in geomagnetism and oceanography led to full acceptance of Wegener's theory, and to a new geophysical discipline of plate tectonics after World War II.

Weil, Simone *(1909–1943)* French philosopher and theologian. Weil, all of whose works were published posthumously, earned a reputation as one of the most incisive and original thinkers of her era. Albert CAMUS, for one, referred to her has "the only great spirit of our time." Weil, whose brother André was a distinguished mathematician, was raised in an agnostic Jewish family. As a youth, she studied under the noted French philosopher Alain. In 1928, she finished first in the entrance examination for the Ecole Normale Supérieure; Simone DE BEAUVOIR finished second. In the 1930s, Weil alternated stints of teaching philosophy with manual labor in factories and fields in order to understand the real needs of the workers. In the mid-1930s, Weil became increasingly drawn to Christianity but refused baptism into the Catholic Church. Her political philosophy, which cannot be categorized as left- or right-wing, is best expressed in *The Need for Roots* (1953), which she wrote in 1943 at the request of the FREE FRENCH organization as a guide to the reconstruction of postwar FRANCE. That same year Weil, who was living in London, fell ill but frequently refused food and medical treatment out of sympathy for the plight of the people of occupied France. Those refusals hastened her death. Other major works by Weil include *Waiting for God* (1951) and *Gravity and Grace* (1952).

Weill, Kurt *(1900–1950)* German-born opera and BROADWAY musical show composer who was best known for *Die Dreigroschenoper* (*The Threepenny Opera*). Dissatisfied with his early training in Berlin under Ferruccio BUSONI and with the limited appeal of sophisticated, abstract music in general, Weill embraced the German aesthetic *Zeitkunst* movement and wrote a kind of "song-play," or "musical theater," as he put it, that infused classical forms with contemporary jazz, cabaret songs, popular dances and topical references. A mocking, sarcastic satire of decadent, bourgeois postwar German life hovered over collaborations with dramatists Georg KAISER, *Der Zar laesst sich photographieren* (*The Czar Has Himself Photographed,* 1927); and with Bertolt BRECHT, *Aufstieg und Fall der Stadt Mahagonny* (*The Rise and Fall of the City of Mahagonny,* 1927–1929) and *Die Dreigroschenoper* (1928). Despite the popularity of the latter opera—songs like "Moritat" ("Mack the Knife") made it the most successful musical production in Germany between the two World Wars—Weill and his wife, the actress Lotte LENYA, fled Nazi persecution in 1933 and after two years in PARIS, came to their permanent home in the U.S. Weill's subsequent Broadway musical shows continued the pattern of broad eclecticism that marked most of his work. With Maxwell ANDERSON he satirized President ROOSEVELT in *Knickerbocker Holiday* (1938). (Its most popular song, "September Song," has become a standard.) With Moss HART he explored themes concerning psychoanalysis in *Lady in the Dark* (1941). With Elmer RICE he depicted tenement life in New York in *Street Scene.* And in *Huckleberry Finn,* unfinished at the time of his death in 1950, he quoted the songs of the Missouri Ozarks. In HOLLYWOOD he reunited with Brecht and scored the Fritz LANG film *You and Me* (1938). Weill's music was frequently pungent, spare, lyric and brutal by turns—and profoundly divided between its serious motivations and sometimes brittle, artificial effects.

Weimar Republic Name generally used to refer to GERMANY and its democratic government during the period from just after the nation's defeat in WORLD WAR I (1918) to shortly after the appointment of Adolf HITLER as chancellor (1933). In February 1919 a national assembly gathered in the German town of Weimar to create a new form of government for the nation. On July 31, 1919, it officially adopted a constitution that provided for a president, a chancellor (prime minister), a two-house legislature and proportional representation. Despite the good intentions of the Weimar constitution, the government was handicapped by complex economic and political problems: heavy war reparations; runaway inflation during the 1920s and the GREAT DEPRESSION during the 1930s; and the proliferation of political parties, including several antidemocratic extremist groups. The democratic socialist Friedrich Ebert served as president from 1919 to 1925; he was succeeded by Field Marshal Paul von HINDENBURG, who held the office until his death in 1933. Gustav STRESEMANN and Heinrich BRUNING were among the prominent statesmen of the Weimar Republic. The strain of social and political turmoil in the early 1930s finally tore the fabric of the republic. In 1932 Hitler's Nazi Party became the single largest party in the legislature, and Hitler demanded to be appointed chancellor. On March 23, 1933—two months after President Hindenburg had appointed him chancellor (Jan. 30)—Hitler suspended the Weimar constitution and thereafter made himself the personal master of Germany.

Weinberg, Steven *(1933–)* American physicist. In 1979, Weinberg shared the NOBEL PRIZE in physics with Sheldon Glashow and Abdus SALAM for work developed independently that concerned two of the four fundamental forces of physics—electromagnetic interaction (which occurs between charged particles) and weak interaction (which explains certain radioactive decay processes). Weinberg, along with his colleagues, formulated a single theory that unified these two forces. Their formulation led the way toward a single theory of strong, electromagnetic, weak and gravitational interactions, as sought by EINSTEIN and Erwin SCHRÖDINGER, among others.

Weingartner, Felix *(1863–1942)* Yugoslavian-born orchestra conductor. He was the first and most important transitional figure between traditions in 19th-century conducting and the modern attitudes of the new century. He was born at Zara (modern Zadar, Yugoslavia) and was influenced early in his career by composers Johannes Brahms and Franz Liszt. He conducted extensively throughout the rest of the century in Danzig (1885–87), Hamburg (1887–89) and at the Vienna Opera in 1908 (succeeding MAHLER). He came to the U.S. for the first time in 1905, later conducting the Boston Opera Company. A prolific composer of six symphonies and eight operas (including a trilogy from Aeschylus), he regarded it as the tragedy of his life that his eclectic style of music was never generally accepted. Although originally in the great 19th-century romantic tradition, he broke with one of its chief exponents, Hans von Bülow, and attacked prevalent excesses in interpretation and performance. He abandoned his former histrionic podium style and adopted a quiet, restrained, dignified manner. The cause of the composer's music, and not the egotism of the conductor, he wrote in his book *On Conducting* (1895), should be the chief priority. Weingartner, a handsome and personable figure, was also an indefatigable editor and writer, pioneering a modern revival of Hector Berlioz and classic editions of the symphonies of Schubert, Beethoven and Schumann. Critic Harold C. Schonberg has written that to many "he remains the most rounded and satisfactory of all conductors in his chosen repertoire."

Weir, Peter *(1944–)* Australian film director; a leading figure in the so-called new wave of Australian motion pictures that began in the 1970s. Weir's movies often have a mystical atmos-

phere; they examine the conflict between social mores and personal values with sympathy for the underdog. Among his films are *The Last Wave* (1977), *Gallipoli* (1981), *The Year of Living Dangerously* (1983), *Dead Poets Society* (1989) and *Green Card* (1990). Weir later became well known for his work on *The Truman Show* (1998) and *Master and Commander: The Far Side of the World* (2003).

Weiss, George M. *(1895–1972)* American baseball executive. Weiss was general manager of the New York Yankees from 1947 to 1960. During this time the Yankees were virtually a dynasty, winning 10 American League pennants and seven World Series. Weiss was later the first president of the New York Mets (1961–66). He was elected to the Baseball Hall of Fame in 1971.

Weiss, Paul Alfred *(1898–1989)* Austrian-born U.S. biologist who won the National Medal of Science for his pioneering work in the theory of cellular development. Among other findings, he established the principle of cellular self-organization and helped prove that nerve cells could replenish themselves in all parts of the body. He taught at the University of CHICAGO for 21 years and was a professor emeritus at Rockefeller University.

Weiss, Peter *(1916–1982)* German-born playwright and novelist. He fled Nazi Germany as a teenager in 1934 and later became a naturalized Swedish citizen. His plays were considered profoundly disturbing. Centering on historical events and taking a Marxist outlook, they were essentially dialogues between representatives of opposing ideas. Weiss was best known for his prize-winning play *Marat/Sade* (1964), set in an insane asylum where inmates depict the 1793 assassination of the French Revolutionary leader Jean-Paul Marat. The play shocked audiences with its graphic violence and helped establish a new genre, **theater of cruelty.**

Weissmuller, Johnny *(1904–1984)* American swimmer and actor. Weissmuller set 67 swimming records during the 1920s. He won five gold medals in the 100-meter and 400-meter individual and 800-meter relay, freestyle events in the 1924 and 1928

OLYMPIC GAMES. He then went on to play the role of TARZAN in some 18 movies. Of the many actors who played the Edgar Rice BURROUGHS hero during the 20th century, Weissmuller was probably the most closely identified with the role.

Weizmann, Chaim *(1874–1952)* Chemist, Zionist leader, first president of Israel (1948–52). Born in Russia, he studied at the University of Freiburg, where he obtained his Ph.D. in 1900. He taught chemistry at the University of Geneva (1901–3) and moved to the faculty of the University of Manchester in 1904. Already a committed Zionist, he soon became a leader of British ZIONISM, visited PALESTINE in 1907 and became a British subject in 1910. During WORLD WAR I, he was director of the Admiralty Laboratories (1916–19). In 1917, Weizmann was instrumental in the creation of the BALFOUR DECLARATION, and the following year he headed the Zionist Commission to Palestine and cofounded the Hebrew University in Jerusalem. He was twice (1920–31, 1935–46) the president of the World Zionist Organization. In that office, he stressed the need for settlement in Palestine as well as for British support of a Jewish homeland. In 1934, he established a research institute at Rehoboth, which later became the world-renowned Weizmann Institute of Science. He returned to British service at the outbreak of WORLD WAR II, serving as adviser to the ministry of supply. When ISRAEL became independent in 1948, Weizmann was elected president, serving in that office until his death.

Welch, Jack *(1935–)* Chief executive officer (CEO) of General Electric (GE) (1981–2001). Born in Salem, Massachusetts, Welch attended the University of Massachusetts, where he received his B.S. in chemical engineering in 1957. He obtained his Ph.D. in chemical engineering from the University of Illinois in 1960. That year, Welch joined GE as a junior engineer in Pittsfield, Massachusetts. Welch's performance at GE soon earned the notice of Reuben Gutoff, a junior executive at the firm, who converted Welch into a national marketer of GE's products and services. Welch's extraordinary success as a salesman for several

GE subsidiaries resulted in his appointment as one of the company's vice presidents in 1972. He was promoted to senior vice president in 1977, vice chairman in 1979 and chairman and CEO in 1981.

As CEO of GE, Welch expanded the corporation's holdings and vastly increased its market value. Shortly after his promotion, Welch sold off GE's less-productive components for $10 billion and spent $19 billion in an effort to acquire companies he believed would soon experience dramatic economic growth. In 1986, Welch persuaded the company to acquire Employers Reinsurance Corporation, a financial services firm, and RCA CORPORATION, which included the television network NATIONAL BROADCASTING COMPANY (NBC). Welch also became known for his efforts to reduce the bureaucracy within GE, which he held was responsible for the lack of dynamism and success he had earlier witnessed within the corporation. Welch's management of GE and it subsidiaries raised the company's value from $12 billion in 1981, to over $280 billion in 2001. In December 2001 GE announced Welch's retirement and granted him a compensation package that included continued access to a company plane, membership in a country club, the firm's box seats at home games of the Boston Red Sox and an apartment in Manhattan. The components of this package became the focus of a SECURITIES and EXCHANGE COMMISSION (SEC) probe in 2003 shortly after his wife filed for divorce and published the details of Welch's retirement in the divorce settlement.

Welensky, Roy (*1907–1991*) Rhodesian statesman. Born in Salisbury (now Harare), he became a railway engineer and trade union leader. In 1938 he founded the Labour Party in Northern Rhodesia (now ZAMBIA) and in 1953 aided in the union of Northern Rhodesia, Southern Rhodesia (now ZIMBABWE) and Nyasaland (now MALAWI) into the Federation of Rhodesia and Nyasaland. He served in a number of federation posts before becoming prime minister in 1956. As head of the government, Welensky advocated interracial cooperation. However, he was unsuccessful in preventing the dissolution of the federation late in 1963. Opposed to Ian SMITH's

declaration of Southern Rhodesian independence from Britain, he retired from politics in 1965.

welfare state Term for the state that guarantees its citizens' economic and social well-being. This policy has applied to democratic governments particularly in the post–World War II period and has addressed such problems as unemployment, illness, disability, old age, housing and social services. The concept of the welfare state is highly developed in the Scandinavian nations and the Netherlands, and was taken for granted in the UNITED KINGDOM from the time of Clement ATTLEE's LABOUR PARTY government until the government of Margaret THATCHER. Manifestations of this approach to social policy include Great Britain's NATIONAL HEALTH SERVICE and unemployment insurance in the U.S. and the U.K. American adaptations of welfare state policies include SOCIAL SECURITY, workers compensation, MEDICAID and MEDICARE.

Welk, Lawrence (*1903–1992*) American band leader. An accordionist, Welk led a six-man band that played on radio in North Dakota in 1925. Welk moved to Chicago during the 1930s to develop his sound, known as "Champagne Music." After 1953 his musicians were heard on radio and seen on television, becoming one of the most popular programs on the air. As musical tastes and social mores changed in the 1960s and later, Welk was the object of many good-natured jokes and satires concerning his "square" music and his central European accent.

Welles, Orson (George Orson Welles) (*1915–1985*) Legendary American actor and director. In his long, spectacular but uneven career, Welles was active in the theater, radio and film. However, his successes all came before he reached the age of 30. He starred on Broadway during his 20s, and also became known to millions as the voice of Lamont Cranston on the radio mystery series *The Shadow*. In 1938, he presented a radio dramatization of H. G. WELLS's *War of the Worlds* that frightened tens of thousands of listeners into thinking that Martians were truly invading Earth. His first film, *CITIZEN KANE*, was re-

Director and actor Orson Welles (LONDON ILLUSTRATED NEWS)

leased in 1941. The film, which he directed, coauthored and starred in, was in 1962 selected as the "best film in motion picture history." In later life, he lived and worked in Europe, taking roles in second-rate films and commercials to allow him to finance his own projects.

Wells, Dickie (William Wells) (*1909–1985*) Jazz trombonist and composer. Wells was one of the leading jazz trombonists of the 1930s and 1940s. He was especially well known for his rhythmic intensity and inventive solos. Wells was raised in Louisville, Kentucky, and first came to New York in the mid-1920s. Over the next two decades, he played with numerous big bands, most notably those led by Fletcher HENDERSON and Count BASIE. Wells remained active as a jazz performer through the 1970s. His compositions include the jazz songs "Sugar Hip" and "Kansas City Strike." He Wrote an autobiography, *The Night People* (1971).

Wells, Edward C. (*1910–1986*) American engineer. His work on the 1935 design for the flap system of the wing of the B-17 Flying Fortress bomber was adopted for use on nearly all U.S.-made jet aircraft. He held 20 patents, including the one for the landing-gear system on the last plane he helped design, Boeing's 767 medium-range passenger jet. He was Boeing's chief engineer when he retired.

Wells, H(erbert) G(eorge) (1866–1946)

British social prophet, novelist, pioneer in science fiction and, in the words of Bertrand RUSSELL, "an important liberator of thought and action." The son of a shopkeeper, Wells's early education and experience ranged from jobs as a draper's assistant, school teacher and textbook writer to study under T. H. Huxley in biology. His first novel, the brilliant *The Time Machine* (1895), was the first literary work in history to suggest the possibility of time travel by means of a *machine*. Integral to the story of a man who travels to the year 30,000,000 (by which time man has become extinct) are the sciences of physics, biology, astronomy and chemistry. In this and succeeding novels and stories in the next five years—including *The Island of Dr. Moreau, The Invisible Man, The War of the Worlds* and *The First Men in the Moon*—he produced his best work. As if echoing the words of the Time Traveller, Wells could say: "With a kind of madness growing upon me, I flung myself into futurity." He kicked away the traces of 19th-century art and ideas and looked to the 20th century and beyond, tackling issues of politics, nuclear war, evolution, interplanetary space travel, mind-altering drugs and new communications technologies. His tendency to sermonize about the ills of man and society came to the fore after the turn of the century in "realistic" novels like *The History of Mr. Polly, Ann Veronica* (both 1909) and *The Shape of Things to Come* (1933). His later years were preoccupied with

British science fiction author H. G. Wells (LIBRARY OF CONGRESS, PRINTS AND PHOTOGRAPHS DIVISION)

causes like the FABIAN SOCIETY and the LEAGUE OF NATIONS. Many of Wells's stories have been adapted for motion pictures, radio and television, beginning in 1918 with an adaptation for the British Gaumont Film Company of *The First Men in the Moon*. That his early optimism about man's progress was replaced late in life by a darker pessimism can be seen in his first and last works. In *The Island of Dr. Moreau* the narrator, Prendrick, concludes that "whatever is more than animal within us" must remain our solace and hope. However, in his last essay, "Mind at the End of Its Tether" (1945), Wells declares that man is doomed because he cannot and will not adapt himself to his technological circumstances. After a long illness, Wells died of cancer in 1946.

Welsh nationalism Political and cultural movement starting among Welsh intellectuals in 1886; favored Welsh language rights, religious equality and local autonomy. The movement, led by Tom Ellis (1859–99) and David LLOYD GEORGE, secured disestablishment of the Church of England (1920) in Wales. Weakened by the challenge of the Labour Party, the movement formed PLAID CYMRU—a political party favoring dominion status for Wales. The party was split between socialists and cultural nationalists, and it turned to violence in the late 1930s. Several of its leaders were imprisoned in 1938. The party gained parliamentary seats only in 1966, and it has held at least two seats in all subsequent elections. Despite failure in the 1979 Devolution Referendum, the movement continued nonviolent action in favor of Welsh-language signs, and opposed English immigration into Welsh-speaking areas. In 1998 British prime minister Tony BLAIR created a regional assembly for Wales. Although the body has no formal power, it is seen by some as a stepping stone toward a Welsh counterpart to the Scottish parliament Blair also created.

Welty, Eudora (1909–2001) American author. Educated at Mississippi State College for Women and the University of Wisconsin, Welty studied advertising at Columbia University in New York City and originally planned to become a commercial artist. She

began writing short stories; her first collection, *A Curtain of Green* (1941), was such a popular success that it enabled her to write full time in her hometown. A regional writer, she is noted for the colloquial accuracy of her dialogue and for her comically understated presentation of absurd rural events. She is the author of the novels *Delta Wedding* (1946) and *The Optimist's Daughter* (1972), as well as collections of short stories, including *The Wide Net* (1943), *The Golden Apples* (1949) and *Thirteen Stories* (1965), *One Time, One Place: Mississippi in the Depression: a Snapshot Album* (1971), *One Writer's Beginnings* (1984) and *Eudora Welty: Photographs* (1989).

Werfel, Franz (1890–1945) Czech-born Jewish novelist and playwright. Werfel, who spent most of his writing career in Austria, was a highly popular novelist and playwright in the era between the two world wars. Werfel served in the Austrian army during World War I, an experience that left him with a deeply held antimilitarist viewpoint. Influenced by EXPRESSIONISM in German drama, Werfel wrote plays including *The Goat Song* (1921) and *Juarez and Maximilian* (1924). Werfel achieved international fame with his novel *The Forty Days of Musa Dagh* (1934), a classic historical novel that portrays Armenian resistance to the Turks in 1915. A subsequent novel, *The Song of Bernadette* (1942), also achieved great popularity for its exploration of inspirational religious themes. Werfel was forced to flee Austria in 1938 to escape the Nazi terror. He settled in the U.S. His final play, *Jacobowsky and the Colonel* (1940), was successfully staged in New York in 1944.

Wertheimer, Max (1880–1943) German psychologist. Wertheimer, along with Kurt KOFFKA and Wolfgang KÖHLER, was a key figure in the development of Gestalt theory as a field of psychological research. Wertheimer's researches helped to demonstrate that humans perceive in terms of immediately structured patterns—termed gestalts—as opposed to continual piecemeal assemblages of the outside world. Wertheimer earned his doctorate in psychology at the University of Würzburg in 1904. He taught for several decades at the Universities of

Frankfurt and Bonn before leaving GERMANY in 1937 to escape Nazi rule. Emigrating to New York, he taught at the New School for Social Research in his final years, applying gestalt theory to social issues. *Productive Thinking* (1945) is his major work.

West, Jerome Alan "Jerry" *(1938–)* American basketball player. West was drafted by the Minneapolis Lakers out of West Virginia University, where he was twice an All-American and 1959 NCAA most valuable player. The team moved before his rookie year, so West spent his entire career with the Los Angeles Lakers. In 1970, he led the league in scoring with 2,309 points and a 31.2 points per game average. An outstanding play making guard, his 2,435 assists place him sixth on the all-time list. A 10-time all-star, he finished his career in 1974 with 25,192 points. Two years after his retirement from active play, West was named coach of the Lakers, a post he held until 1979. That same year, he was named to the Basketball Hall of Fame. From 1982 to 2002 West served as general manager for the Lakers, and helped assemble the talented "Showtime" offense that featured Earvin "Magic" Johnson, as well as the three-time NBA championship teams led by Shaquille O'Neal and Kobe Bryant. In 2002 West left the Lakers to become the general manager of the Memphis Grizzlies.

West, Mae *(1892–1980)* American stage, film and nightclub comedienne known for her sex appeal and saucy, suggestive wit. West's trademarks were her tight gowns, blond hair, sultry voice, suggestive manner and racy double-entendres. Her line, "Why don't you come up and see me sometime?" became one of the most often repeated phrases of its day. Mae West's career spanned more than 60 years, but her heyday was in the 1920s and '30s. She was born in Brooklyn, New York, and performed in VAUDEVILLE while still a child. She acted in several Broadway musicals before starring in *Sex* (1926), which she also wrote, produced and directed. The play caused an uproar; when West was arrested and jailed on obscenity charges, she became an instant celebrity and enjoyed great success in several more plays over the next few years. West made her film debut in HOLLYWOOD in *Night After Night* (1932)

with George RAFT and Constance Cummings, and emerged as a bona fide movie star in *She Done Him Wrong* (1933, with Cary GRANT) and *I'm No Angel* (1933), for which she wrote her own dialogue. Her suggestive performances in these films led the film industry to strengthen the HAYS CODE in 1934. Among her other films were *Belle of the Nineties* (1934); her popularity peaked with *My Little Chickadee* (1940, with W. C. FIELDS). She later appeared in the movie *Myra Breckenridge* (1970). Her autobiography is *Goodness Had Nothing to Do with It* (1959).

West, Nathanael (Nathan Weinstein) *(1903–1940)* American writer. West graduated from Brown University in 1924. His experience as a night manager in a New York City hotel led to the novel *Miss Lonelyhearts* (1933). During the 1930s West worked as a HOLLYWOOD screenwriter and gained inspiration for *The Day of the Locust* (1939). The juxtaposition of disillusion and despair for society with compassion and humor for humanity characterizes his work. His *Complete Works* were published in 1957.

West, Rebecca (Cecily Isabel Fairfield) *(1892–1983)* British novelist, critic and journalist. Born and educated in Edinburgh, West was briefly an actress in London before turning to journalism. She adopted her pseudonym when she was 19 after the heroine in Ibsen's *Rosmersholm*. West was a committed feminist, and her first works appeared in such periodicals as *The Freewoman* and *The Clarion*. Her review of H. G. WELLS's *Marriage* (1912) brought about their meeting and a stormy 10-year relationship during which their son Anthony West (1914–87) was born. Many of her early pieces have been collected into *The Young Rebecca* (1982). West's incisive works of nonfiction include *Henry James* (1916); *Black Lamb and Grey Falcon* (1941), which details a trip she took through YUGOSLAVIA in 1937; *The Meaning of Treason* (1947), which evolved from articles on the NUREMBERG TRIALS commissioned by *The New Yorker;* and *1900* (1982). West's novels include *The Return of Soldier* (1918), *The Thinking Reed* (1936), *The Fountain Overflows* (1956), which is the first of three semiautobiographical novels;

and *The Birds Fall Down* (1966). The unfinished *Sunflower,* which draws upon her experiences with Wells and with Lord BEAVERBROOK, was published posthumously in 1986. Her fiction intelligently explores her characters' motivations and feelings. West, who had married Henry Maxwell Andrews in 1930, remained active and pugnacious to the end of her life, continuing to write and even appearing briefly in the 1981 film *Reds*. In 1959 she was made dame commander in the Order of the British Empire.

West African Cease-Fire Monitoring Group (ECOMOG) A monitoring force created in 1990 by the ECONOMIC COMMUNITY OF WEST AFRICAN STATES (ECOWAS) to help bring an end to the civil war in LIBERIA. Led by NIGERIA, ECOWAS member states had begun to express concern about the effects that a continued and intensifying Liberian civil war could have on the region of West Africa, and decided to serve as an "honest broker" in the conflict. They established ECOMOG, which comprised approximately 4,000 troops from the ECOWAS nations of GAMBIA, GHANA, GUINEA, NIGERIA and SIERRA LEONE to attempt to bring stability and security to the war-torn West African country. In 1997 shortly after the election of Liberian president Charles TAYLOR, ECOMOG forces left Liberia to much international acclaim, and the monitoring group was set to disband. However, an outbreak of civil war in nearby Sierra Leone led Nigeria to transfer 700 of its ECOMOG forces to that country. There it helped to reinstate the nation's deposed president, Ahmed Kabbah, and repel repeated rebel assaults until a UN-sponsored peace-keeping force was dispatched. Shortly after ECOMOG assumed this additional monitoring role, ECOWAS governments met and concurred that the force should be granted a permanent status and budget, so it could be immediately available to restore peace and order to any country in the region that became the victim of internal strife. ECOMOG has since served as a peace-keeping force in Guinea (1999), where the government came under attack from a rebel chieftain, and along the Guinea-Liberian border (2001) to stop the flow of weapons, aid and personnel to rebels seeking to overthrow Taylor. By the end of 2001 Nigerian president Olusegun Obsanajo announced that his country alone had spent over $12 billion for the maintenance of ECOMOG, and questioned its continued utility. However, two years after this statement, a new ECOMOG contingent was dispatched to Liberia in April 2003 to restore order to the country following Taylor's resignation and departure into exile.

West Bank An area of west of the Jordan river, formerly Jordanian territory. Captured by ISRAEL in the 1967 SIX DAY WAR, it has been occupied and administered by Israel ever since. JORDAN's King HUSSEIN renounced Jordanian claims to the West Bank in 1988. However, the Palestinian Liberation Organization has demanded an end of the Israeli occupation and the establishment of a Palestinian homeland in the West Bank region. The INTIFADA (Palestinian uprising) against Israeli rule that began in the late 1980s was centered in the West Bank. Although the West Bank was one of two regions designated in the 1993 Oslo Accords to fall under the jurisdiction of the PALESTINIAN AUTHORITY (PA), the outbreak of violence in the area since 2000 has prevented progress toward the goals established by the Oslo Accords and subsequent agreements (see INTIFADA II).

Western European Union (WEU) Created in 1955 after the failure of the proposed EUROPEAN DEFENSE COMMUNITY, the WEU permitted the rearming of WEST GERMANY by including that country in an expanded version of the 1948 Brussels Pact—a defensive alliance among the UNITED KINGDOM, FRANCE, BELGIUM, the NETHERLANDS and LUXEMBOURG. This arrangement allowed West German military units to take part in the country's defense and to contribute to the defense of Western Europe against the perceived Soviet threat during the COLD WAR. However, to calm French fears about the threat of a renewal of German militarism, the WEU regulated the rearmament of the German armed forces, the *Bundeswehr,* by completely subordinating them to the supreme commander of the NORTH ATLANTIC TREATY ORGANIZATION (NATO) forces and by prohibiting West Germany from possessing or developing nuclear, biological or chemical weapons.

Following its creation, the WEU faded into insignificance, as its defensive obligations were met by the NATO alliance. However, in 1984 French president François Mitterrand tried to resurrect the WEU as a vehicle for promoting greater security cooperation among its members and strengthening what many referred to as the "European pillar" of the Atlantic alliance. By 1987 the European Council, the governing body of the European Community, had endorsed Mitterrand's plan, and WEU members began efforts to create a permanent standing WEU force independent of NATO. These measures of greater European defense cooperation received additional impetus with the end of the cold war, the collapse of the Soviet Union, U.S. president George H. W. BUSH's 1991 decision to reduce American military commitments in western Europe and the acceleration of the trend toward European economic and political integration in the 1990s. The Maastricht Treaty of February 1992, which endorsed the creation of a COMMON FOREIGN AND SECURITY POLICY (CFSP) for the emerging EUROPEAN UNION (EU), designated the WEU as the nucleus of greater military cooperation among the member states of the EU. Starting with the nucleus of a Franco-German Eurocorps formed in 1993, this military contingent of the EU was expanded to include units from Spain, Belgium, and Luxembourg by 1995.

Initially the U.S. expressed its appreciation for the increased European willingness to bear a greater burden for defense that the WEU represented. However, officials in the Clinton administration began to express concern that if the WEU became the military arm of the EU, it would thereby weaken the U.S.-European military alliance, produce a rivalry between the U.S. and its European allies and waste resources through the duplication of tasks. These concerns appeared to be given greater credence following the SAINT MALO CONFERENCE in 1997, where British prime minister Tony BLAIR and French president Jacques CHIRAC proposed the creation of an EU force designed for missions beyond Europe's borders. However, it remains unclear how specifically the EU and the WEU will incorporate their duties with the Franco-British force advocated at

the Saint Malo Conference, or the rapid-reaction force envisioned at the December 1999 Helsinki Conference.

Western Sahara Located on the Atlantic coast of northwestern Africa, Western Sahara covers an area of 102,676 square miles. Spain, which ruled Western Sahara from 1926 to 1976, crushed a revolt (1957–58), stopped a liberation movement (1967–70), rejected a UNITED NATIONS–proposed self-determination referendum for the country (1966) and dismissed claims to the country by MOROCCO and MAURITANIA. In 1976 Spain formally ended its control and partitioned the country between Morocco and Mauritania. Morocco occupied the entire country when Mauritania withdrew its claim in 1979. A Western Sahara nationalist movement declared independence as the SAHARAWI ARAB DEMOCRATIC REPUBLIC in 1976 and fought Morocco for control during the 1980s. Although both sides accepted a UN peace plan in 1988, fighting erupted again in 1989. In 1991 a UN-sponsored cease-fire took effect, which called for an internationally supervised referendum within six months. As of 2004 this vote had yet to occur. In 2001 the group POLISARIO attempted to accelerate the independence of Western Sahara by releasing several Moroccan prisoners. By September 2003 nearly 1,000 Moroccan prisoners had been returned.

West Indies Federation A union of 10 British Colonies—ANTIGUA, BARBADOS, DOMINICA, GRENADA, JAMAICA, MONSERRAT, ST. CHRISTOPHER-NEVIS and Anguilla, ST. LUCIA, ST. VINCENT and TRINIDAD AND TOBAGO—established in 1958. The idea for a federation comprised of Barbados, Jamaica, Trinidad and Tobago and the Leeward and Windward Islands arose in 1947, and finally came to fruition in 1958 with its parliament at Port-of-Spain, Trinidad. In Jamaica, particularly, it was felt that the British were attempting to saddle the wealthier areas of the Caribbean with the poorer ones; and led by Jamaican Prime Minister Sir Alexander BUSTAMENTE, opposition to the federation grew. Following Jamaica's and then Trinidad and Tobago's secession and subsequent independence, the federation ended in 1962. Barbados became independent in 1966. The lesser islands banded together loosely as the West Indies Associate States, but by the 1980s, all had achieved independence except St. Christopher-Nevis, from which Anguilla separated itself in 1980.

Westland affair Internal British government arguments over the fate of Britain's failing Westland Helicopter Co. broke into the open in January 1986 with the leak of sensitive cabinet letters. The letters suggested that the government had decided to sell the firm to an American company rather than to a European consortium that had made a higher bid. This revelation prompted the resignation of Defense Minister Michael HESELTINE and of the industry minister, it also compromised the traditional neutrality of the civil service and undermined the reputation of Prime Minister Margaret THATCHER, who was accused of deeper involvement than she admitted.

Westmoreland, William Childs *(1914–2005)* American general, commander of U.S. forces during the VIETNAM WAR. Born in Spartanburg County, S.C., Westmoreland graduated from West Point in 1936. He was a combat officer in World War II and the Korean War. Returning to the U.S., he was promoted to the rank of general, commanded an airborne division and served as superintendent of West Point (1960–63). After the outbreak of the Vietnam War, he was appointed head of the Military Assistance Command (MACV) (1964), commanding U.S. forces in the field in South Vietnam. Continuing to direct U.S. efforts until 1968, and presiding over American involvement as it grew from several thousand advisers to over 500,000 soldiers, Westmoreland became the focus of much public animosity toward the war. Returned to Washington, D.C., in 1968, he served as army chief of staff until 1972, when he retired from active duty. He later criticized the JOHNSON administration's handling of the war, claiming that he could have defeated North Vietnam after the TET OFFENSIVE if the administration had let him attack communist sanctuaries in Laos, Cambodia and North Vietnam. He brought a libel suit against CBS after a 1982 CBS documentary charged that he had

manipulated intelligence data during the war. The suit was settled out of court in 1985. Westmoreland is the author of *A Soldier Reports* (1976).

Weston, Edward *(1886–1958)* American photographer. Weston is widely regarded as one of the greatest American photographers of the 20th century. A master craftsman with a superb aesthetic eye, Weston became famous for his photographic studies of natural forms such as shells, cacti, peppers, clouds and human nudes. In the 1930s, he founded a school of photography known as "f64," after the smallest camera lens opening—thus signifying the school's emphasis on fine technique. Major published collections of photographs by Weston include the two-volume *Daybooks of Edward Weston* (1961, 1966) and *Edward Weston: Fifty Years* (1979).

West Pakistan See PAKISTAN.

West Side Story A landmark in American musical theater; arguably, with *SHOW BOAT* (1927), *PORGY AND BESS* (1935) and *OKLAHOMA!* (1943), among the greatest of all American music-dramas. It premiered in New York at the Winter Garden Theater on September 26, 1957, and ran for 732 performances. Leonard BERNSTEIN and Stephen SONDHEIM wrote the songs, Arthur Laurents wrote the book and Jerome ROBBINS choreographed the dancing. Basically, it was a variant of *Romeo and Juliet:* Verona was replaced by New York's West Side; the lovers were Maria and Tony; and the feuding families of the Montagues and the Capulets were transformed into rival juvenile gangs—Puerto Rican "Sharks" and American "Jets." Despite its impressive achievement, many critics and audiences at the time were annoyed at its violence, bitter humor and unhappy ending. ("Although the material is horrifying," wrote Brooks ATKINSON, "the workmanship is admirable.") The songs were, by turns, crude "Gee, Officer Krupke"), raucous ("America") and sentimental ("Tonight" and "Maria"). The tender "Wedding Song" remains one of its most effective moments. The dances had an edgy, finger-snapping pulse reflective of the frenetic rhythms of city streets. After several successful revivals, a film adaptation was made in

1961, directed by Robert Wise and Jerome Robbins, starring Natalie Wood and Richard Beymer as Maria and Tony. It won 10 ACADEMY AWARDS, including one as best picture. In 1969 *West Side Story* entered the regular repertory of the distinguished Vienna opera house, the Volksoper.

West Wing The American television drama series created by Aaron Sorkin for the NATIONAL BROADCASTING CORPORATION (NBC) (1999–2006). *The West Wing* examines the private and public activities of fictional U.S. president Josiah Bartlett (played by Martin Sheen) and the members of his Oval Office staff and family. While the writers of *The West Wing* regularly developed their own story lines, they occasionally altered the script of an episode or the plot developments of a season to accommodate new domestic and international events. In the aftermath of the terrorist attacks of **September 11, 2001**, *The West Wing* aired an unscheduled episode called "Isaac and Ishmael" in which White House staff members talked with students who had won a trip to the White House shortly after a "fictional" terrorist attack had occurred on the U.S., and attempted to convince these students of the need for greater understanding of Islam. In its first four years on NBC, *The West Wing* won 24 Emmy Awards. At the end of the 2002–03 television season, Sorkin announced he would no longer serve as the show's executive producer because of growing creative differences with other producers, particularly John Wells, over where to take the focus and story lines of *The West Wing.*

Weygand, Maxime *(1867–1965)* French general. Born in Brussels, he attended the military college at St. Cyr and became a career army officer. During WORLD WAR I and until 1923, he was chief of staff to Marshal FOCH, and in 1920 he reorganized the Polish army and successfully repelled Soviet attacks. His distinguished career included posts as high commissioner of Syria (1923–24), military educator (1924–29) and chief of the French general staff (1930–35). Early in WORLD WAR II he was commander of Middle Eastern forces (1939–40), and was recalled to France to serve as supreme French commander in May

1940. Unable to prevent the fall of France, Weygand served the VICHY government as commander in North Africa (1940) and governor general of Algeria (1941). Suspected of RESISTANCE sympathies, he was imprisoned by the Germans from 1942 to 1945. Returning to France, he was tried and acquitted of charges of collaboration with Germany.

Whale, James *(1896–1957)* British-born film and theatrical director. Whale began his career as a cartoonist before becoming drawn to the theater while serving in a German prisoner of war camp during WORLD WAR I. After a successful stint as a theater director in London in the 1920s, Whale was invited to HOLLYWOOD to make a film adaptation of the play *Journey's End* (1930). Whale's most memorable films were in the horror genre—FRANKENSTEIN (1931), *The Old Dark House* (1932). *The Invisible Man* (1933) and *The Bride of Frankenstein* (1935). Whale gave up his Hollywood career in 1941 to devote himself to painting. His life was fictionalized in the 1998 film *Gods and Monsters.*

Wharton, Edith (Edith Newbold Jones) *(1862–1937)* American novelist of society and manners, whose *The Age of Innocence* won a PULITZER PRIZE in 1920. Born into a socially prominent New York family, she grew up in the social milieu of many of her works—a world of "first families" whose wealth and position were declining under the impact of modern industrial democracy. She married Edward Wharton in 1885 and began a writing career that scored its first big success with *The House of Mirth* in 1905. Two years later she moved to France, where she spent the rest of her life, although many of her subsequent works continued to have American settings. Her wide range of tone and subject was impressive. In *The House of Mirth* and *The Custom of the Country* (1913) she explored with cool, detached prose the tragedy that threatened the pleasure-loving society of the idle rich. "A frivolous society can acquire dramatic significance only through what its frivolity destroys," she wrote. "Its tragic implication lies in its power of debasing people and ideals." In two of her finest works, *Ethan Frome* (1911) and *Summer* (1917), she wielded a more severe prose style to il-

luminate the stunted lives of New England farmers and villagers. And she used her magnificent horror stories as vehicles for her strongest feminist concerns. The stock devices of vampire ("Bewitched"), ghost ("The Lady Maid's Bell") and witch cult ("All Souls") represent the sexual repression and social injustice endured by women. In the opinion of biographer R. W. B. Lewis, Wharton was without peer in her generation in the ability to depict "the modes of entrapment, betrayal, and exclusion devised for women in the first decades of the American and European twentieth century."

Wheldon, Sir Huw Prys *(1916–1986)* BRITISH BROADCASTING CORPORATION executive. Wheldon joined the BBC in 1952 as a television publicity officer, but later worked on many children's shows and documentaries. Deeply committed to the arts, he was responsible for "Monitor," the first arts program on British TV. As managing director of BBC television (1968–75), he was a major influence on British television programming. His assumption of that post marked the first time that a programmer was given overall control of British television.

Whirlaway *(1938–1953)* American race horse; one of the standard-bearers of the great Calumet era, during which seven Calumet horses in less than two decades won the Kentucky Derby. Known for his long, elegant tail, Whirlaway was ridden by Eddie ARCARO to victories in the Kentucky Derby, Preakness and Belmont, becoming only the fifth horse in history to win racing's Triple Crown.

White, Byron R(aymond) *(1917–2002)* Associate justice, U.S. Supreme Court (1962–1993). A graduate of the University of Colorado and Yale Law School, and a Rhodes Scholar at Oxford University, White gained the nickname of "Whizzer" for his exploits on the football field and played professional football for one year after college before enrolling at Oxford. He continued to play professional football while attending Yale Law School before a navy career in World War II. White worked as a law clerk for Supreme Court Chief Justice Frederick VINSON before joining a large Denver law firm.

A Democrat, he worked in the presidential campaign of John F. KENNEDY, who appointed him to the Supreme Court in 1962. Although initially perceived as a member of the liberal majority of the WARREN Court, White's views seemed to grow more conservative, until he was perceived as a member of the conservative bloc in the later part of his career on the REHNQUIST Court. In 1993 White retired from the Supreme Court. He was replaced later that year by President William Jefferson CLINTON's nominee Ruth Bader Ginsburg.

White, Eartha Mary Magdalene *(1876–1974)* American social and community activist. After schooling in New York City, she returned south and started several successful businesses (1905–30). In 1900 she joined Booker T. WASHINGTON to found the National Negro Business League. In 1928 she founded the Clara White Mission, a community house that became the focus of black relief work and a WPA headquarters during the GREAT DEPRESSION. Her work in organizing the proposed 1941 march on Washington led to Presidential Order 8802 banning discrimination in federal hiring for defense and government. In 1967 White founded the Eartha M. White Nursing Home.

White, Edward *(1930–1967)* U.S. astronaut. With *Gemini 4* White became the first American to walk in space on June 3, 1965. Attached to his spacecraft by a long tether, White floated out into the vast vacuum of space while fellow crewmember James MCDIVITT took some of the most stunning photographs of the space program. White tested a small gas handgun to propel himself for part of his 10-minute extravehicular activity (EVA), gaining better control than just pushing off could do. The two returned to Earth after four days in orbit. With Gus GRISSOM and Roger CHAFFEE, White was scheduled to make the fist flight in the APOLLO series that would ultimately land human beings on the moon. But as the three sat sealed and strapped inside the *Apollo 1* cabin during a dry-run test, a sudden spark from an electrical short resulted in an instant inferno, raging through the pure-oxygen atmosphere. Grissom, Chaffee and White never had a chance to get out. White was buried at West Point.

White, E(lwyn) B(rooks) *(1899–1985)* American author and essayist. White was widely regarded as one of the most engaging prose stylists in 20th-century American literature; for most of his writing career he was associated with THE NEW YORKER. White—along with James THURBER—was principal in shaping the magazine's tone and direction. Among the best-known of his many books was *The Elements of Style* (first edition, 1959), a guide to correct English usage that drew upon the privately printed notes of Cornell English Professor William Strunk. In its various editions, the book became a staple of the curriculum in high school and college English classes. White was also the author of three books for children that came to be regarded as classics: *Stuart Little, Charlotte's Web* (1952) and *The Trumpet of the Swan* (1970). White was awarded a special PULITZER PRIZE in 1978.

White, Patrick (Victor Martindale) *(1912–1990)* Anglo-Australian author. Born in London of Australian parents, White grew up in Australia but was educated in England at Cheltenham and King's College, Cambridge. After serving in the RAF in WORLD WAR II, he returned permanently to Australia in 1947. His first published work was a collection of verse written before 1930, *The Ploughman and Other Poems* (1935), and his first novel was *Happy Valley* (published in London, 1939; in the U.S., 1940). *The Aunt's Story* (1948) was acclaimed in the U.K. and the U.S., but was generally ignored in Australia. It was *The Tree of Man* (1955), a realistic family saga of a couple establishing a farm in the Australian outback, that established his reputation and drew comparisons to the work of Leo Tolstoy and D. H. LAWRENCE. Subsequent celebrated works include. *Voss* (1957), *The Vivisectors* (1970) and the *Eye of the Storm* (1973). White was awarded the NOBEL PRIZE for literature in 1973. Later works include the self-portrait, *Flaws in the Glass* (1981), and the novel *Memoirs of Many in One* (1986). White was also a playwright.

White, Ryan *(1971–1990)* American AIDS activist. An Indiana teenager who was a hemophiliac, Ryan White was diagnosed with AIDS in 1984. He was shunned by his classmates and banned from classes. He sued the Kokomo, Indiana, school system and was readmitted. Later, his family moved to Cicero, Indiana, where he found greater acceptance. His story was made into a television movie, and Ryan became an articulate and important spokesman for PWAs (people with AIDS). His funeral was attended by more than 1,500 people, including First Lady Barbara BUSH and singers Michael JACKSON and Elton JOHN.

White, Theodore H(arold) *(1915–1986)* American political writer. One of the most influential journalists of his time, he won early recognition while reporting from China for such publications as the *Manchester Guardian,* the *Boston Globe* and *Time* magazine. His book *The Making of the President 1960* was one of the seminal works of modern political reporting. The book became a huge best seller for which White won a PULITZER PRIZE. He wrote three further *Making of the President* books in 1964, 1968 and 1972. He had planned to write about the 1976 election, but the WATERGATE scandal led him to write *Breach of Faith: The Fall of Richard Nixon.* He later wrote a personal memoir entitled *In Search of History.*

White, Walter Francis *(1893–1955)* Black American leader and author. White was a strong force in the promotion of racial justice in the U.S., as described in his autobiography *A Man Called White* (1948). His other books include *Fire in the Flint* (1924), *Flight* (1926), *A Rising Wind* (1945) and *How Far the Promised Land* (1955). He was secretary of the NATIONAL ASSOCIATION FOR THE ADVANCEMENT OF COLORED PEOPLE (1931–55).

Whitehead, Alfred North *(1861–1947)* British mathematician and philosopher. A graduate of Trinity College, Cambridge, and teacher at Cambridge (until 1922), the University of London (1911–24) and Harvard University (1924–37), Whitehead is known primarily for his contributions to the fields of mathematics, logic, metaphysics and the philosophy of science. His three-volume work *Principia Mathematica* (1910–13), written with his protege Bertrand RUSSELL, remains a milestone in the field of logic. In *Process and Reality* (1929), Whitehead created a complex vocabulary to formulate his concept of reality, which he termed the "philosophy of organism."

Whiteman, Paul *(1891–1967)* American musician. A highly successful leader of JAZZ orchestras and bands, Whiteman conducted two transcontinental symphonic jazz concert tours of the United States between 1924 and 1926, the year his musicians toured the major capitals of Europe. With his work in symphonic music, he became a highly regarded link between classical and jazz forms. He was one of George GERSHWIN's most effective supporters, and conducted the first performance of Gershwin's RHAPSODY IN BLUE, which was composed for Whiteman's band.

Whites Name given to the anti-Bolshevik forces at the time of the RUSSIAN CIVIL WAR. The majority of Whites were Social Revolutionaries, right-wing Social Democrats who disagreed with the MENSHEVIK party, and other rightists. The White Army was first formed among the Don Cossacks and was led by General Lavr KORNILOV and the former czarist chief of staff, Anton DENIKIN. In 1919 General Nicholas YUDENICH, advised by the British, marched from Estonia to take Petrograd. This was unsuccessful; once back in Estonia, his forces disintegrated. As a result, Denikin withdrew and handed over his position to General Peter WRANGEL. Wrangel was defeated, and his forces evacuated from the south of Russia in 1920. By 1922 the Reds had taken Vladivostok, the last stronghold of the Whites. The Whites were unsuccessful because they lacked any leadership of the caliber mustered by the Reds, had no sense of a common purpose and were unable to generate peasant support.

Whiting, Margaret *(1924–)* American popular singer. The daughter of composer Richard WHITING and singer-actress Barbara Whiting, she began her singing career while still in high school, performing in 1941 with Johnny MERCER. Gifted with fine vocal quality and a lively interpretive style, Whiting had her greatest successes during the 1940s. Her first hit, "That Old Black Magic," was followed in 1943 by "My Ideal" and in 1944 by one of her most outstanding records, "Moonlight in Vermont." Her career continued to flourish in the early 1950s, but waned later in the decade. She continued to perform throughout the years that followed, touring with other figures from the 1940s into the 1990s.

Whiting, Richard *(1891–1938)* American composer. A native of Los Angeles, he was mainly self-taught as a pianist and composer. He first gained notice as a composer of scores for Broadway musicals, beginning with *George White's Scandals of 1919* and *Toot Sweet* (both, 1919). Other stage scores included *Take a Chance* (1932), which contained such memorable songs as "Eadie Was a Lady" and "You're an Old Smoothie." His many movie musical scores include *Close Harmony* (1929), *Ready, Willing and Able* 1937) and *Hollywood Hotel* (1938), for which he composed the famous "Hooray for Hollywood." Among his other well-known songs are "Japanese Sandman," "Ain't We Got Fun," "My Ideal" (later a hit record by his daughter, Margaret WHITING) and "Too Marvelous for Words."

Whitlam, Gough (Edward Gough Whitlam) *(1916–)* Prime minister of AUSTRALIA (1972–75). Whitlam was born and educated in Sydney and served in the Royal Australian Air Force before becoming a barrister. He was elected a Labour M.P. in 1952, and established his reputation as a moderate. Whitlam served as deputy leader of the Australian Labour Party from 1960 to 1967, when he succeeded A. A. Calwell as party leader. Labour won the 1972 elections, though without a majority in the Senate, and Whitlam became prime minister, serving until 1975. His tenure was a difficult one. He was unable to enact any Labour measures due to the LIBERAL-dominated senate, and there was dissention in his party over the inflation and high unemployment of the time. Whitlam was forced to discharge his deputy prime minister and his energy minister. 1975, Sir John Kerr, the governor-general, dismissed the government and called for a general election. The Australian Labor Party lost the 1976 election, but Whitlam remained party leader. In the following year, Labour lost again and Whitlam stepped down

from the leadership. He became Australia's ambassador to UNESCO in 1983.

Whittaker, Charles E(vans) *(1901–1973)* Associate justice, U.S. Supreme Court (1957–62). A native of Kansas, Whittaker attended the Kansas City Law School. A Republican, he was appointed a U.S. district court judge in 1954 and was elevated to the U.S. Court of Appeals for the Eighth Circuit by President EISENHOWER in 1956. In 1957, Eisenhower nominated Whittaker to the Supreme Court. Whittaker generally aligned himself with the conservative minority of the WARREN Court, but was not always consistent in his opinions. He resigned after five years for health reasons and maintained an active public life until his death in 1973.

Who, The British ROCK and roll band, founded in 1964. The Who ranked just behind the BEATLES and the ROLLING STONES as one of the three major bands to emerge from the "British Invasion" that swept rock and roll audiences around the world in the 1960s. The original personnel of the Who were Roger Daltrey, vocals; John Entwhistle, bass; Pete Townshend, guitar and Keith Moon, drums. Moon died in 1978 and was replaced by drummer Kenney Jones; the remaining three musicians have continued on as members of the Who to the present day, although Townshend and Daltrey have also pursued solo musical projects. The Who is best known for its driving, slashing rock style featuring the powerful guitar solos of Townshend and the melodramatic vocals of Daltrey. Its biggest hit singles include "My Generation" (1965), "I Can See For Miles" (1967), "Pinball Wizard" (1969), "See Me, Feel Me" (1970) and "Won't Get Fooled Again" (1971). *Tommy* (1969), a rock opera, remains the band's most successful album. *Quadrophenia* (1979) was the soundtrack to a feature film of the same name; *The Kids are Alright* (1979) was the soundtrack to a film documentary of the band. The Who continues to record and mount major live tours.

Who's Afraid of Virginia Woolf? *(1962)* Acclaimed play by American playwright Edward ALBEE. *Who's Afraid of Virginia Woolf* was a dramatic hit on Broadway in 1962 and earned wide-

spread fame for its author. The play is a biting portrayal of a long-time marriage between a professor and his vitriolic and seductive wife that has decayed into mutual hatred between the spouses. A younger married couple that witnesses this hatred—during the course of an evening's visit—is thereby compelled to face the hypocrisy and fear that governs their own union as well. *Who's Afraid of Virginia Woolf* was adapted into a 1966 film directed by Mike NICHOLS and starring Richard BURTON and Elizabeth TAYLOR, who won a Best Actress Award for her role as Martha, the professor's wife.

Wiener, Norbert *(1894–1964)* American mathematician. Wiener is considered one of the most extraordinary mathematicians to be born in the U.S. A child prodigy, his diverse interests included studying mathematical logic with Bertrand RUSSELL. In 1919 Wiener accepted a post at the Massachusetts Institute of Technology, where he remained throughout his stellar career. Among his vast body of singular achievements is his theory of stochastic (random) processes and Brownian motion. He also delved into the work of Fourier, such as the Fourier transforms. He also developed the subject he dubbed "cybernetics." This involves the mathematical analysis of the flow of information in such systems as mechanics and biology, and the analogies between them. Also of import was his work on quantum mechanics.

Wiesel, Elie (Eliezer Wiesel) *(1928–)* Romanian-born Jewish author who won the 1986 Nobel Peace Prize. Wiesel is a remarkable writer who has earned both literary acclaim and an international following for his role as a spokesman for peace and justice. Raised in a pious Hasidic family, Wiesel's world was shattered by the HOLOCAUST, which claimed his father, mother and sister among the 6 million JEWS murdered by the Nazis during WORLD WAR II. Wiesel, a young boy, survived internment in the death camps and came to Paris as a refugee after the war. He worked for over a decade as a journalist before publishing *Night* (1958), his only autobiographical work, which told movingly of the Holocaust horrors. Since then, Wiesel's writing output has been prodigious, including novels such as *Dawn* (1962), *The Gates of the Forest* (1964), *A Beggar in Jerusalem* (1968) and *The Fifth Son* (1983), as well as plays, essays, biblical interpretations and studies of the rabbinical Hasidic masters. In 1978, Wiesel was named by President Jimmy CARTER as chairman of the President's Commission on the Holocaust, on which he served through 1987. Wiesel has been an outspoken opponent of prejudice and injustice in the USSR, South Africa and other areas of the world. He also stirred political controversy by opposing the visit of President Ronald REAGAN to the German army cemetery at Bitburg in 1985. Wiesel has served as the Andrew W. Mellon Professor in the Humanities at Boston University since 1976. Throughout the 1990s Wiesel received numerous honors for his literary and humanitarian work, including the International Brotherhood Award (1990), the Literature Arts award of the National Foundation for Jewish Culture (1992), the Ellis Island Medal of Honor (1992), the Primo Levi Award (1992) and the Yitzhak Rabin Peacemaker Award (1998). Since *The Fifth Son,* Wiesel has brought out several additional fictional and nonfictional works, including The *Six Days of Destruction* (1989), *The Forgotten* (1995), *All Rivers Run to the Sea; Memoirs* (1995), *Memoir of Two Voices* (1996) and *From the Kingdom of Memory* (1996).

Wiesenthal, Simon *(1908–2005)* Born in Russia, Wiesenthal trained an architect and engineer. Most of his family died in Nazi CONCENTRATION CAMPS during WORLD WAR II. Wiesenthal survived and vowed to dedicate his life to bringing Nazi war criminals to justice. In 1961 he founded the Jewish Documentation Center in Vienna. The center documents HOLOCAUST deaths and gathers information on Nazis still at large. He was instrumental in the capture of many Nazis, including Adolf EICHMANN. In recognition of his crusade to bring Nazi war criminals to justice, Wiesenthal received numerous international honors, including the U.S. Congressional Gold Medal (1980), the Austrian Cross of Honor of the Sciences and Arts (1993) and the U.S. Presidential Medal of Freedom (2000). In 2004 Wiesenthal was made a knight of the British Empire (KBE) by Queen Elizabeth II.

Wigner, Eugene Paul *(1902–1995)* Hungarian-American physicist. After receiving his doctorate in engineering in 1925 at the Berlin Institute of Technology, Wigner moved to the U.S. in 1930 and took a post at Princeton, where he was appointed chair of theoretical physics. He remained there until his retirement in 1971. Among his many fundamental contributions to quantum and nuclear physics is his early work on chemical reactions and the spectra of compounds. In the 1930s Wigner shed light on the nuclear force that binds neutrons and protons. He was later involved in the early stages of nuclear reactors, which led to the first controlled nuclear chain reaction. In 1963, Wigner shared the NOBEL PRIZE for physics with Maria Goeppert Mayer and J. Hans Jensen.

Wilbur, Richard *(1921–)* American poet and recipient of the Pulitzer Prize (1956 and 1988) and National Book Award (1956). Wilbur was born in New York City and studied literature at Amherst College, where he received his B.A. in 1942. Upon graduating, he began training as a U.S. Army cryptographer and served in WORLD WAR II (1939–45), but was transferred to the infantry because of suspicions that Wilbur's leftist affiliations during his college days would make him unreliable as a code-breaker. At the end of the war, Wilbur returned to the U.S. and enrolled in Harvard University. While at Harvard he published his first collection of poetry, *The Beautiful Changes* (1947), received his M.A. and taught in the university's renowned Harvard Fellows program until 1954. In 1950, Wilbur brought out his second poetry collection, *Ceremony,* which established his reputation as one of America's most prominent poets. Wilbur left Harvard in 1954 and taught at Wellesley College for one year before accepting a position at Wesleyan University. While teaching English literature and poetry at Wesleyan, Wilbur helped improve the libretto for Leonard Bernstein's musical *Candide* (1956) and published his third collection of poems, *Things of This World* (1956), for which he received the Pulitzer Prize and the National Book Award. He also helped found the Wesleyan University Poetry Series in 1959, which soon became renowned for its introduction of young American poets through its publishing program. Poets in the series included Robert Bly, James Dickey, Richard Howard and James Wright. In 1987 after publishing several additional collections of poetry, as well as translating such classical works as *Beowolf,* Wilbur was named the poet laureate of the U.S., succeeding Robert Penn Warren in that position. A year later, he received his second Pulitzer Prize for *New and Collected Poems.*

Wilder, Billy (Samuel Wilder) *(1906–2002)* American film writer, director and producer. Born in Vienna, Wilder briefly studied law, became a reporter for a Berlin newspaper and began screenwriting in GERMANY in 1929. Wilder fled Hitler's Germany, moved to France where he directed his first film in 1933 and emigrated to the U.S. later that year. He soon developed a reputation for cynical, sophisticated and sharply comedic scripts. Among his early Hollywood works were *Bluebeard's Eighth Wife* (1938), *Ninotchka* (1939) and *The Major and the Minor* (1942), a popular farce that marked his American directorial debut. He established his ability with the film noir genre in *Double Indemnity* (1944), which was followed by the fiercely brilliant ACADEMY AWARD-winning drama *The Lost Weekend* (1945). Wilder won his second best director Oscar for the melodrama *Sunset Boulevard* (1950). Among his later works are the comedies *The Seven Year Itch* (1955), *Some Like it Hot* (1959), *The Apartment* (1960; Academy Award), *Irma La Douce* (1963), *The Fortune Cookie* (1966) and *Buddy, Buddy* (1981). Wilder's final screenplay before his death was the 1995 remake of *Sabrina.*

Wilder, Thornton *(1897–1975)* American playwright and novelist. A teacher by profession, Wilder first gained recognition as a writer with his philosophical novel *The Bridge of San Luis Rey,* which won the 1927 PULITZER PRIZE. In 1938 he made theatrical history and received his second Pulitzer with the nonrealistically constructed play *Our Town,* which used a narrator and improvised staging. His next prize-winning play, *The Skin of Our Teeth* (1942), combined allegory and farce to present human history through the story of a suburban New Jersey family. All of his major writing reflects his concern with man's place in the universe. Other novels include *The Ides of March* (1948), and other dramas include *Three Plays for Bleecker Street* (1962). His last work, *Theophilus North* (1973), is a semiautobiographical story of a retired teacher.

Wilhelm II (*1859–1941*) King of Prussia and kaiser (emperor) of GERMANY, reigned 1888–1918. Wilhelm, who was later to be known as Kaiser Wilhelm, was born in Berlin, the son of Emperor Frederick III and Princess Victoria of England. Frederick III had ruled only three months when he died of cancer and Wilhelm succeeded. Wilhelm was intent on building up the Prussian army and the Prussian profile in the world. Although he had been a childhood admirer of Chancellor Bismarck (1815–98), Wilhelm dismissed Bismarck in 1890, preferring to surround himself with more malleable advisers. Wilhelm's arrogance and provocative behavior alienated Britain, France and Russia, and the kaiser began to gear up for what he thought would be a short, preventative war. When Archduke Franz FERDINAND was assassinated in 1914 and WORLD WAR I began, even Italy, the third member of the Triple Alliance, fought against Germany and Austria. Wilhelm was eclipsed by his generals as the war continued, and on their advice he fled to Holland in 1918. At the 1919 PARIS PEACE CONFERENCE, it was requested of Queen Wilhelmina of Holland that he be returned. She refused, and Wilhelm remained in Doorn with his second wife, Princess Hermine of Reuss. At the advent of World War II, Winston CHURCHILL offered him asylum in England, and Adolph HITLER had offered to allow him to return to one of his estates in Germany, but Wilhelm died in Holland.

Wilkins, Roy (*1901–1981*) American campaigner for CIVIL RIGHTS, head of the NATIONAL ASSOCIATION FOR THE ADVANCEMENT OF COLORED PEOPLE (NAACP) from 1931 to 1977. A diplomatic but indefatigable crusader for racial integration and social justice through constitutional means, he fought the doctrines of black separatism and white supremacy alike. The grandson of a Mississippi slave, Wilkins joined the NAACP while a student at the University of Minnesota. After graduating in 1923, he worked as a journalist for a black newspaper in Kansas City, Missouri, while rising through the ranks of the NAACP. He became leader of the organization in 1931 and guided it through its strongest years. During the 1930s he successfully campaigned for antilynching laws in the South. He was the chief architect of the legal onslaught on school segregation that resulted in the 1954 BROWN V. BOARD OF EDUCATION decision outlawing "separate but equal" public schools. He was also a moving force behind the passage of the CIVIL RIGHTS ACT OF 1964.

Will, George F. (*1941–*) American political columnist, commentator and author. A thoughtful and eloquent spokesman for traditional CONSERVATISM, Will began his career on the staff of Senator Gordon Allott (R., Colo.) before joining the NATIONAL REVIEW as Washington editor in 1973. In 1974, Will began a regular column for *The WASHINGTON POST* and two years later was named a contributing editor to *Newsweek*. Will also acted as an informal campaign adviser to President Ronald REAGAN in 1980. Will promotes conservative viewpoints in his journalism; since the 1980s he has been featured on the weekly news analysis program *This Week With David Brinkley*. He is the author of several books, including *The Pursuit of Happiness and Other Sobering Thoughts* (1978); *Suddenly: The American Idea Abroad and At Home, 1986–1990* (1990) and *Political Essays* (1990). He has also revealed his passion for and knowledge of baseball in *Men at Work: The Craft of Baseball* (1990). In 1976 Will received the Pulitzer Prize for commentary in recognition of his work as a newspaper columnist. Will's later published works include an assessment of the American political scene—*Restoration: Congress, Term Limits and the Recovery of Deliberative Democracy* (1992)—and two collections of his columns—*The Leveling Wind: Politics, the Culture, and Other News, 1990–1994* (1994), and *The Woven Figure: Conservatism and America's Fabric, 1994–1997* (1997).

Williams, Betty (*1943–*) Northern Irish peace activist. (See Mairead CORRIGAN.)

Williams, Edward Bennett (*1920–1988*) American trial lawyer; a Washington, D.C., insider whose clients included many controversial and even notorious figures. Among Williams's best-known clients were Teamsters leaders Jimmy HOFFA and Dave BECK, Senator Joseph MCCARTHY, mobster Frank Costello, fugitive financier Robert Vesco and U.S. Representative Adam Clayton POWELL. Politically active, Williams was a liberal Republican until 1964. That year, he became a Democrat because of the Republicans' treatment of Nelson A. ROCKEFELLER and their nomination of Barry GOLDWATER. He was on good terms with all presidents in the years that followed, except Jimmy CARTER; he led the "Dump Carter" movement in 1980. At the time of his death he headed the law firm of Williams & Connolly and was owner of the Baltimore Orioles baseball team.

Williams, Eric (Eustace) (*1911–1981*) Historian, politician, prime minister of TRINIDAD AND TOBAGO (1962–81). He was widely regarded as the father of British West Indian independence. A graduate of Oxford University, he received his Ph.D. (1938) for a thesis later published as *Capitalism and Slavery* (1944), which became a classic in the field. After teaching history at Howard University in Washington (1939–53), he returned to Trinidad and Tobago, where he quickly became a leader in the independence movement. He founded the People's National Movement (PNM) in 1955, and the following year became chief minister in the colonial government. He was elected prime minister of the newly independent nation of Trinidad and Tobago in 1962. As prime minister, he helped transform the islands from a chain of poverty-stricken sugar colonies into a modern industrialized state.

Williams, Garth (*1912–1996*) American children's book illustrator. Williams studied art at the Westminster School of Art and the Royal Academy of Art in London, winning the 1936 Prix de Rome. After WORLD WAR II he returned to New York and began working as a magazine artist, primarily for the NEW YORKER. He achieved fame for his pencil drawings in E. B. WHITE's children's book *Stuart Little* (1945). The 70 books he illustrated include 11 by Margaret Wise Brown and all of Laura Ingalls Wilder's *Little House* series, as well as many others by prominent children's writers. His pencil drawings and paintings are by turns delicately realistic and whimsical.

Williams, Hank *(1923–1953)* American country music composer, vocalist, guitarist. Williams is widely acknowledged as the greatest star—and most influential composer—in the history of American country music. The story of his life, which saw his rise from small-time musician in Montgomery, Alabama, to star of Nashville's Grand Ole Opry in the early 1950s, has become the stuff of legend, not to mention a biographical Hollywood film, *Your Cheatin' Heart* (1964). In the final years of his meteoric career, Williams was plagued by a failed marriage coupled with alcohol and drug abuse. He died of a heart attack at age 29. His classic songs include "Your Cheatin' Heart," "Honky Tonkin'," "I'm So Lonesome I Could Cry," "Jambalaya," "Hey, Good Lookin'," "Cold, Cold Heart" and "I'll Never Get Out Of This World Alive." His son, Hank Williams, Jr., is also a major country music star. (See also COUNTRY AND WESTERN MUSIC.)

Williams, John (Towner) *(1932–)* American film score composer. Commercially one of the most successful HOLLYWOOD composers ever, Williams has written the music for eight of Hollywood's top-fifteen biggest-grossing movies: *Jaws* (1975), *Star Wars* (1977), *Close Encounters of the Third Kind* (1977), *The Empire Strikes Back* (1980), *Raiders of the Lost Ark* (1981), E.T. (1982), *Return of the Jedi* (1983) and *Home Alone* (1990). Born in Flushing, New York, Williams studied music at Juilliard and then at UCLA. His first Hollywood project was for a film titled *Because They're Young* (1960); he has since scored more than 40 movies, including *The Killers, Valley of the Dolls* and *The Poseidon Adventure*. By the mid-1970s he had become one of the most sought-after composers in Hollywood. His notable collaborations with producer George LUCAS and director Steven SPIELBERG subsequently earned him five ACADEMY AWARDS for best original score. In 1980 he was named conductor of the Boston Pops Orchestra, although his tenure there was not without contro-

versy. In 1993 Williams left the Boston Pops and accepted the title of Laureate Conductor. Williams's latest Academy Award for Best Score came in 1993 for his work on the Holocaust drama, *Schindler's List* (1992), which also won him a 1994 Grammy Award for Best Instrumental Composition for a Motion Picture or Television. He received the same award in 1998 and 1999 for his work on the films *Savings Private Ryan* (1998) and *Angela's Ashes* (1999), respectively.

Williams, Mary Lou (Mary Elfrieda Scruggs) *(1910–1981)* American JAZZ pianist, arranger and composer. During her 50–year career she was associated with most of the well-known jazz musicians of the time. Versatile and influential, she was regarded almost as a barometer of musical style, playing and excelling in RAGTIME, DIXIELAND, SWING, BEBOP and sacred jazz music. She made a number of recordings, including such numbers as *Walkin' but Swingin'* and *Froggy Bottom.* She wrote such songs as "Roll 'Em" and "Camel Hop" for Benny GOODMAN.

Williams, Paul Revere *(1895–1980)* American architect. The first African-American member and fellow of the American Institute of Architects, he practiced in Los Angeles from 1915–73. He is known for the sumptuous southern California homes he designed for important figures in the film industry, beautifully detailed structures executed in a number of period styles including Georgian, Colonial, Tudor, Mediterranean and Norman. One of his most significant designs is the Litton Industries Building (originally the M.C.A. Building), an award-winning Beverly Hills landmark built in the mid-1930s. Among Williams's other designs are the Grave of the Unknown Sailor in Pearl Harbor, the Polo Lounge at the Beverly Hills Hotel and elements of the Los Angeles International Airport.

Williams, Raymond *(1921–1988)* British cultural historian. In such works as *Culture and Society* (1958) and *The Country and the City* (1973) Williams examined the relationship between literature and society from a leftist perspective. His books also included novels and a major critical biography of author George ORWELL

(1971). Williams was professor of drama at Cambridge University from 1974 to 1983.

Williams, Robin (McLaurin) *(1952–)* American comedian, actor, and winner of the Academy Award for Best Supporting Actor (1997). Born in Chicago, Illinois, Williams studied drama at the renowned Juilliard School of New York City. Williams left Juilliard for California, where he was cast as Mork, an alien, in a spin-off show called *Mork and Mindy,* which followed the life of Mork as he attempted to discover more about Earth and report back to his leader, Orson. Williams gained nationwide recognition and an Academy Award nomination for his role as military disc-jockey (DJ) Adrian Cronauer in the comedy *Good Morning Vietnam* (1987). Williams's appearance as preparatory school instructor John Keating in *Dead Poets Society* (1989) was equally successful, earning him another Academy Award nomination. *The Fisher King* (1991), in which he played a depressed man obsessed with his quest to find the Holy Grail, earned him additional accolades and a third Academy Award nomination.

In 1992 he provided the voice for the genie character in Disney's commercially successful animated film *Aladdin* (1992). Other films in the same child-oriented genre were to come: *Mrs. Doubtfire* (1993), in which he played a man who disguises himself as a nanny to see his kids who are in the custody of his ex-wife; *Jumanji* (1995), about a man caught in a board game; and *Flubber* (1997), in which he depicted a scientist who discovers a gravity-defying substance. In the meantime Williams continued to work in adult-oriented films, including *The Birdcage* (1996), in which he played a gay father whose son has become engaged to the daughter of a conservative senator, and *Good Will Hunting* (1997), in which he depicted a psychologist seeking to aid a troubled genius. It was for his performance in *Good Will Hunting* that Williams received his first Academy Award for Best Supporting Actor in 1997.

Williams, Roger J. *(1893–1988)* U.S. biochemist and nutritionist; discovered the growth-promoting vitamin pantothenic acid. For more than four decades Williams directed the

University of Texas laboratory that was credited with the discovery of more vitamins and their variants than any other lab in the world. His older brother, Robert R. Williams, was the scientist who isolated vitamin B-1.

Williams, Shirley Vivien Teresa Brittain (1930–) British politician. The daughter of the author Vera BRITTAIN, Williams served as secretary to the FABIAN SOCIETY from 1960 to 1964, when she was elected to Parliament. She held various junior ministerial posts, and served as secretary of state for prices and consumer protection from 1974 to 1976, and for education and science from 1976 to 1979, when she lost her seat. In 1981, along with Roy JENKINS, William RODGERS and David OWEN, she left the LABOUR PARTY and formed the SOCIAL DEMOCRATIC PARTY, serving as its president in 1982. She was considered the most left-wing of the moderate "GANG OF FOUR." Williams was reelected to Parliament in a by-election in 1981, but was unseated in the general election of 1983. In 1993 Williams reentered Parliament as a life peer in the House of Lords. In 2001 she was elected leader of the Liberal Democrats in the House of Lords.

Williams, Tennessee (Thomas Lanier Williams) (1911–1983) American playwright, generally considered one of the greatest of all 20th-century American writers for the stage. Raised in Mississippi, he was catapulted to fame in 1945 with the performance of his first successful play, *The Glass Menagerie.* His plays, usually set in his native South and often partly autobiographical, frequently dealt with the loss of beauty, the harshness of reality and the appeal of illusion. In addition to *The Glass Menagerie,* the most notable of his 24 plays were *A Streetcar Named Desire* (1947) and *Cat on a Hot Tin Roof* (1955), both of which won PULITZER PRIZES. Williams also won four Drama Critics Circle Awards. His plays after *The Night of the Iguana* (1961), however, were received less favorably by both critics and audiences, and his career declined. In his later years, Williams suffered from alcoholism, drug addition and mental illness, but he continued to write. He died by choking on a bottle cap. In its decadent atmosphere and dark intensity, his work is often compared to that of William FAULKNER and

American playwright Tennessee Williams, 1963 (NEW YORK WORLD-TELEGRAM AND *THE SUN* NEWSPAPER COLLECTION, LIBRARY OF CONGRESS, PRINTS AND PHOTOGRAPHS DIVISION)

Eugene O'NEILL. Among leading American actors who gained distinction in his plays or in screen adaptations of them were Marlon BRANDO, Burl IVES, Paul NEWMAN and Elizabeth TAYLOR.

Williams, Ted (Samuel) (1918–2002) American baseball player. Obsessed by the art of hitting, Williams translated his studies into six American League batting championships, a total surpassed only by Ty COBB. He spent 20 seasons with the Boston Red Sox, twice interrupted for military service, and amassed a total of 521 home runs and a batting average of .344. His left-handed swing is regarded as one of the most classic in the history of the game. Williams's temper was as legendary as his stance, as he had little patience for writers, fans or most other ballplayers. He retired in 1960 and was named to the Hall of Fame in 1966. From 1969 to 1972, he was manager of the Washington Senators/Texas Rangers. Williams's death in 2002 stirred controversy among his family members and baseball fans when his son and executor of his estate, John Henry Williams, cryogenically froze his father's corpse, despite claims by relatives and friends that Ted Williams wished to be cremated.

Williams, William Carlos (1883–1963) American poet and novelist.

Williams was born in Rutherford, New Jersey, and received an M.D. from the University of Pennsylvania Medical School in 1906. While practicing medicine in Rutherford, he published poetry in Ezra POUND's anthology *Des Imagistes* (1914) and in the periodicals *Poetry, The Egotist* and *The Little Review.* He also coedited *Contact* (1920–23). Influenced by IMAGISM as well as CUBISM and SURREALISM, Williams used consciously plain language to reveal the beauty of everyday objects and surroundings. His well-known poems include "January Morning" (1917), "The Great Figure" (1921), "The Red Wheelbarrow" (1923); his long poem "Paterson" is considered his masterwork. His short stories were collected in *The Farmer's Daughters* (1961), and his novels include *White Mule* (1937), *In the Money* (1940) and *The Buildup* (1952). Although retiring from medicine in 1951, following a stroke, Williams wrote copiously until his death. In 1963 he won the PULITZER PRIZE and the Gold Medal of the National Institute of Arts and Letters.

Willis, Frances E. (1899–1983) The first woman career officer in the U.S. Foreign Service to serve as a U.S. ambassador. Commissioned in the Foreign Service in 1927, she was named by President Dwight D. EISENHOWER to head the U.S. embassy in SWITZERLAND in 1953. In 1957 Eisenhower appointed her ambassador to NORWAY. In 1961 President John F. KENNEDY appointed her ambassador to Ceylon (now SRI LANKA), where she served until her retirement in 1964.

Willkie, Wendell (Wendell Lewis Willkie) (1892–1944) American lawyer and presidential candidate. Willkie attracted national attention during the GREAT DEPRESSION as president and chief executive officer of the Commonwealth and Southern Corporation, a giant utility holding company, and as a crusader for the LEAGUE OF NATIONS and against the KU KLUX KLAN and two policies of the NEW DEAL: the Public Utility Holding Company Act and the TENNESSEE VALLEY AUTHORITY. While acknowledging past abuses in the management of utilities, Willkie opposed public ownership and excessive federal control. His winning of the Republican presidential nomination in

1940 over better-known candidates such as Thomas E. DEWEY and Robert A. TAFT was remarkable, considering that many of his best friends never knew that he had changed party affiliation and that he did not actively campaign until May, too late to enter many primaries. His victory was due to his reputation in the business community, his support from several key Republicans, his personal charisma and his strong stand for aid to England after Germany's easy conquest of the Continent. In the election Willkie polled a larger popular vote than any other Republican candidate before Eisenhower, but lost to F. D. ROOSEVELT by a wide margin.

Following the election, Willkie worked to unite the country behind aid to Britain. He supported Roosevelt's LEND-LEASE proposal and became the president's good will ambassador to the Middle East, the Soviet Union and China. His "Report to the People" radio broadcast upon his return to the United States was estimated to have had a larger audience than any speech except Roosevelt's following the attack on PEARL HARBOR. His theme became one of encouraging colonial peoples to join the West in a global partnership based on economic, racial and political justice. Willkie campaigned for the 1944 Republican presidential nomination, but lost in the Wisconsin primary and withdrew from the race. Excluded by Dewey from an active role, Willkie attempted to influence the party with a series of newspaper articles entitled a "Proposed Platform" in which he called for antilynching laws, an extension of Social Security, and a world organization in which the small states would have real power. Campaigning weakened him, and he died after a series of heart attacks.

Wills, Garry *(1934–)* American journalist, educator and author. Wills is a conservative commentator who has occasionally embraced liberal issues. While writing for the *National Review,* he adopted an anti-Vietnam War, pro–Civil Rights stance and moved on to write for *Esquire.* Wills developed the theory of "the convenient state," which posits that a confluence of interests rather than an enforcing authority holds things together. He writes a nationally syndicated column, "The Outrider," and is a professor of American culture and public policy at Northwestern University. His books include *Confessions of a Conservative* (1979), *Explaining America* (1981) and *The Kennedy Imprisonment* (1982). In 1993 Wills received the Pulitzer Prize for general nonfiction.

Wilson, Charles Thomson Rees *(1869–1959)* Scottish physicist. The son of a sheep farmer, Wilson studied physics at Cambridge University. There he began experiments to duplicate cloud formation in the laboratory. He observed the effect of X rays on cloud formation. In 1911 he perfected the cloud chamber, for which he won the NOBEL PRIZE for physics in 1927. The cloud chamber became an indispensable aid to research into subatomic particles and, with the addition of a magnetic field, made different particles distinguishable by the curvature of their tracks. Returning to the study of real clouds, Wilson also investigated atmospheric electricity and developed a sensitive electrometer to measure it. He was able to determine the electric structure of thunderclouds.

Wilson, Colin *(1931–)* English novelist, philosopher and literary critic. Wilson is a prolific writer whose central interests—as expressed in both his fiction and his nonfiction works—revolve around the evolutionary potential of humankind and the unique and startling capacities of the brain. Wilson won international acclaim for his first book, *The Outsider* (1956), an analysis of existential alienation and its role in 20th-century philosophy and literature. He has since written over 40 more books, including the novel *The Philosopher's Stone* (1968), the scholarly compendium *The Occult: A History* (1971) and a biographical study, *Aleister Crowley: The Nature of the Beast* (1987). In the 1990s, Wilson's published works—*Alien Dawn* (1998) and *Devil's Party* (2000)—focused on the occult.

Wilson, Edmund *(1895–1972)* American social and literary critic, widely considered the foremost critic of his time. Wilson was the son of an affluent lawyer and one-time attorney general in Red Bank, New Jersey. Early on he was exposed to the literary life, contributing to Princeton University's *Nassau Literary Magazine* and befriending F. Scott FITZGERALD. In 1920 Wilson became managing editor of *Vanity Fair* (1920–1921). A year later he was hired as the drama critic for *The New Republic* and in 1926 he was named associate editor of the magazine. During this decade his influential essays helped determine the literary fate of some of the 20th century's greatest writers, including Henry JAMES, Ernest HEMINGWAY, Eugene O'NEILL and Willa CATHER. In the 1930s he became a political activist of sorts, writing articles condemning LIBERALISM and hailing the principles of COMMUNISM. But his reputation as a leading critic and man of letters continued into the 1940s when he became book critic for THE NEW YORKER (1944–48). Over the years his pieces were collected in volumes such as *Axel's Castle* (1931), *The American Jitters: A Year of the Slump* (1932), *The Wound and the Bow* (1941) and *The Shores of Light* (1952). In spite of his controversial political status and opposition to paying taxes, Wilson was awarded the Presidential Medal of Freedom in 1953.

Wilson, Edward Osborne *(1929–)* American entomologist, ecologist and sociobiologist. Wilson emerged as a controversial household name in 1975, when he argued that "a single strong thread does indeed run from the conduct of termite colonies and turkey brotherhoods to the social behavior of man." In his earlier work as an entomologist, he restricted his theories to the organization of social insects such as ants, which was comprehensively outlined in the 1971 publication of his *Insect Societies.* However, when he extrapolated to include human behavior in his sociobiological belief system, his viewpoint was dismissed by many. In 1990 Wilson collaborated with Bert Hoelldobler on *The Ants,* a sociobiological account of ant life. It won the Pulitzer Prize later that year.

Wilson, Harold Albert *(1874–1964)* British-born physicist and educator. Educated in England, Wilson taught in London, Montreal and Glasgow before taking a professorship at Rice Institute in Houston (1912–47). He achieved fame for his verification of the electromagnetic equations of such forebears as Albert EINSTEIN. His books include *The Mysteries of the Atom: Electricity* (1934).

Wilson, (James) Harold *(1916–1995)* British politician, prime minister of the UNITED KINGDOM (1964–70, 1974–76). Born in Yorkshire, Wilson was educated at Wirral Grammar School and Jesus College, Oxford, where he later lectured in economics. During WORLD WAR II, Wilson was a civil servant in the Ministry of Fuel, and was elected to Parliament as a Labour member in 1945. He served as president of the Board of Trade from 1947 to 1951, and in 1954 joined the LABOUR PARTY's parliamentary committee. During Hugh GAITSKELL's party leadership, Wilson was the party's mouthpiece on economic matters and was considered the leader of Labour's left wing. Wilson succeeded Gaitskell as party leader in 1963 and became prime minister following the 1964 elections, which Labour won by a narrow margin. By the following year, his majority in Parliament had increased nearly 100 percent. Wilson balanced the budget and heightened the role of prime minister in global affairs, but he was castigated by the press and in the 1970 elections the Conservatives were voted into power. Wilson became prime minister again in 1974, following Edward HEATH's inability to cope with economic strife and labor strikes. Wilson placated labor with the "social compact" agreement with trade unions, which gained him a sufficient majority in the elections later in the year; he also devalued the pound, froze prices and wages and raised taxes in an attempt to bolster the economy. He resigned unexpectedly in 1976 and was succeeded by James CALLAGHAN. Wilson was knighted that year and named a baron in 1983, thus entering the House of Lords.

Wilson, Lanford (Eugene) *(1937–)* Pulitzer-Prize-winning American playwright, product of the off-off-Broadway theater scene in the 1960s. He was born in Lebanon, Missouri (subsequent location for several plays), and grew up in the towns of Springfield and Ozark, Missouri, where he finished high school. Early plans to be a painter and illustrator were abandoned when he discovered that he could write. He migrated to New York in the summer of 1962 and soon had a number of short plays produced at the Caffe Cino, an important independent theater in the growing "off-off-Broadway" movement in GREENWICH VILLAGE. He found there an atmosphere of theatrical experimentation denied writers on Broadway—or even on off-Broadway. An early play, *Home Free!* (1964), was directed by Marshall W. Mason, with whom Wilson formed a productive professional relationship. Subsequent plays of this period included *Balm in Gilead* (1965), *Rimers of Eldritch* (1966) and *The Gingham Dog* (1968). They forged the Wilson style—disparate groups of people peopling late-night diners, town squares and hotel rooms, each character representing a counterpoint of dreams, false hopes and crippling reality. Numerous plots and dialogues unfold simultaneously, and the action seems to repeat and double back on itself. Realism and a more poetic symbolism become a shifting figure-ground relationship. In 1968 Wilson and Mason cofounded the Circle Repertory Company, which he has described as "sort of a loose collective of writers and designers and actors and directors, presently located in Greenwich Village." It has premiered many of his subsequent plays, *The Hot L Baltimore* (1973), *The Mound Builders* (1975), *Burn This* (1986) and the so-called Talley Trilogy—*Fifth of July* (1978), *Talley's Folly* (1980) and *A Tale Told* (1981). The trilogy tells the story of the Talley family over several generations and is set in Lebanon, Missouri. The second play won Wilson a PULITZER PRIZE in 1980. Wilson continued to produce plays throughout the 1990s, such as *Redwood Curtain* (1993) and *Book of Days* (1998). Although many of his plays have been staged on television, to date none of them have been adapted for motion pictures. He cites playwrights Tennessee WILLIAMS and Brendan BEHAN as important influences on his work; in turn, younger playwrights like David Mamet acknowledge Wilson's impact upon them.

Wilson, Margaret *(1882–1976)* American author. Wilson was educated at the University of Chicago and went to India as a Presbyterian missionary. She wrote many articles and gave numerous lectures on life in India, especially on the treatment of Indian women. In India she met Douglas Turner, a British criminologist, and they were married. Wilson continued her writing, and in 1924 won the PULITZER PRIZE for fiction for her novel *The Able McLaughlins,* which she claimed was a true account of life in the Traer, Iowa, community where she grew up. Her writing continued with other novels and the nonfiction *The Crime of Punishment.* This was based on her study of the British criminal system which her husband headed. The book was widely hailed and as widely criticized for its sharp denunciation of the system.

Wilson, Teddy *(1912–1986)* American jazz pianist and arranger. Wilson was one of the most popular—and critically acclaimed—JAZZ pianists of the 20th century. His style was marked by restraint, elegance and depth of feeling. Wilson was raised in Alabama and first won renown for his playing in the Chicago area in the early 1930s, including a stint with a band led by Louis ARMSTRONG. Wilson then moved to New York where he achieved national fame through his work with various bands led by Benny GOODMAN. Wilson also led his own small jazz combos and became a favored accompanist for jazz vocalists, including Ella FITZGERALD and Billie HOLIDAY. Wilson remained active on the New York jazz scene through the 1970s and participated in several reunion concerts by the Benny Goodman band.

Wilson, Woodrow *(1856–1924)* American educator, author, governor of New Jersey and 28th president of the U.S. The son of a Presbyterian minister, the future president was named Thomas Woodrow Wilson at birth. He moved with his family from Virginia to Georgia, South Carolina and North Carolina in his youth, and first attended college at Davidson in North Carolina in 1873. The bulk of his undergraduate education, however, took place at Princeton, where he graduated with a B.A. in 1879. Wilson returned to the South to study law at the University of Virginia and practice law in Atlanta, Georgia, then studied history and political science at Johns Hopkins University in Baltimore, where he was awarded his Ph.D. in 1886. After brief teaching appointments at Bryn Mawr

College in Pennsylvania and Wesleyan University in Connecticut, he accepted a full professorship of jurisprudence and political science at Princeton, where he remained until 1910.

An influential writer in his field and on education subjects, Wilson became president of Princeton in 1902. His knowledge of political theory led to ambitions for practical political influence, and in 1910 he resigned from the university and successfully ran for the governorship of New Jersey as a Democrat. Only two years later, in 1912, he became the Democratic nominee for president on the basis of support from William Jennings BRYAN; he won the general election when dissension between supporters of Theodore ROOSEVELT and William Howard TAFT split the REPUBLICAN PARTY.

Reelected by a slight margin in 1916, Wilson oversaw the American involvement in WORLD WAR I. On April 2, 1917, he reluctantly asked Congress to declare war on Germany, which it did on April 6. In 1918 Wilson formulated the famous FOURTEEN POINTS that he thought would make the world "safe for democracy." Peace came with the TREATY OF VERSAILLES on January 18, 1919, and because this was negotiated according to Wilson's formulations he was awarded the NOBEL PRIZE for peace in that year. The treaty included establishment of a LEAGUE OF NATIONS, but for lack of a clause to guarantee U.S. supremacy on war votes it was not ratified in the U.S. Senate. Wilson launched a concentrated campaign to secure ratification of the League of Nations idea, but it failed to sway the Senate. Bitterly disappointed and taxed by overwork, in October 1919 he suffered a stroke from which he never fully recovered.

Winchell, Walter (*1897–1972*) American columnist and radio commentator. During the 1930s and 1940s Winchell had the most popular radio show and newspaper column in the country. He is regarded as the creator of the modern gossip column. Originally a vaudeville performer, he began writing columns for *The Vaudeville News* and *Billboard* in the early 1920s Then, after five years as entertainment editor for the *Evening Graphic,* he joined the staff of *The Mirror* (1929) in New York City. His melodramatic,

slang-filled items on show business people and politicians reflected his personal views. His column and popularity had faded by 1960.

Windgassen, Wolfgang (*1914–1974*) German singer. Windgassen is most often associated with his regular performances in the Wagnerian heldentenor roles at the BAYREUTH FESTIVAL. He made his operatic debut in Verdi's *La Forza del Destino* in 1941 and achieved widespread fame with his performance in the title role of *Parsifal* at Bayreuth in 1951. His major roles included Tristan in *Tristan und Isolde* and title roles in *Tannhäuser* and *Lohengrin.*

Windscale accident (*October 7–10, 1957*) A fire in Great Britain's Windscale Pile No. 1 plutonium production plant (later renamed SELLAFIELD) caused the escape of as much as 20,000 curies of radioactive iodine, the largest known release of radioactive gases. More than 30 cancer cases were eventually linked to the incident, but the British government did not acknowledge the accident's scope until 1978. Along with CHERNOBYL and THREE MILE ISLAND, Windscale entered the lexicon of the late 20th century as a symbol of the potential for disaster in nuclear power.

Windsor, duchess of (Wallis Warfield Simpson) (*1896–1986*) An American divorcee, she was at the heart of a British constitutional crisis in 1936, when it became known that King EDWARD VIII, a 41-year-old bachelor, wished to marry her and have her crowned queen. His family, the government and the Church of England were violently opposed, leading to his abdication in December 1936. He was given the title duke of Windsor, and she became duchess when they married in 1937. The couple lived outside England the rest of their lives as international socialites. She and the duke returned to England in 1976 to attend a ceremony commemorating the duke's mother, and upon their deaths, both were buried there.

Windsor, duke of See EDWARD VIII.

Winfrey, Oprah (*1954– *) American daytime television talk show hostess and movie actress. Born in Kosciusko,

Talk show host, actress and media tycoon Oprah Winfrey (PHOTOFEST)

Mississippi, Winfrey's career in television began in 1973 when she was hired at the Nashville television station WTVF as a reporter and news anchor. In 1976 Winfrey was hired as coanchor of prime-time news programs at television station WJZ in Baltimore, Maryland. Two years later, WJZ named her the cohost of its weekly local talk show, *People Are Talking.* Winfrey's ability to stimulate animated conversation prompted Chicago television station WLS to hire her in 1984 to host its *AM Chicago,* a half-hour show suffering from dwindling ratings. By the end of the year she had transformed *AM Chicago* into Chicago's most discussed local television program, which was soon renamed *The Oprah Winfrey Show.* Winfrey's skills on the small screen brought her to the attention of director Steven Spielberg, who cast her as Sofia in his 1985 adaptation of the Alice Walker novel *The Color Purple.*

In 1986, Winfrey's star continued to rise, as her talk show entered national syndication, and she received nominations for an Academy and a Golden Globe Award for her performance in *The Color Purple.* 1986 was also the year Winfrey decided to found Harpo Productions, Inc., a television and film production company that would allow her to advance her own projects. In 1988 Harpo purchased her talk show from Capitol Cities/ABC, giving Winfrey complete control over its production, syndication and topics. In 1989 Harpo released its first miniseries, *The Women of Brewster Place,* followed by several made-for-television movies, such as *There Are No Children Here* (1993), and

Before Women Had Wings (1997). Winfrey starred in all three films.

In 1998 Winfrey appeared as Sethe, one of the primary characters in Harpo's first motion picture, an adaptation of Toni Morrison's Pulitzer Prize–winning novel *Beloved*. While the movie received several positive reviews, it failed to equal the critical acclaim and commercial appeal of *The Color Purple*. The year 1998 was also when Winfrey helped found the entertainment media company Oxygen Media and introduced her audiences to Dr. Phil McGraw, a self-described "life strategist." Dr. Phil became known for his "straight-shooting" advice to her audience members. In 2000 Oxygen Media launched the cable-based and female-oriented Oxygen Network, on which Winfrey debuted the 12-part *Oprah Goes Online* to instruct viewers on using the resources of the INTERNET. In the same year Winfrey and Heart Magazines began production of the monthly *O, The Oprah Magazine*, a periodical designed to offer additional lifestyle suggestions, as well as health, fashion, education and entertainment information. In 2002 Harpo Productions gave McGraw his own nationally syndicated television series, *Dr. Phil*, which has since become the second-most-watched daytime talk show.

Wingate, Orde (Orde Charles Wingate) *(1903–1944)* British general. A colorful career army officer, famous for his brilliantly unorthodox style, Wingate was commissioned in the Royal Artillery in 1922. From 1928 to 1933 he served in the Sudan. On special duty in PALESTINE (1936–39), he organized Jewish guerrilla squads against Arab sabotage. During WORLD WAR II, he again called on his tactical cunning in leading the "Gideon's Force" guerrillas against the Italians in Ethiopia in 1940–41. He is best known for his subsequent guerrilla activities in Burma. In 1942–43 Wingate trained and led an Anglo-Indian force known as the "Chindits," harassing Japanese forces from behind their own lines. Promoted to the rank of major general in command of airborne strikes into Burma in 1944, he was killed in an airplane crash shortly thereafter.

Winston, Henry *(1911–1986)* American Communist Party chairman. Born into a family of Mississippi sharecroppers, he was active in the Southern Youth Negro Congress before joining the U.S. Communist Party in 1933. Convicted in 1949 under the Smith Act of conspiring to teach and advocate forcible overthrow of the U.S. government, he was jailed upon his surrender in 1956. He went blind before winning his release in 1961. He served as chairman of the Communist Party, U.S.A. from 1966 until his death.

Winter War See RUSSO-FINNISH WAR OF 1939–40.

Witte, Count Sergei Yulyevich *(1849–1915)* Russian statesman. In 1892 Witte was appointed minister of transport and from 1892 to 1903 was minister of finance. He encouraged industrial growth in RUSSIA by protectionist tariffs, large foreign loans and the large-scale building of railways. From 1903 to 1906 Witte was prime minister. He was in charge of negotiating the peace treaty with Japan at Portsmouth, New Hampshire. As a moderate conservative, Witte was attacked by both liberals and the extreme right. After his dismissal by the czar, he continued as an independent member of the council of state.

Wittgenstein, Ludwig Josef Johann *(1889–1951)* Austrian-born philosopher. Wittgenstein was one of the most influential philosophers of the 20th century. Born in Vienna, he trained as an engineer in his native land and at the University of Manchester in Britain before switching to the study of philosophy at Cambridge University in 1912. At Cambridge, his major mentor was Bertrand RUSSELL, whose interests in mathematics and the foundations of logic were shared by Wittgenstein. Wittgenstein's interest in language as an expression of experience was evidenced by the patronage he provided during this period—out of his inherited family funds—to poets Rainer Maria RILKE and George TRAKL. During WORLD WAR I, he served in the Austrian army. His first major work was the *Tractatus Logico-Philosophicus* (1922), which argued that logical truth was no more than tautology, that language functions as a "picture" of reality and that certain aspects of reality cannot be said, only shown. Yet, Wittgenstein asserted, "the world is everything that is the case." Other works by Wittgenstein include *Philosophical Investigations* (1935) and *Remarks on the Foundations of Mathematics* (1956). Wittgenstein taught at Cambridge University for most of the final decades of his life. Wittgenstein's brother **Paul Wittgenstein** was a noted concert pianist who lost his right arm in World War I. Several composers subsequently wrote new works for Paul Wittgenstein; among these is Maurice RAVEL's Concerto for the Left Hand.

Wodehouse, P(elham) G(renville) "Plum" *(1881–1975)* British-born comic author. Most of Wodehouse's works are parodies of life among the British aristocracy of the 1920s and '30s. Dubbed "the Master" by Evelyn WAUGH, he is best known for his novels featuring Bertie Wooster, a bumbling but likeable aristocrat, and Jeeves, his discreet and capable valet. His work is rich in simile, as well as fractured fragments of schoolboy knowledge. During WORLD WAR II Wodehouse made several humorous broadcasts that some officials considered treasonous. He was exonerated in later years. After the war he moved to the U.S. and became a citizen, settling on Long Island, where he continued to turn out his popular books for an appreciative trans-Atlantic readership. The England that he depicted in fact bore little relation to the actual place, but evolved in his work into a land where time stood still. Wodehouse also wrote numerous articles, essays, plays, screenplays and lyrics. He was knighted in 1975, shortly before his death.

Wolf, Christa *(1929–)* German novelist and literary critic. Wolf is one of the leading novelists to have been published in communist EAST GERMANY prior to the 1990 German reunification. Born in Landsberg an der Warthe, Wolf was educated at the Universities of Jena and Leipzig. She won immediate critical praise for her first novel, *Divided Heaven* (1963), which explored the psychological and social effects caused by the division of the German nation. This theme was again successfully pursued in Wolf's next novel, *The Quest for Crista T.* (1968). *The Reader and the Writer* (1972) is a collection of critical essays. Wolf's more recent

works include *No Place on Earth* (1979) and *Cassandra: A Novel and Four Essays* (1983). Following Germany's reunification, Wolf briefly became a target of criticism for her early support of communism in East Germany. Since the fall of East Germany, she has published several works, including *What Remains* (1990), *On the Way to Taboo* (1994) and *Medea's Voices* (1996).

Wolfe, Thomas Clayton *(1900–1938)* One of the most important of modern American novelists. In his fiction Wolfe described at length his hometown of Asheville under the name Altamont. His father was a stonecutter and his mother the proprietor of a boarding house, as are the Gants in *Look Homeward, Angel* (1929). Like Eugene Gant in that novel, young Thomas Wolfe worked at odd jobs, absorbed his father's love of poetry and was attentive to the stories told by his mother's boarders. In 1916 Wolfe enrolled at the University of North Carolina, where his creative energies were devoted to the theater until his graduation in 1920. Wolfe benefited from the presence there of the Carolina Playmakers and the lectures of the group's founder, Frederick Koch. After graduation he completed an M.A. program at Harvard before heading to New York City with a play under his arm in 1922.

During the late 1920s he was deeply influenced by Aline Bernstein, the Esther Jack of his novels. Wolfe's plays were never professionally produced, a fact that he rued for the rest of his life. While subsisting on a teaching job at New York University, he began to spin out the expansive novels on which his reputation now rests. *Look Homeward, Angel* appeared in 1929 after substantial editorial trimming by Maxwell PERKINS. Presented with a long and chaotic manuscript, Perkins helped Wolfe set aside independent episodes and sometimes revise them into short stories. The novel that resulted was a great success, and it was followed by an important second novel, *Of Time and the River* (1935), *The Web and the Rock* (1939), *You Can't Go Home Again* (1940) and distinguished collections of short stories.

Wolfe never indulged in the experiments with style common in the work of his contemporaries, such as William FAULKNER. His fame rests instead on a panoramic vision of the South, an enthusiasm for travel and appetite for life and a continuing interest in relations between different social classes and the members of extended families.

Wolfe, Thomas "Tom" Kenerly *(1931–)* American journalist, social critic and novelist. Wolfe achieved a rare blending of critical acclaim and popular acceptance in his writing career. He first won fame in the 1960s as a primary proponent of the NEW JOURNALISM, as a frequent contributor to *Esquire* and other magazines and as the author of books such as *The Kandy-Kolored Tangerine-Flake Streamline Baby* (1965), a collection of pieces on pop culture, and *The Electric Kool-Aid Acid Test* (1968), an account of Ken KESEY and the Merry Pranksters. Wolfe has continued as a prolific writer, with works including *From Bauhaus to Our House* (1981), a study of modern architectural trends, and the novel *The Bonfire of the Vanities* (1987), a bitter satire on greed and ambition in Manhattan. In 1998 Wolfe published a novel, *A Man in Field* and *I Am Charlotte Simmons* in 2004.

Wolff, Karl Friedrich Otto *(1900–1984)* Nazi SS general, head of the personal staff of SS Reichsführer Heinrich HIMMLER. During 1943–44 Wolff commanded the German forces in ITALY, and in 1945 he negotiated the surrender of German troops in Italy to the Allies. Wolff escaped prosecution in the NUREMBERG TRIALS after the war. However, in 1962 he was arrested and charged by the Munich state prosecutor with complicity in the deaths of 300,000 JEWS at the Treblinka death camp. He was convicted and sentenced to 15 years' imprisonment but was released after six years because of poor health.

women's movements Women's, or feminist, movements are, generally speaking, political organizations initiated by women to expand their rights and role in society. In the United States, women began campaigning for suffrage, or the right to vote, in the early 1800s. In 1890, the two major U.S. organizations seeking the vote and women's equality joined to form the National American Woman Suffrage Association (NAWSA). At the beginning of the 20th century, suffragists (sometimes called suffragettes) in the United States and Great Britain intensified their efforts, planning marches and distributing literature in support of their cause. Many women were ridiculed, arrested and jailed. Important figures in the struggle for suffrage include Susan B. Anthony (1820–1906) and the Englishwoman Emmeline PANKHURST (1857–1928). In the United States, the Nineteenth Amendment to the Constitution, granting women the right to vote, was adopted in 1920. In Great Britain, women were granted the vote in 1928. In many other countries, such as France, the fight for suffrage continued into the 1940s. NAWSA evolved into the League of Women Voters, which continues to disseminate information on political issues.

Other social issues that motivated women to action in the early 20th century were birth control and temperance. Women who supported temperance, or the abolition of alcoholic beverages, were frequently scorned as puritanical fanatics, but their involvement in the issue often began after they had suffered domestic violence at the hands of drunken husbands. The movement was later taken up by religious organizations and became less a women's issue than a moral one. In the early 1900s the dissemination of birth control, or even related, information was illegal. Believing that uncontrolled pregnancies contributed to poverty, Margaret SANGER led a movement to provide contraceptive information to women, and organized the National Birth Control League, which later became Planned Parenthood. She was jailed in 1916 when she attempted to open a clinic in Brooklyn, New York, but by 1923 she had successfully sponsored several clinics in the United States.

Although many feminists continued their efforts on behalf of increased rights for women, the next wave of society-wide feminist activity did not occur until the 1960s. Important catalysts at this time were *The Feminine Mystique* (1963) by Betty FRIEDAN and *The Second Sex* (1949) by Simone DE BEAUVOIR. Both books analyzed women's roles as determined by society. Among the spokeswomen who emerged at the time are Gloria STEINEM, author and founder of *MS. Magazine*, and Germaine GREER, who

American women demonstrate outside the White House for the right to vote. 1916. (LIBRARY OF CONGRESS. PRINTS AND PHOTOGRAPHS DIVISION)

wrote about women's issues. Women began forming "consciousness raising groups," informal gatherings in which they discussed their problems, and also political organizations to fight for equal rights.

In 1961 President KENNEDY established the Commission on the Status of Women, which exposed the barriers to women in many fields, the disparity between women's and men's salaries and women's lesser civil rights. Many organizations were formed to address these issues, including the National Organization for Women (NOW) in 1966, the Women's Equity Action League in 1968 and the National Women's Political Caucus in 1971. These groups were able to effect many legal gains for women, including the Equal Pay Act of 1963; Title VII of the CIVIL RIGHTS ACT OF 1964, which outlawed job discrimination on the basis of sex as well as race; Title IX of the Education Amendments of 1972, which prohibited federally funded colleges and universities from discriminating against women; and the Equal Credit Opportunity Act of 1975. The EQUAL RIGHTS AMENDMENT (ERA) to the Constitution was passed by Congress in 1972 and sent to states for passage, but only 35 of the necessary 38 states approved the ERA by the 1982 deadline.

The impact of the women's movement is evident in the United States, most particularly in the American workforce. In 1987, 57 percent of American women worked outside of the home; yet as recently as 1987, women's salaries were still 70 percent of those earned by men. Women continue to struggle for equal salaries and for access to fields of employment from which they are still barred. The overall number of employed women continued to rise throughout the 1990s and early 2000s, reaching an average of 63.3 million female workers for the 2003 fiscal year and leading to marked increases in women's employment in such traditionally male-dominated fields as the construction industry. However, with the economic decline of 2001–03, female employment in some professions decreased. There was a 750,000-woman decline in the manufacturing sector and a 900,000-woman decline in the consumer goods sector. (See also FEMINISM.)

Wonder, Stevie (Steveland Judkins Morris) *(1950–)* Blind American singer-composer. Born in Detroit's black ghetto, Wonder was discovered playing the harmonica and dancing at age 10 and had his first gold hit at age 13. He then learned other instruments—piano, drums, organ and synthesizer. A consummate musician, he composed, performed and arranged his own albums. Hit singles include "You Are the Sunshine of My Life" (1972), "Living for the City" (1973) and "I Wish" (1977). He has also composed film scores and championed the movement against APARTHEID in South Africa. In the course of his music career, Wonder has received numerous honors, including induction into the Rock 'n' Roll Hall of Fame in 1989, the Grammy Awards' Lifetime Achievement Award in 1996 and 22 additional Grammy Awards for his composition of songs such as "For Your Love" from his album *Conversation Peace* (1995). Wonder also collaborated on musical scores and songs for two Spike Lee motion pictures: *Jungle Fever* (1991) and *Bamboozled* (2000).

Wood, Grant *(1891–1942)* American painter. He attended the Art Institute of Chicago and traveled to Europe, where he studied in Paris. During his European travels in the late 1920s, Wood was struck by the meticulous realism of such northern Renaissance painters as the Van Eycks. Returning to the U.S., he adopted this almost magical Flemish realism to portray quintessentially American subjects such as the famous *American Gothic* (1930, Art Institute of Chicago) and *Daughters of Revolution* (1932, Cincinnati Art Museum). His brilliantly incisive portraits and simplified, stylized landscapes put Wood in the forefront of regionalist painting in the U.S.

Wood, Sir Henry J(oseph) *(1869–1944)* British conductor. Born in London, Wood studied the organ and conducting at the Royal Academy of Music. He began conducting in 1888 and served in a number of minor conducting posts before being appointed conductor of the newly formed Promenade concerts in 1895. For the next 49 years, Wood directed the popular nightly performances in London each fall, playing the standard repertoire, British composers and many modern composers. Wood also conducted the Queen's Hall Orchestra in Saturday concerts that began in 1897. He later developed an interest in Russian music as well. Wood was knighted in 1911 and became a professor at the Royal Academy of Music in 1923. A thoroughly British conductor, he performed in the U.S. but turned down the post of director of the Boston Symphony in 1918. He was one of the most beloved and influential figures on the British classical music scene.

Woodcock, George *(1904–1979)* British labor leader, secretary of the TRADES UNION CONGRESS (TUC) (1960–69). As head of Britain's labor movement, Woodcock attempted to steer unions toward a broader role in the making of national economic policy. He also stressed the need for Britain to be more competitive in world markets.

Woodcock, Leonard (Freel) *(1911–2001)* American labor leader and diplomat. Born in Providence, R.I., Woodcock grew up in Europe and returned to the U.S. where he attended Wayne State University, Detroit. He began work at a Detroit auto parts factory in 1933, joined the United Automobile Workers (UAW) and became active in the union. Appointed administrative assistant to union president Walter REUTHER in 1946, he rose in the union hierarchy and was elected an international vice president in 1955. Upon Reuther's death in 1970, Woodcock succeeded to the UAW's presidency. A skilled negotiator, he helped to negotiate a number of important auto industry contracts before leaving the UAW (union rules made him ineligible for a third term) in 1977. Closely allied with the Democratic Party, Woodcock was appointed head of the U.S. Liaison Office in Beijing by President Jimmy CARTER in 1979. When diplomatic relations between the U.S. and CHINA were established later that year, Woodcock became ambassador. After leaving that post in 1981, he took up a teaching post at the University of Michigan.

Woodhouse, Barbara *(1910–1988)* British dog trainer. Woodhouse publicized her training techniques in the BBC's *Training Dogs the Woodhouse Way* and became an international celebrity in the late 1970s and early 1980s.

Woodruff, Robert Winship *(1889–1985)* Atlanta businessman. As head of the COCA-COLA Co. from 1923 to 1955, he transformed it from a debt-ridden, one-product soda fountain business into an international financial empire. A dynamic promoter and salesman, he created a network of independent bottlers and distributors that eventually made Coke available almost everywhere in the world. During World War II he turned millions of American servicemen into Coke drinkers by making the product available to them at a nickel a bottle. After he retired, he remained influential as a director until 1984. Enormously wealthy, he was a prominent philanthropist and donated an estimated $350 million to Emory University and other Atlanta institutions.

Woods, "Tiger" *(1975–)* American professional golfer. Born Eldrick Woods in Cypress, California, Woods was nicknamed "Tiger" after a Vietnamese soldier, Vuong Dang Phong, who befriended his father, Green Beret Lieutenant Colonel Earl Woods. After learning golf as a young child, Woods entered and won the Optimist International Junior World Championships in 1983 and proceeded to win the Optimist title six times (1983, 1984, and 1987–90). Between 1991 and 1996, Woods won three U.S. Junior Amateur Championships (1991–93) and three U.S. Amateur Championships (1994–96), becoming the youngest golfer to win both competitions. In 1992 Woods made his first foray into the world of professional golfing at the Nissan Los Angeles Open. Two years later Woods accepted an athletic scholarship at Stanford University, where he helped the team to an NCAA golfing title in 1996. In the summer of that year, Woods announced he would be leaving Stanford to join the Professional Golfing Association (PGA). The following year, after winning two relatively minor tournaments on the PGA tour, Woods became the youngest golfer to win the Masters (one of the four major PGA tournaments). In June 1997 Woods became the top-ranked professional golfer in the world, the youngest male golfer to achieve that position. Since 1997, Woods has won 39 PGA major events, including two PGA Championships (1999–2000), the U.S. Open (2000, 2002), the Masters (2001, 2002), the

Golf champion Tiger Woods. 2002 (PHOTOFEST)

British Open (2002), and the World Golf Championship-Accenture Match Play Championship (2003). He has twice set the record for the most money won on the PGA tour—in 1999 with $6,616,585, and in 2000 with $9,188,321—and has been named PGA Tour Player of the Year six times (1997, and 1999–2003). In 2000, Woods had his most productive year to date, winning nine PGA Tour events and 11 tournaments overall. By the end of 2003, Woods had won $39,777,265 in PGA Tour events and earned a total of $48,613,450 in tournaments throughout the world.

Woodson, Carter Godwin *(1875–1950)* Black American historian, editor and educator. Soon after receiving his Ph.D. from Harvard in 1912, Woodson founded the Association for the Study of Afro-American Life and History. One of the association's primary goals was to train black historians; its *The Journal of Negro History* flourished for 30 years under Woodson's direction. His educational posts included dean of the college of liberal arts at Howard University in Washington, D.C., and dean of West Virginia State College. He also founded a black-oriented publishing concern, Associated Publishers, and authored *The Negro in Our History* (1922) and *A Century of Negro Migration* (1918).

Woodstock *(1969)* Legendary ROCK music festival during the summer of 1969. Promoters put together a concert

Poster for Woodstock, a music festival held for three days on Max Yasgur's farm in Bethel, N.Y., 1969 (LIBRARY OF CONGRESS, PRINTS AND PHOTOGRAPHS DIVISION)

featuring such groups as JEFFERSON AIRPLANE; the WHO; CROSBY, STILLS AND NASH; Arlo GUTHRIE and others—expecting a turnout of 10,000 to 20,000. In fact, some 300,000 to 400,000 people converged on a farm near Woodstock, New York, on the wet, rainy weekend of August 15–17. Although facilities were completely overburdened and attendees shared food, liquor and drugs, no violence was reported. The Woodstock weekend is remembered as the ultimate BE-IN, the high point of the HIPPIE era and the culmination of the 1960s COUNTERCULTURE movement.

Woodward and Bernstein American journalists Robert Woodward (1943–) and Carl Bernstein (1944–). While working as reporters for the *Washington Post,* this pair of award-winning journalists investigated and exposed the WATERGATE scandal. They coauthored *All the President's Men* (1974) and *The Final Days* (1976), which dealt with the scandal and its aftermath. Woodward became the *Post's* metropolitan editor in 1979 and assistant managing editor in 1981. His other books include *The Brethren* (1979), *Wired* (1984), *Veil: The Secret Wars of the CIA* (1987), *The Agenda* (1995) *The Choice* (1997), *The Commanders* (2002) and *Bush at War*

(2002). Bernstein served as Washington bureau chief for ABC from 1979 to 1981, and as an ABC New York City correspondent from 1981 to 1984.

Woolcott, Alexander *(1887–1943)* American drama critic, columnist, radio commentator, actor and renowned wit. Woolcott was one of the best-known American journalists of the 1920s and 1930s and emerged as an oft-quoted member of the group of New York–based celebrity raconteurs known as the Algonquin Round Table (due to their frequent social meetings at the Algonquin Hotel). Woolcott, who was born in New Jersey and attended Hamilton College, became the drama critic of *The New York Times* in 1914. He later contributed to numerous other newspapers and also wrote a column, "Shouts and Murmurs," for THE NEW YORKER. Woolcott acted the role of Sheridan Whiteside (based on Woolcott himself) in a road company production of the George S. KAUFMAN and Moss HART classic comedy *The Man Who Came to Dinner* (1937). He also was a commentator on the CBS radio network in the 1930s.

Woolf, Virginia *(1882–1941)* English novelist, essayist, diarist, literary critic and feminist; one of the premier figures in all of 20th-century British literature. The daughter of prominent 19th-century literary critic Leslie Stephen, Woolf never received a formal university education but easily took her part as a key member of the BLOOMSBURY GROUP of British intellectuals that flourished from the 1910s to the 1930s. In the 1920s, Woolf became one of the foremost practitioners of the fictional technique known as STREAM OF CONSCIOUSNESS. Her major works include the novels *Mrs. Dalloway* (1925), *To the Lighthouse* (1927) and *The Waves* (1931), the feminist study *A Room of One's Own* (1929) and the posthumous *A Writer's Diary* (1953). With husband, the economist **Leonard Woolf,** she founded the **Hogarth Press,** a small but influential literary publishing house that published many of her own works. Woolf suffered from bouts of depression and mental instability throughout her life. She took her life by drowning herself in the River Ouse near her home in Sussex.

Wootton, Barbara Frances (Baroness Wootton of Abinger) *(1897–*

1988) British social scientist. Wootton challenged conventional wisdom in fields ranging from economics to sociology to criminology. Her experiences as a lay magistrate for nearly half a century and as chair of juvenile courts in London for 16 years formed the basis for her seminal work *Social Science and Social Pathology* (1959). She was a member of four royal commissions and was one of four women among the first life peers created in 1958.

Workers' Opposition Opposition, mainly from trade unionists with the Bolshevik Party, that in 1920 criticized the bureaucratic control of industry by the government and the central party organs and advocated the establishment of an All-Russian Congress of Producers to run the country's economy. At the 10th Party Congress (1921) the opposition was condemned, and a resolution was carried forbidding "factionalism." The Workers' Opposition was alleged to have continued during the following year. Most of the Workers' Opposition leaders were expelled from the party, and all the known leaders, except Alexandra KOLLONTAY, disappeared during the GREAT PURGE.

Works Progress Administration NEW DEAL agency that employed thousands of unemployed Americans during the GREAT DEPRESSION. When President Franklin D. ROOSEVELT took office in 1933 the U.S. was in the midst of its worst economic downturn, with one-quarter of the workforce unemployed. FDR took the then-radical step of creating government agencies to employ thousands, paying their salaries with borrowed money. Established in 1935, the Works Progress Administration (later called the Work Projects Administration) employed thousands in public construction jobs. The federal government helped localities build bridges, highways, and courthouses. Artists, musicians and writers were also employed by the government, which established programs to assist artists, the theater and symphony orchestras. The WPA's FEDERAL WRITERS' PROJECT is best known for its series of guidebooks for each of the U.S. states.

World Bank International bank that encourages investment in developing nations. The bank, formally known as the **International Bank for Recon-**

struction and Development, was established along with the International Monetary Fund at the BRETTON WOODS CONFERENCE in 1944, during World War II. Although the initial purpose of the bank was the reconstruction of war-torn member nations, it later shifted its emphasis toward making loans to the governments of developing nations. The bank's funds are supplied by contributions from the 44 member nations and also from the proceeds of bond sales. The bank makes loans to developing nations who are facing hardships because of balance of payment problems or trade problems. The bank has encountered controversy in the third world by requiring borrowers to adopt austerity budgets as a condition for receiving these loans. Since the 1990s, the World Bank has increased its efforts to support social services in developing nations. By 2003 such funding accounted for 22% of the bank's annual budget.

World Council of Churches International organization of some 340 Protestant and Orthodox churches. With headquarters in Geneva, Switzerland, the group fosters interchurch cooperation and Christian unity and attempts to relate church activities to worldwide problems. While the WCC constitution was drafted in 1937, the group was not formed until after World War II, at the Amsterdam Conference of 1948. Among the areas in which the WCC is active are education, missionary activities, aid to the poor, help for refugees, study of religio-social issues, promotion of world peace, work for social justice and promotion of ecumenism. Its views are stated in recommendations to its member churches, which are not legally obliged to follow its lead, but which are given the opportunity to act in concert regarding matters of common concern. The WCC's activities and interests are bound up with nearly every part of Christian service on an international scale. The organization is administered by six presidents and a 145-member central committee, the members of which are elected by the WCC's diverse member churches. The group meets annually, and assemblies of representatives from member churches are held once every six or seven years.

World Health Organization (WHO) Agency of the UNITED NA-

TIONS. Founded in 1948, WHO has the mission of improving health care throughout the world, particularly in developing countries. WHO's activities include the prevention of disease, the establishment of standards for food and medicine, the identification and classification of diseases and the sponsoring of medical research. The agency's main headquarters are in Geneva, Switzerland. In 2003 the WHO worked to contain the outbreak of Sudden Acute Respiratory Syndrome (SARS), a disease that infected regions of China and several cities in Canada. In 2005 the WHO was working to contain an outbreak of the deadly avian flu in Asia.

World Trade Center (WTC) A business complex owned by the Port Authority of New York and New Jersey. Consisting of seven buildings located on 16 acres in downtown New York City, the WTC was best known for its two towers (One and Two World Trade Center), which had heights of 1,368 and 1,362 feet, respectively. Built by Japanese-American architect Minoru YAMASAKI, construction on the WTC began on August 5, 1966, under the supervision of the architectural firm Emery Roth & Sons. After receiving suggestions from the Port Authority to make Tower One and Two taller than the previously envisioned 90 stories, Yamasaki and his colleagues utilized a tubular steel and aluminum framework emanating from the core of each tower to allow for the buildings' expansion to the previously unheard of height of 110 stories. The WTC was formally opened on April 4, 1973, and by the 1990s it had become a tourist attraction and a mainstay of the New York financial district, housing investment firms, insurance corporations and international companies.

Because of its symbolic association with the economic trend of GLOBALIZATION, the WTC became the target of Islamic fundamentalists opposed to Western economic and cultural penetration of Islamic societies. On February 26, 1993, a bomb exploded in the underground garage of Tower One that killed six and injured over 1,000 people, but failed to destroy the tower and kill its occupants through structural damage and the release of cyanide gas, as the planners of the attack had envisioned. Six members of radical Islamic terrorist groups were captured and ar-

rested in connection with this attack. By 1998 all had received sentences totaling 240 years. The second attack on the towers came in the morning of SEPTEMBER 11, 2001, when an airplane crashed into each of the two towers. The structural damage inflicted by the planes' impact and explosion caused Tower One and Tower Two's complete collapse, as well as the destruction of another building in the complex, Seven World Trade Center.

After a massive cleanup of the site that began almost immediately after the attacks, the Port Authority began to consider plans for the future of the site. Despite protests that the terrorist attacks had shown the dangers of erecting tall skyscrapers in the downtown area, the Port Authority announced that it would not rule out the construction of similarly tall buildings on the WTC site. On December 19, 2003, the Port Authority announced that the Freedom Tower, the tallest building planned on the WTC site, would contain 70 stories and measure 1,776 feet, in commemoration of the year the U.S. declared its independence. The proposed building was designed by a team of architects headed by Daniel Libeskind. The Port Authority also opened a contest for the design of a memorial to commemorate the attacks of September 11. In December 2003, after reviewing over 5,000 entries, it selected "Reflecting Absence," a proposal by Michael Arad and Peter Walker, which envisioned a part of the WTC complex as a place of repose and reflection.

World Trade Organization (WTO) An international organization charged with regulating trade and commercial practices between nations. Between 1986 and 1994, negotiations began at the Uruguay meeting (or "round") of the members of the GENERAL AGREEMENT ON TRADE AND TARIFFS (GATT), an organization formed in 1947 to promote free trade in the world. These talks had the goal of replacing the ad-hoc bilateral agreements negotiated under GATT with a new international body capable of regulating and improving the flow of international trade. The new body would also address such issues as intellectual property and trade in services that had not been covered under GATT. By 1993 these negotiations had established the framework of the WTO. The new organization formally came into existence on January 1, 1995, with headquarters in Geneva, Switzerland, and more than 120 member countries.

Since its creation, the WTO has continued many of the trade-related activities begun under GATT, as well as making advances in other regulatory aspects of international commerce. Any state that is involved in the WTO must extend "Most Favored Nation" trading status (the most advantageous trading arrangements that a nation has with any of its trading partners) to all the organization's members. In 1997 the WTO sponsored a summit conference seeking to establish regulations governing international telecommunications, which resulted in a 69-member accord that substantially reduced protectionist legislation favoring domestic telecommunications corporations. However, the WTO has also become the target of protest groups that denounce the process of globalization promoted by the WTO for benefiting large transnational corporations at the expense of local firms, consumers and workers. Opponents of the WTO, such as the French activist José BOVE, have repeatedly organized protests against the organization's annual meetings, such as the WTO conference held at Seattle, Washington, in November 1999; Sydney, Australia, in November 2002; and Cancun, Mexico, in September 2003. As of 2005 150 nations had joined the WTO.

World War I *(1914–1918)* Although the assassination in SERBIA of the heir to the Austro-Hungarian throne was the event that sparked the beginning of the so-called Great War, international tensions and competition had been mounting for many years (see BALKAN WARS). On July 28, 1914, the AUSTRO-HUNGARIAN EMPIRE declared war on Serbia. RUSSIA began mobilizing troops along the German border, and GERMANY declared war on Russia and its ally, FRANCE. Immediately German armies went into action against France, planning to conquer it in a few months and then to turn the powerful German military machine against Russia. When German troops disregarded the neutrality of LUXEMBOURG and BELGIUM by invading these countries to sweep through France from the northeast, Great Britain joined France to repel the invaders. The Central Powers of Austria-Hungary and Ger-

World War I German high command: (left to right) Hindenburg, Kaiser Wilhelm II and General Ludendorff (LIBRARY OF CONGRESS, PRINTS AND PHOTOGRAPHS DIVISION)

many, later joined by the OTTOMAN EMPIRE (Turkey) and BULGARIA, were aligned against the Allies of France, Great Britain, Serbia, Russia, and Belgium, which were later joined by ITALY, ROMANIA, PORTUGAL, Montenegro, JAPAN, AUSTRALIA, the U.S., and 20 other countries. Within a month German divisions reached the outskirts of Paris, but the retreating French rallied and counterattacked (see MARNE, FIRST BATTLE OF THE), driving the Germans back to the north. For the next four years the opposing armies faced each other, sometimes only a few hundred feet apart, in a long line extending from the North Sea to Switzerland (see WORLD WAR I ON THE WESTERN FRONT). Bloody battles were fought at YPRES, Artois, on the SOMME, in the Meuse Valley and the Argonne Forest and elsewhere (see VERDUN, BATTLE OF) with staggering losses on both sides, but basically the line remained stationary until the fall of 1918. Austro-Hungarian troops had to face the Russians on their eastern border (see WORLD WAR I ON THE EASTERN FRONT) and Italians in the south (see WORLD WAR I ON THE ITALIAN FRONT), while they subdued Serbia and Montenegro (see WORLD WAR I IN THE BALKANS). When its navy could no longer operate from the North Sea (see JUTLAND, BATTLE OF), Germany resorted to unrestricted submarine warfare. This so angered the Americans that they declared war on Germany on April 6, 1917; although it was some time before they could send large numbers of men and material, their entry into the conflict gave the Allies a great moral boost. Despite a defeat at Gallipoli (see DARDANELLES CAMPAIGN). Britain remained master of the seas by protecting the Suez Canal (see WORLD WAR I IN EGYPT), and this enabled it to seize German colonies in Africa, to supply its armies in the Middle East (see WORLD WAR I IN

MESOPOTAMIA; WORLD WAR I IN PALESTINE), and to transport troops from its COMMONWEALTH countries. When Russia dropped out of the war in 1917 (see BOLSHEVIK REVOLUTION), the Germans were able to transfer troops from the eastern front to help the Austro-Hungarians and the Turks, whose empires were crumbling, but even fresh troops could not break the stalemate on the Western Front. As the French, British, and Americans slowly, doggedly drove the Germans back to the "Hindenburg Line," Bulgaria fell, the Ottoman Empire sued for peace and Austria-Hungary collapsed. The war-weary Germans revolted, and their kaiser and generals were forced to sign an armistice on November 11, 1918. The ensuing Treaty of VERSAILLES and other treaties changed the geographical face of Europe and the Middle East and brought about numerous political, economic and social changes. The war had seen the introduction of tanks, airplanes and poison gas and had caused enormous suffering and destruction wherever it was fought. More than 10 million persons had died, and many more were injured. (See also RUSSO-POLISH WAR OF 1919–20; TURKISH WAR OF INDEPENDENCE; ZEEBRUGGE RAID.)

World War I battlefield, 1918 (LIBRARY OF CONGRESS, PRINTS AND PHOTOGRAPHS DIVISION)

Yorkshire regiment in France (LIBRARY OF CONGRESS, PRINTS AND PHOTOGRAPHS DIVISION)

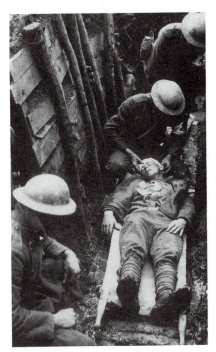

Life and death in the trenches, 1918 (LIBRARY OF CONGRESS, PRINTS AND PHOTOGRAPHS DIVISION)

World War I in Egypt *(1914–1917)*

As soon as the OTTOMAN EMPIRE (Turkey) announced that it was entering World War I against the Allies, Great Britain declared Egypt a British protectorate and deposed the pro-German ruler. Egypt's SUEZ CANAL was an essential lifeline and had to be protected at all costs; both the Turks and the Germans were anxious to gain control of the canal. In February 1915, three Turkish forces approached the canal by different routes, but the British had already fortified the western bank; the Turks were driven away with heavy losses. A year later the British began to fortify the eastern bank of the canal along an 80-mile stretch and to secure the Sinai Desert. As they slowly made their way north toward El Arish on the border with PALESTINE, they laid railroad tracks and a water pipeline. In July 1916, they were attacked by a sizable Turkish force, but again the Turks were severely beaten, and many prisoners were taken. By December that year, the British were within 20 miles of their destination, which was garrisoned by Turkish troops, who withdrew without a fight. Two Turkish contingents still remained in Egypt, but they were dispatched by surprise attacks by the British Camel Corps. By 1917, the last Turkish forces were gone from Egypt, and the Suez Canal was no longer in danger.

World War I in Mesopotamia *(1914–1918)*

Shortly after the OTTOMAN EMPIRE (Turkey) entered World War I in November 1914, on the side of the Central Powers, the British sent a small force from India to the head of the PERSIAN GULF to establish a British sphere of influence in Mesopotamia to protect INDIA and EGYPT. The troops were ordered to move northward up the gulf to seize BAGHDAD eventually. At first the British forces were successful against the Turkish forces, but when the Anglo-French armies failed on the Gallipoli peninsula (see DARDANELLES CAMPAIGN), Turkish divisions were rushed to Mesopotamia. The British were driven back to Kut-el-Amara, which was surrounded and besieged. Several relief expeditions were dispatched, but they were unable to break through the Turkish lines. After a 143-day siege, the British surrendered in April 1916. The following year Allied reinforcements and gunboats were sent to the Persian gulf, and the British quickly established themselves on both sides of the Tigris River as they proceeded north. After heavy fighting, Kut-el-Amara was captured, and the retreating Turks were pursued up the river to Baghdad. To prevent any counterattacks, the British continued their pursuit of the fleeing Turks and so gained control of most of Mesopotamia, including the Baghdad-Samara Railroad. Although all this action did not have great strategic significance for the war as a whole, it did boost the sagging morale of the Allies and dealt the Ottoman Empire a blow from which it never recovered.

World War I in Palestine *(1917–1918)*

Once the British had driven the Turks from EGYPT (see WORLD WAR I IN EGYPT), they continued to pursue their enemy north into Palestine. Their first two efforts to capture the stronghold of Gaza failed, but the third under the command of Edmund H. H. ALLENBY succeeded. Earlier he had captured Beersheba to the east, and after the victory at Gaza his men proceeded northward, meeting little resistance until they reached Lydda, a junction point on the railroad between Jaffa and Jerusalem. After fierce fighting they dislodged the Turks and effectively cut their forces in two. The British next took Jaffa on the coast and then turned east toward Jerusalem, which was strongly fortified. Allenby devised a plan to surround the city and take all the outposts. This involved much hard fighting in difficult terrain and bad weather. After reinforcements arrived, an assault was made on the Holy City on December 8, 1917, and the next day the Turks surrendered. However, they regrouped and attempted to retake Jerusalem two weeks later, but to no avail. Gradually the British drove them from the hills and into what was then called Syria. Palestine became a British protectorate after centuries of Turkish rule.

World War I in the Balkans *(1915–1918)*

The Balkan peninsula in southeastern Europe had long been seething with nationalistic rivalries and competing territorial desires (see BALKAN WARS). Although the AUSTRO-HUNGARIAN EMPIRE declared war on the Balkan state of SERBIA on July 28, 1914 (see WORLD WAR I), it was not until after combined Austro-Hungarian and German forces had driven the Russians from Galacia (see WORLD WAR I ON THE EASTERN FRONT) that the Austrians turned their attention to Serbia and invaded it from the north. In October 1915, BULGARIA joined the Central Powers (GERMANY, Austro-Hungary, and the OTTOMAN EMPIRE) and promptly launched an invasion of Serbia from the south; Bulgarian troops were crushed by superior numbers and firepower. The Austrians then moved against Serbia's neighbor, Montenegro, and captured its capital in January 1916. Bulgarian and Austrian armies next invaded ALBANIA from the north and east, but failed to drive an Italian force from the southern region. ROMANIA wavered for two years, debating which side was most apt to win the war; in August 1916, it decided to join the Allies and declared war on the Central Powers. Romanian troops invaded Transylvania in Hungary with initial success but were soon pushed back by two German armies. Soon Romania itself was overrun by Bulgarians and Germans. In Greece, the Allies seized control of the telegraph and postal systems, the Greek navy and large stores of munitions from the army and blockaded the coast. A French and British expeditionary force in Salonica, in northern Greece, made sure that Greece maintained its neutrality in the war, but it made no move against the Bulgarians in Macedonia until September 1918. Reinforced by exiled Serbian soldiers and Greek troops, the Allies attacked on three fronts and within two weeks captured the major Bulgarian strong points. Bulgaria soon sued for peace and agreed to an unconditional surrender. The Allies continued their advance northward as they liberated both Serbia and Montenegro. Romanian forces reentered the Balkan war arena and helped drive the Austro-Hungarian and German soldiers from its borders and southern Russia. The pro-German rulers of the Balkan states (present day Albania, Greece, Romania, Bulgaria, YUGOSLAVIA, and the European part of Turkey) were deposed, and the fate of the states was decided at the forthcoming peace conference. (See also HUNGARIAN REVOLUTION OF 1918).)

World War I on the eastern front

(1914–1917) When Austria-Hungary declared war on SERBIA on July 28, 1914 (see WORLD WAR I). Russia began to mobilize its armies despite Germany's protests; on August 1, 1914, the two countries were at war. Russian troops invaded East Prussia but were badly defeated at the Battle of Tannenberg (August 29–30, 1914), where many prisoners and materiel were seized by the Germans, and at the Battle of Masurian Lakes (September 9–14, 1914). The Russians were more successful in Galacia (southeast Poland and western Ukraine) against the Austro-Hungarian forces, from whom they wrested key passes in the Carpathian Mountains and captured the capital city, Lemberg (Lvov) and the fortress city of Przemysl in early 1915. During the previous fall German armies had twice invaded Russian Poland and had twice failed to capture Warsaw, although they did control western Poland. By the winter of 1915, the opposing forces were facing each other from trenches along a 900-mile front. In May that year combined Austro-Hungarian and German armies struck in Galicia; their heavy artillery routed the Russians from their mountain strongholds; Lemberg and Przemysl were retaken. Then the Germans launched a major offensive, called "Hindenburg's Drive" after the brilliant strategist General Paul von HINDENBURG (1847–1934), to drive the Russians out of Poland. By encircling maneuvers, they threatened to trap the Russians, who hastily retreated, leaving Warsaw, Brest-Litovsk, Vilna and part of Lithuania to the enemy. A year later, in June 1916, the Russians began an offensive against Austria-Hungary in the area of the Styr and Sereth (Siretul) Rivers and succeeded in advancing 20 to 50 miles along a 250-mile front; they were halted only when their supplies gave out. Meanwhile, discontent over the corrupt government of the czar was increasing in Russia; in March 1917, the czar's regime was toppled (see BOLSHEVIK REVOLUTION; FEBRUARY REVOLUTION). The new Russian government quickly made peace with GERMANY, and the war on the eastern front ended.

World War I on the Italian front

(1915–1918) Italy remained neutral until May 23, 1915, when it decided to join the Allies and fight its traditional enemy, Austria-Hungary (see WORLD WAR I). The Italian army took the offensive in the Isonzo River valley, but the Austrians had already fortified the peaks in that mountainous area, and the Italians were unable to make any tangible headway, although they made assault after assault. They did manage to cross the river in the Caporetto area in the fall of 1915 and in 1916 captured Gorizia. The following year the Italians pushed forward again in several places, and the Germans, fearing their Austrian allies might withdraw, sent reinforcements. This turned the tide. After a heavy bombardment, the demoralized Italian troops began to retreat from Caporetto, and the retreat soon became a rout that stopped only when the army reached the Piave River. The other large-scale action on the Italian front occurred in the Trentino alpine area to the west where the Austrians launched an offensive in 1916 against ill-prepared Italian outposts. The Austrians swept across the border, and it seemed possible that they might seize Venice and cut off the armies on the Isonzo. However, an Italian force holding a commanding position on Monte Ciove held firm against overwhelming odds and stopped the Austrian advance. This offensive weakened Austria's eastern front and permitted the Russians to invade its territory in the Styr and Sereth (Siretul) Rivers region (see WORLD WAR I ON THE EASTERN FRONT). In November 1918, the Austrians surrendered to an Italian general whose troops had beaten them at Vittoria Veneto, and under the peace terms Italy regained Trieste and other territory the Austrians had seized in previous wars.

World War I on the western front

(1914–1918) At the beginning of World War I, the rapid and powerful German advance through Belgium and northeastern France was stopped by the French and British in September 1914 (see MARNE, FIRST BATTLE OF THE), and the German armies were forced back beyond the Aisne River. In the north the Allies contended with the Germans for control of Ypres in southwestern Belgium and the English Channel ports, while in the southeast the Germans were driven back to the mountains. By December 1914, both sides had dug into a series of fortified trenches almost 600 miles long and

stretching from Ostend (Oostende, Belgium) to Douai, Saint-Quentin, Rheims, Verdun, Saint-Mihiel and Lunéville (northeastern French towns) and then south to the Swiss border. This battle line remained almost stationary for the next four years; although there were frequent bombardments and waves of soldiers sent out of the trenches ("over the top") against the enemy, the gains in territory were insignificant, but the losses in lives were very high. Life in the trenches was miserable for all; many novels and memoirs have described the horror, mud, cold and filth of that trench warfare. In 1916, the Germans launched a major offensive against the strongest Allied fortress (see VERDUN, BATTLE OF); there the French held fast. Another German offensive was repulsed by the Allies in July 1918, and was followed by a massive counterattack in which the Allies under Marshal Ferdinand FOCH drove the Germans out of most of France and Belgium; a counteroffensive by American troops pushed the Germans from the Argonne Forest and Saint-Mihiel. The Western Front moved eastward as the war drew to a close.

World War II (*1939–1945*) The principal Axis power—GERMANY—felt cheated by the harsh terms of the Treaty of VERSAILLES (see WORLD WAR I) and was eager to regain or expand its territories. Germany had become fascist, and was ruled by a military dictatorship—under Adolf HITLER it began to disregard treaties and commit acts of aggression. It remilitarized the RHINELAND in 1935, annexed AUSTRIA and subsequently CZECHOSLOVAKIA's SUDETENLAND in 1938 and occupied Czechoslovakia in 1939 (see MEMEL, INSURRECTION AT). Also fascist, Italy under Benito MUSSOLINI conquered Ethiopia (see ITALO-ETHIOPIAN WAR OF 1935–36) and seized Albania in 1939. Japan invaded Manchuria in 1931 and began an undeclared war against China (see SINO-JAPANESE WAR OF 1937–45). Most of the world wanted peace and watched these warlike acts with apprehension. When Hitler's troops invaded Poland (see BLITZKRIEG), Great Britain and France had to honor their agreement to protect the Poles, although it was too late to save them. At first Russia sided with the Axis powers and seized the Baltic states and Finland (see

RUSSO-FINNISH WAR OF 1939–40), but in 1941 Hitler turned on his former ally and invaded Russian territory (see WORLD WAR II ON THE RUSSIAN FRONT). After conquering Poland (September 1939), Hitler turned his energies westward; Britain and France had declared war on Germany on September 3, 1939. Hitler's mechanized, powerful armies swept through Denmark and invaded Norway (see NORWAY, GERMANY INVASION OF). A month later, May of 1940, German Nazi troops marched on Holland, Belgium and Luxembourg, broke through France's defensive MAGINOT LINE (see FRANCE, BATTLE OF), and seized ports on the English Channel while dislodging a British expeditionary force (see DUNKIRK, EVACUATION OF). After occupying northern France and setting up the puppet VICHY government in the south, the Germans used their Luftwaffe (air force) to attempt to bomb Great Britain into submission, but without success (see BATTLE OF BRITAIN). By the end of 1939, the war had expanded into the Balkan peninsula (see WORLD WAR II IN THE BALKANS) and to North Africa, where the Italians invaded Egypt. Although the U.S. remained neutral, it did set up a lend-lease agreement with Britain, whereby food and supplies were shipped across the Atlantic in armed convoys to protect them from German U-boats or submarines (see ATLANTIC, BATTLE OF THE). The year 1941 was grim for Britain as it faced the Axis powers alone until Russia was invaded by the Germans and the U.S. naval base at PEARL HARBOR was attacked by the Japanese. In early 1942, Japan rapidly expanded its "Great East Asia Co-prosperity Sphere," but the Americans recovered quickly from their initial defeat and began to demolish the Japanese naval strength (see WORLD WAR II IN THE PA-

CIFIC). Germany's Afrika Korps was beaten at EL ALAMEIN in northern Egypt (see NORTH AFRICAN CAMPAIGN), and the lifeline of the SUEZ CANAL was preserved. The British, joined by FREE FRENCH and American forces, which landed in Algeria and French Morocco, drove the Axis troops out of Africa by May 1943. The supposed German victory in Russia turned into defeat at STALINGRAD (Volgograd) in early 1943, and the Allies invaded SICILY and Italy from their North African bases (see WORLD WAR II ON THE ITALIAN FRONT). The leaders of the Allies (chiefly Britain, France, Canada, Australia, Russia, Belgium, the Netherlands, China and the U.S.) met at a number of conferences to decide future strategy and objective and to sign the United Nations declaration. In the east, the Japanese fought doggedly against Chinese, American, British, and Australian forces in Burma (see BURMA CAMPAIGN) and the Pacific islands, but only in China were they successful (see WORLD WAR II IN CHINA). German-occupied Europe was severely bombed by the Allies before they landed troops to liberate the area (see NORMANDY, INVASION OF; WORLD WAR II ON THE WESTERN FRONT). By the end of 1944, an Allied victory was assured and, with some grievous setbacks (see BULGE, BATTLE OF THE), the Russians, Americans and British advanced steadily on BERLIN, Germany's capital, from the east and the west. Their forces met at Torgau in Saxony (later part of East Germany) on April 25, 1945, and a few days later Hitler and his mistress-turned-wife presumably killed themselves in a bunker in Berlin. Germany surrendered unconditionally on May 7, 1945. After U.S. ATOMIC BOMBS devastated two of its large cities, HIROSHIMA and NAGASAKI, Japan surrendered on August 14, 1945. The U.S. and the

French citizens weep as the Nazis march into Paris, 1940. (LIBRARY OF CONGRESS, PRINTS AND PHOTOGRAPHS DIVISION)

Hundreds of cities in Europe and Asia suffered damage like that inflicted on this German city. (LIBRARY OF CONGRESS, PRINTS AND PHOTOGRAPHS DIVISION)

USSR emerged as superpowers after this most terrible of wars, in which millions of soldiers, sailors, airmen, marines and civilians died in air aids, U-boat sinkings, rocket attacks, concentration camps, death marches and bloody battles, and from disease, starvation, torture and forced labor.

World War II in China (*1941–1945*) CHINA, which had been at war with JAPAN for many years (see SINO-JAPANESE WAR OF 1937–45), entered World War II on the side of the Allies in late 1941. Most of the Chinese coast was in the hands of the Japanese, and the Chinese armies in the interior were supplied by material trucked in over the BURMA ROAD. When the road was sealed off in 1942 (see BURMA CAMPAIGN), supplies were flown into China over the Himalayan "hump" by expert British and American fliers. The U.S. Fourteenth Air Force set up bases in southeastern China, from which it effectively carried out bombing raids on Japanese shipping: U.S. general Joseph "Vinegar Joe" STILWELL served as chief of staff of American forces for CHIANG KAI-SHEK, supreme Allied commander of air and land forces in the Chinese war theater. In the spring of 1944, the Japanese mounted a new large offensive. First they occupied Honan Province, whose armies had fled, and then moved south along the rail line from Hangzhou (Hankow) to Canton. The Japanese

forces traveled by night to try to avoid the FLYING TIGERS, P-40 fighter planes flown by the U.S. Volunteer Group in China, which unremittingly bombed and strafed their lines of march. Each time a Chinese force opposed the Japanese, it was overcome. By November 1944, the Japanese had fulfilled their objective of controlling the railroad from Indochina north to Beijing and had taken eight Chinese provinces. In the north, however, they did not fare so well, for the Chinese Communist Eighth Route Army and peasant militia used guerrilla tactics to harass their garrisons and strongholds. Later, when the war ended, the Chinese Communists would demand the surrender of the Japanese and take over their arms. Despite large amounts of British and American aid, the corrupt and strife-ridden Chinese Nationalist government at Qongqing (Chungking) never took an initiative against the Japanese, preferring instead to reserve its best troops for possible use against the Communists.

World War II in the Balkans (*1939–1941*) Benito MUSSOLINI, ITALY'S dictator, dreamed of a glorious Italian empire obtained with the help of his fascist ally in GERMANY, Adolf HITLER. In April 1939, Italian troops invaded and soon conquered Albania, and from there they invaded GREECE in October 1940. The Greeks, however, were far better soldiers than the Ital-

ians, who were soon chased back to Albania. In August 1940, Russia demanded two provinces from ROMANIA, and HUNGARY demanded control of Transylvania; both demands were met reluctantly by the pro-German dictators of Romania and Transylvania. To make sure of his allies on the Balkan peninsula, Hitler sent German troops into Hungary and Romania in January 1941 and into Bulgaria shortly afterward. YUGOSLAVIA'S leaders signed a pact making them Nazi puppets, but its army objected and resolved to fight. On April 6, 1941, the Luftwaffe (German air force), accompanied by troops, attacked both Yugoslavia and Greece, neither of which could counter the superior German arms and forces. Yugoslavia was overrun in 11 days; its capital, Belgrade, was bombed mercilessly in "Operation Punishment"; and the remnants of the Yugoslavian army fled to the mountains, from which they waged damaging guerrilla warfare against the Nazis during the next three years. A British expeditionary force had been sent to aid the Greeks, but the most it could do was fight delaying actions. Greek forces surrendered in Albania on April 20, 1941, and in Greece proper four days later. The British were evacuated to Crete, but the Germans pursued them, and the Luftwaffe pounded this island into submission after a 10-day aerial and naval battle. TURKEY signed a friendship treaty with Germany and granted the Germans passage through the DARDANELLES. The loss of the Balkans was a severe blow to Britain as it struggled alone against the Nazi war machine.

World War II in the Middle East

(1941) Britain sought to prevent the Middle East from falling into the hands of the Axis powers in World War II. In IRAQ, whose government had become pro-German, the British landed forces at BASRA and Habbaniyah, their air base west of BAGHDAD. The Iraqis flooded the land between the Tigris and Euphrates Rivers to thwart the British advance on Baghdad. After three weeks of scattered fighting, Iraqi resistance collapsed, and the British secured Baghdad. About a week later, on June 8, 1941, FREE FRENCH forces, supported by British COMMONWEALTH troops, invaded SYRIA and LEBANON from PALESTINE and Trans-Jordan; British forces from Iraq invaded Syria soon afterward. At the Lebanese city of Sidon, VICHY French forces resisted the invaders until British bombardments drove them out. Westward-moving Allied armies captured the Syrian cities of Aleppo and Latakia. The Germans made air strikes against the Allies without much success. An armistice was signed at Acre (Akko, Israel) on July 14, 1941; the Free French and British occupied Syria and Lebanon for the remainder of the war. In Iran, German technicians helped operate the oil fields, which the British wanted to control. In late summer of 1941, the Allies carried out an invasion of Iran with remarkable speed; Soviet troops moved down both sides of the Caspian Sea and seized major ports, while Soviet planes bombed Tehran; British forces invaded from Iraq and seized oil fields; the minuscule Iranian naval force was sunk. The Allied campaign ended successfully about four days after it began; Britain had gained its objectives with little loss of life and materiel.

World War II in the Pacific

(1941–1945) Hours after their surprise attack on PEARL HARBOR, Japanese bombers destroyed most of the U.S. planes on the ground at a field outside Manila in the Philippines; three days later they sank three British battleships in the Gulf of Siam. With little to stop them, the Japanese then seized WAKE and GUAM islands and the British base at HONG KONG and invaded the PHILIPPINES in full force. BATAAN and CORREGIDOR in the Philippines held out for almost five months before they fell. In February 1942, after the surrender of THAILAND, the Japanese moved down the Malay Peninsula and seized the British port of SINGAPORE, where they took 70,000 troops captive. Java, Borneo, Bali, Sumatra, Timor and BURMA fell in turn until the Japanese occupied all East Asia. PORT MORESBY on New Guinea was their next target; from there they planned to attack AUSTRALIA. But the indecisive **Battle of the Coral Sea** (May 7–8, 1942) between the Japanese and American fleets prevented this from happening. Then the tide turned in the **Battle of Midway** (June 4, 1942), which was fought almost entirely by planes that tried to sink each other's warships; the Japanese suffered heavy losses. Afterward the Americans took the offensive; they won GUADALCANAL after a bloody six-month fight in the jungles there (August 7, 1942–February 9, 1943) and Papua in New Guinea. In 1943, the Japanese were cleared out of the Aleutian Islands off Alaska. The SOLOMON, Gilbert (Kiribati) and Marshall Islands were seized next by the Allies in large-scale amphibious operations supported by air and naval bombardments. Saipan, Tinian and Guam in the Marianas were taken in August 1944. The Americans were now within flying distance of Japan, which they bombed repeatedly. On October 20, 1944, American forces landed on LEYTE in the Philippines, and U.S. general Douglas MACARTHUR, supreme Allied commander in the Southwest Pacific, announced "I have returned." One of the greatest naval engagements of all times was fought in the Gulf of Leyte on October 23–26, 1944; the Japanese were defeated, but the fighting on land continued for four months before the Philippines were completely liberated. IWO JIMA was captured by U.S. Marines in March 1945, and Okinawa was invaded the next month; there the Japanese resisted for over two months. In July 1945, the Allies sent Japan an ultimatum with terms that had been determined at the POTSDAM

The Japanese delegation arrives for the official surrender ceremonies ending World War II. 1945.
(LIBRARY OF CONGRESS, PRINTS AND PHOTOGRAPHS DIVISION)

CONFERENCE, but the Japanese ignored it. The agonizing American decision was then made to use the newly developed ATOMIC BOMB. On August 6, 1945, one such bomb was dropped on the Japanese city of HIROSHIMA, 90 percent of which was leveled, with about 130,000 persons killed or injured. A second bomb fell on NAGASAKI on August 9, 1945, ruining a third of this Japanese city and killing or wounding about 75,000 persons. Five days later Japan's emperor HIROHITO overruled his military advisers and accepted the peace terms of Potsdam.

World War II on the Italian front
(1943–1945) After defeating the Axis forces in the NORTH AFRICAN CAMPAIGN, the Allies turned their attention to Italy. On July 10, 1943, thousands of American and British soldiers landed under the cover of darkness on the shores of southern SICILY. They took the Germans and Italians garrisoned there by complete surprise and, within hours, gained control of 150 miles of the coast. After one battle at the Gela beachhead, Allied troops swept across the island, captured Palermo and by August 17, 1943, secured all of Sicily. Meanwhile, the Italian dictator, Benito MUSSOLINI, had been deposed, and his successor had sued for peace, which was granted on September 3, 1943, the same day the British landed on the toe of the Italian peninsula. Six days later U.S. forces made a large amphibious landing at Salerno, expecting little resistance. Adolf HITLER, Germany's dictator, had sent German troops to occupy strategic places in Italy, and they fought the Allied invaders ruthlessly. Slowly the Allies moved up the peninsula, seized Naples, and by December 1943, reached CASSINO Pass, south of Rome, which the Germans had fortified. Some of the toughest fighting of the war occurred in this mountainous terrain. In an effort to outflank the Germans, another Allied force was sent ashore at the Anzio beachhead, but German reinforcements arrived, and the Allies had to struggle to maintain their foothold. Finally, in May 1944, they overcame the Germans at Anzio and Cassino Pass and advanced northward again. Rome was liberated on June 4, 1944, and Florence two months later. The Allies, however, were stopped at the German

Gothic Line stretching across the Alps in northern Italy. A stalemate developed during which time Italian partisans harassed the Germans wherever they were stationed. In April 1945, Allied forces crossed the Po River, and partisan forces seized Milan, Genoa and Venice. Mussolini was captured by partisans as he tried to flee the country and was summarily shot to death with his mistress. On April 29, 1945, the Germans in Italy surrendered; shortly after the partisans handed over their arms and dissolved their resistance movement.

World War II on the Russian front *(1941–1945)* Although the USSR had entered World War II as an Axis power and had defeated FINLAND (see RUSSO-FINNISH WAR OF 1939–40) and absorbed the Baltic states, its Soviet leaders realized that Adolf HITLER, the German führer (leader), was not to be trusted. There was worldwide surprise when three German armies, supported by Romanian, Hungarian, Italian, Finnish, Slovak and Spanish troops, invaded Russia on June 22, 1941. Even more surprise was shown at the valiant resistance displayed by Soviet soldiers and civilians. Hitler had expected to overrun Russia in four to six weeks, but he had underrated his opponents, the vast distances to be covered in Russia and the scarcity of good roads and railroads there. At first the Germans were successful as they swept eastward in their tanks and armored vehicles against the retreating Russians. The city of LENINGRAD (St. Petersburg) was surrounded and besieged for two harrowing years; KIEV

Field Marshal Wilhelm Keitel signs surrender terms for the German army. 1945. (LIBRARY OF CONGRESS. PRINTS AND PHOTOGRAPHS DIVISION)

fell, and half a million Soviet soldiers were killed or taken prisoner; the rich agricultural and industrial region of the Ukraine fell into German hands; Nazi troops were within sight of Moscow. But then winter set in, and the war bogged down. In the spring of 1942, the Germans resumed their offensive, intending to conquer the Caucasus region and its oil fields, but they were stopped at STALINGRAD (Volgograd). The city was bombed to rubble, but the Russians fought stubbornly from house to house, factory to factory. In mid-November 1942, the Russian military high command assembled its remaining troops, which began to advance upon Stalingrad from the north and south. The two Russian forces met behind the German lines, trapping the enemy's army in the smoldering city. All efforts to break out failed, and on February 2, 1943, the Germans surrendered. The victory at Stalingrad was the turning point of the war; thereafter the Russians took the offensive and drove the retreating Nazis, who slaughtered and destroyed as they withdrew, from their country. By 1944, Russian troops had control of the Baltic states, eastern Poland, the Ukraine, Romania, Bulgaria and Finland. Early in 1945, they conquered East Prussia, Czechoslovakia and eastern Germany, and in April that year they took BERLIN, Germany's capital. As Napoleon I (1769–1821) had done before him, Hitler had underestimated the will of the Russian people and the severity of the Russian winters.

World War II on the western front *(1944–1945)* Although British and American bombers had struck the principal industrial centers of Germany during 1942 and 1943 in World War II, it was not until the successful Allied landing on France's Normandy beaches in June 1944 (see NORMANDY, INVASION OF) that a western front was established on European soil. The mechanized U.S. Third Army moved southward into the Loire River valley and then proceeded east toward German-occupied Paris, which was liberated on August 25, 1944. A month later the American forces had advanced eastward to the Moselle River, had captured the fortress city of Liège and were at the German border near

Aachen, while the British had recaptured Brussels and Antwerp in Belgium and another Allied force had landed in southern France and was making its way north. But lack of supplies, especially fuel, slowed the Allied advance to a standstill until the continental harbors and ports could be reopened. An attempt to seize the RHINE bridge at Arnhem in the Netherlands failed in September 1944. Three months later the Germans launched a surprise offensive against the weak American line at the Ardennes Forest (see BULGE, BATTLE OF THE), hoping to divide and conquer the Allied forces, but this last strike failed. In February 1945, the Allies again went on the offensive, cleared the retreating Germans from the west banks of the Rhine River, crossed the river at REMAGEN and later other places and trapped some 300,000 German troops in the RUHR Valley. Thereafter the Western Front moved rapidly eastward toward Berlin.

World Wide Web See INTERNET.

Wortman, Sterling (*1923–1981*) American plant geneticist and a leading figure in the so-called GREEN REVOLUTION. Wortman experimented with grain production and developed high-yielding grains. He was also a vice president and president of the influential Rockefeller Foundation.

Wozniak, Stephen (*1950– *) American computer engineer and cofounder of APPLE COMPUTERS. Born in Sunnyvale, California, Wozniak demonstrated an interest in electronic devices during his childhood years when he and his friends began building intercoms that would transmit sound between their houses. Although he studied computer science at the University of California at Berkeley, Wozniak left that institution before graduating to work in the Hewlett-Packard (HP) computer division. During his time at HP, Wozniak encountered Steven JOBS, a fellow HP employee and computer aficionado, at meetings of the Homebrew Computer Club of Palo Alto, California. In 1975 Wozniak and Jobs began working on a new computer design in their spare time, which they named the Apple I. The design proved popular in the area, and Jobs and Wozniak sold 600 of the new machines. After the success of the machine, Jobs

and Wozniak left their jobs at HP and founded Apple Computers in April 1976. Jobs and Wozniak quickly expanded their operations, introducing new computer models, such as the Apple II, and began to produce a variety of software for their machines.

In 1981 shortly after he was involved in a plane crash, Wozniak left Apple Computers. His departure also followed the complete failure of Apple's latest release, the Apple III, whose serious design flaws forced its recall from stores. Wozniak used his two-year "sabbatical" from the company to complete his college education and obtain a B.S. in both computer science and engineering from Berkeley in 1982. After returning to the company in 1983 and helping to design the new Apple computer—Macintosh—Wozniak permanently left his position as Apple's vice president of research and development in 1985 to pursue others commercial ventures.

Wozzeck Landmark modern opera by Viennese composer Alban BERG (1925). With Claude DEBUSSY's *Pelléas et Mélisande* it is regarded as the greatest opera of the 20th century. It was adapted from a play by Georg Buechner, *Woyzeck* (1836). Based on the real-life trial and beheading of a Leipzig murderer, Buechner's play depicted the doomed love of a downtrodden soldier for the mistress, Marie. With the appearance of a rival, a drum-major, Woyzeck kills Marie and drowns himself in a pool. Berg's opera employed the musical device of the "Sprechstimme," a kind of song-speech devised by mentor Arnold SCHOENBERG in his song-cycle *Pierrot Lunaire* (1912). The brooding atmosphere of terror and derangement, the swooping vocal lines against stark, atonal harmonies, the bewildering profusions of all manner of instrumental ensembles—military bands, restaurant orchestras, chamber orchestras, and strange instruments like an out-of-tune piano and an accordion—confused and outraged audiences and critics at the first performances in Berlin and Prague in 1925 and 1926. Venomous attacks called the stage action "an insane asylum" and the music "a capital offense." However, by the time Leopold STOKOWSKI introduced it to America in 1931 its cause-celebre status was changing into that of a bona

fide modern classic. By the mid-1950s it had entered the repertory of the Metropolitan Opera. Despite its potential cacophony it has exerted a strange fascination for audiences. "Even the non-technical listener," critic Ernest Newman has said, "finds himself, perhaps for the first time in his life, taking a vast amount of nontonal music and not merely not wincing at it but being engrossed by it." Philosophically, it expresses Buechner's and Berg's acceptance of life on its own terms. "One must love mankind in order to penetrate the particular existence of each thing," Buechner wrote. "There must be nothing too common or too ugly. The most insignificant of faces can make a deeper impression than the mere sensation of beauty."

WPA See WORKS PROGRESS ADMINISTRATION.

Wragg, Harry (*1902–1985*) British jockey. Wragg rode from the end of World War I until 1946. During his career as a trainer, from 1947 until 1983, he won six English classics, with only the Oaks eluding him.

Wrangel, Baron Peter Nikolayevich (*1878–1928*) General. Following service in the RUSSO-JAPANESE WAR and WORLD WAR I, he joined the anti-Bolshevik forces of General Anton DENIKIN. After Denikin's defeat in November 1919 he was left in command of the disorganized White army. He advanced against the BOLSHEVIKS but was forced to retreat, and the remnants of his troops were evacuated from Sevastopol to Turkey in 1920. He spent the rest of his life in Belgium.

Wright, Frank Lloyd (*1867–1959*) American architect. Wright, considered by some as one of America's most imaginative architects, left a wealth of striking architectural forms. He studied civil engineering at the University of Wisconsin from 1884 to 1888, when he was apprenticed to CHICAGO architects Louis Sullivan and Dankmar Adler and soon became their chief draftsman. He left in 1893 to build his own practice, but continued to show Sullivan's influence in attempts to bring harmony to a building's function, form and location.

Wright's unique style soon brought him the extreme in praise and scorn usually reserved for politicians. The Unity Temple in Oak Park, Illinois, was the first public building in the United States to show its concrete construction. Wright planned many "prairie-style" houses in and around Chicago. Prairie-style buildings permit the open spaces inside to expand into the outdoors through the use of terraces and porches. The Willitts house in Highland Park, Illinois, is shaped like a cross, with rooms arranged so that they seem to flow into each other. The Robie house in Chicago appears to be a series of horizontal layers floating in the air. The Johnson Wax building in Racine, Wisconsin, gave the same impression of streamlined style as Wright's other products of the late 1930s. The building featured a smooth, curved exterior of glass and brick. One of his most famous buildings was Fallingwater at Mill Run, Pennsylvania. Another was the Imperial hotel in Tokyo completed in 1922, one of the major buildings to survive the terrible earthquake of the next year.

While Wright's influence was felt internationally, he remained a Midwesterner at heart. In 1932 Wright established the Taliesin Fellowship where architectural students were paid to live and work with Wright in the summer at TALIESIN, Wright's home in Spring Green, Wisconsin, and in the winter at Taliesin West, his home in Scottsdale, Arizona. He continued to design controversial buildings such as the Guggenheim Museum in New York City, a daring spiral structure (1959).

Wright, J. Skelly *(1911–1988)* U.S. judge; an enemy of segregation whose landmark 1960 desegregation order integrated public schools and public transportation in New Orleans. Reviled by many southerners as a traitor to his race, Wright later served as a judge on the U.S. court of appeals for the District of Columbia, where he championed the cause of the poor, particularly those of the inner cities.

Wright, Peter *(1916–1995)* British counterintelligence agent, author of *Spycatcher.* Wright joined MI5 in 1955 as a scientific adviser in electronics. Following the defection of Kim PHILBY (1963), Wright headed the seven-man committee that investigated Soviet infiltration of British intelligence. He retired from MI5 in 1976 and later moved to Australia. His controversial book *Spycatcher* (1985), a purported expose of the British intelligence services, was banned in Britain for several years under the Official Secrets Act and was the subject of fierce legal battles in Britain and Australia (1986–87). Among other things, Wright claimed that Sir Roger Hollis had been a Soviet agent—the so-called Fifth Man.

Wright, Richard *(1908–1960)* American novelist and social critic. The son of black sharecroppers, Wright was an errand boy in Memphis when he borrowed his white employer's library card and steeped himself in the work of such socially conscious writers as Theodore DREISER and Sinclair LEWIS. During the Depression of the 1930s he joined the FEDERAL WRITERS PROJECT and directed the Federal Negro Theater. His collection of stories *Uncle Tom's Children* (1938) won a prize as best book submitted by anyone in the project. As Harlem editor of the *Daily Worker* (1940), he displeased fellow communists, which led to a troubled disaffiliation from party and eventually to expatriation from America. Considered by many the most important black writer of his time, he also wrote his autobiography, *Black Boy* (1945), and several books about the lives of blacks around the world.

Wright, Sewall *(1889–1988)* American geneticist who is widely regarded as the foremost U.S. evolutionary theorist of the 20th century. Together with R. A. Fisher and J. B. S. HALDANE of Great Britain, he founded the field of population genetics, thus providing a mathematical underpinning for the 19th-century theories of Charles Darwin and Gregor Mendel. The fourth and final volume of his magnum opus, *Evolution and the Genetics of Populations*, was published in 1968.

Wright, Willard Huntington (S. S. Van Dine) *(1883–1939)* New York art and literary critic whose detective novels in the 1920s and 1930s (written under the pseudonym S. S. Van Dine) were among the most famous and influential works in modern American crime fiction. Wright was born in Charlottesville, Virginia, educated at Harvard and worked from 1907 to 1923 as a critic for magazines like *Smart Set* and *Town Topics.* His first book, *Europe After 8:15,* was a series of witty social and artistic observations written in collaboration with H. L. MENCKEN and George Jean Nathan. He suffered a nervous breakdown in 1923 and for the next few years turned his interests to the "recreational pursuits" of the detective story. From 1926 to 1939 under the "Van Dine" name, he wrote the 12 "Philo Vance" detective novels that secured his fame. Vance was Wright's alter-ego, a curious mixture of incisive intellect, great artistic erudition, exotic, eclectic tastes and a haughty, pretentious manner. In the preface to his groundbreaking anthology, *The Great Detective Stories* (1927), Wright formulated a series of "rules" for the genre, demanding the same kind of consistency and craft commonly applied to classical literary forms. Although at the time of his death from thrombosis in 1939 he had grown tired of Vance and had outlived his popularity, he was, for a few years at least, according to scholar Howard Haycraft, "the best known American writer of the detective story since Poe."

Wright brothers Orville (1871–1948) Wilbur (1867–1912) Wright, pioneers in powered aircraft. They first became interested in the possibility of powered flight in the 1890s, after hearing about the glider flights of the German aviation pioneer Otto Lilienthal. In their Dayton, Ohio, bicycle repair shop and factory, the Wrights, very able mechanics, were experimenting (most called it tinkering) with kites and gliders and every other aspect of aerodynamics. In their efforts to learn about every discovery having to do with flight, it was said they read every book in the Dayton public library pertaining to aerodynamics. They built a wind tunnel, the world's first, and developed their own science of flying, drawing up valuable tables of wind current and drift and noting other discoveries. They discovered the use of the aileron, probably the single most important discovery they made in preparation for the world's first flight of a heavier-than-air craft at Kitty Hawk, North Carolina (December 17, 1903). They chose Kitty Hawk because their investigations showed that its air currents were probably the best for their purposes. They continued their experiments at Dayton.

The record-breaking flights of Wilbur in the United States and Orville in France brought them world fame, as well as orders from government and private organizations. They formed the

American Wright Company in 1909. After Wilbur's death, Orville retired from the business to engage in private research. In 1948, the year of Orville's death, their historic Kitty Hawk plane was installed at the Smithsonian Institution. The house where Orville was born and their bicycle shop laboratory were bought by Henry FORD and moved to his Greenfield Village in Michigan, where they were restored and put on public display.

Wu, John C. H. *(1899–1986)* Chinese statesman. A leading cultural figure in the Chinese Nationalist government, he was the principal author of the Nationalist Constitution in 1946. He later served as a judge of the Permanent Court of Arbitration at the Hague.

Wunderlich, Fritz *(1930–1966)* German lyric tenor, known for his sensitive singing in the operas of Wolfgang Amadeus Mozart, Gioacchino Rossini and Goetano Donizetti and the operettas of Otto Nicolai and Franz Lehar. Wunderlich, whose professional career lasted a brief 11 years, is widely acknowledged as possessing one of the most beautiful voices of any singer of his generation. His first professional appearance was in 1955, at the Wurttemberg State Opera in Stuttgart, in a supporting role in Wagne'r *Die Meistersinger;* soon after, he gained acclaim when he substituted for another singer as Tamino in Mozart's *The Magic Flute.* Wunderlich sang in Germany, Austria (at the SALZBURG FESTIVAL) and Britain. He died at age 36 when he fell down a staircase in Heidelberg, just one month before his scheduled American debut. His voice has been preserved in numerous recordings.

Wye River Memorandum A document signed by Israeli prime minister Benjamin NETANYAHU and PALESTINIAN AUTHORITY (PA) president Yassir ARAFAT. Meeting with U.S. President William Jefferson CLINTON, as well as King HUSSEIN of Jordan, at the Wye Plantation in the U.S. state of Maryland, Arafat and Netanyahu signed an agreement on October 23, 1998, that provided for a three-stage release of 750 Palestinian prisoners by Israel and a gradual end to the Israeli military occupation of the West Bank. In return Arafat promised to use his authority over Palestinian Arabs to halt violence and terrorist attacks against Israeli citizens. However, following a clash between protesting Palestinian Arabs and Israeli police over Israel's refusal to release an estimated 2,500 Palestinian prisoners, Netanyahu denounced Arafat for not arresting those responsible for the violence, and suspended Israel's adherence to the Wye River agreement on the grounds that the PA had not fulfilled its side of the bargain. In May 1999 the agreements were reinstated following Netanyahu's replacement as prime minister by Ehud BARAK, who modified the memorandum in a September 1999 meeting with Arafat at the Egyptian resort town of Sharm-el-Sheik.

Wyeth, Andrew *(1917–)* American painter; the son of renowned American artist, muralist and children's book illustrator Newell Convers WYETH (1882–1944). The vast majority of Andrew's canvases depict people and landscapes from his native Pennsylvania or from Maine, where the painter had a summer home. His paintings are generally simple in form and subject matter but exhibit technical virtuosity and convey an emotional impact. Wyeth's most famous work is *Christina's World* (1948). In the 1980s, nude studies completed by Wyeth in the latter decades of his life were exhibited for the first time. In 1990 he was awarded the Congressional Gold Medal of Honor.

Wyeth, Nathaniel Convers (Newell Convers Wyeth) *(1920–1990)* U.S. engineer. In the 1970s, while working for E.I. du Pont de Nemours & Co., he invented the plastic soda bottle. The bottle, made from polyethylene terephthalate (PET), quickly became the industry standard as it did not contaminate its contents as earlier plastic bottles had. By 1990 15 billion of the PET bottles were being produced annually. He was also a brother of artist Andrew Wyeth and son of the late illustrator N. C. Wyeth.

Wyeth, N(ewell) C(onvers) *(1882–1944)* American painter noted for his book and magazine illustrations. Influenced by the picturesque, colonial flavor of his native Needham, Massachusetts, Wyeth began his art training at the Massachusetts Normal Art School and later studied with illustrator Howard Pyle in Wilmington, Delaware. Wyeth sold his first *Saturday Evening Post* cover in 1903. After a trip West that produced a notable series of western paintings (1906–07), Wyeth settled in Chadds Ford, Pennsylvania. Generations of Wyeths and a number of other painters, notably Frank Schoonover, lived and worked there. From 1903 until his death, Wyeth produced nearly 4,000 works, including important murals such as the "Pilgrim" series for the Metropolitan Life Insurance Company in New York (1939), numerous magazine and newspaper illustrations and magnificent work for the Scribner's Classics series, beginning with *Treasure Island* (1911)—arguably the most famous book illustrations by any American artist in the 20th century. Wyeth was elected to the National Academy in 1941.

Wyler, William *(1902–1981)* Hollywood film director whose career spanned nearly 50 years. Born in Alsace (then part of Germany, now in France) to a Swiss family, he immigrated to the U.S. to work for UNIVERSAL PICTURES (1922). He held a number of jobs in the movie business before directing his first feature film in 1925. His career took off when he left Universal to work for Samuel GOLDWYN (1936). Wyler was most successful in filming adaptations of the works of well-known novelists and playwrights. A notoriously demanding director, he insisted on the best performances possible from his actors and actresses, 14 of whom won ACADEMY AWARDS for their roles in his films. He himself received 12 best-director nominations, winning the award three times. Among his most notable films were *Dodsworth* (1936), *Wuthering Heights* (1939), *The Little Foxes, Mrs. Miniver* (1942), *The Best Years of Our Lives* (1946), *The Big Country* (1958), *Ben-Hur* (1959) and *Funny Girl* (1968).

Wyndham-White, Eric *(1913–1980)* British economist. He was an expert in world trade and commerce. For 20 years (1948–69) he was the executive secretary and director-general of the General Agreement on Tariffs and Trade (GATT), the Swiss-based international agency set up after World War II to establish rules for world trade. He was considered one of the main architects of post-war cooperation among governments to promote international trade and economic growth, and also played an important role in the **Kennedy round** of trade negotiations that led to reductions in import tariffs (1967).

Wynne, Greville Maynard *(1944–1990)* British businessman and spy. Wynne worked for the British secret intelligence service MI6 during the height of the COLD WAR in the 1960s. He spent 18 months in a Soviet prison after being arrested on espionage charges in Budapest in 1962. Although he was sentenced to eight years in prison, he was released in 1964 in exchange for a Soviet spy being held by the British. He detailed his experiences in two books, *The Man from Moscow* (1967) and *The Man from Odessa.*

Wyszyński, Stefan *(1901–1981)* Roman Catholic cardinal, primate of POLAND (1949–81). Ordained a priest in 1924, Wyszyński was a distinguished scholar, receiving a doctorate in sociology and canon law from Lublin's Catholic University in 1929. He took an active part in the RESISTANCE during WORLD WAR II, and after the war (1946) he was named bishop of Lublin. In 1949 he was appointed archbishop of Gniezno and Warsaw and primate of Poland, and in 1953 he was elevated to the office of cardinal. He was imprisoned by the pro-Soviet Polish regime from 1953 to 1956. After his release, he worked to achieve reconciliation between the church and the communist government, thus strengthening the church's position within Poland. With the rise of the SOLIDARITY movement, he met often with Lech WAŁESA and government officials, becoming an active force in mediating disputes between the unions and the Polish authorities.

X

X-Files, The A science-fiction television series on the Fox Broadcasting Corporation's network (1993–2002). Created by Chris Carter, the show premiered on September 10, 1993, and focused on FBI agent Dana Scully (played by Gillian Anderson), who was assigned to observe fellow FBI agent Fox Mulder (played by David Duchovny) and his investigations into allegedly paranormal incidents. Although she initially dismissed (and on occasion disproved) Mulder's theories about government conspiracies and alien abductions, Scully eventually concurred with his assessments. While the series' episodes initially adopted a format similar to that of *The Twilight Zone,* in which Mulder and Scully would investigate and solve cases within each installment, *The X-Files* soon began to revolve around Mulder's increasing belief in a government-led conspiracy to conceal the evidence of visitations by alien life forms in exchange for high-end technology. In the course of their continuing investigations on this subject, both agents were abducted by aliens, although in the case of Duchovny's character, the abduction was meant to afford him a permanent exit from the series. The show also produced a movie—*X Files: Fight the Future* (1998)—and a short-lived spin-off series (*The Lone Gunmen,* 2001) that explored the investigatory lives of three minor characters within the series. In the 2001–02 season, despite the return of Mulder and the introduction of new FBI agents—John Doggett (played by Robert Patrick) and Monica Reyes (played by Annabeth Gish)—the series' ratings began to decline, and Carter announced the season would be the show's last. Over its nine seasons, *The X-Files* won 15 Emmy Awards.

Xi'an Incident (Sian Incident) Kidnapping of CHIANG KAI-SHEK by ZHANG XUELIANG in the city of XIAN in 1936. At the time, Chiang was planning to attack and destroy Chinese communist forces in northwestern China and had traveled to Xian to announce the offensive. The powerful warlord Zhang feared a split in China that would jeopardize the country's opposition to Japanese aggression. The bold kidnapping forced Chiang to agree to cooperate with the communists. After announcing this agreement, Chiang was released in December 1936, and the period of uneasy cooperation between communist and Nationalist forces lasted until the end of WORLD WAR II. The truce also allowed the communists to regroup, gather strength and position themselves to take over the government of China in 1949.

Xinjiang (Sinkiang) Region of western China under the control of the Qing (Ch'ing [Manchu]) dynasty (1644–1911), Yang Zengxin (1911–28), Nationalist China (1928–49) and the People's Republic of China (PRC, 1949–). The majority of the territory's inhabitants are UIGHURS, an Islamic and Turkic people also found in the neighboring states of KAZAKHSTAN, KYRGYZSTAN, TURKMENISTAN and UZBEKISTAN. Ruled by the centralized rule of the Qing dynasty for nearly three centuries, Xinjiang came under the control of the Han Chinese warlord Yang Zengxin shortly after the collapse of Qing rule in 1911. In 1928 Yang was assassinated, and the territory briefly enjoyed a certain degree of autonomy while nominally acknowledging the political authority of the Nationalist Chinese government of CHIANG KAI-SHEK (Jiang Jieshi). In 1933 and 1944 Uighur tribesmen within the territory led unsuccessful insurrections against Chinese rule.

In 1949 the Chinese Communist Party (CCP) overthrew the Nationalist regime and began to assert its control over Xinjiang and incorporate the region into the PRC. The introduction of communist rule sparked conflict between the Uighurs and the Han Chinese settlers whom the PRC had dispatched to the territory. Tensions increased markedly as PRC officials attempted to bring all mosques and MADRASSAS (Islamic schools) in predominantly Muslim Xinjiang under state control. As the PRC consolidated its control over the region, the more lucrative jobs were given to Han Chinese, creating a socioeconomic cleavage between the two ethnic groups. In an effort to ameliorate these conflicts, the government in Beijing designated the province an Autonomous Region (the Xinjiang-Uighur Autonomous Region, or XUAR) within the PRC in 1955. However, the XUAR remained under the strict control of the CCP, rendering illusory the region's autonomy. Also, allegations of political, cultural and religious repression within the XUAR have been regularly issued by such human-rights NONGOVERNMENTAL ORGANIZATIONS (NGOs) as AMNESTY INTERNATIONAL and Human Rights Watch.

By the end of the 1980s, this mistreatment of Uighurs inside Xinjiang became a severe problem for the PRC. Following the successful efforts of the MUJAHIDEEN, or Islamic freedom fighters, in AFGHANISTAN to force the withdrawal of Soviet forces from their country in 1989, Uighurs within the XUAR began to demand either true autonomy or full independence. When the PRC responded to these demands with increased repression, Uighur nationalists launched a guerrilla campaign against the PRC that included the kidnapping and execution of government officials. In 1991 the independence of former Soviet republics such as KAZAKHSTAN and UZBEKISTAN, which contained Uighur minorities, fanned the flames of Uighur nationalism in Xinjiang. Throughout the 1990s, the PRC repeatedly alleged that Uighur rebel bands were receiving assistance from such Central Asian Islamic terrorist organizations as the East Turkestan Islamic Movement and the Home of East Turkestan Youth. In 1997 a series of terrorist bombings in China was traced by the government in Beijing to Uighur bands. Following an explosion in a Chinese shopping center in the XUAR in October 2001, the PRC began to intensify repression of Uighur nationalism.

X-ray A form of energy—electromagnetic radiation—with an extremely short wavelength. X-rays are produced naturally by the sun, but were only discovered in 1895 by German physicist Wilhelm Roentgen. Because of its short wavelength, X-rays can penetrate all but the densest materials. Artificially generated X-rays have a myriad of medical, scientific and industrial applications. They have become indispensable in the diagnosis of injury and disease. They

are also used to shrink and destroy cancerous tumors. However, overexposure to X-rays can cause cancers.

X series aircraft Experimental rocket-powered aircraft. Developed by the U.S. to test and expand the limits of aircraft, the single-seat planes set records for speed and altitude. The prototype **X-1** was designed to reach supersonic speeds. The sleek winged craft was launched from the belly of a B-29. Powered by a liquid oxygen and ethyl alcohol engine, it first went beyond the speed of sound (Mach 1) on October 14, 1947, piloted by Colonel Charles E. (Chuck) YEAGER. The next in the series was the **X-2**, taken aloft by a B-50 bomber. The first of these aluminum-steel planes with stainless steel wings exploded on its maiden test flight, killing pilot Skip Ziegler and a member of the B-50 crew. In subsequent flights, the aircraft achieved speeds of Mach 2.93 and a height of 126,200 ft. On its last flight on September 27, 1956, pilot Milburn Apt flew the plane at Mach 3.196 (2,094 mph) before crashing. The **X-15**, the last in the series, was a joint project of the air force, the navy and the National Advisory Committee for Aeronautics (later the NATIONAL AERONAUTICS AND SPACE ADMINISTRATION). It had a wingspan of 22 ft. and was crafted of stainless steel and titanium covered by a chrome-nickel alloy and coated with a silicon-based substance to reduce the temperature of its skin at supersonic speeds. Its seat was capable of ejecting at speeds up to Mach 4 and altitudes to 120,000 ft. With a rocket engine producing 57,300 lbs. of thrust, powered by a liquid oxygen and anhydrous ammonia fuel, the X-15 was launched from the underside of a Boeing B-52 wing. The first flight, on June 8, 1959, was piloted by A. Scott CROSSFIELD, who had also acted as a project adviser. After two other 1959 flights using older engines, the first flight to employ the full one-million horsepower XLR-99 engine was made by Crossfield on November 15, 1960. Flights continued

until 1967, pushing the X-15 to higher altitudes and greater speeds. On August 22, 1963, a NASA pilot set the aircraft's altitude record at 67 miles (353,760 ft). The speed record of Mach 6.7 (4,520 mph) was set by U.S. Air Force pilot William J. (Pete) Knight on October 3, 1967. The X-series is still underway, its latest development being the Joint Strike Fighter.

Xu Jiatun (Hsü Chia-t'un) (1916–) Chinese political figure. Born in Jiangsu Province, Xu became director of the HONG KONG branch of China's official Xinhua news agency in 1983 and is China's chief representative in Hong Kong. Prior to his arrival in Hong Kong in 1983 he held a variety of party and government posts in Jiangsu. He served as a member of the 11th (1977–82) and 12th (1982–85) central committees and in 1985 became a member of the Central Advisory Committee. As head of the local branch of the Chinese Communist Party (the Hong Kong and Macau Work Committee), he revamped the party and recruited local businesspeople and professionals. He served as vice chairman of the committee drafting the basic law for the Hong Kong special administrative region after 1985 and has been an outspoken critic of local demands for democratic reform. In 1990, a year after the Chinese government's brutal suppression of the TIANANMEN SQUARE MASSACRE, Xu defected to the U.S. rather than face probable punishment for his support of the student demonstrations.

Xu Xiangqian (Hsü Hsiang-chien) (1901–1990) Chinese military leader. He joined the COMMUNIST PARTY in the 1920s and participated in the epic LONG MARCH from southeast to northwest CHINA in 1934 and 1935. After the founding of the People's Republic of China in 1949, he was named army chief of staff. In 1955, Chairman MAO named him one of 10 marshals of China's Red Army. He later served as defense minister (1978–81).

Y

Yablonski, Joseph *(1910–1969)* American labor leader. Born in Pittsburgh, he began working in the mines at the age of 15. Joining the United Mine Workers (UMW), he rose to be president of the Pittsburgh district (1958), but in 1966 was forced to resign by union president "Tony" BOYLE. While acting as the union's head lobbyist in Washington, Yablonski became increasingly enraged at abuses in the union, and in 1969 he announced his candidacy for the union's presidency. After Boyle's reelection, Yablonski charged fraud and on December 30, 1969, he, his wife and daughter were murdered in a gangland-style execution. In 1975 Boyle was convicted as a coconspirator in the Yablonski family killing.

Yacoub, Talaat *(1943?–1988)* Palestinian leader; head of the PALESTINE Liberation Front, a small hard-line guerrilla faction. In 1981 the group split in half, with one group remaining loyal to Yacoub and the other to Abul Abbas. The Abbas group was responsible for the 1985 hijacking of the Italian cruise ship ACHILLE LAURO. Yacoub denounced the hijackers as "pirates."

Yadin, Yigael *(1917–1984)* Israeli archaeologist, military hero and politician. Yadin used his knowledge of biblical history and ancient fortifications to outwit an Egyptian force in the ARAB-ISRAELI WAR OF 1948–49. He subsequently played a major role in organizing the Israeli army in its formative years. As an archaeologist, he obtained the Dead Sea Scrolls and other ancient manuscripts and led the excavations at the fortress of Masada. He served as deputy prime minister under Menachem BEGIN from 1977 to 1981.

Yagoda, Genrikh Grigorevich *(1891–1937)* Soviet political official. He became deputy chairman of the GPU in 1924 and chief of the security police in 1934. He was responsible for the first purge. In 1936 he was dismissed, having been accused of slackness by STALIN. He was a defendant at the show trial of the "Anti-Soviet bloc of Rightists and Trotskyites" and in 1937 was executed.

Yahya Khan, Agha Muhammad *(1917–1980)* Military ruler of PAKISTAN *(1969–71).* A career army officer, he became commanding general of the Pakistani army in 1966. In 1969 he was appointed to lead the country under martial law; he became president later that year. His presidency was marked by civil war (see BANGLADESH) and the simultaneous INDO-PAKISTANI WAR OF 1971; Pakistan lost both wars. Yahya Khan was forced out of office in 1971 and spent five years under house arrest.

Yakovlev, Aleksandr Sergeyevich *(1906–1989)* Leading Soviet designer of WORLD WAR II fighter planes and postwar military and civilian aircraft. Among the best-known Yakovlev planes in service at the time of his death were the vertical takeoff YAK-38, known by Western military experts as the Forger, and the 120-seat YAK-38 short-haul passenger jet.

Yalow, Rosalyn Sussman *(1921–)* American physicist. Since 1947 Yalow has worked as a physicist at the Bronx Veterans Administration Hospital in New York City. Together with Solomon A. Berson in the 1950s, she developed the technique of radioimmunoassay (RIA), which enables the detection of minute substances in plasma and other bodily tissues. This duo's collaborative efforts, which lasted 22 years, began by using radioisotopes to measure blood volume, assess the distribution of serum protein in bodily tissues and diagnose thyroid disease. Their subsequent investigations into diabetes led to their published description of RIA in 1959. The many uses for RIA include detecting drugs in bodily fluids or tissues, screening blood for the hepatitis virus, early cancer detection and measuring levels of neurotransmitters and hormones. In 1977 she shared the 1977 NOBEL PRIZE for physiology or medicine.

Yalta Conference World War II summit meeting held by Great Britain's Winston CHURCHILL, the USSR's Joseph STALIN and the U.S.'s Franklin D. ROOSEVELT and their staffs at the Black Sea resort town of Yalta, February 4–11, 1945. Among the agreements arrived at was the Soviet promise to declare war against JAPAN 30 days after the surrender of GERMANY. In return, the U.S. agreed to grant the USSR southern SAKHALIN Island and the Kuril Islands,

The "Big Three" at the Yalta Conference (left to right): Winston Churchill, Franklin Roosevelt, and Joseph Stalin, 1945 (LIBRARY OF CONGRESS, PRINTS AND PHOTOGRAPHS DIVISION)

lost in the RUSSO-JAPANESE WAR, and a zone of occupation in Korea. Germany's unconditional surrender was again demanded and its postwar occupation by the "Big Three" and France was settled. The leaders also agreed to convene a conference later that year to make plans for the UNITED NATIONS. In addition, the three powers endorsed the reorganization of an independent Poland, the establishment of free elections in Poland and the fixing of Polish boundaries. Most of the Yalta Conference agreements were arrived at in secret, and a complete text was not published until 1947. This secrecy, together with what some considered excessive concessions to the Soviets by Roosevelt, later brought the American president a great deal of criticism at home and abroad.

Yamamoto, Isoruko *(1884–1943)* Japanese admiral. Born at Nagaoka, he was educated in Japan and in the U.S. at Harvard University. Naval attache to Washington from 1925 to 1927, he was made assistant naval minister in 1936. Appointed commander in chief of the navy in 1939, he maintained that only quick destruction of the U.S. fleet could assure JAPAN's wartime success, and he was the force behind the 1941 attack on PEARL HARBOR. An advocate of strong naval air power, he achieved early victories in WORLD WAR II, but was halted in 1942 at the battle of the CORAL SEA and at MIDWAY. Yamamoto was chief of Japan's Pacific operations until his plane was shot down by American fighters on April 18, 1943.

Yamasaki, Minoru *(1912–1986)* Japanese-American architect. He de-

signed more than 300 structures, among them the Federal Science Pavilion at the 1962 Seattle World's Fair. He was perhaps best known as the designer of New York's colossal twin towers, the World Trade Center.

Yamashita, Tomoyuki *(188?–1946)* Japanese general. A career officer, he served in the RUSSO-JAPANESE WAR, WORLD WAR I and the SINO-JAPANESE WAR OF 1937–45. A leading Japanese commander during WORLD WAR II, he led troops in northern CHINA in 1939 and headed the successful Malayan campaign in 1941 that resulted in the surrender of SINGAPORE in February 1942. Commanding Japanese forces in the PHILIPPINES, he took BATAAN and CORREGIDOR in 1944, but was overwhelmed by the Allied invasion under General Douglas MACARTHUR. He surrendered in 1945, was tried for atrocities committed by his troops, found guilty and hanged in 1946.

Yanaev, Gennady *(1937–)* Soviet politician and president of the UNION OF SOVIET SOCIALIST REPUBLICS (USSR) (August 1991). Born in Perevoz, Yanaev joined the Communist Party of the Soviet Union (CPSU) in 1962, and a year later was designated second secretary of the Communist Party in Ukraine's Obkom region. He was promoted to first secretary a year later.

In 1968 Yanaev was named chairman of the committee of USSR Youth Organizations and vice chairman of the Presidium of the Union of Soviet Associations for Friendship and Cultural Relations with Foreign Countries. After 18 years of participation in Soviet

youth and cultural activities, Yanaev became secretary of the Trades Union Federation of the USSR and became vice chairman in 1988. In 1990 he became vice president of the Soviet Union, a position recently created by Soviet president Mikhail GORBACHEV, also advancing to the Central Committee of the CPSU and the Politburo, the country's executive governing body. In the summer of 1991 after learning that Gorbachev planned to sign a Treaty of Union on August 20, 1991, that would grant the republics greater autonomy, Yanaev joined a conspiracy designed to block the proposed treaty and overthrow Gorbachev.

On August 19, 1991, Yanaev and his cohorts placed Gorbachev under house arrest at his Crimean summer house. The coup's leaders then immediately announced that Yanaev would replace Gorbachev as president of the USSR. However, this coup by hardliners immediately encountered resistance from Yeltsin and other political and military leaders from the various republics, and the conspiracy unraveled within three days. Yanaev was arrested and charged with conspiracy against the Soviet president. Although the Soviet Union ceased to exist on December 25, 1991, the trials of Yanaev and his fellow conspirators began in 1993. A general amnesty proclaimed by Yeltsin in 1994 saved Yanaev from having to serve time in prison.

Yao Wenyuan See GANG OF FOUR.

Yardley, Norman *(1915–1989)* English cricketer. He played for Cambridge and for Yorkshire, and captained the England eleven 14 times, beginning in 1947. During his career he scored a total of 18,173 runs. He served as chairman of the selectors committee for England in 1951 and 1952; he also remained active as president of the Yorkshire Cricket Club from 1981 through 1984.

Yaroslavsky, Yemelyan Mikhailovich (Miney Izrailevich Gubelman) *(1878–1943)* Jewish politician active in the Russian Social Democratic Labor Party from 1898, for which he was imprisoned and exiled. As a supporter of LENIN he was involved in the BOLSHEVIK REVOLUTION of 1917, but in 1918 he became critical of Lenin's policies and joined the Left Communists. He became a supporter of STALIN and the official historian of the COMMUNIST PARTY in the USSR and was instrumental in falsifying the history of the party. He was also a militant atheist. He wrote *Twenty-five Years of Soviet Power,* which was published in 1943.

Yastrzemski, Michael "Carl" (Yaz) *(1939–)* American baseball player. In his 23 years with the Boston Red Sox, Yastrzemski became the first American League player to reach both the 3,000 hit and 400 homer plateau. An 18-time All Star, he was an outstanding fielder, with seven Gold Gloves, and was the winner of three batting titles. His most memorable season was 1967, when he was the league's Most Valuable Player as he led the Red Sox through a four-team pennant race in the final weeks of the season, to their first title in 21 seasons. Although he hit .400 in the series, the Sox fell short of the championship. He retired at the age of 43 in 1982. Yaz was named to the Hall of Fame in 1989.

Ydigoras Fuentes, Miguel *(1895– 1982)* President of GUATEMALA (1958– 63). A right-wing general, he was overthrown in a coup by junior army officers.

Yeager, Charles Elwood "Chuck" *(1923–)* American test pilot. Yeager was the first pilot to break the sound barrier, flying at a speed of 700 miles per hour in his Bell-X-1 aircraft in 1947. He had served as a fighter pilot in WORLD WAR II. As a test pilot after the war, he first broke the sound barrier, then a speed record, flying at 1,650 miles per hour in 1953. His accomplishments contributed to the training of the first astronauts in the U.S. space program.

Yeats, John Butler *(1839–1922)* Irish portrait painter. The father of William Butler YEATS, he began his career as a barrister. Turning to painting in 1867, he studied art in London. Yeats returned to Ireland in 1902 and from then until 1907, he painted many portraits of literary figures involved in the IRISH LITERARY REVIVAL. He journeyed to New York in 1907 and stayed for the rest of his life, while his famous sons remained in Ireland.

Yeats, William Butler *(1865– 1939)* Irish poet, dramatist, essayist, memoirist and national figure. Yeats, who won the NOBEL PRIZE for literature in 1923, is universally regarded as one of the greatest poets of the 20th century. His poetic output, which began in the 1880s and continued until his death, spanned the schools of symbolism and MODERNISM but ultimately transcended them all. Yeats possessed not only great lyric gifts but also a remarkably unique vision that encompassed Celtic myth and romance, Western and Eastern occult and mystical traditions and the political aspirations of the Irish people. Major poetic works by Yeats include *The Wanderings of Oisin and Other Poems* (1889), *Last Poems* (1939) and *Collected Poems* (1950). In addition, Yeats was a gifted poetic dramatist who, with Lady Augusta GREGORY and John SYNGE, helped found the ABBEY THEATRE in Dublin. Plays by Yeats include *The Countess Cathleen* (1899) and *Deirdre* (1906). He also collected and wrote numerous fictional adaptations of Celtic legends. From 1922 to 1928, Yeats served by appointment as a senator of the Irish Free State. *A Vision* (1937) is a highly fascinating and idiosyncratic account of Yeats's mystical beliefs, while *Autobiographies* (1955) contains much revelatory material on his life. (See also IRELAND, IRISH LITERARY REVIVAL.)

Irish poet. essayist. dramatist and Nobel Prize winner William Butler Yeats (LIBRARY OF CONGRESS. PRINTS AND PHOTOGRAPHS DIVISION)

Ye Jianying *(1897–1986)* Chinese army officer. A survivor of the LONG MARCH OF 1934–35, he was CHINA's defense minister from 1975 to 1978. He also held the ceremonial post of head of state from 1978 to 1983. His retirement as head of state, purportedly due to ill health, was widely seen as buttressing the faction led by DENG XIAOPING. As the most renowned survivor of the military old guard, Ye had come to symbolize the entrenched conservatism that Deng was trying to eliminate.

Yeltsin, Boris Nikolayevich *(1931–)* Russian political figure. Born in the Ural Mountains, the son of peasants, Yeltsin was educated as a civil engineer. He joined the COMMUNIST PARTY and quickly rose in its ranks, becoming party leader in his home region of Sverdlovsk. In the mid-1980s, new Soviet leader Mikhail GORBACHEV chose Yeltsin to head the Moscow party organization; Yelsin also became a member of the ruling Politburo. Soon Yeltsin began to criticize Gorbachev for what he saw as the sluggish pace of economic reform in Soviet society, which caused Gorbachev to dismiss him from the party leadership. In 1989 Yeltsin's political career was resurrected as popular disaffection with political leadership swept him into the Soviet parliament as a deputy from Moscow. A fiery populist and passionate spokesman for reform, Yeltsin became the leader of the opposition, the Interregional Deputies Group. In 1990 he was elected to the powerful position of president of the Russian Republic and soon resigned from the Communist Party. Yeltsin constantly chided Gorbachev for slowness in reform while strongly advocating decentralization, privatization and the promotion of a free market economy.

On August 19, 1991, a conspiracy engineered by hard-liners placed Gorbachev under house arrest in his Crimean residence and established a new government. Yeltsin responded by denouncing the coup, and organizing Russian resistance against the newly installed president, Gennady YANAEV. As a result of the efforts of Yeltsin and a group of supporters in the army, the plot failed, and Gorbachev was released and returned to the Kremlin.

Following the coup's failure, Yeltsin began to mount a campaign to bring an end to the Soviet Union. On December

8, 1991, a week after Ukraine voted to secede from the USSR, the presidents of BELARUS, RUSSIA and UKRAINE jointly established the COMMONWEALTH OF Independent STATES (CIS)—a voluntary confederation among newly independent republics that would preserve their political, economic and military cooperation. Creation of the CIS helped force Gorbachev to resign as Soviet president and announce his country's dissolution on December 25, 1991, leaving Yeltsin's Russian Federation to inherit most of the defunct Soviet Union's assets and responsibilities.

As president of the newly independent Russian state, Yeltsin's top priority was to reform his country's ailing economy. Seeking to stimulate economic growth and investment through the rapid conversion from a command to a free-market economy, Yeltsin ended price controls, reduced government expenditures and began selling off most government-owned industries and property.

To avert efforts mounted by his political opponents to remove him from power, Yeltsin unconstitutionally dissolved both houses of the Russian legislature on September 21, 1993, and called for new parliamentary elections as well as a referendum on a new constitution increasing the president's powers. Refusing to disband, the members of both houses remained in the White House (the legislative building), declared Yeltsin in violation of the Russian constitution and designated his vice president, General Alexander RUTSKOI, president of Russia. On October 3, after paramilitary forces loyal to Rutskoi seized government buildings in Moscow, Yeltsin ordered loyal forces to fire on the White House and capture the rebellious forces. The following day Rutskoi and his accomplices were arrested, and the attempted coup was thwarted.

In the mid-1990s, Yeltsin ordered a forceful military response to a campaign by Islamic rebels in CHECHNYA, a Russian autonomous province in Central Asia, to obtain independence for the province. The conflict in Chechnya resulted in the deaths of thousands of Chechen civilians, created hundreds of thousands of refugees and caused declining support for Yeltsin at home and around the world. Yeltsin's reputation at home and abroad further suffered from the exponential growth of organized crime and unemployment throughout Russia.

After winning reelection to the presidency in 1996, Yeltsin's victory was marred by a chronic instability in the office of prime minister. Between November 1996 and August 1999, Yeltsin appointed a total of five men to the office, dismissing some for failed policies and others for fear they would challenge him in the next presidential election. This period of ministerial instability coincided with foreign policy setbacks, such as the admission of the former WARSAW PACT members POLAND, HUNGARY and the CZECH REPUBLIC to NATO.

Interestingly, the last man Yeltsin appointed to the office of prime minister did indeed develop a rival center of power within the Kremlin. Designated the new premier in August 1999, former domestic intelligence chief Vladimir PUTIN soon acquired public support for his swift and strong response to renewed military and terrorist attacks from Chechen rebels in August and September 1999, which resulted in a Russian military invasion of **Chechnya** in October. On December 31 of that year, citing his poor health rather than his continually declining popularity, Yeltsin announced his immediate resignation as Russian president, and designated Putin as his hand-picked successor.

Yemen Located at the mouth of the Red Sea, on the southwestern tip of the Arabian Peninsula, Yemen covers an area of about 207,000 square miles; until recently, the area was divided into the two separate countries of **North Yemen** (pro-Western) and **South Yemen** (pro-Soviet). Gaining its independence from the OTTOMAN EMPIRE in 1918, North Yemen's absolute monarch Muhammad al-Badr was overthrown in 1962 and the Yemen Arab Republic proclaimed. Civil war erupted (1962–68), followed by governments influenced by Saudi Arabia in the 1970s. An independent South Yemen was formed by joining the British colony of ADEN and the British protectorate of South Arabia in 1967. When the country became a Marxist state (the People's Republic of Yemen) in 1970, thousands fled to North Yemen, thereby precipitating conflict between the two Yemens that lasted for years. War erupted twice during the 1970s. The two countries united as the Republic of Yemen in May 1990, with General Ali Abdullah Saleh of North Yemen as the first president. After opposing the 1991 U.S. invasion of IRAQ to liberate KUWAIT, Yemen allied itself with the U.S. in 2001 in U.S. president George W. BUSH's "War on Terror." In 2002

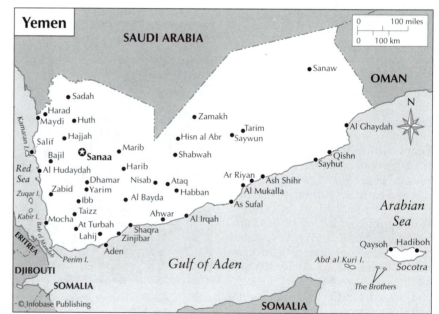

YEMEN

1918	North Yemen becomes independent.
1947	Yemen joins the UN.
1962	Army officers seize power, set up the Yemen Arab Republic (YAR), sparking civil war between royalists supported by Saudi Arabia and republicans backed by Egypt.
1963	The civil war becomes an international conflict as Egyptian troops land in Yemen to aid the republican forces and the Saudis lend arms and equipment to the royalists.
1967	Formation of South Yemen, comprising Aden and former Protectorate of South Arabia.
1970	New constitution is promulgated; name of the republic is changed to People's Democratic Republic of Yemen (PDRY).
1971	Thousands flee to north following crackdown on dissidents.
1970s	Border clashes between YAR and PDRY; cease-fire brokered by Arab League.
1990	North Yemen and South Yemen merge into a single nation, the Republic of Yemen; General Ali Abdallah Saleh, president of North Yemen, becomes the first president.
1991	Yemen condemns the UN coalition's offensive against Iraq; the people of Yemen ratify the new constitution by a large majority.
2000	Yemen and Saudi Arabia announce their boundary agreement; drought strikes Yemen; terrorists bomb the USS *Cole* in the harbor port of Aden, killing 17 and injuring 39 U.S. military personnel.
2001	Saleh visits the U.S. and assures President Bush that Yemen is a partner in the international fight against terrorism.
2002	Yemen expels more than 100 Islamic scholars as part of a crackdown on suspected al-Qaeda members.

Yemen expelled more than 100 foreign Islamic soldiers in a crackdown on suspected terrorists.

Yerkes, Robert Mearns (1876–1956) American psychobiologist. An expert on ape psychology, Yerkes was responsible for army psychological testing during WORLD WAR I. After earning his Ph.D. at Harvard, he developed the Department of Comparative Animal Psychology there. Following the war he joined the Yale faculty (1924–56) developing the Yale Laboratories of Primate Biology at Orange Park, Florida (1929), renamed the Yerkes Laboratories in 1942.

Yevtushenko, Yevgeny Aleksandrovich (1933–) Russian poet. The poem *Babi Yar* (1961), in which he denounced Nazi and Russian ANTI-SEMITISM, made Yevtushenko internationally famous. Encompassing both personal and social-political themes, his poetry is characterized by a concern for human suffering and oppression. Although a loyal communist, his attacks on STALINISM have caused government censure. Nevertheless, he was allowed to travel widely in the West. In 1995 Yevtushenko published *Don't Die Before You're Dead*, a memoir and a narrative of Boris YELTSIN's victory over the August 1991 hard-liner coup against President Mikhail GORBACHEV.

Yezhov, Nicholas Ivanovich (1895–1939?) Soviet Communist Party official. He joined the COMMUNIST PARTY after the RUSSIAN REVOLUTION but was not well known until 1934, when he became a member of the central committee. He was appointed chairman of the commission of party control and from 1936 to 1938 was chief of security police (NKVD), directing the GREAT PURGE (Yezhovshchina). He was succeeded by Lavrenti BERIA in 1938 and disappeared in 1939.

Yom Kippur War See ARAB-ISRAELI WAR OF 1973.

Yonai, Mitsumasa (1880–1948) Japanese naval official. An admiral, he was naval minister at various times from 1937–45. He vainly attempted to stop the warfare in CHINA in 1937 and later opposed Japanese ties with the AXIS powers and JAPAN's plans for war with the Allies (see SINO-JAPANESE WAR OF 1937–45). As premier during the first half of 1940, he fostered expansionist pressures in French INDOCHINA and the Dutch East Indies. Serving as naval minister during the last year of WORLD WAR II, he pressed his nation to sue for peace.

Yorkshire Ripper case Case involving the serial murder of 13 young women in Yorkshire in the north of England in the late 1970s. In 1981, following a lengthy and controversial search, Peter B. Sutcliffe, a 35-year-old truck driver from Bradford in West Yorkshire, was arrested and charged with the murders. He was found in a car with a prostitute and was armed with a hammer and a knife, items that had been used to brutalize previous victims. Sutcliffe confessed to the 13 murders and to seven other attempted murders, but pleaded not guilty by reason of "diminished responsibility." His defense claimed that he had heard voices telling him to kill prostitutes, which eight of his victims had been. Sutcliffe was found guilty and sentenced to life in prison.

Yoshida, Shigeru (*1878–1967*) Japanese statesman. A career diplomat, Yoshida received a law degree from Tokyo Imperial University in 1906, entered the foreign service and served as ambassador to Italy (1930–32) and Great Britain (1936–39). An advocate of conciliation, he was imprisoned in 1945 for attempting to negotiate peace. After JAPAN's surrender, he headed the Liberal Party, becoming premier in 1946 and holding the post for the majority of time until 1954. Probably the most important figure in postwar Japanese politics, he was supported by the occupying American forces in his administration of the constitution of 1947, his implementation of land reform and his revamping of Japan's shattered economy. As premier, he also negotiated the end of occupation and promulgated treaties with the U.S. and other Allied powers.

Youlou, Fulbert (*1917–1972*) First president of the People's Republic of the CONGO (1960–63). Before independence, he served as premier and minister of agriculture of the French Congo. Strongly pro-Western, he spent three years in office as president of the newly independent nation. He was deposed amid charges of corruption and later went into exile in Spain.

Youmans, Vincent (*1898–1946*) American composer. Born in New York City, he began composing and producing musicals while in the navy during World War I. After the war he worked as a pianist and song-plugger. He scored his first Broadway hit with *Two Little Girls in Blue* (1921), with lyrics by Ira GERSHWIN. After that, many stage successes followed, making him one of the most important Broadway composers of the 1920s and 1930s. These included *No, No, Nanette* (1925), *Hit the Deck* (1927), *Great Day!* (1929) and *Take a Chance* (1932). His movie credits include the classic *Flying Down to Rio* (1933). Among his best-known songs are *Tea for Two, I Want to Be Happy, More Than You Know,* and *Time on My Hands.* The successful early 1970s revival of *No, No, Nanette* helped to again focus attention on Youmans' music.

Young, Cy (Denton True Young) (*1867–1955*) American baseball pitcher for whom the Best Pitcher of the Year award is named. Young began his career in the National League with Cleveland in 1890 and continued with St. Louis from 1899 to 1900. He went to the American League with Boston from 1901 to 1908, and ended his playing career with the Cleveland Indians from 1909 to 1911 and the Boston Braves (of the National League) in 1912. His record of 511 wins still stands. He pitched a perfect game in 1904, and was a 20-game winner 16 times and 30-game winner 15 times. He was inducted into the Baseball Hall of Fame in 1937.

Young, John (*1930– *) U.S. astronaut; as a veteran of six spaceflights, Young has logged over 835 hours in space. His first mission was a pilot for *Gemini 3* (March 23, 1965); with fellow astronaut Gus GRISSOM he tested the first manned spacecraft to maneuver in orbit. Young's second space mission was *Gemini 10* (July 18–21, 1966), during which he served as commander with pilot Michael Collins. The GEMINI missions had been in preparation for America's APOLLO Moon series, and in May 1969 Young served as command module pilot for *Apollo 10* (May 18–26, 1969), a mission that took its crew of Young and fellow astronauts Thomas STAFFORD and Eugene CERNAN into lunar orbit with Young waiting aboard the command module. Stafford and Cernan approached to within 10 miles of the lunar surface, but the mission was only an elaborate dress rehearsal for a lunar landing and no touchdown on the moon was made.

Young finally made it to the Moon as commander of *Apollo 16* (April 16–27, 1972) when he and fellow astronaut Charles Duke spent three days on the lunar surface while command module pilot Thomas Mattingly orbited overhead. Moving over to the U.S. SPACE SHUTTLE program, Young's next command was aboard America's first Space Shuttle flight STS-1 (April 12–14, 1981), with Robert Crippen as pilot. His last spaceflight to date was Shuttle mission STS-9 (November 28–December 8, 1983), the first flight to carry the European-built Spacelab. Young had also been scheduled to command the Shuttle launch of the Hubble Space Telescope in 1986 when the CHALLENGER tragedy forced a postponement of the mission. From 1987 to 1996 Young served as an assistant to the director of the Johnson Space Center (JSC). Since 1996 Young has served as special assistant to the director of the JSC for Engineering, Operations and Safety.

Young, Lester (*1909–1959*) American tenor saxophonist. Young, one of jazzdom's great stylists, coined a uniquely light, lyrical sound and improvisational approach. Until Young appeared in the late 1930s as a featured soloist with the Count BASIE Band, virtually all horn players sought an extroverted, bravura style best epitomized in the exuberant work of Young's contemporary and fellow tenor saxophonist, Coleman HAWKINS; indeed, Young's flowing melodism can be thought of as the *yin* contrasting to the *yang* of Hawkins's muscular assertiveness. Young attributed his unique sound to his efforts to replicate the melodious sound of Paul WHITEMAN saxophonist Frankie Trumbauer, who played "C melody saxophone," an instrument slightly smaller than Young's tenor saxophone. In addition to productive stints with Basie, Young achieved success in a number of small group recordings, including seminal collaborations with singer Billie HOLIDAY, who dubbed Young "The President" or "Prez," a tribute to Young's preeminence as an instrumental soloist. Young's beautiful sound and ethereal yet bluesy improvisations have been pivotal influences on such prominent yet varied saxophonists as Stan GETZ, Zoot SIMS and Sonny Rollins. Sadly, Young's playing deteriorated in his later years, which were marred by personal and legal problems.

Young, Whitney M(oore, Jr.)
(1921–1971) American Civil Rights leader. Born in Lincoln Ridge, Kentucky, Young studied at the University of Minnesota, obtained an M.A. and embarked upon a career in social work. Young held a variety of positions with the URBAN LEAGUE from 1947 to 1954. He was dean of Atlanta University's School of Social Work from 1954 to 1961, leaving to become the Urban League's executive director. As the group's leader throughout the tumultuous 1960s he turned the organization from a social services agency into an activist group. He sponsored anti-poverty and job-training programs, but was widely criticized by militants for his cooperative rather than confrontational style. Under his leadership, the Urban League grew into a large and effective organization that was favored by the nonviolent wing of the CIVIL RIGHTS MOVEMENT and well funded by liberal individuals and corporations. Young drowned while at a beach resort in Lagos, Nigeria; he had been there for a conference.

Young Guard (Molodaya Gvardiya)
Organization of about 100 KOMSOMOL members that existed from September to December 1942 in Krasnodon, UKRAINE, during WORLD WAR II ON THE RUSSIAN FRONT. The group showed much heroism against the occupying Germans but was betrayed by an informer; most of its members were arrested, tortured and murdered. The novelist Alexander A. FADEYEV describes the group in *The Young Guard* (1946, rev. 1951).

Young Plan *(1929)* A plan for revising GERMANY's WORLD WAR I reparations payments. The DAWES PLAN (1924) had revised the payment schedule set up by the 1919 VERSAILLES Treaty, but by 1929 Germany was unable to meet its payments under the Dawes Plan. Conceived by an international committee headed by Owen D. Young, the Young Plan reduced Germany's debts and made them payable over a 58.5–year period. It took effect in 1930, but the GREAT DEPRESSION soon made it impossible for Germany to comply. Adolf HITLER abrogated the Young Plan after he became chancellor in 1933.

Young Turks Coalition of various reform groups in the OTTOMAN EMPIRE opposed to the reactionary regime of Sultan ABDUL HAMID II. In July 1908 army officers belonging to this group revolted in Salonika (now Thessaloniki, Greece), demanding liberal reforms. In 1908 the influential Young Turk organization, the Committee of Union and Progress (CUP), forced Abdul Hamid to restore the 1876 constitution and recall the parliament. In 1909 the CUP overthrew the sultan after an attempted counterrevolution, and set up Mohammed V (1844–1918) as sultan. Some of the CUP leaders, including ENVER BEY, Mehmed TALAAT and Ahmed DJEMAL, took a more nationalistic position than some liberal members, who had returned from exile in 1908, and favored alliance with Germany. Enver and Talaat continued to dominate Turkish politics until late 1918.

Yourcenar, Marguerite (Marguerite de Crayencour) *(1907–1987)* Belgian-born author. She was a novelist, playwright, poet, classicist and translator. She grew up in France, but moved to the U.S. in the 1940s and became a citizen. In 1980, she became the first woman to be elected to the French Academy. She was best known to English-speaking readers for her 1951 novel *Memoirs of Hadrian*.

Ypres, battles of Three important WORLD WAR I military encounters, fought in and around the medieval Belgian city of Ypres. The first battle occurred from October 12 to November 11, 1914, and formed the last of the "race to the sea" engagements in which Germany attempted to turn the flank of the Allies. The German move toward the Channel ports of Dunkirk and Calais in northern France was halted by the British Expeditionary Force, with aid from Belgium and France. A costly battle, it resulted in about 100,000 casualties on each side. The second engagement took place from April 22 to May 24, 1915. In the course of this unsuccessful assault against the British line, the Germans won an unenviable place in history by using poison gas for the first time. The Allies suffered about 65,000 casualties, the Germans some 35,000. The third battle of Ypres, also known as PASSCHENDAELE, lasted from July 31 to November 10, 1917. The British, seeking to break the German line, were hampered by mud and rain; their troops advanced only five miles during all this time, capturing a ridge and the town of Passchendaele. This dirty, hard-fought campaign consumed some 310,000 Allied and about 260,000 German lives. Fighting continued in and around the city of Ypres throughout 1918.

Yuan Shih-k'ai (Yuan Shikai)
(1859–1916) Chines political figure, president of China (1912–16). He began his career in the military in 1880, and served as the Chinese resident in Korea from 1885–94. Yuan served in the Sino-Japanese War, and thereafter was in charge of creating a modern military force for CHINA. A protégé of the dowager empress Tz'u-hsi (Cizi), he was her viceroy in Pechili Province from 1901–07 and was forced to resign from the army at her death in 1908. At the outbreak of revolution in 1911, he returned to the Ch'ing (Qing) court, where he was called upon to defend the empire. However, he quickly moved to consolidate his own power, encouraging the abdication of the emperor PU-YI in February 1912 and the resignation of Sun YAT-SEN, first president of the Republic of China, in his favor a few months later. Yuan assumed dictatorial powers, dissolved the parliament in 1914 and attempted to restore the monarchy with himself as emperor in 1916. His plans were thwarted almost immediately when rebellion at home and opposition abroad forced him to restore the republic, and he died shortly thereafter.

Yudenich, Nicholas Nikolayevich
(1862–1933) General commanding a Russian force in the war against Japan (1905) and during WORLD WAR I. In 1919 he led a White Russian army (based on the Baltic) against Petrograd but was defeated and driven back. He died in exile. (See also WHITES.)

Yugoslavia (Federal Republic of Yugoslavia) Yugoslavia covered an

YUGOSLAVIA

1918	(Dec. 1) Kingdom of Serbs, Croats and Slovenes proclaimed.
1919	Communist Party of Yugoslavia (CPY) is formed.
1929	Kingdom renamed Yugoslavia; King Alexander imposes dictatorship.
1934	(Oct. 9) King Alexander is assassinated by Croat separatists.
1937	Josip Broz (Marshal Tito) becomes head of the CPY.
1941	(April) Yugoslavia is overrun by the Nazis.
1945	(Nov. 29) Monarchy is abolished and the Federative People's Republic of Yugoslavia is established, modeled along Soviet lines.
1948	(June) Tito breaks with the USSR.
1961	Yugoslavia becomes a founding member of the Nonaligned Movement.
1980	(May 4) Tito dies and power is assumed by a collective leadership.
1981	(May) Albanian population in Serbia's province of Kosovo stages uprising in protest of the Serbian administration.
1989	(Jan. 19) Amid growing ethnic unrest, Yugoslavia's collective presidency chooses Ante Markovic to be prime minister.
1991–92	Croatia, Slovenia, Macedonia and Bosnia-Herzegovina declare independence; civil war and ethnic conflict break out.
1992–95	Civil war in Bosnia.
1999	NATO air strikes against Serbia to halt attacks on Albanians in Kosovo.
2000	Slobodan Milošević is ousted in national elections and Vojislav Kostunica becomes president; Milošević is arrested.
2001	Milošević is placed in the custody of the International Court of Justice in The Hague.
2002	Serbia and Montenegro reach an agreement, negotiated through the European Union, to replace the Federal Republic of Yugoslavia with a loose union called Serbia and Montenegro; both republics will be allowed to vote on full independence in three years (March).
2003	Yugoslavia's parliament consigns the Federal Republic to history by approving a new constitutional charter for the union of Serbia and Montenegro.

area of 98,739 square miles in south central Europe. After World War I disparate regions were carved from the ruins of the OTTOMAN and AUSTRO-HUNGARIAN Empires and united to form the Kingdom of Serbs, Croats and Slovenes (1918). In 1929 the kingdom was renamed Yugoslavia, and Serbian king Alexander became dictator, igniting Croat-Serb hostilities. The king was assassinated by Croat separatists in 1934, and Prince Paul governed the country as regent until Germany invaded and partitioned Yugoslavia in 1941. Resistance was carried out by the mainly Serbian, anticommunist CHETNIKS under Draža MIHAILOVIĆ and by the left-wing PARTISANS under Josip Broz (Marshal TITO). The Allies supported the formation of a provisional government under Tito in 1943, and the monarchy was abolished in 1945. Tito introduced a socialist system patterned after the Soviet Union, but followed an independent policy and did not join the WARSAW PACT. The country was named the Socialist Federal Republic of Yugoslavia in 1974. After Tito's death in 1980 the country was governed by a Serbian-dominated collective leadership that curbed provincial autonomy. As a result, ethnic rivalries intensified. Yugoslavia was torn apart by the independence campaigns of Macedonia (1991) CROATIA (1991–92), SLOVENIA (1991–92) and BOSNIA AND HERZEGOVINA (1992–95) and the ethnic conflict in the Serbian province of KOSOVO (1999). In 1992 Serbia and Montenegro united to form the Federal Republic of Yugoslavia. However, by 2003 the two provinces chose to decentralize their political union and changed the name of their

Yugoslavia, 1945–1991

joint government to Serbia and Montenegro. In 2006 Serbia and Montenegro decided to sever their union.

Yukawa, Hideki (1907–1981) Japanese physicist. He was educated at Kyoto and Osaka Universities, receiving his doctorate in 1938. He also taught at both universities. Yukawa's work involved the structure of the atom and subatomic particles. He was puzzled by the fact that electrons and protons could exist together in the same atom; normally, charged particles like these repel one another. In 1935, Yukawa predicted the existence of mesons, subatomic particles intermediate in mass between electrons and protons. These mesons were the "glue" that held the atom together. Over the next 12 years, his hypothesis was confirmed by other scientists. In 1949, Yukawa was awarded the NOBEL PRIZE in physics—the first Japanese to win a Nobel Prize. He was director of Kyoto University's Research

Institute for Fundamental Physics from 1954 until his retirement in 1970. In his later years he opposed atomic energy research because he believed that it would not be used for peaceful purposes.

Yun Po Sun (1898–1990) South Korean politician. He served as president of SOUTH KOREA from 1960 to 1962, resigning following a military coup by Major General PARK CHUNG HEE. He retired from politics in 1967 after losing two elections to Park and became a strong critic of Park's government. He was tried in 1979 for supporting dissident organizations. His two-year sentence was forgiven because of his age.

Yuon, Konstantin (1875–1958) Russian painter. A pupil of Mstislav Dobrzhinsky, Yuon was later a member of the WORLD OF ART society. One of his best-known paintings is *A Sunny Spring Day*, executed in a neoclassical style. Yuon was first chairman of the Union of Soviet Artists.

Yutkevich, Sergei (1904–1985) Soviet film director. He won two Cannes Film Festival prizes, including the 1956 best director for his version of Shakespeare's *Othello*. Best known in his own country for a series of films dealing with the life of LENIN, he was honored with the title Hero of Socialist Labor in 1974.

Z

Zabern Incident *(1913)* International incident that occurred in the town of Zabern (now Saverne) in Alsace, then under German rule. A German officer made insulting public remarks about Alsatians. This led to rioting and the arrest of 29 civilians. The German Reichstag voted 293 to 55 to censure the army for its conduct. However, Chancellor BETHMANN-HOLLWEG and Kaiser WILHELM II chose to ignore the vote—an ominous indication of the army's political influence on the eve of WORLD WAR I.

Zaccagnini, Benigno *(1912–1989)* Italian politician. From 1975 to 1980 he was the secretary of ITALY's dominant Christian Democratic Party. He played a key role in forging a "historic compromise" that resulted in a brief alliance with the Italian Communist Party. Known as "the upright man" of the scandal-plagued Christian Democrats, he remained influential after his resignation, heading a leftist faction of the party.

Zacharias, Jerrold R(elnach) *(1905–1986)* American nuclear physicist. He directed the engineering division of the MANHATTAN PROJECT, which developed the first atomic bomb during WORLD WAR II. After the war, while director of the Massachusetts Institute of Technology's Laboratory of Nuclear Science, he designed the world's first atomic clock. In 1956, he formed the Physical Science Study Committee, which revolutionized the teaching of high school physics in the U.S.

Zaharias, Babe See Babe DIDRIKSON.

Zahir Shah, Mohammad *(1914–)* King of AFGHANISTAN (1933–73). Born in KABUL, Zahir Shah received his education in France. In 1933, following the assassination of his father, Muhammed Nader Shah, Zahir Shah returned to Afghanistan to assume the throne and govern the state. While he managed to preserve his country's independence and neutrality during WORLD WAR II, the emergence of the U.S. and Soviet Union as superpowers helped convince the king of the need to modernize Afghanistan in order to preserve its independence from them. To this end he recruited foreign advisers to modernize the country's agriculture, educational institutions, industry, communications, economy and armed forces. By 1964 Zahir Shah had also decided to reform the Afghan central government by introducing a new constitution that provided for a parliament elected by universal adult suffrage, established free and open elections and guaranteed civil liberties to men and women alike.

A faction in the Afghan ruling elite led by Muhammed Daud, the cousin of the king and prime minister from 1953 to 1963, sought to end Afghanistan's neutrality by aligning it with the Soviet Union. In 1973, while Shah was in Italy recovering from medical treatment for an eye condition, Daud orchestrated Zahir Shah's overthrow and installed himself as the new head of state.

In 2001, following the overthrow of the TALIBAN, a fundamentalist Islamic group that had governed Afghanistan since 1996, Zahir Shah's name surfaced in international circles as the head of a transition government until the advent of a constitution accepted by the majority of the country. The former monarch declined this offer and unilaterally announced that he had no desire to return to the throne. But he suggested that U.S. military officials, who controlled much of Afghanistan, support the convening of the LOYA JIRGA, a traditional political assembly consisting of tribal leaders and prominent personalities, which could form an interim government. Shah threw his support to the U.S.-backed Hamid KARZAI, the leader chosen by this transitional body, who was elected president of Afghanistan in July 2002.

Zaire See CONGO, DEMOCRATIC REPUBLIC OF THE.

Zaleski, August *(1883–1972)* Polish statesman. Zaleski was POLAND's foreign minister from 1926 to 1932. He served as chairman of the Council of the LEAGUE OF Nations in 1930. Two weeks after the German invasion of POLAND (1939) he was again named foreign minister, and subsequently went to London with the Polish government in exile. A strong anticommunist, he remained in London after WORLD WAR II, and was president of the Polish Republic in Exile from 1947 until his death in 1972.

Zambia (Republic of Zambia) Zambia is a landlocked country in southern Africa, covering an area of 290,507 square miles. Known during the colonial era as Northern Rhodesia, the area

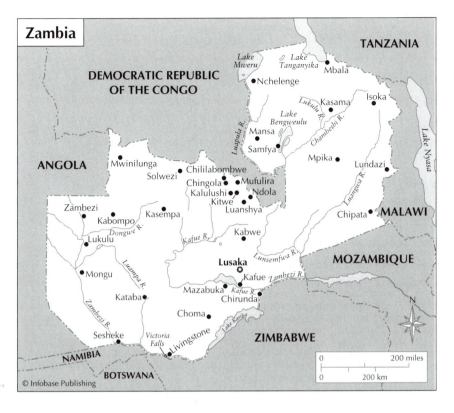

Zambia

TANZANIA

DEMOCRATIC REPUBLIC
OF THE CONGO

Lake Mweru   *Lake Tanganyika*   Mbala

Nchelenge

ANGOLA

Mwinilunga

Kasama   Isoka

Lukulu R.

Lake Bengweulu

Mansa   *Chambeshi R.*

Samfya

Mpika   Lundazi

Solwezi   Chililabombwe

Chingola   Mufulira

Kalulushi   Ndola

Kitwe

Zambezi   Luanshya

Kabompo   Kasempa

Dongwe R.

Lukulu   *Kafue R.*   Kabwe

Chipata   MALAWI

Lake Nyasa

Luapula R.

Luangwa R.

MOZAMBIQUE

Mongu   *Lunsemfwa R.*

Luanpa R.   Lusaka

Kataba   Kafue   *Zambezi R.*

Mazabuka   *Kafue R.*

Chirunda

Choma   *Lake Kariba*

Zambezi R.   ZIMBABWE

Sesheke   *Victoria Falls*   Livingstone

NAMIBIA   N

BOTSWANA

© Infobase Publishing

0   200 miles

0   200 km

was administered by the British South Africa Company until 1924, then by the British government (until 1953), which developed its mining industry (primarily copper) during the 1920s–40s. The country was part of the Central African Federation from 1953 to 1963. With the formation of the AFRICAN NATIONAL CONGRESS (1951), nationalistic feelings strengthened. Zambia became an independent republic in 1964, with Kenneth KAUNDA as its only president. Zambia has played a major foreign policy role in Africa by supporting independence movements in several countries as well as through its attempts to settle the SOUTH AFRICA conflict. Kaunda's one-party rule was challenged in the early 1990s, and there were calls for him to step down. In 1991 Kaunda was defeated in the country's first free presidential elections by Frederick Chiluba. In 2003 former Zambian president Frederick Chiluba was charged with 59 criminal counts, including abuse of the powers of the presidency.

Zamora, Ricardo *(1901–1978)* Legendary Spanish soccer player. Zamora was goalie on the Spanish national team from 1920 to 1936. In 20 of his 46 in-

ternational matches, he allowed no goals by the opposing team. This feat prompted a newspaper reporter to write, "There are only two gatekeepers—St. Peter in heaven and Ricardo Zamora on earth."

Zamyatin, Yevgeny Ivanovich *(1884–1937)* Russian neorealist writer. A Bolshevik in his early life, Zamytatin became critical of the regime after the revolution. His 20th-century novel *My* (*We;* tr. 1925) anticipated HUXLEY's *Brave New World* and Orwell's *1984,* and also prophesied the reign of STALIN, which estranged him from the authorities. He lived in France from 1931.

ZANU (Zimbabwe African National Union) Organization founded in 1963 by former ZAPU members to force the Rhodesian government to grant black majority rule (see ZIMBABWE). It was immediately banned. The failure of the Geneva talks on RHODESIA's future (1976) led to increased guerrilla activity up to 1979, when the ban was lifted. In the 1980 elections, ZANU won 57 seats and 63 percent of the vote. Its leader, Robert MUGABE, became leader of a coalition government that included ZAPU members.

Zanuck, Darryl F(rancis) *(1902–1979)* American motion picture producer. After service in World War I, Zanuck worked as a scriptwriter for WARNER BROS. in HOLLYWOOD. He rose to head of production for Warners and played a key role in the talking picture revolution of the late 1920s and early 1930s. In 1933 he left Warner Brothers and founded his own Twentieth Century Pictures with Joseph M. Schenck, and in 1935 he combined with the ailing Fox Films to establish TWENTIETH CENTURY-FOX, serving as vice president in charge of production until 1956. He spent several years as an independent producer but returned to the studio in the mid-1960s, retiring in 1971. In a career of some 40 years, he created screen stars and made many popular film classics from gangster movies to musicals, social-problem melodramas and historical epics. Notable films that he produced included *Little Caesar* (1931), *Forty-Second Street* (1933), *The Grapes of Wrath* (1940), *All About Eve* (1950) and *The Longest Day* (1962). He won ACADEMY AWARDS for *How Green Was My Valley* (1941) and *Gentleman's Agreement* (1947).

Zanzibar Island off the coast of East Africa; now part of the nation of TANZANIA. In 1890 the United Kingdom established a protectorate over Zanzibar. At the time, the population consisted of Muslims (descended from Arab traders), who formed the ruling class; Indians; and black Africans. Zanzibar gained independence in 1963; its first prime minister and head of state were both Arabs. The following year they were overthrown by left-wing black revolutionaries. The revolutionaries established a one-party state, nationalized the Arab holdings and declared a republic. As a result, most of the Arab and Indian population left the country. Zanzibar merged with Tanganyika to form the new nation of Tanzania in 1964.

Zanzibar Rebellion of 1964 In 1963, Britain granted independence to the island of **Zanzibar**, whose governmental power was in the hands of two Arab-dominated political parties and whose head of state was an Arab sultan. On January 12, 1964, the government was overthrown in a violent

---

ZAMBIA

1911	Northern Rhodesia formed by merger of two British protectorates.
1951	African National Congress (ANC) founded to resist white settler domination of Central African Federation.
1964	Northern Rhodesia becomes independent Republic of Zambia, with David Kaunda as first president.
1968	Kaunda issues Mulungushi Declaration announcing state takeover of 51% ownership in 25 major companies through the Industrial Development Corporation.
1969	Kaunda sponsors Lusaka Manifesto condemning South Africa and Rhodesia but calling for peaceful change instead of confrontation to eliminate racism.
1973	Kaunda signs into law new constitution establishing Zambia as a "one party participating democracy"; Rhodesia closes border with Zambia.
1974	Kaunda nationalizes country's two major mining companies.
1975	Tan Zam rail link between Dar es Salaam and Kapiri Mposhi opens.
1976	State of emergency declared as depressed copper prices cause severe economic difficulties.
1986	South African planes raid Lusaka and other targets in pursuit of ANC rebels.
1990	Food riots erupt over doubled price of cornmeal; Kaunda announces national referendum on multiparty political system; after 27 years in prison, newly released Nelson Mandela visits Zambia to attend strategy meeting of ANC.
1991	Kaunda is defeated in presidential elections that, by a wide margin, bring to power the Movement for Multiparty Democracy (MMD) led by Frederick Chiluba.
1996	The government introduces an amendment to the constitution limiting presidents to two terms, preventing Kaunda from standing for president; Chiluba and the MMD are reelected.
1997	The army attempts a coup and Kaunda is arrested on suspicion of being involved.
1998	The MMD wins local elections.
2000	In less than a week, more than 60,000 refugees flee into Zambia to escape fighting in the Democratic Republic of Congo (December).
2002	Levy Mwanawasa is sworn in as president amid opposition protests over alleged fraud.
2003	Former president Chiluba is arrested and charged with corruption.
2005	President Mwanawasa fends off challenges to the leadership of his ruling party, paving the way for his candidature in 2006 presidential polling. Zambia declares a national disaster and appeals for food aid due to the extensive drought gripping the country.

---

leftist rebellion by black African nationalists, some of whom had been trained in Communist China. A people's republic was declared; the Arab parties were banned; thousands of Arabs were arrested and imprisoned, and their property was confiscated; and the sultan was sent into exile. The new government, directed by the Afro-Shirazi party (whose supporters were black Africans), initiated land reforms and measures to abolish class privileges. To stabilize and strengthen its economy, Zanzibar merged (1964) with TANGANYIKA to form the United Republic of TANZANIA under the leadership of President Julius NYERERE.

Zapata, Emiliano (1879–1919) Mexican revolutionary and peasant leader in the MEXICAN REVOLT OF 1914–15. An Indian, Zapata championed land reform. He raised arms against dictator Porfirio DÍAZ in the MEXICAN CIVIL WAR OF 1911 and then with Pancho VILLA, rebelled against DÍAZ's successors, Francisco Madero, Victoriano Huerta and Venustiano Carranza. He was eventually assassinated on Carranza's orders.

Zapatista National Liberation Army (Ejército Zapatista de Liberación Nacional [EZLN]) A paramilitary revolutionary group that operates out of the Mexican state of Chiapas. Named after the legendary Mexican revolutionary Emiliano ZAPATA, the EZLN was created in November 1983 to coordinate the efforts of native Chiapas groups that were dissatisfied with their political, economic and social conditions and organized opposition to the Mexican government. The EZLN is most famous for its campaign against the NORTH AMERICAN FREE TRADE AGREEMENT (NAFTA), which it denounced as a threat to the well-being of Chiapas's indigenous people. On January 2, 1994, the day after NAFTA came into effect, EZLN guerrillas seized several cities in Chiapas and announced their intention to march on the nation's capital, Mexico City. In an effort to avert social conflicts, Mexico's president, Carlos Salinas de GORTARI, quickly proposed a ceasefire to permit negotiations between the government and the EZLN. Between 1994 and 1996, EZLN emissaries met with members of Salinas's government and that of his successor, Ernesto ZEDILLO PONCE DE LEÓN, in an effort to reach a settlement. In the San Andrés Agreement signed on February 16, 1996, the Mexican government pledged to amend its constitution to increase the autonomy of native peoples in Mexico, such as those of Chiapas.

While this agreement initially appeared to satisfy both sides, Zedillo delayed the agreement's implementation then announced that it would have to be modified. In response, EZLN leaders dispersed their forces in preparation for renewing their rebellion against the government. Zedillo dispatched military units throughout Chiapas in an effort to eradicate the EZLN's base of support. Between 1997 and 2000 the Mexican army and progovernment paramilitary forces repeatedly raided Chiapas in an effort to capture EZLN supporters, leading to the deaths of insurgents as well as innocent civilians. Despite efforts by President Vicente Fox after 2000 to settle the conflict with the EZLN, no durable agreement was reached.

Zappa, Frank (Francis Vincent Zappa, Jr.) *(1940–1993)* American ROCK and roll songwriter, instrumental composer, guitarist and vocalist. Zappa became a widely known COUNTERCULTURE figure in the 1960s after forming the satiric and innovative rock band. The Mothers of Invention. Notable albums by this band include *Freak Out* (1966), *Burnt Weenie Sandwich* (1969), and *Weasels Ripped My Flesh* (1970). From 1970, Zappa issued a large number of albums—such as *Bongo Fury* (1975), *Sheik Yerbouti* (1979), and *Does Humor Belong in Music* (1986)—that featured constantly shifting musical personnel and explored JAZZ, electronic music, 1950s rock and roll, and PUNK ROCK. Zappa, who in interviews displayed a caustic wit directed at all social and artistic pretensions, became a leading spokesman against censorship of rock music. His two children, daughter Moon Unit and son Dweezil, have also made pop recordings.

ZAPU (Zimbabwe African People's Union) Organization founded in 1961 by Joshua NKOMO with the aim of achieving black majority rule in RHODESIA (later ZIMBABWE). It was banned and undertook guerrilla activities with ZANU in a Patriotic Front alliance. In the 1980 elections, against the hopes and expectations of Western governments, it won only 20 seats. In 1982 and after, ZANU alleged that ZAPU sought to overthrow the government. ZAPU claimed that ZANU committed atrocities in order to intimidate ZAPU. Nkomo fled Zimbabwe in 1983.

Zedillo Ponce de León, Ernesto *(1951–)* Mexican politician and president of Mexico (1994–2000). As a high official in the Mexican Central Bank, Zedillo was the architect of the Mexican government's response to the 1982 national debt crisis. After Carlos SALINAS DE GORTARI, was elected president of Mexico in 1988, he chose Zedillo as his minister of budget and planning. As minister, Zedillo oversaw the Mexican government's successful effort to reduce the country's inflation rate. In 1992 Zedillo became minister of education, and instituted a new program to transfer greater authority to the Mexican states for funding schools and development of curricula.

In 1994 Zedillo succeeded Salinas in a close presidential election as the candidate of the Institutional Revolutionary Party (PRI).

As president of Mexico, Zedillo sought to stimulate Mexican exports by devaluing the peso, which wreaked havoc on the country's currency and led to a massive influx of foreign (and primarily U.S.) loans in an effort to shore up the peso and restore fiscal stability. This financial crisis led Salinas to harshly criticize his political heir, something unprecedented in Mexican politics. Later in his presidency, Zedillo retaliated by announcing on national television that an investigation into the murder of former PRI presidential candidate Luis Donaldo Colosio had implicated Salinas's brother Raúl.

In 2000, after several efforts to reduce corruption within the Mexican government, Zedillo was succeeded as president by Vicente FOX, the PAN candidate, marking the first time that an opposition candidate had defeated the PRI in presidential elections.

Zeebrugge Raid *(1918)* After German forces invaded Belgium in 1914 at the start of WORLD WAR I, the Germans converted the Belgian port of Zeebrugge into a U-boat (submarine) base for preying upon Allied shipping in the North Sea and Atlantic Ocean. On the night of April 22–23, 1918, a daring British naval force under the command of Sir Roger J. B. Keyes raided the port, sank three old cruisers filled with cement in the harbor channel and knocked out some of the submarine operations, although three U-boats did manage to make their way out the next day. At the same time a British raid on the Belgian port of Ostend (Oostende) was unsuccessful. On May 9–10, 1918, however, a similar raid by Keyes and his men closed Ostend's harbor, whose entrance was blocked with a sunken cruiser.

Zeffirelli, Franco *(1923–)* Italian-born opera and motion picture director. After a troubled childhood—he was born illegitimate and could not take his father's name, Corsi (the name *Zeffirelli* is a reference to Mozart's opera *Cosi fan tutte*)—he studied architecture and fought in the RESISTANCE in the hills around Florence during WORLD WAR II. A screening of Laurence OLIVIER's *Henry V* and an association with Italian opera and film director Luchino VISCONTI confirmed his ambitions to work on stage and screen. In the late 1940s he designed stage productions for Visconti. By the mid-1950s he was a successful opera director, guiding the careers of such luminaries as Maria CALLAS and Joan SUTHERLAND. He is most famous for his theatrically oriented movies, including the Shakespearean films—*The Taming of the Shrew* (1967), *Romeo and Juliet* (1968), *Hamlet* (1990)—and such opera films as *Otello* (1987) and *La Traviata*. In 1995 he directed the film adaptation of the Charlotte Brönte novel *Jane Eyre* and *Tea with Mussolini* in 1999. He has been criticized for a style he describes in his autobiography, *Zeffirelli* (1986), as "lavish in scale and unashamedly theatrical." He defended this theatricality in an interview: "From my childhood I remember the little troupes of players who would perform with lamps on the floor before them, throwing diabolical shadows on the walls. These performers were the true descendants of the world of Boccaccio. I've always believed more in their fantasies than in anything else. I am always irritated by those who say 'art' must be difficult and only for an elite few. I think culture—especially opera and Shakespeare—must be available to as many people as possible. All my training has been a preparation for the one medium that can do that—the motion picture."

Zeller, André *(1898–1979)* French army officer. Zeller was one of four retired generals who tried to take over ALGERIA by military force in 1961, in an abortive attempt to prevent Algerian independence. He was arrested, stripped of his rank and sentenced to 15 years in prison for treason. Five years later he was pardoned by President Charles DE GAULLE as part of an amnesty.

zemstva Name for institutions of local self-government for European Russia and the Ukraine, established in 1864 during the period of the Great Reforms. The aim of the *zemstva* was to provide social and economic services. Although they were limited from time to time in their authority and revenues and were dominated by the nobility, their existence and liberal influence achieved much in the fields of education, communications, agriculture and health. The authority of the *zemstva* was increased after the FEBRUARY REVOLUTION of 1917, but they were replaced by Soviets after the Bolshevik seizure of power. (See also ZEMSTVO UNION.)

Zemstvo Union The union or association of *zemstva* and their professional employees, which acted as a body campaigning for social reform and supported revolutionary activity in 1904–05 and 1917. The *zemstva* were introduced in 1864 as elected local government assemblies at the provincial and county level. They were elected by all classes, from the peasants upward; they had power to levy taxes and to spend on schools, roads and public health. Much of their effort at social amelioration was obstructed by the central government. They were abolished in 1918. (See also ZEMSTVA.)

Zeppelin A rigid cigar-shaped dirigible invented by Ferdinand, Graf von Zeppelin (1838–1917) and first flown by him on July 2, 1900. His original airship was a 419-foot-long vehicle of aluminum filled with hydrogen gas, covered with fabric and powered by twin 16-hp engines. The invention was met with great enthusiasm in Germany, where passenger-carrying airships flew some 100,000 miles from 1909 to 1914. During WORLD WAR I, German Zeppelins made extensive bombing raids, and some 40 of the slow-flying dirigibles were brought down by Allied fire. At war's end, they resumed commercial service. The Zeppelin program was virtually eliminated after the HINDENBURG DISASTER in 1937.

Zhang Chungqiao (Chang Chung-chao) See GANG OF FOUR.

Zhang Xueliang (Chang Hsüehliang) *(1902–2001)* Chinese military and political figure. Born in northeastern CHINA, he was the son of Zhang Zuolin, a powerful warlord popularly known as the Old Marshal. When his father was assassinated by the Japanese in 1928, Zhang, also known as the Young Marshal, inherited his father's army of 200,000 and his status as one of China's most influential warlords. In 1936, Zhang precipitated the XIAN INCIDENT by briefly kidnapping CHIANG KAISHEK. Zhang thus played the leading role in preventing a Chinese civil war and in presenting a united front to Japan. Given the opportunity to flee with MAO TSE-TUNG, Zhang instead chose to abandon his wealth and power and to stay with his old friend Chiang, who had him arrested and tried by a military court. Sentenced to house arrest, he remained under surveillance on the mainland and later on TAIWAN. In his 80s, Zhang was finally granted a measure of freedom. He is widely viewed as an example of selfless patriotism and heroism to the Chinese people.

Zhao, Ziyang (Chao Tzu-yang) *(1919–2005)* Chinese politician, prime minister of the People's Republic of China (1980–87) and general secretary of the Chinese Communist Party (CCP) (1987–89). Born in Henan (Honan) Province, Zhao joined the CCP in 1938 during its struggle against the Japanese occupation of China. He joined the new Communist government following the declaration of the PRC in October 1949. Zhao established a reputation for loyalty to the party, becoming the first secretary of the CCP in Guangdong. But he fell victim to the CULTURAL REVOLUTION (1966–76), which sought to prevent the creation of an elitist and hierarchical society. Zhao was reassigned to manual labor in rural China. In the early 1970s Zhao was one of several CCP officers rehabilitated and restored to their former positions. Zhao received an additional promotion in 1975, when he was designated the chief administrator of Sichuan (Szechuan) Province. In Sichuan Zhao was responsible for improving the territory's agricultural and industrial output. He also won election to the Politburo, the ruling body of the CCP, first as an alternate member in 1977 and finally a full member in 1979. In 1980 Zhao left his position as chief administrator of Sichuan to succeed Hua Guofeng as prime minister. In 1987, Zhao became general secretary of the CCP, and was succeeded as prime minister by LI PENG.

During the spring 1989 protests of prodemocracy advocates in Beijing's Tiananmen Square, Zhao openly expressed sympathy for the students who were demanding political reforms. In response, the hard-liners who dominated the Politburo removed Zhao as general secretary. During the government's brutal repression of the student protests in June 1989, Zhao was placed under house arrest. But Zhao remained an active force in Chinese politics. In 1997 he arranged for the circulation of a petition at the CCP's congress calling for the immediate adoption of democratic reforms and the formal admission that the repression of student demonstrators in 1989 had been a mistake.

Zhdanov, Andrei Alexandrovich (*1896–1948*) Soviet politician. From 1934 to 1944, he was first secretary of the Leningrad Party, holding also the secretaryship of the central committee. As secretary he was in charge of ideological affairs. He introduced strict political control and extreme nationalism into the arts and opposed Western cultural influences. *Decisions of the Central Committee . . . on Literature and Art,* published by the Communist Party of the Soviet Union in 1951, is an English text of the decrees initiated by Zhdanov. He wrote *Essays on Literature, Philosophy, and Music* (1905). He participated in the defense of Leningrad (see LENINGRAD, SIEGE OF) during World War II, and organized the establishment of the COMINFORM in 1947. He died in 1948, and in 1953 a group of Jewish doctors was accused of his murder, but the charges were dropped after Stalin's death.

Zhirinovsky, Vladimir (*1946– *) Russian politician and head of the ultranationalist Liberal Democratic Party (LDP). Born in Alma-Ata in the Soviet republic of Kazakhstan, Zhirinovsky became a professor at Moscow State University, where he taught courses on law and was a member of its Institute of Asian and African Countries. After serving on the Transcaucasian General Staff for two years, Zhirinovsky joined the Soviet Society of Friendship and Cultural Relations' Committee for Peace. In 1983 he became the legal consultant for Mir Publications, a government-supported publishing house. During the second half of the 1980s, Zhirinovsky turned toward politics during Soviet leader Mikhail GORBACHEV's policy of glasnost ("openness"). In 1989 he helped to found and became chairman of the Liberal Democratic Party (LDP), which espoused an extreme brand of Russian nationalism. In 1991 he ran as the LDP's candidate for the presidency of the Russian Soviet Federated Socialist Republic (RSFSR), one of the 15 constituent republics of

the USSR. Although he lost the race to Boris YELTSIN, the LDP became a powerful force in the Russian Duma (parliament), particularly after Russia obtained its independence from the defunct Soviet Union in December 1991. Two years later, Zhirinovsky won election as an LDP candidate to the Duma, where he became a parliamentary ally of President Boris Yeltsin and his successor, Vladimir PUTIN. Since entering the Duma, Zhirinovsky has continually advocated a string of ultranationalist foreign and domestic policies. He caused a stir by demanding that the U.S. return Alaska to Russia. He called for a harsh Russian response to NATO's air-strikes in 1999 against Serbia over the dispute in its province of KOSOVO. In 2000, Zhirinovsky became the deputy chairman of the Duma.

Zhivkov, Todor (*1911–1998*) Bulgarian political leader. A member of the Communist Party from 1932, he was a PARTISAN leader during WORLD WAR II. Elected to the national assembly in 1945, he became a candidate member of the central committee of the party that same year and a full member three years later. He was named to the central committee secretariat in 1950 and to the Politburo in 1951. In a steady rise to power, Zhivkov became first secretary of the central committee in 1954, premier in 1961 and chairman of the council of state (president) in 1971. Maintaining close ties with the Soviet Union, he built the Bulgarian economy by stimulating the industrial sector and provided the country with stability for about two decades. In late 1989, however, amid worsening economic conditions and a wave of anticommunist feeling that swept Eastern Europe, he and his fellow hard-liners were ousted from office. The disgraced Zhivkov, once the most pro-Moscow leader in the Soviet bloc, soon renounced communism and apologized for his longtime policies.

Zhou Enlai (Chou En-lai) (*1898–1976*) Chinese political leader; premier of the People's Republic of CHINA (1949–76). Born in Zhejiang (Chekiang) province of an upperclass family, he attended a Japanese university from 1917 to 1919. Imprisoned briefly in 1920 for

his participation in the MAY FOURTH MOVEMENT, Zhou went to France later that year to study. There he was impressed with European radicalism and cofounded the Chinese Communist Party and the Chinese Communist Youth Group. Returning to China in 1924, he joined the KUOMINTANG (KMT), which was then cooperating with the Communists, and organized labor groups in SHANGHAI, opening the city to CHIANG Kai-shek's forces. When Chiang broke with the Communists, Zhou was imprisoned and released. He then journeyed to Nanchang, where he took part in an abortive 1927 uprising. He made several trips to Moscow, participating in Communist Party congresses. Important in the political and military policy of the Chinese Communist Party, Zhou became a leading adviser to MAO ZEDONG and participated in the LONG MARCH of 1934–35. An able negotiator with a broad knowledge of the Eastern and Western worlds, he negotiated Chiang's release from the XIAN INCIDENT (1936), served as a liaison officer for the communists in Chongqing (Chunking) during the SINO-JAPANESE WAR (1937–45) and represented the Communists in civil war mediation talks with the U.S. (1945–47).

Upon the establishment of the People's Republic of China in 1949, Zhou became premier, holding this position until his death. He also served as foreign minister from 1949 to 1958. He was instrumental in procuring the Sino-Soviet friendship treaty of 1950 and was China's chief representative at the Geneva Conference of 1954 and the Bandung Conference of 1955. Zhou used his skills to stay in power through the upheavals of the GREAT LEAP FORWARD (1958) and the CULTURAL REVOLUTION (1966–70). Emerging from these troubled times, he spent much of the early 1970s securing a rapprochement with the U.S. and remained China's major international spokesman until his death.

Zhou Yang (Chou Yang) (*1907–1989*) Chinese Communist official. One of the Communist Party's leading arbiters of literature in CHINA for nearly 60 years, he held several influential posts in the 1950s and 1960s, including vice minister of culture. He was purged along with many other intellectuals during the CULTURAL REVOLUTION but was rehabilitated in 1977. Although he had initially supported strong party control of literature and had participated in the purges of other intellectuals, later in his life he became a champion of artistic freedom.

Zhu De (Chu Teh) *(1886–1976)* Chinese military leader. Born in Sichuan (Szechwan), he attended the Yenan Military Academy, where he joined SUN YAT-SEN's Revolutionary Party in 1909. Graduating in 1911, he entered the army and soon participated in the overthrow of the Qing (Ch'ing) dynasty. A warlord from 1916 to 1920, he traveled to Europe in 1922, meeting ZHOU ENLAI and joining the newly formed Chinese Communist Party. Expelled from Germany in 1925 for his radical activities, Zhu journeyed to the USSR and then returned to CHINA. After CHIANG KAI-SHEK purged the Communists from the KUOMINTANG in 1927, Zhu led the NANCHANG UPRISING and thus played a key role in forming the Red Army. The following year he and his followers combined with the forces of MAO ZEDONG in Jiangxi (Kiangsi). Zhu then led his troops in the LONG MARCH (1934–35). He commanded the Communist forces in the SINO-JAPANESE WAR (1937–45) and the CHINESE CIVIL WAR (1946–49). After the establishment of the People's Republic of China in 1949, Zhu continued to hold the post of commander in chief until he left the military in 1954 to serve in various high political offices.

Zhukov, Georgi Konstantinovich *(1896–1974)* Marshal of the Soviet Union. He joined the Red Army in 1918 and the COMMUNIST PARTY in 1919. During WORLD WAR II he was at first chief of the general staff and subsequently deputy commissar of defense and deputy supreme commander in chief of the Soviet armed forces. He was prominent in the planning of Soviet operations and is particularly remembered in the defense of Moscow (1941), the SIEGE OF STALINGRAD (1942), the relief of LENINGRAD (1943) and the advance toward GERMANY (1943–44). On May 8, 1945, he received the surrender of the German High Command in Berlin, but in 1946 he was removed from the post by STALIN, and after a brief period as commander in chief, land forces, and

Marshal Zhukov (center) decorates Field Marshal Montgomery with the Russian Order of Victory. 1945. (LIBRARY OF CONGRESS, PRINTS AND PHOTOGRAPHS DIVISION)

deputy minister of the armed forces, he was sent into semiretirement.

He again became a first deputy minister of defense upon Stalin's death in 1953 and in 1955 was appointed minister of defense. He took KHRUSHCHEV's side against MALENKOV, KAGANOVICH and MOLOTOV, and he became a full member of the Presidium upon their expulsion in 1957. However, he was himself expelled from the Presidium and the central committee and was dismissed as minister of defense later that year. In 1964 he was partially rehabilitated after the fall of Khrushchev and was awarded the Order of Lenin (1966).

Zia ul-Haq, Muhammad *(1924–1988)* Pakistani politician. A career army officer, Zia overthrew prime minister Zulfikar Ali BHUTTO in a bloodless coup in 1979. Zia soon reinstated Islamic penal laws, imposed martial law and postponed elections indefinitely. A referendum in 1985 supported Zia for president. Buoyed by this result, Zia lifted martial law and allowed opposition parties to form and elections to take place. Three years of political unrest followed. On August 17, 1988, a transport plane carrying Zia, the U.S. ambassador and Pakistani officials mysteriously crashed; all were killed.

Ziaur Rahman *(1931–1981)* President of BANGLADESH (1975–81). In November 1975, Bangladesh's army chief of staff, General Ziaur Rahman, assumed control of the country after the assassination of President Mujibur

RAHMAN; Ziaur was sworn in as president in April 1977. He was credited with bringing some stability to Bangladesh, but on May 30, 1981, Ziaur was assassinated in an attempted coup by a group of army officers led by Major General Manzur Ahmed. The rebellion was quelled, and on June 2 the government announced that Manzur had been killed by enraged guards.

Ziegfeld Follies Musical comedy extravaganzas staged in New York City by the American showman Florenz Ziegfeld beginning in 1907. Modeled on the Parisian revues at the Folies-Bergere, the Follies featured lavish musical numbers, top-flight comedians, gorgeous showgirls dubbed the "Ziegfeld Girls," opulent sets and spectacular costumes. These immensely popular shows were produced annually until Ziegfeld's death in 1932 and were staged on an irregular basis until 1957. Often imitated, the Follies provided a model for the variety shows that were among television's earliest hits.

Zimbabwe Zimbabwe, a landlocked republic located in southern Africa, covers an area of 150,764 square miles; known successively as **Southern Rhodesia** (1911–64), **Rhodesia** (1964–79) and **Zimbabwe Rhodesia** (1979–80). The country was administered by the British South Africa Company until 1923, when it was granted self-government and annexed by the British Crown. Led by Prime Minister Ian SMITH, the country declared its independence as Rhodesia in 1965.

Zimbabwe

African nationalist organizations ZANU and ZAPU, banned by the white minority government, went underground and pursued guerrilla warfare during the 1960s and 1970s. In 1979 an agreement between the white government and African nationalists was reached at the British-organized Lancaster House Conference, which provided for a transition to independence based on majority rule. In 1980 Zimbabwe became an independent republic within the British COMMONWEALTH, with Robert MUGABE as prime minister. In 1987 he became the country's first executive president. Internationally, Zimbabwe has worked toward the stabilization of Africa and an end to APARTHEID in neighboring SOUTH AFRICA. Zimbabwe has experienced a severe economic crisis because of the combination of a drought in 2002 and political conflicts between white landowners and black sharecroppers who were supported by Mugabe. In 2002 Mugabe was reelected amid protests by opposition parties and foreign observers who claimed voter fraud and violence by the ZANU party. Zimbabwe was suspended by the Commonwealth in 2003 owing to the

ZIMBABWE	
1897	Final defeat of Shona and Ndebele tribes by British South Africa Company under Cecil Rhodes.
1922	Settlers vote to form self-governing British colony named Rhodesia.
1931	Land Apportionment Act reserves all mining rights and 50% of total land area for whites, who are under 5% of population.
1934	Original African National Congress founded in South Africa and Rhodesia.
1953	British form Central African Federation from Rhodesia and other colonies.
1963	CAF broken up as Zambia and Malawi move toward independence; nationalist movement in Rhodesia splits along tribal lines—ZANU represents majority Shona; ZAPU the less populous Ndebele.
1965	White government under Ian Smith unilaterally declares independence; British impose economic embargo; ZANU and ZAPU wage limited guerrilla war.
1972	Full-scale war begins.
1976	ZANU under Robert Mugabe and ZAPU under Joshua Nkomo form Patriotic Front to negotiate with Smith government and British.
1979	Lancaster House Agreement paves way for majority rule.

(Table continues)

ZIMBABWE (CONTINUED)

1980	Zimbabwe created as a republic within the Commonwealth; Mugabe elected prime minister; huge independence celebration features Western pop stars.
1982	Nkomo and ZAPU members expelled from government; intertribal violence breaks out.
1985	Mugabe reelected; South Africa raids ANC bases inside Zimbabwe.
1987	Zimbabwe clashes with rebels from Mozambique.
1988	Nkomo and Mugabe reach agreement; ZANU and ZAPU merged.
1990	Mugabe reelected again; calls for one-party system.
1992	President Mugabe announces that the government will seize commercial farms, breaking an earlier promise to confiscate only derelict and underutilized farms.
1994	Productive farms are seized without compensation.
1995	Legislative elections take place in which Mugabe's party, ZANU-PF, gains all but two seats in the House of Assembly; opposition parties boycott the elections and opposition leader Sithole is arrested; severe drought produces food shortages.
1996	President Mugabe wins another six-year term in an election in which only one-third of eligible voters participate.
1998	Riots and demonstrations result from high food and petroleum prices.
1999	Critics of the Mugabe government are brutally mistreated; a new opposition party, the Movement for Democratic Change (MDC), is formed.
2000	The MDC wins 57 seats in parliament, although Mugabe's ZANU-PF retains control with 93 seats; in a national referendum, voters reject a proposal to give Mugabe greater powers; the government begins to arrest opposition legislators.
2001	The government demands that judges opposed to land seizures resign and expels foreign journalists.
2002	Mugabe wins another term; the opposition and foreign observers allege widespread ballot irregularities and violence; the government seizes some 2,900 farmsteads owned by whites; a severe economic crisis hits the country.
2003	A general strike leads to the arrest of thousands; MDC leader Morgan Tsvangirai is arrested twice; Zimbabwe leaves the Commonwealth.
2005	The ruling ZANU-PF Party wins two-thirds of votes in legislative elections that the opposition MDC charges are rigged; tens of thousands of shanty dwellings are destroyed in a campaign that the UN says leaves about 700,000 homeless; the United States labels Zimbabwe one of six "outposts of tyranny"; Zimbabwe denies the statement.

escalation of violence, including the government's destruction of thousands of shanty dwellings, leaving many homeless.

Zimbalist, Efrem, Sr. (1890–1985) Russian-born violin virtuoso. Zimbalist was one of the major concert violinists of the 20th century. He made his American debut with the Boston Symphony Orchestra in 1911 and continued to play in public for more than 40 years. In 1928 he joined the faculty of the newly formed Curtis Institute of Music in Philadelphia, and was the institute's director from 1941 to 1968. He also composed. His son, Efrem Zimbalist, Jr., was a television actor, as was his granddaughter, Stephanie Zimbalist.

Zimmermann telegram Secret telegram sent from Berlin by Arthur Zimmermann, GERMANY's foreign secretary, to Count Johann von Bernstorff, Germany's ambassador to the U.S., on January 16, 1917. Composed in a numerical code, it was intercepted and deciphered by the British, who turned it over to the U.S. Its text indicated that if Germany and the

U.S. were to go to war, Germany would seek to gain Mexico as an ally by promising the return of Texas, New Mexico and Arizona after a German victory. Released to the press by President Woodrow WILSON on March 1, 1917, the Zimmerman telegram caused a public outcry and helped to convince many to favor America's entry into WORLD WAR I.

Zinn, Walter Henry *(1906–2000)* Canadian-American physicist. Zinn moved to the U.S. in 1930 and received a Ph.D. from Columbia University in 1934. He continued research there in collaboration with Leo SZILARD, investigating atomic fission. In 1938 he became a U.S. citizen. A year later, Zinn and Szilard demonstrated that uranium underwent fission when bombarded with neutrons and that part of the mass was converted into energy according to Albert EINSTEIN's famous formula, "$E = mc^2$." This work led Zinn into research during the construction of the ATOMIC BOMB in WORLD WAR II (see MANHATTAN PROJECT). After the war, Zinn worked on the design of an atomic reactor and in 1951 built the first breeder reactor.

Zinoviev, Grigori Yevseyevich Radomyslsky *(1883–1936)* Soviet politician. He joined the Social Democratic Labor Party in 1901 and its BOLSHEVIK faction in 1903. He emigrated after the 1905 Revolution and accompanied Lenin on his return to Russia after the February 1917 Revolution, but he was not in agreement with the APRIL THESES, the OCTOBER REVOLUTION or the Treaty of BREST-LITOVSK. He was chairman of the Petrograd Soviet after the October Revolution, became a candidate member of the Politburo in 1919, was a full member from 1921 to 1926 and was chairman of the executive committee of the Communist International from 1919 to 1926. After Lenin's death he first opposed TROTSKY and then joined him against STALIN. He was falsely accused of complicity in the murder of Sergei KIROV and in 1935 was sentenced to 10 years' imprisonment. He was retried in the great treason trial (1936) and executed. He became notorious in British politics with the publication (1924) of a letter, allegedly by him, urging supporters in Great Britain to prepare for violent insurrection. This contributed materially to Ramsay MACDONALD's electoral defeat and the deterioration of British-Soviet relations.

Zinoviev letter Letter allegedly written by Grigori Yevseyevich Radomyslsky ZINOVIEV, the head of the Soviet Comintern, to the British Communist Party. It called for revolution in Great Britain provoked by acts of sedition. The letter was published in the English press in 1924 and was the cause of a great deal of antileftist feeling. The letter was quite possibly a forgery. In any event, it was certainly a factor in the defeat of Ramsay MACDONALD's Labour government and the victory of the Conservatives in the 1924 British elections and in the deterioration of British-Soviet relations.

Zionism Movement for the return of a Jewish nation to PALESTINE. It dates back to the 6th-century B.C. beginning of the Diaspora and, later, to the Roman destruction of Jerusalem in 70 A.D. Zionism was mainly a cultural movement until the very end of the 19th century, when it became a worldwide political cause. Its modern manifestation was largely prompted by the widespread ANTI-SEMITISM of 19th-century Europe. In 1897 Theodore HERZL convened the first World Jewish Congress in Basel, Switzerland, to promote the idea of a Jewish home in Palestine guaranteed by public law, and modern Zionism was born. While there was some opposition from assimilated JEWS, who feared for their status, from fundamentalists, who believed only the Messiah could create such a state, and from those who favored an immediate Jewish homeland in some other part of the world, the Zionist movement gathered strength in the early part of the 20th century. Chaim WEIZMANN assumed leadership of the movement and was a key figure in securing the BALFOUR DECLARATION OF 1917, which assured British support. The LEAGUE OF NATIONS followed with its mandate for Palestine in 1922. During the period of the British mandate, increasing tensions and violence between Jews and Arabs and Britain's shifting interpretation of the declaration led to splits among Zionists. Vladimir Jabotinsky's Revisionists demanded large and immediate Jewish immigration, while the General Zionists continued to favor compromise. After WORLD WAR II the horrors of the HOLOCAUST caused an intensification of Zionist activities, and Jewish refugees poured into Palestine. A UNITED NATIONS plan to partition Palestine was accepted, and on May 14, 1948, the state of ISRAEL was proclaimed. Since the creation of Israel, Zionists have largely centered their activities on promoting immigration, education, cultural matters and fund-raising.

Zita (Zita Maria Grazia Adelgonda Michela Raffaella Gabriella Giuseppina Antonia Luisa Agnese of Bourbon-Parma) *(1892–1989)* Last empress of the Hapsburg empire of AUSTRIA-HUNGARY. In 1911 she married Archduke Karl, who was crowned emperor of Austria-Hungary following the death of his uncle, Franz Josef, in 1916. Karl was forced to relinquish his imperial rights following the Allied victory in WORLD WAR I, and died in 1922. Thereafter, Zita lived an austere life in a Franciscan convent in Switzerland. (See also AUSTRO-HUNGARIAN EMPIRE.)

Zorach, William *(1887–1966)* American sculptor. Born in Lithuania, he and his family immigrated to the U.S. in 1891 and settled near Cleveland. He studied at the Cleveland Institute of Art (1902–05) and New York's National Academy of Design (1908–10) before traveling to Paris, where he studied from 1910 to 1911. At first a painter, his work in Paris showed the influence of FAUVISM, and the pictures he painted after his return to the U.S. have many of the characteristics of CUBISM. In 1922 Zorach turned to sculpture, in which he had no formal training. Working directly in carved stone or wood and sometimes in cast metal, he created figures that are noted for their simplified monumentality. Zorach created a number of important sculptural commissions, among them for the RADIO CITY MUSIC HALL, New York City (*Spirit of the Dance*, 1932), the NEW YORK WORLD'S FAIR (*Builders of the Future*, 1939) and the MAYO CLINIC, Rochester, Minnesota (1954). His best-known works include *Mother and Child* (Metropolitan Museum, New York City) and *Pegasus* (Whitney Museum, New York City). A popular teacher at New York's Art Students League, he was the author of *Zorach Explains Sculpture* (1947).

Zoshchenko, Mikhail Mikhailovich *(1895–1958)* Ukrainian satirical writer. From 1921 he began to gain popularity with his short stories depicting the bewilderment and disbelief of the ordinary citizen in Soviet Russia. In 1946 he was the main target of Andrei ZHDANOV's attacks when the latter began his campaign to impose absolute party control over cultural life. He was expelled from the Union of Soviet Writers and his works were banned. His books include *Youth Restored* (1933), *Russia Laughs* (tr. 1935), *The Woman Who Could Not Read* (tr. 1940) and *The Wonderful Dog* (tr. 1942).

Zuckerman, Yitzhak *(1915?–1981)* Leader of the Polish RESISTANCE movement during WORLD WAR II. Zuckerman was the last commander of the Jewish uprising against the Nazis in the Warsaw ghetto in 1943–44 (see WARSAW UPRISING). He led the ghetto's survivors to safety through the city's sewer system. He was later part of an underground network that transported Jewish survivors to the Mediterranean coast and thence to PALESTINE. He settled in Palestine (now ISRAEL) after the war, and later helped establish a Tel Aviv museum memorializing the HOLOCAUST.

Zukor, Adolph *(1873–1976)* Zukor was perhaps the most ambitious, most powerful and most successful of all the HOLLYWOOD movie studio moguls. Born in Risce, Hungary, he immigrated to New York's Lower East Side at the age of 15 in 1888. By 1912 he had worked his way up from store sweeper, fur salesman and theater owner to successful film distributor. With Daniel Frohman he formed one of the first important production studios, Famous Players, with the express intent of bringing famous stage stars to feature-length movies. After several mergers and an active campaign to acquire theaters, Zukor transformed the studio into PARAMOUNT PICTURES, serving as its president until 1936. His policy of integrating production, distribution and exhibition under one corporate roof revolutionized a chaotic system. Zukor helped put the industry on a sound economic footing by creating a reliable supply and constant demand, at the same time making it a respectable, legitimate business. Zukor eventually became chairman of the board and for the remainder of his days was the gray eminence of the corporation, downplaying to the very end his status as the greatest of all the moguls—but attesting to that in his autobiography *The Public Is Never Wrong* (1953). In 1949 his "contributions to the industry" earned Zukor a special ACADEMY AWARD. Having once sworn to outlive his enemies, he lived to the age of 103.

Zweig, Stefan *(1881–1942)* Austrian-born Jewish novelist, story writer, poet, playwright and biographer. Zweig was a gifted and versatile writer who was one of the most popular German-language writers in the decades between the two world wars. His works for the theater include the pacifist play *Jeremias* (1917) and an adaptation of *Volpone* (1926), from the Elizabethan playwright Ben Jonson. As a popular biographer, he romanticized subjects ranging from the Renaissance humanist Erasmus of Rotterdam (1934) to the Spanish explorer Ferdinand Magellan (1938). His best-known work of fiction is the novella *The Royal Game* (1944). *The World of Yesterday* (1943) is his autobiography. Zweig's lyric adaptations of Jewish folktales were collected in *Legends* (1945). Due to his Jewish background, Zweig was compelled to flee Austria. In despair over the Nazi conquests, Zweig committed suicide in Brazil in 1942.

Zworykin, Vladimir Kosma *(1889–1982)* Russian-American physicist who made a number of contributions to electron optics and invented the first electronic scanning television camera—the iconoscope. Zworykin studied electrical engineering at St. Petersburg, graduated in 1912 and served in WORLD WAR I as a radio officer in the Russian army. He moved to America in 1919 and joined the Westinghouse Electric Corporation in 1920 and the Radio Corporation of America (RCA) in 1929; that year he successfully transmitted a picture from a television camera onto a cathode-ray tube.

Bibliography

Bailey, Paul J. *China in the Twentieth Century,* 2nd edition. Oxford, U.K.: Blackwell Publishers, 2001.

Brose, Eric Dorne. *A History of Europe in the Twentieth Century.* New York & Oxford: Oxford University Press, 2004.

Bulliet, Richard. *The Earth and Its Peoples: A Global History,* 3rd edition. Boston: Houghton Mifflin, 2000.

Cleveland, William L. *A History of the Modern Middle East.* New York: Westnew Press, 1999.

Cook, Nicholas and Anthony Pople. *The Cambridge History of Twentieth-Century Music.* Cambridge: Cambridge University Press, 2004.

Crossley, Pamela. *Global Society: The World since 1900.* Boston, Mass.: Houghton Mifflin, 2003.

Duus, Peter. *The Cambridge History of Japan,* vol. 6, *The Twentieth Century.* Cambridge: Cambridge University Press, 1989.

Howard, Michael and Wm. Roger Louis. *The Oxford History of the Twentieth Century.* New York and Oxford: Oxford University Press, 2000.

Keylor, William R. *The Twentieth Century World and Beyond: An International History since 1900,* 5th edition. New York & Oxford: Oxford University Press, 2005.

Oxford University Press. *A World of Nations: The International Order since 1945.* New York and Oxford: Oxford University Press, 2003.

Lamb, David. *The Africans.* New York: Vintage Press, 1987.

Maltby, Richard. *Passing Parade: A History of Popular Culture in the Twentieth Century.* New York and Oxford: Oxford University Press, 1989.

Narins, Brigham. *Notable Scientists from 1900 to the Present.* New York: Thomson Gale, 2001.

Overfield, James. *Sources in Twentieth-Century Global History.* Boston: Houghton Mifflin, 2001.

Patterson, James T. *America in the Twentieth Century,* 5th edition. New York: Wadsworth, 1999.

Rowbotham, Sheila. A *Century of Women: The History of Women in Britain and the United States in the Twentieth Century.* New York: Penguin, 2000.

Service, Robert. *A History of Twentieth-Century Russia.* Cambridge, Mass.: Harvard University Press, 1999.

Shillington, Kevin. *History of Africa.* London: Palgrave MacMillan, 1995.

Sitkoff, Harvard. *Perspectives on Modern America: Making Sense of the Twentieth Century.* Oxford and New York: Oxford University Press, 2000.

Tarling, Nicholas, ed. *The Cambridge History of Southeast Asia,* Vol. 2, *The Nineteenth and Twentieth Centuries.* Cambridge: Cambridge University Press, 1992.

Index

Boldface page numbers indicate primary discussions. *Italic* page numbers indicate illustrations.